Better Reading Two:

LITERATURE

Better Reading Two

FOURTH EDITION

LITERATURE

introduction to short stories, drama, and poetry

Walter Blair

UNIVERSITY OF CHICAGO

John Gerber

STATE UNIVERSITY OF IOWA

Eugene Garber

STATE UNIVERSITY OF IOWA

Scott, Foresman and Company

CONTENTS

Part One

....

MAJOR ASPECTS OF LITERATURE

Part Two

SOME WAYS OF
EVALUATING LITERATURE

Part Three

....

CASEBOOK

The following titles were given by the editors to excerpts from longer works: "Storm on Jackson's Island," "On a Ship at Sea," "A Fierce Rush of All the Winds," "Keats' 'On First Looking into Chapman's Homer,' " "Coleridge's 'Kubla Khan,' " "Kipling's Politics," "Vaughan's Platonism," "The Novel and the Romance," "Aeneas' Journey to the Underworld," "Analytic Psychology and Art"

CHRONOLOGICAL LIST OF
AUTHORS AND LITERARY TYPES

Poetry

Foreword

This fourth edition of *Better Reading 2*, like earlier editions, is designed to help students increase their skill in understanding and evaluating fiction, drama, and poetry. The changes in this edition reflect our conviction that the introductory study of literature in American colleges and universities has gained markedly in the last few years in both scope and depth. Below we describe the overall plan of the book, the function of each part, and, for users of earlier editions, the changes and additions we have made.

Part One has as its object helping the student understand the nature of imaginative literature in general, not of one but of all three types—fiction, drama, and poetry. The starting point is a contrast between "fact" and "fiction"—between informative prose and imaginative writing, which shows how the writer of fiction, drama, or poetry characteristically invests with esthetic values material which the scientist or historian uses factually. Next the basic materials of a literary work are discussed: action, characters, setting, and language. Part One concludes with a study of the elements which give unity and coherence to the basic materials: tone, point of view, atmosphere, and meaning. The notable change in this section is the addition of discussions of point of view and atmosphere. This part also contains new selections by Christina Rossetti, Emily Dickinson, and Eudora Welty.

We have changed Part Two considerably in an effort to give the student a more systematic presentation of the important ways in which a literary work can be evaluated. We have divided critical approaches into two kinds, those that concentrate on formal excellence and those that deal primarily with content. We believe it important that the student be encouraged to use a variety of critical methods and to avoid the rigidity and injustice which come from using the same method with every work. To give the student a chance to see critics and writers using various kinds of evaluation, we provide new critical selections by Nathaniel Hawthorne, John Middleton Murry, Maud Bodkin, George Orwell, and John Smith Harrison.

Part Three, a casebook on "Heart of Darkness," is entirely new. This study of Conrad's story has three important functions: it provides a summary of the means of analysis and evaluation that the student has learned, it provides the opportunity for a study in depth, and it affords the student the opportunity to formulate specific critical premises of his own. That students may begin with some common basis for their evaluation of the story, we provide the following: Conrad's "Congo Diary," excerpts from Book VI of Vergil's *Aeneid,* and selections by Northrop Frye, Carl J. Jung, John Stuart Mill, Harold J. Laski, Walter Lippmann, and Blaise Pascal.

Part Four, an anthology of short stories, plays, and poems, remains essentially the same, though Edward Albee's provocative play *The American Dream* is a notable addition. An introductory discussion of each genre points out its main characteristics, and headnotes for particular works or groups of works are provided when needed.

Because of the influence of contemporaneous audiences in shaping plays, each drama is preceded by a relevant historical discussion. Here, as elsewhere in the book, the selections range from the distant past to the present.

Two indexes are included at the end of the book. "Glossary and Index of Critical Terms" defines terms or cites passages in the text which treat them. Because many terms are valuable for communicating different insights and evaluations, many of the most useful ones are included. "Index of Titles and Authors" indicates passages included and also provides essential facts and vital statistics about the authors.

To our colleagues and to the many teachers and students who have used the earlier editions of this book, we give our sincere thanks for helpful suggestions. We also wish to thank the many authors and publishers who have permitted us to include selections from their books.

W.B.   J.G.   E.G.

PART ONE

Major Aspects of Literature

Introduction: 'Fact' versus 'Fiction'

A natural question at the beginning of a study of the reading of fiction, drama, and poetry is, "What is it that literature does that factual prose does not do?" Common sense suggests that we may answer this question, in part at least, by contrasting the purposes and achievements of a literary work on the one hand and of a factual account on the other. Let us compare two selections dealing with the same general subject, the Oedipus complex as it manifests itself in the child. Our first selection has been drawn from the science of psychology; the second is a short story.

Sigmund Freud, THE OEDIPUS COMPLEX

Now you will be impatiently waiting to hear what this Oedipus complex comprises. The name tells you: you all know the Greek myth of King Oedipus, whose destiny it was to slay his father and to wed his mother, who did all in his power to avoid the fate prophesied by the oracle, and who in self-punishment blinded himself when he discovered that in ignorance he had committed both these crimes. I trust that many of you have yourselves experienced the profound effect of the tragic drama fashioned by Sophocles from this story. The Attic poet's work portrays the gradual discovery of the deed of Oedipus, long since accomplished, and brings it slowly to light by skilfully prolonged enquiry, constantly fed by new evidence; it has thus a certain resemblance to the course of a psycho-analysis. In the dialogue the deluded mother-wife, Jocasta, resists the continuation of the enquiry; she points out that many people in their dreams have mated with their mothers, but that dreams are of no account. To us [as psychologists] dreams are of much account, especially typical dreams which occur in many people; we have no doubt that the dream Jocasta speaks of is intimately related to the shocking and terrible story of the myth. . . .

There is no possible doubt that one of the most important sources of the sense of guilt which so often torments neurotic people is to be found in the Oedipus complex. More than this: in 1913, under the title of *Totem und Tabu*, I published a study of the earliest forms of religion and morality in which I expressed a suspicion that perhaps the sense of guilt of mankind as a whole, which is the ultimate source of religion and morality, was acquired in the beginnings of history through the Oedipus complex. . . .

Now what does direct observation of children, at the period of object-choice before the latency period, show us in regard to the Oedipus complex? Well, it is easy to see that the little man wants his mother all to himself, finds his father in the way, becomes restive when the latter takes upon himself to caress her, and shows his satisfaction when the father goes away or is absent. He often expresses his feelings directly in words and promises his mother to marry her; this may not seem much in comparison with the deeds of Oedipus, but it is enough in fact; the kernel of each is the same. Observation is often rendered puzzling by the circumstance that the same child on other occasions as this period will display great affection for the father; but such contrasting—or, better, *ambivalent*—states of feeling, which in adults would lead to conflicts, can be tolerated alongside one another in the child for a long time, just as later on they dwell together permanently in the unconscious. One might try to object that the little boy's behaviour is due to egoistic motives and does not justify the conception of an erotic complex; the mother looks after all the child's needs and consequently it is to the child's interest that she should trouble herself about no one else. This too is quite correct; but it is soon clear that in this, as in similar dependent situations, egoistic interests only provide the occasion on which the erotic impulses seize. When the little boy shows the most open sexual curiosity about his mother, wants to sleep with her at night, insists on being in the room while she is dressing, or even attempts physical acts of seduction, as the mother so often observes and laughingly relates, the erotic nature of this attachment to her is established without a doubt. Moreover, it should not be forgotten that a mother looks after a little daughter's needs in the same way without producing this effect; and that often enough a father eagerly vies with her in trouble for the boy without succeeding in winning the same importance in his eyes as the mother. In short, the factor of sex preference is not to be eliminated from the situation by any criticisms. From the point of view of the boy's egoistic interests it would merely be foolish if he did not tolerate two people in his service rather than only one of them. . . .

Clearly, in this passage Freud's purpose is to demonstrate factually the existence in the male child of an erotic impulse toward the mother. This impulse and the patterns of behavior through which it expresses itself Freud calls the Oedipus complex, after Sophocles' great tragedy. The play, Freud finds, is a dramatization of this great fact of our psychic lives. What we want to notice here with particular care is that Freud, as a psychologist, a scientist, builds his argument on fact, on the empirically observable: certain elements in Sophocles' drama, certain actions and attitudes of the male child, significant differences in the behavior of the female child, and the responses of the parents. When these observations, these facts, are carefully weighed and fitted together, they demonstrate and define the psychological complex which Freud wants us to accept.

Further, we should note this: Not only are the materials factual, but the organization of them is methodical and inductive. The demonstration proceeds this way: The existence and general nature of the Oedipus complex is hypothesized; then the hypothesis is shown to account for important behavioral patterns within the family. It is proved sound inductively. Freud not only marshals his evidence carefully but also successfully meets the obvious objection that the little boy's behavior is merely due to egoistic motives. At this point his differentiation between the behavior of boys and girls is telling. And note that Freud, the scientist, does not dodge the more questionable of his observations, i.e., the boy's marks of affection for his father and the complicating factor of parental sex preferences, but demonstrates that these, too, can be logically accounted for.

Observe what Freud has not done. He has not invented any characters, events or conversations. His interest is not in the particular, but in the general. For the scientist must formulate his laws, his governing concepts on the basis not of the individual, the exceptional, but on the basis of the typical. "To us [as psychologists]," says Freud, "dreams are of much account, especially typical dreams which occur in many people. . . ." Nor does Freud reveal his emotional reaction to his material. Surely, the reader feels a certain intellectual intensity, call it fervor if you like—the keen and probing mind fashioning from the welter of experience a universal law—but it is the excitement of the dedicated scientist. The language that Freud uses is chosen for its precision, not for its emotive qualities. In short, Freud does not attempt to render experience dramatic and immediate nor imbue it with the unique colors of the artistic imagination.

It would be dangerous to generalize about the nature of all factual prose, using this single example. Indeed, the classification of some literature presents vexing problems. The existence of works in which the demarcation between fact and fiction is hazy should not, however, discourage us from setting down the basic characteristics of each. Let us concentrate for the moment on fact. The writer of factual prose, be he scientist, historian, newspaper man, or whatever, deals primarily with the observable, with what can be verified by the senses. Though he may establish hypotheses, come to conclusions, or support opinions, he must arrive at his position through an orderly consideration of the facts. He stands firmly on the ground of actual experience—dates, occurrences, documents, statistics.

However, imaginative literature—fiction, drama, and poetry (each "fiction" of a sort)—typically differs from factual writing. With Freud's analysis of the Oedipus complex, let us contrast the following short story.

Frank O'Connor, MY OEDIPUS COMPLEX

Father was in the army all through the war—the first war, I mean—so, up to the age of five, I never saw much of him, and what I saw did not worry me. Sometimes I woke and there was a big figure in khaki peering down at me in the candlelight. Sometimes in the early morning I heard the slamming of the front door and the clatter of nailed boots down the cobbles of the lane. These were Father's entrances and exits. Like Santa Claus, he came and went mysteriously.

In fact, I rather liked his visits, though it was an uncomfortable squeeze between Mother and him when I got into the big bed in the early morning. He smoked,

Reprinted from *The Stories of Frank O'Connor* by Frank O'Connor, by permission of Alfred A. Knopf, Inc. Copyright 1950, 1952 by Frank O'Connor. Canadian distribution rights by permission of Harold Matson Company.

which gave him a pleasant musty smell, and shaved, an operation of astounding interest. Each time he left a trail of souvenirs—model tanks and Gurkha knives with handles made of bullet cases, and German helmets and cap badges and button-sticks, and all sorts of military equipment—carefully stowed away in a long box on top of the wardrobe, in case they ever came in handy. There was a bit of the magpie about Father; he expected everything to come in handy. When his back was turned, Mother let me get a chair and rummage through his treasures. She didn't seem to think so highly of them as he did.

The war was the most peaceful period of my life. The window of my attic faced southeast. My mother had curtained it, but that had small effect. I always woke with the first light and, with all the responsibilities of the previous day melted, feeling myself rather like the sun, ready to illumine and rejoice. Life never seemed so simple and clear and full of possibilities as then. I put my feet out from under the clothes—I called them Mrs. Left and Mrs. Right—and invented dramatic situations for them in which they discussed the problems of the day. At least Mrs. Right did; she was very demonstrative, but I hadn't the same control of Mrs. Left, so she mostly contented herself with nodding agreement.

They discussed what Mother and I should do during the day, what Santa Claus should give a fellow for Christmas, and what steps should be taken to brighten the home. There was that little matter of the baby, for instance. Mother and I could never agree about that. Ours was the only house in the terrace without a new baby, and Mother said we couldn't afford one till Father came back from the war because they cost seventeen and six. That showed how simple she was. The Geneys up the road had a baby, and everyone knew they couldn't afford seventeen and six. It was probably a cheap baby, and Mother wanted something really good, but I felt she was too exclusive. The Geneys' baby would have done us fine.

Having settled my plans for the day, I got up, put a chair under the attic window, and lifted the frame high enough to stick out my head. The window overlooked the front gardens of the terrace behind ours, and beyond these it looked over a deep valley to the tall, red-brick houses terraced up the opposite hillside, which were all still in shadow, while those at our side of the valley were all lit up, though with long strange shadows that made them seem unfamiliar; rigid and painted.

After that I went into Mother's room and climbed into the big bed. She woke and I began to tell her of my schemes. By this time, though I never seem to have noticed it, I was petrified in my nightshirt, and I thawed as I talked until, the last frost melted, I fell asleep beside her and woke again only when I heard her below in the kitchen, making the breakfast.

After breakfast we went into town; heard Mass at St. Augustine's and said a prayer for Father, and did the shopping. If the afternoon was fine we either went for a walk in the country or a visit to Mother's great friend in the convent, Mother St. Dominic. Mother had them all praying for Father, and every night, going to bed, I asked God to send him back safe from the war to us. Little, indeed, did I know what I was praying for!

One morning, I got into the big bed, and there, sure enough, was Father in his usual Santa Claus manner, but later, instead of uniform, he put on his best blue suit, and Mother was as pleased as anything. I saw nothing to be pleased about, because, out of uniform, Father was altogether less interesting, but she only beamed, and explained that our prayers had been answered, and off we went to Mass to thank God for having brought Father safely home.

The irony of it! That very day when he came in to dinner he took off his boots and put on his slippers, donned the dirty old cap he wore about the house to save him from colds, crossed his legs, and began to talk gravely to Mother, who looked anxious. Naturally, I disliked her looking anxious, because it destroyed her good looks, so I interrupted him.

"Just a moment, Larry!" she said gently.

This was only what she said when we had boring visitors, so I attached no importance to it and went on talking.

"Do be quiet, Larry!" she said impatiently. "Don't you hear me talking to Daddy?"

This was the first time I had heard those ominous words, "talking to Daddy," and I couldn't help feeling that if this was how God answered prayers, he couldn't listen to them very attentively.

"Why are you talking to Daddy?" I asked with as great a show of indifference as I could muster.

"Because Daddy and I have business to discuss. Now, don't interrupt again!"

In the afternoon, at Mother's request, Father took me for a walk. This time we went into town instead of out to the country, and I thought at first, in my usual optimistic way, that it might be an improvement. It was nothing of the sort. Father and I had quite different notions of a walk in town. He had no proper interest in trams, ships, and horses, and the only thing that seemed to divert him was talking to fellows as old as himself. When I wanted to stop he simply went on, dragging me behind him by the hand; when he wanted to stop I had no alternative but to do the same. I noticed that it seemed to be a sign that he wanted to stop for a long time whenever he leaned against a wall. The second time I saw him do it I got wild. He seemed to be settling himself forever. I pulled him by the coat and trousers, but, unlike Mother who, if you were too persistent, got into a wax and said: "Larry, if you don't behave yourself, I'll give you a good slap," Father had an extraordinary capacity for amiable inattention. I sized him up and wondered would I cry, but he seemed to be too remote to be annoyed even by that. Really, it was like going for a walk with a mountain! He either ignored the wrenching and pummeling entirely, or else glanced down with a grin of amusement from his peak. I had never met anyone so absorbed in himself as he seemed.

At teatime, "talking to Daddy" began again, complicated this time by the fact that he had an evening paper, and every few minutes he put it down and told Mother something new out of it. I felt this was foul play. Man for man, I was prepared to compete with him any time for Mother's attention, but when he had it all made up for him by other people it left me no chance. Several times I tried to change the subject without success.

"You must be quiet while Daddy is reading, Larry," Mother said impatiently.

It was clear that she either genuinely liked talking to Father better than talking to me, or else that he had some terrible hold on her which made her afraid to admit the truth.

"Mummy," I said that night when she was tucking me up, "do you think if I prayed hard God would send Daddy back to the war?"

She seemed to think about that for a moment.

"No, dear," she said with a smile. "I don't think he would."

"Why wouldn't he, Mummy?"

"Because there isn't a war any longer, dear."

"But, Mummy, couldn't God make another war, if He liked?"

"He wouldn't like to, dear. It's not God who makes wars, but bad people."

"Oh!" I said.

I was disappointed about that. I began to think that God wasn't quite what he was cracked up to be.

Next morning I woke at my usual hour, feeling like a bottle of champagne. I put out my feet and invented a long conversation in which Mrs. Right talked of the trouble she had with her own father till she put him in the Home. I didn't quite know what the Home was but it sounded the right place for Father. Then I got my chair and stuck my head out of the attic window. Dawn was just breaking, with a guilty air that made me feel I had caught it in the act. My head bursting with stories and schemes, I stumbled in next door, and in the half-darkness scrambled into the big bed. There was no room at Mother's side so I had to get between her and Father. For the time being I had forgotten about him, and for several minutes I sat bolt upright, racking my brains to know what I could do with him. He was taking up more than his fair share of the bed, and I couldn't get comfortable, so I gave him several kicks that made him grunt and stretch. He made room all right, though. Mother waked and felt for me. I settled back comfortably in the warmth of the bed with my thumb in my mouth.

"Mummy!" I hummed, loudly and contentedly.

"Sssh! dear," she whispered. "Don't wake Daddy!"

This was a new development, which threatened to be even more serious than "talking to Daddy." Life without my early-morning conferences was unthinkable.

"Why?" I asked severely.

"Because poor Daddy is tired."

This seemed to me a quite inadequate reason, and I was sickened by the sentimentality of her "poor Daddy." I never liked that sort of gush; it always struck me as insincere.

"Oh!" I said lightly. Then in my most winning tone: "Do you know where I want to go with you today, Mummy?"

"No, dear," she sighed.

"I want to go down the Glen and fish for thornybacks with my new net, and then I want to go out to the Fox and Hounds, and—"

"Don't-wake-Daddy!" she hissed angrily, clapping her hand across my mouth.

But it was too late. He was awake, or nearly so. He grunted and reached for the matches. Then he stared incredulously at his watch.

"Like a cup of tea, dear?" asked Mother in a meek, hushed voice I had never heard her use before. It sounded almost as though she were afraid.

"Tea?" he exclaimed indignantly. "Do you know what the time is?"

"And after that I want to go up to Rathcooney Road," I said loudly, afraid I'd forget something in all those interruptions.

"Go to sleep at once, Larry!" she said sharply.

I began to snivel. I couldn't concentrate, the way that pair went on, and smothering my early-morning schemes was like burying a family from the cradle.

Father said nothing, but lit his pipe and sucked it, looking out into the shadows without minding Mother or me. I knew he was mad. Every time I made a remark Mother hushed me irritably. I was mortified. I felt it wasn't fair; there was even something sinister in it. Every time I had pointed out to her the waste of making two beds when we could both sleep in one, she had told me it was healthier like that, and now here was this man, this stranger, sleeping with her without the least regard for her health!

He got up early and made tea, but though he brought Mother a cup he brought none for me.

"Mummy," I shouted, "I want a cup of tea, too."

"Yes, dear," she said patiently. "You can drink from Mummy's saucer."

That settled it. Either Father or I would have to leave the house. I didn't want to drink from Mother's saucer; I wanted to be treated as an equal in my own home, so, just to spite her, I drank it all and left none for her. She took that quietly, too.

But that night when she was putting me to bed she said gently:

"Larry, I want you to promise me something."

"What is it?" I asked.

"Not to come in and disturb poor Daddy in the morning. Promise?"

"Poor Daddy" again! I was becoming suspicious of everything involving that quite impossible man.

"Why?" I asked.

"Because poor Daddy is worried and tired and he doesn't sleep well."

"Why doesn't he, Mummy?"

"Well, you know, don't you, that while he was at the war Mummy got the pennies from the Post Office?"

"From Miss MacCarthy?"

"That's right. But now, you see, Miss MacCarthy hasn't any more pennies, so Daddy must go out and find us some. You know what would happen if he couldn't?"

"No," I said, "tell us."

"Well, I think we might have to go out and beg for them like the poor old woman on Fridays. We wouldn't like that, would we?"

"No," I agreed. "We wouldn't."

"So you'll promise not to come in and wake him?"

"Promise."

Mind you, I meant that. I knew pennies were a serious matter, and I was all against having to go out and beg like the old woman on Fridays. Mother laid out all my toys in a complete ring round the bed so that, whatever way I got out, I was bound to fall over one of them.

When I woke I remembered my promise all right. I got up and sat on the floor and played—for hours, it seemed to me. Then I got my chair and looked out the attic window for more hours. I wished it was time for Father to wake; I wished someone would make me a cup of tea. I didn't feel in the least like the sun; instead, I was bored and so very, very cold! I simply longed for the warmth and depth of the big featherbed.

At last I could stand it no longer. I went into the next room. As there was still no room at Mother's side I climbed over her and she woke with a start.

"Larry," she whispered, gripping my arm very tightly, "what did you promise?"

"But I did, Mummy," I wailed, caught in the very act. "I was quiet for ever so long."

"Oh, dear, and you're perished!" she said sadly, feeling me all over. "Now, if I let you stay will you promise not to talk?"

"But I want to talk, Mummy," I wailed.

"That has nothing to do with it," she said with a firmness that was new to me. "Daddy wants to sleep. Now, do you understand that?"

I understood it only too well. I wanted to talk, he wanted to sleep—whose house was it, anyway?

"Mummy," I said with equal firmness, "I think it would be healthier for Daddy to sleep in his own bed."

That seemed to stagger her, because she said nothing for a while.

"Now, once for all," she went on, "you're to be perfectly quiet or go back to your own bed. Which is it to be?"

The injustice of it got me down. I had convicted her out of her own mouth of inconsistency and unreasonableness, and she hadn't even attempted to reply. Full of spite, I gave Father a kick, which she didn't notice but which made him grunt and open his eyes in alarm.

"What time is it?" he asked in a panic-stricken voice, not looking at Mother but at the door, as if he saw someone there.

"It's early yet," she replied soothingly. "It's only the child. Go to sleep again. . . . Now, Larry," she added, getting out of bed, "you've wakened Daddy and you must go back."

This time, for all her quiet air, I knew she meant it, and knew that my principal rights and privileges were as good as lost unless I asserted them at once. As she lifted me, I gave a screech, enough to wake the dead, not to mind Father. He groaned.

"That damn child! Doesn't he ever sleep?"

"It's only a habit, dear," she said quietly, though I could see she was vexed.

"Well, it's time he got out of it," shouted Father, beginning to heave in the bed. He suddenly gathered all the bedclothes about him, turned to the wall, and then looked back over his shoulder with nothing showing only two small, spiteful, dark eyes. The man looked very wicked.

To open the bedroom door, Mother had to let me down, and I broke free and dashed for the farthest corner, screeching. Father sat bolt upright in bed.

"Shut up, you little puppy!" he said in a choking voice.

I was so astonished that I stopped screeching. Never, never had anyone spoken to me in that tone before. I looked at him incredulously and saw his face convulsed with rage. It was only then that I fully realized how God had codded me, listening to my prayers for the safe return of this monster.

"Shut up, you!" I bawled, beside myself.

"What's that you said?" shouted Father, making a wild leap out of the bed.

"Mick, Mick!" cried Mother. "Don't you see the child isn't used to you?"

"I see he's better fed than taught," snarled Father, waving his arms wildly. "He wants his bottom smacked."

All his previous shouting was as nothing to these obscene words referring to my person. They really made my blood boil.

"Smack your own!" I screamed hysterically. "Smack your own! Shut up! Shut up!"

At this he lost his patience and let fly at me. He did it with the lack of conviction you'd expect of a man under Mother's horrified eyes, and it ended up as a mere tap, but the sheer indignity of being struck at all by a stranger, a total stranger who had cajoled his way back from the war into our big bed as a result of my innocent intercession, made me completely dotty. I shrieked and shrieked, and danced in my bare feet, and Father, looking awkward and hairy in nothing but a short grey army shirt, glared down at me like a mountain out for murder. I think it must have been then that I realized he was jealous too. And there stood Mother in her nightdress, looking as if her heart was broken between us. I hoped she felt as she looked. It seemed to me that she deserved it all.

From that morning out my life was a hell. Father and I were enemies, open and avowed. We conducted a series of skirmishes against one another, he trying to steal my time with Mother and I his. When she was sitting on my bed, telling me a story, he took to looking for some pair of old boots which he alleged he had left behind him at the beginning of the war. While he talked to Mother I played loudly with my toys to show my total lack of concern. He created a terrible scene one evening when he came in from work and found me at his box, playing with his regimental badges, Gurkha knives and button-sticks. Mother got up and took the box from me.

"You mustn't play with Daddy's toys unless he lets you, Larry," she said severely. "Daddy doesn't play with yours."

For some reason Father looked at her as if she had struck him and then turned away with a scowl.

"Those are not toys," he growled, taking down the box again to see had I lifted anything. "Some of those curios are very rare and valuable."

But as time went on I saw more and more how he managed to alienate Mother and me. What made it worse was that I couldn't grasp his method or see what attraction he had for Mother. In every possible way he was less winning than I. He had a common accent and made noises at his tea. I thought for a while that it might be the newspapers she was interested in, so I made up bits of news of my own to read to her. Then I thought it might be the smoking, which I personally thought attractive, and took his pipes and went round the house dribbling into them till he caught me. I even made noises at my tea, but Mother only told me I was disgusting. It all seemed to hinge round that unhealthy habit of sleeping together, so I made a point of dropping into their bedroom and nosing round, talking to myself, so that they wouldn't know I was watching them, but they were never up to anything that I could see. In the end it beat me. It seemed to depend on being grown-up and giving people rings, and I realized I'd have to wait.

But at the same time I wanted him to see that I was only waiting, not giving up the fight. One evening when he was being particularly obnoxious, chattering away well above my head, I let him have it.

"Mummy," I said, "do you know what I'm going to do when I grow up?"

"No dear," she replied. "What?"

"I'm going to marry you," I said quietly.

Father gave a great guffaw out of him, but he didn't take me in. I knew it must only be pretence. And Mother, in spite of everything, was pleased. I felt she was probably relieved to know that one day Father's hold on her would be broken.

"Won't that be nice?" she said with a smile.

"It'll be very nice," I said confidently. "Because we're going to have lots and lots of babies."

"That's right, dear," she said placidly. "I think we'll have one soon, and then you'll have plenty of company."

I was no end pleased about that because it showed that in spite of the way she gave in to Father she still considered my wishes. Besides, it would put the Geneys in their place.

It didn't turn out like that, though. To begin with, she was very preoccupied— I supposed about where she would get the seventeen and six—and though Father took to staying out late in the evenings it did me no particular good. She stopped taking me for walks, became as touchy as blazes, and smacked me for nothing at all. Sometimes I wished I'd never mentioned the confounded baby—I seemed to have a genius for bringing calamity on myself.

And calamity it was! Sonny arrived in the most appalling hullabaloo—even that much he couldn't do without a fuss—and from the first moment I disliked him. He was a difficult child—so far as I was concerned he was always difficult—and demanded far too much attention. Mother was simply silly about him, and couldn't see when he was only showing off. As company he was worse than useless. He slept all day, and I had to go round the house on tiptoe to avoid waking him. It wasn't any longer a question of not waking Father. The slogan now was "Don't-wake-Sonny!" I couldn't understand why the child wouldn't sleep at the proper time, so whenever Mother's back was turned I woke him. Sometimes to keep him awake I pinched him as well. Mother caught me at it one day and gave me a most unmerciful flaking.

One evening, when Father was coming in from work, I was playing trains in the front garden. I let on not to notice him; instead, I pretended to be talking to myself, and said in a loud voice: "If another bloody baby comes into this house, I'm going out."

Father stopped dead and looked at me over his shoulder.

"What's that you said?" he asked sternly.

"I was only talking to myself," I replied, trying to conceal my panic. "It's private."

He turned and went in without a word. Mind you, I intended it as a solemn warning, but its effect was quite different. Father started being quite nice to me. I could understand that, of course. Mother was quite sickening about Sonny. Even at mealtimes she'd get up and gawk at him in the cradle with an idiotic smile, and tell Father to do the same. He was always polite about it, but he looked so puzzled you could see he didn't know what she was talking about. He complained of the way Sonny cried at night, but she only got cross and said that Sonny never cried except when there was something up with him—which was a flaming lie, because Sonny never had anything up with him, and only cried for attention. It was really painful to see how simple-minded she was. Father wasn't attractive, but he had a fine intelligence. He saw through Sonny, and now he knew that I saw through him as well.

One night I woke with a start. There was someone beside me in the bed. For one wild moment I felt sure it must be mother, having come to her senses and left Father for good, but then I heard Sonny in convulsions in the next room, and Mother saying: "There! There! There!" and I knew it wasn't she. It was Father. He was lying beside me, wide awake, breathing hard and apparently as mad as hell.

After a while it came to me what he was mad about. It was his turn now. After turning me out of the big bed, he had been turned out himself. Mother had no consideration now for anyone but that poisonous pup, Sonny. I couldn't help feeling sorry for Father. I had been through it all myself, and even at that age I was magnanimous. I began to stroke him down and say: "There! There!" He wasn't exactly responsive.

"Aren't you asleep either?" he snarled.

"Ah, come on and put your arm around us, can't you?" I said, and he did, in a sort of way. Gingerly, I suppose, is how you'd describe it. He was very bony but better than nothing.

At Christmas he went out of his way to buy me a really nice model railway.

Immediately we notice that O'Connor, in contrast to Freud, is communicating an imagined experience. Where Freud has covered a large number of typical family situations, O'Connor confines the scope of his story to one particular family. Whereas Freud cites actual words, actions, and attitudes of children and parents, O'Connor invents conversations and incidents. The most obvious difference between the two selections, then, is simply this: Freud presents the typical and real, O'Connor the specific and imaginary. But there is also an important difference in the organizations of the two selections. Freud proceeds from a generalization to the inductive evidence that substantiates the generalization, pausing as he sees fit to answer objections and elaborate potentially difficult observations. O'Connor proceeds chronologically, shaping his incidents into a story and at the same time developing the psychological antagonism between the boy and the father. Throughout, the different intentions of the two writers lead to differences in selection and arrangement. Freud wishes to convince and inform, O'Connor to tell a meaningful story.

As a result, when we read the short story, we react differently from the way we react when we read Freud's analysis. While reading Freud, we react intellectually, we try to understand and evaluate the argument. While reading the short story, we react both intellectually and emotionally, we have a sense of sharing an experience. We share the dismay of the boy, the irritation of the father, and the discomfort of the mother caught between the two.

At least part of our emotional reaction comes about because O'Connor, unlike Freud, shows his own feelings about his subject matter. The details and the wording indicate what the author's emotions are. Leo Stein suggested a contrast that we notice in these selections when he said:

Art is the union of man and nature; its realities are essentially man-made. Science is the separation of man and nature, so far as in a man's universe this is possible. Science tries to see things as a . . . robot intelligence, would see them. It prefers the testimony of a registering apparatus . . . to the testimony of "a simple separate person." But without that simple separate person, there is no art.

To sum up, O'Connor, the artist, unlike Freud, the scientist, does not hesitate to invent, recreate. We see his imagination at work covering the bare skeletal "fact" of psychological conflict with the flesh and integument of "fiction": memorable characters, vivid incidents and conversations, humor, and a touch of pathos.

These, then, are some of the differences between one literary and one factual handling of similar materials. How many of the contrasts noticed between the selection from Freud, on the one hand, and from O'Connor, on the other, will be found if similar contrasts are made between other parallel factual and literary accounts? What generalizations are possible about the aims and the methods of imaginative authors, whether they write fiction or drama or poetry? What do these generalizations mean to you as readers? These are questions which you are to try to solve as you study the selections which follow.

Your purpose as you read the following two selections—one factual, one imaginative—and answer the questions about them is to test and supplement what has been said in the previous pages about the aims and methods of imaginative literature.

Encyclopaedia Britannica

DANDELION

DANDELION *(Taraxacum officinale)* and related species, perennial herbs belonging to the family Compositae *(q.v.)*. The plant has a wide range, being found in Europe and central Asia. Elsewhere it has become a cosmopolitan and

From *Encyclopædia Britannica*, Encyclopædia Britannica, Inc., 1964.

pestiferous weed, especially in North America. The leaves form a spreading
rosette on the very short stem; they are smooth, of a bright shining green,
sessile and tapering downward. The name dandelion is derived from the French
dent-de-lion (lion's tooth), an appellation given on account of the toothlike lobes
of the leaves. The long taproot makes it somewhat difficult to eradicate. The
flower stalks (scapes) are smooth, leafless, hollow and numerous. The flowers
bloom nearly throughout the year. The flower heads are golden yellow, and
reach one and one-half to two inches in width; the florets are all strap-shaped.
The fruits are olive or dull yellow in colour, and are each surmounted by a long
beak, on which rests a pappus of delicate white hairs, which occasions the ready
dispersal of the fruit by the wind; each fruit contains one seed. The globes
formed by the plumed fruits are nearly two inches in diameter. The involucre
consists of an outer spreading (or reflexed) and an inner erect row of bracts.
In all parts of the plant a milky juice is present. The root externally is brown
and wrinkled, internally white, with a yellow centre and concentric paler rings.
It is two inches to one foot long, and about one-fourth inch to one-half inch in
diameter. . . . The eradication of dandelions is easy if few plants are involved.
Digging the roots is the most effective. If infestation is severe a spray of 2,4-D
applied in warm sunlight is fatal, but it must cover the foliage.

James Russell Lowell

TO THE DANDELION

Dear common flower, that grow'st beside the way,
Fringing the dusty road with harmless gold,
   First pledge of blithesome May,
Which children pluck, and, full of pride, uphold,
   High-hearted buccaneers, o'erjoyed that they   5
An Eldorado in the grass have found,
    Which not the rich earth's ample round
   May match in wealth,—thou art more dear to me
   Than all the prouder summer-blooms may be.

Gold such as thine ne'er drew the Spanish prow   10
Through the primeval hush of Indian seas,
   Nor wrinkled the lean brow
Of age, to rob the lover's heart of ease,

'Tis the spring's largess, which she scatters now
To rich and poor alike, with lavish hand,   15
    Though most hearts never understand
To take it at God's value, but pass by
The offered wealth with unrewarded eye.

Thou art my tropics and mine Italy;
To look at thee unlocks a warmer clime;   20
    The eyes thou givest me
Are in the heart, and heed not space or time:
    Not in mid June the golden cuirassed bee
Feels a more summer-like warm ravishment
    In the white lily's breezy tent,   25
    His fragrant Sybaris, than I, when first
From the dark green thy yellow circles burst.

Then think I of deep shadows on the grass,
Of meadows where in sun the cattle graze,
    Where, as the breezes pass,   30
The gleaming rushes lean a thousand ways,
    Of leaves that slumber in a cloudy mass,
Or whiten in the wind, of waters blue
    That from the distance sparkle through
    Some woodland gap, and of a sky above,   35
    Where one white cloud like a stray lamb doth move.

My childhood's earliest thoughts are linked with thee;
The sight of thee calls back the robin's song,
    Who, from the dark old tree
Beside the door, sang clearly all day long,   40
    And I, secure in childish piety,   .
Listened as if I heard an angel sing
    With news from heaven, which he could bring
    Fresh every day to my untainted ears,
    When birds and flowers and I were happy peers.   45

How like a prodigal doth nature seem,
When thou, for all thy gold, so common art!
    Thou teachest me to deem
More sacredly of every human heart,
    Since each reflects in joy its scanty gleam   50
Of heaven and could some wondrous secret show
    Did we but pay the love we owe,
    And with a child's undoubting wisdom look
    On all these living pages of God's book. (1844; 1845)

QUESTIONS

1. What do the writers of the *Britannica* selection seem to suppose the reader of their article is looking for? How have they organized the information about the dandelion? How does the organization reflect the purpose of the article?

2. What is the purpose of Lowell's poem? Lowell once wrote of nature "as a strengthener and consoler, a wholesome tonic for a mind ill at ease with itself . . . correcting it with rebuke or lifting it away from its unmanly depression. . . ." Does the poem embody such a view of nature? How is the poem organized? Toward what climax of feeling or thought does it progress?

3. Account for the differences in detail in the two pieces. What qualities of the dandelion are emphasized in each? Would it have been appropriate for Lowell to introduce the etymology of the word *dandelion*? Explain.

4. What is the attitude of the writers of the encyclopedia article toward the dandelion? Do they find it beautiful, useful, a nuisance, or what? What is Lowell's attitude toward the dandelion? Does Lowell take in account the fact that many people do not value the dandelion? How?

5. Discuss the differences between the kinds of language used in the two pieces of writing. How is this difference, in your opinion, related to the contrasting aims and methods of the writers?

So far the contrasts you have found between factual writing and imaginative writing have been relatively easy ones to formulate because the factual passages involved have been "purely" factual. Some factual works, however, have aims and appeals in some ways like those of literature. Histories and biographies are likely to offer us entertainment, excitement, and vivid depictions of characters and actions. How do such writings as these contrast with stories, plays, and poems?

To answer this question, contrast a passage from *The Life of Brutus* by the famous Greek biographer Plutarch with a passage from Shakespeare's *Julius Caesar*. Both passages concern the same characters and practically the same events, and both selections are by masters, and differences, therefore, will not result from the ineptitude of either author. If you have read *Julius Caesar*, you will recall what happened before these passages begin: Julius Caesar, having won fame as a military leader and a governor, attained the height of his glory in 44 B.C., when he was made dictator of Rome "for life." Some Romans became fearful that he had won too much power. A group therefore conspired against him, led by Brutus, a high-minded but somewhat impractical idealist. On March 15, the conspirators slew Caesar. Most of the conspirators wanted to slay Antony also, but they were dissuaded by Brutus. Both passages begin with a meeting of the conspirators following the assassination.

Plutarch

from THE LIFE OF BRUTUS

When this was done, they came to talk of Cæsar's will and testament, and of his funerals and tomb. Then Antonius thinking good his testament should be read openly, and also that his body should be honourably buried, and not in hugger-mugger, lest the people might thereby take occasion to be worse offended if they did otherwise: Cassius stoutly spake against it.

But Brutus went with the motion, and agreed unto it: wherein it seemeth he committed a second fault. For the first fault he did was, when he would not consent to his fellow-conspirators, that Antonius should be slain. And therefore he was justly accused, that thereby he had saved and strengthened a strong and grievous enemy of their conspiracy. The second fault was, when he agreed that Cæsar's funerals should be as Antonius would have them: the which indeed marred all. For first of all, when Cæsar's testament was openly read among them, whereby it appeared that he bequeathed unto every citizen of Rome, seventy-five drachmas a man, and that he left his gardens and arbours unto the people, which he had on this side of the river of Tiber, in the place where now the temple of Fortune is built: the people then loved him, and were marvellous sorry for him.

Afterwards when Cæsar's body was brought into the market-place, Antonius making his funeral oration in praise of the dead, according to the ancient custom of Rome, and perceiving that his words moved the common people to compassion: he framed his eloquence to make their hearts yearn the more, and taking Cæsar's gown all bloody in his hand, he laid it open to the sight of them all, shewing what a number of cuts and holes it had upon it.

Therewithal the people fell presently into such a rage and mutiny, that there was no more order kept amongst the common people. For some of them cried out, Kill the murtherers: others plucked up forms, tables, and stalls about the market-place, as they had done before at the funerals of Clodius, and having laid them all on a heap together, they set them on fire, and thereupon did put the body of Cæsar, and burnt it in the midst of the most holy places. And furthermore, when the fire was thoroughly kindled, some here, some there, took burning firebrands, and ran with them to the murderers' houses that had killed him, to set them afire. Howbeit the conspirators, foreseeing the danger before, had wisely provided for themselves and fled.

William Shakespeare

from THE TRAGEDY OF JULIUS CAESAR

Act III, Scene i. Rome. Before the Capitol.

(*Enter a* SERVANT)
BRUTUS. Soft! who comes here? A friend of Antony's.
SERVANT. Thus, Brutus, did my master bid me kneel;
    Thus did Mark Antony bid me fall down;
    And, being prostrate, thus he bade me say: 125
    Brutus is noble, wise, valiant, and honest;
    Cæsar was mighty, bold, royal, and loving;
    Say I love Brutus, and I honor him;
    Say I fear'd Cæsar, honor'd him, and lov'd him.
    If Brutus will vouchsafe that Antony   130
    May safely come to him, and be resolv'd
    How Cæsar hath deserv'd to lie in death,
    Mark Antony shall not love Cæsar dead
    So well as Brutus living; but will follow
    The fortunes and affairs of noble Brutus   135
    Thorough the hazards of this untrod state
    With all true faith. So says my master Antony.
BRUTUS. Thy master is a wise and valiant Roman;
    I never thought him worse.
    Tell him, so please him come unto this place,   140
    He shall be satisfied, and, by my honor,
    Depart untouch'd.
  SERVANT.   I'll fetch him presently. (*Exit*)
BRUTUS. I know that we shall have him well to friend.
CASSIUS. I wish we may, but yet have I a mind
    That fears him much, and my misgiving still   145
    Falls shrewdly to the purpose.
(*Re-enter* ANTONY)
BRUTUS. But here comes Antony. Welcome, Mark Antony!
ANTONY. O mighty Cæsar! dost thou lie so low?
    Are all thy conquests, glories, triumphs, spoils,
    Shrunk to this little measure? Fare thee well!   150
    I know not, gentlemen, what you intend,

---

122. *Soft!* an interjection meaning "Wait!" **126.** *honest,* honorable. **131.** *be resolv'd,* have his doubts dispelled. **136.** *Thorough,* a dissyllabic form of "through." **140.** *so please him,* if it please him. **142.** *presently,* immediately. **143.** *to friend,* as a friend. **145.** *still,* always. **146.** *shrewdly,* mischievously. Hence the meaning is "When I have misgivings, they always turn out to be mischievously correct."

Who else must be let blood, who else is rank;
If I myself, there is no hour so fit
As Cæsar's death's hour, nor no instrument
Of half that worth as those your swords, made rich   155
With the most noble blood of all this world.
I do beseech ye, if you bear me hard,
Now, whilst your purpled hands do reek and smoke,
Fulfil your pleasure. Live a thousand years,
I shall not find myself so apt to die;   160
No place will please me so, no mean of death,
As here by Cæsar, and by you cut off,
The choice and master spirits of this age.

BRUTUS. O Antony, beg not your death of us.
Though now we must appear bloody and cruel,   165
As, by our hands and this our present act,
You see we do, yet see you but our hands
And this the bleeding business they have done.
Our hearts you see not; they are pitiful;
And pity to the general wrong of Rome—   170
As fire drives out fire, so pity pity—
Hath done this deed on Cæsar. For your part,
To you our swords have leaden points, Mark Antony:
Our arms, in strength of malice, and our hearts
Of brothers' temper, do receive you in   175
With all kind love, good thoughts, and reverence.

CASSIUS. Your voice shall be as strong as any man's
In the disposing of new dignities.

BRUTUS. Only be patient till we have appeas'd
The multitude, beside themselves with fear,   180
And then we will deliver you the cause
Why I, that did love Cæsar when I struck him,
Have thus proceeded.

ANTONY.   I doubt not of your wisdom.
Let each man render me his bloody hand.
First, Marcus Brutus, will I shake with you;   185
Next, Caius Cassius, do I take your hand;
Now, Decius Brutus, yours; now yours, Metellus;
Yours, Cinna; and, my valiant Casca, yours;
Though last, not least in love, yours, good Trebonius.
Gentlemen all,—alas, what shall I say?   190

---

152. *let blood*, bled. An allusion to "bleeding" as a remedy for illness. *rank*, diseased from repletion. The remedy was blood-letting. **157.** *bear me hard*, bear a grudge against me. **158.** *purpled hands*, blood-covered hands. **159.** *Live*, if I live. **160.** *apt*, ready. **161.** *mean*, means. **162.** *by Caesar*, beside Caesar. **174.** *in strength of malice*, violent in enmity. **178.** *dignities*, offices. **181.** *deliver*, report.

My credit now stands on such slippery ground
That one of two bad ways you must conceit me,
Either a coward or a flatterer.
That I did love thee, Cæsar, O, 'tis true;
If then thy spirit look upon us now,   195
Shall it not grieve thee dearer than thy death,
To see thy Antony making his peace,
Shaking the bloody fingers of thy foes,
Most noble! in the presence of thy corse?
Had I as many eyes as thou hast wounds,   200
Weeping as fast as they stream forth thy blood,
It would become me better than to close
In terms of friendship with thine enemies.
Pardon me, Julius! Here wast thou bay'd, brave hart;
Here didst thou fall; and here thy hunters stand,   205
Sign'd in thy spoil, and crimson'd in thy Lethe.
O world, thou wast the forest to this hart;
And this, indeed, O world, the heart of thee.
How like a deer, strucken by many princes,
Dost thou here lie!   210

CASSIUS. Mark Anthony,—

ANTONY.   Pardon me, Caius Cassius.
The enemies of Cæsar shall say this;
Then, in a friend, it is cold modesty.

CASSIUS. I blame you not for praising Cæsar so;
But what compact mean you to have with us?   215
Will you be prick'd in number of our friends;
Or shall we on, and not depend on you?

ANTONY. Therefore I took your hands, but was indeed
Sway'd from the point, by looking down on Cæsar.
Friends am I with you all and love you all.   220
Upon this hope, that you shall give me reasons
Why and wherein Cæsar was dangerous.

BRUTUS. Or else were this a savage spectacle.
Our reasons are so full of good regard
That were you, Antony, the son of Cæsar,   225
You should be satisfied.

ANTONY.   That's all I seek;
And am, moreover, suitor that I may
Produce his body to the market-place;

191. *credit*, honor. 192. *conceit*, believe. 196. *dearer*, more keenly. 202. *close*, compromise.
204. *bay'd*, brought to bay. *hart*, a stag (a pun upon "heart" and "hart" is involved). 206.
Sign'd in, marked with the signs of. *Lethe*, oblivion, hence, death. 213. *modesty*, moderation.
215. *compact*, agreement. 216. *prick'd*, marked. 224. *full . . . regard*, worthy of approval,
well considered. 228. *Produce*, bring forward.

And in the pulpit, as becomes a friend,
Speak in the order of his funeral.   230
BRUTUS. You shall, Mark Antony.
CASSIUS.   Brutus, a word with you.
(*Aside to* BRUTUS) You know not what you do. Do not consent
That Antony speak in his funeral.
Know you how much the people may be mov'd
By that which he will utter?
BRUTUS.   By your pardon.   235
I will myself into the pulpit first,
And show the reason of our Cæsar's death.
What Antony shall speak, I will protest
He speaks by leave and by permission,
And that we are contented Cæsar shall   240
Have all true rites and lawful ceremonies.
It shall advantage more than do us wrong.
CASSIUS. I know not what may fall; I like it not.
BRUTUS. Mark Antony, here, take you Cæsar's body.
You shall not in your funeral speech blame us,   245
But speak all good you can devise of Cæsar,
And say you do't by our permission;
Else shall you not have any hand at all
About his funeral. And you shall speak
In the same pulpit whereto I am going,   250
After my speech is ended.
ANTONY.   Be it so.
I do desire no more.
BRUTUS. Prepare the body then, and follow us. (*Exeunt all but* ANTONY)
ANTONY. O, pardon me, thou bleeding piece of earth,
That I am meek and gentle with these butchers!   255
Thou art the ruins of the noblest man
That ever lived in the tide of times.
Woe to the hand that shed this costly blood!
Over thy wounds now do I prophesy,
Which, like dumb mouths, do ope their ruby lips,   260
To beg the voice and utterance of my tongue:
A curse shall light upon the limbs of men;
Domestic fury and fierce civil strife
Shall cumber all the parts of Italy;
Blood and destruction shall be so in use   265
And dreadful objects so familiar
That mothers shall but smile when they behold

230. *order,* course. 238. *protest,* make known. 242. *advantage,* benefit. 243. *fall,* befall.
257. *tide of times,* the ebb and flow of the ages. 264. *cumber,* encumber, burden. 266.
objects, sights.

Their infants quarter'd with the hands of war;
All pity chok'd with custom of fell deeds;
And Cæsar's spirit, ranging for revenge,   270
With Ate by his side come hot from hell,
Shall in these confines with a monarch's voice
Cry "Havoc," and let slip the dogs of war
That this foul deed shall smell above the earth
With carrion men, groaning for burial.   275
(Enter OCTAVIUS' SERVANT*)*
You serve Octavius Cæsar, do you not?
SERVANT. I do, Mark Antony.
ANTONY. Cæsar did write for him to come to Rome.
SERVANT. He did receive his letters, and is coming;
And bid me say to you by word of mouth—   280
O Cæsar!—*(Seeing the body)*
ANTONY. Thy heart is big; get thee apart and weep.
Passion, I see, is catching; for mine eyes,
Seeing those beads of sorrow stand in thine,
Began to water. Is thy master coming?   285
SERVANT. He lies to-night within seven leagues of Rome.
ANTONY. Post back with speed and tell him what hath chanc'd.
Here is a mourning Rome, a dangerous Rome,
No Rome of safety for Octavius yet;
Hie hence, and tell him so. Yet, stay a while;   290
Thou shalt not back till I have borne this corse
Into the market-place. There shall I try,
In my oration, how the people take
The cruel issue of these bloody men;
According to the which, thou shalt discourse   295
To young Octavius of the state of things.
Lend me your hand. *(Exeunt with Cæsar's body)*

Scene II. *Rome. The Forum.*

(Enter BRUTUS *and* CASSIUS, *with the* PLEBEIANS*)*
PLEBEIANS. We will be satisfied! Let us be satisfied!
BRUTUS. Then follow me, and give me audience, friends.
Cassius, go you into the other street,
And part the numbers.
Those that will hear me speak, let 'em stay here;   5

268. *quarter'd*, slaughtered. 269. *fell*, cruel. 271. *Ate*, goddess of vengeance. 272. *confines*, regions. 273. *"Havoc,"* a cry which meant "Kill without quarter." *let slip*, unleash. 274. *That*, so that. 275. *carrion*, dead and putrefying. 283. *Passion*, sorrow. 286. *lies*, is camped. 292. *try*, experiment to discover. 294. *issue*, deed. 295. *the which*, public sentiment.
ACT III, SCENE II. 1. *satisfied*, completely informed. 4. *part the numbers*, divide the crowd.

Those that will follow Cassius, go with him;
And public reasons shall be rendered
Of Cæsar's death.
1. PLEBEIAN.   I will hear Brutus speak.
2. PLEBEIAN. I will hear Cassius; and compare their reasons,
When severally we hear them rendered.   10
(Exit CASSIUS, *with some of the* PLEBEIANS. BRUTUS *goes into the pulpit)*
3. PLEBEIAN. The noble Brutus is ascended; silence!
BRUTUS. Be patient till the last.

Romans, countrymen, and lovers! hear me for my cause, and be silent,
that you may hear; believe me for mine honor, and have respect to
mine honor, that you may believe; censure me in your wisdom, and
awake your senses, that you may the better judge. If there be any
in this assembly, any dear friend of Cæsar's, to him I say, that Brutus'
love to Cæsar was no less than his. If then that friend demand why
Brutus rose against Cæsar, this is my answer: Not that I lov'd
Cæsar less, but that I lov'd Rome more. Had you rather Cæsar were
living and die all slaves, than that Cæsar were dead, to live all free-
men? As Cæsar lov'd me, I weep for him; as he was fortunate, I rejoice at it; as he was valiant, I honor him; but, as he was ambitious,
I slew him. There is tears for his love; joy for his fortune; honor for
his valor; and death for his ambition. Who is here so base that would
be a bondman? If any, speak; for him have I offended. Who is here
so rude that would not be a Roman? If any, speak; for him have I
offended. Who is here so vile that will not love his country? If any,
speak; for him have I offended. I pause for a reply.   37
ALL. None, Brutus, none.
BRUTUS. Then none have I offended. I have done no more to Cæsar than
you shall do to Brutus. The question of his death is enroll'd in the
Capitol; his glory not extenuated, wherein he was worthy, nor his
offences enforc'd, for which he suffered death.   44
(Enter ANTONY *and others, with Cæsar's body)*
Here comes his body, mourn'd by Mark Antony; who, though he had
no hand in his death, shall receive the benefit of his dying, a place in
the commonwealth; as which of you shall not? With this I depart,
that, as I slew my best lover for the good of Rome, I have the same
dagger for myself, when it shall please my country to need my death.
ALL. Live, Brutus! live, live!   53
1. PLEBEIAN. Bring him with triumph home unto his house.
2. PLEBEIAN. Give him a statue with his ancestors.   55
3. PLEBEIAN. Let him be Cæsar.

---

10. *severally*, individually. **17.** *censure*, judge. **18.** *senses*, intellectual powers. **34.** *rude*,
boorish. **41.** *question of . . . enroll'd.* The reasons for his death are recorded. **42.** *extenuated*,
understated. **43.** *enforc'd*, exaggerated.

....

4. PLEBEIAN.   Cæsar's better parts
   Shall be crown'd in Brutus.
1. PLEBEIAN.   We'll bring him to his house
   With shouts and clamors.
BRUTUS.   My countrymen,—
2. PLEBEIAN. Peace, silence! Brutus speaks.
1. PLEBEIAN.   Peace, ho!
BRUTUS. Good countrymen, let me depart alone,   60
   And, for my sake, stay here with Antony.
   Do grace to Cæsar's corpse, and grace his speech
   Tending to Cæsar's glories, which Mark Antony,
   By our permission, is allow'd to make.
   I do entreat you, not a man depart   65
   Save I alone, till Antony have spoke. *(Exit)*
1. PLEBEIAN. Stay, ho! and let us hear Mark Antony.
3. PLEBEIAN. Let him go up into the public chair;
   We'll hear him. Noble Antony, go up.
ANTONY. For Brutus' sake, I am beholding to you. *(Goes into the pulpit)*   70
4. PLEBEIAN. What does he say of Brutus?
3. PLEBEIAN.   He says, for Brutus' sake,
   He finds himself beholding to us all.
4. PLEBEIAN. 'Twere best he speak no harm of Brutus here.
1. PLEBEIAN. This Cæsar was a tyrant.
3. PLEBEIAN.   Nay, that's certain:
   We are blest that Rome is rid of him.   75
2. PLEBEIAN. Peace! let us hear what Antony can say.
ANTONY. You gentle Romans,—
ALL.   Peace, ho! let us hear him.
ANTONY. Friends, Romans, countrymen, lend me your ears!
   I come to bury Cæsar, not to praise him.
   The evil that men do lives after them;   80
   The good is oft interred with their bones.
   So let it be with Cæsar. The noble Brutus
   Hath told you Cæsar was ambitious;
   If it were so, it was a grievous fault,
   And grievously hath Cæsar answer'd it.   85
   Here, under leave of Brutus and the rest
   (For Brutus is an honorable man;
   So are they all, all honorable men),
   Come I to speak in Cæsar's funeral.
   He was my friend, faithful and just to me;   90
   But Brutus says he was ambitious,
   And Brutus is an honorable man.

---

70. *beholding,* beholden. **85.** *answer'd it,* paid for it. **90.** *just,* exact and punctual.

He hath brought many captives home to Rome,
Whose ransoms did the general coffers fill;
Did this in Cæsar seem ambitious?   95
When that the poor have cried, Cæsar hath wept;
Ambition should be made of sterner stuff.
Yet Brutus says he was ambitious,
And Brutus is an honorable man.
You all did see that on the Lupercal   100
I thrice presented him a kingly crown,
Which he did thrice refuse. Was this ambition?
Yet Brutus says he was ambitious,
And, sure, he is an honorable man.
I speak not to disprove what Brutus spoke,   105
But here I am to speak what I do know.
You all did love him once, not without cause;
What cause withholds you then to mourn for him?
O judgement! thou art fled to brutish beasts.
And men have lost their reason! Bear with me;   110
My heart is in the coffin there with Cæsar,
And I must pause till it come back to me.
1. PLEBEIAN. Methinks there is much reason in his sayings.
2. PLEBEIAN. If thou consider rightly of the matter.
Cæsar has had great wrong.
3. PLEBEIAN.   Has he not, masters?   115
I fear there will a worse come in his place.
4. PLEBEIAN. Mark'd ye his words? He would not take the crown;
Therefore 'tis certain he was not ambitious.
1. PLEBEIAN. If it be found so, some will dear abide it.
2. PLEBEIAN. Poor soul! his eyes are red as fire with weeping. 120
3. PLEBEIAN. There's not a nobler man in Rome than Antony.
4. PLEBEIAN. Now mark him, he begins again to speak.
ANTONY. But yesterday the word of Cæsar might
Have stood against the world. Now lies he there,
And none so poor to do him reverence.   125
O masters, if I were dispos'd to stir
Your hearts and minds to mutiny and rage,
I should do Brutus wrong, and Cassius wrong,
Who, you all know, are honorable men.
I will not do them wrong; I rather choose   130
To wrong the dead, to wrong myself and you,
Than I will wrong such honorable men.
But here's a parchment with the seal of Cæsar;

---

94. *general coffers*, public treasury. **119.** *dear abide it*, pay dearly for it. **125.** *to do*, as to do.

I found it in his closet; 'tis his will.
Let but the commons hear this testament—   135
Which (pardon me) I do not mean to read—
And they would go and kiss dead Cæsar's wounds
And dip their napkins in his sacred blood,
Yea, beg a hair of him for memory,
And, dying, mention it within their wills,   140
Bequeathing it as a rich legacy
Unto their issue.

4. PLEBEIAN. We'll hear the will. Read it, Mark Antony.

ALL. The will, the will! we will hear Cæsar's will.

ANTONY. Have patience, gentle friends, I must not read it; 145
It is not meet you know how Cæsar lov'd you.
You are not wood, you are not stones, but men:
And, being men, hearing the will of Cæsar,
It will inflame you, it will make you mad.
'Tis good you know not that you are his heirs;   150
For, if you should, O, what would come of it!

4. PLEBEIAN. Read the will; we'll hear it, Antony.
You shall read us the will, Cæsar's will.

ANTONY. Will you be patient? Will you stay a while?
I have o'ershot myself to tell you of it.   155
I fear I wrong the honorable men
Whose daggers have stabb'd Cæsar; I do fear it.

4. PLEBEIAN. They were traitors; honorable men!

ALL. The will! the testament!

2. PLEBEIAN. They were villains, murderers. The will! read the will.   160

ANTONY. You will compel me, then, to read the will?
Then make a ring about the corpse of Cæsar,
And let me show you him that made the will.
Shall I descend? and will you give me leave?

ALL. Come down.   165

2. PLEBEIAN. Descend.

3. PLEBEIAN. You shall have leave.

(ANTONY comes down from the pulpit)

4. PLEBEIAN. A ring; stand round.

1. PLEBEIAN. Stand from the hearse, stand from the body.

2. PLEBEIAN. Room for Antony, most noble Antony.   170

ANTONY. Nay, press not so upon me; stand far off.

ALL. Stand back; room; bear back!

ANTONY. If you have tears, prepare to shed them now.
You all do know this mantle; I remember

---

134. *closet*, private room. 135. *commons*, common people. 138. *napkins*, handkerchiefs.
169. *hearse*, bier.

The first time ever Cæsar put it on.   175
'Twas on a summer's evening, in his tent,
That day he overcame the Nervii.
Look, in this place ran Cassius' dagger through;
See what a rent the envious Casca made;
Through this the well-beloved Brutus stabb'd,   180
And as he pluck'd his cursed steel away,
Mark how the blood of Cæsar followed it,
As rushing out of doors, to be resolv'd
If Brutus so unkindly knock'd, or no;
For Brutus, as you know, was Cæsar's angel.   185
Judge, O you gods, how dearly Cæsar lov'd him!
This was the most unkindest cut of all;
For when the noble Cæsar saw him stab,
Ingratitude, more strong than traitors' arms,
Quite vanquish'd him. Then burst his mighty heart;   190
And, in his mantle muffling up his face,
Even at the base of Pompey's statue,
Which all the while ran blood, great Cæsar fell.
O, what a fall was there, my countrymen!
Then I, and you, and all of us fell down,   195
Whilst bloody treason flourish'd over us.
O, now you weep, and I perceive you feel
The dint of pity. These are gracious drops.
Kind souls, what, weep you when you but behold
Our Cæsar's vesture wounded? Look you here: *(Lifting Cæsar's mantle)*
Here is himself, marr'd, as you see, with traitors.   201
1. PLEBEIAN. O piteous spectacle!
2. PLEBEIAN. O noble Cæsar!
3. PLEBEIAN. O woeful day!
4. PLEBEIAN. O traitors, villains!   205
1. PLEBEIAN. O most bloody sight!
2. PLEBEIAN. We will be reveng'd!
ALL.   Revenge! About!
   Seek! Burn! Fire! Kill! Slay!
   Let not a traitor live!
ANTONY. Stay, countrymen.   210
1. PLEBEIAN. Peace there! hear the noble Antony.
2. PLEBEIAN. We'll hear him, we'll follow him, we'll die with him.
ANTONY. Good friends, sweet friends, let me not stir you up
   To such a sudden flood of mutiny.   215
   They that have done this deed are honorable.

---

179. *envious,* malicious. **183.** *resolv'd,* assured. **185.** *angel,* guardian spirit. **198.** *dint,* impact. **215.** *mutiny,* disorder.

What private griefs they have, alas, I know not,
That made them do it; they are wise and honorable,
And will, no doubt, with reasons answer you.
I come not, friends, to steal away your hearts.   220
I am no orator, as Brutus is;
But, as you know me all, a plain blunt man
That love my friend; and that they know full well
That gave me public leave to speak of him;
For I have neither wit, nor words, nor worth,   225
Action, nor utterance, nor the power of speech
To stir men's blood; I only speak right on.
I tell you that which you yourselves do know;
Show you sweet Cæsar's wounds, poor, poor, dumb mouths,
And bid them speak for me. But were I Brutus,   230
And Brutus Antony, there were an Antony
Would ruffle up your spirits, and put a tongue
In every wound of Cæsar, that should move
The stones of Rome to rise and mutiny.
ALL. We'll mutiny.   235
1. PLEBEIAN. We'll burn the house of Brutus!
3. PLEBEIAN. Away, then! come, seek the conspirators.
ANTONY. Yet hear me, countrymen; yet hear me speak.
ALL. Peace, ho! hear Antony, most noble Antony!
ANTONY. Why, friends, you go to do you know not what.   240
  Wherein hath Cæsar thus deserv'd your loves?
  Alas, you know not; I must tell you, then.
  You have forgot the will I told you of.
ALL. Most true. The will! Let's stay and hear the will.
ANTONY. Here is the will, and under Cæsar's seal.   245
  To every Roman citizen he gives,
  To every several man, seventy-five drachmas.
2. PLEBEIAN. Most noble Cæsar! We'll revenge his death.
3. PLEBEIAN. O royal Cæsar!
ANTONY. Hear me with patience.   250
ALL. Peace, ho!
ANTONY. Moreover, he hath left you all his walks,
  His private arbors and new-planted orchards,
  On this side Tiber; he hath left them you,
  And to your heirs forever, common pleasures,   255
  To walk abroad, and recreate yourselves.
  Here was a Cæsar! When comes such another?

---

225. *wit*, intelligence. 226. *Action*, gesture. *utterance*, good delivery. 232. *ruffle up*, arouse.
247. *drachmas*, Roman coins, each worth only about nineteen cents, but with a high purchasing power. 253. *orchards*, gardens. 255. *common pleasures*, parks.

1. PLEBEIAN. Never, never! Come, away, away!
   We'll burn his body in the holy place,
   And with the brands fire the traitors' houses.   260
   Take up the body.
2. PLEBEIAN. Go fetch fire!
3. PLEBEIAN. Pluck down benches!
4. PLEBEIAN. Pluck down forms, windows, anything!
(Exeunt PLEBEIANS *with the body)*
ANTONY. Now let it work. Mischief, thou art afoot.   265
   Take thou what course thou wilt!

QUESTIONS

1. State as specifically as you can the purposes of a typical biographer. To what extent does Plutarch achieve these purposes? Can you find, in this passage, any support for the claim of some that Plutarch was one of the "great" biographers?

2. (a) Plutarch says that Antony, in his talk with the conspirators, urged that Cæsar's will be made public. He also indicates that the will was read before the funeral address was delivered. What purposes of biography required that he set down these details?

(b) Shakespeare, by contrast, includes no mention of the will in Antony's conversation with the conspirators. Furthermore, he shows Antony first making public the contents of the will at the time when he delivers his funeral address. What purposes of drama—as distinguished from the purposes of biography—justified these manipulations?

3. Plutarch does not quote directly the remarks of any of the characters; Shakespeare quotes all their words throughout. Considering the different aims of the two authors, how may this difference be justified? (We don't want this answer: You don't have a play unless people talk.) Note, for instance, the protests of Cassius—III, i. 144-146, 211, 214-217, 232-235, 243.

4. Contrast the language employed by the two authors. How are the differences you find related to the differences between their aims?

5. Here are a few passages in the drama which parallel nothing in the biography and which, therefore, Shakespeare apparently invented. How did the invention and handling of each passage contribute to the drama—in other words, what justified his inventing the additional action?

(a) Antony's servant conveys Antony's regards and exacts a promise that Antony will not be harmed by the conspirators (III, i, 123-137). It may be helpful to compare these lines with Antony's speech (III, i, 151-163).

(b) Antony addresses the dead Cæsar (III, i, 148-150, 194-210, 254-275), converses with Octavius' servant (III, i, 276-296), and comments upon the results of his funeral address (III, ii, 265-266).

264. *forms,* long benches.

(c) Brutus makes a speech and the populace reacts to it (III, ii, 1-76). Contrast Antony's speech and the public reaction.

(d) Antony not only shows Cæsar's gown and the "number of cuts and holes it had upon it"; he points out exactly which hole was made by each of the conspirators (III, ii, 178-190).

6. (a) Granville Barker classifies Shakespeare's Brutus, Cassius, and Antony, respectively, as "the idealist, the egoist, and the opportunist." He says that "the contrast between them, the action and reaction of one upon the other, is most carefully contrived." Are his statements about these men and the contrast between them justified by this scene? Contrast the way Plutarch portrays them in his biography, and explain why his treatment has to be different.

(b) E. K. Chambers sees the conflict between Brutus and Antony as "righteousness massed against efficiency and showing itself clearly impotent in the unequal contest." "Had we only to do with the fate of individuals," he continues, "it might pass. But the selection of the artist makes the puppets more than individuals. They stand for spiritual forces, and in the spiritual order the triumph of efficiency over righteousness is tragic stuff." What does he mean? How valid is the claim as a statement about the play? As a statement about Plutarch's biography? What does your consideration of play and biography in this light suggest about the aims and methods of imaginative literature?

7. Why is it more difficult to formulate differences between Plutarch's biography and Shakespeare's scenes than between (a) the *Encyclopædia Britannica* writer and Lowell, (b) Freud and O'Connor?

8. On the basis of your reading so far, what generalizations are possible about (a) aims and methods of authors of imaginative works? (b) the values to the reader of imaginative literature?

9. What do your generalizations imply about an appropriate way to read fiction, drama, and poetry as contrasted with an appropriate way to read factual works?

Action

Your contrasts between factual writing and imaginative writing have shown you what the latter, in some instances at least, may do. As you read other imaginative works, you will, of course, enlarge your list of possible achievements. Just now it is enough to say that typical imaginative literature may effectively show human feelings, motives, actions, and experience; that such literature may embody an emotional interpretation—the author's interpretation—of life; and that imaginative literature, therefore, may affect not only the thoughts but also the feelings of the reader.

How does an author shape his writings so they will do these things?—that is the next question for you to consider. The world, as we know it, is a collection of varied scenes thronging with multitudes of people whose characters and actions vary greatly. The author, looking at the world in his own individual way, is eager to represent and interpret it in a story, a drama, or a poem. How will he go about his task?

He will, of course, select characters, action, and scenes. Suppose that he decides that he will write about one man of the many he knows in life and in books: suppose that he decides to write about Andrew Jackson. A scientific biographer of Jackson might feel impelled to set down every detail about Jackson ascertainable from birth to death. The imaginative author, by contrast, might treat only a few hours in Jackson's life (as Vachel Lindsay did in his poem, "Old, Old, Old Andrew Jackson"). And certainly the imaginative writer would include only those details, real and imagined, which he thought significant for his representation and interpretation. Every imaginative author thus selects and arranges details, and uses words as well as he can, to communicate his insights to the reader. He strives to make all the elements in his work, all his technical procedures, contribute to his saying what he has to say.

Your purpose as you study the rest of this section is to learn about the technique of the author—the selection, the arrangement, and the handling of the matter of life in fiction, drama, and poetry. In other words you will be studying the craftsmanship used in managing important elements in imaginative literature. The elements to be studied will include *Action, Characters, Setting, Language, Tone, Point of View, Atmosphere,* and *Meaning.*

SELECTION AND ARRANGEMENT OF ACTION

The action in an imaginative work ordinarily is not chosen or set down in an aimless and unthinking fashion. Rarely does a storyteller follow a character from his birth to his death: usually he follows him through only a few years, days, or even minutes. And even when his narrative covers a brief period, the author usually leaves out many details. Probably very few authors would say, for instance: "Pete awoke at seven, yawned, scratched his nose, cleared his throat, decided that he must get up, crawled out of the left side of bed, donned his slippers, went to the closet and got his bathrobe, went to the bathroom, took a shower, shaved, returned to the bedroom, dressed . . ." and so on interminably. A much wiser author might skip all these dull and meaningless details and simply write, "Next morning Pete, at the office, began work on the big deal." —A moment's examination of almost any imaginative work will show that the author has taken for granted some incidents, merely referred to others, and recounted still others in great detail. Often authors take still other liberties and arrange occurrences in orders which do not follow the order of time. For instance, an author may outline his whole story and then go back to the start and cover the same time span for a second time; or he may confine his narrative to a single scene and outline what has gone before and imply what will follow.

Such omissions, simplifications, and manipulations are justified if they help the author create a work with more form, and therefore with more articulated meaning and impact, than life has. When an author selects and arranges the action so that every gesture, every fleeting thought, every movement, and every deed has been related to a perceivable scheme or pattern, he has made a good start toward expressing such an articulated meaning. (The pattern itself, quite often, will have an implied meaning.) And when he has so handled other elements in the story—character and setting, for instance—as to make them, too, contribute their share to the whole work, the artist will have achieved his aim.

How, then, may an author select and arrange the action so that it will follow such a pattern? He may "plot" his narrative in such a way as to make it both complete and economical. His "plot," as we call a patterned series of interrelated happenings, will be complete if it tells one story from beginning to end. The completeness will be perceivable if the action adds up to a single significant change or lack of change, and if reasons may be found for the narrative's beginning, developing, and ending exactly as it does. The account will be economical if, as Edgar Allan Poe has put it in describing a perfect plot, "no part can be displaced without ruin to the whole." Aristotle, who, though a philosopher, had a good deal of common sense, suggested long ago that a patterned narrative— a plot—"must represent one action, a complete whole, with its several incidents so closely connected that the transposal or withdrawal of any one of them will disjoin and dislocate the whole."

PATTERNS OF ACTION

An author may create such a unified work in various ways. A detective story offers a completed line of action when it shows a brilliant sleuth who has been confronted with a problem working out a solution. The pattern properly starts with the problem and the detective, the development properly consists of a growing comprehension of the solution, and a proper ending is the solution of the problem. Another unified story may trace the growing love of a character for another from its beginning to an ending wherein the character's great love is proved beyond a doubt. Still another complete story—a typical one by Poe, say— may tell of a graduated development of some emotion, terror perhaps, which ends when the emotion reaches a crescendo. In still another unified story, an ambitious character may decide to reach some goal, he may then strive to reach it, and the story may conclude when the goal is reached. Thus action which adds up to a completely developed knowledge, a completely developed attitude, a completely developed emotion, or a completely developed achievement, may be a complete and economical whole. A scheme of this sort might be pictured thus: ⸻ The rising line would represent a graduated change.

Another type of story might tell of a character or situation which does *not* change. Suppose the leading character is a rascal at the start of the story, that most of the action consists of people's trying to convert him, and that, at the end, he continues to be a reprobate. The significant fact would be that the character remains the same throughout the story, and perhaps the picture would be this one: ____

Still another type of unified narrative might, by contrast, be pictured thus: ⌒⌒Such a "two part" or "complex" narrative would involve a reversal. There is such a reversal in the scenes from *Julius Caesar* (pp. 18-29): during the first (rising) part of the action, Brutus wins over the mob, then comes a turning point, or climax, and during the second (falling) part of the action, Antony, Brutus' rival, wins the mob's approval. In another such schematized narrative, after a character has been deceived for a time, he may catch a glimpse of truth, and from that time on his comprehension may grow. In still another, an emotion may change: terror, say, may be supplanted by bravery. Or a character, after progressing toward his goal, may fail. Such complex developments would contrast with the simple development of an attitude, or knowledge, or emotion, or achievement, described a couple of paragraphs ago. The counterpart of the reprobate story discussed above would, of course, be a narrative in which a character undergoes conversion.

CONFLICT

All three kinds of action patterns, more often than not, will involve one or more conflicts, contests between opposing forces—man versus nature, perhaps, man versus society, man versus "fate." Or the conflict may be an "internal" one—between two parts of a man's nature. In the simple scheme, one force will consistently move toward victory; in the "unchanging" scheme, a stubborn force will successfully resist change; in the complex scheme, one force will win for a time, and then the opposing force will gain the upper hand and go on to triumph.

In many narratives, not one but several strands such as these are followed to completion. In Steinbeck's *The Grapes of Wrath*, for instance, the characters battle against an economic situation and are rather consistently defeated; they triumph over the obstacles of nature as they make their way to California; and they gradually comprehend their problem and its solution.

An imaginative writer who deals with action, then, copes with the problem of finding some complete and economical scheme for plotting and relating his incidents. A careful reader has the task of seeing what the incidents in a narrative are and how the author gives—or fails to give—unity to the pattern of action.

This is a simple account in verse of the exciting and sad adventures of the woman Frankie and the man who "done her wrong." It has been memorized and sung by thousands of people, both educated and uneducated, who are evidently fascinated by the story and the way it is told. Who wrote the first version (about 1888), nobody knows, and nobody knows how the words went in that first version because people have sung it from memory and some have consciously or unconsciously changed it.

This does not mean—as the reader will see—that the account in the form presented below is not well handled.

Anonymous

FRANKIE AND JOHNNY

Frankie and Johnny were lovers, O, how that couple could love.
Swore to be true to each other, true as the stars above.
He was her man, but he done her wrong.

Frankie she was his woman, everybody knows.
She spent one hundred dollars for a suit of Johnny's clothes.   5
He was her man, but he done her wrong.

Frankie and Johnny went walking, Johnny in his bran' new suit,
"O good Lawd," says Frankie, "but don't my Johnny look cute?"
He was her man, but he done her wrong.

Frankie went down to Memphis; she went on the evening train.   10
She paid one hundred dollars for Johnny a watch and chain.
He was her man, but he done her wrong.

Frankie went down to the corner, to buy a glass of beer;
She says to the bartender, "Has my loving man been here?
He is my man; he wouldn't do me wrong."   15

"Ain't going to tell you no story, ain't going to tell you no lie,
I seen your man 'bout an hour ago with a girl named Alice Fry.
If he's your man, he's doing you wrong."

Frankie went back to the hotel, she didn't go there for fun,
Under her long red kimono she toted a forty-four gun.   20
He was her man, he was doing her wrong.

Frankie went down to the hotel, looked in the window so high,
There was her lovin' Johnny a-lovin' up Alice Fry;
He was her man, he was doing her wrong.

Frankie threw back her kimono; took out the old forty-four;   25
Roota-toot-toot, three times she shot, right through that hotel door.
She shot her man, 'cause he done her wrong.

Johnny grabbed off his Stetson. "O good Lawd, Frankie, don't shoot."
But Frankie put her finger on the trigger, and the gun went roota-toot-toot.
He was her man, but she shot him down.   30

"Roll me over easy, roll me over slow,
Roll me over easy, boys, 'cause my wounds is hurting me so,
I was her man, but I done her wrong."

With the first shot Johnny staggered; with the second shot he fell;
When the third bullet hit him, there was a new man's face in hell.   35
He was her man, but he done her wrong.

"Oh, bring on your rubber-tired hearses, bring on your rubber-tired hacks,
They're takin' Johnny to the buryin' groun' but they'll never bring him back.
He was my man, but he done me wrong."

ACTION

1. Does the action in this narrative have a unified pattern? If not, prove that it does not. If so, state the exact nature of the unity and justify your answer by referring to the text.

2. What do the repetitions and the variations in the final lines of all the stanzas accomplish in the telling of the story? Precisely how?

3. Lines 1-12 set forth the situation and acquaint us with each of the lovers. How do they do this? Thereafter, the rest of the narrative is presented in a series of scenes. How many scenes are there? How can you account for the relative length of the development of each? Is the omission of some events justified or unjustified?

4. Which of the following does Johnny have: vanity, good taste, impeccable manners, fickleness, complete lack of moral sense, gratitude? Point out passages which lead you to draw your conclusions about him. How do his qualities make possible some of the action? What kind of person is Frankie? Relate her qualities to the events in the poem.

5. Are some stanzas unnecessary? Would you suggest rearranging any of the stanzas? Why or why not?

6. One version of the song adds the following four stanzas to the stanzas we have given:

The judge he said to the jury, "It's plain as plain can be.
This woman shot her man, so it's murder in the second degree.
He was her man, though he done her wrong."

Now it wasn't murder in the second degree, it wasn't murder in the third.
Frankie simply dropped her man, like a hunter drops a bird.
He was her man, but he done her wrong.

"Oh, put me in that dungeon. Oh, put me in that cell.
Put me where the northeast wind blows from the southwest corner of hell.
I shot my man 'cause he done me wrong."

Frankie walked up to the scaffold, calm as a girl could be,
She turned her eyes to heaven and said, "Good Lord, I'm coming to thee.
He was my man, and I done him wrong."

How would the addition of these stanzas change the whole nature of the narrative? Would the new pattern be a unified one? How might Frankie's remark in the final line be justified as the culmination of the development which these stanzas trace?

7. In your opinion, does the action in this poem by itself account for the poem's continued fascination? If not, how would you account for the popularity of "Frankie and Johnny"?

Lord Dunsany by his own account devoted ninety-seven per cent of his life to athletic activities and only three per cent to writing. Included in the "athletic activities" was his service in the Boer War and World War I. Although his writing seemingly occupied a small part of his time, he was a prolific author of plays and short stories. The combination of melodrama and fantasy in this play, his most famous, is found in many of his works.

Lord Dunsany

A NIGHT AT AN INN

CHARACTERS

A. E. SCOTT-FORTESCUE (THE TOFF) *a dilapidated gentleman*
WILLIAM JONES (BILL)
ALBERT THOMAS *merchant sailors*
JACOB SMITH (SNIGGERS)
1ST PRIEST OF KLESH
2ND PRIEST OF KLESH
3RD PRIEST OF KLESH
KLESH

From *Plays of Gods and Men,* by Lord Dunsany. Courtesy of G. P. Putnam's Sons and Putnam and Company, Ltd.

The Curtain rises on a room in an inn. SNIGGERS *and* BILL *are talking.* THE TOFF *is reading a paper.* ALBERT *sits a little apart.*

SNIGGERS. What's his idea, I wonder?

BILL. I don't know.

SNIGGERS. And how much longer will he keep us here?

BILL. We've been here three days.

SNIGGERS. And 'aven't seen a soul.

BILL. And a pretty penny it cost us when he rented the pub.

SNIGGERS. 'Ow long did 'e rent the pub for?

BILL. You never know with him.

SNIGGERS. It's lonely enough.

BILL. 'Ow long did you rent the pub for, Toffy?

(THE TOFF *continues to read a sporting paper; he takes no notice of what is said*)

SNIGGERS. 'E's such a toff.

BILL. Yet 'e's clever, no mistake.

SNIGGERS. Those clever ones are the beggars to make a muddle. Their plans are clever enough, but they don't work, and then they make a mess of things much worse than you or me.

BILL. Ah!

SNIGGERS. I don't like this place.

BILL. Why not?

SNIGGERS. I don't like the looks of it.

BILL. He's keeping us here because here those niggers can't find us. The three heathen priests what was looking for us so. But we want to go and sell our ruby soon.

ALBERT. There's no sense in it.

BILL. Why not, Albert?

ALBERT. Because I gave those black devils the slip in Hull.

BILL. You give 'em the slip, Albert?

ALBERT. The slip, all three of them. The fellows with the gold spots on their foreheads. I had the ruby then, and I give them the slip in Hull.

BILL. How did you do it, Albert?

ALBERT. I had the ruby and they were following me . . .

BILL. Who told them you had the ruby? You didn't show it?

ALBERT. No . . . But they kind of know.

SNIGGERS. They kind of know, Albert?

ALBERT. Yes, they know if you've got it. Well, they sort of mouched after me, and I tells a policeman and he says, O they were only three poor niggers and they wouldn't hurt me. Ugh! When I thought of what they did in Malta to poor old Jim.

BILL. Yes, and to George in Bombay before we started.

SNIGGERS. Ugh!

BILL. Why didn't you give 'em in charge?

ALBERT. What about the ruby, Bill?

BILL. Ah!

ALBERT. Well, I did better than that. I walks up and down through Hull. I walks slow enough. And then I turns a corner and I runs. I never sees a corner but I turns it. But sometimes I let a corner pass just to fool them. I twists about like a hare. Then I sits down and waits. No priests.

SNIGGERS. What?

ALBERT. No heathen black devils with gold spots on their face. I gave 'em the slip.

BILL. Well done, Albert.

SNIGGERS (after a sigh of content). Why didn't you tell us?

ALBERT. 'Cause 'e won't let you speak. 'E's got 'is plans and 'e thinks we're silly folk. Things must be done 'is way. And all the time I've give 'em the slip. Might 'ave 'ad one o' them crooked knives in him before now but for me who give 'em the slip in Hull.

BILL. Well done, Albert.

SNIGGERS. Do you hear that, Toffy? Albert has give 'em the slip.

THE TOFF. Yes, I hear.

SNIGGERS. Well, what do you say to that?

THE TOFF. O . . . Well done, Albert.

ALBERT. And what a' you going to do?

THE TOFF. Going to wait.

ALBERT. Don't seem to know what 'e's waiting for.

SNIGGERS. It's a nasty place.

ALBERT. It's getting silly, Bill. Our money's gone and we want to sell the ruby. Let's get on to a town.

BILL. But 'e won't come.

ALBERT. Then we'll leave him.

SNIGGERS. We'll be all right if we keep away from Hull.

ALBERT. We'll go to London.

BILL. But 'e must 'ave 'is share.

SNIGGERS. All right. Only let's go. (To THE TOFF) We're going, do you hear? Give us the ruby.

THE TOFF. Certainly.

(He gives them a ruby from his waistcoat pocket: it is the size of a small hen's egg. He goes on reading his paper)

ALBERT. Come on, Sniggers. (Exeunt ALBERT and SNIGGERS)

BILL. Good-bye, old man. We'll give you your fair share, but there's nothing to do here, no girls, no halls, and we must sell the ruby.

THE TOFF. I'm not a fool, Bill.

BILL. No, no, of course not. Of course you ain't, and you've helped us a lot. Good-bye. You'll say good-bye?

THE TOFF. Oh, yes. Good-bye.

(Still reads paper. Exit BILL. THE TOFF puts a revolver on the table beside him and goes on with his paper)

SNIGGERS *(out of breath)*. We've come back, Toffy.

THE TOFF. So you have.

ALBERT. Toffy—how did they get here?

THE TOFF. They walked, of course.

ALBERT. But it's eighty miles.

SNIGGERS. Did you know they were here, Toffy?

THE TOFF. Expected them about now.

ALBERT. Eighty miles.

BILL. Toffy, old man—what are we to do?

THE TOFF. Ask Albert.

BILL. If they can do things like this there's no one can save us but you, Toffy —I always knew you were a clever one. We won't be fools any more. We'll obey you, Toffy.

THE TOFF. You're brave enough and strong enough. There isn't many that would steal a ruby eye out of an idol's head, and such an idol as that was to look at, and on such a night. You're brave enough, Bill. But you're all three of you fools. Jim would have none of my plans and where's Jim? And George. What did they do to him?

SNIGGERS. Don't, Toffy!

THE TOFF. Well, then, your strength is no use to you. You want cleverness; or they'll have you the way that they had George and Jim.

ALL. Ugh!

THE TOFF. Those black priests would follow you round the world in circles, year after year, till they got the idol's eye. And if we died with it they'd follow our grandchildren. That fool thinks he can escape men like that by running round three streets in the town of Hull.

ALBERT. God's truth, *you* 'aven't escaped them, because they're *'ere*.

THE TOFF. So I supposed.

ALBERT. You *supposed!*

THE TOFF. Yes, I believe there's no announcement in the Society papers. But I took this country seat especially to receive them. There's plenty of room if you dig; it is pleasantly situated and what is most important it is in a very quiet neighbourhood. So I am at home to them this afternoon.

BILL. Well, you're a deep one.

THE TOFF. And remember you've only my wits between you and death, and don't put your futile plans against those of an educated gentleman.

ALBERT. If you're a gentleman, why don't you go about among gentlemen instead of the likes of us?

THE TOFF. Because I was too clever for them as I am too clever for you.

ALBERT. Too clever for them?

THE TOFF. I never lost a game of cards in my life.

BILL. You never lost a game?

THE TOFF. Not when there was money on it.

BILL. Well, well.

THE TOFF. Have a game of poker?

ALL. No, thanks.

THE TOFF. Then do as you're told.

BILL. All right, Toffy.

SNIGGERS. I saw something just then. Hadn't we better draw the curtains?

THE TOFF. No.

SNIGGERS. What?

THE TOFF. Don't draw the curtains.

SNIGGERS. O all right.

BILL. But Toffy, they can see us. One doesn't let the enemy do that. I don't see why . . .

THE TOFF. No, of course you don't.

BILL. O all right, Toffy. *(All begin to pull out revolvers)*

THE TOFF *(putting his own away)*. No revolvers, please.

ALBERT. Why not?

THE TOFF. Because I don't want any noise at my party. We might get guests that hadn't been invited. *Knives* are a different matter.

(All draw knives. THE TOFF *signs to them not to draw them yet.* TOFFY *has already taken back his ruby)*

BILL. I think they're coming, Toffy.

THE TOFF. Not yet.

ALBERT. When will they come?

THE TOFF. When I am quite ready to receive them. Not before.

SNIGGERS. I should like to get this over.

THE TOFF. Should you? Then we'll have them now.

SNIGGERS. Now?

THE TOFF. Yes. Listen to me. You shall do as you see me do. You will all pretend to go out. I'll show you how. I've got the ruby. When they see me alone they will come for their idol's eye.

BILL. How can they tell like this which of us has it?

THE TOFF. I confess I don't know, but they seem to.

SNIGGERS. What will you do when they come in?

THE TOFF. I shall do nothing.

SNIGGERS. What?

THE TOFF. They will creep up behind me. Then my friends, Sniggers and Bill and Albert, who gave them the slip, will do what they can.

BILL. All right, Toffy. Trust us.

THE TOFF. If you're a little slow you will see enacted the cheerful spectacle that accompanied the demise of Jim.

SNIGGERS. Don't, Toffy. We'll be there all right.

THE TOFF. Very well. Now watch me. *(He goes past the windows to the inner door* R.; *he opens it inwards. Then under cover of the open door he slips down on his knee and closes it, remaining on the inside, appearing to have gone out. He signs to the others who understand. Then he appears to reënter in the same manner)* Now, I shall sit with my back to the door. You go out one by one so far as our friends can make out. Crouch very low to be on the safe side. They mustn't see you through the window. *(*BILL *makes his sham exit)* Remember, no revolvers. The police are, I believe, proverbially inquisitive.

(The other two follow BILL. *All three are now crouching inside the door* R. THE TOFF *puts the ruby beside him on the table. He lights a cigarette. The door in back opens so slowly that you can hardly say at what moment it began.* THE TOFF *picks up his paper. A* NATIVE OF INDIA *wriggles along the floor ever so slowly, seeking cover from chairs. He moves* L. *where* THE TOFF *is. The three sailors are* R. SNIGGERS *and* ALBERT *lean forward.* BILL's *arm keeps them back. An armchair had better conceal them from the* INDIAN. *The black* PRIEST *nears* THE TOFF. BILL *watches to see if any more are coming. Then he leaps forward alone [he has taken his boots off] and knifes the* PRIEST. *The* PRIEST *tries to shout but* BILL's *left hand is over his mouth.* THE TOFF *continues to read his sporting paper. He never looks round.)*

BILL *(sotto voce)*. There's only one, Toffy. What shall we do?

THE TOFF *(without turning his head)*. Only one?

BILL. Yes.

THE TOFF. Wait a moment. Let me think. *(Still apparently absorbed in his paper)* Ah, yes. You go back, Bill. We must attract another guest. Now are you ready?

BILL. Yes.

THE TOFF. All right. You shall now see my demise at my Yorkshire residence. You must receive guests for me. *(He leaps up in full view of the window, flings up both arms and falls on the floor near the dead* PRIEST.*)* Now be ready. *(His eyes close)*

(There is a long pause. Again the door opens, very, very slowly. Another PRIEST *creeps in. He has three golden spots upon his forehead. He looks round, then he creeps up to his companion and turns him over and looks inside each of his clenched hands. Then he looks at the recumbent* TOFF. *Then he creeps towards him.* BILL *slips after him and knifes him like the other with his left hand over his mouth)*

BILL *(sotto voce)*. We've only got two, Toffy.

THE TOFF. Still another.

BILL. What'll we do?

THE TOFF *(sitting up)*. Hum.

BILL. This is the best way, much.

THE TOFF. Out of the question. Never play the same game twice.

BILL. Why not, Toffy?

THE TOFF. Doesn't work if you do.

BILL. Well?

THE TOFF. I have it, Albert. You will now walk into the room. I showed you how to do it.

ALBERT. Yes.

THE TOFF. Just run over here and have a fight at this window with these two men.

ALBERT. But they're——

THE TOFF. Yes, they're dead, my perspicuous Albert. But Bill and I are going to resuscitate them——Come on. (BILL *picks up a body under the arms)* That's right, Bill. *(Does the same)* Come and help us, Sniggers. (SNIGGERS *comes)* Keep low, keep low. Wave their arms about, Sniggers. Don't show yourself. Now, Albert, over you go. Our Albert is slain. Back you get, Bill. Back, Sniggers. Still, Albert. Mustn't move when he comes. Not a muscle.

(A face appears at the window and stays for some time. Then the door opens and looking craftily round the third PRIEST *enters. He looks at his companions' bodies and turns round. He suspects something. He takes up one of the knives and with a knife in each hand he puts his back to the wall. He looks to the left and right)*

THE TOFF. Come on, Bill. *(The* PRIEST *rushes to the door.* THE TOFF *knifes the last* PRIEST *from behind)* A good day's work, my friends.

BILL. Well done, Toffy. Oh, you are a deep one.

ALBERT. A deep one if ever there was one.

SNIGGERS. There ain't any more, Bill, are there?

THE TOFF. No more in the world, my friend.

BILL. Aye, that's all there are. There were only three in the temple. Three priests and their beastly idol.

ALBERT. What is it worth, Toffy? Is it worth a thousand pounds?

THE TOFF. It's worth all they've got in the shop. Worth just whatever we like to ask for it.

ALBERT. Then we're millionaires, now.

THE TOFF. Yes, and what is more important, we no longer have any heirs.

BILL. We'll have to sell it now.

ALBERT. That won't be easy. It's a pity it isn't small and we had half a dozen. Hadn't the idol any other on him?

BILL. No, he was green jade all over and only had this one eye. He had it in the middle of his forehead, and was a long sight uglier than anything else in the world.

SNIGGERS. I'm sure we ought all to be very grateful to Toffy.

BILL. And indeed we ought.

ALBERT. If it hadn't 'ave been for him——

BILL. Yes, if it hadn't 'a' been for old Toffy . . .

SNIGGERS. He's a deep one.

THE TOFF. Well, you see, I just have a knack of foreseeing things.

SNIGGERS. I should think you did.

BILL. Why, I don't suppose anything happens that our Toff doesn't foresee. Does it, Toffy?

THE TOFF. Well, I don't think it does, Bill. I don't think it often does.

BILL. Life is no more than just a game of cards to our old Toff.

THE TOFF. Well, we've taken these fellows' trick.

SNIGGERS *(going to the window)*. It wouldn't do for any one to see them.

THE TOFF. O nobody will come this way. We're all alone on a moor.

BILL. Where will we put them?

THE TOFF. Bury them in the cellar, but there's no hurry.

BILL. And what then, Toffy?

THE TOFF. Why, then we'll go to London and upset the ruby business. We have really come through this job very nicely.

BILL. I think the first thing that we ought to do is to give a little supper to old Toffy. We'll bury these fellows to-night.

ALBERT. Yes, let's.

SNIGGERS. The very thing.

BILL. And we'll all drink his health.

ALBERT. Good old Toffy.

SNIGGERS. He ought to have been a general or a premier. *(They get bottles from cupboard, etc.)*

THE TOFF. Well, we've earned our bit of a supper. *(They sit down)*

BILL *(glass in hand)*. Here's to old Toffy who guessed everything.

ALBERT AND SNIGGERS. Good old Toffy.

BILL. Toffy who saved our lives and made our fortunes.

ALBERT AND SNIGGERS. Hear. Hear.

THE TOFF. And here's to Bill who saved me twice to-night.

BILL. Couldn't have done it but for your cleverness, Toffy.

SNIGGERS. Hear, hear. Hear, hear.

ALBERT. He foresees everything.

BILL. A speech, Toffy. A speech from our general.

ALL. Yes, a speech.

SNIGGERS. A speech.

THE TOFF. Well, get me some water. This whiskey's too much for my head, and I must keep it clear till our friends are safe in the cellar.

BILL. Water. Yes, of course. Get him some water, Sniggers.

SNIGGERS. We don't use water here. Where shall I get it?

BILL. Outside in the garden. *(Exit SNIGGERS)*

ALBERT. Here's to fortune.

BILL. Here's to Albert Thomas Esquire.

ALBERT. And William Jones Esquire. *(Reënter SNIGGERS terrified)*

THE TOFF. Hullo, here's Jacob Smith Esquire, J. P., alias Sniggers, back again.

SNIGGERS. Toffy, I've been a thinking about my share in that ruby. I don't want it, Toffy, I don't want it.

THE TOFF. Nonsense, Sniggers, nonsense.

SNIGGERS. You shall have it, Toffy, you shall have it yourself, only say Sniggers has no share in this 'ere ruby. Say it, Toffy, say it.

BILL. Want to turn informer, Sniggers?

SNIGGERS. No, no. Only I don't want the ruby, Toffy . . .

THE TOFF. No more nonsense, Sniggers; we're all in together in this. If one hangs we all hang; but they won't outwit me. Besides, it's not a hanging affair; they had their knives.

SNIGGERS. Toffy, Toffy, I always treated you fair, Toffy. I was always one to say, Give Toffy a chance. Take back my share, Toffy.

THE TOFF. What's the matter? What are you driving at?

SNIGGERS. Take it back, Toffy.

THE TOFF. Answer me; what are you up to?

SNIGGERS. I don't want my share any more.

BILL. Have you seen the police? *(ALBERT pulls out his knife)*

THE TOFF. No, no knives, Albert.

ALBERT. What then?

THE TOFF. The honest truth in open court, barring the ruby. We were attacked.

SNIGGERS. There's no police.

THE TOFF. Well, then, what's the matter?

BILL. Out with it.

SNIGGERS. I swear to God . . .

ALBERT. Well?

THE TOFF. Don't interrupt.

SNIGGERS. I swear I saw something *what I didn't like.*

THE TOFF. What you didn't like?

SNIGGERS *(in tears)*. O Toffy, Toffy, take it back. Take my share. Say you take it.

THE TOFF. What has he seen?

(Dead silence only broken by SNIGGERS' *sobs. Then stony steps are heard. Enter a hideous* IDOL. *It is blind and gropes its way. It gropes its way to the ruby and picks it up and screws it into a socket in the forehead.* SNIGGERS *still weeps softly; the rest stare in horror. The* IDOL *steps out, not groping. Its steps move off, then stop)*

THE TOFF. O great heavens!

ALBERT *(in a childish, plaintive voice)*. What is it, Toffy?

BILL. Albert, it is that obscene idol *(in a whisper)* come from India.

ALBERT. It is gone.

BILL. It has taken its eye.

SNIGGERS. We are saved.

OFF, A VOICE *(with outlandish accent)*. Meestaire William Jones. Able Seaman.

*(*THE TOFF *has never spoken, never moved. He only gazes stupidly in horror)*

BILL. Albert, Albert, what is this? *(He rises and walks out. One moan is heard.* SNIGGERS *goes to window. He falls back sickly)*

ALBERT *(in a whisper)*. What has happened?

SNIGGERS. I have seen it. I have seen it. O I have seen it. *(He returns to table)*

THE TOFF *(laying his hand very gently on* SNIGGERS' *arm, speaking softly and winningly)*. What was it, Sniggers?

SNIGGERS. I have seen it.

ALBERT. What?

SNIGGERS. O!

VOICE. Meestaire Albert Thomas, Able Seaman.

ALBERT. Must I go, Toffy? Toffy, must I go?

SNIGGERS *(clutching him).* Don't move.
ALBERT *(going).* Toffy, Toffy. *(Exit)*
VOICE. Meestaire Jacob Smith, Able Seaman.
SNIGGERS. I can't go, Toffy. I can't go. I can't do it. *(He goes)*
VOICE. Meestaire Arnold Everett Scott-Fortescue, late Esquire, Able Seaman.
THE TOFF. I did not foresee it. *(Exit)*

ACTION

1. What has happened before the curtain rises? How are we informed of the preceding action? How is this action important to the play?

2. At what point does the "reversal" occur? State the nature of the action before and after this point. What preparation has there been for the reversal?

3. Before the priests enter, how do the words and actions of the other characters show (a) their fear, (b) the likelihood of their fear?

4. What qualities do the Toff and his followers have which make possible their victory over the priests? What qualities does the god have which account for his eventual triumph? How are these qualities shown?

5. Why should the Toff and his followers be called off the stage, one by one, in the order in which they are called? What is shown by their way of going?

6. Suggest the exact nature of the setting, the lighting, the costuming, and the acting which you believe would be best for this play. Support your suggestions with references to the text.

7. Compare this pattern of action with that of "Frankie and Johnny."

Characters

The problems of personality and the human emotions are usually dealt with deeply and in detail in imaginative literature. Hence one reason for the fascination of such literature is that, in it, most readers may meet many kinds of people unfamiliar to them in life. Again, they may come to know even familiar kinds of characters more intimately in books than they do in actuality. Knowing of people's interest in human nature, and fascinated themselves by it, authors as a rule make personalities—characters—their qualities and feelings, important elements in their works.

So important is personality in fiction, drama, and poetry that a character or an emotion at times may suffice to give a work its essential unity. Some novels, stories, and plays in which the action is not patterned but miscellaneous may be unified because one great character appears throughout (*Gil Blas,* for instance). Some character sketches are unified, despite the fact that they present no happenings in detail, because they offer insights concerning characters. And many lyrical poems, although they record no happenings, are unified by the expression of an emotion and—to some extent—the personality experiencing the emotion. (For example, see Keats' "Ode on a Grecian Urn," p. 766.) In many imaginative works, therefore, the writer takes care to show the reader what the character is— his qualities, his likes and dislikes, how he lives and what he does. The sum total of such traits is the *character*. *Characterization* is the technique used by the writer to make these qualities known.

PERSONALITY OF THE CHARACTER

The reader who studies characters and characterization in a work should ask and answer three questions. The first is: What are the qualities—the characteristics—of the characters in the work? The reader, in other words, has the problem of describing the personality of each of the figures, major or minor, who appear in the work. Some characters, of course, will be nothing more than isolated traits or types or, perhaps, representatives of professions (e.g., a jealous man, a lover of sports, a housemaid). Others will be more complex, and several adjectives will be needed to describe them. If characters have several traits, the reader needs to see not only what those traits are but also how they are related. In some characters, all other traits will be subordinated to one dominating motive, drive, or passion (e.g., Macbeth, or Ahab in *Moby Dick*). Some will have qualities which contend for mastery; and their contending drives or motives may result from a single characteristic, or one contending drive may result from another. Some characters will be, essentially, contending drives—personalities which threaten to split under trying circumstances. (Hamlet, for example). Whatever the traits or combinations of traits, the reader needs to discern what they are and what they cause the characters to like and dislike, to want to do and to shrink from doing.

INDICATIONS OF PERSONALITY

A second question with which the reader copes is: How has the work indicated these qualities? For the author must, obviously, have the technical skill required to acquaint us with his creations, and if he is not to be obvious or monotonous, he will vary his methods. He may, for instance, *describe* a person in such a way as to indicate that he is arrogant or intelligent, or that he dislikes capitalists and likes women. The character's features, his dress, his gestures, the timbre and inflections of his voice, his facial expressions—all or any of these may be so delineated as to show us what he is. Or an author may characterize by *direct statement:* "Jones, of course, was an utter fool." He may indicate a character's traits by picturing his *surroundings:* "He lived in a huge and showy mansion, which was cared for by armies of servants." He may convey to us what a character is like by quoting his *dialog:* both what he says and the kind of words in which he expresses himself will offer clues. He may tell us the character's *thoughts,* or he may give us the *opinions of others* about him. He may show us a trait by showing us an *action*. Often he will use not one but a combination of these methods to acquaint us with a character. And we as readers should note what methods an author uses to indicate what his characters are like.

FUNCTION OF THE CHARACTERS AND CHARACTERIZATION

A third question about characters and characterization with which the reader is concerned is: What is their function in the work? For they may be related to the action, to life, and to the interpretation of life which a work provides.

Unlike a painter or sculptor, the author—in most works—will not show his people frozen in one position. In imaginative literature, characters do things. They are intimately related to the patterns of action which you considered in the last series of exercises. Interrelationships in the action almost always come about as a result of characters—because authors and readers logically relate certain kinds of characters in certain situations with certain actions. If, for instance, an author introduces a dishonest character, and then shows him, when tempted, lying to his mother, cheating in an examination, and deceiving his sweetheart, we say that it is "logical" or "in character" for such a character, when tempted, to do such things. Our experience with similar individuals, in life, has shown us that such actions are logically probable. *A characterization, therefore, may prepare for a particular action.* Sometimes such preparation will be pretty simple: if the character's only chore is to say, "Tea is served, madam," it will be enough for the author simply to indicate that he is a butler. If, by contrast, the character is to be shown vacillating between kind acts and cruel ones, the author will need to equip him with traits which prepare for such vacillations.

Again, *a characterization may prepare for a change—a reversal*—which is at the heart of a pattern of action. Here is a play about Jane Roe, who loves her husband in Act I and who deliberately scalds the poor man with a pot of boiling tea in Act III. She may be given qualities which motivate both actions—the loving and the scalding—at the proper moments in the play. It will be important for the reader to see exactly how the author's portrayal prepares or fails to prepare for her changing behavior.

In some works, *a character may offer signs of the progress and the completion of the narrative pattern.* Often the "exhaustion," so to speak, of possible actions for characters accompanies the working out of such a pattern. In such works, as Elizabeth Bowen has said:

Characters . . . promote, by showing, the advance of the plot. How? By the advances, from act to act, in their action. By their showing (by emotional and physical changes) the effects both of action and the passage of time. The diminution of the character's alternatives shows . . . advance—by the end of the novel the character's alternatives, many at the beginning, have been reduced to almost none . . . the character has, like the silkworm at work on the cocoon, spun itself out. . . . Throughout the novel, each character is expending potentiality.

Her remarks, of course, hold good for short stories, plays, and narrative poems, as well as for novels.

Some qualities will be given to characters, on occasion, merely to make them "lifelike." Aware that readers cannot become interested in mere puppets on a string put through their paces by their creator, an author often endows his figures with traits which have no relationship to the action but which make them seem real. Of course, in a work containing several characters, the minor characters may do perfectly well if they are not *un*lifelike; and in a work which has action or setting sufficiently exciting, characters may be shown who have very few lifelike traits. Often, however, an author will take pains to give his creatures qualities which give the impression of life—and the reader should note that the characterization has this function.

Finally, some *characters may be given some traits which make them attractive or unattractive to the reader*—better than the reader, like the reader, or worse than the reader. Such traits practically always will be assigned to the protagonist (hero or heroine) and the antagonist (villain)—if there is one. Enough universal and enough specific traits will be assigned to them so that the reader will follow with interest their trials and their tribulations, their triumphs and their joys, and so that he will feel that there is meaning in their defeats or their triumphs. The physical aspects of the characters, their moral codes, their philosophies, their associations with good or bad friends, the way other characters feel about them, all will offer clues to the attitude readers are expected to adopt toward them. Note, for instance, how Stevenson shows the nature of the infamous Mr. Hyde:

Mr. Hyde was pale and dwarfish, he gave an impression of deformity without any nameable malformation, he had a displeasing smile, he had borne himself to the lawyer with a sort of murderous mixture of timidity and boldness, and he spoke with a husky, whispering and somewhat broken voice; all these were points against him, but not all of these together could explain the hitherto unknown disgust, loathing and fear with which Mr. Utterson regarded him. "There must be something else," said the perplexed gentleman. "There is something more, if I could find a name for it. God bless me, the man seems hardly human! Something troglodytic, shall we say? . . . or is it the mere radiance of a foul soul that thus transpires through, and transfigures, its clay continent? The last, I think, for, O my poor old Harry Jekyll, if I ever read Satan's signature upon a face, it is on that of your new friend."—*The Strange Case of Dr. Jekyll and Mr. Hyde.*

Not only does the endowment of characters with sympathetic or unsympathetic qualities interest the reader; it also helps the author give his work meanings. The nature of these qualities will help him show the reader how he is interpreting the people and the events which his story, his drama, or his poem portrays.

The reader, then, who intelligently studies the characters and the characterization in an imaginative work will notice what the characters are like, how the author reveals those qualities, and what function each detail performs. The following selections are to be read with these ideas in mind.

Robert Penn Warren is well known not only as a writer of fiction and poetry but also as a literary critic and teacher. His experience as a student of literary works has undoubtedly made him a very self-conscious artist—one who knows, as he writes, what he is doing and why he is doing it. The following story creates a memorable character; and in order to accomplish this in so short a story, it makes excellent use of a number of characterizing devices. In addition to the grandfather, the reader comes to know the narrator well—an important matter since it is through his eyes that the grandfather is seen.

Robert Penn Warren

WHEN THE LIGHT GETS GREEN

My grandfather had a long white beard and sat under the cedar tree. The beard, as a matter of fact, was not very long and not white, only gray, but when I was a child and was away from him at school during the winter, I would think of him, not seeing him in my mind's eye, and say: He has a long white beard. Therefore, it was a shock to me, on the first morning back home, to watch him lean over the dresser toward the wavy green mirror, which in his always shadowy room reflected things like deep water riffled by a little wind, and clip his gray beard to a point. It is gray and pointed, I would say then, remembering what I had thought before.

He turned his face to the green wavy glass, first one side and then the other in quarter profile, and lifted the long shears, which trembled a little, to cut the beard. His face being turned like that, with his good nose and pointed gray beard, he looked like General Robert E. Lee, without any white horse to ride. My grandfather had been a soldier, too, but now he wore blue-jean pants and when he leaned over like that toward the mirror, I couldn't help but notice how small his hips and backsides were. Only they weren't just small, they were shrunken. I noticed how the blue jeans hung loose from his suspenders and loose off his legs and down around his shoes. And in the morning when I noticed all this about his legs and backsides, I felt a tight feeling in my stomach like when you walk behind a woman and see the high heel of her shoe is worn and twisted and jerks her ankle every time she takes a step.

Always before my grandfather had finished clipping his beard, my Uncle Kirby came to the door and beat on it for breakfast. "I'll be down in just a minute, thank you, sir," my grandfather said. My uncle called him Mr. Barden.

"Mr. Barden, breakfast is ready." It was because my Uncle Kirby was not my real uncle, having married my Aunt Lucy, who lived with my grandfather. Then my grandfather put on a black vest and put his gold watch and chain in the vest and picked up his cob pipe from the dresser top, and he and I went down to breakfast, after Uncle Kirby was already downstairs.

When he came into the dining room, Aunt Lucy was sitting at the foot of the table with the iron coffee pot on a plate beside her. She said, "Good morning, Papa."

"Good morning, Lucy," he said, and sat down at the head of the table, taking one more big puff off his pipe before laying it beside his plate.

"You've brought that old pipe down to breakfast again," my aunt said, while she poured the bright-looking coffee into the cups.

"Don't it stink," he always said.

My uncle never talked at breakfast, but when my grandfather said that, my uncle always opened his lips to grin like a dog panting, and showed his hooked teeth. His teeth were yellow because he chewed tobacco, which my grandfather didn't do, although his beard was yellow around the mouth from smoking. Aunt Lucy didn't like my uncle to chew, that was the whole trouble. So she rode my grandfather for bringing his pipe down, all in fun at first before she got serious about it. But he always brought it down just the same, and said to her, "Don't it stink."

After we ate, my uncle got up and said, "I got to get going," and went out through the kitchen where the cook was knocking and sloshing around. If it had rained right and was a good tobacco-setting season, my grandfather went off with me down to the stable to get his mare, for he had to see the setting. We saddled up the mare and went across the lot, where limestone bunched out of the ground and cedar trees and blue grass grew out of the split rock. A branch of cold water with minnows in it went through the lot between rocks and under the cedar trees; it was where I used to play before I got big enough to go to the river with the niggers to swim.

My grandfather rode across the lot and over the rise back of the house. He sat up pretty straight for an old man, holding the bridle in his left hand, and in his right hand a long hickory tobacco stick whittled down to make a walking cane. I walked behind him and watched the big straw hat he wore waggle a little above his narrow neck, or how he held the stick in the middle, firm and straight up like something carried in a parade, or how smooth and slow the muscles in the mare's flanks worked as she put each hoof down in the ground, going up hill. Sassafras bushes and blackberry bushes grew thick along the lane over the rise. In summer, tufts of hay would catch and hang on the dry bushes and showed that the hay wagons had been that way; but when we went that way in setting time, just after breakfast, the blackberry blooms were hardly gone, only a few rusty patches of white left, and the sassafras leaves showed still wet with dew or maybe the rain.

From the rise we could look back on the house. The shingles were black with damp, and the whitewash grayish, except in spots where the sun already struck it and it was drying. The tops of the cedar trees, too, were below us, very dark green and quiet. When we crossed the rise, there were the fields going down toward the river, all checked off and ready for setting, very even, only for the gullies where brush was piled to stop the washing. The fields were reddish from the wet, not yet steaming. Across them, the green woods and the sycamores showing white far off told where the river was.

The hands were standing at the edge of the field under the trees when we got there. The little niggers were filling their baskets with the wet plants to drop, and I got me a basket and filled it. My Uncle Kirby gave me fifty cents for dropping plants, but he didn't give the little niggers that much, I remember. The hands and women stood around waiting a minute, watching Uncle Kirby, who always fumed around, waving his dibble, his blue shirt already sticking to his arms with sweat. "Get the lead out," he said. The little niggers filled faster, grinning with their teeth at him. "Goddam, get the lead out!" My grandfather sat on his mare under the trees, still holding the walking cane, and said, "Why don't you start 'em, sir?"

Then, all of a sudden, they all moved out into the field, scattering out down the rows, the droppers first, and after a minute the setters, who lurched along, never straightening up, down the rows toward the river. I walked down my row, separating out the plants and dropping them at the hills, while it got hotter and the ground steamed. The sun broke out now and then, making my shadow on the ground, then the cloud would come again, and I could see its shadow drifting at me on the red field.

My grandfather rode very slow along the edge of the field to watch the setting, or stayed still under the trees. After a while, maybe about ten o'clock, he would leave and go home. I could see him riding the mare up the rise and then go over the rise; or if I was working the other way toward the river, when I turned round at the end, the lane would be empty and nothing on top the rise, with the cloudy, blue-gray sky low behind it.

The tobacco was all he cared about, now we didn't have any horses that were any real good. He had some silver cups, only one real silver one though, that his horses won at fairs, but all that was before I was born. The real silver one, the one he kept on his dresser and kept string and old minnie balls and pins and things in, had *1859* on it because his horse won it then before the War, when he was a young man. Uncle Kirby said horses were foolishness, and Grandfather said, yes, he reckoned horses were foolishness, all right. So what he cared about now was the tobacco. One time he was a tobacco-buyer for three years, but after he bought a lot of tobacco and had it in his sheds, the sheds burned up on him. He didn't have enough insurance to do any good and he was a ruined man. After that all his children, he had all girls and his money was gone, said about him, "Papa's just visionary, he tried to be a tobacco-buyer but he's too visionary and not practical." But he always said, "All tobacco-buyers are sons-of-bitches, and three years is enough of a man's life for him to be a son-of-a-bitch, I reckon." Now he was old, the corn could get the rust or the hay get rained on for all he cared, it was Uncle Kirby's worry, but all summer, off and on, he had to go down to the tobacco field to watch them sucker or plow or worm, and sometimes he pulled a few suckers himself. And when a cloud would blow up black in summer, he got nervous as a cat, not knowing whether it was the rain they needed or maybe a hail storm coming that would cut the tobacco up bad.

Mornings he didn't go down to the field, he went out under the cedar tree where his chair was. Most of the time he took a book with him along with his pipe, for he was an inveterate reader. His being an inveterate reader was one of the things made his children say he was visionary. He read a lot until his eyes went bad the summer before he had his stroke, then after that, I read to him some, but not as much as I ought. He used to read out loud some from Macaulay's *History of England* or Gibbon's *Decline and Fall*, about Flodden Field or about how the Janizaries took Constantinople amid great slaughter and how the Turk surveyed the carnage and quoted from the Persian poet about the lizard keeping the courts of the mighty. My grandfather knew some poetry, too, and he said it to himself when he didn't have anything else to do. I lay on my back on the ground, feeling the grass cool and tickly on the back of my neck, and looked upside down into the cedar tree where the limbs were tangled and black-green like big hairy fern fronds with the sky blue all around, while he said some poetry. Like the "Isles of Greece, the Isles of Greece, where burning Sappho loved and sung." Or like "Roll on, thou deep and dark blue ocean, roll."

But he never read poetry, he just said what he already knew. He only read history and *Napoleon and His Marshals*, having been a soldier and fought in the War himself. He rode off and joined the cavalry, but he never told me whether he took the horse that won the real silver cup or not. He was with Forrest before Forrest was a general. He said Forrest was a great general, and if they had done what Forrest wanted and cleaned the country ahead of the Yankees, like the Russians beat Napoleon, they'd whipped the Yankees sure. He told me about Fort Donelson, how they fought in the winter woods, and how they got away with Forrest at night, splashing through the cold water. And how the dead men looked in the river bottoms in winter, and I lay on my back on the grass, looking up in the thick cedar limbs, and thought how it was to be dead.

After Shiloh was fought and they pushed the Yankees down in the river, my grandfather was a captain, for he raised a cavalry company of his own out of West Tennessee. He was a captain, but he never got promoted after the War; when I was a little boy everybody still called him Captain Barden, though they called lots of other people in our section Colonel and Major. One time I said to him: "Grandpa, did you ever kill any Yankees?" He said: "God-a-mighty, how do I know?" So, being little, I thought he was just a captain because he never killed anybody, and I was ashamed. He talked about how they took Fort Pillow, and the drunk niggers under the bluff. And one time he said niggers couldn't stand a charge or stand the cold steel, so I thought maybe he killed some of them. But then I thought, niggers don't count, maybe.

He only talked much in the morning. Almost every afternoon right after dinner, he went to sleep in his chair, with his hands curled up in his lap, one of them holding the pipe that still sent up a little smoke in the shadow, and his head propped back on the tree trunk. His mouth hung open, and under the hairs of his mustache, all yellow with nicotine, you could see his black teeth and his lips that were wet and pink like a baby's. Usually I remember him that way, asleep.

I remember him that way, or else trampling up and down the front porch, nervous as a cat, while a cloud blew up and the trees began to rustle. He tapped his walking cane on the boards and whistled through his teeth with his breath and kept looking off at the sky where the cloud and sometimes the lightning was. Then of a sudden it came, and if it was rain he used to go up to his room and lie down; but if it came hail on the tobacco, he stayed on the front porch, not trampling any more, and watched the hail rattle off the roof and bounce soft on the grass. "God-a-Mighty," he always said, "bigger'n minnie balls," even when it wasn't so big.

In 1914, just before the war began, it was a hot summer with the tobacco mighty good but needing rain. And when the dry spell broke and a cloud blew up, my grandfather came out on the front porch, watching it like that. It was mighty still, with lightning way off, so far you couldn't hardly hear the thunder. Then the leaves began to ruffle like they do when the light gets green, and my grandfather said to me, "Son, it's gonna hail." And he stood still. Down in the pasture, that far off, you could see the cattle bunching up and the white horse charging across the pasture, looking bright, for the sun was shining bright before the cloud struck it all at once. "It's gonna hail," my grandfather said. It was dark, with jagged lightning and the thunder high and steady. And there the hail was.

He just turned around and went in the house. I watched the hail bouncing, then I heard a noise and my aunt yelled. I ran back in the dining room where the noise was, and my grandfather was lying on the floor with the old silver pitcher he dropped and a broken glass. We tried to drag him, but he was too heavy; then my Uncle Kirby came up wet from the stable and we carried my grandfather upstairs and put him on his bed. My aunt tried to call the doctor even if the lightning might hit the telephone. I stayed back in the dining room and picked up the broken glass and the pitcher and wiped up the floor with a rag. After a while Dr. Blake came from town; then he went away.

When Dr. Blake was gone, I went upstairs to see my grandfather. I shut the door and went in his room, which was almost dark, like always, and quiet because the hail didn't beat on the roof any more. He was lying on his back in the feather-bed, with a sheet pulled up over him, lying there in the dark. He had his hands curled loose on his stomach, like when he went to sleep in his chair holding the pipe. I sat on a split-bottom chair by the bed and looked at him: he had his eyes shut and his mouth hung loose, but you couldn't hear his breathing. Then I quit looking at him and looked round the room, my eyes getting used to the shadow. I could see his pants on the floor, and the silver cup on the dresser by the mirror, which was green and wavy like water.

When he said something, I almost jumped out of my skin, hearing his voice like that. He said, "Son, I'm gonna die." I tried to say something, but I couldn't.

And he waited, then he said, "I'm on borrowed time, it's time to die." I said, "No!" so sudden and loud I jumped. He waited a long time and said, "It's time to die. Nobody loves me." I tried to say, "Grandpa, I love you." And then I did say it all right, feeling like it hadn't been me said it, and knowing all of a sudden it was a lie, because I didn't feel anything. He just lay there; and I went downstairs.

It was sunshiny in the yard, the clouds gone, but the grass was wet. I walked down toward the gate, rubbing my bare feet over the slick cold grass. A hen was in the yard and she kept trying to peck up a piece of hail, like a fool chicken will do after it hails; but every time she pecked, it bounced away from her over the green grass. I leaned against the gate, noticing the ground on one side the posts, close up, was still dry and dusty. I wondered if the tobacco was cut up bad, because Uncle Kirby had gone to see. And while I looked through the gate down across the pasture where everything in the sun was green and shiny with wet and the cattle grazed, I thought about my grandfather, not feeling anything. But I said out loud anyway, "Grandpa, I love you."

My grandfather lived four more years. The year after his stroke they sold the farm and moved away, so I didn't stay with them any more. My grandfather died in 1918, just before the news came that my Uncle Kirby was killed in France, and my aunt had to go to work in a store. I got the letter about my grandfather, who died of flu, but I thought about four years back, and it didn't matter much.

CHARACTERS AND ACTION

1. How are the following physical details, presented in the opening two paragraphs, valuable in characterizing the grandfather: (a) the nature of his reflection in the mirror, (b) the resemblance to Robert E. Lee, (c) his shrunken hips?

2. What additional aspects of grandfather's character are later revealed by (a) the account of his visit to the fields, (b) the indication of his taste in reading, (c) his statements about the Civil War, (d) his way of going to sleep, (e) his reaction to a storm? The first of these is characterization by detailing an action. What other techniques for characterization are employed in this story?

3. Indicate the attitudes toward the old man of (a) the uncle, (b) the aunt. Point out passages showing these attitudes. Why are these important for characterization?

4. What statements may be made about the narrator's character on the basis of what he says concerning (a) his way of recalling the old man when away from him at school, (b) the particular quality of the "tight feeling" in his stomach indicated in paragraph 2, (c) the things he notices when he goes out to watch the setting? What does his language indicate about him?

5. How has what has gone before prepared for (a) the grandfather having a stroke when he does, (b) his saying what he does to the boy after the stroke, (c) the boy's replying as he does, (d) the narrator's reaction to the news of the old man's death?

6. Discuss the kinds of characters represented here. Are they type characters? Are they complex? Are they sympathetic characters? Justify your answers.

In a picture gallery on an upper floor of a mansion in Ferrara, two men are talking. One is the duke, the owner of the mansion. The other is an envoy of a count whose daughter the duke is about to marry. The pair seat themselves before a portrait of the duke's deceased wife, and the poem tells what the duke says about the painting, his "last duchess," and the forthcoming marriage. (Any words which may have been uttered by the envoy are not recorded, but at one point the duke refers to an expression he notices on the envoy's face.) We learn about two characters—one directly, one indirectly. The things the duke says and the way he says them both characterize him and unfold a revealing story about him. What he says about his dead wife familiarizes us with her, and in the end the duke draws a picture of her which is much more favorable than he suspects. Every word of this poem is packed with implications: as William Lyon Phelps has said, "The whole poem contains only fifty-six lines, but it could easily be expanded into a three-volume novel." As a result, of course, the reader should carefully consider every word and what it implies.

Robert Browning

MY LAST DUCHESS

Ferrara

That's my last Duchess painted on the wall,
Looking as if she were alive; I call
That piece a wonder, now: Fra Pandolf's hands
Worked busily a day, and there she stands.
Will't please you sit and look at her? I said   5
"Fra Pandolf" by design, for never read
Strangers like you that pictured countenance,
The depth and passion of its earnest glance,
But to myself they turned (since none puts by
The curtain I have drawn for you, but I)   10
And seemed as they would ask me, if they durst,
How such a glance came there; so, not the first
Are you to turn and ask thus. Sir, 'twas not
Her husband's presence only, called that spot
Of joy into the Duchess' cheek: perhaps   15
Fra Pandolf chanced to say "Her mantle laps

Over my Lady's wrist too much," or "Paint
Must never hope to reproduce the faint
Half-flush that dies along her throat"; such stuff
Was courtesy, she thought, and cause enough   20
For calling up that spot of joy. She had
A heart . . . how shall I say? . . . too soon made glad,
Too easily impressed; she liked whate'er
She looked on, and her looks went everywhere.
Sir, 'twas all one! My favor at her breast,   25
The dropping of the daylight in the West,
The bough of cherries some officious fool
Broke in the orchard for her, the white mule
She rode with round the terrace—all and each
Would draw from her alike the approving speech,   30
Or blush, at least. She thanked men,—good; but thanked
Somehow . . . I know not how . . . as if she ranked
My gift of a nine-hundred-years-old name
With anybody's gift. Who'd stoop to blame
This sort of trifling? Even had you skill   35
In speech—(which I have not)—to make your will
Quite clear to such an one, and say "Just this
Or that in you disgusts me; here you miss
Or there exceed the mark"—and if she let
Herself be lessoned so, nor plainly set   40
Her wits to yours, forsooth, and made excuse,
—E'en then would be some stooping, and I choose
Never to stoop. Oh, Sir, she smiled, no doubt,
Whene'er I passed her; but who passed without
Much the same smile? This grew; I gave commands;   45
Then all smiles stopped together. There she stands
As if alive. Will't please you rise? We'll meet
The company below, then. I repeat,
The Count your Master's known munificence
Is ample warrant that no just pretence   50
Of mine for dowry will be disallowed;
Though his fair daughter's self, as I avowed
At starting, is my object. Nay, we'll go
Together down, Sir! Notice Neptune, though,
Taming a sea-horse, thought a rarity,   55
Which Claus of Innsbruck cast in bronze for me.

CHARACTERS AND ACTION

1. The word *last* in line 1 should be stressed. What does the stress indicate about the duke's attitude toward his late wife?

2. The "Fra" in line 3 is a "brother"—a monk. "I said *'Fra* Pandolf' by design," says the duke. What is suggested by this emphasis on the religious nature of the painter in the speech to the envoy? What is the reader to deduce from these facts: (a) even a monk was allowed only one day to paint the portrait, (b) only the duke puts by the curtain which ordinarily covers the painting, (c) the duke carefully quotes (ll. 16-19) what he believes the monk said while painting.

3. In lines 22-34, the duke offers examples to show that his wife "had a heart . . . too soon made glad." What do the examples indicate about her likings? Do the examples justify a critic's suggestion that "she was one of those lovely women whose kindness and responsiveness are as natural as sunlight"? Why or why not?

4. Precisely what does the duke seem to feel was wrong with the responsiveness of his former wife? What does the nature of his displeasure show about his character?

5. Why—according to lines 34-43—did the duke never reveal his displeasure to the woman? What does his justification of his silence show about him?

6. Says line 45: "I gave commands." What were the commands? (A knowledge of the history of Ferrara may help answer this, if considered in connection with the rather grim line which follows: "Then all smiles stopped together.") How does your knowledge of the character justify your interpretation?

7. What is to be learned about the duke from his remarks (ll. 48-53) concerning the dowry and his love for the count's daughter?

8. Since a duke was supposed to walk before a commoner, why did the duke say, "Nay, we'll go together down, Sir!"?

9. Why, as the poem closes, does the duke call attention to the particular piece of statuary mentioned in lines 54-56? What bearing does his singling out of this work of art have upon this question: What were the motives for the whole conversation here recorded? Was the duke trying to tell the envoy something indirectly? If so, what?

10. Summarize what you have learned about the characters of the duke and the duchess. Generalize about the methods of characterization in the poem.

11. Contrast the methods and the functions of characterization here with those in "When the Light Gets Green" (p. 49).

Setting

The setting of "My Last Duchess" (p. 55) is the picture gallery on an upper floor of the duke's palace in Ferrara, Italy, at an unspecified time. That of "My Oedipus Complex" (p. 4) is Ireland in the period of World War I and just after it. That of Act III, Scene I, of *Julius Caesar* (p. 18) is "Rome. Before the

Capitol," in 44 B.C. The setting includes the details of background set forth in the narrative, the drama, or the poem. Such details may be presented at length or briefly. They may be concentrated at one point in the work or, as is more frequent these days, doled out bit by bit. Almost always a consideration of the employment of such details will be valuable for the reader.

The reader of poetry, fiction, or drama will find it illuminating to notice exactly how the author's handling of such details gives or fails to give that illusion of reality which is indispensable if imaginative works are to create interest and sympathy. More important, he should consider whether the details of time, of place, of social milieu, of emotional atmosphere, are functional or not—that is, whether they contribute to the unfolding of the action, to the representation of character, and to the achievement of the work as a whole.

SETTING AS THE SHAPER OF EVENTS

The great novelist and critic, Henry James, once said that he could not conceive of "a passage of description that is not in its intention narrative," and certainly it is clear that details in a scene may often be vital circumstances in a fictional work or in a poem which tells a story. The lay of the land may actually determine some of the action in accounts of treasure hunts ("The Gold Bug" and *Treasure Island*), stories of pursuits (*The Thirty-nine Steps*), or narratives of journeys (*The Odyssey*, "The Midnight Ride of Paul Revere," *Huckleberry Finn*). At one point in *Les Miserables*, Hugo carefully describes the battlefield of Waterloo; at one point in *Henry Esmond*, Thackeray tells of the disposition of troops at Blenheim: in each instance the data show why a battle had to follow a predetermined pattern. So important is topography in many detective stories that their publishers often print maps as frontispieces. Not only topography but also climate and soil may determine events—as in many of Robert Frost's New England poems and Rölvaag's *Giants in the Earth*. In stories of men in conflict with nature, the setting itself, in a sense, becomes a character—the antagonist.

SETTING AS AN ADJUNCT TO PLOT AND CHARACTERIZATION

Even in works wherein the setting does not notably shape events, the author—as the alert reader should see—often uses scenes to help tell his story. In such works, in other words, setting becomes an adjunct in showing important changes and developments. By calling attention to the lengthening of shadows, or to the coming of autumn, or to the growth of weeds in a garden, an author may be showing the passage of time. A character's sense of novelty in an unchanged scene may betoken a change in the character himself. An example is Hawthorne's passage about Minister Dimmesdale in *The Scarlet Letter*:

As he drew near the town, he took an impression of change from the series of familiar objects. . . . There, indeed, was each former trace of the street, as he remembered it, and all the peculiarities of the houses, with the due multitude of gable-peaks, and a weathercock at every point where his memory suggested one. Not the less, however, came this importunately obtrusive sense of change. . . . A similar impression struck him most remarkably, as he passed under the walls of his own church. The edifice had so very strange, and yet so familiar, an aspect, that Mr. Dimmesdale's mind vibrated between two ideas; either that he had seen it in a dream hitherto, or that he was merely dreaming about it now.

A character's sense of change in a scene which remains the same, in another narrative, may show a shift in thought and feeling: witness the difference between the initial description and the final description of the same nighttime scene in Keats' "Ode to a Nightingale." And in still another narrative, an author may show the reader the effect of a happening by emphasizing changes in a scene—for instance, a decaying house may indicate that the family living in it has deteriorated ("The Fall of the House of Usher").

Scene is often an adjunct, not only to plot, but also to character portrayal. A reader often comes to know a character by noticing how the author describes the character's dwelling, or by considering how an environment which has been described would be likely to shape the character's personality. Not only the physical climate but also the intellectual and moral climate, as revealed by the author, may clarify motives and possible actions. The words "Ancien Regime" beneath the title in Browning's poem, "The Laboratory," help explain why the heroine chose to get revenge by poisoning a successful rival; and at the start of "The Outcasts of Poker Flat," John Oakhurst, gambler, notices "a change in the moral atmosphere since the preceding night . . . a Sabbath lull in the air" which heralds his ejection, by request, from the mining town. Again, the nature of a character may be revealed to the reader by the author's record of what the character notices in a scene: a businessman may see a waterfall as a source of power, a painter may see it as an arrangement of colors, a poet may see it as a symbol expressive of some high truth.

THE EMOTIONAL QUALITY OF SETTING

Speaking of one way of writing a story, Robert Louis Stevenson said, "You may take a certain atmosphere and get action and persons to express and realize it. I'll give you an example—*The Merry Men*. There I began with the feeling of one of those islands on the west coast of Scotland, and I gradually developed the story to express the sentiment with which that coast affected me." Although this recipe probably is an unusual one for an author to follow, it does suggest one thing which setting may do—in the actual world or the world of books: it may arouse emotions. In many plays the manipulation of lighting has this effect. In many stories and poems, the author records certain details in the landscape which body forth an emotional state. Some poems communicate the thought and feeling of a poet simply by presenting appropriate details. An "atmosphere" thus created may correspond to the moods of the characters. Or it may heighten the representation of their emotions by a contrast. Consider the passage in *Moby Dick* which tells of the feelings of a crew after their boats have been smashed by the whale:

Judge, then, to what pitches of inflamed, distracted fury the minds of the whale's more desperate hunters were impelled, when amid the chips of chewed boats, and the sinking limbs of torn comrades, they swam out of the white curds of the whale's direful wrath into the serene, exasperating sunlight, that smiled on, as if at a birth or a bridal.

Here and in some other narratives the setting, in addition to showing emotions, underlines important meanings or themes. All these facts about the possible usefulness of setting mean that the reader who is interested in the craftsmanship of a work will notice how the author's management of this element contributes to the telling of a story, the representation of the motives and actions of a character, the emotional overtones and the implications of the work.

This is a remarkably compressed story of revenge and of the emotions which accompanied that revenge. The opening sentence tells of the vow of the narrator to avenge an insult. The rest of the first paragraph tells what conditions were to be fulfilled in order to secure satisfactory revenge. The rest of the story tells how the conditions were fulfilled and how both the narrator and his victim felt about the happenings. There is only enough characterization to create sympathy at the start for the narrator and as the story progresses, for the helpless victim. Although the details of setting are relatively scant, study will show that they were selected and handled with unusual skill.

Edgar Allan Poe

THE CASK OF AMONTILLADO

The thousand injuries of Fortunato I had borne as I best could; but when he ventured upon insult, I vowed revenge. You, who so well know the nature of my soul, will not suppose, however, that I gave utterance to a threat. *At length* I would be avenged; this was a point definitively settled; but the very definitiveness with which it was resolved precluded the idea of risk. I must not only punish, but punish with impunity. A wrong is unredressed when retribution overtakes its redresser. It is equally unredressed when the avenger fails to make himself felt as such to him who has done the wrong.

It must be understood that neither by word nor deed had I given Fortunato cause to doubt my good-will. I continued, as was my wont, to smile in his face, and he did not perceive that my smile *now* was at the thought of his immolation.

He had a weak point, this Fortunato, although in other regards he was a man to be respected and even feared. He prided himself on his connoisseurship in wine. Few Italians have the true virtuoso spirit. For the most part their enthusiasm is adopted to suit the time and opportunity, to practice imposture upon the British and Austrian millionaires. In painting and gemmary Fortunato, like his countrymen, was a quack; but in the matter of old wines he was sincere. In this respect I did not differ from him materially: I was skillful in the Italian vintages myself, and bought largely whenever I could.

It was about dusk one evening, during the supreme madness of the carnival season, that I encountered my friend. He accosted me with excessive warmth, for he had been drinking much. The man wore motley. He had on a tight-fitting parti-striped dress, and his head was surmounted by the conical cap and bells. I was so pleased to see him that I thought I should never have done wringing his hand.

I said to him: "My dear Fortunato, you are luckily met. How remarkably well you are looking to-day! But I have received a pipe of what passes for Amontillado, and I have my doubts."

"How?" said he. "Amontillado? A pipe? Impossible! And in the middle of the carnival!"

"I have my doubts," I replied; "and I was silly enough to pay the full Amontillado price without consulting you in the matter. You were not to be found, and I was fearful of losing a bargain."

"Amontillado!"

"I have my doubts."

"Amontillado!"

"And I must satisfy them."

"Amontillado!"

"As you are engaged, I am on my way to Luchesi. If any one has a critical turn, it is he. He will tell me—"

"Luchesi cannot tell Amontillado from sherry."

"And yet some fools will have it that his taste is a match for your own."

"Come, let us go."

"Whither?"

"To your vaults."

"My friend, no; I will not impose upon your good-nature. I perceive you have an engagement. Luchesi—"

"I have no engagement; come."

"My friend, no. It is not the engagement, but the severe cold with which I perceive you are afflicted. The vaults are insufferably damp. They are incrusted with niter."

"Let us go, nevertheless. The cold is merely nothing. Amontillado! You have been imposed upon. And as for Luchesi, he cannot distinguish sherry from Amontillado."

Thus speaking, Fortunato possessed himself of my arm. Putting on a mask of black silk, and drawing a *roquelaure* closely about my person, I suffered him to hurry me to my palazzo.

There were no attendants at home; they had absconded to make merry in honor of the time. I had told them that I should not return until the morning, and had given them explicit orders not to stir from the house. These orders were sufficient, I well knew, to insure their immediate disappearance, one and all, as soon as my back was turned.

I took from their sconces two flambeaux, and, giving one to Fortunato, bowed him through several suites of rooms to the archway that led into the vaults. I passed down a long and winding staircase, requesting him to be cautious as he followed. We came at length to the foot of the descent, and stood together on the damp ground of the catacombs of the Montresors.

The gait of my friend was unsteady, and the bells upon his cap jingled as he strode.

"The pipe?" said he.

"It is farther on," said I; "but observe the white webwork which gleams from these cavern walls."

He turned towards me, and looked into my eyes with two filmy orbs that distilled the rheum of intoxication.

"Niter?" he asked at length.

"Niter," I replied. "How long have you had that cough?"

"Ugh! ugh! ugh!—ugh! ugh! ugh!—ugh! ugh! ugh!—ugh! ugh! ugh!— ugh! ugh! ugh!"

My poor friend found it impossible to reply for many minutes.

"It is nothing," he said, at last.

"Come," I said, with decision, "we will go back; your health is precious. You are rich, respected, admired, beloved; you are happy, as once I was. You are a man to be missed. For me it is no matter. We will go back; you will be ill, and I cannot be responsible. Besides, there is Luchesi—"

"Enough," he said; "the cough is a mere nothing; it will not kill me. I shall not die of a cough."

"True—true," I replied; "and, indeed, I had no intention of alarming you unnecessarily; but you should use all proper caution. A draught of this Medoc will defend us from the damps."

Here I knocked off the neck of a bottle which I drew from a long row of its fellows that lay upon the mold.

"Drink," I said, presenting him the wine.

He raised it to his lips with a leer. He paused and nodded to me familiarly, while his bells jingled.

"I drink," he said, "to the buried that repose around us."

"And I to your long life."

He again took my arm and we proceeded.

"These vaults," he said, "are extensive."

"The Montresors," I replied, "were a great and numerous family."

"I forget your arms."

"A huge human foot d'or, in a field azure; the foot crushes a serpent rampant whose fangs are imbedded in the heel."

"And the motto?"

"Nemo me impune lacessit."[1]

"Good!" he said.

The wine sparkled in his eyes and the bells jingled. My own fancy grew warm with the Medoc. We had passed through walls of piled bones, with casks and puncheons intermingling, into the inmost recesses of the catacombs. I paused again, and this time I made bold to seize Fortunato by an arm above the elbow.

"The niter!" I said; "see, it increases. It hangs like moss upon the vaults. We are below the river's bed. The drops of moisture trickle among the bones. Come, we will go back ere it is too late. Your cough—"

"It is nothing," he said; "let us go on. But first, another draught of the Medoc."

I broke and reached him a flagon of De Grâve. He emptied it at a breath. His eyes flashed with a fierce light. He laughed and threw the bottle upward with a gesticulation I did not understand.

I looked at him in surprise. He repeated the movement—a grotesque one.

"You do not comprehend?" he said.

"Not I," I replied.

"Then you are not of the brotherhood."

"How?"

"You are not of the masons."

"Yes, yes," I said; "yes, yes."

"You? Impossible! A mason?"

"A mason," I replied.

"A sign," he said.

"It is this," I answered, producing a trowel from beneath the folds of my *roquelaure*.

"You jest!" he exclaimed, recoiling a few paces. "But let us proceed to the Amontillado."

"Be it so," I said, replacing the tool beneath the cloak, and again offering him my arm. He leaned upon it heavily. We continued our route in search of the Amontillado. We passed through a range of low arches, descended, passed on, and, descending again, arrived at a deep crypt, in which the foulness of the air caused our flambeaux rather to glow than flame.

At the most remote end of the crypt there appeared another less spacious. Its walls had been lined with human remains, piled to the vault overhead, in the fashion of the great catacombs of Paris. Three sides of this interior crypt

---

1. No one injures me with impunity.

were still ornamented in this manner. From the fourth the bones had been thrown down, and lay promiscuously upon the earth, forming at one point a mound of some size. Within the wall thus exposed by the displacing of the bones we perceived a still interior recess, in depth about four feet, in width three, in height six or seven. It seemed to have been constructed for no especial use within itself, but formed merely the interval between two of the colossal supports of the roof of the catacombs, and was backed by one of their circumscribing walls of solid granite.

It was in vain that Fortunato, uplifting his dull torch, endeavored to pry into the depth of the recess. Its termination the feeble light did not enable us to see.

"Proceed," I said; "herein is the Amontillado. As for Luchesi—"

"He is an ignoramus," interrupted my friend, as he stepped unsteadily forward, while I followed immediately at his heels. In an instant he had reached the extremity of the niche, and, finding his progress arrested by the rock, stood stupidly bewildered. A moment more and I had fettered him to the granite. In its surface were two iron staples, distant from each other about two feet, horizontally. From one of these depended a short chain, from the other a padlock. Throwing the links about his waist, it was but the work of a few seconds to secure it. He was too much astounded to resist. Withdrawing the key, I stepped back from the recess.

"Pass your hand," I said, "over the wall; you cannot help feeling the niter. Indeed it is *very* damp. Once more let me *implore* you to return. No? Then I must positively leave you. But I must first render you all the little attentions in my power."

"The Amontillado!" ejaculated my friend, not yet recovered from his astonishment.

"True," I replied: "the Amontillado."

As I said these words I busied myself among the pile of bones of which I have before spoken. Throwing them aside, I soon uncovered a quantity of building stone and mortar. With these materials and with the aid of my trowel, I began vigorously to wall up the entrance of the niche.

I had scarcely laid the first tier of the masonry when I discovered that the intoxication of Fortunato had in a great measure worn off. The earliest indication I had of this was a low, moaning cry from the depth of the recess. It was *not* the cry of a drunken man. There was then a long and obstinate silence. I laid the second tier, and the third, and the fourth; and then I heard the furious vibrations of the chain. The noise lasted for several minutes, during which, that I might harken to it with the more satisfaction, I ceased my labors and sat down upon the bones. When at last the clanking subsided, I resumed the trowel, and finished without interruption the fifth, the sixth, and the seventh tier. The wall was now nearly upon a level with my breast. I again paused, and, holding the flambeaux over the masonwork, threw a few feeble rays upon the figure within.

A succession of loud and shrill screams, bursting suddenly from the throat of the chained form, seemed to thrust me violently back. For a brief moment I hesitated, I trembled. Unsheathing my rapier, I began to grope with it about the recess; but the thought of an instant reassured me. I placed my hand upon the solid fabric of the catacombs and felt satisfied. I reapproached the wall. I replied to the yells of him who clamored. I re-echoed, I aided, I surpassed them in volume and in strength. I did this, and the clamorer grew still.

It was now midnight, and my task was drawing to a close. I had completed the eighth, the ninth, and the tenth tier. I had finished a portion of the last and the eleventh; there remained but a single stone to be fitted and plastered in. I struggled with its weight; I placed it partially in its destined position. But now there came from out the niche a low laugh that erected the hairs upon my head. It was succeeded by a sad voice, which I had difficulty in recognizing as that of the noble Fortunato. The voice said:

"Ha! ha! ha!—he! he!—a very good joke indeed, an excellent jest. We will have many a rich laugh about it at the palazzo—he! he! he!—over our wine— he! he! he!"

"The Amontillado!" I said.

"He! he! he!—he! he! he!—yes, the Amontillado. But is it not getting late? Will not they be awaiting us at the palazzo,—the Lady Fortunato and the rest? Let us be gone."

"Yes," I said, "let us be gone."

"For the love of God, Montresor!"

"Yes," I said, "for the love of God!"

But to these words I harkened in vain for a reply. I grew impatient. I called aloud:

"Fortunato!"

No answer. I called again.

"Fortunato!"

No answer still. I thrust a torch through the remaining aperture and let it fall within. There came forth in return only a jingling of the bells. My heart grew sick—on account of the dampness of the catacombs. I hastened to make an end of my labor. I forced the last stone into its position; I plastered it up. Against the new masonry I re-erected the old rampart of bones. For the half of a century no mortal has disturbed them. *In pace requiescat!*[1]

SETTING, ACTION, AND CHARACTERS

1. What is the value, for the story, of presenting the first brief scene (par. 3, p. 61) "about dusk one evening, during the supreme madness of the carnival season"? Why is Fortunato's carnival costume appropriate for this story? In what two ways does the carnival help make Montresor's revenge possible?

2. In the last paragraph on page 61, the narrator first mentions the "insufferably damp" vaults "incrusted with niter." His expressed concern, of course, is not sincerely felt; he is being ironic. Point out other examples of irony—in the contrast between the scenes outside and inside the vaults, the names of the

---

1. May he rest in peace.

characters, the dialogue. What quality of Montresor does this irony underline? Why is such underlining desirable in motivating the action?

3. A few paragraphs later, Montresor calls attention to "the white webwork" on the walls. Why, in terms of the story, should he not talk instead of white crystals? The white material is identified as "niter." What chemical properties and uses of niter make continued emphasis upon it desirable?

4. A passage on page 63 concerns the coat of arms of the Montresors. Why are they particularly appropriate for the family of the character in this story?

5. Comment in detail upon the value for the narrative of the elements in the setting set forth on pages 63-65.

6. Trace Fortunato's changing emotions from the beginning to his final cry. What is indicated by Montresor's remark in the last paragraph, "My heart grew sick—on account of the dampness of the catacombs"?

7. Generalize about Poe's use of setting as an adjunct to this narrative.

8. What are the characteristics of Montresor and Fortunato? How are they shown? How are they related to the action?

9. Compare Poe's handling of setting with that of O'Connor, page 4; Dunsany, page 36; and Warren, page 49.

One of the most admired opening chapters in English fiction is the first chapter of *Bleak House,* a book which Dickens wrote between 1851 and 1853. Critics have pointed out that the chapter is an extraordinarily meaningful overture to the long and complicated story that follows. As G. K. Chesterton has noted, in the opening paragraphs, "we have the feeling that it is not only a beginning; we have the feeling that the author sees the conclusion and the whole." The vivid and unified description evokes an unforgettable atmosphere. It does more: it initiates an attack (which is to be developed during the course of the whole angry novel) upon a widespread evil.

Charles Dickens

IN CHANCERY

LONDON. Michaelmas Term lately over, and the Lord Chancellor sitting in Lincoln's Inn Hall. Implacable November weather. As much mud in the streets, as if the waters had but newly retired from the face of the earth, and it would not be wonderful to meet a Megalosaurus, forty feet long or so, waddling like an elephantine lizard up Holborn Hill. Smoke lowering down from chimney-pots, making a soft black drizzle, with flakes of soot in it as big as full-grown snowflakes—gone into mourning, one might imagine, for the death of the sun. Dogs, undistinguishable in mire. Horses, scarcely better; splashed to their very blinkers. Foot passengers, jostling one another's umbrellas, in a general infection of ill-temper, and losing their foothold at street-corners, where tens of thousands of other foot passengers have been slipping and sliding since the day broke (if this day ever broke), adding new deposits to the crust upon crust of mud, sticking at those points tenaciously to the pavement, and accumulating at compound interest.

Fog everywhere. Fog up the river, where it flows among green aits and meadows; fog down the river, where it rolls defiled among the tiers of shipping, and the waterside pollutions of a great (and dirty) city. Fog on the Essex marshes, fog on the Kentish heights. Fog creeping into the cabooses of collier-brigs; fog lying out on the yards, and hovering in the rigging of great ships; fog drooping on the gunwales of barges and small boats. Fog in the eyes and throats of ancient Greenwich pensioners, wheezing by the fire-side of their wards; fog in the stem and bowl of the afternoon pipe of the wrath-ful skipper, down in his close cabin, fog cruelly pinching the toes and fingers of his shivering little 'prentice boy on deck. Chance people on the bridges peeping over the parapets into a nether sky of fog, with fog all round them, as if they were up in a balloon, and hanging in the misty clouds.

Gas looming through the fog in divers places in the streets, much as the sun may, from the spongy fields, be seen to loom by husbandman and ploughboy. Most of the shops lighted two hours before their time—as the gas seems to know, for it has a haggard and unwilling look.

The raw afternoon is rawest, and the dense fog is densest, and the muddy streets are muddiest, near that leaden-headed old obstruction, appropriate orna-ment for the threshold of a leaden-headed old corporation: Temple Bar. And hard by Temple Bar, in Lincoln's Inn Hall, at the very heart of the fog, sits the Lord High Chancellor in his High Court of Chancery.

Never can there come fog too thick, never can there come mud and mire too deep, to assort with the groping and floundering condition which this High Court of Chancery, most pestilent of hoary sinners, holds, this day, in the sight of heaven and earth.

On such an afternoon, if ever, the Lord High Chancellor ought to be sitting here—as here he is—with a foggy glory round his head, softly fenced in with crimson cloth and curtains, addressed by a large advocate with great whiskers, a little voice, and an interminable brief, and outwardly directing his contempla-tion to the lantern in the roof, where he can see nothing but fog. On such an afternoon, some score of members of the High Court of Chancery bar ought to be—as here they are—mistily engaged in one of the ten thousand stages of an endless cause, tripping one another up on slippery precedents, groping knee-deep in technicalities, running their goat-hair and horse-hair warded heads against walls of words, and making a pretence of equity with serious faces, as players might. On such an afternoon, the various solicitors in the cause, some two or three of whom have inherited it from their fathers, who made a fortune by it, ought to be—as are they not?—ranged in a line, in a long matted well (but you might look in vain for truth at the bottom of it), between the registrar's red table and the silk gowns, with bills, cross-bills, answers, rejoinders, injunctions, affidavits, issues, references to masters, masters' reports, mountains of costly nonsense, piled before them. Well may the court be dim, with wasting candles here and there; well may the fog hang heavy in it, as if it would never get out; well may the stained glass windows lose their color, and admit no light of day into the place; well may the uninitiated from the streets, who peep in through the glass panes in the door, be deterred from entrance by its owlish aspect, and by the drawl languidly echoing to the roof from the padded dais where the Lord High Chancellor looks into the lantern that has no light in it, and where the attendant wigs are all stuck in a fog-bank! This is the Court of Chancery; which has its decaying houses and its blighted lands in every shire; which has its worn-out lunatic in every madhouse, and its dead in every churchyard; which has its ruined suitor, with his slipshod heels and threadbare dress, borrowing and begging through the round of every man's acquaintance; which gives to moneyed might, the means abundantly of wearying out the right; which so exhausts finances, patience, courage, hope; so overthrows the brain and breaks the heart; that there is not an honorable man among its practitioners who would not give—who does not often give—the warning, "Suffer any wrong that can be done you, rather than come here!"

Who happen to be in the Lord Chancellor's court this murky afternoon besides the Lord Chancellor, the counsel in the cause, two or three counsel who are never in any cause, and the well of solicitors before mentioned? There is the registrar below the Judge, in wig and gown; and there are two or three maces, or petty bags, or privy purses, or whatever they may be, in legal court suits. These are all yawning; for no crumb of amusement ever falls from *Jarndyce and Jarndyce* (the cause in hand), which was squeezed dry years upon years ago. The short-hand writers, the reporters of the court, and the reporters of the newspapers, invariably decamp with the rest of the regulars when Jarndyce and Jarndyce comes on. Their places are a blank. Standing, on a seat at the side of the hall, the better to peer into the curtained sanctuary, is a little mad old woman in a squeezed bonnet, who is always in court, from its sitting to its rising, and always expecting some incomprehensible judgment to be given in her favor. Some say she really is or was, a party to a suit; but no one knows for certain, because no one cares. She carries some small litter in a reticule which she calls her documents; principally consisting of paper matches and dry lavender. A sallow prisoner has come up, in custody, for the half-dozenth time, to make a personal application "to purge himself of his contempt;" which, being a solitary surviving executor who has fallen into a state of conglomeration about accounts of which it is not pretended that he had ever any knowledge, he is not at all likely ever to do. In the meantime his prospects in life are ended. Another ruined suitor, who periodically appears from Shropshire, and breaks out into efforts to address the Chancellor at the close of the day's business, and who can by no means be made to understand that the Chancellor is legally ignorant of his existence after making it desolate for a quarter of a century, plants himself in a good place and keeps an eye on the Judge, ready to call out "My Lord!" in a voice of sonorous complaint, on the instant of his rising. A few lawyers' clerks and others who know this suitor by sight, linger, on the chance of his furnishing some fun, and enlivening the dismal weather a little.

Jarndyce and Jarndyce drones on. This scarecrow of a suit has, in course of time, become so complicated, that no man alive knows what it means. The parties to it understand it least; but it has been observed that no two Chancery lawyers can talk about it for five minutes, without coming to a total disagreement as to all the premises. Innumerable children have been born into the cause; innumerable young people have married into it; innumerable old people have died out of it. Scores of persons have deliriously found themselves made parties in Jarndyce and Jarndyce, without knowing how or why; whole families have inherited legendary hatreds with the suit. The little plaintiff or defendant, who was promised a new rocking-horse when Jarndyce and Jarndyce should be settled, has grown up, possessed himself of a real horse, and trotted away into the other world. Fair wards of court have faded into mothers and grandmothers; a long procession of Chancellors has come in and gone out; the legion of bills in the suit have been transformed into mere bills of mortality; there are not three Jarndyces left upon the earth perhaps, since old Tom Jarndyce in despair blew his brains out at a coffee-house in Chancery Lane; but Jarndyce and Jarndyce still drags its dreary length before the Court, perennially hopeless.

Jarndyce and Jarndyce has passed into a joke. That is the only good that has ever come of it. It has been death to many, but it is a joke in the profession. Every master in Chancery has had a reference out of it. Every Chancellor was "in it," for somebody or other, when he was counsel at the bar. Good things have been said about it by blue-nosed, bulbous-shoed old benchers, in select port-wine committee after dinner in hall. Articled clerks have been in the habit of fleshing their legal wit upon it. The last Lord Chancellor handled it neatly, when, correcting Mr. Blowers the eminent silk gown who said that such a thing might happen when the sky rained potatoes, he observed. "or when we get through Jarndyce and Jarndyce, Mr. Blowers;"—a pleasantry that particularly tickled the maces, bags, and purses.

How many people out of the suit, Jarndyce and Jarndyce has stretched forth its unwholesome hand to spoil and corrupt, would be a very wide question. From the master, upon whose impaling files reams of dusty warrants in Jarndyce and Jarndyce have grimly writhed into many shapes; down to the copying-clerk in the Six Clerks' Office, who has copied his tens of thousands of Chancery-folio-pages under that eternal heading; no man's nature has been made better by it. In trickery, evasion, procrastination, spoliation, botheration, under false pretences, of all sorts, there are influences that can never come to good. The very solicitors' boys who have kept the wretched suitors at bay, by protesting time out of mind that Mr. Chizzle, Mizzle, or otherwise, was particularly engaged and had appointments until dinner, may have got an extra moral twist and shuffle into themselves out of Jarndyce and Jarndyce. The receiver in the cause has acquired a goodly sum of money by it, but has acquired too a distrust of his own mother, and a contempt for his own kind. Chizzle, Mizzle, and otherwise have lapsed into a habit of vaguely promising themselves that they will look into that outstanding little matter, and see what can be done for Drizzle—who was not well used—when Jarndyce and Jarndyce shall be got out of the office. Shirking and sharking, in all their many varieties, have been sown broadcast by the ill-fated cause; and even those who have contemplated its history from the outermost circle of such evil, have been insensibly tempted into a loose way of letting bad things alone to take their own bad course, and a loose belief that if the world go wrong, it was, in some offhand manner, never meant to go right.

Thus, in the midst of the mud and at the heart of the fog, sits the Lord High Chancellor in his High Court of Chancery.

SETTING, ACTION, AND CHARACTERS

1. The opening paragraph deals with mud, the second with fog, the third with gas. How does the choice of details in each bind all three together?

2. In the fourth and fifth paragraphs, the author pictures the High Court of Chancery. What is the business of this court? What is the author's view of the court and its activities? What details in the picture give the court an atmosphere akin to that of the opening three paragraphs of the selection?

3. Says Edgar Johnson: "The fog . . . is both literal and allegorical. It is the sooty London fog, but it covers all England, and it is the fog of obstructive procedures and outmoded institutions and selfish interests and obscure thinking as well." Indicate how these meanings are enforced by the following: (a) the Megalosaurus of paragraph 1, (b) the indications about the extent of the fog in paragraph 2, (c) the particularly raw afternoon, dense fog, and muddy streets near the court.

4. In paragraph 6, what relationship is established between the surrounding fog and the Lord High Chancellor, the members of the court, the solicitors, and the attendants? How is the sentence which is made up of a series of clauses beginning with the words *well may*—each describing an aspect of the scene—related to the final sentence in the paragraph?

5. How have the details about the case of Jarndyce and Jarndyce been prepared for in the description preceding their introduction?

6. The "very wide question" with which the novel is to be concerned, as stated by Dickens, is, "How many people out of the suit, Jarndyce and Jarndyce has stretched forth its unwholesome hand to spoil and corrupt?" Morton D. Zabel has remarked, "Scarcely a noun or adjective in this opening chapter leaves the nature of that doom unsuggested." What words do you think he has in mind? What is that doom to be?

In this poem, one of the finest by a great nineteenth-century poet, almost everything accomplished is the result of the author's depiction of a setting. The setting is the English countryside in the autumn. This scene changes in a simple but highly meaningful fashion as the poem moves through its three brief stanzas. As a result of Keats' selection and handling of details, the setting subtly indicates the thought and the feeling of the poet.

John Keats

TO AUTUMN

Season of mists and mellow fruitfulness,
    Close bosom-friend of the maturing sun;
Conspiring with him how to load and bless
    With fruit the vines that round the thatch-eaves run;
To bend with apples the moss'd cottage-trees,   5
    And fill all fruit with ripeness to the core;
        To swell the gourd, and plump the hazel shells
With a sweet kernel; to set budding more,
    And still more, later flowers for the bees,
    Until they think warm days will never cease,   10
        For Summer has o'er-brimm'd their clammy cells.

Who hath not seen thee oft amid thy store?
    Sometimes whoever seeks abroad may find
Thee sitting careless on a granary floor,
    Thy hair soft-lifted by the winnowing wind;   15
Or on a half-reap'd furrow sound asleep,
    Drows'd with the fume of poppies, while thy hook
        Spares the next swath and all its twinèd flowers;
And sometimes like a gleaner thou dost keep
    Steady thy laden head across a brook;   20
    Or by a cider-press, with patient look,
        Thou watchest the last oozings, hours by hours.

Where are the songs of Spring? Ay, where are they?
    Think not of them, thou hast thy music too,—
While barrèd clouds bloom the soft-dying day,   25
    And touch the stubble-plains with rosy hue;
Then in a wailful choir the small gnats mourn
    Among the river sallows, borne aloft
        Or sinking as the light wind lives or dies;
And full-grown lambs loud bleat from hilly bourn;   30

Hedge-crickets sing; and now with treble soft
The redbreast whistles from a garden-croft;
And gathering swallows twitter in the skies.

SETTINGS, ACTION, AND CHARACTERS

1. Which word best summarizes the concept of autumn chiefly developed in stanza 1: mists, mellow fruitfulness, bless? How do the verbs contribute to the expression of this concept? What is noteworthy about the verbs? the aspects of the scene emphasized? What details do not contribute to this concept?

2. Contrast the selection of details in Keats' first stanza with the selection of details in this stanza:

> O gorgeous Autumn-tide, to thee I sing!
> O thou art fairer, warmer, far, I ween,
> Than is the time of blossom-dappled Spring,
> Or Winter with red hearth and snowy scene.
> Now meadows erstwhile wondrous green
> Are dotted here and there with rain-greyed corn
>   In shocks, and in between,
>   The ground is black. Against the cloudy sky,
> Black trees lift shivering leaves on high,
>   And night brings frosts and chill is every morn.
> O Autumn, drenched with color, thee I sing—
> And praise the fruits and leaves that thou dost bring.

3. What phase of autumn is depicted in stanza 2? What chronological progress is traced through these sets of lines: 12-15, 16-18, 19-20, 21-22? Suggest a summarizing word for the phenomena described in stanza 2.

4. Read line 22 aloud, and you will see that the sounds suggest weariness. Do other details in the stanza also suggest weariness? Be specific.

5. Sum up the contrasts between the picture of autumn in stanzas 2 and 3.

6. Stanza 3 begins by asking where the songs of Spring are. How does the inferred answer prepare for the concept of autumn given in this stanza? What is this concept, and what details enforce it?

7. How would the substitution of the following details spoil the impression of autumn set forth in stanza 3: "quick-passing" for "soft-dying" (25), "snarl" for "mourn" (27), "music" for "treble" (31)?

8. How does the last stanza justify these details in stanza 1: mists, conspiring, think, clammy?

9. What other relationships are there between the three stanzas? Why would it be undesirable to change the order of the stanzas?

10. What conclusions can you draw from "To Autumn" about the poet's character? How is it related to what happens in the poem?

11. Can you find any meaning in this poem? If so, state it, and suggest how the selection and handling of details in the setting contribute to it.

Language

Language used in imaginative works bodies forth the action. the setting, and the characters; it withholds or gives emphasis, emotional colorations, and interpretations. Therefore, the reader does well to notice how the author's manner of using words, phrases, sentences, and rhythms relates to the achievement of the story, the drama, or the poem.

WORDS, ACTION, AND SETTINGS

In portraying either action or setting, the author may use language to convey emphasis and vividness, and to suggest emotional interpretations. If, for instance, he tells us merely, "After the three individuals departed, they encountered two other individuals," thereby he relegates this encounter to an unimportant place. The account is unemphatic for two reasons—(1) because it is brief, and (2) because it is abstract. And if the encounter is actually unimportant in the particular chain of events being presented, the reader notes that the language is appropriately handled.

But suppose the event were an important one—how might the author use words to emphasize it? Note what Ernest Hemingway does in the following passage:

The three of them started for the door, and I watched them go. They were good-looking young fellows, wore good clothes. . . . As they turned out of the door to the right, I saw a closed car come across the square toward them. The first thing a pane of glass went and the bullet smashed into the row of bottles on the show case wall to the right. I heard the gun going and bop, bop, bop, there were bottles smashing all along the wall.

I jumped behind the bar on the left and could see over the edge. The car was stopped and there were two fellows crouched down by it. One had a Thompson gun and the other had a sawed-off automatic shotgun. . . . One of the boys was spread out on the sidewalk, face down, just outside the big window that was smashed. The other two were behind one of the Tropical beer ice wagons. . . . One of the boys shot from the rear corner of the wagon and it ricocheted off the sidewalk. . . . You could see the buckshot marks all over the sidewalk like silver splatters.—*To Have and Have Not*

Here emphasis is achieved because the incident is treated at some length. Moreover, the author uses few abstract words such as "individuals," "departed," and "encountered." Rather, he uses *concrete words* which specify details in the happening, for instance, "closed car," "smashed," "ricocheted." Such image-bearing words convey sensory impressions, achieve vividness, and therefore give the passage more emotional impact than an abstract (and hence neutral) account possibly could have. Quintilian, the famous Roman critic, long ago pointed out that "he who says that a city is captured . . . makes no impression on the feelings." "It is less impressive to tell the whole at once," he added, "than to specify the different particulars." A stanza shows how the poet Shakespeare "specified the different particulars" by using concrete words:

> When icicles hang by the wall,
>   And Dick the shepherd blows his nail,
> And Tom bears logs into the hall,
>   And milk comes frozen home in pail,
> When blood is nipped and ways be foul,
> Then nightly sings the staring owl,
> Tu-whit, tu-who! a merry note,
> While greasy Joan doth keel the pot.

WORDS WHICH EVOKE EMOTIONS

But it should be noticed that in using concrete words, both authors are *selective*. Hemingway has said that the writer's problem is to set down "the real thing, the sequence of motion and fact which make the emotion. . . . If you get so you can give that to people then you are a writer." The author—not only Hemingway but any writer—therefore leaves out details irrelevant to such a sequence. The quiet sunlight on the square where the encounter took place, the beggars asleep in the sunlight (actually described by Hemingway in an earlier scene) here would spoil the record of tense and vicious action. Similarly, Shakespeare leaves out of his stanza a number of details which are characteristic of winter but not of the emotional concept of the season he is presenting.

Concrete words, and abstract ones as well—furthermore, are often valuable not only for denotations, or dictionary meanings, but also for their connotations, or *emotional associations.* You will see the importance of our accretions of feelings about certain words if you consider these possible (though not desirable) substitutions in the Hemingway passage: "disappeared" for "went," and "broke" for "smashed" in sentence 4; "shattering" for "smashing" in sentence 5; "leaped" for "jumped" in sentence 6; "squatted" for "crouched" in sentence 7; and "wrecked" for "smashed" in sentence 9. Substitutions in Shakespeare's poem will show that connotations there are also important for the expression of emotion.

FIGURATIVE PHRASES

When, however, selected concrete words will not convey with sufficient precision the exact emotional quality of a scene, the author may use phrases or sentences making *poetic comparisons*. Figures of speech—metaphors, similes, hyperboles, and others—are valuable chiefly because they indicate the nature of an emotion. The phrase "buckshot marks . . . like silver splatters" in the passage by Hemingway is a figurative one: literally, the marks are lead splatters, but the author figuratively compares them with silver. This particular simile is more valuable for its vividness than its emotional freighting, but compare a sailor's memory of his first impression of the East, in Joseph Conrad's *Youth:*

And this is how I see the East. I have seen its secret places and have looked into its very soul; but now I see it always from a small boat, a high outline of mountains, blue and afar in the morning; like a faint mist at noon; a jagged wall of purple at sunset. I have the feel of the oar in my hand, the vision of a scorching blue sea in my eyes. And I see a bay, a wide bay, smooth as glass and polished like ice, shimmering in the dark. A red light burns far off upon the gloom of the land, and the night is soft and warm. We drag at the oars with aching arms, and suddenly a puff of wind, a puff faint and tepid and laden with strange odors of blossoms, of aromatic wood, comes out of the still night—the first sigh of the East on my face. That I can never forget. It was impalpable and enslaving, like a charm, like a whispered promise of mysterious delight.

There are many concrete words here—Conrad once defined his task thus: "by the power of the written word, to make you hear, to make you feel . . . before all, to make you *see*." But the end of such vividness, he went on to say, is to hold up a fragment of experience, "to show its vibration, its color, its form and through its movement, its form, its color, reveal the substance of its truth— disclose the inspiring secret: the stress and passion within the core of each convincing moment." The concrete words in the passage contribute much to the revelation of the "stress and passion" here—the impression of the East as "impalpable and enslaving"; but the figurative phrases contribute even more. The narrator who has achingly rowed across a seemingly shoreless "scorching blue sea" conveys his delight by telling how mountains changed from a figurative "faint mist at noon" to a palpable and cool-colored shape at sunset—figuratively, "a jagged wall of purple." He conveys his emotion when he tells how, storm-tossed and sun-parched, he looked at last upon a dark wide bay—figuratively, "smooth as glass and polished like ice." The "soft and warm" night figuratively suggests rest for his tired body. And the figurative characterization of the breeze as "the first sigh of the East . . . impalpable and enslaving, like a charm, like a whispered promise of mysterious delight" gives more than a vivid account of a puff of wind: it conveys emotion by subtly likening this welcome haven to an entrancing yet enigmatic woman. Thus figures of speech help define an emotion precisely.

SENTENCES AND RHYTHMS

A comparison between the passage by Hemingway and that by Conrad will suggest that, in addition to words and phrases, *sentences* and *rhythms* are important elements for representing action, settings, and emotions. The simple sentences and compound sentences, with a minimum number of modifiers, which make up the first passage are appropriate for describing rapid action. More complex sentences with numerous appositions and figurative phrases which savor details, are appropriate for Conrad's lyrical account. In Hemingway's paragraphs, a large proportion of one-syllable words which frequently cluster accented syllables ("wóre goód clóthes," "clósed cár cóme," "gláss wént," "shów cáse wáll," "bóp, bóp, bóp," "fáce dówn," "béer icé wágons," etc.) achieve a staccato rhythm corresponding to the action. As writing comes nearer to poetry in expressing emotion, it tends to approach regular rhythms like those in poetry; therefore, Conrad's emotional passage is, for prose, remarkably close at times to iambic and anapestic verse. (See the consideration of rhythms in the introduction to poetry, pp. 705-707). At an opposite extreme from the Hemingway passage is Shakespeare's stanza, with its regular use (after the opening line) of iambic rhythm. Between these two extremes, all sorts of variations are available to the author.

Not only *accent patterns* but also *sound patterns* figure in one kind of rhythmical arrangement—one in which the handling of consonants and vowels suggests the kind of action or the scene. A simple example is the "bop, bop, bop" of the Hemingway passage—wherein the sounds imitate those of gun explosions. The consonants *b* and *p* here used—like hard *c, d, g, k,* and *t*—as a matter of fact, are called "explosives," because you pronounce them by closing your mouth and exploding them with your breath. Note how the use of such consonants helps Tennyson imitate the progress of a knight in his clanking armor:

> Dry clashed his harness on the icy caves
> And barren chasms, and all left and right
> The bare black cliff clanged round him. . . .

But contrast with this Herrick's

> Whenas in silks my Julia goes,
> Then, then, methinks, how sweetly flows
> That liquefaction of her clothes.

Here a predominance of "continuous consonants," so called because they may be prolonged indefinitely (drawn from "sibilants"—soft *c, f, s, v, z*—and "liquids"—*l, m, n, r, ng*), imitates the smooth movement of the lady in silks. And vowels as well as consonants may, at times, be so managed that, as Pope puts it, the sound will "seem an echo of the sense." Compare the vowels (as well as the consonants) in these passages:

The huge round stone resulting with a bound,
Thunders impetuous down and smokes along the ground.
—POPE, Odyssey, XI

. . . the spires
Pricked with incredible pinnacles into heaven.
—TENNYSON, Holy Grail

Such suggestions by sound of sense are called *onomatopoeia*. Finally, there will be times, of course, when sound patterns are not used to imitate actions or scenes but to achieve sheer harmony which helps convey an emotion. At such times the author will use sounds of various sorts which blend melodiously.

LANGUAGE AND CHARACTERIZATION

In descriptions of the physical appearances or gestures of characters. an author uses language in ways comparable to those employed in describing action or scenes. Language is also important for characterization, in ways which we have not so far considered, when the work quotes the character—in first person narratives or in passages of dialog. Here, of course, the choice of words, the figures of speech, the sentences and rhythms may be useful because they are in keeping.

The connotations or associations of words used in dialog are as important as they are in descriptive passages, though in a rather different way. Here what might be called *"social" connotations* loom large. As H. J. C. Grierson remarks, words have *"color"*:

I mean by "color" the associations which gather around a word by long usage. The meaning provides the first nucleus for this, and then come all the accidental circumstances connected with our experience of the word—the people who use it, the places in which we have heard it, the other words and ideas it tends to evolve. And so we find that, against our will, some words are vulgarized, savor (for we might speak of "taste" as well as "color") of the streets and the music-hall; others are homely, though anything but vulgar, are redolent . . . of home, of familiar objects and experiences, of the farm-yard, the fishing-boat and the workshop; others are pedantic, schoolmaster's words that no healthy boy would ever use on the playground . . . . and other words are dignified, learned but not pedantic, for a learned word is only pedantic when it takes the place of a simpler or more obvious one . . . . and again others are lovely exotics that only the poets have ventured to use: "At length burst in the *argent* revelry."

"Color" in words shows itself when a sailor says, "We shipped a sea that carried away our pinnace and our binnacle," and a landsman says "A heavy wave broke over our ship." It shows itself when a pompous man mouths what Thoreau called "bad words—words like 'tribal' and 'ornamentation,' which drag their tails behind them." It shows itself when a politician uses words which fill the air with glittering but not very meaningful generalities. The coloration of a character's words shows us something about her when she addresses her mother: whether she calls her Hazel, Mom, Maw, Mother, or Mother Darling, we shall learn something about the character from the form of address. The kinds of words a character uses may show whether he is educated or unread, whether he has a sense of humor or is humorless, whether he is sensitive or crass, refined or vulgar, intelligent or stupid.

Figurative phrases or sentences used in dialog may also suggest much about the nature of the character. They may, by their allusions, suggest the character's background: witness how Huck Finn, born and reared in a river town, describes a room mussed up by his "pap"—"And when they come to look at that spare room they had to take soundings before they could navigate it." Trite figures may indicate unimaginativeness; literary figures, bookishness; original figures, imaginativeness; profane figures, irreligion; inept figures, a lack of a sense of proportion or a sense of humor; and so on.

Sentences, too, are important. In passages representing conversations or thoughts, authors often imitate the qualities of talk or of the thought processes. Perhaps they do this by suggesting the fumbling for words, the ambiguity, the repetition, the irrelevancies we hear in speech or notice in our thinking. Or they may construct sentences which have a fragmentary quality, awkwardness of arrangement, a frequent use of *and* and *but*. Sometimes the constructions are not only lifelike but also characteristic of certain kinds of people—for instance, bad grammar for the uneducated man, choppy sentences for the decisive man, fragmentary sentences—never finished—for the indecisive character, orotund and long sentences for the orator.

These, according to the nature of the work, will be more or less stenographic. They will never be completely literal transcriptions, however, because the author has to select and condense talk or thought, like everything else in his literary work. Furthermore, the adaptation of such material must be in tune with the style of the whole work. Thus if the work is a poem, although the speech may have definite lifelike qualities (see "My Last Duchess," p. 55, for instance), it will naturally be far more condensed and far more rhythmical than speech is. Or if the work is a drama, the author may allow some characters to speak lifelike prose, and forfeit the right to be realistically lifelike as he allows other characters to speak in the heightened style of blank verse. (See, for instance, *The Tragedy of Julius Caesar*, p. 18.)

Mark Twain once wrote this summary of part of *The Adventures of Huckleberry Finn*: "An ignorant village boy, Huck Finn, son of the town drunkard . . . has run away from his persecuting father, and from a persecuting good widow who wishes to make a nice, truth-telling, respectable boy of him; and with him a slave . . . has also escaped." In the following selection from *The Adventures of Huckleberry Finn*, Huck and the slave, Jim, are on Jackson's Island. They have taken shelter in a cave because Jim, after watching the behavior of some young birds, has predicted the coming of a rainstorm.

Samuel L. Clemens

STORM ON JACKSON'S ISLAND

Pretty soon it darkened up, and begun to thunder and lighten; so the birds was right about it. Directly it begun to rain, and it rained like all fury, too, and I never see the wind blow so. It was one of these regular summer storms. It would get so dark that it looked all blue-black outside, and lovely; and the rain would thrash along by so thick that the trees off a little ways looked dim and spider-webby; and here would come a blast of wind that would bend the trees down and turn up the pale underside of the leaves; and then a perfect ripper of a gust would follow along and set the branches to tossing their arms as if they was just wild; and next, when it was just about the bluest and blackest—*fst!* it was as bright as glory, and you'd have a little glimpse of treetops a-plunging about away off yonder in the storm, hundreds of yards further than you could see before; dark as sin again in a second, and now you'd hear the thunder let go with an awful crash, and then go rumbling, grumbling, tumbling, down the sky towards the under side of the world, like rolling empty barrels down-stairs— where it's long stairs and they bounce a good deal, you know.

LANGUAGE, CHARACTER, AND SETTING

1. What qualities in Huck's character may be deduced from his way of writing? How are the qualities appropriate for a character who has acted in the way indicated by Twain's synopsis? Precisely what qualities of his language indicate these traits?

2. Edgar Lee Masters has questioned the appropriateness of Huck's language in other parts of the book in this series of questions: "Would Huck, in speaking of his feeling, say 'very well satisfied'? Would he not rather say, 'and feelin' all right'? . . . Would he not say 'et' instead of 'eat'? Would he not say 'the lightning showed her very plain,' instead of 'the lightning showed her very distinct'?" What is Masters' criterion? Might he have drawn any examples from this passage? If so, cite some examples. Do you agree or disagree with his criticism? Why?

3. Comment upon the relative number of concrete and abstract words here. What is noteworthy about the verbs which Huck uses?

4. What figures of speech do you find in this passage? Is the use of so many figures of speech in character? Are they the sort an uneducated river-town boy would be likely to use? Do they help make the scene vivid? Why or why not? What is Huck's feeling about the storm, and to what extent do the figures of speech indicate it?

5. Discuss the words, *"fst!"* and "you'd hear the thunder let go with an awful crash, and then go rumbling, grumbling, tumbling" in relation to (a) Huck's character, (b) their value in this description.

6. Are the sentences formed more like those in talk or those in written discourse? Cite details which support your answer. How appropriate for Huck is their length? kind? arrangement?

7. Discuss the rhythms in the passage. How would you describe them? Are they useful to characterize Huck, to indicate his feelings, or to make vivid the scene?

The language of a scene from a play as old as *The Tempest* (c. 1611) offers some difficulties to students not familiar with the diction of Shakespeare's period. Such difficulties, however, may easily be overcome with the help of a small footnote glossary such as the one here supplied. Once you have understood the few unfamiliar words, you will find that this opening scene of one of the dramatist's late plays shows much about what a genius can do with words. The ship is one bearing Alonso, King of Naples; Sebastian, his brother; Antonio, the Duke of Milan; Ferdinand, Alonso's son; and Gonzalo, "an honest old Counsellor."

William Shakespeare

ON A SHIP AT SEA

Act I, Scene I: *On a ship at sea; a tempestuous noise of thunder and lightning heard. Enter a* SHIP-MASTER *and a* BOATSWAIN.

MASTER. Boatswain!

BOATSWAIN. Here, master: what cheer?

MASTER. Good, speak to the mariners. Fall to 't, yarely, or we run ourselves aground! Bestir, bestir! (*Exit, blowing his whistle*)

(*Enter* MARINERS)

2. *Master*, the captain. **3.** *Good*, my good fellow. *Fall to 't, yarely*, go about it, quickly.

BOATSWAIN. Heigh, my hearts! cheerly, cheerly, my hearts! yare, yare! Take in the topsail. Tend to the master's whistle. Blow, till thou burst thy wind, if room enough!

(Enter ALONSO, SEBASTIAN, ANTONIO, FERDINAND, GONZALO, *and others)*

ALONSO. Good boatswain, have care. Where's the master? Play the men.   11

BOATSWAIN. I pray now, keep below.

ANTONIO. Where is the master, bos'n?

BOATSWAIN. Do you not hear him? You mar our labor. Keep your cabins: you do assist the storm.

GONZALO. Nay, good, be patient.

BOATSWAIN. When the sea is. Hence! What cares these roarers for the name of king? To cabin! Silence! Trouble us not.

GONZALO. Good, yet remember whom thou hast aboard.   21

BOATSWAIN. None that I more love than myself. You are a counsellor; if you can command these elements to silence, and work the peace of the present, we will not hand a rope more; use your authority. If you cannot, give thanks you have lived so long, and make yourself ready in your cabin for the mischance of the hour, if it so hap. Cheerly, good hearts! Out of our way, I say. *(Exit)*   29

GONZALO. I have great comfort from this fellow; methinks he hath no drowning mark upon him; his complexion is perfect gallows. Stand fast, good Fate, to his hanging: make the rope of his destiny our cable, for our own doth little advantage. If he be not born to be hanged, our case is miserable. *(Exeunt)*   36

(Re-enter BOATSWAIN*)*

BOATSWAIN. Down with the topmast! Yare! Lower, lower! Bring her to try with main-course. *(A cry within)* A plague upon this howling! they are louder than the weather or our office.   40

(Re-enter SEBASTIAN, ANTONIO, *and* GONZALO*)*

BOATSWAIN. Yet, again! what do you here? Shall we give o'er and drown? Have you a mind to sink?

SEBASTIAN. A pox o' your throat, you bawling, blasphemous, incharitable dog!

BOATSWAIN. Work you then.

ANTONIO. Hang, cur! hang, you insolent noisemaker! We are less afraid to be drowned than thou art.

GONZALO. I'll warrant him for drowning; though the ship were no stronger than a nutshell.   51

6. *my hearts!* the equivalent of the more modern "my hearties." *cheerly,* with good cheer. 7. *Take in the topsail.* This was done in order to check the drift to leeward. 8. *Tend,* attend. *Blow . . . enough!* This speech is addressed to the wind. *if room enough,* if there is enough open sea. 11. *Play the men,* act as men should. 19. *roarers,* both roaring waves and bullies. 24. *work the peace of the present,* create peace immediately. 33. *the rope of his destiny,* the hangman's rope. 37. *Down with the topmast!* This is struck to take the weight from aloft and halt the drift leeward. 38. *Bring . . . main-course,* keep her close to the wind. 40. *our office,* our commands. 49. *for,* against.

The Shakespearean Theater

BOATSWAIN. Lay her a-hold, a-hold! set her two courses off to sea again;
   lay her off.
(Enter MARINERS *wet)*
MARINERS. All lost! to prayers, to prayers! all lost!   55
BOATSWAIN. What, must our mouths be cold?
GONZALO. The king and prince at prayers! let's assist them,
   For our case is as theirs.
SEBASTIAN.   I'm out of patience.
ANTONIO. We are merely cheated of our lives by drunkards:
   This wide-chapp'd rascal—would thou mightst lie drowning   60
   The washing of ten tides!
GONZALO.   He'll be hang'd yet,
   Though every drop of water swear against it
   And gape at widest to glut him.

Model of Globe Theatre used as basis for drawing by permission of John Cranford Adams
and Irwin Smith.
52. *Lay her a-hold . . . off*, keep her to the wind, set her foresail and her mainsail to carry
her to sea. **59.** *merely*, utterly. **60.** *wide-chapp'd*, big-mouthed.

(A confused noise within) 'Mercy on us!'—
    'We split, we split!'—'Farewell my wife and children!'—
    'Farewell, brother!'—'We split, we split, we split!'   65
ANTONIO. Let's all sink with the king.
SEBASTIAN. Let's take leave of him. *(Exeunt* ANTONIO *and* SEBASTIAN*)*
GONZALO. Now would I give a thousand furlongs of sea for an acre of
    barren ground, long heath, brown furze, any thing. The wills above be
    done! but I would fain die a dry death. *(Exeunt)*

LANGUAGE, SETTING, CHARACTERS, AND ACTION

1. The Shakespearean theater was, by our standards, quite bare of scenery.
How did Shakespeare make use of words and actions to evoke a vivid sense of
the setting?

2. Do the seamen talk as seamen should? Is there any evidence that Shakespeare took any pains to make them do so?

3. Critic Samuel Johnson said, "It may be observed of Gonzalo that, being
the only good man that appears with the king, he is the only man that preserves
his cheerfulness in the wreck. . . ." How does his way of talking indicate his
cheerfulness?

4. A sailor, writing of the boatswain, has called him "a grand old seadog,"
and has claimed that in this brief passage "we learn to know him as thoroughly
as though he lived and moved in our presence." Do you agree? Comment upon
line 60.

5. A scholar has cited lines 1-9 as an instance of Shakespeare's rhythmical
prose. How might he demonstrate that it is rhythmical? What value does
rhythmical prose have here?

6. Coleridge has pointed out that this scene has been appropriately handled
for the start of a romantic and imaginative play. "It is the bustle of a tempest,"
he says, "from which the real horrors are abstracted; therefore it is poetical,
though not in strictness natural, and it is purposely restrained from concentrating
the interest in itself, but used merely as an induction or tuning for what is to
follow." Do you agree or disagree? Why?

These lines from Homer's *Odyssey*, Book V, describe how Odysseus (Ulysses) en-

countered a storm loosed by Neptune. Ulysses, the King of Ithaca, had left his wife

and his young son to fight in the Trojan War. Troy had finally been taken in the tenth

year of the conflict, and Ulysses had started his long voyage home. Just before our

selection begins, he had left Calypso's Isle on a raft and had sailed along, pleasantly

enough, for seventeen days. Neptune, the god of the sea, then had sighted him and had announced that he would harass the wanderer. The passage tells of the storm which followed.

Homer

TRANSLATOR: *William Cullen Bryant*

'A FIERCE RUSH OF ALL THE WINDS'

He [Neptune] spoke, and round about him called the clouds
And roused the ocean, wielding in his hand
The trident, summoned all the hurricanes
Of all the winds, and covered earth and sky
At once with mists, while from above, the night   5
Fell suddenly. The east wind and the south
Rushed forth at once, with the strong-blowing west,
And the clear north rolled up his mighty waves.
Ulysses trembled in his knees and heart,
And thus to his great soul, lamenting, said: 10
    "What will become of me? unhappy man!
I fear that all the goddess said was true,
Foretelling what disasters should o'ertake
My voyage, ere I reach my native land.
Now are her words fulfilled. Now Jupiter   15
Wraps the great heaven in clouds and stirs the deep
To tumult! Wilder grow the hurricanes
Of all the winds, and now my fate is sure.
Thrice happy, four times happy they, who fell
On Troy's wide field, warring for Atreus' sons: 20
O, had I met my fate and perished there,
That very day on which the Trojan host,
Around the dead Achilles, hurled at me
Their brazen javelins! I had then received
Due burial and great glory with the Greeks;   25
Now must I die a miserable death."
    As thus he spoke, upon him, from on high,
A huge and frightful billow broke; it whirled
The raft around, and far from it he fell.
His hands let go the rudder; a fierce rush   30
Of all the winds together snapped in twain
The mast; far off the yard and canvas flew
Into the deep; the billow held him long
Beneath the waters, and he strove in vain

Quickly to rise to air from that huge swell   35
Of ocean, for the garments weighed him down
Which fair Calypso gave him. But. at length,
Emerging, he rejected from his throat
The bitter brine that down his forehead streamed.
Even then, though hopeless with dismay, his thought   40
Was on the raft, and, struggling through the waves,
He seized it, sprang on board, and seated there
Escaped the threatened death. Still to and fro
The rolling billows drove it. As the wind
In autumn sweeps the thistles o'er the field,   45
Clinging together, so the blasts of heaven
Hither and thither drove it o'er the sea.

LANGUAGE

1. Any author translating a poem tries, of course, to capture in his own language the qualities of the original. Bryant says, "The style of Homer is simple, and he has been praised for fire and rapidity of narrative . . . . Homer . . . wrote in idiomatic Greek, and . . . should have been translated into idiomatic English." How well does Bryant's translation live up to this theory of his about the ideal translation?

2. Bryant criticized Cowper's translation of this poem for its lack of simplicity, its lack of "fire and rapidity." "Almost every sentence," he continued, "is stiffened by some clumsy inversion; stately phrases are used when simpler ones were at hand, and would have rendered the meaning of the original better. The entire version . . . is cold and constrained . . . ." With these points in mind, compare the following lines from Cowper's translation with lines 19-26 of Bryant's version:

> Thrice blest, and more than thrice, Achaia's sons
> At Ilium slain for the Atridae' sake!
> Ah, would to heav'n that, dying, I had felt
> That day the stroke of fate, when me the dead
> Achilles guarding, with a thousand spears
> Troy's furious host assail'd! Funereal rites
> I then had shared, and praise from ev'ry Greek,
> Whom now the most inglorious death awaits.

3. Compare lines 27-39 of Bryant's translation with the following prose version written by S. H. Butcher and A. Lang:

Even as he spake, the great wave smote down upon him, driving on in terrible wise, that the raft reeled again. And far therefrom he fell, and lost the helm from his hand; and the fierce blast of the jostling winds came and brake his mast in the midst, and sail and yardarm fell afar in the deep. Long time the water kept him under, nor could he speedily rise from beneath the rush of the mighty wave: for the garments hung heavy which fair Calypso gave him. But late and at length he came up, and spat forth from his mouth the bitter salt water, which ran down in streams from his head.

4. What is extraordinary about the figurative language in Bryant's passage? What values do you find in the kinds of figures here used?

5. Contrast Bryant's language with that of Keats in "To Autumn," page 71. How do the contrasts which you find relate to the differing purposes of the two authors?

The author of this poem believes in making his writings dramatic. "Everything written," he once said, "is as good as it is dramatic." Here he sets forth the drama of a New England farmer's thoughts and emotions as the farmer hears a nighttime storm raging outside his home. The concrete words, the figures of speech, and the rhythms show how a modern poet uses language to convey an emotion.

Robert Frost

STORM-FEAR

When the wind works against us in the dark,
And pelts with snow
The lower chamber window on the east,
And whispers with a sort of stifled bark,
The beast,   5
"Come out! Come out!"—
It costs no inward struggle not to go,
Ah, no!
I count our strength,
Two and a child,   10
Those of us not asleep subdued to mark
How the cold creeps as the fire dies at length,—
How drifts are piled,
Dooryard and road ungraded,
Till even the comforting barn grows far away,   15

And my heart owns a doubt
Whether 'tis in us to arise with day
And save ourselves unaided.

LANGUAGE, CHARACTERS, SETTING, AND ACTION

1. What can you learn about the character of the speaker of these lines from the kind of words he uses? Be specific.

2. Compared with this vivid figurative description of the storm, what would a vivid literal description lack? In your answer, take account of the following figures of speech: (a) "the wind works against us in the dark"; (b) "whispers with a sort of stifled bark,/The beast"; (c) "How the cold creeps as the fire dies at length"; (d) "the comforting barn." Is it true, as Professor Lawrence Thompson has suggested, that here "words and images bring the attention to focus on the emotional sense which underlies the poem"?

3. What is the pattern of the action here presented? What change is there in the speaker's attitude? How is this change shown?

4. What is peculiar about the rhythmical structure? Is the peculiarity you find in any way appropriate to what is being expressed? Develop your answer. Does the use of rhyme help or hinder the development of the thought?

5. Contrast the use of figurative language in "Storm-Fear" with that in "Storm on Jackson's Island" (p. 79) and in "A Fierce Rush of All the Winds" (p. 84).

The Author and the Work:

Feeling and Focus

In a literary work, as a rule, the elements (action, characters, settings, and language) are so adapted and integrated as to form a harmonious whole. To you, the reader, this whole is of the utmost importance. When you read a complex sentence, you may find it useful to notice the parts of speech which form it. But it is hardly conceivable that you will be satisfied to stop with your perception of the parts. Instead, you will want to re-imbed the words in the whole sentence so that you may sense the emotional effect and come to grips with the meaning.

Similarly, when you read a story, a drama, or a poem, you are not satisfied with an analysis of its separate elements. You are not likely to want to stop before perceiving the accomplishment of the whole work. Actually, it may be argued that you have not "taken in" the work at all until you have considered the factors unifying the work, (1) the author as the work reveals him and (2) the meaning of the work. This section deals with the former of these matters; the next section will deal with the latter.

In the preceding sections dealing with action, characters, setting, and language, we have, of course, been talking about the author's choices. But we have yet to speak directly of the ways in which the writer leaves his personal stamp upon his work as a sort of esthetic trademark. Some critics have claimed that the great writer ought to be impersonal. T. S. Eliot has said, "Poetry . . . is not the expression of personality, but an escape from personality." We accept the implication that the writer deals with large issues. But even as the writer in his art transcends the perplexities of his personal life, he paradoxically infuses into his work a highly individual element. Our common talk of literature attests to this fact. We speak of Swiftian irony, Chaucerian humor, Shakespearean style, Keatsian sensitivity. Dantesque vividness. Even in the work of Émile Zola, who claimed for himself scientific objectivity, the plight of the common man elicits an unmistakable smouldering indignation. This unique quality, quintessence, of the writer's work is sometimes called his world view. Such a phrase indicates aptly the scope and complexity of attitudes that a writer brings to his work. But the discriminating reader will want to be more analytical. In the discussion that follows we examine three of the main ways in which an author enters his work: (1) through the personal attitudes revealed in the work—*tone*; (2) through choice of the sensibility that sifts and filters the experience—*point of view*; and (3) through the overall aspects and the emotional aura of the author's world—*atmosphere*.

Tone

THE NATURE OF TONE

Suppose that you, a new student on a college campus, go to one of those parties called mixers, where students are supposed to get to know each other. The gathering may be fitfully enlivened by students who exchange gossip or tell stories of first days on a college campus. Looking for a group to join, you hear the beginning of an anecdote and step closer to listen. You have not met the storyteller. You listen to his voice, watch his face, and attend to the matter of the story. After a very few moments you will know how to take the story.

It is a humorous story about the discomfort of a farm boy trying to outfit himself stylishly at a men's store. You have detected on the speaker's face a certain mischievous smile, heard in his voice a deliberate comic drawling, and seen him imitate the awkwardness of the rural shopper. You have been comprehending the *tone* of the story, the teller's attitude toward his materials. You may or may not like the speaker's tone. You may think him amusing, or you may think him supercilious and his story cruel. The important initial fact is that because you have successfully evaluated a certain timbre of voice, certain intonations, and certain gestures, you know how to take the story.

Catching the tone of a literary work is similar except that, of course, you cannot watch the writer's facial expressions and gestures. There are only the words on the page. But, like the storyteller at the party, the author is a personality with his own peculiar tastes, bents, prejudices, and emotions. When he creates an imaginative work about the world as he sees it, almost inevitably—consciously or unconsciously—he reveals certain aspects of his personality. And you, if you are an alert reader, will, so to speak, hear the voicing. You will come to know the tone, which may be defined as the *personal attitudes and emotions revealed in the work*.

When Thomas Wolfe speaks, in *Of Time and the River*, of "the lusty, vulgar and sweet-singing voice of Geoffrey Chaucer," of "Thackeray's sentimental gallantry," and of "acid and tart-humored Horace," he is considering the tone of each author. Young Walt Whitman had the tone of his early works in mind when he spoke of "shouting his barbaric yawp over the roofs of the world."

We have said that tone in literature must be revealed through the author's use of language—in short, through style. In one of his short stories, Sherwood Anderson spoke of the advantage early storytellers had over moderns whose stories are printed: "They were both storytellers and actors. As they talked they modulated their voices, made gestures with their hands. . . . All our modern fussing with style is an attempt to do the same thing." His point is that through style, through careful choice of details, words, and phrases, the writer conveys his feelings about elements in his work. Great care must have gone into Robert Louis Stevenson's choices in the following description of his fictionalized version of the poet Villon in the short story "A Lodging for the Night":

The poet was a rag of a man, dark, little and lean, with hollow cheeks and thin black locks. He carried his four-and-twenty years with feverish animation. Greed had made folds about his eyes, evil smiles had puckered his mouth. The wolf and pig struggled together in his face. It was an eloquent, sharp, ugly, earthy countenance. His hands were small and prehensile, with fingers knotted like a cord; and they were continually flickering in front of him in violent and expressive pantomime.

Every word conveys to the reader Stevenson's distaste for this character. Notice the animal images and the description of facial distortions, both of which reveal the brutalization of what might have been a sensitive and delicate artist.

Actions as well as characters will be interpreted in ways that reveal the author's attitude toward them. If, for instance, he says that a character "smirked," he will imply a different attitude from the one implied by his saying that the character "giggled" or "laughed wryly." Contrast "walked" with "minced," "marched," "stalked," and "trod": each, used in relationship to other revealing words, will help show approval or disapproval. All the devices of language which we have considered (pp. 73-78) may, in fact, be called upon by the author to communicate his feelings.

The tone of an author in parts of a work or throughout a whole work then may be, for instance, broadly comic, witty, ironic, satirical, disinterested, disillusioned, sentimental, idealistic, or tragic. Whatever it is, it will provide his commentary upon the people, the emotions, and the action presented in the work. All this means that a literary work involves not merely a number of elements but an author's emotional interpretation of them. It means that a work is, in miniature, a copy of the world as the author sees it, and that the tone which pervades his commentary upon that world gives the work unity. It means that the author tacitly asks the reader to join him in feeling as he does about this world and the things that happen in it.

THE IMPORTANCE OF TONE TO THE READER

As readers, we are therefore faced with the necessity of coöperating with the author. We must become aware of what he feels, and, in order to share his imaginative experience with him, we must feel as he does. We must join the storyteller, the dramatist, or the poet in liking and disliking. If he is sympathetic, we must be so, or if he is ironic, we must follow his lead.

But such coöperation between reader and author does not mean that our critical sense is completely numbed while we read. As Gordon Hall Gerould shrewdly remarks:

Somewhat as the writer in the act of composition must control his imagination, if he is to accomplish anything of value, rejecting this as wrong and choosing that as right, we can . . . . recognize that the guide to life whom we are following has here made a misstep or there quite badly stumbled. Only the naïf playgoer fails to observe a certain detachment as he watches a spectacle on the stage. The wiser auditor may be absorbed in the drama, and certainly he must let his imagination respond to that of playwright and actors; but he is at the same time able to evaluate the effect produced—even the effect on his own feelings. He does not try to shoot the villain. Just so the experienced reader keeps his critical judgment awake while he yields himself to the guidance of the author. Nor is his enjoyment lessened by so doing. Indeed, he comes into closer association with the writer, and participates more fully in the imaginative processes by which the story has been made, if he combines such control with sympathetic absorption.

Gerould is speaking of the reading of fiction, but obviously the reading of drama and poetry also requires this combination of warm sympathy and cool detachment.

Your task, then, is to perceive as exactly as possible the nature of the tone in any literary work. By noting the author's choice of details, words, and phrases, you should learn what feelings are expressed and how the author has expressed them. You should be aware of what the author requires of you in the way of sympathy, and so far as is possible, you should imaginatively share the author's attitudes and emotions. You should also, in the end, see what the tone of the work does to give it its emotional impact, its emotional unity.

Point of View[1]

THE NATURE OF POINT OF VIEW

In the preceding discussion of tone we have been assuming that the voice which we hear, so to speak, is actually the voice of the writer. Although the author often communicates with us directly and openly, he may assume a guise. Kipling, for instance, in his early tales of India, assumed the role of a sophisticated member of the ruling group, learned in the ways of men and women and in the intricacies of British colonial government and army life. One gets the impression, not of the real twenty-two-year-old Kipling, but of the worldly, wise, philosophical, witty club member that the young author pretended to be.

Or, more obviously, the writer may create a character to tell his tale for him. It is Huck Finn who tells the story of the memorable trip down the Mississippi, not his creator Mark Twain. Clearly it is necessary to ask whose voice we hear, whose eyes we look through. When we have answered this question, we have described the *fictional point of view*, or what some critics have called "the narrative vantage point" or "the angle of vision." But it would be a mistake to let the metaphorical phrase *angle of vision* lead us to think of point of view merely as a *place* from which the experience is seen. For we, the readers, do not see and experience the literary event *from a certain place* but rather, to use a phrase preferred by some critics, through a certain *center of consciousness*. The nature of this center has an effect on the content and impact of the work that would be hard to exaggerate. Let us return for a moment to our example of the student storyteller at the freshman icebreaker. The student may have chosen to let the discomforted farm-boy shopper tell his own story, in other words, may have assumed the character of the farm boy for the purpose of entertaining his friends with this anecdote. Or the student may have pretended to tell the story in the role of the disdainful and ironic clerk that waited on the yokel. How different in the two versions would be the choice of details, the diction, and the whole impact of the story. Just so, the author determines a great deal about

1. Other aspects of point of view are discussed on pp. 341-344.

the entire emotional cast of his work through his choice of point of view. It would be well for us to look at the basic varieties of point of view. Though the point of view or center of consciousness of each work is unique, the establishment of certain general categories will be useful.

THE BASIC VARIETIES OF POINT OF VIEW

The first distinction to be made between narrators involves simply the matter of grammatical person. Does the narrator refer to himself as "I"? If so, we have a *first person* narrator; if not, a *third person* narrator. Within each grammatical class there are two major types of narrators and hence altogether four varieties of narrators which we wish to discuss here: (1) the third person reporter, (2) the third person omniscient narrator, (3) the author as first person narrator, and (4) the dramatized first person narrator.

The Third Person Reporter

The third person reporter views everything from the outside. The purest use of the third person reporter occurs in the typical drama, for when we go to the theater or when we read a play, we hear only the voices of the characters. We see the characters' actions. We hear no narrator at all. Poets and fiction writers who use the reportorial third person sometimes approach the objectivity of drama. Look back at "Frankie and Johnny" (p. 34), for instance. The writer uses a narrator who is almost as thoroughly effaced as is the dramatist from his play. But other authors will use a reporter who comments, who offers explicit interpretations. Look back at the selection from *Bleak House* (p. 66). Though the narrator, like the narrator of "Frankie and Johnny," does not enter the mind of any character, he does comment, make clear his feelings. Such a narrator is often called *intrusive*. Obviously the emotional quality of a work depends to a great extent on whether the writer chooses to have his reporter convey information objectively or intrude his feelings.

The Third Person Omniscient Narrator

Making use of a convention, some third person narrators tell us about things which they cannot see or hear: They tell us what characters think and feel. They are said to be omniscient. But as Wayne C. Booth says in *The Rhetoric of Fiction,* "Observers . . . , commenting or silent, . . . can be either privileged to know what could not be learned by strictly natural means or limited to realistic vision and inference. Complete privilege is what we usually call omniscience. But there are many kinds of privilege, and very few 'omniscient' narrators are allowed to know or show as much as their authors know." As Booth implies, omniscience is an unhandy term, for when applied to a narrator, it means that he knows everything, can report what is going on in any character's mind at any time. Most writers do not use such all-knowing narrators. Privilege is clearly the better term, with omniscience, as Booth says, defined as a very special kind of privilege, the privilege to know all.

The important thing for us to notice about the privileged narrator at this point is simply that by invading the mind of one or more characters, he provides us with other vantage points from which to view the experience. He opens more windows onto the scene, so to speak. Look at the following paragraph from Stephen Crane's "The Bride Comes to Yellow Sky." It pictures newlyweds on a train:

> To the minds of the pair, their surroundings reflected the glory of their marriage that morning in San Antonio; this was the environment of their new estate; and the man's face in particular beamed with an elation that made him appear ridiculous to the Negro porter. This individual at times surveyed them from afar with an amused and superior grin. On other occasions he bullied them with skill in ways that did not make it exactly plain to them that they were being bullied. He subtly used all the manners of the most unconquerable kind of snobbery. He oppressed them; but of this oppression they had small knowledge, and they speedily forgot that infrequently a number of travellers covered them with stares of derisive enjoyment. Historically there was supposed to be something infinitely humorous in their situation.

Here we see how things appear to both the bride and groom, and also how the couple appears to the porter. The privilege of the narrator enriches the experience of the train ride. Even in this paragraph, though, the narrator's privilege is limited. We can easily surmise from the expressions on their faces what the other passengers think of the couple, but the narrator does not enter their minds. As Booth observes, the truly omniscient narrator, one with unlimited privilege, is rare.

The Author as First Person Narrator

As we said earlier, any narrator who refers to himself as "I" is a first person narrator. But that merely settles the matter of grammatical person. What we really want to know is who the "I" is. For the moment, let us oversimplify by saying that the "I" has one of two possible identities. Either he is the author or he is an imaginary character, like Huck Finn, whom the author has invented to tell the story. Some critics claim that there is no such thing in literature as an "I" who is precisely the author. They say that even the "I" in the lyric poem is not really the poet but an idealized version of the poet: the perfect lover, the most sincere mourner, etc. The point is well taken, but in order to develop workable categories, we must insist, even if somewhat imprecisely, that some "I" narrators have essentially the voices of their creators and that others are obviously invented characters clearly distinguishable from their creators.

The narrator who is essentially the author speaks with great authority; his story has to a high degree the qualities of verisimilitude and immediacy. We feel that we are listening to one who was there when it happened and knows just how it was. Though it would be naïve to suppose that Frank O'Connor's "My Oedipus Complex" (p. 4) is an actual personal recollection, the story has many of the qualities of autobiography, a real-life remembrance.

One special category of first person narrators should be mentioned at this point. Some narrators speak not so much for the writer himself as for a large group of which the writer pretends to be or actually is a member. Such a narrator might conveniently be called a *choric narrator*, functioning not only to advance the narrative but also to comment from the point of view of some community large or small, as do the choruses in Greek tragedy. Faulkner uses this kind of narrator in his famous story "A Rose for Emily." John Crowe Ransom uses it in "Bells for John Whiteside's Daughter" (p. 806).

The Dramatized First Person Narrator

The dramatized first person narrator is called by some critics the *persona* (Latin for the mask worn by actors in classical drama). It is useful to keep in mind the notion of a mask, for it makes metaphorically vivid the fact that the writer when using the dramatized first person narrator is hiding behind, actually speaking through, an assumed identity. But, as you will have foreseen, merely seeing a narrator as an identity that the writer has assumed does not exhaust our interest in the particular ways this kind of narrator can function. What we want to discover are the special emotional qualities that such narrators lend to a work. If you will look back at Browning's "My Last Duchess" (p. 55), you can readily see how the personality of the Duke pervades the poem, enveloping the whole in an aura of sickening jealousy, possessiveness, and egoism. The effect that Montresor, the narrator of Poe's "The Cask of Amontillado" (p. 60), has on that story is similar. In contrast, Huck Finn is winning and lovable, and he leavens his story with that fine comic mixture of naïveté and wisdom that in large part makes the novel so memorable. In short, the use of the dramatized first person narrator provides the writer with opportunities for striking emotional coloration.

THE IMPORTANCE OF POINT OF VIEW

In the preface to *Roderick Hudson,* James says of his novel:

The centre of interest throughout "Roderick" is in Rowland Mallet's consciousness, and the drama is the very drama of that consciousness—which I had of course to make sufficiently acute in order to enable it, like a set and lighted scene, to hold the play. By making it acute, meanwhile, one made its own movement—or rather, strictly, its movement in the particular connexion—interesting; this movement really being quite the stuff of one's thesis. It had, naturally, Rowland's consciousness, not to be *too* acute—which would have disconnected it and made it superhuman: the beautiful little problem was to keep it connected, connected intimately, with the general human exposure, and thereby bedimmed and befooled and bewildered, anxious, restless, fallible, and yet to endow it with such intelligence that the appearances reflected in it, and constituting together there the situation and the "story," should become by that fact intelligible.

James, perhaps more than any other writer, was fascinated with problems of point of view, and he articulated that fascination brilliantly. Notice the effects that he ascribes to his choice of Rowland Mallet as the center of consciousness of the novel:

The drama of the book is the drama of Rowland's consciousness. The change in Rowland's consciousness is the theme of the book. Characterization depends on the way Rowland sees people. The action or plot is structured by the reflection of events in Rowland's mind.

The tone that the writer himself takes toward his material is affected by Rowland's mind.

Though not every writer explores the effects of point of view as systematically as James did, the fact remains that there is always a center of consciousness through which the literary experience passes and that consciousness will help shape, as James pointed out, setting, tone, meaning, characterization, and plot—every element of a literary work. You can demonstrate for yourself the truth of this proposition if you will look back at "My Last Duchess" and ask yourself what changes in plot, characterization, setting, tone, and meaning might have occurred had Browning chosen to tell the story from the point of view of the Duchess just before she was murdered.

Point of view, then, is an important unifying element in any literary work. Your task is to identify the center of consciousness, define it clearly by asking yourself the important questions: Who is the narrator? Does he comment and evaluate or merely report? Is he privileged to look into the minds of the characters? What special emotional qualities does he give to the work? When you have answered these questions, you can perceive how the point of view shapes and unifies the other elements of the work.

Atmosphere

THE NATURE OF ATMOSPHERE

Critics use the term "atmosphere" to express two quite different but related concepts. Both concepts have to do with an overall achievement of the action, characters, setting, language, and tone of an imaginative work. But by "atmosphere" some critics mean the general pervasive feeling aroused *in the reader* by these elements, while other critics mean the particular world *in the work* which these elements create.[1] Many critics talk, naturally enough, about both the stimulus in the work and the response of the reader. Edgar Allan Poe, so he said, started to write his stories and poems with the atmosphere as response (which he called the effect) in mind; he then turned to atmosphere as world, "inventing such incidents, combining such events, and discussing them in such tone as may best serve him in establishing this preconceived effect." Either use of the term is correct, but it is important for you to know which you are employing because very different matters are involved in each usage. To determine what atmosphere as response is, you consider your own reaction; to determine what atmosphere as stimulus is, you consider the elements in the work.

The idea of atmosphere as world needs some further consideration. An author in the process of creating his work creates his own world. However, unlike our "real" world, the writer's world has its own coherence, its own logic and inner consistency. Rene Welleck and Austin Warren speak of such a world as the novelist creates it:

> The great novelists all have such a world—recognizable as overlapping the empirical world but distinct in its self-coherent intelligibility. Sometimes it is a world which can be mapped out in some area of the globe—like Trollope's counties and cathedral towns, Hardy's Wessex; but sometimes . . . it is not. . . . Dickens' world can be identified with London; Kafka's with old Prague: but both worlds are so "projected," so creative and created . . . that the identifications seem rather irrelevant. . . .
>
> This world or *Kosmos* of a novelist—this pattern or structure or organism, which includes the plot, characters, setting, world-view, "tone"—is what we must scrutinize when we attempt to compare a novel with life.

Not only novelists but also short story writers, dramatists, and poets create worlds. In a work of any sort the atmosphere as a world may be described by setting forth the aspects of the work—events, personages, scenes, and tone—which give the writer's world its emotional quality.

The atmosphere of "The Cask of Amontillado" (p. 60) for instance, is compounded of the vaults below a castle, damp, unlighted, webbed with niter; the drunken Fortunato stumbling nearer and nearer to destruction; and the vengeful and sardonic Montresor coldly and cleverly leading him to his ruin. Van Wyck Brooks tells of settings, actions, and characters in other horror tales by Poe as he describes their atmosphere in *The World of Washington Irving*:

> There was scarcely even a glimmer of sunlight in this world of sorrow and desolation, of shadow, disaster, horror, revenge and crime, a world overhung with the sable wings of lunacy, perversity, hysteria, of sickness, hypochondria, ruin, dissolution, and death. The typical heroes of these tales were victims of neuroses who shared no relationships or interests with the rest of the race, who had forgotten, if they

1. Critics give the word "mood" even more meanings: (1) what we have called "tone"; (2) the emotional effect upon the reader; (3) "atmosphere" in both senses. The signification of the term, consequently, has become blurred.

ever possessed, any ties with humankind and whose habits and surroundings reflected and partook of their disorder. The women . . . were mysteriously stricken and wasted away with maladies that were obscure and fatal.

THE IMPORTANCE OF ATMOSPHERE

Poe, it will be recalled, created his world with the aim of achieving a certain effect. Few other authors proceed in such a fashion, and it is useless, therefore, to try to formulate any general rule about the place of atmosphere in the creative process. What we can say about atmosphere in the created work, though, is this: It unifies and artistically limits the writer's world. For instance, imagine Montresor and Fortunato running across Huck Finn in the wine vault, or imagine the Duke of Ferrara having a beer in that bar where Frankie went to ask about Johnny. Such imaginary transferences are not primarily grotesque because they involve anachronisms but because in them a character steps from his own world into an alien one, where he cannot really exist at all.

Your job in analyzing atmosphere is to discover the special qualities of the writer's world. What kinds of people populate it and what kinds do not? What kinds of things characteristically happen there—violence and revenge, as in Poe's world, or subtle, sometimes almost imperceptible shifts in attitude, as in Henry James' world? What kinds of settings—the raw frontier towns of a Twain or the brooding seas of a Melville or a Conrad—are typical?

You need not read the entire canon of a writer's work to discover atmosphere. In fact, each work has its own atmosphere, and some writers, like Shakespeare, are masters at creating remarkably different atmospheres for their various works. To note carefully the nature of this amalgam in a group of works or a single work is to see an important unifying aspect of the author's achievement.

In the two poems that follow, delicate and memorable emotional effects are achieved by the careful adjustment of artistic elements, especially tone and point of view. Though both poems deal with the same basic situation, the recent death of a woman, the final effects are quite different.

Christina Rossetti

AFTER DEATH

The curtains were half drawn, the floor was swept
  And strewn with rushes, rosemary and may
  Lay thick upon the bed on which I lay,

Where through the lattice ivy-shadows crept.
He leaned above me, thinking that I slept 5
 And could not hear him; but I heard him say,
 'Poor child, poor child': and as he turned away
Came a deep silence, and I knew he wept.
He did not touch the shroud, or raise the fold
 That hid my face, or take my hand in his, 10
  Or ruffle the smooth pillows for my head:
  He did not love me living; but once dead
 He pitied me; and very sweet it is
To know he still is warm though I am cold. (1849; 1904)

Emily Dickinson

THE LAST NIGHT THAT SHE LIVED

The last Night that She lived
It was a Common Night
Except the Dying—this to Us
Made Nature different

We noticed smallest things— 5
Things overlooked before
By this great light upon our Minds
Italicized—as 'twere.

As We went out and in
Between Her final Room 10
And Rooms where Those to be alive
Tomorrow were, a Blame

That Others could exist
While She must finish quite
A Jealousy for Her arose 15
So nearly infinite—

Reprinted by permission of the publishers from Thomas H. Johnson, Editor, *The Poems of Emily Dickinson.* The Belknap Press of Harvard University Press, copyright, 1951, 1955 by The President and Fellows of Harvard College.

We waited while She passed—
It was a narrow time—
Too jostled were Our Souls to speak
At length the notice came.   20

She mentioned, and forgot—
Then lightly as a Reed
Bent to the Water, struggled scarce—
Consented, and was dead—

And We—We placed the Hair—   25
And drew the Head erect—
And then an awful leisure was
Belief to regulate— (c. 1866; 1890)

QUESTIONS

1. Who are the narrators? Classify them according to the types that have been discussed.

2. Are the narrators merely reporters or do they intrude to express their own emotions? Contrast the primary emotions felt by each. Is there any evidence that the narrators are suppressing some emotions? If so, cite it.

3. Would you agree that one poem deals with the meaning of death and the other with unrequited love and that these differences in theme are accounted for by the poets' selection of different points of view? Argue for your answer.

4. Are these poems essentially without characterization in the ordinary sense of the word? Or does the tone of each poem give a sense of character?

5. The rendering of a delicate tone requires on the part of the poet very careful choice of words and phrases. What words in each poem seem to you especially well chosen? What does the word *narrow* mean in stanza five of "The Last Night That She Lived"? What about the words *warm* and *cold* in the last line of "After Death"? Do they mean one thing only?

6. In "After Death" how should you take the phrase in the last line, "very sweet it is"? Do you judge it to be sincere or bitterly ironic? How do you know?

7. Characterize the atmosphere of each poem. Which poem makes greater use of setting to create atmosphere?

The two poems that follow, like the previous pair, deal with an aspect of death. This time the poets explore not the relationship of intimates separated by death but the effect of death on the casual bystander. And again, despite the common materials, the final effects of the two poems are distinctly different.

W. H. Auden

MUSÉE DES BEAUX ARTS

About suffering they were never wrong,
The Old Masters: how well they understood
Its human position; how it takes place
While someone else is eating or opening a window or just walking dully along;
How, when the aged are reverently, passionately waiting   5
For the miraculous birth, there always must be
Children who did not specially want it to happen, skating
On a pond at the edge of the wood:
They never forgot
That even the dreadful martyrdom must run its course   10
Anyhow in a corner, some untidy spot
Where the dogs go on with their doggy life and the torturer's horse
Scratches its innocent behind on a tree.

In Brueghel's *Icarus*, for instance; how everything turns away
Quite leisurely from the disaster; the ploughman may   15
Have heard the splash, the forsaken cry,
But for him it was not an important failure; the sun shone
As it had to on the white legs disappearing into the green
Water; and the expensive delicate ship that must have seen
Something amazing, a boy falling out of the sky,   20
Had somewhere to get to and sailed calmly on. (1940)

Karl Shapiro

AUTO WRECK

Its quick soft silver bell beating, beating,
And down the dark one ruby flare
Pulsing out red light like an artery,
The ambulance at top speed floating down

Past beacons and illuminated clocks   5
Wings in a heavy curve, dips down,
And brakes speed, entering the crowd.
The doors leap open, emptying light;
Stretchers are laid out, the mangled lifted
And stowed into the little hospital.   10
Then the bell, breaking the hush, tolls once,
And the ambulance with its terrible cargo
Rocking, slightly rocking, moves away,
As the doors, and afterthought, are closed.

We are deranged, walking among the cops   15
Who sweep glass and are large and composed.
One is still making notes under the light.
One with a bucket douches ponds of blood
Into the street and gutter.
One hangs lanterns on the wrecks that cling,   20
Empty husks of locusts, to iron poles.

Our throats were tight as tourniquets,
Our feet were bound with splints, but now
Like convalescents intimate and gauche,
We speak through sickly smiles and warn   25
With the stubborn saw of common sense,
The grim joke and the banal resolution.
The traffic moves around with care,
But we remain, touching a wound
That opens to our richest horror.   30

Already old, the question Who shall die?
Becomes unspoken Who is innocent?
For death in war is done by hands;
Suicide has cause and stillbirth, logic.
And cancer, simple as a flower, blooms.   35
But this invites the occult mind,
Cancels our physics with a sneer,
And spatters all we knew of dénouement
Across the expedient and wicked stones. (1942)

QUESTIONS

1. Who are the narrators? If you decide that each voice is essentially the poet's own, what differences in point of view nevertheless remain?

2. One poem has definite narrative elements; the other offers a general statement, then justifies it with examples. What is the relationship between these structural differences and the differences in point of view?

3. What, in addition to the narrative elements, structures "Auto Wreck"? Is the poem what James referred to as the drama of a consciousness, of the change and movement in that consciousness? Whose consciousness?

4. Babette Deutsch has said this about the tone of Shapiro's poetry: "The prominence of feeling in his work is one of the elements that distinguish it from that of Auden, the cogitative contemporary from whom he learned so much." Judging from these two poems, do you find this evaluation justified? Explain.

5. Each poem deals with people who merely happen to be nearby when tragic death occurs. But these people are characterized quite differently in the two poems. What is the relationship between these differences in characterization and the different attitudes that the narrators take toward the bystanders?

6. What is the effect of scene on tone and atmosphere in these two poems? Why is a series of more or less static tableaux suitable for one poem and dramatic movement for the other?

7. Which poem seems more philosophically settled in its conclusion? Account for this difference. How do action, tone, and point of view in part determine theme?

8. Metaphor, imagery, and allusion are powerful creators of atmosphere. What is the effect in "Auto Wreck" of such metaphors as "one ruby flare/ Pulsing out red light like an artery" and "wrecks that cling,/Empty husks of locusts, to iron poles"? Identify the artistic, religious, and mythical allusions in "Musée des Beaux Arts." What do they contribute?

The two stories that follow deal, again, with some aspect of death. Like the pair of poems by Christina Rossetti and Emily Dickinson, the first focuses on one who must experience death and the second on those who remain behind after death.

Alphonse Daudet

THE DEATH OF THE DAUPHIN

The little Dauphin is ill—the Dauphin is going to die. In all the churches the Host is elevated and tall candles burn for the recovery of the royal child. The streets of the ancient residence are sad and silent, the bells are mute, citizens peer curiously through the palace gratings, porters talk in solemn tones in the courts.

All the palace is astir. Chamberlains and majordomos hurry up and down the marble steps; the galleries are thronged with pages; courtiers in silken robes pass from group to group, asking the news in smothered accents. On the broad stairways weeping maids of honor bow low, and wipe their eyes with beautiful embroidered kerchiefs.

An assemblage of robed doctors gathers in the orangery. Through the glasses they can be seen waving their long black sleeves and inclining doctorally their perukes. Before the door walk the tutor and riding-master of the little Dauphin. They are waiting for decisions of the faculty. The riding-master swears like a trooper, the tutor quotes Horace. From the stable comes a long, plaintive neigh. It is the little Dauphin's chestnut, who, forgotten by the grooms, calls sadly from his empty crib.

And the king—where is the king? Shut up all alone at the farther end of the palace. Kings must not be seen to weep. Not so, however, the queen. Seated by the Dauphin's side, her lovely face all bathed in tears, she sobs before us all like the veriest serving-woman.

In his lace bed lies the little Dauphin. He is whiter than the pillow upon which his head reclines. They believe that he is asleep; but no, he is not asleep. The little Dauphin turns to his mother. "Madame the queen, why do you weep? Do you believe, like the rest, that I am going to die?" The queen tries to answer; sobs choke her utterance.

"Do not weep, madame the queen. You forget that I am the Dauphin; Dauphins do not die thus." The queen sobs more piteously. The little Dauphin is frightened. "Halloo!" exclaims he, "I do not want to die! Order instantly forty stout lansquenets to keep guard around our bed. Set a hundred large guns to watch night and day before our windows. And woe to Death should he dare approach us!"

To humor the royal child the queen makes a sign. In a twinkling, cannon are heard rolling in the court; forty stout lansquenets with their partisans range themselves around the room. They are old troopers and their mustaches are gray. The Dauphin recognizes one. "Lorrain!" he cries. The old soldier draws closer. "Let me look at your big sword. If Death comes for me you will kill him, will you not?" "Yes, monseigneur." And two big tears roll down his tanned cheeks.

The priest approaches the Dauphin. He speaks long in subdued tones and holds up the crucifix. The Dauphin shows surprise. Suddenly he interrupts him. "I see what you mean, monsieur the abbé; but would not my little friend Beppo die in my place if we pay him plenty of money?" The priest continues to speak. The Dauphin looks more and more surprised. When the priest ceases, he says, with a sigh, "All that is very sad, monsieur the abbé, but there is one comfort for me. When I get to the paradise of the stars I shall still be the Dauphin. The good God is my cousin, and will treat me according to my rank."

Then he turned to his mother, and said, "Let them bring my best clothes— the ermine doublet and velvet pumps. I want to make myself smart for the angels, and enter paradise dressed like the Dauphin." Again the priest bends over the Dauphin, and speaks to him in low tones. In the midst of the discourse the royal child interrupts him angrily: "What! it is nothing, then, to be a Dauphin, after all!" and refusing to hear more, he turns his head to the wall and weeps bitterly.   (1869)

Eudora Welty

A CURTAIN OF GREEN

Every day one summer in Larkin's Hill, it rained a little. The rain was a regular thing, and would come about two o'clock in the afternoon.

One day, almost as late as five o'clock, the sun was still shining. It seemed almost to spin in a tiny groove in the polished sky, and down below, in the trees along the street and in the rows of flower gardens in the town, every leaf reflected the sun from a hardness like a mirror surface. Nearly all the women sat in the windows of their houses, fanning and sighing, waiting for the rain.

Mrs. Larkin's garden was a large, densely grown plot running downhill behind the small white house where she lived alone now, since the death of her husband. The sun and the rain that beat down so heavily that summer had not kept her from working there daily. Now the intense light like a tweezers picked out her clumsy, small figure in its old pair of men's overalls rolled up at the sleeves and trousers, separated it from the thick leaves, and made it look strange and yellow as she worked with a hoe—over-vigorous, disreputable, and heedless.

Within its border of hedge, high like a wall, and visible only from the upstairs windows of the neighbors, this slanting, tangled garden, more and more over-abundant and confusing, must have become so familiar to Mrs. Larkin that quite possibly by now she was unable to conceive of any other place. Since the accident in which her husband was killed, she had never once been seen anywhere else. Every morning she might be observed walking slowly, almost timidly, out of the white house, wearing a pair of the untidy overalls, often with her hair streaming and tangled where she had neglected to comb it. She would wander about for a little while at first, uncertainly, deep among the plants and wet with their dew, and yet not quite putting out her hand to touch anything. And then a sort of sturdiness would possess her—stabilize her; she would stand still for a moment, as if a blindfold were being removed; and then she would kneel in the flowers and begin to work.

She worked without stopping, almost invisibly, submerged all day among the thick, irregular, sloping beds of plants. The servant would call her at dinnertime, and she would obey; but it was not until it was completely dark that she would truthfully give up her labor and with a drooping, submissive walk appear at the house, slowly opening the small low door at the back. Even the rain would bring only a pause to her. She would move to the shelter of the pear tree, which in mid-April hung heavily almost to the ground in brilliant full leaf, in the center of the garden.

It might seem that the extreme fertility of her garden formed at once a preoccupation and a challenge to Mrs. Larkin. Only by ceaseless activity could she cope with the rich blackness of this soil. Only by cutting, separating, thinning and tying back in the clumps of flowers and bushes and vines could she have kept them from over-reaching their boundaries and multiplying out of all reason. The daily summer rains could only increase her vigilance and her already excessive energy. And yet, Mrs. Larkin rarely cut, separated, tied back. . . . To a certain extent, she seemed not to seek for order, but to allow an over-flowering, as if she consciously ventured forever a little farther, a little deeper, into her life in the garden.

She planted every kind of flower that she could find or order from a catalogue—planted thickly and hastily, without stopping to think, without any regard for the ideas that her neighbors might elect in their club as to what constituted an appropriate vista, or an effect of restfulness, or even harmony of color. Just to what end Mrs. Larkin worked so strenuously in her garden, her neighbors could not see. She certainly never sent a single one of her fine flowers to any of them. They might get sick and die, and she would never send a flower. And if she thought of *beauty* at all (they regarded her stained overalls, now almost of a color with the leaves), she certainly did not strive for it in her garden. It was impossible to enjoy looking at such a place. To the neighbors gazing down from their upstairs windows it had the appearance of a sort of jungle, in which the slight, heedless form of its owner daily lost itself.

At first, after the death of Mr. Larkin—for whose father, after all, the town had been named—they had called upon the widow with decent frequency. But she had not appreciated it, they said to one another. Now, occasionally, they looked down from their bedroom windows as they brushed studiously at their hair in the morning; they found her place in the garden, as they might have run their fingers toward a city on a map of a foreign country, located her from their distance almost in curiosity, and then forgot her.

Early that morning they had heard whistling in the Larkin garden. They had recognized Jamey's tune, and had seen him kneeling in the flowers at Mrs. Larkin's side. He was only the colored boy who worked in the neighborhood by the day. Even Jamey, it was said, Mrs. Larkin would tolerate only now and then. . . .

Throughout the afternoon she had raised her head at intervals to see how fast he was getting along in his transplanting. She had to make him finish before it began to rain. She was busy with the hoe, clearing one of the last patches of uncultivated ground for some new shrubs. She bent under the sunlight, chopping in blunt, rapid, tireless strokes. Once she raised her head far back to stare at the flashing sky. Her eyes were dull and puckered, as if from long impatience or bewilderment. Her mouth was a sharp line. People said she never spoke.

But memory tightened about her easily, without any prelude of warning or even despair. She would see promptly, as if a curtain had been jerked quite unceremoniously away from a little scene, the front porch of the white house, the shady street in front, and the blue automobile in which her husband approached, driving home from work. It was a summer day, a day from the summer before. In the freedom of gaily turning her head, a motion she was now forced by memory to repeat as she hoed the ground, she could see again the tree that was going to fall. There had been no warning. But there was the enormous tree, the fragrant chinaberry tree, suddenly tilting, dark and slow like a cloud, leaning down to her husband. From her place on the front porch she had spoken in a soft voice to him, never so intimate as at that moment, "You can't be hurt." But the tree had fallen, had struck the car exactly so as to crush him to death. She had waited there on the porch for a time afterward, not moving at all— in a sort of recollection—as if to reach under and bring out from obliteration her protective words and to try them once again . . . so as to change the whole happening. It was accident that was incredible, when her love for her husband was keeping him safe.

She continued to hoe the breaking ground, to beat down the juicy weeds. Presently she became aware that hers was the only motion to continue in the whole slackened place. There was no wind at all now. The cries of the birds had hushed. The sun seemed clamped to the side of the sky. Everything had stopped once again, the stillness had mesmerized the stems of the plants, and all the leaves went suddenly into thickness. The shadow of the pear tree in the center of the garden lay callous on the ground. Across the yard, Jamey knelt, motionless.

"Jamey!" she called angrily.

But her voice hardly carried in the dense garden. She felt all at once terrified, as though her loneliness had been pointed out by some outside force whose finger parted the hedge. She drew her hand for an instant to her breast. An obscure fluttering there frightened her, as though the force babbled to her, The bird that flies within your heart could not divide this cloudy air . . . She stared without expression at the garden. She was clinging to the hoe, and she stared across the green leaves toward Jamey.

A look of docility in the Negro's back as he knelt in the plants began to infuriate her. She started to walk toward him, dragging the hoe vaguely through the flowers behind her. She forced herself to look at him, and noticed him closely for the first time—the way he looked like a child. As he turned his head a little to one side and negligently stirred the dirt with his yellow finger, she saw, with a sort of helpless suspicion and hunger, a soft, rather deprecating smile on his face; he was lost in some impossible dream of his own while he was transplanting the little shoots. He was not even whistling; even that sound was gone.

She walked nearer to him—he must have been deaf!—almost stealthily bearing down upon his laxity and his absorption, as if that glimpse of the side of his face, that turned-away smile, were a teasing, innocent, flickering and beautiful vision—some mirage to her strained and wandering eyes.

Yet a feeling of stricture, of a responding hopelessness almost approaching ferocity, grew with alarming quickness about her. When she was directly behind him she stood quite still for a moment, in the queer sheathed manner she had before beginning her gardening in the morning. Then she raised the hoe above her head; the clumsy sleeves both fell back, exposing the thin, unsunburned whiteness of her arms, the shocking fact of their youth.

She gripped the handle tightly, tightly, as though convinced that the wood of the handle could feel, and that all her strength could indent its surface with pain. The head of Jamey, bent there below her, seemed witless, terrifying, wonderful, almost inaccessible to her, and yet in its explicit nearness meant surely for destruction, with its clustered hot woolly hair, its intricate, glistening ears, its small brown branching streams of sweat, the bowed head holding so obviously and so deadly its ridiculous dream.

Such a head she could strike off, intentionally, so deeply did she know, from the effect of a man's danger and death, its cause in oblivion; and so helpless was she, too helpless to defy the workings of accident, of life and death, of unaccountability. . . . Life and death, she thought, gripping the heavy hoe, life and death, which now meant nothing to her but which she was compelled continually to wield with both her hands, ceaselessly asking, Was it not possible to compensate? to punish? to protest? Pale darkness turned for a moment through the sunlight, like a narrow leaf blown through the garden in a wind.

In that moment, the rain came. The first drop touched her upraised arm. Small, close sounds and coolness touched her.

Sighing, Mrs. Larkin lowered the hoe to the ground and laid it carefully among the growing plants. She stood still where she was, close to Jamey, and listened to the rain falling. It was so gentle. It was so full—the sound of the end of waiting.

In the light from the rain, different from sunlight, everything appeared to gleam unreflecting from within itself in its quiet arcade of identity. The green of the small zinnia shoots was very pure, almost burning. One by one, as the rain reached them, all the individual little plants shone out, and then the branching vines. The pear tree gave a soft rushing noise, like the wings of a bird alighting. She could sense behind her, as if a lamp were lighted in the night, the signal-like whiteness of the house. Then Jamey, as if in the shock of realizing the rain had come, turned his full face toward her, questions and delight intensifying his smile, gathering up his aroused, stretching body. He stammered some disconnected words, shyly.

She did not answer Jamey or move at all. She would not feel anything now except the rain falling. She listened for its scattered soft drops between Jamey's words, its quiet touching of the spears of the iris leaves, and a clear sound like a bell as it began to fall into a pitcher the cook had set on the doorstep.

Finally, Jamey stood there quietly, as if waiting for his money, with his hand trying to brush his confusion away from before his face. The rain fell steadily. A wind of deep wet fragrance beat against her.

Then as if it had swelled and broken over a daily levee, tenderness tore and spun through her sagging body.

It has come, she thought senselessly, her head lifting and her eyes looking without understanding at the sky which had begun to move, to fold nearer in softening, dissolving clouds. It was almost dark. Soon the loud and gentle night of rain would come. It would pound upon the steep roof of the white house. Within, she would lie in her bed and hear the rain. On and on it would fall, beat and fall. The day's work would be over in the garden. She would lie in bed, her arms tired at her sides and in motionless peace: against that which was inexhaustible, there was no defense.

Then Mrs. Larkin sank in one motion down into the flowers and lay there, fainting and streaked with rain. Her face was fully upturned, down among the plants, with the hair beaten away from her forehead and her open eyes closing at once when the rain touched them. Slowly her lips began to part. She seemed to move slightly, in the sad adjustment of a sleeper.

Jamey ran jumping and crouching about her, drawing in his breath alternately at the flowers breaking under his feet and at the shapeless, passive figure on the ground. Then he became quiet, and stood back at a little distance and looked in awe at the unknowing face, white and rested under its bombardment. He remembered how something had filled him with stillness when he felt her standing there behind him looking down at him, and he would not have turned around at that moment for anything in the world. He remembered all the while the oblivious crash of the windows next door being shut when the rain started. . . . But now, in this unseen place, it was he who stood looking at poor Mrs. Larkin.

He bent down and in a horrified, piteous, beseeching voice he began to call her name until she stirred.

"Miss Lark'! Miss Lark'!"

Then he jumped nimbly to his feet and ran out of the garden.

QUESTIONS

1. Before beginning an analysis of the two stories, attempt simply to describe your emotional reaction to each story.

2. Now seek the causes of the emotional impact of each story. Who are the narrators? What privilege does each have? What is the relationship in each story between tone and privilege?

3. Point out exactly where shifts in point of view occur in "A Curtain of Green." What do these shifts achieve? What is the value, for instance, of the assignment of the point of view to the neighbors early in the story?

4. What effect is achieved by the author's denying the narrator of "The Death of the Dauphin" the privilege of entering any character's mind? Consider whose mind Daudet might have chosen to let his narrator enter. What would the danger have been?

5. Which narrator takes the more ironic tone toward his characters? Is the irony sardonic, pathetic, or what? Explain.

6. Define the nature of the conflict in each story. Locate the reversal in each. How do these elements of structure contribute to the atmosphere of the stories?

7. Katherine Anne Porter once characterized Eudora Welty's work as a "particular kind of story, where external act and the internal voiceless life of the human imagination almost meet and mingle on the mysterious threshold between dream and waking." Does this description characterize the atmosphere of "A Curtain of Green"? Explain. Work out your own description of the atmosphere of Daudet's story.

8. In both stories, scene plays an important part in creating atmosphere. Account for the fact that in one story the most important centers of scenic focus are things and in the other people.

9. Characterize the style of each story. Which is the more lyrical, the more metaphorical? Is the style of each suited to the particular narrator? Explain.

Meanings

In "Wakefield," Nathaniel Hawthorne tells the story of a crafty Londoner who "under pretense of going a journey, took lodgings in the next street to his own house, and there, unheard of by his wife or friends, and without the shadow of a reason for such self-banishment, dwelt upwards of twenty years." Then, caught in a shower near his home one afternoon, he ascended his own steps once more and passed into his house—as if his long absence had been nothing but a little joke at his wife's expense. The story of Wakefield ends thus:

> This happy event—supposing it to be such—could only have occurred at an unpremeditated moment. We will not follow our friend across the threshold. He has left us much food for thought, a portion of which shall lend its wisdom to a moral, and be shaped into a figure. Amid the seeming confusion of our mysterious world, individuals are so nicely adjusted to a system, and systems to one another and to a whole, that, by stepping aside for a moment, a man exposes himself to a fearful risk of losing his place forever. Like Wakefield, he may become, as it were, the Outcast of the Universe.

Were you to read the entire story you would have little trouble in discovering how its form and tone have prepared for this conclusion. But the conclusion itself rather obviously involves something besides just form and tone.

This ending has converted the whole story into a springboard for something more general than the particular action, characters, and settings which up to this point the author has portrayed. Hawthorne's concern has broadened beyond a *single* event. The concern now is with *all* events in which an individual steps outside his own little system of human affections. Hawthorne has caused you to shift your attention from Wakefield to man, and in so doing has made it clear that he is concerned not only with Wakefield but with himself and his readers.

As a reader, therefore, you are no longer simply a spectator watching a little drama play itself out; to a certain extent, at least, you are in the drama yourself.

Let us put it another way. A story, a play, a poem, if it is to give the illusion of reality, must be about a particular experience taking place at one time and in one place and involving certain particular people. But though this experience may be in many ways unique, it can at the same time be representative of experiences which all of us have or will have. And to the degree that the affairs portrayed in a literary work are representative of your affairs the work can be said to have meaning for you. If you want a more formal definition, it might run something like this: the meaning of a literary work for you is that insight into human affairs which it offers and which you find useful in understanding your experience.

At this point someone is bound to ask whether a work can have meanings which the author did not intend it to have. The answer is yes. For hundreds of years people have been finding various worth-while meanings in *Hamlet* and *Othello* and *Twelfth Night* that Shakespeare undoubtedly never knew were there. Every reader applies poetical, fictional, and dramatic representations to himself in the light of his own background, interests, and information. Indeed, the same reader coming to a work at two different times and in different moods may apply its representations to himself in two quite different fashions. Possibly you yourself have said of a book, "I got a lot more meaning out of it the second time I read it." By this, you indicate that your experience with life and literature has led you to see more implications in the book and more applications of the work to human affairs than you saw during your first reading. Actually, what meaning the author has in mind is unimportant unless the literary work makes it clear—and makes it clear, moreover, to you and other readers. Your task, therefore, is to find whatever clues to meaning there are in the work and to follow them through to their implications for you. Note that the implications are to be found *in the works*—that you should discover meanings in what the author has written as well as in your interpretations.

How do you discover meanings? There is no one answer to such a question, for the process of discovery changes with every work you read. There are certain guideposts to meaning, however, and these you should look for as you read. They are (1) statements of meaning provided by the author and expressed either directly by him or indirectly through one of his characters; (2) relations and conflicts of the characters which are representative of broader relations and conflicts. Let us examine these more closely.

STATEMENTS OF MEANING

Statements of meaning may be of four kinds: explicit, ironic, symbolic, and mythical. Of these the first is by far the easiest to detect. In an *explicit statement* of meaning the author simply tells you, or has an attractive character expressing his point of view tell you, what the meaning is which he has in mind. The example given from "Wakefield" shows you how it is done in a short story. Notice how Wordsworth does it in one stanza from "The Tables Turned":

> One impulse from a vernal wood
> May teach you more of man,
> Of moral evil and of good,
> Than all the sages can.

For an example of a meaning stated by an attractive character in a play, examine the ending to Ibsen's *An Enemy of the People*. Ibsen has dramatized the story of a Dr. Stockman, who discovers that the water in the town's Municipal Baths is polluted. But because the Baths provide the main income for the townsmen, Stockman is reviled and persecuted by the authorities, the local paper, his father-in-law, who threatens to disinherit his wife and children, and the public in general, who brand him "an enemy of the people." For a while, Dr. Stockman considers the possibility of fleeing to America, but in the end he decides to stay and fight the thing out. The last few lines then run like this:

MRS. STOCKMAN. Let us hope it won't be the wolves *[narrow-minded leaders of the people]* that will drive you out of the country, Thomas.

DR. STOCKMAN. Are you out of your mind, Katherine? Drive me out! Now—when I am the strongest man in the town!

MRS. STOCKMAN. The strongest—now?

DR. STOCKMAN. Yes, and I will go so far as to say that now I am the strongest man in the world.

MORTEN *[his son]*. I say!

DR. STOCKMAN *(lowering his voice)*. Hush! You mustn't say anything about it yet; but I have made a great discovery.

MRS. STOCKMAN. Another one?

DR. STOCKMAN. Yes. *(Gathers them around him, and says confidentially)* It is this, let me tell you—that the strongest man in the world is he who stands most alone.

MRS. STOCKMAN *(smiling and shaking her head)*. Oh, Thomas, Thomas.

PETRA *(encouragingly, as she grasps her father's hands)*. Father!

Ironic statements are not so frequent, but their possibility should be kept in mind. In such a statement the author will say playfully, or allow an unattractive character to say seriously, exactly the opposite to what the author means. This is the same sort of thing which you do when you growl on a cold, rainy afternoon. "This is a fine day!" You indicate by your tone rather than by your words what you mean. Likewise the author indicates by his tone that his statement is to be taken ironically.[1]

---

1. Notice how important tone is to the right perception of meaning. It is especially so when meaning is communicated through the characters. As a reader, you can never be certain that any character is speaking directly for the author, but you may be completely certain that those characters which the author has made attractive to you are more likely to give voice to his real convictions than those which he has made unattractive. Thus Cordelia in *King Lear* is much more likely to express Shakespeare's true sentiments than are Goneril and Regan, her base and quite unattractive sisters.

No one could possibly miss the ironic intent of Mark Twain in the *Connecticut Yankee* when he writes:

If you take a nation of sixty millions, where average wages are two dollars per day, three days' wages taken from each individual will provide three hundred and sixty million dollars and pay the government's expenses. In my day, in my own country, this money was collected from imports, and the citizen imagined that the foreign importer paid it, and it made him comfortable to think so, whereas, in fact, it was paid by the American people, and was so equally distributed and exactly distributed among them that the annual cost to the one-hundred-millionaire and the annual cost to the sucking child of the day laborer was precisely the same—each paid six dollars. Nothing could be equaler than that, I reckon.

Symbolic statements are those in which the meaning is communicated in figurative language. Such a statement may be a single simile or metaphor; sometimes it is an analogy which carries through a paragraph or a series of paragraphs; and sometimes, as in works like *Pilgrim's Progress* and *Gulliver's Travels,* the symbolism carries through an entire work. If you have read Melville's *Moby Dick* you will recall that the main character, Ahab, with his wooden leg and lightning scar, goes clumping through the novel not only as a sea captain but as an animated metaphor representing what is defiant in mankind. The following paragraphs are from the same book. To understand their meaning you must recognize that the land represents what man knows, the sea what he still does not know. Melville addresses the reader directly in this symbolic statement:

Consider the subtleness of the sea; how its most dreaded creatures glide under water, unapparent for the most part, and treacherously hidden beneath the loveliest tints of azure. Consider also the devilish brilliance and beauty of many of its most remorseless tribes, as the dainty embellished shape of many species of sharks. Consider, once more, the universal cannibalism of the sea; all whose creatures prey upon each other, carrying on eternal war since the world began.

Consider all this; and then turn to this green, gentle, and most docile earth; consider them both, the sea and the land; and do you not find a strange analogy to something in yourself? For as this appalling ocean surrounds the verdant land, so in the soul of man lies one insular Tahiti, full of peace and joy, but encompassed by all the horrors of the half known life. God help thee! Push not off from that isle, thou canst never return!

Sometimes meaning is conveyed through a *mythical statement. Myth,* a term frequently used in contemporary criticism, was used by Aristotle to denote plot or narrative structure. Today, it is still at times used with this meaning. It is also used to denote an imagined story as opposed to a factual one, in contrast with history, say, or science. However, it is used most frequently today to mean a traditional story, or set of references, or attitude, or—by extension—a modern version of such a story. It is often associated with folklore, psychology, or religion, for it may explain phenomena of nature, the origins of man, religious rites, the beliefs or customs of a people. Heroes, demigods, or gods often figure in myths. Thus the comic story of how Paul Bunyan logged North Dakota, the tragic story of Oedipus (pp. 511-554), and the reverent stories recounted in *Paradise Lost* and *Paradise Regained* are all, in this broad sense, myths. Emerson pointed out how meanings in time become associated with mythology: "the legend is tossed from believer to poet, from poet to believer, everybody adding a grace or dropping a fault or rounding the form, until it gets an ideal truth."

Thus mythology is often important for the evocation of both feeling and meaning, providing metaphors or symbols on a large scale which have deeply significant implications. Coleridge, in an expanded translation of a passage by Schiller, suggests that even after belief in myths dies, they still have evocative power and meaning:

> They live no longer in the faith of reason!
> But still the heart doth need a language, still
> Doth the old instinct bring back the old names. . . .

Therefore, as William York Tindale remarks, "Serving the individual as it once served the group, myth may unite him with tradition or society, and, in literature, while uniting the conscious mind with the unconscious, myth may express the inner by the outer, the present by the past."

A particularly clear and effective use of myth gives depth to the poem "Palladium," by Matthew Arnold:

Matthew Arnold, **PALLADIUM**

> Set where the upper streams of Simois flow
> Was the Palladium, high 'mid rock and wood;
> And Hector was in Ilium, far below,
> And fought, and saw it not—but there it stood!
>
> It stood, and sun and moonshine rain'd their light   5
> On the pure columns of its glen-built hall.
> Backward and forward rolled the waves of fight
> Round Troy—but while this stood, Troy could not fall.
>
> So, in its lovely moonlight, lives the soul.
> Mountains surround it, and sweet virgin air;   10

Cold plashing, past it, crystal waters roll;
We visit it by moments, ah, too rare!

We shall renew the battle in the plain
Tomorrow;—red with blood will Xanthus be;
Hector and Ajax will be there again,   15
Helen will come upon the wall to see.

Then we shall rust in shade, or shine in strife,
And fluctuate 'twixt blind hopes and blind despairs,
And fancy that we put forth all our life,
And never know how with the soul it fares.   20

Still doth the soul, from its lone fastness high,
Upon our life a ruling effluence send.
And when it fails, fight as we will, we die;
And while it lasts, we cannot wholly end.

It is possible that the meaning of this poem can be deciphered by one un-
acquainted with Grecian mythology, but the meaning and the appeal certainly
will be enriched if the reader knows the lore to which the poem refers. The
Palladium was a statue of Pallas Athene, a goddesss who was the protector of
civilized life and the embodiment of purity and reason. During the building of
Troy, this image had fallen from heaven, and its power was such that as long
as it stood on a hill above the city, the city could not fall. Hector, the Trojan,
and Ajax, the Greek, heroes both, fought in Ilium (Troy) without decisive
results, therefore, as long as the statue stood. The image, sunlit or moonlit,
high on the forested hill where the pure headwaters of the Simois River rolled,
is contrasted with the Trojan battlefield below where the Xanthus River is red
with the blood of war. The image is likened by Arnold to the soul, which also
stands aloof, seldom thought upon, though it actually rules our lives. In the
story of the Trojan War, the statue was stolen, and thereafter Troy fell. Thus
the two concluding lines,

And when it fails, fight as we will, we die;
And while it lasts, we cannot wholly end.

Professor Douglas Bush calls this poem "perhaps the most firm and finely
rounded of Arnold's many poems in which morality is touched by emotion."
In it, he continues, "a classical symbol or example gives to the presentation of
ethical ideas a distinctness, a substantial unity, an aura of noble associations. . . ."
    Some critics use the term *myth* to denote not only classic stories but also
mythlike fictions of various authors. They talk, for instance, of Faulkner's
"myth of the South," a mythlike account of Southern history. Employed with

such a meaning, the term must be used with the utmost caution, but at times (as in some of the criticism of Faulkner) it helps define important meanings of imaginative works.

RELATIONS AND CONFLICTS

Not all meanings are easy to discover since many authors, especially the modern ones, are reluctant to be explicit. They feel that a statement of meaning often results in artless banality and gives the impression that they underrate the reader's intelligence and sensitivity. In a competent literary work, they contend, meaning should emerge clearly enough without its being stated. Now it is quite true that the meaning of a poem or a short story or a passage in a play or novel may be readily apparent; yet in many instances rereading will be required, and in the case of works like T. S. Eliot's poems and Joyce's novels many rereadings will be necessary. What are the signposts to meaning in works where there are no statements of it? The answer is the relations and conflicts of the characters—inner conflicts or outer ones involving such relations as those between a person and his environment, a person and other persons, a person and his God.

We say relations and conflicts rather than action, settings, or characters because a concentration on the latter tends to emphasize the unique characteristics of what is being portrayed rather than its representative characteristics. For example, the exact action related by Conrad in his *Nigger of the "Narcissus"* will never occur again; the setting in this particular crew's quarters will never be duplicated, and, naturally, these exact characters will never navigate the seas. Yet the *relations* among these men are of the things that, in the words of Henry James, "we cannot possibly *not* know, sooner or later, in one way or another." Motivated by a common fear of the big, burly Negro, a quarrelsome crew is gradually bound together in a tightly cohesive unit. Is this development of a relation among people unique? Are quarreling nations ever bound together by fear of a common foe? Have you and a brother or sister ever begun pulling together when faced by an obstreperous outsider? Generalizations such as those suggested are almost inevitable for the reader of this novel.

A simple formula, then, for seeing how relations and conflicts imply meanings, might be the following:

Step One: See whether the important relations or conflicts are representative of ones which you encounter or might encounter in actual life. A Superman scrap, for example, in which that dauntless character wins because of his steel muscles and X-ray vision would be ruled out; ruled in would be the conflict in Huckleberry Finn's mind over whether he should surrender Jim, the runaway slave, to the authorities. (Note that in real life you are no more likely to meet Huckleberry Finn than Superman but that you can't miss encountering an inner conflict like Huck's between what he knows the community wants him to do and what his feelings urge him to do.)

Step Two: Convert the particular persons, places, and action in the relation or conflict into their respective classes or categories (e.g., substitute mankind for Huck Finn, death in general for the death of one man, nature for a woods at twilight).[1]

Although at first such a process may sound rather mechanical, it is precisely the procedure you employ unconsciously in reading a work in which the meaning is readily discernible. Here, all we are suggesting is that in the tougher cases you make your unconscious process conscious. Notice how you might handle the following poem by Whitman:

Walt Whitman, WHEN I HEARD THE LEARN'D ASTRONOMER

When I heard the learn'd astronomer,
When the proofs, the figures, were ranged in columns before me,
When I was shown the charts and diagrams, to add, divide, and measure them,
When I sitting heard the astronomer where he lectured with much applause in
    the lecture-room,
How soon unaccountable I became tired and sick,   5
Till rising and gliding out I wander'd off by myself,
In the mystical moist night-air, and from time to time,
Look'd up in perfect silence at the stars.

Step One: The conflict is in the mind of the poet. On the one hand he is sickened by an explanation of the stars; on the other he views the stars themselves in perfect silence. This seems representative of conflicts that we all have had. (Whether our reactions have been the same makes no difference; the point is that the conflict is a common one.)

Step Two: The poet can be generalized into man; the stars into nature; the the astronomer's charts, figures, and the like into an explanation of nature.

All you need to do now is to find some congenial phrasing for the meaning as you have come to perceive it. A sentence like this might do the job: Nature itself is more satisfying to man than his own explanations of it.

LEVELS OF MEANING

In the preceding paragraphs we have been concerned with what meaning is and how you find it. You should not suppose, however, that all works are equally rich in meaning. Indeed, it might be argued that many notable works of literature possess no meaning at all as we have defined it. Works designed simply to excite us, to re-create a mood or a feeling, works centered about an

1. This little formula, of course, will not work in those poems and occasional prose pieces where the author is using a private set of symbols. In such cases you will have to consult your own good sense, other works by the same author, or commentaries by or on the author.

emotion rather than people and ideas, these are the ones with little meaning. Yet this is not to say that such works give no pleasure. Think, for instance, of Dunsany's *A Night at an Inn* (p. 36) or Poe's story "The Pit and the Pendulum" or Coleridge's poem "Kubla Khan" (p. 194). Meaning of a certain kind, in short, is not necessary for a literary experience.

In those cases, however, where the author is more interested in studying how people think and feel and act than he is in simply evoking a mood, you can be sure of at least one level of meaning. This is the overall level of meaning or what we shall call theme. When you ask about a work, "What's the point of all this?" you are asking in effect for its theme. Often a work will have no other meaning than its theme. This certainly is true of Aesop's fables and of Jesus' parables. It is true also of many short stories and poems (for instance, "When I Heard the Learn'd Astronomer" has only a theme).

Longer works, since they touch on more relations of men and portray more conflicts, are almost bound to have more than one level of meaning. These secondary levels can be of two kinds: (1) they can be meanings which apply to the work as a whole and thus constitute subthemes, or (2) they can be meanings which emerge from sections of the work, indeed from stanzas or paragraphs, and have sometimes only a distant relation to the theme. For a complex example of a work with theme and subthemes you might sometime turn to Whitman's "Passage to India." On the surface, he is dealing with the West and the East, suddenly brought closer because of the Suez Canal, the transatlantic cables, and the transcontinental railroads. But in doing this, he is also dealing symbolically with science and wisdom, with the rational and the mystical, with the body and the soul, with man's soul and God. It would be hard to say which is the major theme and which are the minor ones in such a poem. Almost any novel affords an example of a work with an overall meaning or meanings and incidental meanings which apply to only small passages. The great ones afford what amounts to a continuous succession of penetrating and provocative insights into your own experience.

There is still another level of meaning, one that is often neither stated nor susceptible of the method of generalizing proposed on page 115. This level deals with the kinds of assumptions which the author makes. In short, what is his philosophic position? Here are typical questions you should ask yourself: What does the author believe about the *nature of man:* is he made in the image of God? has he free will? is he a creature of blind chance? is he dominated by reason or impulse? What does the author believe about the *nature of society:* does he think the strong man should rule? the rich? the capable? the majority? the working class? What does he believe about the *nature of the universe:* is there a Divine purpose behind it? is it working according to laws? is it accidental or capricious? What is the *nature of truth:* is it something beyond our senses which we can never prove but perceive through intuition, our reason, or the Bible? or is it something that we agree upon only after the scientific process of observation, hypothesis, verification, and conclusion? The ability to discern an author's fundamental assumptions will not come overnight, nor is it likely to come through the reading of a single work. But ultimately, if you are to be able to say that you understand thoroughly the meaning of a poem or novel or play, you must be able to push beneath its themes and subsidiary meanings to this level of basic assumptions.

For illustration, let us return once more to "Wakefield." You will recall that the theme was stated at the end in this fashion:

> Amid the seeming confusion of our mysterious world, individuals are so nicely adjusted to a system, and systems to one another and to a whole, that by stepping aside for a moment, a man exposes himself to a fearful risk of losing his place forever.

What does this imply about the nature of man? That he becomes a free agent at his peril and, therefore, that he is substantially without freedom of the will. What is assumed about the nature of society? Nothing about the proper or desirable form of society, but the implication is that whatever the form, there is little chance of changing it. What is implied about the nature of the universe? Hawthorne apparently is suggesting here that cosmic events are but a long sequence of cause and effect. This philosophy of predestination, determinism, fatalism—call it what you will—is more strongly suggested in another passage from the same story:

> Would that I had a folio to write, instead of an article of a dozen pages! Then might I exemplify how an influence beyond our control lays its strong hand on every deed which we do, and weaves its consequences into an iron tissue of necessity.

What is the nature of truth? Obviously Hawthorne is assuming that there is some superhuman and, undoubtedly, supernatural power which controls our destiny. Presumably, therefore, ultimate truth must lie beyond the range of our five senses. Whether such truth may be discerned by intuition, by reason, or through Scriptures, he does not say. There is a strong suspicion from the tone of the story that he does not believe it can be discerned at all.

It would be a mistake to build up these particular questions into a monotonous pattern, a little ritual which you go through every time you read a literary work that seems to have some meaning. These are representative, however, of the more searching type of question you should ask of any thoughtful work of art. Use them, modify them, adapt them, discard them as you see fit. Use your common sense—but don't be content until you have exhausted all the possible levels of meaning.

Even as a young man Nathaniel Hawthorne thought long and deeply about sin and its effects upon men's lives. In one fashion or another the subject gets into all of his novels and short stories. The idea for "The Minister's Black Veil," he says, came from an account of a New England clergyman by the name of Joseph Moody, who ever after accidentally killing a beloved friend hid his face from the world in the same manner as here related of the Reverend Mr. Hooper. The story has always been one of Hawthorne's more popular ones, and many persons have speculated about its meaning. (See p. 153 for an analysis by Richard Fogle.)

Nathaniel Hawthorne

THE MINISTER'S BLACK VEIL

The sexton stood in the porch of Milford meeting-house, pulling busily at the bell-rope. The old people of the village came stooping along the street. Children, with bright faces, tripped merrily beside their parents, or mimicked a graver gait, in the conscious dignity of their Sunday clothes. Spruce bachelors looked sidelong at the pretty maidens, and fancied that the Sabbath sunshine made them prettier than on week days. When the throng had mostly streamed into the porch, the sexton began to toll the bell, keeping his eye on the Reverend Mr. Hooper's door. The first glimpse of the clergyman's figure was the signal for the bell to cease its summons.

"But what has good Parson Hooper got upon his face?" cried the sexton in astonishment.

All within hearing immediately turned about, and beheld the semblance of Mr. Hooper, pacing slowly his meditative way towards the meeting-house. With one accord they started, expressing more wonder than if some strange minister were coming to dust the cushions of Mr. Hooper's pulpit.

"Are you sure it is our parson?" inquired Goodman Gray of the sexton.

"Of a certainty it is good Mr. Hooper," replied the sexton. "He was to have exchanged pulpits with Parson Shute, of Westbury; but Parson Shute sent to excuse himself yesterday, being to preach a funeral sermon."

The cause of so much amazement may appear sufficiently slight. Mr. Hooper, a gentlemanly person, of about thirty, though still a bachelor, was dressed with due clerical neatness, as if a careful wife had starched his band, and brushed the weekly dust from his Sunday's garb. There was but one thing remarkable in his appearance. Swathed about his forehead, and hanging down over his face, so low as to be shaken by his breath, Mr. Hooper had on a black veil. On a nearer view it seemed to consist of two folds of crape, which entirely concealed his features, except the mouth and chin, but probably did not intercept his sight, further than to give a darkened aspect to all living and inanimate things. With this gloomy shade before him, good Mr. Hooper walked onward, at a slow and quiet pace, stooping somewhat, and looking on the ground, as is customary with abstracted men, yet nodding kindly to those of his parishioners who still waited on the meeting-house steps. But so wonder-struck were they that his greeting hardly met with a return.

"I can't really feel as if good Mr. Hooper's face was behind that piece of crape," said the sexton.

"I don't like it," muttered an old woman, as she hobbled into the meeting-house. "He has changed himself into something awful, only by hiding his face."

"Our parson has gone mad!" cried Goodman Gray, following him across the threshold.

A rumor of some unaccountable phenomenon had preceded Mr. Hooper into the meeting-house, and set all the congregation astir. Few could refrain from twisting their heads towards the door; many stood upright, and turned directly about; while several little boys clambered upon the seats, and came down again with a terrible racket. There was a general bustle, a rustling of the women's gowns and shuffling of the men's feet, greatly at variance with that hushed repose which should attend the entrance of the minister. But Mr. Hooper appeared not to notice the perturbation of his people. He entered with an almost noiseless step, bent his head mildly to the pews on each side, and bowed as he passed his oldest parishioner, a white-haired great-grandsire, who occupied an arm-chair in the centre of the aisle. It was strange to observe how slowly this venerable man became conscious of something singular in the appearance of his pastor. He seemed not fully to partake of the prevailing wonder, till Mr. Hooper had ascended the stairs, and showed himself in the pulpit, face to face with his congregation, except for the black veil. That mysterious emblem was never once withdrawn. It shook with his measured breath, as he gave out the psalm; it threw its obscurity between him and the holy page, as he read the Scriptures; and while he prayed, the veil lay heavily on his uplifted countenance. Did he seek to hide it from the dread Being whom he was addressing?

Such was the effect of this simple piece of crape, that more than one woman of delicate nerves was forced to leave the meeting-house. Yet perhaps the pale-faced congregation was almost as fearful a sight to the minister, as his black veil to them.

Mr. Hooper had the reputation of a good preacher, but not an energetic one: he strove to win his people heavenward by mild, persuasive influences, rather than to drive them thither by the thunders of the Word. The sermon which he now delivered was marked by the same characteristics of style and manner as the general series of his pulpit oratory. But there was something, either in the sentiment of the discourse itself, or in the imagination of the auditors, which made it greatly the most powerful effort that they had ever heard from their pastor's lips. It was tinged, rather more darkly than usual, with the gentle gloom of Mr. Hooper's temperament. The subject had reference to secret sin, and those sad mysteries which we hide from our nearest and dearest, and would fain conceal from our own consciousness, even forgetting that the Omniscient can detect them. A subtle power was breathed into his words. Each member of the congregation, the most innocent girl, and the man of hardened breast, felt as if the preacher had crept upon them, behind his awful veil, and discovered their hoarded iniquity of deed or thought. Many spread their clasped hands on their bosoms. There was nothing terrible in what Mr. Hooper said, at least, no violence; and yet, with every tremor of his melancholy voice, the hearers quaked. An unsought pathos came hand in hand with awe. So sensible were the audience of some unwonted attribute in their minister, that they longed for a breath of wind to blow aside the veil, almost believing that a stranger's visage would be discovered, though the form, gesture, and voice were those of Mr. Hooper.

At the close of the services, the people hurried out with indecorous confusion, eager to communicate their pent-up amazement, and conscious of lighter spirits the moment they lost sight of the black veil. Some gathered in little circles, huddled closely together, with their mouths all whispering in the centre; some went homeward alone, wrapt in silent meditation; some talked loudly, and profaned the Sabbath day with ostentatious laughter. A few shook their sagacious heads, intimating that they could penetrate the mystery; while one or two affirmed that there was no mystery at all, but only that Mr. Hooper's eyes were so weakened by the midnight lamp, as to require a shade. After a brief interval, forth came good Mr. Hooper also, in the rear of his flock. Turning his veiled face from one group to another, he paid due reverence to the hoary heads, saluted the middle aged with kind dignity as their friend and spiritual guide, greeted the young with mingled authority and love, and laid his hands on the little children's heads to bless them. Such was always his custom on the Sabbath day. Strange and bewildered looks repaid him for his courtesy. None, as on former occasions, aspired to the honor of walking by their pastor's side. Old Squire Saunders, doubtless by an accidental lapse of memory, neglected to invite Mr. Hooper to his table, where the good clergyman had been wont to bless the food, almost every Sunday since his settlement. He returned, therefore, to the parsonage, and, at the moment of closing the door, was observed to look back upon the people, all of whom had their eyes fixed upon the minister. A sad smile gleamed faintly from beneath the black veil, and flickered about his mouth, glimmering as he disappeared.

"How strange," said a lady, "that a simple black veil, such as any woman might wear on her bonnet, should become such a terrible thing on Mr. Hooper's face!"

"Something must surely be amiss with Mr. Hooper's intellects," observed her husband, the physician of the village. "But the strangest part of the affair is the effect of this vagary, even on a sober-minded man like myself. The black veil, though it covers only our pastor's face, throws its influence over his whole person, and makes him ghostlike from head to foot. Do you not feel it so?"

"Truly do I," replied the lady; "and I would not be alone with him for the world. I wonder he is not afraid to be alone with himself!"

"Men sometimes are so," said her husband.

The afternoon service was attended with similar circumstances. At its conclusion, the bell tolled for the funeral of a young lady. The relatives and friends were assembled in the house, and the more distant acquaintances stood about the door, speaking of the good qualities of the deceased, when their talk was interrupted by the appearance of Mr. Hooper, still covered with his black veil. It was now an appropriate emblem. The clergyman stepped into the room where the corpse was laid. and bent over the coffin, to take a last farewell of his deceased parishioner. As he stooped, the veil hung straight down from his forehead, so that, if her eyelids had not been closed forever, the dead maiden might have seen his face. Could Mr. Hooper be fearful of her glance, that he so hastily caught back the black veil? A person who watched the interview between the dead and living, scrupled not to affirm, that, at the instant when the clergyman's features were disclosed, the corpse had slightly shuddered, rustling the shroud and muslin cap, though the countenance retained the composure of death. A superstitious old woman was the only witness of this prodigy. From the coffin Mr. Hooper passed into the chamber of the mourners, and thence to the head of the staircase, to make the funeral prayer. It was a tender and heart-dissolving prayer, full of sorrow, yet so imbued with celestial hopes, that the music of a heavenly harp, swept by the fingers of the dead, seemed faintly to be heard among the saddest accents of the minister. The people trembled, though they but darkly understood him when he prayed that they, and himself, and all of mortal race, might be ready, as he trusted this young maiden had been, for the dreadful hour that should snatch the veil from their faces. The bearers went heavily forth, and the mourners followed, saddening all the street, with the dead before them, and Mr. Hooper in his black veil behind.

"Why do you look back?" said one in the procession to his partner.

"I had a fancy," replied she, "that the minister and the maiden's spirit were walking hand in hand."

"And so had I, at the same moment," said the other.

That night, the handsomest couple in Milford village were to be joined in wedlock. Though reckoned a melancholy man, Mr. Hooper had a placid cheerfullness for such occasions, which often excited a sympathetic smile where livelier merriment would have been thrown away. There was no quality of his disposition which made him more beloved than this. The company at the wedding awaited his arrival with impatience, trusting that the strange awe, which had gathered over him throughout the day, would now be dispelled. But such was not the result. When Mr. Hooper came, the first thing that their eyes rested on was the same horrible black veil, which had added deeper gloom to the funeral, and could portend nothing but evil to the wedding. Such was its immediate effect on the guests that a cloud seemed to have rolled duskily from beneath the black crape, and dimmed the light of the candles. The bridal pair stood up before the minister. But the bride's cold fingers quivered in the tremulous hand of the bridegroom, and her deathlike paleness caused a whisper that the maiden who had been buried a few hours before was come from her grave to be married. If ever another wedding were so dismal, it was that famous one where they tolled the wedding knell. After performing the ceremony, Mr. Hooper raised a glass of wine to his lips, wishing happiness to the new-married couple in a strain of mild pleasantry that ought to have brightened the features of the guests, like a cheerful gleam from the hearth. At that instant, catching a glimpse of his figure in the looking-glass, the black veil involved his own spirit in the horror with which it overwhelmed all others. His frame shuddered, his lips grew white, he spilt the untasted wine upon the carpet, and rushed forth into the darkness. For the Earth, too, had on her Black Veil.

The next day, the whole village of Milford talked of little else than Parson Hooper's black veil. That, and the mystery concealed behind it, supplied a topic for discussion between acquaintances meeting in the street, and good women gossiping at their open windows. It was the first item of news that the tavern-keeper told to his guests. The children babbled of it on their way to school. One imitative little imp covered his face with an old black handkerchief, thereby so affrighting his playmates that the panic seized himself, and he well-nigh lost his wits by his own waggery.

It was remarkable that of all the busybodies and impertinent people in the parish, not one ventured to put the plain question to Mr. Hooper, wherefore he did this thing. Hitherto, whenever there appeared the slightest call for such interference, he had never lacked advisers, nor shown himself averse to be guided by their judgment. If he erred at all, it was by so painful a degree of self-distrust, that even the mildest censure would lead him to consider an indifferent action as a crime. Yet, though so well acquainted with this amiable weakness, no individual among his parishioners chose to make the black veil a subject of friendly remonstrance. There was a feeling of dread, neither plainly confessed nor carefully concealed, which caused each to shift the responsibility upon another, till at length it was found expedient to send a deputation of the church, in order to deal with Mr. Hooper about the mystery, before it should grow into a scandal. Never did an embassy so ill discharge its duties. The minister received them with friendly courtesy, but became silent, after they were seated, leaving to his visitors the whole burden of introducing their important business. The topic, it might be supposed, was obvious enough. There was the black veil swathed round Mr. Hooper's forehead, and concealing every feature above his placid mouth, on which, at times, they could perceive the glimmering of a melancholy smile. But that piece of crape, to their imagination, seemed to hang down before his heart, the symbol of a fearful secret between him and them. Were the veil but cast aside, they might speak freely of it, but not till then. Thus they sat a considerable time, speechless, confused, and shrinking uneasily from Mr. Hooper's eye, which they felt to be fixed upon them with an invisible glance. Finally, the deputies returned abashed to their constituents, pronouncing the matter too weighty to be handled, except by a council of the churches, if, indeed, it might not require a general synod.

But there was one person in the village unappalled by the awe with which the black veil had impressed all beside herself. When the deputies returned without an explanation, or even venturing to demand one, she, with the calm energy of her character, determined to chase away the strange cloud that appeared to be settling around Mr. Hooper, every moment more darkly than before. As his plighted wife, it should be her privilege to know what the black veil concealed. At the minister's first visit, therefore, she entered upon the subject with a direct simplicity, which made the task easier both for him and her. After he had seated himself, she fixed her eyes steadfastly upon the veil, but could discern nothing of the dreadful gloom that had so overawed the multitude: it was but a double fold of crape, hanging down from his forehead to his mouth, and slightly stirring with his breath.

"No," said she aloud, and smiling, "there is nothing terrible in this piece of crape, except that it hides a face which I am always glad to look upon. Come, good sir, let the sun shine from behind the cloud. First lay aside your black veil: then tell me why you put it on."

Mr. Hooper's smile glimmered faintly.

"There is an hour to come," said he, "when all of us shall cast aside our veils. Take it not amiss, beloved friend, if I wear this piece of crape till then."

"Your words are a mystery, too," returned the young lady. "Take away the veil from them, at least."

"Elizabeth, I will," said he, "so far as my vow may suffer me. Know, then, this veil is a type and a symbol, and I am bound to wear it ever, both in light and darkness, in solitude and before the gaze of multitudes, and as with strangers, so with my familiar friends. No mortal eye will see it withdrawn. This dismal shade must separate me from the world: even you, Elizabeth, can never come behind it!"

"What grievous affliction hath befallen you," she earnestly inquired, "that you should thus darken your eyes forever?"

"If it be a sign of mourning," replied Mr. Hooper, "I, perhaps, like most other mortals, have sorrows dark enough to be typified by a black veil."

"But what if the world will not believe that it is the type of an innocent sorrow?" urged Elizabeth. "Beloved and respected as you are, there may be whispers that you hide your face under the consciousness of secret sin. For the sake of your holy office, do away this scandal!"

The color rose into her cheeks as she intimated the nature of the rumors that were already abroad in the village. But Mr. Hooper's mildness did not forsake him. He even smiled again—that same sad smile, which always appeared like a faint glimmering of light, proceeding from the obscurity beneath the veil.

"If I hide my face for sorrow, there is cause enough," he merely replied; "and if I cover it for secret sin, what mortal might not do the same?"

And with this gentle, but unconquerable obstinacy did he resist all her entreaties. At length Elizabeth sat silent. For a few moments she appeared lost in thought, considering, probably, what new methods might be tried to withdraw her lover from so dark a fantasy, which, if it had no other meaning, was perhaps a symptom of mental disease. Though of a firmer character than his own, the tears rolled down her cheeks. But, in an instant, as it were, a new feeling took the place of sorrow: her eyes were fixed insensibly on the black veil, when, like a sudden twilight in the air, its terrors fell around her. She arose, and stood trembling before him.

"And do you feel it then, at last?" said he mournfully.

She made no reply, but covered her eyes with her hand, and turned to leave the room. He rushed forward and caught her arm.

"Have patience with me, Elizabeth!" cried he, passionately. "Do not desert me, though this veil must be between us here on earth. Be mine, and hereafter there shall be no veil over my face, no darkness between our souls! It is but a mortal veil—it is not for eternity! O! you know not how lonely I am, and how frightened, to be alone behind my black veil. Do not leave me in this miserable obscurity forever!"

"Lift the veil but once, and look me in the face," said she.

"Never! It cannot be!" replied Mr. Hooper.

"Then farewell!" said Elizabeth.

She withdrew her arm from his grasp, and slowly departed, pausing at the door, to give one long shuddering gaze, that seemed almost to penetrate the mystery of the black veil. But, even amid his grief, Mr. Hooper smiled to think that only a material emblem had separated him from happiness, though the horrors, which it shadowed forth, must be drawn darkly between the fondest of lovers.

From that time no attempts were made to remove Mr. Hooper's black veil, or, by a direct appeal, to discover the secret which it was supposed to hide. By persons who claimed a superiority to popular prejudice, it was reckoned merely an eccentric whim, such as often mingles with the sober actions of men other-wise rational, and tinges them all with its own semblance of insanity. But with the multitude, good Mr. Hooper was irreparably a bugbear. He could not walk the street with any peace of mind, so conscious was he that the gentle and timid would turn aside to avoid him, and that others would make it a point of hardihood to throw themselves in his way. The impertinence of the latter class compelled him to give up his customary walk at sunset to the burial ground; for when he leaned pensively over the gate, there would always be faces behind the gravestones, peeping at his black veil. A fable went the rounds that the stare of the dead people drove him thence. It grieved him, to the very depth of his kind heart, to observe how the children fled from his approach, breaking up their merriest sports, while his melancholy figure was yet afar off. Their instinctive dread caused him to feel more strongly than aught else, that a preternatural horror was interwoven with the threads of the black crape. In truth, his own antipathy to the veil was known to be so great, that he never willingly passed before a mirror, nor stooped to drink at a still fountain, lest, in its peaceful bosom, he should be affrighted by himself. This was what gave plausibility to the whispers, that Mr. Hooper's conscience tortured him for some great crime too horrible to be entirely concealed, or otherwise than so obscurely intimated. Thus, from beneath the black veil, there rolled a cloud into the sunshine, an ambiguity of sin or sorrow, which enveloped the poor minister, so that love or sympathy could never reach him. It was said that ghost and fiend consorted with him there. With self-shudderings and outward terrors, he walked continually in its shadow, groping darkly within his own soul, or gazing through a medium that saddened the whole world. Even the lawless wind, it was believed, respected his dreadful secret, and never blew aside the veil. But still good Mr. Hooper sadly smiled at the pale visages of the wordly throng as he passed by.

Among all its bad influences, the black veil had the one desirable effect, of making its wearer a very efficient clergyman. By the aid of his mysterious emblem—for there was no other apparent cause—he became a man of awful power over souls that were in agony for sin. His converts always regarded him with a dread peculiar to themselves, affirming, though but figuratively, that, before he brought them to celestial light, they had been with him behind the black veil. Its gloom, indeed, enabled him to sympathize with all dark affections. Dying sinners cried aloud for Mr. Hooper, and would not yield their breath till he appeared; though ever, as he stooped to whisper consolation, they shuddered at the veiled face so near their own. Such were the terrors of the black veil, even when Death had bared his visage! Strangers came long distances to attend service at his church, with the mere idle purpose of gazing at his figure, because it was forbidden them to behold his face. But many were made to quake ere they departed! Once, during Governor Belcher's administration, Mr. Hooper was appointed to preach the election sermon. Covered with his black veil, he stood before the chief magistrate, the council, and the representatives, and wrought so deep an impression, that the legislative measures of that year were characterized by all the gloom and piety of our earliest ancestral sway.

In this manner, Mr. Hooper spent a long life, irreproachable in outward act, yet shrouded in dismal suspicions; kind and loving, though unloved, and dimly feared; a man apart from men, shunned in their health and joy, but ever summoned to their aid in mortal anguish. As years wore on, shedding their snows above his sable veil, he acquired a name throughout the New England churches, and they called him Father Hooper. Nearly all his parishioners, who were of mature age when he was settled, had been borne away by many a funeral: he had one congregation in the church, and a more crowded one in the churchyard; and having wrought so late into the evening, and done his work so well, it was now good Father Hooper's turn to rest.

Several persons were visible by the shaded candle-light, in the death chamber of the old clergyman. Natural connections he had none. But there was the decorously grave, though unmoved physician, seeking only to mitigate the last pangs of the patient whom he could not save. There were the deacons, and other eminently pious members of his church. There, also, was the Reverend Mr. Clark, of Westbury, a young and zealous divine, who had ridden in haste to pray by the bedside of the expiring minister. There was the nurse, no hired handmaiden of death, but one whose calm affection had endured thus long in secrecy, in solitude, amid the chill of age, and would not perish, even at the dying hour. Who, but Elizabeth! And there lay the hoary head of good Father Hooper upon the death pillow, with the black veil still swathed about his brow, and reaching down over his face, so that each more difficult gasp of his faint breath caused it to stir. All through life that piece of crape had hung between him and the world: it had separated him from cheerful brother-hood and woman's love, and kept him in that saddest of all prisons, his own heart; and still it lay upon his face, as if to deepen the gloom of his darksome chamber, and shade him from the sunshine of eternity.

For some time previous, his mind had been confused, wavering doubtfully between the past and the present, and hovering forward, as it were, at intervals, into the indistinctness of the world to come. There had been feverish turns, which tossed him from side to side, and wore away what little strength he had. But in his most convulsive struggles, and in the wildest vagaries of his intellect, when no other thought retained its sober influence, he still showed an awful solicitude lest the black veil should slip aside. Even if his bewildered soul could have forgotten, there was a faithful woman at his pillow, who, with averted eyes, would have covered that aged face, which she had last beheld in the comeliness of manhood. At length the death-stricken old man lay quietly in the torpor of mental and bodily exhaustion, with an imperceptible pulse, and breath that grew fainter and fainter, except when a long, deep, and irregular inspiration seemed to prelude the flight of his spirit.

The minister of Westbury approached the bedside.

"Venerable Father Hooper," said he, "the moment of your release is at hand. Are you ready for the lifting of the veil that shuts in time from eternity?"

Father Hooper at first replied merely by a feeble motion of his head; then, apprehensive, perhaps, that his meaning might be doubtful, he exerted himself to speak.

"Yea," said he, in faint accents, "my soul hath a patient weariness until that veil be lifted."

"And is it fitting," resumed the Reverend Mr. Clark, "that a man so given to prayer, of such a blameless example, holy in deed and thought, so far as mortal judgment may pronounce; is it fitting that a father in the church should leave a shadow on his memory, that may seem to blacken a life so pure? I pray you, my venerable brother, let not this thing be! Suffer us to be gladdened by your triumphant aspect as you go to your reward. Before the veil of eternity be lifted, let me cast aside this black veil from your face!"

And thus speaking, the Reverend Mr. Clark bent forward to reveal the mystery of so many years. But, exerting a sudden energy, that made all the beholders stand aghast, Father Hooper snatched both his hands from beneath the bedclothes, and pressed them strongly on the black veil, resolute to struggle, if the minister of Westbury would contend with a dying man.

"Never!" cried the veiled clergyman. "On earth, never!"

"Dark old man!" exclaimed the affrighted minister, "with what horrible crime upon your soul are you now passing to the judgment?"

Father Hooper's breath heaved; it rattled in his throat; but, with a mighty effort, grasping forward with his hands, he caught hold of life, and held it back till he should speak. He even raised himself in bed; and there he sat, shivering with the arms of death around him, while the black veil hung down, awful, at that last moment, in the gathered terrors of a lifetime. And yet the faint, sad smile, so often there, now seemed to glimmer from its obscurity, and linger on Father Hooper's lips.

"Why do you tremble at me alone?" cried he, turning his veiled face round the circle of pale spectators. "Tremble also at each other! Have men avoided me, and women shown no pity, and children screamed and fled, only for my black veil? What, but the mystery which it obscurely typifies, has made this piece of crape so awful? When the friend shows his inmost heart to his friend; the lover to his best beloved; when man does not vainly shrink from the eye of his Creator, loathsomely treasuring up the secret of his sin; then deem me a monster, for the symbol beneath which I have lived, and die! I look around me, and, lo! on every visage a Black Veil!"

While his auditors shrank from one another, in mutual affright, Father Hooper fell back upon his pillow, a veiled corpse, with a faint smile lingering on the lips. Still veiled, they laid him in his coffin, and a veiled corpse they bore him to the grave. The grass of many years has sprung up and withered on that grave, the burial stone is moss-grown, and good Mr. Hooper's face is dust; but awful is still the thought that it mouldered beneath the Black Veil!

THE WHOLE WORK

Action

1. How does Hawthorne manage the beginning to make it dramatic?

2. What are the time breaks in the story? Why does plausibility depend upon the elapse of a considerable amount of time?

Characters

3. How completely are the various age, social, and occupational classes of the community represented?

4. Are the reactions to the black veil probable? Do any seem overdone?

5. Is Mr. Hooper's character delineated well enough so that his wearing of the veil seems plausible? Why does Hawthorne not tell us the nature of Mr. Hooper's secret sin? Is Mr. Hooper an attractive character or an eccentric?

Setting

6. Why should a small town be a more useful setting for this story than a farm or a large city?

Language

7. What differences do you notice between Hawthorne's language and that of a typical modern short story? Why is Hawthorne's language more suitable for this subject than that of (a) Ernest Hemingway? (b) Robert Penn Warren?

Tone

8. Does Hawthorne seem to feel that Mr. Hooper's wearing of the veil is a silly business? Explain your answer.

Point of View

9. Characterize the narrator. What would have happened to the story if Hawthorne had allowed the narrator to enter the mind of Mr. Hooper?

Atmosphere

10. What kind of world has Hawthorne created here? Many of the details of the tale invite us to describe the atmosphere metaphorically, in terms of colors and lighting. Explain.

Meaning

11. Which relation is stressed: the mental or moral conflict within the man? the relation between man and nature? the relation between man and other men? the relation between man and God? Are they all present? Give examples where possible.

12. What does the black veil symbolize? Whom does the Reverend Mr. Hooper symbolize? What is ironic about the fact that the veil frightens people whereas what the veil symbolizes ordinarily does not?

13. What ambiguity in meaning does Professor Fogle see in the story? (Read his evaluation of it, pp. 153-157.)

14. Do you agree that such an ambiguity exists? If so, do you think it makes the story less or more interesting? less or more illuminating about the nature of man? Explain your answers.

"The Love Song of J. Alfred Prufrock" is a longer and much more complicated poem than "When I Heard the Learn'd Astronomer" on page 116. Basically, however, the same techniques that were helpful in understanding Whitman's poem can be used. Readers generally agree that it is one of Eliot's best, both because it makes a considerable impact emotionally and because its details are so loaded with meaning that it can be reread many times and still not be completely mastered. Like "My Last

Duchess'' (p. 55) it is a dramatic monologue—the rendition of the thoughts of a character.

T. S. Eliot

THE LOVE SONG OF
J. ALFRED PRUFROCK

S'io credesse che mia risposta fosse
A persona che mai tornasse al mondo,
Questa fiamma staria senza piu scosse.
Ma perciocche giammai di questo fondo
Non torno vivo alcun, s'i'odo il vero,
Senza tema d'infamia ti rispondo.[1]

Let us go then, you and I,
When the evening is spread out against the sky
Like a patient etherized upon a table;
Let us go, through certain half-deserted streets,
The muttering retreats   5
Of restless nights in one-night cheap hotels
And sawdust restaurants with oyster-shells:
Streets that follow like a tedious argument
Of insidious intent
To lead you to an overwhelming question . . .   10
Oh, do not ask, 'What is it?'
Let us go and make our visit.

In the room the women come and go
Talking of Michelangelo.

The yellow fog that rubs its back upon the window-panes,   15
The yellow smoke that rubs its muzzle on the window-panes

1. *S'io . . . rispondo.* If I could believe that my answer might be to a person who should ever return into the world, this flame would stand without more quiverings; but inasmuch as, if I hear the truth, never from this depth did any living man return, without fear of infamy I answer thee (from Dante's *Inferno*, Canto XXVII, ll. 61-66).

Licked its tongue into the corners of the evening,
Lingered upon the pools that stand in drains,
Let fall upon its back the soot that falls from chimneys,
Slipped by the terrace, made a sudden leap,   20
And seeing that it was a soft October night,
Curled once about the house, and fell asleep.

And indeed there will be time
For the yellow smoke that slides along the street,
Rubbing its back upon the window-panes;   25
There will be time, there will be time
To prepare a face to meet the faces that you meet;
There will be time to murder and create,
And time for all the works and days of hands
That lift and drop a question on your plate;   30
Time for you and time for me,
And time yet for a hundred indecisions,
And for a hundred visions and revisions,
Before the taking of a toast and tea.

In the room the women come and go   35
Talking of Michelangelo.

And indeed there will be time
To wonder, 'Do I dare?' and, 'Do I dare?'
Time to turn back and descend the stair,
With a bald spot in the middle of my hair—   40
(They will say: 'How his hair is growing thin!')
My morning coat, my collar mounting firmly to the chin,
My necktie rich and modest, but asserted by a simple pin—
(They will say: 'But how his arms and legs are thin!')
Do I dare   45
Disturb the universe?
In a minute there is time
For decisions and revisions which a minute will reverse.

For I have known them all already, known them all:—
Have known the evenings, mornings, afternoons,   50
I have measured out my life with coffee spoons;
I know the voices dying with a dying fall
Beneath the music from a farther room.
    So how should I presume?

And I have known the eyes already, known them all—   55
The eyes that fix you in a formulated phrase,

And when I am formulated, sprawling on a pin,
When I am pinned and wriggling on the wall,
Then how should I begin
To spit out all the butt-ends of my days and ways?   60
  And how should I presume?

And I have known the arms already, known them all—
Arms that are braceleted and white and bare
(But in the lamplight, downed with light brown hair!)
Is it perfume from a dress   65
That makes me so digress?
Arms that lie along a table, or wrap about a shawl.
  And should I then presume?
  And how should I begin?

                . . . .

Shall I say, I have gone at dusk through narrow streets   70
And watched the smoke that rises from the pipes
Of lonely men in shirt-sleeves, leaning out of windows? . . .
I should have been a pair of ragged claws
Scuttling across the floors of silent seas.

                . . . .

And the afternoon, the evening, sleeps so peacefully!   75
Smoothed by long fingers,
Asleep . . . tired . . . or it malingers,
Stretched on the floor, here beside you and me.
Should I, after tea and cakes and ices,
Have the strength to force the moment to its crisis?   80
But though I have wept and fasted, wept and prayed,
Though I have seen my head (grown slightly bald) brought in
        upon a platter,
I am no prophet—and here's no great matter;
I have seen the moment of my greatness flicker,
And I have seen the eternal Footman hold my coat, and snicker, 85
And in short, I was afraid.

And would it have been worth it, after all,
After the cups, the marmalade, the tea,
Among the porcelain, among some talk of you and me,
Would it have been worth while,   90
To have bitten off the matter with a smile,
To have squeezed the universe into a ball
To roll it toward some overwhelming question,
To say: 'I am Lazarus, come from the dead,
Come back to tell you all, I shall tell you all'—   95

If one, settling a pillow by her head,
    Should say: 'That is not what I meant at all,
    That is not it, at all.'

          .   .   .   .   .   .

And would it have been worth it, after all,
Would it have been worth while,   100
After the sunsets and the dooryards and the sprinkled streets,
After the novels, after the teacups, after the skirts that trail along
        the floor—
And this, and so much more?—
It is impossible to say just what I mean!
But as if a magic lantern threw the nerves in patterns on a screen: 105
Would it have been worth while
If one, settling a pillow or throwing off a shawl,
And turning toward the window, should say:
    'That is not it at all,
    That is not what I meant, at all.'   110

          .   .   .   .   .   .

No! I am not Prince Hamlet, nor was meant to be;
Am an attendant lord, one that will do
To swell a progress, start a scene or two,
Advise the prince; no doubt, an easy tool,
Deferential, glad to be of use,   115
Politic, cautious, and meticulous;
Full of high sentence, but a bit obtuse;
At times, indeed, almost ridiculous—
Almost, at times, the Fool.

I grow old . . . I grow old . . .   120
I shall wear the bottoms of my trousers rolled.

Shall I part my hair behind? Do I dare to eat a peach?
I shall wear white flannel trousers, and walk upon the beach.
I have heard the mermaids singing, each to each.

I do not think that they will sing to me.   125

I have seen them riding seaward on the waves
Combing the white hair of the waves blown back
When the wind blows the water white and black.

We have lingered in the chambers of the sea
By sea-girls wreathed with seaweed red and brown   130
Till human voices wake us, and we drown.

THE WHOLE WORK

Action and Structure

1. What is the situation here that gives the poem a surface unity? (To answer this you must first realize that the "you" of the poem is that part of Prufrock's personality which is social, outgoing, and active. The "I" of the poem is that part which is shy, retiring, introspective, and fearful. Apparently before the poem opens the active self [the "you"] has suggested to the retiring self [the "I"] that they go into the room where the "women come and go." For convenience we shall hereafter refer to the "I" or the shy, fearful self as Prufrock.)

2. What is Prufrock's attitude at the beginning of the poem? At the end? Show the main stages by which he moves from the initial to the final position. (It might be well not to try to answer this question until you have answered the various parts of question 16.)

Characters

3. Describe Prufrock's appearance. What does it imply about his character?

4. What does his name suggest about him? Consider each part of the name.

5. How does he characterize himself? (See lines 111-119 especially.)

6. What is added to our understanding of him by the allusions to John the Baptist (lines 81-83), Lazarus (lines 94-95), and Hamlet (lines 111-119)?

7. Summarize Prufrock as a person, being as orderly and specific as you can.

8. What are the basic characteristics of the women in the poem?

Setting

9. What is the setting of the poem? How is it of value? Can you hazard a guess about why Eliot does not give us the setting in more detail?

Language

10. Would you say that the poem is written in formal, informal, or vulgate diction? Cite specific words and sentences to prove your claim.

11. Contemporary poetry is often described as being so compressed in form that the connections and transitions we are accustomed to in prose and in older poetry get squeezed out. Is this true of "Prufrock"? Explain your answer.

12. What characteristics of the language clearly distinguish "Prufrock" from a prose selection that has simply been set up in uneven lines and stanzas?

Tone

13. How can the tone of the poem best be characterized?

Point of View

14. Is this poem the kind of work that James describes as the drama of a consciousness? Do any important changes or recognitions occur in the center of consciousness during the progress of the poem? Explain.

Atmosphere

15. Presumably the world of this poem is a modern city in the second decade of the twentieth century, say London, with that yellow fog. But the epigraph suggests Hell. Where are we? What is the atmosphere?

Meaning

16. Let these questions help you to discover the meaning of each stanza:
Lines 1-12. How does Prufrock make clear that he does not want to visit the room where the women are even though he says, "Let us go and make our visit"?
Lines 13-14. What is apparently repelling about the women?
Lines 15-34. With what does he identify himself in these lines and how does he rationalize his indecisiveness?
Lines 35-36. What effect is gained by repeating these two lines?
Lines 37-48. How does Prufrock come to believe that even the slightest action will be embarrassing and self-defeating?
Lines 49-54. How does Prufrock characterize the society in which he has been living a kind of half-life? Why does the very thought of it make him more incapable of action?
Lines 55-69. Show how these lines suggest more positively his shyness and terror and yet indicate that the thought of the visit is not so dreadful that he can come to an easy decision about it.
Lines 70-74. Why does Prufrock recall the "lonely men in shirt-sleeves" at this point in the poem? What do they mean to him?
Lines 75-86. What quality in the evening does he envy?
Lines 87-98. What is he afraid will happen if he tells "all"? What is meant by "all"?
Lines 99-110. How is this stanza related to the preceding one?
Lines 111-119. Is Prufrock's analysis of himself accurate? What is the importance of this section in the poem as a whole?
Lines 120-131. What is Prufrock going to do and with what does he identify himself in these closing lines of the poem?
17. What clues to the overall meaning of the poem are provided by the quotation from Dante? by the title of the poem?
18. Is Eliot advocating anything (e.g., action rather than inaction) or is he simply stating a problem? Defend your answer.
19. What is behind Prufrock's predicament? Is Eliot saying anyone or anything is to blame?
20. How typical of modern man is Prufrock? In what ways can you generalize from his problem to the problem of man in the modern world? Do not answer this in a glib sentence or two. Think out your answer and make it as orderly, specific, and informative as you can.
21. Summarize the meaning of the poem as briefly but as cogently as you can.

PART TWO

Some Ways of Evaluating Literature

Introduction

So far, you have considered what makes literature what it is, you have examined certain aspects of its form and craftsmanship, and you have tried to become more sensitive to tone and atmosphere and more aware of meanings. But now consider this problem: A sad tale from a journal that we might call *True Heartaches* has everything that we have talked about so far—action, characters, setting, language, tone, point of view, atmosphere, and meanings—yet no one with any judgment at all would say that this melancholy piece of prose has the same power over the reader as, for example, a story by Hawthorne or William Faulkner. Think of some other combinations: a play by Shakespeare versus a soap opera, a poem by Robert Frost versus a jingle on a valentine, a novel by Joseph Conrad versus a science fiction thriller. In each instance the elements we observed and described in the last section are present. What, then, makes the difference between the good work and the poor one? To supply a few answers for such a question is the purpose of this section.

In other words, we might say that in the last section we were thinking about literature in a quantitative way. We wanted to discover what the main aspects of a piece of writing are and how many of them there are. Now we are interested in looking at literature qualitatively. We want to know what makes one story better than another, one play better than another, one poem better than another.

There is, of course, no one way of measuring works of art because we all use different yardsticks. Loosely we call the yardstick "taste." More specifically, a yardstick is a compound of our likes and dislikes, our desires and needs, our preconceptions, our knowledge and wisdom and experience—everything, in short, that makes up our particular psycho-physiological being. Since we are all different, we like different things, and since we like different things, we are not going to agree wholly on what makes one piece of literature better than another. Let us try to clear this up with a simple example.

You and your friends visit an automobile showroom. On anything involving weight, number, or size you can agree perfectly because you all use the same methods of measurement. You all agree that the model on display, a hardtop, weighs so many pounds, has a wheelbase of so many inches, has eight cylinders, and is gold and white in color. There are many details like these on which there is not the slightest difference of opinion. But—and here is where you start arguing—you say this is just the car that you have been waiting for, whereas the others say they wouldn't have it if the dealer gave it to them. What has happened? The conversation has passed from observation and description to evaluation. And, in the process of evaluation, you are all employing different standards. You want the car because you have always wanted a gold and white hardtop. Friend A wants a Volkswagen because he is thinking of economy;

Friend B wants a car with greater speed; and Friend C disagrees with you out of sheer cussedness. The Romans, not the Greeks in this case, had a word for it: *de gustibus non est disputandum,* "there is no arguing about tastes."

Something of the same situation prevails when we try to argue with a friend that one poem is better than another, or one play is better than another. Maybe the friend will agree; and then maybe he won't. We might as well face up frankly to the fact that there is no single rule or set of rules which you can use in evaluating literature. Nor are the authors of this book going to recommend any single rule or set of rules. Rather, they hope to show you a number of standards which people have used over a long period of time and have found satisfying. Literary criticism is not the completely chaotic affair that the Roman proverb might suggest. It is not a case of every man for himself. Just as a great many people *will* agree with you that a gold and white hardtop is the right car, so many will agree with you that the books you like are good books and the poems you dislike are poor poems. Many people agree on standards, but not all people. It would be a dull world if they did.

You may ask, why worry about standards? Won't I reach the same conclusions whether I am conscious of my standards or not? There are several answers to this. You may come to the same conclusions, to be sure, but it is doubtful that you will understand them so well. An estimate of twenty inches means something to you only if you know what inches are; the statement "this is a good book" has meaning only as you know what you mean by goodness. Furthermore, it is quite possible that through a knowledge of standards you will reach a sounder and more defensible conclusion, that you will see many things in a literary work that you would otherwise miss. Knowing your criterion in literary evaluation is analogous to knowing your major premise in an argument. It is building from a known rather than an unknown. It stops silly criticisms before they begin. A friend of yours says he does not like Wolfe's *Of Time and the River* because it is too long. Does he realize that his criterion or major premise is that "all long books are bad"? A knowledge of standards, in short, makes for thoughtful evaluations which will be more satisfying to you and more acceptable to your friends.

To emphasize that we are considering methods of evaluation in this section, we shall refer to our standards as "yardsticks." We are interested in measurement, not an enumeration of parts or devices or problems. Our main question is: What are the yardsticks which readers most commonly use in evaluating literature? In considering each we shall try to discover what it is, how it operates, and what its peculiar advantages and disadvantages are.

Essentially there are two kinds of yardsticks: yardsticks of form and yardsticks of content. Such a division needs no elaborate explanation. Some readers, and notably among them critics who call themselves formalists, focus their attention primarily on the purely esthetic aspects of a work such as style, structure, tone, and atmosphere. Other readers are more interested in what the writer reveals about the universe, society, and human nature. Probably the ideal reader attends carefully to all of these elements.

EVALUATING FORM

Artistry in Details

By the standard of pleasure in artistic details, a work is good if it provides enough pleasurable moments through effectively handled details to compensate for the time spent on it. For many readers, a single moment of intense pleasure is enough to justify an otherwise rather tedious book or poem.

This is the yardstick of the hedonist, the type of person who believes that one should like or dislike things for themselves, that values lie in feelings of pleasure and pain. As Walter Pater points out, it is not the fruit of experience that is important, but the experience itself. In using such a yardstick, therefore, you read not to learn facts or to weigh moral concepts or to discover what real life is like, but to find as much delight in the present as you can. Your basic assumption is that all pleasure is good, and all pain bad.

Many Americans find this a difficult yardstick to employ. Most of us are so trained in the concepts of "usefulness," of making every minute count toward something else, that we find it hard to value experience for its own sake. Automobile riding is pleasant because it gets us some place; swimming provides good exercise; reading is useful because through it we learn something that someday we may be able to use. Rarely do we enjoy automobile riding just because it is automobile riding, swimming just because it is swimming, and so on. Ahead of almost everything we do is some future and often indefinite goal. Experience is usually a means, seldom an end. Someone has said that the only times that we ever really live in the present are when we take an ocean cruise or when we fall in love. Then, we surrender ourselves to the moment and enjoy it. This is the attitude that must be taken toward reading if we are to employ the standard of pleasure in artistic details.

What can provide this pleasure? This is hard to answer, for it can be almost anything. Furthermore, it will not be the same thing in quite the same way for any two persons. Probably the best way to answer the question is to take a poem (for the sake of space only; a short story, play, or novel would do as well) and discover what some of the elements are which might give pleasure.

Robert Frost, **STOPPING BY WOODS ON A SNOWY EVENING**

Whose woods these are I think I know.
His house is in the village though;

He will not see me stopping here
To watch his woods fill up with snow.

My little horse must think it queer   5
To stop without a farmhouse near
Between the woods and frozen lake
The darkest evening of the year.

He gives his harness bells a shake
To ask if there is some mistake.   10
The only other sound's the sweep
Of easy wind and downy flake.

The woods are lovely, dark and deep.
But I have promises to keep,
And miles to go before I sleep,   15
And miles to go before I sleep.

You may find your pleasure here primarily in the language, in the sort of things discussed in the section on Language (pp. 73-78). After the generalizations of international arguments and the exaggerations of movie advertisements, you may find relief in the simple, concrete terms of this poem. Or the sound patterns may be especially appealing. Here are simple four-beat lines which proceed quietly—just as they should to suggest a woods on a snowy evening. You may enjoy reading the lines aloud and listening to the play on *o*'s and *r*'s and *s*'s. The rhymes are clear and obvious, yet not forced. Notice how the last word in the third line of each stanza except the last establishes the rhyme for the next stanza. You may find it satisfying that the ending of the third line of the last stanza does *not* introduce a new rhyme, thus indicating that the poem is being closed off. You may find the semirefrain in the last stanza a quietly melodic device which is appropriate to the feeling and meaning.

The poem may give you special pleasure in what it calls to mind. Possibly you have had a similar experience which is suggested by these lines. Or possibly the poem suggests what you nostalgically look back upon as a simpler and more delightful age when men did have time to relax before hurrying on because there are "promises to keep." Or possibly phrases or single words call to mind associations which you treasure. "Harness bells" may suggest your grandfather's farm with the barn smelling sweetly of hay and the cherry tree in the front yard afoam with blossoms.

You may find enjoyment in the pattern of the work, the four stanzas of four lines each. There may be a neatness and compression here that you like. Or you may be pleased by the ease of comprehension made possible by the fact that the elements of the poem fit so comfortably within the structure. Or you may like a pattern like this because it is brief, because you can give a maximum amount of your attention to it and yet not tire before you reach its end. Or you may enjoy the pattern of the contrast established between the horse and the man. The horse, a being with a material sense of values, is indignant at the stop because it serves no useful purpose. In the first stanza, the man with his sensory delight in an experience for its own sake is the master—he stops the horse. In the second stanza, the horse shows a mental reaction—he is puzzled. In the third stanza, he exhibits physical impatience—he gives his harness bells a shake. In the fourth stanza, he is successful—he has reminded the man of his promises in the world of affairs, and the man, surrendering, does what the horse has been urging him to do—drives on. Or, finally, you may find delight in the pattern because of the interplay of variety and repetition. The meter is the same throughout; so are the line lengths, the stanza form, and, with one exception, the rhyme pattern. But within this relatively unvaried structure are subtle variations in sound values. Notice, moreover, that even though the structure remains the same, the lines perceptibly change in tempo. The speed accelerates up to the third line of the third stanza, when a reversal takes place. By the time the last two lines are reached, you are reading the poem very slowly indeed.

These are only a few of the details in this poem that may give you pleasurable moments. In the case of a play or a piece of fiction, it might be a single character, one or two well-written descriptions, a moving scene or speech, an unexpected yet plausible twist in plot. Many critics deride the use of this yardstick and say that it results only in simple-minded impressionism. Admittedly, evaluation according to this method can be subjective and undisciplined. Indeed, the person using this yardstick may talk about himself as much as he talks about the work. He may even hypnotize himself and others into thinking the work had a more powerful effect upon him than it really had. All this must be recognized and guarded against. But, as you discovered from the example given above, pleasurable moments can be the result of detailed and analytical reading. The method, therefore, need not simply be a subjective operation which results in a Zane Grey novel seeming to be as good as one written by Thomas Hardy. There are different kinds of pleasure, varying from a superficial emotional titillation to the deeply compelling satisfaction coming from an awareness of the greatest artistic achievement. The quantitative criteria are the number and duration of the pleasurable moments; the qualitative criteria are the intensity and nature of the pleasure itself. When these are all taken into consideration, the yardstick of artistry in details affords a standard for mature and defensible judgments. Even if it did not, it would still be valuable in that it brings to our attention the fact that reading can be delightful for its own sake.

QUESTIONS

1. Think back over the works that you have read which on the whole did not interest you but which had details in them that you enjoyed and that you still remember. What kinds of details were these: action, bits of characterization, description, dialog, or what?

2. What kinds of details are likely to give most pleasure to the person who

has read very little? (Refer to the kinds mentioned in the analysis of "Stopping by Woods on a Snowy Evening.") An appreciation of which details is likely to come only after one becomes more sophisticated in literary matters? Reread the Frost poem. Which details give you most pleasure?

You will probably agree that Saki's story below, "The Open Window," has little if any moral or philosophical content. Yet the piece continues to be a favorite with many readers. What are the details that give pleasure? What elements of characterization, dialog, and plot account for the special effect of the story? Do you think the point of view well chosen? Why?

Saki

THE OPEN WINDOW

"My aunt will be down presently, Mr. Nuttel," said a very self-possessed young lady of fifteen; "in the meantime you must try and put up with me."

Framton Nuttel endeavoured to say the correct something which should duly flatter the niece of the moment without unduly discounting the aunt that was to come. Privately he doubted more than ever whether these formal visits on a succession of total strangers would do much towards helping the nerve cure which he was supposed to be undergoing.

"I know how it will be," his sister had said when he was preparing to migrate to this rural retreat; "you will bury yourself down there and not speak to a living soul, and your nerves will be worse than ever from moping. I shall just give you letters of introduction to all the people I know there. Some of them, as far as I can remember, were quite nice."

Framton wondered whether Mrs. Sappleton, the lady to whom he was presenting one of the letters of introduction, came into the nice division.

"Do you know many of the people round here?" asked the niece, when she judged that they had had sufficient silent communion.

"Hardly a soul," said Framton. "My sister was staying here, at the rectory, you know, some four years ago, and she gave me letters of introduction to some of the people here."

He made the last statement in a tone of distinct regret.

"Then you know practically nothing about my aunt?" pursued the self-possessed young lady.

"Only her name and address," admitted the caller. He was wondering whether Mrs. Sappleton was in the married or widowed state. An undefinable something about the room seemed to suggest masculine habitation.

"Her great tragedy happened just three years ago," said the child; "that would be since your sister's time."

"Her tragedy?" asked Framton; somehow in this restful country spot tragedies seemed out of place.

"You may wonder why we keep that window wide open on an October afternoon," said the niece, indicating a large French window that opened on to a lawn.

"It is quite warm for the time of the year," said Framton; "but has that window got anything to do with the tragedy?"

"Out through that window, three years ago to a day, her husband and her two young brothers went off for their day's shooting. They never came back. In crossing the moor to their favourite snipe-shooting ground they were all three engulfed in a treacherous piece of bog. It had been that dreadful wet summer, you know, and places that were safe in other years gave way suddenly without warning. Their bodies were never recovered. That was the dreadful part of it." Here the child's voice lost its self-possessed note and became falteringly human. "Poor aunt always thinks that they will come back some day, they and the little brown spaniel that was lost with them, and walk in at that window just as they used to do. That is why the window is kept open every evening till it is quite dusk. Poor dear aunt, she has often told me how they went out, her husband with his white waterproof coat over his arm, and Ronnie, her youngest brother, singing, 'Bertie, why do you bound?' as he always did to tease her, because she said it got on her nerves. Do you know, sometimes on still, quiet evenings like this, I almost get a creepy feeling that they will all walk in through that window——"

She broke off with a little shudder. It was a relief to Framton when the aunt bustled into the room with a whirl of apologies for being late in making her appearance.

"I hope Vera has been amusing you?" she said.

"She has been very interesting," said Framton.

"I hope you don't mind the open window," said Mrs. Sappleton briskly; "my husband and brothers will be home directly from shooting, and they always come in this way. They've been out for snipe in the marshes today, so they'll make a fine mess over my poor carpets. So like you men-folk, isn't it?"

She rattled on cheerfully about the shooting and the scarcity of birds, and the prospects for duck in the winter. To Framton it was all purely horrible. He made a desperate but only partially successful effort to turn the talk on to a less ghastly topic; he was conscious that his hostess was giving him only a fragment of her attention, and her eyes were constantly straying past him to the open window and the lawn beyond. It was certainly an unfortunate coincidence that he should have paid his visit on this tragic anniversary.

"The doctors agree in ordering me complete rest, an absence of mental excitement, and avoidance of anything in the nature of violent physical exercise," announced Framton, who laboured under the tolerably widespread delusion that total strangers and chance acquaintances are hungry for the least detail of one's ailments and infirmities, their cause and cure. "On the matter of diet they are not so much in agreement," he continued.

"No?" said Mrs. Sappleton, in a voice which only replaced a yawn at the last moment. Then she suddenly brightened into alert attention—but not to what Framton was saying.

"Here they are at last!" she cried. "Just in time for tea, and don't they look as if they were muddy up to the eyes!"

Framton shivered slightly and turned towards the niece with a look intended to convey sympathetic comprehension. The child was staring out through the open window with dazed horror in her eyes. In a chill shock of nameless fear Framton swung round in his seat and looked in the same direction.

In the deepening twilight three figures were walking across the lawn towards the window; they all carried guns under their arms, and one of them was additionally burdened with a white coat hung over his shoulders. A tired brown spaniel kept close at their heels. Noiselessly they neared the house, and then a hoarse young voice chanted out of the dusk: "I said, Bertie, why do you bound?"

Framton grabbed wildly at his stick and hat; the hall-door, the gravel-drive, and the front gate were dimly noted stages in his headlong retreat. A cyclist coming along the road had to run into the hedge to avoid imminent collision.

"Here we are, my dear," said the bearer of the white mackintosh, coming in through the window; "fairly muddy, but most of it's dry. Who was that who bolted out as we came up?"

"A most extraordinary man, a Mr. Nuttel," said Mrs. Sappleton; "could only talk about his illness, and dashed off without a word of good-bye or apology when you arrived. One would think he had seen a ghost."

"I expect it was the spaniel," said the niece calmly; "he told me he had a horror of dogs. He was once hunted into a cemetery somewhere on the banks of the Ganges by a pack of pariah dogs, and had to spend the night in a newly dug grave with the creatures snarling and grinning and foaming just above him. Enough to make any one lose their nerve."

Romance at short notice was her specialty.

Internal Consistency

Critics who apply the yardstick of internal consistency to a piece of work take as their basic premise that the work of art is a unique product of the human genius and should be judged by criteria which are applicable to it and to it alone. Who the writer is or what the individual effect of the work on the reader is, are matters which are irrelevant. The problem here is to discover what the relation of the parts is to the whole and to one another. The competent work, presumably, is the one in which the parts are so consistent and harmonious that the work as a totality is an organism in which no part could be changed without detriment to the whole work.

Although the nature of the internal consistency varies with each work, in its largest terms it is always a matter of congruity between form and content. In the case of the lyric poem, to take one example, it is a matter of seeing whether the words, lines, stanzas, and overall form harmonize with the material and ideas. Let us examine briefly the following very simple lyric.

John Masefield, **CARGOES**

Quinquireme of Nineveh from distant Ophir,
Rowing home to haven in sunny Palestine,
With a cargo of ivory,
And apes and peacocks,
Sandalwood, cedarwood, and sweet white wine.   5

Stately Spanish galleon coming from the Isthmus,
Dipping through the Tropics by the palm-green shores,
With a cargo of diamonds,
Emeralds, amethysts,
Topazes, and cinnamon, and gold moidores.   10

Dirty British coaster with salt-caked smoke stack,
Butting through the Channel in the mad March days,
With a cargo of Tyne coal,
Road-rail, pig-lead,
Firewood, iron-ware, and cheap tin trays.   15

In the first stanza here, the material is exotic and romantically delightful. Notice how all matters of form correspond: the words are melodic, the connotations appealing, the lines smoothly flowing. As we come closer to the present, as we do in the second stanza, the material, though attractive, is somewhat less exotic. Notice that the sounds are somewhat less melodic, the connotations less enchanting, and the lines slightly less liquid. Then, when the material becomes contemporary, as it does in the third stanza, a marked change takes place. The words are stubby and monosyllabic; the connotations are distasteful; and the lines are jerky. Note, too, that the color images, brilliant and sparkling at the start, are replaced by dull, drab ones at the end.

The stanzas give the material both unity and coherence. Unity is achieved through a repetition of stanza form. Since the poet is merely listing three details, and not even presenting them in complete sentences, he must find a way to hold them together. He does this through a precise paralleling of material. In each stanza the first line is devoted to the ship, the second to its motion and location, and the next three to the cargo. The number of stanzas indicates the number of concepts; the arrangement indicates movement from past to present, from the romantic to the workaday. For these reasons and others, we may say that in "Cargoes" Masefield has achieved harmony between form and content, and that according to the standard of internal consistency this poem ranks high.

There is too little space here to make a similar analysis of a longer work, but we can suggest some of the elements which might have to be considered. In the novel, play, short story, epic, or narrative poem, the reader ordinarily focuses his attention upon people. The primary question is what happens to them: Do they remain the same? Make a simple change? Change and then reverse themselves? Or make a series of changes? Only as you know what happens to them can you determine whether they have been consistent.

The first step is to determine what state of affairs prevails at the opening of the work: Who are the people? What are their essential characteristics? What are the conflicts within their minds? What are the conflicts which face them with outside forces? What is the nature of the world they live in—whimsical? romantic? realistic but responsive to human effort? realistic and unresponsive to human effort? Once you know the answers to questions like these, you can determine whether what the characters do and say is plausible or probable.

Note that internal consistency is not dependent upon lifelike action unless the air of reality has been established at the beginning. For example, what Ulysses does in the *Odyssey* is quite plausible in the world which Homer creates. The accomplishments of Swift's Gulliver, of Barrie's Peter Pan, and of Melville's Ahab are plausible and probable, too, in the worlds of the books in which they appear. But imagine Gulliver or Peter Pan on the main street of Sinclair Lewis' Gopher Prairie, and you have inconsistency carried to an absurdity. Consistency is not truth to life; it is a matter of the characters thinking, speaking, and acting in a manner which seems harmonious with their natures and setting.

Where there is no change in the characters of the short story, narrative poem, or one-act play, an analysis of internal consistency is a matter of seeing that what occurs is in accord with the basic motives of the people and the nature of the circumstances. Even in very short works, however, changes may take place. Three familiar lyrical patterns, for example, are as follows: One, the poet repeats explicitly or in figures the same emotion: I'm sad; I'm sad; how sad I am. Two, the poet explores various aspects of his thought-emotion: I'm sad for a number of reasons; how sad I am; my sadness will end only when I win my love Three, the poet's feeling changes: I'm sad; as I sit and think about it, a new thought comes to me; now my sadness is gone. For consistency, the potential change in the second case and the actual change in the third must be plausible in the light of the poet's nature and original disturbance.

In the novel and longer play changes inevitably take place. In Hawthorne's short story about Wakefield, the main character remains the same throughout: canny, egotistic, and cruel. His consistency lies in the fact that he does remain the same. In *The Scarlet Letter*, however, all of the main characters because of sin and a resulting sense of isolation change rather markedly. The consistency here comes in the fact that the change grows logically out of the circumstances and the temperaments of the characters. The attitudes and actions of Hester Prynne at the end of the book are not at all what they were at the beginning, but the shift is both plausible and probable. There are other concerns of the novel and play many of which were suggested in our analysis of "Cargoes." Just as in the lyrical poem, the words, sentences, and larger structural units of the novel should be suited to the sense, and should fit into the main artistic pattern. A nice problem in an analysis of *Moby Dick*, for instance, is whether the scientific and historical material on whales is intellectually or artistically justifiable in the light of the form and content of the whole.

The advantages of this "formal" or "organic" yardstick are numerous. It brings attention to bear upon the work itself and in doing so eliminates a great many irrelevancies that sometimes occupy our attention and get us no place. As the formalistic critic points out, what difference does it make in reading Byron's *Don Juan* that Byron had a club foot or swam the Hellespont? Or of what importance is it to the intrinsic worth of the poem that it reminds you of Marlowe's "Hero and Leander" or of the man your great-aunt Tillie married? In making you concentrate upon the work itself, this method of evaluation is likely to make you conscious of many aspects of a literary work which you never noticed before. Furthermore, this mode of criticism is likely to result in a more disciplined and a more precise kind of statement. There is no excuse for vague impressions, for well-meaning but often weak-minded "appreciation." In many ways this method takes over the spirit and the method of scientific inquiry and adapts them to literary evaluation.

The system also has fairly serious drawbacks. It is doubtful, for example, that it provides any criterion for making comparative judgments. When you use it, you are concerned only with the unique work itself. Indeed, when pushed to its logical extreme, the method involves only description and not evaluation at all. Evaluation gets in only when the description of the work conforms to what you think is excellent. But your notion of excellence must come from other sources. To put it another way, the function of this method is to show that the parts of a work are related harmoniously to the whole and to one another. One might well ask, then, what if they are? By this method there would be no answer except that they are. By introducing the yardstick of artistry in details, however, one might go on to say: This work is good because anything which is harmonious and consistent gives me esthetic pleasure. I like a forward pass cleanly executed, an aria well sung, a novel without inconsistencies.

Another drawback is that the method tends to result in such an emphasis upon structure that matters like mood, color, connotation, and melody are almost ignored. Inattention to such elements is not enforced by the method; it is simply a habit which many of its practitioners fall into—with the result that their handling of literary works becomes a series of problems in mental acrobatics and these persons themselves become desensitized to the emotional effects which give literature its distinctive quality.

Each of the analyses in the following group of selections illustrates for you the type of criticism which we have just been describing. Notice how in each essay the critic concentrates his attention on the work itself in an attempt to bring out the internal consistency and the relationship of parts that less observant readers might miss.

Robert Herrick

UPON JULIA'S CLOTHES

Whenas in silks my Julia goes,
Then, then, methinks, how sweetly flows
The liquefaction of her clothes.

Next, when I cast mine eyes, and see
That brave vibration, each way free,   5
Oh, how that glittering taketh me!

Earl Daniels

HERRICK'S
"UPON JULIA'S CLOTHES"

Superficially, the poem is obvious to the point of seeming to depreciate analysis, not to be worth it. A pretty girl moves through six lines, for a moment only catches an observer's eye, passes, and is gone. So slight is the impact of the experience that he writes not about the girl but about her clothes. Costume

Reprinted from *The Explicator*, March 1943. By permission.

is defined by silks, and each stanza is centered in a single quality of silk in movement, and in light ("liquefaction," line 3, and "glittering," line 6). The positions of these words in the last lines of each stanza should be noted and, more particularly, the increased sharpness lent to "glittering" by the necessity, here, of pronunciation in two syllables only: the vowel sound of an acute and pointed short "i" is closed tightly in by consonants, "g" and "t" in one syllable, "tr" and "ng" in the other. The stab of that word, a superb mine-eyes-dazzle effect, suggests the poem is not so simple as it seems: that Julia-in-clothes is more important than clothes, the apparent subject; that the observer is more deeply moved than he wants a careless reader to suppose, possibly than he himself knows.

Attention to sound and movement reveals the implications of the single word "glittering" to be a clue worth following. The poem is Julia and Julia's clothes. But each stanza contains lines (I, 2; II, 1, 3) which turn to the observer, and seem to hint in sound and movement at a central ironic contrast between the states of mind of the observer and the girl. The Julia lines flow, as easy and as liquid as the smooth silks which dress and conceal a lovely body. But the observer lines throb unevenly; they start and stop; they image the excitement and disturbance of the poet. It may not be too far-fetched to wonder if they are not symbol for the quickened beating of a heart, the surprised catch of breath, in the presence of beauty, especially beauty of a woman. An attentive reader now begins to understand it is not Julia's clothes but Julia herself who is the subject of the poem; and the poem begins to grow and to take on new richness of meaning. To be especially noted is the contrast in stanza I between lines 1 and 2: In line 1, word ripples into word, sound into sound, the caesural pause is so slight as to be almost not noticeable; in line 2, the opening repetition of "Then, then," where each word must be distinctly separated by pauses, where vowels are imbedded between inescapable consonants, announces a change, further stressed by the parenthetical "methinks." (Even the parenthesis plays its part here.) Only as this line, toward the end, moves to Julia and her costume does it begin to glide, to be liquefied again. The point is Julia moves through the poem serene, untouched; she may not even know the poet has so much as seen her. But he is in a different situation, for though he is ostensibly doing nothing more than writing a pretty lyric about a pretty dress, yet he reveals, in the sound, the movement, the pace of his words, how deeply he has been stirred by what seems so unimportant.

This makes for a basic ironic contrast, central to the poem: the ironic contrast between the girl and the man. Is it the irony of man (male) set over against woman (female)—a contrast as old as the Garden of Eden itself—or is it the profounder suggestion of the situation of man (not *a man*) in the presence of beauty—beauty here, as so often, being symbolized by a woman? I am reasonably certain that by implication and suggestion, by the subtlest of overtones, both ideas are in their way present, contributing rich values for a poem too often looked upon as too slight for serious consideration. Herrick has too long suffered from that kind of treatment.

Archibald MacLeish

ARS POETICA

A poem should be palpable and mute
As a globed fruit

Dumb
As old medallions to the thumb

Silent as the sleeve-worn stone   5
Of casement ledges where the moss has grown—

A poem should be wordless
As the flight of birds

A poem should be motionless in time
As the moon climbs   10

Leaving, as the moon releases
Twig by twig the night-entangled trees,

Leaving, as the moon behind the winter leaves,
Memory by memory the mind—

A poem should be motionless in time   15
As the moon climbs

A poem should be equal to:
Not true

For all the history of grief
An empty doorway and a maple leaf   20

For love
The leaning grasses and two lights above the sea—

A poem should not mean
But be

From *Collected Poems of Archibald MacLeish 1917–1952*, Houghton Mifflin Company.

Donald Stauffer

MacLEISH'S "ARS POETICA"

However we may interpret its significance, Mr. MacLeish has unmistakably given us his first demand in five overlapping adjectives: a poem should be palpable, mute, dumb, silent, and wordless. There can be no doubt that in these lines Mr. MacLeish has wished to give a general statement of the necessary qualities, or quality, of a poem. But immediately these ideas—and a quality must necessarily be an idea abstracted from some thing or some things more complex—are illustrated concretely, in images that might have been drawn from Keats or Tennyson or Rossetti, and we have in the first section a globed fruit, old medallions, stone, and birds in flight. This tendency to think of the idea, or the quality, in concrete terms is carried even further by the modifying adjectives and phrases that will compel a more vivid realization of the object imagined as so very quiet. A poem is as silent as a stone. Such a comparison might be overlooked because we have heard the phrase "still as a stone" so often. Therefore, to rouse our attention, the poem is as silent as a particular worn stone; and to make us believe that it is worn the coined adjective "sleeve-worn" (akin to "thread-bare"? worn by sleeves resting upon it? worn out at elbow and cuff, like a sleeve?) turns us to yet another image from concrete experience. And then the sleeve-worn stone is particularized and modified by a tangible ledge, which in turn is modified by a tangible casement, and the whole is modified by an arresting specific detail, designed to catch or convince our imagination: "where the moss has grown."

The other sections develop in like fashion, but in place of the four similitudes of the first section, the second section repeats the same image—that a poem in some way is like the moon—four times. Here again the particular interpretation may vary from reader to reader, although most would probably feel that a poem wakens in the reader's consciousness memory after memory, complex, minute, and exact, just as moonlight, against the motionless, durable, illimitable night, etches out twigs and leaves and innumerable silhouettes. But all readers would agree that the writer is saying a poem is timeless, although even this idea is seemingly given more tangible form by translating it from time to space— "*motionless* in time." Particularly interesting is the device of suggesting time-lessness through repetition rather than through change of images. In this section the final pair of lines mirrors the first, so that we are meant to feel, in the changeless concrete image of the moon, that time has not elapsed, or that if it has, it has made no difference, for the end and the beginning are the same.

The third section continues the minuet between meaning and its concrete embodiment. The first and fourth pairs of lines are direct statements, and as such, considered purely by themselves rather than in the light of the whole, are not poetic because they defy this very law of concreteness that the poem is designed to proclaim. Most readers would agree that they present the argument that a poem does not state its meaning directly, syllogistically, logically, rationally; its meaning rather exists in the recognition of unstated, sometimes unformulated, equivalences between its concrete symbols and what they symbolize. In this last section of the poem, the two middle pairs of lines are excellent illustrations of the doctrine of concreteness which Mr. MacLeish has so unconcretely expounded in the first pair and the last. Within a poem we come upon an empty doorway and a maple leaf; in the crucible of our imagination these objects assume a general significance and become "all the history of grief." Similarly the leaning grasses and two lights above the sea become in our minds the symbols of love. This is the way poetry works. The significance of a poem to any individual reader need be no less sharp than the significance of a mathematical proposition, though within limits this significance may vary from reader to reader as the mathematical proposition cannot do. But the *technique* of expressing significance in poetry demands sharp, specific *detail*. The concrete symbols, the things of this world as we know it—these are the invariable stuff of poetry, as, to the same extent, they need be of no other form of verbal communication. Poetry must operate through such concrete symbols.

Richard Fogle

HAWTHORNE'S
"THE MINISTER'S BLACK VEIL"[1]

Hawthorne's characteristic fusion of surface simplicity and underlying complexity is perhaps nowhere more clearly evident than in "The Minister's Black Veil," a brief, highly typical, and thoroughly successful story. It is subtitled "A Parable," and the outer meaning of the parable is abundantly clear. An apparently blameless minister inexplicably dons a black veil and wears it throughout his lifetime, despite many well-meant pleas to cast it off. On his deathbed he reveals its secret and its justification:

> "What, but the mystery which it obscurely typifies, has made this piece of crape so awful? When the friend shows his inmost heart to his friend; the lover to his best beloved; when man does not vainly shrink from the eye of his Creator, loathsomely treasuring up the secret of his sin; then

Reprinted from Richard Harter Fogle, *Hawthorne's Fiction*, copyright 1952, by the University of Oklahoma Press. Reprinted by kind permission of the publisher.
1. "The Minister's Black Veil" appears on page 119.

deem me a monster, for the symbol beneath which I have lived, and die!
I look around me, and, lo! on every visage a Black Veil!"

The moral is impressive; but as a proposition it is not difficult to grasp,
however it may wind and reverberate within the deeps of the imagination. The
veil as the visible symbol of secret sin was suggested by Hawthorne's reading
in New England history and legend. The veil's solid actuality has the effect of
isolating the minister from human society, which unhappy result presumably
differs only in degree from the self-isolation of every living soul. The minister
is Everyman, bearing his lonely fate in order to demonstrate a tragic truth.

The moral is explicit and orthodox. The explicit statement, however, leads to
more than a single possibility. The self-imposed martyrdom of Father Hooper
must correspond with some deep necessity of his nature. He who isolates himself
in the outward fact must already have performed the deed in spirit. The act of
donning the veil has in it something of caprice; it is entirely out of proportion
to any obvious necessity or benefit. By it the minister forfeits the affection of
his congregation, the chance of human love and marriage, and the sympathy of
society in general—and to what end? No note of triumph sounds for him. With
remorseless consistency, Hawthorne pursues him even into the grave. "Still veiled,
they laid him in his coffin, and a veiled corpse they bore him to the grave. The
grass of many years has sprung up and withered on that grave, the burial-stone
is moss-green, and good Mr. Hooper's face is dust; but awful still is the thought
that it mouldered beneath the Black Veil!"

One may feel that the veil is less representative of mankind than of the
eccentricity of the minister himself, who severs himself from men either through
perverse pride or through some other obscure and tragic compulsion. His preoccupation with sin has blunted his perceptions of the normal and the good, which
lie as ready to his hand as evil. In rejecting the love of his betrothed, Elizabeth,
he casts away a gift of inestimable value in order to satisfy a wild obsession.

If we continue with this reading of the story, we shall take Elizabeth to
exemplify the normal and well-ordered human being, as Mr. Hooper represents
the abnormal, who has lost the power of seeing life steadily and whole. The
"calm energy" of her character, her "direct simplicity," contrast with the
"gentle, but unconquerable obstinacy" of the minister, whom her good counsel
fails to persuade, and with his infatuated love of mystification. Hawthorne
inherited the psychology, but not the theology nor the morality of his Puritan
ancestors; and Elizabeth is more likely to represent his ideal than is the gloomy
and sin-crazed Hooper.

Which, then, of these two interpretations shall we accept? Both, I believe—they
are both in the story. Either presents its difficulties. If we take "The Minister's
Black Veil" at its face value as a homily on secret sin, we are confronted with
the apparent disproportion between the act and its causes. The minister himself
is to outward gaze the gentlest and least sinful of men; and we have no vivid
sense of that presence of Evil which would necessitate so heroic an object

lesson. But if we wholly accede to the second interpretation, which makes the steady view of life, the *aurea mediocritas,* the highest good, then the tone and emphasis of the story remain to be explained. It is too deeply gloomy and intense to harmonize fully with such a moral, which should demand a certain dry sparkle and lightness.

This ambivalence of meaning is realized in ambiguity, which occurs with unusual frequency in "The Minister's Black Veil." Here its most marked effect is to maintain a balance between subjective and objective in the portrait of the minister, to invite us inside his character while excluding us from any final certainty about it, and, of course, to preserve the objectivity of the narrator, who simultaneously offers and reserves his judgment. Thus, for example, we do not quite know what Mr. Hooper saw through the veil, "which entirely concealed his features, except the mouth and chin, but *probably* did not intercept his sight, further than to give a darkened aspect to all living and inanimate things." The word "probably" bars us from certainty on the point. Again, as the minister preaches for the first time from beneath the veil, it "lay heavily on his uplifted countenance. Did he seek to hide it from the dread Being whom he was addressing?" Hawthorne proposes the question, but does not answer it.

Pressed by Elizabeth to expound the meaning of the veil, Mr. Hooper will reply only darkly. " 'If it be sign of mourning,' " says he, " 'I, perhaps, like most other mortals, have sorrows dark enough to be typified by a black veil.' " When she further relates the scandalous whispers in the village that he hides his face from consciousness of secret sin, he will not deny the imputation. " 'If I hide my face for sorrow, there is cause enough,' " he merely replies; " 'and if I cover it for secret sin, what mortal might not do the same?' " Hawthorne holds out the suggestion that the veil is a penance for an actual and serious crime, while at the same time permitting no real grounds for it. The vulgar interpret the meaning vulgarly, the complacent complacently, and men of good will regretfully. The calm good sense of Elizabeth forces her to regard the veil as the emblem of a tragic but unbased obsession. She believes at first that " 'there is nothing terrible in this piece of crape' " but at length yields to its influence, not from a dread of the veil itself, but of what the veil tells her of her lover's state of mind.

The mystery of the veil is hidden to the end among these artfully contrived ambiguities. As Elizabeth leaves him, "Mr. Hooper smiled to think that only a material emblem had separated him from happiness, though the horrors, which it shadowed forth, must be drawn darkly between the fondest of lovers." It is confusing to have the symbol detached from its meaning in this fashion; and the passage calls up another consideration. If the veil alone has separated the minister from happiness, what are we to do with "the horrors, which it shadowed forth?" Surely it is they which shut him off from earthly good. The effect is at once to assert and to cast doubt on the reality of what the veil portrays but also hides. And the smile itself, shining dimly from beneath the black cloth, emphasizes in its self-irony the ambiguity of the minister's character.

The veil has varying effects on different minds and different levels of society.

To those who claimed a superiority to popular prejudice, it is merely "an eccentric whim." In the multitude it occasions either impertinence or superstitious dread, reactions equally grievous to its unhappy wearer. It is whispered that the veil is the obscure intimation of a horrible crime; and there are hints of supernatural forces:

> Thus, from beneath the black veil, there rolled a cloud into the sunshine, *an ambiguity of sin or sorrow,* which enveloped the poor minister, so that love or sympathy could never reach him. *It was said* that ghost and fiend consorted with him there. With self-shudderings and outward terrors, he walked continually in its shadow, groping darkly within his own soul, or gazing through a medium that saddened the whole world. Even the lawless wind, *it was believed,* respected his dreadful secret, and never blew aside the veil. But still good Mr. Hooper sadly smiled at the pale visages of the worldly throng as he passed by.

In one respect, however, the veil makes Mr. Hooper a more efficient clergyman, for it allows him to "sympathize with all dark affections." His words are imbued with its gloomy power, and he can bring sinners to the light denied to him. Yet here as well the effects of the veil are ambiguous. His converts regard the minister with dread, not with love or joy, even though they owe their redemption to him. "Dying sinners cried aloud for Mr. Hooper, and would not yield their breath till he appeared; though ever, as he stooped to whisper consolation, they shuddered at the veiled face so near their own." Hawthorne summarizes the twofold influence of the veil in a climactic ambiguity which embodies its dualism in a series of antitheses: "In this manner Mr. Hooper spent a long life, irreproachable in outward act, yet shrouded in dismal suspicions; kind and loving, though unloved, and dimly feared; a man apart from men, shunned in their health and joy, but ever summoned to their aid in mortal anguish."

This dubiety persists in the final scene at the deathbed, despite the explicit pronouncement with which the scene ends. As the minister lies dying, the veil still rests upon his face, stirred slightly by his faint breath. "All through life that piece of crape had hung between him and the world; it had separated him from cheerful brotherhood and woman's love, and kept him in that saddest of all prisons, his own heart; and still it lay upon his face, as if to deepen the gloom of his darksome chamber, and shade him from the sunshine of eternity." If, however, the veil is emblematic of the common plight of man, why should it isolate its wearer with a poignancy unfelt by other men and leave him lonely and alone? We have no sense in the story that all men feel as does Mr. Hooper; they are portrayed, in fact, as a cohesive band, united if only in dread of the fearful veil. Even the minister's colleague, praying by his bedside, rather cruelly misunderstands its significance. Or, on the other hand, is it possible that we can go further afield and determine that the message of the veil *is* representative and universal: that the failure to recognize it is simply the last and most chilling proof of man's imprisonment within himself? If this latter interpretation is the true one, we must conclude that Hawthorne's emphasis upon the problem as embodied in Mr. Hooper has made it impossible for him to deal with it in other characters. To achieve unity of composition his canvas can contain only one important figure. In order to present the tragic isolation of one man, Hawthorne is obliged to consider society as a solid group arrayed against his hero, ignoring for the time being the fact that this hero is Everyman.

We conclude, then, without arriving at a clear decision about the meaning of the tale, but with a sense of depths unplumbed, of rich potentialities not fully realized. The discrepancies between the two interpretations which have been outlined here must go unreconciled. Their mutual presence can, I think, be satisfactorily explained in two ways—one psychological, and one esthetic— separable, and yet closely related. In the first place, these discrepancies represent the faculties of Hawthorne's own psychology, the heart and the head. His heart, his imagination, the inherited bent of his Puritan ancestry—all his instincts, in short—bind him in sympathy with the possessed minister, who broods over the vague and bottomless abyss of Evil. But his head, his intellect, is with the calm and steady-minded Elizabeth, who is unable to look upon the minister's vow as other than a sad but groundless whim. The ancestral Hawthorne stands beside the nineteenth-century Hawthorne in "The Minister's Black Veil," and their voices do not wholly harmonize.

Second, Hawthorne does not force a reconciliation which he has not, in Keats's words, "proved upon his pulses." Having chosen the symbol of the black veil and invented an action for it, he refrains from pushing the reader to a single conclusion. The minister himself believes the veil to be an emblem of the secret sin that poisons the souls of all mankind, but we are not compelled to accept his reading of the matter. We may, if we like, consider it rather a veil upon his understanding, whose gloomy shade conceals from the eyes behind it as much as it discloses. As it casts its shadow over the bright and various colors of the material world—colors distinct to every unhandicapped observer— so does it darken the vision of the spiritual eye.

The imagination, however, playing freely over the theme, will not content itself to remain within the limits of any single meaning. Beneath the explicit statement, the clear and simple outline of the tale, lie the irony of the minister's smile and the ambiguity of almost every incident. In "The Minister's Black Veil" the moral constitutes the framework; but it is merely an element of the completed structure.

QUESTIONS

1. What is the main point of each of the critical selections? Do you think any of the authors overstates his case, finding meanings and relationships of parts that can be seen only by a stretch of the imagination? Which of these aspects of the literary work of art do you find these critics especially emphasizing: economy, unity, emphasis and subordination, point of view, organization, action, characterization, setting, language, tone, rhythm, sound patterns, compactness, figurativeness, intensity of effect? Which of these aspects get almost no consideration? Can you account for your answers to the last two questions?

2. On pages 141-142 we itemized a number of aspects of Frost's "Stopping by Woods on a Snowy Evening" which might give a reader pleasure. Take these elements, now, and see whether they fit together harmoniously and whether the poem as a whole is internally consistent.

3. Make an analysis of (a) *A Night at an Inn,* page 36; (b) "My Last Duchess," page 55; (c) "The Cask of Amontillado," page 60; (d) "To Autumn," page 71. Cite enough specific details to prove that the work is or is not internally consistent.

The two stories that follow deal with a change in the attitude of the chief character toward a woman. Compare the two and evaluate them according to the yardstick of internal consistency. In which of the two stories are changes in the characters' attitudes better accounted for? Explain in detail. Which has the more consistent tone, the more cohesive atmosphere? Determine whether the various elements of each work are woven into a unified whole.

Norbert Davis

BUILD ME A BUNGALOW SMALL

William Martin stepped out on the three worn planks that served the cabin as a front porch and looked all around and saw nothing but trees. That was just fine with him. It was not that he was fond of trees as such. He wasn't. He considered them nonfunctional and a waste of lumber, but at the moment he vastly preferred them to people.

He was tall and dark, a little gaunt in the face and stooped in the shoulders, and his black hair was clipped in a crew cut. He was wearing a red flannel shirt and brand-new khaki pants and shoe pacs. Standing there on the porch, he drew in a long, luxurious breath of mountain air—thin and dry with a sharp, cold tingle in it.

The air tasted very good. Martin tried some more of it and then pounded his chest, Tarzan style. He jumped down off the porch and did a complicated series of crouched, whirling shifts and then caught an imaginary football and kicked it. He was right at the apex of his punt when he saw the man watching him, and he very nearly went over backward.

"Oops!" he said, waving his arms violently to catch his balance. "I didn't see—I didn't think there was anyone—Hello."

The man was leaning against the fender of a dust-colored sedan that blended perfectly into the dried brown of the brush along the twisted, narrow road. He was dressed in brown, too, and he was smoking a brown, hand-rolled cigarette. He was squat and blocky and bowlegged, and he was scowling. He looked as if he had been born with a great many suspicions and had lived to see every single one of them confirmed.

"Your name Martin?" he asked.

"Yes."

"You leased this cabin from the owner for three weeks?"

"Yes."

"You understand that he don't own the land the cabin sits on. Just the cabin itself. The land is part of this state park and can't be sold."

"I understand that."

"Keep it in mind. You're a tenant here by sufferance. In case you don't savvy that, it means you can stay here as long as you behave yourself. My name's Bradwell. I'm the state ranger in charge."

"Well," said Martin uncertainly. "Hello."

"How drunk are you now?"

"I'm not drunk at all!" Martin denied indignantly. "I was just feeling good, that's all—just taking a little morning workout to—to—"

"If I catch you plastered and passed out around here, you're going to wake up with a shovel in your hand on the road gang. And don't sling garbage around in the brush. Bury it. All of it. Deep. And don't build fires except in the fireplace in the cabin, and don't smoke away from this clearing. And don't drive over twenty on these park roads. And leave the animals alone. They got more right to be here than you have."

"Okay," said Martin. "Okay, okay, okay."

Bradwell got back in his car. The sound of its motor was a muted, smooth murmur.

"I'll be seeing you," he said. "Often. Keep that in mind, too."

The sedan slid silently away.

"Huh," said Martin.

He breathed in deeply again, trying to retrieve his exuberant mood. It eluded him, and he looked around exploratively. He spotted a path that angled crookedly away from the cabin, and he started following it.

The trees closed in instantly on him, and the silence and the solitude were soothing balm. He began to whistle softly and jauntily to himself. He kept on whistling until he walked around a curve and came face to face with a deer.

This was not a small deer, and it was in no way fragile or dainty. It was equipped with antlers, and it was tall enough so that when it held its head up it could look Martin right in the eye, and that was just what it was doing.

"Shoo," said Martin. "Scram. Get out of here."

The deer came a step closer.

"Boo!" Martin shouted. "Beat it!"

The deer lowered its head and pawed the ground. The hoof was sharp enough to leave a clean, deep groove in the dirt. It snorted.

"Well," said Martin. "Okay. If that's the way you feel."

He backed around the curve and started toward the cabin. The deer snorted again—right behind him. Martin walked a lot faster. He was perspiring. He sneaked a glance over his shoulder. The antlers were about a yard from his back, and they were approaching a lot faster than he was receding.

"*Yike!*" Martin gasped.

He ran. He ran like a rabbit. And behind him he could hear those sharply sinister snorts getting closer and closer.

Crashing out into the clearing, he sailed around the cabin, leaning hard on the turns. He reached the porch in one last ten-foot leap. There was a camp chair leaning against the wall beside the door, and he swung it up over his shoulder and whirled around—at bay.

It was then that he heard the high-pitched, uproarious shriek of laughter. The deer had stopped a dozen feet from the porch. It was regarding Martin with an offended expression, and now it turned its head to look toward the laughter. Martin dropped the chair as though it had suddenly become red-hot. He picked it up and dropped it again and then kicked it furiously.

The laughter died in a series of gurgling gasps. "I'm sorry!" the girl said. "I really shouldn't have—" She started up again, bending over and holding her sides. She had shiny black hair with a thin red ribbon tied in it. She was tall, and she was wearing dungarees and moccasins and a man's white shirt. She was very tanned, and she had startlingly blue eyes and a short, straight nose with a little tilt to it.

She straightened up painfully. "You should have seen your face when you came around the cabin. It was really—Oh, Dagwood! You big fool, you!"

The deer stalked up to her and lowered its antlers and snorted.

The girl slapped at it. "Oh, get away. I haven't anything for you to eat." She smiled up at Martin. "They call him Dagwood because he's always hungry, and he'll eat absolutely anything. Dagwood, you pest. Go away."

She seized him expertly by an antler, turned him around, and slapped him on the haunch. Dagwood sailed over a bush and disappeared in three more graceful bounces.

The girl walked up to the porch. "Hello. My name is Carol Carter. I'm staying at the Bracken cabin. It's over that way a half mile. You're William Martin, aren't you?"

"Yes."

"The Greys told me they were renting their cabin to you. They said you were an architect."

"Did they?"

"Yes. They said you wanted to come up here to be alone while you finished some important work."

"But you didn't believe them, did you?"

"What?" said Carol.

"You didn't believe them when they told you I wanted to be alone."

Carol lost her smile. "Oh. Well—are you mad at me? I apologize for laughing. I shouldn't have. I know you were scared to death."

"Is there anything else you know about me besides my name and my business and my state of mind?"

"I know you've got a nasty temper."

"There's something you can do to avoid that."

"What?" Carol asked.

"Leave."

"Oh. Well—well, I mean . . ."

"Goodby, now."

"Goodby," said Carol soberly.

She turned around and walked on along the road. She walked well—erect and graceful, very quick and light on her feet.

"Faugh!" Martin snarled. "The next time I'll pick the city zoo or the Union Station."

Martin had set himself up in business in the sunlight at the side of the cabin. He and his paraphernalia were spread all over the camp chair and two collapsible bridge tables. He had red ink and black ink and white ink and six different kinds of pens: squares, triangles, compasses, dividers, rulers, erasers and slide rules, and dozens of sectional plans and blue, checked master sheets—all placed precisely where he wanted them. He was a happy man.

He consulted one of the slide rules and found the answer he needed and began to print it in slanted, neat figures.

"Hello," said Carol.

Martin's pen jerked.

"Oh, I'm sorry," said Carol.

Martin blotted carefully and began to erase.

"Let me help—" said the girl.

Martin stopped erasing and looked at her.

"I said I was sorry," Carol said defensively. "And I'm sorry I laughed at you a while ago. What else can I say?"

"Plenty, I'm afraid."

"Now, look," said Carol. "I'm just trying to be neighborly. I came over here this morning with the best intentions in the world. I was going to show you how the Greys' stove worked. They asked me to. They were worried about how you'd make out, because they knew you weren't married, and they didn't know whether or not you could cook for yourself. I was even going to ask you over to dinner tonight. Of course, we call it supper."

"How odd!"

"Look," said Carol. "Relax. I'm not that repulsive. We got off to a bad start, but can't you sort of skip it? You'll find it's lonesome up here. No one comes up in the fall, because they don't realize how swell the weather is."

"What are you doing up here?"

Carol smiled. "That's better. I had pneumonia last winter, and I came up here in the spring to rest for three months, and I just sort of lingered. I like it. What are you working on?"

"A plan for a small home."

"You've got a lot of plans just for that?"

Martin explained reluctantly: "These are master plans to be used on a lot of small homes to be built all at once in a big subdivision. Each house has to have the same over-all requirements, but they have to be incidentally variable, so that each one can be made to look different."

"Sounds complicated."

"It is. It's a Kreiger-Croft Construction Company project. If I can satisfy them, there's plenty in it for me. I've done some work for them before, but nothing as big as this will be."

"You're up here to concentrate, eh?"

"That was the idea, at least. I got tired of trying to think while contractors and frustrated homeowners and building inspectors pound on my desk."

"I see. Can I look at the master sheet?"

"You can't visualize from a blueprint."

"I can so. I took two years of architecture in art school. . . . Say, this is cute! Now if you put a—"

Martin threw his slide rule on the ground.

"All right," Carol said quickly. "All right."

"Artists," Martin muttered. "Now it's artists. That's all I needed."

"Architecture is an art."

"It is not! It's a science! Do I look like some boob who hangs out in a garret?"

"No, and artists don't, either. Just remember that I happen to be one."

"Ha."

"I am, and I'm pretty good, too."

"Ha."

"Are you always this way?" Carol asked. "You pack around just about the nastiest disposition I've run across."

"It's a device," Martin explained carefully. "It's a device I employ so people will leave me alone long enough for me to get a little work done. But sometimes it doesn't work. There are people who are so dumb they don't get the idea."

"Meaning me?" Carol said thoughtfully. "You don't like me?"

"Now you're smartening up."

"You want me to go away?"

"You're right on the beam."

Carol swallowed. "All right. But I think you could have been a little more polite about it all."

"Oh, go drown yourself somewhere."

Carol walked away. She walked slowly this time; all her bounce had gone.

Martin picked up the slide rule and looked at it in an antagonistic manner. "Ummm," he said uneasily, using it to scratch his head. "Well."

He went back to work, but most of the flavor seemed to have simmered out of his house plans. He stalled around for a while and then got up and went in the back door of the cabin. He came out a moment later, carrying a long-handled spade in one hand and a dripping paper sack of garbage in the other.

Holding the sack well away from him, he paced up the slope back of the cabin. Finding a site that suited him, he put the sack down and started digging.

He dug steadily for about a half hour. He had made a trench, then, about two feet deep and a foot and a half wide. He figured this would be large enough to hold a week's deposit of garbage, and he stopped and leaned on the spade handle, contemplating his handiwork.

Somebody pushed him—hard. The spade tangled his feet up, and he went headlong over it and fell flat on his face in the ditch. He scrambled frantically, rolled over and sat up.

Dagwood snorted at him.

"You get out of here!" Martin yelled furiously.

He scrambled up and swung awkwardly with the spade. It didn't miss Dagwood by more than fifteen feet. Dagwood bounced this way and that way on his spring-steel legs, shook his antlers coyly, and then paused, ready for more fun and games.

Martin ran at him. "Get out of here! You get off this property!"

Dagwood glided over a bush and flicked his white tail tauntingly. That did it. Martin lost what remained of his perspective. He took off after Dagwood like a bat from the belfry.

Dagwood danced happily all around the clearing twice and then took off up the path with Martin thundering grimly behind. Dagwood teased him along for a couple of hundred yards and then casually melted away into the brush.

Martin stumbled over to a fallen tree trunk and collapsed. He had a bad case of the gulps—an affliction which often seizes lowlanders who exert themselves unduly at high altitudes—and he sat and gasped for ten minutes before his heart stopped booming in his ears.

Finally he got up and went drearily down the path again, helping himself along with the spade. He came out into the clearing and stopped short, frozen numb with horror.

Here was Dagwood again. He had tipped over both card tables, and he was chewing meditatively on a large number of sheets of blue, checked paper.

"Oh, no," Martin groaned. "No!"

Dagwood stopped chewing and glanced at him inquiringly.

"Drop those plans!" Martin shrieked.

Dagwood started chewing again.

Martin howled. He threw the spade and ran after it. He picked it up en route and cut a vicious swath in the air with it. Dagwood bounced jauntily away, carrying the blue sheets like a banner.

"I'll kill you!" Martin promised fervently, fighting his way through brush. "I'll spatter your brains—"

They went up hill and down dale. They went around in two circles. They went through a bramble patch, some poison oak, and a small growth of cockleburs. Martin fell down three times, and when he got up the third time Dagwood was gone again.

Martin went right on, anyway, staggering. "Where are you?" he roared. "I'll tear you limb from limb! I'll murder you in cold blood!"

He stumbled down a rock-strewn slope, burst through a waist-high barrier of brush, and very nearly fell down the fourth time. He caught his balance and stood there, swaying and strangling, staring unbelievingly at a painter's easel. It was sitting all by itself in the clearing.

"Oh," said Martin, fighting for breath. "You! Carol Carter! Where are you?"

His voice dropped into the silence. There was no answer, not even an echo. "Hey!" said Martin.

He listened, and then he heard the faint, infinitely alluring chuckle of running water. Realizing suddenly that he had a mouth like a blast furnace, he dragged his feet across the clearing and fought through some more brush.

He didn't even see the stream until his feet went out from under him, and he sat down with a dull thud on the bank. His feet were hanging over a deep, dark pool where the water circled hungrily like a slow-motion whirlpool, and abruptly it didn't seem inviting at all.

Martin stared at the bank opposite him. It was steep and studded with sharp rocks, and someone had slipped on it. Someone had left fresh, frantically clawed gouges in the dirt.

"Hey!" said Martin, scared now. "Hey, Carol! Where are you? Where—"

The water chuckled gruesomely beneath him.

Martin's voice went up a queasy notch. "Carol! Carol! Are you all right?"

He slid down the bank and stared into the water. He couldn't see anything but his own reflection.

"Hey?" he said, putting everything into a last appeal. There was no answer save the ghoulish gurgle of the water.

Martin scrambled back up the bank. He ran first to his left and then to his right and then hightailed it over the hill. It was very heavy going now. His feet didn't track, and he seemed to have an irrepressible urge to fall down every twenty yards. He lost the spade and his sense of direction, and it was approximately a century before he came out on a narrow, rutted road. He whirled around groggily twice, picked a direction, and started running all over again.

He was still going when Bradwell's dusty sedan pulled up silently alongside of him.

"Oh!" said Martin. "Listen—listen—"

Bradwell said: "I warned you what would happen to you if I caught you plastered."

Martin clutched the car door. "Listen. Carol Carter. Drowned."

"What?" Bradwell barked.

"Drowned. Pool. Back there."

"You mean that little pool where she paints?"

Martin nodded numbly. "Dangerous. Steep bank."

"You're crazy."

"No. Slipped on bank. Hit her head on rock. Drowned."

"Get in here," said Bradwell.

Martin fell into the front seat and held his head in his hands, completely blown out. Bradwell put the sedan into reverse, slammed it backward into the brush, and cramped the wheels expertly.

"No!" Martin protested. "Other way."

"Shut up. I know the way."

The sedan popped out of the brush, jittered sideways on the ruts, and picked up speed in a breathless spurt.

"Should never have said that," Martin muttered. "Never, never."

"Said what?" Bradwell asked absently.

"What I said to her. Oh, no. No."

"Pipe down. I'm busy."

The roadside brush swished past them in a brown, splattered blur. Suddenly it fell eerily away on one side, and Bradwell stood on the brakes.

"Huh?" said Martin. "This isn't—"

"I know. That's your cabin there, you dope. Someone is in it. I saw something move in the window."

"Never mind," Martin said. "It's just that damned Dagwood again."

"It ain't Dagwood," said Bradwell. "He don't break into cabins—not since I caught him tryin' it once and fanned his rear end good with a lath. Come on. We'll take a look."

"No! I'm not going—"

Bradwell reached over the back of the seat and came up with an efficient-looking .30-30 saddle carbine. "Yes, you are. You're going to march right up that path ahead of me. Get."

Martin marched up the path, and opened the front door of the cabin cautiously.

"Hello," Carol called. "I'm in the kitchen."

Martin tore across the room and hung limply in the kitchen doorway, staring with bulged, incredulous eyes. Carol had just started washing his dirty dishes.

"Here I am again," she said. "I'm really a pig for punishment."

Martin tiptoed across the floor and touched her arm gingerly. She wasn't a phantom. "Whew!" he said.

"What's the matter?" Carol asked casually. "Is your conscience bothering you?"

Martin rallied a little. "Weren't you up at that pool a while ago? Why didn't you answer me when I called?"

"Yes, I was up at the pool, and I didn't answer you for two good reasons. Reason number one: I didn't have any clothes on."

"What?" said Martin blankly.

"I had taken a sun bath, and I was just about to dunk myself in the pool to cool off when you came howling around. I had to scramble for cover. Reason number two: You scared me with all those threats about murder and tearing the limb from limb. I thought you'd gone clear off your trolley. I finally figured out what you thought from your actions, but by that time you were gone with the wind. So I came over here."

Martin said, "I wasn't threatening you. I was just going to murder Dagwood because he chewed up my plans."

"What was that, again?" Bradwell demanded. "I told you to leave the animals around here alone."

"Relax. I didn't catch him."

"How do I know you didn't?"

"You know he didn't," Carol said, "because Dagwood is outside the back door right now, waiting to be fed." She nodded at Martin. "I came back before, mad as I was, to warn you that you mustn't leave any important paper lying around outside, because Dagwood likes the taste of it. He chews it like tobacco. But when I came back, you were gone."

"I was digging a garbage ditch."

"I know. I gathered up your plans then and put them in the cabin. Dagwood ran off with some scratch sheets. I put your plans in on the table."

"Yeah," said Bradwell. "I'm lookin' at 'em. . . . Say, this is going to be a neat layout. Who's going to build bungalows like this, Martin? How much do they want for a down payment on one?"

"Later," Martin said absently. "Later. Anyway, I'm going to buy the first one."

"You don't need a house," Bradwell informed him. "You ain't married."

"Well, I can get married, can't I?" Martin asked. He hesitated, watching Carol. "Can't I?"

Carol glanced sideways at him.

"Well," said Martin shamefacedly, "a person can say things—I mean, he can sort of fly off the handle and say things and then—and then he can suddenly sort of see the light and change his—"

Carol smiled slightly. "Take this lettuce leaf out to Dagwood."

"A leaf?" Martin said exuberantly. "One little leaf? No! We'll give him the whole head! We wouldn't want to turn him away hungry. Dagwood is a very fine deer and a credit to the community. Here, Dagwood. Here you are, old boy, old pal."

Maxim Gorky

BOLESS

An acquaintance of mine once told me the following story:

"While still a student at Moscow I happened to be living alongside one of those—well, she was a Polish woman, Teresa by name. A tall, powerfully built brunet with heavy, bushy eyebrows, and a large coarse, vulgar face, as if carved out with an ax—the animal gleam of her eyes, the deep bass voice, the gait and manners of a cabman, and her immense strength like that of a market-woman, inspired me with an inexpressible horror. I lived in the garret of the house, and her room was opposite mine. I never opened my door when I knew that she was in. But this, of course, happened very rarely. Sometimes I chanced to meet her on the landing, staircase, or in the yard, and she would look at me with a smile which seemed to me cynical and rapacious. Occasionally I saw her in her cups, with bleary eyes, her hair and clothes in disorder and with a particularly loathsome smile. On such occasions she would meet my eye with an impudent stare and say:

" 'How are you, Pan Student?'[1]

"And her stupid laugh would increase my dislike for her still more. I would have liked nothing better than to change my quarters in order to get rid of her proximity, but my room was so nice, and the view from my window was so fine, the street below so quiet and peaceful, that I concluded to endure it.

"One morning after I had dressed and was sprawling on the cot, trying to invent some sort of an excuse for not attending my classes, the door of my room suddenly opened, and the disgusting bass voice of the Polish woman sounded from the threshold:

" 'Good morning, Pan Student!'

" 'What is it you wish?' I asked her. I saw she looked confused and had in her face a kind of pleading expression, something unusual with her.

" 'You see, Pan Student, I came to beg you to do me a great favor. Don't refuse me, please!'

"Lying there on my cot I thought that it was just some pretext or other to make my further acquaintance. Take care, my boy!

" 'You see, I have to send a letter to my native country,' she continued in a supplicating, low, tremulous voice.

" 'Well,' I thought, 'the devil take you. If you wish I will write it for you.' And springing to my feet I sat down to the table, took some paper and said: 'Well, come nearer; sit down and dictate.'

"She came over; sat down cautiously on the edge of the chair and looked at me in rather a guilty way.

" 'To whom shall I write?'

" 'To Boleslav Kapshat, in the town Sventsiani, on the Warsaw railroad.'

" 'Well, what shall I write? Speak.'

" 'My dearest Boless, my heart's delight, my beloved. May the Mother of God protect you! My golden heart, why have you not written for so long a time to your sorrowing dove, Teresa—'

"I could hardly keep from laughing. A sorrowing dove, indeed! Almost six feet tall, with the fists of a prize-fighter, and a face so black that it seemed as if the 'dove' had been sweeping chimneys all her life and had never thoroughly washed herself. But I somehow kept my face straight and asked:

---

1. Pan is Polish for Mister.

" 'Who is this Bolesst?'

" 'Boless, Pan Student,' she replied, seemingly offended because of my mis-pronouncing the name. 'He is my affianced.'

" 'Affianced!'

" 'And why are you so astonished? Can not I, a girl, have an affianced?'

"She—a girl! well, this beats everything I ever heard. Oh, well, who can tell about such matters! Everything is possible in this world.

" 'And have you been long engaged?'

" 'The sixth year.'

" 'Oh, oh!' I thought and then said aloud: 'Well, go ahead with your letter.'

"And I must confess—so tender and loving was this message—that I would have willingly exchanged places with this Boless had the fair correspondent been any one else but Teresa.

" 'I thank you from my inmost soul for your favor, Pan Student,' Teresa said, bowing low. 'Can I in any way be of service to you?'

" 'No, thank you.'

" 'But maybe the Pan's shirts or trousers need mending?'

"This made me quite angry. I felt that this mastodon in petticoats was making the blood mount to my cheeks, and I told her quite sharply that her services were not required; and she departed.

"Two weeks or so passed. One evening I was sitting at my window, softly whistling and thinking hard how to get away from myself. I felt very bored. The weather was as nasty as it could be. To go out that evening was out of the question, and having nothing better to do I began from sheer ennui a course of self-analysis. This proved dull enough work, but there was nothing else to do. Suddenly the door opened, thank God! Some one was coming to see me.

" 'Are you very busy just now, Pan Student?'

" 'Teresa! H'm—' I thought I would have preferred any one at all to her. Then I said aloud:

" 'No, what is it you want now?'

" 'I wish to ask the Pan Student to write me another letter.'

" 'Very well. Is it again to Boless you wish me to write?'

" 'No, this time I want you to write a letter from Boless to me.'

" 'Wha-at?'

" 'I beg your pardon, Pan Student. How stupid of me! It is not for me, this letter, but for a friend of mine, a man acquaintance; he has a fiancée. Her name is like mine, Teresa. He does not know how to write, so I want the Pan Student to write for him a letter to that Teresa—'

"I looked at her. She seemed very confused and frightened, and her fingers trembled. And tho I failed at first to understand what was the matter with her I at last understood.

" 'Look here, my lady,' I said to her. 'You have been telling me a pack of lies. There are no Bolesses nor Teresas among your acquaintances. It is only a pretext for coming in here. I tell you outright that there is no use of coming sneaking around me, as I do not wish to have anything to do with you. Do you understand?'

"She grew very red in the face and I saw that she was strangely frightened and confused, and moved her lips so oddly, wishing to say something, without being able to say it. And somehow I began to think that I had misjudged her a little. There was something behind all this. But what?

" 'Pan Student,' she suddenly began, but broke off, and turning toward the door, walked out of the room.

"I remained with a very unpleasant feeling in my heart. I heard her shut her own door with a bang; evidently the poor girl was very angry—I thought the matter over and decided to go in to her and induce her to return; I would write her the letter she wished.

"I entered her room. She was sitting at the table with her head pressed in her hands.

" 'Teresa,' I said, 'will you listen to me a moment?'

"Whenever I come to this turn of the story I always feel very awkward and embarrassed. But let us return to my narrative. Seeing that she did not reply I repeated:

" 'Listen to me, my girl—'

"She sprang to her feet, came close up to me, with eyes flashing, and placing her two hands on my shoulders she began to whisper, or rather to hum in her deep bass voice:

" 'Look you here, Pan Student. What of it, what of it if there is no Boless? And what if there is no Teresa? What difference does it make to you? Is it so hard for you to draw a few lines on the paper! Oh, you! And I thought you such a good fellow, such a nice fair-haired little boy. Yes, it is true—there is no Boless, and there is no Teresa, there is only me! Well, what of it?'

" 'Allow me,' I said, greatly disconcerted by this reception. 'What is it you are saying? Is there no Boless?'

" 'Yes, there is none. But what of it?'

" 'And no Teresa either?'

" 'No, no Teresa either; that is, yes, I am her.'

"I could not understand a word. I stared straight into her eyes, trying to determine which of us two had lost our reason. And she returned once more to the table, rummaged for some time in the drawer, and coming back to me said in an offended tone:

" 'Here is the letter you wrote for me, take it back. You do not wish to write me a second one anyway. Others will probably be kinder than you and would do so.'

"I recognized the letter she held out to me as the one I wrote for her to Boless. Humph!

" 'Look here, Teresa,' I said to her. 'Will you please explain to me what it all means? Why do you ask people to write letters for you when you do not find it necessary even to post them?'

" 'Post them? Where to?'

" 'Why, to this Boless, of course.'

" 'But he does not exist!'

"I really could not understand a word. There was nothing left for me to do but to spit and walk out of the room. But she explained herself.

" 'Well, what of it?' she began in an offended voice. 'He does not exist. He does not, so,' and she extended her hands as if she could not herself clearly understand why he did not exist in reality. 'But I want him to. Am I not as much of a human being as the others? Of course I—I know— But it does no harm to any one, that I am writing to him—'

" 'Allow me—to whom?'

" 'To Boless, of course.'

" 'But he does not exist.'

" 'Oh, Mother of God! What if he does not exist? He does not; still to me he does. And Teresa—this is myself, and he replies to my letters, and I write to him again.'

"I understood. I felt so sick at heart, so ashamed of myself to know that alongside of me, only three paces removed, lived a human being who had no one in the whole world to love and sympathize with her, and that this being had to invent a friend for herself.

" 'Here you have written a letter from me to Boless, and I gave it to another to read, and when I hear it read it really begins to seem to me as if there is a Boless. And then I ask that a letter be written from Boless to Teresa—that is to me. And when such a letter is written and is read to me then I am almost entirely convinced that there is a Boless, and that makes my life easier.'

"Yes, the devil take it all," continued my acquaintance. "To make a long story short I began from that time on to write with the greatest punctuality twice a week letters to Boless and vice versa. I wrote splendid replies to her. She used to listen to my reading of those epistles and to weep in her bass voice. In return for this she used to mend my clothes and darn my socks.

"Three months later she was thrown into prison for some reason or other and by now she must surely be dead."

My acquaintance blew the ashes from his cigaret, looked thoughtfully at the sky, and concluded:

"Y-e-s, the more a human being has drunk of the cup of bitterness the more ardently he longs for sweetness. And we, enveloped in our worn-out virtues and gazing at each other through the haze of self-sufficiency and convinced of our righteousness, fail to understand it.

"And the whole affair turns out very stupid, and very cruel. Fallen people we say—but who and what are those fallen ones? First of all they are human beings of the very same bone and blood, of the very same flesh and nerves as ourselves. We have been told the very same thing for whole ages, day in and day out. And we listen and—and the devil alone knows how stupid it all is! In reality we, too, are but fallen people and more deeply fallen too, probably— into the abyss of self-sufficiency, convinced of our own sinlessness and superiority, the superiority of our own nerves and brains over the nerves and brains of those who are only less crafty than we are, and who can not, as we can, feign a goodness they do not possess—but enough of this. It is all so old and stale— so old and stale indeed that one is ashamed to speak of it—"

Literary Mode

Everyone who enjoys literature is aware that there are various kinds of works. He brings to his appreciation of each work certain minimum expectations. If he reads a poem, he expects rhythm and heightened language. If he attends a play, he expects to hear and see people acting on some kind of stage. If he reads a short story or a novel, he expects characters, a sense of place, and a story of some sort. In short, the major kinds of imaginative literature are pretty well agreed on: poetry, drama, and fiction—and each affords pleasures peculiar to its species. One does not expect rhyme in novels or theatrical scenery in poems.

But within the basic genres of poetry, drama, and fiction, the great variety of individual works, many quite different even in their basic intentions, is at first glance bewildering. Polonius boasts that the traveling players who visit Elsinore are "The best actors in the world, either for tragedy, comedy, history, pastoral, pastoral-comical, historical-pastoral, tragical-historical, tragical-comical-historical-pastoral, scene individable, or poem unlimited: . . ." Even if some of the fatuous old man's dramatic modes are bogus, the matter of literary kind has become greatly complicated since Aristotle could speak of the two kinds of drama: tragedy and comedy (see *Poetics*, p. 553). And if we began to add such innovations since Shakespeare's time as naturalistic drama, expressionistic drama, and "absurd" drama, our list would become extensive indeed.

The careful student of literature, then, will not be content merely to classify a work as poetry, drama, or fiction. He will wish to discover which specific mode or genre the work belongs to. He will measure the work according to the yardstick of literary mode, seeking to determine how well the work exploits the potentialities of its particular form and how well the work compares with the most excellent of its kind. In addition, the careful student will note in what ways the writer departs from the usual characteristics of the mode in which he is working. In other words, the pleasures for the student of literary mode, like the pleasures of the concert-goer, are twofold: he enjoys the familiar pattern and he enjoys the surprises, the variations which are played against the pattern. In an age when we place such a high premium on originality, we should be careful not to overlook the value of literary traditions. We should not think that the great artist is necessarily an innovator. Shakespeare and Milton worked within familiar and long established modes.

The yardstick of literary mode must be used with care, of course. One must not allow his fondness for a particular mode to blind him to the value of others. Nor should one stumble into the pitfall of dogmatism, as did certain inflexible proponents of the dramatic "unities" of Aristotle.

If you wish to evaluate a particular work as a specimen of a literary class, you must first determine which class or mode the work belongs to and define the mode, noting its characteristic form and qualities. Then you must appraise the particular work in terms of your expectations. Suppose, for example, you were studying epigrams. You might arrive at this basic definition: "An epigram is a short poem that ends with a point of wit." You would further determine that the epigram characteristically contains social satire or personal abuse. Its style is often colloquial, its meter deliberately loose, sometimes almost doggerel, though in many epigrams you discover a good deal of polish—witty parallelism and antithesis and a conciseness often approaching the proverb or aphorism. It is unusual, you find, for an epigram to be lyrical or sententious.

Below are eight epigrams for you to evaluate according to the yardstick of mode. Which seem to you to make the most ingenious use of the mode, at once satisfying your formal expectations and providing you with pleasant surprises? In short, which are the best epigrams, the most epigrammatic? Do any of the poems seem to you excellent though atypical, that is, unepigrammatic?

Marcus Valerius Martialis
TRANSLATOR: *Samuel Johnson*

A HINTED WISH

> You told me, Maro, whilst you live
> You'd not a single penny give,
> But that, whene'er you chanct to die,
> You'd leave a handsome legacy:
> You must be mad beyond redress,   5
> If my next wish you cannot guess!

John Heywood

JACK AND HIS FATHER

> Jack (quoth his father) how shall I ease take?
> If I stand, my legs ache; and if I kneel

My knees ache; if I go, then my feet ache;
If I lie, my back ach'th; if I sit, I feel
My hips ache; and lean I never so weel,   5
My elbows ache. Sir (quoth Jack) pain to exile,
Since all these ease not, best ye hang awhile.

Sir Thomas Wyatt

OF HIS RETURN FROM SPAIN

Tagus, farewell, that westward with thy streams
Turns up the grains of gold already tried;
For I with spur and sail go seek the Temes,
Gainward the sun, that showeth her wealthy pride;
And to the town that Brutus sought by dreams,   5
Like bended moon that leans her lusty side,
My king, my country, I seek, for whom I live—
O mighty Jove, the winds for this me give!

Ben Jonson

TO DOCTOR EMPIRIC

When men a dangerous disease did 'scape
Of old, they gave a cock to Aesculape;
Let me give two, that doubly am got free:
From my disease's danger, and from thee.

Timothy Kendall

OF FUSCUS, A DRUNKARD

A certain man in physic skilled
To F. spake in this wise:
F., drink not overmuch; take heed!
For drink will lose your eyes.
He paused upon this sentence given,   5
And pondered what was spoke,
And when he had bethought him, thus

At last his mind he broke:
I will by drinking lose mine eyes!
Quoth he, 'tis better so   10
Than for to keep them for the worms
To gnaw them out below.

Lord Byron

THE WORLD IS A BUNDLE OF HAY

The world is a bundle of hay,
    Mankind are the asses who pull;
Each tugs it a different way,
    And the greatest of all is John Bull.

Ambrose Bierce

THE POLITICIAN

Let patriots manipulate
The tiller of the Ship of State;
Be mine the humble, useful toil
To work the tiller of the soil.

J. V. Cunningham

EPIGRAM

The Elders at their services begin
With paper offerings. They release from sin
The catechumens on the couches lying
In visions, testimonies, prophesying:
Not, "Are you saved?" they ask, but in informal   5
Insistent query, "Brother, are you normal?"

From *The Exclusions of a Rhyme* by J. V. Cunningham, Alan Swallow, Denver, 1960.

Hawthorne is accounted by many critics America's finest writer of the romance, a literary mode somewhat out of fashion in this age of realism. In the "Preface" to *The House of the Seven Gables* below, Hawthorne offers his own definition of the romance. Note carefully what he says about the relationship of the romance to such things as probability, atmosphere, moral content, setting, characterization, the marvelous, the picturesque, and the legendary. Apply this definition of the romance to "The Minister's Black Veil" (p. 119). Contrast the romance to the realistic fiction that you have been studying. What are the peculiar qualities and advantages of each mode?

Nathaniel Hawthorne

"PREFACE" TO
THE HOUSE OF THE SEVEN GABLES

When a writer calls his work a Romance, it need hardly be observed that he wishes to claim a certain latitude, both as to its fashion and material, which he would not have felt himself entitled to assume had he professed to be writing a Novel. The latter form of composition is presumed to aim at a very minute fidelity, not merely to the possible, but to the probable and ordinary course of man's experience. The former—while, as a work of art, it must rigidly subject itself to laws, and while it sins unpardonably so far as it may swerve aside from the truth of the human heart—has fairly a right to present that truth under circumstances, to a great extent, of the writer's own choosing or creation. If he think fit, also, he may so manage his atmospherical medium as to bring out or mellow the lights and deepen and enrich the shadows of the picture. He will be wise, no doubt, to make a very moderate use of the privileges here stated, and, especially, to mingle the Marvellous rather as a slight, delicate, and evanescent flavor, than as any portion of the actual substance of the dish offered to the public. He can hardly be said, however, to commit a literary crime even if he disregard this caution.

In the present work, the author has proposed to himself—but with what success, fortunately, it is not for him to judge—to keep undeviatingly within his immunities. The point of view in which this tale comes under the Romantic definition lies in the attempt to connect a bygone time with the very present that is flitting away from us. It is a legend prolonging itself, from an epoch now gray in the distance, down into our own broad daylight, and bringing along with it some of its legendary mist, which the reader, according to his pleasure, may either disregard, or allow it to float almost imperceptibly about the characters and events for the sake of a picturesque effect. The narrative, it may be, is woven of so humble a texture as to require this advantage, and, at the same time, to render it the more difficult of attainment.

Many writers lay very great stress upon some definite moral purpose, at which they profess to aim their works. Not to be deficient in this particular, the author has provided himself with a moral,—the truth, namely, that the wrong-doing of one generation lives into the successive ones, and, divesting itself of every temporary advantage, becomes a pure and uncontrollable mischief; and he would feel it a singular gratification if this romance might effectually convince mankind—or, indeed, any one man—of the folly of tumbling down an avalanche of ill-gotten gold, or real estate, on the heads of an unfortunate posterity, thereby to maim and crush them, until the accumulated mass shall be scattered abroad in its original atoms. In good faith, however, he is not sufficiently imaginative to flatter himself with the slightest hope of this kind. When romances do really teach anything, or produce any effective operation, it is usually through a far more subtle process than the ostensible one. The author has considered it hardly worth his while, therefore, relentlessly to impale the story with its moral as with an iron rod,—or, rather, as by sticking a pin through a butterfly,—thus at once depriving it of life, and causing it to stiffen in an ungainly and unnatural attitude. A high truth, indeed, fairly, finely, and skilfully wrought out, brightening at every step, and crowning the final development of a work of fiction, may add an artistic glory, but is never any truer, and seldom any more evident, at the last page than at the first.

The reader may perhaps choose to assign an actual locality to the imaginary events of this narrative. If permitted by the historical connection,—which, though slight, was essential to his plan,—the author would very willingly have avoided anything of this nature. Not to speak of other objections, it exposes the romance to an inflexible and exceedingly dangerous species of criticism, by bringing his fancy-pictures almost into positive contact with the realities of the moment. It has been no part of his object, however, to describe local manners, nor in any way to meddle with the characteristics of a community for whom he cherishes a proper respect and a natural regard. He trusts not to be considered as unpardonably offending by laying out a street that infringes upon nobody's private rights, and appropriating a plot of land which had no visible owner, and building a house of materials long in use for constructing castles in the air. The personages of the tale—though they give themselves out to be of ancient stability and considerable prominence—are really of the author's own making, or, at all events, of his own mixing; their virtues can shed no lustre, nor their defects redound, in the remotest degree, to the discredit of the venerable town of which they profess to be inhabitants. He would be glad, therefore, if— especially in the quarter to which he alludes—the book may be read strictly as a Romance, having a great deal more to do with the clouds overhead than with any portion of the actual soil of the County of Essex.

EVALUATING CONTENT

Escape

If you measure by the yardstick of escape, the literary work which causes you to forget yourself and the circumstances of your own life is by that fact good. You probably employ this yardstick oftener than you think, for in a world full of perplexities and frustrations it is natural for you and everyone else to want to slip away into a land where men are men and women are exquisite creatures in slinky black evening dresses. Writing that is most successful in effecting escape ordinarily involves adventure, love, crimebusting, or humor.

"A shot rang out in the Silver Star saloon!" There's the beginning of adventure. You can visualize the rest: the mustachioed barkeeper; the beetle-browed villain with his shoestring necktie; the strong, silent hero (inevitably called Tex); his faithful but comically stupid "pardner"; the fresh-faced girl who can ride with the best of 'em; and honest John, her father. The story, if it is excellent as escape, is exciting, fast-moving, tense, and not too complicated. The villain— curse his dirty heart!—gets his just deserts, and Tex gets the girl. A few implausibilities in the story will not bother you if events move fast enough to keep your interest. In general, you demand the same qualities of all adventure stories, whether you read them in books or magazines, see them in plays or movies or on television. Whether it is cloak-and-dagger stuff, sports stories, sagas of the air and sea, or science fiction, you want movement, suspense, and thrills. You want a happy ending. You want uncomplicated characters that are clearly either good or bad. Especially, you want the exotic scene and the unfamiliar adventure. The writers in the pulp magazines may satisfy you, but the great romanticists are sure to do so: Cooper, Scott, Stevenson, Dumas, Hugo.

Romances need not necessarily be set at so fast a tempo as adventure fiction. Indeed, the good ones, you probably feel, are at their best when they are quiet: a hushed night with a silver moon riding overhead, a man and a girl, the soft splashing of a fountain, a whispered "I love you." The old formula is always adequate: boy meets girl, boy loses girl, boy gets girl.

In detective fiction, you expect the excitement, suspense, and physical action of the adventure story, plus, possibly, a boy-girl routine that is interesting but not so absorbing that it interferes with the solution of the crime. In romance and adventure, you know the villain from the outset; in the detective stories you are not so sure. The fun comes in finding out. And the more you are fooled the better you like it. In a sense, therefore, the detective story combines the appeals of the adventure and the romance and adds to them a type of mystery which tantalizes the intellect. That detective stories are considered good reading is evidenced by the fact that Sherlock Holmes, Perry Mason, Hercule Poirot, and Mike Hammer are probably the best-known characters of modern fiction.

Poems which help us best to escape from the complexities of modern life have, curiously enough, almost none of the qualities which we have been considering with regard to fiction and drama. The most popular escapist poetry is quiet, soothing, melodic. It is nonintellectual, questions nothing about life, death, or immortality. By such a standard, Longfellow is greater than Whitman, Poe than Emerson, and Tennyson than Wordsworth. You might be able to point out exceptions to these generalizations in the form of poems like Harte's "Heathen Chinee" and ballads like "Frankie and Johnny" (p. 34), but it would generally hold that readers wanting escape through poetry prefer something like Longfellow's "The Day Is Done" with its famous final stanza:

> And the night shall be filled with music,
> And the cares, that infest the day,
> Shall fold their tents, like the Arabs,
> And as silently steal away.

Humor allows you to escape into the world of the incongruous where things happen in unexpected and amusing ways, and where even the language itself is full of surprises. Even when the characters in a humorous situation seem to suffer excruciatingly, you as reader feel no pain, for the incongruity of the context makes you feel detached and superior. This, you say, is not life, and so you don't identify yourself with it, at least not sufficiently to feel concern for the characters who are suffering.

It has been the custom for many teachers and literary sophisticates to pooh-pooh escapist reading and to decry the standard by which it can be measured and considered good. Their point is that other and more serious works of art bring richer pleasure and a better understanding of actual experience. The point is well taken. The *continual* practice of identifying yourself with a hero or heroine who always comes off triumphantly, while satisfying to the ego, is quite likely to make you less capable of handling real-life situations, where choices between right and wrong are not so clear-cut and where happy endings are often the exception rather than the rule. Yet there is some defense for considering escapist reading good reading. At one time or another, all of us need relaxation; we cannot always go to the movies or play golf. On such occasions, Sherlock Holmes or Longfellow may be just what the doctor ordered.

QUESTIONS

1. How do you account for the popularity of the Sherlock Holmes stories? Would you say that more recent detective fiction like that by Ellery Queen and Erle Stanley Gardner is more absorbing? What elements have been added or have been dropped in these newer works?

2. Is "The Cask of Amontillado" (p. 60) good as escapist reading? Is "To Autumn" (p. 71)? Is *A Night at an Inn* (p. 36)? In each case give reasons for your answer.

3. Why is prose fiction more popular as escape reading than poetry?

4. Of the reading which you do that is unconnected with school work, how much of it rates high by this standard?

5. What do you think would be the effect upon society if we read nothing but good escapist literature? If we read no escapist literature?

Are the following selections by Davis and Browning good according to the yardstick of escape? Can either be construed as something more than escapist reading? Does either embody a serious meaning or take a genuine interest in human nature? Explain. Compare these two selections as escape reading with "The Minister's Black Veil" (p. 119).

H. L. Davis

THE ELECTRIC BULLDOG

The electric bulldog, a new and improved electronic version of the Frankenstein-Apprenti-Sorcier myth as it has been re-created back in, I believe Cincinnati, or maybe it was Cleveland. It was Ohio, anyway, and this is it:

There was a technical expert of some kind who lived in whichever of the places it was, and he had been working out a variety of new uses for the photoelectric cell for some local industrial plant. For one reason and another, the requirements of the plant didn't give him as much scope to spread out in as his imagination required, so he began tinkering with it around home, and, to show what he could really do when the hobbles were taken off, he confected a small sensitized platform on his front porch from which a little railroad track led through a trap door in the wall into his bedroom. The platform was marked off plainly, and the paper boy had orders to drop the morning paper in it. When the paper was dropped, the trap door opened, a cast-iron bulldog rolled out along the track and picked it up, and rolled back inside and deposited it at the master's bedside. On being patted on the head, the faithful animal wagged its tail, rolled out of sight under the bed, and was through for the day. No feeding, no defleaing, no fighting other dogs, no barking at night, no nothing. Just pure service, and nothing to pay for it except a few cents a month for the electricity.

From "Hesperiana," by H. L. Davis, in the *Rocky Mountain Herald*, Denver, Colorado, May 12, 1945.

Well, it worked, and people gawped at it and stood lined up along the curb to watch while the paper boy touched the magic spring of a morning, and then they got to dropping things on their own account—bread-wrappers, old shoes, anything at all, just to see the bulldog roll out and perform, and since it was piling up a big light bill and wearing the contraption out for nothing, the inventor turned it off and went on to more practical things and forgot all about it. During spring housecleaning, somebody apparently turned it on again. He didn't know it at the time. He found it out one night when, returning home from somewhere with some light-hearted friends and turning to call a gay farewell to them from the porch, he stuck his foot into the area that had been designed for the paper. Before he had time to finish the farewell, the trap door opened, the bulldog rolled purposefully out behind him, grabbed him by the ankle, threw him flat on his face, and started back inside, dragging him.

There was not light enough for his friends to see what the trouble was. For a minute or two they weren't quite sure there was any. It might, they thought, be merely another of his gags. He was always pulling them. Then the bulldog hauled his leg in through the trap door, leaving a sort of corolla of torn pants-leg and epidermis frilled around it, until he was in clear up to his crotch. That wouldn't go through. The dog set itself for a fresh start and almost split him lengthwise trying to force him. He screamed for help, and his friends began to realize vaguely what was happening. They rushed up onto the porch and laid hold on him to pull him loose. There were four of them against one electric bulldog, but the bulldog made them dig. First they gained an inch; then he made it back, and a couple more with it; then they strung out tandem and took a death grip on the inventor, who was stretched a foot beyond his normal stature and cracking in the middle, and laid in on one desperate and concerted surge. The house gave, the track gave, the bulldog gave, and the inventor screamed bloody murder. Then all the fuses blew out, and they reeled back into the street, still clutching him, and fell in a heap on top of him.

He was in bed for three weeks thereafter as a result of his injuries, but that isn't the ending that the Ohio story-telling convention leaves it with. In some states it would be, with possibly the addition of a moral about tinkering with buzz-saws, or something on that dark and Sophoclean order. Where the Ohio narrative comes to rest is on the visit of the attending physician, which took place the following morning. The physician was pretty savage about being called out to minister to a patient who was, obviously, the victim of his own idiocy, and took occasion, on leaving, to offer a number of sarcastic remarks on the mentality of a man who would be so asinine as to stick his foot into a place that everybody else in town knew about, had seen work, and had sense enough to stay clear of. He departed, mentioning that if such a thing happened again the inventor could do his own doctoring. There was a painful silence in the sick chamber for a few moments, followed by a crash and a scream from the porch. Then the trap door opened and in came the bulldog, its jaws firmly clenched on the doctor's leg.

Robert Browning

THE LABORATORY

Ancien Régime

Now that I, tying thy glass mask tightly,
May gaze through these faint smokes curling whitely,
As thou pliest thy trade in this devil's-smithy—
Which is the poison to poison her, prithee?

He is with her, and they know that I know   5
Where they are, what they do; they believe my tears flow
While they laugh, laugh at me, at me fled to the drear
Empty church, to pray God in, for them!—I am here.

Grind away, moisten and mash up thy paste,
Pound at thy powder—I am not in haste!   10
Better sit thus, and observe thy strange things,
Than go where men wait me and dance at the King's.

That in the mortar—you call it a gum?
Ah, the brave tree whence such gold oozings come!
And yonder soft phial, the exquisite blue,   15
Sure to taste sweetly—is that poison too?

Had I but all of them, thee and thy treasures,
What a wild crowd of invisible pleasures!
To carry pure death in an earring, a casket,
A signet, a fan-mount, a filigree basket!   20

Soon, at the King's, a mere lozenge to give,
And Pauline should have just thirty minutes to live!
But to light a pastile, and Elise, with her head
And her breast and her arms and her hands, should drop dead!

Quick—is it finished? The color's too grim!   25
Why not soft like the phial's, enticing and dim?
Let it brighten her drink, let her turn it and stir,
And try it and taste, ere she fix and prefer!

What a drop! She's not little, no minion like me!
That's why she ensnared him; this never will free   30

The soul from those masculine eyes—say "no!"
To that pulse's magnificent come-and-go.

For only last night, as they whispered, I brought
My own eyes to bear on her so, that I thought
Could I keep them one half minute fixed, she would fall   35
Shriveled; she fell not; yet this does it all!

Not that I bid you spare her the pain;
Let death be felt and the proof remain;
Brand, burn up, bite into its grace—
He is sure to remember her dying face!   40

Is it done? Take my mask off! Nay, be not morose;
It kills her, and this prevents seeing it close:
The delicate droplet, my whole fortune's fee!
If it hurts her, beside, can it ever hurt me?

Now, take all my jewels, gorge gold to your fill,   45
You may kiss me, old man, on my mouth if you will!
But brush this dust off me, lest horror it brings
Ere I know it—next moment I dance at the King's! (1844)

Biography

In an earlier section entitled "The Author and the Work," we discussed the ways in which an author enters his work and pointed out those elements—tone, point of view, and atmosphere—which especially reveal the author's attitudes. But we did not, at that point, ask the question that logically follows: *Why* did the author choose those particular materials and fashion his work in that unique way? The question, of course, is an enormous one, and no one can provide a perfect answer though a host of investigators offer their contributions—psychologists, historians, sociologists, literary critics, and others. Perhaps the findings of the biographer are the most promising, for the very heart of the biographer's inquiry is the discovery of the innermost qualities of the man. "The best biographers," says Wilmarth S. Lewis, "burst through the time barrier. In spite of all the handicaps of differing speech and customs, they are able to convey to us the essence of the people that they are writing about." And certainly modern literary criticism is blest with abundant and excellent biographical studies—E. M. W. Tillyard's work on Milton and Leon Edel's work on Henry James, to mention only two of the very best.

But the study of the relationship between the biography of the author and the author's work is complicated by two questions. First, does the biographer always reveal the essence of the man? Second, is the essence of the man the same as the essence of the man's work? Let us explore each question, not to discredit biographical criticism but to set carefully its limitations.

One need only read the various accounts of Caesar as man and ruler to see that no single interpretation of his character is generally accepted. Plutarch relates that Caesar put away the crown that Antony offered him only after paid applauders failed to arouse the crowd to urge him to accept it. Appian maintains that Caesar rejected the crown indignantly and that it was his enemies who tried to make it appear that he coveted kingship. Dante, and the Middle Ages in general, reckoned Caesar one of the greatest of men. Shakespeare portrayed him as autocratic, diseased, and superstitious. Shaw made him humane and wise. The essential character of the literary artist is often no easier to fix, for he is usually much less accessible than the public figure. Opinions vary and records are often pitifully fragmentary. We shall, for instance, never know with certainty much about Shakespeare's life and personality.

The other difficulty, as we have suggested, is that there is no simple one-to-one relationship between the artist's personality and his work. Pascal has said, "When we see a natural style, we are astonished and delighted; for we expected to see an author, and we find a man." The implication is that the excellent artist will make a straightforward revelation of himself in his work, but it is not always so. Molière, for instance, who married an actress eighteen years younger than he, satirized in his comedies foolish old men who court young women. He also satirized hypochondriacs and doctors, while he sought vainly from the latter a cure for his tuberculosis. In this case the artist seems to punish the man in his plays; the man is the self, the artist the antiself.

Although we must keep these cautions in mind, biographical studies can be especially valuable in establishing the personal circumstances that surrounded the creation of a literary work. Biographers can answer basic questions. Where was the writer when he wrote the work in question? Whom was he with? What were they talking about? What was he reading? Do his letters or conversations reveal what his intentions were? How does this work fit into the overall pattern of his artistic development? Does the work draw on the writer's experiences? Are his characters fashioned wholly or in part from family or acquaintances? The answers to such questions, though they may not tell us directly whether the work is good or bad, are well worth pursuing, for they enrich our understanding of the work and put us in a better position to evaluate it.

Below are Keats' sonnet "On First Looking into Chapman's Homer" and J. Middleton Murry's account of the circumstances that surrounded the composition of the poem. Note the great variety of biographical elements that Murry brings to bear in his analysis of the poem. The final test of the success of Murry's study is whether or not your reading of the poem is richer for it.

John Keats

ON FIRST LOOKING INTO CHAPMAN'S HOMER

Much have I traveled in the realms of gold,
And many goodly states and kingdoms seen;
Round many western islands have I been
Which bards in fealty to Apollo hold.
Oft of one wide expanse had I been told   5
That deep-browed Homer ruled as his demesne;
Yet did I never breathe its pure serene
Till I heard Chapman speak out loud and bold:
Then felt I like some watcher of the skies
When a new planet swims into his ken;   10
Or like stout Cortez when with eagle eyes
He stared at the Pacific—and all his men
Looked at each other with a wild surmise—
Silent, upon a peak in Darien. (1815; 1816)

J. Middleton Murry

KEATS' "ON FIRST LOOKING INTO CHAPMAN'S HOMER"

Keats's sonnet *On First Looking into Chapman's Homer* holds a position of peculiar significance in his work as a whole: for several reasons: because it is one of the finest sonnets in the English language; because it is the first entirely successful poem that he wrote; because he wrote it very early in his poetic career—in the very month, October 1816, in which he became twenty-one, and decided, to his guardian's consternation, to abandon medicine for poetry; because it was to take him many months, even of his brief and crowded poetic life, to reach such assured mastery again; and finally because he wrote it very quickly. There are not many poems so well worth studying as this one.

But before we study it let us have in mind the story of its composition. We owe the story to the friend of his youth, Charles Cowden Clarke, his young schoolmaster and intimate. The poem was written in October 1816. In 1816 Keats had left school some five years; he had served his apprenticeship to Hammond the surgeon at Edmonton, and had been living for some time in the Borough, studying for a diploma in medicine at Guy's Hospital, and also writing verses.

Keats and Cowden Clarke were in the habit of meeting together for literary discussion. One day in October Clarke was lent a copy of Chapman's *Homer* in folio, and Keats was immediately summoned over in the evening to Clarke's lodging in Clerkenweil to share the feast. They read Chapman together till dawn; then Keats went home to his lodgings in the Borough, two miles away. At 10 o'clock in the morning Clarke found the sonnet on his breakfast table. . . .

What is the impression produced by the sonnet upon us? Impressions of this sort are hard to define: but here one seems to be predominant and recognizable.

We receive an impression of excitement so intense that the declared and actual subject of the poem is as it were dissolved away by it. It is almost impossible not to forget that it is all about a book—Chapman's translation of *Homer*. There is a direct communication of emotion, which grows swifter and swifter, till in the final picture of Cortez, half visual, half abstract, it touches a consummation: the image is not merely stamped upon our minds by the emotional force of the poem, but the image gathers up, clinches, makes tangible, the emotional content of the poem. Cortez on the peak—it is the perfect culmination of the sonnet. All that the sonnet really means is crammed into that final image: it is the flower of the plant, the purpose and the essence of the created thing. . . .

. . . We are conscious of a certain discrepancy between the emotional content of the poem and its ostensible cause: . . . for the reader of the poem Chapman's *Homer* is as it were dissolved away in the intensity of the emotion it has excited. That noble book, in its own quiddity, passes out of question; its function is not its own self-existence, but rather to be a symbol of something beyond itself, a point of crystallization for a condition of thought and feeling which existed in independence of it. Chapman's *Homer*, we feel, has served the office of a spark to ignite a highly combustible gas in the poet's mind into a flash of incandescence. The force of the explosion is as great as the flame is beautiful.

Of so much a sensitive reader is conscious through a simple submission of his mind to the isolated sonnet. But if he goes farther and reads it no longer in isolation, but in its native setting among Keats's poetry of this period— that is to say, if he reads it in its place in Keats's first volume of poetry—the immediate impression becomes more definite. He becomes aware, at first perhaps only vaguely, that this particular sonnet, besides being the one perfect poem in that uneven and exciting book, is a crystallization of a mood of thought and feeling which exists in solution throughout the volume. In the sonnet Keats succeeded in expressing, with a strange completeness and concision, a complex condition of thought and feeling which finds imperfect and partial utterance in nearly all his serious poems of the same period.

The condition is not easy to describe, it needs to be demonstrated; but we may call it, provisionally, the ardour of exploration and the excitement of discovery.

We are first aware of it as a baffled ardour to explore two different realms— Poetry and Nature. In the *Epistle to George Felton Mathew*, written in November 1815, Keats cries:

> Far different cares
> Beckon me sternly from soft 'Lydian airs',
> And hold my faculties so long in thrall,
> That I am oft in doubt whether at all
> I shall again see Phoebus in the morning . . .

He was working at medicine in the Borough. The Borough was a dirty place, and the lodgings of medical students there, to judge by Dickens's account of Bob Sawyer's rooms in Lant Street, took the colour of their surroundings. In the same *Epistle* Keats laments that even if he had the time for poetry he could not write it there:

> But might I now each passing moment give
> To the coy muse, with me she would not live
> In this dark city.

The darkness and the gloom forbid. From the first quotation it is already apparent that for Keats Nature and Poetry are one. 'Soft Lydian airs' are the virtual equivalent of 'seeing Phoebus in the morning'. The idea that he might be the poet of a city of dreadful night never entered his head. Nature and Poetry are one; and he is chained prisoner from both. Again:

> O Solitude! if I must with thee dwell,
>   Let it not be among the jumbled heap
>   Of murky buildings; climb with me the steep,—
> Nature's observatory—whence the dell,
> Its flowery slopes, its river's crystal swell,
>   May seem a span . . .

Perhaps he had broken his bonds for a moment and climbed out of the dingy Borough. His escape is more certain in a sonnet of the early summer, 1816:

> To one who has been long in city pent,
>   'Tis very sweet to look into the fair
>   And open face of heaven—to breathe a prayer
> Full in the smile of the blue firmament.

What had happened? He had found his way to Hampstead Heath; and not merely to Nature and Poetry in the simple sense, but not long after to the company of a poet. Cowden Clarke had shown some of Keats's verses to Leigh Hunt. Hunt had been, as he himself tells us, 'fairly surprised with the truth of their ambition and ardent grappling with nature' (*The Examiner*, December 1st, 1816), and had invited Keats to his cottage in the Vale of Health on the Heath. To Hunt's cottage Keats went often, in the autumn of 1816, and stayed long. (Even his first visit, says Clarke, was prolonged into three morning calls.) He departed reluctantly. . . .

Hunt had published a poem of his—the sonnet to *Solitude*—on May 6th, 1816, in *The Examiner*. No doubt to Keats, as to any common slave of the inkpot, publication was a tangible evidence of vocation. His mind forsook his gallipots, once and for all. He must be with Nature and Poetry. He walked the Heath; he stood tiptoe upon his little hill, by the gate which leads from the Heath to the field by Ken Wood. It was not enough. He must go away. And away he went, to Margate—to something he had not seen before, the sea. In August he wrote an *Epistle* to his brother George:

> Full many a dreary hour have I past,
> My brain bewilder'd, and my mind o'ercast
> With heaviness; in seasons when I've thought
> No sphery strains by me could e'er be caught
> From the blue dome . . .

Again Nature and Poetry are one: the sphery strains are caught direct from the blue dome. All his three *Epistles:* to Mathew, to George, to Cowden Clarke, are concerned with a single theme, his consuming ambition to write poetry and his conviction that poetry is somehow directly created in the poet's soul by Nature. Nature is poetry—'The poetry of earth is never dead'—but to his knowledge of Nature one thing is now added—the ocean. 'E'en now,' he writes to George:

> E'en now I'm pillow'd on a bed of flowers
> That crowns a lofty cliff, which proudly towers
> Above the ocean-waves . . .

So in his *Epistle* the simple fact; in his sonnet of the same time to the same brother George, he tells of the significance.

> The ocean with its vastness, its blue green,
>   Its ships, its rocks, its caves, its hopes, its fears,—
>   Its voice mysterious, which whoso hears
> Must think on what will be, and what has been. . . .

So the ardour of exploration and the excitement of discovery become threefold: of the beauty of Nature, of the beauty of poetry, and of his own power to utter the beauty of Nature in poetry. And as his excitement gathers, so does his confidence in his own powers. In the sonnet *Great spirits now on earth are sojourning*, there is no mistaking the reference of:

> And other spirits there are standing apart
>   Upon the forehead of the age to come;
> These, these will give the world another heart,
>   And other pulses.

It is to himself.

Now let us take stock of our materials—what we have gathered towards the making of the Chapman sonnet. The moment is apt, for that spirit 'standing apart upon the forehead of the age to come' is curiously reminiscent of Cortez on his peak in Darien. We have the ardour of exploration, the excitement of discovery: of Nature, of Poetry, and of Keats's own powers of poetry. We have an ocean, that speaks to him unutterable things, upon which he looks down from a lofty cliff. We have, if not a planet, a moon, to whom he cries:

> O Maker of sweet poets, dear delight
> Of this fair world, and all its gentle livers;

whom he had first described in *Calidore*,

> Lovely the moon in ether, all alone,

and later as 'with a gradual swim, coming into the blue with all her light'.

The discovery of poetry—the thing in itself and his own powers of it—the discovery of the moon, the discovery of the ocean. Since Nature and Poetry are one to him, why should not all these be the same? But how to express these as discoveries? The moon had been discovered—why not a new planet? The ocean had been discovered—why not the ocean when it was unknown? . . .

. . . By these devious ways we have followed Cortez-Keats while he has climbed the steep to the peak in Darien to discover with wondering eyes the dim ocean before him. With him we stare at the Pacific: it is not exactly Chapman's *Homer*, but rather his vast and rolling idea of poetry, and his own poetry to be; and if we are at all his men we feel the tremor of a wild surmise: surely not less thrilling because the peak in Darien is found in the final inquiry to be situated somewhere between the cliffs of Margate and the heights of Hampstead Heath.

But what can we claim to have accomplished by this investigation? To have explained a great poem? Assuredly not. The act of composing the sonnet on Chapman's *Homer* remains unique and beyond analysis. But we can, I think, fairly claim to have substantiated the theory that the composition of a *great* poem is but a final conscious act supervening upon a long process of unconscious elaboration.

Can we, with the help of our evidence, more clearly define the nature of this process? What elements can we distinguish in it?

First and foremost, a predominant, constantly recurring complex of thought and emotion. Throughout the period of unconscious elaboration Keats had been continually discovering more and more of what was to him the highest reality: Nature, Poetry, the Nature of Poetry; and the continual discovery was accompanied by an incessant emotional excitement. Whether his successive acts of discovery can properly be called 'thoughts' will depend upon the philosophy of the man describing them; but 'thoughts' they shall be for us, as they were for Keats:

> There came
> Thought after thought to nourish up the flame
> Within my breast . . .

These successive thoughts (which some would call intuitions), accompanied by an incessant emotional excitement, form what Coleridge calls 'a predominant passion'—more exactly a persistent process of thought-emotion.

Second, in the service of this persistent thought-emotion the specific poetic-creative faculty has been continually at work to find means of expression for it. These means of expression are chiefly images derived from a series of particular sense-perceptions. Thus, the poet's first perception of the moon:

> Lovely the moon in ether, all alone

is refined to a subtler perception of her

> Lifting her silver rim
> Above a cloud, and with a gradual swim
> Coming into the blue with all her light.

And this sense-perception is used to enable the poet to grasp his own thought of the nature of poetry. The smooth and lovely motion of the moon is a quality of the poetry he conceives:

> More strange, more beautiful, more smooth, more regal
> Than wings of swans, than doves, than dim-seen eagle.

So the image of the moon becomes an image of his thought of poetry.

Again, he sees the sea for the first time, and that perception of the sea, with its attendant emotion, enables him once again to grasp his main thought with its emotion. The image of the vast ocean also becomes an image of his vast 'idea' of poetry. Nay more, the very sound of the sea,

> which whoso hears
> Must think on what will be, and what has been,

enables him to make audible, as the sight of the sea to make visible his thought. Again, another aspect of his thought is grasped through the vision of himself standing alone on a cliff (at Margate) or on a hill (at Hampstead), staring with wondering eyes at the prospect before him. He is 'a spirit standing apart upon the forehead of the age to come'.

So the poet's mind has been accumulating through successive acts of sense-perception a series of images which can be assimilated into the main process of his thought and act as surrogates for it. And the condition of this assimilation is an emotional and qualitative correspondence. His perception of the moon is a delighted discovery, so is his perception of the ocean—in both the hidden loveliness of an unknown reality is revealed to him; therefore, both in the qualities discovered and in the emotion awakened in discovering them, these sense-discoveries are analogous to the main thought—discovery of the nature of poetry. With his senses he discovers Nature, with his thoughts he discovers the nature of poetry.

His two crowning sense-discoveries were those of the moon and sea, and those are instantly pressed into the service of his thought: the images of the moon and the ocean can serve at will to embody the objects of his thought. And he is able to think more exactly concerning the nature of poetry because the sensuous images of moon and ocean are become true symbols of the reality about which he is thinking. So that in the process of unconscious elaboration the continually progressing thought is given ever fresh definition and substance by the images it is able to assimilate; and, on the other hand, the images acquire a thought-content. The thought steadily gains focus and intensity; the images significance.

Suddenly this complex of thought and images, which is working itself towards an organic unity, is ejected into poetic form. What occasions this sudden birth? The dominant thought, with its attendant emotion, is given a final focus by a particular event. The discovery of the nature of poetry, which had been going on for months, is consummated by the discovery of Chapman's *Homer*. Utterance becomes urgent, necessary, inevitable. The means are at hand—images long since assimilated to that dominant thought-emotion, of which the discovery of Chapman is the final instance and occasion.

But there is a final creative act. If this unconscious preparation were all, we should imagine Keats in his sestet saying: 'Then felt I—as I did when I discovered the moon, as I did when I discovered the ocean.' But the moon was discovered long ago, and so was the ocean. It will not do. It must be: 'Then felt I—as a man who discovers a new planet, as a man who discovers a new ocean.' Then to his need came the memory of Robertson's *America*, which he had read as a schoolboy. An inexact memory—for as Tennyson pointed out, it was Balboa, not Cortez, who stared at the Pacific—but one definite enough to give the final perfection to his imagery.

Of the last act of poetic creation there is nothing to say. We cannot explain it; but it is no longer utterly miraculous. We have seen at least how the main materials lay ready prepared for the final harmonious ordering; part, and not the least part, of the final harmony had already been achieved; we may fairly say that the actual composition of this great poem was but the conscious last of a whole series of unconscious acts of poetic creation. And we may hazard the guess that it is this long period of unconscious preparation which distinguishes the great poem from the merely good one; that this is the reason why, in a great poem, the subject seems to be dissolved away in the incandescence of the emotion it kindles; and, finally, that this is the reason why the depths of significance in a great poem are inexhaustible.

Psychology

The use of psychology for the study of literature can lead in several directions. We can talk about the psychology of the author and his creative processes, about the psychological insights embodied in his work, or about the psychological effect of the work on the reader. It would be convenient for us if it worked like this: The writer observes in himself a certain psychological complex, he creates a character in his work whose psyche contains the same complex, and finally the reader, through empathy, experiences this mental state. If such were the case, we would have only one thing to analyze—the complex—and we would discern it in identical form in author, work, and audience. But in actuality such simple equivalences do not exist. The author reshapes his experience as he weaves it into his work or he creates characters and mental states vastly different from any that he has actually known. And audiences will often misunderstand, or sometimes understand better than the writer himself, a psychological type that the writer has created. The unemotional nihilist Bazarov, hero of Turgenev's famous novel *Fathers and Sons,* was judged by most contemporary Russian readers to be the very type of inhuman intellectualism, yet Turgenev had intended him to be admirable. Necessarily, then, we must discuss separately the focuses of psychological investigation—author, work, and audience —and suggest possible interrelationships.

If we turn our attention to the writer, we can study the creative process itself as it typically takes place in the mind of any writer, or we may study the mind and creative habits of a particular writer. In the former category are esthetic theories of the past and modern theories like those of Sigmund Freud and Carl Jung. The basic question involves the source of the creative impulse. Generally, the ancients thought of the poet as a *vates,* a seer or prophet inspired by the muses or gods, though Aristotle emphasized the importance of reason and conscious craftsmanship. Later, Christian writers like Milton and Blake believed themselves inspired by God. Modern theories are more purely psychological. Freud saw the source of literary creativity as the egotistical satisfactions of infantile daydreaming. Jung, too, made use of the concept of fantasy but saw the creative mind more evenly balanced between attitudes of introversion and extroversion—in-looking and out-looking. Clearly, the present state of psychological inquiry does not permit us to define with certainty the creative process. But what is useful for us in these speculations is the establishment of the two strata of the human mind that may be at work in the creation of literature, the conscious and the unconscious. And as a kind of rough working principle, we may say that for romantic works that contain a large element of the dreamlike or fantastic, like Coleridge's "Rime of the Ancient Mariner" or Kafka's stories, we are justified in bringing to bear the concepts of psychoanalysis. Whereas for more realistic works we will do better to attend principally to the conscious intentions of the writer.

Such distinctions between works bring us to consider the mind of a particular writer. Again, our studies would be greatly simplified if a system of psychological types were agreed on. But even if it were, we could never fully describe the unique mental qualities of a given writer by classifying him as a certain type. In fact, the most convincing studies of the psychology of an individual author are those that combine the insights of psychoanalysis with a close study of the writer's life. For the careful researcher, then, the assumption that Poe was a sexually impotent neurotic will be an oversimplification. He will want to study the psychological significance of Poe's unhappy childhood, his unfortunate romance with Sarah Elmira Royster, his undisciplined life at the University of Virginia, as well as his strange marriage to Virginia Clemm, a fourteen-year-old cousin. Not only will the thorough psychological study combine psychoanalysis and biography but it will also bring the writer's work into its interpretations. Biographers of Hawthorne, and notably Newton Arvin, have seen in his fiction evidences of the man's preoccupation with guilt and withdrawal. The value for us of the psychological study of the individual author is apparent. It helps explain for us the source of typical characters, themes, and atmosphere.

When we shift our focus to the work itself and study psychological types or states of mind embodied in it, we can use the insights of psychology to arrive at a critical evaluation. For what we ask is how convincing the psychological elements of the work are. What we look for are coherent patterns of emotion and motivation. Our judgment, of course, is not much affected by the crudeness of the contemporary psychological theories that the writer had to work with. Certainly Ben Jonson's theory of humors is outdated, but he transcended the limitations of his theory to create memorable and psychologically credible characters. Laurence Sterne in composing *Tristram Shandy* seems consciously to have used Locke's theory of association, the self-generated flow of images and ideas in the human mind, but the mental meanderings of Sterne's eccentric hero are transformed somehow into something far richer than a mere illustration of Locke's psychological concepts. Similarly, the acute psychological insight of such writers as Auden, Joyce, and Lawrence does not depend finally on the validity of the theories of Freud and Jung, whom they studied.

Keeping in mind that the mental states and emotions in lyric poetry are amenable to psychological evaluation, just as characters in the narrative or drama, let us formulate some questions to use when applying the yardstick of psychological insight to literature. Are characters and mental states in the work psychologically consistent? This question does not imply that the work must be static but that psychological shifts be credible. You may wish to recall your evaluation of the stories by Davis and Gorky (pp. 158-171). Is the psychological content rich, or are the characters uninteresting stereotypes and the emotional states sentimental or oversimplified? What, for instance, keeps J. Alfred Prufrock in Eliot's poem (p. 130) from being a mere caricature of the middle-aged fop? Do the psychological elements seem true to human nature? This question does not imply that only realistic literature can be psychologically sound. For example, Hawthorne's tales and romances have many nonrealistic elements in them. Yet few writers have given us such thoughtful and penetrating analyses of what happens to the human mind and emotions when a human being commits what he considers to be a sinful act. Even Poe's wild tales of horror cast light on what could happen to any of us in a moment of abnormal stress.

When we turn finally to the psychological study of the effect of literature on the audience, we are again faced with conflicting theories about the essence of the esthetic experience. In an earlier section entitled "Escape" we discussed the simple pleasure that a reader gets from identifying with the hero. It does seem, therefore, that Freud tells part of the truth when he says that the artist creates for us a pleasant fantasy which we can participate in without feeling ashamed. But such a theory does not set literature in a very high place. Longinus says in his famous essay *On the Sublime,* "When a passage is pregnant in suggestion, when it is hard, nay impossible, to distract the attention from it, and when it takes a strong and lasting hold on the memory, then we may be sure that we have lighted on the true Sublime." What is this esthetic experience that Longinus implies is certainly more than pleasant escapism? The Italian critic Benedetto Croce has said, "artistic representations arouse pleasure and pain in their infinite shades of variety. We tremble with anxiety, we rejoice, we fear, we laugh, we weep, we desire, with the personages of a drama or of a romance. . . . But these feelings are not such as would be aroused by the real fact outside art. . . . And it is natural that they do not trouble and afflict us as passionately as those of real life. . . ." One psychological function of literature, then, is to enrich our emotional lives without requiring of us the actual pain and trial that attend such emotions in real life. Aristotle seems to say much the same thing when he assigns to tragedy the function of arousing and then purging the emotions of pity and fear. Jung suggests that the artist organizes for us symbolically our deepest instincts and the primordial images in our unconscious, but here the discussion verges on myth, which we will discuss at length in the following section. What we note finally is this: Though there is not general agreement about the essence of the esthetic experience, it does seem certain that one legitimate yardstick of literary value is audience reaction. Provided that we guard against mere escapism or mere emotionalism, a deep response felt by many sensitive readers suggests greatness in a literary work.

Possibly the chief danger in the use of the yardstick of psychological insight, particularly as it applies to the artist and to his work, lies in the tendency to place a higher value upon perceptions of abnormal behavior than on those of normal behavior. A probing treatment of a psychotic seems much more significant to many of us (probably because the material is more striking) than a conscientious treatment of an average person. This is an unfortunate tendency because it can badly distort our evaluations.

In a chapter on a method of criticism he calls "Formism," Stephen C. Pepper in his provocative *The Basis of Criticism in the Arts* identifies human value with what is normal in human behavior. The greatest literature, he says, is that which deals with norms, which penetrates to basic actions and traits. Most of us would agree that psychological insight is most likely to result from those works which cast light upon the typical and even commonplace in human behavior.

Below are Coleridge's "Kubla Khan" and Maud Bodkin's psychological analysis of the poem. Drawing heavily on the writings of Jung, the critic attempts to bring into a meaningful relationship the creative process of Coleridge, the psychological symbols in the poem, and the response of the reader. Such an analysis, if it is successful, does not dissipate our feelings about the poem by explaining them away; rather it deepens our awareness and understanding of the poem's enchantment.

Samuel Taylor Coleridge

KUBLA KHAN

In Xanadu did Kubla Khan
A stately pleasure-dome decree:
Where Alph, the sacred river, ran
Through caverns measureless to man
    Down to a sunless sea.   5
So twice five miles of fertile ground
With walls and towers were girdled round:
And here were gardens bright with sinuous rills,
Where blossomed many an incense-bearing tree;
And here were forests ancient as the hills,   10

Enfolding sunny spots of greenery.
But oh! that deep romantic chasm which slanted
Down the green hill athwart a cedarn cover!
A savage place! as holy and enchanted
As e'er beneath a waning moon was haunted   15
By woman wailing for her demon-lover!
And from this chasm, with ceaseless turmoil seething,
As if this earth in fast thick pants were breathing
A mighty fountain momently was forced;
Amid whose swift half-intermitted burst   20
Huge fragments vaulted like rebounding hail,
Or chaffy grain beneath the thresher's flail:
And 'mid these dancing rocks at once and ever
It flung up momently the sacred river.
Five miles meandering with a mazy motion   25
Through wood and dale the sacred river ran,
Then reached the caverns measureless to man,
And sank in tumult to a lifeless ocean:
And 'mid this tumult Kubla heard from far
Ancestral voices prophesying war!   30

    The shadow of the dome of pleasure
    Floated midway on the waves;
    Where was heard the mingled measure
    From the fountain and the caves.
It was a miracle of rare device,   35
A sunny pleasure-dome with caves of ice!
    A damsel with a dulcimer
    In a vision once I saw:
    It was an Abyssinian maid,
    And on her dulcimer she played,   40
    Singing of Mount Abora.
    Could I revive within me,
    Her symphony and song,
    To such a deep delight 'twould win me,
That with music loud and long,   45
I would build that dome in air,
That sunny dome! those caves of ice!
And all who heard should see them there,
And all should cry, Beware! Beware!
His flashing eyes, his floating hair!   50
Weave a circle round him thrice,
And close your eyes with holy dread,
For he on honey-dew hath fed,
And drunk the milk of Paradise. (1797; 1816)

Maud Bodkin

COLERIDGE'S ''KUBLA KHAN''

The study of the pattern which appears in different forms in the poetic representation of Paradise and Hades, or of Heaven and Hell, may be introduced by means of a brief examination of Coleridge's dream poem, *Kubla Khan*. We may again make use of the research into sources contained in Professor Lowes's book, *The Road to Xanadu*.

As before, I will assume that the reader is familiar with the poem, or has ready access to it, and will quote only such lines as are needed for direct illustration of the argument. I would suggest that for the moment we should put aside any psychological curiosity, or memory of psychological discussions, concerning the poem as a product of a dream, and should consider only the experience that arises naturally when the poem is read under conditions which allow of complete concentration, or absorption within the communicated experience. We may examine first the closing lines as felt within such a reading of the whole poem:

> A damsel with a dulcimer
> In a vision once I saw:
> It was an Abyssinian maid,
> And on her dulcimer she played,
> Singing of Mount Abora.
> Could I revive within me,
> Her symphony and song,
>   To such a deep delight 'twould win me,
> That with music loud and long,
> I would build that dome in air,
> That sunny dome! those caves of ice!
> And all who heard should see them there,
> And all should cry, Beware! Beware!
> His flashing eyes, his floating hair!
> Weave a circle round him thrice,
> And close your eyes with holy dread,
> For he on honey-dew hath fed,
> And drunk the milk of Paradise.

What are the main elements of the experience communicated by these lines? We are aware of the poet, terrible in the power of his vision, of the damsel, and her song that excites in him the divine frenzy, and of the content of the

From *Archetypal Patterns in Poetry: Psychological Studies of Imagination* by Maud Bodkin, Oxford University Press, London, 1934.

inspired vision—a dome and caves, which the sequence of the poem seems to identify with the previously mentioned pleasure-dome on the green hill crowned by blossoming watered gardens, and with the caverns through which the sacred river ran to the sunless sea. When we have felt these things, both the phrases and the images, in their relations and full emotional quality, in such fashion as our stored memories and emotional resources make possible, we are in a position to question those memories, or add to them from the researches of others. What is the history behind these phrases and images?

The most obvious reference is perhaps to the *Paradise Lost* of Milton. Here the whole plan of river, mount, and garden is paralleled. We recall:

> Southward through Eden went a river large,
> Nor chang'd his course, but through the shaggy hill
> Pass'd underneath ingulf'd, for God had thrown
> That mountain as his garden-mould high rais'd
> Upon the rapid current, which, through veins
> Of porous earth with kindly thirst updrawn,
> Rose a fresh fountain, and with many a rill
> Water'd the garden; thence united fell
> Down the steep glade, and met the nether flood,

and again, the passage presenting, among other spots of famed loveliness, the pseudo-Paradise of Mount Amara:

> Not that fair field
> Of Enna, where Proserpine gathering flow'rs,
> Herself a fairer flower, by gloomy Dis
> Was gather'd, which cost Ceres all that pain
> To seek her through the world; nor that sweet grove
> Of Daphne by Orontes, and the inspir'd
> Castalian spring, might with this Paradise
> Of Eden strive; . . .

> Nor where Abassin kings their issue guard,
> Mount Amara, though this by some suppos'd
> True Paradise under the Ethiop line
> By Nilus' head, enclos'd with shining rock,
> A whole day's journey high,

Lowes has pointed out the probable origin of the name, Abora, in Coleridge's poem, through confluence of "the hill, Amara"—of which both Coleridge and Milton had read in the *Pilgrimage* of Purchas—with the names "Abola" and "Astaboras," which occur frequently in a narrative by James Bruce, *Travels to Discover the Source of the Nile,* which Coleridge knew well. Lowes has discovered different descriptions which Coleridge had read of fountains—one in Florida which "threw up, from dark rocky caverns below, tons of water every minute, forming a bason . . . and a creek . . . which meanders six miles through green meadows"; another that with terrific noise and tremor of the earth threw up a flood which formed a river that left fragments of rock in heaps at places where ridges opposed its course. These fountains seem to have coalesced with Bruce's description of the sacred river, Nile, that also, in Abyssinia, had its fountains, by which their discoverer stood in rapture. Moreover Coleridge had read the speculations of ancient writers concerning the identity of the Nile with one of those four rivers that, as stated in Genesis, went out of Eden. He had, Lowes believes, read an account by Moses bar Cepha of those rivers of Paradise descending through huge chasms and subterranean channels to boil up far away; also an account of the Nile, plunging "through chasms inaccessible to man." He had read, and loved, Burnet's "grand Miltonic romance": the *Telluris Theoria Sacra,* according to which subterranean waters, the Deep whose foundations, Genesis tells us, were broken up at the Deluge, shall again be loosed at the last catastrophe, and meanwhile persist, an illimitable ocean, lifeless and sunless, beneath the upper lands and waters of the world. He had found the Nile and the Alpheus—whose confluent names no doubt explain "Alph, the sacred river"— associated by Pausanias as rivers flowing underground and reappearing; in Seneca's writings he had found them associated also with the idea of a nether ocean, a hidden sea.

Thus, with Lowes's help,[1] we gather some of the accumulated memories behind the vision of the fountain and caverns, the engulfed river and sunless sea. The question then arises concerning these images: what is their emotional significance, to Coleridge, to ourselves, and to the men who fashioned the more mythical of them in their earliest form? Or shall we rather say, to us, as participating in the European Mind? It will, however, be convenient first to have before us the result of Lowes's researches concerning one more image, that of the maid charming the poet with her song.

Lowes finds reason to believe that, together with the passage from Purchas's *Pilgrimage* to which Coleridge alludes in his note to the poem—the passage describing the Khan Kubla's palace and garden—there was present in the poet's mind a passage from the *Pilgrimes* of Purchas, describing the palace and garden of Aloadine, the Old Man of the Mountain. Into this palace, Purchas relates, youths previously instructed concerning the sensual Paradise of Mahomet were brought in a drugged sleep, given wine, milk and honey to drink, served by "goodly Damosels skilfull in Songs and Instruments of Musicke and to make Sports and Delights unto men whatsoever they could imagine." When the youths had enjoyed these pleasures four or five days, they were again carried forth in sleep. Afterwards they believed themselves to have been in Paradise, and so cherished the memory of its delights that in fighting for Aloadine they contemned their lives. This passage, Lowes considers, partly determines the appearance in Coleridge's poem both of the singing damsel and of the figure exciting terror,

---

1. The references are all in chapter xix of *The Road to Xanadu.*

with flashing eyes and floating hair, who had fed on the milk and honey-dew of Paradise.

We may accept this suggestion so far as it harmonizes with what is naturally conveyed by the words of the poem. The wild longing of the youths for the lost delights of their supposed Paradise does so harmonize with the description of the poet and his longing; but to me it came with a shock of surprise that Lowes, in summing up the sequence of the poem's images, should refer to the figure with flashing eyes as "the Tartar youth." [2] Within the poem this figure, whatever its origin, has clearly become the poet who, could he recall the music of his dream, would so rebuild his vision that all who heard should behold it also, and cry out in fear and wonder. . . .

It is, I think, the expression of longing in the cry "Could I revive within me" that strikes the keynote of my experience of the whole poem, together with the suggestion of ecstasy in imaginative fulfilment, in the lines that follow:

> To such a deep delight 'twould win me,
> That with music loud and long,
> I would build that dome in air,

I can identify faint visual images of the shining dome and flowery landscape around it, the gleam of water in sunlight above, and darkness of water, and great lines of overhanging cavern, below. The meaning and value of the passages of description for me, however, is hardly at all in the faint visual images aroused: it is in the far-reaching suggestiveness, so much harder to explore, that belongs to the words, and clings also about these image fragments.

The singing damsel of the poem I never spontaneously visualize, but as I fastened questioningly upon the reference to her, I caught a glimpse of a face, generalized, it seemed, from pictures by Rossetti and by Watts, and the phrase flashed "the dweller in the innermost." With the last lines of the poem came an image of the poet—very indistinct visually, rather an organic image of posture, with a suggestion of dizziness; since "floating hair," for me, mediates a reference to the whirling dance of a dervish. When I gave time, the lines arose in my mind: "He that knows the power of the dance dwells in God; for he has learnt that Love can slay!" Also I half recalled sayings of Plato concerning the divine insanity of the poet. The faint visual and motor image of the poet in his ecstasy included a circle of dancers moving around him with gestures of awe and reverence.

This seems as much as I need give as an indication, through such images as one can describe, of the nature of the individual existence of the poem in my mind. However that in the mind of my reader may vary, both in the terms of its imagery and in these deeper associations that underlie the images, it will, I assume, show in some manner the pattern that I have indicated in my distinctive terms: a presentation of sunlit gardens above and dark caverns below

2. *Op. cit.*, p. 409.

—an image corresponding in some degree to the traditional ideas of Paradise and Hades—recognized as the vision of a poet inspired by the music of a mysterious maiden.

With this pattern in mind let us turn to the poem to which, we observed, *Kubla Khan* seems most closely related, the *Paradise Lost* of Milton. I would ask the reader to recall Milton's poem, focusing his memory of it at those lines already quoted, in which Milton views his Paradise, as it were, obliquely through a simile, negative in form but bearing an important relation to the poem's whole story:

> Not that fair field
> Of Enna, where Prosérpine gathering flow'rs,
> Herself a fairer flower, by gloomy Dis
> Was gather'd, which cost Ceres all that pain
> To seek her through the world; . . .
> . . . might with this Paradise
> Of Eden strive . . .

These lines Professor Bailey has said[3] might be chosen for their amazing beauty to represent Milton rather than any others. If the reader will recall or refer to them in their place in the poem he will feel with what effect their simplicity of diction follows the richly ornate verse in which Milton has celebrated the beauty of his Paradise. Direct description has done its utmost, but in the slow-moving monosyllables, "all that pain to seek her through the world," we have, as Bailey says, "a simplicity akin to silence"—a silence that vibrates with the very pulse of the longing that created Paradise, so that within it whatever vision description may have kindled takes on more poignant significance.

Another relation which helps to make this simile of central importance in the experience of the poem is that which links it with the crisis of the tale as told by Milton. When the tempter appears, to lead Eve to the fruit of that forbidden tree whose taste "brought death into the world," he finds her, as Proserpine was found by gloomy Dis, among the flowers, herself the "fairest unsupported flower." The pattern is evidently reproduced deliberately by Milton, and one discerns in it, I think, the kind of significance I have called archetypal. As Proserpine moved in beauty through the flowery field of Enna, a symbol of transient spring loveliness threatened by the powers of the underworld—of dark,

---

3. *Milton*, p. 170 (Home Univ. Lib.). The "amazing beauty" of these lines—which Matthew Arnold also selected for a place among his supreme passages—seems to be due . . . to the way in which the emotional significance of the whole poem converges upon them, especially when they return to mind after the poem is well known. The "amazement" is, I think, the result in consciousness of relations felt though not explicitly recognized. One feels, and is thrilled by, the beauty of the whole poem as focused at that particular passage, just as in looking at a landscape from a chosen viewpoint one rejoices in the satisfying pattern made by its lines from that angle, though without realizing all the interrelations of visual impression and latent motor imagery that make that aspect so delightful.

cold, and death—so Milton's Eve also stands amid flowers, a symbol of the frailty of earthly joy and loveliness before the Powers of Evil. It is as though the poet's feeling divined the relation of the concepts of Heaven and Hell to the images of spring's beauty and of the darkness under the earth whence beauty comes forth and to which it returns. In the communicated experience, at all events, one finds, through this binding of the tale to the myth-image, that the pattern stands clear, of Satan struggling upwards from his tremendous cavern below the realm of Chaos, to waylay the flower-like Eve in her walled Paradise and make her an inmate of his Hell, even as Pluto rose from beneath the earth to carry off Proserpine from her flowery meadow.

If, still keeping in view the pattern experienced in *Kubla Khan,* we look in Milton's poem for the setting of his vision of Paradise, or of Heaven and Hell, we find, recurring at the poem's main divisions, the figure of the poet himself and of the muse that inspires him; and the passages that constitute this setting of the vision are perhaps of the whole communicated experience the part which we feel most poignantly to-day.

Gilbert Murray has suggested, and Professor Grierson has endorsed the suggestion,[4] that for Milton the poet, as distinct from the thinker, his poem was to him chiefly "a sanctuary of escape" from the pain and disappointment of life. We feel that he dwells lovingly within his pictured Paradise, yet perhaps the note of love sounds never so clearly as when he describes that sacred hill of Sion, whose image he links with that of the classical haunt of the Muses.

Thus, at the opening of the poem, Milton calls upon the heavenly Muse that "on the secret top of Oreb, or of Sinai" inspired Moses:

> Or, if Sion hill
> Delight thee more, and Siloa's brook that flow'd
> Fast by the oracle of God; I thence
> Invoke thy aid. . . .

But it is at the beginning of the third book, when the poem passes from blind Hell, and Satan labouring through night and chaos, to Heaven and the vision of God "High thron'd above all highth," that the poet, calling in his darkness upon the heavenly light, tells intimately of his own joy in poetry:

> Yet not the more
> Cease I to wander where the Muses haunt
> Clear spring, or shady grove, or sunny hill,
> Smit with the love of sacred song; but chief
> Thee, Sion, and the flowery brooks beneath,
> That wash thy hallow'd feet, and warbling flow,
> Nightly I visit:

· · · · ·

---

4. *Cross Currents in English Literature of the XVIIth Century* (Chatto & Windus, 1929), p. 266.

> Then feed on thoughts, that voluntary move
> Harmonious numbers . . .

And once more, before telling through the mouth of Raphael the story of Creation, Milton calls upon the Muse, the eternal Wisdom, who will not fail him, and again tells in his own person of the poet's secret bliss:

> On evil days though fall'n, and evil tongues;
> In darkness, and with dangers compass'd round,
> And solitude; yet not alone, while thou
> Visit'st my slumbers nightly, or when morn
> Purples the east: still govern thou my song,
> Urania . . .

The moving beauty of these passages brings it about that as we recall the poem, the whole vision of Paradise, of Hell beneath and Heaven above, is set, as was the vision of Coleridge, within our emotional awareness of the poet who sings, not alone, but inspired by the song of another—a feminine figure for whose origin we must go far back in the history of the poetic imagination. . . .

I would venture here again to utilize something of my own experience, presenting it only as an individual mode of approach to what may be truth of general validity.

In my experience the lines describing the fountain forced upward with turmoil, "as if this earth in fast thick pants were breathing," are closely linked with the passage in the *Phaedo* picturing the vast cavern where the measureless flood swings and surges, the wind swinging with it like the breath of a living creature drawn forth and in. That this image was actually operative in Coleridge's mind, determining the picture and phrases of his dream poem, we certainly cannot say. It may have been rather the aptness of the simile to express an imaginative spectator's response that has brought into both pictures a reference to the tumultuous breathing of the earth. Within those travellers' descriptions which Lowes exhibits as sources of the phrases of Coleridge's poem, was there also latent an organic response to the natural phenomenon witnessed, as to an expression of a living creature's force? We have, to judge from, in these descriptions, only the strong note of wonder: "the inchanting and amazing chrystal fountain," "he was astonished by an inexpressible rushing noise . . . and tremor of the earth . . . and saw, with amazement, the floods rushing upward many feet high." Whatever organic response may have been present within the recorded amazement of the traveller, to Coleridge, sharing it as he read, some sense of the passion of a living thing was evidently conveyed.

Elements of organic response which remain latent and undiscoverable in our conscious apprehensions we are now learning to explore by means of the analysis of experiences of dreams and reverie in which the same apprehended objects occur. Some time after I had read, with a certain excitement, Plato's description of the swinging flood in Tartarus—and had compared it with that other description in the myth of Er (*Republic*, 614), of the souls coming to the "ghostly place where were two open Mouths of the Earth hard by each other, and also above, two Mouths of the Heaven"—I had a dream which appeared closely connected with Plato's description, and with the fascination it had for me.

In the dream I found myself walking along the street of a sea-side town. Looking between the houses in the direction of the sea, I saw a vast cavern mouth which appeared as an opening both into earth and sky. I knew that through it one could pass into all the elements, earth, water, and air; but it was being boarded up almost completely. Only through some cracks between the boards, jets of water flowed. I was sorry about the boarding up, thinking how dull it would be then for me and all the people in the houses.

As I recalled the dream on waking, I thought of Plato's strange mouths of Earth and Heaven; but, seeking for more personal associations, I came upon a memory from childish days of a certain semicircular grated opening in a wall, through which a stream flowed. On the other side of the high wall were private grounds which I never visited. The water appearing and flowing through the bars of the low curved opening had mystery and fascination for me; so that when we walked with the nurse in that direction I would look forward to coming to the place and be disappointed if we turned back short of it. Another spot I recalled as equally exciting to visit in those days was the lock on a certain canal, where I could watch the runnels of water that forced a way between the planks of the sluice-gates, just as did the water in my dream.

As I recall those early memories in relation to the dream-images, I seem to recognize the note of feeling that unites them with my apprehension of Plato's image, and also with that of Coleridge. It is a brooding wonder at the water's movement, and sympathy with it as with a thing alive. I do not know whether if I underwent a Freudian analysis the daily repeated pressure of the analyst's expectations would enable me to produce in relation to these memories further associations connected with the living body, its functions and secretions, that may have been latent within the childish wonder. If such were present I cannot by my own method of inquiry recover them. What I do seem to recover is the note of a wonder more naïve and unquestioning—a consciousness more utterly surrendered to its object—than any apprehension of my adult everyday consciousness could be. In the trance of the infantile memory as revived by the dream, I seem to share with the flowing water a kind of sub-human life—a life of elemental feeling, from which, the dream seems to say, the higher socialized life must not be completely shut off, or it turns dull and arid.

The hypothesis suggested, then, by my experience is that the magic, or fascination, which a reader may feel in such a description as that of the fountain of Coleridge, depends, at least in part, upon the presence, within his apprehension of the lines, of a factor of feeling of a more primitive character than pertains to ordinary adult consciousness. I have spoken of this feeling as an organic response. The child in presence of the moving water does not so much think, in terms of socialized consciousness, as feel the reaction of her own body, a reaction involving no doubt an immature sexuality, concerning which Freudian researches have taught us something, but involving also other elements, both of instinctual character, and of tensions and stresses shared with beings below the animal level. This factor of organic feeling, which invites our scientific curiosity to carry its analysis farther, should be identifiable, I think, by any reader who has the aptitude both for deep and full response to poetry, and for analysing that response.

I think that such a reader need never fear that acquaintance with the probings and discussions of the psycho-analyst can in any way mar for him the delight of poetry. Rather this delight is increased if, by help of psycho-analysis, the mind is set free from inhibitions—from false shame or misgiving in realizing any association of sexual, or other primitive, character that has a natural place within the response to the poem. The Freudian reiterations concerning sexual origins leave us unmoved, observes a literary critic, since it is "a commonplace of psychology" "that all the elements of consciousness are directly or indirectly interrelated"; and that "distant echoes of a psycho-physiological nature" united with the higher processes of the mind "in an obscure harmony."[5] Enjoyment of the beauty of poetry is spoiled only if certain of these psycho-physiological echoes are emphasized, as though they were somehow more real than all the other elements with which in a mature mind they are fused—as though these other elements that contribute to the actually experienced response were a mere evasion or disguise of those few primitive elements newly identified by the analyst.

The same reflections apply to the consideration of the cavern image. Examining my own response to the cavern image, as it occurs in Coleridge's poem, I find a complex of reminiscence, including memories of damp dark cellars and of a deep well, regarded with fearful interest in childhood; also, fused with these, images of caverns and underground castle-vaults, goblin-tenanted, which I gathered from an absorbed reading of fairy-tales. These memories include no recognizable trace of reference to the womb. If, however, we accept the view that the earliest conscious apprehensions are conditioned by yet earlier responses of the organism—unconscious "prehensions," in Whitehead's phrase, inherited by later conscious "occasions"—we have a means for conceiving how the earliest experiences of the infant in relation to the mother's body, especially the violent adventure of birth, may help to determine the first conscious reactions to dark enclosed places, and may contribute psycho-physiological echoes to dreams and to the play of fancy.

Let us now review the results that have so far emerged from the discussion. We have noted in the poem of *Kubla Khan* an image-pattern of mountain-garden and caverned depths, of waters rising and falling, which we have seen also in *Paradise Lost*, and have followed back in Greek and Hebrew literature. When we examine the experience communicated by poetry and myth showing this image-pattern, we may, it is suggested, discern a corresponding pattern of emotion. Changeful and subtly interrelated as these patterns of emotion and imagery are found to be, yet the image of the watered garden and the mountain

---

5. Louis Cazamian, *Criticism in the Making* (Macmillan, 1929), pp. 95–6.

height show some persistent affinity with the desire and imaginative enjoyment of supreme well-being, or divine bliss, while the cavern depth appears as the objectification of an imaginative fear—an experience of fascination it may be, in which the pain of fear is lost in the relief of expression; in other instances the horror of loss and frustration symbolized by depth, darkness, and enclosing walls sounds its intrinsic note of pain even through the opposing gain and triumph that poetic expression achieves.

. . . we traced a pattern of rising and sinking vitality, a forward urge and backward swing of life, reflected in an imagery deployed in time—an imagery in which winds and waters played their part— . . . we find an emotional pattern . . . presented statically, in imagery of fixed spatial relation—the mountain standing high in storm and sunlight, the cavern unchanging, dark, below, waters whose movement only emphasizes these steadfast relations of height and depth.

Myth

In an earlier section entitled "Meanings" (p. 109) we discussed briefly the nature of myth and the ways in which myth can be embodied in literature. Now we are concerned with how the concept of myth can be used as a yardstick to measure the excellence of certain literary works.

We may begin by elaborating our earlier definition of myth. Every myth has these basic qualities: it is nonrational, idealized, and communal. Philip Wheelwright puts it more eloquently: "Myth is an expression of a profound sense of togetherness—a togetherness not merely upon the plane of intellect, as is primarily the case among fellow-scientists, but a togetherness of feeling and of action and of wholeness of living." The power of a myth, then, depends on its expressiveness, its ability to bind us together with a shared sense of some essential element of human destiny. This definition can be illustrated by the myth of the Garden of Eden and the eating of the apple. Certainly the myth is nonrational, so much so that the rationalist Thomas Paine found it abhorrent and absurd. All elements of the story are idealized: the bounty of God, the beauty of the garden, the subtleness of the serpent, the frailty of Eve, and the justice of God's judgment. Many generations have shared the meaning of the myth. Even today, when the concept of original sin has been challenged by environmentalists and Freudian theorists concerned with the origins of guilt, this old and simple story still has the power to organize for many their deep feelings about human imperfection.

Turning from the nature of myth to the forms that it may take in literary works, we make a very simple distinction. Some writers use myths already formulated, already part of the traditions of the culture, though they often rework or modernize these legends. Other writers create their own myths. Perhaps the most massive and celebrated modern use of traditional myth is that in James Joyce's

Ulysses. Though Joyce eliminates from his novel the heroic elements of Homer's epic, he still finds that the adventures and trials of Leopold Bloom closely parallel those of Odysseus, whose modern counterpart he is. Hemingway, on the other hand, is said by many critics, including Robert Penn Warren, to have created his own myth of the honorable but defeated hero: Jake Barnes in *The Sun Also Rises,* Robert Jordan in *For Whom the Bell Tolls,* or Ole Anderson in "The Killers" (p. 453)—men who live bravely according to a code of tough Stoicism, uncorrupted yet destroyed by a world without ideals. The question could be raised: How can a writer create a myth since, by definition, a myth is the common property of the whole community or culture? The answer is that the writer gives mythical expression to feelings and apprehensions already in the minds of his audience—in the case of Hemingway, the sense of a loss of values and cultural coherence after World War I.

The presence of mythical elements, whether traditional or newly created by the writer, by no means insures that a work is profound. Any careful observer can see the myth of the Old West that the TV "horse operas" are based on—the invulnerability of the heroic lawman, the violent eradication of the badman, etc. The Old West was not like that, of course, but historical accuracy is not the real issue. What debases the myth of the TV western are the childish moral over-simplifications, naïve hero worship, and, some would say, the idealization of violence. Shakespeare in his history plays often departed from the facts, but he embodied in these plays the great and profound myth of earthly governance based on a universal order divinely ordained.

The great danger in using the concept of myth to evaluate literature is the pitfall of overingeniousness. Myth and message hunters find mythological elements in everything and often pervert the intentions of the writer. (Poor Huck Finn becomes the guilt-ridden conscience of the race drifting with his dark alter ego toward the sea of death.) Mythological content for such critics becomes the only test of greatness. The contrast between Shakespeare's history plays and TV westerns should warn us that differences in many other elements—language, plot, and characterization, for example—help account for the relative value of these works. But if we use it with caution, the concept of myth can suggest some legitimate and important questions. Does the use of a traditional myth help the writer shape his material and bring out its significance? Look again at Arnold's "Palladium" (p. 113). Does the writer elevate his plot or his characters symbolically to a universal and mythical significance? Think of the mythical quests of such unlike characters as Ahab and Don Quixote. Or consider Sinclair Lewis' *Babbitt* which attacks the *false* myth of materialistic and social success.

If we are willing to assign to the poet the high place of prophet or seer, as the ancients did, we may look to him to do what Joyce's young artist-hero Stephen Daedalus claimed he would do: "I go to encounter . . . the reality of experience and to forge in the smithy of my soul the uncreated conscience of my race." Probably such claims will seem immodest to most modern readers. But we can at least claim for some writers the function of revealing and evaluating for us the myths that embody our deepest feelings about the human condition.

In the following analysis of Christopher Fry's A Phoenix Too Frequent (p. 619),

Mark Ashin studies Fry's use of mythical elements. Ashin finds that the phoenix legend

suggested to Fry certain symbols and certain elements of characterization and plot,

as well as the title. You may wish to study and discuss the myth itself, seeking to

discover the enduring vitality of its symbolism.

Mark Ashin

FRY'S A PHOENIX TOO FREQUENT

Only a literary scholar would want to trace the story of *A Phoenix Too Frequent* [see the play on p. 619] back through Jeremy Taylor, the seventeenth century divine, to its source in Petronius' tale of the gentlewoman of Ephesus in order to study the transformations which have occurred in the treatment of the story in the course of twenty centuries. And perhaps only a scholar would care to place in their context the lines from the Roman epigram writer, Martial, as quoted by Robert Burton, which serve as the epigraph to the play. However, the choice of the title, in addition to revealing the characteristically pungent wit of Christopher Fry, also shows the poet's attitude toward the central incident of the drama. Therefore, it seems appropriate to ask not the scholar but the young student what the title means and what kind of attitude it does reveal. In order to understand the title and its relevance for this play, a knowledge of the phoenix legend is required.

Briefly, the legend is as follows: The phoenix was an Arabian bird which had the power of living for five hundred years. It was a unique specimen, since at any given time only one member of the species was ever alive. At the end of its life span, the phoenix built a nest of fragrant spices, laid its egg within and then set fire to the nest, supposedly by a rapid beating of its wings. Thus, the old phoenix was burned to death, but from its ashes a new bird came to life to continue the lineal cycle. In ancient and modern literature, the phoenix has been used by both imaginative and religious writers as a symbol of resurrection—of life coming from death.

In Fry's play, the phoenix obviously refers to the resurrection of love, not only in the very tomb of the deceased husband, Virilius, but with his dead body as the condition of its survival. Dynamene, who had come to the tomb to die for grief, offers her husband's corpse as a substitute for the body her new lover has lost. What attitude are we to take toward this surprising, some might say grisly, turn of events? Even her lover at first calls the offer "terrible, horrible." In fact, it would be possible to find people who would react with shock and moral dismay at the narrative of a widow whose vow of eternal fidelity to her husband is dissolved in the course of a single night by the attractions of a handsome, witty soldier who happens to stumble into the tomb where she is grieving. For these people, the sudden resurrection of love in the heart of the beautiful widow would be an excuse either for didactic denunciation or for cynical reflections about the inconstancy of women. They would consider the rebirth of this phoenix of love too frequent indeed.

But what is the appropriate attitude to take toward the central incident of the play? What can reconcile us to the suddenness with which Dynamene, under the influence of wine and masculine charm, turns from the cold morbidity of death to the engrossing passion for life? If we can only once feel deeply that life itself is a genuine miracle, then we cannot be too surprised at any true manifestation of its quickening power. Life rises from death in every form and aspect of being and resurrection is an act worthy of rejoicing. Then why should we question the miracle of love awakening in the very house of death? Dynamene gives the play's answer to the moralist in her reply to her lover:

> How little you can understand. I loved
> His life not his death. And now we can give his death
> The power of life. Not horrible: wonderful!
> Isn't it so? That I should be able to feel
> He moves again in the world, accomplishing
> Our welfare? It's more than my grief could do.

Far from being too frequent, the phoenix cannot be reborn often enough.

The beginning of the play prepares the way for the presentation of this attitude toward life and death and introduces the paradoxical and effervescent gaiety which characterizes Fry's metaphysical fooling. The stage directions describe an underground tomb practically in darkness and the line of trees on which dangle the bodies of the hanged men whom Tegeus has to guard until morning. But instead of the dolorous or macabre atmosphere which this setting should inspire, we are introduced to the comical chattering of the lively servant, Doto, whose attitude toward her mistress' suicidal intentions is feelingly expressed in the words:

> Honestly, I would rather have to sleep
> With a bald bee-keeper who was wearing his boots
> Than spend more days fasting and thirsting and crying
> In a tomb.

Doto's earthy reminiscences about her "recurring" lovers and her uncle's hardware shop and the good pair of shoes she once gave away without thinking provide an atmosphere in which it would be impossible to take a resolve of death seriously, even if it came from somebody more committed to death than Dynamene appears to be. She awakes from her dream in which her husband, Virilius, became a ship with a "white, scrubbed deck," to realize her insufficiency to the task she has set herself:

> Already I have disfigured
> My vigil. My cynical eyelids have soon dropped me
> In a dream.

Her exaggerated praise of her husband's punctilious and precise virtues leaves the reader with the impression that she is goading herself on to her sacrifice with rationalized incentives and that, in reality, she is a lover of life and its wonders.

> What a mad blacksmith creation is
> Who blows his furnaces until the stars fly upward
> And iron Time is hot and politicians glow
> And bulbs and roots sizzle into hyacinth
> And orchis, and the sand puts out the lion,
> Roaring yellow, and oceans bud with porpoises,
> Blenny, tunny and the almost unexisting
> Blindfish; . . .

The entrance of Tegeus, who becomes immediately intrigued with the seeming spectacle of uncorrupted devotion and perfect integrity, soon provides the motive for Dynamene's return to life. The middle of the play presents a sequence of discoveries in the course of which the two find out how wonderfully compatible they are. After the initial exchange of insults by Dynamene and mouth-filling oaths of innocence by Tegeus, they discover the similarity of their tastes in art, in wine, and in witty talk about all manner of subjects. Dynamene recognizes her helplessness in the grip of her natural instincts:

> Oh, how the inveterate body,
> Even when cut from the heart, insists on leaf,
> Puts out, with a separate meaningless will,
> Fronds to intercept the thankless sun.
> How it does, oh, how it does. And how it confuses
> The nature of the mind.

Tegeus, now renamed Chromis because "it has a breadlike sound," and she thinks of him "as a crisp loaf," manages with his wit and rhetoric to complete the work of regeneration and revivification. In what seems no time at all, they rush through the stages from compatibility to affection to passionate love. His arguments against remaining faithful to the memory of her husband are irresistible and soon her vows, the fear of ridicule, and the prickings of shame are wiped out in the wonder of their love. Just before she surrenders, Dynamene tries to understand herself:

> What appears
> Is so unlike what is. And what is madness

> To those who only observe, is often wisdom
> To those to whom it happens.

It is this swift resurrection of love in the tomb which best exemplifies the dramatist's attitude toward life as something always new and always miraculous. ". . . In my plays I want to look at life—at the commonplaces of existence—as if we had just turned a corner and run into it for the first time."

The phoenix symbolism of new life arising from the ashes of death comes to a climax with the turn of events at the end of the play where, in order to save her lover, Dynamene offers her husband's corpse as a substitute for the one he has lost. However, this episode merely puts into sharp focus what has already been said in the play about the quickening power of the instinct for life. If we can accept the sudden blossoming of love which we have just seen, we can go on to accept Dynamene's argument that her offer will give her husband's death "the power of life." And it is significant that after the lovers accept this resolution to their difficulty, the dramatist gives the last line to the unquench-able Doto, the voice of primitive life, who appears on the steps of the tomb calling out a toast to "The master. Both the masters."

Society

Frank Norris, the American naturalistic novelist, once wrote that the greatest novel is the one with a purpose. A gripping narrative is not enough; neither is insight into the motives of the main characters. What still is needed is an intent on the part of the author to show how men under given conditions operate. Norris himself tried to do this in a trilogy about the raising, trading, and consumption of wheat. Simplified, his point was that this great nourisher of mankind, instead of being a blessing to everyone it touches, is almost invari-ably a curse, because of the way men fight for the riches it brings.

That literature can be a criticism of life in a sociological sense is a relatively new idea. It became strongly apparent in England when Dickens' novels brought home to thousands the wretched conditions in London slums and prisons. In this country, as early a writer as Cooper touched upon economic matters, but it was not until the time of Twain, Howells, Norris, and Dreiser that social problems gained widespread treatment in imaginative literature. During the twentieth century many writers have used social issues as the main themes of their works: Shaw, Orwell, Malraux, Silone, Dos Passos, and others.

But we should not think that only recent literature has significant sociological content. Admittedly, modern writers have addressed themselves to social prob-lems more self-consciously than writers of the past, but every literary work in important ways reflects the culture that it is a part of. As W. Witte says:

. . . literature communicates significant experience. Now experience, of whatever order it may be, does not take place in a social vacuum. The life of the individual who has the experience is not a separate, self-sufficient entity; it is one particular thread in the larger fabric of the society in which he happens to live. It does not matter whether the individual's attitude towards that society is one of acquiescence or approval, or whether it is that of a rebel: as weft or warp, he remains part of the pattern. The society to which he belongs, even when he rebels against it, surrounds him and colours his view of the world.

The recognition of this social element in literature led in the nineteenth century to two enormously influential theories, both of which postulated that art is essentially an effect of certain sociological causes. Hippolyte Taine, the theoretical father of modern naturalism, saw literature as a product of race, environment, and "moment" (the pressure of the cumulative forces of the past). Karl Marx believed that literature is merely a part of a fragile cultural "superstructure" erected on the basic structure of economic conditions.

It is not necessary to accept an exclusively sociological theory, however, to justify inquiries into the social content of literature. We prefer Witte's view of the relationship between society and writer: society "colours his view of the world," not *determines* it, as Marx and Taine would have us believe. Society presents to the writer three important patterns or sets of beliefs which we will illustrate briefly: (1) mores, the customs and conventions that prescribe manners and regulate social intercourse; (2) the economic structure that determines the distribution of material wealth; and (3) the political structure that determines the ascription and use of governmental powers. Every society has also as part of its culture an ethic and a world view, often based on religion, but these aspects will be discussed in separate sections that follow.

Any analysis of the cultural elements in a literary work becomes unavoidably involved in unnatural separations. Mores, economics, and politics are interrelated and take a common hue from ethical and philosophical assumptions. We may take as an example John Steinbeck's famous novel *The Grapes of Wrath*. We can study with great profit the folkways and customs of the displaced Okies, the Joads: their great faith in family solidarity and in the soil, the engaging mixture in them of rural naïveté and ingenuity, their speech, their dress, their treatment of strangers, etc. We can study the economic conditions depicted in the novel: drought, foreclosure of farms, cruel exploitation by California fruit growers, the sharp division between haves and have-nots, etc. We can study the political elements in the book: the effects of the wedding of the government and the capitalist, an interlude of almost primitive communal life in a federal compound, the chauvinistic groups that ally themselves with the fruit growers, the labor agitation, etc. All of these studies would be necessary for the student who wished to understand fully this provocative novel. But the thorough student would not stop here; he would form of these individual findings a statement of the writer's unifying vision of his culture. Alfred Kazin sums up the achievement of the novel this way:

. . . the book brought the crisis [the depression] that had severed Americans from their history back into it by recalling what they had lost through it. It gave them a design, a sense of control, where out of other depression novels they could get only the aimless bombardment of rage. . . . It was as if Steinbeck, out of the simplicity of his indignation, had been just primitive enough to call men back to their humanity, to remind depression America that a culture is only the sum total of the human qualities that make it up. . . .

In discussing the social revelations of the literary work, then, we must keep firmly in mind that we are speaking of elements that must be reimbedded in the larger pattern of the work. For the great danger of the sociological yardstick is that it may lead us to begin thinking of literary works as social documents. We would then value only those works with political and economic implications that accord with our own ideas. But it is the richness and breadth of the cultural vision as one aspect of the work that we seek to discover.

The *Prologue* to the *Canterbury Tales* is generally regarded as one of the masterpieces of literary portraiture. Robert Kilburn Root has said, "the peculiar greatness of the *Prologue* may be said to reside in the vividness of its individual portraiture, and in the representative character of the whole series of portraits as a true picture of English life in the fourteenth century. . . . We behold not only the individual, but the type; the abstract type is made visible and real as embodied in the individual."

The great portrait painter, then, and by extension the great literary artist, weaves into his work three levels of details: the unique, the culturally typical, and the universal. At this point we are interested in the culturally typical. We will use the portraits reprinted in Part Four (p. 718-725) to illustrate how richly Chaucer revealed the society he knew.

The Knight and Squire are representatives of the chivalric ideal. The Knight is a seasoned warrior, having fought against heathens in Africa, Asia Minor, Russia, and Lithuania. He is religious and humble. The Squire has been in a few skirmishes, but his fighting has been to impress his lady, for he is the typical courtly lover. His accomplishments include fluting, riding, composing, drawing, jousting, and dancing. In short, the two men, for Chaucer and for his contemporary readers, represented the chivalric ideal of service to God, king, and lady.

From the portraits of the Prioress and the Friar and from other portraits not included in this book—Monk, Parson, Summoner, and Pardoner—we get a fairly complete picture of the ecclesiastical types in Chaucer's England. Apart from the valuable information about the ecclesiastical hierarchy, what is most interesting to note is Chaucer's revelation of the growing worldliness of the various kinds of churchmen. Though the Prioress is a sympathetic character, we can easily detect the encroachments of this world upon her eminently feminine soul: her coyness, her pretentious but bad French, her excessive mannerliness and tenderness, and the feminine eccentricities of her habit. The Friar is a much more extreme case of corruption. He uses his ecclesiastical powers to satisfy his appetite for women and money. He does not serve the poor, the supposed function of the various orders of mendicant friars, but hangs about taverns and the houses of the rich. From Chaucer's portraits of ecclesiastics we come to understand the religious ideals of his time and the regrettable departures from those ideals.

The Wife of Bath and the Miller represent the rising middle class of Chaucer's England. The Wife is a member of the urban mercantile class; the Miller, though technically a member of the old feudal order, has a great deal of independence and a lucrative monopoly on the preparation of grain in his locality. Both love money and good living. The Wife, more citified, has social pretensions. She must be first in order of precedence at the offering in her parish church. She likes men and travel, in combination if possible. The Miller is coarser. He likes noise, physical violence, and dirty jokes. But for Chaucer the common characteristics of these two are their vitality, worldliness, and aggressive materialism.

If you studied in detail all of the portraits and tales in *The Canterbury Tales*, you would come to a remarkably full understanding of the social, economic, and political conditions and of the cultural ideals of fourteenth-century England. Though you cannot expect to find this richness of social revelation in every work, you may always ask, as one legitimate measure of literary excellence: How convincingly does the writer explore the relationship between man and society? What does the writer reveal about the effects of customs and manners, the economic and the political system on character? In short, how rich is the writer's cultural design, how comprehensive his view?

Below are Kipling's "Recessional" and Orwell's criticism of Kipling's political position. To understand fully the implications of the essay, which is partly defense and partly attack, you should note carefully Orwell's distinctions between Liberal, Conservative, and Fascist. Why does Orwell hold that the stereotyped Liberal criticism of Kipling is shallow and hypocritical? What, according to Orwell, are Kipling's virtues and defects as a social observer? You will find it useful when you study "The Man Who Would Be King" (p. 378) to return to this essay by Orwell.

Rudyard Kipling

RECESSIONAL

God of our fathers, known of old,
Lord of our far-flung battle-line,
Beneath whose awful Hand we hold

From *The Five Nations* by Rudyard Kipling. Reprinted by permission of Mrs. Kipling, Doubleday, Doran and Co., Inc., and the Macmillan Co. of Canada Limited.

Dominion over palm and pine—
Lord God of Hosts, be with us yet,   5
Lest we forget—lest we forget!

The tumult and the shouting dies;
   The Captains and the Kings depart:
Still stands Thine ancient sacrifice,
   An humble and a contrite heart.   10
Lord God of Hosts, be with us yet,
Lest we forget—lest we forget!

Far-called, our navies melt away;
   On dune and headland sinks the fire:
Lo, all our pomp of yesterday   15
   Is one with Nineveh and Tyre!
Judge of the Nations, spare us yet,
Lest we forget—lest we forget!

If, drunk with sight of power, we loose
   Wild tongues that have not Thee in awe,   20
Such boastings as the Gentiles use,
   Or lesser breeds without the Law—
Lord God of Hosts, be with us yet,
Lest we forget—lest we forget!

For heathen heart that puts her trust   25
   In reeking tube and iron shard,
All valiant dust that builds on dust,
   And guarding, calls not Thee to guard,
For frantic boast and foolish word—
Thy Mercy on Thy People, Lord! (1897)

George Orwell

KIPLING'S POLITICS

It was a pity that Mr. Eliot should be so much on the defensive in the long essay with which he prefaces this selection of Kipling's poetry, but it was not to be avoided, because before one can even speak about Kipling one has to clear away a legend that has been created by two sets of people who have not read his works. Kipling is in the peculiar position of having been a byword for fifty years. During five literary generations every enlightened person has despised him, and at the end of that time nine-tenths of those enlightened persons are forgotten and Kipling is in some sense still there. Mr. Eliot never satisfactorily explains this fact, because in answering the shallow and familiar charge that Kipling is a "Fascist", he falls into the opposite error of defending him where he is not defensible. It is no use pretending that Kipling's view of life, as a whole, can be accepted or even forgiven by any civilized person. It is no use claiming, for instance, that when Kipling describes a British soldier beating a "nigger" with a cleaning rod in order to get money out of him, he is acting merely as a reporter and does not necessarily approve what he describes. There is not the slightest sign anywhere in Kipling's work that he disapproves of that kind of conduct—on the contrary, there is a definite strain of sadism in him, over and above the brutality which a writer of that type has to have. Kipling is a jingo imperialist, he is morally insensitive and æsthetically disgusting. It is better to start by admitting that, and then to try to find out why it is that he survives while the refined people who have sniggered at him seem to wear so badly.

And yet the "Fascist" charge has to be answered, because the first clue to any understanding of Kipling, morally or politically, is the fact that he was *not* a Fascist. He was further from being one than the most humane or the most "progressive" person is able to be nowadays. An interesting instance of the way in which quotations are parroted to and fro without any attempt to look up their context or discover their meaning is the line from *Recessional,* "Lesser breeds without the Law". This line is always good for a snigger in pansy-left circles. It is assumed as a matter of course that the "lesser breeds" are "natives", and a mental picture is called up of some pukka sahib in a pith helmet kicking a coolie. In its context the sense of the line is almost the exact opposite of this. The phrase "lesser breeds" refers almost certainly to the Germans, and especially the pan-German writers, who are "without the Law" in the sense of being lawless, not in the sense of being powerless. The whole poem, conventionally thought of as an orgy of boasting, is a denunciation of power politics, British as well as German. Two stanzas are worth quoting (I am quoting this as politics, not as poetry):

> "If, drunk with sight of power, we loose
> Wild tongues that have not Thee in awe,
> Such boastings as the Gentiles use,
> Or lesser breeds without the Law—
> Lord God of hosts, be with us yet,
> Lest we forget—lest we forget!
>
> "For heathen heart that puts her trust
> In reeking tube and iron shard,

> All valiant dust that builds on dust,
> And guarding, calls not Thee to guard,
> For frantic boast and foolish word—
> Thy mercy on Thy People, Lord!"

Much of Kipling's phraseology is taken from the Bible, and no doubt in the second stanza he had in mind the text from Psalm cxxvii.: "Except the Lord build the house, they labour in vain that build it; except the Lord keep the city, the watchman waketh but in vain." It is not a text that makes much impression on the post-Hitler mind. No one, in our time, believes in any sanction greater than military power; no one believes that it is possible to overcome force except by greater force. There is no "law", there is only power. I am not saying that that is a true belief, merely that it is the belief which all modern men do actually hold. Those who pretend otherwise are either intellectual cowards, or power-worshippers under a thin disguise, or have simply not caught up with the age they are living in. Kipling's outlook is pre-Fascist. He still believes that pride comes before a fall and that the gods punish *hubris*. He does not foresee the tank, the bombing plane, the radio and the secret police, or their psychological results.

But in saying this, does not one unsay what I said above about Kipling's jingoism and brutality? No, one is merely saying that the nineteenth-century imperialist outlook and the modern gangster outlook are two different things. Kipling belongs very definitely to the period 1885-1902. The Great War and its aftermath embittered him, but he shows little sign of having learned anything from any event later than the Boer War. He was the prophet of British Imperialism in its expansionist phase (even more than his poems, his solitary novel, *The Light That Failed*, gives you the atmosphere of that time) and also the unofficial historian of the British Army, the old mercenary army which began to change its shape in 1914. All his confidence, his bouncing vulgar vitality, sprang out of limitations which no Fascist or near-Fascist shares.

Kipling spent the later part of his life in sulking, and no doubt it was political disappointment rather than literary vanity that accounted for this. Somehow history had not gone according to plan. After the greatest victory she had ever known, Britain was a lesser world power than before, and Kipling was quite acute enough to see this. The virtue had gone out of the classes he idealised, the young were hedonistic or disaffected, the desire to paint the map red had evaporated. He could not understand what was happening, because he had never had any grasp of the economic forces underlying imperial expansion. It is notable that Kipling does not seem to realise, any more than the average soldier or colonial administrator, that an empire is primarily a money-making concern. Imperialism as he sees it is a sort of forcible evangelizing. You turn a Gatling gun on a mob of unarmed "natives", and then you establish "the law", which includes roads, railways and a court-house. He could not foresee, therefore, that the same motives which brought the Empire into existence would end by destroying it. It was the same motive, for example, that caused the Malayan jungles to be cleared for rubber estates, and which now causes those estates to be handed over intact to the Japanese. The modern totalitarians know what they are doing, and the nineteenth-century English did not know what they were doing. Both attitudes have their advantages, but Kipling was never able to move forward from one into the other. His outlook, allowing for the fact that after all he was an artist, was that of the salaried bureaucrat who despises the "box-wallah" and often lives a lifetime without realizing that the "box-wallah" calls the tune.

But because he identifies himself with the official class, he does possess one thing which "enlightened" people seldom or never possess, and that is a sense of responsibility. The middle-class Left hate him for this quite as much as for his cruelty and vulgarity. All left-wing parties in the highly industrialized countries are at bottom a sham, because they make it their business to fight against something which they do not really wish to destroy. They have internationalist aims, and at the same time they struggle to keep up a standard of life with which those aims are incompatible. We all live by robbing Asiatic coolies, and those of us who are "enlightened" all maintain that those coolies ought to be set free; but our standard of living, and hence our "enlightenment", demands that the robbery shall continue. A humanitarian is always a hypocrite, and Kipling's understanding of this is perhaps the central secret of his power to create telling phrases. It would be difficult to hit off the one-eyed pacifism of the English in fewer words than in the phrase, "making mock of uniforms that guard you while you sleep". It is true that Kipling does not understand the economic aspect of the relationship between the highbrow and the blimp. He does not see that the map is painted red chiefly in order that the coolie may be exploited. Instead of the coolie he sees the Indian Civil Servant; but even on that plane his grasp of function, of who protects whom, is very sound. He sees clearly that men can only be highly civilized while other men, inevitably less civilized, are there to guard and feed them.

How far does Kipling really identify himself with the administrators, soldiers and engineers whose praises he sings? Not so completely as is sometimes assumed. He had travelled very widely while he was still a young man, he had grown up with a brilliant mind in mainly philistine surroundings, and some streak in him that may have been partly neurotic led him to prefer the active man to the sensitive man. The nineteenth-century Anglo-Indians, to name the least sympathetic of his idols, were at any rate people who did things. It may be that all that they did was evil, but they changed the face of the earth (it is instructive to look at a map of Asia and compare the railway system of India with that of the surrounding countries), whereas they could have achieved nothing, could not have maintained themselves in power for a single week, if the normal Anglo-Indian outlook had been that of, say, E. M. Forster. Tawdry and shallow though it is, Kipling's is the only literary picture that we possess of nineteenth-century Anglo-India, and he could only make it because he was just coarse enough to be able to exist and keep his mouth shut in clubs and regimental messes. But he did not greatly resemble the people he admired. I know from several private sources that many of the Anglo-Indians who were Kipling's contemporaries did not like or approve of him. They said, no doubt truly, that he knew nothing about India, and on the other hand, he was from their point of view too much of a highbrow. While in India he tended to mix with "the wrong" people, and because of his dark complexion he was wrongly suspected of having a streak of Asiatic blood. Much in his development is traceable to his having been born in India and having left school early. With a slightly different background he might have been a good novelist or a superlative writer of music-hall songs. But how true is it that he was a vulgar flag-waver, a sort of publicity agent for Cecil Rhodes? It is true, but it is not true that he was a yes-man or a time-server. After his early days, if then, he never courted public opinion. Mr. Eliot says that what is held against him is that he expressed unpopular views in a popular style. This narrows the issue by assuming that "unpopular" means unpopular with the intelligentsia, but it is a fact that Kipling's "message" was one that the big public did not want, and, indeed, has never accepted. The mass of the people, in the 'nineties as now, were anti-militarist, bored by the Empire and only unconsciously patriotic. Kipling's official admirers are and were the "service" middle class, the people who read *Blackwood's*. In the stupid early years of this century, the blimps, having at last discovered someone who could be called a poet and who was on their side, set Kipling on a pedestal, and some of his more sententious poems, such as *If*, were given almost Biblical status. But it is doubtful whether the blimps have ever read him with attention, any more than they have read the Bible. Much of what he says they could not possibly approve. Few people who have criticised England from the inside have said bitterer things about her than this gutter patriot. As a rule it is the British working class that he is attacking, but not always. That phrase about "the flannelled fools at the wicket and the muddied oafs at the goal" sticks like an arrow to this day, and it is aimed at the Eton and Harrow match as well as the Cup-Tie Final. Some of the verses he wrote about the Boer War have a curiously modern ring, so far as their subject-matter goes. *Stellenbosch*, which must have been written about 1902, sums up what every intelligent infantry officer was saying in 1918, or is saying now, for that matter. . . .

One reason for Kipling's power as a good bad poet I have already suggested—his sense of responsibility, which made it possible for him to have a world-view, even though it happened to be a false one. Although he had no direct connection with any political party, Kipling was a Conservative, a thing that does not exist nowadays. Those who now call themselves Conservatives are either Liberals, Fascists or the accomplices of Fascists. He identified himself with the ruling power and not with the opposition. In a gifted writer this seems to us strange and even disgusting, but it did have the advantage of giving Kipling a certain grip on reality. The ruling power is always faced with the question, "In such and such circumstances, what would you *do*?", whereas the opposition is not obliged to take responsibility or make any real decisions. Where it is a permanent and pensioned opposition, as in England, the quality of its thought deteriorates accordingly. Moreover, anyone who starts out with a pessimistic, reactionary view of life tends to be justified by events, for Utopia never arrives and "the gods of the copybook headings", as Kipling himself put it, always return. Kipling sold out to the British governing class, not financially but emotionally. This warped his political judgment, for the British ruling class were not what he imagined, and it led him into abysses of folly and snobbery, but he gained a corresponding advantage from having at least tried to imagine what action and responsibility are like. It is a great thing in his favour that he is not witty, not "daring", has no wish to *épater les bourgeois*. He dealt largely in platitudes, and since we live in a world of platitudes, much of what he said sticks. Even his worst follies seem less shallow and less irritating than the "enlightened" utterances of the same period, such as Wilde's epigrams or the collection of cracker-mottoes at the end of *Man and Superman*. (1942)

Morality

Within the last one hundred years or so certain theorists have proclaimed that the function of literature is solely esthetic, or sociological, or psychologically therapeutic. But such exclusive theories are distinctly modern. The great students and practitioners of literature in the past—men like Aristotle, Dante, Milton, and Johnson—have always held that one important function of literature is to uphold moral behavior. According to Matthew Arnold, the great English critic, the desire of great writers is to "educe and cultivate what is best and noblest in themselves." Speaking of the classical Greek poets whom he especially admired, Arnold pointed out that from them we can learn "how unspeakably superior is the effect of one moral impression left by a great action treated as a whole, to the effect produced by the most striking simple thought or by the happiest image." The implication is that the great artist organizes his whole work around a central moral principle. This same view of the essentially ethical function of literature is stoutly defended today by humanist critics like Douglas Bush, who has said of literature, "the ultimate end [of reading literature], according to my creed, is that literature is ethical, that it makes us better."

Few would disagree that literature with the power to bring out the best in us has a high claim to greatness. In fact, the only real claim that any source of moral principles has upon us is its ability to lead us to ultimate good. But we cannot apply so abstract a concept to specific literary works. We need to define what the ultimate good is and derive from that definition a moral system capable of informing us of the rightness of thinking and acting in particular cases. Such a system is called an ethic. If there were a universally accepted ethic, the problem of the moral evaluation of literature would be greatly simplified. Our only disagreements about the excellence of a particular work would involve matters of presentation, how forcefully the work dramatizes the particular moral principle that it embodies. But there is no universal ethic. The vexing question is simply this: How can we apply the yardstick of morality when the nature of the yardstick (the ethic) is not agreed upon?

Suppose we said that certain basic moral principles appeal to all men and, looking to Aristotle's great *Nicomachean Ethics*, listed such cardinal attributes as courage, temperance, honor, justice, mercy, wisdom, friendship, moderation, and contemplation. Such a list would certainly have great appeal for most men in western civilization. But an adherent to the ethic of one of the great eastern religions like Buddhism, Hinduism, or Taoism, might offer a list of basic moral attributes with significant differences: simplicity, gentleness, compassion, self-denial, passivity, and mystical meditation. Such attributes, of course, are not unadmired in the western world. Great writers as different as Thoreau and T. S. Eliot have found Oriental philosophies an important source of spiritual sustenance. But the point is that no single list of cardinal virtues is truly universal.

In fact, western civilization itself has conflicting ethical traditions. Hedonists and Epicureans find the highest ethical good in the pursuit of pleasure and the avoidance of pain. The ethic of the Utilitarians, notably Jeremy Bentham and John Stuart Mill, was similar though less individualistic. They spoke of the greatest possible happiness for the greatest number of people. In the eighteenth century the idea of a sort of sixth "moral sense" was popular; the good man was the sensitive man easily moved to compassion and benevolence. Naturalists, like Herbert Spencer, find the highest good in conforming to nature, adapting oneself to one's environment. Certain modern theorists, influenced by the findings of psychoanalysis, insist on the avoidance of repression and the liberation of the creative forces of the instincts, the libido. Perhaps the most influential ethical tradition of the western world is Humanism. Based on the teachings of Socrates, Plato, and Aristotle, Humanism postulates that the highest good for man is the development and use of his most human attribute, the one that distinguishes him from all else in creation: reason. For Aristotle, reason has two main functions: to contemplate the universe and to regulate the lower impulses. So great was the appeal of Humanism as it was embodied in classical literature that during the late Middle Ages and the Renaissance it virtually transformed the Christian ethic, leavening faith with reason and otherworldliness with a sense of the orderliness and goodness of this world.

We have, of course, traced only the broad outline of the diversity of ethical thought in the western world. But it is enough to make us realize that readers come to literature with a great variety of moral convictions. Even so, our yardstick of ethical insight need not be a hopelessly relative thing. We must begin by admitting that any reader will tend to approve those works that embody an ethic like his own; but we can go on to say that any work is valuable that dramatizes clearly and powerfully a set of moral convictions. In fact, only the dogmatic reader rejects as pernicious every work embracing ethical principles different from his own. An Irish patriot or a Catholic will not approve of the decision of Stephen Daedalus in James Joyce's *Portrait of the Artist as a*

Young Man to break allegiance with the church and with Ireland, but he can appreciate the moral fervor of the young man and the seriousness of his decision. A Christian of traditional beliefs cannot easily sanction the emphasis on sexual freedom in the novels of D. H. Lawrence, but he may value the insight into the evil consequences of harsh repression. Such a reader may also have mixed feelings about Fry's *A Phoenix Too Frequent* (p. 619) and Mark Ashin's defense of the play (p. 207). But the point is that the generous reader welcomes the chance to enrich his knowledge of all ethical positions and the opportunity to test his own convictions by seriously studying views both traditional and unorthodox.

If we can agree that one's moral life is richer for accepting the challenge to encounter a variety of ethical positions, then we have a real basis for measuring literature according to the yardstick of moral worth. The attempt to make such an evaluation raises several basic questions. Is the moral position of the work clear? Does the writer honestly explore the logical implications of his moral position? Some critics, for instance, find the moral content of Wordsworth's "Ode: Intimations of Immortality from Recollections of Early Childhood" (p. 756) unclear. They say that the praise of the receptivity of the child is sentimental. Others find the "Beauty is truth, truth beauty" formula in Keats' "Ode on a Grecian Urn" (p. 766) a moral equivocation. Does the writer's ethic take into account the great complexity of human experience? No serious reader is engaged by the silly and platitudinous verse that too often appears in the columns of our newspapers and magazines. Sinclair Lewis has T. Cholmondelay Frink, the newspaper poet in *Babbitt*, compose the following lyric:

I sat alone and groused and thunk, and scratched my head and sighed and wunk, and groaned, "There still are boobs, alack, who'd like the old-time gin-mill back; that den that makes a sage a loon, the vile and smelly old saloon!" I'll never miss their poison booze, whilst I the bubbling spring can use, that leaves my head at merry morn as clear as any babe new-born!

Unfortunately the piece is not much worse than many of the kind it burlesques. Another question involves the way in which the writer presents moral content. Does he maintain dramatic and artistic interest or does he lapse into mere moralizing? Some critics have found that Tennyson's view of his role as public poet led him on occasion to write little moralistic essays in verse instead of poetry. The great neoclassic poets like Dryden and Pope raised their moralistic poetry to the level of great art through the great precision of their language and imagery as well as through the wisdom of their utterances.

Certainly, then, one legitimate measure of greatness in a literary work is its ability to heighten our moral perception, to lead us to reëxamine our own convictions.

Browning's "The Bishop Orders His Tomb at St. Praxed's Church" and Stuart Tave's

analysis of the moral elements of the poem follow. Tave finds the bishop thoroughly sensuous and materialistic, yet not contemptible. Compare with Tave's view the following comment by Ruskin: "I know no other piece of modern English prose or poetry in which there is so much told, as in these lines, of the Renaissance spirit—its worldliness, inconsistency, pride, hypocrisy, ignorance of itself, love of art, of luxury, and of good Latin." After formulating your own judgment of the moral content of the poem, speculate about the reaction of others whose moral convictions differ from yours. For example, how would a Hedonist judge the bishop? A Naturalist? A Christian Humanist?

Robert Browning

THE BISHOP ORDERS HIS TOMB AT SAINT PRAXED'S CHURCH

Rome, 15—

Vanity, saith the preacher, vanity!
Draw round my bed; is Anselm keeping back?
Nephews—sons mine . . . ah, God, I know not! Well—
She, men would have to be your mother once,
Old Gandolf envied me, so fair she was!   5
What's done is done, and she is dead beside,
Dead long ago, and I am Bishop since,
And as she died so must we die ourselves,
And thence ye may perceive the world's a dream.
Life, how and what is it? As here I lie   10
In this state-chamber, dying by degrees,
Hours and long hours in the dead night, I ask,
"Do I live, am I dead?" Peace, peace seems all.
Saint Praxed's ever was the church for peace;
And so, about this tomb of mine. I fought   15
With tooth and nail to save my niche, ye know—
Old Gandolf cozened me, despite my care;
Shrewd was that snatch from out the corner South
He graced his carrion with, God curse the same!
Yet still my niche is not so cramped but thence   20
One sees the pulpit o' the epistle-side,
And somewhat of the choir, those silent seats,

And up into the aëry dome where live
The angels, and a sunbeam's sure to lurk;
And I shall fill my slab of basalt there,   25
And 'neath my tabernacle take my rest,
With those nine columns round me, two and two,
The odd one at my feet where Anselm stands:
Peach-blossom marble all, the rare, the ripe
As fresh-poured red wine of a mighty pulse.   30
—Old Gandolf with his paltry onion-stone,
Put me where I may look at him! True peach,
Rosy and flawless; how I earned the prize!
Draw close; that conflagration of my church—
What then? So much was saved if aught were missed!   35
My sons, ye would not be my death? Go dig
The white-grape vineyard where the oil-press stood,
Drop water gently till the surface sink,
And if ye find . . . Ah, God, I know not, I! . . .
Bedded in store of rotten fig-leaves soft,   40
And corded up in a tight olive-frail,
Some lump, ah, God, of *lapis lazuli,*
Big as a Jew's head cut off at the nape,
Blue as a vein o'er the Madonna's breast . . .
Sons, all have I bequeathed you, villas, all,   45
That brave Frascati villa with its bath,
So, let the blue lump poise between my knees,
Like God the Father's globe on both his hands
Ye worship in the Jesu Church so gay,
For Gandolf shall not choose but see and burst!   50
Swift as a weaver's shuttle fleet our years;
Man goeth to the grave, and where is he?
Did I say basalt for my slab, sons? Black—
'Twas ever antique-black I meant! How else
Shall ye contrast my frieze to come beneath?   55
The bas-relief in bronze ye promised me,
Those Pans and Nymphs ye wot of, and perchance
Some tripod, thyrsus, with a vase or so,
The Savior at his sermon on the mount,
Saint Praxed in a glory, and one Pan   60
Ready to twitch the Nymph's last garment off,
And Moses with the tables . . . but I know
Ye mark me not! What do they whisper thee,
Child of my bowels, Anselm? Ah, ye hope
To revel down my villas while I gasp   65
Bricked o'er with beggar's moldy travertine
Which Gandolf from his tomb-top chuckles at!

Nay, boys, ye love me—all of jasper, then!
'Tis jasper ye stand pledged to, lest I grieve.
My bath must needs be left behind, alas!   70
One block, pure green as a pistachio-nut,
There's plenty jasper somewhere in the world—
And have I not Saint Praxed's ear to pray
Horses for ye, and brown Greek manuscripts,
And mistresses with great smooth marbly limbs? 75
—That's if ye carve my epitaph aright
Choice Latin, picked phrase, Tully's every word,
No gaudy ware like Gandolf's second line—
Tully, my masters? Ulpian serves his need!
And then how I shall lie through centuries,   80
And hear the blessed mutter of the Mass,
And see God made and eaten all day long,
And feel the steady candle-flame, and taste
Good strong thick stupefying incense-smoke!
For as I lie here, hours of the dead night,   85
Dying in state and by such slow degrees,
I fold my arms as if they clasped a crook,
And stretch my feet forth straight as stone can point,
And let the bedclothes, for a mortcloth, drop
Into great laps and folds of sculptor's work; 90
And as yon tapers dwindle, and strange thoughts
Grow, with a certain humming in my ears
About the life before I lived this life,
And this life too, popes, cardinals, and priests,
Saint Praxed at his sermon on the mount,   95
Your tall pale mother with her talking eyes,
And new-found agate urns as fresh as day,
And marble's language, Latin pure, discreet—
Aha, ELUCESCEBAT quoth our friend?
No Tully, said I, Ulpian at the best!   100
Evil and brief hath been my pilgrimage.
All *lapis,* all, sons! Else I give the Pope
My villas! Will ye ever eat my heart?
Ever your eyes were as a lizard's quick,
They glitter like your mother's for my soul, 105
Or ye would heighten my impoverished frieze,
Piece out its starved design, and fill my vase
With grapes, and add a visor and a term,
And to the tripod ye would tie a lynx
That in his struggle throws the thyrsus down, 110
To comfort me on my entablature
Whereon I am to lie till I must ask,

"Do I live, am I dead?" There, leave me, there!
For ye have stabbed me with ingratitude
To death—ye wish it—God, ye wish it! Stone— 115
Gritstone, a-crumble! Clammy squares which sweat
As if the corpse they keep were oozing through—
And no more *lapis* to delight the world!
Well, go! I bless ye. Fewer tapers there,
But in a row; and, going, turn your backs— 120
Aye, like departing altar-ministrants,
And leave me in my church, the church for peace,
That I may watch at leisure if he leers—
Old Gandolf—at me, from his onion-stone,
As still he envied me, so fair she was! (1845) 125

Stuart M. Tave

BROWNING'S
"THE BISHOP ORDERS HIS
TOMB AT SAINT PRAXED'S CHURCH"

The bishop is a man who has held spiritual office, and who has led a full and enjoyable worldly life. He is a priest who has struggled successfully with his ecclesiastical rival, Gandolf, for the affections of the fair woman who bore his so-called "nephews." He has lived well in handsome villas; he has accumulated the good things of this world. Nor has he been above a little sly purloining to acquire his goods: the *lapis lazuli* missing from his church after a fire, it now develops, is secretly buried in his vineyard. Even now, on his deathbed, his chief thought is for his worldly remains, the elaborate tomb that will outshine Gandolf once again. The tomb itself is an incongruous mixture of flesh and spirit, the near naked nymph and the sermon on the mount, as his dying words are a mixture of Biblical quotations on the vanity of earthly life and an intense desire to hold fast to vanity beyond death.

But if the bishop is a worldly man, he is not a contemptible man. If, as a bishop, the body has occupied him over much, there is no sign that he has been gross in his pleasures. If he has loved flesh, he has not been a promiscuous lover. He has tasted pleasure finely. His interests extend to Greek manuscripts and the niceties of Latin style; he is a connoisseur of the fine arts. His great redeeming quality is that he is not a hypocrite in grain. He has perhaps fooled the world, but he has not fooled himself. He has a protective ingenuousness, an insensibility to his spiritual failings that is an odd contrast to his sensitive physical perceptiveness. He is not repentant on his deathbed; other than the platitudes he recites automatically there is no sign that he has any strong consciousness of wrongdoing. What he has done he has done from his heart; he has loved his life and he is rejoicing in the physical accompaniments of his death. He expects his tomb to delight the world; it is a prize he has earned.

The bishop lives and dies a consistent sensuous man, lives and dies with his body. It is the bath of the Frascati villa that he remembers most, it is the bath that he regrets he cannot take with him. Experience comes to him through the physical senses, and he dwells upon it with relish, with an intense pleasure expressed in the imagery of his speech. He loves the large, full, unadulterated, and perfect sensation: "mistresses with great smooth marbly limbs"; their size, touch, and heroic texture are all present to him; he rolls the liquids, *r*'s and *l*'s, with caressing feeling. Nothing but the finest material satisfies him, marbly limbs in life, a marble tomb in death, "marble's language" for his epitaph: "Choice Latin, picked phrase"—Latin becomes a material to be fingered, fine fruit—"No gaudy ware," "Latin pure." Images of fine food, images of sound, smell, and taste, of sight, and above all, of touch, the most intimate of the senses, pervade his speech.

His tomb must have physical room. In physical images he has fought, "tooth and nail," with Gandolf to save his niche, not with entire success because Gandolf has died earlier and made his shrewd "snatch." Still, the bishop rejoices, he is not so "cramped," but he will enjoy, after death, sight of the epistle-side of the pulpit, of somewhat of the choir (he is very precise in perception), and of the aëry dome, where (among the angels) "a sunbeam's sure to lurk." The colors of the tomb are brilliant, individually and in contrast. The surrounding nine columns, perfect in number (the trinity of trinities) and perfectly placed, will be "Peach-blossom marble all." They are living fruits to him, "the rare, the ripe/As fresh-poured red wine of a mighty pulse." And again he turns over in his mouth the luscious liquid consonants. He delights in returning to a word, to savor the thing and the sound again: "True peach,/Rosy and flawless." The columns are a fruit color, which is in turn a wine color. Old Gandolf used onion-stone. The green jasper that the bishop later asks for wildly is a nut color, "One block, pure green as a pistachio-nut." All colors of his tomb he must have in their utmost intensity. The slab of basalt later becomes "antique-black," because "How else/Shall ye contrast my frieze to come beneath?" The *lapis lazuli*—he loves the word—is the purest, tenderest, and most intense physical blue, "Blue as a vein o'er the Madonna's breast." (The bishop notices the details of religious art; he also recalls most the *color* of the brown Greek manuscripts.) The *lapis lazuli* is the heaviest physical "lump," again presented with an intense tactile image of the body, "Big as a Jew's head cut off at the nape." It is to rest in poise in contact with his body, "between my knees,/Like God the Father's globe on both his hands." And its present secret place he describes in a series of images again intense with fruit, color, and close touch.

> Go dig
> The white-grape vineyard where the oil-press stood,

> Drop water gently till the surface sink,
> And if ye find . . . Ah, God, I know not, I! . . .
> Bedded in a store of rotten fig-leaves soft,
> And corded up in a tight olive-frail,
> Some lump . . .

The striking figure on the frieze, because so oddly contrasted with the Savior, St. Praxed, and Moses, is the Pan "Ready to twitch the Nymph's last garment off"—again the last, poised moment of tactile experience. The bas-relief itself, of course, is literally open to the touch.

With this blessed abode before his imagination he contemplates the prolonged satisfaction of sensuousness:

> . . . how I shall lie through centuries,
> And *hear* the blessed mutter of the Mass,
> And *see* God made and eaten all day long,
> And *feel* the steady candle-flame, and *taste*
> Good strong thick stupefying incense-smoke!

There are few words that do not carry weight in these lines, none in that slow and heavy climactic line of rapt satiety. And so the bishop grows luxuriously from his present body into that eternal, beautiful, statuesque body that he shall be, in a series of tactile images:

> I fold my arms as if they clasped a crook,
> And stretch my feet forth straight as stone can point,
> And let the bedclothes, for a mortcloth, drop
> Into great laps and folds of sculptor's work.

This is his heaven. His hell, if his sons do not fulfill his desires, will be a hell of starvation and things unpleasant to the touch. The frieze will have a "starved" design. The bishop will have no easy comfort in his niche; he will suffocate, "gasp/Bricked o'er with beggar's moldy travertine." His tomb will be

> Gritstone, a-crumble! Clammy squares which sweat
> As if the corpse they keep were oozing through.

But his vision of hell is momentary only. The bishop is dying well, dying as he lived, tasting the experience moment by moment. He begins his speech by dwelling on death, slowly revolving all the derivatives of the word, "dead . . . Dead . . . died . . . die . . . dying . . . dead . . . dead" (ll. 6-13), applying them to the mother of his sons, to the world at large, to the night, to himself. He is "dying by degrees,/Hours and long hours," not in pain. He is poised: "Do I live, am I dead?" He is at peace. "Peace, peace seems all,/Saint Praxed's ever was the church for peace." The bishop's ear delights in softness and silence: the church, the silent seats he will see from his niche, the blessed mutter of the Mass, the talking eyes of his dead beloved. And so after his brief vision of hell he returns to his peace. He reduces the number of tapers, but has them arranged carefully, and directs the ceremony of the departure of his sons. In peace he enjoys his death and his life; the distinction is lost, as it must be for so ingenuous and entire a materialist.

Philosophy

When we speak of a yardstick of philosophical insight, we are using the term *philosophical* in a broad sense. We mean to signify the great range of ideas expressed in literature, from the vast skein of metaphysical speculation in *Moby Dick* to the simple concept in Whitman's "When I Heard the Learn'd Astronomer" (p. 116) that scientific truth is not the ultimate truth. The enormous difference in philosophical complexity between Melville's novel and Whitman's poem suggests a qualification: The yardstick of philosophical insight is not equally applicable to all literary works. Look at Shelley's sonnet "Ozymandias" (p. 762). The idea of the poem can be simply stated: Time mocks and destroys the works of the mighty and the proud. No one reading the poem is likely to feel that the philosophical content is either original or very profound, though he will probably agree that it is true. What makes the poem memorable is not the idea but the dramatization of the idea and the selection of details. This does not mean that we are ever altogether excused from attending to the ideas in short and simple works. Here is another poem:

Anonymous, **THE VOYAGE OF LIFE**

Life is but a journey free
Upon a fair and feastful sea
Where sunbright fish and freshets of rain
Are every farer's easy gain

Speak not to me of endless strife,
Of the fateful journey that is life.
I see horizons wide and white,
Unbroken arches, hope's bright light.

Quite apart from matters of imagery, diction, and tone, the idea of the poem is fatuous. Many great poets have seen life metaphorically as a sea journey, but none have reveled in absolute absence of struggle.

Philosophical ideas in literary works almost always have ethical implications. The writer may begin by exploring such things as the meaning of change, the nature of time, the nature of man, the relationship between man and God, the relationship between God and nature, etc., but probably he will end by implying some judgment about human conduct. (The ethical implication of Shelley's "Ozymandias" is roughly this: Do not attempt to achieve immortality through earthly works.) However, since we have discussed the moral insights of literature in the preceding section, we confine ourselves here, if somewhat arbitrarily, to those ideas in literature that deal primarily with the nature of things: God, man, nature, time, death, immortality, etc.

We have said that the yardstick of philosophical insight is most useful for evaluating those works in which the author self-consciously addresses himself to more or less complex philosophical ideas. But we have not said exactly how the yardstick is to be used. For instance, do we expect of a philosophical poem, say Yeats' "Among School Children" (p. 796), the same sort of logical exactness that we expect of an actual piece of philosophical writing like Aristotle's *Metaphysics*? Obviously not. How do we apply the yardstick of philosophical insight then? Eliot, writing about Dante's *Divine Comedy* and about philosophical poetry in general, says this:

Without doubt, the effort of the philosopher proper, the man who is trying to deal with ideas in themselves, and the effort of the poet, who may be trying to realize ideas, cannot be carried on at the same time. But this is not to deny that poetry can be in some sense philosophic. The poet can deal with philosophic ideas, not as matter for argument, but as matter for inspection. The original form of a philosophy cannot be poetic. But poetry can be penetrated by a philosophic idea. . . . Dante, more than any other poet, has succeeded in dealing with his philosophy, not as a theory (in the modern and not the Greek sense of that word) or as his own comment or reflection, but in terms of something perceived.

From these remarks by Eliot we may attempt to formulate a statement about the philosophical content of imaginative literature: Philosophical ideas in their naked, abstract form are not imaginative literature, but if, as in Dante's *Divine Comedy*, they are transformed into a world of memorable places, people, and events, then they are artistically *realized*, objectified.

For the student who wishes to evaluate a literary work according to the yardstick of philosophical insight, the question is not how much philosophical content the work has but how well the philosophical content and the dramatic or the sensually perceptible elements are integrated. Think of the philosophical ideas as a shapely scaffolding upon which the writer fashions an integument of certain colors and textures. In the consummate work the scaffolding will be perfectly sufficient to support and shape the visible surfaces. If the scaffolding is overelaborate and shows through the surface, then we may charge the work with being overintellectualized (Samuel Johnson's main criticism of the poetry of Donne and the seventeenth-century metaphysical poets). If the scaffolding is not firm, then we may charge the work with being too sensuous or too emotional or both (a common criticism of a great deal of Romantic poetry).

The chief danger in this yardstick lies in its current popularity. Too often overingenious critics find vast mythical structures, allegories, and metaphysical schemata in works that are essentially much simpler than they would have us believe. We have already mentioned the unfortunate distortions of *Huckleberry Finn*. Another danger involves the question of belief. What do we say to the agnostic who hesitates to read Dante's *Divine Comedy*? He feels that he will not get much from the work because he does not believe in Heaven, Hell, and Purgatory. The answer is that belief, of course, intensifies enjoyment, but is not absolutely necessary. One need not accept the philosophical ideas and the theological tenets of a great work to appreciate its excellent integration of abstract concept and vivid details or to learn a great deal from it about man's condition.

In evaluating the literary work according to the yardstick of philosophical insight, we formulate and evaluate as best we can the themes, the philosophical ideas; then we try to determine how artistically the ideas have been demonstrated. What is the writer trying to tell us about the nature of man, the nature of God, the purpose and design of the universe? Are his ideas oversimplifications or are they capable of accounting in one way for the complexity of human experience? How skillfully has the writer dramatized his ideas, made them memorable in terms of action, character, and scene or, as Eliot says, "in terms of something *perceived*"?

In the following analysis of several poems by Henry Vaughan, John Smith Harrison studies the influence of Platonic philosophy on both the ideas and the images of the poet. The complete text of "The World" is on p. 740. With Vaughan's "The Retreat" compare Wordsworth's "Ode: Intimations of Immortality from Recollections of Early Childhood" (p. 756). Which poem, do you feel, explores and dramatizes more convincingly the idea of the preëxistence of the soul?

John Smith Harrison

VAUGHAN'S PLATONISM

In the work of Vaughan and Spenser two distinct phases of another form of Platonic idealism are presented: one in which the poet looks back upon eternity as a fact of the soul's past experience, and the other in which he directs a forward glance to the future when the soul shall find its eternal rest.

In the expression of his sense of eternity, Vaughan recurs to the doctrine of the preëxistence of the soul as it is expounded in Plato. In Vaughan this idea is felt as an influence either affording the substance of his thought or determining the nature of his imagery. The idea which Vaughan carries over into his own poetry is found in Plato's account in the "Phædrus" of the preëxistence of the soul in a world of pure ideas before its descent into the body. "There was a time," says Plato, "when with the rest of the happy band they [i.e. the human souls] saw beauty shining in brightness: we philosophers following in the train of Zeus, others in company with other gods; and then we beheld the beatific vision and were initiated into a mystery which may be truly called most blessed, celebrated by us in our state of innocence, before we had any experience of evils to come, when we were admitted to the sight of apparitions innocent and simple and calm and happy, which we held shining in pure light, pure ourselves and not yet enshrined in that living tomb which we carry about, now that we are imprisoned in the body, like an oyster in his shell." ("Phaedrus," 250.)

This idea occurs in two forms in Vaughan. In "The Retreat" the reminiscence of a past is described as a fact of Vaughan's religious experience. He longs to travel back to the time when, in his purity, he was nearer to God than he is now in his sinful state.

> "Happy those early days, when I
> Shin'd in my angel-infancy!
> Before I understood this place
> Appointed for my second race,
> Or taught my soul to fancy ought
> But a white, celestial thought;
> When yet I had not walk'd above
> A mile or two from my first love,
> And looking back—at that short space—
> Could see a glimpse of His bright face;
> When on some gilded cloud, or flow'r,
> My gazing soul would dwell an hour,
> And in those weaker glories spy
> Some shadows of eternity;
> Before I taught my tongue to wound
> My conscience with a sinful sound,
> Or had the black art to dispence
> A sev'ral sin to ev'ry sense,
> But felt through all this fleshly dress
> Bright shoots of everlastingness.
> O how I long to travel back,
> And tread again that ancient track!
> That I might once more reach that plain,
> Where first I left my glorious train:

> From whence th' enlighten'd spirit sees
> That shady City of palm-trees.
> But ah! my soul with too much stay
> Is drunk, and staggers in the way!
> Some men a forward motion love,
> But I by backward steps would move;
> And when this dust falls to the urn,
> In that state I came, return."

The second form of this idea appears in Vaughan's poem called "Corruption." Man is represented as enjoying the happiness of innocence in the garden of Eden, where he was in close touch with the beauties of heaven. Here he had a glimpse of his heavenly birth; but when, by reason of sin, he was forced to leave that place, he found earth and heaven no longer friendly.

> "Sure, it was so. Man in those early days
>   Was not all stone and earth;
> He shin'd a little, and by those weak rays
>   Had some glimpse of his birth.
> He saw heaven o'er his head, and knew from whence
>   He came, condemnèd, hither;
> And, as first love draws strongest, so from hence
>   His mind sure progress'd thither.
> Things here were strange unto him; sweat and till;
>   All was a thorn or weed.

> This made him long for home, as loth to stay
>   With murmurers and foes;
> He sigh'd for Eden, and would often say
>   'Ah! what bright days were those!'
> Nor was heav'n cold unto him: for each day
>   The valley or the mountain
> Afforded visits, and still Paradise lay
>   In some green shade or fountain.
> Angels lay leiger here: each bush, and cell,
>   Each oak, and highway knew them;
> Walk but the fields, or sit down at some well,
>   And he was sure to view them."

In this poem, although there is no such parallelism with the account of a pre-existent state as it is given in Plato, the fundamental idea is the same as that of "The Retreat." Vaughan describes man's life in Eden as one of closer intimacy with his celestial home than his lot on earth affords him, just as he had described the experience of his own "angel-infancy" and its contrast to his earthly life. In both poems is present the conviction that the human soul once lived in a state of pure innocence; and in both is heard the note of regret at the loss of this through sin.

In Vaughan's poem, "The World," the influence of Plato's account of the preëxistent life of the soul is felt only in affording the character of the imagery which Vaughan has used to express his idea. In the "Phaedrus" Plato describes the progress of the soul in its sight of the eternal ideas in the heaven of heavens. Each soul, represented as a charioteer guiding a pair of winged horses, is carried about by the revolution of the spheres, and during the progress it beholds the ideas. The souls of the gods have no difficulty in seeing these realities; "but of the other souls," says Plato, "that which follows God best and is likest to him lifts the head of the charioteer into the outer world, and is carried round in the revolution, troubled indeed by the steeds, and with difficulty beholding true being; while another only rises and falls, and sees, and again fails to see by reason of the unruliness of the steeds. The rest of the souls are also longing after the upper world, and they all follow, but not being strong enough they are carried round below the surface, plunging, treading on one another, each striving to be first; and there is confusion and perspiration and the extremity of effort; and many of them are lamed, or have their wings broken, through the ill-driving of the charioteers." ("Phaedrus," 248.)

In this account of the revolution of the soul about the eternal realities of true being, Vaughan found the suggestion for his poem, "The World." Instead of the revolution of the soul about true being, he describes the revolution of time about eternity. The figure of the charioteer is absent, too, but it is by the use of the "wing" that those who make the revolution about eternity mount up into the circle, just as in Plato. Time in the poem also is represented as being "driven about by the spheres." Such coincidences of imagery show that Vaughan found in Plato's fanciful account of the soul's preëxistent life in heaven the medium through which he expressed his view of the relation of the life of the present day world to that of eternity. At first he pictures the revolution of the world about the great ring of light which he calls eternity:

> "I saw Eternity the other night,
> Like a great ring of pure and endless light,
>   All calm, as it was bright;
> And round beneath it, Time in hours, days, years,
>   Driv'n by the spheres
> Like a vast shadow mov'd: in which the world
>   And all her train were hurl'd."

He then describes the lover busied in his trifles,—his lute, his fancies, and his delights. Next moves the statesman, pursued by the shouts of multitudes. The next to follow are the miser and the epicure.

"The doting lover in his quaintest strain
　　　　Did there complain;
Near him, his lute, his fancy, and his flights,
　　　　Wit's sour delights;
With gloves, and knots, the silly snares of pleasure
　　　　Yet his dear treasure,
All scatter'd lay, while he his eyes did pour
　　　　Upon a flow'r.

"The darksome statesman, hung with weights and woe,
Like a thick midnight fog, mov'd there so slow,
　　　　He did nor stay, nor go;
Condemning thoughts—like sad eclipses—scowl
　　　　Upon his soul,
And clouds of crying witnesses without
　　　　Pursued him with one shout.

"The fearful miser on a heap of rust
Sate pining all his life there, did scarce trust
　　　　His own hands with the dust,
Yet would not place one piece above, but lives
　　　　In fear of thieves.
Thousands there were as frantic as himself,
　　　　And hugg'd each one his pelf;
The downright epicure plac'd heav'n in sense,
　　　　And scorn'd pretence;
While others, slipp'd into a wide excess,
　　　　Said little less;
The weaker sort slight, trivial wares enslave,
　　　　Who think them brave;
And poor, despisèd Truth sate counting by
　　　　Their victory."

At this point Vaughan ends his catalogue of human types and comments upon the unwillingness of the many to soar up into the ring by the aid of the wing.

"Yet some, who all this while did weep and sing,
And sing, and weep, soar'd up into the ring;
　　　　But most would use no wing.
O fools—said I—thus to prefer dark night
　　　　Before true light!
To live in grots and caves, and hate the day
　　　　Because it shows the way;
The way, which from this dead and dark abode
　　　　Leads up to God."

PART THREE

Casebook

Introduction

In the foregoing sections you have been increasing your skill in the analysis and evaluation of literature. You took works apart to see how the author shaped or failed to shape into a pleasing unity the basic elements: action, character, setting, language, tone, point of view, atmosphere, and meaning. Then you undertook to measure the value of various works according to certain critical yardsticks, yardsticks representing your emotional and intellectual expectations —artistry in details, internal consistency, faithfulness to a literary mode, escape, and various kinds of insights: biographical, psychological, mythological, sociological, moral, and philosophical. The uses of these yardsticks were exemplified in essays by critics with varied interests.

By now it should be clear that most works yield more to certain kinds of inquiry than to others. For instance, one may find the language, the tone, and the philosophical implications of George Herbert's short lyric "Virtue" (p. 734) fascinating, but one will find little to say about its characterization or its psychological insights. Some works, however, are esthetically so rich and intellectually so ample that you can explore every element fully and apply every critical yardstick profitably—*The Iliad, Oedipus Rex, The Aeneid, The Divine Comedy, King Lear, Paradise Lost,* and *War and Peace,* to mention only a few examples. The tale that follows, Conrad's "Heart of Darkness," is that kind of work. It therefore affords a chance to bring to bear many critical approaches.

After the text of the story, we have provided a number of questions about the basic elements and their relationships. Since these questions are by no means exhaustive, you would do well to review Part One and the materials provided in Part Two for the yardsticks of artistry in details and internal consistency so that you can fully analyze and evaluate the structure, the formal excellence of the story. Finally, there are several essays and associated questions which are again related to a number of critical yardsticks studied in the previous sections. Never is an essay offered as a comprehensive and exact consideration of certain elements in the story. Rather, the essays are intended to suggest *some* of the important ways of considering the work. For example, the essay by Jung will lead to a discussion of the psychological significance of a great deal of the imagery and action of the story, but a psychological analysis of the manager or of Marlow will require other psychological data.

In short, this intensive study of "Heart of Darkness" suggests, though it does not exhaust, the varied ways of approaching a single work.

Joseph Conrad

HEART OF DARKNESS

The *Nellie*, a cruising yawl, swung to her anchor without a flutter of the sails, and was at rest. The flood had made, the wind was nearly calm, and being bound down the river, the only thing for it was to come to and wait for the turn of the tide.

The sea-reach of the Thames stretched before us like the beginning of an interminable waterway. In the offing the sea and the sky were welded together without a joint, and in the luminous space the tanned sails of the barges drifting up with the tide seemed to stand still in red clusters of canvas sharply peaked, with gleams of varnished sprits. A haze rested on the low shores that ran out to sea in vanishing flatness. The air was dark above Gravesend, and farther back still seemed condensed into a mournful gloom, brooding motionless over the biggest, and the greatest, town on earth.

The Director of Companies was our captain and our host. We four affectionately watched his back as he stood in the bows looking to seaward. On the whole river there was nothing that looked half so nautical. He resembled a pilot, which to a seaman is trustworthiness personified. It was difficult to realize his work was not out there in the luminous estuary, but behind him, within the brooding gloom.

Between us there was, as I have already said somewhere, the bond of the sea. Besides holding our hearts together through long periods of separation, it had the effect of making us tolerant of each other's yarns—and even convictions. The Lawyer—the best of old fellows—had, because of his many years and many virtues, the only cushion on deck, and was lying on the only rug. The Accountant had brought out already a box of dominoes, and was toying architecturally with the bones. Marlow sat cross-legged right aft, leaning against the mizzen-mast. He had sunken cheeks, a yellow complexion, a straight back, an ascetic aspect, and, with his arms dropped, the palms of hands outwards, resembled an idol. The director, satisfied the anchor had good hold, made his way aft and sat down amongst us. We exchanged a few words lazily. Afterwards there was silence on board the yacht. For some reason or other we did not begin that game of dominoes. We felt meditative, and fit for nothing but placid staring. The day was ending in a serenity of still and exquisite brilliance. The water shone pacifically; the sky, without a speck, was a benign immensity of unstained light; the very mist on the Essex marshes was like a gauzy and radiant fabric, hung from the wooded rises inland, and draping the low shores in diaphanous folds. Only the gloom to the west, brooding over the upper reaches, became more somber every minute, as if angered by the approach of the sun.

And at last, in its curved and imperceptible fall, the sun sank low, and from glowing white changed to a dull red without rays and without heat, as if about to go out suddenly, stricken to death by the touch of that gloom brooding over a crowd of men.

Forthwith a change came over the waters, and the serenity became less brilliant but more profound. The old river in its broad reach rested unruffled at the decline of day, after ages of good service done to the race that peopled its banks, spread out in the tranquil dignity of a waterway leading to the uttermost ends of the earth. We looked at the venerable stream not in the vivid flush of a short day that comes and departs forever, but in the august light of abiding memories. And indeed nothing is easier for a man who has, as the phrase goes, "followed the sea" with reverence and affection, than to evoke the great spirit of the past upon the lower reaches of the Thames. The tidal current runs to and fro in its unceasing service, crowded with memories of men and ships it had borne to the rest of home or to the battles of the sea. It had known and served all the men of whom the nation is proud, from Sir Francis Drake to Sir John Franklin, knights all, titled and untitled—the knights-errant of the sea. It had borne all the ships whose names are like jewels flashing in the night of time, from the *Golden Hind* returning with her round flanks full of treasure, to be visited by the Queen's Highness and thus pass out of the gigantic tale to the *Erebus* and *Terror*, bound on other conquests—and that never returned. It had known the ships and the men. They had sailed from Deptford, from Greenwich, from Erith—the adventurers and the settlers; kings' ships and the ships of men on 'Change; captains, admirals, the dark "interlopers" of the Eastern trade, and the commissioned "generals" of East India fleets. Hunters for gold or pursuers of fame, they all had gone out on that stream, bearing the sword, and often the torch, messengers of the might within the land, bearers of a spark from the sacred fire. What greatness had not floated on the ebb of that river into the mystery of an unknown earth! . . . The dreams of men, the seed of commonwealths, the germs of empires.

The sun set; the dusk fell on the stream, and lights began to appear along the shore. The Chapman lighthouse, a three-legged thing erect on a mud-flat, shone strongly. Lights of ships moved in the fairway—a great stir of lights going up and going down. And farther west on the upper reaches the place of the monstrous town was still marked ominously on the sky, a brooding gloom in sunshine, a lurid glare under the stars.

"And this also," said Marlow suddenly, "has been one of the dark places on the earth."

He was the only man of us who still "followed the sea." The worst that could be said of him was that he did not represent his class. He was a seaman, but he was a wanderer, too, while most seamen lead, if one may so express it, a sedentary life. Their minds are of the stay-at-home order, and their home is always with them—the ship; and so is their country—the sea. One ship is very much like another, and the sea is always the same. In the immutability of their surroundings the foreign shores, the foreign faces, the changing immensity of life, glide past, veiled not by a sense of mystery but by a slightly disdainful ignorance; for there is nothing mysterious to a seaman unless it be the sea itself, which is the mistress of his existence and as inscrutable as Destiny. For the rest, after his hours of work, a casual stroll or a casual spree on shore suffices to unfold for him the secret of a whole continent, and generally he finds the secret not worth knowing. The yarns of seamen have a direct simplicity, the whole meaning of which lies within the shell of a cracked nut. But Marlow was not typical (if his propensity to spin yarns be excepted), and to him the meaning of an episode was not inside like a kernel but outside, enveloping the tale which brought it out only as a glow brings out a haze, in the likeness of one of these misty halos that sometimes are made visible by the spectral illumination of moonshine.

His remark did not seem at all surprising. It was just like Marlow. It was accepted in silence. No one took the trouble to grunt even; and presently he said, very slow—

"I was thinking of very old times, when the Romans first came here, nineteen hundred years ago—the other day. . . . Light came out of this river since—you say Knights? Yes; but it is like a running blaze on a plain, like a flash of light-ning in the clouds. We live in the flicker—may it last as long as the old earth keeps rolling! But darkness was here yesterday. Imagine the feelings of a com-mander of a fine—what d'ye call 'em—trireme in the Mediterranean, ordered suddenly to the north; run overland across the Gauls in a hurry; put in charge of one of these craft the legionaries—a wonderful lot of handy men they must have been, too—used to build, apparently by the hundred, in a month or two, if we may believe what we read. Imagine him here—the very end of the world, a sea the color of lead, a sky the color of smoke, a kind of ship about as rigid as a concertina—and going up this river with stores, or orders, or what you like. Sand-banks, marshes, forests, savages,—precious little to eat fit for a civilized man, nothing but Thames water to drink. No Falernian wine here, no going ashore. Here and there a military camp lost in a wilderness, like a needle in a bundle of hay—cold, fog, tempests, disease, exile, and death,—death skulking in the air, in the water, in the bush. They must have been dying like flies here. Oh, yes—he did it. Did it very well, too, no doubt, and without thinking much about it either, except afterwards to brag of what he had gone through in his time, perhaps. They were men enough to face the darkness. And perhaps he was cheered by keeping his eye on a chance of promotion to the fleet at Ravenna by and by, if he had good friends in Rome and survived the awful climate. Or think of a decent young citizen in a toga—perhaps too much dice, you know—coming out here in the train of some prefect, or tax-gatherer, or trader even, to mend his fortunes. Land in a swamp, march through the woods, and in some inland post feel the savagery, the utter savagery, had closed round him,—all that mysterious life of the wilderness that stirs in the forest, in the jungles, in the hearts of wild men. There's no initiation either into such mysteries. He has to live in the midst of the incomprehensible, which is also detestable. And it has a fascination, too, that goes to work upon him. The fascination of the abomination—you know, imagine the growing regrets, the longing to escape, the powerless disgust, the surrender, the hate."

He paused.

"Mind," he began again, lifting one arm from the elbow, the palm of the hand outwards, so that, with his legs folded before him, he had the pose of a Buddha preaching in European clothes and without a lotus-flower—"Mind, none of us would feel exactly like this. What saves us is efficiency—the devotion to efficiency. But these chaps were not much account, really. They were no colonists; their administration was merely a squeeze, and nothing more, I suspect. They were conquerors, and for that you want only brute force—nothing to boast of, when you have it, since your strength is just an accident arising from the weakness of others. They grabbed what they could get for the sake of what was to be got. It was just robbery with violence, aggravated murder on a great scale, and men going at it blind—as is very proper for those who tackle a darkness. The conquest of the earth, which mostly means the taking it away from those who have a different complexion or slightly flatter noses than ourselves, is not a pretty thing when you look into it too much. What redeems it is the idea only. An idea at the back of it; not a sentimental pretense but an idea; and an unselfish belief in the idea—something you can set up, and bow down before, and offer a sacrifice to. . . ."

He broke off. Flames glided in the river, small green flames, red flames, white flames, pursuing, overtaking, joining, crossing each other—then separating slowly or hastily. The traffic of the great city went on in the deepening night upon the sleepless river. We looked on, waiting patiently—there was nothing else to do till the end of the flood; but it was only after a long silence, when he said, in a hesitating voice, "I suppose you fellows remember I did once turn fresh-water sailor for a bit," that we knew we were fated, before the ebb began to run, to hear one of Marlow's inconclusive experiences.

"I don't want to bother you much with what happened to me personally," he began, showing in this remark the weakness of many tellers of tales who seem so often unaware of what their audience would best like to hear; "yet to understand the effect of it on me you ought to know how I got out there, what I saw, how I went up that river to the place where I first met the poor chap. It was the farthest point of navigation and the culminating point of my experience. It seemed somehow to throw a kind of light on everything about me—and into my thoughts. It was somber enough, too—and pitiful—not extraordinary in any way —not very clear either. No, not very clear. And yet it seemed to throw a kind of light.

"I had then, as you remember, just returned to London after a lot of Indian Ocean, Pacific, China Seas—a regular dose of the East—six years or so, and I was loafing about, hindering you fellows in your work and invading your homes, just as though I had got a heavenly mission to civilize you. It was very fine for a time, but after a bit I did get tired of resting. Then I began to look for a ship—

I should think the hardest work on earth. But the ships wouldn't even look at me. And I got tired of that game, too.

"Now when I was a little chap I had a passion for maps. I would look for hours at South America, or Africa, or Australia, and lose myself in all the glories of exploration. At that time there were many blank spaces on the earth, and when I saw one that looked particularly inviting on a map (but they all look that) I would put my finger on it and say, When I grow up I will go there. The North Pole was one of these places, I remember. Well, I haven't been there yet, and shall not try now. The glamour's off. Other places were scattered about the Equator, and in every sort of latitude all over the two hemispheres. I have been in some of them, and . . . well, we won't talk about that. But there was one yet— the biggest, the most blank, so to speak—that I had a hankering after.

"True, by this time it was not a blank space any more. It had got filled since my childhood with rivers and lakes and names. It had ceased to be a blank space of delightful mystery—a white patch for a boy to dream gloriously over. It had become a place of darkness. But there was in it one river especially, a mighty big river, that you could see on the map, resembling an immense snake uncoiled, with its head in the sea, its body at rest curving afar over a vast country, and its tail lost in the depths of the land. And as I looked at the map of it in a shop-window, it fascinated me as a snake would a bird—a silly little bird. Then I remembered there was a big concern, a Company for trade on that river. Dash it all! I thought to myself, they can't trade without using some kind of craft on that lot of fresh water—steamboats! Why shouldn't I try to get charge of one? I went on along Fleet Street, but could not shake off the idea. The snake had charmed me.

"You understand it was a Continental concern, that Trading society; but I have a lot of relations living on the Continent, because it's cheap and not so nasty as it looks, they say.

"I am sorry to own I began to worry them. This was already a fresh departure for me. I was not used to getting things that way, you know. I always went my own road and on my own legs where I had a mind to go. I wouldn't have believed it of myself; but, then—you see—I felt somehow I must get there by hook or by crook. So I worried them. The men said 'My dear fellow,' and did nothing. Then—would you believe it?—I tried the women. I, Charlie Marlow, set the women to work—to get a job. Heavens! Well, you see, the notion drove me. I had an aunt, a dear enthusiastic soul. She wrote: 'It will be delightful. I am ready to do anything, anything for you. It is a glorious idea. I know the wife of a very high personage in the Administration, and also a man who has lots of influence with,' etc., etc. She was determined to make no end of fuss to get me appointed skipper of a river steamboat, if such was my fancy.

"I got my appointment—of course; and I got it very quick. It appears the Company had received news that one of their captains had been killed in a scuffle with the natives. This was my chance, and it made me the more anxious to go. It was only months and months afterwards, when I made the attempt to recover what was left of the body, that I heard the original quarrel arose from a misunderstanding about some hens. Yes, two black hens. Fresleven—that was the fellow's name, a Dane—thought himself wronged somehow in the bargain, so he went ashore and started to hammer the chief of the village with a stick. Oh, it didn't surprise me in the least to hear this, and at the same time to be told that Fresleven was the gentlest, quietest creature that ever walked on two legs. No doubt he was; but he had been a couple of years already out there engaged in the noble cause, you know, and he probably felt the need at last of asserting his self-respect in some way. Therefore he whacked the old nigger mercilessly, while a big crowd of his people watched him, thunderstruck, till some man—I was told the chief's son—in desperation at hearing the old chap yell, made a tentative jab with a spear at the white man—and of course it went quite easy between the shoulder-blades. Then the whole population cleared into the forest, expecting all kinds of calamities to happen, while, on the other hand, the steamer Fresleven commanded left also in a bad panic, in charge of the engineer, I believe. Afterwards nobody seemed to trouble much about Fresleven's remains, till I got out and stepped into his shoes. I couldn't let it rest, though; but when an opportunity offered at last to meet my predecessor, the grass growing through his ribs was tall enough to hide his bones. They were all there. The supernatural being had not been touched after he fell. And the village was deserted, the huts gaped black, rotting, all askew within the fallen enclosures. A calamity had come to it, sure enough. The people had vanished. Mad terror had scattered them, men, women, and children, through the bush, and they had never returned. What became of the hens I don't know either. I should think the cause of progress got them, anyhow. However, through this glorious affair I got my appointment, before I had fairly begun to hope for it.

"I flew around like mad to get ready, and before forty-eight hours I was crossing the Channel to show myself to my employers, and sign the contract. In a very few hours I arrived in a city that always makes me think of a whited sepulcher. Prejudice no doubt. I had no difficulty in finding the Company's offices. It was the biggest thing in the town, and everybody I met was full of it. They were going to run an over-sea empire, and make no end of coin by trade.

"A narrow and deserted street in deep shadow, high houses, innumerable windows with venetian blinds, a dead silence, grass sprouting between the stones, imposing carriage archways right and left, immense double doors standing ponderously ajar. I slipped through one of these cracks, went up a swept and ungarnished staircase, as arid as a desert, and opened the first door I came to. Two women, one fat and the other slim, sat on straw-bottomed chairs, knitting black wool. The slim one got up and walked straight at me—still knitting with down-cast eyes—and only just as I began to think of getting out of her way, as you would for a somnambulist, stood still, and looked up. Her dress was as plain as an umbrella-cover, and she turned round without a word and preceded me into a waiting-room. I gave my name, and looked about. Deal table in the middle, plain chairs all around the walls, on one end a large shining map, marked with all the colors of a rainbow. There was a vast amount of red—good to see at any time, because one knows that some real work is done in there, a deuce of a lot of blue, a little green, smears of orange, and, on the East Coast, a purple patch, to show where the jolly pioneers of progress drink the jolly lager-beer. However, I wasn't going into any of these. I was going into the yellow. Dead in the center. And the river was there—fascinating—deadly—like a snake. Ough! A door opened, a white-haired secretarial head, but wearing a compassionate expression, appeared, and a skinny forefinger beckoned me into the sanctuary. Its light was dim, and a heavy writing-desk squatted in the middle. From behind that structure came out an impression of pale plumpness in a frock-coat. The great man himself. He was five feet six, I should judge, and had his grip on the handle-end of ever so many millions. He shook hands, I fancy, murmured vaguely, was satisfied with my French. *Bon voyage.*

"In about forty-five seconds I found myself again in the waiting-room with the compassionate secretary, who, full of desolation and sympathy, made me sign some document. I believe I undertook amongst other things not to disclose any trade secrets. Well, I am not going to.

"I began to feel slightly uneasy. You know I am not used to such ceremonies, and there was something ominous in the atmosphere. It was just as though I had been let into some conspiracy—I don't know—something not quite right; and I was glad to get out. In the outer room the two women knitted black wool feverishly. People were arriving, and the younger one was walking back and forth introducing them. The old one sat on her chair. Her flat cloth slippers were propped up on a foot-warmer, and a cat reposed on her lap. She wore a starched white affair on her head, had a wart on one cheek, and silver-rimmed spectacles hung on the tip of her nose. She glanced at me above the glasses. The swift and indifferent placidity of that look troubled me. Two youths with foolish and cheery countenances were being piloted over, and she threw at them the same quick glance of unconcerned wisdom. She seemed to know all about them and about me, too. An eerie feeling came over me. She seemed uncanny and fateful. Often far away there I thought of these two, guarding the door of Darkness, knitting black wool as for a warm pall, one introducing, introducing continuously to the unknown, the other scrutinizing the cheery and foolish faces with unconcerned old eyes. *Ave!* Old knitter of black wool. *Morituri te salutant.* Not many of those she looked at ever saw her again—not half, by a long way.

"There was yet a visit to the doctor. 'A simple formality,' assured me the secretary, with an air of taking an immense part in all my sorrows. Accordingly a young chap wearing his hat over the left eyebrow, some clerk I suppose,— there must have been clerks in the business, though the house was as still as a house in a city of the dead—came from somewhere upstairs, and led me forth. He was shabby and careless, with inkstains on the sleeves of his jacket, and his cravat was large and billowy, under a chin shaped like the toe of an old boot. It was a little too early for the doctor, so I proposed a drink, and thereupon he developed a vein of joviality. As we sat over our vermouths he glorified the Company's business, and by and by I expressed casually my surprise at him not going out there. He became very cool and collected all at once. 'I am not such a fool as I look, quoth Plato to his disciples,' he said sententiously, emptied his glass with great resolution, and we rose.

"The old doctor felt my pulse, evidently thinking of something else the while. 'Good, good for there,' he mumbled, and then with a certain eagerness asked me whether I would let him measure my head. Rather surprised, I said Yes, when he produced a thing like calipers and got the dimensions back and front and every way, taking notes carefully. He was an unshaven little man in a threadbare coat like a gaberdine, with his feet in slippers, and I thought him a harmless fool. 'I always ask leave, in the interests of science, to measure the crania of those going out there,' he said. 'And when they come back, too?' I asked. 'Oh, I never see them,' he remarked; 'and, moreover, the changes take place inside, you know.' He smiled, as if at some quiet joke. 'So you are going out there. Famous. Interesting, too.' He gave me a searching glance, and made another note. 'Ever any madness in your family?' he asked, in a matter-of-fact tone. I felt very annoyed. 'Is that question in the interests of science, too?' 'It would be,' he said, without taking notice of my irritation, 'interesting for science to watch the mental changes of individuals, on the spot, but . . .' 'Are you an alienist?' I interrupted. 'Every doctor should be—a little,' answered that original, imperturbably. 'I have a little theory which you Messieurs who go out there must help me to prove. This is my share in the advantages my country shall reap from the possession of such a magnificent dependency. The mere wealth I leave to others. Pardon my questions, but you are the first Englishman coming under my observation . . .' I hastened to assure him I was not in the least typical. 'If I were,' said I, 'I wouldn't be talking like this with you.' 'What you say is rather profound, and probably erroneous,' he said, with a laugh. 'Avoid irritation more than exposure to the sun. Adieu. How do you English say, eh? Good-by. Ah! Good-by. Adieu. In the tropics one must before everything keep calm.' . . . He lifted a warning forefinger. . . . '*Du calme, du calme. Adieu.*'

"One thing more remained to do—say good-by to my excellent aunt. I found her triumphant. I had a cup of tea—the last decent cup of tea for many days— and in a room that most soothingly looked just as you would expect a lady's drawing-room to look, we had a long quiet chat by the fireside. In the course of these confidences it became quite plain to me I had been represented to the wife of the high dignitary, and goodness knows to how many more people besides, as an exceptional and gifted creature—a piece of good fortune for the Company—a man you don't get hold of every day. Good heavens! and I was going to take charge of a two-penny-half-penny river-steamboat with a penny whistle attached! It appeared, however, I was also one of the Workers, with a capital—you know. Something like an emissary of light, something like a lower sort of apostle. There had been a lot of such rot let loose in print and talk just about that time, and the excellent woman, living right in the rush of all that humbug, got carried off her feet. She talked about 'weaning those ignorant millions from their horrid ways,' till, upon my word, she made me quite uncomfortable. I ventured to hint that the Company was run for profit.

" 'You forget, dear Charlie, that the laborer is worthy of his hire,' she said, brightly. It's queer how out of touch with truth women are. They live in a world of their own, and there has never been anything like it, and never can be. It is too beautiful altogether, and if they were to set it up it would go to pieces before the first sunset. Some confounded fact we men have been living contentedly with ever since the day of creation would start up and knock the whole thing over.

"After this I got embraced, told to wear flannel, be sure to write often, and so on—and I left. In the street—I don't know why—a queer feeling came to me that I was an impostor. Odd thing that I, who used to clear out for any part of the world at twenty-four hours' notice, with less thought than most men give to the crossing of a street, had a moment—I won't say of hesitation, but of startled pause, before this commonplace affair. The best way I can explain it to you is by saying that, for a second or two, I felt as though, instead of going to the center of a continent, I were about to set off for the center of the earth.

"I left in a French steamer, and she called in every blamed port they have out there, for, as far as I could see, the sole purpose of landing soldiers and custom-house officers. I watched the coast. Watching a coast as it slips by the ship is like thinking about an enigma. There it is before you—smiling, frowning, inviting, grand, mean, insipid, or savage, and always mute with an air of whispering, Come and find out. This one was almost featureless, as if still in the making, with an aspect of monotonous grimness. The edge of a colossal jungle, so dark-green as to be almost black, fringed with white surf, ran straight, like a ruled line, far, far away along a blue sea whose glitter was blurred by a creeping mist. The sun was fierce, the land seemed to glisten and drip with steam. Here and there grayish-whitish specks showed up clustered inside the white surf, with a flag flying above them perhaps. Settlements some centuries old, and still no bigger than pinheads on the untouched expanse of their background. We pounded along, stopped, landed soldiers; went on, landed custom-house clerks to levy toll in what looked like a God-forsaken wilderness, with a tin shed and a flag-pole lost in it; landed more soldiers—to take care of the custom-house clerks, presumably. Some, I heard, got drowned in the surf; but whether they did or not, nobody seemed particularly to care. They were just flung out there, and on we went. Every day the coast looked the same, as though we had not moved; but we passed various places—trading places—with names like Gran' Bassam, Little Popo; names that seemed to belong to some sordid farce acted in front of a sinister backcloth. The idleness of a passenger, my isolation amongst all these men with whom I had no point of contact, the oily and languid sea, the uniform somberness of the coast, seemed to keep me away from the truth of things, within the toil of a mournful and senseless delusion. The voice of the surf heard now and then was a positive pleasure, like the speech of a brother. It was something natural, that had its reason, that had a meaning. Now and then a boat from the shore gave one a momentary contact with reality. It was paddled by black fellows. You could see from afar the white of their eyeballs glistening. They shouted, sang; their bodies streamed with perspiration; they had faces like grotesque masks—these chaps; but they had bone, muscle, a wild vitality, an intense energy of movement, that was as natural and true as the surf along their coast. They wanted no excuse for being there. They were a great comfort to look at. For a time I would feel I belonged still to a world of straightforward facts; but the feeling would not last long. Something would turn up to scare it away. Once, I remember, we came upon a man-of-war anchored off the coast. There wasn't even a shed there, and she was shelling the bush. It appears the French had one of their wars going on thereabouts. Her ensign dropped limp like a rag; the muzzles of the long six-inch guns stuck out all over the low hull; the greasy, slimy swell swung her up lazily and let her down, swaying her thin masts. In the empty immensity of earth, sky, and water, there she was, incomprehensible, firing into a continent. Pop, would go one of the six-inch guns; a small flame would dart and vanish, a little white smoke would disappear, a tiny projectile would give a feeble screech—and nothing happened. Nothing could happen. There was a touch of insanity in the proceeding, a sense of lugubrious drollery in the sight; and it was not dissipated by somebody on board assuring me earnestly there was a camp of natives—he called them enemies!—hidden out of sight somewhere.

"We gave her her letters (I heard the men in that lonely ship were dying of fever at the rate of three a day) and went on. We called at some more places with farcical names, where the merry dance of death and trade goes on in a still and earthy atmosphere as of an overheated catacomb; all along the formless coast bordered by dangerous surf, as if Nature herself had tried to ward off intruders; in and out of rivers, streams of death in life, whose banks were rotting into mud, whose waters, thickened into slime, invaded the contorted mangroves, that seemed to writhe at us in the extremity of an impotent despair. Nowhere did we stop long enough to get a particularized impression, but the general sense of vague and oppressive wonder grew upon me. It was like a weary pilgrimage amongst hints for nightmares.

"It was upward of thirty days before I saw the mouth of the big river. We anchored off the seat of the government. But my work would not begin till some two hundred miles farther on. So as soon as I could I made a start for a place thirty miles higher up.

"I had my passage on a little sea-going steamer. Her captain was a Swede, and knowing me for a seaman, invited me on the bridge. He was a young man, lean, fair, and morose, with lanky hair and a shuffling gait. As we left the miserable little wharf, he tossed his head contemptuously at the shore. 'Been living there?' he asked. I said, 'Yes.' 'Fine lot these government chaps—are they not?' he went on, speaking English with great precision and considerable bitterness. 'It is funny what some people will do for a few francs a month. I wonder what becomes of that kind when it goes up-country?' I said to him I expected to see that soon. 'So-o-o!' he exclaimed. He shuffled athwart, keeping one eye ahead vigilantly. 'Don't be too sure,' he continued. 'The other day I took up a man who hanged himself on the road. He was a Swede, too.' 'Hanged himself! Why, in God's name?' I cried. He kept on looking out watchfully. 'Who knows? The sun was too much for him, or the country perhaps.'

"At last we opened a reach. A rocky cliff appeared, mounds of turned-up earth by the shore, houses on a hill, others with iron roofs, amongst a waste of excavations, or hanging to the declivity. A continuous noise of the rapids above hovered over this scene of inhabited devastation. A lot of people, mostly black and naked, moved about like ants. A jetty projected into the river. A blinding sunlight drowned all this at times in a sudden recrudescence of glare. 'There's your Company's station,' said the Swede, pointing to three wooden barrack-like structures on the rocky slope. 'I will send your things up. Four boxes did you say? So. Farewell.'

"I came upon a boiler wallowing in the grass, then found a path leading up the hill. It turned aside for the bowlders, and also for an undersized railway-truck lying there on its back with its wheels in the air. One was off. The thing looked as dead as the carcass of some animal. I came upon more pieces of decaying machinery, a stack of rusty rails. To the left a clump of trees made a shady spot, where dark things seemed to stir feebly. I blinked, the path was steep. A horn tooted to the right, and I saw the black people run. A heavy and dull detonation shook the ground, a puff of smoke came out of the cliff, and that was all. No change appeared on the face of the rock. They were building a railway. The cliff was not in the way or anything; but this objectless blasting was all the work going on.

"A slight clinking behind me made me turn my head. Six black men advanced in a file, toiling up the path. They walked erect and slow, balancing small baskets full of earth on their heads, and the clink kept time with their footsteps. Black rags were wound round their loins, and the short ends behind waggled to and fro like tails. I could see every rib, the joints of their limbs were like knots in a rope; each had an iron collar on his neck, and all were connected together with a chain whose bights swung between them, rhythmically clinking. Another report from the cliff made me think suddenly of that ship of war I had seen firing into a continent. It was the same kind of ominous voice; but these men could by no stretch of imagination be called enemies. They were called criminals, and the outraged law, like the bursting shells, had come to them, an insoluble mystery from the sea. All their meager breasts panted together, the violently dilated nostrils quivered, the eyes stared stonily up-hill. They passed me within six inches, without a glance, with that complete, deathlike indifference of unhappy savages. Behind this raw matter one of the reclaimed, the product of the new forces at work, strolled despondently, carrying a rifle by its middle. He had a uniform jacket with one button off, and seeing a white man on the path, hoisted his weapon to his shoulder with alacrity. This was simple prudence, white men being so much alike at a distance that he could not tell who I might be. He was speedily reassured, and with a large, white rascally grin, and a glance at his charge, seemed to take me into partnership in his exalted trust. After all, I also was a part of the great cause of these high and just proceedings.

"Instead of going up, I turned and descended to the left. My idea was to let that chain-gang get out of sight before I climbed the hill. You know I am not particularly tender; I've had to strike and to fend off. I've had to resist and to attack sometimes—that's only one way of resisting—without counting the exact cost, according to the demands of such sort of life as I had blundered into. I've seen the devil of violence, and the devil of greed, and the devil of hot desire; but, by all the stars! these were strong, lusty, red-eyed devils, that swayed and drove men—men, I tell you. But as I stood on this hillside, I foresaw that in the blinding sunshine of that land I would become acquainted with a flabby, pretending, weak-eyed devil of a rapacious and pitiless folly. How insidious he could be, too, I was only to find out several months later and a thousand miles farther. For a moment I stood appalled, as though by a warning. Finally I descended the hill, obliquely, towards the trees I had seen.

"I avoided a vast artificial hole somebody had been digging on the slope, the purpose of which I found it impossible to divine. It wasn't a quarry or a sand-pit, anyhow. It was just a hole. It might have been connected with the philanthropic desire of giving the criminals something to do. I don't know. Then I nearly fell into a very narrow ravine, almost no more than a scar in the hillside. I discovered that a lot of imported drainage-pipes for the settlement had been tumbled in there. There wasn't one that was not broken. It was a wanton smash-up. At last I got under the trees. My purpose was to stroll into the shade for a moment; but no sooner within than it seemed to me I had stepped into the gloomy circle of some Inferno. The rapids were near, and an uninterrupted, uniform, headlong, rushing noise filled the mournful stillness of the grove, where not a breath stirred, not a leaf moved, with a mysterious sound—as though the tearing pace of the launched earth had suddenly become audible.

"Black shapes crouched, lay, sat between the trees leaning against the trunks, clinging to the earth, half coming out, half effaced within the dim light, in all the attitudes of pain, abandonment, and despair. Another mine on the cliff went off, followed by a slight shudder of the soil under my feet. The work was going on. The work! And this was the place where some of the helpers had withdrawn to die.

"They were dying slowly—it was very clear. They were not enemies, they were not criminals, they were nothing earthly now,—nothing but black shadows of disease and starvation, lying confusedly in the greenish gloom. Brought from all the recesses of the coast in all the legality of time contracts, lost in uncongenial surroundings, fed on unfamiliar food, they sickened, became inefficient, and were then allowed to crawl away and rest. These moribund shapes were free as air—and nearly as thin. I began to distinguish the gleam of the eyes under the trees. Then, glancing down, I saw a face near my hand. The black bones reclined at full length with one shoulder against the tree, and slowly the eyelids rose and the sunken eyes looked up at me, enormous and vacant, a kind of blind, white flicker in the depths of the orbs, which died out slowly. The man seemed young— almost a boy—but you know with them it's hard to tell. I found nothing else to do but to offer him one of my good Swede's ship's biscuits I had in my pocket. The fingers closed slowly on it and held—there was no other movement and no other glance. He had tied a bit of white worsted round his neck— Why? Where did he get it? Was it a badge—an ornament—a charm—a propitiatory act? Was there any idea at all connected with it? It looked startling round his black neck, this bit of white thread from beyond the seas.

"Near the same tree two more bundles of acute angles sat with their legs drawn up. One, with his chin propped on his knees, stared at nothing, in an intolerable and appalling manner: his brother phantom rested its forehead, as if overcome with a great weariness; and all about others were scattered in every pose of contorted collapse, as in some picture of a massacre or a pestilence. While I stood horror-struck, one of these creatures rose to his hands and knees, and went off on all-fours towards the river to drink. He lapped out of his hand, then sat up in the sunlight, crossing his shins in front of him, and after a time let his woolly head fall on his breastbone.

"I didn't want any more loitering in the shade, and I made haste towards the station. When near the buildings I met a white man, in such an unexpected elegance of get-up that in the first moment I took him for a sort of vision. I saw a high starched collar, white cuffs, a light alpaca jacket, snowy trousers, a clean necktie, and varnished boots. No hat. Hair parted, brushed, oiled, under a green-lined parasol held in a big white hand. He was amazing, and had a penholder behind his ear.

"I shook hands with this miracle, and I learned he was the Company's chief accountant, and that all the book-keeping was done at this station. He had come out for a moment, he said, 'to get a breath of fresh air.' The expression sounded wonderfully odd, with its suggestion of sedentary desk-life. I wouldn't have mentioned the fellow to you at all, only it was from his lips that I first heard the name of the man who is so indissolubly connected with the memories of that time. Moreover, I respected the fellow. Yes; I respected his collars, his vast cuffs, his brushed hair. His appearance was certainly that of a hairdresser's dummy; but in the great demoralization of the land he kept up his appearance. That's backbone. His starched collars and got-up shirt-fronts were achievements of character. He had been out nearly three years; and, later, I could not help asking him how he managed to sport such linen. He had just the faintest blush, and said modestly, 'I've been teaching one of the native women about the station. It was difficult. She had a distaste for the work.' Thus this man had verily accomplished something. And he was devoted to his books, which were in apple-pie order.

"Everything else in the station was in a muddle,—heads, things, buildings. Strings of dusty niggers with splay feet arrived and departed; a stream of manufactured goods, rubbishy cottons, beads, and brass-wire set into the depths of darkness, and in return came a precious trickle of ivory.

"I had to wait in the station for ten days—an eternity. I lived in a hut in the yard, but to be out of the chaos I would sometimes get into the accountant's office. It was built of horizontal planks, and so badly put together that, as he bent over his high desk, he was barred from neck to heels with narrow strips of sunlight. There was no need to open the big shutter to see. It was hot there, too; big flies buzzed fiendishly, and did not sting, but stabbed. I sat generally on the floor, while, of faultless appearance (and even slightly scented), perching on a high stool, he wrote, he wrote. Sometimes he stood up for exercise. When a trucklebed with a sick man (some invalid agent from up-country) was put in there, he exhibited a gentle annoyance. 'The groans of this sick person,' he said, 'distract my attention. And without that it is extremely difficult to guard against clerical errors in this climate.'

"One day he remarked, without lifting his head, 'In the interior you will no doubt meet Mr. Kurtz.' On my asking who Mr. Kurtz was, he said he was a first-class agent; and seeing my disappointment at this information, he added slowly, laying down his pen, 'He is a very remarkable person.' Further questions elicited from him that Mr. Kurtz was at present in charge of a trading post, a very important one, in the true ivory-country, at 'the very bottom of there. Sends in as much ivory as all the others put together. . . .' He began to write again. The sick man was too ill to groan. The flies buzzed in a great peace.

"Suddenly there was a growing murmur of voices and a great tramping of feet. A caravan had come in. A violent babble of uncouth sounds burst out on the other side of the planks. All the carriers were speaking together, and in the midst of the uproar the lamentable voice of the chief agent was heard 'giving it up' tearfully for the twentieth time that day. . . . He rose slowly. 'What a frightful row,' he said. He crossed the room gently to look at the sick man, and returning, said to me, 'He does not hear.' 'What! Dead?' I asked, startled. 'No, not yet,' he answered, with great composure. Then, alluding with a toss of the head to the tumult in the stationyard, 'When one has got to make correct entries, one comes to hate those savages—hate them to the death.' He remained thoughtful for a moment. 'When you see Mr. Kurtz,' he went on, 'tell him for me that everything here'—he glanced at the desk—'is very satisfactory. I don't like to write to him—with those messengers of ours you never know who may get hold of your letter—at that Central Station.' He stared at me for a moment with his mild, bulging eyes. 'Oh, he will go far, very far,' he began again. 'He will be a somebody in the Administration before long. They, above—the Council in Europe, you know—mean him to be.'

"He turned to his work. The noise outside had ceased, and presently in going out I stopped at the door. In the steady buzz of flies the homeward-bound agent was lying flushed and insensible; the other, bent over his books, was making correct entries of perfectly correct transactions; and fifty feet below the doorstep I could see the still tree-tops of the grove of death.

"Next day I left that station at last, with a caravan of sixty men, for a two-hundred-mile tramp.

"No use telling you much about that. Paths, paths, everywhere; a stamped-in network of paths spreading over the empty land, through long grass, through burnt grass, through thickets, down and up chilly ravines, up and down stony hills ablaze with heat; and a solitude, a solitude, nobody, not a hut. The population had cleared out a long time ago. Well, if a lot of mysterious niggers armed with all kinds of fearful weapons suddenly took to traveling on the road between Deal and Gravesend, catching the yokels right and left to carry heavy loads for them, I fancy every farm and cottage thereabouts would get empty very soon.

Only here the dwellings were gone, too. Still I passed through several abandoned villages. There's something pathetically childish in the ruins of grass walls. Day after day, with the stamp and shuffle of sixty pair of bare feet behind me, each pair under a sixty-lb. load. Camp, cook, sleep, strike camp, march. Now and then a carrier dead in harness, at rest in the long grass near the path, with an empty water-gourd and his long staff lying by his side. A great silence around and above. Perhaps on some quiet night the tremor of far-off drums, sinking, swelling, a tremor vast, faint; a sound weird, appealing, suggestive, and wild— and perhaps with as profound a meaning as the sound of bells in a Christian country. Once a white man in an unbuttoned uniform, camping on the path with an armed escort of lank Zanzibars, very hospitable and festive—not to say drunk. Was looking after the upkeep of the road, he declared. Can't say I saw any road or any upkeep, unless the body of a middle-aged Negro, with a bullet-hole in the forehead, upon which I absolutely stumbled three miles farther on, may be considered as a permanent improvement. I had a white companion, too, not a bad chap, but rather too fleshy and with the exasperating habit of fainting on the hot hillsides, miles away from the least bit of shade and water. Annoying, you know, to hold your own coat like a parasol over a man's head while he is coming-to. I couldn't help asking him once what he meant by coming there at all. 'To make money, of course. What do you think?' he said, scornfully. Then he got fever, and had to be carried in a hammock slung under a pole. As he weighed sixteen stone I had no end of rows with the carriers. They jibbed, ran away, sneaked off with their loads in the night—quite a mutiny. So, one evening, I made a speech in English with gestures, not one of which was lost to the sixty pairs of eyes before me, and the next morning I started the hammock off in front all right. An hour afterwards I came upon the whole concern wrecked in a bush—man, hammock, groans, blankets, horrors. The heavy pole had skinned his poor nose. He was very anxious for me to kill somebody, but there wasn't the shadow of a carrier near. I remembered the old doctor—'It would be interesting for science to watch the mental changes of individuals, on the spot.' I felt I was becoming scientifically interesting. However, all that is to no purpose. On the fifteenth day I came in sight of the big river again, and hobbled into the Central Station. It was on a back water surrounded by scrub and forest, with a pretty border of smelly mud on one side, and on the three others enclosed by a crazy fence of rushes. A neglected gap was all the gate it had, and the first glance at the place was enough to let you see the flabby devil was running that show. White men with long staves in their hands appeared languidly from amongst the buildings, strolling up to take a look at me, and then retired out of sight somewhere. One of them, a stout, excitable chap with black mustaches, informed me with great volubility and many digressions, as soon as I told him who I was, that my steamer was at the bottom of the river. I was thunderstruck. What, how, why? Oh, it was 'all right.' The 'manager himself' was there. All quite correct. 'Everybody had behaved splendidly! splendidly!'—'you must,' he said in agitation, 'go and see the general manager at once. He is waiting!'

"I did not see the real significance of that wreck at once. I fancy I see it now, but I am not sure—not at all. Certainly the affair was too stupid—when I think of it—to be altogether natural. Still. . . . But at the moment it presented itself simply as a confounded nuisance. The steamer was sunk. They had started two days before in a sudden hurry up the river with the manager on board, in charge of some volunteer skipper, and before they had been out three hours they tore the bottom out of her on stones, and she sank near the south bank. I asked myself what I was to do there, now my boat was lost. As a matter of fact, I had plenty to do in fishing my command out of the river. I had to set about it the very next day. That, and the repairs when I brought the pieces to the station, took some months.

"My first interview with the manager was curious. He did not ask me to sit down after my twenty-mile walk that morning. He was commonplace in complexion, in feature, in manners, and in voice. He was of middle size and of ordinary build. His eyes, of the usual blue, were perhaps remarkably cold, and he certainly could make his glance fall on one as trenchant and heavy as an ax. But even at these times the rest of his person seemed to disclaim the intention. Otherwise there was only an indefinable, faint expression of his lips, something stealthy—a smile—not a smile—I remember it, but I can't explain. It was unconscious, this smile was, though just after he had said something it got intensified for an instant. It came at the end of his speeches like a seal applied on the words to make the meaning of the commonest phrase appear absolutely inscrutable. He was a common trader, from his youth up employed in these parts—nothing more. He was obeyed, yet he inspired neither love nor fear, nor even respect. He inspired uneasiness. That was it! Uneasiness. Not a definite mistrust—just uneasiness— nothing more. You have no idea how effective such a . . . a . . . faculty can be. He had no genius for organizing, for initiative, or for order even. That was evident in such things as the deplorable state of the station. He had no learning, and no intelligence. His position had come to him—why? Perhaps because he was never ill. . . . He had served three terms of three years out there. . . . Because triumphant health in the general rout of constitutions is a kind of power in itself. When he went home on leave he rioted on a large scale—pompously. Jack ashore —with a difference—in externals only. This one could gather from his casual talk. He originated nothing, he could keep the routine going—that's all. But he was great. He was great by this little thing that it was impossible to tell what could control such a man. He never gave that secret away. Perhaps there was nothing within him. Such a suspicion made one pause—for out there there were no external checks. Once when various tropical diseases had laid low almost every 'agent' in the station, he was heard to say, 'Men who come out here should have no entrails.' He sealed the utterance with that smile of his, as though it had been a door opening into a darkness he had in his keeping. You fancied you had seen things—but the seal was on. When annoyed at meal-times by the constant quarrels of the white men about precedence, he ordered an immense round table to be made, for which a special house had to be built. This was the station's mess-room. Where he sat was the first place—the rest were nowhere. One felt this to be his unalterable conviction. He was neither civil nor uncivil. He was quiet. He allowed his 'boy'—an overfed young Negro from the coast—to treat the white men, under his very eyes, with provoking insolence.

"He began to speak as soon as he saw me. I had been very long on the road. He could not wait. Had to start without me. The up-river stations had to be relieved. There had been so many delays already that he did not know who was dead and who was alive, and how they got on—and so on, and so on. He paid no attention to my explanations, and, playing with a stick of sealing-wax, repeated several times that the situation was 'very grave, very grave.' There were rumors that a very important station was in jeopardy, and its chief, Mr. Kurtz, was ill. Hoped it was not true. Mr. Kurtz was . . . I felt weary and irritable. Hang Kurtz, I thought. I interrupted him by saying I had heard of Mr. Kurtz on the coast. 'Ah! So they talk of him down there,' he murmured to himself. Then he began again, assuring me Mr. Kurtz was the best agent he had, an exceptional man, of the greatest importance to the Company; therefore I could understand his anxiety. He was, he said, 'very, very uneasy.' Certainly he fidgeted on his chair a good deal, exclaimed, 'Ah, Mr. Kurtz!' broke the stick of sealing-wax and seemed dumfounded by the accident. Next thing he wanted to know 'how long it would take to.' . . . I interrupted him again. Being hungry, you know, and kept on my feet too, I was getting savage. 'How can I tell?' I said. 'I haven't even seen the wreck yet—some months, no doubt.' All this talk seemed to me so futile. 'Some months,' he said. 'Well, let us say three months before we can make a start. Yes. That ought to do the affair.' I flung out of his hut (he lived all alone in a clay hut with a sort of veranda) muttering to myself my opinion of him. He was a chattering idiot. Afterwards I took it back when it was borne in upon me startlingly with what extreme nicety he had estimated the time requisite for the 'affair.'

"I went to work the next day, turning, so to speak, my back on that station. In that way only it seemed to me I could keep my hold on the redeeming facts of life. Still, one must look about sometimes; and then I saw this station, these men strolling aimlessly about in the sunshine of the yard. I asked myself sometimes what it all meant. They wandered here and there with their absurd long staves in their hands, like a lot of faithless pilgrims bewitched inside a rotten fence. The word 'ivory' rang in the air, was whispered, was sighed. You would think they were praying to it. A taint of imbecile rapacity blew through it all, like a whiff from some corpse. By Jove! I've never seen anything so unreal in my life. And outside, the silent wilderness surrounding this cleared speck on the earth struck me as something great and invincible, like evil or truth, waiting patiently for the passing away of this fantastic invasion.

"Oh, these months! Well, never mind. Various things happened. One evening a grass shed full of calico, cotton prints, beads, and I don't know what else, burst into a blaze so suddenly that you would have thought the earth had opened to let an avenging fire consume all that trash. I was smoking my pipe quietly by my dismantled steamer, and saw them all cutting capers in the light, with their arms lifted high, when the stout man with mustaches came tearing down to the river, a tin pail in his hand, assured me that everybody was 'behaving spendidly, splendidly,' dipped about a quart of water and tore back again. I noticed there was a hole in the bottom of his pail.

"I strolled up. There was no hurry. You see the thing had gone off like a box of matches. It had been hopeless from the very first. The flame had leaped high, driven everybody back, lighted up everything—and collapsed. The shed was already a heap of embers glowing fiercely. A nigger was being beaten near by. They said he had caused the fire in some way; be that as it may, he was screeching most horribly. I saw him, later, for several days, sitting in a bit of shade looking very sick and trying to recover himself: afterwards he arose and went out—and the wilderness without a sound took him into its bosom again. As I approached the glow from the dark I found myself at the back of two men, talking. I heard the name of Kurtz pronounced, then the words, 'take advantage of this unfortunate accident.' One of the men was the manager. I wished him a good evening. 'Did you ever see anything like it—eh? it is incredible,' he said, and walked off. The other man remained. He was a first-class agent, young, gentlemanly, a bit reserved, with a forked little beard and a hooked nose. He was stand-offish with the other agents, and they on their side said he was the manager's spy upon them. As to me, I had hardly ever spoken to him before. We got into talk, and by and by we strolled away from the hissing ruins. Then he asked me to his room, which was in the main building of the station. He struck a match, and I perceived that this young aristocrat had not only a silver-mounted dressing-case but also a whole candle all to himself. Just at that time the manager was the only man supposed to have any right to candles. Native mats covered the clay walls; a collection of spears, assegais, shields, knives was hung up in trophies. The business intrusted to this fellow was the making of bricks—so I had been informed; but there wasn't a fragment of a brick anywhere in the station, and he had been there more than a year—waiting. It seems he could not make bricks without something. I don't know what—straw, maybe. Anyway, it could not be found there, and as it was not likely to be sent from Europe, it did not appear clear to me what he was waiting for. An act of special creation perhaps. However, they were all waiting—all the sixteen or twenty pilgrims of them—for something; and upon my word it did not seem an un-congenial occupation, from the way they took it, though the only thing that ever came to them was disease—as far as I could see. They beguiled the time by back-biting and intriguing against each other in a foolish kind of way. There was an air of plotting about that station, but nothing came of it, of course. It was as unreal as everything else—as the philanthropic pretense of the whole concern, as their talk, as their government, as their show of work. The only real feeling was a desire to get appointed to a trading-post where ivory was to be had, so that they could earn percentages. They intrigued and slandered and hated each other only on that account.—but as to effectually lifting a little finger—oh, no. By heavens! there is something after all in the world allowing one man to steal a horse while another must not look at a halter. Steal a horse straight out. Very well. He has done it. Perhaps he can ride. But there is a way of looking at a halter that would provoke the most charitable of saints into a kick.

"I had no idea why he wanted to be sociable, but as we chatted in there it suddenly occurred to me the fellow was trying to get at something—in fact, pumping me. He alluded constantly to Europe, to the people I was supposed to know there—putting leading questions as to my acquaintances in the sepulchral city, and so on. His little eyes glittered like mica discs—with curiosity—though he tried to keep up a bit of superciliousness. At first I was astonished, but very soon I became awfully curious to see what he would find out from me. I couldn't possibly imagine what I had in me to make it worth his while. It was very pretty to see how he baffled himself, for in truth my body was full only of chills, and my head had nothing in it but that wretched steamboat business. It was evident he took me for a perfectly shameless prevaricator. At last he got angry, and, to conceal a movement of furious annoyance, he yawned. I rose. Then I noticed a small sketch in oils, on a panel, representing a woman, draped and blindfolded, carrying a lighted torch. The background was somber—almost black. The movement of the woman was stately, and the effect of the torch-light on the face was sinister.

"It arrested me, and he stood by civilly, holding an empty half-pint champagne bottle (medical comforts) with the candle stuck in it. To my question he said Mr. Kurtz had painted this—in this very station more than a year ago—while waiting for means to go to his trading-post. 'Tell me, pray,' said I, 'who is this Mr. Kurtz?'

"'The chief of the Inner Station,' he answered in a short tone, looking away. 'Much obliged,' I said, laughing. 'And you are the brickmaker of the Central Station. Every one knows that.' He was silent for a while. 'He is a prodigy,' he said at last. 'He is an emissary of pity, and science, and progress, and devil knows what else. We want,' he began to declaim suddenly, 'for the guidance of the cause intrusted to us by Europe, so to speak, higher intelligence, wide sympathies, a singleness of purpose.' 'Who says that?' I asked. 'Lots of them,' he replied. 'Some even write that; and so *he* comes here, a special being, as you ought to know.' 'Why ought I to know?' I interrupted, really surprised. He paid no attention. 'Yes. To-day he is chief of the best station, next year he will be assistant-manager, two years more and . . . but I daresay you know what he will be in two years' time. You are of the new gang—the gang of virtue. The same people who sent him specially also recommended you. Oh, don't say no. I've my own eyes to trust.' Light dawned upon me. My dear aunt's influential acquaintances were producing an unexpected effect upon that young man. I nearly burst into a laugh. 'Do you read the Company's confidential correspondence?' I asked. He hadn't a word to say. It was great fun. 'When Mr. Kurtz,' I continued, severely, 'is General Manager, you won't have the opportunity.'

"He blew the candle out suddenly, and we went outside. The moon had risen. Black figures strolled about listlessly, pouring water on the glow, whence proceeded a sound of hissing; steam ascended in the moonlight, the beaten nigger groaned somewhere. 'What a row the brute makes!' said the indefatigable man with the mustaches, appearing near us. 'Serves him right. Transgression—punishment—bang! Pitiless, pitiless. That's the only way. This will prevent all conflagrations for the future. I was just telling the manager. . . .' He noticed my companion, and became crestfallen all at once. 'Not in bed yet,' he said, with a kind of servile heartiness; 'it's so natural. Ha! Danger—agitation.' He vanished. I went on to the river-side, and the other followed me. I heard a scathing murmur at my ear, 'Heap of muffs—go to.' The pilgrims could be seen in knots gesticulating, discussing. Several had still their staves in their hands. I verily believe they took these sticks to bed with them. Beyond the fence the forest stood up spectrally in the moonlight, and through the dim stir, through the faint sounds of that lamentable courtyard, the silence of the land went home to one's very heart—its mystery, its greatness, the amazing reality of its concealed life. The hurt nigger moaned feebly somewhere near by, and then fetched a deep sigh that made me mend my pace away from there. I felt a hand introducing itself under my arm. 'My dear sir,' said the fellow, 'I don't want to be misunderstood, and especially by you, who will see Mr. Kurtz long before I can have that pleasure. I wouldn't like him to get a false idea of my disposition. . . .'

"I let him run on, this papier-mâché Mephistopheles, and it seemed to me that if I tried I could poke my forefinger through him, and would find nothing inside but a little loose dirt, maybe. He, don't you see, had been planning to be assistant-manager by and by under the present man, and I could see that the coming of that Kurtz had upset them both not a little. He talked precipitately, and I did not try to stop him. I had my shoulders against the wreck of my steamer, hauled up on the slope like a carcass of some big river animal. The smell of mud, of primeval mud, by Jove! was in my nostrils, the high stillness of primeval forest was before my eyes; there were shiny patches on the black creek. The moon had spread over everything a thin layer of silver—over the rank grass, over the mud, upon the wall of matted vegetation standing higher than the wall of a temple, over the great river I could see through a somber gap glittering, glittering, as it flowed broadly by without a murmur. All this was great, expectant, mute, while the man jabbered about himself. I wondered whether the stillness on the face of the immensity looking at us two were meant as an appeal or as a menace. What were we who had strayed in here? Could we handle that dumb thing, or would it handle us? I felt how big, how confoundedly big, was that thing that couldn't talk, and perhaps was deaf as well. What was in there? I could see a little ivory coming out from there, and I had heard Mr. Kurtz was in there. I had heard enough about it, too—God knows! Yet somehow it didn't bring any image with it—no more than if I had been told an angel or a fiend was in there. I believed it in the same way one of you might believe there are inhabitants in the planet Mars. I knew once a Scotch sailmaker who was certain, dead sure, there were people in Mars. If you asked him for some idea how they looked and behaved, he would get shy and mutter something about 'walking on all-fours.' If you as much as smiled, he would—though a man of sixty-four—offer to fight you. I would not have gone so far as to fight for Kurtz, but I went for him near enough to a lie. You know I hate, detest, and can't bear a lie, not because I am straighter than the rest of us, but simply because it appalls me. There is a taint of death, a flavor of mortality in lies—which is exactly what I hate and detest in the world—what I want to forget. It makes me miserable and sick, like biting something rotten would do. Temperament, I suppose. Well, I went near enough to it by letting the young fool there believe anything he liked to imagine as to my influence in Europe. I became in an instant as much of a pretense as the rest of the bewitched pilgrims. This simply because I had a notion it somehow would be of help to that Kurtz whom at the time I did not see—you understand. He was just a word for me. I did not see the man in the name any more than you do. Do you see him? Do you see the story? Do you see anything? It seems to me I am trying to tell you a dream—making a vain attempt, because no relation of a dream can convey the dream-sensation, that commingling of absurdity, surprise, and bewilderment in a tremor of struggling revolt, that notion of being captured by the incredible which is of the very essence of dreams. . . ."

He was silent for a while.

". . . No, it is impossible; it is impossible to convey the life-sensation of any given epoch of one's existence—that which makes its truth, its meaning—its subtle and penetrating essence. It is impossible. We live, as we dream—alone. . . ."

He paused again as if reflecting, then added—

"Of course in this you fellows see more than I could then. You see me, whom you know. . . ."

It had become so pitch dark that we listeners could hardly see one another. For a long time already he, sitting apart, had been no more to us than a voice. There was not a word from anybody. The others might have been asleep, but I was awake. I listened, I listened on the watch for the sentence, for the word, that would give me the clew to the faint uneasiness inspired by this narrative that seemed to shape itself without human lips in the heavy night-air of the river.

". . . Yes—I let him run on," Marlow began again, "and think what he pleased about the powers that were behind me. I did! And there was nothing behind me! There was nothing but that wretched, old, mangled steamboat I was leaning against, while he talked fluently about 'the necessity for every man to get on.' 'And when one comes out here, you conceive, it is not to gaze at the moon.' Mr. Kurtz was a 'universal genius,' but even a genius would find it easier to work with 'adequate tools—intelligent men.' He did not make bricks—why, there was a physical impossibility in the way—as I was well aware; and if he did secretarial work for the manager, it was because 'no sensible man rejects wantonly the confidence of his superiors.' Did I see it? I saw it. What more did I want? What I really wanted was rivets, by heaven! Rivets. To get on with the work— to stop the hole. Rivets I wanted. There were cases of them down at the coast —cases—piled up—burst—split! You kicked a loose rivet at every second step in that station yard on the hillside. Rivets had rolled into the grove of death. You could fill your pockets with rivets for the trouble of stooping down—and there wasn't one rivet to be found where it was wanted. We had plates that would do, but nothing to fasten them with. And every week the messenger, a lone negro, letter-bag on shoulder and staff in hand, left our station for the coast. And

several times a week a coast caravan came in with trade goods—ghastly glazed
calico that made you shudder only to look at it; glass beads, valued about a penny
a quart, confounded spotted cotton handkerchiefs. And no rivets. Three carriers
could have brought all that was wanted to set that steamboat afloat.

"He was becoming confidential now, but I fancy my unresponsive attitude
must have exasperated him at last, for he judged it necessary to inform me he
feared neither God nor devil, let alone any mere man. I said I could see that very
well, but what I wanted was a certain quantity of rivets—and rivets were what
really Mr. Kurtz wanted, if he had only known it. Now letters went to the coast
every week.... 'My dear sir,' he cried, 'I write from dictation.' I demanded rivets.
There was a way—for an intelligent man. He changed his manner; became very
cold, and suddenly began to talk about a hippopotamus; wondered whether
sleeping on board the steamer (I stuck to my salvage night and day) I wasn't
disturbed. There was an old hippo that had the bad habit of getting out on the
bank and roaming at night over the station grounds. The pilgrims used to turn
out in a body and empty every rifle they could lay hands on at him. Some even
had sat up o' nights for him. All this energy was wasted, though. 'That animal
has a charmed life,' he said; 'but you can say this only of brutes in this country.
No man—you apprehend me?—no man here bears a charmed life.' He stood
there for a moment in the moonlight with his delicate hooked nose set a little
askew, and his mica eyes glittering without a wink, then, with a curt good night,
he strode off. I could see he was disturbed and considerably puzzled, which made
me feel more hopeful than I had been for days. It was a great comfort to turn
from that chap to my influential friend, the battered, twisted, ruined, tin-pot
steamboat. I clambered on board. She rang under my feet like an empty Huntley
& Palmer biscuit-tin kicked along a gutter; she was nothing so solid in make,
and rather less pretty in shape, but I had expended enough hard work on her
to make me love her. No influential friend would have served me better. She
had given me a chance to come out a bit—to find out what I could do. No, I don't
like work. I had rather laze about and think of all the fine things that can be
done. I don't like work—no man does—but I like what is in the work,—the
chance to find yourself. Your own reality—for yourself, not for others—what no
other man can ever know. They can only see the mere show, and never can tell
what it really means.

"I was not surprised to see somebody sitting aft, on the deck, with his legs
dangling over the mud. You see I rather chummed with the few mechanics there
were in that station, whom the other pilgrims naturally despised—on account of
their imperfect manners, I suppose. This was the foreman—a boiler-maker by
trade—a good worker. He was a lank, bony, yellow-faced man, with big intense
eyes. His aspect was worried, and his head was as bald as the palm of my hand;
but his hair in falling seemed to have stuck to his chin, and had prospered in
the new locality, for his beard hung down to his waist. He was a widower with
six young children (he had left them in charge of a sister of his to come out
there), and the passion of his life was pigeon-flying. He was an enthusiast and
a connoisseur. He would rave about pigeons. After work hours he used sometimes

to come over from his hut for a talk about his children and his pigeons; at work, when he had to crawl in the mud under the bottom of the steamboat, he would tie up that beard of his in a kind of white serviette he brought for the purpose. It had loops to go over his ears. In the evening he could be seen squatted on the bank rinsing that wrapper in the creek with great care, then spreading it solemnly on a bush to dry.

"I slapped him on the back and shouted, 'We shall have rivets!' He scrambled to his feet exclaiming, 'No! Rivets!' as though he couldn't believe his ears. Then in a low voice, 'You . . . eh?' I don't know why we behaved like lunatics. I put my finger to the side of my nose and nodded mysteriously. 'Good for you!' he cried, snapped his fingers above his head, lifting one foot. I tried a jig. We capered on the iron deck. A frightful clatter came out of that hulk, and the virgin forest on the other bank of the creek sent it back in a thundering roll upon the sleeping station. It must have made some of the pilgrims sit up in their hovels. A dark figure obscured the lighted doorway of the manager's hut, vanished, then, a second or so after, the doorway itself vanished, too. We stopped, and the silence driven away by the stamping of our feet flowed back again from the recesses of the land. The great wall of vegetation, an exuberant and entangled mass of trunks, branches, leaves, boughs, festoons, motionless in the moonlight, was like a rioting invasion of soundless life, a rolling wave of plants, piled up, crested, ready to topple over the creek, to sweep every little man of us out of his little existence. And it moved not. A deadened burst of mighty splashes and snorts reached us from afar, as though an ichthyosaurus had been taking a bath of glitter in the great river. 'After all,' said the boiler-maker in a reasonable tone, 'why shouldn't we get the rivets?' Why not, indeed? I did not know of any reason why we shouldn't. 'They'll come in three weeks,' I said, confidently.

"But they didn't. Instead of rivets there came an invasion, an infliction, a visitation. It came in sections during the next three weeks, each section headed by a donkey carrying a white man in new clothes and tan shoes, bowing from that elevation right and left to the impressed pilgrims. A quarrelsome band of footsore sulky niggers trod on the heels of the donkeys; a lot of tents, campstools, tin boxes, white cases, brown bales would be shot down in the courtyard, and the air of mystery would deepen a little over the muddle of the station. Five such installments came, with their absurd air of disorderly flight with the loot of innumerable outfit shops and provision stores, that, one would think, they were lugging, after a raid, into the wilderness for equitable division. It was an inextricable mess of things decent in themselves but that human folly made look like the spoils of thieving.

"This devoted band called itself the Eldorado Exploring Expedition, and I believe they were sworn to secrecy. Their talk, however, was the talk of sordid buccaneers: it was reckless without hardihood, greedy without audacity, and cruel without courage; there was not an atom of foresight or of serious intention in the whole batch of them, and they did not seem aware these things are wanted for the work of the world. To tear treasure out of the bowels of the land was their desire, with no more moral purpose at the back of it than there is in burglars breaking into a safe. Who paid the expenses of the noble enterprise I don't know; but the uncle of our manager was leader of that lot.

"In exterior he resembled a butcher in a poor neighborhood, and his eyes had a look of sleepy cunning. He carried his fat paunch with ostentation on his short legs, and during the time his gang infested the station spoke to no one but his nephew. You could see these two roaming about all day long with their heads close together in an everlasting confab.

"I had given up worrying myself about the rivets. One's capacity for that kind of folly is more limited than you would suppose. I said Hang!—and let things slide. I had plenty of time for meditation, and now and then I would give some thought to Kurtz. I wasn't very interested in him. No. Still, I was curious to see whether this man, who had come out equipped with moral ideas of some sort, would climb to the top after all and how he would set about his work when there."

II .

"One evening as I was lying flat on the deck of my steamboat, I heard voices approaching—and there were the nephew and the uncle strolling along the bank. I laid my head on my arm again, and had nearly lost myself in a doze, when somebody said in my ear, as it were: 'I am as harmless as a little child, but I don't like to be dictated to. Am I the manager—or am I not? I was ordered to send him there. It's incredible.' . . . I became aware that the two were standing on the shore alongside the forepart of the steamboat, just below my head. I did not move; it did not occur to me to move: I was sleepy. 'It *is* unpleasant,' grunted the uncle. 'He has asked the Administration to be sent there,' said the other, 'with the idea of showing what he could do; and I was instructed accordingly. Look at the influence that man must have. Is it not frightful?' They both agreed it was frightful, then made several bizarre remarks: 'Make rain and fine weather—one man—the Council—by the nose'—bits of absurd sentences that got the better of my drowsiness, so that I had pretty near the whole of my wits about me when the uncle said, 'The climate may do away with this difficulty for you. Is he alone there?' 'Yes,' answered the manager; 'he sent his assistant down the river with a note to me in these terms: "Clear this poor devil out of the country, and don't bother sending more of that sort. I had rather be alone than have the kind of men you can dispose of with me." It was more than a year ago. Can you imagine such impudence!' 'Anything since then?' asked the other, hoarsely. 'Ivory,' jerked the nephew; 'lots of it—prime sort—lots—most annoying, from him.' 'And with that?' questioned the heavy rumble. 'Invoice,' was the reply fired out, so to speak. Then silence. They had been talking about Kurtz.

"I was broad awake by this time, but, lying perfectly at ease, remained still, having no inducement to change my position. 'How did that ivory come all this way?' growled the elder man, who seemed very vexed. The other explained that it had come with a fleet of canoes in charge of an English half-caste clerk Kurtz had with him; that Kurtz had apparently intended to return himself, the station being by that time bare of goods and stores, but after coming three hundred miles, had suddenly decided to go back, which he started to do alone in a small dugout with four paddlers, leaving the half-caste to continue down the river with the ivory. The two fellows there seemed astounded at anybody attempting such a thing. They were at a loss for an adequate motive. As to me, I seemed to see Kurtz for the first time. It was a distinct glimpse: the dugout, four paddling savages, and the lone white man turning his back suddenly on the headquarters, on relief, on thoughts of home—perhaps; setting his face towards the depths of the wilderness, towards his empty and desolate station. I did not know the motive. Perhaps he was just simply a fine fellow who stuck to his work for its own sake. His name, you understand, had not been pronounced once. He was 'that man.' The half-caste, who, as far as I could see, had conducted a difficult trip with great prudence and pluck, was invariably alluded to as 'that scoundrel.' The 'scoundrel' had reported that the 'man' had been very ill —had recovered imperfectly. . . . The two below me moved away then a few paces, and strolled back and forth at some little distance. I heard: 'Military post—doctor—two hundred miles—quite alone now—unavoidable delays—nine months—no news—strange rumors.' They approached again, just as the manager was saying, 'No one, as far as I know, unless a species of wandering trader—a pestilential fellow, snapping ivory from the natives.' Who was it they were talking about now? I gathered in snatches that this was some man supposed to be in Kurtz's district, and of whom the manager did not approve. 'We will not be free from unfair competition till one of these fellows is hanged for an example,' he said. 'Certainly,' grunted the other; 'get him hanged! Why not? Anything—anything can be done in this country. That's what I say; nobody here, you understand, *here,* can endanger your position. And why? You stand the climate—you outlast them all. The danger is in Europe; but there before I left I took care to—' They moved off and whispered, then their voices rose again. 'The extraordinary series of delays is not my fault. I did my best.' The fat man sighed. 'Very sad.' 'And the pestiferous absurdity of his talk,' continued the other; 'he bothered me enough when he was here. "Each station should be like a beacon on the road towards better things, a center for trade, of course, but also for humanizing, improving, instructing." Conceive you—that ass! And he wants to be manager! No, it's—' Here he got choked by excessive indignation, and I lifted my head the least bit. I was surprised to see how near they were—right under me. I could have spat upon their hats. They were looking on the ground, absorbed in thought. The manager was switching his leg with a slender twig: his sagacious relative lifted his head. 'You have been well since you came out this time?' he asked. The other gave a start. 'Who? I? Oh! Like a charm—like a charm. But the rest—oh, my goodness! All sick. They die so quick, too, that I haven't the time to send them out of the country—it's incredible!' 'H'm. Just so,' grunted the uncle. 'Ah! my boy, trust to this—I say, trust to this.' I saw him extend his short flipper of an arm for a gesture that took in the forest, the creek, the mud, the river,—seemed to beckon with a dishonoring flourish before the sunlit face of the land a treacherous appeal to the lurking death, to the hidden evil, to the profound darkness of its heart. It was so startling that I leaped to my feet and looked back at the edge of the forest, as though I had expected an answer of some sort to that black display of confidence. You know the foolish notions that come to one sometimes. The high stillness confronted these two figures with its ominous patience, waiting for the passing away of a fantastic invasion.

"They swore aloud together—out of sheer fright, I believe—then pretending not to know anything of my existence, turned back to the station. The sun was low; and leaning forward side by side, they seemed to be tugging painfully uphill their two ridiculous shadows of unequal length, that trailed behind them slowly over the tall grass without bending a single blade.

"In a few days the Eldorado Expedition went into the patient wilderness, that closed upon it as the sea closes over a diver. Long afterwards the news came that all the donkeys were dead. I know nothing as to the fate of the less valuable animals They, no doubt, like the rest of us, found what they deserved. I did not inquire. I was then rather excited at the prospect of meeting Kurtz very soon. When I say very soon I mean it comparatively. It was just two months from the day we left the creek when we came to the bank below Kurtz's station.

"Going up that river was like traveling back to the earliest beginnings of the world, when vegetation rioted on the earth and the big trees were kings. An empty stream, a great silence, an impenetrable forest. The air was warm, thick, heavy, sluggish. There was no joy in the brilliance of sunshine. The long stretches of the waterway ran on, deserted, into the gloom of overshadowed distances. On silvery sandbanks hippos and alligators sunned themselves side by side. The broadening waters flowed through a mob of wooded islands; you lost your way on that river as you would in a desert, and butted all day long against shoals, trying to find the channel, till you thought yourself bewitched and cut off forever from everything you had known once—somewhere—far away—in another existence perhaps. There were moments when one's past came back to one, as it will sometimes when you have not a moment to spare to yourself; but it came in the shape of an unrestful and noisy dream, remembered with wonder amongst the overwhelming realities of this strange world of plants, and water, and silence. And this stillness of life did not in the least resemble a peace. It was the stillness of an implacable force brooding over an inscrutable intention. It looked at you with a vengeful aspect. I got used to it afterwards; I did not see it any more; I had no time. I had to keep guessing at the channel; I had to discern, mostly by inspiration, the signs of hidden banks; I watched for sunken stones; I was learning to clap my teeth smartly before my heart flew out, when I shaved by a fluke some infernal sly old snag that would have ripped the life out of the tin-pot steamboat and drowned all the pilgrims; I had to keep a look-out for the signs of dead wood we could cut up in the night for next day's steaming. When you have to attend to things of that sort, to the mere incidents of the surface, the reality—the reality, I tell you—fades. The inner truth is hidden—luckily, luckily. But I felt it all the same; I felt often its mysterious stillness watching me at my monkey tricks, just as it watches you fellows performing on your respective tight-ropes for—what is it? half-a-crown a tumble—"

"Try to be civil, Marlow," growled a voice, and I knew there was at least one listener awake besides myself.

"I beg your pardon. I forgot the heartache which makes up the rest of the price. And indeed what does the price matter, if the trick be well done? You do your tricks very well. And I didn't do badly either, since I managed not to sink that steamboat on my first trip. It's a wonder to me yet. Imagine a blind-folded man set to drive a van over a bad road. I sweated and shivered over that business considerably, I can tell you. After all, for a seaman, to scrape the bottom of the thing that's supposed to float all the time under his care is the unpardonable sin. No one may know of it, but you never forget the thump—eh? A blow on the very heart. You remember it, you dream of it, you wake up at night and think of it—years after—and go hot and cold all over. I don't pretend to say that steamboat floated all the time. More than once she had to wade for a bit, with twenty cannibals splashing around and pushing. We had enlisted some of these chaps on the way for a crew. Fine fellows—cannibals—in their place. They were men one could work with, and I am grateful to them. And, after all, they did not eat each other before my face: they had brought along a provision of hippo-meat which went rotten, and made the mystery of the wilderness stink in my nostrils. Phoo! I can sniff it now. I had the manager on board and three or four pilgrims with their staves—all complete. Sometimes we came upon a station close by the bank, clinging to the skirts of the unknown, and the white men rushing out of a tumble-down hovel, with great gestures of joy and surprise and welcome, seemed very strange—had the appearance of being held there captive by a spell. The word ivory would ring in the air for a while—and on we went again into the silence, along empty reaches, round the still bends, between the high walls of our winding way, reverberating in hollow claps the ponderous beat of the stern-wheel. Trees, trees, millions of trees, massive, im-mense, running up high; and at their foot, hugging the bank against the stream, crept the little begrimed steamboat, like a sluggish beetle crawling on the floor of a lofty portico. It made you feel very small, very lost, and yet it was not al-together depressing, that feeling. After all, if you were small, the grimy beetle crawled on—which was just what you wanted it to do. Where the pilgrims imagined it crawled to I don't know. To some place where they expected to get something, I bet! For me it crawled towards Kurtz—exclusively; but when the steam-pipes started leaking we crawled very slow. The reaches opened before us and closed behind, as if the forest had stepped leisurely across the water to bar the way for our return. We penetrated deeper and deeper into the heart of darkness. It was very quiet there. At night sometimes the roll of drums behind the curtain of trees would run up the river and remain sustained faintly, as if hovering in the air high over our heads, till the first break of day. Whether it meant war, peace, or prayer we could not tell. The dawns were heralded by the descent of a chill stillness; the wood-cutters slept, their fires burned low; the snapping of a twig would make you start. We were wanderers on a pre-historic earth, on an earth that wore the aspect of an unknown planet. We could have fancied ourselves the first of men taking possession of an accursed inheritance, to be subdued at the cost of profound anguish and of excessive toil. But suddenly, as we struggled round a bend, there would be a glimpse of rush walls, of peaked grass-roofs, a burst of yells, a whirl of black limbs, a mass of hands clapping, of feet stamping, of bodies swaying, of eyes rolling, under the droop of heavy and motionless foliage. The steamer toiled along slowly on the edge of a black and incomprehensible frenzy. The prehistoric man was cursing us, praying to us, welcoming us—who could tell? We were cut off from the comprehension of our surroundings; we glided past like phantoms, wondering and secretly appalled, as sane men would be before an enthusiastic outbreak in a madhouse. We could not understand because we were too far and could not remember, because we were traveling in the night of first ages, of those ages that are gone, leaving hardly a sign—and no memories.

"The earth seemed unearthly. We are accustomed to look upon the shackled form of a conquered monster, but there—there you could look at a thing monstrous and free. It was unearthly, and the men were— No, they were not inhuman. Well, you know, that was the worst of it—this suspicion of their not being inhuman. It would come slowly to one. They howled and leaped, and spun, and made horrid faces; but what thrilled you was just the thought of their humanity—like yours—the thought of your remote kinship with this wild and passionate uproar. Ugly. Yes, it was ugly enough; but if you were man enough you would admit to yourself that there was in you just the faintest trace of a response to the terrible frankness of that noise, a dim suspicion of there being a meaning in it which you—you so remote from the night of first ages—could comprehend. And why not? The mind of man is capable of anything—because everything is in it, all the past as well as all the future. What was there after all? Joy, fear, sorrow, devotion, valor, rage—who can tell?— but truth—truth stripped of its cloak of time. Let the fool gape and shudder— the man knows, and can look on without a wink. But he must at least be as much of a man as these on the shore. He must meet that truth with his own true stuff—with his own inborn strength. Principles won't do. Acquisitions, clothes, pretty rags—rags that would fly off at the first good shake. No; you want a deliberate belief. An appeal to me in this fiendish row—is there? Very well; I hear; I admit, but I have a voice, too, and for good or evil mine is the speech that cannot be silenced. Of course, a fool, what with sheer fright and fine sentiments, is always safe. Who's that grunting? You wonder I didn't go ashore for a howl and a dance? Well, no—I didn't. Fine sentiments, you say? Fine sentiments, be hanged! I had no time. I had to mess about with whitelead and strips of woolen blanket helping to put bandages on those leaky steampipes—I tell you. I had to watch the steering, and circumvent those snags, and get the tinpot along by hook or by crook. There was surface-truth enough in these things to save a wiser man. And between whiles I had to look after the savage who was fireman. He was an improved specimen; he could fire up a vertical boiler. He was there below me, and, upon my word, to look at him was as edifying as seeing a dog in a parody of breeches and a feather hat, walking on his hind-legs. A few months of training had done for that really fine chap. He squinted at the steam-gauge and at the water-gauge with an evident effort of intrepidity—and he had filed teeth, too, the poor devil, and the wool of his pate shaved into queer patterns, and three ornamental scars on each of his cheeks. He ought to have been clapping his hands and stamping his feet on the bank, instead of which he was hard at work, a thrall to strange witch-craft, full of improving knowledge. He was useful because he had been instructed; and what he knew was this—that should the water in that transparent thing disappear, the evil spirit inside the boiler would get angry through the greatness of his thirst, and take a terrible vengeance. So he sweated and fired up and watched the glass fearfully (with an impromptu charm, made of rags, tied to his arm, and a piece of polished bone, as big as a watch, stuck flat-ways through his lower lip), while the wooden banks slipped past us slowly, the short noise was left behind, the interminable miles of silence—and we crept on, towards Kurtz. But the snags were thick, the water was treacherous and shallow, the boiler seemed indeed to have a sulky devil in it, and thus neither that fireman nor I had any time to peer into our creepy thoughts.

"Some fifty miles below the Inner Station we came upon a hut of reeds, an inclined and melancholy pole, with the unrecognizable tatters of what had been a flag of some sort flying from it, and a neatly stacked woodpile. This was unexpected. We came to the bank, and on the stack of firewood found a flat piece of board with some faded pencil-writing on it. When deciphered it said: 'Wood for you. Hurry up. Approach cautiously.' There was a signature, but it was illegible—not Kurtz—a much longer word. 'Hurry up.' Where? Up the river? 'Approach cautiously.' We had not done so. But the warning could not have been meant for the place where it could be only found after approach. Something was wrong above. But what—and how much? That was the question. We commented adversely upon the imbecility of that telegraphic style. The bush around said nothing, and would not let us look very far, either. A torn curtain of red twill hung in the doorway of the hut, and flapped sadly in our faces. The dwelling was dismantled; but we could see a white man had lived there not very long ago. There remained a rude table—a plank on two posts; a heap of rubbish reposed in a dark corner, and by the door I picked up a book. It had lost its covers, and the pages had been thumbed into a state of extremely dirty softness; but the back had been lovingly stitched afresh with white cotton thread, which looked clean yet. It was an extraordinary find. Its title was, *An Inquiry into some Points of Seamanship*, by a man Towser, Towson—some such name—Master in his Majesty's Navy. The matter looked dreary reading enough, with illustrative diagrams and repulsive tables of figures, and the copy was sixty years old. I handled this amazing antiquity with the greatest possible tenderness, lest it should dissolve in my hands. Within, Towson or Towser was inquiring earnestly into the breaking strain of ships' chains and tackle, and other such matters. Not a very enthralling book; but at the first glance you could see there a singleness of intention, an honest concern for the right way of going to work, which made these humble pages, thought out so many years ago, luminous with another than a professional light. The simple old sailor, with his talk of chains and purchases, made me forget the jungle and the pilgrims in a delicious sensation of having come upon something unmistakably real. Such a book being there was wonderful enough; but still more astounding were the notes penciled in the margin, and plainly referring to the text. I couldn't believe my eyes! They were in cipher! Yes, it looked like cipher. Fancy a man lugging with him a book of that description into this nowhere and studying it—and making notes—in cipher at that! It was an extravagant mystery.

"I had been dimly aware for some time of a worrying noise, and when I lifted my eyes I saw the wood pile was gone, and the manager, aided by all the pilgrims, was shouting at me from the river-side. I slipped the book into my pocket. I assure you to leave off reading was like tearing myself away from the shelter of an old and solid friendship.

"I started the lame engine ahead. 'It must be this miserable trader—this intruder,' exclaimed the manager, looking back malevolently at the place we had left. 'He must be English,' I said. 'It will not save him from getting into trouble if he is not careful,' muttered the manager darkly. I observed with assumed innocence that no man was safe from trouble in this world.

"The current was more rapid now, the steamer seemed at her last gasp, the stern-wheel flopped languidly, and I caught myself listening on tiptoe for the next beat of the boat, for in sober truth I expected the wretched thing to give up every moment. It was like watching the last flickers of a life. But still we crawled. Sometimes I would pick out a tree a little way ahead to measure our progress towards Kurtz by, but I lost it invariably before we got abreast. To keep the eyes so long on one thing was too much for human patience. The manager displayed a beautiful resignation. I fretted and fumed and took to arguing with myself whether or no I would talk openly with Kurtz; but before I could come to any conclusion it occurred to me that my speech or my silence, indeed any action of mine, would be a mere futility. What did it matter what any one knew or ignored? What did it matter who was manager? One gets sometimes such a flash of insight. The essentials of this affair lay deep under the surface, beyond my reach, and beyond my power of meddling.

"Towards the evening of the second day we judged ourselves about eight miles from Kurtz's station. I wanted to push on; but the manager looked grave, and told me the navigation up there was so dangerous that it would be advisable, the sun being very low already, to wait where we were till next morning. Moreover, he pointed out that if the warning to approach cautiously were to be followed, we must approach in daylight—not at dusk, or in the dark. This was sensible enough. Eight miles meant nearly three hours' steaming for us, and I could also see suspicious ripples at the upper end of the reach. Nevertheless, I was annoyed beyond expression at the delay, and most unreasonably, too, since one night more could not matter much after so many months. As we had plenty of wood, and caution was the word, I brought up in the middle of the stream. The reach was narrow, straight, with high sides like a railway cutting. The dusk came gliding into it long before the sun had set. The current ran smooth and swift, but a dumb immobility sat on the banks. The living trees, lashed together by the creepers and every living bush of the undergrowth, might have been changed into stone, even to the slenderest twig, to the lightest leaf. It was not sleep—it seemed unnatural, like a state of trance. Not the faintest sound of any kind could be heard. You looked on amazed, and began to suspect yourself of being deaf—then the night came suddenly, and struck you blind as well. About three in the morning some large fish leaped, and the loud splash made me jump as though a gun had been fired. When the sun rose there was a white fog, very warm and clammy, and more blinding than the night. It did not shift or drive; it was just there, standing all round you like something solid. At eight or nine, perhaps, it lifted as a shutter lifts. We had a glimpse of the towering multitude of trees, of the immense matted jungle, with the blazing little ball of the sun hanging over it—all perfectly still—and then the white shutter came down again, smoothly, as if sliding in greased grooves. I ordered the chain, which we had begun to heave in, to be paid out again. Before it stopped running with a muffled rattle, a cry, a very loud cry, as of infinite desolation, soared slowly in the opaque air. It ceased. A complaining clamor, modulated in savage discords, filled our ears. The sheer unexpectedness of it made my hair stir under my cap. I don't know how it struck the others: to me it seemed as though the mist itself had screamed, so suddenly, and apparently from all sides at once, did this tumultuous and mournful uproar arise. It culminated in a hurried outbreak of almost intolerably excessive shrieking, which stopped short, leaving us stiffened in a variety of silly attitudes, and obstinately listening to the nearly as appalling and excessive silence. 'Good God! What is the meaning—' stammered at my elbow one of the pilgrims,—a little fat man, with sandy hair and red whiskers, who wore side-spring boots, and pink pajamas tucked into his socks. Two others remained open-mouthed a whole minute, then dashed into the little cabin, to rush out incontinently and stand darting scared glances, with Winchesters at 'ready' in their hands. What we could see was just the steamer we were on, her outlines blurred as though she had been on the point of dissolving, and a misty strip of water, perhaps two feet broad, around her—and that was all. The rest of the world was nowhere, as far as our eyes and ears were concerned. Just nowhere. Gone, disappeared; swept off without leaving a whisper or a shadow behind.

"I went forward, and ordered the chain to be hauled in short, so as to be ready to trip the anchor and move the steamboat at once if necessary. 'Will they attack?' whispered an awed voice. 'We will be all butchered in this fog,' murmured another. The faces twitched with the strain, the hands trembled slightly, the eyes forgot to wink. It was very curious to see the contrast of expressions of the white men and of the black fellows of our crew, who were as much strangers to that part of the river as we, though their homes were only eight hundred miles away. The whites, of course, greatly discomposed, had besides a curious look of being painfully shocked by such an outrageous row. The others had an alert, naturally interested expression; but their faces were essentially quiet, even those of the one or two who grinned as they hauled at the chain. Several exchanged short, grunting phrases, which seemed to settle the matter to their satisfaction. Their headman, a young, broad-chested black, severely draped in dark-blue fringed cloths, with fierce nostrils and his hair all done up artfully in oily ringlets, stood near me. 'Aha!' I said, just for good fellowship's sake. 'Catch 'em,' he snapped, with a bloodshot widening of his eyes and a flash of sharp teeth—'catch 'im. Give 'im to us.' 'To you, eh?' I asked; 'what would you do with them?' 'Eat 'im!' he said, curtly, and, leaning his elbow on the rail, looked out into the fog in a dignified and profoundly pensive attitude. I would no doubt have been properly horrified, had it not occurred to me that he and his chaps must be very hungry: that they must have been growing increasingly hungry for at least this month past. They had been engaged for six months (I don't think a single one of them had any clear idea of time, as we at the end of countless ages have. They still belonged to the beginnings of time—had no inherited experience to teach them as it were), and of course, as long as there was a piece of paper written over in accordance with some farcical law or other made down the river, it didn't enter anybody's head to trouble how they would live. Certainly they had brought with them some rotten hippo-meat, which couldn't have lasted very long, anyway, even if the pilgrims hadn't, in the midst of a shocking hullabaloo, thrown a considerable quantity of it overboard. It looked like a high-handed proceeding; but it was really a case of legitimate self-defense. You can't breathe dead hippo waking, sleeping, and eating, and at the same time keep your precarious grip on existence. Besides that, they had given them every week three pieces of brass wire, each about nine inches long; and the theory was they were to buy their provisions with that currency in river-side villages. You can see how *that* worked. There were either no villages, or the people were hostile, or the director, who like the rest of us fed out of tins, with an occasional old he-goat thrown in, didn't want to stop the steamer for some more or less recondite reason. So, unless they swallowed the wire itself, or made loops of it to snare the fishes with, I don't see what good their extravagant salary could be to them. I must say it was paid with a regularity worthy of a large and honorable trading company. For the rest, the only thing to eat—though it didn't look eatable in the least—I saw in their possession was a few lumps of some stuff like half-cooked dough, of a dirty lavender color, they kept wrapped in leaves, and now and then swallowed a piece of, but so small that it seemed done more for the looks of the thing than for any serious purpose of sustenance. Why in the name of all the gnawing devils of hunger they didn't go for us— they were thirty to five—and have a good tuck-in for once, amazes me now when I think of it. They were big powerful men, with not much capacity to weigh the consequences, with courage, with strength, even yet, though their skins were no longer glossy and their muscles no longer hard. And I saw that something restraining, one of those human secrets that baffle probability, had come into play there. I looked at them with a swift quickening of interest—not because it occurred to me I might be eaten by them before very long, though

I own to you that just then I perceived—in a new light, as it were—how unwholesome the pilgrims looked, and I hoped, yes, I positively hoped, that
my aspect was not so—what shall I say?—so—unappetizing: a touch of fantastic vanity which fitted well with the dream-sensation that pervaded all my
days at that time. Perhaps I had a little fever, too. One can't live with one's
finger everlastingly on one's pulse. I had often 'a little fever,' or a little touch
of other things—the playful paw-strokes of the wilderness, the preliminary
trifling before the more serious onslaught which came in due course. Yes; I
looked at them as you would on any human being, with a curiosity of their
impulses, motives, capacities, weaknesses, when brought to the test of an inexorable physical necessity. Restraint! What possible restraint? Was it superstition, disgust, patience, fear—or some kind of primitive honor? No fear can
stand up to hunger, no patience can wear it out, disgust simply does not exist
where hunger is; and as to superstition, beliefs, and what you may call principles, they are less than chaff in a breeze. Don't you know the devilry of lingering starvation, its exasperating torment, its black thoughts, its somber and
brooding ferocity? Well, I do. It takes a man all his inborn strength to fight
hunger properly. It's really easier to face bereavement, dishonor, and the per-
dition of one's soul—than this kind of prolonged hunger. Sad, but true. And
these chaps, too, had no earthly reason for any kind of scruple. Restraint! I
would just as soon have expected restraint from a hyena prowling amongst the
corpses of a battlefield. But there was the fact facing me—the fact dazzling, to
be seen, like the foam on the depths of the sea, like a ripple on an unfathomable
enigma, a mystery greater—when I thought of it—than the curious, inexplicable note of desperate grief in this savage clamor that had swept by us on the
river-bank, behind the blind whiteness of the fog.

"Two pilgrims were quarreling in hurried whispers as to which bank.
'Left.' 'No, no; how can you? Right, right, of course.' 'It is very serious,' said the
manager's voice behind me; 'I would be desolated if anything should happen
to Mr. Kurtz before we came up.' I looked at him, and had not the slightest
doubt he was sincere. He was just the kind of man who would wish to preserve
appearances. That was his restraint. But when he muttered something about
going on at once, I did not even take the trouble to answer him. I knew, and he
knew, that it was impossible. Were we to let go our hold of the bottom, we
would be absolutely in the air—in space. We wouldn't be able to tell where
we were going to—whether up or down stream, or across—till we fetched
against one bank or the other,—and then we wouldn't know at first which it
was. Of course I made no move. I had no mind for a smash-up. You couldn't
imagine a more deadly place for a ship-wreck. Whether drowned at once or not,
we were sure to perish speedily in one way or another. 'I authorize you to take
all the risks,' he said, after a short silence. 'I refuse to take any,' I said, shortly;
which was just the answer he expected, though its tone might have surprised
him. 'Well, I must defer to your judgment. You are captain,' he said, with
marked civility. I turned my shoulder to him in sign of my appreciation, and
looked into the fog. How long would it last? It was the most hopeless look-out.

The approach to this Kurtz grubbing for ivory in the wretched bush was beset by as many dangers as though he had been an enchanted princess sleeping in a fabulous castle. 'Will they attack, do you think?' asked the manager, in a confidential tone.

"I did not think they would attack, for several obvious reasons. The thick fog was one. If they left the bank in their canoes they would get lost in it, as we would be if we attempted to move. Still, I had also judged the jungle of both banks quite impenetrable—and yet eyes were in it, eyes that had seen us. The river-side bushes were certainly very thick; but the undergrowth behind was evidently penetrable. However, during the short lift I had seen no canoes anywhere in the reach—certainly not abreast of the steamer. But what made the idea of attack inconceivable to me was the nature of the noise—of the cries we had heard. They had not the fierce character boding immediate hostile intention. Unexpected, wild, and violent as they had been, they had given me an irresistible impression of sorrow. The glimpse of the steamboat had for some reason filled those savages with unrestrained grief. The danger, if any, I expounded, was from our proximity to a great human passion let loose. Even extreme grief may ultimately vent itself in violence—but more generally takes the form of apathy. . . .

"You should have seen the pilgrims stare! They had no heart to grin, or even to revile me: but I believe they thought me gone mad—with fright, maybe. I delivered a regular lecture. My dear boys. it was no good bothering. Keep a look-out? Well, you may guess I watched the fog for the signs of lifting as a cat watches a mouse; but for anything else our eyes were of no more use to us than if we had been buried miles deep in a heap of cotton-wool. It felt like it, too—choking. warm, stifling. Besides. all I said, though it sounded extravagant, was absolutely true to fact. What we afterwards alluded to as an attack was really an attempt at repulse. The action was very far from being aggressive—it was not even defensive. in the usual sense: it was undertaken under the stress of desperation, and in its essence was purely protective.

"It developed itself, I should say, two hours after the fog lifted, and its commencement was at a spot, roughly speaking, about a mile and a half below Kurtz's station. We had just floundered and flopped round a bend, when I saw an islet, a mere grassy hummock of bright green, in the middle of the stream. It was the only thing of the kind; but as we opened the reach more, I perceived it was the head of a long sandbank. or rather of a chain of shallow patches stretching down the middle of the river. They were discolored, just awash, and the whole lot was seen just under the water, exactly as a man's backbone is seen running down the middle of his back under the skin. Now, as far as I did see, I could go to the right or to the left of this. I didn't know either channel, of course. The banks looked pretty well alike, the depth appeared the same; but as I had been informed the station was on the west side, I naturally headed for the western passage.

"No sooner had we fairly entered it than I became aware it was much narrower than I had supposed. To the left of us there was the long uninterrupted shoal, and to the right a high, steep bank heavily overgrown with bushes. Above the bush the trees stood in serried ranks. The twigs overhung the current thickly, and from distance to distance a large limb of some tree projected rigidly over the stream. It was then well on in the afternoon, the face of the forest was gloomy, and a broad strip of shadow had already fallen on the water. In this shadow we steamed up—very slowly, as you may imagine. I sheered her well inshore—the water being deepest near the bank, as the sounding-pole informed me.

"One of my hungry and forbearing friends was sounding in the bows just below me. This steamboat was exactly like a decked scow. On the deck, there were two little teak-wood houses, with doors and windows. The boiler was in the fore-end, and the machinery right astern. Over the whole there was a light roof, supported on stanchions. The funnel projected through that roof, and in front of the funnel a small cabin built of light planks served for a pilot-house. It contained a couch, two camp-stools, a loaded Martini-Henry leaning in one corner, a tiny table, and the steering-wheel. It had a wide door in front and a broad shutter at each side. All these were always thrown open, of course. I spent my days perched up there on the extreme fore-end of that roof, before the door. At night I slept, or tried to, on the couch. An athletic black belonging to some coast tribe, and educated by my poor predecessor, was the helmsman. He sported a pair of brass earrings, wore a blue cloth wrapper from the waist to the ankles, and thought all the world of himself. He was the most unstable kind of fool I had ever seen. He steered with no end of a swagger while you were by; but if he lost sight of you, he became instantly the prey of an abject funk, and would let that cripple of a steamboat get the upper hand of him in a minute.

"I was looking down at the sounding-pole, and feeling much annoyed to see at each try a little more of it stick out of that river, when I saw my poleman give up the business suddenly, and stretch himself flat on the deck, without even taking the trouble to haul his pole in. He kept hold on it though, and it trailed in the water. At the same time the fireman, whom I could also see below me, sat down abruptly before his furnace and ducked his head. I was amazed. Then I had to look at the river mighty quick, because there was a snag in the fairway. Sticks, little sticks, were flying about—thick: they were whizzing before my nose, dropping below me, striking behind me against my pilot-house. All this time the river, the shore, the woods, were very quiet—perfectly quiet. I could only hear the heavy splashing thump of the stern-wheel and the patter of these things. We cleared the snag clumsily. Arrows, by Jove! We were being shot at! I stepped in quickly to close the shutter on the land-side. That fool-helmsman, his hands on the spokes, was lifting his knees high, stamping his feet, champing his mouth, like a reined-in horse. Confound him! And we were staggering within ten feet of the bank. I had to lean right out to swing the heavy shutter, and I saw a face amongst the leaves on the level with my own, looking at me very fierce and steady; and then suddenly, as though a veil had been removed from my eyes, I made out, deep in the tangled gloom, naked breasts, arms, legs, glaring eyes,—the bush was swarming with human limbs in movement, glistening, of bronze color. The twigs shook, swayed, and rustled, the arrows flew out of them, and then the shutter came to. 'Steer her straight.' I said to the helmsman. He held his head rigid, face forward; but his eyes rolled, he kept on lifting and setting down his feet gently, his mouth foamed a little. 'Keep quiet!' I said in a fury. I might just as well have ordered a tree not to sway in the wind. I darted out. Below me there was a great scuffle of feet on the iron deck; confused exclamations; a voice screamed, 'Can you turn back?' I caught sight of a V-shaped ripple on the water ahead. What? Another snag! A fusillade burst out under my feet. The pilgrims had opened with their Winchesters, and were simply squirting lead into that bush. A deuce of a lot of smoke came up and drove slowly forward. I swore at it. Now I couldn't see the ripple or the snag either. I stood in the doorway, peering, and the arrows came in swarms. They might have been poisoned, but they looked as though they wouldn't kill a cat. The bush began to howl. Our wood-cutters raised a warlike whoop; the report of a rifle just at my back deafened me. I glanced over my shoulder, and the pilot-house was yet full of noise and smoke when I made a dash at the wheel. The fool-nigger had dropped everything, to throw the shutter open and let off that Martini-Henry. He stood before the wide opening, glaring, and I yelled at him to come back, while I straightened the sudden twist out of that steamboat. There was no room to turn even if I had wanted to, the snag was somewhere very near ahead in that confounded smoke, there was no time to lose, so I just crowded her into the bank—right into the bank, where I knew the water was deep.

"We tore slowly along the overhanging bushes in a whirl of broken twigs and flying leaves. The fusillade below stopped short, as I had foreseen it would when the squirts got empty. I threw my head back to a glinting whizz that traversed the pilot-house, in at one shutter-hole and out at the other. Looking past that mad helmsman, who was shaking the empty rifle and yelling at the shore, I saw vague forms of men running bent double, leaping, gliding, distinct, incomplete, evanescent. Something big appeared in the air before the shutter, the rifle went overboard, and the man stepped back swiftly, looked at me over his shoulder in an extraordinary, profound, familiar manner, and fell upon my feet. The side of his head hit the wheel twice, and the end of what appeared a long cane clattered round and knocked over a little camp-stool. It looked as though, after wrenching that thing from somebody ashore he had lost his balance in the effort. The thin smoke had blown away, we were clear of the snag, and looking ahead I could see that in another hundred yards or so I would be free to sheer off, away from the bank; but my feet felt so very warm and wet that I had to look down. The man had rolled on his back and stared straight up at me; both his hands clutched that cane. It was the shaft of a spear that, either thrown or lunged through the opening, had caught him in the side just below the ribs; the blade had gone in out of sight, after making a frightful gash; my shoes were full; a pool of blood lay very still, gleaming dark-red under the wheel; his eyes shone with an amazing luster. The fusillade burst out again. He looked at me anxiously, gripping the spear like something precious, with an air of being afraid I would try to take it away from him. I had to make an effort to free my eyes from his gaze and attend to steering. With one hand I felt above my head for the line of the steam whistle, and jerked out screech after screech hurriedly. The tumult of angry and warlike yells was checked instantly, and then from the depths of the woods went out such a tremulous and prolonged wail of mournful fear and utter despair as may be imagined to follow the flight of the last hope from the earth. There was a great commotion in the bush; the shower of arrows stopped, a few dropping shots rang out sharply—then silence, in which the languid beat of the stern-wheel came plainly to my ears. I put the helm hard a-starboard at the moment when the pilgrim in pink pajamas, very hot and agitated, appeared in the doorway. 'The manager sends me—' he began in an official tone, and stopped short. 'Good God!' he said, glaring at the wounded man.

"We two whites stood over him, and his lustrous and inquiring glance enveloped us both. I declare it looked as though he would presently put to us some question in an understandable language; but he died without uttering a sound, without moving a limb, without twitching a muscle. Only in the very last moment, as though in response to some sign we could not see, to some whisper we could not hear, he frowned heavily, and that frown gave to his black death-mask an inconceivably somber, brooding, and menacing expression. The luster of inquiring glance faded swiftly into vacant glassiness. 'Can you steer?' I asked the agent eagerly. He looked very dubious; but I made a grab at his arm, and he understood at once I meant him to steer whether or no. To tell you the truth, I was morbidly anxious to change my shoes and socks. 'He is dead,' murmured the fellow, immensely impressed. 'No doubt about it,' said I, tugging like mad at the shoe-laces. 'And by the way, I suppose Mr. Kurtz is dead as well by this time.'

"For the moment that was the dominant thought. There was a sense of extreme disappointment, as though I had found out I had been striving after something altogether without a substance. I couldn't have been more disgusted if I had traveled all this way for the sole purpose of talking with Mr. Kurtz. Talking with . . . I flung one shoe overboard, and became aware that that was exactly what I had been looking forward to—a talk with Kurtz. I made the strange discovery that I had never imagined him as doing, you know, but as discoursing. I didn't say to myself, 'Now I will never see him,' or 'Now I will never shake him by the hand,' but, 'Now I will never hear him.' The man presented himself as a voice. Not of course that I did not connect him with some sort of action. Hadn't I been told in all the tones of jealousy and admiration that he had collected, bartered, swindled, or stolen more ivory than all the other agents together? That was not the point. The point was in his being a gifted creature, and that of all his gifts the one that stood out preëminently, that carried with it a sense of real presence, was his ability to talk, his words— the gift of expression, the bewildering, the illuminating, the most exalted and the most contemptible, the pulsating stream of light, or the deceitful flow from the heart of an impenetrable darkness.

"The other shoe went flying unto the devil-god of that river. I thought, by Jove! it's all over. We are too late; he has vanished—the gift has vanished, by means of some spear, arrow, or club. I will never hear that chap speak after all,—and my sorrow had a startling extravagance of emotion, even such as I had noticed in the howling sorrow of these savages in the bush. I couldn't have felt more lonely desolation somehow, had I been robbed of a belief or had missed my destiny in life. . . . Why do you sigh in this beastly way, somebody? Absurd? Well, absurd. Good Lord! mustn't a man ever— Here, give me some tobacco.". . .

There was a pause of profound stillness, then a match flared, and Marlow's lean face appeared, worn, hollow, with downward folds and drooped eyelids, with an aspect of concentrated attention; and as he took vigorous draws at his pipe, it seemed to retreat and advance out of the night in the regular flicker of the tiny flame. The match went out.

"Absurd!" he cried. "This is the worst of trying to tell. . . . Here you all are, each moored with two good addresses, like a hulk with two anchors, a butcher round one corner, a policeman round another, excellent appetites, and temperature normal—you hear—normal from year's end to year's end. And you say, Absurd! Absurd be—exploded! Absurd! My dear boys, what can you expect from a man who out of sheer nervousness had just flung overboard a pair of new shoes! Now I think of it, it is amazing I did not shed tears. I am, upon the whole, proud of my fortitude. I was cut to the quick at the idea of having lost the inestimable privilege of listening to the gifted Kurtz. Of course I was wrong. The privilege was waiting for me. Oh, yes, I heard more than enough. And I was right, too. A voice. He was very little more than a voice. And I heard—him—it—this voice—other voices—all of them were so little more than voices—and the memory of that time itself lingers around me, impalpable, like a dying vibration of one immense jabber, silly, atrocious, sordid, savage, or simply mean, without any kind of sense. Voices, voices—even the girl herself—now—"

He was silent for a long time.

"I laid the ghost of his gifts at last with a lie," he began, suddenly. "Girl! What? Did I mention a girl? Oh, she is out of it—completely. They—the women I mean—are out of it—should be out of it. We must help them to stay in that beautiful world of their own, lest ours gets worse. Oh, she had to be out of it. You should have heard the disinterred body of Mr. Kurtz saying, 'My Intended.' You would have perceived directly then how completely she was out of it. And the lofty frontal bone of Mr. Kurtz! They say the hair goes on growing sometimes, but this—ah—specimen, was impressively bald. The wilderness had patted him on the head, and, behold, it was like a ball—an ivory ball; it had caressed him, and—lo!—he had withered; it had taken him, loved him, embraced him, got into his veins, consumed his flesh, and sealed his soul to its own by the inconceivable ceremonies of some devilish initiation. He was its spoiled and pampered favorite. Ivory? I should think so. Heaps of it, stacks of it. The old mud shanty was bursting with it. You would think there was not a single tusk left either above or below the ground in the whole country. 'Mostly fossil,' the manager had remarked, disparagingly. It was no more fossil than I am; but they call it fossil when it is dug up. It appears these niggers do bury the tusks sometimes—but evidently they couldn't bury this parcel deep enough to save the gifted Mr. Kurtz from his fate. We filled the steamboat with it, and had to pile a lot on the deck. Thus he could see and enjoy as long as he could see, because the appreciation of this favor had remained with him to the last. You should have heard him say, 'My ivory.' Oh, yes, I heard him. 'My Intended, my ivory, my station, my river, my—' everything belonged to him. It made me hold my breath in expectation of hearing the wilderness burst into a prodigious peal of laughter that would shake the fixed stars in their places. Everything belonged to him—but that was a trifle. The thing was to know what he belonged to, how many powers of darkness claimed him for their own. That was the reflection that made you creepy all over. It was impossible—it was not good for one either—trying to imagine. He had taken a high seat amongst the devils of the land—I mean literally. You can't understand. How could you?—with solid pavement under your feet, surrounded by kind neighbors ready to cheer you or to fall on you, stepping delicately between the butcher and the policeman, in the holy terror of scandal and gallows and lunatic asylums—how can you imagine what particular region of the first ages a man's untrammeled feet may take him into by the way of solitude—utter solitude without a policeman—by the way of silence—utter silence, where no warning voice of a kind neighbor can be heard whispering of public opinion? These little things make all the great difference. When they are gone you must fall back upon your own innate strength, upon your own capacity for faithfulness. Of course you may be too much of a fool to go wrong—too dull even to know you are being assaulted by the powers of darkness. I take it, no fool ever made a bargain for his soul with the devil: the fool is too much of a fool, or the devil too much of a devil—I don't know which. Or you may be such a thunderingly exalted creature as to be altogether deaf and blind to anything but heavenly sights and sounds. Then the earth for you is only a standing place—and whether to be like this is your loss or your gain I won't pretend to say. But most of us are neither one nor the other. The earth for us is a place to live in, where we must put up with sights, with sounds, with smells, too, by Jove!—breathe dead hippo, so to speak, and not be contaminated. And there, don't you see? your strength comes in, the faith in your ability for the digging of unostentatious holes to bury the stuff in— your power of devotion, not to yourself, but to an obscure, back-breaking business. And that's difficult enough. Mind, I am not trying to excuse or even explain—I am trying to account to myself for—for—Mr. Kurtz—for the shade of Mr. Kurtz. This initiated wraith from the back of Nowhere honored me with its amazing confidence before it vanished altogether. This was because it could speak English to me. The original Kurtz had been educated partly in England, and—as he was good enough to say himself—his sympathies were in the right place. His mother was half-English, his father was half-French. All Europe contributed to the making of Kurtz; and by and by I learned that, most appropriately, the International Society for the Suppression of Savage Customs had intrusted him with the making of a report, for its future guidance. And he had written it, too. I've seen it. I've read it. It was eloquent, vibrating with eloquence, but too high-strung, I think. Seventeen pages of close writing he had found time for! But this must have been before his—let us say—nerves, went wrong, and caused him to preside at certain midnight dances ending with unspeakable rites, which—as far as I reluctantly gathered from what I heard at various times—were offered up to him—do you understand?—to Mr. Kurtz himself. But it was a beautiful piece of writing. The opening para-graph, however, in the light of later information, strikes me now as ominous. He began with the argument that we whites, from the point of development we had arrived at, 'must necessarily appear to them [savages] in the nature of supernatural beings—we approach them with the might as of a deity,' and so on, and so on. 'By the simple exercise of our will we can exert a power for good practically unbounded,' etc. etc. From that point he soared and took me with him. The peroration was magnificent, though difficult to remember, you know. It gave me the notion of an exotic Immensity ruled by an august Benevolence. It made me tingle with enthusiasm. This was the unbounded power of elo-quence—of words—of burning noble words. There were no practical hints to interrupt the magic current of phrases, unless a kind of note at the foot of the last page, scrawled evidently much later, in an unsteady hand, may be regarded as the exposition of a method. It was very simple, and at the end of that moving appeal to every altruistic sentiment it blazed at you, luminous and terrifying, like a flash of lightning in a serene sky: 'Exterminate all the brutes!' The curious part was that he had apparently forgotten all about the valuable post-scriptum, because, later on, when he in a sense came to himself, he repeatedly entreated me to take good care of 'my pamphlet' (he called it), as it was sure to have in the future a good influence upon his career. I had full information about all these things, and, besides, as it turned out, I was to have the care of his memory. I've done enough for it to give me the indisputable right to lay it, if I choose, for an everlasting rest in the dustbin of progress, amongst all the sweepings and, figuratively speaking, all the dead cats of civilization. But then, you see, I can't choose. He won't be forgotten. Whatever he was, he was not common. He had the power to charm or frighten rudimentary souls into an aggravated witch-dance in his honor; he could also fill the small souls of the pilgrims with bitter misgivings: he had one devoted friend at least, and he had conquered one soul in the world that was neither rudimentary nor tainted with self-seeking. No; I can't forget him, though I am not prepared to affirm the fellow was exactly worth the life we lost in getting to him. I missed my late helmsman awfully,—I missed him even while his body was still lying in the pilot-house. Perhaps you will think it passing strange this regret for a savage who was no more account than a grain of sand in a black Sahara. Well, don't you see, he had done something, he had steered; for months I had him at my back—a help—an instrument. It was a kind of partnership. He steered for me—I had to look after him, I worried about his deficiencies, and thus a subtle bond had been created, of which I only became aware when it was suddenly broken. And the intimate profundity of that look he gave me when he received his hurt remains to this day in my memory—like a claim of distant kinship affirmed in a supreme moment.

"Poor fool! If he had only left that shutter alone. He had no restraint, no restraint—just like Kurtz—a tree swayed by the wind. As soon as I had put on a dry pair of slippers, I dragged him out, after first jerking the spear out of his side, which operation I confess I performed with my eyes shut tight. His heels leaped together over the little door-step; his shoulders were pressed to my breast; I hugged him from behind desperately. Oh! he was heavy, heavy; heavier than any man on earth, I should imagine. Then without more ado I tipped him overboard. The current snatched him as though he had been a wisp of grass, and I saw the body roll over twice before I lost sight of it forever. All the pilgrims and the manager were then congregated on the awning-deck about the pilot-house, chattering at each other like a flock of excited magpies, and there was a scandalized murmur at my heartless promptitude. What they wanted to keep that body hanging about for I can't guess. Embalm it, maybe. But I had also heard another, and a very ominous, murmur on the deck below. My friends the wood-cutters were likewise scandalized, and with a better show of reason—though I admit that the reason itself was quite inadmissible. Oh, quite! I had made up my mind that if my late helmsman was to be eaten, the fishes alone should have him. He had been a very second-rate helmsman while alive, but now he was dead he might have become a first-class temptation, and possibly cause some startling trouble. Besides, I was anxious to take the wheel, the man in pink pajamas showing himself a hopeless duffer at the business.

"This I did directly the simple funeral was over. We were going half-speed, keeping right in the middle of the stream, and I listened to the talk about me. They had given up Kurtz, they had given up the station; Kurtz was dead, and the station had been burnt—and so on—and so on. The red-haired pilgrim was beside himself with the thought that at least this poor Kurtz had been properly avenged. 'Say! We must have made a glorious slaughter of them in the bush. Eh? What do you think? Say?' He positively danced, the bloodthirsty little gingery beggar. And he had nearly fainted when he saw the wounded man! I could not help saying, 'You made a glorious lot of smoke, anyhow.' I had seen, from the way the tops of the bushes rustled and flew, that almost all the shots had gone too high. You can't hit anything unless you take aim and fire from the shoulder; but these chaps fired from the hip with their eyes shut. The retreat, I maintained—and I was right—was caused by the screeching of the steam-whistle. Upon this they forgot Kurtz, and began to howl at me with indignant protests.

"The manager stood by the wheel murmuring confidentially about the necessity of getting well away down the river before dark at all events, when I saw in the distance a clearing on the river-side and the outlines of some sort of building. 'What's this?' I asked. He clapped his hands in wonder. 'The station!' he cried. I edged in at once, still going half-speed.

"Through my glasses I saw the slope of a hill interspersed with rare trees and perfectly free from undergrowth. A long decaying building on the summit was half buried in the high grass; the large holes in the peaked roof gaped black from afar; the jungle and the woods made a background. There was no enclosure or fence of any kind; but there had been one apparently, for near the house half-a-dozen slim posts remained in a row, roughly trimmed, and with their upper ends ornamented with round carved balls. The rails, or whatever there had been between, had disappeared. Of course the forest surrounded all that. The river-bank was clear, and on the water-side I saw a white man under a hat like a cartwheel beckoning persistently with his whole arm. Examining the edge of the forest above and below, I was almost certain I could see movements—human forms gliding here and there. I steamed past prudently, then stopped the engines and let her drift down. The man on the shore began to shout, urging us to land. 'We have been attacked,' screamed the manager. 'I know—I know. It's all right.' yelled back the other, as cheerful as you please. 'Come along. It's all right. I am glad.'

"His aspect reminded me of something I had seen—something funny I had seen somewhere. As I maneuvered to get alongside, I was asking myself, 'What does this fellow look like?' Suddenly I got it. He looked like a harlequin. His clothes had been made of some stuff that was brown holland probably, but it was covered with patches all over, with bright patches, blue, red and yellow,— patches on the back, patches on the front, patches on elbows, on knees; colored binding around his jacket, scarlet edging at the bottom of his trousers; and the sunshine made him look extremely gay and wonderfully neat withal, because you could see how beautifully all this patching had been done. A beardless, boyish face, very fair, no features to speak of, nose peeling, little blue eyes, smiles and frowns chasing each other over that open countenance like sunshine and shadow on a wind-swept plain. 'Look out, captain!' he cried; 'there's a snag lodged in her last night.' 'What! Another snag?' I confess I swore shamefully. I had nearly holed my cripple, to finish off that charming trip. The harlequin on the bank turned his little pug-nose up to me. 'You English?' he asked, all smiles. 'Are you?' I shouted from the wheel. The smiles vanished, and he shook his head as if sorry for my disappointment. Then he brightened up. 'Never mind!' he cried, encouragingly. 'Are we in time?' I asked. 'He is up there,' he replied, with a toss of the head up the hill, and becoming gloomy all of a sudden. His face was like the autumn sky, overcast one moment and bright the next.

"When the manager, escorted by the pilgrims, all of them armed to the teeth, had gone to the house this chap came on board. 'I say, I don't like this. These natives are in the bush,' I said. He assured me earnestly it was all right. 'They are simple people,' he added; 'well, I am glad you came. It took me all my time to keep them off.' 'But you said it was all right,' I cried. 'Oh, they meant no harm,' he said; and as I stared he corrected himself, 'Not exactly.' Then vivaciously, 'My faith, your pilot-house wants a clean-up!' In the next breath he advised me to keep enough steam on the boiler to blow the whistle in case of any trouble. 'One good screech will do more for you than all your rifles. They are simple people,' he repeated. He rattled away at such a rate he quite overwhelmed me. He seemed to be trying to make up for lots of silence, and actually hinted, laughing, that such was the case. 'Don't you talk with Mr. Kurtz?' I said. 'You don't talk with that man—you listen to him,' he exclaimed with severe exaltation. 'But now—' He waved his arm, and in the twinkling of an eye was in the uttermost depths of despondency. In a moment he came up again with a jump, possessed himself of both my hands, shook them continuously, while he gabbled: 'Brother sailor . . . honor . . . pleasure . . . delight . . . introduce myself . . . Russian . . . son of an arch-priest . . . government of Tambov. . . . What? Tobacco! English tobacco; the excellent English tobacco! Now, that's brotherly. Smoke? Where's a sailor that does not smoke?'

"The pipe soothed him, and gradually I made out he had run away from school, had gone to sea in a Russian ship; ran away again; served some time in English ships; was now reconciled with the arch-priest. He made a point of that. 'But when one is young one must see things, gather experience, ideas; enlarge the mind.' 'Here!' I interrupted. 'You can never tell! Here I met Mr. Kurtz,' he said, youthfully solemn and reproachful. I held my tongue after that. It appears he had persuaded a Dutch trading house on the coast to fit him out with stores and goods, and had started for the interior with a light heart, and no more idea of what would happen to him than a baby. He had been wandering about that river for nearly two years alone, cut off from everybody and everything. 'I am not so young as I look. I am twenty-five,' he said. 'At first old Van Shuyten would tell me to go to the devil,' he narrated with keen enjoyment; 'but I stuck to him, and talked and talked, till at last he got afraid I would talk the hind-leg off his favorite dog, so he gave me some cheap things and a few guns, and told me he hoped he would never see my face again. Good old Dutchman, Van Shuyten. I've sent him one small lot of ivory a year ago, so that he can't call me a little thief when I get back. I hope he got it. And for the rest I don't care. I had some wood stacked for you. That was my old house. Did you see?'

"I gave him Towson's book. He made as though he would kiss me, but restrained himself. 'The only book I had left, and I thought I had lost it,' he said, looking at it ecstatically. 'So many accidents happen to a man going about alone, you know. Canoes get upset sometimes—and sometimes you've got to clear out so quick when the people get angry.' He thumbed the pages. 'You made notes in Russian?' I asked. He nodded. 'I thought they were written in cipher,' I said. He laughed, then became serious. 'I had lots of trouble to keep these people off,' he said. 'Did they want to kill you?' I asked. 'Oh, no!' he cried, and checked himself. 'Why did they attack us?' I pursued. He hesitated, then said shamefacedly, 'They don't want him to go.' 'Don't they?' I said curiously.

He nodded a nod full of mystery and wisdom. 'I tell you,' he cried, 'this man has enlarged my mind.' He opened his arms wide, staring at me with his little blue eyes that were perfectly round."

III

"I looked at him, lost in astonishment. There he was before me, in motley, as though he had absconded from a troupe of mimes, enthusiastic, fabulous. His very existence was improbable, inexplicable, and altogether bewildering. He was an insoluble problem. It was inconceivable how he had existed, how he had succeeded in getting so far, how he had managed to remain—why he did not instantly disappear. 'I went a little farther,' he said, 'then still a little farther—till I had gone so far that I don't know how I'll ever get back. Never mind. Plenty time. I can manage. You take Kurtz away quick—quick—I tell you.' The glamour of youth enveloped his parti-colored rags, his destitution, his loneliness, the essential desolation of his futile wanderings. For months—for years—his life hadn't been worth a day's purchase; and there he was gallantly, thoughtlessly alive, to all appearance indestructible solely by the virtue of his few years and of his unreflecting audacity. I was seduced into something like admiration—like envy. Glamour urged him on, glamour kept him unscathed. He surely wanted nothing from the wilderness but space to breathe in and to push on through. His need was to exist, and to move onwards at the greatest possible risk, and with a maximum of privation. If the absolutely pure, uncalculating, unpractical spirit of adventure had ever ruled a human being, it ruled this be-patched youth. I almost envied him the possession of this modest and clear flame. It seemed to have consumed all thought of self so completely, that even while he was talking to you, you forgot that it was he—the man before your eyes—who had gone through these things. I did not envy him his devotion to Kurtz, though. He had not meditated over it. It came to him and he accepted it with a sort of eager fatalism. I must say that to me it appeared about the most dangerous thing in every way he had come upon so far.

"They had come together unavoidably, like two ships becalmed near each other, and lay rubbing sides at last. I suppose Kurtz wanted an audience, because on a certain occasion, when encamped in the forest, they had talked all night, or more probably Kurtz had talked. 'We talked of everything,' he said, quite transported at the recollection. 'I forgot there was such a thing as sleep. The night did not seem to last an hour. Everything! Everything! . . . Of love, too.' 'Ah, he talked to you of love!' I said, much amused. 'It isn't what you think,' he cried, almost passionately. 'It was in general. He made me see things—things.'

"He threw his arms up. We were on deck at the time, and the headman of my wood-cutters, lounging near by, turned upon him his heavy and glittering eyes. I looked around, and I don't know why, but I assure you that never, never before, did this land, this river, this jungle, the very arch of this blazing sky, appear to me so hopeless and so dark, so impenetrable to human thought, so pitiless to human weakness. 'And, ever since, you have been with him, of course?' I said.

"On the contrary. It appears their intercourse had been very much broken by various causes. He had, as he informed me proudly, managed to nurse Kurtz through two illnesses (he alluded to it as you would to some risky feat), but as a rule Kurtz wandered alone far in the depths of the forest. 'Very often coming to this station, I had to wait days and days before he would turn up,' he said. 'Ah, it was worth waiting for!—sometimes.' 'What was he doing? exploring or what?' I asked. 'Oh, yes, of course'; he had discovered lots of villages, a lake, too—he did not know exactly in what direction; it was danger-ous to inquire too much—but mostly his expeditions had been for ivory. 'But he had no goods to trade with by that time,' I objected. 'There's a good lot of cartridges left even yet,' he answered, looking away. 'To speak plainly, he raided the country,' I said. He nodded. 'Not alone, surely!' He muttered something about the villages round that lake. 'Kurtz got the tribe to follow him, did he?' I suggested. He fidgeted a little. 'They adored him,' he said. The tone of these words was so extraordinary that I looked at him searchingly. It was curious to see his mingled eagerness and reluctance to speak of Kurtz. The man filled his life, occupied his thoughts, swayed his emotions. 'What can you expect?' he burst out; 'he came to them with thunder and lightning, you know—and they had never seen anything like it—and very terrible. He could be very terrible. You can't judge Mr. Kurtz as you would an ordinary man. No, no, no! Now—just to give you an idea—I don't mind telling you he wanted to shoot me, too, one day—but I don't judge him.' 'Shoot you!' I cried. 'What for?' 'Well, I had a small lot of ivory the chief of that village near my house gave me. You see I used to shoot game for them. Well, he wanted it, and wouldn't hear reason. He declared he would shoot me unless I gave him the ivory and then cleared out of the country, because he could do so, and had a fancy for it, and there was nothing on earth to prevent him killing whom he jolly well pleased. And it was true, too. I gave him the ivory. What did I care! But I didn't clear out. No, no, I couldn't leave him. I had to be careful, of course, till we got friendly again for a time. He had his second illness then. Afterwards I had to keep out of the way; but I didn't mind. He was living for the most part in those villages on the lake. When he came down to the river, sometimes he would take to me, and sometimes it was better for me to be careful. This man suffered too much. He hated all this, and somehow he couldn't get away. When I had a chance I begged him to try and leave while there was time; I offered to go back with him. And he would say yes, and then he would remain; go off on another ivory hunt; disappear for weeks; forget himself amongst these people—forget himself—you know.' 'Why! he's mad,' I said. He protested indignantly. Mr. Kurtz couldn't be mad. If I had heard him talk, only two days ago, I wouldn't dare hint at such a thing. . . . I had taken up my binoculars while we talked, and was looking at the shore, sweep-ing the limit of the forest at each side and at the back of the house. The con-sciousness of there being people in that bush, so silent, so quiet—as silent and quiet as the ruined house on the hill—made me uneasy. There was no sign on the face of nature of this amazing tale that was not so much told as suggested to me in desolate exclamations, completed by shrugs, in interrupted phrases, in hints ending in deep sighs. The woods were unmoved, like a mask —heavy, like the closed door of a prison—they looked with their air of hidden knowledge, of patient expectation, of unapproachable silence. The Russian was explaining to me that it was only lately that Mr. Kurtz had come down to the river, bringing along with him all the fighting men of that lake tribe. He had been absent for several months—getting himself adored, I suppose—and had come down unexpectedly, with the intention to all appearance of making a raid either across the river or down stream. Evidently the appetite for more ivory had got the better of the—what shall I say?—less material aspirations. However he had got much worse suddenly. 'I heard he was lying helpless, and so I came up—took my chance,' said the Russian. 'Oh, he is bad, very bad.' I directed my glass to the house. There were no signs of life, but there was the ruined roof, the long mud wall peeping above the grass, with three little square window-holes, no two of the same size; all this brought within reach of my hand, as it were. And then I made a brusque movement, and one of the re-maining posts of that vanished fence leaped up in the field of my glass. You remember I told you I had been struck at the distance by certain attempts at ornamentation. rather remarkable in the ruinous aspect of the place. Now I had suddenly a nearer view, and its first result was to make me throw my head back as if before a blow. Then I went carefully from post to post with my glass, and I saw my mistake. These round knobs were not ornamental but symbolic; they were expressive and puzzling, striking and disturbing—food for thought and also for vultures if there had been any looking down from the sky; but at all events for such ants as were industrious enough to ascend the pole. They would have been even more impressive, those heads on the stakes, if their faces had not been turned to the house. Only one, the first I had made out, was facing my way. I was not so shocked as you may think. The start back I had given was really nothing but a movement of surprise. I had expected to see a knob of wood there, you know. I returned deliberately to the first I had seen—and there it was, black, dried, sunken, with closed eye-lids,—a head that seemed to sleep at the top of that pole, and with the shrunken dry lips showing a narrow white line of the teeth, was smiling, too, smiling continuously at some endless and jocose dream of that eternal slumber.

"I am not disclosing any trade secrets. In fact, the manager said afterwards that Mr. Kurtz's methods had ruined the district. I have no opinion on that point, but I want you clearly to understand that there was nothing exactly profitable in these heads being there. They only showed that Mr. Kurtz lacked restraint in the gratification of his various lusts, that there was something wanting in him—some small matter which, when the pressing need arose, could not be found under his magnificent eloquence. Whether he knew of this deficiency himself I can't say. I think the knowledge came to him at last—only at the very last. But the wilderness had found him out early, and had taken on him a terrible vengeance for the fantastic invasion. I think it had whispered to him things about himself which he did not know, things of which he had no conception till he took counsel with this great solitude—and the whisper had proved irresistibly fascinating. It echoed loudly within him because he was hollow at the core. . . . I put down the glass, and the head that had appeared near enough to be spoken to seemed at once to have leaped away from me into inaccessible distance.

"The admirer of Mr. Kurtz was a bit crestfallen. In a hurried indistinct voice he began to assure me he had not dared to take these—say, symbols—down. He was not afraid of the natives; they would not stir till Mr. Kurtz gave the word. His ascendancy was extraordinary. The camps of these people surrounded the place, and the chiefs came every day to see him. They would crawl. . . . 'I don't want to know anything of the ceremonies used when approaching Mr. Kurtz,' I shouted. Curious, this feeling that came over me that such details would be more intolerable than those heads drying on the stakes under Mr. Kurtz's windows. After all, that was only a savage sight, while I seemed at one bound to have been transported into some lightless region of subtle horrors, where pure, uncomplicated savagery was a positive relief, being something that had a right to exist—obviously—in the sunshine. The young man looked at me with surprise. I suppose it did not occur to him that Mr. Kurtz was no idol of mine. He forgot I hadn't heard of any of these splendid monologues on, what was it? on love, justice, conduct of life—or what not. If it had come to crawling before Mr. Kurtz, he crawled as much as the veriest savage of them all. I had no idea of the conditions, he said: these heads were the heads of rebels. I shocked him excessively by laughing. Rebels! What would be the next definition I was to hear? There had been enemies, criminals, workers—and these were rebels. Those rebellious heads looked very subdued to me on their sticks. 'You don't know how such a life tries a man like Kurtz,' cried Kurtz's last disciple. 'Well, and you?' I said. 'I! I! I am a simple man. I have no great thoughts. I want nothing from anybody. How can you compare me to . . . ?' His feelings were too much for speech, and suddenly he broke down. 'I don't understand,' he groaned, 'I've been doing my best to keep him alive and that's enough. I had no hand in all this. I have no abilities. There hasn't been a drop of medicine or a mouthful of invalid food for months here. He was shamefully abandoned. A man like this, with such ideas. Shamefully! Shamefully! I—I—haven't slept for the last ten nights. . . .'

"His voice lost itself in the calm of the evening. The long shadows of the forest had slipped downhill while we talked, had gone far beyond the ruined hovel, beyond the symbolic row of stakes. All this was in the gloom, while we down there were yet in the sunshine, and the stretch of the river abreast of the clearing glittered in a still and dazzling splendor, with a murky and overshadowed bend above and below. Not a living soul was seen on the shore. The bushes did not rustle.

"Suddenly round the corner of the house a group of men appeared, as though they had come up from the ground. They waded waist-deep in the grass, in a compact body, bearing an improvised stretcher in their midst. Instantly, in the emptiness of the landscape, a cry arose whose shrillness pierced the still air like a sharp arrow flying straight to the very heart of the land; and, as if by enchantment, streams of human beings—of naked human beings—with spears in their hands, with bows, with shields, with wild glances and savage movements, were poured into the clearing by the dark-faced and pensive forest. The bushes shook, the grass swayed for a time, and then everything stood still in attentive immobility.

" 'Now, if he does not say the right thing to them we are all done for,' said the Russian at my elbow. The knot of men with the stretcher had stopped, too, halfway to the steamer, as if petrified. I saw the man on the stretcher sit up, lank and with an uplifted arm, above the shoulders of the bearers. 'Let us hope that the man who can talk so well of love in general will find some particular reason to spare us this time,' I said. I resented bitterly the absurd danger of our situation, as if to be at the mercy of that atrocious phantom had been a dishonoring necessity. I could not hear a sound, but through my glasses I saw the thin arm extended commandingly, the lower jaw moving, the eyes of that apparition shining darkly far in its bony head that nodded with grotesque jerks. Kurtz—Kurtz—that means short in German—don't it? Well, the name was as true as everything else in his life—and death. He looked at least seven feet long. His covering had fallen off, and his body emerged from it pitiful and appalling as from a winding-sheet. I could see the cage of his ribs all astir, the bones of his arm waving. It was as though an animated image of death carved out of old ivory had been shaking its hand with menaces at a motionless crowd of men made of dark and glittering bronze. I saw him open his mouth wide—it gave him a weirdly voracious aspect, as though he had wanted to swallow all the air, all the earth, all the men before him. A deep voice reached me faintly. He must have been shouting. He fell back suddenly. The stretcher shook as the bearers staggered forward again, and almost at the same time I noticed that the crowd of savages was vanishing without any perceptible movement of retreat, as if the forest that had ejected these beings so suddenly had drawn them in again as the breath is drawn in a long aspiration.

"Some of the pilgrims behind the stretcher carried his arms—two shotguns, a heavy rifle, and a light revolver-carbine—the thunderbolts of that pitiful Jupiter. The manager bent over him murmuring as he walked beside his head. They laid him down in one of the little cabins—just a room for a bedplace and a camp-stool or two, you know. We had brought his belated correspondence, and a lot of torn envelopes and open letters littered his bed. His hand roamed feebly amongst these papers. I was struck by the fire of his eyes and the composed languor of his expression. It was not so much the exhaustion of disease. He did not seem in pain. This shadow looked satiated and calm, as though for the moment it had had its fill of all the emotions.

"He rustled one of the letters, and looking straight in my face said, 'I am glad.' Somebody had been writing to him about me. These special recommendations were turning up again. The volume of tone he emitted without effort, almost without the trouble of moving his lips, amazed me. A voice! a voice! It was grave, profound, vibrating, while the man did not seem capable of a whisper. However, he had enough strength in him—factitious no doubt —to very nearly make an end of us, as you shall hear directly.

"The manager appeared silently in the doorway; I stepped out at once and he drew the curtain after me. The Russian, eyed curiously by the pilgrims, was staring at the shore. I followed the direction of his glance.

"Dark human shapes could be made out in the distance, flitting indistinctly against the gloomy border of the forest, and near the river two bronze figures, leaning on tall spears, stood in the sunlight under fantastic head-dresses of spotted skins, warlike and still in statuesque repose. And from right to left along the lighted shore moved a wild and gorgeous apparition of a woman.

"She walked with measured steps, draped in striped and fringed cloths, treading the earth proudly, with a slight jingle and flash of barbarous orna-ments. She carried her head high; her hair was done in the shape of a helmet; she had brass leggings to the knee, brass wire gauntlets to the elbow, a crimson spot on her tawny cheek, innumerable necklaces of glass beads on her neck; bizarre things, charms, gifts of witch-men, that hung about her, glittered and trembled at every step. She must have had the value of several elephant tusks upon her. She was savage and superb, wild-eyed and magnificent; there was something ominous and stately in her deliberate progress. And in the hush that had fallen suddenly upon the whole sorrowful land, the immense wilderness, the colossal body of the fecund and mysterious life seemed to look at her, pensive, as though it had been looking at the image of its own tenebrous and passionate soul.

"She came abreast of the steamer, stood still, and faced us. Her long shadow fell to the water's edge. Her face had a tragic and fierce aspect of wild sorrow and of dumb pain mingled with the fear of some struggling, half-shaped resolve. She stood looking at us without a stir, and like the wilderness itself, with an air of brooding over an inscrutable purpose. A whole minute passed, and then she made a step forward. There was a low jingle, a glint of yellow metal, a sway of fringed draperies, and she stopped as if her heart had failed her. The young fellow by my side growled. The pilgrims murmured at my back. She looked at us all as if her life had depended upon the unswerving steadiness of her glance. Suddenly she opened her bared arms and threw them up rigid above her head, as though in an uncontrollable desire to touch the sky, and at the same time the swift shadows darted out on the earth, swept around on the river, gathering the steamer into a shadowy embrace. A formid-able silence hung over the scene.

"She turned away slowly, walked on, following the bank, and passed into the bushes to the left. Once only her eyes gleamed back at us in the dusk of the thickets before she disappeared.

" 'If she had offered to come aboard I really think I would have tried to shoot her,' said the man of patches, nervously. 'I have been risking my life every day for the last fortnight to keep her out of the house. She got in one day and kicked

Casebook

. . . .

286

up a row about those miserable rags I picked up in the storeroom to mend
my clothes with. I wasn't decent. At least it must have been that, for she talked
like a fury to Kurtz for an hour, pointing at me now and then. I don't understand the dialect of this tribe. Luckily for me, I fancy Kurtz felt too ill that day
to care, or there would have been mischief. I don't understand. . . . No—it's
too much for me. Ah, well, it's all over now.'

"At this moment I heard Kurtz's deep voice behind the curtain: 'Save me!
—save the ivory, you mean. Don't tell me. Save *me!* Why, I've had to save you.
You are interrupting my plans now. Sick! Sick! Not so sick as you would like
to believe. Never mind. I'll carry my ideas out yet—I will return. I'll show you
what can be done. You with your little peddling notions—you are interfering
with me. I will return. I . . .'

"The manager came out. He did me the honor to take me under the arm and
lead me aside. 'He is very low, very low,' he said. He considered it necessary
to sigh, but neglected to be consistently sorrowful. 'We have done all we could
for him—haven't we? But there is no disguising the fact, Mr. Kurtz has done
more harm than good to the Company. He did not see the time was not ripe
for vigorous action. Cautiously, cautiously—that's my principle. We must be
cautious yet. The district is closed to us for a time. Deplorable! Upon the
whole, the trade will suffer. I don't deny there is a remarkable quantity of
ivory   mostly fossil. We must save it, at all events—but look how precarious
the position is—and why? Because the method is unsound.' 'Do you,' said I,
looking at the shore, 'call it "unsound method"?' 'Without doubt,' he exclaimed
hotly. 'Don't you?' . . . 'No method at all,' I murmured after a while. 'Exactly,'
he exulted. 'I anticipated this. Shows a complete want of judgment. It is my
duty to point it out in the proper quarter.' 'Oh,' said I, 'that fellow—what's
his name?—the brickmaker, will make a readable report for you.' He appeared
confounded for a moment. It seemed to me I had never breathed an atmosphere so vile, and I turned mentally to Kurtz for relief—positively for relief.
'Nevertheless I think Mr. Kurtz is a remarkable man,' I said with emphasis.
He started, dropped on me a cold heavy glance, said very quietly, 'he *was,*'
and turned his back on me. My hour of favor was over; I found myself lumped
along with Kurtz as a partisan of methods for which the time was not ripe:
I was unsound! Ah! but it was something to have at least a choice of nightmares.

"I had turned to the wilderness really, not to Mr. Kurtz, who, I was ready
to admit, was as good as buried. And for a moment it seemed to me as if I also
were buried in a vast grave full of unspeakable secrets. I felt an intolerable
weight oppressing my breast, the smell of the damp earth, the unseen presence
of victorious corruption, the darkness of an impenetrable night. . . . The
Russian tapped me on the shoulder. I heard him mumbling and stammering
something about 'brother seaman—couldn't conceal—knowledge of matters
that would affect Mr. Kurtz's reputation.' I waited. For him evidently Mr.
Kurtz was not in his grave; I suspect that for him Mr. Kurtz was one of the
immortals. 'Well!' said I at last, 'speak out. As it happens, I am Mr. Kurtz's
friend—in a way.'

"He stated with a good deal of formality that had we not been 'of the same profession,' he would have kept the matter to himself without regard to consequences. 'He suspected there was an active ill will towards him on the part of these white men that—' 'You are right,' I said, remembering a certain conversation I had overheard. 'The manager thinks you ought to be hanged.' He showed a concern at this intelligence which amused me at first. 'I had better get out of the way quietly,' he said, earnestly. 'I can do no more for Kurtz now, and they would soon find some excuse. What's to stop them? There's a military post three hundred miles from here.' 'Well, upon my word,' said I, 'perhaps you had better go if you have any friends amongst the savages near by.' 'Plenty,' he said. 'They are simple people—and I want nothing, you know.' He stood biting his lip, then: 'I don't want any harm to happen to these whites here, but of course I was thinking of Mr. Kurtz's reputation—but you are a brother seaman and—' 'All right,' said I, after a time. 'Mr. Kurtz's reputation is safe with me.' I did not know how truly I spoke.

"He informed me, lowering his voice, that it was Kurtz who had ordered the attack to be made on the steamer. 'He hated sometimes the idea of being taken away—and then again. . . . But I don't understand these matters. I am a simple man. He thought it would scare you away—that you would give it up, thinking him dead. I could not stop him. Oh, I had an awful time of it this last month.' 'Very well,' I said. 'He is all right now.' 'Ye-e-es,' he muttered, not very convinced apparently. 'Thanks,' said I; 'I shall keep my eyes open.' 'But quiet—eh?' he urged, anxiously. 'It would be awful for his reputation if anybody here—' I promised a complete discretion with great gravity. 'I have a canoe and three black fellows waiting not very far. I am off. Could you give me a few Martini-Henry cartridges?' I could, and did, with proper secrecy. He helped himself, with a wink at me, to a handful of my tobacco. 'Between sailors—you know—good English tobacco.' At the door of the pilot-house he turned round—'I say, haven't you a pair of shoes you could spare?' He raised one leg. 'Look.' The soles were tied with knotted strings sandal-wise under his bare feet. I rooted out an old pair, at which he looked with admiration before tucking them under his left arm. One of his pockets (bright red) was bulging with cartridges, from the other (dark blue) peeped 'Towson's Inquiry,' etc., etc. He seemed to think himself excellently well equipped for a renewed encounter with the wilderness. 'Ah! I'll never, never meet such a man again. You ought to have heard him recite poetry—his own, too, it was, he told me. Poetry!' He rolled his eyes at the recollection of these delights. 'Oh, he enlarged my mind!' 'Good-by,' said I. He shook hands and vanished in the night. Sometimes I ask myself whether I had ever really seen him— whether it was possible to meet such a phenomenon! . . .

"When I woke up shortly after midnight his warning came to my mind with its hint of danger that seemed, in the starred darkness, real enough to make me get up for the purpose of having a look round. On the hill a big fire burned, illuminating fitfully a crooked corner of the station-house. One of the

agents with a picket of a few of our blacks, armed for the purpose, was keeping
guard over the ivory; but deep within the forest, red gleams that wavered,
that seemed to sink and rise from the ground amongst confused columnar
shapes of intense blackness, showed the exact position of the camp where
Mr. Kurtz's adorers were keeping their uneasy vigil. The monotonous beating
of a big drum filled the air with muffled shocks and a lingering vibration. A
steady droning sound of many men chanting each to himself some weird
incantation came out from the black, flat wall of the woods as the humming
of bees comes out of a hive, and had a strange narcotic effect upon my half-
awake senses. I believe I dozed off leaning over the rail, till an abrupt burst
of yells, an overwhelming outbreak of a pent-up and mysterious frenzy, woke
me up in a bewildered wonder. It was cut short all at once, and the low droning
went on with an effect of audible and soothing silence. I glanced casually
into the little cabin. A light was burning within, but Mr. Kurtz was not
there.

"I think I would have raised an outcry if I had believed my eyes. But I
didn't believe them at first—the thing seemed so impossible. The fact is I was
completely unnerved by a sheer blank fright, pure abstract terror, unconnected
with any distinct shape of physical danger. What made this emotion so
overpowering was—how shall I define it?—the moral shock I received, as if
something altogether monstrous, intolerable to thought and odious to the
soul, had been thrust upon me unexpectedly. This lasted of course the merest
fraction of a second, and then the usual sense of commonplace, deadly danger,
the possibility of a sudden onslaught and massacre, or something of the kind,
which I saw impending, was positively welcome and composing. It pacified
me, in fact, so much, that I did not raise an alarm.

"There was an agent buttoned up inside an ulster and sleeping on a chair
on deck within three feet of me. The yells had not awakened him; he snored
very slightly; I left him to his slumbers and leaped ashore. I did not betray
Mr. Kurtz—it was ordered I should never betray him—it was written I should
be loyal to the nightmare of my choice. I was anxious to deal with this
shadow by myself alone,—and to this day I don't know why I was so jealous
of sharing with any one the peculiar blackness of that experience.

"As soon as I got on the bank I saw a trail—a broad trail through the grass.
I remember the exultation with which I said to myself, 'He can't walk—he is
crawling on all-fours—I've got him.' The grass was wet with dew. I strode
rapidly with clenched fists. I fancy I had some vague notion of falling upon
him and giving him a drubbing. I don't know. I had some imbecile thoughts.
The knitting old woman with the cat obtruded herself upon my memory as a
most improper person to be sitting at the other end of such an affair. I saw a
row of pilgrims squirting lead in the air out of Winchesters held to the hip.
I thought I would never get back to the steamer, and imagined myself living
alone and unarmed in the woods to an advanced age. Such silly things—you
know. And I remember I confounded the beat of the drum with the beating
of my heart, and was pleased at its calm regularity.

"I kept to the track though—then stopped to listen. The night was very clear; a dark blue space, sparkling with dew and starlight, in which black things stood very still. I thought I could see a kind of motion ahead of me. I was strangely cocksure of everything that night. I actually left the track and ran in a wide semicircle (I verily believe chuckling to myself) so as to get in front of that stir, of that motion I had seen—if indeed I had seen anything. I was circumventing Kurtz as though it had been a boyish game.

"I came upon him, and, if he had not heard me coming, I would have fallen over him, too, but he got up in time. He rose, unsteady, long, pale, indistinct, like a vapor exhaled by the earth, and swayed slightly, misty and silent before me; while at my back the fires loomed between the trees, and the murmur of many voices issued from the forest. I had cut him off cleverly; but when actually confronting him I seemed to come to my senses, I saw the danger in its right proportion. It was by no means over yet. Suppose he began to shout? Though he could hardly stand, there was still plenty of vigor in his voice. 'Go away—hide yourself,' he said, in that profound tone. It was very awful. I glanced back. We were within thirty yards from the nearest fire. A black figure stood up, strode on long black legs, waving long black arms, across the glow. It had horns—antelope horns, I think—on its head. Some sorcerer, some witch-man, no doubt: it looked fiend-like enough. 'Do you know what you are doing?' I whispered. 'Perfectly,' he answered, raising his voice for that single word: it sounded to me far off and yet loud, like a hail through a speaking-trumpet. If he makes a row we are lost, I thought to myself. This clearly was not a case for fisticuffs, even apart from the very natural aversion I had to beat that Shadow—this wandering and tormented thing. 'You will be lost,' I said—'utterly lost.' One gets sometimes such a flash of inspiration, you know. I did say the right thing, though indeed he could not have been more irretrievably lost than he was at this very moment, when the foundations of our intimacy were being laid—to endure—to endure—even to the end—even beyond.

" 'I had immense plans,' he muttered irresolutely. 'Yes,' said I; 'but if you try to shout I'll smash your head with—' There was not a stick or a stone near. 'I will throttle you for good,' I corrected myself. 'I was on the threshold of great things,' he pleaded, in a voice of longing, with a wistfulness of tone that made my blood run cold. 'And now for this stupid scoundrel—' 'Your success in Europe is assured in any case,' I affirmed, steadily. I did not want to have the throttling of him, you understand—and indeed it would have been very little use for any practical purpose. I tried to break the spell—the heavy, mute spell of the wilderness—that seemed to draw him to its pitiless breast by the awakening of forgotten and brutal instincts, by the memory of gratified and monstrous passions. This alone, I was convinced, had driven him out to the edge of the forest, to the bush, towards the gleam of fires, the throb of drums, the drone of weird incantations; this alone had beguiled his unlawful soul beyond the bounds of permitted aspirations. And, don't you see, the terror of the position was not in being knocked on the head—though I had a very lively sense of that danger, too—but in this, that I had to deal with a being to whom I could not appeal in the name of anything high or low. I had, even like the niggers, to invoke him—himself—his own exalted and incredible degradation. There was nothing either above or below him, and I knew it. He had kicked himself loose of the earth. Confound the man! he had kicked the very earth to pieces. He was alone, and I before him did not know whether I stood on the ground or floated in the air. I've been telling you what we said—repeating the phrases we pronounced—but what's the good? They were common everyday words—the familiar, vague sounds exchanged on every waking day of life. But what of that? They had behind them, to my mind, the terrific suggestiveness of words heard in dreams, of phrases spoken in nightmares. Soul! If anybody had ever struggled with a soul, I am the man. And I wasn't arguing with a lunatic either. Believe me or not, his intelligence was perfectly clear—concentrated, it is true, upon himself with horrible intensity, yet clear; and therein was my only chance—barring, of course, the killing him there and then, which wasn't so good, on account of unavoidable noise. But his soul was mad. Being alone in the wilderness, it had looked within itself, and, by heavens! I tell you, it had gone mad. I had—for my sins, I suppose—to go through the ordeal of looking into it myself. No eloquence could have been so withering to one's belief in mankind as his final burst of sincerity. He struggled with himself, too. I saw it,—I heard it. I saw the inconceivable mystery of a soul that knew no restraint, no faith, and no fear, yet struggling blindly with itself. I kept my head pretty well; but when I had him at last stretched on the couch, I wiped my forehead, while my legs shook under me as though I had carried half a ton on my back down that hill. And yet I had only supported him, his bony arm clasped round my neck—and he was not much heavier than a child.

"When next day we left at noon, the crowd, of whose presence behind the curtain of trees I had been acutely conscious all the time, flowed out of the woods again, filled the clearing, covered the slope with a mass of naked, breathing, quivering, bronze bodies. I steamed up a bit, then swung downstream, and two thousand eyes followed the evolutions of the splashing, thumping, fierce river-demon beating the water with its terrible tail and breathing black smoke into the air. In front of the first rank, along the river, three men, plastered with bright red earth from head to foot, strutted to and fro restlessly. When we came abreast again, they faced the river, stamped their feet, nodded their horned heads, swayed their scarlet bodies; they shook towards the fierce river-demon a bunch of black feathers, a mangy skin with a pendent tail—something that looked like a dried gourd; they shouted periodically together strings of amazing words that resembled no sounds of human language; and the deep murmurs of the crowd, interrupted suddenly, were like the responses of some satanic litany.

"We had carried Kurtz into the pilot-house: there was more air there. Lying on the couch, he stared through the open shutter. There was an eddy in the mass of human bodies, and the woman with helmeted head and tawny cheeks rushed out to the very brink of the stream. She put out her hands, shouted something, and all that wild mob took up the shout in a roaring chorus of articulated, rapid, breathless utterance.

" 'Do you understand this?' I asked.

"He kept on looking out past me with fiery, longing eyes, with a mingled expression of wistfulness and hate. He made no answer, but I saw a smile, a smile of indefinable meaning, appear on his colorless lips that a moment after twitched convulsively. 'Do I not?' he said slowly, gasping, as if the words had been torn out of him by a supernatural power.

"I pulled the string of the whistle, and I did this because I saw the pilgrims on deck getting out their rifles with an air of anticipating a jolly lark. At the sudden screech there was a movement of abject terror through that wedged mass of bodies. 'Don't! don't you frighten them away,' cried some one on deck disconsolately. I pulled the string time after time. They broke and ran, they leaped, they crouched, they swerved, they dodged the flying terror of the sound. The three red chaps had fallen flat, face down on the shore, as though they had been shot dead. Only the barbarous and superb woman did not so much as flinch, and stretched tragically her bare arms after us over the somber and glittering river.

"And then that imbecile crowd down on the deck started their little fun, and I could see nothing more for smoke.

"The brown current ran swiftly out of the heart of darkness, bearing us down towards the sea with twice the speed of our upward progress; and Kurtz's life was running swiftly, too, ebbing, ebbing out of his heart into the sea of inexorable time. The manager was very placid, he had no vital anxieties now, he took us both in with a comprehensive and satisfied glance: the 'affair' had come off as well as could be wished. I saw the time approaching when I would be left alone of the party of 'unsound method.' The pilgrims looked upon me with disfavor. I was, so to speak, numbered with the dead. It is strange how I accepted this unforeseen partnership, this choice of nightmares forced upon me in the tenebrous land invaded by these mean and greedy phantoms.

"Kurtz discoursed. A voice! a voice! It rang deep to the very last. It survived his strength to hide in the magnificent folds of eloquence the barren darkness of his heart. Oh, he struggled! he struggled! The wastes of his weary brain were haunted by shadowy images now—images of wealth and fame revolving obsequiously round his unextinguishable gift of noble and lofty expression. My Intended, my station, my career, my ideas—these were the subjects for the occasional utterances of elevated sentiments. The shade of the original Kurtz frequented the bedside of the hollow sham, whose fate it was to be buried presently in the mold of primeval earth. But both the diabolic love and the unearthly hate of the mysteries it had penetrated fought for the possession of that soul satiated with primitive emotions, avid of lying fame, of sham distinction, of all the appearances of success and power.

"Sometimes he was contemptibly childish. He desired to have kings meet him at railway stations on his return from some ghastly Nowhere, where he intended to accomplish great things. 'You show them you have in you something that is really profitable, and then there will be no limits to the recognition of your ability,' he would say. 'Of course you must take care of the motives —right motives—always.' The long reaches that were like one and the same reach, monotonous bends that were exactly alike, slipped past the steamer, with their multitude of secular trees looking patiently after this grimy fragment of another world, the forerunner of change, of conquest, of trade, of massacres, of blessings. I looked ahead—piloting. 'Close the shutter,' said Kurtz suddenly one day; 'I can't bear to look at this.' I did so. There was a silence. 'Oh, but I will wring your heart yet!' he cried at the invisible wilderness.

"We broke down—as I had expected—and had to lie up for repairs at the head of an island. This delay was the first thing that shook Kurtz's confidence. One morning he gave me a packet of papers and a photograph—the lot tied together with a shoestring. 'Keep this for me,' he said. 'This noxious fool' (meaning the manager) 'is capable of prying into my boxes when I am not looking.' In the afternoon I saw him. He was lying on his back with closed eyes, and I withdrew quietly, but I heard him mutter, 'Live rightly, die, die. . . .' I listened. There was nothing more. Was he rehearsing some speech in his sleep, or was it a fragment of a phrase from some newspaper article? He had been writing for the papers and meant to do so again, 'for the furthering of my ideas. It's a duty.'

"His was an impenetrable darkness. I looked at him as you peer down at a man who is lying at the bottom of a precipice where the sun never shines. But I had not much time to give him, because I was helping the engine-driver to take to pieces the leaky cylinders, to straighten a bent connecting-rod, and in other such matters. I lived in an infernal mess of rust, filings, nuts, bolts, spanners, hammers, ratchet-drills—things I abominate, because I don't get on with them. I tended the little forge we fortunately had aboard; I toiled wearily in a wretched scrap-heap—unless I had the shakes too bad to stand.

"One evening coming in with a candle I was startled to hear him say a little tremulously, 'I am lying here in the dark waiting for death.' The light was within a foot of his eyes. I forced myself to murmur, 'Oh, nonsense!' and stood over him as if transfixed.

"Anything approaching the change that came over his features I have never seen before, and hope never to see again. Oh, I wasn't touched. I was fascinated. It was as though a veil had been rent. I saw on that ivory face the expression of somber pride, of ruthless power, of craven terror—of an intense and hopeless despair. Did he live his life again in every detail of desire, temptation, and surrender during that supreme moment of complete knowledge? He cried in a whisper at some image, at some vision—he cried out twice, a cry that was no more than a breath—

" 'The horror! The horror!' "

"I blew the candle out and left the cabin. The pilgrims were dining in the mess-room, and I took my place opposite the manager, who lifted his eyes to give me a questioning glance, which I successfully ignored. He leaned back, serene, with that peculiar smile of his sealing the unexpressed depths of his meanness. A continuous shower of small flies streamed upon the lamp, upon the cloth, upon our hands and faces. Suddenly the manager's boy put his insolent black head in the doorway, and said in a tone of scathing contempt—

" 'Mistah Kurtz—he dead.'

"All the pilgrims rushed out to see. I remained, and went on with my dinner. I believe I was considered brutally callous. However, I did not eat much. There was a lamp in there—light, don't you know—and outside it was so beastly, beastly dark. I went no more near the remarkable man who had pronounced a judgment upon the adventures of his soul on this earth. The voice was gone. What else had been there? But I am of course aware that next day the pilgrims buried something in a muddy hole.

"And then they very nearly buried me.

"However, as you see I did not go to join Kurtz there and then. I did not. I remained to dream the nightmare out to the end, and to show my loyalty to Kurtz once more. Destiny. My destiny! Droll thing life is—that mysterious arrangement of merciless logic for a futile purpose. The most you can hope from it is some knowledge of yourself—that comes too late—a crop of unextinguishable regrets. I have wrestled with death. It is the most unexciting contest you can imagine. It takes place in an impalpable grayness, with nothing underfoot, with nothing around, without spectators, without clamor, without glory, without the great desire of victory, without the great fear of defeat, in a sickly atmosphere of tepid skepticism, without much belief in your own right, and still less in that of your adversary. If such is the form of ultimate wisdom, then life is a greater riddle than some of us think it to be. I was within a hair's breadth of the last opportunity for pronouncement, and I found with humiliation that probably I would have nothing to say. This is the reason why I affirm that Kurtz was a remarkable man. He had something to say. He said it. Since I had peeped over the edge myself, I understand better the meaning of his stare, that could not see the flame of the candle, but was wide enough to embrace the whole universe, piercing enough to penetrate all the hearts that beat in the darkness. He had summed up—he had judged. 'The horror!' He was a remarkable man. After all, this was the expression of some sort of belief; it had candor, it had conviction, it had a vibrating note of revolt in its whisper, it had the appalling face of a glimpsed truth—the strange commingling of desire and hate. And it is not my own extremity I remember best—a vision of grayness without form filled with physical pain, and a careless contempt for the evanescence of all things—even of this pain itself. No! It is his extremity that I seem to have lived through. True, he had made that last stride, he had stepped over the edge, while I had been permitted to draw back my hesitating foot. And perhaps in this is the whole difference; perhaps all the wisdom, and all truth, and all sincerity, are just compressed into the inappreciable moment of time in which we step over the threshold of the invisible. Perhaps! I like to think my summing-up would not have been a word of careless contempt. Better his cry—much better. It was an affirmation, a moral victory paid for by innumerable defeats, by abominable terrors, by abominable satisfactions. But it was a victory! That is why I have remained loyal to Kurtz to the last, and even beyond, when a long time after I heard once more, not his own voice, but the echo of his magnificent eloquence thrown to me from a soul as translucently pure as a cliff of crystal.

"No, they did not bury me, though there is a period of time which I remember mistily, with a shuddering wonder, like a passage through some inconceivable world that had no hope in it and no desire. I found myself back in the sepulchral city resenting the sight of people hurrying through the streets to filch a little money from each other, to devour their infamous cookery, to gulp their unwholesome beer, to dream their insignificant and silly dreams. They trespassed upon my thoughts. They were intruders whose knowledge of life was to me an irritating pretense, because I felt so sure they could not possibly know the things I knew. Their bearing, which was simply the bearing of commonplace individuals going about their business in the assurance of perfect safety, was offensive to me like the outrageous flauntings of folly in the face of a danger it is unable to comprehend. I had no particular desire to enlighten them, but I had some difficulty in restraining myself from laughing in their faces, so full of stupid importance. I daresay I was not very well at that time. I tottered about the streets—there were various affairs to settle— grinning bitterly at perfectly respectable persons. I admit my behavior was inexcusable, but then my temperature was seldom normal in these days. My dear aunt's endeavors to 'nurse up my strength' seemed altogether beside the mark. It was not my strength that wanted nursing, it was my imagination that wanted soothing. I kept the bundle of papers given me by Kurtz, not knowing exactly what to do with it. His mother had died lately, watched over, as I was told, by his Intended. A clean-shaved man, with an official manner and wearing gold-rimmed spectacles, called on me one day and made inquiries, at first circuitous, afterwards suavely pressing, about what he was pleased to denominate certain 'documents.' I was not surprised, because I had had two rows with the manager on the subject out there. I had refused to give up the smallest scrap out of that package, and I took the same attitude with the spectacled man. He became darkly menacing at last, and with much heat argued that the Company had the right to every bit of information about its 'territories.' And said he, 'Mr. Kurtz's knowledge of unexplored regions must have been necessarily extensive and peculiar—owing to his great abilities and to the deplorable circumstances in which he had been placed: therefore—' I assured him Mr. Kurtz's knowledge, however extensive, did not bear upon the problems of commerce or administration. He invoked then the name of science. 'It would be an incalculable loss, if,' etc., etc. I offered him the report on the 'Suppression of Savage Customs,' with the postscriptum torn off. He took it up eagerly, but ended by sniffing at it with an air of contempt. 'This is not what we had a right to expect,' he remarked. 'Expect nothing else,' I said. 'There are only private letters.' He withdrew upon some threat of legal proceedings, and I saw him no more; but another fellow, calling himself Kurtz's cousin, appeared two days later, and was anxious to hear all the details about his dear relative's last moments. Incidentally he gave me to understand that Kurtz had been essentially a great musician. 'There was the making of an immense success,' said the man, who was an organist, I believe, with lank gray hair flowing over a greasy coat-collar. I had no reason to doubt his statement; and to this day I am unable to say what was Kurtz's profession, whether he ever had any—which was the greatest of his talents. I had taken him for a painter who wrote for the papers, or else for a journalist who could paint—but even the cousin (who took snuff during the interview) could not tell me what he had been—exactly. He was a universal genius—on that point I agreed with the old chap, who thereupon blew his nose noisily into a large cotton handkerchief and withdrew in senile agitation, bearing off some family letters and memoranda without importance. Ultimately a journalist anxious to know something of the fate of his 'dear colleague' turned up. This visitor informed me Kurtz's proper sphere ought to have been politics 'on the popular side.' He had furry straight eyebrows, bristly hair cropped short, an eye-glass on a broad ribbon, and, becoming expansive, confessed his opinion that Kurtz really couldn't write a bit—'but heavens! how that man could talk. He electrified large meetings. He had faith—don't you see?—he had the faith. He could get himself to believe anything—anything. He would have been a splendid leader of an extreme party.' 'What party?' I asked. 'Any party,' answered the other. 'He was an—an—extremist.' Did I not think so? I assented. Did I know, he asked, with a sudden flash of curiosity, 'what it was that had induced him to go out there?' 'Yes,' said I, and forthwith handed him the famous Report for publication, if he thought fit. He glanced through it hurriedly, mumbling all the time, judged 'it would do,' and took himself off with this plunder.

"Thus I was left at last with a slim packet of letters and the girl's portrait. She struck me as beautiful—I mean she had a beautiful expression. I know that the sunlight can be made to lie, too, yet one felt that no manipulation of light and pose could have conveyed the delicate shade of truthfulness upon those features. She seemed ready to listen without mental reservation, without suspicion, without a thought for herself. I concluded I would go and give her back her portrait and those letters myself. Curiosity? Yes; and also some other feeling perhaps. All that had been Kurtz's had passed out of my hands: his soul, his body, his station, his plans, his ivory, his career. There remained only his memory and his Intended—and I wanted to give that up, too, to the past, in a way—to surrender personally all that remained of him with me to that oblivion which is the last word of our common fate. I don't defend myself. I had no clear perception of what it was I really wanted. Perhaps it was an impulse of unconscious loyalty, or the fulfillment of one of those

ironic necessities that lurk in the facts of human existence. I don't know.
I can't tell. But I went.

"I thought his memory was like the other memories of the dead that ac-
cumulate in every man's life—a vague impress on the brain of shadows that
had fallen on it in their swift and final passage; but before the high and
ponderous door, between the tall houses of a street as still and decorous as
a well-kept alley in a cemetery, I had a vision of him on the stretcher, opening
his mouth voraciously, as if to devour all the earth with all its mankind. He
lived then before me; he lived as much as he had ever lived—a shadow insatiable
of splendid appearances, of frightful realities; a shadow darker than the
shadow of the night, and draped nobly in the folds of a gorgeous eloquence.
The vision seemed to enter the house with me—the stretcher, the phantom-
bearers, the wild crowd of obedient worshipers, the gloom of the forest, the
glitter of the reach between the murky bends, the beat of the drum, regular
and muffled like the beating of a heart—the heart of a conquering darkness.
It was a moment of triumph for the wilderness, an invading and vengeful
rush which, it seemed to me, I would have to keep back alone for the salvation
of another soul. And the memory of what I had heard him say afar there,
with the horned shapes stirring at my back, in the glow of fires, within the
patient woods, those broken phrases came back to me, were heard again in
their ominous and terrifying simplicity. I remembered his abject pleading,
his abject threats, the colossal scale of his vile desires, the meanness, the
torment, the tempestuous anguish of his soul. And later on I seemed to see
his collected languid manner, when he said one day, 'This lot of ivory now is
really mine. The Company did not pay for it. I collected it myself at a very
great personal risk. I am afraid they will try to claim it as theirs though. H'm.
It is a difficult case. What do you think I ought to do—resist? Eh? I want no
more than justice.' . . . He wanted no more than justice—no more than justice.
I rang the bell before a mahogany door on the first floor, and while I waited
he seemed to stare at me out of the glassy panel—stare with that wide and
immense stare embracing, condemning, loathing all the universe. I seemed to
hear the whispered cry, 'The horror! The horror!'

"The dusk was falling. I had to wait in a lofty drawing room with three
long windows from floor to ceiling that were like three luminous and bedraped
columns. The bent gilt legs and backs of the furniture shone in indistinct
curves. The tall marble fireplace had a cold and monumental whiteness. A
grand piano stood massively in a corner; with dark gleams on the flat surfaces
like a somber and polished sarcophagus. A high door opened—closed. I rose.

"She came forward, all in black, with a pale head, floating towards me in the
dusk. She was in mourning. It was more than a year since his death, more
than a year since the news came; she seemed as though she would remember
and mourn forever. She took both my hands in hers and murmured, 'I had
heard you were coming.' I noticed she was not very young—I mean not
girlish. She had a mature capacity for fidelity, for belief, for suffering. The

room seemed to have grown darker, as if all the sad light of the cloudy evening had taken refuge on her forehead. This fair hair, this pale visage, this pure brow, seemed surrounded by an ashy halo from which the dark eyes looked out at me. Their glance was guileless, profound, confident, and trustful. She carried her sorrowful head as though she were proud of that sorrow, as though she would say, I—I alone know how to mourn him as he deserves. But while we were still shaking hands, such a look of awful desolation came upon her face that I perceived she was one of those creatures that are not the playthings of Time. For her he had died only yesterday. And, by Jove! the impression was so powerful that for me, too, he seemed to have died only yesterday—nay, this very minute. I saw her and him in the same instant of time—his death and her sorrow—I saw her sorrow in the very moment of his death. Do you understand? I saw them together—I heard them together. She had said, with a deep catch of the breath, 'I have survived' while my strained ears seemed to hear distinctly, mingled with her tone of despairing regret, the summing up whisper of his eternal condemnation. I asked myself what I was doing there, with a sensation of panic in my heart as though I had blundered into a place of cruel and absurd mysteries not fit for a human being to behold. She motioned me to a chair. We sat down. I laid the packet gently on the little table, and she put her hand over it. . . . 'You knew him well,' she murmured, after a moment of mourning silence.

" 'Intimacy grows quickly out there,' I said. 'I knew him as well as it is possible for one man to know another.'

" 'And you admired him,' she said. 'It was impossible to know him and not to admire him. Was it?'

" 'He was a remarkable man,' I said, unsteadily. Then before the appealing fixity of her gaze, that seemed to watch for more words on my lips, I went on, 'It was impossible not to—'

" 'Love him,' she finished eagerly, silencing me into an appalled dumbness. 'How true! how true! But when you think that no one knew him so well as I! I had all his noble confidence. I knew him best.'

" 'You knew him best,' I repeated. And perhaps she did. But with every word spoken the room was growing darker, and only her forehead, smooth and white, remained illumined by the unextinguishable light of belief and love.

" 'You were his friend,' she went on. 'His friend,' she repeated, a little louder. 'You must have been, if he had given you this, and sent you to me. I feel I can speak to you—and oh! I must speak. I want you—you have heard his last words—to know I have been worthy of him. . . . It is not pride. . . . Yes! I am proud to know I understood him better than any one on earth—he told me so himself. And since his mother died I have had no one—no one—to—to—'

"I listened. The darkness deepened. I was not even sure he had given me the right bundle. I rather suspect he wanted me to take care of another batch of his papers which, after his death, I saw the manager examining under the lamp. And the girl talked, easing her pain in the certitude of my sympathy; she talked as thirsty men drink. I had heard that her engagement with Kurtz had been disapproved by her people. He wasn't rich enough or something. And indeed I don't know whether he had not been a pauper all his life. He had given me some reason to infer that it was his impatience of comparative poverty that drove him out there.

" '. . . Who was not his friend who had heard him speak once?' she was saying. 'He drew men towards him by what was best in them.' She looked at me with intensity. 'It is the gift of the great,' she went on, and the sound of her low voice seemed to have the accompaniment of all the other sounds, full of mystery, desolation, and sorrow, I had ever heard—the ripple of the river, the soughing of the trees swayed by the wind, the murmurs of the crowds, the faint ring of incomprehensible words cried from afar, the whisper of a voice speaking from beyond the threshold of an eternal darkness. 'But you have heard him! You know!' she cried.

" 'Yes, I know,' I said with something like despair in my heart, but bowing my head before the faith that was in her, before that great and saving illusion that shone with an unearthly glow in the darkness, in the triumphant darkness from which I could not have defended her—from which I could not even defend myself.

" 'What a loss to me—to us!'—she corrected herself with beautiful generosity; then added in a murmur, 'To the world.' By the last gleams of twilight I could see the glitter of her eyes, full of tears—of tears that would not fall.

" 'I have been very happy—very fortunate—very proud,' she went on. 'Too fortunate. Too happy for a little while. And now I am unhappy for—for life.'

"She stood up; her fair hair seemed to catch all the remaining light in a glimmer of gold. I rose, too.

" 'And of all this,' she went on, mournfully, 'of all his promise, and of all his greatness, of his generous mind, of his noble heart, nothing remains— nothing but a memory. You and I—'

" 'We shall always remember him,' I said, hastily.

" 'No!' she cried. 'It is impossible that all this should be lost—that such a life should be sacrificed to leave nothing—but sorrow. You know what vast plans he had. I knew of them, too—I could not perhaps understand—but others knew of them. Something must remain. His words, at least, have not died.'

" 'His words will remain,' I said.

" 'And his example,' she whispered to herself. 'Men looked up to him— his goodness shone in every act. His example—'

" 'True,' I said; 'his example, too. Yes, his example. I forgot that.'

" 'But I do not. I cannot—I cannot believe—not yet. I cannot believe that I shall never see him again, that nobody will see him again, never, never, never.'

"She put out her arms as if after a retreating figure, stretching them black and with clasped pale hands across the fading and narrow sheen of the window. Never see him! I saw him clearly enough then. I shall see this eloquent phantom as long as I live, and I shall see her, too, a tragic and familiar Shade, resembling in this gesture another one, tragic also, and bedecked with powerless charms, stretching bare brown arms over the glitter of the infernal stream, the stream of darkness. She said suddenly very low, 'He died as he lived.'

" 'His end,' said I, with dull anger stirring in me, 'was in every way worthy of his life.'

" 'And I was not with him,' she murmured. My anger subsided before a feeling of infinite pity.

" 'Everything that could be done—' I mumbled.

" 'Ah, but I believed in him more than any one on earth—more than his own mother, more than—himself. He needed me! Me! I would have treasured every sigh, every word, every sign, every glance.'

"I felt like a chill grip on my chest. 'Don't,' I said, in a muffled voice.

" 'Forgive me. I—I—have mourned so long in silence—in silence. . . . You were with him—to the last? I think of his loneliness. Nobody near to understand him as I would have understood. Perhaps no one to hear. . . .'

" 'To the very end,' I said, shakily. 'I heard his very last words. . . .' I stopped in a fright.

" 'Repeat them,' she murmured in a heart-broken tone. 'I want—I want—something—something—to—live with.'

"I was on the point of crying at her, 'Don't you hear them?' The dusk was repeating them in a persistent whisper all around us, in a whisper that seemed to swell menacingly like the first whisper of a rising wind. 'The horror! The horror!'

" 'His last word—to live with,' she insisted. 'Don't you understand I loved him—I loved him—I loved him!'

"I pulled myself together and spoke slowly.

" 'The last word he pronounced was—your name.'

"I heard a light sigh and then my heart stood still, stopped dead short by an exulting and terrible cry, by the cry of inconceivable triumph and of unspeakable pain. 'I knew it—I was sure!' . . . She knew. She was sure. I heard her weeping; she had hidden her face in her hands. It seemed to me that the house would collapse before I could escape, that the heavens would fall upon my head. But nothing happened. The heavens do not fall for such a trifle. Would they have fallen, I wonder, if I had rendered Kurtz that justice which was his due? Hadn't he said he wanted only justice? But I couldn't. I could not tell her. It would have been too dark—too dark altogether. . . ."

Marlow ceased, and sat apart, indistinct and silent, in the pose of a meditating Buddha. Nobody moved for a time. "We have lost the first of the ebb," said the Director, suddenly. I raised my head. The offing was barred by a black bank of clouds, and the tranquil waterway leading to the uttermost ends of the earth flowed somber under an overcast sky—seemed to lead into the heart of an immense darkness. (1903)

QUESTIONS

1. "Heart of Darkness" is a "frame story," i.e., a story told by a narrator to listeners introduced in the opening scene, then shown at the conclusion. The narrative of Marlow's trip, in other words, is framed by the setting on the Thames and the conversations aboard the *Nellie*. What is the relationship between the frame and the interior narrative? Point out the interruptions of Marlow's narrative that remind us of the circumstances indicated in the frame. Do the interruptions seem appropriate, well-timed? Why or why not?

2. What characteristics distinguish Marlow from the others aboard the *Nellie*? What are the values for the story of his distinctive qualities?

3. How valid is the objection that Marlow's visit to the city (pp. 242-245) is essentially irrelevant because the story is about a journey up the Congo River? (To answer this you need to indicate precisely what the story is about.) Relate the geographical progress of Marlow's journey up the Congo to other important progressions.

4. Like most writers, Conrad often defines one character by relating him to others. This is particularly true of the employees of the Company in the Congo. What are the relationships between Marlow, the chief accountant at the first station, Kurtz, the manager of the central station, the first-class agent, the boiler-maker, the manager's uncle, the pilgrims, the native fireman, the native helmsman, and the cannibal crew?

5. What is the function of the fantastically dressed young Russian, Kurtz' admirer? Why is his appearance appropriate?

6. Is Kurtz' Intended a beautiful idealist, an egotistical fool, or what? Is Marlow's visit with her loosely tacked on or is it a genuinely functional epilog? Explain.

7. The most important setting in the story, of course, is the Congo itself, the immense wilderness that the narrative vividly represents. What is the function of the wilderness? Along the perimeters of the wilderness there is some variety: the company stations, the changeful river, the Russian's crude hut of reeds, the white fog, and Kurtz' camp with the heads on stakes. What do these scenic elements contribute to the meaning of the story? What are the functions of these settings: the Thames, the city like "a whited sepulchre," the company offices, and the home of Kurtz' Intended?

8. Characterize Marlow's style, analyze his diction, his propensity to repeat certain sounds, his sentence structure and rhythms, and his use of figurative speech. Why should it not be more straightforward and economical? What is the relationship between language and atmosphere? In answering these questions, consider this remark of the narrator about Marlow: ". . . to him the meaning of an episode was not inside like a kernel but outside, enveloping the tale which brought it out only as a glow brings out a haze, in the likeness of one of these misty halos that sometimes are made visible by the spectral illumination of moonshine."

9. What is Marlow's general tone, i.e., his attitude toward himself and his adventure? Find examples of varieties in tone: Are there instances of wit, irony, and sarcasm? Does Marlow use hyperbole and understatement? Is he ever sentimental? What is the attitude of the frame narrator toward Marlow?

10. Technically the story has two point of view characters, the frame narrator and Marlow, the latter, of course, the more important. However, Marlow often speculates imaginatively about the feelings and thoughts of others: the manager, the young Russian, Kurtz, Kurtz' Intended, and even, though to a lesser degree, the native crew members. Find these instances of empathy. Are they convincing? Do they enrich the meaning of the story? Explain.

11. Earlier, atmosphere was defined as the unique world that the writer creates to unify his materials. What common atmospheric elements pull together such disparate scenes as those in the Company offices, the Congo, and the house of Kurtz' Intended?

12. Most of the essays that follow will lead you to discussions of the various meanings and levels of meaning of the story. At this point sum up your understanding of the story by stating precisely what Marlow learned in the Congo and the aftermath of his journey. Justify your answer by citing relevant passages.

FORM

In the selection below, Northrop Frye distinguishes two types of prose fiction, the novel and the romance. Though his primary purpose is to define each, he steps aside briefly to defend the romance against modern detractors. Your job is to determine whether "Heart of Darkness" is primarily novel or primarily romance, and to see how such a discrimination of the mode is valuable. It is a matter of historical interest to know what tradition Conrad was working in, but more important are the implications that the choice of mode has for such things as action, character, and meaning.

Northrop Frye

THE NOVEL AND THE ROMANCE

In assigning the term fiction to the genre of the written word, in which prose tends to become the predominating rhythm, we collide with the view that the real meaning of fiction is falsehood or unreality. Thus an autobiography

Reprinted from *Anatomy of Criticism*, by Northrop Frye, by permission of Princeton University Press, 1957.

coming into a library would be classified as non-fiction if the librarian believed the author, and as fiction if she thought he was lying. It is difficult to see what use such a distinction can be to a literary critic. Surely the word fiction, which, like poetry, means etymologically something made for its own sake, could be applied in criticism to any work of literary art in a radically continuous form, which almost always means a work of art in prose. Or, if that is too much to ask, at least some protest can be entered against the sloppy habit of identifying fiction with the one genuine form of fiction which we know as the novel. . . .

When we start to think seriously about the novel, not as fiction, but as a form of fiction, we feel that its characteristics, whatever they are, are such as make, say, Defoe, Fielding, Austen, and James central in its tradition, and Borrow, Peacock, Melville, and Emily Brontë somehow peripheral. This is not an estimate of merit: we may think *Moby Dick* "greater" than *The Egoist* and yet feel that Meredith's book is closer to being a typical novel. Fielding's conception of the novel as a comic epic in prose seems fundamental to the tradition he did so much to establish. In novels that we think of as typical, like those of Jane Austen, plot and dialogue are closely linked to the conventions of the comedy of manners. The conventions of *Wuthering Heights* are linked rather with the tale and the ballad. They seem to have more affinity with tragedy, and the tragic emotions of passion and fury, which would shatter the balance of tone in Jane Austen, can be safely accommodated here. So can the supernatural, or the suggestion of it, which is difficult to get into a novel. The shape of the plot is different: instead of manoeuvering around a central situation, as Jane Austen does, Emily Brontë tells her story with linear accents, and she seems to need the help of a narrator, who would be absurdly out of place in Jane Austen. Conventions so different justify us in regarding *Wuthering Heights* as a different form of prose fiction from the novel, a form which we shall here call the romance. Here again we have to use the same word in several different contexts, but romance seems on the whole better than tale, which appears to fit a somewhat shorter form.

The essential difference between novel and romance lies in the conception of characterization. The romancer does not attempt to create "real people" so much as stylized figures which expand into psychological archetypes. It is in the romance that we find Jung's libido, anima, and shadow reflected in the hero, heroine, and villain respectively. That is why the romance so often radiates a glow of subjective intensity that the novel lacks, and why a suggestion of allegory is constantly creeping in around its fringes. Certain elements of character are released in the romance which make it naturally a more revolutionary form than the novel. The novelist deals with personality, with characters wearing their *personae* or social masks. He needs the framework of a stable society, and many of our best novelists have been conventional to the verge of fussiness. The romancer deals with individuality, with characters *in vacuo* idealized by revery, and, however conservative he may be, something nihilistic and untamable is likely to keep breaking out of his pages.

The prose romance, then, is an independent form of fiction to be distinguished from the novel and extracted from the miscellaneous heap of prose works now covered by that term. Even in the other heap known as short stories one can isolate the tale form used by Poe, which bears the same relation to the full romance that the stories of Chekhov or Katherine Mansfield do to the novel. "Pure" examples of either form are never found; there is hardly any modern romance that could not be made out to be a novel, and vice versa. The forms of prose fiction are mixed, like racial strains in human beings, not separable like the sexes. In fact the popular demand in fiction is always for a mixed form, a romantic novel just romantic enough for the reader to project his libido on the hero and his anima on the heroine, and just novel enough to keep these projections in a familiar world. It may be asked, therefore, what is the use of making the above distinction, especially when, though undeveloped in criticism, it is by no means unrealized. It is no surprise to hear that Trollope wrote novels and William Morris romances.

The reason is that a great romancer should be examined in terms of the conventions he chose. William Morris should not be left on the side lines of prose fiction merely because the critic has not learned to take the romance form seriously. Nor, in view of what has been said about the revolutionary nature of the romance, should his choice of that form be regarded as an "escape" from his social attitude. If Scott has any claims to be a romancer, it is not good criticism to deal only with his defects as a novelist. The romantic qualities of *The Pilgrim's Progress,* too, its archetypal characterization and its revolutionary approach to religious experience, make it a well-rounded example of a literary form: it is not merely a book swallowed by English literature to get some religious bulk in its diet. Finally, when Hawthorne, in the preface to *The House of the Seven Gables,* insists that his story should be read as romance and not as novel, it is possible that he meant what he said, even though he indicates that the prestige of the rival form has induced the romancer to apologize for not using it.

Romance is older than the novel, a fact which has developed the historical illusion that it is something to be outgrown, a juvenile and undeveloped form. The social affinities of the romance, with its grave idealizing of heroism and purity, are with the aristocracy . . . . It revived in the period we call Romantic as part of the Romantic tendency to archaic feudalism and a cult of the hero, or idealized libido. In England the romances of Scott and, in less degree, the Brontës, are part of a mysterious Northumbrian renaissance, a Romantic reaction against the new industrialism in the Midlands, which also produced the poetry of Wordsworth and Burns and the philosophy of Carlyle. It is not surprising, therefore, that an important theme in the more bourgeois novel should be the parody of the romance and its ideals. The tradition established by *Don Quixote* continues in a type of novel which looks at a romantic situation from its own point of view, so that the conventions of the two forms make up an ironic compound instead of a sentimental mixture. Examples range from *Northanger Abbey* to *Madame Bovary* and *Lord Jim.*

The tendency to allegory in the romance may be conscious, as in *The Pilgrim's*

Progress, or unconscious, as in the very obvious sexual mythopoeia in William Morris. The romance, which deals with heroes, is intermediate between the novel, which deals with men, and the myth, which deals with gods. Prose romance first appears as a late development of Classical mythology, and the prose Sagas of Iceland follow close on the mythical Eddas. The novel tends rather to expand into a fictional approach to history. The soundness of Fielding's instinct in calling *Tom Jones* a history is confirmed by the general rule that the larger the scheme of a novel becomes, the more obviously its historical nature appears. As it is creative history, however, the novelist usually prefers his material in a plastic, or roughly contemporary state, and feels cramped by a fixed historical pattern. *Waverley* is dated about sixty years back from the time of writing and *Little Dorrit* about forty years, but the historical pattern is fixed in the romance and plastic in the novel, suggesting the general principle that most "historical novels" are romances. Similarly a novel becomes more romantic in its appeal when the life it reflects has passed away: thus the novels of Trollope were read primarily as romances during the Second World War. It is perhaps the link with history and a sense of temporal context that has confined the novel, in striking contrast to the world-wide romance, to the alliance of time and Western man.

QUESTIONS

1. What, according to Frye, is the typical shape of the plot of a novel? Of a romance? Is "Heart of Darkness" shaped "around a central situation" or is it "linear"?

2. Are Conrad's characters, in Frye's terms, "real people" or idealized people? Is it possible to assign allegorical values to any characters in the story?

3. Does Conrad use the historical elements in his work as Frye says the novelist typically does? Explain.

4. What does Frye believe are the typical psychological values for the reader of a novel? Of a romance? Try in these terms to characterize your own reaction to the work.

5. Frye claims that Conrad's *Lord Jim* is an "ironic compound" of novel and romance. Would you argue that the same is true of "Heart of Darkness"? Explain.

6. How does the consideration of the mode of "Heart of Darkness" assist in its evaluation?

SOURCES

Conrad's journey to the Congo not only provided him with experiences for "Heart of Darkness," but proved a turning point in his career. The long and dangerous illness which followed his adventure caused him to take stock of his former life and to seriously consider turning from seafaring to writing. The diary below, therefore, is a valuable document for the study of both the man and the fictionalized account of his adventures in Africa.

Joseph Conrad

INTRODUCTION: *Richard Curle*

"THE CONGO DIARY"

Introduction

The diary kept by Joseph Conrad in the Congo in 1890, or such of it as has survived (for there is no saying whether there was more or not), is contained in two small black penny notebooks, and is written in pencil. One carries his initials, J. C. K.—Joseph Conrad Korzeniowski. The first entry is dated June 13, 1890, but in the second notebook dates are practically discarded, and it is impossible to say when the last entry was made. And names of places, also, are practically discarded in the second notebook, while abounding in the first, so that, though we can see that the diary was begun at Matadi, we cannot discover where it was ended. The last place mentioned is Lulanga, far up the great sweep of the Congo River to the north of the Equator, but there remain some twenty-four pages of the diary beyond that entry in which no name whatsoever appears. It must, indeed, have been continued into the very heart of that immense darkness where the crisis of his story, "Heart of Darkness," is unfolded. We know from "A Personal Record" that he reached ultimately somewhere to the neighbourhood of Stanley Falls, and Stanley Falls are farther from Lulanga than Lulanga is from Stanley Pool.

And it is in this same book that we can read how the Polish boy, when nine years of age, looking upon a map of Africa, had put his finger upon its unexplored centre, and had said to himself, "When I grow up I shall go *there*." Go there he did, and these notebooks are the first expression of his fulfilled resolve. . . .

The following is a reproduction of the first notebook alone—not, however, of the list of names, persons, books, stores, and the calculations that fill the last pages—consisting of thirty-two manuscript pages, not all of which are full, and twelve of which are further curtailed by Conrad's sectional drawings of the day's march. The given spelling and abbreviations have been adhered to throughout—they help to heighten its true flavour—but the paragraphing and the punctuation have been freely altered.

As to the appended footnotes, their chief purpose has been to show how closely some of the earlier pages of "Heart of Darkness" are a recollection of Conrad's own Congo journey. This story was serialized in *Blackwood's Magazine* between February and April, 1899, and I remember Conrad telling me that its 40,000 words occupied only about a month in writing. When we consider the painful, slow labour with which he usually composed, we can perceive how intensely vivid his memories of this experience must have been, and, to judge from the parallel passages, how intensely actual. But then the notebook only goes to prove the almost self-evident contention that much of Conrad's work is founded upon autobiographical remembrance. Conrad himself wrote of this story in his Author's Note to the new edition of the "Youth" volume in which it appeared: " 'Heart of Darkness' is quite as authentic in fundamentals as 'Youth' . . . it is experience pushed a little (and only a little) beyond the actual facts of the case." If only he had kept a diary of his meeting and association with Kurtz! . . .

. . . One would argue, indeed, that he must have consulted the diary when writing the story, but Mrs. Conrad assures me that it was not so. Twice had she saved it from the wastepaper basket, and probably by the time "Heart of Darkness" came to be written Conrad had forgotten all about it, or did not dream that it had survived. He never spoke to me of it, and I never heard of its existence until after his death.

The second notebook, which is an entirely technical account of Congo navigation, written, no doubt, in relation to the then river charts, is not printed here, simply because it has no personal or literary interest. . . .

No other diary of Conrad's is extant, and I am very sceptical as to whether he ever kept another. He was not at all that type of man, and his piercing memory for essentials was quite sufficient for him to recreate powerfully vanished scenes and figures for the purposes of his work. In 1890, of course, he had published nothing, and though we know that the unfinished MS. (seven chapters) of "Almayer's Folly" accompanied him on his Congo journey—"A Personal Record" describes how it was nearly lost on the river—yet it is doubtful whether he seriously envisaged its appearance in print at a future date. It was largely the breakdown of Conrad's health, due to this very trip, that caused him finally to abandon the sea, and if he had not abandoned the sea, how could he have become a novelist in the accepted sense? Unless we assume that genius must always find means of full expression—a big assumption and quite beyond proof— we owe it really to an accident that Conrad adopted writing as a career. Without this journey, and, therefore, without this diary, where would have been the great Conrad novels?

The Diary

Arrived at Matadi[1] on the 13th of June, 1890.
Mr. Gosse, chief of the station (O. K.) retaining us for some reason of his own.

---

1. On his voyage from Europe presumably.

Made the acquaintance of Mr. Roger Casement,[2] which I should consider as a great pleasure under any circumstances and now it becomes a positive piece of luck. Thinks, speaks well, most intelligent and very sympathetic.

Feel considerably in doubt about the future. Think just now that my life amongst the people (white) around here cannot be very comfortable. Intend avoid acquaintances as much as possible.

Through Mr. R. C. have made the acquain[ce] of Mr. Underwood, the Manager of the English Factory (Hatton & Cookson) in Kalla Kalla. Av[ge] com[al]—hearty and kind. Lunched there on the 21st.

24th. Gosse and R. C. gone with a large lot of ivory down to Boma. On G.['s] return intend to start up the river. Have been myself busy packing ivory in casks. Idiotic employment. Health good up to now.

Wrote to Simpson, to Gov. B., to Purd.,[3] to Hope,[4] to Capt. Froud,[5] and to Mar.[6] Prominent characteristic of the social life here; people speaking ill of each other.[7]

Saturday, 28th June. Left Matadi with Mr. Harou[8] and a caravan of 31 men.[9] Parted with Casement in a very friendly manner. Mr. Gosse saw us off as far as the State station.

First halt, M'poso. 2 Danes in Company.[10]

Sund[ay], 29th. Ascent of Pataballa sufficiently fatiguing. Camped at 11 A.M. at Nsoke river. Mosquitos [always spelt thus].

Monday, 30th. To Congo da Lemba after passing black rocks. Long ascent. Harou giving up.[11] Bother. Camp bad. Water far. Dirty. At night Harou better.

Tuesday, 1st July. Left early in a heavy mist, marching towards Lufu river. Part route through forest on the sharp slope of a high mountain. Very long descent. Then market place from where short walk to the bridge (good) and

2. Afterwards the notorious Sir Roger Casement, who was hanged for treason on August 3, 1916—the very date on which Conrad died eight years later. At this period Casement was in the employ of a commercial firm in the Congo. In 1898 he became British Consul in the Congo Free State. **3.** Probably Captain Purdy, an acquaintance of Conrad. **4.** Conrad's old friend, now living in Essex, Mr. G. F. W. Hope. In 1900 Conrad dedicated "Lord Jim" to Mr. and Mrs. Hope, "with grateful affection after many years of friendship." **5.** The then Secretary of the London Ship-Master's Society. See "A Personal Record" (Concord Edition), p. 7. "Dear Captain Froud—it is impossible not to pay him the tribute of affectionate familiarity at this distance of years—had very sound views as to the advancement of knowledge and status for the whole body of the officers of the mercantile marine." **6.** Probably Marguerite Poradowska, his aunt. **7.** This was also a failing of the white men at the "Central Station" in "Heart of Darkness." **8.** Harou was an official of the Etat Indépendant du Congo Belge. **9.** Compare "Heart of Darkness," p. [250]: "Next day I left that station at last with a caravan of 60 men for a 200-mile tramp." On 13 out of the 19 travelling days taken by Conrad on this overland journey he kept a record of the distance covered, and it totals 197½ miles. [The page numbers in brackets correspond to this book's pagination of "Heart of Darkness."] **10.** Curiously enough, the identity of these two Danes was discovered by Monsieur G. Jean-Aubry in Brussels early in 1925. Not knowing that they were mentioned in the diary, he omitted to take names or particulars. **11.** He seems to have been constantly unwell and one may compare "Heart of Darkness," p. [251]: "I had a white companion too, not a bad chap, but rather too fleshy, and with the exasperating habit of fainting on the hot hillsides, miles away from the least bit of shade or water."

camp. V. G. Bath. Clear river. Feel well. Harou all right. 1st chicken, 2 P.[M.] No sunshine to-day.

Wednesday, 2nd July.   Started at 5:30 after a sleepless night. Country more open. Gently undulating hills. Road good, in perfect order. (District of Lukungu.) Great market at 9:30. Bought eggs and chickens. Feel not well to-day. Heavy cold in the head. Arrived at 11 at Banza Manteka. Camped on the market place. Not well enough to call on the missionary. Water scarce and bad. Camp^g place dirty. 2 Danes still in Company.

Thursday, 3rd July. Left at 6 A.M. after a good night's rest. Crossed a low range of hills and entered a broad valley, or rather plain, with a break in the middle. Met an off^{er} of the State inspecting. A few minutes afterwards saw at a camp^g place the dead body of a Backongo. Shot?[12] Horrid smell.

Crossed a range of mountains, running N. W.—S. E. by a low pass. Another broad flat valley with a deep ravine through the centre. Clay and gravel. Another range parallel to the first mentioned, with a chain of low foothills running close to it. Between the two came to camp on the banks of the Luinzono river. Camp^g place clean. River clear. Gov^t Zanzibari[13] with register. Canoe. 2 Danes camp^g on the other bank. Health good.

General tone of landscape gray-yellowish (dry grass) with reddish patches (soil) and clumps of dark green vegetation scattered sparsely about. Mostly in steep gorges between the high mountains or in ravines cutting the plain.[14]

Noticed Palma Christi—Oil Palm. Very straight, tall and thick trees in some places. Name not known to me. Villages quite invisible. Infer their existence from calbashes [sic] suspended to palm trees for the "Malafu." Good many caravans and travellers. No women, unless on the market place.

Bird notes charming. One especially a flute-like note. Another, kind of "boom" ressembling [sic] the very distant baying of a hound. Saw only pigeons and a few green parroquets. Very small and not many. No birds of prey seen by me.[15]

Up to 9 A.M. sky clouded and calm. Afterwards gentle breeze from the Nth generally and sky clearing. Nights damp and cool. White mists on the hills up about half way. Water effects very beautiful this morning. Mists generally raising before sky clears.

Distance 15 miles. General direction N. N. E.—S. S. W.

Friday, 4th July.   Left camp at 6 A.M. after a very unpleasant night. Marching

---

12. Compare "Heart of Darkness," p. [251]: "Once a white man in an unbuttoned uniform camping on the path . . . was looking after the upkeep of the road, he declared. Can't say I saw any road or any upkeep, unless the body of a middle-aged negro with a bullet-hole in the forehead, upon which I absolutely stumbled three miles further on, may be considered as a permanent improvement." **13.** Compare "Heart of Darkness," p. [251], in which he mentioned his meeting with a white man, who was accompanied by "an armed escort of lank Zanzibaris." **14.** In "Heart of Darkness," p. [250], the country of the march is described as "a stamped-in network of paths spreading over the empty land, through long grass, through burnt grass, through thickets, down and up hilly ravines, up and down stony hills ablaze with heat." **15.** These natural history observations are curious, as Conrad practically never showed the slightest interest in such subjects.

across a chain of hills and then in a maze of hills. At 8:15 opened out into an undulating plain. Took bearings of a break in the chain of mountains on the other side. Bearing N. N. E. Road passes through that. Sharp ascents up very steep hills not very high. The higher mountains recede sharply and show a low hilly country. At 9:30 market place. At 10 passed R. Lukanga and at 10:30 camped on the Mpwe R.

To-day's march. Direction N. N. E.$\frac{1}{2}$.—N. Dist^{ce} 13 miles.

Saw another dead body lying by the path in an attitude of meditative repose.[16]

In the evening three women, of whom one albino, passed our camp; horrid chalky white with pink blotches; red eyes; red hair; features very negroid and ugly. Mosquitos. At night when the moon rose heard shouts and drumming in distant villages.[17] Passed a bad night.

Saturday, 5th July. Left at 6:15. Morning cool, even cold, and very damp. Sky densely overcast. Gentle breeze from N. E. Road through a narrow plain up to R. Kwilu. Swift flowing and deep, 50 yds. wide. Passed in canoes. After^{ds} up and down very steep hills intersected by deep ravines. Main chain of heights running mostly N. W.—S. E. or W. and E. at times. Stopped at Manyamba. Camp^g place bad—in a hollow—water very indifferent. Tent set at 10:15. N. N. E. Dist^{ce} 12 m.

To-day fell into a muddy puddle—beastly! The fault of the man that carried me. After camp^g went to a small stream, bathed and washed clothes. Getting jolly well sick of this fun.

To-morrow expect a long march to get to Nsona, 2 days from Manyanga. No sunshine to-day.

Sunday, 6th July. Started at 5:40. The route at first hilly, then, after a sharp descent, traversing a broad plain. At the end of it a large market place. At 10 sun came out. After leaving the market passed another plain, then, walking on the crest of a chain of hills, passed 2 villages and at 11 arrived at Nsona. Village invisible.

Direction about N. N. E. Distance 18 miles.

In this camp (Nsona) there is a good camp^g place. Shady, water far and not very good. This night no mosquitos owing to large fires, lit all round our tent. Afternoon very close: night clear and starry.

Monday, 7th July. Left at 6, after a good night's rest, on the road to Inkandu, which is some distance past Lukunga Govt. station. Route very accidented.[18] Succession of round steep hills. At times walking along the crest of a chain of hills. Just before Lukunga our carriers took a wide sweep to the southward till the station bore Nth. Walking through long grass for 1½ hours. Crossed a broad river about 100 feet wide and 4 deep.

16. The most "Conradesque" phrase in the diary. **17.** Compare "Heart of Darkness," p. [251]: "Perhaps on some quiet night the tremor of far-off drums, sinking, swelling, a tremor vast, faint; a sound weird, appealing, suggestive, and wild—and perhaps with as profound a meaning as the sound of bells in a Christian country." **18.** An odd Gallicism. Conrad knew French long before he knew English; moreover, he was naturally talking much French at this time.

After another ½ hour's walk through manioc plantations in good order
rejoined our route to the E^d of the Lukunga sta^on, walking along an undulating
plain towards the Inkandu market on a hill. Hot, thirsty and tired. At 11 arrived
on the m^ket place. About 200 people. Business brisk. No water; no camp^g place.
After remaining for one hour left in search of a resting place. Row with carriers.
No water. At last about 1½ P.M. camped on an exposed hill side near a muddy
creek. No shade. Tent on a slope. Sun heavy. Wretched.

Direction N. E. by N.—Distance 22 miles.

Night miserably cold. No sleep. Mosquitos.

Tuesday, 8th July. Left at 6 A.M. About ten minutes from camp left main
Gov^t path for the Manyanga track. Sky overcast. Rode up and down all the
time, passing a couple of villages. The country presents a confused wilderness
of hills, landslips on their sides showing red. Fine effect of red hill covered in
places by dark green vegetation. ½ hour before beginning the descent got a
glimpse of the Congo. Sky clouded.

To-day's march—3 h. General direction N. by E. Dist^ce 9½ miles.

Arrived at Manyanga at 9 A.M. Received most kindly by Messrs. Heyn and
Jaeger. Most comfortable and pleasant halt.

Stayed here till the 25. Both have been sick. Most kindly care taken of us.
Leave with sincere regrets.

Friday, the 25th July, 1890. Left Manyanga at 2½ P.M. with plenty of
hammock carriers. H. lame and not in very good form. Myself ditto but not
lame. Walked as far as Mafiela and camped—2 h.

Saturday, 26th. Left very early. Road ascending all the time. Passed villages.
Country seems thickly inhabited. At 11 arrived at large market place. Left at
noon and camped at 1 P.M.

General direction E ½ N-W ½ S. Sun visible at 8 A.M. Very hot. Distance
18 miles.

Sunday, 27th. Left at 8 A.M. Sent luggage carriers straight on to Luasi, and
went ourselves round by the Mission of Sutili. Hospitable reception by Mrs.
Comber. All the missio. absent. The looks of the whole establishment eminently
civilized and very refreshing to see after the lots of tumbled down hovels in
which the State & Company agents are content to live. Fine buildings. Position
on a hill. Rather breezy.

Left at 3 P.M. At the first heavy ascent met Mr. Davis, Miss., returning from
a preaching trip. Rev. Bentley away in the south with his wife. This being off
the road, no section given.[19]

Distance traversed about 15 miles. Gen. direction E. N. E.

At Luasi we get on again on to the Gov^t road.

Camped at 4½ P.M. with Mr. Heche in company. To-day no sunshine. Wind
remarkably cold. Gloomy day.

Monday, 28th. Left camp at 6:30 after breakfasting with Heche. Road at

19. Sections of the days' marches, with numerous names on them, were given under the
following dates: July 3rd, 4th, 5th, 6th, 7th, 8th, 25th, 28th, 29th, 30th, 31st, August 1st.

first hilly. Then walking along the ridges of hill chains with valleys on both sides. The country more open and there is much more trees[20] growing in large clumps in the ravines.

Passed Nzungi and camped, 11, on the right bank of the Ngoma, a rapid little river with rocky bed. Village on a hill to the right.

General direction E. N. E.—Distance 14 miles.

No sunshine. Gloomy cold day. Squalls.

Tuesday, 29th. Left camp at 7, after a good night's rest. Continuous ascent; rather easy at first. Crossed wooded ravines and the river Lunzadi by a very decent bridge. At 9 met Mr. Louette escorting a sick agent of the comp[y] back to Matadi. Looking very well. Bad news from up the river. All the steamers disabled—one wrecked.[21] Country wooded. At 10:30 camped at Inkissi.

General direction E. N. E.—Dist[ce] 15 miles.

Sun visible at 6:30. Very warm day.

Inkissi River very rapid; is about 100 yards broad. Passage in canoes. Banks wooded very densely, and valley of the river rather deep, but very narrow.

To-day did not set the tent, but put up in Gov[t] shimbek. Zanzibari[22] in charge —very obliging. Met ripe pineapple for the first time. On the road to-day passed a skeleton tied up to a post. Also white man's grave—no name—heap of stones in the form of a cross. Health good now.

Wednesday, 30th. Left at 6 A.M. intending to camp at Kinfumu. Two hours sharp walk brought me to Nsona na Nsefe. Market. ½ hour after Harou arrived very ill with billious [*sic*] attack and fever. Laid him down in Gov[t] shimbek.

Dose of ipec[a]. Vomiting bile in enormous quantities. At 11 gave him 1 gramme of quinine and lots of hot tea. Hot fit ending in heavy perspiration. At 2 P.M. put him in hammock and started for Kinfumu. Row with carriers all the way.[23] Harou suffering much through the jerks of the hammock. Camped at a small stream. At 4 Harou better; fever gone.

General direction N. E. by E. ½ E. Distance 13 miles.

Up till noon sky clouded and strong N. W. wind very chilling. From 1 P.M. to 4 P.M. sky clear and a very hot day. Expect lots of bother with carriers tomorrow. Had them all called and made a speech, which they did not understand.[24] They promise good behaviour.

Thursday, 31st. Left at 6. Sent Harou ahead, and followed in ½ an hour.[25] Road presents several sharp ascents, and a few others easier but rather long.

20. One of the few un-English phrases in the diary. By 1890 Conrad had been a British subject for six years, but he never learnt the language until he was grown up. **21.** Compare "Heart of Darkness," p. [251]: "One of them [the white men at the Central Station] . . . informed me with great volubility and many digressions . . . that my steamer was at the bottom of the river." **22.** See note [13], p. [308]. **23.** Compare "Heart of Darkness," p. [251]: "Then he [the white man with him] got fever, and had to be carried in a hammock slung under a pole. As he weighed sixteen stone I had no end of rows with the carriers." **24.** Compare "Heart of Darkness," p. [251]: ". . . one evening, I made a speech in English with gestures, not one of which was lost to the sixty pairs of eyes before me." **25.** Compare "Heart of Darkness," p. [251]: ". . . the next morning I started the hammock off in front all right."

Notice in places sandy surface soil instead of hard clay as heretofore; think however that the layer of sand is not very thick and that the clay would be found under it. Great difficulty in carrying Harou. Too heavy—bother![26] Made two long halts to rest the carriers. Country wooded in valleys and on many of the ridges.

At 2:30 P.M. reached Luila at last, and camped on right bank. Breeze from S. W.

General direction of march about N. E. ½ E. Distance, est^d 16 miles.

Congo very narrow and rapid. Kinzilu rushing in. A short distance up from the mouth, fine waterfall. Sun rose red. From 9 A.M. infernally hot day. Harou very little better. Self rather seedy. Bathed. Luila about 60 feet wide. Shallow.

Friday, 1st of August, 1890. Left at 6:30 A.M. after a very indifferently passed night. Cold, heavy mists. Road in long ascents and sharp dips all the way to Mfumu Mbé. After leaving there, a long and painful climb up a very steep hill; then a long descent to Mfumu Kono, where a long halt was made. Left at 12:30 P.M. towards Nselemba. Many ascents. The aspect of the country entirely changed. Wooded hills with openings. Path almost all the afternoon thro' a forest of light trees with dense undergrowth.

After a halt on a wooded hillside, reached Nselemba at 4:10 P.M. Put up at Gov^t shanty. Row between the carriers and a man, stating himself in Gov^t employ, about a mat. Blows with sticks raining hard. Stopped it.

Chief came with a youth about 13 suffering from gun-shot wound in the head. Bullet entered about an inch above the right eyebrow, and came out a little inside the roots of the hair, fairly in the middle of the brow in a line with the bridge of the nose. Bone not damaged apparently. Gave him a little glycerine to put on the wound made by the bullet on coming out.

Harou not very well. Mosquitos—frogs—beastly! Glad to see the end of this stupid tramp. Feel rather seedy. Sun rose red. Very hot day. Wind Sth.

General direction of march N. E. by N. Distance about 17 miles.[27]

QUESTIONS

1. Our most obvious interest is in the sources that the diary provides for many of the details in "Heart of Darkness." In his notes, Richard Curle points out several important parallels between diary and story but perhaps not all of them. Find possible sources, for instance, for: (a) the occasional dead carriers that Marlow sees on the trek from the first station to the central station (p. 251), (b) the stakes mounted with heads at Kurtz' camp (p. 282), (c) the circum-

26. Compare "Heart of Darkness," p. [251]: ". . . he [the white man with him] weighed sixteen stone. . . ." **27.** The journey from Matadi to this point by Stanley Pool took nineteen travelling days. Compare "Heart of Darkness," p. [251]: "On the fifteenth day I came in sight of the big river [Congo] again and hobbled into the Central Station."

stances surrounding the death of Fresleven (p. 242). Point out instances of Conrad's adaptation of his experiences to the course of his narrative.

2. It is interesting to note some of the experiences of the journey that Conrad did not use in the story. Account for the omission of: (a) the missionaries, (b) the numerous market places, (c) the beautiful birdsongs, (d) the long pleasant rest at Manyanga.

3. Conrad actually reached Kinchassa ("the Central Station") the day after the diary ends, August 2, 1890, and set sail up river the following day, the third. What does Conrad accomplish by having Marlow delayed two months at the Central Station? It actually took Conrad twenty-eight days to steam from Kinchassa to Stanley Falls, as far inland as he ever went. Why does Conrad make Marlow's trip to Kurtz' camp two months long?

4. Are the tone and atmosphere of the diary carried directly over into the story, or are there significant differences?

The following excerpts from Vergil's *Aeneid*, Book VI, describe Aeneas' descent to the underworld. Aeneas and a loyal group of followers escaped the sack of Troy, built a fleet of ships, and set sail. At this point in the story Aeneas and his Trojan followers have already had many adventures. As we pick up the narrative here in Book VI, Aeneas and his followers have finally reached the western shore of Italy at Cumae, south of the site of Rome. Already the Sibyl has foretold that there must be another war and that Aeneas must encounter "a new Achilles" (Turnus, king of the Rutuli) before he can found Rome. Undismayed, Aeneas petitions the Sibyl to help him gain entrance to the underworld. There he hopes to speak to his father, Anchises, who died during the voyage from Troy to Italy.

Publius Vergilius Maro
TRANSLATOR: *C. Day Lewis*

AENEAS' JOURNEY TO THE UNDERWORLD

Thus he was making petition, his hands upon the altar,
When the Sibyl began to speak:—

Reprinted by permission of Harold Matson Company, Inc. and The Hogarth Press Ltd. from *The Aeneid of Virgil*, translated by C. Day Lewis. Copyright 1952.

O child of a goddess' womb,
Trojan son of Anchises, the way to Avernus is easy;
Night and day lie open the gates of death's dark kingdom: 5
But to retrace your steps, to find the way back to daylight—
That is the task, the hard thing. A few, because of Jove's
Just love, or exalted to heaven by their own flame of goodness,
Men born from gods, have done it. Between, there lies a forest,
And darkly winds the river Cocytus round the place.   10
But if so great your love is, so great your passion to cross
The Stygian waters twice and twice behold black Tartarus,
If your heart is set on this fantastic project,
Here's what you must do first. Concealed in a tree's thick shade
There is a golden bough—gold the leaves and the tough stem—   15
Held sacred to Proserpine: the whole wood hides this bough
And a dell walls it round as it were in a vault of shadow.
Yet none is allowed to enter the land which earth conceals
Save and until he has plucked that gold-foil bough from the tree.
Fair Proserpine ordains that it should be brought to her   20
As tribute. When a bough is torn away, another
Gold one grows in its place with leaves of the same metal.
So keep your eyes roving above you, and when you have found the bough
Just pull it out: that branch will come away quite easily
If destiny means you to go; otherwise no amount of   25
Brute force will get it, nor hard steel avail to hew it away.
Also—and this you know not—the lifeless corpse of a friend
Is lying unburied, a dead thing polluting your whole expedition,
While you are lingering here to inquire about fate's decrees.
Before anything else, you must give it proper burial and make   30
Sacrifice of black sheep: only when you are thus
Purified, shall you see the Stygian groves and the regions
Not viable to the living. . . .
     This done, Aeneas hastened to follow the Sibyl's directions.
A deep, deep cave there was, its mouth enormously gaping,   35
Shingly, protected by the dark lake and the forest gloom:
Above it, no winged creatures could ever wing their way
With impunity, so lethal was the miasma which
Went fuming up from its black throat to the vault of heaven:
Wherefore the Greeks called it Avernus, the Birdless Place.   40
Here the Sibyl first lined up four black-skinned bullocks,
Poured a libation of wine upon their foreheads, and then,
Plucking the topmost hairs from between their brows, she placed
These on the altar fires as an initial offering,
Calling aloud upon Hecate, powerful in heaven and hell.   45
While others laid their knives to these victims' throats, and caught
The fresh warm blood in bowls, Aeneas sacrificed

A black-fleeced lamb to Night, the mother of the Furies,
And her great sister, Earth, and a barren heifer to Proserpine.
Then he set up altars by night to the god of the Underworld,   50
Laying upon the flames whole carcases of bulls
And pouring out rich oil over the burning entrails.
But listen!—at the very first crack of dawn, the ground
Underfoot began to mutter, the woody ridges to quake,
And a baying of hounds was heard through the half-light: the   55
    goddess was coming,
Hecate. The Sibyl cried:—
                              Away! Now stand away,
You uninitiated ones, and clear the whole grove!
But you, Aeneas, draw your sword from the scabbard and fare forth!
Now you need all your courage, your steadfastness of heart.   60
    So much she said and, ecstatic, plunged into the opened cave mouth:
Unshrinking went Aeneas step for step with his guide.
    You gods who rule the kingdom of souls! You soundless shades!
Chaos, and Phlegethon! O mute wide leagues of Nightland!—
Grant me to tell what I have heard! With your assent   65
May I reveal what lies deep in the gloom of the Underworld!
    Dimly through the shadows and dark solitudes they wended,
Through the void domiciles of Dis, the bodiless regions:
Just as, through fitful moonbeams, under the moon's thin light,
A path lies in a forest, when Jove has palled the sky   70
With gloom, and the night's blackness has bled the world of colour.
See! At the very porch and entrance way to Orcus
Grief and ever-haunting Anxiety make their bed:
Here dwell pallid Diseases, here morose Old Age,
With Fear, ill-prompting Hunger, and squalid Indigence,   75
Shapes horrible to look at, Death and Agony;
Sleep, too, which is the cousin of Death; and Guilty Joys,
And there, against the threshold, War, the bringer of Death:
Here are the iron cells of the Furies, and lunatic Strife
Whose viperine hair is caught up with a headband soaked in blood.   80
    In the open a huge dark elm tree spreads wide its immemorial
Branches like arms, whereon, according to old wives' tales,
Roost the unsolid Dreams, clinging everywhere under its foliage.
Besides, many varieties of monsters can be found
Stabled here at the doors—Centaurs and freakish Scyllas,   85
Briareus with his hundred hands, the Lernaean Hydra
That hisses terribly and the flame-throwing Chimaera,
Gorgons and Harpies, and the ghost of three-bodied Geryon.
Now did Aeneas shake with a spasm of fear, and drawing
His sword, offered its edge against the creatures' onset: 90
Had not his learned guide assured him they were but incorporeal

Existences floating there, forms with no substance behind them,
He'd have attacked them, and wildly winnowed with steel mere shadows.
    From here is the road that leads to the dismal waters of Acheron.
Here a whirlpool boils with mud and immense swirlings   95
Of water, spouting up all the slimy sand of Cocytus.
A dreadful ferryman looks after the river crossing,
Charon: appallingly filthy he is, with a bush of unkempt
White beard upon his chin, with eyes like jets of fire;
And a dirty cloak draggles down, knotted about his shoulders.   100
He poles the boat, he looks after the sails, he is all the crew
Of that rust-coloured wherry which takes the dead across—
An ancient now, but a god's old age is green and sappy.
This way came fast and streaming up to the bank the whole throng:
Matrons and men were there, and there were great-heart heroes   105
Finished with earthly life, boys and unmarried maidens,
Young men laid on the pyre before their parents' eyes;
Multitudinous as the leaves that fall in a forest
At the first frost of autumn, or the birds that out of the deepsea
Fly to land in migrant flocks, when the cold of the year   110
Has sent them overseas in search of a warmer climate.
So they all stood, each begging to be ferried across first,
Their hands stretched out in longing for the shore beyond the river.
But the surly ferryman embarks now this, now that group,
While others he keeps away at a distance from the shingle. . . .   115
    And look! yonder was roaming the helmsman, Palinurus,
Who, on their recent voyage, while watching the stars, had fallen
From the afterdeck, thrown off the ship there in mid-passage.
A sombre form in the deep shadows, Aeneas barely
Recognised him; then accosted:—   120
                            Which of the gods, Palinurus,
Snatched you away from us and made you drown in the mid-sea?
Oh, tell me! For Apollo, whom never before had I found
Untruthful, did delude my mind with this one answer,
Foretelling that you would make your passage to Italy   125
Unharmed by sea. Is it thus he fulfils a sacred promise?
    Palinurus replied:—
                            The oracle of Phoebus has not tricked you,
My captain, son of Anchises; nor was I drowned by a god.
It was an accident: I slipped, and the violent shock   130
Of my fall broke off the tiller to which I was holding firmly
As helmsman, and steering the ship. By the wild seas I swear
That not on my own account was I frightened nearly so much as
Lest your ship, thus crippled, its helmsman overboard,
Lose steerage-way and founder amid the mountainous waves.   135
Three stormy nights did the South wind furiously drive me along

Over the limitless waters: on the fourth day I just
Caught sight of Italy, being lifted high on a wave crest.
Little by little I swam to the shore. I was all but safe,
When, as I clung to the rough-edged cliff top, my fingers crooked   140
And my soaking garments weighing me down, some barbarous natives
Attacked me with swords, in their ignorance thinking that I was a rich prize.
Now the waves have me, the winds keep tossing me up on the shore again. . . .
    Aeneas looked back on a sudden: he saw to his left a cliff
Overhanging a spread of battlements, a threefold wall about them,   145
Girdled too by a swift-running stream, a flaming torrent—
Hell's river of fire, whose current rolls clashing rocks along.
In front, an enormous portal, the door-posts columns of adamant,
So strong that no mortal violence nor even the heaven-dwellers
Can broach it: an iron tower stands sheer and soaring above it,   150
Whereupon Tisiphone sits, wrapped in a bloodstained robe,
Sleeplessly, day-long, night-long, guarding the forecourt there.
From within can be heard the sounds of groaning and brutal lashing,
Sounds of clanking iron, of chains being dragged along.
Scared by the din, Aeneas halted; he could not move:—   155
    What kinds of criminals are these? Speak, lady! What punishments
Afflict them, that such agonised sounds rise up from there?
    Then the Sibyl began:—
                    O famous lord of the Trojans,
No righteous soul may tread that threshold of the damned: 160
But, when Hecate appointed me to the Avernian grove,
She instructed me in heaven's punishments, showed me all.
Here Rhadamanthus rules, and most severe his rule is,
Trying and chastising wrongdoers, forcing confessions
From any who, on earth, went gleefully undetected—   165
But uselessly, since they have only postponed till death their atonement.
At once Tisiphone, the avenger, scourge in hand,
Pounces upon the guilty, lashing them, threatening them
With the angry snakes in her left hand, and calls up her bloodthirsty sisters.
Then at last the hinges screech, the infernal gates   170
Grind open. Do you see the sentry, who she is,
Posted over the forecourt? the shape that guards the threshold?
Within, there dwells a thing more fierce—the fifty-headed
Hydra, with all its black throats agape. Then Tartarus
Goes sheer down under the shades, an abyss double in depth   175
The height that Olympus stands above a man gazing skyward.
Here Earth's primaeval offspring, the breed of Titans, who
Were hurled down by Jove's lightning, writhe in the bottomless pit.
Here have I seen the twin sons of Aloeus, the gigantic
Creatures who sought to pull down heaven itself with their own   180
Bare hands, and to unseat Jove from his throne above.

Salmoneus too have I seen undergoing the rigorous sentence
Imposed when he mimicked the thunder and lightning of Jove almighty:
Drawn by a four-horse team and shaking a lighted torch,
He would go through Greece exulting, even through the middle of Elis   185
City, claiming the homage due to the gods alone—
Madman, to copy the nonpareil lightning, the thunderstorm
With a rumble of bronze wheels and a clatter of hard-hoofed horses!
But the Father almighty, among his serried storm clouds, launched
A weapon—no torches, no smoky light of farthing dips   190
Was this—and hurled the blasphemer down with the wind of its passage. . . .

[The Words of Anchises]

. . . See over there the Decii, the Drusi, Torquatus
With merciless axe, Camillus with the standards he recovered.
See those twin souls, resplendent in duplicate armour: now
They're of one mind, and shall be as long as the Underworld holds them; 195
But oh, if ever they reach the world above, what warfare,
What battles and what carnage will they create between them—
Caesar descending from Alpine strongholds, the fort of Monoecus,
His son-in-law Pompey lined up with an Eastern army against him.
Lads, do not harden yourselves to face such terrible wars!   200
Turn not your country's hand against your country's heart!
You, be the first to renounce it, my son of heavenly lineage,
You be the first to bury the hatchet! . . .
That one shall ride in triumph to the lofty Capitol,
The conqueror of Corinth, renowned for the Greeks he has slain.   205
That one shall wipe out Argos and Agamemnon's Mycenae,
Destroying an heir of Aeacus, the seed of warrior Achilles,
Avenging his Trojan sires and the sacrilege done to Minerva.
Who could leave unnoticed the glorious Cato, Cossus,
The family of the Gracchi, the two Scipios—thunderbolts   210
In war and death to Libya; Fabricius, who had plenty
In poverty; Serranus, sowing his furrowed fields?
Fabii, where do you lead my lagging steps? O Fabius,
The greatest, you the preserver of Rome by delaying tactics!
Let others fashion from bronze more lifelike, breathing images—   215
For so they shall—and evoke living faces from marble;
Others excel as orators, others track with their instruments
The planets circling in heaven and predict when stars will appear.
But, Romans, never forget that government is your medium!
Be this your art:—to practise men in the habit of peace,   220
Generosity to the conquered, and firmness against aggressors. . . .
                    So far and wide, surveying all,
They wandered through that region, those broad and hazy plains.

After Anchises had shown his son over the whole place
And fired his heart with passion for the great things to come,   225
He told the hero of wars he would have to fight one day,
Told of the Laurentines and the city of Latinus,
And how to evade, or endure, each crisis upon his way.
   There are two gates of Sleep: the one is made of horn,
They say, and affords the outlet for genuine apparitions: 230
The other's a gate of brightly-shining ivory; this way
The Shades send up to earth false dreams that impose upon us.
Talking, then, of such matters, Anchises escorted his son
And the Sibyl as far as the ivory gate and sent them through it.
Aeneas made his way back to the ships and his friends with all speed,   235
Then coasted along direct to the harbour of Caieta.
The ships, anchored by the bows, line the shore with their sterns.

QUESTIONS

1. A great many readers have seen Marlow's adventure in the Congo as essentially a trip to the underworld. Obviously, unlike Odysseus, Aeneas, and Dante, Marlow is not literally in Hades, but there are striking similarities between the Congo and the classical underworld as Vergil describes it in the selection above. Indicate similarities in setting and atmosphere.

2. Find parallels in "Heart of Darkness" for the following elements in *The Aeneid*: (a) the rites that Aeneas must perform before entering the underworld; (b) the Sibyl, guardian of the entrance to the underworld; (c) the allegorical figures of Disease, Hunger, etc.; (d) the throngs of pleading shadowy figures along the banks of the infernal river; (e) Palinurus; (f) Salmoneus.

3. Note that Anchises in the Elysian fields points out to Aeneas the spirits of great Romans confined in the underworld until their destiny calls them up to play their parts in the drama of the Roman empire. Anchises counsels peace and the cultivation of the art of government, but he foresees civil war and strife. Does Marlow, like Aeneas, learn lessons of empire? What empires are either dramatized or discussed in "Heart of Darkness"? How are they differentiated?

4. Is Kurtz' Intended a citizen of the world or is she, too, one of the dead?

5. What value does a consideration of this possible "source" have as a means of leading to an appreciation of Conrad's story?

PSYCHOLOGY

The writings of Jung have found greater favor with many artists and critics than those of Freud because Jung does not depend so much on neuroses to explain the activity of the artist. The selection below contains the broad outlines of his theory of the collective unconscious, particularly as it applies to the creative process. The selection also throws light on the nature of the reader's response to the work that embodies what Jung calls primordial images.

Carl Jung

ANALYTIC PSYCHOLOGY AND ART

Notwithstanding its manifold difficulties, the task of discussing the relation of analytical psychology to poetic art provides me with a not unwelcome occasion for defining my standpoint in regard to a much debated question; namely, the relation between psychology and art in general. In spite of their incommensurability both provinces are closely inter-related, and these connexions cannot remain unexplored. For they originate in the fact that art in practice is a psychological activity, and, in so far as this is the case, it actually requires a psychological consideration. Art, like every other human activity proceeds from psychic motives, and from this angle, it is a proper object for psychology. But this conclusion also involves a very obvious limitation in the application of the psychological view-point: only that aspect of art which consists in the process of artistic form can be an object of psychology; whereas that which constitutes the essential nature of art must always lie outside its province. This other aspect, namely, the problem what is art in itself, can never be the object of a psychological, but only of an æsthetico-artistic method of approach. . . .

But in what does the autonomous creative complex consist? Of this we can know next to nothing so long as the completed work offers us no insight into its foundations. The work gives us a finished picture in the widest sense. This picture is accessible to analysis just in so far as we are able to appreciate it as a symbol. But if we are unable to discover any symbolic value in it, we have thereby ascertained that, for us at least, it means no more than what it obviously says—in other words, so far as we are concerned it is no more than it seems. I use the word 'seems', because it is conceivable that our own bias forbids a wider appreciation of it. At all events in the latter case we can find no motive and no point of attack for analysis. In the former case, however, a phrase of Gerhart Hauptmann will come to our minds almost with the force of an axiom: 'Poetry means the distant echo of the primitive word behind our veil of words.' Translated into psychological language our first question should run: to what primordial image of the collective unconscious can we trace the image we see developed in the work of art?

From "On the Relation of Analytical Psychology to Poetic Art" in *Contributions to Analytic Psychology* by Carl J. Jung. Translated by H. G. Baynes. Reprinted by permission of Harcourt, Brace and Company, 1928.

This question demands elucidation in more than one respect. As already observed, the case I have assumed is that of a symbolical art-work; a work, therefore, of which the source is not to be found in the personal unconscious of the author, but in that sphere of unconscious mythology, the primordial contents of which are the common heritage of mankind. Accordingly, I have termed this sphere the collective unconscious, thus distinguishing it from a personal unconscious which I regard as the totality of those psychic processes and contents that are not only accessible to consciousness, but would often be conscious were they not subject to repression because of some incompatibility that keeps them artificially suppressed beneath the threshold of consciousness. From this sphere art also receives tributaries, dark and turbid though they be; but if they become a major factor they make the work of art a symptomatic rather than a symbolical product. This kind of art might conceivably be left without injury or regret to the Freudian purgative method.

In contrast to the personal unconscious, which in a sense is a relatively superficial layer immediately below the conscious threshold, the collective unconscious is quite unadapted for consciousness under normal conditions, and hence by no analytical technique can it be brought to conscious recollection, being neither repressed nor forgotten. In itself the collective unconscious cannot be said to exist at all; that is to say, it is nothing but a possibility, that possibility in fact which from primordial time has been handed down to us in the definite form of mnemic images, or expressed in anatomical formations in the very structure of the brain. It does not yield innate ideas, but inborn possibilities of ideas, which also set definite bounds to the most daring phantasy. It provides categories of phantasy-activity, ideas *a priori* as it were, the existence of which cannot be ascertained except by experience. In finished or shaped material they appear only as the regulative principle of its shaping, *i.e.*, only through the conclusion derived *a posterior* from the perfected work of art are we able to reconstruct the primitive foundation of the primordial image. The primordial image or archetype is a figure, whether it be a dæmon, man, or process, that repeats itself in the course of history wherever creative phantasy is freely manifested. Essentially, therefore, it is a mythological figure. If we subject these images to a closer investigation, we discover them to be the formulated resultants of countless typical experiences of our ancestors. They are, as it were, the psychic residua of numberless experiences of the same type. They depict millions of individual experiences in the average, presenting a kind of picture of the psychic life distributed and projected into the manifold shapes of the mythological pandemonium. These mythological forms, however, are in themselves themes of creative phantasy that still await their translation into conceptual language, of which there exist as yet only laborious beginnings. These concepts, for the most part still to be created, could provide us with an abstract scientific understanding of the unconscious processes that are the roots of the primordial images. Each of these images contains a piece of human psychology and human destiny, a relic of suffering or delight that has happened countless times in our ancestral story, and on the average follows ever the same course. It is like a deeply graven river-bed in the soul, in which the waters of life, that had spread hitherto with groping and uncertain course over wide but shallow surfaces, suddenly become a mighty river. This happens when that particular chain of circumstances is encountered which from immemorial time has contributed to the laying down of the primordial image. The moment when the mythological situation appears is always characterized by a peculiar emotional intensity; it is as though chords in us were touched that had never resounded before, or as though forces were unloosed, of the existence of which we had never even dreamed. The struggle of adaptation is laborious, because we have constantly to be dealing with individual, *i.e.* atypical conditions. No wonder then, that at the moment when a typical situation occurs, we feel suddenly aware of an extraordinary release, as though transported, or caught up as by an overwhelming power. At such moments we are no longer individuals, but the race; the voice of all mankind resounds in us. The individual man is never able to use his powers to their fullest range, unless there comes to his aid one of those collective presentations we call ideals that liberates in his soul all the hidden forces of instinct, to which the ordinary conscious will alone can never gain access. The most effective ideals are always more or less transparent variants of the archetype. This is proved by the fact that these ideals lend themselves so readily to allegorization, *e.g.* the motherland as the mother. In this kind of figurative expression the allegory itself has not the smallest motive-power; this has its source in the symbolic value of the motherland-idea. The corresponding archetype in this case is the so-called '*participation mystique*' of the primitive with the soil on which he dwells, and which alone contains the spirit of his ancestors. Exile spells misery.

Every relation to the archetype, whether through experience or the mere spoken word, is 'stirring', *i.e.* it is impressive, it calls up a stronger voice than our own. The man who speaks with primordial images speaks with a thousand tongues; he entrances and overpowers, while at the same time he raises the idea he is trying to express above the occasional and the transitory into the sphere of the ever-existing. He transmutes personal destiny into the destiny of mankind, thus evoking all those beneficent forces that have enabled mankind to find a rescue from every hazard and to outlive the longest night.

That is the secret of effective art. The creative process, in so far as we are able to follow it at all, consists in an unconscious animation of the archetype, and in a development and shaping of this image till the work is completed. The shaping of the primordial image is, as it were, a translation into the language of the present which makes it possible for every man to find again the deepest springs of life which would otherwise be closed to him. Therein lies the social importance of art; it is constantly at work educating the spirit of the age, since it brings to birth those forms in which the age is most lacking. Recoiling from the unsatisfying present the yearning of the artist reaches out to that primordial image in the unconscious which is best fitted to compensate the insufficiency and one-sidedness of the spirit of the age. The artist seizes this image, and in the work of raising it from deepest unconsciousness he brings it into relation with conscious values, thereby transforming its shape, until it can be accepted by his contemporaries according to their powers.

The nature of the work of art permits conclusions to be drawn concerning the character of the period from which it sprang. What was the significance of realism and naturalism to their age? What was the meaning of romanticism, or Hellenism? They were tendencies of art which brought to the surface that unconscious element of which the contemporary mental atmosphere had most need. The artist as educator of his time—much could be said about that to-day.

People and times, like individual men, have their peculiar tendencies or attitudes. The very word 'attitude' betrays the necessary one-sidedness that every definite tendency postulates. Where there is direction there must also be exclusion. But exclusion means that certain definite psychic elements that could participate in life are denied their right to live through incompatibility with the general attitude. The normal man can endure the general tendency without much injury. But the man who takes to the by-streets and alley-ways because, unlike the normal man, he cannot endure the broad high-way, will be the first to discover those elements that lie apart from the main streets, and that await a new participation in life.

The artist's relative lack of adaptation becomes his real advantage; for it enables him to keep aloof from the high-ways, the better to follow his own yearning and to find those things of which the others are deprived without noticing it. Thus, as in the case of the single individual whose one-sided conscious attitude is corrected by unconscious reactions towards self-regulation, art also represents a process of mental self-regulation in the life of nations and epochs.

I am aware that I have only been able to give certain intuitive perceptions, and these only in the barest outlines. But I may perhaps hope that what I have been obliged to omit, namely, the concrete application to poetic works, has been furnished by your own thoughts, thus giving flesh and blood to my abstract intellectual frame.

QUESTIONS

1. Elsewhere, Jung distinguishes two kinds of literary works: those which the writer produces self-consciously according to certain preconceived intellectual intentions and those which the writer produces under compulsion. These latter works, says Jung, "positively impose themselves on the author; his hand is, as it were, seized, and his pen writes things that his mind perceives with amazement." To this second kind of work the concept of the collective unconscious is especially applicable, Jung claims. What evidence do Curle's remarks above provide that "Heart of Darkness" falls into this second category?

2. Jung tells us that the work that draws images from the collective unconscious will be symbolic. Is "Heart of Darkness" a symbolic work? Explain.

3. Jung says that we expect the primordial image to recur in many works (to be essentially mythological). What light does the comparison between the excerpts from *The Aeneid* and "Heart of Darkness" throw on this matter?

4. We encounter the mythological situation with "a peculiar emotional intensity." Characterize your own emotional reaction to the story. To what passages are you especially responsive? Why these passages?

5. Attack or defend the following statement: "In Jungian terms, 'Heart of Darkness' is a reaction to the rationalism, the materialism, the shallow optimism, and the superficial progressivism that pervaded England and the Continent at the end of the nineteenth century; for it re-creates the myth of the Dionysian element in man, the dark irrational."

6. Look back at Maud Bodkin's discussion of "Kubla Khan" (p. 196). Find similarities in the imagery of "Heart of Darkness" and "Kubla Khan." What psycho-physiological echoes would Maud Bodkin sense in Conrad's story? How valuable would her comments be?

SOCIETY

In the selections that follow, two great English political philosophers discuss the basis of liberty. Mill emphasizes the principle of noninterference, Laski equality. For us, who live in an ideological age, there is a prophetic ring to Mill's statement written a century ago, that the relationship between society and the individual "is likely soon to make itself recognized as the vital question of the future."

John Stuart Mill

from "ON LIBERTY"

Introductory

The subject of this Essay is not the so-called Liberty of the Will, so unfortunately opposed to the misnamed doctrine of Philosophical Necessity; but Civil, or Social Liberty: the nature and limits of the power which can be legitimately exercised by society over the individual. A question seldom stated, and hardly ever discussed, in general terms, but which profoundly influences the practical controversies of the age by its latent presence, and is likely soon to make itself recognized as the vital question of the future. It is so far from being new, that,

From Alburey Castell, ed., *Mill's On Liberty* (Appleton–Century–Crofts, 1947).

in a certain sense, it has divided mankind, almost from the remotest ages; but in the stage of progress into which the more civilized portions of the species have now entered, it presents itself under new conditions, and requires a different and more fundamental treatment. . . .

The object of this Essay is to assert one very simple principle, as entitled to govern absolutely the dealings of society with the individual in the way of compulsion and control, whether the means used be physical force in the form of legal penalties, or the moral coercion of public opinion. That principle is, that the sole end for which mankind are warranted, individually or collectively, in interfering with the liberty of action of any of their number, is self-protection. That the only purpose for which power can be rightfully exercised over any member of a civilized community, against his will, is to prevent harm to others. His own good, either physical or moral, is not a sufficient warrant. He cannot rightfully be compelled to do or forbear because it will be better for him to do so, because it will make him happier, because, in the opinions of others, to do so would be wise, or even right. These are good reasons for remonstrating with him, or reasoning with him, or persuading him, or entreating him, but not for compelling him, or visiting him with any evil in case he do otherwise. To justify that, the conduct from which it is desired to deter him, must be calculated to produce evil to some one else. The only part of the conduct of any one, for which he is amenable to society, is that which concerns others. In the part which merely concerns himself, his independence is, of right, absolute. Over himself, over his own body and mind, the individual is sovereign.

It is, perhaps, hardly necessary to say that this doctrine is meant to apply only to human beings in the maturity of their faculties. We are not speaking of children, or of young persons below the age which the law may fix as that of manhood or womanhood. Those who are still in a state to require being taken care of by others, must be protected against their own actions as well as against external injury. For the same reason, we may leave out of consideration those backward states of society in which the race itself may be considered as in its nonage. The early difficulties in the way of spontaneous progress are so great, that there is seldom any choice of means for overcoming them; and a ruler full of the spirit of improvement is warranted in the use of any expedients that will attain an end, perhaps otherwise unattainable. Despotism is a legitimate mode of government in dealing with barbarians, provided the end be their improvement, and the means justified by actually effecting that end. Liberty, as a principle, has no application to any state of things anterior to the time when mankind have become capable of being improved by free and equal discussion. Until then, there is nothing for them but implicit obedience to an Akbar or a Charlemagne, if they are so fortunate as to find one. But as soon as mankind have attained the capacity of being guided to their own improvement by conviction or persuasion (a period long since reached in all nations with whom we need here concern ourselves), compulsion, either in the direct form or in that of pains and penalties for non-compliance, is no longer admissible as a means to their own good, and justifiable only for the security of others.

Harold Laski

from ''A PLEA FOR EQUALITY''

Without equality, I say, there cannot be liberty. All history goes to show that interdependence. For if liberty means the continuous power of expansion in the human spirit, it is rarely present save in a society of equals. Where there are rich and poor, educated and uneducated, we find always masters and servants. To be rich is to be powerful; to be educated is to have authority. To live in subordination by reason of poverty or ignorance is to be like a tree in the shade which perishes because it cannot reach the light. Poverty and ignorance benumb the faculties and depress the energies of men. It is, of course, true that there are those who by the very strength of the conditions which suppress them are goaded to conquest of their environment. But with ordinary men this is not the case. On the contrary, the sense of inferiority which an unequal society inflicts upon them deprives them of that hope which is the spur of effort. They remain contented with a condition in which they cannot make the best of themselves. The distance which separates them from the wealthy and the cultured is so vast they they are never stimulated to make the effort to overpass it. They remain uncivilized because power and consideration are objects too refined for their understanding. They are satisfied with the crude in arts and letters, the brutal in sensual pleasures, the material and the vulgar in objects of desire. And because of their inferiority, they are judged incapable of advancement. Aristocracies, whether of wealth or birth, have never understood the secret of this degradation. In part, they have accepted it as proof of their own superiority; and in part they have welcomed it as a safeguard of their security. They take the deference they are accorded as the proof of their inherent worth; and they do not examine into the causes of its reception.

Aristocracies, historically, have always suffered from an incapacity for ideas. They cannot share the wants or the instincts of the rest of the society of which they are a part. And they always fail, accordingly, to realize that the desire of equality is one of the most permanent passions of mankind. At the very birth of political science, Aristotle had already seen that a failure to satisfy it is one of the major causes of revolutions; it is not less so today. For where there are wide differences in the habits of men, there are wide differences in their thoughts. To think differently is to lose hold of a basis of social unity. A house divided against itself, the Bible says, cannot stand; a nation divided into rich and poor is a house divided against itself. It is only where men have an equal interest in the result of the common effort that there is a bond of genuine fellowship between them. A realization of unequal interest means, inevitably, the growth of a sense of injustice. That sense fastens itself upon the perception of an unequal return to effort; and an abyss is precipitated between classes of which, in the end, revolution is always the outcome.

It appears, therefore, that the less obvious the differences between men in the gain of living, the greater the bond of fellowship between them. And in a society like our own the differences between men are intensified by the fact that they are rarely referable to rational principle. We have wealthy men and women who have never contributed a day's effort to the sum of productivity; and we have poor men and women who have never known relaxation from unremitting toil. Wealth, with us, is so often the result of accident, of corruption, of a power to satisfy demand not inherently social in character, that there is little relation between its possession and a criterion of social benefit. The economic inequalities of society, that is to say, do not so explain themselves that men can regard them as just. Those who support them as necessary are always on the defensive; and they are always occupied in searching for possible concessions to the poor whereby they can be the better preserved. Philanthropy and social legislation are the taxes the rich must pay to keep the poor in order; and instead of a stimulus to cease from poverty they act as an incentive to remain in a routine where the service performed prevents by its character the emergence of a civilized quality in the performer. Our inegalitarian system corrodes the conscience of the rich by extracting ransom from them; and it destroys the creativeness of the poor by emphasizing their inferiority in the very conference of benefit. The rich hate the process of giving, and the poor hate them because they are compelled to receive. . . .

There is, moreover, a psychological result of inequality upon which too much stress can hardly be laid. Inequality divides our society into men who give and men who receive orders. The second class, being deprived of initiative, is robbed of the possibility of freedom. Its members spend their lives as prisoners of an inescapable routine they have had no part in making. When their life is compared with that of their governors, whose power of self-controlled initiative is continuous and unbroken, it is obvious enough that distinctiveness of personality has there little chance of survival. And the orders received are irresponsible since, in general, they are born, not of function, but of the possession of wealth. The farm laborer, the domestic servant, the factory worker realize in a high degree that definition of an animate tool which Aristotle insisted was the quintessence of slavery. In the psychological sphere their experience means a continuous inhibition of natural impulse, a want of room to experiment with themselves, which is disastrous to the expansion of personality. Economic equality, for them, would mean the end of government by a narrow oligarchy of wealth whose sole purpose in life is personal pleasure or personal gain. We can understand the need for obedience to a doctor, a tax collector, a policeman. There, as we can realize, the rules they enforce are born of principles of which they, not less than we, are servants; and their relation to the result is a disinterested one. But the orders of the narrow group who own economic power are rarely disinterested and never born of principle unless they choose so to make them. The result is the loss of freedom in those whom they command because they dictate the rules of authority to ends in which their servants cannot share.

QUESTIONS

1. Mill excuses from the doctrine of noninterference rulers of backward societies. Would he, therefore, approve the Company's treatment of the natives, as it is described in "Heart of Darkness"? Explain.

2. What probably would be Mill's judgment of Marlow's notion (p. 240) that it is "the idea" that redeems the conquest of primitive people? What idea is Marlow talking about?

3. Are there any Europeans in Conrad's Congo whose aim is to civilize the natives? What hints are there concerning the Company propaganda about its goals in the Congo?

4. Does "Heart of Darkness" support Laski's claims about the results of poverty and ignorance?

5. The accumulation of wealth, according to Laski, rarely results in social benefit. Is this true of the Company's activities in Conrad's Congo?

6. In these terms evaluate the Company hierarchy itself, apart from the question of its treatment of the natives.

7. Citing the writings of several explorers who were in the Congo at about the same time as Conrad, Lucién Levy-Bruhl in *Primitive Mentality* assesses the white man's power over the natives this way: "It therefore seems incorrect to state, as has so frequently been done, that primitives fear and respect nothing but force. . . . That which inspires fear and respect in them is mystic force, that of unseen powers whose cooperation the white man knows how to secure, and this alone it is which makes his implements and weapons effective and irresistible." Does this seem accurate to you? What characters, if any, consciously use the superstitions of the natives to manipulate them?

MORALITY

Earlier, in the introduction to the "Morality" section (p. 219), we indicated the difficulty that one has in formulating an ethic which can command something like universal acceptance. Walter Lippmann in the selection below offers a definition of virtue which he believes discovers the inner principle of moral behavior.

Walter Lippmann

"VIRTUE"

It can be shown, I think, that those qualities which civilized men, regardless of their theologies and their allegiances, have agreed to call virtues, have disinterestedness as their inner principle. I am not talking now about the eccentric virtues which at some time or other have been held in great esteem. I am not talking about the virtue of not playing cards, or of not drinking wine, or of not eating beef, or of not eating pork, or of not admitting that women have legs. These little virtues are historical accidents which may or may not once have had a rational origin. I am talking about the central virtues which are esteemed by every civilized people. I am talking about such virtues as courage, honor, faithfulness, veracity, justice, temperance, magnanimity, and love.

They would not be called virtues and held in high esteem if there were no difficulty about them. There are innumerable dispositions which are essential to living that no one takes the trouble to praise. Thus it is not accounted a virtue if a man eats when he is hungry or goes to bed when he is ill. He can be depended upon to take care of his immediate wants. It is only those actions which he cannot be depended upon to do, and yet are highly desirable, that men call virtuous. They recognize that a premium has to be put upon certain qualities if men are to make the effort which is required to transcend their ordinary impulses. The premium consists in describing these desirable and rarer qualities as virtues. For virtue is that kind of conduct which is esteemed by God, or public opinion, or that less immediate part of a man's personality which he calls his conscience.

To transcend the ordinary impulses is, therefore, the common element in all virtue. Courage, for example, is the willingness to face situations from which it would be more or less natural to run away. No one thinks it is courageous to run risks unwittingly. The drunken driver of an automobile, the boy playing with a stick of dynamite, the man drinking water which he does not know is polluted, all take risks as great as those of the most renowned heroes. But the fact that they do not know the risks, and do not, therefore, have to conquer the fear they would feel if they did know them, robs their conduct of all courage. The test is not the uselessness or even the undesirability of their acts. It is useless to go over Niagara Falls in a barrel. But it is brave, assuming the performer to be in his right mind. It is a wicked thing to assassinate a king. But if it is not done from ambush, it is brave, however wicked and however useless.

Because courage consists in transcending normal fears, the highest kind of courage is cold courage; that is to say, courage in which the danger has been fully realized and there is no emotional excitement to conceal the danger. The world instantly recognized this in Colonel Lindbergh's flight to Paris. He flew alone; he was not an impetuous fool, but a man of the utmost sobriety of judgment. He had no companion to keep his courage screwed up; he knew exactly what he was doing, yet apparently he did not realize the rewards which were in store for him. The world understood that here was somebody who was altogether braver than the average sensual man. For Colonel Lindbergh did not merely conquer the Atlantic Ocean; he conquered those things in himself which the rest of us would have found unconquerable.

The cold courage of a man like Noguchi who, though in failing health, went into one of the unhealthiest parts of Africa to study a deadly disease, could come only from a nature which was overwhelmingly interested in objects outside itself. Noguchi must have known exactly how dangerous it was for him to go to Africa, and exactly how horrible was the disease to which he exposed himself. To have gone anyway is really to have cared for science in a way which very few care for anything so remote and impersonal. But even courage like Lindbergh's and Noguchi's is more comprehensible than the kind of courage which anonymous men have displayed. I am thinking of the four soldiers at the Walter Reed Hospital who let themselves be used for the study of typhoid fever. They did not even have Lindbergh's interest in performing a great feat or Noguchi's interest in science to buoy them up and carry them past the point where they might have faltered. Their courage was as near to absolute courage as it is possible to imagine, and I who think this cannot even recall their names.

To understand the inwardness of courage would be, I think, to have understood almost all the other important virtues. It is "not only the chiefest virtue and most dignifies the haver," but it embodies the principle of all virtue, which is to transcend the immediacy of desire and to live for ends which are transpersonal. Virtuous action is conduct which responds to situations that are more extensive, more complicated, and take longer to reach their fulfillment, than the situations to which we instinctively respond. An infant knows neither vice nor virtue because it can respond only to what touches it immediately. A man has virtue insofar as he can respond to a larger situation.

He has honor if he holds himself to an ideal of conduct though it is inconvenient, unprofitable, or dangerous to do so. He has veracity if he says and believes what he thinks is true though it would be easier to deceive others or himself. He is just if he acknowledges the interests of all concerned in a transaction and not merely his own apparent interest. He is temperate if, in the presence of temptation, he can still prefer Philip sober to Philip drunk. He is magnanimous if, as Aristotle says, he cares "more for truth than for opinion," speaks and acts openly, will not live at the will of another, except it be a friend, does not recollect injuries, does not care that he should be praised or that others should be blamed, does not complain or ask for help in unavoidable or trifling calamities. For such a man, as the word 'magnanimous' itself implies, is "conversant with great matters."

A man who has these virtues has somehow overcome the inertia of his impulses. Their disposition is to respond to the immediate situation, and not merely to the situation at the moment, but to the most obvious fragment of it, and not only to the most obvious fragment, but to that aspect which promises instant pleasure or pain. To have virtue is to respond to larger situations and to longer stretches of time and without much interest in their immediate result in convenience and pleasure. It is to overcome the impulses of immaturity, to detach one's self from the objects that preoccupy it and from one's own preoccupations. There are many virtues in the catalogues of the moralists, and they have many different names. But they have a common principle, which is detachment from that which is apparently pleasant or unpleasant, and they have a common quality, which is disinterestedness, and they spring from a common source, which is maturity of character.

Few men, if any, possess virtue in all its varieties because few men are wholly matured to the core of their being. We are for the most part like fruit which is partly ripened: there is sourness and sweetness in our natures. This may be due to the casualness of our upbringing; it may be due to unknown congenital causes; it may be due to functional and organic disease, to partial inferiorities of mind and body. But it is due also to the fact that we can give our full attention only to a few phases of our experience. With the equipment at our disposal we are forced to specialize and to neglect very much. Hence the mature scientist with petty ambitions and ignoble timidities. Hence the realistic states-man who is a peevish husband. Hence the man who manages his affairs in masterly fashion and bungles every personal relationship when he is away from his office. Hence the loyal friend who is a crooked politician, the kind father who is a merciless employer, the champion of mankind who is an intolerable companion. If any of these could carry over into all their relationships the qualities which have made them distinguished in some, they would be wholly adult and wholly good. It would not be necessary to imagine the ideal character, for he would already exist.

It is out of these practical virtues that our conception of virtue has been formed. We may be sure that no quality is likely to have become esteemed as a virtue which did not somewhere and sometime produce at least the appearance of happiness. The virtues are grounded in experience; they are not idle sugges-tions inadvertently adopted because somebody took it into his head one fine day to proclaim a new ideal. There are, to be sure, certain residual and obsolete virtues which no longer correspond to anything in our own experience and now seem utterly arbitrary and capricious. But the cardinal virtues correspond to an experience so long and so nearly universal among men of our civilization, that when they are understood they are seen to contain a deposited wisdom of the race.

QUESTIONS

1. Consider Marlow, the manager, and Kurtz. Which of these men had the most disinterested motives in coming to Africa? Did their goals change? Explain.

2. Which characters in the story must conquer fear and overcome their basic impulses? Do not overlook the unexpected restraint of the cannibal crew.

3. In what sense does the story dramatize Lippmann's contention that true courage is the conquest not of external things but of the self?

4. Evaluate the conduct of the various employees of the Company in terms of Lippmann's definition of the just man.

5. In so barren and uncomfortable a place as the Congo, we hardly expect the virtue of temperance to be in question, for we tend to associate intemperance with luxury. Yet intemperance plays a great part in the story. How?

6. Is Marlow's lie to Kurtz' Intended a moral lapse, a departure from the virtue of veracity as Lippmann defines it, or can the lie be excused in terms of some higher moral claim? Explain.

7. Lippmann lists a number of possible explanations for the lack of virtue in men: upbringing, heredity, disease, and so forth. Try to assign a cause or causes for those in the story who have fallen from virtue. Are there causes that Lippmann does not mention?

PHILOSOPHY

Since Blaise Pascal, the great seventeenth-century French mathematician, physicist, and religious philosopher, died at the age of thirty-nine before he could finish his most famous work, the *Pensées*, we have only fragments of it. Beginning with a disillusioned analysis of the inadequacies of human reason and the miseries of human life, Pascal proceeds to defend Christian beliefs and the necessity of faith.

Blaise Pascal

"MAN'S DISPROPORTION"

. . . Let man then contemplate the whole of nature in her full and grand majesty, and turn his vision from the low objects which surround him. Let him gaze on that brilliant light, set like an eternal lamp to illumine the universe; let the earth appear to him a point in comparison with the vast circle described by the sun; and let him wonder at the fact that this vast circle is itself but a very fine point in comparison with that described by the stars in their revolution round the firmament. But if our view be arrested there, let our imagination pass beyond; it will sooner exhaust the power of conception than nature that of supplying material for conception. The whole visible world is only an imperceptible atom in the ample bosom of nature. No idea approaches it. We may enlarge our conceptions beyond all imaginable space; we only produce atoms in comparison with the reality of things. It is an infinite sphere, the centre of which is everywhere, the circumference nowhere. In short it is the greatest sensible mark of the almighty power of God, that imagination loses itself in that thought.

Returning to himself, let man consider what he is in comparison with all existence; let him regard himself as lost in this remote corner of nature; and

From "Man's Disproportion" in *Pensées* by Blaise Pascal, translated by W. F. Trotter. Reprinted by permission of E. P. Dutton & Co., Inc., and J. M. Dent and Sons Ltd: Publishers. Copyright 1931.

from the little cell in which he finds himself lodged, I mean the universe, let him estimate at their true value the earth, kingdoms, cities, and himself. What is a man in the Infinite?

But to show him another prodigy equally astonishing, let him examine the most delicate things he knows. Let a mite be given him, with its minute body and parts incomparably more minute, limbs with their joints, veins in the limbs, blood in the veins, humours in the blood, drops in the humours, vapours in the drops. Dividing these last things again, let him exhaust his powers of conception, and let the last object at which he can arrive be now that of our discourse. Perhaps he will think that here is the smallest point in nature. I will let him see therein a new abyss. I will paint for him not only the visible universe, but all that he can conceive of nature's immensity in the womb of this abridged atom. Let him see therein an infinity of universes, each of which has its firmament, its planets, its earth, in the same proportion as in the visible world; in each earth animals, and in the last mites, in which he will find again all that the first had, finding still in these others the same thing without end and without cessation. Let him lose himself in wonders as amazing in their littleness as the others in their vastness. For who will not be astounded at the fact that our body, which a little while ago was imperceptible in the universe, itself imperceptible in the bosom of the whole, is now a colossus, a world, or rather a whole, in respect of the nothingness which we cannot reach? He who regards himself in this light will be afraid of himself, and observing himself sustained in the body given him by nature between those two abysses of the Infinite and Nothing, will tremble at the sight of these marvels; and I think that, as his curiosity changes into admiration, he will be more disposed to contemplate them in silence than to examine them with presumption.

For in fact what is man in nature? A Nothing in comparison with the Infinite, an All in comparison with the Nothing, a mean between nothing and everything. Since he is infinitely removed from comprehending the extremes, the end of things and their beginning are hopelessly hidden from him in an impenetrable secret; he is equally incapable of seeing the Nothing from which he was made, and the Infinite in which he is swallowed up.

What will he do then, but perceive the appearance of the middle of things, in an eternal despair of knowing either their beginning or their end. All things proceed from the Nothing, and are borne towards the Infinite. Who will follow these marvellous processes? The Author of these wonders understands them. None other can do so.

Through failure to contemplate these Infinites, men have rashly rushed into the examination of nature, as though they bore some proportion to her. It is strange that they have wished to understand the beginnings of things, and thence to arrive at the knowledge of the whole, with a presumption as infinite as their object. For surely this design cannot be formed without presumption or without a capacity infinite like nature.

If we are well informed, we understand that, as nature has graven her image and that of her Author on all things, they almost all partake of her double infinity. Thus we see that all the sciences are infinite in the extent of their researches. For who doubts that geometry, for instance, has an infinite infinity of problems to solve? They are also infinite in the multitude and fineness of their premises; for it is clear that those which are put forward as ultimate are not self-supporting, but are based on others which, again having others for their support, do not permit of finality. But we represent some as ultimate for reason, in the same way as in regard to material objects we call that an indivisible point beyond which our senses can no longer perceive anything, although by its nature it is infinitely divisible.

Of these two Infinites of science, that of greatness is the most palpable, and hence a few persons have pretended to know all things. "I will speak of the whole," said Democritus.

But the infinitely little is the least obvious. Philosophers have much oftener claimed to have reached it, and it is here they have all stumbled. This has given rise to such common titles as *First Principles, Principles of Philosophy*, and the like, as ostentatious in fact, though not in appearance, as that one which blinds us, *De omni scibili*.

We naturally believe ourselves far more capable of reaching the centre of things than of embracing their circumference. The visible extent of the world visibly exceeds us; but as we exceed little things, we think ourselves more capable of knowing them. And yet we need no less capacity for attaining the Nothing than the All. Infinite capacity is required for both, and it seems to me that whoever shall have understood the ultimate principles of being might also attain to the knowledge of the Infinite. The one depends on the other, and one leads to the other. These extremes meet and reunite by force of distance, and find each other in God, and in God alone.

Let us then take our compass; we are something, and we are not everything. The nature of our existence hides from us the knowledge of first beginnings which are born of the Nothing; and the littleness of our being conceals from us the sight of the Infinite.

Our intellect holds the same position in the world of thought as our body occupies in the expanse of nature.

Limited as we are in every way, this state which holds the mean between two extremes is present in all our impotence. Our senses perceive no extreme. Too much sound deafens us; too much light dazzles us; too great distance or proximity hinders our view. Too great length and too great brevity of discourse tend to obscurity; too much truth is paralysing. (I know some who cannot understand that to take four from nothing leaves nothing.) First principles are too self-evident for us; too much pleasure disagrees with us. Too many concords are annoying in music; too many benefits irritate us; we wish to have the wherewithal to over-pay our debts. *Beneficia eo usque læta sunt dum videntur exsolvi posse; ubi multum antevenere, pro gratia odium redditur.* We feel neither extreme heat nor extreme cold. Excessive qualities are prejudicial to us and not perceptible by the senses; we do not feel but suffer them. Extreme youth and extreme age hinder the mind, as also too much and too little education.

In short, extremes are for us as though they were not, and we are not within their notice. They escape us, or we them.

This is our true state; this is what makes us incapable of certain knowledge and of absolute ignorance. We sail within a vast sphere, ever drifting in uncertainty, driven from end to end. When we think to attach ourselves to any point and to fasten to it, it wavers and leaves us; and if we follow it, it eludes our grasp, slips past us, and vanishes for ever. Nothing stays for us. This is our natural condition, and yet most contrary to our inclination; we burn with desire to find solid ground and an ultimate sure foundation whereon to build a tower reaching to the Infinite. But our whole groundwork cracks, and the earth opens to abysses.

Let us therefore not look for certainty and stability: Our reason is always deceived by fickle shadows; nothing can fix the finite between the two Infinites, which both enclose and fly from it.

If this be well understood, I think that we shall remain at rest, each in the state wherein nature has placed him. As this sphere which has fallen to us as our lot is always distant from either extreme, what matters it that man should have a little more knowledge of the universe? If he has it, he but gets a little higher. Is he not always infinitely removed from the end, and is not the duration of our life equally removed from eternity, even if it lasts ten years longer?

In comparison with these Infinites all finites are equal, and I see no reason for fixing our imagination on one more than on another. The only comparison which we make of ourselves to the finite is painful to us.

If man made himself the first object of study, he would see how incapable he is of going further. How can a part know the whole? But he may perhaps aspire to know at least the parts to which he bears some proportion. But the parts of the world are all so related and linked to one another, that I believe it impossible to know one without the other and without the whole.

Man, for instance, is related to all he knows. He needs a place wherein to abide, time through which to live, motion in order to live, elements to compose him, warmth and food to nourish him, air to breathe. He sees light; he feels bodies; in short, he is in a dependent alliance with everything. To know man, then, it is necessary to know how it happens that he needs air to live, and, to know the air, we must know how it is thus related to the life of man, etc. Flame cannot exist without air; therefore to understand the one, we must understand the other.

Since everything then is cause and effect, dependent and supporting, mediate and immediate, and all is held together by a natural though imperceptible chain, which binds together things most distant and most different, I hold it equally impossible to know the parts without knowing the whole, and to know the whole without knowing the parts in detail.

[The eternity of things in itself or in God must also astonish our brief duration. The fixed and constant immobility of nature, in comparison with the continual change which goes on within us, must have the same effect.]

And what completes our incapability of knowing things, is the fact that they are simple, and that we are composed of two opposite natures, different in kind, soul and body. For it is impossible that our rational part should be other than spiritual; and if any one maintain that we are simply corporeal, this would far more exclude us from the knowledge of things, there being nothing so inconceivable as to say that matter knows itself. It is impossible to imagine how it should know itself.

So if we are simply material, we can know nothing at all; and if we are composed of mind and matter, we cannot know perfectly things which are simple, whether spiritual or corporeal. Hence it comes that almost all philosophers have confused ideas of things, and speak of material things in spiritual terms, and of spiritual things in material terms. For they say boldly that bodies have a tendency to fall, that they seek after their centre, that they fly from destruction, that they fear the void, that they have inclinations, sympathies, antipathies, all of which attributes pertain only to mind. And in speaking of minds, they consider them as in a place, and attribute to them movement from one place to another; and these are qualities which belong only to bodies.

Instead of receiving the ideas of these things in their purity, we colour them with our own qualities, and stamp with our composite being all the simple things which we contemplate.

Who would not think, seeing us compose all things of mind and body, but that this mixture would be quite intelligible to us? Yet it is the very thing we least understand. Man is to himself the most wonderful object in nature; for he cannot conceive what the body is, still less what the mind is, and least of all how a body should be united to a mind. This is the consummation of his difficulties, and yet it is his very being.

QUESTIONS

1. Pascal finds it instructive for man to consider himself in relation to the enormity of nature. Find similar elements in "Heart of Darkness."

2. Do Marlow and Pascal share common views about the possibilities of progress through scientific discovery and exploration?

3. In characterizing the human intellect, Pascal says, "too much truth is paralysing." What does he mean? Are any characters in "Heart of Darkness" paralyzed by too much truth?

4. In view of the hopelessness of discovering ultimate truth, Pascal advises that we "remain at rest." Does Marlow accept such a doctrine of philosophical impassivity? Explain.

5. What evidence do you find that Marlow accepts the traditional view of man as part body and part spirit? Look at the episode of Kurtz' attempt to return to his native admirers (pp. 288-290).

6. Though Pascal is writing philosophy and Conrad fiction, do you find similarities in tone and imagery? Do you find the last sentence of the story philosophically symbolic? Explain.

PART FOUR

Types of Literature

The Short Story

Although all imaginative literature interprets human qualities, emotions, motives, and values, different forms interpret them in different ways. Fictional works, dramas, and poems all have their peculiar limitations and possibilities. Therefore, in order to see clearly and judge wisely what each particular work offers, the reader should know something about the nature of each of these forms. Hereafter. works in this book will be introduced and grouped according to type. This arrangement will help you consider, in turn, the *special qualities* of short stories. dramas, and poems as types in addition to the more *general literary qualities* of the works here printed.

We start, then, with a form of prose fiction, ordinarily the easiest of all forms to understand and to enjoy. Primitive men by campfires, children in nurseries, and traveling men in smoking cars obviously appreciate some kinds of imaginative narratives in prose without paying much attention to their structure. But most readers and listeners will find that even such narratives—and others as well—can be most thoroughly appreciated by understanding not only the materials but also the methods involved. And they will find that some works—often the best ones—demand careful attention to the technique as well as to the material in order to be understood or appreciated at all.

Students often have tried to classify fiction, and several categories have been suggested—for example. the novel. the novella. the novellette. the long short story, the short story, the short short story, and the anecdote. Rigid distinctions between these are unsatisfactory because most of them break down. Many scholars, as a result, have stopped worrying about them, and we may well follow their example. For us, two points about the type here represented— the short story—are important: (1) It is short, usually a good deal less than ten thousand words and seldom more than thirty-five thousand or so. (2) It is. nevertheless, a story rather than a part of a story—a complete work with a discoverable unity comparable to that found in other forms. The problem of the short story writer. then, is to combine rigid economy with unity, and a problem for the reader is to see this combination.

ECONOMY

Contrasted with the novel, the short story is less complex in its picturing of life, more swift in the accomplishment of its task. Economy constrains the author to confine his pattern of action by giving a detailed account of one episode or even of part of what would be a complete action in a novel—the beginning, the middle, *or* the end—rather than all three. (Other parts of the action, of course, may be implied or briefly summarized.) The author ordinarily limits the number of characters introduced: often he portrays only one character or a small group of characters. And even leading characters are not likely to be endowed with a large number of traits. Settings, too, in contrast to those in the novel, are limited in number: a short story with a panoramic view comparable to that in Tolstoy's wide-ranging *War and Peace* is inconceivable.

As a rule, the brevity of the short story brings a similar limitation upon its tone and its meanings. Whereas the novelist may range from pathos to scorn and from scorn to ridicule in various parts of his book, in a given story, the short story writer is likely to voice only one emotional attitude. And whereas the novelist may give his work complex multiple meanings, the short story writer is likely to develop rather simpler and fewer meanings. In such ways as these, the short story shows the result of economy, and the reader should notice how simplifications and cuts keep it within bounds.

UNITY

A short story, nevertheless, should be a complete whole, fused according to some principle or principles. In reading a work of this sort, you are obliged, therefore, to see what the nature of the whole work is and how each element contributes to its final achievement. You will find it useful to consider these questions: Is it unified? If not, why not? If so, what is the precise nature of its unity? And how is the unity achieved? You need not, of course, consider these questions in this order, but you do well to attend to all of them.

Critics, you will find, have suggested a variety of ways of getting at the heart of a short story. Some urge you to consider the single effect it has upon the reader, some to discover the single intention upon the part of the author, some to study the story itself as a concrete object which is a fusion of several parts. Your study of Part Two will suggest to you that these ways are not contradictory, but that they represent varied approaches. Since any of them or all of them may help you discern the nature of the unity of a story, you may find it useful to consider each in turn.

(1) What is the effect of the story upon you? As far back as 1842, Edgar Allan Poe, who wrote the first careful discussion of the prose tale, saw the short story as a stimulus to a response on the part of the reader. With "a certain unique or single effect" in mind, the author, said Poe, "then invents such incidents—he then combines such events, and discusses them in such tone as may best serve . . . in establishing the preconceived effect." In using this approach, you read the story and note what is memorable about it—precisely what it gave you, an idea, perhaps, an attitude, an insight into life or character, or an emotion. You then consider how, exactly, that particular story and the manner of its telling established such an effect.

(2) What is the apparent intention of the author, and how does that intention influence his handling of elements and details? (The word *apparent* is appropriate here, since readers who do not happen to be mind readers can never be certain about the intention of the author.) Carl Grabo, among other

critics, finds it useful to start with "the inception of the story"—so far as it can be discovered through hints in the narrative—and then to go on to "the method of story development by which the author realizes his intent." In using this approach, you look for whatever signs there are of the germinal interest which apparently led the author to write the story, and then see how everything in the narrative contributed. Mr. Grabo (perhaps a bit too neatly) divides stories into five classes—"stories of action, character, setting, idea, and emotional effect." If you find this classification (or some similar one) satisfactory, you classify the story, formulate an accurate statement about the exact nature of the dominant element (if you can find one), and then note how all other elements are made to help develop it.

(3) What is the unique content of the story itself, and how does its form contribute to the setting forth of this unique content? In using this approach, you aim at the definition of the whole story, and then at the discovery of the interrelations through which the parts function to create that story. Here your reading makes possible answers to questions such as: What happens? To whom? Where? Why? How? Perhaps your conclusions make possible the formulation of the unique features of the work in a sentence beginning, "This is the story of how . . ." and going on to answer the questions listed above. Having formulated such a sentence, you may notice in detail how the handling of characters, action, settings, language, tone, and symbols of meaning are related to the unfolding of such a narrative.

EMPHASIS AND SUBORDINATION

Any serious study of a story will take into account, then, not only the nature of its unity but also the methods whereby such unity is achieved. In other words, you attempt to discover what is emphasized and what is subordinated for the achievement of the effect, the realization of the author's intention, and the creation of an artistic entity. Some elements and details will be stressed, some will be played down, in ways which have been discussed as we talked of action, characters, setting, language, tone, point of view, atmosphere, and meanings (pp. 31-135). Also important is the point of view from which the story is unfolded.

Emphasis in a story may be achieved by length of treatment, by repetition, by memorable phrasing, and by particularization. The very fact that more space is devoted to one matter than to another in a short story (as in fact in any literary work) emphasizes that matter. Other things being equal, a character or scene introduced with a curt sentence or phrase will receive less stress than one introduced by several long paragraphs. Again, repetition of any item makes for prominence. If an author says, on page one of his story, "John was dishonest"; on page three, "that lying John"; on page seven, "Since John instinctively avoided the truth," the idea that John was something other than veracious is pretty well underlined. And, of course, a phrase which is particularly vivid or poetic or unusual can make a detail or series of details stand out.

Very valuable for emphasis, of course, is particularization—the use of detail, of concrete words. A happening which is portrayed in all its particulars, or a series of happenings in which each event is explicitly presented, will thereby be emphasized. That which is generalized, by contrast, is subordinated. Edgar Allan Poe, for instance, in "The Pit and the Pendulum," as Bliss Perry has noticed, "paints with extraordinary vividness the sensations and thoughts" of the chief character, but he gives this character "absolutely no individuality, save possibly in the ingenuity by means of which he finally escapes." In this tale, therefore, the emotions, because they are particularized, become a main element, while the characterization, because it is generalized, is subordinated. A character, on the other hand, stands out when he is given a number of vivid physical qualities or a number of unusual traits. Setting, too, will loom large or small in a story in accordance with the number of concrete details about it given to the reader. Even the theme of a story, abstract idea though it is, will be emphasized largely by particularization of certain sorts. We quickly discover that a story is an allegory when we note that the personified virtues and vices have concrete qualities which stand for ideas. Similarly, the vivid details in a symbolical story stress the relationship between the story and the meaning it is developing.

Thus some elements may be emphasized, some "de-emphasized" or subordinated, in well-wrought short stories—all in the interest of unity. By noticing the lengthy developments, the repetition, the striking language, the use of concrete details, we as readers may learn a great deal about the way the narrative has been unified—fused into a single composition.

POINT OF VIEW

The aspects of point of view considered earlier (p. 91) were important for the study of poetry, fiction, and drama. We outlined the principal characteristics of the four basic types of narrators: (1) the third person reporter, (2) the third person omniscient narrator, (3) the author as first person, and (4) the dramatized first person narrator. At this point we want to explore more fully than we did in the earlier discussion two aspects of point of view relevant, not to the study of drama, but to poetry and particularly to fiction: distance and reliability.

Distance

The distant narrator is not necessarily physically removed from the scene and the action he describes, though he may be. He is emotionally distant, i.e., he does not indicate his feelings. Look back at "The Death of the Dauphin" (p. 102). The narrator of the story seems to be saying, "I merely report to you what happened, I do not comment, I do not react." If we conceive a full spectrum of degrees of emotional commitment, at the end opposite from the distant narrator will stand the sympathetic narrator. Recall Marlow in "Heart of Darkness." So strong is his emotional reaction to certain elements of his story that, on one occasion at least, he offends his audience aboard the *Nellie*. The onlooker of "The Death of the Dauphin" and Marlow can serve, then, as representatives of the distant narrator and the emotionally involved narrator, respectively.

Between these extremes there is much variety. Suppose, for example, that the narrator prefers to stay emotionally out of his story, for the most part, but wishes on occasion to reveal his judgment of certain elements. He may use irony, as does the narrator of "The Minister's Black Veil" when he says (p. 121), "A few shook their sagacious heads, intimating that they could penetrate the mystery; . . ." Such a narrator is relatively distant. He sets the protection of his irony between himself and a full emotional response to his story, but he is more committed than Daudet's narrator. For another example, look at the narrator of Robert Penn Warren's story "When the Light Gets Green" (p. 49). Throughout most of the story, you recall, the narrator sympathizes with the feelings he had as a boy about his grandfather. But when the old man is stricken and later dies, the boy fails to react, and the narrator does not tell us directly how he now feels. Yet a great deal of pathos, a sense of real loss, slips into the story. It is as though the narrator said through clenched teeth, "I must not become sentimental here at the end, but you will understand how I feel." Still the distance of this narrator is little compared to that of Daudet's or Hawthorne's narrator. He becomes distant, not because he is unwilling to respond, but in order to avoid being offensive. Finally there is Marlow, who insistently reveals and often even analyzes his emotional reactions for us.

There is not necessarily a connection between distance and any one of the four basic kinds of narrators. However, there is a special problem involving distance and the first person narrator who is a character in his own story. Look again at "When the Light Gets Green." There are, in a sense, two first persons: "I" as boy, the character, and "I" as man, the narrator. Though the narrator generally views the boy with sympathy, the two are not the same—age and perspective separate them. The distinction is clear, in such a statement as, ". . . I read to him some, but not as much as I ought." (p. 52). The difference between "I" as character and "I" as narrator is greater in Frank O'Connor's "My Oedipus Complex" (p. 4) and even greater in a story that you will read later, "Araby" (p. 436).

The narrators of eighteenth-century fiction and of Gothic and Victorian fiction often joined freely with their characters in weeping, feeling terror, pity, and love. In the twentieth century, however, we like to think ourselves tougher and more objective and tend to prefer distant narrators. You need not, perhaps should not, determine your favorite kind of narrator—great fiction can be written either way. But it is important that you understand the matter of distance; you must perceive the degree of the narrator's emotional commitment before you can accurately assess tone and the emotional colorations of the story.

Reliability

The reliable narrator is one whose account of the story we can trust—his interpretations, if he provides any, as well as his narration of the facts. Unlike distance, the concept of reliability does not apply to all the basic kinds of narrators. The third person reporter (whether offering commentary or not), the third person narrator whose privilege includes inside and outside views, and the first person as author are narrators whom we can almost certainly trust. To illustrate this fact, let us return to some fiction that you have read. We do not, for example, question the reliability of the reporter of Hawthorne's "The Minister's Black Veil," nor do we distrust the narrator of Eudora Welty's "A Curtain of Green." (Though the story contains point of view characters who are not perfectly knowledgeable—the neighbors and Jamie—the fact remains that the narrator can get free of such points of view to produce a reliable report.) And finally, we do not question the reliability of the narrator-author of "My Oedipus Complex"; by definition he speaks for the author.

The question of reliability, then, pertains to only two kinds of narrators, the third person narrator whose privilege is limited to a single point of view and the dramatized first person narrator. The problem, then, is easy to see— these narrators are imprisoned in a consciousness, a sensibility, which is not the writer's own. It may be an exquisite sensibility, like Marlow's, attuned to every nuance of meaning and therefore eminently reliable, but it may be the consciousness of a child, of an idiot, or of a warped or diseased person. In these latter cases the writer is asking us to take an ironic view of what the narrator reports. We should, in other words, be careful to differentiate our own perceptions and reactions from those of the point of view character. Look at the narrator of Saki's "The Open Window" (p. 143). By staying quite close to Framton's point of view until the very end of the story, he allows us to share with Framton the illusion that the dead have returned. Montresor, the narrator of Poe's "The Cask of Amontillado" (p. 60), is a more striking example. We can probably rely on his account of the proceedings in the wine vault, but we cannot accept his reactions, colored as they are by the diseased pleasure of revenge. So warped is Montresor's mind that we even wonder whether there are any real injuries to avenge.

You may ask the question: What is the writer's motive for using an unreliable narrator and thus distorting his material? Why not tell the story straight? There are several possible motives. One of the common themes in literature, as you know, is the disparity between appearance and reality. By creating the unreliable narrator, the writer invites you to use your sense of irony, to become intellectually engaged in differentiating the values reflected by the distorting mind and your own mind. In this sense, seeing through the unreliable account to the real significances is an exercise in practical philosophy. The unreliable narrator also provides psychological insight. You have a chance to watch an imperfect intelligence or a diseased mind at work—in the case of Montresor the mind of one obsessed with pride and revenge. And finally, the unreliable narrator can be a device by which the writer artfully withholds or disguises essential information, thus creating mystery and suspense.

By studying the author's choice of a point of view, the distance and reliability of his narrator, we as readers can see what that choice enables the author to tell and to omit, to emphasize and to subordinate; we can also see what effect the choice has upon the author's ordering of the action. Thus, like other devices which determine emphasis and subordination, the point of view offers useful clues concerning the achievement of the effect of the story, the author's intention, and the story's unique content and form.

In addition to the short stories that follow here, you might wish to turn back and reconsider those you studied in Parts One and Two: Frank O'Connor, "My Oedipus Complex" (p. 4); Robert Penn Warren, "When the Light Gets Green" (p. 49); Edgar Allan Poe, "The Cask of Amontillado" (p. 60); Alphonse Daudet, "The Death of the Dauphin" (p. 102); Eudora Welty, "A Curtain of Green" (p. 104); Nathaniel Hawthorne, "The Minister's Black Veil" (p. 119); Saki, "The Open Window" (p. 143); Maxim Gorky, "Boless" (p. 166); and H. L. Davis, "The Electric Bulldog" (p. 179).

THE BOOK OF RUTH

Now it came to pass in the days when the judges ruled, that there was a famine in the land. And a certain man of Beth-lehem-judah went to sojourn in the country of Moab, he, and his wife, and his two sons. And the name of the man was Elimelech, and the name of his wife Naomi, and the name of his two sons Mahlon and Chilion, Ephrathites of Beth-lehem-judah. And they came into the country of Moab, and continued there.

And Elimelech Naomi's husband died; and she was left, and her two sons. And they took them wives of the women of Moab; the name of the one was Orpah, and the name of the other Ruth: and they dwelled there about ten years. And Mahlon and Chilion died also both of them; and the woman was left of her two sons and her husband.

Then she arose with her daughters-in-law, that she might return from the country of Moab; for she had heard in the country of Moab how that the Lord had visited His people in giving them bread. Wherefore she went forth out of the place where she was, and her two daughters-in-law with her; and they went on the way to return unto the land of Judah. And Naomi said unto her two daughters-in-law, "Go, return each to her mother's house: the Lord deal kindly with you, as ye have dealt with the dead, and with me. The Lord grant you that ye may find rest, each of you in the house of her husband." Then she kissed them; and they lifted up their voice, and wept. And they said unto her, "Surely we will return with thee unto thy people."

And Naomi said, "Turn again, my daughters: why will ye go with me? are there yet any more sons in my womb, that they may be your husbands? Turn again, my daughters, go your way; for I am too old to have an husband. If I should say, I have hope, if I should have an husband also to-night, and should also bear sons; would ye tarry for them till they were grown? would ye stay for them from having husbands? nay, my daughters, for it grieveth me much for your sakes that the hand of the Lord is gone out against me."

And they lifted up their voice, and wept again: and Orpah kissed her mother-in-law; but Ruth clave unto her. And she said, "Behold, thy sister-in-law is gone back unto her people, and unto her gods: return thou after thy sister-in-law." And Ruth said, "Intreat me not to leave thee, or to return from following after thee: for whither thou goest, I will go; and where thou lodgest, I will lodge: thy people shall be my people, and thy God my God: where thou diest, will I die, and there will I be buried: the Lord do so to me, and more also, if ought but death part thee and me."

When she saw that she was steadfastly minded to go with her, then she left speaking unto her. So they two went until they came to Beth-lehem. And it came to pass, when they were come to Beth-lehem, that all the city was moved about them, and they said, "Is this Naomi?" And she said unto them, "Call me not Naomi, call me Mara: for the Almighty hath dealt very bitterly with me. I went out full, and the Lord hath brought me home again empty: why then call ye me Naomi, seeing the Lord hath testified against me, and the Almighty hath afflicted me?"

So Naomi returned, and Ruth the Moabitess, her daughter-in-law, with her, which returned out of the country of Moab: and they came to Beth-lehem in the beginning of barley harvest. And Naomi had a kinsman of her husband's, a mighty man of wealth, of the family of Elimelech; and his name was Boaz. And Ruth the Moabitess said unto Naomi, "Let me now go to the field, and glean ears of corn after him in whose sight I shall find grace." And she said unto her, "Go, my daughter." And she went, and came, and gleaned in the field after the reapers: and her hap was to light on a part of the field belonging unto Boaz. who was of the kindred of Elimelech.

And, behold, Boaz came from Beth-lehem, and said unto the reapers, "The Lord be with you." And they answered him, "The Lord bless thee." Then said Boaz unto his servant that was set over the reapers. "Whose damsel is this?" And the servant that was set over the reapers answered and said, "It is the Moabitish damsel that came back with Naomi out of the country of Moab: and she said, I pray you, let me glean and gather after the reapers among the sheaves: so she came, and hath continued even from the morning until now, that she tarried a little in the house."

Then said Boaz unto Ruth, "Hearest thou not, my daughter? Go not to glean in another field, neither go from hence, but abide here fast by my maidens: let thine eyes be on the field that they do reap, and go thou after them: have I not charged the young men that they shall not touch thee? and when thou art athirst, go unto the vessels, and drink of that which the young men have drawn."

Then she fell on her face, and bowed herself to the ground, and said unto him, "Why have I found grace in thine eyes, that thou shouldest take knowledge of me, seeing I am a stranger?"

And Boaz answered and said unto her, "It hath fully been shewed me, all that thou hast done unto thy mother-in-law since the death of thine husband: and how thou hast left thy father and thy mother, and the land of thy nativity, and art come unto a people which thou knewest not heretofore. The Lord recompense thy work, and a full reward be given thee of the Lord God of Israel, under whose wings thou art come to trust."

Then she said, "Let me find favor in thy sight, my lord; for that thou hast comforted me, and for that thou hast spoken friendly unto thine hand-maid, though I be not like unto one of thine handmaidens."

And Boaz said unto her, "At mealtime come thou hither, and eat of the bread, and dip thy morsel in the vinegar." And she sat beside the reapers: and he reached her parched corn, and she did eat, and was sufficed, and left. And when she was risen up to glean, Boaz commanded his young men, saying, "Let her glean even among the sheaves, and reproach her not: and let fall also some of the handfuls of purpose for her, and leave them, that she may glean them, and rebuke her not."

So she gleaned in the field until even, and beat out that she had gleaned: and it was about an ephah of barley. And she took it up, and went into the city: and her mother-in-law saw what she had gleaned: and she brought forth, and gave to her that she had reserved after she was sufficed. And her mother-in-law said unto her, "Where hast thou gleaned to-day? and where wroughtest thou? blessed be he that did take knowledge of thee."

And she shewed her mother-in-law with whom she had wrought, and said, "The man's name with whom I wrought to-day is Boaz." And Naomi said unto her daughter-in-law, "Blessed be he of the Lord, who hath not left off His kindness to the living and to the dead." And Naomi said unto her, "The man is near of kin unto us, one of our next kinsmen."

And Ruth the Moabitess said, "He said unto me also, Thou shalt keep fast by my young men, until they have ended all my harvest."

And Naomi said unto Ruth her daughter-in-law, "It is good, my daughter, that thou go out with his maidens, that they meet thee not in any other field." So she kept fast by the maidens of Boaz to glean unto the end of barley harvest and of wheat harvest; and dwelt with her mother-in-law.

Then Naomi her mother-in-law said unto her, "My daughter, shall I not seek rest for thee, that it may be well with thee? And now is not Boaz of our kindred, with whose maidens thou wast? Behold, he winnoweth barley to-night in the threshing-floor. Wash thyself therefore, and anoint thee, and put thy raiment upon thee, and get thee down to the floor: but make not thyself known unto the man, until he shall have done eating and drinking. And it shall be, when he lieth down, that thou shalt mark the place where he shall lie, and thou shalt go in, and uncover his feet, and lay thee down; and he will tell thee what thou shalt do."

And she said unto her, "All that thou sayest unto me I will do."

And she went down unto the floor, and did according to all that her mother-in-law bade her. And when Boaz had eaten and drunk, and his heart was merry, he went to lie down at the end of the heap of corn: and she came softly, and uncovered his feet, and laid her down. And it came to pass at midnight, that the man was afraid, and turned himself: and, behold, a woman lay at his feet. And he said, "Who art thou?" And she answered, "I am Ruth thine handmaid: spread therefore thy skirt over thine handmaid; for thou art a near kinsman."

And he said, "Blessed be thou of the Lord, my daughter: for thou hast shewed more kindness in the latter end than at the beginning, inasmuch as thou followedst not young men, whether poor or rich. And now, my daughter, fear not; I will do to thee all that thou requirest: for all the city of my people doth know that thou art a virtuous woman. And now it is true that I am thy near kinsman: howbeit there is a kinsman nearer than I. Tarry this night, and it shall be in the morning, that if he will perform unto thee the part of a kinsman, well; let him do the kinsman part: but if he will not do the part of a kinsman to thee, then will I do the part of a kinsman to thee, as the Lord liveth: lie down until the morning."

And she lay at his feet until the morning: and she rose up before one could know another. And he said, "Let it not be known that a woman came into the floor." Also he said, "Bring the vail that thou hast upon thee, and hold it." And when she held it, he measured six measures of barley, and laid it on her: and she went into the city.

And when she came to her mother-in-law, she said, "Who art thou, my daughter?" And she told her all that the man had done to her. And she said, "These six measures of barley gave he me; for he said to me, Go not empty unto thy mother-in-law." Then said she, "Sit still, my daughter, until thou know how the matter will fall: for the man will not be in rest, until he have finished the thing this day."

Then went Boaz up to the gate, and sat him down there: and, behold, the kinsman of whom Boaz spake came by; unto whom he said, "Ho, such a one! turn aside, sit down here." And he turned aside, and sat down. And he took ten men of the elders of the city, and said, "Sit ye down here." And they sat down. And he said unto the kinsman, "Naomi, that is come again out of the country of Moab, selleth a parcel of land, which was our brother Elimelech's: and I thought to advertise thee, saying, Buy it before the inhabitants, and before the elders of my people. If thou wilt redeem it, redeem it: but if thou wilt not redeem it, then tell me, that I may know: for there is none to redeem it beside thee; and I am after thee."

And he said, "I will redeem it."

Then said Boaz, "What day thou buyest the field of the hand of Naomi, thou must buy it also of Ruth the Moabitess, the wife of the dead, to raise up the name of the dead upon his inheritance."

And the kinsman said, "I cannot redeem it for myself, lest I mar mine own inheritance: redeem thou my right to thyself; for I cannot redeem it." Now this was the manner in former time in Israel concerning redeeming and concerning changing, for to confirm all things; a man plucked off his shoe, and gave it to his neighbor: and this was a testimony in Israel. Therefore the kinsman said unto Boaz, "Buy it for thee." So he drew off his shoe.

And Boaz said unto the elders, and unto all the people, "Ye are witnesses this day, that I have bought all that was Elimelech's, and all that was Chilion's and Mahlon's, of the hand of Naomi. Moreover, Ruth the Moabitess, the wife of Mahlon, have I purchased to be my wife, to raise up the name of the dead upon his inheritance, that the name of the dead be not cut off from among his brethren, and from the gate of his place: ye are witnesses this day."

And all the people that were in the gate, and the elders, said, "We are witnesses. The Lord make the woman that is come into thine house like Rachel and like Leah, which two did build the house of Israel: and do thou worthily in Ephratah, and be famous in Beth-lehem: and let thy house be like the house of Pharez, whom Tamar bore unto Judah, of the seed which the Lord shall give thee of this young woman."

So Boaz took Ruth, and she was his wife: and when he went in unto her, the Lord gave her conception, and she bare a son. And the women said unto Naomi, "Blessed be the Lord, which hath not left thee this day without a kinsman, that his name may be famous in Israel. And he shall be unto thee a restorer of thy life, and a nourisher of thine old age: for thy daughter-in-law, which loveth thee, which is better to thee than seven sons, hath born him." And Naomi took the child, and laid it in her bosom, and became nurse unto it. And the women her neighbors gave it a name, saying, "There is a son born to Naomi"; and they called his name Obed: he is the father of Jesse, the father of David.   (c. 450 B.C.)

Giovanni Boccaccio

THE FALCON

You must know, then, that Coppo di Borghese Domenichi, who was of our days and maybe is yet a man of great worship and authority in our city and illustrious and worthy of eternal renown, much more for his fashions and his merit than for the nobility of his blood, being grown full of years, delighted oftentimes to discourse with his neighbours and others of things past, the which he knew how to do better and more orderly and with more memory and elegance of speech than any other man. Amongst other fine things of his, he was used to tell that there was once in Florence a young man called Federigo, son of Messer Filippo Alberighi, and renowned for deeds of arms and courtesy over every other bachelor in Tuscany, who, as betideth most gentlemen, became enamoured of a gentlewoman named Madam Giovanna, in her day held one of the fairest and sprightliest ladies that were in Florence; and to win her love, he held jousts and tourneyings and made entertainments and gave gifts and spent his substance without any stint; but she, being no less virtuous than fair, recked nought of these things done for her nor of him who did them. Federigo spending thus far beyond his means and gaining nought, his wealth, as lightly happeneth, in course of time came to an end and he abode poor, nor was aught left him but a poor little farm, on whose returns he lived very meagrely, and to boot a falcon he had, one of the best in the world. Wherefore, being more in love than ever and him seeming he might no longer make such a figure in the city as he would fain do, he took up his abode at Campi, where his farm was, and there bore his poverty with patience, hawking whenas he might and asking of no one.

Federigo being thus come to extremity, it befell one day that Madam Giovanna's husband fell sick and seeing himself nigh upon death, made his will, wherein, being very rich, he left a son of his, now well grown, his heir, after which, having much loved Madam Giovanna, he substituted her to his heir, in case his son should die without lawful issue, and died. Madam Giovanna, being thus left a widow, betook herself that summer, as is the usance of our ladies, into the country with her son to an estate of hers very near that of Federigo; wherefore it befell that the lad made acquaintance with the latter and began to take delight in hawks and hounds, and having many a time seen his falcon flown and being strangely taken therewith, longed sore to have it, but dared not ask it of him, seeing it so dear to him. The thing standing thus, it came to pass that the lad fell sick, whereat his mother was sore concerned, as one who had none but him and loved him with all her might, and abode about him all day, comforting him without cease; and many a time she asked him if there were aught he desired, beseeching him tell it her, for that, and it might be gotten, she would contrive that he should have it. The lad, having heard these offers many times repeated, said, "Mother mine, an you could procure me to have Federigo's falcon, methinketh I should soon be whole."

The lady, hearing this, bethought herself awhile and began to consider how she should do. She knew that Federigo had long loved her and had never gotten of her so much as a glance of the eye; wherefore quoth she in herself, "How shall I send or go to him to seek of him this falcon, which is, by all I hear, the best that ever flew and which, to boot, maintaineth him in the world? And how can I be so graceless as to offer to take this from a gentleman who hath none other pleasure left?" Perplexed with this thought and knowing not what to say, for all she was very certain of getting the bird, if she asked for it, she made no reply to her son, but abode silent. However, at last, the love of her son so got the better of her that she resolved in herself to satisfy him, come what might, and not to send, but to go herself for the falcon and fetch it to him. Accordingly she said to him, "My son, take comfort and bethink thyself to grow well again, for I promise thee that the first thing I do to-morrow morning I will go for it and fetch it to thee." The boy was rejoiced at this and showed some amendment that same day.

Next morning, the lady, taking another lady to bear her company, repaired, by way of diversion, to Federigo's little house and enquired for the latter, who, for that it was no weather for hawking nor had been for some days past, was then in a garden he had, overlooking the doing of certain little matters of his, and hearing that Madam Giovanna asked for him at the door, ran thither, rejoicing and marvelling exceedingly. She, seeing him come, rose and going with womanly graciousness to meet him, answered his respectful salutation with "Give you good day, Federigo!" then went on to say, "I am come to make thee amends for that which thou hast suffered through me, in loving me more than should have behooved thee; and the amends in question is this that I purpose to dine with thee this morning familiarly, I and this lady my companion." "Madam," answered Federigo humbly, "I remember me not to have ever received any ill at your hands, but on the contrary so much good that, if ever I was worth aught, it came about through your worth and the love I bore you; and assuredly, albeit you have come to a poor host, this your gracious visit is far more precious to me than it would be an it were given me to spend over again as much as that which I have spent aforetime." So saying, he shamefastly received her into his house and thence brought her into his garden, where, having none else to bear her company, he said to her, "Madam, since there is none else here, this good woman, wife of yonder husbandman, will bear you company, whilst I go see the table laid."

Never till that moment, extreme as was his poverty, had he been so dolorously sensible of the straits to which he had brought himself for the lack of those riches he had spent on such disorderly wise. But that morning, finding he had nothing wherewithal he might honourably entertain the lady for love of whom he had aforetime entertained folk without number, he was made perforce aware of his default and ran hither and thither, perplexed beyond measure, like a man beside himself, inwardly cursing his ill fortune, but found neither money nor aught he might pawn. It was now growing late and he having a great desire to entertain the gentle lady with somewhat, yet choosing not to have recourse to his own labourer, much less anyone else, his eye fell on his good falcon, which he saw on his perch in his little saloon; whereupon, having no other resource, he took the bird and finding him fat, deemed him a dish worthy of such a lady. Accordingly, without more ado, he wrung the hawk's neck and hastily caused a little maid of his pluck it and truss it and after put it on the spit and roast it diligently. Then, the table laid and covered with very white cloths, whereof he had yet some store, he returned with a blithe countenance to the lady in the garden and told her that dinner was ready, such as it was in his power to provide. Accordingly, the lady and her friend, arising, betook themselves to table and in company with Federigo, who served them with the utmost diligence, ate the good falcon, unknowing what they did.

Presently, after they had risen from table and had abidden with him awhile in cheerful discourse, the lady, thinking it time to tell that wherefore she was come, turned to Federigo and courteously bespoke him, saying, "Federigo, I doubt not a jot but that, when thou hearest that which is the especial occasion of my coming hither, thou wilt marvel at my presumption, remembering thee of thy past life and of my virtue, which latter belike thou reputedst cruelty and hardness of heart; but, if thou hadst or hadst had children, by whom thou mightest know how potent is the love one beareth them, meseemeth certain that thou wouldst in part hold me excused. But, although thou hast none, I, who have one child, cannot therefore escape the common laws to which other mothers are subject and whose enforcements it behooveth me ensue, need must I, against my will and contrary to all right and seemliness, ask of thee a boon, which I know is supremely dear to thee (and that with good reason, for that thy sorry fortune hath left thee none other delight, none other diversion, none other solace), to wit, thy falcon, whereof my boy is so sore enamoured that, an I carry it not to him, I fear me his present disorder will be so aggravated that there may presently ensue thereof somewhat whereby I shall lose him. Wherefore I conjure thee—not by the love thou bearest me and whereto thou art nowise beholden, but by thine own nobility, which in doing courtesy hath approved itself greater than in any other—that it please thee give it to me, so by the gift I may say I have kept my son alive and thus made him forever thy debtor."

Federigo, hearing what the lady asked and knowing that he could not oblige her, for that he had given her the falcon to eat, fell a-weeping in her presence, ere he could answer a word. The lady at first believed that his tears arose from grief at having to part from his good falcon and was like to say that she would not have it. However, she contained herself and awaited what Federigo should reply, who, after weeping awhile, made answer thus: "Madam, since it pleased God that I should set my love on you, I have in many things reputed fortune contrary to me and have complained of her; but all the ill turns she hath done me have been a light matter in comparison with that which she doth me at this present and for which I can never more be reconciled to her, considering that you are come hither to my poor house, whereas you deigned not to come while I was rich, and seek of me a little boon, the which she hath so wrought that I cannot grant you; and why this cannot be I will tell you briefly. When I heard that you, of your favour, were minded to dine with me, I deemed it a right thing and a seemly, having regard to your worth and the nobility of your station, to honour you, as far as in me lay, with some choicer victual than that which is commonly set before other folk; wherefore, remembering me of the falcon which you ask of me and of his excellence, I judged him a dish worthy of you. This very morning, then, you have had him roasted upon the trencher, and indeed I had accounted him excellently well bestowed; but now, seeing that you would fain have had him on the other wise, it is so great a grief to me that I cannot oblige you therein that methinketh I shall never forgive my self therefor." So saying, in witness of this, he let cast before her the falcon's feathers and feet and beak.

The lady, seeing and hearing this, first blamed him for having, to give a woman to eat, slain such a falcon, and after inwardly much commended the greatness of his soul, which poverty had not availed nor might anywise avail to abate. Then, being put out of all hope of having the falcon and fallen therefore in doubt of her son's recovery, she took her leave and returned, all disconsolate, to the latter, who, before many days had passed, whether for chagrin that he could not have the bird or for this his disorder was e'en fated to bring him to that pass, departed this life, to the inexpressible grief of his mother. After she had abidden awhile full of tears and affliction, being left very rich and yet young, she was more than once urged by her brothers to marry again, and albeit she would fain not have done so, yet, finding herself importuned and calling to mind Federigo's worth and his last magnificence, to wit, the having slain such a falcon for her entertainment, she said to them, "I would gladly, an it liked you, abide as I am; but, since it is your pleasure that I take a second husband, certes I will never take any other, an I have not Federigo degli Alberighi." Whereupon her brothers, making mock of her, said, "Silly woman that thou art, what is this thou sayest? How canst thou choose him, seeing he hath nothing in the world?" "Brothers mine," answered she, "I know very well that it is as you say; but I would liefer have a man that lacketh of riches than riches that lack of a man." Her brethren, hearing her mind and knowing Federigo for a man of great merit, poor though he was, gave her, with all her wealth, to him, even as she would; and he, seeing himself married to a lady of such worth and one who he had loved so dear and exceedingly rich, to boot, became a better husband of his substance and ended his days with her in joy and solace.   (1353)

Voltaire

MEMNON
THE PHILOSOPHER

Memnon one day took it into his head to become a great philosopher. There are few men who have not, at some time or other, conceived the same wild project. Says Memnon to himself, To be a perfect philosopher, and of course to be perfectly happy, I have nothing to do but to divest myself entirely of passions; and nothing is more easy, as everybody knows. In the first place, I will never be in love; for, when I see a beautiful woman, I will say to myself, These cheeks will one day grow wrinkled, these eyes be encircled with vermilion, that bosom become flabby and pendant, that head bald and palsied. Now I have only to consider her at present in imagination, as she will afterwards appear; and certainly a fair face will never turn my head.

In the second place, I will be always temperate. It will be in vain to tempt me with good cheer, with delicious wines, or the charms of society. I will have only to figure to myself the consequences of excess, an aching head, a loathing stomach, the loss of reason, of health, and of time: I will then only eat to supply the waste of nature; my health will be always equal, my ideas pure and luminus. All this is so easy that there is no merit in accomplishing it.

But, says Memnon, I must think a little of how I am to regulate my fortune: why, my desires are moderate, my wealth is securely placed with the Receiver General of the finances of Nineveh: I have wherewithal to live independent; and that is the greatest of blessings. I shall never be under the cruel necessity of dancing attendance at court; I will never envy anyone, and nobody will envy me; still all this is easy. I have friends, continued he, and I will preserve them, for we shall never have any difference; I will never take amiss anything they may say or do; and they will behave in the same way to me.—There is no difficulty in all this.

Having thus laid his little plan of philosophy in his closet, Memnon put his head out of the window. He saw two women walking under the plane trees near his house. The one was old and appeared quite at her ease. The other was young, handsome, and seemingly much agitated: she sighed, she wept, and seemed on that account still more beautiful. Our philosopher was touched, not, to be sure, with the beauty of the lady (he was too much determined not to feel any uneasiness of that kind), but with the distress which he saw her in. He came down stairs and accosted the young Ninevite in the design of consoling her with philosophy. That lovely person related to him, with an air of the greatest simplicity, and in the most affecting manner, the injuries she sustained from an imaginary uncle; with what art he had deprived her of some imaginary property, and of the violence which she pretended to dread from him. "You appear to me," said she, "a man of such wisdom, that if you will condescend to come to my house and examine into my affairs, I am persuaded you will be able to draw me from the cruel embarrassment I am at present involved in." Memnon did not hesitate to follow her, to examine her affairs philosophically, and to give her sound counsel.

The afflicted lady led him into a perfumed chamber, and politely made him sit down with her on a large sofa, where they both placed themselves opposite to each other, in the attitude of conversation, their legs crossed; the one eager in telling her story, the other listening with devout attention. The lady spoke with downcast eyes, whence there sometimes fell a tear, and which, as she now and then ventured to raise them, always met those of the sage Memnon. Their discourse was full of tenderness, which redoubled as often as their eyes met. Memnon took her affairs exceedingly to heart, and felt himself every instant more and more inclined to oblige a person so virtuous and so unhappy.—By degrees, in the warmth of conversation, they ceased to sit opposite; they drew nearer; their legs were no longer crossed. Memnon counselled her so closely, and gave her such tender advices, that neither of them could talk any longer of business, nor well knew what they were about.

At this interesting moment, as may easily be imagined, who should come in but the uncle; he was armed from head to foot, and the first thing he said was, that he would immediately sacrifice, as was just, the sage Memnon and his niece; the latter, who made her escape, knew that he was well enough disposed to pardon, provided a good round sum were offered to him. Memnon was obliged to purchase his safety with all he had about him. In those days people were happy in getting so easily quit. America was not then discovered, and distressed ladies were not nearly so dangerous as they are now.

Memnon, covered with shame and confusion, got home to his own house; there he found a card inviting him to dinner with some of his intimate friends. If I remain at home alone, said he, I shall have my mind so occupied with this vexatious adventure, that I shall not be able to eat a bit, and I shall bring upon myself some disease. It will therefore be prudent in me to go to my intimate friends, and partake with them of a frugal repast. I shall forget, in the sweets of their society, the folly I have this morning been guilty of. Accordingly he attends the meeting; he is discovered to be uneasy at something, and he is urged to drink and banish care. A little wine, drunk in moderation, comforts the heart of god and man: so reasons Memnon the philosopher, and he becomes intoxicated. After the repast, play is proposed. A little play, with one's intimate friends, is a harmless pastime:—he plays and loses all that is in his purse, and four times as much on his word. A dispute arises on some circumstance in the game, and the disputants grow warm: one of his intimate friends throws a dicebox at his head and strikes out one of his eyes. The philosopher Memnon is carried home to his house, drunk and penniless, with the loss of an eye.

He sleeps out his debauch, and when his head has got a little clear, he sends his servant to the Receiver General of the finances of Nineveh to draw a little money to pay his debt of honour to his intimate friends. The servant returns and informs him, that the Receiver General had that morning been declared a fraudulent bankrupt, and that by this means an hundred families are reduced to poverty and despair. Memnon, almost beside himself, puts a plaster on his eye and a petition in his pocket, and goes to court to solicit justice from the king against the bankrupt. In the saloon he meets a number of ladies, all in the highest spirits, and sailing along with hoops four and twenty feet in circumference. One of them, who knew him a little, eyed him askance, and cried aloud, "Ah! what a horrid monster!" Another, who was better acquainted with him, thus accosts him, "Good-morrow, Mr. Memnon, I hope you are very well, Mr. Memnon: La! Mr. Memnon, how did you lose your eye?" and turning upon her heel, she tripped away without waiting an answer.

Memnon hid himself in a corner, and waited for the moment when he could throw himself at the feet of the monarch. That moment at last arrived. Three times he kissed the earth, and presented his petition. His gracious majesty received him very favourably, and referred the paper to one of his satraps, that he might give him an account of it. The satrap takes Memnon aside, and says to him with a haughty air and satyrical grin. "Hark ye, you fellow with the one eye, you must be a comical dog indeed, to address yourself to the king rather than to me; and still more so, to dare to demand justice against an honest bankrupt, whom I honour with my protection, and who is nephew to the waiting-maid of my mistress. Proceed no further in this business, my good friend, if you wish to preserve the eye you have left."

Memnon having thus, in his closet, resolved to renounce women, the excesses of the table, play and quarreling, but especially having determined never to go to court, had been in the short space of four and twenty hours duped and robbed by a gentle dame, had got drunk, had gamed, had been engaged in a quarrel, had got his eye knocked out, and had been at court, where he was sneered at and insulted.

Petrified with astonishment, and his heart broken with grief, Memnon returns homeward in despair. As he was about to enter his house, he is repulsed by a number of officers who are carrying out his furniture for the benefit of his creditors; he falls down almost lifeless under a plane tree. There he finds the fair dame of the morning, who was walking with her dear uncle; and both set up a loud laugh on seeing Memnon with his plaster. The night approached, and Memnon made his bed on some straw near the walls of his house. Here the ague seized him, and he fell asleep in one of the fits, when a celestial spirit appeared to him in a dream.

It was all resplendent with light; it had six beautiful wings, but neither feet nor head, nor tail, and could be likened to nothing. "What art thou?" said Memnon.

"Thy good genius," replied the spirit.

"Restore to me then my eye, my health, my fortune, my reason," said Memnon; and he related how he had lost them all in one day.

"These are adventures which never happen to us in the world we inhabit," said the spirit.

"And what world do you inhabit?" said the man of affliction.

"My native country," replied the other, "is five hundred millions of leagues distant from the sun, in a little star near Sirius, which you see from hence."

"Charming country!" said Memnon. "And are there indeed with you no jades to dupe a poor devil, no intimate friends that win his money and knock out an eye to him, no fraudulent bankrupts, no satraps, that make a jest of you while they refuse you justice?"

"No," said the inhabitant of the star, "we have nothing of what you talk of; we are never duped by women, because we have none among us; we never commit excesses at table, because we neither eat nor drink; we have no bankrupts, because with us there is neither silver nor gold; our eyes cannot be knocked out because we have not bodies in the form of yours; and satraps never do us injustice, because in our world we are all equal."

"Pray, my Lord," then said Memnon, "without women and without eating how do you spend your time?"

"In watching," said the genius, "over the other worlds that are entrusted to us; and I am now come to give you consolation."

"Alas!" replied Memnon, "why did you not come yesterday to hinder me from committing so many indiscretions?"

"I was with your elder brother Hassan," said the celestial being. "He is still more to be pitied than you are. His most gracious Majesty, the Sultan of the Indies, in whose court he has the honour to serve, has caused both his eyes to be put out for some small indiscretion; and he is now in a dungeon, his hands and feet loaded with chains."

"'Tis a happy thing truly," said Memnon, "to have a good genius in one's family, when out of two brothers one is blind of an eye, the other blind of both; one stretched upon straw, the other in a dungeon."

"Your fate will soon change," said the animal of the star. "It is true, you will never recover your eye but, except that, you may be sufficiently happy if you never again take it into your head to be a perfect philosopher."

"Is it then impossible?" said Memnon.

"As impossible as to be perfectly wise, perfectly strong, perfectly powerful, perfectly happy. We ourselves are very far from it. There is a world indeed where all this takes place; but, in a hundred thousand millions of worlds dispersed over the regions of space, everything goes on by degrees. There is less philosophy and less enjoyment in the second than in the first, less in the third than in the second, and so forth till the last in the scale, where all are completely fools."

"I am afraid," said Memnon, "that our little terraqueous globe here is the madhouse of those hundred thousand millions of worlds, of which your Lordship does me the honour to speak."

"Not quite," said the spirit, "but very nearly: everything must be in its proper place."

"But are those poets and philosophers wrong, then, who tell us that everything is for the best?"

"No, they are right, when we consider things in relation to the gradation of the whole universe."

"Oh! I shall never believe it till I recover my eye again," said the poor Memnon.   (1750)

Prosper Mérimée

MATEO FALCONE

Coming out of Porto-Vecchio, and turning northwest toward the interior of the island, the ground rises somewhat rapidly, and, after a three hours' walk along winding paths, blocked by huge rocky boulders, and sometimes cut by ravines, you come to the edge of a wide *mâquis*. The *mâquis*, or high plateau, is the home of the Corsican shepherds and of all those who wish to escape the police. I would have you understand that the Corsican peasant sets fire to a stretch of woodland to save himself the trouble of manuring his fields. If the flames spread further than they should, so much the worse. In any case, he is sure of a good crop if he sows on this ground, which has been fertilised by the ashes of the trees which grew on it. When the corn has been harvested, they leave the straw, because it takes too much time to gather it up. The roots of the burned trees, which have been left in the ground undamaged, put forth very thick shoots in the following spring, and these shoots, before many years, attain a height of seven or eight feet. It is this sort of undergrowth which is called a *mâquis*. It is composed of all sorts of trees and shrubs mingled and tangled every whichway. A man has to hew his way through with an axe, and there are *mâquis* so thick and tangled that even wild rams cannot penetrate them.

If you have killed a man, go into the *mâquis* of Porto-Vecchio with a good gun and powder and shot. You will live there quite safely, but don't forget to bring along a brown cloak and hood for your blanket and mattress. The shepherds will give you milk, cheese, and chestnuts, and you need not trouble your head about the law or the dead man's relatives, except when you are compelled to go down into the town to renew your ammunition.

When I was in Corsica in 18—, Mateo Falcone's house stood half a league away from the *mâquis*. He was a fairly rich man for that country. He lived like a lord, that is to say, without toil, on the produce of his flocks, which the nomadic shepherds pastured here and there on the mountains. When I saw him, two years later than the incident which I am about to relate, he did not seem to be more than fifty years of age.

Picture a small, sturdy man, with jet-black curly hair, a Roman nose, thin lips, large piercing eyes, and a weather-beaten complexion. His skill as a marksman was extraordinary, even in this country, where everyone is a good shot. For instance, Mateo would never fire on a wild ram with small shot, but at a hundred and twenty paces he would bring it down with a bullet in its head or its shoulder, just as he fancied. He used his rifle at night as easily as in the daytime, and I was given the following illustration of his skill, which may seem incredible, perhaps, to those who have never travelled in Corsica. He placed a lighted candle behind a piece of transparent paper as big as a plate, and aimed at it from eighty paces away. He extinguished the candle, and a moment later, in utter darkness, fired and pierced the paper three times out of four.

With this extraordinary skill Mateo Falcone had gained a great reputation. He was said to be a good friend and a dangerous enemy. Obliging and charitable, he lived at peace with all his neighbors around Porto-Vecchio. But they said of him that once, at Corte, whence he had brought home his wife, he had quickly freed himself of a rival reputed to be as fearful in war as in love. At any rate, people gave Mateo the credit for a certain shot which had surprised his rival shaving in front of a small mirror hung up in his window. The matter was hushed up and Mateo married the girl. His wife Giuseppa presented him at first, to his fury, with three daughters, but at last came a son whom he christened Fortunato, the hope of the family and the heir to its name. The girls were married off satisfactorily. At a pinch their father could count on the daggers and rifles of his sons-in-law. The son was only ten years old, but already gave promise for the future.

One autumn day, Mateo and his wife set forth to visit one of his flocks in a clearing on the *mâquis*. Little Fortunato wanted to come along, but the clearing was too far off, and moreover, someone had to stay to look after the house. His father refused to take him. We shall see that he was sorry for this afterwards.

He had been gone several hours, and little Fortunato lay stretched out quietly in the sunshine, gazing at the blue mountains, and thinking that next Sunday he would be going to town to have dinner with his uncle, the magistrate, when he was suddenly startled by a rifle shot. He rose and turned toward the side of the plain whence the sound had come. Other shots followed, fired at irregular intervals, and they sounded nearer and nearer, till finally, he saw a man on the path which led from the plain up to Mateo's house. He wore a mountaineer's peaked cap, had a beard, and was clad in rags. He dragged himself along with difficulty, leaning on his gun. He had just been shot in the thigh. The man was an outlaw from justice, who, having set out at nightfall to buy ammunition in the town, had fallen on the way into an ambuscade of Corsican gendarmes. After a vigorous defense, he had succeeded in making his escape, but the gendarmes had pursued him closely and fired at him from rock to rock. He had been just ahead of the soldiers, and his wound made it impossible for him to reach the *mâquis* without being captured.

He came up to Fortunato and asked:

"Are you Mateo Falcone's son?"

"Yes, I am."

"I'm Gianetto Sanpiero. The yellow necks are after me. Hide me, for I can go no farther."

"But what will my father say, if I hide you without his permission?"

"He will say that you did the right thing."

"How can I be sure of that?"

"Quick! Hide me! Here they come!"

"Wait till my father comes back."

"How the devil can I wait? They'll be here in five minutes. Come now, hide me, or I shall kill you."

Fortunato replied as cool as a cucumber:

"Your rifle is not loaded, and there are no cartridges in your pouch."

"I have my stiletto."

"But can you run as fast as I can?"

He bounded out of the man's reach.

"You are no son of Mateo Falcone. Will you let me be captured in front of his house?"

The child seemed touched.

"What will you give me if I hide you?" he said, coming nearer to him.

The fugitive felt in a leather wallet that hung from his belt, and took out a five-franc piece which he had been saving, no doubt, to buy powder. Fortunato smiled when he saw the piece of silver. He snatched it and said to Gianetto:

"Have no fear."

He made a large hole at once in a haystack beside the house. Gianetto huddled down in it, and the boy covered him up so as to leave a little breathing space, and yet so that no one could possibly suspect that a man was hidden there. He showed his ingenious wild cunning by another trick. He fetched a cat and her kittens and put them on top of the haystack, so that anyone who passed would think that it had not been disturbed for a long time. Then he noticed some bloodstains on the path in front of the house and covered them over carefully with dust. When he had finished, he lay down again in the sun looking as calm as ever.

A few minutes later, six men in brown uniforms with yellow collars, led by an adjutant, stopped in front of Mateo's door. The adjutant was a distant cousin of Falcone. (You know that degrees of kindred are traced farther in Corsica than anywhere else.) His name was Tiodoro Gamba. He was an energetic man, much feared by the outlaws, many of whom he had already hunted down.

"Good morning, little cousin," he said, accosting Fortunato. "How you have grown! Did you see a man go by just now?"

"Oh, I'm not as tall as you are yet, cousin," replied the child with an innocent smile.

"It won't take long. But, tell me, didn't you see a man go by?"

"Did I see a man go by?"

"Yes, a man with a black velvet peaked cap and a waistcoat embroidered in red and yellow?"

"A man with a black velvet peaked cap, and a waistcoat embroidered in red and yellow?"

"Yes. Hurry up and answer me, and don't keep repeating my questions."

"Monsieur the Curé went by this morning on his horse Pierrot. He enquired after papa's health, and I said to him that——"

"You are making a fool of me, you limb of the devil! Tell me at once which way Gianetto went. He's the man we're looking for, and I'm sure he went this way."

"How do you know?"

"How do I know? I know you've seen him."

"Can I see people pass by in my sleep?"

"You weren't asleep, you rascal. Our shots would wake you."

"So you think, cousin, that your rifles make all that hullaballoo? My father's rifle makes much more noise."

"The devil take you, you little scamp. I am positive that you have seen Gianetto. Maybe you've hidden him, in fact. Here, boys, search the house and see if our man isn't there. He could only walk on one foot, and he has too much sense, the rascal, to try and reach the *mâquis* limping. Besides, the trail of blood stops here."

"What will papa say?" asked Fortunato. "What will he say when he discovers that his house has been searched during his absence?"

"Do you realise that I can make you change your tune, you rogue?" cried the adjutant, as he pulled his ear. "Perhaps you will have something more to say when I have thrashed you with the flat of my sword."

Fortunato laughed in derision.

"My father is Mateo Falcone," he said meaningly.

"Do you realise, you rascal, that I can haul you off to Corte or to Bastia? I shall put you in a dungeon on straw, with your feet in irons, and I'll have your head chopped off unless you tell me where to find Gianetto Sanpiero."

The child laughed again derisively at this silly threat. He repeated:

"My father is Mateo Falcone."

"Adjutant, don't get us into trouble with Mateo," muttered one of the gendarmes.

You could see that Gamba was embarrassed. He whispered to his men, who had already searched the house thoroughly. This was not a lengthy matter, for a Corsican hut consists of one square room. There is no furniture other than a table, benches, chests, cooking utensils, and weapons. Meanwhile, little Fortunato was stroking the cat, and seemed to take a malicious satisfaction in the discomfiture of his cousin and the gendarmes.

One gendarme approached the haystack. He looked at the cat and carelessly stuck a bayonet into the hay, shrugging his shoulders as if he thought the precaution absurd. Nothing stirred, and the child's face remained perfectly calm.

The adjutant and his men were desperate. They looked seriously out across the plain, as if they were inclined to go back home, when their leader, satisfied that threats would make no impression on Falcone's son, decided to make a final attempt, and see what coaxing and gifts might do.

"Little cousin," said he, "I can see that your eyes are open. You'll get on in life. But you are playing a risky game with me, and, if it weren't for the trouble it would give my cousin Mateo, God help me if I wouldn't carry you off with me."

"Nonsense!"

"But, when my cousin returns, I am going to tell him all about it, and he'll horsewhip you till the blood comes because you've been telling me lies."

"How do you know?"

"You'll see! . . . But see here! Be a good boy, and I'll give you a present."

"I advise you to go and look for Gianetto in the *mâquis*, cousin. If you hang about here much longer, it will take a cleverer man than you to catch him." The adjutant took a silver watch worth ten dollars out of his pocket. He noticed that little Fortunato's eyes sparkled as he looked at it, and he dangled the watch out to him at the end of its steel chain as he said:

"You scamp, wouldn't you like to have a watch like this hanging round your neck, and to strut up and down the streets of Porto-Vecchio as proud as a peacock? Folk would ask you what time it was and you would say, 'Look at my watch!'"

"When I'm a big boy, my uncle, the magistrate, will give me a watch."

"Yes, but your uncle's son has one already—not as fine as this, to be sure—but he is younger than you are."

The boy sighed.

"Well, would you like this watch, little cousin?"

Fortunato kept eyeing the watch out of the corner of his eye, like a cat that has been given a whole chicken to play with. It does not dare to pounce upon it, because it is afraid folk are laughing at it, but it turns its eyes away now and then so as to avoid temptation, and keeps licking its lips, as much as to say to its master: "What a cruel trick to play on a cat!" And yet Gamba seemed to be really offering him the watch. Fortunato did not hold out his hand, but said with a bitter smile:

"Why are you mocking me?"

"I swear that I am not mocking you. Only tell me where Gianetto is, and the watch is yours."

Fortunato smiled incredulously and fixed his dark eyes on those of the adjutant, trying to read them to see if the man could be trusted.

"May I lose my epaulettes," cried the adjutant, "if I do not give you the watch on this one condition! My men are witnesses, and I cannot back out of it."

As he spoke, he held the watch nearer and nearer till it almost touched the pale cheek of the boy, whose face clearly showed the struggle going on in his heart between greed and the claims of hospitality. His bare breast heaved till he was almost suffocated. Meanwhile the watch dangled and twisted and even touched the tip of his nose. Little by little, his right hand rose toward it, the tips of his fingers touched it, and the whole weight of it rested on his hand, although the adjutant still had it by the chain. . . . The face of the watch was blue. . . . The case was newly burnished. . . . It flamed like fire in the sun. . . . The temptation was too great.

Fortunato raised his left hand and pointed with his thumb over his shoulder to the haystack on which he was leaning. The adjutant understood him at once and let go the end of the chain. Fortunato felt that he was now sole possessor of the watch. He leaped away like a deer, and paused ten paces from the haystack which the gendarmes began to tumble over at once.

It was not long before they saw the hay begin to stir and a bleeding man came out with a stiletto in his hand. But when he tried to rise to his feet, his congealed wound prevented him from standing. He fell down. The adjutant flung himself upon his prey and wrested the stiletto from his grasp. He was speedily trussed up, in spite of his resistance, bound securely, and flung on the ground like a bundle of sticks. He turned his head toward Fortunato who had drawn near again.

"Son of . . . !" he exclaimed, more in contempt than in anger.

The child threw him the piece of silver, realising that he no longer deserved it, but the fugitive paid no attention to it. He merely said quietly to the adjutant:

"My dear Gamba, I cannot walk. You must carry me to town."

"You were running as fast as a kid just now," retorted his captor, roughly. "But don't worry! I'm so glad to have caught you that I could carry you a league on my own back without feeling it. Anyhow, my friend, we'll make a litter for you out of branches and your cloak. We'll find horses at the farm at Crespoli."

"Very well," said the prisoner. "I suppose you will put a little straw on the litter to make it easier for me."

While the gendarmes were busy, some making a crude litter of chestnut boughs, and others dressing Gianetto's wound, Mateo Falcone and his wife suddenly appeared at a turn of the path which led from the *mâquis*. His wife came first, bowed low beneath the weight of a huge sack of chestnuts, while her husband strolled along, carrying a gun in one hand, and another slung over his shoulder. It is beneath a man's dignity to carry any other burden than his weapons.

As soon as he saw the soldiers, Mateo's first thought was that they must have come to arrest him. But there was no reason for it. He had no quarrel with the forces of law and order. He had an excellent reputation. He was "well thought of," as they say, but he was a Corsican, and a mountaineer, and there are very few Corsican mountaineers who, if they search their past sufficiently, cannot find some peccadillo, a rifle shot or a thrust with a stiletto or some other trifle. Mateo had a clearer conscience than most of his friends, for it was at least ten years since he had pointed a rifle at a man; but all the same it behooved him to be cautious, and he prepared to put up a good defense, if necessary.

"Wife," he said, "put down your sack and be on your guard."

She obeyed at once. He gave her the gun from his shoulder belt, as it seemed likely that it might be in his way. He cocked the other rifle, and advanced in a leisurely manner toward the house, skirting the trees beside the path, and ready, at the least sign of hostility, to throw himself behind the largest trunk and fire from cover. His wife followed close behind him, holding her loaded rifle and his cartridges. It was a good wife's duty, in case of trouble, to reload her husband's arms.

The adjutant, on his side, was much troubled at seeing Mateo advance upon him so with measured steps, pointing his rifle, and keeping his finger on the trigger.

"If it should happen," thought he, "that Gianetto turns out to be Mateo's relative or friend, and he wishes to defend him, two of his bullets will reach us as sure as a letter goes by post, and if he aims at me, in spite of our kinship . . . !"

In his perplexity, he put the best face he could on the matter, and went forward by himself to meet Mateo and tell him all that had happened, greeting him like an old friend. But the short distance between him and Mateo seemed fearfully long.

"Hello, there, old comrade!" he cried out. "How are you? I'm your cousin Gamba."

Mateo stood still and said not a word. As the other man spoke, he slowly raised the barrel of his rifle so that, by the time the adjutant came up to him, it was pointing to the sky.

"Good-day, brother," said the adjutant, holding out his hand. "It's an age since I've seen you."

"Good-day, brother."

"I just stopped by to pass the time of day with you and cousin Pepa. We've had a long march to-day, but we can't complain, for we've made a famous haul. We've just caught Gianetto Sanpiero."

"Heaven be praised!" exclaimed Giuseppa. "He stole one of our milch goats a week ago."

Gamba was delighted at her words.

"Poor devil!" said Mateo, "he was hungry."

"The chap fought like a lion," pursued the adjutant, somewhat annoyed. "He killed one of my men, and as if that were not enough, broke Corporal Chardon's arm; not that it matters, he's only a Frenchman. . . . Then he hid himself so cleverly that the devil himself couldn't find him. If it hadn't been for my little cousin Fortunato, I should never have found him."

"Fortunato?" cried Mateo.

"Fortunato?" echoed Giuseppa.

"Yes! Gianetto was hidden in your haystack over there, but my little cousin soon showed up his tricks. I shall tell his uncle, the magistrate, and he'll send him a fine present as a reward. And both his name and yours shall be in the report that I'm sending to the Public Prosecutor."

"Damn you!" muttered Mateo under his breath.

They had now rejoined the gendarmes. Gianetto was already laid on his litter, and they were all ready to start. When he saw Mateo in Gamba's company, he smiled oddly; then, turning toward the door of the house, he spat at the threshold.

"The house of a traitor!"

It was asking for death to call Falcone a traitor. A quick stiletto thrust, and no need of a second, would have instantly wiped out the insult. But Mateo's only movement was to put his hand to his head as if he were stunned.

Fortunato had gone into the house when he saw his father coming. Presently he reappeared with a bowl of milk, which he offered with downcast eyes to Gianetto.

"Keep away from me!" thundered the outlaw.

Then, turning to one of the gendarmes, he said:

"Comrade, will you give me a drink?"

The gendarme put the flask in his hand, and the outlaw drank the water given him by the man with whom he had just been exchanging rifle shots. Then he requested that his hands might be tied crossed on his breast instead of behind his back.

"I would rather," he said, "lie comfortably."

They gratified his request. Then, at a sign from the adjutant, saying good-bye to Mateo, who vouchsafed no answer, they set off quickly toward the plain.

Ten minutes passed before Mateo opened his mouth. The child looked uneasily, first at his mother, then at his father, who was leaning on his gun and gazing at him with an expression of concentrated fury.

"You begin well," said Mateo at last, in a calm voice, terrifying enough to those who knew the man.

"Father!" cried the boy, with tears in his eyes, coming nearer as if to throw himself at his father's knee.

"Out of my sight!" Mateo shouted.

The child stopped short a few paces away from his father, and sobbed.

Giuseppa approached him. She had just noticed the watch-chain hanging out of his shirt.

"Who gave you that watch?" she asked sternly.

"My cousin, the adjutant."

Falcone snatched the watch and flung it against a stone with such violence that it was shattered into a thousand fragments.

"Woman," he said, "is this a child of mine?"

Giuseppa's brown cheeks flushed brick red.

"What are you saying, Mateo? Do you realise to whom you are speaking?"

"Yes, perfectly well. This child is the first traitor in my family."

Fortunato redoubled his sobs and choking, and Falcone kept watching him like a hawk. At last he struck the ground with the butt of his rifle, then flung it across his shoulder, returned to the path which led toward the *mâquis*, and commanded Fortunato to follow him. The child obeyed.

Giuseppa ran after Mateo and clutched his arm.

"He is your son," she said in a trembling voice, fixing her dark eyes on those of her husband, as if to read all that was passing in his soul.

"Leave me," replied Mateo. "I am his father."

Giuseppa kissed her son and went back weeping into the house. She flung herself on her knees before an image of the Blessed Virgin and prayed fervently. Falcone walked about two hundred paces along the path, and went down a little ravine where he stopped. He tested the ground with the butt of his rifle, and found it soft and easy to dig. The spot seemed suitable for his purpose.

"Fortunato, go over to that big rock."

The boy did as he was told. He knelt down.

"Father, Father, do not kill me!"

"Say your prayers!" shouted Mateo in a terrible voice.

The boy, stammering and sobbing, recited the Our Father and the Apostles' Creed. The father said "Amen!" in a firm voice at the end of each prayer.

"Are those all the prayers you know?"

"I know the Hail Mary, too, and the Litany my aunt taught me, Father."

"It is long, but never mind."

The boy finished the Litany in a stifled voice.

"Have you finished?"

"Oh, Father, forgive me! Forgive me! I'll never do it again. I'll beg my cousin, the magistrate, ever so hard to pardon Gianetto!"

He kept beseeching his father. Mateo loaded his gun and took aim.

"God forgive you!" he said.

The boy made a desperate effort to rise and clasp his father's knees, but he had no time. Mateo fired and Fortunato fell stone-dead.

Without glancing at the body, Mateo returned to the house to fetch a spade with which to dig his son's grave. He had only gone a few steps along the path when he met Giuseppa, running, for she had been alarmed by the rifle shot.

"What have you done?" she cried.

"Justice!"

"Where is he?"

"In the ravine. I am going to bury him. He died a Christian. I shall have a Mass said for him. Send word to my son-in-law, Tiodoro Bianchi, that he is to come and live with us." (1829)

Robert Louis Stevenson

MARKHEIM

"Yes," said the dealer, "our windfalls are of various kinds. Some customers are ignorant, and then I touch a dividend on my superior knowledge. Some are dishonest," and here he held up the candle, so that the light fell strongly on his visitor, "and in that case," he continued, "I profit by my virtue."

Markheim had but just entered from the daylight streets, and his eyes had not yet grown familiar with the mingled shine and darkness in the shop. At these pointed words, and before the near presence of the flame, he blinked painfully and looked aside.

The dealer chuckled, "You come to me on Christmas-day," he resumed, "when you know that I am alone in my house, put up my shutters, and make a point of refusing business. Well, you will have to pay for that; you will have to pay for my loss of time, when I should be balancing my books; you will have to pay, besides, for a kind of manner that I remark in you to-day very strongly. I am the essence of discretion, and ask no awkward questions; but when a customer can not look me in the eye, he has to pay for it." The dealer once more chuckled; and then, changing to his usual business voice, though still with a note of irony, "You can give, as usual, a clean account of how you came into the possession of the object?" he continued. "Still your uncle's cabinet? A remarkable collector, sir!"

And the little, pale, round-shouldered dealer stood almost on tip-toe, looking over the top of his gold spectacles, and nodding his head with every mark of disbelief. Markheim returned his gaze with one of infinite pity, and a touch of horror.

"This time," said he, "you are in error. I have not come to sell, but to buy. I have no curios to dispose of; my uncle's cabinet is bare to the wainscot; even were it still intact, I have done well on the Stock Exchange, and should more likely add to it than otherwise, and my errand to-day is simplicity itself. I seek a Christmas-present for a lady," he continued, waxing more fluent as he struck into the speech he had prepared; "and certainly I owe you every excuse for thus disturbing you upon so small a matter. But the thing was neglected yesterday; I must produce my little compliment at dinner; and, as you very well know, a rich marriage is not a thing to be neglected."

There followed a pause, during which the dealer seemed to weigh this statement incredulously. The ticking of many clocks among the curious lumber of the shop, and the faint rushing of the cabs in a near thoroughfare, filled up the interval of silence.

"Well, sir," said the dealer, "be it so. You are an old customer after all; and if, as you say, you have the chance of a good marriage, far be it from me to be an obstacle. Here is a nice thing for a lady now," he went on, "this hand-glass—fifteenth century, warranted; comes from a good collection, too; but I reserve the name, in the interests of my customer, who was just like yourself, my dear sir, the nephew and sole heir of a remarkable collector."

The dealer, while he thus ran on in his dry and biting voice, had stooped to take the object from its place; and, as he had done so, a shock had passed through Markheim, a start both of hand and foot, a sudden leap of many tumultuous passions to the face. It passed as swiftly as it came, and left no trace beyond a certain trembling of the hand that now received the glass.

"A glass," he said, hoarsely, and then paused, and repeated it more clearly. "A glass? For Christmas? Surely not?"

"And why not?" cried the dealer. "Why not a glass?"

Markheim was looking upon him with an indefinable expression. "You ask me why not?" he said. "Why, look here—look in it—look at yourself! Do you like to see it? No! nor I—nor any man."

The little man had jumped back when Markheim had so suddenly confronted him with the mirror; but now, perceiving there was nothing worse on hand, he chuckled. "Your future lady, sir, must be pretty hard favored," said he.

"I ask you," said Markheim, "for a Christmas-present, and you give me this—this damned reminder of years, and sins and follies—this hand-conscience! Did you mean it? Had you a thought in your mind? Tell me. It will be better for you if you do. Come, tell me about yourself. I hazard a guess now, that you are in secret a very charitable man?"

The dealer looked closely at his companion. It was very odd, Markheim did not appear to be laughing; there was something in his face like an eager sparkle of hope, but nothing of mirth.

"What are you driving at?" the dealer asked.

"Not charitable?" returned the other, gloomily. "Not charitable; not pious; not scrupulous; unloving, unbeloved; a hand to get money, a safe to keep it. Is that all? Dear God, man, is that all?"

"I will tell you what it is," began the dealer, with some sharpness, and then broke off again into a chuckle. "But I see this is a love match of yours, and you have been drinking the lady's health."

"Ah!" cried Markheim, with a strange curiosity. "Ah, have you been in love? Tell me about that."

"I," cried the dealer. "I in love! I never had the time, nor have I the time to-day for all this nonsense. Will you take the glass?"

"Where is the hurry?" returned Markheim. "It is very pleasant to stand here talking; and life is so short and insecure that I would not hurry away from any pleasure—no, not even from so mild a one as this. We should rather cling, cling to what little we can get, like a man at a cliff's edge. Every second is a cliff, if you think upon it—a cliff a mile high—high enough, if we fall, to dash us out of every feature of humanity. Hence it is best to talk pleasantly. Let us talk of each other; why should we wear this mask? Let us be confidential. Who knows, we might become friends?"

"I have just one word to say to you," said the dealer. "Either make your purchase, or walk out of my shop."

"True, true," said Markheim. "Enough fooling. To business. Show me something else."

The dealer stooped once more, this time to replace the glass upon the shelf, his thin blonde hair falling over his eyes as he did so. Markheim moved a little nearer, with one hand in the pocket of his great-coat; he drew himself up and filled his lungs; at the same time many different emotions were depicted together on his face—terror, horror, and resolve, fascination and a physical repulsion; and through a haggard lift of his upper lip, his teeth looked out.

"This, perhaps, may suit," observed the dealer; and then, as he began to re-arise, Markheim bounded from behind upon his victim. The long, skewer-like dagger flashed and fell. The dealer struggled like a hen, striking his temple on the shelf, and then tumbled on the floor in a heap.

Time had some score of small voices in that shop, some stately and slow as was becoming to their great age; others garrulous and hurried. All these told out the seconds in an intricate chorus of tickings. Then the passage of a lad's feet, heavily running on the pavement, broke in upon these smaller voices and startled Markheim into the consciousness of his surroundings. He looked about him awfully. The candle stood on the counter, its flame solemnly wagging in a draught; and by that inconsiderable movement, the whole room was filled with noiseless bustle and kept heaving like a sea: the tall shadows nodding, the gross blots of darkness swelling and dwindling as with respiration, the faces of the portraits and the china gods changing and wavering like images in water. The inner door stood ajar, and peered into that league of shadows with a long slit of daylight like a pointing finger.

From these fear-stricken rovings, Markheim's eyes returned to the body of his victim, where it lay both humped and sprawling, incredibly small and strangely meaner than in life. In these poor, miserly clothes, in that ungainly attitude, the dealer lay like so much sawdust. Markheim had feared to see it, and, lo! it was nothing. And yet, as he gazed, this bundle of old clothes and pool of blood began to find eloquent voices. There it must lie; there was none to work the cunning hinges or direct the miracle of locomotion—there it must lie till it was found. Found! ay, and then? Then would this dead flesh lift up a cry that would ring over England, and fill the world with the echoes of pursuit. Ay, dead or not, this was still the enemy. "Time was that when the brains were out," he thought; and the first word struck into his mind. Time, now that the deed was accomplished—time, which had closed for the victim, had become instant and momentous for the slayer.

The thought was yet in his mind, when, first one and then another, with every variety of pace and voice—one deep as the bell from a cathedral turret, another ringing on its treble notes the prelude of a waltz—the clocks began to strike the hour of three in the afternoon.

The sudden outbreak of so many tongues in that dumb chamber staggered him. He began to bestir himself, going to and fro with the candle, beleaguered by moving shadows, and startled to the soul by chance reflections. In many rich mirrors, some of home designs, some from Venice or Amsterdam, he saw his face repeated and repeated, as it were an army of spies; his own eyes met and detected him; and the sound of his own steps, lightly as they fell, vexed the surrounding quiet. And still as he continued to fill his pockets, his mind accused him, with a sickening iteration, of the thousand faults of his design. He should have chosen a more quiet hour; he should have prepared an alibi; he should not have used a knife; he should have been more cautious, and only bound and gagged the dealer, and not killed him; he should have been more bold, and killed the servant also; he should have done all things otherwise; poignant regrets, weary, incessant toiling of the mind to change what was unchangeable, to plan what was now useless, to be the architect of the irrevocable past. Meanwhile, and behind all this activity, brute terrors, like scurrying of rats in a deserted attic, filled the more remote chambers of his brain with riot; the hand of the constable would fall heavy on his shoulder, and his nerves would jerk like a hooked fish; or he beheld, in galloping defile, the dock, the prison, the gallows, and the black coffin.

Terror of the people in the street sat down before his mind like a besieging army. It was impossible, he thought, but that some rumor of the struggle must have reached their ears and set on edge their curiosity; and now, in all the neighboring houses, he divined them sitting motionless and with uplifted ear—solitary people, condemned to spend Christmas dwelling alone on memories of the past, and now startlingly recalled from that tender exercise; happy family parties, struck into silence round the table, the mother still with raised finger: every degree and age and humor, but all, by their own hearths, prying and hearkening and weaving the rope that was to hang him. Sometimes it seemed to him he could not move too softly; the clink of the tall Bohemian goblets rang out loudly like a bell; and alarmed by the bigness of the ticking, he was tempted to stop the clocks. And then, again, with a swift transition of his terrors, the very silence of the place appeared a source of peril, and a thing to strike and freeze the passer-by; and he would step more boldly, and bustle aloud among the contents of the shop, and imitate, with elaborate bravado, the movements of a busy man at ease in his own house.

But he was now so pulled about by different alarms that, while one portion of his mind was still alert and cunning, another trembled on the brink of lunacy. One hallucination in particular took a strong hold on his credulity. The neighbor hearkening with white face beside his window, the passer-by arrested by a horrible surmise on the pavement—these could at worst suspect, they could not know; through the brick walls and shuttered windows only sounds could penetrate. But here, within the house, was he alone? He knew he was; he had watched the servant set forth sweethearting, in her poor best, "out for the day" written in every ribbon and smile. Yes, he was alone, of course; and yet, in the bulk of empty house above him, he could surely hear a stir of delicate footing—he was surely conscious, inexplicably conscious of some presence. Ay, surely; to every room and corner of the house his imagination followed it; and now it was a faceless thing, and yet had eyes to see with; and again it was a shadow of himself; and yet again behold the image of the dead dealer, reinspired with cunning and hatred.

At times, with a strong effort, he would glance at the open door which still seemed to repel his eyes. The house was tall, the skylight small and dirty, the day blind with fog; and the light that filtered down to the ground story was exceedingly faint, and showed dimly on the threshold of the shop. And yet, in that strip of doubtful brightness, did there not hang wavering a shadow?

Suddenly, from the street outside, a very jovial gentleman began to beat with a staff on the shop-door, accompanying his blows with shouts and railleries in which the dealer was continually called upon by name. Markheim, smitten into ice, glanced at the dead man. But no! he lay quite still; he was fled away far beyond earshot of these blows and shoutings; he was sunk beneath seas of silence; and his name, which would once have caught his notice above the howling of a storm, had become an empty sound. And presently the jovial gentleman desisted from his knocking and departed.

Here was a broad hint to hurry what remained to be done, to get forth from this accusing neighborhood, to plunge into a bath of London multitudes, and to reach, on the other side of day, that haven of safety and apparent innocence—his bed. One visitor had come: at any moment another might follow and be more obstinate. To have done the deed, and yet not to reap the profit, would be too abhorrent a failure. The money, that was now Markheim's concern; and as a means to that, the keys.

He glanced over his shoulder at the open door, where the shadow was still lingering and shivering; and with no conscious repugnance of the mind, yet with a tremor of the belly, he drew near the body of his victim. The human character had quite departed. Like a suit half-stuffed with bran, the limbs lay scattered, the trunk doubled, on the floor; and yet the thing repelled him. Although so dingy and inconsiderable to the eye, he feared it might have more significance to the touch. He took the body by the shoulders, and turned it on its back. It was strangely light and supple, and the limbs, as if they had been broken, fell into the oddest postures. The face was robbed of all expression; but it was as pale as wax, and shockingly smeared with blood about one temple. That was, for Markheim, the one displeasing circumstance. It carried him back, upon the instant, to a certain fair day in a fisher's village: a gray day, a piping wind, a crowd upon the street, the blare of brasses, the booming of drums, the nasal voice of a ballad singer; and a boy going to and fro, buried over head in the crowd and divided between interest and fear, until, coming out upon the chief place of concourse, he beheld a booth and a great screen with pictures, dismally designed, garishly colored: Brownrigg with her apprentice; the Mannings with their murdered guest; Weare in the death-grip of Thurtell; and a score besides of famous crimes. The thing was as clear as an illusion; he was once again that little boy; he was looking once again, and with the same sense of physical revolt, at these vile pictures; he was still stunned by the thumping of the drums. A bar of that day's music returned upon his memory; and at that, for the first time, a qualm came over him, a breath of nausea, a sudden weakness of the joints, which he must instantly resist and conquer.

He judged it more prudent to confront than to flee from these considerations; looking the more hardily in the dead face, bending his mind to realize the nature and greatness of his crime. So little awhile ago that face had moved with every change of sentiment, that pale mouth had spoken, that body had been all on fire with governable energies; and now, and by his act, that piece of life had been arrested, as the horologist, with interjected finger, arrests the beating of the clock. So he reasoned in vain; he could rise to no more remorseful consciousness; the same heart which had shuddered before the painted effigies of crime, looked on its reality unmoved. At best, he felt a gleam of pity for one who had been endowed in vain with all those faculties that can make the world a garden of enchantment, one who had never lived and who was now dead. But a penitence, no, with a tremor.

With that, shaking himself clear of these considerations, he found the keys and advanced toward the open door of the shop. Outside, it had begun to rain smartly; and the sound of the shower upon the roof had banished silence. Like some dripping cavern, the chambers of the house were haunted by an incessant echoing, which filled the ear and mingled with the ticking of the clocks. And, as Markheim approached the door, he seemed to hear, in answer to his own cautious tread, the steps of another foot withdrawing up the stair. The shadow still palpitated loosely on the threshold. He threw a ton's weight of resolve upon his muscles, and drew back the door.

The faint, foggy daylight glimmered dimly on the bare floor and stairs; on the bright suit of armor posted, halbert in hand, upon the landing; and on the dark wood-carvings, and framed pictures that hung against the yellow panels of the wainscot. So loud was the beating of the rain through all the house that, in Markheim's ears, it began to be distinguished into many different sounds. Footsteps and sighs, the tread of regiments marching in the distance, the chink of money in the counting, and the creaking of doors held stealthily ajar, appeared to mingle with the patter of the drops upon the cupola and the gushing of the water in the pipes. The sense that he was not alone grew upon him to the verge of madness. On every side he was haunted and begirt by presences. He heard them moving in the upper chambers; from the shop, he heard the dead man getting to his legs; and as he began with a great effort to mount the stairs, feet fled quietly before him and followed stealthily behind. If he were but deaf, he thought, how tranquilly he would possess his soul. And then again, and hearkening with every fresh attention, he blessed himself for that unresisting sense which held the outposts and stood a trusty sentinel upon his life. His head turned continually on his neck; his eyes, which seemed starting from their orbits, scouted on every side, and on every side were half-rewarded as with the tail of something nameless vanishing. The four-and-twenty steps to the first floor were four-and-twenty agonies.

On that first story, the doors stood ajar, three of them like three ambushes, shaking his nerves like the throats of cannon. He could never again, he felt, be sufficiently immured and fortified from men's observing eyes; he longed to be home, girt in by walls, buried among bedclothes, and invisible to all but God. And at that thought he wondered a little, recollecting tales of other murderers and the fear they were said to entertain of heavenly avengers. It was not so, at least, with him. He feared the laws of nature, lest, in their callous and immutable procedure, they should preserve some damning evidence of his crime. He feared tenfold more, with a slavish, superstitious terror, some scission in the continuity of man's experience, some willful illegality of nature. He played a game of skill, depending on the rules, calculating consequence from cause; and what if nature, as the defeated tyrant overthrew the chess-board, should break the mold of their succession? The like had befallen Napoleon (so writers said) when the winter changed the time of its appearance. The like might befall Markheim: the solid walls might become transparent and reveal his doings like those of bees in a glass hive; and stout planks might yield under his foot like quicksands and detain him in their clutch; ay, and there were soberer accidents that might destroy him; if, for instance, the house should fall and imprison him beside the body of his victim; or the house next door should fly on fire, and the firemen invade him from all sides. These things he feared; and, in a sense, these things might be called the hands of God reached forth against sin. But about God himself he was at ease; his act was doubtless exceptional, but so were his excuses, which God knew; it was there, and not among men, that he felt sure of justice.

When he had got safe into the drawing-room, and shut the door behind him, he was aware of a respite from alarms. The room was quite dismantled, uncarpeted besides, and strewn with packing cases and incongruous furniture; several great pier-glasses, in which he beheld himself at various angles, like an actor on the stage; many pictures, framed and unframed, standing with their faces to the wall; a fine Sheraton sideboard, a cabinet of marquetry, and a great old bed, with tapestry hangings. The windows opened to the floor; but by great good fortune the lower part of the shutters had been closed, and this concealed him from the neighbors. Here, then, Markheim drew in a packing case before the cabinet, and began to search among the keys. It was a long business, for there were many; and it was irksome, besides; for, after all, there might be nothing in the cabinet, and time was on the wing. But the closeness of the occupation sobered him. With the tail of his eye he saw the door—even glanced at it from time to time directly, like a besieged commander pleased to verify the good estate of his defenses. But in truth he was at peace. The rain falling in the street sounded natural and pleasant. Presently, on the other side, the notes of a piano were wakened to the music of a hymn, and the voices of many children took up the air and words. How stately, how comfortable was the melody! How fresh the youthful voices! Markheim gave ear to it smilingly, as he sorted out the keys; and his mind was thronged with answerable ideas and images; church-going children and the pealing of the high organ; children afield, bathers by the brookside, ramblers on the brambly common, kite-flyers in the windy and cloud-navigated sky; and then, at another cadence of the hymn, back again to church, and the somnolence of summer Sundays, and the high genteel voice of the parson (which he smiled a little to recall) and the painted Jacobean tombs, and the dim lettering of the Ten Commandments in the chancel.

And as he sat thus, at once busy and absent, he was startled to his feet. A flash of ice, a flash of fire, a bursting gush of blood, went over him, and then he stood transfixed and thrilling. A step mounted the stair slowly and steadily, and presently a hand was laid upon the knob, and the lock clicked, and the door opened.

Fear held Markheim in a vice. What to expect he knew not, whether the dead man walking, or the official ministers of human justice, or some chance witness blindly stumbling in to consign him to the gallows. But when a face was thrust into the aperture, glanced round the room, looked at him, nodded and smiled as if in friendly recognition, and then withdrew again, and the door closed behind it, his fear broke loose from his control in a hoarse cry. At the sound of this the visitant returned.

"Did you call me?" he asked, pleasantly, and with that he entered the room and closed the door behind him.

Markheim stood and gazed at him with all his eyes. Perhaps there was a film upon his sight, but the outlines of the newcomer seemed to change and waver like those of the idols in the wavering candle-light of the shop; and at times he thought he knew him; and at times he thought he bore a likeness to himself; and always, like a lump of living terror, there lay in his bosom the conviction that this thing was not of the earth and not of God.

And yet the creature had a strange air of the common-place, as he stood looking on Markheim with a smile; and when he added: "You are looking for the money, I believe?" it was in the tones of everyday politeness.

Markheim made no answer.

"I should warn you," resumed the other, "that the maid has left her sweet-heart earlier than usual and will soon be here. If Mr. Markheim be found in this house, I need not describe to him the consequences."

"You know me?" cried the murderer.

The visitor smiled. "You have long been a favorite of mine," he said; "and I have long observed and often sought to help you."

"What are you?" cried Markheim: "the devil?"

"What I may be," returned the other, "can not affect the service I propose to render you."

"It can," cried Markheim; "it does! Be helped by you? No, never; not by you! You do not know me yet, thank God, you do not know me!"

"I know you," replied the visitant, with a sort of kind severity or rather firmness. "I know you to the soul."

"Know me!" cried Markheim. "Who can do so? My life is but a travesty and slander on myself. I have lived to belie my nature. All men do; all men are better than this disguise that grows about and stifles them. You see each dragged away by life, like one whom bravos have seized and muffled in a cloak. If they had their own control—if you could see their faces, they would be altogether different, they would shine out for heroes and saints! I am worse than most; myself is more overlaid; my excuse is known to me and God. But, had I the time, I could disclose myself."

"To me?" inquired the visitant.

"To you before all," returned the murderer. "I supposed you were intelligent. I thought—since you exist—you would prove a reader of the heart. And yet you would propose to judge me by my acts! Think of it; my acts! I was born and I have lived in a land of giants; giants have dragged me by the wrists since I was born out of my mother—the giants of circumstance. And you would judge me by my acts! But can you not look within? Can you not understand that evil is hateful to me? Can you not see within me the clear writing of conscience, never blurred by any willful sophistry, although too often disregarded? Can you not read me for a thing that surely must be common as humanity—the unwilling sinner?"

"All this is very feelingly expressed," was the reply, "but it regards me not. These points of consistency are beyond my province, and I care not in the least by what compulsion you may have been dragged away, so as you are but carried in the right direction. But time flies; the servant delays, looking in the faces of the crowd and at the pictures on the hoardings, but still she keeps moving nearer; and remember, it is as if the gallows itself was striding toward you through the Christmas streets! Shall I help you; I, who know all? Shall I tell you where to find the money?"

"For what price?" asked Markheim.

"I offer you the service for a Christmas gift," returned the other.

Markheim could not refrain from smiling with a kind of bitter triumph. "No," said he, "I will take nothing at your hands; if I were dying of thirst, and it was your hand that put the pitcher to my lips, I should find the courage to refuse. It may be credulous, but I will do nothing to commit myself to evil."

"I have no objection to a death-bed repentance," observed the visitant.

"Because you disbelieve their efficacy!" Markheim cried.

"I do not say so," returned the other; "but I look on these things from a different side, and when the life is done my interest falls. The man has lived to serve me, to spread black looks under color of religion, or to sow tares in the wheat-field, as you do, in a course of weak compliance with desire. Now that he draws so near to his deliverance, he can add but one act of service—to repent, to die smiling, and thus to build up in confidence and hope the more timorous of my surviving followers. I am not so hard a master. Try me. Accept my help. Please yourself in life as you have done hitherto; please yourself more amply, spread your elbows at the board; and when the night begins to fall and the curtains to be drawn, I tell you, for your greater comfort, that you will find it even easy to compound your quarrel with your conscience, and to make a truckling peace with God. I came but now from such a deathbed, and the room was full of sincere mourners, listening to the man's last words: and when I looked into that face, which had been set as a flint against mercy, I found it smiling with hope."

"And do you, then, suppose me such a creature?" asked Markheim. "Do you think I have no more generous aspirations than to sin, and sin, and sin, and, at last, sneak into heaven? My heart rises at the thought. Is this, then, your experience of mankind? or is it because you find me with red hands that you presume such baseness? and is this crime of murder indeed so impious as to dry up the very springs of good?"

"Murder is to me no special category," replied the other. "All sins are murder, even as all life is war. I behold your race, like starving mariners on a raft, plucking crusts out of the hands of famine and feeding on each other's lives. I follow sins beyond the moment of their acting; I find in all that the last consequence is death; and to my eyes, the pretty maid who thwarts her mother with such taking graces on a question of a ball, drips no less visibly with human gore than such a murderer as yourself. Do I say that I follow sins? I follow virtues also; they differ not by the thickness of a nail, they are both scythes for the reaping angel of Death. Evil, for which I live, consists not in action but in character. The bad man is dear to me; not the bad act, whose fruits, if we could follow them far enough down the hurtling cataract of the ages, might yet be found more blessed than those of the rarest virtues. And it is not because you have killed a dealer, but because you are Markheim, that I offered to forward your escape."

"I will lay my heart open to you," answered Markheim. "This crime on which you find me is my last. On my way to it I have learned many lessons; itself is a lesson, a momentous lesson. Hitherto I have been driven with revolt to what I would not; I was a bond-slave to poverty, driven and scourged. There are robust virtues that can stand in these temptations; mine was not so: I had a thirst of pleasure. But to-day, and out of this deed, I pluck both warning and riches—both the power and a fresh resolve to be myself. I become in all things a free actor in the world; I begin to see myself all changed, these hands the agents of good, this heart at peace. Something comes over me out of the past; something of what I have dreamed on Sabbath evenings to the sound of the church organ, of what I forecast when I shed tears over noble books, or talked, an innocent child, with my mother. There lies my life; I have wandered a few years, but now I see once more my city of destination."

"You are to use this money on the Stock Exchange, I think?" remarked the visitor; "and there, if I mistake not, you have already lost some thousands?"

"Ah," said Markheim, "but this time I have a sure thing."

"This time, again, you will lose," replied the visitor, quietly.

"Ah, but I keep back the half!" cried Markheim.

"That also you will lose," said the other.

The sweat started upon Markheim's brow. "Well, then, what matter?" he exclaimed. "Say it be lost, say I am plunged again in poverty, shall one part of me, and that the worse, continue until the end to override the better? Evil and good run strong in me, haling me both ways. I do not love the one thing,

I love all. I can conceive great deeds, renunciations, martyrdoms; and though I be fallen to such a crime as murder, pity is no stranger to my thoughts. I pity the poor; who knows their trials better than myself? I pity and help them; I prize love, I love honest laughter; there is no good thing nor true thing on earth but I love it from my heart. And are my vices only to direct my life, and my virtues to lie without effect, like some passive lumber of the mind? Not so; good, also, is a spring of acts."

But the visitant raised his finger. "For six-and-thirty years that you have been in this world," said he, "through many changes of fortune and varieties of humor, I have watched you steadily fall. Fifteen years ago you would have started at a theft. Three years back you would have blenched at the name of murder. Is there any crime, is there any cruelty or meanness, from which you still recoil?—five years from now I shall detect you in the fact! Downward, downward, lies your way; nor can anything but death avail to stop you."

"It is true," Markheim said, huskily, "I have in some degree complied with evil. But it is so with all: the very saints, in the mere exercise of living, grow less dainty, and take on the tone of their surroundings."

"I will propound to you one simple question," said the other; "and as you answer, I shall read to you your moral horoscope. You have grown in many things more lax; possibly you do right to be so; and at any account, it is the same with all men. But granting that, are you in any one particular, however trifling, more difficult to please with your own conduct, or do you go in all things with a looser rein?"

"In any one?" repeated Markheim, with an anguish of consideration. "No," he added, with despair, "in none! I have gone down in all."

"Then," said the visitor, "content yourself with what you are, for you will never change; and the words of your part on this stage are irrevocably written down."

Markheim stood for a long while silent, and indeed it was the visitor who first broke the silence. "That being so," he said, "shall I show you the money?"

"And grace?" cried Markheim.

"Have you not tried it?" returned the other. "Two or three years ago, did I not see you on the platform of revival meetings, and was not your voice the loudest in the hymn?"

"It is true," said Markheim; "and I see clearly what remains for me by way of duty. I thank you for these lessons from my soul: my eyes are opened, and I behold myself at last for what I am."

At this moment, the sharp note of the door-bell rang through the house; and the visitant, as though this were some concerted signal for which he had been waiting, changed at once in his demeanor.

"The maid!" he cried. "She has returned, as I forewarned you, and there is now before you one more difficult passage. Her master, you must say, is ill; you must let her in, with an assured but rather serious countenance—no smiles, no overacting, and I promise you success! Once the girl within, and the door closed, the same dexterity that has already rid you of the dealer will relieve you of this last danger in your path. Thenceforward you have the whole evening—the whole night, if needful—to ransack the treasures of the house and to make good your safety. This is help that comes to you with the mask of danger. Up!" he cried: "up, friend; your life hangs trembling in the scales; up, and act!"

Markheim steadily regarded his counsellor. "If I be condemned to evil acts," he said, "there is still one door of freedom open—I can cease from action. If my life be an ill thing, I can lay it down. Though I be, as you say truly, at the beck of every small temptation, I can yet, by one decisive gesture, place myself beyond the reach of all. My love of good is damned to barrenness; it may, and let it be! But I have still my hatred of evil; and from that, to your galling disappointment, you shall see that I can draw both energy and courage."

The features of the visitor began to undergo a wonderful and lovely change; they brightened and softened with a tender triumph; and, even as they brightened, faded and dislimned. But Markheim did not pause to watch or understand the transformation. He opened the door and went downstairs very slowly, thinking to himself. His past went soberly before him; he beheld it as it was, ugly and strenuous like a dream, random as chance-medley—a scene of defeat. Life, as he thus reviewed it, tempted him no longer; but on the further side he perceived a quiet haven for his bark. He paused in the passage, and looked into the shop, where the candle still burned by the dead body. It was strangely silent. Thoughts of the dealer swarmed into his mind, as he stood gazing. And then the bell once more broke out into impatient clamor.

He confronted the maid upon the threshold with something like a smile.

"You had better go for the police," said he: "I have killed your master."

(1885)

Rudyard Kipling

THE MAN WHO WOULD BE KING

"Brother to a prince and fellow to a beggar if he be found worthy."

The law, as quoted, lays down a fair conduct of life, and one not easy to follow. I have been fellow to a beggar again and again under circumstances which prevented either of us finding out whether the other was worthy. I have still to be brother to a prince, though I once came near to kinship with what might have been a veritable king and was promised the reversion of a kingdom—army, law-courts, revenue and policy all complete. But today I greatly fear that my king is dead, and if I want a crown I must go and hunt it for myself.

The beginning of everything was in a railway train upon the road to Mhow from Ajmir. There had been a Deficit in the Budget, which necessitated traveling not second-class, which is only half as dear as first-class, but by intermediate, which is very awful indeed. There are no cushions in the intermediate class, and the population are either intermediate, which is Eurasian, or native, which for a long night journey is nasty, or loafer, which is amusing though intoxicated. Intermediates do not patronize refreshment-rooms. They carry their food in bundles and pots, and buy sweets from the native sweetmeat sellers, and drink the roadside water. That is why in the hot weather intermediates are taken out of the carriages dead, and in all weathers are most properly looked down upon.

My particular intermediate happened to be empty till I reached Nasirabad, when a huge gentleman in shirt-sleeves entered and, following the custom of intermediates, passed the time of day. He was a wanderer and a vagabond like myself, but with an educated taste for whisky. He told tales of things he had seen and done, of out-of-the-way corners of the Empire into which he had penetrated, and of adventures in which he risked his life for a few days' food. "If India was filled with men like you and me, not knowing more than the crows where they'd get their next day's rations, it isn't seventy millions of revenue the land would be paying—it's seven hundred millions," said he; and as I looked at his mouth and chin I was disposed to agree with him. We talked politics—the politics of loaferdom that sees things from the underside where the lath and plaster is not smoothed off—and we talked postal arrangements because my friend wanted to send a telegram back from the next station to Ajmir, which is the turning-off place from the Bombay to the Mhow line as you travel westward. My friend had no money beyond eight annas which he wanted for dinner, and I had no money at all, owing to the hitch in the Budget before mentioned. Further, I was going into a wilderness where, though I should resume touch with the Treasury, there were no telegraph offices. I was, therefore, unable to help him in any way.

"We might threaten a station-master to make him send a wire on tick," said my friend, "but that'd mean inquiries for you and for me, and I've got my hands full these days. Did you say you were traveling back along this line within any days?"

"Within ten," I said.

"Can't you make it eight?" said he. "Mine is rather urgent business."

"I can send your telegram within ten days if that will serve you," I said.

"I couldn't trust the wire to fetch him now I think of it. It's this way. He leaves Delhi on the 23d for Bombay. That means he'll be running through Ajmir about the night of the 23d."

"But I'm going into the Indian Desert," I explained.

"Well *and* good," said he. "You'll be changing at Marwar Junction to get into Jodhpore territory—you must do that—and he'll be coming through Marwar Junction in the early morning of the 24th by the Bombay Mail. Can you be at Marwar Junction on that time? 'Twon't be inconveniencing you, because I know that there's precious few pickings to be got out of those Central India States— even though you pretend to be correspondent of the *Backwoodsman*."

"Have you ever tried that trick?" I asked.

"Again and again, but the Residents find you out, and then you get escorted to the Border before you've time to get your knife into them. But about my friend here. I *must* give him word o' mouth to tell him what's come to me or else he won't know where to go. I would take it more than kind of you if you was to come out of Central India in time to catch him at Marwar Junction, and say to him: 'He has gone south for the week.' He'll know what that means. He's a big man with a red beard, and a great swell he is. You'll find him sleeping like a gentleman with all his luggage round him in a second-class compartment. But don't you be afraid. Slip down the window and say: 'He has gone south for the week,' and he'll tumble. It's only cutting your time of stay in those parts by two days. I ask you as a stranger—going to the west," he said with emphasis.

"Where have *you* come from?" said I.

"From the East," said he, "and I am hoping that you will give him the message on the square—for the sake of my mother as well as your own."

Englishmen are not usually softened by appeals to the memory of their mothers, but for certain reasons, which will be fully apparent, I saw fit to agree.

"It's more than a little matter," said he, "and that's why I ask you to do it— and now I know that I can depend on you doing it. A second-class carriage at Marwar Junction, and a red-haired man asleep in it. You'll be sure to remember. I get out at the next station, and I must hold on there till he comes or sends me what I want."

"I'll give the message if I catch him," I said, "and for the sake of your mother as well as mine I'll give you a word of advice. Don't try to run the Central India

States just now as the correspondent of the *Backwoodsman*. There's a real one knocking about here, and it might lead to trouble."

"Thank you," said he simply, "and when will the swine be gone? I can't starve because he's ruining my work. I wanted to get hold of the Degumber Rajah down here about his father's widow, and give him a jump."

"What did he do to his father's widow, then?"

"Filled her up with red pepper and slippered her to death as she hung from a beam. I found that out myself and I'm the only man that would dare going into the state to get hush-money for it. They'll try to poison me, same as they did in Chortumna when I went on the loot there. But you'll give the man at Marwar Junction my message?"

He got out at a little roadside station, and I reflected. I had heard, more than once, of men personating correspondents of newspapers and bleeding small native states with threats of exposure, but I had never met any of the caste before. They lead a hard life, and generally die with great suddenness. The native states have a wholesome horror of English newspapers, which may throw light on their peculiar methods of government, and do their best to choke correspondents with champagne, or drive them out of their mind with four-in-hand barouches. They do not understand that nobody cares a straw for the internal administration of native states so long as oppression and crime are kept within decent limits, and the ruler is not drugged, drunk or diseased from one end of the year to the other. Native states were created by Providence in order to supply picturesque scenery, tigers and tall writing. They are the dark places of the earth, full of unimaginable cruelty, touching the Railway and the Telegraph on one side, and on the other the days of Harun-al-Raschid. When I left the train I did business with divers kings, and in eight days passed through many changes of life. Sometimes I wore dress clothes and consorted with princes and politicals, drinking from crystal and eating from silver. Sometimes I lay out upon the ground and devoured what I could get from a plate made of a flapjack, and drank the running water, and slept under the same rug as my servant. It was all in the day's work.

Then I headed for the Great Indian Desert upon the proper date, as I had promised, and the night mail set me down at Marwar Junction, where a funny little happy-go-lucky, native-managed railway runs to Jodhpore. The Bombay Mail from Delhi makes a short halt at Marwar. She arrived as I got in, and I had just time to hurry to her platform and go down the carriages. There was only one second-class on the train. I slipped the window and looked down upon a flaming red beard, half-covered by a railway rug. That was my man, fast asleep, and I dug him gently in the ribs. He woke with a grunt and I saw his face in the light of the lamps. It was a great and shining face.

"Tickets again?" said he.

"No," said I. "I am to tell you that he is gone south for the week. He is gone south for the week!"

The train had begun to move out. The red man rubbed his eyes. "He has gone south for the week," he repeated. "Now that's just like his impidence. Did he say that I was to give you anything? 'Cause I won't."

"He didn't," I said and dropped away, and watched the red lights die out in the dark. It was horribly cold because the wind was blowing off the sands. I climbed into my own train—not an intermediate carriage this time—and went to sleep.

If the man with the beard had given me a rupee I should have kept it as a memento of a rather curious affair. But the consciousness of having done my duty was my only reward.

Later on I reflected that two gentlemen like my friends could not do any good if they foregathered and personated correspondents of newspapers, and might, if they "stuck up" one of the little rat-trap states of Central India or Southern Rajputana, get themselves into serious difficulties. I therefore took some trouble to describe them as accurately as I could remember to people who would be interested in deporting them: and succeeded, so I was later informed, in having them headed back from the Degumber borders.

Then I became respectable, and returned to an office where there were no kings and no incidents except the daily manufacture of a newspaper. A newspaper office seems to attract every conceivable sort of person to the prejudice of discipline. Zenana-mission ladies arrive, and beg that the editor will instantly abandon all his duties to describe a Christian prize-giving in a back slum of a perfectly inaccessible village; colonels who have been overpassed for commands sit down and sketch the outline of a series of ten, twelve or twenty-four leading articles on Seniority versus Selection; missionaries wish to know why they have not been permitted to escape from their regular vehicles of abuse and swear at a brother missionary under special patronage of the editorial we; stranded theatrical companies troop up to explain that they cannot pay for their advertisements, but on their return from New Zealand or Tahiti will do so with interest; inventors of patent punkah-pulling machines, carriage couplings, and unbreakable swords and axletrees call with specifications in their pockets and hours at their disposal; tea companies enter and elaborate their prospectuses with the office pens; secretaries of ball committees clamor to have the glories of their last dance more fully expounded; strange ladies rustle in and say: "I want a hundred lady's cards printed *at once*, please," which is manifestly part of an editor's duty; and every dissolute ruffian that ever tramped the Grand Trunk Road makes it his business to ask for employment as a proofreader. And, all the time, the telephone bell is ringing madly, and kings are being killed on the Continent, and empires are saying "You're another," and Mister Gladstone is calling down brimstone upon the British Dominions, and the little black copy boys are whining *"kaa-pi chay-ha-yeh"* (copy wanted) like tired bees, and most of the paper is as blank as Modred's shield.

But that is the amusing part of the year. There are other six months wherein none ever come to call, and the thermometer walks inch by inch up to the top of the glass, and the office is darkened to just above reading light, and the press machines are red-hot to touch, and nobody writes anything but accounts of amusements in the hill-stations, or obituary notices. Then the telephone becomes a tinkling terror, because it tells you of the sudden deaths of men and women that you knew intimately, and the prickly heat covers you as with a garment, and you sit down and write: "A slight increase of sickness is reported from the Khuda Janta Khan District. The outbreak is purely sporadic in its nature, and thanks to the energetic efforts of the district authorities, is now almost at an end. It is, however, with deep regret we record the death, etc."

Then the sickness really breaks out, and the less recording and reporting the better for the peace of the subscribers. But the empires and kings continue to divert themselves as selfishly as before, and the foreman thinks that a daily paper really ought to come out once in twenty-four hours, and all the people at the hill-stations in the middle of their amusements say: "Good gracious! Why can't the paper be sparkling? I'm sure there's plenty going on up here."

That is the dark half of the moon, and as the advertisements say, "must be experienced to be appreciated."

It was in that season, and a remarkably evil season, that the paper began running the last issue of the week on Saturday night, which is to say Sunday morning, after the custom of a London paper. This was a great convenience, for immediately after the paper was put to bed the dawn would lower the thermometer from 96° to almost 84° for half an hour, and in that chill—you have no idea how cold is 84° on the grass until you begin to pray for it—a very tired man could set off to sleep ere the heat roused him.

One Saturday night it was my pleasant duty to put the paper to bed alone. A king or courtier or a courtesan or a community was going to die or get a new constitution, or do something that was important on the other side of the world, and the paper was to be held open till the latest possible minute in order to catch the telegram. It was a pitchy black night, as stifling as a June night can be, and the *loo*, the red-hot wind from the westward, was booming among the tinder-dry trees and pretending that the rain was on its heels. Now and again a spot of almost boiling water would fall on the dust with the flop of a frog, but all our weary world knew that was only pretense. It was a shade cooler in the press-room than the office, so I sat there while the type clicked and clicked, and the night-jars hooted at the windows, and the all but naked compositors wiped the sweat from their foreheads and called for water. The thing that was keeping us back, whatever it was, would not come off, though the *loo* dropped and the last type was set, and the whole round earth stood still in the choking heat, with its finger on its lip, to await the event. I drowsed, and wondered whether the telegraph was a blessing, and whether this dying man or struggling people was aware of the inconvenience the delay was causing. There was no special reason beyond the heat and worry to make tension, but as the clock hands crept up to three o'clock and the machines spun their flywheels two and three times to see that all was in order, before I said the word that would set them off, I could have shrieked aloud.

Then the roar and rattle of the wheels shivered the quiet into little bits. I rose to go away, but two men in white clothes stood in front of me. The first one said: "It's him!" The second said: "So it is!" And they both laughed almost as loudly as the machinery roared, and mopped their foreheads. "We see there was a light burning across the road and we were sleeping in that ditch there for coolness, and I said to my friend here: 'The office is open. Let's come along and speak to him as turned us back from the Degumber State,' " said the smaller of the two. He was the man I had met in the Mhow train, and his fellow was the red-bearded man of Marwar Junction. There was no mistaking the eyebrows of the one or the beard of the other.

I was not pleased, because I wished to go to sleep, not to squabble with loafers. "What do you want?" I asked.

"Half an hour's talk with you cool and comfortable, in the office," said the red-bearded man. "We'd *like* some drink—the contrack doesn't begin yet, Peachey, so you needn't look—but what we really want is advice. We don't want money. We ask you as a favor, because you did us a bad turn about Degumber."

I led from the press-room to the stifling office with the maps on the walls, and the red-haired man rubbed his hands. "That's something like," said he. "This was the proper shop to come to. Now, sir, let me introduce to you Brother Peachey Carnehan, that's him, and Brother Daniel Dravot, that is *me*, and the less said about our professions the better, for we have been most things in our time. Soldier, sailor, compositor, photographer, proofreader, street preacher, and correspondents of the *Backwoodsman*, when we thought the paper wanted one. Carnehan is sober, and so am I. Look at us first and see that's sure. It will save you cutting into my talk. We'll take one of your cigars apiece, and you shall see us light it."

I watched the test: The men were absolutely sober, so I gave them each a tepid peg.

"Well *and* good," said Carnehan of the eyebrows, wiping the froth from his mustache. "Let me talk now, Dan. We have been all over India, mostly on foot. We have been boiler-fitters, engine-drivers, petty contractors, and all that, and we have decided that India isn't big enough for such as us."

They certainly were too big for the office. Dravot's beard seemed to fill half the room and Carnehan's shoulders the other half, as they sat on the big table. Carnehan continued: "The country isn't half worked out because they that governs it won't let you touch it. They spend all their blessed time in governing it, and you can't lift a spade, nor chip a rock, nor look for oil, nor anything like that without all the Government saying: 'Leave it alone and let us govern.' Therefore, such as it is, we will let it alone, and go away to some other place where a man isn't crowded and can come to his own. We are not little men, and there is nothing that we are afraid of except drink, and we have signed a contrack on that. *Therefore* we are going away to be kings."

"Kings in our own right," muttered Dravot.

"Yes, of course," I said. "You've been tramping in the sun, and it's a very warm night, and hadn't you better sleep over the notion? Come tomorrow."

"Neither drunk nor sunstruck," said Dravot. "We have slept over the notion half a year, and require to see books and atlases, and we have decided that there is only one place now in the world that two strong men can Sar-a-*whack*. They call it Kafiristan. By my reckoning it's top right-hand corner of Afghanistan, not more than three hundred miles from Peshawar. They have two-and-thirty heathen idols there, and we'll be the thirty-third. It's a mountainous country, and the women of those parts are very beautiful."

"But that is provided against in the contrack," said Carnehan. "Neither women nor liquor, Daniel."

"And that's all we know, except that no one has gone there and they fight, and in any place where they fight a man who knows how to drill men can always be a king. We shall go to those parts and say to any king we find: 'D'you want to vanquish your foes?' and we will show him how to drill men; for that we know better than anything else. Then we will subvert that king and seize his throne and establish a dy-nasty."

"You'll be cut to pieces before you're fifty miles across the border," I said. "You have to travel through Afghanistan to get to that country. It's one mass of mountains and peaks and glaciers, and no Englishman has been through it. The people are utter brutes, and even if you reached them you couldn't do anything."

"That's more like," said Carnehan. "If you could think us a little more mad we would be more pleased. We have come to you to know about this country, to read a book about it, and to be shown maps. We want you to tell us that we are fools and to show us your books."

He turned to the bookcases.

"Are you at all in earnest?" I said.

"A little," said Dravot sweetly. "As big a map as you have got, even if it's all blank where Kafiristan is, and any books you've got. We can read, though we aren't very educated."

I uncased the big thirty-two-miles-to-the-inch map of India, and two smaller Frontier maps, hauled down volume Inf-Kan of the *Encyclopaedia Britannica*, and the men consulted them.

"See here!" said Dravot, his thumb on the map. "Up to Jagdallak, Peachey and me know the road. We was there with Roberts's Army. We'll have to turn off to the right at Jagdallak through Laghmann territory. Then we get among the hills—fourteen thousand feet—fifteen thousand—it will be cold work there, but it don't look very far on the map."

I handed him Wood on the *Sources of the Oxus*. Carnehan was deep in the *Encyclopaedia*.

"They're a mixed lot," said Dravot reflectively; "and it won't help us to know the names of their tribes. The more tribes the more they'll fight, and the better for us. From Jagdallak to Ashang. H'mm!"

"But all the information about the country is as sketchy and inaccurate as can be," I protested. "No one knows anything about it really. Here's the file of the *United Services' Institute*. Read what Bellew says."

"Blow Bellew!" said Carnehan. "Dan, they're an all-fired lot of heathens, but this book here says they think they're related to us English."

I smoked while the men pored over Raverty, Wood, the maps and the *Encyclopaedia.*

"There is no use your waiting," said Dravot politely. "It's about four o'clock now. We'll go before six o'clock if you want to sleep, and we won't steal any of the papers. Don't you sit up. We're two harmless lunatics, and if you come tomorrow evening down to the Serai we'll say good-by to you."

"You *are* two fools," I answered. "You'll be turned back at the frontier or cut up the minute you set foot in Afghanistan. Do you want any money or a recommendation down-country? I can help you to the chance of work next week."

"Next week we shall be hard at work ourselves, thank you," said Dravot. "It isn't so easy being a king as it looks. When we've got our kingdom in going order we'll let you know, and you can come up and help us to govern it."

"Would two lunatics make a contrack like that?" said Carnehan, with sub-dued pride, showing me a greasy half-sheet of note-paper on which was written the following. I copied it, then and there, as a curiosity:

> This Contract between me and you persuing witnesseth in the name of God—Amen and so forth.
>
> | | |
> |---|---|
> | (One) | That me and you will settle this matter together: *i.e.,* to be Kings of Kafiristan. |
> | (Two) | That you and me will not, while this matter is being settled, look at any liquor, nor any woman black, white or brown, so as to get mixed up with one or the other harmful. |
> | (Three) | That we conduct ourselves with dignity and discretion, and if one of us gets into trouble the other will stay by him. |
>
> Signed by you and me this day.
> Peachey Taliaferro Carnehan.
> Daniel Dravot.
> Both Gentlemen at Large.

"There was no need for the last article," said Carnehan, blushing modestly; "but it looks regular. Now you know the sort of men that loafers are—we *are* loafers, Dan, until we get out of India—and *do* you think that we would sign a contrack like that unless we was in earnest? We have kept away from the two things that make life worth having."

"You won't enjoy your lives much longer if you are going to try this idiotic adventure. Don't set the office on fire," I said, "and go away before nine o'clock."

I left them still poring over the maps and making notes on the back of the "contrack." "Be sure to come down to the Serai tomorrow," were their parting words.

The Kumharsen Serai is the great four-square sink of humanity where the strings of camels and horses from the North load and unload. All the nationalities of Central Asia may be found there, and most of the folk of India proper. Balkh and Bokhara there meet Bengal and Bombay, and try to draw eye-teeth. You can buy ponies, turquoises, Persian pussy-cats, saddlebags, fat-tailed sheep and musk in the Kumharsen Serai, and get many strange things for nothing. In the afternoon I went down there to see whether my friends intended to keep their word or were lying about drunk.

A priest attired in fragments of ribbons and rags stalked up to me, gravely twisting a child's paper whirligig. Behind him was his servant bending under the load of a crate of mud toys. The two were loading up two camels, and the inhabitants of the Serai watched them with shrieks of laughter.

"The priest is mad," said a horse-dealer to me. "He is going up to Kabul to sell toys to the Amir. He will either be raised to honor or have his head cut off. He came in here this morning and has been behaving madly ever since."

"The witless are under the protection of God," stammered a flat-cheeked Usbeg in broken Hindi. "They foretell future events."

"Would they could have foretold that my caravan would have been cut up by the Shinwaris almost within shadow of the Pass!" grunted the Eusufzai agent of a Rajputana trading-house whose goods had been feloniously diverted into the hands of other robbers just across the border, and whose misfortunes were the laughing-stock of the bazaar. "Ohé, priest, whence come you and whither do you go?"

"From Roum have I come," shouted the priest, waving his whirligig; "from Roum, blown by the breath of a hundred devils across the sea! O thieves, robbers, liars, the blessing of Pir Khan on pigs, dogs and perjurers! Who will take the Protected of God to the north to sell charms that are never still to the Amir? The camels shall not gall, the sons shall not fall sick, and the wives shall remain faithful while they are away, of the men who give me place in their caravan. Who will assist me to slipper the King of the Roos with a golden slipper with a silver heel? The protection of Pir Khan be upon his labors!" He spread out the skirts of his gabardine and pirouetted between the lines of tethered horses.

"There starts a caravan from Peshawar to Kabul in twenty days, *Huzrut*," said the Eusufzai trader. "My camels go therewith. Do thou also go and bring us good-luck."

"I will go even now!" shouted the priest. "I will depart upon my winged camels, and be at Peshawar in a day! Ho! Hazar Mir Khan," he yelled to his servant, "drive out the camels, but let me first mount my own."

He leaped on the back of his beast as it knelt, and, turning round to me, cried: "Come thou also, Sahib, a little along the road, and I will sell thee a charm—an amulet that shall make thee King of Kafiristan."

Then the light broke upon me, and I followed the two camels out of the Serai till we reached open road and the priest halted.

"What d'you think o' that?" said he in English. "Carnehan can't talk their patter, so I've made him my servant. He makes a handsome servant. 'Tisn't for nothing that I've been knocking about the country for fourteen years. Didn't I do that talk neat? We'll hitch on to a caravan at Peshawar till we get to Jagdallak, and then we'll see if we can get donkeys for our camels. and strike into Kafiristan. Whirligigs for the Amir, O Lor'! Put your hand under the camel-bags and tell me what you feel."

I felt the butt of a Martini, and another and another.

"Twenty of 'em," said Dravot placidly. "Twenty of 'em, and ammunition to correspond, under the whirligigs and the mud dolls."

"Heaven help you if you are caught with those things!" I said. "A Martini is worth her weight in silver among the Pathans."

"Fifteen hundred rupees of capital—every rupee we could beg, borrow, or steal—are invested on these two camels," said Dravot. "We won't get caught. We're going through the Khaiber with a regular caravan. Who'd touch a poor mad priest?"

"Have you got everything you want?" I asked, overcome with astonishment.

"Not yet, but we shall soon. Give us a memento of your kindness. *Brother.* You did me a service yesterday. and that time in Marwar. Half my kingdom shall you have, as the saying is." I slipped a small charm compass from my watch-chain and handed it up to the priest.

"Good-by," said Dravot, giving me his hand cautiously. "It's the last time we'll shake hands with an Englishman these many days. Shake hands with him, Carnehan," he cried, as the second camel passed me.

Carnehan leaned down and shook hands. Then the camels passed away along the dusty road, and I was left alone to wonder. My eye could detect no failure in the disguises. The scene in the Serai attested that they were complete to the native mind. There was just the chance, therefore, that Carnehan and Dravot would be able to wander through Afghanistan without detection. But, beyond, they would find death, certain and awful death.

Ten days later a native friend of mine, giving me the news of the day from Peshawar, wound up his letter with: "There has been much laughter here on account of a certain mad priest who is going in his estimation to sell petty gauds and insignificant trinkets which he ascribes as great charms to H. H. the Amir of Bokhara. He passed through Peshawar and associated himself to the Second Summer caravan that goes to Kabul. The merchants are pleased because through superstition they imagine that such mad fellows bring good fortune."

The two, then, were beyond the border. I would have prayed for them, but that night a real king died in Europe, and demanded an obituary notice.

The wheel of the world swings through the same phases again and again. Summer passed and winter thereafter, and came and passed again. The daily paper continued and I with it, and upon the third summer there fell a hot night, a night-issue, and a strained waiting for something to be telegraphed from the other side of the world, exactly as had happened before. A few great men had died in the past two years. the machines worked with more clatter and some of the trees in the office garden were a few feet taller. But that was all the difference.

I passed over to the press-room, and went through just such a scene as I have already described. The nervous tension was stronger than it had been two years before and I felt the heat more acutely. At three o'clock I cried "Print off," and turned to go, when there crept to my chair what was left of a man. He was bent into a circle, his head was sunk between his shoulders, and he moved his feet one over the other like a bear. I could hardly see whether he walked or crawled—this rag-wrapped, whining cripple who addressed me by name, crying that he was come back. "Can you give me a drink?" he whimpered. "For the Lord's sake, give me a drink!"

I went back to the office, the man following with groans of pain, and I turned up the lamp.

"Don't you know me?" he gasped, dropping into a chair, and he turned his drawn face, surmounted by a shock of gray hair, to the light.

I looked at him intently. Once before had I seen eyebrows that met over the nose in an inch-broad black band, but for the life of me I could not tell where.

"I don't know you," I said, handing him the whisky. "What can I do for you?"

He took a gulp of the spirit raw, and shivered in spite of the suffocating heat.

"I've come back," he repeated; "and I was the King of Kafiristan—me and Dravot—crowned kings we was! In this office we settled it—you setting there and giving us the books. I am Peachey—Peachey Taliaferro Carnehan, and you've been setting here ever since—O Lord!"

I was more than a little astonished and expressed my feelings accordingly.

"It's true," said Carnehan, with a dry cackle, nursing his feet, which were wrapped in rags. "True as gospel, kings we were, with crowns upon our heads— me and Dravot—poor Dan—oh, poor, poor Dan, that would never take advice, not though I begged of him!"

"Take the whisky," I said, "and take your own time. Tell me all you can recollect of everything from beginning to end. You got across the border on your camels, Dravot dressed as a mad priest, and you his servant. Do you remember that?"

"I ain't mad—yet, but I shall be that way soon. Of course I remember. Keep looking at me, or maybe my words will go all to pieces. Keep looking at me in my eyes and don't say anything."

I leaned forward and looked into his face as steadily as I could. He dropped one hand upon the table and I grasped it by the wrist. It was twisted like a bird's claw, and upon the back was a ragged, red, diamond-shaped scar.

"No, don't look there. Look at *me*," said Carnehan. "That comes afterwards. but for the Lord's sake don't distrack me. We left with that caravan, me and Dravot playing all sorts of antics to amuse the people we were with. Dravot used to make us laugh in the evening when all the people was cooking their dinners—cooking their dinners, and . . . what did they do then? They lit little fires with sparks that went into Dravot's beard, and we all laughed—fit to die. Little red fires they was, going into Dravot's big red beard—so funny." His eyes left mine and he smiled foolishly.

"You went as far as Jagdallak with that caravan," I said at a venture, "after you had lit those fires. To Jagdallak. where you turned off to try to get into Kafiristan."

"No, we didn't neither. What are you talking about? We turned off before Jagdallak, because we heard the roads was good. But they wasn't good enough for our two camels—mine and Dravot's. When we left the caravan Dravot took off all his clothes and mine too, and said we would be heathen, because the Kafirs didn't allow Mohammedans to talk to them. So we dressed betwixt and between, and such a sight as Daniel Dravot I never saw yet nor expect to see again. He burned half his beard, and slung a sheepskin over his shoulder, and shaved his head into patterns. He shaved mine, too, and made me wear outrageous things to look like a heathen. That was in a most mountainous country, and our camels couldn't go along any more because of the mountains. They were tall and black, and coming home I saw them fight like wild goats—there are lots of goats in Kafiristan. And these mountains, they never keep still, no more than the goats. Always fighting they are, and don't let you sleep at night."

"Take some more whisky," I said very slowly. "What did you and Daniel Dravot do when the camels could go no farther because of the rough roads that led into Kafiristan?"

"What did which do? There was a party called Peachey Taliaferro Carnehan that was with Dravot. Shall I tell you about him? He died out there in the cold. Slap for the bridge fell old Peachey, turning and twisting in the air like a penny whirligig that you can sell to the Amir.—No; they was two for three ha'pence, those whirligigs, or I am much mistaken and woeful sore. And then these camels were no use, and Peachey said to Dravot: 'For the Lord's sake. let's get out of this before our heads are chopped off,' and with that they killed the camels all among the mountains, not having anything in particular to eat, but first they took off the boxes with the guns and the ammunition, till two men came along driving four mules. Dravot up and dances in front of them, singing: 'Sell me four mules.' Says the first man: 'If you are rich enough to buy you are rich enough to rob'; but before ever he could put his hand to his knife Dravot breaks his neck over his knee, and the other party runs away. So Carnehan loaded the mules with the rifles that was taken off the camels, and together we starts forward into those bitter cold mountainous parts, and never a road broader than the back of your hand."

He paused for a moment, while I asked him if he could remember the nature of the country through which he had journeyed.

"I am telling you as straight as I can, but my head isn't as good as it might be. They drove nails through it to make me hear better how Dravot died. The country was mountainous and the mules were most contrary, and the inhabitants was dispersed and solitary. They went up and up, and down and down, and that other party, Carnehan, was imploring of Dravot not to sing and whistle so loud, for fear of bringing down the tremenjus avalanches. But Dravot says that if a king couldn't sing it wasn't worth being king, and whacked the mules over the rump, and never took no heed for ten cold days. We came to a big level valley all among the mountains, and the mules were near dead, so we killed them, not having anything in special for them or us to eat. We sat upon the boxes, and played odd and even with the cartridges that was jolted out.

"Then ten men with bows and arrows ran down that valley chasing twenty men with bows and arrows, and the row was tremenjus. They was fair men— fairer than you or me—with yellow hair and remarkable well built. Says Dravot, unpacking the guns: 'This is the beginning of the business. We'll fight for the ten men,' and with that he fires two rifles at the twenty men, and drops one of them at two hundred yards from the rock where we was sitting. The other men began to run, but Carnehan and Dravot sits on the boxes picking them off at all ranges, up and down the valley. Then we goes up to the ten men that had run across the snow, too, and they fires a footy little arrow at us. Dravot he shoots above their heads and they all falls down flat. Then he walks over them and kicks them, and then he lifts them up and shakes hands all around to make them friendly like. He calls them and gives them the boxes to carry, and waves his hand for all the world as though he was king already. They take the boxes and him across the valley and up the hill into a pine wood on the top, where there was half a dozen big stone idols. Dravot he goes to the biggest—a fellow they call Imbra—and lays a rifle and a cartridge at his feet, rubbing his nose respectful with his own nose, patting him on the head, and saluting in front of it. He turns round to the men and nods his head, and says 'That's all right. I'm in the know, too, and all these old jim-jams are my friends.' Then he opens his mouth and points down it, and when the first man brings him food, he says— 'No'; and when the second man brings him food, he says—'No'; but when one of the old priests and the boss of the village brings him food, he says—'Yes,' very haughty, and eats it slow. That was how we came to our first village, without any trouble, just as though we had tumbled from the skies. But we tumbled from one of those damned rope-bridges, you see, and you couldn't expect a man to laugh much after that."

"Take some more whisky and go on," I said. "That was the first village you came into. How did you get to be king?"

"I wasn't king," said Carnehan. "Dravot he was the king, and a handsome man he looked with the gold crown on his head and all. Him and the other party stayed in that village, and every morning Dravot sat by the side of old Imbra, and the people came and worshiped. That was Dravot's order. Then a lot of men came into the valley, and Carnehan and Dravot picks them off with the rifles before they knew where they was, and runs down into the valley and up again the other side, and finds another village, same as the first one, and the people all falls down flat on their faces, and Dravot says, 'Now what is the trouble between you two villages?' and the people points to a woman, as fair as you or me, that was carried off, and Dravot takes her back to the first village and counts up the dead—eight there was. For each dead man Dravot pours a little milk on the ground and waves his arms like a whirligig and 'That's all right,' says he. Then he and Carnehan takes the big boss of each village by the arm and walks them down into the valley, and shows them how to scratch a line with a spear right down the valley, and gives each a sod of turf from both sides o' the line. Then all the people comes down and shouts like the devil and all, and Dravot says, 'Go and dig the land, and be fruitful and multiply,' which they did, though they didn't understand. Then we asks the names of things in their lingo—bread and water and fire and idols and such, and Dravot leads the priest of each village up to the idol, and says he must sit there and judge the people, and if anything goes wrong he is to be shot.

"Next week they was all turning up the land in the valley as quiet as bees and much prettier, and the priests heard all the complaints and told Dravot in dumb show what it was about. 'That's just the beginning,' says Dravot. 'They think we're gods.' He and Carnehan picks out twenty good men and shows them how to click off a rifle and form fours, and advance in line, and they was very pleased to do so, and clever to see the hang of it. Then he takes out his pipe and his baccy-pouch and leaves one at one village and one at the other, and off we two goes to see what was to be done in the next valley. That was all rock, and there was a little village there, and Carnehan says,—'Send 'em to the old valley to plant,' and takes 'em there and gives 'em some land that wasn't took before. They were a poor lot, and we blooded 'em with a kid before letting 'em into the new kingdom. That was to impress the people, and then they settled down quiet, and Carnehan went back to Dravot, who had got into another valley all snow and ice and most mountainous. There was no people there and the army got afraid, so Dravot shoots one of them, and goes on till he finds some people in a village, and the army explains that unless the people wants to be killed they had better not shoot their little matchlocks; for they had matchlocks. We makes friends with the priest and I stays there alone with two of the army, teaching the men how to drill, and a thundering big chief comes across the snow with kettle-drums and horns twanging, because he heard there was a new god kicking about. Carnehan sights for the brown of the men half a mile across the snow and wings one of them. Then he sends a message to the chief that, unless he wished to be killed, he must come and shake hands with me and leave his arms behind. The chief comes alone first, and Carnehan shakes hands with him and whirls his arms about same as Dravot used, and very much surprised that chief was, and strokes my eyebrows. Then Carnehan goes alone to the chief and asks him in dumb show if he had an enemy he hated. 'I have,' said the chief. So Carnehan weeds out the pick of his men, and sets the two of the army to show them drill and at the end of two weeks the men can maneuver about as well as volunteers. So he marches with the chief to a great big plain on the top of a mountain, and the chief's men rushes into a village and takes it; we three Martinis firing into the brown of the enemy. So we took the village too, and I gives the chief a rag from my coat, and says, 'Occupy till I come,' which was Scriptural. By way of a reminder, when me and the army was eighteen hundred yards away, I drops a bullet near him standing on the snow, and all the people falls flat on their faces. Then I sends a letter to Dravot, wherever he be by land or by sea."

At the risk of throwing the creature out of train I interrupted, "How could you write a letter up yonder?"

"The letter? Oh! The letter! Keep looking at me between the eyes, please. It was a string-talk letter, that we'd learned the way of it from a blind beggar in the Punjab."

I remembered that there had once come to the office a blind man with a knotted twig and a piece of string which he wound round the twig according to some cipher of his own. He could, after the lapse of days or hours, repeat the sentence which he had reeled up. He had reduced the alphabet to eleven primitive sounds; and tried to teach me his method, but failed.

"I sent that letter to Dravot," said Carnehan; "and told him to come back because this kingdom was growing too big for me to handle, and then I struck for the first valley, to see how the priests were working. They called the village we took along with the chief, Bashkai, and the first village we took Er-Heb. The priests at Er-Heb was doing all right, but they had a lot of pending cases about land to show me, and some men from another village had been firing arrows at night. I went out and looked for that village and fired four rounds at it from a thousand yards. That used all the cartridges I cared to spend, and I waited for Dravot, who had been away two or three months, and I kept my people quiet.

"One morning I heard the devil's own noise of drums and horns, and Dan Dravot marches down the hill with his army and a tail of hundreds of men, and, which was the most amazing—a great gold crown on his head. 'My Gord, Carnehan,' says Daniel, 'this is a tremenjus business, and we've got the whole country as far as it's worth having. I am the son of Alexander by Queen Semiramis, and you're my younger brother and a god too! It's the biggest thing we've ever seen. I've been marching and fighting for six weeks with the army, and every footy little village for fifty miles has come in rejoiceful; and more than that, I've got the key of the whole show, as you'll see, and I've got a crown for you! I told 'em to make two of 'em at a place called Shu, where the gold lies in the rock like suet in mutton. Gold I've seen, and turquoise I've kicked out of the cliffs, and there's garnets in the sands of the river, and here's a chunk of amber that a man brought me. Call up all the priests and, here, take your crown.'

"One of the men opens a black hair bag and I slips the crown on. It was too small and too heavy, but I wore it for the glory. Hammered gold it was—five-pound weight, like a hoop of a barrel.

"'Peachey,' says Dravot, 'we don't want to fight no more. The craft's the trick, so help me!' and he brings forward that same chief that I left at Bashkai—Billy Fish we called him afterwards, because he was so like Billy Fish that drove the big tank-engine at Mach on the Bolan in the old days. 'Shake hands with him,' says Dravot, and I shook hands and nearly dropped, for Billy Fish gave me the grip. I said nothing, but tried him with the fellowcraft grip. He answers all right, and I tried the master's grip, but that was a slip. 'A fellowcraft he is!' I says to Dan. 'Does he know the word?' 'He does,' says Dan, 'and all the priests know. It's a miracle! The chiefs and the priests can work a fellowcraft lodge in a way that's very like ours, and they've cut the marks on the rocks, but they don't know the third degree, and they've come to find out. It's Gord's truth. I've known these long years that the Afghans knew up to the fellowcraft degree, but this is a miracle. A god and a grand-master of the craft am I, and a lodge in the third degree I will open, and we'll raise the head priests and the chiefs of the villages.'

" 'It's against all the law,' I says, 'holding a lodge without warrant from any one; and we never held office in any lodge.'

" 'It's a master-stroke of policy,' says Dravot. 'It means running the country as easy as a four-wheeled bogy on a down grade. We can't stop to inquire now, or they'll turn against us. I've forty chiefs at my heel, and passed and raised according to their merit they shall be. Billet these men on the villages, and see that we run up a lodge of some kind. The temple of Imbra will do for the lodge room. The women must make aprons as you show them. I'll hold a levee of chiefs tonight and lodge tomorrow.'

"I was fair run off my legs, but I wasn't such a fool as not to see what a pull this craft business gave us. I showed the priests' families how to make aprons of the degrees, but for Dravot's apron the blue border and marks was made of turquoise lumps on white hide, not cloth. We took a great square stone in the temple for the master's chair, and little stones for the officers' chairs, and painted the black pavement with white squares, and did what we could to make things regular.

"At the levee which was held that night on the hillside with big bonfires, Dravot gives out that him and me were gods and sons of Alexander, and past grand-masters in the craft, and was come to make Kafiristan a country where every man should eat in peace and drink in quiet, and specially obey us. Then the chiefs come round to shake hands, and they was so hairy and white and fair it was just shaking hands with old friends. We gave them names according as they were like men we had known in India—Billy Fish, Holly Dilworth, Pikky Kargan that was bazaar-master when I was at Mhow, and so on and so on.

"*The* most amazing miracle was at lodge next night. One of the old priests was watching us continuous, and I felt uneasy, for I knew we'd have to fudge the ritual, and I didn't know what the men knew. The old priest was a stranger come in from beyond the village of Bashkai. The minute Dravot puts on the master's apron that the girls had made for him, the priest fetches a whoop and a howl, and tries to overturn the stone that Dravot was sitting on. 'It's all up now,' I says. 'That comes of meddling with the craft without warrant!' Dravot never winked an eye, not when ten priests took and tilted over the grand-master's chair—which was to say the stone of Imbra. The priest begins rubbing the bottom of it to clear away the black dirt, and presently he shows all the other priests the master's mark, same as was on Dravot's apron, cut into the stone. Not even the priests of the temple of Imbra knew it was there. The old chap falls flat on his face at Dravot's feet and kisses 'em. 'Luck again,' says Dravot, across the lodge to me, 'they say it's the missing mark that no one could understand the why of. We're more than safe now.' Then he bangs the butt of his gun for a gavel and says: 'By virtue of the authority vested in me by my own right hand and the help of Peachey, I declare myself Grand-Master of all Freemasonry in Kafiristan in this the mother lodge o' the country, and King of Kafiristan equally with Peachey!' At that he puts on his crown and I puts on mine—I was doing senior warden—and we opens the lodge in most ample form. It was an amazing miracle! The priests moved in lodge through the first two degrees almost without telling, as if the memory was coming back to them. After that Peachey and Dravot raised such as was worthy—high priests and chiefs of far-off villages. Billy Fish was the first, and I can tell you we scared the soul out of him. It was not in any way according to ritual, but it served our turn. We didn't raise more than ten of the biggest men because we didn't want to make the degree common. And they was clamoring to be raised.

" 'In another six months,' says Dravot, 'we'll hold another communication and see how you are working.' Then he asks them about their villages, and learns that they was fighting one against the other and were fair sick and tired of it. And when they wasn't doing that they was fighting with the Mohammedans. 'You can fight those when they come into our country,' says Dravot. 'Tell off every tenth man of your tribes for a frontier guard, and send two hundred at a time to this valley to be drilled. Nobody is going to be shot or speared any more so long as he does well, and I know that you won't cheat me because you're white people—sons of Alexander—and not like common, black Mohammedans. You are *my* people, and by God,' says he, running off into English at the end—'I'll make a damned fine nation of you, or I'll die in the making!'

"I can't tell all we did for the next six months, because Dravot did a lot I couldn't see the hang of, and he learned their lingo in a way I never could. My work was to help the people plow, and now and again go out with some of the army and see what the other villages were doing, and make 'em throw rope bridges across the ravines which cut up the country horrid. Dravot was very kind to me, but when he walked up and down in the pine wood pulling that bloody red beard of his with both fists I knew he was thinking plans I could not advise him about and I just waited for orders.

"But Dravot never showed me disrespect before the people. They were afraid of me and the army, but they loved Dan. He was the best of friends with the priests and the chiefs; but any one could come across the hills with a complaint and Dravot would hear him out fair and call four priests together and say what was to be done. He used to call in Billy Fish from Bashkai and Pikky Kargan from Shu, and an old chief we called Kefuzelum—it was like enough to his real name—and held councils with 'em when there was any fighting to be done in small villages. That was his Council of War, and the four priests of Bashkai, Shu, Khawak and Madora was his Privy Council. Between the lot of 'em they sent me, with forty men and twenty rifles, and sixty men carrying turquoises, into the Ghorband country to buy those hand-made Martini rifles that come out of the Amir's workshops at Kabul, from one of the Amir's Herati regiments that would have sold the very teeth out of their mouths for turquoises.

"I stayed in Ghorband a month, and gave the Governor there the pick of my baskets for hush-money, and bribed the colonel of the regiment some more, and between the two and the tribes people, we got more than a hundred hand-made Martinis, a hundred good Kohat Jezails that'll throw to six hundred yards, and forty man-loads of very bad ammunition for the rifles. I came back with what I had, and distributed 'em among the men that the chiefs sent in to me to drill. Dravot was too busy to attend to those things, but the old army that we first made helped me, and we turned out five hundred men that could drill, and two hundred that knew how to hold arms pretty straight. Even those cork-screwed, hand-made guns was a miracle to them. Dravot talked big about powder-shops and factories, walking up and down in the pine wood when the winter was coming on.

" 'I won't make a nation,' says he. 'I'll make an empire! These men aren't niggers; they're English! Look at their eyes—look at their mouths. Look at the way they stand up. They sit on chairs in their own houses. They're the Lost Tribes, or something like it, and they've grown to be English. I'll take a census in the spring if the priests don't get frightened. There must be fair two million of 'em in these hills. The villages are full o' little children. Two million people— two hundred and fifty thousand fighting men—and all English! They only want the rifles and a little drilling. Two hundred and fifty thousand men, ready to cut in on Russia's right flank when she tries for India! Peachey, man,' he says, chewing his beard in great hunks, 'we shall be emperors—emperors of the earth. Rajah Brooke will be a suckling to us. I'll treat with the Viceroy on equal terms. I'll ask him to send me twelve picked English—twelve that I know of—to help us govern a bit. There's Mackray, Sergeant-pensioner at Segowli—many's the good dinner he's given me, and his wife a pair of trousers. There's Donkin, the Warder of Tounghoo Jail; there's hundreds that I could lay my hands on if I was in India. The Viceroy shall do it for me. I'll send a man through in the spring for those men, and I'll write for a dispensation from the grand lodge for what I've done as grand master. That—and all the Sniders that'll be thrown out when the native troops in India take up the Martini. They'll be worn smooth, but they'll do for fighting in these hills. Twelve English, a hundred thousand Sniders run through the Amir's country in driblets—I'd be content with twenty thousand in one year—and we'd be an empire. When everything was shipshape, I'd hand over the crown—this crown I'm wearing now—to Queen Victoria on my knees, and she'd say: "Rise up, Sir Daniel Dravot." Oh, it's big! It's big, I tell you! But there's so much to be done in every place—Bashkai, Khawak, Shu, and everywhere else.'

" 'What is it?' I says. 'There are no more men coming in to be drilled this autumn. Look at those fat, black clouds. They're bringing the snow.'

" 'It isn't that,' says Daniel, putting his hand very hard on my shoulder; 'and I don't wish to say anything that's against you, for no other living man would have followed me and made me what I am as you have done. You're a first-class commander-in-chief, and the people know you; but—it's a big country, and somehow you can't help me, Peachey, in the way I want to be helped.'

" 'Go to your blasted priests, then!' I said, and I was sorry when I made that remark, but it did hurt me sore to find Daniel talking so superior when I'd drilled all the men, and done all he told me.

" 'Don't let's quarrel, Peachey,' says Daniel without cursing. 'You're a king too, and the half of this kingdom is yours; but can't you see, Peachey, we want cleverer men than us now—three or four of 'em, that we can scatter about for our deputies. It's a huge great state, and I can't always tell the right thing to do, and I haven't time for all I want to do, and here's the winter coming on and all.' He put half his beard into his mouth, and it was as red as the gold of his crown.

" 'I'm sorry, Daniel,' says I. 'I've done all I could. I've drilled the men and shown the people how to stack their oats better; and I've brought in those tin-ware rifles from Ghorband—but I know what you're driving at. I take it kings always feel oppressed that way.'

" 'There's another thing, too,' says Dravot, walking up and down. 'The winter's coming and these people won't be giving much trouble, and if they do we can't move about. I want a wife.'

" 'For Gord's sake leave the women alone!' I says. 'We've both got all the work we can, though I *am* a fool. Remember the contrack and keep clear o' women.'

" 'The contrack only lasted till such time as we was kings; and kings we have been these months past,' says Dravot, weighing his crown in his hand. 'You go get a wife too, Peachey, a nice, strappin', plump girl that'll keep you warm in the winter. They're prettier than English girls, and we can take the pick of 'em. Boil 'em once or twice in hot water, and they'll come as fair as chicken and ham.'

" 'Don't tempt me!' I says. 'I will not have any dealings with a woman, not till we are a dam' side more settled than we are now. I've been doing the work o' two men and you've been doing the work o' three. Let's lie off a bit, and see if we can get some better tobacco from Afghan country and run in some good liquor; but no women.'

" 'Who's talking o' *women?*' says Dravot. 'I said *wife*—a queen to breed a king's son for the king. A queen out of the strongest tribe, that'll make them your blood-brothers, and that'll lie by your side and tell you all the people thinks about you and their own affairs. That's what I want.'

" 'Do you remember that Bengali woman I kept at Mogul Serai when I was a plate layer?' says I. 'A fat lot o' good she was to me. She taught me the lingo and one or two other things; but what happened? She ran away with the station master's servant and half my month's pay. Then she turned up at Dadur Junction in tow of a half-caste, and had the impidence to say I was her husband—all among the drivers in the running-shed.'

" 'We've done with that,' says Dravot. 'These women are whiter than you or me, and a queen I will have for the winter months.'

" 'For the last time o' asking, Dan, do *not*,' I says. 'It'll only bring us harm. The Bible says that kings ain't to waste their strength on women, 'specially when they've got a new raw kingdom to work over.'

" 'For the last time of answering I will,' says Dravot, and he went away through the pine-trees looking like a big red devil. The low sun hit his crown and beard on one side, and the two blazed like hot coals.

"But getting a wife was not as easy as Dan thought. He put it before the Council, and there was no answer till Billy Fish said he'd better ask the girls. Dravot damned them all round. 'What's wrong with me?' he shouts, standing by the idol Imbra. 'Am I a dog or am I not enough of a man for your wenches? Haven't I put the shadow of my hand over this country? Who stopped the last Afghan raid?' It was me really, but Dravot was too angry to remember. 'Who bought your guns? Who repaired the bridges? Who's the grand master of the sign cut in the stone?' and he thumped his hand on the block that he used to sit on in lodge, and at council, which opened like lodge always. Billy Fish said nothing and no more did the others. 'Keep your hair on, Dan,' said I, 'and ask the girls. That's how it's done at home, and these people are quite English.'

" 'The marriage of the king is a matter of state,' says Dan, in a white-hot rage, for he could feel, I hope, that he was going against his better mind. He walked out of the council room, and the others sat still, looking at the ground.

" 'Billy Fish,' says I to the Chief of the Bashkai, 'what's the difficulty here? A straight answer to a true friend.' 'You know,' says Billy Fish. 'How should a man tell you, who knows everything? How can daughters of men marry gods or devils? It's not proper.'

"I remembered something like that in the Bible; but if, after seeing us as long as they had, they still believed we were gods, it wasn't for me to undeceive them.

" 'A god can do anything,' says I. 'If the king is fond of a girl he'll not let her die.' 'She'll have to,' said Billy Fish. 'There are all sorts of gods and devils in these mountains, and now and again a girl marries one of them and isn't seen any more. Besides, you two know the mark cut in the stone. Only the gods know that. We thought you were men till you showed the sign of the master.'

"I wished then that we had explained about the loss of the genuine secrets of a Master Mason at the first go-off; but I said nothing. All that night there was a blowing of horns in a little dark temple half-way down the hill and I heard a girl crying fit to die. One of the priests told us that she was being prepared to marry the king.

" 'I'll have no nonsense of that kind,' says Dan. 'I don't want to interfere with your customs, but I'll take my own wife.' 'The girl's a little bit afraid,' says the priest. 'She thinks she's going to die, and they are aheartening her up down in the temple.'

" 'Hearten her very tender, then,' says Dravot, 'or I'll hearten you with the butt of a gun so that you'll never want to be heartened again.' He licked his lips, did Dan, and stayed up walking about more than half the night, thinking of the wife that he was going to get in the morning. I wasn't any means comfortable, for I knew that dealings with a woman in foreign parts though you was crowned king twenty times over, could not but be risky. I got up very early in the morning while Dravot was asleep, and I saw the priests talking together in whispers, and the chiefs talking together, too, and they looked at me out of the corners of their eyes.

" 'What is up, Fish?' I says to the Bashkai man, who was wrapped up in his furs and looking splendid to behold.

" 'I can't rightly say,' says he; 'but if you can induce the king to drop all this nonsense about marriage you'll be doing him and me and yourself a great service.'

" 'That I do believe,' says I. 'But sure, you know, Billy, as well as me, having fought against and for us, that the king and me are nothing more than two of the finest men that God Almighty ever made. Nothing more, I do assure you.'

" 'That may be,' says Billy Fish, 'and yet I should be sorry if it was.' He sinks his head upon his great fur coat for a minute and thinks. 'King,' says he, 'be you man or god or devil, I'll stick by you today. I have twenty of my men with me, and they will follow me. We'll go to Bashkai until the storm blows over.'

"A little snow had fallen in the night, and everything was white except the greasy fat clouds that blew down and down from the north. Dravot came out with his crown on his head, swinging his arms and stamping his feet, and looking more pleased than Punch.

" 'For the last time drop it, Dan,' says I in a whisper. 'Billy Fish here says that there will be a row.'

" 'A row among my people!' says Dravot. 'Not much. Peachey, you're a fool not to get a wife too. Where's the girl?' says he with a voice as loud as the braying of a jackass. 'Call up all the chiefs and priests, and let the emperor see if his wife suits him.'

"There was no need to call any one. They were all there leaning on their guns and spears round the clearing in the center of the pine wood. A deputation of priests went down to the little temple to bring up the girl, and the horns blew fit to wake the dead. Billy Fish saunters round and gets as close to Daniel as he could, and behind him stood his twenty men with matchlocks. Not a man of them under six feet. I was next to Dravot, and behind me was twenty men of the regular army. Up comes the girl, and a strapping wench she was, covered with silver and turquoises, but white as death, and looking back every minute at the priests.

" 'She'll do,' said Dan, looking her over. 'What's to be afraid of, lass? Come and kiss me.' He puts his arm round her. She shuts her eyes, gives a bit of a squeak, and down goes her face in the side of Dan's flaming red beard.

" 'The slut's bitten me!' says he, clapping his hand to his neck; and sure enough his hand was red with blood. Billy Fish and two of his matchlock-men catches hold of Dan by the shoulders and drags him into the Bashkai lot, while the priests howls in their lingo, 'Neither god nor devil but a man!' I was all taken aback, for a priest cut at me in front, and the army began firing into the Bashkai men.

" 'God A'mighty!' says Dan. 'What is the meaning o' this?'

" 'Come back! Come away!' says Billy Fish. 'Ruin and mutiny is the matter. We'll break for Bashkai if we can.'

"I tried to give some sort of orders to my men—the men o' the regular army—but it was no use, so I fired into the brown of 'em with an English Martini and drilled three beggars in a line. The valley was full of shouting, howling creatures, and every soul was shrieking, 'Not a god nor a devil but only a man!' The Bashkai troops stuck to Billy Fish all they were worth, but their matchlocks wasn't half as good as the Kabul breech-loaders, and four of them dropped. Dan was bellowing like a bull, for he was very wrathy; and Billy Fish had a hard job to prevent him running out at the crowd.

" 'We can't stand,' said Billy Fish. 'Make a run for it down the valley! The whole place is against us.' The matchlock-men ran, and we went down the valley in spite of Dravot's protestations. He was swearing horribly and crying out that he was a king. The priests rolled great stones on us, and the regular army fired hard, and there wasn't more than six men, not counting Dan, Billy Fish and me, that came down to the bottom of the valley alive.

"Then they stopped firing and the horns in the temple blew again. 'Come away—for Gord's sake come away!' says Billy Fish. 'They'll send runners out to all the villages before ever we get to Bashkai. I can protect you there, but I can't do anything now.'

"My own notion is that Dan began to go mad in his head from that hour. He stared up and down like a stuck pig. Then he was all for walking back alone and killing the priests with his bare hands, which he could have done. 'An emperor am I,' says Daniel, 'and next year I shall be a knight of the queen.'

" 'All right, Dan,' says I; 'but come along now while there's time.'

" 'It's your fault,' says he, 'for not looking after your army better. There was mutiny in the midst, and you didn't know—you damned engine-driving, plate-laying, missionaries'-pass hunting hound!' He sat upon a rock and called me every foul name he could lay tongue to. I was too heartsick to care, though it was all his foolishness that brought the smash.

" 'I'm sorry, Dan,' says I, 'but there's no accounting for natives. This business is our Fifty-Seven. Maybe we'll make something out of it yet, when we've got back to Bashkai.'

" 'Let's get to Bashkai, then,' says Dan, 'and by God, when I come back here again I'll sweep the valley so there isn't a bug in a blanket left!'

"We walked all that day, and all that night Dan was stumping up and down on the snow, chewing his beard and muttering to himself.

" 'There's no hope o' getting clear,' says Billy Fish. 'The priests will have sent runners to the villages to say that you are only men. Why didn't you stick on as gods till things was more settled? I'm a dead man.' says Billy Fish, and he throws himself down on the snow and begins to pray to his gods.

"Next morning we was in a cruel bad country—all up and down, no level ground at all, and no food either. The six Bashkai men looked at Billy Fish hungry-wise as if they wanted to ask something, but they said never a word. At noon we came to the top of a flat mountain all covered with snow, and when we climbed up into it, behold, there was an army in position waiting in the middle!

" 'The runners have been very quick,' says Billy Fish, with a little bit of a laugh. 'They are waiting for us.'

"Three or four men began to fire from the enemy's side, and a chance shot took Daniel in the calf of the leg. That brought him to his senses. He looks across the snow at the army, and sees the rifles that we had brought into the country.

" 'We're done for,' says he. 'They are Englishmen, these people—and it's my blasted nonsense that has brought you to this. Get back, Billy Fish, and take your men away; you've done what you could, and now cut for it. Carnehan,' says he, 'shake hands with me and go along with Billy. Maybe they won't kill you. I'll go and meet 'em alone. It's me that did it. Me, the king!' "

" 'Go!' says I. 'Go to Hell, Dan. I'm with you here. Billy Fish, you clear out and we two will meet those folk.'

" 'I'm a chief,' says Billy Fish quite quiet. 'I stay with you. My men can go.'

"The Bashkai fellows didn't wait for a second word but ran off, and Dan and me and Billy Fish walked across to where the drums were drumming and the horns were horning. It was cold—awful cold. I've got that cold in the back of my head now. There's a lump of it there."

The punkah-coolies had gone to sleep. Two kerosene lamps were blazing in the office, and the perspiration poured down my face and splashed on the blotter as I leaned forward. Carnehan was shivering, and I feared that his mind might go. I wiped my face, took a fresh grip of the piteously mangled hands and said, "What happened after that?"

The momentary shift of my eyes had broken the clear current.

"What was you pleased to say?" whined Carnehan. "They took them without any sound. Not a little whisper all along the snow, not though the king knocked down the first man that set hand on him—not though old Peachey fired his last cartridge into the brown of 'em. Not a single solitary sound did those swines make. They just closed up tight, and I tell you their furs stunk. There was a man called Billy Fish, a good friend of us all, and they cut his throat, Sir, then and there, like a pig; and the king kicks up the bloody snow and says:—'We've had a dashed fine run for our money. What's coming next?' But Peachey, Peachey Taliaferro, I tell you, Sir, in confidence as betwixt two friends, he lost his head, Sir. No, he didn't either. The king lost his head, so he did, all along o' one of those cunning rope-bridges. Kindly let me have the paper-cutter, Sir. It tilted this way. They marched him a mile across that snow to a rope-bridge over a ravine with a river at the bottom. You may have seen such. They prodded him behind like an ox. 'Damn your eyes!' says the king. 'D' you suppose I can't die like a gentleman?' He turns to Peachey—Peachey that was crying like a child. 'I've brought you to this, Peachey,' says he. 'Brought you out of your happy life to be killed in Kafiristan, where you was late commander-in-chief of the emperor's forces. Say you forgive me, Peachey.' 'I do,' says Peachey. 'Fully and freely do I forgive you, Dan.' 'Shake hands, Peachey,' says he. 'I'm going now.' Out he goes, looking neither right nor left, and when he was plumb in the middle of those dizzy dancing ropes, 'Cut, you beggars,' he shouts; and they cut, and old Dan fell, turning round and round and round, twenty thousand miles, for he took half an hour to fall till he struck the water, and I could see his body caught on a rock with the gold crown close beside.

"But do you know what they did to Peachey between two pine-trees? They crucified him, Sir, as Peachey's hands will show. They used wooden pegs for his hands and his feet; and he didn't die. He hung there and screamed; and they took him down next day and said it was a miracle that he wasn't dead. They took him down—poor old Peachey that hadn't done them any harm—that hadn't done them any . . ."

He rocked to and fro and wept bitterly, wiping his eyes with the back of his scarred hands and moaning like a child for some ten minutes.

"They was cruel enough to feed him up in the temple, because they said he was more of a god than old Daniel that was a man. Then they turned him out on the snow, and told him to go home; and Peachey came home in about a year, begging along the roads quite safe; for Daniel Dravot he walked before and said: 'Come along, Peachey. It's a big thing we're doing.' The mountains they danced at night, and the mountains they tried to fall on Peachey's head, but Dan he held up his hand, and Peachey came along bent double. He never let go of Dan's hand, and he never let go of Dan's head. They gave it to him as a present in the temple, to remind him not to come again. and though the crown was pure gold, and Peachey was starving, never would Peachey sell the same. You knew Dravot, Sir! You knew Right Worshipful Brother Dravot! Look at him now!"

He fumbled in the mass of rags round his bent waist; brought out a black horsehair bag embroidered with silver thread; and shook therefrom onto my table—the dried, withered head of Daniel Dravot! The morning sun that had long been paling the lamps struck the red beard and blind, sunken eyes; struck, too, a heavy circlet of gold studded with raw turquoises, that Carnehan placed tenderly on the battered temples.

"You behold now," said Carnehan, "the Emperor in his habit as he lived— the King of Kafiristan with his crown upon his head. Poor old Daniel that was a monarch once!"

I shuddered, for, in spite of defacements manifold, I recognized the head of the man of Marwar Junction. Carnehan rose to go. I attempted to stop him. He was not fit to walk abroad. "Let me take away the whisky and give me a little money," he gasped. "I was a king once. I'll go to the deputy commissioner and ask to set in the poor-house till I get my health. No, thank you, I can't wait till you get a carriage for me. I've urgent private affairs—in the south—at Marwar."

He shambled out of the office and departed in the direction of the deputy commissioner's house. That day at noon I had occasion to go down the blinding hot Mall, and I saw a crooked man crawling along the white dust of the road-side, his hat in his hand, quavering dolorously after the fashion of street-singers at home. There was not a soul in sight, and he was out of all possible earshot of the houses. And he sang through his nose, turning his head from right to left:

> "The Son of Man goes forth to war,
> A golden crown to gain:
> His blood-red banner streams afar—
> Who follows in his train?"

I waited to hear no more, but put the poor wretch into my carriage and drove him off to the nearest missionary for eventual transfer to the asylum. He repeated the hymn twice while he was with me, whom he did not in the least recognize, and I left him singing it to the missionary.

Two days later I inquired after his welfare of the superintendent of the asylum.

"He was admitted suffering from sunstroke. He died early yesterday morning." said the superintendent. "Is it true that he was half an hour bareheaded in the sun at midday?"

"Yes," said I; "but do you happen to know if he had anything upon him by any chance when he died?"

"Not to my knowledge," said the superintendent.

And there the matter rests.   (1888)

Anton Chekhov

THE DARLING

Olenka, the daughter of the retired collegiate assessor, Plemyanniakov, was sitting in her back porch, lost in thought. It was hot, the flies were persistent and teasing, and it was pleasant to reflect that it would soon be evening. Dark rainclouds were gathering from the east, and bringing from time to time a breath of moisture in the air.

Kukin, who was the manager of an open-air theater called the Tivoli, and who lived in the lodge, was standing in the middle of the garden looking at the sky.

"Again!" he observed despairingly. "It's going to rain again! Rain every day, as though to spite me. I might as well hang myself! Its ruin! Fearful losses every day."

He flung up his hands, and went on, addressing Olenka:

"There! That's the life we lead, Olga Semyonovna. It's enough to make one cry. One works and does one's utmost; one wears oneself out, getting no sleep at night, and racks one's brain what to do for the best. And then what happens? To begin with, one's public is ignorant, boorish. I give them the very best operetta, a dainty masque, first rate music-hall artists. But do you suppose that's what they want! They don't understand anything of that sort. They want a clown; what they ask for is vulgarity. And then look at the weather! Almost every evening it rains. It started on the tenth of May, and it's kept it up all May

From *The Darling and Other Stories*, translated by Constance Garnett. Reprinted by permission of The Macmillan Company and Chatto and Windus.

and June. It's simply awful! The public doesn't come, but I've to pay the rent just the same, and pay the artists."

The next evening the clouds would gather again, and Kukin would say with an hysterical laugh:

"Well, rain away, then! Flood the garden, drown me! Damn my luck in this world and the next! Let the artists have me up! Send me to prison!—to Siberia!—the scaffold! ha, ha, ha!"

And next day the same thing.

Olenka listened to Kukin with silent gravity, and sometimes tears came into her eyes. In the end his misfortunes touched her; she grew to love him. He was a small thin man, with a yellow face, and curls combed forward on his forehead. He spoke in a thin tenor; as he talked his mouth worked on one side, and there was always an expression of despair on his face; yet he aroused a deep and genuine affection in her. She was always fond of some one, and could not exist without loving. In earlier days she had loved her papa, who now sat in a darkened room, breathing with difficulty; she had loved her aunt who used to come every other year from Bryansk; and before that, when she was at school, she had loved her French master. She was a gentle, soft-hearted, compassionate girl, with mild, tender eyes and very good health. At the sight of her full rosy cheeks, her soft white neck with a little dark mole on it, and the kind, naïve smile, which came into her face when she listened to anything pleasant, men thought, "Yes, not half bad," and smiled too, while lady visitors could not refrain from seizing her hand in the middle of a conversation, exclaiming in a gush of delight, "You darling!"

The house in which she had lived from her birth upwards, and which was left her in her father's will, was at the extreme end of the town, not far from the Tivoli. In the evenings and at night she could hear the band playing, and the crackling and banging of fireworks, and it seemed to her that it was Kukin struggling with his destiny, storming the entrenchments of his chief foe, the indifferent public; there was a sweet thrill at her heart, she had no desire to sleep, and when he returned home at daybreak, she tapped softly at her bedroom window, and showing him only her face and one shoulder through the curtain, she gave him a friendly smile. . . .

He proposed to her, and they were married. And when he had a closer view of her neck and her plump, fine shoulders, he threw up his hands, and said:

"You darling!"

He was happy, but as it rained on the day and night of his wedding, his face still retained an expression of despair.

They got on very well together. She used to sit in his office, to look after things in the Tivoli, to put down the accounts and pay the wages. And her rosy cheeks, her sweet, naïve, radiant smile, were to be seen now at the office window, now in the refreshment bar or behind the scenes of the theater. And already she used to say to her acquaintances that the theater was the chief and most important thing in life, and that it was only through the drama that one could derive true enjoyment and become cultivated and humane.

"But do you suppose the public understands that?" she used to say. "What they want is a clown. Yesterday we gave *Faust Inside Out,* and almost all the boxes were empty; but if Vanitchka and I had been producing some vulgar thing, I assure you the theater would have been packed. Tomorrow Vanitchka and I are doing *Orpheus in Hell.* Do come."

And what Kukin said about the theater and the actors she repeated. Like him she despised the public for their ignorance and their indifference to art; she took part in the rehearsals, she corrected the actors, she kept an eye on the behavior of the musicians, and when there was an unfavorable notice in the local paper, she shed tears, and then went to the editor's office to set things right.

The actors were fond of her and used to call her "Vanitchka and I," and "the darling"; she was sorry for them and used to lend them small sums of money, and if they deceived her, she used to shed a few tears in private, but did not complain to her husband.

They got on well in the winter too. They took the theater in the town for the whole winter, and let it for short terms to a Little Russian company, or to a conjurer, or to a local dramatic society. Olenka grew stouter, and was always beaming with satisfaction, while Kukin grew thinner and yellower, and continually complained of their terrible losses, although he had not done badly all the winter. He used to cough at night, and she used to give him hot raspberry tea or lime-flower water, to rub him with eau de Cologne and to wrap him in her warm shawls.

"You're such a sweet pet!" she used to say with perfect sincerity, stroking his hair. "You're such a pretty dear!"

Towards Lent he went to Moscow to collect a new troupe, and without him she could not sleep, but sat all night at her window, looking at the stars, and she compared herself to the hens, who are awake all night and uneasy when the cock is not in the henhouse. Kukin was detained in Moscow, and wrote that he would be back at Easter, adding some instructions about the Tivoli. But on the Sunday before Easter, late in the evening, came a sudden ominous knock at the gate; some one was hammering on the gate as though on a barrel—boom, boom boom! The drowsy cook went flopping with her bare feet through the puddles, as she ran to open the gate.

"Please open," said some one outside in a thick bass. "There is a telegram for you."

Olenka had received telegrams from her husband before, but this time for some reason she felt numb with terror. With shaking hands she opened the telegram and read as follows:

> Ivan Petrovitch died suddenly today. Awaiting immate instructions fufuneral Tuesday.

That was how it was written in the telegram—"fufuneral," and the utterly incomprehensible word "immate." It was signed by the stage manager of the operatic company.

"My darling!" sobbed Olenka. "Vanitchka, my precious, my darling! Why did I ever meet you! Why did I know you and love you! Your poor heart-broken Olenka is all alone without you!"

Kukin's funeral took place on Tuesday in Moscow, Olenka returned home on Wednesday, and as soon as she got indoors she threw herself on her bed and sobbed so loudly that it could be heard next door, and in the street.

"Poor darling!" the neighbors said, as they crossed themselves. "Olga Semyo-novna, poor darling! How she does take on!"

Three months later Olenka was coming home from mass, melancholy and in deep mourning. It happened that one of her neighbors, Vassily Andreitch Pustovalov, returning home from church, walked back beside her. He was the manager at Babakayev's, the timber merchant's. He wore a straw hat, a white waistcoat, and a gold watch-chain, and looked more like a country gentleman than a man in trade.

"Everything happens as it is ordained, Olga Semyonovna," he said gravely, with a sympathetic note in his voice; "and if any of our dear ones die, it must be because it is the will of God, so we ought to have fortitude and bear it submissively."

After seeing Olenka to her gate, he said good-by and went on. All day afterwards she heard his sedately dignified voice, and whenever she shut her eyes she saw his dark beard. She liked him very much. And apparently she had made an impression on him too, for not long afterwards an elderly lady, with whom she was only slightly acquainted, came to drink coffee with her, and as soon as she was seated at table began to talk about Pustovalov, saying that he was an excellent man whom one could thoroughly depend upon, and that any girl would be glad to marry him. Three days later Pustovalov came himself. He did not stay long, only about ten minutes, and he did not say much, but when he left, Olenka loved him—loved him so much that she lay awake all night in a perfect fever, and in the morning she sent for the elderly lady. The match was quickly arranged, and then came the wedding.

Pustovalov and Olenka got on very well together when they were married.

Usually he sat in the office till dinnertime, then he went out on business, while Olenka took his place, and sat in the office till evening, making up accounts and booking orders.

"Timber gets dearer every year; the price rises twenty per cent," she would say to her customers and friends. "Only fancy we used to sell local timber, and now Vassitchka always has to go for wood to the Mogilev district. And the freight!" she would add, covering her cheeks with her hands in horror. "The freight!"

It seemed to her that she had been in the timber trade for ages and ages, and that the most important and necessary thing in life was timber; and there was something intimate and touching to her in the very sound of words such as "baulk," "post," "beam," "pole," "scantling," "batten," "lath," "plank," etc.

At night when she was asleep she dreamed of perfect mountains of planks and boards, and long strings of wagons, carting timber somewhere far away. She dreamed that a whole regiment of six-inch beams forty feet high, standing on end, was marching upon the timber-yard; that logs, beams, and boards knocked together with the resounding crash of dry wood, kept falling and getting up again, piling themselves on each other. Olenka cried out in her sleep, and Pustovalov said to her tenderly: "Olenka, what's the matter, darling? Cross yourself!"

Her husband's ideas were hers. If he thought the room was too hot, or that business was slack, she thought the same. Her husband did not care for entertainments, and on holidays he stayed at home. She did likewise.

"You are always at home or in the office," her friends said to her. "You should go to the theater, darling, or to the circus."

"Vassitchka and I have no time to go to theaters," she would answer sedately. "We have no time for nonsense. What's the use of these theaters?"

On Saturdays Pustovalov and she used to go to the evening service; on holidays to early mass, and they walked side by side with softened faces as they came home from church. There was a pleasant fragrance about them both, and her silk dress rustled agreeably. At home they drank tea, with fancy bread and jams of various kinds, and afterwards they ate pie. Every day at twelve o'clock there was a savory smell of beet-root soup and of mutton or duck in their yard, and on fast-days of fish, and no one could pass the gate without feeling hungry. In the office the samovar was always boiling, and customers were regaled with tea and cracknels. Once a week the couple went to the baths and returned side by side, both red in the face.

"Yes, we have nothing to complain of, thank God," Olenka used to say to her acquaintances. "I wish every one were as well off as Vassitchka and I."

When Pustovalov went away to buy wood in the Mogilev district, she missed him dreadfully, lay awake and cried. A young veterinary surgeon in the army, called Smirnin, to whom they had let their lodge, used sometimes to come in in the evening. He used to talk to her and play cards with her, and this entertained her in her husband's absence. She was particularly interested in what he told her of his home life. He was married and had a little boy, but was separated from his wife because she had been unfaithful to him, and now he hated her and used to send her forty roubles a month for the maintenance of their son. And hearing of all this, Olenka sighed and shook her head. She was sorry for him.

"Well, God keep you," she used to say to him at parting, as she lighted him down the stairs with a candle. "Thank you for coming to cheer me up, and may the Mother of God give you health."

And she always expressed herself with the same sedateness and dignity, the same reasonableness, in imitation of her husband. As the veterinary surgeon was disappearing behind the door below, she would say:

"You know, Vladimir Platonitch, you'd better make it up with your wife. You should forgive her for the sake of your son. You may be sure the little fellow understands."

And when Pustovalov came back, she told him in a low voice about the veterinary surgeon and his unhappy home life, and both sighed and shook their heads and talked about the boy, who, no doubt, missed his father, and by some strange connection of ideas, they went up to the holy ikons, bowed to the ground before them and prayed that God would give them children.

And so the Pustovalovs lived for six years quietly and peaceably in love and complete harmony.

But behold! one winter day after drinking hot tea in the office, Vassily Andreitch went out into the yard without his cap on to see about sending off some timber, caught cold and was taken ill. He had the best doctors, but he grew worse and died after four months' illness. And Olenka was a widow once more.

"I've nobody, now you've left me, my Darling," she sobbed, after her husband's funeral. "How can I live without you, in wretchedness and misery! Pity me, good people, all alone in the world!"

She went about dressed in black with long "weepers," and gave up wearing hat and gloves for good. She hardly ever went out, except to church, or to her husband's grave, and led the life of a nun. It was not till six months later that she took off the weepers and opened the shutters of the windows. She was some-times seen in the mornings, going with her cook to market for provisions, but what went on in her house and how she lived now could only be surmised. People guessed, from seeing her drinking tea in her garden with the veterinary surgeon, who read the newspaper aloud to her, and from the fact that, meeting a lady she knew at the post office, she said to her:

"There is no proper veterinary inspection in our town, and that's the cause of all sorts of epidemics. One is always hearing of people's getting infection from the milk supply, or catching diseases from horses and cows. The health of domestic animals ought to be as well cared for as the health of human beings."

She repeated the veterinary surgeon's words, and was of the same opinion as he about everything. It was evident that she could not live a year without some attachment, and had found new happiness in the lodge. In any one else this would have been censured, but no one could think ill of Olenka; everything she did was so natural. Neither she nor the veterinary surgeon said anything to other people of the change in their relations, and tried, indeed, to conceal it, but without success, for Olenka could not keep a secret. When he had visitors, men serving in his regiment, and she poured out tea or served the supper, she would begin talking of the cattle plague, of the foot and mouth disease, and of the municipal slaughter-houses. He was dreadfully embarrassed, and when the guests had gone, he would seize her by the hand and hiss angrily:

"I've asked you before not to talk about what you don't understand. When we veterinary surgeons are talking among ourselves, please don't put your word in. It's really annoying."

And she would look at him with astonishment and dismay, and ask him in alarm: "But, Voloditchka, what *am* I to talk about?"

And with tears in her eyes she would embrace him, begging him not to be angry, and they were both happy.

But this happiness did not last long. The veterinary surgeon departed, departed forever with his regiment, when it was transferred to a distant place—to Siberia, it may be. And Olenka was left alone.

Now she was absolutely alone. Her father had long been dead, and his arm-chair lay in the attic, covered with dust and lame of one leg. She got thinner and plainer, and when people met her in the street they did not look at her as they used to, and did not smile to her; evidently her best years were over and left behind, and now a new sort of life had begun for her, which did not bear thinking about. In the evening Olenka sat in the porch, and heard the band playing and the fireworks popping in the Tivoli, but now the sound stirred no response. She looked into her yard without interest, thought of nothing, wished for nothing, and afterwards, when night came on she went to bed and dreamed of her empty yard. She ate and drank as it were unwillingly.

And what was worst of all, she had no opinions of any sort. She saw the objects about her and understood what she saw, but could not form any opinion about them, and did not know what to talk about. And how awful it is not to have any opinions! One sees a bottle, for instance, or the rain, or a peasant driving in his cart, but what the bottle is for, or the rain, or the peasant, and what is the meaning of it, one can't say, and could not even for a thousand roubles. When she had Kukin, or Pustovalov, or the veterinary surgeon, Olenka could explain everything, and give her opinion about anything you like, but now there was the same emptiness in her brain and in her heart as there was in her yard outside. And it was as harsh and as bitter as wormwood in the mouth.

Little by little the town grew in all directions. The road became a street, and where the Tivoli and the timber-yard had been there were new turnings and houses. How rapidly time passes! Olenka's house grew dingy, the roof got rusty, the shed sank on one side, and the whole yard was overgrown with docks and stinging-nettles. Olenka herself had grown plain and elderly; in summer she sat in the porch, and her soul, as before, was empty and dreary and full of bitter-ness. In winter she sat at her window and looked at the snow. When she caught the scent of spring, or heard the chime of the church bells, a sudden rush of memories from the past came over her, there was a tender ache in her heart, and her eyes brimmed over with tears; but this was only for a minute, and then came emptiness again and the sense of the futility of life. The black kitten, Briska, rubbed against her and purred softly, but Olenka was not touched by these feline caresses. That was not what she needed. She wanted a love that would absorb her whole being, her whole soul and reason—that would give her ideas and an object in life, and would warm her old blood. And she would shake the kitten off her skirt and say with vexation:

"Get along; I don't want you!"

And so it was, day after day and year after year, and no joy, and no opinions. Whatever Mavra, the cook, said she accepted.

One hot July day, towards evening, just as the cattle were being driven away, and the whole yard was full of dust, some one suddenly knocked at the gate. Olenka went to open it herself and was dumbfounded when she looked out: she saw Smirnin, the veterinary surgeon, gray-headed, and dressed as a civilian. She suddenly remembered everything. She could not help crying and letting her head fall on his breast without uttering a word, and in the violence of her feeling she did not notice how they both walked into the house and sat down to tea.

"My dear Vladimir Platonitch! What fate has brought you?" she muttered, trembling with joy.

"I want to settle here for good, Olga Semyonovna," he told her. "I have resigned my post, and have come to settle down and try my luck on my own account. Besides, it's time for my boy to go to school. He's a big boy. I am reconciled with my wife, you know."

"Where is she?" asked Olenka.

"She's at the hotel with the boy, and I'm looking for lodgings."

"Good gracious, my dear soul! Lodgings? Why not have my house? Why shouldn't that suit you? Why, my goodness, I wouldn't take any rent!" cried Olenka in a flutter, beginning to cry again. "You live here, and the lodge will do nicely for me. Oh, dear! how glad I am!"

Next day the roof was painted and the walls were whitewashed, and Olenka, with her arms akimbo, walked about the yard giving directions. Her face was beaming with her old smile, and she was brisk and alert as though she had waked from a long sleep. The veterinary's wife arrived—a thin, plain lady, with short hair and a peevish expression. With her was her little Sasha, a boy of ten, small for his age, blue-eyed, chubby, with dimples in his cheeks. And scarcely had the boy walked into the yard when he ran after the cat, and at once there was the sound of his gay, joyous laugh.

"Is that your puss, Auntie?" he asked Olenka. "When she has little ones, do give us a kitten. Mamma is awfully afraid of mice."

Olenka talked to him, and gave him tea. Her heart warmed and there was a sweet ache in her bosom, as though the boy had been her own child. And when he sat at the table in the evening, going over his lessons, she looked at him with deep tenderness and pity as she murmured to herself:

"You pretty pet! . . . my precious! . . . Such a fair little thing, and so clever."

" 'An island is a piece of land which is entirely surrounded by water,' " he read aloud.

"An island is a piece of land," she repeated, and this was the first opinion to which she gave utterance with positive conviction after so many years of silence and dearth of ideas.

Now she had opinions of her own, and at supper she talked to Sasha's parents, saying how difficult the lessons were at the high schools, but that yet the high school was better than a commercial one, since with a high school education all careers were open to one, such as being a doctor or an engineer.

Sasha began going to the high school. His mother departed to Harkov to her sister's and did not return; his father used to go off every day to inspect cattle, and would often be away from home for three days together, and it seemed to Olenka as though Sasha was entirely abandoned, that he was not wanted at home, that he was being starved, and she carried him off to her lodge and gave him a little room there.

And for six months Sasha had lived in the lodge with her. Every morning Olenka came into his bedroom and found him fast asleep, sleeping noiselessly with his hand under his cheek. She was sorry to wake him.

"Sashenka," she would say mournfully, "get up, Darling. It's time for school."

He would get up, dress and say his prayers, and then sit down to breakfast, drink three glasses of tea, and eat two large cracknels and half a buttered roll. All this time he was hardly awake and a little ill-humored in consequence.

"You don't quite know your fable, Sashenka," Olenka would say, looking at him as though he were about to set off on a long journey. "What a lot of trouble I have with you! You must work and do your best, Darling, and obey your teachers."

"Oh, do leave me alone!" Sasha would say.

Then he would go down the street to school, a little figure, wearing a big cap and carrying a satchel on his shoulder. Olenka would follow him noiselessly.

"Sashenka!" she would call after him, and she would pop into his hand a date or a caramel. When he reached the street where the school was, he would feel ashamed of being followed by a tall, stout woman; he would turn round and say:

"You'd better go home, Auntie. I can go the rest of the way alone."

She would stand still and look after him fixedly till he had disappeared at the school gate.

Ah, how she loved him! Of her former attachments not one had been so deep; never had her soul surrendered to any feeling so spontaneously, so disinterestedly, and so joyously as now that her maternal instincts were aroused. For this little boy with the dimple in his cheek and the big school cap she would have given her whole life, she would have given it with joy and tears of tenderness. Why? Who can tell why?

When she had seen the last of Sasha, she returned home, contented and serene, brimming over with love; her face, which had grown younger during the last six months, smiled and beamed; people meeting her looked at her with pleasure.

"Good morning, Olga Semyonovna, Darling. How are you, Darling?"

"The lessons at the high school are very difficult now," she would relate at the market. "It's too much; in the first class yesterday they gave him a fable to learn by heart, and a Latin translation and a problem. You know it's too much for a little chap."

And she would begin talking about the teachers, the lessons, and the school books, saying just what Sasha said.

At three o'clock they had dinner together: in the evening they learned their lessons together and cried. When she put him to bed, she would stay a long time making the cross over him and murmuring a prayer; then she would go to bed and dream of that far-away, misty future when Sasha would finish his studies and become a doctor or an engineer, would have a big house of his own with horses and a carriage, would get married and have children. . . . She would fall asleep still thinking of the same thing, and tears would run down her cheeks from her closed eyes, while the black cat lay purring beside her: "Mrr, mrr, mrr."

Suddenly there would come a loud knock at the gate.

Olenka would wake up breathless with alarm, her heart throbbing. Half a minute later would come another knock.

"It must be a telegram from Harkov," she would think, beginning to tremble from head to foot. "Sasha's mother is sending for him from Harkov. . . . Oh, mercy on us!"

She was in despair. Her head, her hands, and her feet would turn chill, and she would feel that she was the most unhappy woman in the world. But another minute would pass, voices would be heard: it would turn out to be the veterinary surgeon coming home from the club.

"Well, thank God!" she would think.

And gradually the load in her heart would pass off, and she would feel at ease. She would go back to bed thinking of Sasha, who lay sound asleep in the next room, sometimes crying out in his sleep:

"I'll give it you! Get away! Shut up!"   (1898)

Stephen Crane

THE BRIDE COMES
TO YELLOW SKY

The great Pullman was whirling onward with such dignity of motion that a glance from the window seemed simply to prove that the plains of Texas were pouring eastward. Vast flats of green grass, dull-hued spaces of mesquit and cactus, little groups of frame houses, woods of light and tender trees, all were sweeping into the east, sweeping over the horizon, a precipice.

A newly married pair had boarded this coach at San Antonio. The man's face was reddened from many days in the wind and sun, and a direct result of his new black clothes was that his brick-colored hands were constantly performing in a most conscious fashion. From time to time he looked down respectfully at his attire. He sat with a hand on each knee, like a man waiting in a barber's shop. The glances he devoted to other passengers were furtive and shy.

The bride was not pretty, nor was she very young. She wore a dress of blue cashmere, with small reservations of velvet here and there, and with steel buttons abounding. She continually twisted her head to regard her puff sleeves, very stiff, straight, and high. They embarrassed her. It was quite apparent that she had cooked, and that she expected to cook, dutifully. The blushes caused by the careless scrutiny of some passengers as she had entered the car were strange to see upon this plain, under-class countenance, which was drawn in placid, almost emotionless lines.

They were evidently very happy. "Ever been in a parlor-car before?" he asked, smiling with delight.

"No," she answered; "I never was. It's fine, ain't it?"

"Great! And then after a while we'll go forward to the diner, and get a big lay-out. Finest meal in the world. Charge a dollar."

"Oh, do they?" cried the bride. "Charge a dollar? Why, that's too much— for us—ain't it, Jack?"

"Not this trip, anyhow," he answered bravely. "We're going to go the whole thing."

Later he explained to her about the trains. "You see, it's a thousand miles from one end of Texas to the other; and this train runs right across it, and never stops but four times." He had the pride of an owner. He pointed out to her the dazzling fittings of the coach; and in truth her eyes opened wider as she contemplated the sea-green figured velvet, the shining brass, silver, and glass, the wood that gleamed as darkly brilliant as the surface of a pool of oil. At one end a bronze figure sturdily held a support for a separated chamber, and at convenient places on the ceiling were frescos in olive and silver.

To the minds of the pair, their surroundings reflected the glory of their marriage that morning in San Antonio; this was the environment of their new estate; and the man's face in particular beamed with an elation that made him appear ridiculous to the negro porter. This individual at times surveyed them from afar with an amused and superior grin. On other occasions he bullied them with skill in ways that did not make it exactly plain to them that they were being bullied. He subtly used all the manners of the most unconquerable kind of snobbery. He oppressed them; but of this oppression they had small knowledge, and they speedily forgot that infrequently a number of travellers covered them with stares of derisive enjoyment. Historically there was supposed to be something infinitely humorous in their situation.

"We are due in Yellow Sky at 3:42," he said, looking tenderly into her eyes.

"Oh, are we?" she said, as if she had not been aware of it. To evince surprise at her husband's statement was part of her wifely amiability. She took from a pocket a little silver watch; and as she held it before her, and stared at it with a frown of attention, the new husband's face shone.

"I bought it in San Anton' from a friend of mine," he told her gleefully.

"It's seventeen minutes past twelve," she said, looking up at him with a kind of shy and clumsy coquetry. A passenger, noting this play, grew excessively sardonic, and winked at himself in one of the numerous mirrors.

At last they went to the dining-car. Two rows of negro waiters, in glowing white suits, surveyed their entrance with the interest, and also the equanimity, of men who had been forewarned. The pair fell to the lot of a waiter who happened to feel pleasure in steering them through their meal. He viewed them with the manner of a fatherly pilot, his countenance radiant with benevolence. The patronage, entwined with the ordinary deference, was not plain to them. And yet, as they returned to their coach, they showed in their faces a sense of escape.

To the left, miles down a long purple slope, was a little ribbon of mist where moved the keening Rio Grande. The train was approaching it at an angle, and the apex was Yellow Sky. Presently it was apparent that, as the distance from Yellow Sky grew shorter, the husband became commensurately restless. His brick-red hands were more insistent in their prominence. Occasionally he was even rather absent-minded and far-away when the bride leaned forward and addressed him.

As a matter of truth, Jack Potter was beginning to find the shadow of a deed weigh upon him like a leaden slab. He, the town marshal of Yellow Sky, a man known, liked, and feared in his corner, a prominent person, had gone to San Antonio to meet a girl he believed he loved, and there, after the usual prayers, had actually induced her to marry him, without consulting Yellow Sky for any part of the transaction. He was now bringing his bride before an innocent and unsuspecting community.

Of course people in Yellow Sky married as it pleased them, in accordance with a general custom; but such was Potter's thought of his duty to his friends, or of their idea of his duty, or of an unspoken form which does not control men in these matters, that he felt he was heinous. He had committed an extraordinary crime. Face to face with this girl in San Antonio, and spurred by his sharp impulse, he had gone headlong over all the social hedges. At San Antonio he was like a man hidden in the dark. A knife to sever any friendly duty, any form, was easy to his hand in that remote city. But the hour of Yellow Sky—the hour of daylight—was approaching.

He knew full well that his marriage was an important thing to his town. It could only be exceeded by the burning of the new hotel. His friends could not forgive him. Frequently he had reflected on the advisability of telling them by telegraph, but a new cowardice had been upon him. He feared to do it. And now the train was hurrying him toward a scene of amazement, glee, and reproach. He glanced out of the window at the line of haze swinging slowly in toward the train.

Yellow Sky had a kind of brass band, which played painfully, to the delight of the populace. He laughed without heart as he thought of it. If the citizens could dream of his prospective arrival with his bride, they would parade the band at the station and escort them, amid cheers and laughing congratulations, to his adobe home.

He resolved that he would use all the devices of speed and plains-craft in making the journey from the station to his house. Once within that safe citadel, he could issue some sort of vocal bulletin, and then not go among the citizens until they had time to wear off a little of their enthusiasm.

The bride looked anxiously at him. "What's worrying you, Jack?"

He laughed again. "I'm not worrying, girl; I'm only thinking of Yellow Sky."

She flushed in comprehension.

A sense of mutual guilt invaded their minds and developed a finer tenderness. They looked at each other with eyes softly aglow. But Potter often laughed the same nervous laugh; the flush upon the bride's face seemed quite permanent.

The traitor to the feelings of Yellow Sky narrowly watched the speeding landscape. "We're nearly there," he said.

Presently the porter came and announced the proximity of Potter's home. He held a brush in his hand, and, with all his airy superiority gone, he brushed Potter's new clothes as the latter slowly turned this way and that way. Potter fumbled out a coin and gave it to the porter, as he had seen others do. It was a heavy and muscle-bound business, as that of a man shoeing his first horse.

The porter took their bag, and as the train began to slow they moved forward to the hooded platform of the car. Presently the two engines and their long string of coaches rushed into the station of Yellow Sky.

"They have to take water here," said Potter, from a constricted throat and in mournful cadence, as one announcing death. Before the train stopped his eye had swept the length of the platform, and he was glad and astonished to see there was none upon it but the station-agent, who, with a slightly hurried and anxious air, was walking toward the water-tanks. When the train had halted, the porter alighted first, and placed in position a little temporary step.

"Come on, girl," said Potter, hoarsely. As he helped her down they each laughed on a false note. He took the bag from the negro, and bade his wife cling to his arm. As they slunk rapidly away, his hang-dog glance perceived that they were unloading the two trunks, and also that the station-agent, far ahead near the baggage-car, had turned and was running toward him, making gestures. He laughed, and groaned as he laughed, when he noted the first effect of his marital bliss upon Yellow Sky. He gripped his wife's arm firmly to his side, and they fled. Behind them the porter stood, chuckling fatuously.

II

The California express on the Southern Railway was due at Yellow Sky in twenty-one minutes. There were six men at the bar of the Weary Gentleman

Saloon. One was a drummer, who talked a great deal and rapidly; three were Texans, who did not care to talk at that time; and two were Mexican sheep-herders, who did not talk as a general practice in the Weary Gentleman Saloon. The barkeeper's dog lay on the board walk that crossed in front of the door. His head was on his paws, and he glanced drowsily here and there with the constant vigilance of a dog that is kicked on occasion. Across the sandy street were some vivid green grass-plots, so wonderful in appearance, amid the sands that burned near them in a blazing sun, that they caused a doubt in the mind. They exactly resembled the grass mats used to represent lawns on the stage. At the cooler end of the railway station, a man without a coat sat in a tilted chair and smoked his pipe. The fresh-cut bank of the Rio Grande circled near the town, and there could be seen beyond it a great plum-colored plain of mesquit.

Save for the busy drummer and his companions in the saloon, Yellow Sky was dozing. The new-comer leaned gracefully upon the bar, and recited many tales with the confidence of a bard who has come upon a new field.

"—and at the moment that the old man fell downstairs with the bureau in his arms, the old woman was coming up with two scuttles of coal, and of course—"

The drummer's tale was interrupted by a young man who suddenly appeared in the open door. He cried: "Scratchy Wilson's drunk, and has turned loose with both hands." The two Mexicans at once set down their glasses and faded out of the rear entrance of the saloon.

The drummer, innocent and jocular, answered: "All right, old man. S'pose he has? Come in and have a drink, anyhow."

But the information had made such an obvious cleft in every skull in the room that the drummer was obliged to see its importance. All had become instantly solemn. "Say," said he, mystified, "what is this?" His three companions made the introductory gesture of eloquent speech; but the young man at the door forestalled them.

"It means, my friend," he answered, as he came into the saloon, "that for the next two hours this town won't be a health resort."

The barkeeper went to the door, and locked and barred it; reaching out of the window, he pulled in heavy wooden shutters, and barred them. Immediately a solemn, chapel-like gloom was upon the place. The drummer was looking from one to another.

"But say," he cried, "what is this, anyhow? You don't mean there is going to be a gun-fight?"

"Don't know whether there'll be a fight or not," answered one man, grimly; "but there'll be some shootin'—some good shootin'."

The young man who had warned them waved his hand. "Oh, there'll be a fight fast enough, if any one wants it. Anybody can get a fight out there in the street. There's a fight just waiting."

The drummer seemed to be swayed between the interest of a foreigner and a perception of personal danger.

"What did you say his name was?" he asked.

"Scratchy Wilson," they answered in chorus.

"And will he kill anybody? What are you going to do? Does this happen often? Does he rampage around like this once a week or so? Can he break in that door?"

"No; he can't break down that door," replied the barkeeper. "He's tried it three times. But when he comes you'd better lay down on the floor, stranger. He's dead sure to shoot at it, and a bullet may come through."

Thereafter the drummer kept a strict eye upon the door. The time had not yet been called for him to hug the floor, but, as a minor precaution, he sidled near to the wall. "Will he kill anybody?" he said again.

The men laughed low and scornfully at the question.

"He's out to shoot, and he's out for trouble. Don't see any good in experimentin' with him."

"But what do you do in a case like this? What do you do?"

A man responded: "Why, he and Jack Potter—"

"But," in chorus the other men interrupted, "Jack Potter's in San Anton'."

"Well, who is he? What's he got to do with it?"

"Oh, he's the town marshal. He goes out and fights Scratchy when he gets on one of these tears."

"Wow!" said the drummer, mopping his brow. "Nice job he's got."

The voices had toned away to mere whisperings. The drummer wished to ask further questions, which were born of an increasing anxiety and bewilderment; but when he attempted them, the men merely looked at him in irritation and motioned him to remain silent. A tense waiting hush was upon them. In the deep shadows of the room their eyes shone as they listened for sounds from the street. One man made three gestures at the barkeeper; and the latter, moving like a ghost, handed him a glass and a bottle. The man poured a full glass of whiskey, and set down the bottle noiselessly. He gulped the whiskey in a swallow, and turned again toward the door in immovable silence. The drummer saw that the barkeeper, without a sound, had taken a Winchester from beneath the bar. Later he saw this individual beckoning to him, so he tiptoed across the room.

"You better come with me back of the bar."

"No, thanks," said the drummer, perspiring; "I'd rather be where I can make a break for the back door."

Whereupon the man of bottles made a kindly but peremptory gesture. The drummer obeyed it, and, finding himself seated on a box with his head below the level of the bar, balm was laid upon his soul at sight of various zinc and copper fittings that bore a resemblance to armor-plate. The barkeeper took a seat comfortably upon an adjacent box.

"You see," he whispered, "this here Scratchy Wilson is a wonder with a gun —a perfect wonder; and when he goes on the wartrail, we hunt out holes— naturally. He's about the last one of the old gang that used to hang out along the river here. He's a terror when he's drunk. When he's sober he's all right—kind of simple—wouldn't hurt a fly—nicest fellow in town. But when he's drunk—whoo!"

There were periods of stillness. "I wish Jack Potter was back from San Anton'," said the barkeeper. "He shot Wilson up once—in the leg—and he would sail in and pull out the kinks in this thing."

Presently they heard from a distance the sound of a shot, followed by three wild yowls. It instantly removed a bond from the men in the darkened saloon. There was a shuffling of feet. They looked at each other. "Here he comes," they said.

III

A man in a maroon-colored flannel shirt, which had been purchased for purposes of decoration, and made principally by some Jewish women on the East Side of New York, rounded a corner and walked into the middle of the main street of Yellow Sky. In either hand the man held a long, heavy, blue-black revolver. Often he yelled, and these cries rang through a semblance of a deserted village, shrilly flying over the roofs in a volume that seemed to have no relation to the ordinary vocal strength of a man. It was as if the surrounding stillness formed the arch of a tomb over him. These cries of ferocious challenge rang against walls of silence. And his boots had red tops with gilded imprints, of the kind beloved in winter by little sledding boys on the hillsides of New England.

The man's face flamed in a rage begot of whiskey. His eyes, rolling, and yet keen for ambush, hunted the still doorways and windows. He walked with the creeping movement of the midnight cat. As it occurred to him, he roared menacing information. The long revolvers in his hands were as easy as straws; they were moved with an electric swiftness. The little fingers of each hand played sometimes in a musician's way. Plain from the low collar of the shirt, the cords of his neck straightened and sank, straightened and sank, as passion moved him. The only sounds were his terrible invitations. The calm adobes preserved their demeanor at the passing of this small thing in the middle of the street.

There was no offer of fight—no offer of fight. The man called to the sky. There were no attractions. He bellowed and fumed and swayed his revolvers here and everywhere.

The dog of the barkeeper of the Weary Gentleman Saloon had not appreciated the advance of events. He yet lay dozing in front of his master's door. At sight of the dog, the man paused and raised his revolver humorously. At sight of the man, the dog sprang up and walked diagonally away, with a sullen head, and growling. The man yelled, and the dog broke into a gallop. As it was about to enter an alley, there was a loud noise, a whistling, and something spat the ground directly before it. The dog screamed, and, wheeling in terror, galloped headlong in a new direction. Again there was a noise, a whistling, and sand was kicked viciously before it. Fear-stricken, the dog turned and flurried like an animal in a pen. The man stood laughing, his weapons at his hips.

Ultimately the man was attracted by the closed door of the Weary Gentleman Saloon. He went to it, and, hammering with a revolver, demanded drink.

The door remaining imperturbable, he picked a bit of paper from the walk, and nailed it to the framework with a knife. He then turned his back contemptuously upon this popular resort and, walking to the opposite side of the street, and spinning there on his heel quickly and lithely, fired at the bit of paper. He missed it by a half-inch. He swore at himself, and went away. Later he comfortably fusilladed the windows of his most intimate friend. The man was playing with this town; it was a toy for him.

But still there was no offer of fight. The name of Jack Potter, his ancient antagonist, entered his mind, and he concluded that it would be a glad thing if he should go to Potter's house, and by bombardment induce him to come out and fight. He moved in the direction of his desire, chanting Apache scalp-music.

When he arrived at it, Potter's house presented the same still front as had the other adobes. Taking up a strategic position, the man howled a challenge. But this house regarded him as might a great stone god. It gave no sign. After a decent wait, the man howled further challenges, mingling with them wonderful epithets.

Presently there came the spectacle of a man churning himself into deepest rage over the immobility of a house. He fumed at it as the winter wind attacks a prairie cabin in the North. To the distance there should have gone the sound of a tumult like the fighting of two hundred Mexicans. As necessity bade him, he paused for breath or to reload his revolvers.

IV

Potter and his bride walked sheepishly and with speed. Sometimes they laughed together shamefacedly and low.

"Next corner, dear," he said finally.

They put forth the efforts of a pair walking bowed against a strong wind. Potter was about to raise a finger to point the first appearance of the new home when, as they circled the corner, they came face to face with a man in a maroon-colored shirt, who was feverishly pushing cartridges into a large revolver. Upon the instant the man dropped his revolver to the ground and, like lightning, whipped another from its holster. The second weapon was aimed at the bridegroom's chest.

There was a silence. Potter's mouth seemed to be merely a grave for his tongue. He exhibited an instinct to at once loosen his arm from the woman's grip, and he dropped the bag to the sand. As for the bride, her face had gone as yellow as old cloth. She was a slave to hideous rites, gazing at the apparitional snake.

The two men faced each other at a distance of three paces. He of the revolver smiled with a new and quiet ferocity.

"Tried to sneak up on me," he said. "Tried to sneak up on me!" His eyes grew more baleful. As Potter made a slight movement, the man thrust his revolver venomously forward. "No; don't you do it, Jack Potter. Don't you move a finger toward a gun just yet. Don't you move an eyelash. The time has come for me to settle with you, and I'm goin' to do it my own way, and loaf along with no interferin'. So if you don't want a gun bent on you, just mind what I tell you."

Potter looked at his enemy. "I ain't got a gun on me, Scratchy," he said. "Honest, I ain't." He was stiffening and steadying, but yet somewhere at the back of his mind a vision of the Pullman floated: the sea-green figured velvet, the shining brass, silver, and glass, the wood that gleamed as darkly brilliant as the surface of a pool of oil—all the glory of the marriage, the environment of the new estate. "You know I fight when it comes to fighting, Scratchy Wilson; but I ain't got a gun on me. You'll have to do all the shootin' yourself."

His enemy's face went livid. He stepped forward, and lashed his weapon to and fro before Potter's chest. "Don't you tell me you ain't got no gun on you, you whelp. Don't tell me no lie like that. There ain't a man in Texas ever seen you without no gun. Don't take me for no kid." His eyes blazed with light, and his throat worked like a pump.

"I ain't takin' you for no kid," answered Potter. His heels had not moved an inch backward. "I'm takin' you for a damn fool. I tell you I ain't got a gun, and I ain't. If you're goin' to shoot me up, you better begin now; you'll never get a chance like this again."

So much enforced reasoning had told on Wilson's rage; he was calmer. "If you ain't got a gun, why ain't you got a gun?" he sneered. "Been to Sunday-school?"

"I ain't got a gun because I've just come from San Anton' with my wife. I'm married," said Potter. "And if I'd thought there was going to be any galoots like you prowling around when I brought my wife home, I'd had a gun, and don't you forget it."

"Married!" said Scratchy, not at all comprehending.

"Yes, married. I'm married," said Potter, distinctly.

"Married?" said Scratchy. Seemingly for the first time, he saw the drooping, drowning woman at the other man's side. "No!" he said. He was like a creature allowed a glimpse of another world. He moved a pace backward, and his arm, with the revolver, dropped to his side. "Is this the lady?" he asked.

"Yes; this is the lady," answered Potter.

There was another period of silence.

"Well," said Wilson at last, slowly, "I s'pose it's all off now."

"It's all off if you say so, Scratchy. You know I didn't make the trouble."
Potter lifted his valise.

"Well, I 'low it's off, Jack," said Wilson. He was looking at the ground.
"Married!" He was not a student of chivalry; it was merely that in the presence
of this foreign condition he was a simple child of the earlier plains. He picked
up his starboard revolver, and, placing both weapons in their holsters, he went
away. His feet made funnel-shaped tracks in the heavy sand.   (1898)

Henry James

MRS. MEDWIN

"Well, we *are* a pair!" the poor lady's visitor broke out to her, at the end
of her explanation, in a manner disconcerting enough. The poor lady was Miss
Cutter, who lived in South Audley Street, where she had an "upper half" so
concise that it had to pass, boldly, for convenient; and her visitor was her half-
brother, whom she had not seen for three years. She was remarkable for a
maturity of which every symptom might have been observed to be admirably
controlled, had not a tendency to stoutness just affirmed its independence. Her
present, no doubt, insisted too much on her past, but with the excuse, sufficiently
valid, that she must certainly once have been prettier. She was clearly not
contented with once—she wished to be prettier again. She neglected nothing that
could produce that illusion, and, being both fair and fat, dressed almost wholly
in black. When she added a little color it was not, at any rate, to her drapery.
Her small rooms had the peculiarity that everything they contained appeared
to testify with vividness to her position in society, quite as if they had been
furnished by the bounty of admiring friends. They were adorned indeed almost
exclusively with objects that nobody buys, as had more than once been remarked
by spectators of her own sex, for herself, and would have been luxurious if

luxury consisted mainly in photographic portraits slashed across with signatures, in baskets of flowers beribboned with the cards of passing compatriots, and in a neat collection of red volumes, blue volumes, alphabetical volumes, aids to London lucidity, of every sort, devoted to addresses and engagements. To be in Miss Cutter's tiny drawing-room, in short, even with Miss Cutter alone—should you by any chance have found her so—was somehow to be in the world and in a crowd. It was like an agency—it bristled with particulars.

That was what the tall, lean, loose gentleman lounging there before her might have appeared to read in the suggestive scene over which, while she talked to him, his eyes moved without haste and without rest. "Oh, come, Mamie!" he occasionally threw off; and the words were evidently connected with the impression thus absorbed. His comparative youth spoke of waste even as her positive—her too positive—spoke of economy. There was only one thing, that is, to make up in him for everything he had lost, though it was distinct enough indeed that this thing might sometimes serve. It consisted in the perfection of an indifference, an indifference at the present moment directed to the plea—a plea of inability, of pure destitution—with which his sister had met him. Yet it had even now a wider embrace, took in quite sufficiently all consequences of queerness, confessed in advance to the false note that, in such a setting, he almost excruciatingly constituted. He cared as little that he looked at moments all his impudence as that he looked all his shabbiness, all his cleverness, all his history. These different things were written in him—in his premature baldness, his seamed, strained face, the lapse from bravery of his long tawny moustache; above all, in his easy, friendly, universally acquainted eye, so much too sociable for mere conversation. What possible relation with him could be natural enough to meet it? He wore a scant, rough Inverness cape and a pair of black trousers, wanting in substance and marked with the sheen of time, that had presumably once served for evening use. He spoke with the slowness helplessly permitted to Americans—as something too slow to be stopped—and he repeated that he found himself associated with Miss Cutter in a harmony worthy of wonder. She had been telling him not only that she couldn't possibly give him ten pounds, but that his unexpected arrival, should he insist on being much in view, might seriously interfere with arrangements necessary to her own maintenance; on which he had begun by replying that he of course knew she had long ago spent her money, but that he looked to her now exactly because she had, without the aid of that convenience, mastered the art of life.

"I'd really go away with a fiver, my dear, if you'd only tell me how you do it. It's no use saying only, as you've always said, that 'people are very kind to you.' What the devil are they kind to you *for?*"

"Well, one reason is precisely that no particular inconvenience has hitherto been supposed to attach to me. I'm just what I am," said Mamie Cutter; "nothing less and nothing more. It's awkward to have to explain to you, which, moreover, I really needn't in the least. I'm clever and amusing and charming." She was uneasy and even frightened, but she kept her temper and met him with a grace of her own. "I don't think you ought to ask me more questions than I ask you."

"Ah, my dear," said the odd young man, "*I've* no mysteries. Why in the world, since it was what you came out for and have devoted so much of your time to, haven't you pulled it off? Why haven't you married?"

"Why haven't *you?*" she retorted. "Do you think that if I had it would have been better for you?—that my husband would for a moment have put up with you? Do you mind my asking you if you'll kindly go *now?*" she went on after a glance at the clock. "I'm expecting a friend, whom I must see alone, on a matter of great importance——"

"And my being seen with you may compromise your respectability or undermine your nerve?" He sprawled imperturbably in his place, crossing again, in another sense, his long black legs and showing, above his low shoes, an absurd reach of parti-coloured sock. "I take your point well enough, but mayn't you be after all quite wrong? If you can't do anything for me couldn't you at least do something *with* me? If it comes to that, I'm clever and amusing and charming too! I've been such an ass that you don't appreciate me. But people like me—I assure you they do. They usually don't know what an ass I've been; they only see the surface, which"—and he stretched himself afresh as she looked him up and down—"you *can* imagine them, can't you, rather taken with? I'm 'what I am' too; nothing less and nothing more. That's true of us as a family, you see. We *are* a crew!" He delivered himself serenely. His voice was soft and flat, his pleasant eyes, his simple tones tending to the solemn, achieved at moments that effect of quaintness which is, in certain connections, socially so known and enjoyed. "English people have quite a weakness for me—more than any others. I get on with them beautifully. I've always been with them abroad. They think me," the young man explained, "diabolically American."

"You!" Such stupidity drew from her a sigh of compassion.

Her companion apparently quite understood it. "Are you homesick, Mamie?" he asked, with wondering irrelevance.

The manner of the question made her for some reason, in spite of her preoccupations, break into a laugh. A shade of indulgence, a sense of other things, came back to her. "You *are* funny, Scott!"

"Well," remarked Scott, "that's just what I claim. But *are* you so homesick?" he spaciously inquired, not as if to a practical end, but from an easy play of intelligence.

"I'm just dying of it!" said Mamie Cutter.

"Why, so am I!" Her visitor had a sweetness of concurrence.

"We're the only decent people," Miss Cutter declared. "And I know. *You* don't—you can't; and I can't explain. Come in," she continued with a return of her impatience and an increase of her decision, "at seven sharp."

She had quitted her seat some time before, and now, to get him into motion, hovered before him while, still motionless, he looked up at her. Something intimate, in the silence, appeared to pass between them—a community of fatigue and failure and, after all, of intelligence. There was a final, cynical humour in it. It determined him, at any rate, at last, and he slowly rose, taking in again as he stood there the testimony of the room. He might have been counting the photographs, but he looked at the flowers with detachment. "Who's coming?"

"Mrs. Medwin."

"American?"

"Dear no!"

"Then what are you doing for her?"

"I work for everyone," she promptly returned.

"For everyone who pays? So I suppose. Yet isn't it only we who do pay?" There was a drollery, not lost on her, in the way his queer presence lent itself to his emphasized plural. "Do you consider that *you* do?"

At this, with his deliberation, he came back to his charming idea. "Only try me, and see if I can't be *made* to. Work me in." On her sharply presenting her back he stared a little at the clock. "If I come at seven may I stay to dinner?"

It brought her round again. "Impossible. I'm dining out."

"With whom?"

She had to think. "With Lord Considine."

"Oh, my eye!" Scott exclaimed.

She looked at him gloomily. "Is *that* sort of tone what makes you pay? I think you might understand," she went on, "that if you're to sponge on me successfully you musn't ruin me. I must have *some* remote resemblance to a lady."

"Yes? But why must *I?*" Her exasperated silence was full of answers, of which, however, his inimitable manner took no account. "You don't understand my real strength; I doubt if you even understand your own. You're clever, Mamie, but you're not so clever as I supposed. However," he pursued, "it's out of Mrs. Medwin that you'll get it."

"Get what?"

"Why, the cheque that will enable you to assist me."

On this, for a moment, she met his eyes. "If you'll come back at seven sharp— not a minute before, and not a minute after, I'll give you two five-pound notes."

He thought it over. "Whom are you expecting a minute after?"

It sent her to the window with a groan almost of anguish, and she answered nothing till she had looked at the street. "If you injure me, you know, Scott, you'll be sorry."

"I wouldn't injure you for the world. What I want to do in fact is really to help you, and I promise you that I won't leave you—by which I mean won't leave London—till I've effected something really pleasant for you. I like you, Mamie, because I like pluck; I like you much more than you like me. I like you very, *very* much." He had at last with this reached the door and opened it, but he remained with his hand on the latch. "What does Mrs. Medwin want of you?" he thus brought out.

She had come round to see him disappear, and in the relief of this prospect she again just indulged him. "The impossible."

He waited another minute. "And you're going to do it?"

"I'm going to do it," said Mamie Cutter.

"Well, then, that ought to be a haul. Call it *three* fivers!" he laughed. "At seven sharp." And at last he left her alone.

II

Miss Cutter waited till she heard the house-door close; after which, in a sightless, mechanical way, she moved about the room, readjusting various objects that he had not touched. It was as if his mere voice and accent had spoiled her form. But she was not left too long to reckon with these things, for Mrs. Medwin was promptly announced. This lady was not, more than her hostess, in the first flush of her youth; her appearance—the scattered remains of beauty manipulated by taste—resembled one of the light repasts in which the fragments of yesterday's dinner figure with a conscious ease that makes up for the want of presence. She was perhaps of an effect still too immediate to be called interesting, but she was candid, gentle and surprised—not fatiguingly surprised, only just in the right degree; and her white face—it was too white—with the fixed eyes, the somewhat touzled hair and the Louis Seize hat, might at the end of the very long neck have suggested the head of a princess carried, in a revolution, on a pike. She immediately took up the business that had brought her, with the air, however, of drawing from the omens then discernible less confidence than she had hoped. The complication lay in the fact that if it was Mamie's part to present the omens, that lady yet had so to colour them as to make her own service large. She perhaps overcoloured, for her friend gave way to momentary despair.

"What you mean is then that it's simply impossible?"

"Oh, no," said Mamie, with a qualified emphasis. "It's *possible*."

"But disgustingly difficult?"

"As difficult as you like."

"Then what can I do that I haven't done?"

"You can only wait a little longer."

"But that's just what I *have* done. I've done nothing else. I'm always waiting a little longer!"

Miss Cutter retained, in spite of this pathos, her grasp of the subject. "*The* thing, as I've told you, is for you first to be seen."

"But if people won't look at me?"

"They will."

"They *will*?" Mrs. Medwin was eager.

"They shall," her hostess went on. "It's their only having heard—without having seen."

"But if they stare straight the other way?" Mrs. Medwin continued to object. "You can't simply go up to them and twist their heads about."

"It's just what I can," said Mamie Cutter.

But her charming visitor, heedless for the moment of this attenuation, had found the way to put it. "It's the old story. You can't go into the water till you swim, and you can't swim till you go into the water. I can't be spoken to till I'm seen, but I can't be seen till I'm spoken to."

She met this lucidity, Miss Cutter, with but an instant's lapse. "You say I can't twist their heads about. But I *have* twisted them."

It had been quietly produced, but it gave her companion a jerk. "They say 'Yes'?"

She summed it up. "All but one. She says 'No.' "

Mrs. Medwin thought; then jumped. "Lady Wantridge?"

Miss Cutter, as more delicate, only bowed admission. "I shall see her either this afternoon or late to-morrow. But she has written."

Her visitor wondered again. "May I see her letter?"

"No." She spoke with decision. "But I shall square her."

"Then how?"

"Well"—and Miss Cutter, as if looking upward for inspiration, fixed her eyes awhile on the ceiling—"well, it will come to me."

Mrs. Medwin watched her—it was impressive. "And will *they* come to you— the others?" This question drew out the fact that they would—so far, at least, as they consisted of Lady Edward, Lady Bellhouse and Mrs. Pouncer, who had engaged to muster, at the signal of tea, on the 14th—prepared, as it were, for the worst. There was of course always the chance that Lady Wantridge might take the field in such force as to paralyse them, though that danger, at the same time, seemed inconsistent with her being squared. It didn't perhaps all quite ideally hang together; but what it sufficiently came to was that if she was the one who could do most *for* a person in Mrs. Medwin's position she was also the one who could do most against. It would therefore be distinctly what our friend familiarly spoke of as "collar-work." The effect of these mixed considera- tions was at any rate that Mamie eventually acquiesced in the idea, hand- somely thrown out by her client, that she should have an "advance" to go on with. Miss Cutter confessed that it seemed at times as if one scarce *could* go on; but the advance was, in spite of this delicacy, still more delicately made— made in the form of a banknote, several sovereigns, some loose silver and two coppers, the whole contents of her purse, neatly disposed by Mrs. Medwin on one of the tiny tables. It seemed to clear the air for deeper intimacies, the fruit of which was that Mamie, lonely, after all, in her crowd, and always more helpful than helped, eventually brought out that the way Scott had been going on was what seemed momentarily to overshadow her own power to do so.

"I've had a descent from him." But she had to explain. "My half-brother— Scott Homer. A wretch."

"What kind of a wretch?"

"Every kind. I lose sight of him at times—he disappears abroad. But he always turns up again, worse than ever."

"Violent?"

"No."

"Maudlin?"

"No."

"Only unpleasant?"

"No. Rather pleasant. Awfully clever—awfully travelled and easy."

"Then what's the matter with him?"

Mamie mused, hesitated—seemed to see a wide past. "I don't know."

"Something in the background?" Then as her friend was silent, "Something queer about cards?" Mrs. Medwin threw off.

"I don't know—and I don't want to!"

"Ah, well, I'm sure *I* don't," Mrs. Medwin returned with spirit. The note of sharpness was perhaps also a little in the observation she made as she gathered herself to go. "Do you mind my saying something?"

Mamie took her eyes quickly from the money on the little stand. "You may say what you like."

"I only mean that anything awkward you may have to keep out of the way does seem to make more wonderful, doesn't it, that you should have got just where you are? I allude, you know, to your position."

"I see." Miss Cutter somewhat coldly smiled. "To my power."

"So awfully remarkable in an American."

"Ah, you like us so."

Mrs. Medwin candidly considered. "But we don't, dearest."

Her companion's smile brightened. "Then why do you come to me?"

"Oh, I like *you!*" Mrs. Medwin made out.

"Then that's it. There are no 'Americans.' It's always 'you.' "

"Me?" Mrs. Medwin looked lovely, but a little muddled.

"*Me!*" Mamie Cutter laughed. "But if you like me, you dear thing, you can judge if I like *you*." She gave her a kiss to dismiss her. "I'll see you again when I've seen her."

"Lady Wantridge? I hope so, indeed. I'll turn up late to-morrow, if you don't catch me first. Has it come to you yet?" the visitor, now at the door, went on.

"No; but it will. There's time."

"Oh, a little less every day!"

Miss Cutter had approached the table and glanced again at the gold and silver and the note, not indeed absolutely overlooked the two coppers. "The balance," she put it, "the day after?"

"That very night, if you like."

"Then count on me."

"Oh, if I didn't——!" But the door closed on the dark idea. Yearningly then, and only when it had done so, Miss Cutter took up the money.

She went out with it ten minutes later, and, the calls on her time being many, remained out so long that at half-past six she had not come back. At that hour, on the other hand, Scott Homer knocked at her door, where her maid, who opened it with a weak pretence of holding it firm, ventured to announce to him, as a lesson well learnt, that he had not been expected till seven. No lesson, none the less, could prevail against his native art. He pleaded fatigue, her, the maid's, dreadful depressing London, and the need to curl up somewhere. If she would just leave him quiet half an hour that old sofa upstairs would do for it, of which he took quickly such effectual possession that when, five minutes later, she peeped, nervous for her broken vow, into the drawing-room, the faithless young woman found him extended at his length and peacefully asleep.

III

The situation before Miss Cutter's return developed in other directions still, and when that event took place, at a few minutes past seven, these circumstances were, by the foot of the stair, between mistress and maid, the subject of some interrogative gasps and scared admissions. Lady Wantridge had arrived shortly after the interloper, and wishing, as she said, to wait, had gone straight up in spite of being told he was lying down.

"She distinctly understood he was there?"

"Oh, yes, ma'am, I thought it right to mention."

"And what did you call him?"

"Well, ma'am, I thought it unfair to *you* to call him anything but a gentleman."

Mamie took it all in, though there might well be more of it than one could quickly embrace. "But if she has had time," she flashed, "to find out he isn't one?"

"Oh, ma'am, she had a quarter of an hour."

"Then she isn't with him still?"

"No, ma'am; she came down again at last. She rang, and I saw her here, and she said she wouldn't wait longer."

Miss Cutter darkly mused. "Yet had already waited——?"

"Quite a quarter."

"Mercy on us!" She began to mount. Before reaching the top, however, she reflected that quite a quarter was long if Lady Wantridge had only been shocked. On the other hand, it was short if she had only been pleased. But how *could* she have been pleased? The very essence of their actual crisis was just that there was no pleasing her. Mamie had but to open the drawing-room door indeed to perceive that this was not true at least of Scott Homer, who was horribly cheerful.

Miss Cutter expressed to her brother without reserve her sense of the constitutional, the brutal selfishness that had determined his mistimed return. It had taken place, in violation of their agreement, exactly at the moment when it was most cruel to her that he should be there, and if she must now completely wash her hands of him he had only himself to thank. She had come in flushed with resentment and for a moment had been voluble; but it would have been striking that, though the way he received her might have seemed but to aggravate, it presently justified him by causing their relation really to take a stride. He had the art of confounding those who would quarrel with him by reducing them to the humiliation of an irritated curiosity.

"What *could* she have made of you?" Mamie demanded.

"My dear girl, she's not a woman who's eager to make too much of anything— anything, I mean, that will prevent her from doing as she likes, what she takes into her head. Of course," he continued to explain, "if it's something she doesn't want to do, she'll make as much as Moses."

Mamie wondered if that was the way he talked to her visitor, but felt obliged to own to his acuteness. It was an exact description of Lady Wantridge, and she was conscious of tucking it away for future use in a corner of her miscellaneous little mind. She withheld, however, all present acknowledgment, only addressing him another question. "Did you really get on with her?"

"Have you still to learn, darling—I can't help again putting it to you—that I get on with everybody? That's just what I don't seem able to drive into you. Only see how I get on with *you*."

She almost stood corrected. "What I mean is, of course, whether——"

"Whether she made love to me? Shyly, yet—or because—shamefully? She would certainly have liked awfully to stay."

"Then why didn't she?"

"Because, on account of some other matter—and I could see it was true—she hadn't time. Twenty minutes—she was here less—were all she came to give you. So don't be afraid I've frightened her away. She'll come back."

Mamie thought it over. "Yet you didn't go with her to the door?"

"She wouldn't let me, and I know when to do what I'm told—quite as much as what I'm not told. She wanted to find out about me. I mean from your little creature; a pearl of fidelity, by the way."

"But what on earth did she come up for?" Mamie again found herself appealing, and, just by that fact, showing her need of help.

"Because she always goes up." Then, as, in the presence of this rapid generalisation, to say nothing of that of such a relative altogether, Miss Cutter could only show as comparatively blank: "I mean she knows when to go up and when to come down. She has instincts; she didn't know whom you might have up here. It's a kind of compliment to you anyway. Why, Mamie," Scott pursued, "you don't know the curiosity we any of us inspire. You wouldn't believe what I've seen. The bigger bugs they are the more they're on the look-out."

Mamie still followed, but at a distance. "The look-out for what?"

"Why, for anything that will help them to live. You've been here all this time without making out then, about them, what I've had to pick out as I can? They're dead, don't you see? And *we're* alive."

"You? Oh!"—Mamie almost laughed about it.

"Well, they're a worn-out old lot, anyhow; they've used up their resources. They do look out; and I'll do them the justice to say they're not afraid—not even of me!" he continued as his sister again showed something of the same irony. "Lady Wantridge, at any rate, wasn't; that's what I mean by her having made love to me. She does what she likes. Mind it, you know." He was by this time fairly teaching her to know one of her best friends, and when, after it, he had come back to the great point of his lesson—that of her failure, through feminine inferiority, practically to grasp the truth that their being just as they were, he and she, was the real card for them to play—when he had renewed that reminder he left her absolutely in a state of dependence. Her impulse to press him on the subject of Lady Wantridge dropped; it was as if she had felt that, whatever had taken place, something would somehow come of it. She was to be, in a manner, disappointed, but the impression helped to keep her over to the next morning, when, as Scott had foretold, his new acquaintance did reappear, explaining to Miss Cutter that she had acted the day before to gain time and that she even now sought to gain it by not waiting longer. What, she promptly intimated she had asked herself, could that friend be thinking of? She must show where she stood before things had gone too far. If she had brought her answer without more delay she wished to make it sharp. Mrs. Medwin? Never! "No, my dear— not I. *There* I stop."

Mamie had known it would be "collar-work," but somehow now, at the beginning, she felt her heart sink. It was not that she had expected to carry the position with a rush, but that, as always after an interval, her visitor's defences really loomed—and quite, as it were, to the material vision—too large. She was always planted with them, voluminous, in the very centre of the passage; was like a person accommodated with a chair in some unlawful place at the theatre. She wouldn't move and you couldn't get round. Mamie's calculation indeed had not been on getting round; she was obliged to recognise that, too foolishly and fondly, she had dreamed of producing a surrender. Her dream had been the fruit of her need; but, conscious that she was even yet unequipped for pressure, she felt, almost for the first time in her life, superficial and crude. She was to be paid—but with what was she, to that end, to pay? She had engaged to find an answer to this question, but the answer had not, according to her promise, "come." And Lady Wantridge meanwhile massed herself, and there was no view of her that didn't show her as verily, by some process too obscure to be traced, the hard depository of the social law. She was no younger, no fresher, no stronger, really, than any of them; she was only, with a kind of haggard fineness, a sharpened taste for life, and, with all sorts of things behind and beneath her, more abysmal and more immoral, more secure and more impertinent. The points she made were two in number. One was that she absolutely declined; the other was that she quite doubted if Mamie herself had measured the job. The thing couldn't be done. But say it *could* be; was Mamie quite the person to do it? To this Miss Cutter, with a sweet smile, replied that she quite understood how little she might seem so. "I'm only one of the persons to whom it has appeared that *you* are."

"Then who are the others?"

"Well, to begin with, Lady Edward, Lady Bellhouse and Mrs. Pouncer."

"Do you mean that they'll come to meet her?"

"I've seen them, and they've promised."

"To come, of course," Lady Wantridge said, "if *I* come."

Her hostess hesitated. "Oh, of course, you could prevent them. But I should take it as awfully kind of you not to. *Won't* you do this for me?" Mamie pleaded.

Her friend looked about the room very much as Scott had done. "Do they really understand what it's *for?*"

"Perfectly. So that she may call."

"And what good will that do her?"

Miss Cutter faltered, but she presently brought it out. "Of course what one hopes is that you'll ask her,"

"Ask her to call?"

"Ask her to dine. Ask her, if you'd be so *truly* sweet, for a Sunday, or some-thing of that sort, and even if only in one of your *most* mixed parties, to Catchmore."

Miss Cutter felt the less hopeful after this effort in that her companion only showed a strange good nature. And it was not the amiability of irony; yet it *was* amusement. "Take Mrs. Medwin into my family?"

"Some day, when you're taking forty others."

"Ah, but what I don't see is what it does for *you*. You're already so welcome among us that you can scarcely improve your position even by forming for us the most delightful relation."

"Well, I know how dear you are," Mamie Cutter replied; "but one has, after all, more than one side, and more than one sympathy. I like her, you know." And even at this Lady Wantridge was not shocked; she showed that ease and blandness which were her way, unfortunately, of being most impossible. She remarked that *she* might listen to such things, because she was clever enough for them not to matter; only Mamie should take care how she went about saying them at large. When she became definite, however, in a minute, on the subject of the public facts, Miss Cutter soon found herself ready to make her own concession. Of course, she didn't dispute *them:* there they were; they were unfortunately on record, and nothing was to be done about them but to— Mamie found it, in truth, at this point, a little difficult.

"Well, what? Pretend already to have forgotten them?"

"Why not, when you've done it in so many other cases?"

"There *are* no other cases so bad. One meets them, at any rate, as they come. Some you can manage, others you can't. It's no use, you must give them up. They're past patching; there's nothing to be done with them. There's nothing, accordingly, to be done with Mrs. Medwin but to put her off." And Lady Wantridge rose to her height.

"Well, you know, I *do* do things," Mamie quavered with a smile so strained that it partook of exaltation.

"You help people? Oh yes, I've known you to do wonders. But stick," said Lady Wantridge with strong and cheerful emphasis, "to your Americans!"

Miss Cutter, gazing, got up. "You don't do justice, Lady Wantridge, to your own compatriots. Some of them are really charming. Besides," said Mamie, "working for mine often strikes me, so far as the interest—the inspiration and excitement, don't you know?—go, as rather too easy. You all, as I constantly have occasion to say, like us so!"

Her companion frankly weighed it. "Yes; it takes that to account for your position. I've always thought of you, nevertheless, as keeping, for their benefit, a regular working agency. They come to you, and you place them. There remains, I confess," her ladyship went on in the same free spirit, "the great wonder——"

"Of how I first placed my poor little self? Yes," Mamie bravely conceded, "when *I* began there was no agency. I just worked my passage. I didn't even come to *you*, did I? You never noticed me till, as Mrs. Short Stokes says,

'I was, 'way up!' Mrs. Medwin," she threw in, "can't get over it." Then, as her friend looked vague: "Over my social situation."

"Well, it's no great flattery to you to say," Lady Wantridge good-humouredly returned, "that she certainly can't hope for one resembling it." Yet it really seemed to spread there before them. "You simply *made* Mrs. Short Stokes."

"In spite of her name!" Mamie smiled.

"Oh, your names———! In spite of everything."

"Ah, I'm something of an artist." With which, and a relapse marked by her wistful eyes into the gravity of the matter, she supremely fixed her friend. She felt how little she minded betraying at last the extremity of her need, and it was out of this extremity that her appeal proceeded. "Have I really had your last word? It means so much to me."

Lady Wantridge came straight to the point. "You mean you depend on it?"

"Awfully!"

"Is it all you have?"

"All. Now."

"But Mrs. Short Stokes and the others—'rolling.' aren't they? Don't they pay up?"

"Ah," sighed Mamie, "if it wasn't for them——!"

Lady Wantridge perceived. "You've had so much?"

"I couldn't have gone on."

"Then what do you do with it all?"

"Oh, most of it goes back to them. There are all sorts, and it's all help. Some of them have nothing."

"Oh, if you feed the hungry," Lady Wantridge laughed, "you're indeed in a great way of business. Is Mrs. Medwin"—her transition was immediate—"really rich?"

"Really. He left her everything."

"So that if I do say 'yes'——"

"It will quite set me up."

"I see—and how much more responsible it makes one! But I'd rather myself give you the money."

"Oh!" Mamie coldly murmured.

"You mean I mayn't suspect your prices? Well, I daresay I don't! But I'd rather give you ten pounds."

"Oh!" Mamie repeated in a tone that sufficiently covered her prices. The question was in every way larger. "Do you *never* forgive?" she reproachfully inquired. The door opened, however, at the moment she spoke, and Scott Homer presented himself.

IV

Scott Homer wore exactly, to his sister's eyes, the aspect he had worn the day before, and it also formed, to her sense, the great feature of his impartial greeting.

"How d'ye do, Mamie? How d'ye do, Lady Wantridge?"

"How d'ye do again?" Lady Wantridge replied with an equanimity striking to her hostess. It was as if Scott's own had been contagious; it was almost indeed as if she had seen him before. *Had* she ever so seen him—before the previous day? While Miss Cutter put to herself this question her visitor, at all events, met the one she had previously uttered.

"Ever 'forgive'?" this personage echoed in a tone that made as little account as possible of the interruption. "Dear, yes! The people I *have* forgiven!" She laughed—perhaps a little nervously; and she was now looking at Scott. The way she looked at him was precisely what had already had its effect for his sister. "The people I can!"

"Can you forgive *me?*" asked Scott Homer.

She took it so easily. "But—what?"

Mamie interposed; she turned directly to her brother. "Don't try her. Leave it so." She had had an inspiration; it was the most extraordinary thing in the world. "Don't try *him*"—she had turned to their companion. She looked grave, sad, strange. "Leave it so." Yes, it was a distinct inspiration, which she couldn't have explained, but which had come, prompted by something she had caught—the extent of the recognition expressed—in Lady Wantridge's face. It had come absolutely of a sudden, straight out of the opposition of the two figures before her—quite as if a concussion had struck a light. The light was helped by her quickened sense that her friend's silence on the incident of the day before showed some sort of consciousness. She looked surprised. "Do you know my brother?"

"*Do* I know you?" Lady Wantridge asked of him.

"No, Lady Wantridge," Scott pleasantly confessed, "not one little mite!"

"Well, then, if you *must* go——!" and Mamie offered her a hand. "But I'll go down with you. Not *you!*" she launched at her brother, who immediately effaced himself. His way of doing so—and he had already done so, as for Lady Wantridge, in respect to their previous encounter—struck her even at the moment as an instinctive, if slightly blind, tribute to her possession of an idea; and as such, in its celerity, made her so admire him and their common wit, that, on the spot, she more than forgave him his queerness. He was right. He could be as queer as he liked! The queerer the better! It was at the foot of the stairs, when she had got her guest down, that what she had assured Mrs. Medwin would come did indeed come. "*Did* you meet him here yesterday?"

"Dear, yes. Isn't he too funny?"

"Yes," said Mamie gloomily. "He *is* funny. But had you ever met him before?"

"Dear, no!"

"Oh!"—and Mamie's tone might have meant many things.

Lady Wantridge, however, after all, easily overlooked it. "I only knew he was one of your odd Americans. That's why, when I heard yesterday, here, that he was up there awaiting your return, I didn't let that prevent thought he might be. He certainly," her ladyship laughed, "*is,*"

"Yes, he's very American," Mamie went on in the same way.

"As you say, we *are* fond of you! Good-bye," said Lady Wantridge.

But Mamie had not half done with her. She felt more and more—or she hoped at least—that she looked strange. She *was*, no doubt, if it came to that, strange. "Lady Wantridge," she almost convulsively broke out, "I don't know whether you'll understand me, but I seem to feel that I must act with you— I don't know what to call it!—responsibly. He *is* my brother."

"Surely—and why not?" Lady Wantridge stared. "He's the image of you!"

"Thank you!"—and Mamie was stranger than ever.

"Oh, he's good-looking. He's handsome, my dear. Oddly—but distinctly!" Her ladyship was for treating it much as a joke.

But Mamie, all sombre, would have none of this. She boldly gave him up. "I think he's awful."

"He is indeed—delightfully. And where *do* you get your ways of saying things? It isn't anything—and the things aren't anything. But it's so droll."

"Don't let yourself, all the same," Mamie consistently pursued, "be carried away by it. The thing can't be done—simply."

Lady Wantridge wondered. " 'Done simply'?"

"Done at all."

"But what can't be?"

"Why, what you might think—from his pleasantness. What he spoke of your doing for him."

Lady Wantridge recalled. "Forgiving him?"

"He asked you if you couldn't. But you can't. It's too dreadful for me, as so near a relation, to have, loyally—loyally to *you*—to say it. But he's impossible."

It was so portentously produced that her ladyship had somehow to meet it. "What's the matter with him?"

"I don't know."

"Then what's the matter with *you?*" Lady Wantridge inquired.

"It's because I *won't* know," Mamie—not without dignity—explained.

"Then *I* won't either!"

"Precisely. Don't. It's something," Mamie pursued, with some inconsequence, "that—somewhere or other, at some time or other—he appears to have done; something that has made a difference in his life."

" 'Something'?" Lady Wantridge echoed again. "What kind of thing?"

Mamie looked up at the light above the door through which the London sky was doubly dim. "I haven't the least idea."

"Then what kind of difference?"

Mamie's gaze was still at the light. "The difference you see."

Lady Wantridge, rather obligingly, seemed to ask herself what she saw. "But I don't see any! It seems, at least," she added, "such an amusing one! And he has such nice eyes."

"Oh, *dear* eyes!" Mamie conceded; but with too much sadness, for the moment, about the connections of the subject, to say more.

It almost forced her companion, after an instant, to proceed. "Do you mean he can't go home?"

She weighed her responsibility. "I only make out—more's the pity!—that he doesn't."

"Is it then something too terrible——?"

She thought again. "I don't know what—for men—*is* too terrible."

"Well then, as you don't know what 'is' for women either—good-bye!" her visitor laughed.

It practically wound up the interview; which, however terminating thus on a considerable stir of the air, was to give Miss Cutter, the next few days, the sense of being much blown about. The degree to which to begin with, she had been drawn—or perhaps rather pushed—closer to Scott was marked in the brief colloquy that, on her friend's departure, she had with him. He had immediately said it. "You'll see if she doesn't ask me down!"

"So soon?"

"Oh, I've known them at places—at Cannes, at Pau, at Shanghai—to do it sooner still. I always know when they will. You *can't* make out they don't love me!" He spoke almost plaintively, as if he wished she could.

"Then I don't see why it hasn't done you more good."

"Why, Mamie," he patiently reasoned, "what more good *could* it? As I tell you," he explained, "it has just been my life."

"Then why do you come to me for money?"

"Oh, they don't give me *that!*" Scott returned.

"So that it only means then, after all, that I, at the best, must keep you up?"

He fixed on her the nice eyes that Lady Wantridge admired. "Do you mean to tell me that already—at this very moment—I am not distinctly keeping *you?*"

She gave him back his look. "Wait till she *has* asked you, and then," Mamie added, "decline."

Scott, not too grossly, wondered. "As acting for *you?*"

Mamie's next injunction was answer enough. "But *before*—yes—call."

He took it in. "Call—but decline. Good."

"The rest," she said, "I leave to you." And she left it, in fact, with such confidence that for a couple of days she was not only conscious of no need to give Mrs. Medwin another turn of the screw, but positively evaded, in her fortitude, the reappearance of that lady. It was not till the third day that she waited upon her, finding her, as she had expected, tense.

"Lady Wantridge *will*——?"

"Yes, though she says she won't."

"She says she won't? O—oh!" Mrs. Medwin moaned.

"Sit tight all the same. I *have* her!"

"But how?"

"Through Scott—whom she wants."

"Your bad brother!" Mrs. Medwin stared. "What does she want of h——?"

"To amuse them at Catchmore. Anything for that. And he *would*. But he sha'n't!" Mamie declared.

"He sha'n't go unless she comes. She must meet you first—You're my condition."

"O—o—oh!" Mrs. Medwin's tone was a wonder of hope and fear. "But doesn't he want to go?"

"He wants what *I* want. She draws the line at you. I draw the line at *him*."

"But she—doesn't she mind that he's bad?"

It was so artless that Mamie laughed. "No; it doesn't touch her. Besides, perhaps he isn't. It isn't as for *you*—people seem not to know. He has settled everything, at all events, by going to see her. It's before her that he's the thing she will have to have."

"Have to?"

"For Sundays in the country. A feature—*the* feature."

"So she has asked him?"

"Yes; and he has declined."

"For *me?*" Mrs. Medwin panted.

"For me," said Mamie, on the doorstep. "But I don't leave him for long." Her hansom had waited. "She'll come."

Lady Wantridge did come. She met in South Audley Street, on the fourteenth, at tea, the ladies whom Mamie had named to her, together with three or four others, and it was rather a masterstroke for Miss Cutter that, if Mrs. Medwin was modestly present, Scott Homer was as markedly not. This occasion, however, is a medal that would take rare casting, as would also, for that matter, even the minor light and shade, the lower relief, of the pecuniary transaction that Mrs. Medwin's flushed gratitude scarce awaited the dispersal of the company munificently to complete. A new understanding indeed, on the spot rebounded from it, the conception of which, in Mamie's mind, had promptly bloomed. "He sha'n't go *now* unless he takes you." Then, as her fancy always moved quicker for her client than her client's own—"Down with him to Catchmore! When he goes to amuse them, *you*," she comfortably declared, "shall amuse them too." Mrs. Medwin's response was again rather oddly divided, but she was sufficiently intelligible when it came to meeting the intimation that this latter would be an opportunity involving a separate fee. "Say," Mamie had suggested, "the same."

"Very well; the same."

The knowledge that it was to be the same had perhaps something to do, also, with the obliging spirit in which Scott eventually went. It was all, at the last, rather hurried—a party rapidly got together for the Grand Duke, who was in England but for the hour, who had good-naturedly proposed himself, and who liked his parties small, intimate and funny. This one was of the smallest, and it was finally judged to conform neither too little nor too much to the other conditions—after a brief whirlwind of wires and counterwires, and an iterated waiting of hansoms at various doors—to include Mrs. Medwin. It was from Catchmore itself that, snatching a moment on the wondrous Sunday afternoon, this lady had the harmonious thought of sending the new cheque. She was in bliss enough, but her scribble none the less intimated that it was Scott who amused them most. He *was* the feature.   (1903)

James Joyce

ARABY

North Richmond Street, being blind, was a quiet street except at the hour when the Christian Brothers' School set the boys free. An uninhabited house of two storeys stood at the blind end, detached from its neighbours in a square ground. The other houses of the street, conscious of decent lives within them, gazed at one another with brown imperturbable faces.

The former tenant of our house, a priest, had died in the back drawing-room. Air, musty from having been long enclosed, hung in all the rooms, and the waste room behind the kitchen was littered with old useless papers. Among these I found a few paper-covered books, the pages of which were curled and damp: *The Abbot*, by Walter Scott, *The Devout Communicant* and *The Memoirs of Vidocq*. I liked the last best, because its leaves were yellow. The wild garden behind the house contained a central apple-tree and a few straggling bushes, under one of which I found the late tenant's rusty bicycle-pump. He had been a very charitable priest; in his will he had left all his money to institutions and the furniture of his house to his sister.

When the short days of winter came, dusk fell before we had well eaten our dinners. When we met in the street, the houses had grown sombre. The space of sky above us was the colour of ever-changing violet, and towards it the lamps of the street lifted their feeble lanterns. The cold air stung us and we played till our bodies glowed. Our shouts echoed in the silent street. The career of our play brought us through the dark muddy lanes behind the houses where we ran the gauntlet of the rough tribes from the cottages, to the back doors of the dark dripping gardens where odours arose from the ashpits, to the dark odorous stables where a coachman smoothed and combed the horse or shook music from the buckled harness. When we returned to the street, light from the kitchen windows had filled the areas. If my uncle was seen turning the corner, we hid in the shadow until we had seen him safely housed. Or if Mangan's sister came out on the doorstep to call her brother in to his tea, we watched her from our shadow peer up and down the street. We waited to see whether she would remain or go in, and, if she remained, we left our shadow and walked up to Mangan's steps resignedly. She was waiting for us, her figure defined by the light from the half-opened door. Her brother always teased her before he obeyed, and I stood by the railings looking at her. Her dress swung as she moved her body, and the soft rope of her hair tossed from side to side.

Every morning I lay on the floor in the front parlour watching her door. The blind was pulled down to within an inch of the sash, so that I could not be seen. When she came out on the doorstep, my heart leaped. I ran to the hall, seized my books, and followed her. I kept her brown figure always in my eye, and, when we came near the point at which our ways diverged, I quickened my pace and passed her. This happened morning after morning. I had never spoken to her, except for a few casual words, and yet her name was like a summons to all my foolish blood.

Her image accompanied me even in places the most hostile to romance. On Saturday evenings, when my aunt went marketing, I had to go to carry some of the parcels. We walked through the flaring streets, jostled by drunken men and bargaining women, amid the curses of labourers, the shrill litanies of shop-boys who stood on guard by the barrels of pigs' cheeks, the nasal chanting of street-singers, who sang a *come-all-you* about O'Donovan Rossa, or a ballad about the troubles in our native land. These noises converged in a single sensation of life for me: I imagined that I bore my chalice safely through a throng of foes. Her name sprang to my lips at moments in strange prayers and praises which I myself did not understand. My eyes were often full of tears (I could not tell why) and at times a flood from my heart seemed to pour itself out into my bosom. I thought little of the future. I did not know whether I would ever speak to her or not, or, if I spoke to her, how I could tell her of my confused adoration. But my body was like a harp, and her words and gestures were like fingers running upon the wires.

One evening I went into the back drawing-room, in which the priest had died. It was a dark rainy evening, and there was no sound in the house. Through one of the broken panes I heard the rain impinge upon the earth, the fine incessant needles of water playing in the sodden beds. Some distant lamp or lighted window gleamed below me. I was thankful that I could see so little. All my senses seemed to desire to veil themselves, and, feeling that I was about to slip from them, I pressed the palms of my hands together until they trembled, murmuring: *'O love! O love!'* many times.

At last she spoke to me. When she addressed the first words to me, I was so confused that I did not know what to answer. She asked me was I going to *Araby*. I forget whether I answered yes or no. It would be a splendid bazaar; she said she would love to go.

"And why can't you?" I asked.

While she spoke, she turned a silver bracelet round and round her wrist. She could not go, she said, because there would be a retreat that week in her convent. Her brother and two other boys were fighting for their caps, and I was alone at the railings. She held one of the spikes, bowing her head towards me. The light from the lamp opposite our door caught the white curve of her neck, lit up her hair that rested there, and, falling, lit up the hand upon the railing. It fell over one side of her dress and caught the white border of a petticoat, just visible as she stood at ease.

"It's well for you," she said.

"If I go," I said, "I will bring you something."

What innumerable follies laid waste my waking and sleeping thoughts after that evening! I wished to annihilate the tedious intervening days. I chafed against the work of school. At night in my bedroom and by day in the classroom her image came between me and the page I strove to read. The syllables of the word *Araby* were called to me through the silence in which my soul luxuriated and cast an Eastern enchantment over me. I asked for leave to go to the bazaar on Saturday night. My aunt was surprised and hoped it was not some Freemason affair. I answered few questions in class. I watched my master's face pass from amiability to sternness; he hoped I was not beginning to idle. I could not call my wandering thoughts together. I had hardly any patience with the serious work of life, which, now that it stood between me and my desire, seemed to me child's play, ugly monotonous child's play.

On Saturday morning I reminded my uncle that I wished to go to the bazaar in the evening. He was fussing at the hallstand, looking for the hat-brush, and answered me curtly:

"Yes, boy, I know."

As he was in the hall, I could not go into the front parlour and lie at the window. I left the house in bad humour and walked slowly towards the school. The air was pitilessly raw, and already my heart misgave me.

When I came home to dinner, my uncle had not yet been home. Still, it was early. I sat staring at the clock for some time, and, when its ticking began to irritate me, I left the room. I mounted the staircase and gained the upper part of the house. The high cold empty gloomy rooms liberated me and I went from room to room singing. From the front window I saw my companions playing below in the street. Their cries reached me weakened and indistinct, and, leaning my forehead against the cool glass, I looked over at the dark house where she lived. I may have stood there for an hour, seeing nothing but the brown-clad figure cast by my imagination, touched discreetly by the lamplight at the curved neck, at the hand upon the railings, and at the border below the dress.

When I came downstairs again, I found Mrs. Mercer sitting at the fire. She was an old garrulous woman, a pawnbroker's widow, who collected used stamps for some pious purpose. I had to endure the gossip of the tea-table. The meal was prolonged beyond an hour, and still my uncle did not come. Mrs. Mercer stood up to go: she was sorry she couldn't wait any longer, but it was after eight o'clock, and she did not like to be out late, as the night air was bad for her. When she had gone, I began to walk up and down the room, clenching my fists. My aunt said:

"I'm afraid you may put off your bazaar for this night of Our Lord."

At nine o'clock I heard my uncle's latchkey in the hall-door. I heard him talking to himself and heard the hall-stand rocking when it had received the weight of his overcoat. I could interpret these signs. When he was midway through his dinner, I asked him to give me the money to go to the bazaar. He had forgotten.

"The people are in bed and after their first sleep now," he said.

I did not smile. My aunt said to him energetically:

"Can't you give him the money and let him go? You've kept him late enough as it is."

My uncle said he was very sorry he had forgotten. He said he believed in the old saying: "All work and no play makes Jack a dull boy." He asked me where I was going, and, when I had told him a second time, he asked me did I know *The Arab's Farewell to His Steed*. When I left the kitchen, he was about to recite the opening lines of the piece to my aunt.

I held a florin tightly in my hand as I strode down Buckingham Street towards the station. The sight of the streets thronged with buyers and glaring with gas recalled to me the purpose of my journey. I took my seat in a third-class carriage of a deserted train. After an intolerable delay the train moved out of the station slowly. It crept onward among ruinous houses and over the twinkling river. At Westland Row Station a crowd of people pressed to the carriage doors; but the porters moved them back, saying that it was a special train for the bazaar. I remained alone in the bare carriage. In a few minutes the train drew up beside an improvised wooden platform. I passed out on to the road and saw by the lighted dial of a clock that it was ten minutes to ten. In front of me was a large building which displayed the magical name.

I could not find any sixpenny entrance, and, fearing that the bazaar would be closed, I passed in quickly through a turnstile, handing a shilling to a weary-looking man. I found myself in a big hall girdled at half its height by a gallery. Nearly all the stalls were closed and the greater part of the hall was in darkness. I recognised a silence like that which pervades a church after a service. I walked into the centre of the bazaar timidly. A few people were gathered about the stalls which were still open. Before a curtain, over which the words *Café Chantant* were written in coloured lamps, two men were counting money on a salver. I listened to the fall of the coins.

Remembering with difficulty why I had come, I went over to one of the stalls and examined porcelain vases and flowered tea-sets. At the door of the stall a young lady was talking and laughing with two young gentlemen. I remarked their English accents and listened vaguely to their conversation.

"O, I never said such a thing!"

"O, but you did!"

"O, but I didn't!"

"Didn't she say that?"

"Yes. I heard her."

"O, there's a . . . fib!"

Observing me, the young lady came over and asked me did I wish to buy anything. The tone of her voice was not encouraging; she seemed to have spoken to me out of a sense of duty. I looked humbly at the great jars that stood like eastern guards at either side of the dark entrance to the stall and murmured:

"No, thank you."

The young lady changed the position of one of the vases and went back to the two young men. They began to talk of the same subject. Once or twice the young lady glanced at me over her shoulder.

I lingered before her stall, though I knew my stay was useless, to make my interest in her wares seem the more real. Then I turned away slowly and walked down the middle of the bazaar. I allowed the two pennies to fall against the sixpence in my pocket. I heard a voice call from one end of the gallery that the light was out. The upper part of the hall was now completely dark.

Gazing up into the darkness, I saw myself as a creature driven and derided by vanity; and my eyes burned with anguish and anger. (1914)

Katherine Mansfield

MISS BRILL

Although it was so brilliantly fine—the blue sky powdered with gold and great spots of light like white wine splashed over the Jardins Publiques—Miss Brill was glad that she had decided on her fur. The air was motionless, but when you opened your mouth there was just a faint chill, like a chill from a glass of iced water before you sip, and now and again a leaf came drifting—from nowhere, from the sky. Miss Brill put up her hand and touched her fur. Dear little thing! It was nice to feel it again. She had taken it out of its box that afternoon, shaken out the moth-powder, given it a good brush, and rubbed the life back into the dim little eyes. "What has been happening to me?" said the sad little eyes. Oh, how sweet it was to see them snap at her again from the red eiderdown! . . . But the nose, which was of some black composition, wasn't at all firm. It must have had a knock, somehow. Never mind—a little dab of black sealing-wax when the time came—when it was absolutely necessary. . . . Little rogue! Yes, she really felt like that about it. Little rogue biting its tail just by her left ear. She could have taken it off and laid it on her lap and stroked it. She felt a tingling in her hands and arms, but that came from walking, she supposed. And when she breathed, something light and sad—no, not sad, exactly—something gentle seemed to move in her bosom.

There were a number of people out this afternoon, far more than last Sunday. And the band sounded louder and gayer. That was because the Season had begun. For although the band played all the year round on Sundays, out of season it was never the same. It was like some one playing with only the family to listen; it didn't care how it played if there weren't any strangers present. Wasn't the conductor wearing a new coat, too? She was sure it was new.

He scraped with his foot and flapped his arms like a rooster about to crow, and the bandsmen sitting in the green rotunda blew out their cheeks and glared at the music. Now there came a little "flutey" bit—very pretty!—a little chain of bright drops. She was sure it would be repeated. It was; she lifted her head and smiled.

Only two people shared her "special" seat: a fine old man in a velvet coat, his hands clasped over a huge carved walking-stick, and a big old woman, sitting upright, with a roll of knitting on her embroidered apron. They did not speak. This was disappointing, for Miss Brill always looked forward to the conversation. She had become really quite expert, she thought, at listening as though she didn't listen, at sitting in other people's lives just for a minute while they talked round her.

She glanced, sideways, at the old couple. Perhaps they would go soon. Last Sunday, too, hadn't been as interesting as usual. An Englishman and his wife, he wearing a dreadful Panama hat and she button boots. And she'd gone on the whole time about how she ought to wear spectacles; she knew she needed them; but that it was no good getting any; they'd be sure to break and they'd never keep on. And he'd been so patient. He'd suggested everything—gold rims, the kind that curved round your ears, little pads inside the bridge. No, nothing would please her. "They'll always be sliding down my nose!" Miss Brill had wanted to shake her.

The old people sat on the bench, still as statues. Never mind, there was always the crowd to watch. To and fro, in front of the flower-beds and the band rotunda, the couples and groups paraded, stopped to talk, to greet, to buy a handful of flowers from the old beggar who had his tray fixed to the railings. Little children ran among them, swooping and laughing; little boys with big white silk bows under their chins, little girls, little French dolls, dressed up in velvet and lace. And sometimes a tiny staggerer came suddenly rocking into the open from under the trees, stopped, stared, as suddenly sat down "flop," until its small high-stepping mother, like a young hen, rushed scolding to its rescue. Other people sat on the benches and green chairs, but they were nearly always the same. Sunday after Sunday, and—Miss Brill had often noticed—there was something funny about nearly all of them. They were odd, silent, nearly all old, and from the way they stared they looked as though they'd just come from dark little rooms or even—even cupboards!

Behind the rotunda the slender trees with yellow leaves down drooping, and through them just a line of sea, and beyond the blue sky with gold-veined clouds.

Tum-tum-tum tiddle-um! tiddle-um! tum tiddley-um tum ta! blew the band.

Two young girls in red came by and two young soldiers in blue met them, and they laughed and paired and went off arm-in-arm. Two peasant women with funny straw hats passed, gravely, leading beautiful smoke-colored donkeys. A cold, pale nun hurried by. A beautiful woman came along and dropped her bunch of violets, and a little boy ran after to hand them to her, and she took them and threw them away as if they'd been poisoned. Dear me! Miss Brill didn't know whether to admire that or not! And now an ermine toque and a gentleman in gray met just in front of her. He was tall, stiff, dignified, and she was wearing the ermine toque she'd bought when her hair was yellow. Now everything, her hair, her face, even her eyes, was the same color as the shabby ermine, and her hand, in its cleaned glove, lifted to dab her lips, was a tiny yellowish paw. Oh, she was so pleased to see him—delighted! She rather thought they were going to meet that afternoon. She described where she'd been—everywhere, here, there, along by the sea. The day was so charming—didn't he agree? And wouldn't he, perhaps? . . . But he shook his head, lighted a cigarette, slowly breathed a great deep puff into her face, and, even while she was still talking and laughing, flicked the match away and walked on. The ermine toque was alone; she smiled more brightly than ever. But even the band seemed to know what she was feeling and played more softly, played tenderly, and the drum beat, "The Brute! The Brute!" over and over. What would she do? What was going to happen now? But as Miss Brill wondered, the ermine toque turned, raised her hand as though she'd seen some one else, much nicer, just over there, and pattered away. And the band changed again and played more quickly, more gayly than ever, and the old couple on Miss Brill's seat got up and marched away, and such a funny old man with long whiskers hobbled along in time to the music and was nearly knocked over by four girls walking abreast.

Oh, how fascinating it was! How she enjoyed it! How she loved sitting here, watching it all! It was like a play. It was exactly like a play. Who could believe the sky at the back wasn't painted? But it wasn't till a little brown dog trotted on solemn and then slowly trotted off, like a little "theater" dog, a little dog that had been drugged, that Miss Brill discovered what it was that made it so exciting. They were all on the stage. They weren't only the audience, not only looking on; they were acting. Even she had a part and came every Sunday. No doubt somebody would have noticed if she hadn't been there; she was part of the performance after all. How strange she'd never thought of it like that before! And yet it explained why she made such a point of starting from home at just the same time each week—so as not to be late for the performance —and it also explained why she had quite a queer, shy feeling at telling her English pupils how she spent her Sunday afternoons. No wonder! Miss Brill nearly laughed out loud. She was on the stage. She thought of the old invalid gentleman to whom she read the newspaper four afternoons a week while he slept in the garden. She had got quite used to the frail head on the cotton pillow, the hollowed eyes, the open mouth and the high pinched nose. If he'd been dead she mightn't have noticed for weeks; she wouldn't have minded. But suddenly he knew he was having the paper read to him by an actress! "An actress!" The old head lifted; two points of light quivered in the old eyes. "An actress—are ye?" And Miss Brill smoothed the newspaper as though it were the manuscript of her part and said gently: "Yes, I have been an actress for a long time."

The band had been having a rest. Now they started again. And what they played was warm, sunny, yet there was just a faint chill—a something, what was it?—not sadness—no, not sadness—a something that made you want to sing. The tune lifted, lifted, the light shone; and it seemed to Miss Brill that in another moment all of them, all the whole company, would begin singing. The young ones, the laughing ones who were moving together, they would begin, and the men's voices, very resolute and brave, would join them. And then she too, she too, and the others on the benches—they would come in with a kind of accompaniment—something low, that scarcely rose or fell, something so beautiful—moving. . . . And Miss Brill's eyes filled with tears and she looked smiling at all the other members of the company. Yes, we understand, we understand, she thought—though what they understood she didn't know.

Just at that moment a boy and a girl came and sat down where the old couple had been. They were beautifully dressed; they were in love. The hero and heroine, of course, just arrived from his father's yacht. And still soundlessly singing, still with that trembling smile, Miss Brill prepared to listen.

"No, not now," said the girl. "Not here, I can't."

"But why? Because of that stupid old thing at the end there?" asked the boy. "Why does she come here at all—who wants her? Why doesn't she keep her silly old mug at home?"

"It's her fu-fur which is so funny," giggled the girl. "It's exactly like a fried whiting."

"Ah, be off with you!" said the boy in an angry whisper. Then: "Tell me, ma petite chère—"

"No, not here," said the girl. "Not *yet*."

.   .   .   .

On her way home she usually bought a slice of honeycake at the baker's. It was her Sunday treat. Sometimes there was an almond in her slice, sometimes not. It made a great difference. If there was an almond it was like carrying home a tiny present—a surprise—something that might very well not have been there. She hurried on the almond Sundays and struck the match for the kettle in quite a dashing way.

But to-day she passed the baker's by, climbed the stairs, went into the little dark room—her room like a cupboard—and sat down on the red eiderdown. She sat there for a long time. The box that the fur came out of was on the bed. She unclasped the necklet quickly; quickly, without looking, laid it inside. But when she put the lid on she thought she heard something crying.   (1920)

Franz Kafka

A HUNGER ARTIST

During these last decades the interest in professional fasting has markedly diminished. It used to pay very well to stage such great performances under one's own management, but today that is quite impossible. We live in a different world now. At one time the whole town took a lively interest in the hunger artist; from day to day of his fast the excitement mounted; everybody wanted to see him at least once a day; there were people who bought season tickets for the last few days and sat from morning till night in front of his small barred cage; even in the nighttime there were visiting hours, when the whole effect was heightened by torch flares; on fine days the cage was set out in the open air, and then it was the children's special treat to see the hunger artist; for their elders he was often just a joke that happened to be in fashion, but the children stood open-mouthed, holding each other's hands for greater security, marveling at him as he sat there pallid in black tights, with his ribs sticking out so prominently, not even on a seat but down among straw on the ground, sometimes giving a courteous nod, answering questions with a constrained smile, or perhaps stretching an arm through the bars so that one might feel how thin it was, and then again withdrawing deep into himself, paying no attention to anyone or anything, not even to the all-important striking of the clock that was the only piece of furniture in his cage, but merely staring into vacancy with half-shut eyes, now and then taking a sip from a tiny glass of water to moisten his lips.

Besides casual onlookers there were also relays of permanent watchers selected by the public, usually butchers, strangely enough, and it was their task to watch the hunger artist day and night, three of them at a time, in case he should have some secret recourse to nourishment. This was nothing but a formality, instituted to reassure the masses, for the initiates knew well enough that during his fast the artist would never in any circumstances, not even under forcible compulsion, swallow the smallest morsel of food; the honor of his profession forbade it. Not every watcher, of course, was capable of understanding this, there were often groups of night watchers who were very lax in carrying out their duties and deliberately huddled together in a retired corner to play cards with great absorption, obviously intending to give the hunger artist the chance of a little refreshment, which they supposed he could draw from some private hoard. Nothing annoyed the artist more than such watchers; they made him miserable; they made his fast seem unendurable; sometimes he mastered his feebleness sufficiently to sing during their watch for as long as he could keep going, to show them how unjust their suspicions were. But that was of little use; they only wondered at his cleverness in being able to fill his mouth even while singing. Much more to his taste were the watchers who sat close up to the bars, who were not content with the dim night lighting of the hall but focused him in the full glare of the electric pocket torch given them by the impresario. The harsh light did not trouble him at all, in any case he could never sleep properly, and he could always drowse a little, whatever the light, at any hour, even when the hall was thronged with noisy onlookers. He was quite happy at the prospect of spending a sleepless night with such watchers; he was ready to exchange jokes with them, to tell them stories out of his nomadic life, anything at all to keep them awake and demonstrate to them again that he had no eatables in his cage and that he was fasting as not one of them could fast. But his happiest moment was when the morning came and an enormous breakfast was brought them, at his expense, on which they flung themselves with the keen appetite of healthy men after a weary night of wakefulness. Of course there were people who argued that this breakfast was an unfair attempt to bribe the watchers, but that was going rather too far, and when they were invited to take on a night's vigil without a breakfast, merely for the sake of the cause, they made themselves scarce, although they stuck stubbornly to their suspicions.

Such suspicions, anyhow, were a necessary accompaniment to the profession of fasting. No one could possibly watch the hunger artist continuously, day and night, and so no one could produce first-hand evidence that the fast had really been rigorous and continuous; only the artist himself could know that, he was therefore bound to be the sole completely satisfied spectator of his own fast. Yet for other reasons he was never satisfied; it was not perhaps mere fasting that had brought him to such skeleton thinness that many people had regretfully to keep away from his exhibitions, because the sight of him was too much for them, perhaps it was dissatisfaction with himself that had worn him down. For he alone knew, what no other initiate knew, how easy it was to fast. It was the easiest thing in the world. He made no secret of this, yet people did not believe him, at the best they set him down as modest, most of them, however, thought he was out for publicity or else was some kind of cheat who found it easy to fast because he had discovered a way of making it easy, and then had the impudence to admit the fact, more or less. He had to put up with all that, and in the course of time had got used to it, but his inner dissatisfaction always rankled, and never yet, after any term of fasting—this must be granted to his credit—had he left the cage of his own free will. The longest period of fasting was fixed by his impresario at forty days, beyond that term he was not allowed to go, not even in great cities, and there was good reason for it, too. Experience had proved that for about forty days the interest of the public could be stimulated by a steadily increasing pressure of advertisement, but after that the town began to lose interest, sympathetic support began notably to fall off; there were of course local variations as between one town and another or one country and another, but as a general rule forty days marked, the limit. So on the fortieth day the flower-bedecked cage was opened, enthusiastic spectators filled the hall, a military band played, two doctors entered the cage to measure the results of the fast, which were announced through a megaphone, and finally two young ladies appeared, blissful at having been selected for the honor, to help the hunger artist down the few steps leading to a small table on which was spread a carefully chosen invalid repast. And at this very moment the artist always turned stubborn. True, he would entrust his bony arms to the outstretched helping hands of the ladies bending over him, but stand up he would not. Why stop fasting at this particular moment, after forty days of it? He had held out for a long time, an illimitably long time; why stop now, when he was in his best fasting form, or rather, not yet quite in his best fasting form? Why should he be cheated of the fame he would get for fasting longer, for being not only the record hunger artist of all time, which presumably he was already, but for beating his own record by a performance beyond human imagination, since he felt that there were no limits to his capacity for fasting? His public pretended to admire him so much, why should it have so little patience with him; if he could endure fasting longer, why shouldn't the public endure it? Besides, he was tired, he was comfortable sitting in the straw, and now he was supposed to lift himself to his full height and go down to a meal the very thought of which gave him a nausea that only the presence of the ladies kept him from betraying, and even that with an effort. And he looked up into the eyes of the ladies who were apparently so friendly and in reality so cruel, and shook his head, which felt too heavy on its strengthless neck. But then there happened yet again what always happened. The impresario came forward, without a word—for the band made speech impossible—lifted his arms in the air above the artist, as if inviting Heaven to look down upon its creature here in the straw, this suffering martyr, which indeed he was, although in quite another sense; grasped him round the emaciated waist, with exaggerated caution, so that the frail condition he was in might be appreciated; and committed him to the care of the blenching ladies, not without secretly giving him a shaking so that his legs and body tottered and swayed. The artist now submitted completely; his head lolled on his breast as if it had landed there by chance; his body was hollowed out; his legs in a spasm of self-preservation clung close to each other at the knees, yet scraped on the ground as if it were not really solid ground, as if they were only trying to find solid ground; and the whole weight of his body, a featherweight after all, relapsed onto one of the ladies, who, looking round for help and panting a little—this post of honor was not at all what she had expected it to be—first stretched her neck as far as she could to keep her face at least free from contact with the artist, then finding this impossible, and her more fortunate companion not coming to her aid but merely holding extended on her own trembling hand the little bunch of knucklebones that was the artist's, to the great delight of the spectators burst into tears and had to be replaced by an attendant who had long been stationed in readiness. Then came the food, a little of which the impresario managed to get between the artist's lips, while he sat in a kind of half-fainting trance, to the accompaniment of cheerful patter designed to distract the public's attention from the artist's condition; after that, a toast was drunk to the public, supposedly prompted by a whisper from the artist in the impresario's ear; the band confirmed it with a mighty flourish, the spectators melted away, and no one had any cause to be dissatisfied with the proceedings, no one except the hunger artist himself, he only, as always.

So he lived for many years, with small regular intervals of recuperation, in visible glory, honored by the world, yet in spite of that troubled in spirit, and all the more troubled because no one would take his trouble seriously. What comfort could he possibly need? What more could he possibly wish for? And if some good-natured person, feeling sorry for him, tried to console him by pointing out that his melancholy was probably caused by fasting, it could happen, especially when he had been fasting for some time, that he reacted with an outburst of fury and to the general alarm began to shake the bars of his cage like a wild animal. Yet the impresario had a way of punishing these outbreaks which he rather enjoyed putting into operation. He would apologize publicly for the artist's behavior, which was only to be excused, he admitted, because of the irritability caused by fasting; a condition hardly to be understood by well-fed people; then by natural transition he went on to mention the artist's equally incomprehensible boast that he could fast for much longer than he was doing; he praised the high ambition, the good will, the great self-denial undoubtedly implicit in such a statement; and then quite simply countered it by bringing out photographs, which were also on sale to the public, showing the artist on the fortieth day of a fast lying in bed almost dead from exhaustion. This perversion of the truth, familiar to the artist though it was, always unnerved him afresh and proved too much for him. What was a consequence of the premature ending of his fast was here presented as the cause of it! To fight against this lack of understanding, against a whole world of non-understanding, was impossible. Time and again in good faith he stood by the bars listening to the impresario, but as soon as the photographs appeared he always let go and sank with a groan back on to his straw, and the reassured public could once more come close and gaze at him.

A few years later when the witnesses of such scenes called them to mind, they often failed to understand themselves at all. For meanwhile the aforementioned change in public interest had set in; it seemed to happen almost overnight; there may have been profound causes for it, but who was going to bother about that; at any rate the pampered hunger artist suddenly found himself deserted one fine day by the amusement seekers, who went streaming past him to other more favored attractions. For the last time the impresario hurried him over half Europe to discover whether the old interest might still survive here and there; all in vain; everywhere, as if by secret agreement, a positive revulsion from professional fasting was in evidence. Of course it could not really have sprung up so suddenly as all that, and many premonitory symptoms which had not been sufficiently remarked or suppressed during the rush and glitter of success now came retrospectively to mind, but it was now too late to take any countermeasures. Fasting would surely come into fashion again at some future date, yet that was no comfort for those living in the present. What, then, was the hunger artist to do? He had been applauded by thousands in his time and could hardly come down to showing himself in a street booth at village fairs, and as for adopting another profession, he was not only too old for that but too fanatically devoted to fasting. So he took leave of the impresario, his partner in an unparalleled career, and hired himself to a large circus; in order to spare his own feelings he avoided reading the conditions of his contract.

A large circus with its enormous traffic in replacing and recruiting men, animals and apparatus can always find a use for people at any time, even for a hunger artist, provided of course that he does not ask too much, and in this particular case anyhow it was not only the artist who was taken on but his famous and long-known name as well, indeed considering the peculiar nature of his performance, which was not impaired by advancing age, it could not be objected that here was an artist past his prime, no longer at the height of his professional skill, seeking a refuge in some quiet corner of a circus, on the contrary, the hunger artist averred that he could fast as well as ever, which was entirely credible, he even alleged that if he were allowed to fast as he liked, and this was at once promised him without more ado, he could astound the world by establishing a record never yet achieved, a statement which certainly provoked a smile among the other professionals, since it left out of account the change in public opinion, which the hunger artist in his zeal conveniently forgot.

He had not, however, actually lost his sense of the real situation and took it as a matter of course that he and his cage should be stationed, not in the middle of the ring as a main attraction, but outside, near the animal cages, on a site that was after all easily accessible. Large and gaily painted placards made a frame for the cage and announced what was to be seen inside it. When the public came thronging out in the intervals to see the animals, they could hardly avoid passing the hunger artist's cage and stopping there for a moment, perhaps they might even have stayed longer had not those pressing behind them in the narrow gangway, who did not understand why they should be held up on their way towards the excitements of the menagerie, made it impossible for anyone to stand gazing quietly for any length of time. And that was the reason why the hunger artist, who had of course been looking forward to these visiting hours as the main achievement of his life, began instead to shrink from them. At first he could hardly wait for the intervals; it was exhilarating to watch the crowds come streaming his way, until only too soon —not even the most obstinate self-deception, clung to almost consciously, could hold out against the fact—the conviction was borne in upon him that these people, most of them, to judge from their actions, again and again, without exception, were all on their way to the menagerie. And the first sight of them from the distance remained the best. For when they reached his cage he was at once deafened by the storm of shouting and abuse that arose from the two contending factions, which renewed themselves continuously, of those who wanted to stop and stare at him—he soon began to dislike them more than the others—not out of real interest but only out of obstinate self-assertiveness, and those who wanted to go straight on to the animals. When the first great rush was past, the stragglers came along, and these, whom nothing could have prevented from stopping to look at him as long as they had breath, raced past with long strides, hardly even glancing at him, in their haste to get to the menagerie in time. And all too rarely did it happen that he had a stroke of luck, when some father of a family fetched up before him with his children, pointed a finger at the hunger artist and explained at length what the phenomenon meant, telling stories of earlier years when he himself had watched similar but much more thrilling performances, and the children, still rather uncomprehending, since neither inside nor outside school had they been sufficiently prepared for this lesson—what did they care about fasting?—yet showed by the brightness of their intent eyes that new and better times might be coming. Perhaps, said the hunger artist to himself many a time, things would be a little better if his cage were set not quite so near the menagerie. That made it too easy for people to make their choice, to say nothing of what he suffered from the stench of the menagerie, the animals' restlessness by night, the carrying past of raw lumps of flesh for the beasts of prey, the roaring at feeding times, which depressed him continually. But he did not dare to lodge a complaint with the management; after all, he had the animals to thank for the troops of people who passed his cage, among whom there might always be one here and there to take an interest in him, and who could tell where they might seclude him if he called attention to his existence and thereby to the fact that, strictly speaking, he was only an impediment on the way to the menagerie.

A small impediment, to be sure, one that grew steadily less. People grew familiar with the strange idea that they could be expected, in times like these, to take an interest in a hunger artist, and with this familiarity the verdict went out against him. He might fast as much as he could, and he did so; but nothing could save him now, people passed him by. Just try to explain to anyone the art of fasting! Anyone who has no feeling for it cannot be made to understand it. The fine placards grew dirty and illegible, they were torn down; the little notice board telling the number of fast days achieved, which at first was changed carefully every day, had long stayed at the same figure, for after the first few weeks even this small task seemed pointless to the staff; and so the artist simply fasted on and on, as he had once dreamed of doing, and it was no trouble to him, just as he had always foretold, but no one counted the days, no one, not even the artist himself, knew what records he was already breaking, and his heart grew heavy. And when once in a time some leisurely passer-by stopped, made merry over the old figure on the board and spoke of swindling, that was in its way the stupidest lie ever invented by indifference and inborn malice, since it was not the hunger artist who was cheating, he was working honestly, but the world was cheating him of his reward.

Many more days went by, however, and that too came to an end. An overseer's eye fell on the cage one day and he asked the attendants why this perfectly good stage should be left standing there unused with dirty straw inside it; nobody knew, until one man, helped out by the notice board, remembered about the hunger artist. They poked into the straw with sticks and found him in it. "Are you still fasting?" asked the overseer, "when on earth do you mean to stop?" "Forgive me. everybody," whispered the hunger artist; only the overseer, who had his ear to the bars, understood him. "Of course," said the overseer, and tapped his forehead with a finger to let the attendants know what state the man was in, "we forgive you." "I always wanted you to admire my fasting," said the hunger artist. "We do admire it," said the overseer, affably. "But you shouldn't admire it," said the hunger artist. "Well then we don't admire it," said the overseer, "but why shouldn't we admire it?" "Because I have to fast, I can't help it," said the hunger artist. "What a fellow you are," said the overseer, "and why can't you help it?" "Because," said the hunger artist, lifting his head a little and speaking, with his lips pursed, as if for a kiss, right into the overseer's ear, so that no syllable might be lost, "because I couldn't find the food I liked. If I had found it, believe me, I should have made no fuss and stuffed myself like you or anyone else." These were his last words, but in his dimming eyes remained the firm though no longer proud persuasion that he was still continuing to fast.

"Well, clear this out now!" said the overseer, and they buried the hunger artist, straw and all. Into the cage they put a young panther. Even the most insensitive felt it refreshing to see this wild creature leaping around the cage that had so long been dreary. The panther was all right. The food he liked was brought him without hesitation by the attendants; he seemed not even to miss his freedom; his noble body, furnished almost to the bursting point with all that it needed, seemed to carry freedom around with it too; somewhere in his jaws it seemed to lurk; and the joy of life streamed with such ardent passion from his throat that for the onlookers it was not easy to stand the shock of it. But they braced themselves, crowded round the cage, and did not want ever to move away.   (1924)

Ernest Hemingway

THE KILLERS

The door of Henry's lunch-room opened and two men came in. They sat down at the counter.

"What's yours?" George asked them.

"I don't know," one of the men said. "What do you want to eat, Al?"

"I don't know," said Al. "I don't know what I want to eat."

Outside it was getting dark. The street-light came on outside the window. The two men at the counter read the menu. From the other end of the counter Nick Adams watched them. He had been talking to George when they came in.

"I'll have a roast pork tenderloin with apple sauce and mashed potatoes," the first man said.

"It isn't ready yet."

"What the hell do you put it on the card for?"

"That's the dinner," George explained. "You can get that at six o'clock." George looked at the clock on the wall behind the counter.

"It's five o'clock."

"The clock says twenty minutes past five," the second man said.

"It's twenty minutes fast."

"Oh, to hell with the clock," the first man said. "What have you got to eat?"

"I can give you any kind of sandwiches," George said. "You can have ham and eggs, bacon and eggs, liver and bacon, or a steak."

"Give me chicken croquettes with green peas and cream sauce and mashed potatoes."

"That's the dinner."

"Everything we want's the dinner, eh? That's the way you work it."

"I can give you ham and eggs, bacon and eggs, liver——"

"I'll take ham and eggs," the man called Al said. He wore a derby hat and a black overcoat buttoned across the chest. His face was small and white and he had tight lips. He wore a silk muffler and gloves.

"Give me bacon and eggs," said the other man. He was about the same size as Al. Their faces were different but they were dressed like twins. Both wore overcoats too tight for them. They sat leaning forward, their elbows on the counter.

"Got anything to drink?" Al asked.

"Silver beer, bevo, ginger-ale," George said.

"I mean you got anything to *drink?*"

"Just those I said."

"This is a hot town," said the other. "What do they call it?"

"Summit."

"Ever hear of it?" Al asked his friend.

"No," said the friend.

"What do you do here nights?" Al asked.

"They eat the dinner," his friend said. "They all come here and eat the big dinner."

"That's right," George said.

"So you think that's right?" Al asked George.

"Sure."

"You're a pretty bright boy, aren't you?"

"Sure," said George.

"Well, you're not," said the other little man. "Is he, Al?"

"He's dumb," said Al. He turned to Nick. "What's your name?"

"Adams."

"Another bright boy," Al said. "Ain't he a bright boy, Max?"

"The town's full of bright boys," Max said.

George put the two platters, one of ham and eggs, the other of bacon and eggs, on the counter. He set down two side-dishes of fried potatoes and closed the wicket into the kitchen.

"Which is yours?" he asked Al.

"Don't you remember?"

"Ham and eggs."

"Just a bright boy," Max said. He leaned forward and took the ham and eggs. Both men ate with their gloves on. George watched them eat.

"What are *you* looking at?" Max looked at George.

"Nothing."

"The hell you were. You were looking at me."

"Maybe the boy meant it for a joke, Max," Al said.

George laughed.

"*You* don't have to laugh," Max said to him. "*You* don't have to laugh at all, see?"

"All right," said George.

"So he thinks it's all right." Max turned to Al. "He thinks it's all right. That's a good one."

"Oh, he's a thinker," Al said. They went on eating.

"What's the bright boy's name down the counter?" Al asked Max.

"Hey, bright boy," Max said to Nick. "You go around on the other side of the counter with your boy friend."

"What's the idea?" Nick asked.

"There isn't any idea."

"You better go around, bright boy," Al said. Nick went around behind the counter.

"What's the idea?" George asked.

"None of your damn business," Al said. "Who's out in the kitchen?"

"The nigger."

"What do you mean the nigger?"

"The nigger that cooks."

"Tell him to come in."

"What's the idea?"

"Tell him to come in."

"Where do you think you are?"

"We know damn well where we are," the man called Max said. "Do we look silly?"

"You talk silly," Al said to him. "What the hell do you argue with this kid for? Listen," he said to George, "tell the nigger to come out here."

"What are you going to do to him?"

"Nothing. Use your head, bright boy. What would we do to a nigger?"

George opened the slit that opened back into the kitchen. "Sam," he called. "Come in here a minute."

The door to the kitchen opened and the nigger came in. "What was it?" he asked. The two men at the counter took a look at him.

"All right, nigger. You stand right there," Al said.

Sam, the nigger, standing in his apron, looked at the two men sitting at the counter. "Yes, sir," he said. Al got down from his stool.

"I'm going back to the kitchen with the nigger and bright boy," he said. "Go on back to the kitchen, nigger. You go with him, bright boy." The little man walked after Nick and Sam, the cook, back into the kitchen. The door shut after them. The man called Max sat at the counter opposite George. He didn't look at George but looked in the mirror that ran along back of the counter. Henry's had been made over from a saloon into a lunch-counter.

"Well, bright boy," Max said, looking into the mirror, "why don't you say something?"

"What's it all about?"

"Hey, Al," Max called. "bright boy wants to know what it's all about."

"Why don't you tell him?" Al's voice came from the kitchen.

"What do you think it's all about?"

"I don't know."

"What do you think?"

Max looked into the mirror all the time he was talking.

"I wouldn't say."

"Hey, Al, bright boy says he wouldn't say what he thinks it's all about."

"I can hear you, all right," Al said from the kitchen. He had propped open the slit that dishes passed through into the kitchen with a catsup bottle. "Listen, bright boy," he said from the kitchen to George. "Stand a little further along the bar. You move a little to the left, Max." He was like a photographer arranging for a group picture.

"Talk to me, bright boy," Max said. "What do you think's going to happen?"

George did not say anything.

"I'll tell you," Max said. "We're going to kill a Swede. Do you know a big Swede named Ole Andreson?"

"Yes."

"He comes here to eat every night, don't he?"

"Sometimes he comes here."

"He comes here at six o'clock, don't he?"

"If he comes."

"We know all that, bright boy," Max said. "Talk about something else. Ever go to the movies?"

"Once in a while."

"You ought to go to the movies more. The movies are fine for a bright boy like you."

"What are you going to kill Ole Andreson for? What did he ever do to you?"

"He never had a chance to do anything to us. He never even seen us."

"And he's only going to see us once," Al said from the kitchen.

"What are you going to kill him for, then?" George asked.

"We're killing him for a friend. Just to oblige a friend, bright boy."

"Shut up," said Al from the kitchen. "You talk too goddam much."

"Well, I got to keep bright boy amused. Don't I, bright boy?"

"You talk too damn much," Al said. "The nigger and my bright boy are amused by themselves. I got them tied up like a couple of girl friends in the convent."

"I suppose you were in a convent?"

"You never know."

"You were in a kosher convent. That's where you were."

George looked up at the clock.

"If anybody comes in you tell them the cook is off, and if they keep after it, you tell them you'll go back and cook yourself. Do you get that, bright boy?"

"All right," George said. "What you going to do with us afterward?"

"That'll depend," Max said. "That's one of those things you never know at the time."

George looked up at the clock. It was a quarter past six. The door from the street opened. A street-car motorman came in.

"Hello, George," he said. "Can I get supper?"

"Sam's gone out," George said. "He'll be back in about half an hour."

"I'd better go up the street," the motorman said. George looked at the clock. It was twenty minutes past six.

"That was nice, bright boy," Max said. "You're a regular little gentleman."

"He knew I'd blow his head off," Al said from the kitchen.

"No," said Max. "It ain't that. Bright boy is nice. He's a nice boy. I like him."

At six-fifty-five George said: "He's not coming."

Two other people had been in the lunch-room. Once George had gone out to the kitchen and made a ham-and-egg sandwich "to go" that a man wanted to take with him. Inside the kitchen he saw Al, his derby hat tipped back, sitting on a stool beside the wicket with the muzzle of a sawed off shotgun resting on the ledge. Nick and the cook were back to back in the corner, a towel tied in each of their mouths. George had cooked the sandwich, wrapped it up in oiled paper, put it in a bag, brought it in, and the man had paid for it and gone out.

"Bright boy can do everything," Max said. "He can cook and everything. You'd make some girl a nice wife, bright boy."

"Yes?" George said. "Your friend, Ole Andreson, isn't going to come."

"We'll give him ten minutes," Max said.

Max watched the mirror and the clock. The hands of the clock marked seven o'clock, and then five minutes past seven.

"Come on, Al," said Max. "We better go. He's not coming."

"Better give him five minutes," Al said from the kitchen.

In the five minutes a man came in, and George explained that the cook was sick.

"Why the hell don't you get another cook?" the man asked. "Aren't you running a lunch-counter?" He went out.

"Come on, Al," Max said.

"What about the two bright boys and the nigger?"

"They're all right."

"You think so?"

"Sure. We're through with it."

"I don't like it," said Al. "It's sloppy. You talk too much."

"Oh, what the hell," said Max. "We got to keep amused, haven't we?"

"You talk too much, all the same," Al said. He came out from the kitchen. The cut-off barrels of the shotgun made a slight bulge under the waist of his too tight-fitting overcoat. He straightened his coat with his gloved hands.

"So long, bright boy," he said to George. "You got a lot of luck."

"That's the truth," Max said. "You ought to play the races, bright boy."

The two of them went out the door. George watched them, through the window, pass under the arc-light and cross the street. In their tight overcoats and derby hats they looked like a vaudeville team. George went back through the swinging-door into the kitchen and untied Nick and the cook.

"I don't want any more of that," said Sam, the cook. "I don't want any more of that."

Nick stood up. He had never had a towel in his mouth before.

"Say," he said. "What the hell?" He was trying to swagger it off.

"They were going to kill Ole Andreson," George said. "They were going to shoot him when he came in to eat."

"Ole Andreson?"

"Sure."

The cook felt the corners of his mouth with his thumbs.

"They all gone?" he asked.

"Yeah," said George. "They're gone now."

"I don't like it," said the cook. "I don't like any of it at all."

"Listen," George said to Nick. "You better go see Ole Andreson."

"All right."

"You better not have anything to do with it at all," Sam, the cook, said. "You better stay way out of it."

"Don't go if you don't want to," George said.

"Mixing up in this ain't going to get you anywhere," the cook said. "You stay out of it."

"I'll go see him," Nick said to George. "Where does he live?"

The cook turned away.

"Little boys always know what they want to do," he said.

"He lives up at Hirsch's rooming-house," George said to Nick.

"I'll go up there."

Outside the arc-light shone through the bare branches of a tree. Nick walked up the street beside the car-tracks and turned at the next arc-light down a side-street. Three houses up the street was Hirsch's rooming-house. Nick walked up the two steps and pushed the bell. A woman came to the door.

"Is Ole Andreson here?"

"Do you want to see him?"

"Yes, if he's in."

Nick followed the woman up a flight of stairs and back to the end of a corridor. She knocked on the door.

"Who is it?"

"It's somebody to see you, Mr. Andreson," the woman said.

"It's Nick Adams."

"Come in."

Nick opened the door and went into the room. Ole Andreson was lying on the bed with all his clothes on. He had been a heavyweight prizefighter and he was too long for the bed. He lay with his head on two pillows. He did not look at Nick.

"What was it?" he asked.

"I was up at Henry's," Nick said, "and two fellows came in and tied up me and the cook, and they said they were going to kill you."

It sounded silly when he said it. Ole Andreson said nothing.

"They put us out in the kitchen," Nick went on. "They were going to shoot you when you came to supper."

Ole Andreson looked at the wall and did not say anything.

"George thought I better come and tell you about it."

"There isn't anything I can do about it," Ole Andreson said.

"I'll tell you what they were like."

"I don't want to know what they were like," Ole Andreson said. He looked at the wall. "Thanks for coming to tell me about it."

"That's all right."

Nick looked at the big man lying on the bed.

"Don't you want me to go and see the police?"

"No," Ole Andreson said. "That wouldn't do any good."

"Isn't there something I could do?"

"No. There isn't anything to do."

"Maybe it was just a bluff."

"No. It ain't just a bluff."

Ole Andreson rolled over toward the wall.

"The only thing is," he said, talking toward the wall, "I just can't make up my mind to go out. I been in here all day."

"Couldn't you get out of town?"

"No," Ole Andreson said. "I'm through with all that running around."

He looked at the wall.

"There ain't anything to do now."

"Couldn't you fix it up some way?"

"No. I got in wrong." He talked in the same flat voice. "There ain't any thing to do. After a while I'll make up my mind to go out."

"I better go back and see George," Nick said.

"So long," said Ole Andreson. He did not look toward Nick. "Thanks for coming around."

Nick went out. As he shut the door he saw Ole Andreson with all his clothes on, lying on the bed looking at the wall.

"He's been in his room all day," the landlady said down-stairs. "I guess he don't feel well. I said to him: 'Mr. Andreson, you ought to go out and take a walk on a nice fall day like this,' but he didn't feel like it."

"He doesn't want to go out."

"I'm sorry he don't feel well," the woman said. "He's an awfully nice man. He was in the ring, you know."

"I know it."

"You'd never know it except from the way his face is," the woman said. They stood talking just inside the street door. "He's just as gentle."

"Well, good-night, Mrs. Hirsch," Nick said.

"I'm not Mrs. Hirsch," the woman said. "She owns the place. I just look after it for her. I'm Mrs. Bell."

"Well, good-night, Mrs. Bell," Nick said.

"Good-night," the woman said.

Nick walked up the dark street to the corner under the arc-light, and then along the car-tracks to Henry's eating-house. George was inside, back of the counter.

"Did you see Ole?"

"Yes," said Nick. "He's in his room and he won't go out."

The cook opened the door from the kitchen when he heard Nick's voice. "I don't even listen to it," he said and shut the door.

"Did you tell him about it?" George asked.

"Sure. I told him but he knows what it's all about."

"What's he going to do?"

"Nothing."

"They'll kill him."

"I guess they will."

"He must have got mixed up in something in Chicago."

"I guess so," said Nick.

"It's a hell of a thing."

"It's an awful thing," Nick said.

They did not say anything. George reached down for a towel and wiped the counter.

"I wonder what he did?" Nick said.

"Double-crossed somebody. That's what they kill them for."

"I'm going to get out of this town," Nick said.

"Yes," said George. "That's a good thing to do."

"I can't stand to think about him waiting in the room and knowing he's going to get it. It's too damned awful."

"Well," said George, "you better not think about it."   (1927)

Katherine Anne Porter

FLOWERING JUDAS

Braggioni sits heaped upon the edge of a straightbacked chair much too small for him, and sings to Laura in a furry, mournful voice. Laura has begun to find reasons for avoiding her own house until the latest possible moment, for Braggioni is there almost every night. No matter how late she is, he will be sitting there with a surly, waiting expression, pulling at his kinky yellow hair, thumbing the strings of his guitar, snarling a tune under his breath. Lupe the Indian maid meets Laura at the door, and says with a flicker of a glance towards the upper room, "He waits."

Laura wishes to lie down, she is tired of her hairpins and the feel of her long tight sleeves, but she says to him, "Have you a new song for me this evening?" If he says yes, she asks him to sing it. If he says no, she remembers his favorite one, and asks him to sing it again. Lupe brings her a cup of chocolate and a plate of rice, and Laura eats at the small table under the lamp, first inviting Braggioni, whose answer is always the same: "I have eaten, and besides, chocolate thickens the voice."

Laura says, "Sing, then," and Braggioni heaves himself into song. He scratches the guitar familiarly as though it were a pet animal, and sings passionately off key, taking the high notes in a prolonged painful squeal. Laura, who haunts the markets listening to the ballad singers, and stops every day to hear the blind boy playing his reed-flute in Sixteenth of September Street, listens to Braggioni with pitiless courtesy, because she dares not smile at his miserable performance. Nobody dares to smile at him. Braggioni is cruel to everyone, with a kind of specialized insolence, but he is so vain of his talents, and so sensitive to slights, it would require a cruelty and vanity greater than his own to lay a finger on the vast cureless wound of his self-esteem. It would require courage, too, for it is dangerous to offend him, and nobody has this courage.

Braggioni loves himself with such tenderness and amplitude and eternal charity that his followers—for he is a leader of men, a skilled revolutionist, and his skin has been punctured in honorable warfare—warm themselves in the reflected glow, and say to each other: "He has a real nobility, a love of humanity raised above mere personal affections." The excess of this self-love has flowed out, inconveniently for her, over Laura, who, with so many others, owes her comfortable situation and her salary to him. When he is in a very good humor, he tells her, "I am tempted to forgive you for being a *gringa. Gringita!*" and Laura, burning, imagines herself leaning forward suddenly, and with a sound back-handed slap wiping the suety smile from his face. If he notices her eyes at these moments he gives no sign.

She knows what Braggioni would offer her, and she must resist tenaciously without appearing to resist, and if she could avoid it she would not admit even to herself the slow drift of his intention. During these long evenings which have spoiled a long month for her, she sits in her deep chair with an open book on her knees, resting her eyes on the consoling rigidity of the printed page when the sight and sound of Braggioni singing threaten to identify themselves with all her remembered afflictions and to add their weight to her uneasy premonitions of the future. The gluttonous bulk of Braggioni has become a symbol of her many disillusions, for a revolutionist should be lean, animated by heroic faith, a vessel of abstract virtues. This is nonsense, she knows it now and is ashamed of it. Revolution must have leaders, and leadership is a career for energetic men. She is, her comrades tell her, full of romantic error, for what she defines as cynicism in them is merely "a developed sense of reality." She is almost too willing to say, "I am wrong, I suppose I don't really understand the principles," and afterward she makes a secret truce with herself, determined not to surrender her will to such expedient logic. But she cannot help feeling that she has been betrayed irreparably by the disunion between her way of living and her feeling of what life should be, and at times she is almost contented to rest in this sense of grievance as a private store of consolation. Sometimes she wishes to run away, but she stays. Now she longs to fly out of this room, down the narrow stairs, and into the street where the houses lean together like conspirators under a single mottled lamp, and leave Braggioni singing to himself.

Instead she looks at Braggioni, frankly and clearly, like a good child who understands the rules of behavior. Her knees cling together under sound blue serge, and her round white collar is not purposely nun-like. She wears the uniform of an idea, and has renounced vanities. She was born Roman Catholic, and in spite of her fear of being seen by someone who might make a scandal of it, she slips now and again into some crumbling little church, kneels on the chilly stone, and says a Hail Mary on the gold rosary she bought in Tehuantepec. It is no good and she ends by examining the altar with its tinsel flowers and ragged brocades, and feels tender about the battered doll-shape of some male saint whose white, lace-trimmed drawers hang limply around his ankles below the hieratic dignity of his velvet robe. She has encased herself in a set of principles derived from her early training, leaving no detail of gesture or of personal taste untouched, and for this reason she will not wear lace made on machines. This is her private heresy, for in her special group the machine is sacred, and will be the salvation of the workers. She loves fine lace, and there is a tiny edge of fluted cobweb on this collar, which is one of twenty precisely alike, folded in blue tissue paper in the upper drawer of her clothes chest.

Braggioni catches her glance solidly as if he had been waiting for it, leans forward, balancing his paunch between his spread knees, and sings with tremendous emphasis, weighing his words. He has, the song relates, no father and no mother, nor even a friend to console him; lonely as a wave of the sea he comes and goes, lonely as a wave. His mouth opens round and yearns sideways, his balloon cheeks grow oily with the labor of song. He bulges marvelously in his expensive garments. Over his lavender collar, crushed upon a purple necktie, held by a diamond hoop: over his ammunition belt of tooled leather worked in silver, buckled cruelly around his gasping middle: over the tops of his glossy yellow shoes Braggioni swells with ominous ripeness, his mauve silk hose stretched taut, his ankles bound with the stout leather thongs of his shoes.

When he stretches his eyelids at Laura she notes again that his eyes are the true tawny yellow cat's eyes. He is rich, not in money, he tells her, but in power, and this power brings with it the blameless ownership of things, and the right to indulge his love of small luxuries. "I have a taste for the elegant refinements," he said once, flourishing a yellow silk handkerchief before her nose. "Smell that? It is Jockey Club, imported from New York." Nonetheless he is wounded by life. He will say so presently. "It is true everythings turns to dust in the hand, to gall on the tongue." He sighs and his leather belt creaks like a saddle girth. "I am disappointed in everything as it comes. Everything." He shakes his head. "You, poor thing, you will be disappointed too. You are born for it. We are more alike than you realize in some things. Wait and see. Some day you will remember what I have told you, you will know that Braggioni was your friend."

Laura feels a slow chill, a purely physical sense of danger, a warning in her blood that violence, mutilation, a shocking death, wait for her with lessening patience. She has translated this fear into something homely, immediate, and sometimes hesitates before crossing the street. "My personal fate is nothing, except as the testimony of a mental attitude," she reminds herself, quoting from some forgotten philosophic primer, and is sensible enough to add, "Anyhow, I shall not be killed by an automobile if I can help it."

"It may be true I am as corrupt, in another way, as Braggioni," she thinks in spite of herself, "as callous, as incomplete," and if this is so, any kind of death seems preferable. Still she sits quietly, she does not run. Where could she go? Uninvited she has promised herself to this place; she can no longer imagine herself as living in another country, and there is no pleasure in remembering her life before she came here.

Precisely what is the nature of this devotion, its true motives, and what are its obligations? Laura cannot say. She spends part of her days in Xochimilco, near by, teaching Indian children to say in English, "The cat is on the mat." When she appears in the classroom they crowd about her with smiles on their wise, innocent, clay-colored faces, crying, "Good morning, my titcher!" in immaculate voices, and they make of her desk a fresh garden of flowers every day.

During her leisure she goes to union meetings and listens to busy important voices quarreling over tactics, methods, internal politics. She visits the prisoners of her own political faith in their cells, where they entertain themselves with counting cockroaches, repenting of their indiscretions, composing their memoirs, writing out manifestoes and plans for their comrades who are still walking about free, hands in pockets, sniffing fresh air. Laura brings them food and cigarettes and a little money, and she brings messages disguised in equivocal phrases from the men outside who dare not set foot in the prison for fear of disappearing into the cells kept empty for them. If the prisoners confuse night and day, and complain, "Dear little Laura, time doesn't pass in this infernal hole, and I won't know when it is time to sleep unless I have a reminder," she brings them their favorite narcotics, and says in a tone that does not wound them with pity, "Tonight will really be night for you," and though her Spanish amuses them, they find her comforting, useful. If they lose patience and all faith, and curse the slowness of their friends in coming to their rescue with money and influence, they trust her not to repeat everything, and if she inquires, "Where do you think we can find money, or influence?" they are certain to answer, "Well, there is Braggioni, why doesn't he do something?"

She smuggles letters from headquarters to men hiding from firing squads in back streets in mildewed houses, where they sit in tumbled beds and talk bitterly as if all Mexico were at their heels, when Laura knows positively they might appear at the band concert in the Alameda on Sunday morning, and no one would notice them. But Braggioni says, "Let them sweat a little. The next time they may be careful. It is very restful to have them out of the way for a while." She is not afraid to knock on any door in any street after midnight, and enter in the darkness, and say to one of these men who is really in danger: "They will be looking for you—seriously—tomorrow morning after six. Here is some money from Vicente. Go to Vera Cruz and wait."

She borrows money from the Roumanian agitator to give to his bitter enemy the Polish agitator. The favor of Braggioni is their disputed territory, and Braggioni holds the balance nicely, for he can use them both. The Polish agitator talks love to her over café tables, hoping to exploit what he believes is her secret sentimental preference for him, and he gives her misinformation which he begs her to repeat as the solemn truth to certain persons. The Roumanian is more adroit. He is generous with his money in all good causes, and lies to her with an air of ingenuous candor, as if he were her good friend and confidant. She never repeats anything they may say. Braggioni never asks questions. He has other ways to discover all that he wishes to know about them.

Nobody touches her, but all praise her gray eyes, and the soft, round under lip which promises gayety, yet is always grave, nearly always firmly closed; and they cannot understand why she is in Mexico. She walks back and forth on her errands, with puzzled eyebrows, carrying her little folder of drawings and music and school papers. No dancer dances more beautifully than Laura walks, and she inspires some amusing, unexpected ardors, which cause little gossip, because nothing comes of them. A young captain who had been a soldier in Zapata's army attempted, during a horseback ride near Cuernavaca, to express his desire for her with the noble simplicity befitting a rude folk-hero: but gently, because he was gentle. This gentleness was his defeat, for when he alighted, and removed her foot from the stirrup, and essayed to draw her down into his arms, her horse, ordinarily a tame one, shied fiercely, reared and plunged away. The young hero's horse careered blindly after his stable-mate, and the hero did not return to the hotel until rather late that evening. At breakfast he came to her table in full charro dress, gray buckskin jacket and trousers with strings of silver buttons down the leg, and he was in a humorous, careless mood. "May I sit with you?" and "You are a wonderful rider. I was terrified that you might be thrown and dragged. I should never have forgiven myself. But I cannot admire you enough for your riding!"

"I learned to ride in Arizona," said Laura.

"If you will ride with me again this morning, I promise you a horse that will not shy with you," he said. But Laura remembered that she must return to Mexico City at noon.

Next morning the children made a celebration and spent their playtime writing on the blackboard, "We lov ar ticher," and with tinted chalks they drew wreaths of flowers around the words. The young hero wrote her a letter: "I am a very foolish, wasteful, impulsive man. I should have first said I love you, and then you would not have run away. But you shall see me again." Laura thought, "I must send him a box of colored crayons," but she was trying to forgive herself for having spurred her horse at the wrong moment.

A brown, shock-haired youth came and stood in her patio one night and sang like a lost soul for two hours, but Laura could think of nothing to do about it. The moonlight spread a wash of gauzy silver over the clear spaces of the garden, and the shadows were cobalt blue. The scarlet blossoms of the Judas tree were dull purple, and the names of the colors repeated themselves automatically in her mind, while she watched not the boy, but his shadow, fallen like a dark garment across the fountain rim, trailing in the water. Lupe came silently and whispered expert counsel in her ear: "If you will throw him one little flower, he will sing another song or two and go away." Laura threw the flower, and he sang a last song and went away with the flower tucked in the band of his hat. Lupe said, "He is one of the organizers of the Typographers Union, and before that he sold corridos in the Merced market, and before that, he came from Guanajuato, where I was born. I would not trust any man, but I trust least those from Guanajuato."

She did not tell Laura that he would be back again the next night, and the next, nor that he would follow her at a certain fixed distance around the Merced market, through the Zócolo, up Francisco I. Madero Avenue, and so along the Paseo de la Reforma to Chapultepec Park, and into the Philosopher's Footpath, still with that flower withering in his hat, and an indivisible attention in his eyes.

Now Laura is accustomed to him, it means nothing except that he is nineteen years old and is observing a convention with all propriety, as though it were founded on a law of nature, which in the end it might well prove to be. He is beginning to write poems which he prints on a wooden press, and he leaves them stuck like handbills in her door. She is pleasantly disturbed by the abstract, unhurried watchfulness of his black eyes which will in time turn easily towards another object. She tells herself that throwing the flower was a mistake, for she is twenty-two years old and knows better; but she refuses to regret it, and persuades herself that her negation of all external events as they occur is a sign that she is gradually perfecting herself in the stoicism she strives to cultivate against that disaster she fears, though she cannot name it.

She is not at home in the world. Every day she teaches children who remain strangers to her, though she loves their tender round hands and their charming opportunist savagery. She knocks at unfamiliar doors not knowing whether a friend or a stranger shall answer, and even if a known face emerges from the sour gloom of that unknown interior, still it is the face of a stranger. No matter what this stranger says to her, nor what her message to him, the very cells of her flesh reject knowledge and kinship in one monotonous word. No. No. No. She draws her strength from this one holy talismanic word which does not suffer her to be led into evil. Denying everything, she may walk anywhere in safety, she looks at everything without amazement.

No, repeats this firm unchanging voice of her blood; and she looks at Braggioni without amazement. He is a great man, he wishes to impress this simple girl who covers her great round breasts with thick dark cloth, and who hides long, invaluably beautiful legs under a heavy skirt. She is almost thin except for the incomprehensible fullness of her breasts, like a nursing mother's, and Braggioni, who considers himself a judge of women, speculates again on the puzzle of her notorious virginity, and takes the liberty of speech which she permits without a sign of modesty, indeed, without any sort of sign, which is disconcerting.

"You think you are so cold, *gringita!* Wait and see. You will surprise yourself some day! May I be there to advise you!" He stretches his eyelids at her, and his ill-humored cat's eyes waver in a separate glance for the two points of light marking the opposite ends of a smoothly drawn path between the swollen curve of her breasts. He is not put off by that blue serge, nor by her resolutely fixed gaze. There is all the time in the world. His cheeks are bellying with the wind of song. "O girl with the dark eyes," he sings, and reconsiders. "But yours are not dark. I can change all that. O girl with the green eyes, you have stolen my heart away!" then his mind wanders to the song, and Laura feels the weight of his attention being shifted elsewhere. Singing thus, he seems harmless, he is quite harmless, there is nothing to do but sit patiently and say "No," when the moment comes. She draws a full breath, and her mind wanders also, but not far. She dares not wander too far.

Not for nothing has Braggioni taken pains to be a good revolutionist and a professional lover of humanity. He will never die of it. He has the malice, the cleverness, the wickedness, the sharpness of wit, the hardness of heart, stipulated for loving the world profitably. *He will never die of it.* He will live to see himself kicked out from his feeding trough by other hungry world-saviors. Traditionally he must sing in spite of his life which drives him to bloodshed, he tells Laura, for his father was a Tuscany peasant who drifted to Yucatan and married a Maya woman: a woman of race, an aristocrat. They gave him the love and knowledge of music, thus: and under the tip of his thumbnail, the strings of the instrument complain like exposed nerves.

Once he was called Delgadito by all the girls and married women who ran after him; he was so scrawny all his bones showed under his thin cotton clothing, and he could squeeze his emptiness to the very backbone with his two hands. He was a poet and the revolution was only a dream then; too many women loved him and sapped away his youth, and he could never find enough to eat anywhere, anywhere! Now he is a leader of men, crafty men who whisper in his ear, hungry men who wait for hours outside his office for a word with him, emaciated men with wild faces who waylay him at the street gate with a timid, "Comrade, let me tell you . . ." and they blow the foul breath from their empty stomachs in his face.

He is always sympathetic. He gives them handfuls of small coins from his own pocket, he promises them work, there will be demonstrations, they must join the unions and attend the meetings, above all they must be on the watch for spies. They are closer to him than his own brothers, without them he can do nothing—until tomorrow, comrade!

Until tomorrow. "They are stupid, they are lazy, they are treacherous, they would cut my throat for nothing," he says to Laura. He has good food and abundant drink, he hires an automobile and drives in the Paseo on Sunday morning, and enjoys plenty of sleep in a soft bed beside a wife who dares not disturb him, and he sits pampering his bones in easy billows of fat, singing to Laura, who knows and thinks these things about him. When he was fifteen, he tried to drown himself because he loved a girl, his first love, and she laughed at him. "A thousand women have paid for that," and his tight little mouth turns down at the corners. Now he perfumes his hair with Jockey Club, and confides to Laura: "One woman is really as good as another for me, in the dark. I prefer them all."

His wife organizes unions among the girls in the cigarette factories, and walks in picket lines, and even speaks at meetings in the evening. But she cannot be brought to acknowledge the benefits of true liberty. "I tell her I must have my freedom, net. She does not understand my point of view."

Laura has heard this many times. Braggioni scratches the guitar and medi-
tates. "She is an instinctively virtuous woman, pure gold, no doubt of that.
If she were not, I should lock her up, and she knows it."

His wife, who works so hard for the good of the factory girls, employs
part of her leisure lying on the floor weeping because there are so many
women in the world, and only one husband for her, and she never knows
where nor when to look for him. He told her: "Unless you can learn to cry
when I am not here, I must go away for good." That day he went away and
took a room at the Hotel Madrid.

It is this month of separation for the sake of higher principles that has
been spoiled not only for Mrs. Braggioni, whose sense of reality is beyond
criticism, but for Laura, who feels herself bogged in a nightmare. Tonight
Laura envies Mrs. Braggioni, who is alone, and free to weep as much as she
pleases about a concrete wrong. Laura has just come from a visit to the
prison, and she is waiting for tomorrow with a bitter anxiety as if tomorrow
may not come, but time may be caught immovably in this hour, with herself
transfixed, Braggioni singing on forever, and Eugenio's body not yet discovered by the guard.

Braggioni says: "Are you going to sleep?" Almost before she can shake
her head, he begins telling her about the May-day disturbances coming on
in Morelia, for the Catholics hold a festival in honor of the Blessed Virgin,
and the Socialists celebrate their martyrs on that day. "There will be two
independent processions, starting from either end of town, and they will
march until they meet, and the rest depends . . ." He asks her to oil and load
his pistols. Standing up, he unbuckles his ammunition belt, and spreads it
laden across her knees. Laura sits with the shells slipping through the cleaning cloth dipped in oil, and he says again he cannot understand why she
works so hard for the revolutionary idea unless she loves some man who is
in it. "Are you not in love with someone?" "No," says Laura. "And no one
is in love with you?" "No." "Then it is your own fault. No woman need go
begging. Why, what is the matter with you? The legless beggar woman in
the Alameda has a perfectly faithful lover. Did you know that?"

Laura peers down the pistol barrel and says nothing, but a long, slow faint-
ness rises and subsides in her; Braggioni curves his swollen fingers around the
throat of the guitar and softly smothers the music out of it, and when she
hears him again he seems to have forgotten her, and is speaking in the
hypnotic voice he uses when talking in small rooms to a listening, close-
gathered crowd. Some day this world, now seemingly so composed and eternal,
to the edges of every sea shall be merely a tangle of gaping trenches, of crashing walls and broken bodies. Everything must be torn from its accustomed
place where it has rotted for centuries, hurled skyward and distributed, cast
down again clean as rain, without separate identity. Nothing shall survive that
the stiffened hands of poverty have created for the rich and no one shall be left
alive except the elect spirits destined to procreate a new world cleansed of
cruelty and injustice, ruled by benevolent anarchy: "Pistols are good, I love

them, cannon are even better, but in the end I pin my faith to good dynamite," he concludes, and strokes the pistol lying in her hands. "Once I dreamed of destroying this city, in case it offered resistance to General Ortíz, but it fell into his hands like an overripe pear."

He is made restless by his own words, rises and stands waiting. Laura holds up the belt to him: "Put that on, and go kill somebody in Morelia, and you will be happier," she says softly. The presence of death in the room makes her bold. "Today, I found Eugenio going into a stupor. He refused to allow me to call the prison doctor. He had taken all the tablets I brought him yesterday. He said he took them because he was bored."

"He is a fool, and his death is his own business," says Braggioni, fastening his belt carefully.

"I told him if he had waited only a little while longer, you would have got him set free," says Laura. "He said he did not want to wait."

"He is a fool and we are well rid of him," says Braggioni, reaching for his hat.

He goes away. Laura knows his mood has changed, she will not see him any more for a while. He will send word when he needs her to go on errands into strange streets, to speak to the strange faces that will appear, like clay masks with the power of human speech, to mutter their thanks to Braggioni for his help. Now she is free, and she thinks, I must run while there is time. But she does not go.

Braggioni enters his own house where for a month his wife has spent many hours every night weeping and tangling her hair upon her pillow. She is weeping now, and she weeps more at the sight of him, the cause of all her sorrows. He looks about the room. Nothing is changed, the smells are good and familiar, he is well acquainted with the woman who comes toward him with no reproach except grief on her face. He says to her tenderly: "You are so good, please don't cry any more, you dear good creature." She says, "Are you tired, my angel? Sit here and I will wash your feet." She brings a bowl of water, and kneeling, unlaces his shoes, and when from her knees she raises her sad eyes under her blackened lids, he is sorry for everything, and bursts into tears. "Ah, yes, I am hungry, I am tired, let us eat something together," he says, between sobs. His wife leans her head on his arm and says, "Forgive me!" and this time he is refreshed by the solemn, endless rain of her tears.

Laura takes off her serge dress and puts on a white linen nightgown and goes to bed. She turns her head a little to one side, and lying still, reminds herself that it is time to sleep. Numbers tick in her brain like little clocks, soundless doors close of themselves around her. If you would sleep, you must not remember anything, the children will say tomorrow, good morning, my teacher, the poor prisoners who come every day bringing flowers to their jailor. 1-2-3-4-5 it is monstrous to confuse love with revolution, night with day, life with death—ah, Eugenio!

The tolling of the midnight bell is a signal, but what does it mean? Get up, Laura, and follow me: come out of your sleep, out of your bed, out of this strange house. What are you doing in this house? Without a word, without fear she rose and reached for Eugenio's hand, but he eluded her with a sharp, sly smile and drifted away. This is not all, you shall see— Murderer, he said, follow me, I will show you a new country, but it is far away and we must hurry. No, said Laura, not unless you take my hand, no; and she clung first to the stair rail, and then to the topmost branch of the Judas tree that bent down slowly and set her upon the earth, and then to the rocky ledge of a cliff, and then to the jagged wave of a sea that was not water but a desert of crumbling stone. Where are you taking me, she asked in wonder but without fear. To death, and it is a long way off, and we must hurry, said Eugenio. No, said Laura, not unless you take my hand. Then eat these flowers, poor prisoner, said Eugenio in a voice of pity, take and eat: and from the Judas tree he stripped the warm bleeding flowers, and held them to her lips. She saw that his hand was fleshless, a cluster of small white petrified branches, and his eye sockets were without light, but she ate the flowers greedily for they satisfied both hunger and thirst. Murderer! said Eugenio, and Cannibal! This is my body and my blood. Laura cried No! and at the sound of her own voice, she awoke trembling, and was afraid to sleep again.   (1930)

William Faulkner

THE BEAR

He was ten. But it had already begun, long before that day when at last he wrote his age in two figures and he saw for the first time the camp where his father and Major de Spain and old General Compson and the others spent two weeks each November and two weeks again each June. He had already inherited then, without ever having seen it, the tremendous bear with one trap-ruined foot which, in an area almost a hundred miles deep, had earned itself a name, a definite designation like a living man.

He had listened to it for years: the long legend of corncribs rifled, of shotes and grown pigs and even calves carried bodily into the woods and devoured, of traps and deadfalls overthrown and dogs mangled and slain, and shotgun and even rifle charges delivered at point-blank range and with no more effect than so many peas blown through a tube by a boy—a corridor of wreckage and destruction beginning back before he was born, through which sped, not fast but rather with the ruthless and irresistible deliberation of a locomotive, the shaggy tremendous shape.

It ran in his knowledge before he ever saw it. It looked and towered in his dreams before he even saw the unaxed woods where it left its crooked print, shaggy, huge, red-eyed, not malevolent but just big—too big for the dogs which tried to bay it, for the horses which tried to ride it down, for the men and the bullets they fired into it, too big for the very country which was its constricting scope. He seemed to see it entire with a child's complete divination before he ever laid eyes on either—the doomed wilderness whose edges were being constantly and punily gnawed at by men with axes and plows who feared it because it was wilderness, men myriad and nameless even to one another in the land where the old bear had earned a name, through which ran not even a mortal animal but an anachronism, indomitable and invincible, out of an old dead time, a phantom, epitome and apotheosis of the old wild life at which the puny humans swarmed and hacked in a fury of abhorrence and fear, like pygmies about the ankles of a drowsing elephant: the old bear solitary, indomitable and alone, widowered, childless, and absolved of mortality —old Priam reft of his old wife and having outlived all his sons.

Until he was ten, each November he would watch the wagon containing the dogs and the bedding and food and guns and his father and Tennie's Jim, the Negro, and Sam Fathers, the Indian, son of a slave woman and a Chickasaw chief, depart on the road to town, to Jefferson, where Major de Spain and the others would join them. To the boy, at seven, eight, and nine, they were not going into the Big Bottom to hunt bear and deer, but to keep yearly rendezvous with the bear which they did not even intend to kill. Two weeks later they would return, with no trophy, no head and skin. He had not expected it. He had not even been afraid it would be in the wagon. He believed that even after he was ten and his father would let him go too, for those two weeks in November, he would merely make another one, along with his father and Major de Spain and General Compson and the others, the dogs which feared to bay at it and the rifles and shotguns which failed even to bleed it, in the yearly pageant of the old bear's furious immortality.

Then he heard the dogs. It was in the second week of his first time in the camp. He stood with Sam Fathers against a big oak beside the faint crossing where they had stood each dawn for nine days now, hearing the dogs. He had heard them once before, one morning last week—a murmur, sourceless, echoing through the wet woods, swelling presently into separate voices which he could recognize and call by name. He had raised and cocked the gun as Sam told him and stood motionless again while the uproar, the invisible course, swept up and past and faded; it seemed to him that he could actually see the deer, the buck, blond, smoke-colored, elongated with speed, fleeing, vanishing, the woods, the gray solitude, still ringing even when the cries of the dogs had died away.

"Now let the hammers down," Sam said.

"You knew they were not coming here too," he said.

"Yes," Sam said. "I want you to learn how to do when you didn't shoot. It's after the chance for the bear or the deer has done already come and gone that men and dogs get killed."

"Anyway," he said, "it was just a deer."

Then on the tenth morning he heard the dogs again. And he readied the too-long, too-heavy gun as Sam had taught him, before Sam even spoke. But this time it was no deer, no ringing chorus of dogs running strong on a free scent, but a moiling yapping an octave too high, with something more than indecision and even abjectness in it, not even moving very fast, taking a long time to pass completely out of hearing, leaving them somewhere in the air that echo, thin, slightly hysterical, abject, almost grieving, with no sense of a fleeing, unseen, smoke-colored, grass-eating shape ahead of it, and Sam, who had taught him first of all to cock the gun and take position where he could see everywhere and then never move again, had himself moved up beside him; he could hear Sam breathing at his shoulder, and he could see the arched curve of the old man's inhaling nostrils.

"Hah," Sam said. "Not even running. Walking."

"Old Ben!" the boy said. "But up here!" he cried, "Way up here!"

"He do it every year," Sam said. "Once. Maybe to see who in camp this time, if he can shoot or not. Whether we got the dog yet that can bay and hold him. He'll take them to the river, then he'll send them back home. We may as well go back too; see how they look when they come back to camp."

When they reached the camp the hounds were already there, ten of them crouching back under the kitchen, the boy and Sam squatting to peer back into the obscurity where they had huddled, quiet, the eyes luminous, glowing at them and vanishing, and no sound, only that effluvium of something more than dog, stronger than dog and not just animal, just beast, because still there had been nothing in front of that abject and almost painful yapping save the solitude, the wilderness, so that when the eleventh hound came in at noon and with all the others watching—even old Uncle Ash, who called himself first a cook—Sam daubed the tattered ear and the raked shoulder with turpentine and axle grease, to the boy it was still no living creature, but the wilderness which, leaning for the moment down, had patted lightly once the hound's temerity.

"Just like a man," Sam said. "Just like folks. Put off as long as she could having to be brave, knowing all the time that sooner or later she would have to be brave to keep on living with herself, and knowing all the time beforehand what was going to happen to her when she done it."

That afternoon, himself on the one-eyed wagon mule which did not mind the smell of blood nor, as they told him, of bear, and with Sam on the other one, they rode for more than three hours through the rapid, shortening winter day. They followed no path, no trail even that he could see; almost at once they were in a country which he had never seen before. Then he knew why Sam had made him ride the mule which would not spook. The sound one stopped short and tried to whirl and bolt even as Sam got down, blowing its breath, jerking and wrenching at the rein, while Sam held it, coaxing it forward with his voice, since he could not risk tying it, drawing it forward while the boy got down from the marred one.

Then, standing beside Sam in the gloom of the dying afternoon, he looked down at the rotted over-turned log, gutted and scored with claw marks and, in the wet earth beside it, the print of the enormous warped two-toed foot. He knew now what he had smelled when he peered under the kitchen where the dogs huddled. He realized for the first time that the bear which had run in his listening and loomed in his dreams since before he could remember to the contrary, and which, therefore, must have existed in the listening and dreams of his father and Major de Spain and even old General Compson, too, before they began to remember in their turn, was a mortal animal, and that if they had departed for the camp each November without any actual hope of bringing its trophy back, it was not because it could not be slain, but because so far they had had no actual hope to.

"Tomorrow," he said.

"We'll try tomorrow," Sam said. "We ain't got the dog yet."

"We've got eleven. They ran him this morning."

"It won't need but one." Sam said. "He ain't here. Maybe he ain't nowhere. The only other way will be for him to run by accident over somebody that has a gun."

"That wouldn't be me," the boy said. "It will be Walter or Major or—"

"It might," Sam said. "You watch close in the morning. Because he's smart. That's how come he has lived this long. If he gets hemmed up and has to pick out somebody to run over, he will pick out you."

"How?" the boy said. "How will he know—" He ceased. "You mean he already knows me, that I ain't never been here before, ain't had time to find out yet whether I—" He ceased again, looking at Sam, the old man whose face revealed nothing until it smiled. He said humbly, not even amazed, "It was me he was watching. I don't reckon he did need to come but once."

The next morning they left the camp three hours before daylight. They rode this time because it was too far to walk, even the dogs in the wagon; again the first gray light found him in a place which he had never seen before, where Sam had placed him and told him to stay and then departed. With the gun which was too big for him, which did not even belong to him, but to Major de Spain, and which he had fired only once—at a stump on the first day, to learn the recoil and how to reload it—he stood against a gum tree beside a little bayou whose black still water crept without movement out of a canebrake and crossed a small clearing and into cane again, where, invisible, a bird—the big woodpecker called Lord-to-God by Negroes—clattered at a dead limb.

It was a stand like any other, dissimilar only in incidentals to the one where he had stood each morning for ten days; a territory new to him, yet no less familiar than that other one which, after almost two weeks, he had come to believe he knew a little—the same solitude, the same loneliness through which human beings had merely passed without altering it, leaving no mark, no scar, which looked exactly as it must have looked when the first ancestor of Sam Fathers' Chickasaw predecessors crept into it and looked about, club or stone ax or bone arrow drawn and poised; different only because, squatting at the edge of the kitchen, he smelled the hounds huddled and cringing beneath it and saw the raked ear and shoulder of the one who, Sam said, had had to be brave once in order to live with herself, and saw yesterday in the earth beside the gutted log the print of the living foot.

He heard no dogs at all. He never did hear them. He only heard the drumming of the woodpecker stop short off and knew that the bear was looking at him. He never saw it. He did not know whether it was in front of him or behind him. He did not move, holding the useless gun, which he had not even had warning to cock and which even now he did not cock, tasting in his saliva that taint as of brass which he knew now because he had smelled it when he peered under the kitchen at the huddled dogs.

Then it was gone. As abruptly as it had ceased, the woodpecker's dry, monotonous clatter set up again, and after a while he even believed he could hear the dogs—a murmur, scarce a sound even, which he had probably been hearing for some time before he even remarked it, drifting into hearing and then out again, dying away. They came nowhere near him. If it was a bear they ran, it was another bear. It was Sam himself who came out of the cane and crossed the bayou, followed by the injured bitch of yesterday. She was almost at heel, like a bird dog, making no sound. She came and crouched against his leg, trembling, staring off into the cane.

"I didn't see him," he said. "I didn't, Sam!"

"I know it," Sam said. "He done the looking. You didn't hear him neither, did you?"

"No," the boy said. "I—"

"He's smart." Sam said. "Too smart." He looked down at the hound, trembling faintly and steadily against the boy's knee. From the raked shoulder a few drops of fresh blood oozed and clung. "Too big. We ain't got the dog yet. But maybe someday. Maybe not next time. But someday."

So I must see him, he thought. *I must look at him.* Otherwise, it seemed to him that it would go on like this forever, as it had gone on with his father and Major de Spain, who was older than his father, and even with old General Compson, who had been old enough to be a brigade commander in 1865. Otherwise, it would go on so forever, next time and next time, after and after and after. It seemed to him that he could never see the two of them, himself and the bear, shadowy in the limbo from which time emerged, becoming time; the old bear absolved of mortality and himself partaking, sharing a little of it, enough of it. And he knew now what he had smelled in the huddled dogs and tasted in his saliva. He recognized fear. *So I will have to see him,* he thought, without dread or even hope. *I will have to look at him.*

It was in June of the next year. He was eleven. They were in camp again, celebrating Major de Spain's and General Compson's birthdays. Although the one had been born in September and the other in the depth of winter and in another decade, they had met for two weeks to fish and shoot squirrels and turkey and run coons and wildcats with the dogs at night. That is, he and Boon Hoggenbeck and the Negroes fished and shot squirrels and ran the coons and cats, because the proved hunters, not only Major de Spain and old General Compson, who spent those two weeks sitting in a rocking chair before a tremendous iron pot of Brunswick stew, stirring and tasting, with old Ash to quarrel with about how he was making it and Tennie's Jim to pour whiskey from the demijohn into the tin dipper from which he drank it, but even the boy's father and Walter Ewell, who were still young enough, scorned such, other than shooting the wild gobblers with pistols for wagers on their marksmanship.

Or, that is, his father and the others believed he was hunting squirrels. Until the third day, he thought that Sam Fathers believed that too. Each morning he would leave the camp right after breakfast. He had his own gun now, a Christmas present. He went back to the tree beside the bayou where he had stood that morning. Using the compass which old General Compson had given him, he ranged from that point; he was teaching himself to be a better-than-fair woodsman without knowing he was doing it. On the second day he even found the gutted log where he had first seen the crooked print. It was almost completely crumbled now, healing with unbelievable speed, a passionate and almost visible relinquishment, back into the earth from which the tree had grown.

He ranged the summer woods now, green with gloom; if anything, actually dimmer than in November's gray dissolution, where, even at noon, the sun fell only in intermittent dappling upon the earth, which never completely dried out and which crawled with snakes—moccasins and water snakes and rattlers, themselves the color of the dappling gloom, so that he would not always see them until they moved, returning later and later, first day, second day, passing in the twilight of the third evening the little log pen enclosing the log stable where Sam was putting up the horses for the night.

"You ain't looked right yet," Sam said.

He stopped. For a moment he didn't answer. Then he said peacefully, in a peaceful rushing burst as when a boy's miniature dam in a little brook gives way, "All right. But how? I went to the bayou. I even found that log again. I—"

"I reckon that was all right. Likely he's been watching you. You never saw his foot?"

"I," the boy said—"I didn't—I never thought—"

"It's the gun," Sam said. He stood beside the fence, motionless—the old man, the Indian, in the battered faded overalls and the five-cent straw hat which in the Negro's race had been the badge of his enslavement and was now the regalia of his freedom. The camp—the clearing, the house, the barn and its tiny lot with which Major de Spain in his turn had scratched punily and evanescently at the wilderness—faded in the dusk, back into the immemorial darkness of the woods. *The gun*, the boy thought. *The gun.*

"Be scared," Sam said. "You can't help that. But don't be afraid. Ain't nothing in the woods going to hurt you unless you corner it, or it smells that you are afraid. A bear or a deer, too, has got to be scared of a coward the same as a brave man has got to be."

The gun, the boy thought.

"You will have to choose," Sam said.

He left the camp before daylight, long before Uncle Ash would wake in his quilts on the kitchen floor and start the fire for breakfast. He had only the compass and a stick for snakes. He could go almost a mile before he would begin to need the compass. He sat on a log, the invisible compass in his invisible hand, while the secret night sounds, fallen still at his movements, scurried again and then ceased for good, and the owls ceased and gave over to the waking of day birds, and he could see the compass. Then he went fast yet still quietly; he was becoming better and better as a woodsman, still without having yet realized it.

He jumped a doe and a fawn at sunrise, walked them out of the bed, close enough to see them—the crash of undergrowth, the white scut, the fawn scudding behind her faster than he had believed it could run. He was hunting right, upwind, as Sam had taught him; not that it mattered now. He had left the gun; of his own will and relinquishment he had accepted not a gambit, not a choice, but a condition in which not only the bear's heretofore inviolable anonymity but all the old rules and balances of hunter and hunted had been abrogated. He would not even be afraid, not even in the moment when the fear would take him completely—blood, skin, bowels, bones, memory from the long time before it became his memory—all save that thin, clear, immortal lucidity which alone differed him from this bear and from all the other bear and deer he would ever kill in the humility and pride of his skill and endurance, to which Sam had spoken when he leaned in the twilight on the lot fence yesterday.

By noon he was far beyond the little bayou, farther into the new and alien country than he had ever been. He was traveling now not only by the old, heavy, biscuit-thick silver watch which had belonged to his grandfather. When he stopped at last, it was for the first time since he had risen from the log at dawn when he could see the compass. It was far enough. He had left the camp nine hours ago; nine hours from now, dark would have already been an hour old. But he didn't think that. He thought. *All right. Yes. But what?* and stood for a moment, alien and small in the green and topless solitude, answering his own question before it had formed and ceased. It was the watch, the compass, the stick—the three lifeless mechanicals with which for nine hours he had fended the wilderness off; he hung the watch and compass carefully on a bush and leaned the stick beside them and relinquished completely to it.

He had not been going very fast for the last two or three hours. He went no faster now, since distance would not matter even if he could have gone fast. And he was trying to keep a bearing on the tree where he had left the compass, trying to complete a circle which would bring him back to it or at least intersect itself, since direction would not matter now either. But the tree was not there, and he did as Sam had schooled him—made the next circle in the opposite direction, so that the two patterns would bisect somewhere, but crossing no print of his own feet, finding the tree at last, but in the wrong place—no bush, no compass, no watch—and the tree not even the tree, because there was a down log beside it and he did what Sam Fathers had told him was the next thing and the last.

As he sat down on the log he saw the crooked print—the warped, tremendous, two-toed indentation which, even as he watched it, filled with water. As he looked up, the wilderness coalesced, solidified—the glade, the tree he sought, the bush, the watch and the compass glinting where a ray of sunshine touched them. Then he saw the bear. It did not emerge, appear; it was just there, immobile, solid, fixed in the hot dappling of the green and windless noon, not as big as he had dreamed it, but as big as he had expected it, bigger, dimensionless, against the dappled obscurity, looking at him where he sat quietly on the log and looked back at it.

Then it moved. It made no sound. It did not hurry. It crossed the glade, walking for an instant into the full glare of the sun; when it reached the other side it stopped again and looked back at him across one shoulder while his quiet breathing inhaled and exhaled three times.

Then it was gone. It didn't walk into the woods, the undergrowth. It faded, sank back into the wilderness as he had watched a fish, a huge old bass, sink and vanish into the dark depths of its pool without even any movement of its fins.

He thought, *It will be next fall.* But it was not next fall, nor the next nor the next. He was fourteen then. He had killed his buck, and Sam Fathers had marked his face with the hot blood, and in the next year he killed a bear. But even before that accolade he had become as competent in the woods as many grown men with the same experience; by his fourteenth year he was a better woodsman than most grown men with more. There was no territory within thirty miles of the camp that he did not know—bayou, ridge, brake, landmark, tree and path. He could have led anyone to any point in it without deviation, and brought them out again. He knew the game trails that even Sam Fathers did not know; in his thirteenth year he found a buck's bedding place, and unbeknown to his father he borrowed Walter Ewell's rifle and lay in wait at dawn and killed the buck when it walked back to the bed, as Sam had told him how the old Chickasaw fathers did.

But not the old bear, although by now he knew its footprints better than he did his own, and not only the crooked one. He could see any one of the three sound ones and distinguish it from any other, and not only by its size. There were other bears within these thirty miles which left tracks almost as large, but this was more than that. If Sam Fathers had been his mentor and the back-yard rabbits and squirrels at home his kindergarten, then the wilderness the old bear ran was his college, the old male bear itself, so long unwifed and childless as to have become its own ungendered progenitor, was his alma mater. But he never saw it.

He could find the crooked print now almost whenever he liked, fifteen or ten or five miles, or sometimes nearer the camp than that. Twice while on stand during the three years he heard the dogs strike its trail by accident; on the second time they jumped it seemingly, the voices high, abject, almost human in hysteria, as on that first morning two years ago. But not the bear itself. He would remember that noon three years ago, the glade, himself and the bear fixed during that moment in the windless and dappled blaze, and it would seem to him that it had never happened, that he had dreamed that too. But it had happened. They had looked at each other, they had emerged from the wilderness old as earth, synchronized to the instant by something more than the blood that moved the flesh and bones which bore them, and touched, pledged something, affirmed, something more lasting than the frail web of bones and flesh which any accident could obliterate.

Then he saw it again. Because of the very fact that he thought of nothing else, he had forgotten to look for it. He was still hunting with Walter Ewell's rifle. He saw it cross the end of a long blow-down, a corridor where a tornado had swept, rushing through rather than over the tangle of trunks and branches as a locomotive would have, faster than he had ever believed it could move, almost as fast as a deer even, because a deer would have spent most of that time in the air, faster than he could bring the rifle sights up with it. And now he knew what had been wrong during all the three years. He sat on a log, shaking and trembling as if he had never seen the woods before nor anything that ran them, wondering with incredulous amazement how he could have forgotten the very thing which Sam Fathers had told him and which the bear itself had proved the next day and had now returned after three years to reaffirm.

And now he knew what Sam Fathers had meant about the right dog, a dog in which size would mean less than nothing. So when he returned alone in April—school was out then, so that the sons of farmers could help with the land's planting, and at last his father had granted him permission, on his promise to be back in four days—he had the dog. It was his own, a mongrel of the sort called by Negroes a fyce, a ratter, itself not much bigger than a rat and possessing that bravery which had long since stopped being courage and had become foolhardiness.

It did not take four days. Alone again, he found the trail on the first morning. It was not a stalk; it was an ambush. He timed the meeting almost as if it were an appointment with a human being. Himself holding the fyce muffled in a feed sack and Sam Fathers with two of the hounds on a piece of a plowline rope, they lay down wind of the trail at dawn of the second morning. They were so close that the bear turned without even running, as if in surprised amazement at the shrill and frantic uproar of the released fyce, turning at bay against the trunk of a tree, on its hind feet; it seemed to the boy that it would never stop rising, taller and taller, and even the two hounds seemed to take a desperate and despairing courage from the fyce, following it as it went in.

Then he realized that the fyce was actually not going to stop. He flung, threw the gun away, and ran; when he overtook and grasped the frantically pin-wheeling little dog, it seemed to him that he was directly under the bear.

He could smell it, strong and hot and rank. Sprawling, he looked up to where it loomed and towered over him like a cloudburst and colored like a thunderclap, quite familiar, peacefully and even lucidly familiar, until he remembered: This was the way he had used to dream about it. Then it was gone. He didn't see it go. He knelt, holding the frantic fyce with both hands, hearing the abashed wailing of the hounds drawing farther and farther away, until Sam came up. He carried the gun. He laid it down quietly beside the boy and stood looking down at him.

"You've done seed him twice now with a gun in your hands," he said. "This time you couldn't have missed him."

The boy rose. He still held the fyce. Even in his arms and clear of the ground, it yapped frantically, straining and surging after the fading uproar of the two hounds like a tangle of wire springs. He was panting a little, but he was neither shaking nor trembling now.

"Neither could you!" he said. "You had the gun! Neither did you!"

"And you didn't shoot," his father said. "How close were you?"

"I don't know, sir," he said. "There was a big wood tick inside his right hind leg. I saw that. But I didn't have the gun then."

"But you didn't shoot when you had the gun," his father said. "Why?"

But he didn't answer, and his father didn't wait for him to, rising and crossing the room, across the pelt of the bear which the boy had killed two years ago and the larger one which his father had killed before he was born, to the bookcase beneath the mounted head of the boy's first buck. It was the room which his father called the office, from which all the plantation business was transacted; in it for the fourteen years of his life he had heard the best of all talking. Major de Spain would be there and sometimes old General Compson, and Walter Ewell and Boon Hoggenback and Sam Fathers and Tennie's Jim, too, were hunters, knew the woods and what ran them.

He would hear it, not talking himself but listening—the wilderness, the big woods, bigger and older than any recorded document of white man fatuous enough to believe he had bought any fragment of it or Indian ruthless enough to pretend that any fragment of it had been his to convey. It was of the men, not white nor black nor red, but men, hunters with the will and hardihood to endure and the humility and skill to survive, and the dogs and the bear and deer juxtaposed and reliefed against it, ordered and compelled by and within the wilderness in the ancient and unremitting contest by the ancient and immitigable rules which voided all regrets and brooked no quarter, the voices quiet and weighty and deliberate for retrospection and recollection and exact remembering, while he squatted in the blazing firelight as Tennie's Jim squatted, who stirred only to put more wood on the fire and to pass the bottle from one glass to another. Because the bottle was always present, so that after a while it seemed to him that those fierce instants of heart and brain and courage and wiliness and speed were concentrated and distilled into that brown liquor which not women, not boys and children, but only hunters drank, drinking not of the blood they had spilled but some condensation of the wild immortal spirit, drinking it moderately, humbly even, not with the pagan's base hope of acquiring the virtues of cunning and strength and speed, but in salute to them.

His father returned with the book and sat down again and opened it. "Listen," he said. He read the five stanzas aloud, his voice quiet and deliberate in the room where there was no fire now because it was already spring. Then he looked up. The boy watched him. "All right," his father said. "Listen." He read again, but only the second stanza this time, to the end of it, the last two lines, and closed the book and put it on the table beside him. "She cannot fade, though thou hast not thy bliss, for ever wilt thou love, and she be fair," he said.

"He's talking about a girl," the boy said.

"He had to talk about something," his father said. Then he said, "He was talking about truth. Truth doesn't change. Truth is one thing. It covers all things which touch the heart—honor and pride and pity and justice and courage and love. Do you see now?"

He didn't know. Somehow it was simpler than that. There was an old bear, fierce and ruthless, not merely just to stay alive, but with the fierce pride of liberty and freedom, proud enough of the liberty and freedom to see it threatened without fear or even alarm; nay, who at times even seemed deliberately to put that freedom and liberty in jeopardy in order to savor them, to remind his old strong bones and flesh to keep supple and quick to defend and preserve them. There was an old man, son of a Negro slave and an Indian king, inheritor on the one side of the long chronicle of a people who had learned humility through suffering, and pride through the endurance which survived the suffering and injustice, and on the other side, the chronicle of a people even longer in the land than the first, yet who no longer existed in the land at all save in the solitary brotherhood of an old Negro's alien blood and the wild and invincible spirit of an old bear. There was a boy who wished to learn humility and pride in order to become skillful and worthy in the woods, who suddenly found himself becoming so skillful so rapidly that he feared he would never become worthy because he had not learned humility and pride, although he had tried to, until one day and as suddenly he discovered that an old man who could not have defined either had led him, as though by the hand, to that point where an old bear and a little mongrel of a dog showed him that, by possessing one thing other, he would possess them both.

And a little dog, nameless and mongrel and many-fathered, grown, yet weighing less than six pounds, saying as if to itself, "I can't be dangerous, because there's nothing much smaller than I am; I can't be fierce, because they would call it just a noise; I can't be humble, because I'm already too close to the ground to genuflect; I can't be proud, because I wouldn't be near enough to it for anyone to know who was casting the shadow, and I don't even know that I'm not going to heaven, because they have already decided that I don't possess an immortal soul. So all I can be is brave. But it's all right. I can be that, even if they still call it just noise."

That was all. It was simple, much simpler than somebody talking in a book about youth and a girl he would never need to grieve over, because he could never approach any nearer her and would never have to get any farther away. He had heard about a bear, and finally got big enough to trail it, and he trailed it four years and at last met it with a gun in his hands and he didn't shoot. Because a little dog—But he could have shot long before the little dog covered the twenty yards to where the bear waited, and Sam Fathers could have shot at any time during that interminable minute while Old Ben stood on his hind feet over them. He stopped. His father was watching him gravely across the spring-rife twilight of the room; when he spoke, his words were as quiet as the twilight, too, not loud, because they did not need to be because they would last, "Courage, and honor, and pride," his father said, "and pity, and love of justice and of liberty. They all touch the heart, and what the heart holds to becomes truth, as far as we know the truth. Do you see now?"

Sam, and Old Ben, and Nip, he thought. And himself too. He had been all right too. His father had said so. "Yes, sir," he said.   (1942)

$\mathscr{S. J. Perelman}$

THE IDOL'S EYE

I had been week-ending with Gabriel Snubbers at his villa, "The Acacias," on the edge of the Downs. Gabriel isn't seen about as much as he used to be; one hears that an eccentric aunt left him a tidy little sum and the lazy beggar refuses to leave his native haunts. Four of us had cycled down from London together: Gossip Gabrilowitsch, the Polish pianist; Downey Couch, the Irish tenor; Frank Falcovsky, the Jewish prowler, and myself, Clay Modelling. Snubbers, his face beaming, met us at the keeper's lodge. His eyes were set in deep rolls of fat for our arrival, and I couldn't help thinking how well they looked. I wondered whether it was because his daring farce, *Mrs. Stebbins' Step-Ins*, had been doing so well at the Haymarket.

"Deuced decent of you chaps to make this filthy trip." he told us, leading us up the great avenue of two stately alms towards the house. "Rum place, this." A surprise awaited us when we reached the house, for the entire left wing had just burned down. Snubbers, poor fellow, stared at it a bit ruefully, I thought.

"Just as well. It was only a plague-spot," sympathized Falcovsky. Snubbers was thoughtful.

"D'ye know, you chaps," he said suddenly, "I could swear an aunt of mine was staying in that wing." Falcovsky stirred the ashes with his stick and un-covered a pair of knitting needles and a half-charred corset.

"No, it must have been the other wing," dismissed Snubbers. "How about a spot of whisky and soda?" We entered and Littlejohn, Snubbers' man, brought in a spot of whisky on a piece of paper which we all examined with interest. A splendid fire was already roaring in the middle of the floor to drive out the warmth.

"Soda?" offered Snubbers. I took it to please him, for Gabriel's cellar was reputedly excellent. A second later I wished that I had drunk the cellar instead. Baking soda is hardly the thing after a three-hour bicycle trip.

"You drank that like a little soldier," he complimented, his little button eyes fastened on me. I was about to remark that I had never drunk a little soldier, when I noticed Littlejohn hovering in the doorway.

"Yes, that will be all," Snubbers waved, "and, oh, by the way, send up to London tomorrow for a new wing, will you?" Littlejohn bowed and left, silently, sleekly Oriental.

"Queer cove, Littlejohn," commented Snubbers. "Shall I tell you a story?" He did, and it was one of the dullest I have ever heard. At the end of it Falcovsky grunted. Snubbers surveyed him suspiciously.

"Why, what's up, old man?" he queried.

"What's up? Nothing's up," snarled Falcovsky. "Can't a man grunt in front of an open fire if he wants to?"

"But . . ." began Snubbers.

"But nothing," Falcovsky grated. "You haven't lived till you've grunted in front of an open fire. Just for that—grunt, grunt, grunt," and he grunted several times out of sheer spite. The baking soda was beginning to tell on Snubbers.

"Remarkable thing happened the other day," he began. "I was pottering about in the garden . . ."

"Why must one always potter around in a garden?" demanded Couch. "Can't you potter around in an armchair just as well?"

"I did once," confessed Snubbers moodily, revealing a whitish scar on his chin. "Gad, sir, what a wildcat she was!" He chewed his wad of carbon paper reminiscently. "Oh, well, never mind. But as I was saying—I was going through some of my great-grandfather's things the other day . . ."

"What things?" demanded Falcovsky.

"His bones, if you must know," Snubbers said coldly. "You know, Great-grandfather died under strange circumstances. He opened a vein in his bath."

"I never knew baths had veins," protested Gabrilowitsch.

"I never knew his great-grandfather had a ba—" began Falcovsky derisively. With a shout Snubbers threw himself on Falcovsky. It was the signal for Pandemonium, the upstairs girl, to enter and throw herself with a shout on Couch. The outcome of the necking bee was as follows: Canadians 12, Visitors 9. Krebs and Vronsky played footie, subbing for Gerber and Weinwald, who were disabled by flying antipasto.

We were silent after Snubbers had spoken; men who have wandered in far places have an innate delicacy about their great-grandfathers' bones. Snubbers' face was a mask, his voice a harsh whip of pain in the stillness when he spoke again.

"I fancy none of you knew my great-grandfather," he said slowly. "Before your time, I daresay. A rare giant of a man with quizzical eyes and a great shock of wiry red hair, he had come through the Peninsular Wars without a scratch. Women loved this impetual Irish adventurer who would rather fight than eat and vice versa. The wars over, he turned toward cookery, planning to devote his failing years to the perfection of the welsh rarebit, a dish he loved. One night he was chafing at The Bit, a tavern in Portsmouth, when he overheard a chance remark from a brawny gunner's mate in his cups. In Calcutta the man had heard native tales of a mysterious idol, whose single eye was a flawless ruby.

" 'Topscuttle my bamberger, it's the size of a bloomin' pigeon's egg!' spat the salt, shifting his quid to his other cheek. 'A bloomin' rajah's ransom and ye may lay to that, mateys!'

"The following morning the *Maid of Hull*, a frigate of the line mounting thirty-six guns, out of Bath and into bed in a twinkling, dropped downstream on the tide, bound out for Bombay, object matrimony. On her as passenger went my great-grandfather, an extra pair of nankeen pants and a dirk his only baggage. Fifty-three days later in Poona, he was heading for the interior of one of the Northern states. Living almost entirely on cameo brooches and the few ptarmigan which fell to the ptrigger of his pfowlingpiece, he at last sighted the towers of Ishpeming, the Holy City of the Surds and Cosines, fanatic Mohammedan warrior sects. He disguised himself as a beggar and entered the gates.

"For weeks my great-grandfather awaited his chance to enter the temple of the idol. They were changing the guard one evening when he saw it. One of the native janissaries dropped his knife. My great-grandfather leaped forward with cringing servility and returned it to him, in the small of his back. Donning the soldier's turban, he quickly slipped into his place. Midnight found him within ten feet of his prize. Now came the final test. He furtively drew from the folds of his robes a plate of curry, a dish much prized by Indians, and set it in a far corner. The guards rushed upon it with bulging squeals of delight. A twist of his wrist and the gem was his. With an elaborately stifled yawn, my great-grandfather left under pretense of going out for a glass of water. The soldiers winked slyly but when he did not return after two hours, their suspicions were aroused. They hastily made a canvass of the places where water was served and their worst fears were realized. The ruby in his burnoose, Great-grandfather was escaping by fast elephant over the Khyber Pass. Dockside loungers in Yarmouth forty days later stared curiously at a mammoth of a man with flaming red hair striding toward the Bull and Bloater Tavern. Under his belt, did they but only know it, lay the Ruby Eye.

"Ten years to that night had passed, and my great-grandfather, in seclusion under this very roof, had almost forgotten his daring escapade. Smoking by the fireplace, he listened to the roar of the wind and reviewed his campaigns. Suddenly he leaped to his feet—a dark face had vanished from the window. Too late my great-grandfather snatched up powder and ball and sent a charge hurtling into the night. The note pinned to the window drained the blood from his face.

"It was the first of a series. Overnight his hair turned from rose-red to snow-white. And finally, when it seemed as though madness were to rob them of their revenge, *they came.*"

Snubbers stopped, his eyes those of a man who had looked beyond life and had seen things best left hidden from mortal orbs. Falcovsky's hand was trembling as he pressed a pinch of snuff against his gums.

"You—you mean?" he quavelled.

"Yes." Snubbers' voice had sunk to a whisper. "He fought with the strength of nine devils, but the movers took away his piano. You see," he added very gently, "Great-grandfather had missed the last four instalments." Gabrilowitsch sighed deeply and arose, his eyes fixed intently on Snubbers.

"And—and the ruby?" he asked softly, his delicate fingers closing around the fire-tongs.

"Oh, *that*," shrugged Snubbers, "I just threw that in to make it interesting."

We bashed in his conk and left him to the vultures.   (1944)

J. D. Salinger

FOR ESMÉ—WITH

LOVE AND SQUALOR

Just recently, by air mail, I received an invitation to a wedding that will take place in England on April 18th. It happens to be a wedding I'd give a lot to be able to get to, and when the invitation first arrived, I thought it might just be possible for me to make the trip abroad, by plane, expenses be hanged. However, I've since discussed the matter rather extensively with my wife, a breathtakingly levelheaded girl, and we've decided against it—for one thing. I'd completely forgotten that my mother-in-law is looking forward to spending the last two weeks in April with us. I really don't get to see Mother Grencher terribly often, and she's not getting any younger. She's fifty-eight. (As she'd be the first to admit.)

All the same, though, wher*ev*er I happen to be, I don't think I'm the type that doesn't even lift a finger to prevent a wedding from flatting. Accordingly, I've gone ahead and jotted down a few revealing notes on the bride as I knew her almost six years ago. If my notes should cause the groom, whom I haven't met, an uneasy moment or two, so much the better. Nobody's aiming to please, here. More, really, to edify, to instruct.

In April of 1944, I was among some sixty American enlisted men who took a rather specialized pre-Invasion training course, directed by British Intelligence, in Devon, England. And as I look back, it seems to me that we were fairly unique, the sixty of us, in that there wasn't one good mixer in the bunch. We were all essentially letter-writing types, and when we spoke to each other out of the line of duty, it was usually to ask somebody if he had any ink he wasn't using. When we weren't writing letters or attending classes, each of us went pretty much his own way. Mine usually led me, on clear days, in scenic circles around the countryside. Rainy days, I generally sat in a dry place and read a book, often just an axe length away from a ping-pong table.

The training course lasted three weeks, ending on a Saturday, a very rainy one. At seven that last night, our whole group was scheduled to entrain for London, where, as rumor had it, we were to be assigned to infantry and air-borne divisions mustered for the D Day landings. By three in the afternoon, I'd packed all my belongings into my barrack bag, including a canvas gas-mask container full of books I'd brought over from the Other Side. (The gas mask itself I'd slipped through a porthole of the *Mauretania* some weeks earlier, fully aware that if the enemy ever *did* use gas I'd never get the damn thing on in time.) I remember standing at an end window of our Quonset hut for a very long time, looking out at the slanting, dreary rain, my trigger finger itching imperceptibly, if at all. I could hear behind my back the uncomradely scratching of many fountain pens on many sheets of V-mail paper. Abruptly, with nothing special in mind, I came away from the window and put on my raincoat, cashmere muffler, galoshes, woollen gloves, and overseas cap (the last of which, I'm still told, I wore at an angle all my own—slightly down over both ears). Then, after synchronizing my wristwatch with the clock in the latrine, I walked down the long, wet cobblestone hill into town. I ignored the flashes of lightning all around me. They either had your number on them or they didn't.

In the center of town, which was probably the wettest part of town, I stopped in front of a church to read the bulletin board, mostly because the featured numerals, white on black, had caught my attention but partly because, after three years in the Army, I'd become addicted to reading bulletin boards. At three-fifteen, the board stated, there would be children's choir practice. I looked at my wristwatch, then back at the board. A sheet of paper was tacked up, listing the names of the children expected to attend practice. I stood in the rain and read all the names, then entered the church.

A dozen or so adults were among the pews, several of them bearing pairs of small-size rubbers, soles up, in their laps. I passed along and sat down in the front row. On the rostrum, seated in three compact rows of auditorium chairs, were about twenty children, mostly girls, ranging in age from about seven to thirteen. At the moment, their choir coach, an enormous woman in tweeds, was advising them to open their mouths wider when they sang. Had anyone, she asked, ever heard of a little dickey-bird that *dared* to sing his charming song without first opening his little beak wide, wide, wide? Apparently nobody ever had. She was given a steady, opaque look. She went on to say that she wanted all her children to absorb the *meaning* of the words they sang, not just *mouth* them, like silly-billy parrots. She then blew a note on her pitch pipe, and the children, like so many underage weight-lifters, raised their hymnbooks.

They sang without instrumental accompaniment—or, more accurately in their case, without any interference. Their voices were melodious and un-sentimental, almost to the point where a somewhat more denominational man than myself might, without straining, have experienced levitation. A couple of the very youngest children dragged the tempo a trifle, but in a way that only the composer's mother could have found fault with. I had never heard the hymn, but I kept hoping it was one with a dozen or more verses. Listening, I scanned all the children's faces but watched one in particular, that of the child nearest me, on the end seat in the first row. She was about thirteen, with straight ash-blond hair of ear-lobe length, an exquisite forehead, and blasé eyes that, I thought, might very possibly have counted the house. Her voice was distinctly separate from the other children's voices, and not just because she was seated nearest me. It had the best upper register, the sweetest-sounding, the surest, and it automatically led the way. The young lady, however, seemed slightly bored with her own singing ability, or perhaps just with the time and place; twice, between verses, I saw her yawn. It was a ladylike yawn, a closed-mouth yawn, but you couldn't miss it; her nostril wings gave her away.

The instant the hymn ended, the choir coach began to give her lengthy opinion of people who can't keep their feet still and their lips sealed tight during the minister's sermon. I gathered that the singing part of the rehearsal was over, and before the coach's dissonant speaking voice could entirely break the spell the children's singing had cast, I got up and left the church.

It was raining even harder. I walked down the street and looked through the window of the Red Cross recreation room, but soldiers were standing two and three deep at the coffee counter, and, even through the glass, I could hear ping-pong balls bouncing in another room. I crossed the street and entered a civilian tearoom, which was empty except for a middle-aged waitress, who looked as if she would have preferred a customer with a dry raincoat. I used a coat tree as delicately as possible, and then sat down at a table and ordered tea and cinnamon toast. It was the first time all day that I'd spoken to anyone. I then looked through all my pockets, including my raincoat, and finally found a couple of stale letters to reread, one from my wife, telling me how the service at Schrafft's Eighty-eighth Street had fallen off, and one from my mother-in-law, asking me to please send her some cashmere yarn first chance I got away from "camp."

While I was still on my first cup of tea, the young lady I had been watching and listening to in the choir came into the tearoom. Her hair was soaking wet, and the rims of both ears were showing. She was with a very small boy, unmistakably her brother, whose cap she removed by lifting it off his head with two fingers, as if it were a laboratory specimen. Bringing up the rear was an efficient-looking woman in a limp felt hat—presumably their governess. The choir member, taking off her coat as she walked across the floor, made the table selection—a good one, from my point of view, as it was just eight or ten feet directly in front of me. She and the governess sat down. The small boy, who was about five, wasn't ready to sit down yet. He slid out of and discarded his reefer; then, with the deadpan expression of a born heller, he methodically went about annoying his governess by pushing in and pulling out his chair several times, watching her face. The governess, keeping her voice down, gave him two or three orders to sit down, and, in effect, stop the monkey business, but it was only when his sister spoke to him that he came around and applied the small of his back to his chair seat. He immediately picked up his napkin and put it on his head. His sister removed it, opened it, and spread it out on his lap.

About the time their tea was brought, the choir member caught me staring over at her party. She stared back at me, with those house-counting eyes of hers, then, abruptly, gave me a small, qualified smile. It was oddly radiant, as certain small, qualified smiles sometimes are. I smiled back, much less radiantly, keeping my upper lip down over a coal-black G.I. temporary filling showing between two of my front teeth. The next thing I knew, the young lady was standing, with enviable poise, beside my table. She was wearing a tartan dress—a Campbell tartan, I believe. It seemed to me to be a wonderful dress for a very young girl to be wearing on a rainy, rainy day. "I thought Americans despised tea," she said.

It wasn't the observation of a smart aleck but that of a truth-lover or a statistics-lover. I replied that some of us never drank anything *but* tea. I asked her if she'd care to join me.

"Thank you," she said. "Perhaps for just a fraction of a moment."

I got up and drew a chair for her, the one opposite me, and she sat down on the forward quarter of it, keeping her spine easily and beautifully straight. I went back—almost hurried back—to my own chair, more than willing to hold up my end of a conversation. When I was seated, I couldn't think of anything to say, though. I smiled again, still keeping my coal-black filling under concealment. I remarked that it was certainly a terrible day out.

"Yes; quite," said my guest, in the clear, unmistakable voice of a small-talk detester. She placed her fingers flat on the table edge, like someone at a séance, then, almost instantly, closed her hands—her nails were bitten down to the quick. She was wearing a wristwatch, a military-looking one that looked rather like a navigator's chronograph. Its face was much too large for her slender wrist. "You were at choir practice," she said matter-of-factly. "I saw you."

I said I certainly had been, and that I had heard her voice singing separately from the others. I said I thought she had a very fine voice.

She nodded. "I know. I'm going to be a professional singer."

"Really? Opera?"

"Heavens, no. I'm going to sing jazz on the radio and make heaps of money. Then, when I'm thirty, I shall retire and live on a ranch in Ohio." She touched the top of her soaking-wet head with the flat of her hand. "Do you know Ohio?" she asked.

I said I'd been through it on the train a few times but that I didn't really know it. I offered her a piece of cinnamon toast.

"No, thank you," she said. "I eat like a bird, actually."

I bit into a piece of toast myself, and commented that there's some mighty rough country around Ohio.

"I know. An American I met told me. You're the eleventh American I've met."

Her governess was now urgently signalling her to return to her own table —in effect, to stop bothering the man. My guest, however, calmly moved her chair an inch or two so that her back broke all possible further communication with the home table. "You go to that secret Intelligence school on the hill, don't you?" she inquired coolly.

As security-minded as the next one, I replied that I was visiting Devonshire for my health.

"*Really*," she said, "I wasn't quite born yesterday, you know."

I said I'd bet she hadn't been, at that. I drank my tea for a moment. I was getting a trifle posture-conscious and I sat up somewhat straighter in my seat.

"You seem quite intelligent for an American," my guest mused.

I told her that was a pretty snobbish thing to say, if you thought about it at all, and that I hoped it was unworthy of her.

She blushed—automatically conferring on me the social poise I'd been missing. "Well. Most of the Americans *I've* seen act like animals. They're forever punching one another about, and insulting everyone, and—You know what one of them did?"

I shook my head.

"One of them threw an empty whiskey bottle through my aunt's window. *Fortunately*, the window was open. But does that sound very intelligent to you?"

It didn't especially, but I didn't say so. I said that many soldiers, all over the world, were a long way from home, and that few of them had had many real advantages in life. I said I'd thought that most people could figure that out for themselves.

"Possibly," said my guest, without conviction. She raised her hand to her wet head again, picked at a few limp filaments of blond hair, trying to cover her exposed ear rims. "My hair is soaking wet," she said. "I look a fright." She looked over at me. "I have quite wavy hair when it's dry."

"I can see that, I can see you have."

"Not actually curly, but quite wavy," she said. "Are you married?"

I said I was.

She nodded. "Are you very deeply in love with your wife? Or am I being too personal?"

I said that when she was, I'd speak up.

She put her hands and wrists farther forward on the table, and I remember wanting to do something about that enormous-faced wristwatch she was wearing—perhaps suggest that she try wearing it around her waist.

"Usually, I'm not terribly gregarious," she said, and looked over at me to see if I knew the meaning of the word. I didn't give her a sign, though, one way or the other. "I purely came over because I thought you looked extremely lonely. You have an extremely sensitive face."

I said she was right, that I *had* been feeling lonely, and that I was very glad she'd come over.

"I'm training myself to be more compassionate. My aunt says I'm a terribly cold person," she said and felt the top of her head again. "I live with my aunt. She's an extremely kind person. Since the death of my mother, she's done everything within her power to make Charles and me feel adjusted."

"I'm glad."

"Mother was an extremely intelligent person. Quite sensuous, in many ways." She looked at me with a kind of fresh acuteness. "Do you find me terribly cold?"

I told her absolutely not—very much to the contrary, in fact. I told her my name and asked for hers.

She hesitated. "My first name is Esmé. I don't think I shall tell you my full name, for the moment. I have a title and you may just be impressed by titles. Americans are, you know."

I said I didn't think I would be, but that it might be a good idea, at that, to hold onto the title for a while.

Just then, I felt someone's warm breath on the back of my neck. I turned around and just missed brushing noses with Esmé's small brother. Ignoring me, he addressed his sister in a piercing treble: "Miss Megley said you must come and finish your tea!" His message delivered, he retired to the chair between his sister and me, on my right. I regarded him with high interest. He was looking very splendid in brown Shetland shorts, a navy-blue jersey, white shirt, and striped necktie. He gazed back at me with immense green eyes. "Why do people in films kiss sideways?" he demanded.

"Sideways?" I said. It was a problem that had baffled me in my childhood. I said I guessed it was because actors' noses are too big for kissing anyone head on.

"His name is Charles," Esmé said. "He's extremely brilliant for his age."

"He certainly has green eyes. Haven't you, Charles?"

Charles gave me the fishy look my question deserved, then wriggled downward and forward in his chair till all of his body was under the table except his head, which he left, wrestler's-bridge style, on the chair seat. "They're orange," he said in a strained voice, addressing the ceiling. He picked up a corner of the tablecloth and put it over his handsome, dead-pan little face.

"Sometimes he's brilliant and sometimes he's not," Esmé said. "Charles, do sit up!"

Charles stayed right where he was. He seemed to be holding his breath.

"He misses our father very much. He was s-l-a-i-n in North Africa."

I expressed regret to hear it.

Esmé nodded. "Father adored him." She bit reflectively at the cuticle of her thumb. "He looks very much like my mother—Charles, I mean. I look exactly like my father." She went on biting at her cuticle. "My mother was quite a passionate woman. She was an extrovert. Father was an introvert. They were quite well mated, though, in a superficial way. To be quite candid, Father really needed more of an intellectual companion than Mother was. He was an extremely gifted genius."

I waited, receptively, for further information, but none came. I looked down at Charles, who was now resting the side of his face on his chair seat. When he saw that I was looking at him, he closed his eyes, sleepily, angelically, then stuck out his tongue—an appendage of startling length—and gave out what in *my* country would have been a glorious tribute to a myopic baseball umpire. It fairly shook the tearoom.

"Stop that," Esmé said, clearly unshaken. "He saw an American do it in a fish-and-chips queue, and now he does it whenever he's bored. Just stop it, now, or I shall send you directly to Miss Megley."

Charles opened his enormous eyes, as sign that he'd heard his sister's threat, but otherwise didn't look especially alerted. He closed his eyes again, and continued to rest the side of his face on the chair seat.

I mentioned that maybe he ought to save it—meaning the Bronx cheer— till he started using his title regularly. That is, if he had a title, too.

Esmé gave me a long, faintly clinical look. "You have a dry sense of humor, haven't you?" she said—wistfully. "Father said I have no sense of humor at all. He said I was unequipped to meet life because I have no sense of humor."

Watching her, I lit a cigarette and said I didn't think a sense of humor was of any use in a real pinch.

"Father said it was."

This was a statement of faith, not a contradiction, and I quickly switched horses. I nodded and said her father had probably taken the long view, while I was taking the short (whatever *that* meant).

"Charles misses him exceedingly," Esmé said, after a moment. "He was an exceedingly lovable man. He was extremely handsome, too. Not that one's appearance matters greatly, but he was. He had terribly penetrating eyes, for a man who was intransically kind."

I nodded. I said I imagined her father had had quite an extraordinary vocabulary.

"Oh, yes; quite," said Esmé. "He was an archivist—amateur, of course."

At that point, I felt an importunate tap, almost a punch, on my upper arm, from Charles' direction. I turned to him. He was sitting in a fairly normal position in his chair now, except that he had one knee tucked under him. "What did one wall say to the other wall?" he asked shrilly. "It's a riddle!"

I rolled my eyes reflectively ceilingward and repeated the question aloud. Then I looked at Charles with a stumped expression and said I gave up.

"Meet you at the corner!" came the punch line, at top volume.

It went over biggest with Charles himself. It struck him as unbearably funny. In fact, Esmé had to come around and pound him on the back, as if treating him for a coughing spell. "Now, stop that," she said. She went back to her own seat. "He tells that same riddle to everyone he meets and has a fit every single time. Usually he drools when he laughs. Now, just stop, please."

"It's one of the best riddles I've heard, though," I said, watching Charles, who was very gradually coming out of it. In response to this compliment, he sank considerably lower in his chair and again masked his face up to the eyes with a corner of the tablecloth. He then looked at me with his exposed eyes, which were full of slowly subsiding mirth and the pride of someone who knows a really good riddle or two.

"May I inquire how you were employed before entering the Army?" Esmé asked me.

I said I hadn't been employed at all, that I'd only been out of college a year but that I liked to think of myself as a professional short-story writer.

She nodded politely. "Published?" she asked.

It was a familiar but always touchy question, and one that I didn't answer just one, two, three. I started to explain how most editors in America were a bunch—

"My father wrote beautifully," Esmé interrupted. "I'm saving a number of his letters for posterity."

I said that sounded like a very good idea. I happened to be looking at her enormous-faced, chronographic-looking wristwatch again. I asked if it had belonged to her father.

She looked down at her wrist solemnly. "Yes, it did," she said. "He gave it to me just before Charles and I were evacuated." Self-consciously, she took her hands off the table, saying, "Purely as a momento, of course." She guided the conversation in a different direction. "I'd be extremely flattered if you'd write a story exclusively for me sometime. I'm an avid reader."

I told her I certainly would, if I could. I said that I wasn't terribly prolific.

"It doesn't have to be terribly prolific! Just so that it isn't childish and silly." She reflected. "I prefer stories about squalor."

"About what?" I said, leaning forward.

"Squalor. I'm extremely interested in squalor."

I was about to press her for more details, but I felt Charles pinching me, hard, on my arm. I turned to him, wincing slightly. He was standing right next to me. "What did one wall say to the other wall?" he asked, not un-familiarly.

"You asked him that," Esmé said. "Now, stop it."

Ignoring his sister, and stepping up on one side of my feet, Charles re-peated the key question. I noticed that his necktie knot wasn't adjusted properly. I slid it up into place, then, looking him straight in the eye, sug-gested, "Meetcha at the corner?"

The instant I'd said it, I wished I hadn't. Charles' mouth fell open. I felt as if I'd struck it open. He stepped down off my foot and, with white-hot dignity, walked over to his own table, without looking back.

"He's furious," Esmé said. "He has a violent temper. My mother had a propensity to spoil him. My father was the only one who didn't spoil him."

I kept looking over at Charles, who had sat down and started to drink his tea, using both hands on the cup. I hoped he'd turn around, but he didn't.

Esmé stood up. "*Il faut que je parte aussi,*" she said, with a sigh. "Do you know French?"

I got up from my own chair, with mixed feelings of regret and confusion. Esmé and I shook hands; her hand, as I'd suspected, was a nervous hand, damp at the palm. I told her, in English, how very much I'd enjoyed her company.

She nodded. "I thought you might," she said. "I'm quite communicative for my age." She gave her hair another experimental touch. "I'm dreadfully sorry about my hair," she said. "I've probably been hideous to look at."

"Not at all! As a matter of fact, I think a lot of the wave is coming back already."

She quickly touched her hair again. "Do you think you'll be coming here again in the immediate future?" she asked. "We come here every Saturday, after choir practice."

I answered that I'd like nothing better but that, unfortunately, I was pretty sure I wouldn't be able to make it again.

"In other words, you can't discuss troop movements," said Esmé. She made no move to leave the vicinity of the table. In fact, she crossed one foot over the other and, looking down, aligned the toes of her shoes. It was a pretty little execution, for she was wearing white socks and her ankles and feet were lovely. She looked up at me abruptly. "Would you like me to write to you?" she asked, with a certain amount of color in her face. "I write ex-tremely articulate letters for a person my—"

"I'd love it." I took out pencil and paper and wrote down my name, rank, serial number, and A.P.O. number.

"I shall write to you first," she said, accepting it, "so that you don't feel *comp*romised in any way." She put the address into a pocket of her dress. "Goodbye," she said, and walked back to her table.

I ordered another pot of tea and sat watching the two of them till they, and the harassed Miss Megley, got up to leave. Charles led the way out, limping tragically, like a man with one leg several inches shorter than the other. He didn't look over at me. Miss Megley went next, then Esmé, who waved to me. I waved back, half getting up from my chair. It was a strangely emotional moment for me.

Less than a minute later, Esmé came back into the tearoom, dragging Charles behind her by the sleeve of his reefer. "Charles would like to kiss you goodbye," she said.

I immediately put down my cup, and said that was very nice, but was she *sure?*

"Yes," she said, a trifle grimly. She let go Charles' sleeve and gave him a rather vigorous push in my direction. He came forward, his face livid, and gave me a loud, wet smacker just below the right ear. Following this ordeal, he started to make a beeline for the door and a less sentimental way of life, but I caught the half belt at the back of his reefer, held on to it, and asked him, "What did one wall say to the other wall?"

His face lit up. "Meet you at the corner!" he shrieked, and raced out of the room, possibly in hysterics.

Esmé was standing with crossed ankles again. "You're quite sure you won't forget to write that story for me?" she asked. "It doesn't have to be *exclu*sively for me. It can—"

I said there was absolutely no chance that I'd forget. I told her that I'd never written a story *for* anybody, but that it seemed like exactly the right time to get down to it.

She nodded. "Make it extremely squalid and moving," she suggested. "Are you at all acquainted with squalor?"

I said not exactly but that I was getting better acquainted with it, in one form or another, all the time, and that I'd do my best to come up to her specifications. We shook hands.

"Isn't it a pity that we didn't meet under less extenuating circumstances?"

I said it was, I said it certainly was.

"Goodbye," Esmé said. "I hope you return from the war with all your faculties intact."

I thanked her, and said a few other words, and then watched her leave the tearoom. She left it slowly, reflectively, testing the ends of her hair for dryness.

This is the squalid, or moving, part of the story, and the scene changes. The people change, too. I'm still around, but from here on in, for reasons I'm not at liberty to disclose. I've disguised myself so cunningly that even the cleverest reader will fail to recognize me.

It was about ten-thirty at night in Gaufurt, Bavaria, several weeks after V-E Day. Staff Sergeant X was in his room on the second floor of the civilian home in which he and nine other American soldiers had been quartered, even before the armistice. He was seated on a folding wooden chair at a small, messy-looking writing table, with a paperback overseas novel open before him, which he was having great trouble reading. The trouble lay with him, not the novel. Although the men who lived on the first floor usually had first grab at the books sent each month by Special Services, X usually seemed to be left with the book he might have selected himself. But he was a young man who had not come through the war with all his faculties intact, and for more than an hour he had been triple-reading paragraphs, and now he was doing it to the sentences. He suddenly closed the book, without marking his place. With his hand, he shielded his eyes for a moment against the harsh, watty glare from the naked bulb over the table.

He took a cigarette from a pack on the table and lit it with fingers that bumped gently and incessantly against one another. He sat back a trifle in his chair and smoked without any sense of taste. He had been chain-smoking for weeks. His gums bled at the slightest pressure of the tip of his tongue, and he seldom stopped experimenting; it was a little game he played, sometimes by the hour. He sat for a moment smoking and experimenting. Then, abruptly, familiarly, and, as usual, with no warning, he thought he felt his mind dislodge itself and teeter, like insecure luggage on an overhead rack. He quickly did what he had been doing for weeks to set things right: he pressed his hands hard against his temples. He held on tight for a moment. His hair needed cutting, and it was dirty. He had washed it three or four times during his two weeks' stay at the hospital in Frankfort on the Main, but it had got dirty again on the long, dusty jeep ride back to Gaufurt. Corporal Z, who had called for him at the hospital, still drove a jeep combat-style, with the windshield down on the hood, armistice or no armistice. There were thousands of new troops in Germany. By driving with his windshield down, combat-style, Corporal Z hoped to show that he was not one of them, that not by a long shot was he some new son of a bitch in the E.T.O.

When he let go of his head, X began to stare at the surface of the writing table, which was a catchall for at least two dozen unopened letters and at least five or six unopened packages, all addressed to him. He reached behind the debris and picked out a book that stood against the wall. It was a book by Goebbels, entitled "Die Zeit Ohne Beispiel." It belonged to the thirty-eight-year-old unmarried daughter of the family that, up to a few weeks earlier, had been living in the house. She had been a low official in the Nazi Party, but high enough, by Army Regulations standards, to fall into an automatic-arrest category. X himself had arrested her. Now, for the third time since he had returned from the hospital that day, he opened the woman's book and read the brief inscription on the flyleaf. Written in ink, in German, in a small, hopelessly sincere handwriting, were the words "Dear God, life is hell." Nothing led up to or away from it. Alone on the page, and in the sickly stillness of the room, the words appeared to have the stature of an uncontestable, even classic indictment. X stared at the page for several minutes, trying, against heavy odds, not to be taken in. Then, with far more zeal than he had done anything in weeks, he picked up a pencil stub and wrote down under the inscription, in English, "Fathers and teachers, I ponder 'What is hell?' I maintain that it is the suffering of being unable to love." He started to write Dostoevski's name under the inscription, but saw—with fright that ran through his whole body—that what he had written was almost entirely illegible. He shut the book.

He quickly picked up something else from the table, a letter from his older brother in Albany. It had been on his table even before he had checked into the hospital. He opened the envelope, loosely resolved to read the letter straight through, but read only the top half of the first page. He stopped after the words "Now that the g.d. war is over and you probably have a lot of time over there, how about sending the kids a couple of bayonets or swastikas . . ." After he'd torn it up, he looked down at the pieces as they lay in the wastebasket. He saw that he had overlooked an enclosed snapshot. He could make out somebody's feet standing on a lawn somewhere.

He put his arms on the table and rested his head on them. He ached from head to foot, all zones of pain seemingly interdependent. He was rather like a Christmas tree whose lights, wired in series, must all go out if even one bulb is defective.

The door banged open, without having been rapped on. X raised his head, turned it, and saw Corporal Z standing in the door. Corporal Z had been X's jeep partner and constant companion from D Day straight through five campaigns of the war. He lived on the first floor and he usually came up to see X when he had a few rumors or gripes to unload. He was a huge, photogenic young man of twenty-four. During the war, a national magazine had photographed him in Hürtgen Forest; he had posed, more than just obligingly, with a Thanksgiving turkey in each hand. "Ya writin' letters?" he asked X. "It's spooky in here, for Chrissake." He preferred always to enter a room that had the overhead light on.

X turned around in his chair and asked him to come in, and to be careful not to step on the dog.

"The what?"

"Alvin. He's right under your feet, Clay. How 'bout turning on the goddam light?"

Clay found the overhead-light switch, flicked it on, then stepped across the puny, servant's-size room and sat down on the edge of the bed, facing his host. His brick-red hair, just combed, was dripping with the amount of water he required for satisfactory grooming. A comb with a fountain-pen clip protruded, familiarly, from the right-hand pocket of his olive-drab shirt.

Over the left-hand pocket he was wearing the Combat Infantrymen's Badge (which, technically, he wasn't authorized to wear), the European Theatre ribbon, with five bronze battle stars in it (instead of a lone silver one, which was the equivalent of five bronze ones), and the pre-Pearl Harbor service ribbon. He sighed heavily and said, "Christ almighty." It meant nothing; it was Army. He took a pack of cigarettes from his shirt pocket, tapped one out, then put away the pack and rebuttoned the pocket flap. Smoking, he looked vacuously around the room. His look finally settled on the radio. "Hey," he said. "They got this terrific show comin' on the radio in a coupla minutes. Bob Hope, and everybody."

X, opening a fresh pack of cigarettes, said he had just turned the radio off.

Undarkened, Clay watched X trying to get a cigarette lit. "Jesus," he said, with spectator's enthusiasm, "you oughta see your goddam hands. Boy, have you got the shakes. Ya know that?"

X got his cigarette lit, nodded, and said Clay had a real eye for detail.

"No kidding, hey. I goddam near fainted when I saw you at the hospital. You looked like a goddam *corpse*. How much weight ya lose? How many pounds? Ya know?"

"I don't know. How was your mail when I was gone? You heard from Loretta?"

Loretta was Clay's girl. They intended to get married at their earliest convenience. She wrote to him fairly regularly, from a paradise of triple exclamation points and inaccurate observations. All through the war, Clay had read all Loretta's letters aloud to X, however intimate they were—in fact, the more intimate, the better. It was his custom, after each reading, to ask X to plot out or pad out the letter of reply, or to insert a few impressive words in French or German.

"Yeah, I had a letter from her yesterday. Down in my room. Show it to ya later," Clay said, listlessly. He sat up straight on the edge of the bed, held his breath, and issued a long, resonant belch. Looking just semi-pleased with the achievement, he relaxed again. "Her goddam brother's gettin' outa the Navy on account of his hip," he said. "He's got this hip, the bastard." He sat up again and tried for another belch, but with below-par results. A jot of alertness came into his face. "Hey. Before I forget. We gotta get up at five tomorrow and drive to Hamburg or someplace. Pick up Eisenhower jackets for the whole detachment."

X, regarding him hostilely, stated that he didn't want an Eisenhower jacket.

Clay looked surprised, almost a trifle hurt. "Oh, they're good! They look good. How come?"

"No reason. Why do we have to get up at five? The war's over, for God's sake."

"I don't know—we gotta get back before lunch. They got some new forms in we gotta fill out before lunch. . . . I asked Bulling how come we couldn't fill 'em out tonight—he's *got* the goddam forms right on his desk. He don't want to open the envelopes yet, the son of a bitch."

The two sat quiet for a moment, hating Bulling.

Clay suddenly looked at X with new—higher—interest than before. "Hey," he said. "Did you know the goddam side of your face is jumping all over the place?"

X said he knew all about it, and covered his tic with his hand.

Clay stared at him for a moment, then said, rather vividly, as if he were the bearer of exceptionally good news, "I wrote Loretta you had a nervous breakdown."

"Oh?"

"Yeah. She's interested as hell in all that stuff. She's majoring in psychology." Clay stretched himself out on the bed, shoes included. "You know what she said? She says nobody gets a nervous breakdown just from the war and all. She says you probably were unstable like, your whole goddam life."

X bridged his hand over his eyes—the light over the bed seemed to be blinding him—and said that Loretta's insight into things was always a joy.

Clay glanced over at him. "Listen, ya bastard," he said. "She knows a goddam sight more psychology than *you* do."

"Do you think you can bring yourself to take your stinking feet off my bed?" X asked.

Clay left his feet where they were for a few don't-tell-me-where-to-put-my-feet seconds, then swung them around to the floor and sat up. "I'm goin' downstairs anyway. They got the radio on in Walker's room." He didn't get up from the bed, though. "Hey. I was just tellin' that new son of a bitch, Bernstein, downstairs. Remember that time I and you drove into Valognes, and we got shelled for about two goddam hours, and that goddam cat I shot that jumped up on the hood of the jeep when we were layin' in that hole? Remember?"

"Yes—don't start that business with that cat again, Clay, God damn it. I don't want to hear about it."

"No, all I mean is I wrote Loretta about it. She and the whole psychology class discussed it. In class and all. The goddam professor and everybody."

"That's fine. I don't want to hear about it, Clay."

"No, you know the reason I took a pot shot at it, Loretta says? She says I was temporarily insane. No kidding. From the shelling and all."

X threaded his fingers, once, through his dirty hair, then shielded his eyes against the light again. "You weren't insane. You were simply doing your duty. You killed that pussycat in as manly a way as anybody could've, under the circumstances."

Clay looked at him suspiciously. "What the hell are you talkin' about?"

"That cat was a spy. You *had* to take a pot shot at it. It was a very clever German midget dressed up in a cheap fur coat. So there was absolutely nothing brutal, or cruel, or dirty, or even—"

"God damn it!" Clay said, his lips thinned. "Can't you ever be *sincere?*"

X suddenly felt sick, and he swung around in his chair and grabbed the wastebasket—just in time.

When he had straightened up and turned toward his guest again, he found him standing, embarrassed, halfway between the bed and the door. X started to apologize, but changed his mind and reached for his cigarettes.

"C'mon down and listen to Hope on the radio, hey," Clay said, keeping his distance but trying to be friendly over it. "It'll do ya good. I mean it."

"You go ahead, Clay. . . . I'll look at my stamp collection."

"Yeah? You got a stamp collection? I didn't know you—"

"I'm only kidding."

Clay took a couple of slow steps toward the door. "I may drive over to Ehstadt later," he said. "They got a dance. It'll probably last till around two. Wanna go?"

"No, thanks. . . . I may practice a few steps in the room."

"O.K. G'night! Take it easy, now, for Chrissake." The door slammed shut, then instantly opened again. "Hey. O.K. if I leave a letter to Loretta under your door? I got some German stuff in it. Willya fix it up for me?"

"Yes. Leave me alone now, God damn it."

"Sure," said Clay. "You know what my mother wrote me? She wrote me she's glad you and I were together and all the whole war. In the same jeep and all. She says my letters are a helluva lot more intelligent since we been goin' around together."

X looked up and over at him, and said, with great effort, "Thanks. Tell her thanks for me."

"I will. G'night!" The door slammed shut, this time for good.

X sat looking at the door for a long while, then turned his chair around toward the writing table and picked up his portable typewriter from the floor. He made space for it on the messy table surface, pushing aside the collapsed pile of unopened letters and packages. He thought if he wrote a letter to an old friend of his in New York there might be some quick, however slight, therapy in it for him. But he couldn't insert his notepaper into the roller properly, his fingers were shaking so violently now. He put his hands down at his sides for a minute, then tried again, but finally crumpled the notepaper in his hand.

He was aware that he ought to get the wastebasket out of the room, but instead of doing anything about it, he put his arms on the typewriter and rested his head again, closing his eyes.

A few throbbing minutes later, when he opened his eyes, he found himself squinting at a small, unopened package wrapped in green paper. It had probably slipped off the pile when he had made space for the typewriter. He saw that it had been readdressed several times. He could make out, on just one side of the package, at least three of his old A.P.O. numbers.

He opened the package without any interest, without even looking at the return address. He opened it by burning the string with a lighted match. He was more interested in watching the string burn all the way down than in opening the package, but he opened it, finally.

Inside the box, a note, written in ink, lay on top of a small object wrapped in tissue paper. He picked out the note and read it.

17, —— Road,

——, Devon

June 7, 1944

Dear Sergeant X,

I hope you will forgive me for having taken 38 days to begin our correspondence but, I have been extremely busy as my aunt has undergone streptococcus of the throat and nearly perished and I have been justifiably saddled with one responsibility after another. However I have thought of you frequently and of the extremely pleasant afternoon we spent in each other's company on April 30, 1944 between 3:45 and 4:15 P.M. in case it slipped your mind.

We are all tremendously excited and overawed about D Day and only hope that it will bring about the swift termination of the war and a method of existence that is ridiculous to say the least. Charles and I are both quite concerned about you; we hope you were not among those who made the first initial assault upon the Cotentin Peninsula. Were you? Please reply as speedily as possible. My warmest regards to your wife.

Sincerely yours,

Esmé

P.S. I am taking the liberty of enclosing my wristwatch which you may keep in your possession for the duration of the conflict. I did not observe whether you were wearing one during our brief association, but this one is extremely water-proof and shock-proof as well as having many other virtues among which one can tell at what velocity one is walking if one wishes. I am quite certain that you will use it to greater advantage in these difficult days than I ever can and that you will accept it as a lucky talisman.

Charles, whom I am teaching to read and write and whom I am finding an extremely intelligent novice, wishes to add a few words. Please write as soon as you have the time and inclination.

HELLO HELLO HELLO HELLO HELLO

HELLO HELLO HELLO HELLO HELLO

LOVE AND KISSES CHALES

It was a long time before X could set the note aside, let alone lift Esmé's father's wristwatch out of the box. When he did finally lift it out, he saw that its crystal had been broken in transit. He wondered if the watch was otherwise undamaged, but he hadn't the courage to wind it and find out. He just sat with it in his hand for another long period. Then, suddenly, almost ecstatically, he felt sleepy.

You take a really sleepy man, Esmé, and he *always* stands a chance of again becoming a man with all his fac—with all his f-a-c-u-l-t-i-e-s intact.

(1950)

Flannery O'Connor

THE LIFE YOU SAVE
MAY BE YOUR OWN

The old woman and her daughter were sitting on their porch when Mr. Shiftlet came up their road for the first time. The old woman slid to the edge of her chair and leaned forward, shading her eyes from the piercing sunset with her hand. The daughter could not see far in front of her and continued to play with her fingers. Although the old woman lived in this desolate spot with only her daughter and she had never seen Mr. Shiftlet before, she could tell, even from a distance, that he was a tramp and no one to be afraid of. His left coat sleeve was folded up to show there was only half an arm in it and his gaunt figure listed slightly to the side as if the breeze were pushing him. He had on a black town suit and a brown felt hat that was turned up in the front and down in the back and he carried a tin tool box by a handle. He came on, at an amble, up her road, his face turned toward the sun which appeared to be balancing itself on the peak of a small mountain.

The old woman didn't change her position until he was almost into her yard; then she rose with one hand fisted on her hip. The daughter, a large girl in a short blue organdy dress, saw him all at once and jumped up and began to stamp and point and make excited speechless sounds.

Mr. Shiftlet stopped just inside the yard and set his box on the ground and tipped his hat at her as if she were not in the least afflicted; then he turned toward the old woman and swung the hat all the way off. He had long black slick hair that hung flat from a part in the middle to beyond the tips of his ears on either side. His face descended in forehead for more than half its length and ended suddenly with his features just balanced over a jutting steel-trap jaw. He seemed to be a young man but he had a look of composed dissatisfaction as if he understood life thoroughly.

"Good evening," the old woman said. She was about the size of a cedar fence post and she had a man's gray hat pulled down low over her head.

The tramp stood looking at her and didn't answer. He turned his back and faced the sunset. He swung both his whole and his short arm up slowly so that they indicated an expanse of sky and his figure formed a crooked cross. The old woman watched him with her arms folded across her chest as if she were the owner of the sun, and the daughter watched, her head thrust forward and her fat helpless hands hanging at the wrists. She had long pink-gold hair and eyes as blue as a peacock's neck.

He held the pose for almost fifty seconds and then he picked up his box and came on to the porch and dropped down on the bottom step. "Lady," he said in a firm nasal voice, "I'd give a fortune to live where I could see me a sun do that every evening."

"Does it every evening," the old woman said and sat back down. The daughter sat down too and watched him with a cautious sly look as if he were a bird that had come up very close. He leaned to one side, rooting in his pants pocket, and in a second he brought out a package of chewing gum and offered her a piece. She took it and unpeeled it and began to chew without taking her eyes off him. He offered the old woman a piece but she only raised her upper lip to indicate she had no teeth.

Mr. Shiftlet's pale sharp glance had already passed over everything in the yard—the pump near the corner of the house and the big fig tree that three or four chickens were preparing to roost in—and had moved to a shed where he saw the square rusted back of an automobile. "You ladies drive?" he asked.

"That car ain't run in fifteen year," the old woman said. "The day my husband died, it quit running."

"Nothing is like it used to be, lady," he said. "The world is almost rotten."

"That's right," the old woman said. "You from around here?"

"Name Tom T. Shiftlet," he murmured, looking at the tires.

"I'm pleased to meet you," the old woman said. "Name Lucynell Crater and daughter Lucynell Crater. What you doing around here, Mr. Shiftlet?"

He judged the car to be about a 1928 or '29 Ford. "Lady," he said, and turned and gave her his full attention, "lemme tell you something. There's one of these doctors in Atlanta that's taken a knife and cut the human heart—the human heart," he repeated, leaning forward, "out of a man's chest and held it in his hand," and he held his hand out, palm up, as if it were slightly weighted with the human heart, "and studied it like it was a day-old chicken, and lady," he said, allowing a long significant pause in which his head slid forward and his clay-colored eyes brightened, "he don't know no more about it than you or me."

"That's right," the old woman said.

"Why, if he was to take that knife and cut into every corner of it, he still wouldn't know no more than you or me. What you want to bet?"

"Nothing," the old woman said wisely. "Where you come from, Mr. Shiftlet?"

He didn't answer. He reached into his pocket and brought out a sack of tobacco and a package of cigarette papers and rolled himself a cigarette, expertly with one hand, and attached it in a hanging position to his upper lip. Then he took a box of wooden matches from his pocket and struck one on his shoe. He held the burning match as if he were studying the mystery of flame while it traveled dangerously toward his skin. The daughter began to make loud noises and to point to his hand and shake her finger at him, but when the flame was just before touching him, he leaned down with his hand cupped over it as if he were going to set fire to his nose and lit the cigarette.

He flipped away the dead match and blew a stream of gray into the evening. A sly look came over his face. "Lady," he said, "nowadays, people'll do anything anyways. I can tell you my name is Tom T. Shiftlet and I come from Tarwater, Tennessee, but you never have seen me before: how you know I ain't lying? How you know my name ain't Aaron Sparks, lady, and I come from Singleberry, Georgia, or how you know it's not George Speeds and I come from Lucy, Alabama, or how you know I ain't Thompson Bright from Toolafalls, Mississippi?"

"I don't know nothing about you," the old woman muttered, irked.

"Lady," he said, "people don't care how they lie. Maybe the best I can tell you is, I'm a man; but listen, lady," he said and paused and made his tone more ominous still, "what is a man?"

The old woman began to gum a seed. "What you carry in that tin box, Mr. Shiftlet?" she asked.

"Tools," he said, put back. "I'm a carpenter."

"Well, if you come out here to work, I'll be able to feed you and give you a place to sleep but I can't pay. I'll tell you that before you begin," she said.

There was no answer at once and no particular expression on his face. He leaned back against the two-by-four that helped support the porch roof. "Lady," he said slowly, "there's some men that some things mean more to them than money." The old woman rocked without comment and the daughter watched the trigger that moved up and down in his neck. He told the old woman then that all most people were interested in was money, but he asked what a man was made for. He asked her if a man was made for money, or what. He asked her what she thought she was made for but she didn't answer, she only sat rocking and wondered if a one-armed man could put a new roof on her garden house. He asked a lot of questions that she didn't answer. He told her that he was twenty-eight years old and had lived a varied life. He had been a gospel singer, a foreman on the railroad, an assistant in an undertaking parlor, and he had come over the radio for three months with Uncle Roy and his Red Creek Wranglers. He said he had fought and bled in the Arm Service of his country and visited every foreign land and that everywhere he had seen people that didn't care if they did a thing one way or another. He said he hadn't been raised thataway.

A fat yellow moon appeared in the branches of the fig tree as if it were going to roost there with the chickens. He said that a man had to escape to the country to see the world whole and that he wished he lived in a desolate place like this where he could see the sun go down every evening like God make it to do.

"Are you married or are you single?" the old woman asked.

There was a long silence. "Lady," he asked finally, "where would you find an innocent woman today? I wouldn't have any of this trash I could just pick up."

The daughter was leaning very far down, hanging her head almost between her knees, watching him through a triangular door she had made in her overturned hair; and she suddenly fell in a heap on the floor and began to whimper. Mr. Shiftlet straightened her out and helped her get back in the chair.

"Is she your baby girl?" he asked.

"My only," the old woman said, "and she's the sweetest girl in the world. I wouldn't give her up for nothing on earth. She's smart too. She can sweep the floor, cook, wash, feed the chickens, and hoe. I wouldn't give her up for a casket of jewels."

"No," he said kindly, "don't ever let any man take her away from you."

"Any man come after her," the old woman said, " 'll have to stay around the place."

Mr. Shiftlet's eye in the darkness was focused on a part of the automobile bumper that glittered in the distance. "Lady," he said, jerking his short arm up as if he could point with it to her house and yard and pump, "there ain't a broken thing on this plantation that I couldn't fix for you, one-arm jackleg or not. I'm a man," he said with a sullen dignity, "even if I ain't a whole one. I got," he said, tapping his knuckles on the floor to emphasize the immensity of what he was going to say, "a moral intelligence!" and his face pierced out of the darkness into a shaft of doorlight and he stared at her as if he were astonished himself at this impossible truth.

The old woman was not impressed with the phrase. "I told you you could hang around and work for food," she said, "if you don't mind sleeping in that car yonder."

"Why listen, Lady," he said with a grin of delight, "the monks of old slept in their coffins!"

"They wasn't as advanced as we are," the old woman said.

The next morning he began on the roof of the garden house while Lucynell, the daughter, sat on a rock and watched him work. He had not been around a week before the change he had made in the place was apparent. He had patched the front and back steps, built a new hog pen, restored a fence, and taught Lucynell, who was completely deaf and had never said a word in her life, to say the word "bird." The big rosy-faced girl followed him everywhere, saying "Burrttddt ddbirrrttdt," and clapping her hands. The old woman watched from a distance, secretly pleased. She was ravenous for a son-in-law.

Mr. Shiftlet slept on the hard narrow back seat of the car with his feet out the side window. He had his razor and a can of water on a crate that served him as a bedside table and he put up a piece of mirror against the back glass and kept his coat neatly on a hanger that he hung over one of the windows.

In the evenings he sat on the steps and talked while the old woman and Lucynell rocked violently in their chairs on either side of him. The old woman's three mountains were black against the dark blue sky and were visited off and on by various planets and by the moon after it had left the chickens. Mr. Shiftlet pointed out that the reason he had improved this plantation was because he had taken a personal interest in it. He said he was even going to make the automobile run.

He had raised the hood and studied the mechanism and he said he could tell that the car had been built in the days when cars were really built. You take now, he said, one man puts in one bolt and another man puts in another bolt and another man puts in another bolt so that it's a man for a bolt. That's why you have to pay so much for a car: you're paying all those men. Now if you didn't have to pay but one man, you could get you a cheaper car and one that had had a personal interest taken in it, and it would be a better car. The old woman agreed with him that this was so.

Mr. Shiftlet said that the trouble with the world was that nobody cared, or stopped and took any trouble. He said he never would have been able to teach Lucynell to say a word if he hadn't cared and stopped long enough.

"Teach her to say something else," the old woman said.

"What you want her to say next?" Mr. Shiftlet asked.

The old woman's smile was broad and toothless and suggestive. "Teach her to say, 'sugarpie,'" she said.

Mr. Shiftlet already knew what was on her mind.

The next day he began to tinker with the automobile and that evening he told her that if she would buy a fan belt, he would be able to make the car run.

The old woman said she would give him the money. "You see that girl yonder?" she asked, pointing to Lucynell who was sitting on the floor a foot away, watching him, her eyes blue even in the dark. "If it was ever a man wanted to take her away, I would say, 'No man on earth is going to take that sweet girl of mine away from me!' but if he was to say, 'Lady, I don't want to take her away, I want her right here,' I would say, 'Mister, I don't blame you none. I wouldn't pass up a chance to live in a permanent place and get the sweetest girl in the world myself. You ain't no fool,' I would say."

"How old is she?" Mr. Shiftlet asked casually.

"Fifteen, sixteen," the old woman said. The girl was nearly thirty but because of her innocence it was impossible to guess.

"It would be a good idea to paint it too," Mr. Shiftlet remarked. "You don't want it to rust out."

"We'll see about that later," the old woman said.

The next day he walked into town and returned with the parts he needed, and a can of gasoline. Late in the afternoon, terrible noises issued from the shed and the old woman rushed out of the house, thinking Lucynell was somewhere having a fit. Lucynell was sitting on a chicken crate, stamping her feet and screaming, "Burrddttt! bddurrddtttt!" but her fuss was drowned out by the car. With a volley of blasts it emerged from the shed, moving in a fierce and stately way. Mr. Shiftlet was in the driver's seat, sitting very erect. He had an expression of serious modesty on his face as if he had just raised the dead.

That night, rocking on the porch, the old woman began her business at once. "You want you an innocent woman, don't you?" she asked sympathetically. "You don't want none of this trash."

"No'm, I don't," Mr. Shiftlet said.

"One that can't talk," she continued, "can't sass you back or use foul language. That's the kind for you to have. Right there," and she pointed to Lucynell sitting cross-legged in her chair, holding both feet in her hands.

"That's right," he admitted. "She wouldn't give me any trouble."

"Saturday," the old woman said, "you and her and me can drive into town and get married."

Mr. Shiftlet eased his position on the steps.

"I can't get married right now," he said. "Everything you want to do takes money and I ain't got any."

"What you need with money?" she asked.

"It takes money," he said. "Some people'll do anything anyhow these days, but the way I think, I wouldn't marry no woman that I couldn't take on a trip like she was somebody. I mean take her to a hotel and treat her. I wouldn't marry the Duchesser Windsor," he said firmly, "unless I could take her to a hotel and give her something good to eat.

"I was raised thataway and there ain't a thing I can do about it. My old mother taught me how to do."

"Lucynell don't even know what a hotel is," the old woman muttered. "Listen here, Mr. Shiftlet," she said, sliding forward in her chair, "you'd be getting a permanent house and a deep well and the most innocent girl in the world. You don't need no money. Lemme tell you something: there ain't any place in the world for a poor disabled friendless drifting man."

The ugly words settled in Mr. Shiftlet's head like a group of buzzards in the top of a tree. He didn't answer at once. He rolled himself a cigarette and lit it and then he said in an even voice, "Lady, a man is divided into parts, body and spirit."

The old woman clamped her gums together.

"A body and a spirit," he repeated. "The body, lady, is like a house: it don't go anywhere; but the spirit, lady, is like a automobile: always on the move, always . . ."

"Listen, Mr. Shiftlet," she said, "my well never goes dry and my house is always warm in the winter and there's no mortgage on a thing about this place. You can go to the courthouse and see for yourself. And yonder under that shed is a fine automobile." She laid the bait carefully. "You can have it painted by Saturday. I'll pay for the paint."

In the darkness, Mr. Shiftlet's smile stretched like a weary snake waking up by a fire. "Yes'm," he said softly.

After a second he recalled himself and said, "I'm only saying a man's spirit means more to him than anything else. I would have to take my wife off for the weekend without no regards at all for cost. I got to follow where my spirit says to go."

"I'll give you fifteen dollars for a weekend trip," the old woman said in a crabbed voice. "That's the best I can do."

"That wouldn't hardly pay for more than the gas and the hotel," he said. "It wouldn't feed her."

"Seventeen-fifty," the old woman said. "That's all I got so it isn't any use you trying to milk me. You can take a lunch."

Mr. Shiftlet was deeply hurt by the word "milk." He didn't doubt that she had more money sewed up in her mattress but he had already told her he was not interested in her money. "I'll make that do," he said, and rose and walked off without treating with her further.

On Saturday the three of them drove into town in the car that the paint had barely dried on and Mr. Shiftlet and Lucynell were married in the Ordinary's office while the old woman witnessed. As they came out of the courthouse, Mr. Shiftlet began twisting his neck in his collar. He looked morose and bitter as if he had been insulted while someone held him. "That didn't satisfy me none," he said. "That was just something a woman in an office did, nothing but paper work and blood tests. What do they know about my blood? If they was to take my heart and cut it out," he said, "they wouldn't know a thing about me. It didn't satisfy me at all."

"It satisfied the law," the old woman said sharply.

"The law," Mr. Shiftlet said, and spit. "It's the law that don't satisfy me."

He had painted the car dark green with a yellow band around it just under the windows. The three of them climbed in the front seat and the old woman said, "Don't Lucynell look pretty? Looks like a baby doll." Lucynell was dressed up in a white dress that her mother had uprooted from a trunk and there was a Panama hat on her head with a bunch of red wooden cherries on the brim. Every now and then her placid expression was changed by a sly isolated little thought like a shoot of green in the desert. "You got a prize!" the old woman said.

Mr. Shiftlet didn't even look at her.

They drove back to the house to let the old woman off and pick up the lunch. When they were ready to leave, she stood staring in the window of the car, with her fingers clenched around the glass. Tears began to seep sideways out of her eyes and run along the dirty creases in her face. "I ain't ever been parted with her for two days before," she said.

Mr. Shiftlet started the motor.

"And I wouldn't let no man have her but you because I seen you would do right. Goodbye, Sugarbaby," she said, clutching at the sleeve of the white dress. Lucynell looked straight at her and didn't seem to see her there at all. Mr. Shiftlet eased the car forward so that she had to move her hands.

The early afternoon was clear and open and surrounded by pale blue sky. The hills flattened under the car one after another and the climb and dip and swerve went entirely to Mr. Shiftlet's head so that he forgot his morning bitterness. He had always wanted an automobile but he had never been able to afford one before. He drove very fast because he wanted to make Mobile by nightfall.

Occasionally he stopped his thoughts long enough to look at Lucynell in the seat beside him. She had eaten the lunch as soon as they were out of the yard and now she was pulling the cherries off the hat one by one and throwing them out the window. He became depressed in spite of the car. He had driven about a hundred miles when he decided that she must be hungry again and at the next small town they came to, he stopped in front of an aluminum-painted eating place called The Hot Spot and took her in and ordered her a plate of ham and grits. The ride had made her sleepy and as soon as she got up on the stool, she rested her head on the counter and shut her eyes. There was no one in The Hot Spot but Mr. Shiftlet and the boy behind the counter, a pale youth with a greasy rag hung over his shoulder. Before he could dish up the food, she was snoring gently.

"Give it to her when she wakes up," Mr. Shiftlet said. "I'll pay for it now."

The boy bent over her and stared at the long pink-gold hair and the half-shut sleeping eyes. Then he looked up and stared at Mr. Shiftlet. "She looks like an angel of Gawd," he murmured.

"Hitch-hiker," Mr. Shiftlet explained. "I can't wait. I got to make Tuscaloosa."

The boy bent over again and very carefully touched his finger to a strand of the golden hair and Mr. Shiftlet left.

He was more depressed than ever as he drove on by himself. The late afternoon had grown hot and sultry and the country had flattened out. Deep in the sky a storm was preparing very slowly and without thunder as if it meant to drain every drop of air from the earth before it broke. There were times when Mr. Shiftlet preferred not to be alone. He felt too that a man with a car had a responsibility to others and he kept his eye out for a hitch-hiker. Occasionally he saw a sign that warned: "Drive carefully. The life you save may be your own."

The narrow road dropped off on either side into dry fields and here and there a shack or a filling station stood in a clearing. The sun began to set directly in front of the automobile. It was a reddening ball that through his windshield was slightly flat on the bottom and top. He saw a boy in overalls and a gray hat standing on the edge of the road and he slowed the car down and stopped in front of him. The boy didn't have his hand raised to thumb the ride, he was only standing there, but he had a small cardboard suitcase and his hat was set on his head in a way to indicate that he had left somewhere for good. "Son," Mr. Shiftlet said, "I see you want a ride."

The boy didn't say he did or he didn't but he opened the door of the car and got in, and Mr. Shiftlet started driving again. The child held the suitcase on his lap and folded his arms on top of it. He turned his head and looked out the window away from Mr. Shiftlet. Mr. Shiftlet felt oppressed. "Son," he said after a minute, "I got the best old mother in the world so I reckon you only got the second best."

The boy gave him a quick dark glance and then turned his face back out the window.

"It's nothing so sweet," Mr. Shiftlet continued, "as a boy's mother. She taught him his first prayers at her knee, she give him love when no other would, she told him what was right and what wasn't, and she seen that he done the right thing. Son," he said, "I never rued a day in my life like the one I rued when I left that old mother of mine."

The boy shifted in his seat but he didn't look at Mr. Shiftlet. He unfolded his arms and put one hand on the door handle.

"My mother was a angel of Gawd," Mr. Shiftlet said in a very strained voice.

"He took her from heaven and giver to me and I left her." His eyes were instantly clouded over with a mist of tears. The car was barely moving.

The boy turned angrily in the seat. "You go to the devil!" he cried. "My old woman is a flea bag and yours is a stinking pole cat!" and with that he flung the door open and jumped out with his suitcase into the ditch.

Mr. Shiftlet was so shocked that for about a hundred feet he drove along slowly with the door still open. A cloud, the exact color of the boy's hat and shaped like a turnip, had descended over the sun, and another, worse looking, crouched behind the car. Mr. Shiftlet felt that the rottenness of the world was about to engulf him. He raised his arm and let it fall again to his breast. "Oh, Lord!" he prayed. "Break forth and wash the slime from this earth!"

The turnip continued slowly to descend. After a few minutes there was a guffawing peal of thunder from behind and fantastic raindrops, like tin-can tops, crashed over the rear of Mr. Shiftlet's car. Very quickly he stepped on the gas and with his stump sticking out the window he raced the galloping shower into Mobile. (1953)

The Drama

Your study of literary craftsmanship in general and of the short story in particular has given you a good start toward understanding and appreciating dramas. Plots in dramas are in many respects like those in short stories: the overall patterns are similar, and the relationships between happening and happening, or between characters and actions, are similar. Moreover, much of what you have learned about setting, language, tone, meanings, and evaluations applies to the reading of plays.

Yet dramatic writing has peculiarities which you must keep in mind if you are to read it well. The unique purpose for which a play is written naturally influences its substance and form. Always you will find it useful to remember that a dramatic work—unless it is that rare thing, a "closet drama"—is a narrative form designed to be interpreted by actors on a stage in a theater. Dramatists as a result write primarily not for the general reader but for people of the theater likely to be concerned with stage presentations—producers, scene designers, directors, actors, and the like. The playwright sets down only what such specialists need—ordinarily mere hints about the scenery, the appearance of characters and the actors, plus everything the characters are to say.

When theatrical folk read dramas, they try to imagine exactly how such notations may be translated into an actual production. When we read a play, we should, to the best of our ability, do the same thing. As Schlegel, a famed critic of drama, says, "In reading dramatic works, our habitual practice is to supply the representation." Like a producer or an actor, in other words, we try to see what is implied by every detail which the author has given us. We form mental images of the theater and of the stage settings, and of the actors

—their appearance, the quality of their voices and intonations, the nature of their gestures and movements. Furthermore, we note the nature of the motivation, of the plot, and of the tone, in ways appropriate for the reading of plays.

This means that we ask and answer—as well as we can—these questions: (1) How has the nature of the theater and of the audience shaped this play? (2) What are the implied thoughts, the feelings, and the motives of the characters in each scene? (3) How are the parts—the acts and scenes—important in the development of the whole play? (4) Is the tone that of tragedy, that of comedy, that of melodrama, that of farce, or a combination?

THEATER AND AUDIENCE

How has the nature of the theater and of the audience shaped this play?
Every drama is designed for performance at a certain time and in a certain place. The limitations and the possibilities of the theater to a large degree determine the substance of a play and shape its form. Clearly, for instance, the dramas presented under the open sky in the orchestral space of a Greek amphitheater (see p. 508) will differ greatly from those produced on the curtained and lighted stage of the modern playhouse. The scenic representation in Greek dramas, for one thing, was very different from scenic representation in modern productions. In the Greek dramas, it was simple and inflexible; in modern plays, it may be as elaborate as is necessary, and it may be completely changed one or more times in a play.

The audience, too, wields its influence. The physical position of the audience in relationship to the stage is bound to be important. In early theaters, down through the time of Shakespeare, the stage was in the midst of the audience or it at least projected into the audience. From that position, as time passed, it gradually receded until it came to be on the rim of a half circle occupied by the spectators. The result, naturally, was a decrease in the intimacy of the relationship between actor and spectator, and consequent changes in the dramas. In addition, audiences have varied from period to period in their make-up: sometimes they have been a cross section of a whole population, again they have been drawn from only one or two social classes. Since every dramatist wrote to please a particular audience, your knowledge of the education, the beliefs, and the psychology of the audience for which any play was written will help you understand the nature of the appeals of the play.

J. Dover Wilson affords an example of the importance of considering the audience. In his interesting study, *What Happens in Hamlet,* he suggests that it was natural for Elizabethans to interpret what happened in ancient Denmark into Elizabethan terms. "A trivial point, it may be said," he remarks, "yet it is one of far-reaching importance. For if Shakespeare and his audience thought of the constitution of Denmark in English terms, then Hamlet was rightful heir to the throne and Claudius a usurper." Understanding this point is vital to the understanding of the whole play. "The usurpation," as Wilson says, "is one of the main factors in the plot of *Hamlet. . . .*"

THOUGHTS, FEELINGS, MOTIVES

What are the implied thoughts, the feelings, and the motives of the charac-ters in each scene?

Because his work is designed not to be told but to be acted, the playwright, perforce, ordinarily uses the distant point of view (see p. 341). In some periods, conventions of the stage—understandings, as it were, between the playwright and the audience—allow the actors to speak their thoughts to the spectators in soliloquies and asides. In most periods, however, these are used sparingly, and in modern times they have almost entirely disappeared. Since the playwright cannot open the heads and breasts of living men and women to permit us to peer into their minds and hearts, he is forced to show motives indirectly by means of speeches and actions.

Such speeches and actions must be examined by the alert reader for impli-cations. What, you must ask yourself, lies behind that speech, that deed? Granted that this is what the character says and does, what is he really thinking and feeling? To answer these questions, you need, obviously, to have a clear idea about the nature of the character: you need to know what his traits are, why he is likely to act as he does, how likely he is to unfold his true thoughts, how articulate he will be in analyzing his motives. But the method of showing characters makes this fairly difficult: you come to know the characters in a play only gradually—speech by speech, happening by happening. This means that you should make an effort from the first scene to draw every possible inference about each character, and that you should keep in mind your deductions and modify them or supplement them when you can. Thus only may you prepare to formulate as precisely as possible the thoughts, the feelings, and the motiva-tions of each character in every scene throughout the drama.

In reading *Hamlet,* for instance, you first encounter Claudius, the usurping king, as he holds a Council Meeting in Act I, Scene ii. You read his words as he takes up a series of problems. You notice his way of talking to various people. You weigh each speech. And if you are as discerning as possible, you note, with Granville Barker, that "his tactless tact, the mellifluous excess of speech, the smiling kindness overdone—such falseness shows that he feels his position to be false." Such an initial perception is supplemented by others as you read on in the play, and when, later, Claudius tries to arrange for Hamlet's execu-tion, you understand the reason.

SCENES RELATED TO THE PLAY

How are the parts—the acts and scenes—important in the development of the whole play?

You recall how important it was, in reading the short story, to become aware of the nature of the whole work. Similarly, in reading a drama, you should be-come aware of the general pattern of the action, and of the relationship to this pattern of all other elements. After reading a drama, you should be able to see whatever foreshadowings there are of the events, and to comprehend the general course of all the action from the beginning to the conclusion.

Not only should you notice the course of the whole play; you should also notice the relationship of the parts—the acts and scenes—to the whole work. The dramatist, as a rule, is forced to divide his story into acts and scenes. A continuous narrative such as you find in some short stories is impossible, and summaries of action are for the most part impractical. This means that the dramatist must leave out many scenes which a fiction writer might portray, that he must be content with brief references to others, and that he must select and fully develop only those scenes which will best set forth the pattern of action which makes up the plot of his drama. Therefore, you will learn much by considering the artistic justification for certain omissions and certain summaries, and, above all, for the complete working out of the chosen scenes. You will find it useful to notice exactly what each scene accomplishes—how, for instance, the opening scene or scenes offer an exposition (i.e., the details the audience needs to understand the initial situation), and how scenes and acts, in order, mark stages in the advancement of the plot to climactic developments, conflicts, or changes. To notice how the play progresses from scene to scene is an important step toward understanding and appreciating the whole work.

TONE IN DRAMA

Is the tone that of tragedy, that of comedy, that of melodrama, that of farce, or a combination?

The playwright, unlike other narrative writers, cannot lift his own voice to interpret the meanings of what he sets before you: the drama is a form in which explicit interpretation is an impossibility. The playwright cannot state directly his judgments of the characters and their deeds; nor can he tell you what he wants his play to signify. However, he probably will choose a dramatic form which will give you important clues concerning his attitude toward his material and the way he wants you to interpret his work. Over the years, dramatists in general have found four chief forms satisfactory for this purpose—tragedy, comedy, melodrama, and farce.[1] When you discover what choice among these forms an author has made, you define the general tone of his play.

The concepts of *tragedy* differ from period to period. Nevertheless, certain qualities of tragedy have been fairly constant. One thing often said of tragedies is that they end unhappily, with the death, as a rule, of the hero or the heroine. Although there are some exceptions, tragedies usually do end disastrously. A playwright,

---

1. At one time and another, dramatists have used other forms—miracle plays, medieval mysteries, tragicomedies, chronicle plays, heroic plays, and so forth. Each type was written during a period or series of periods during which it appealed to contemporary audiences. The four forms which we have listed are more enduring. Furthermore, they will suffice for our present purposes.

however, cannot make a tragedy simply by tacking on an unhappy conclusion. Other things are important, indeed more important, notably a preparation for the ending which indicates its inevitability and a treatment of a subject which in the minds of the immediate audience is highly serious. The conclusion of a tragedy, in other words, must be the logical outcome of the struggle of the protagonist against his opponents or against himself in a given situation. And the central conflict must be a struggle which the audience believes is significant —man against the gods, say, or against fate, or against the promptings of his own character. Furthermore, such a conflict must be treated, not playfully, but seriously.

Since it treats a vital conflict seriously, a tragedy as a rule is found to have universal significance. You, the reader, note that the plight of the protagonist is similar to a plight in which you may find yourself—that the problems of the play, whether ancient or modern, are in a sense your problems, too. As a result, you find a meaning for yourself in the inevitable outcome. Furthermore, you probably find that not only the meaning but also the emotional effect is universal: you pity the suffering protagonist and share his terror of the inescapable catastrophe.

Although, like tragedy, *comedy* has taken many forms during the ages, ordinarily it does not so deeply engage the sympathies of the audience or the reader as does tragedy. Some comedies, as a matter of fact, do not arouse much sympathy or much dislike for the characters: they ridicule or satirize their traits, their manners, and their foibles. Therefore, the appeal of these plays is largely an intellectual one—an appeal to the audience's or the reader's sense of the incongruous. Other comedies do, it is true, arouse sympathy for some characters, dislike for others; and their author hopes that after sharing the troubles of the attractive characters, the audience will share their delight in a happy ending. Even in such comedies, though, there will be no life and death struggles such as tragedies portray. The ending, as a matter of fact, will often show that the difficulties after all were not nearly so serious as the characters took them to be. The mood will not be desperate and grim but easy-going and good-natured. Most comedies will not, however, be exclusively intellectual or emotional in appeal: they will be a combination in which one appeal predominates. Thus the intellectual element predominates in Ben Jonson's *The Alchemist* or Noel Coward's *Private Lives*, but there are some emotional elements in each; and the emotional element predominates in Shakespeare's *As You Like It* and in Philip Barry's *The Philadelphia Story*, though not to the complete exclusion of satire.

Regardless of the proportions of intellectual and emotional appeal, a comedy (if the author succeeds) will not very deeply stir the audience which views it. The audience will not be moved to pity and terror but—at most—to sympathy mingled with amusement. It will be amiable and tolerant of the sympathetic characters, rather than violently partisan. Nevertheless, you will find that the best comedies have their universal qualities. You will see that, like tragedies, they reveal human nature and comment upon human philosophy, human values. Although they portray man in his lighter moments, they often say very important things about him.

Melodrama and *farce* are counterparts, respectively, of tragedy and comedy —counterparts, however, on a lower level. The lowness of the level is evident in the nature of the conflicts they portray, the emphasis they place upon action, their lack of significant commentary, and their appeal. The conflicts they portray are external rather than internal, trivial rather than important, temporary rather than universal. Melodramas and farces are crammed with action, action, however, which is often developed at the expense of characterization. Therefore, they contain little serious consideration of life and its problems, and they appeal in rather obvious ways to the heart and to the mind of the audience and of the reader.

Melodrama does deal, to be sure, with some situations which at the time appear to be serious or painful—passion, danger of death, even bad fortune. But the characters involved tend to be types who may be quickly classified as black-hearted and white-souled, and if you are familiar with melodrama, once you have so classified them, you will have little trouble guessing what will happen to them. These figures—the brave hero, the true-blue heroine, the scheming villain, his brutish henchmen, and others—will clash in scenes which are chiefly designed to deliver a series of thrills and (as a rule) to straighten out all difficulties in a final scene. If the characters have to be made inconsistent to make some of these thrills possible, the playwright makes them inconsistent. The plot is episodic rather than unified—with each episode delivering a punch. It lacks the inevitability one finds in tragedy: if a wrenching of logic is needed to provide the thrill of a happy ending, the author wrenches away without flinching. Thus, really, the author takes neither the characters nor the action very seriously. His chief aim is to provide thrills for the paying customers.

Farce, by contrast, is built not for a series of thrills but for frequent and hilarious laughs. Like melodrama, farce dispenses with subtlety. It thrives upon exaggeration—of the ridiculous qualities of its characters, of broadly comic actions. Its characters as a rule are not amalgams of several traits: they are exaggerated types such as the stuffy business tycoon, the windy politician, the giggling spinster ruthlessly trying to entrap a man, the haughty society dowager, and the like. Such figures are placed in an impossible situation or series of situations and then are manipulated through an episodic series of scenes each of which (so the author hopes) builds up to a point where the audience howls with laughter. And, of course, neither the author nor the audience takes the characters and the action very seriously.

At times melodramatic or farcical scenes occur in tragedies or comedies. When they do, you should note the clash of tones, the shift in interest, and the effect upon the drama as a whole. Such variations are not necessarily bad: witness the broadly comic scene provided by the drunken porter immediately following the murder of the king in *Macbeth.*

Of course, it is not enough simply to classify a play as tragedy, comedy, melodrama, or farce. So to classify a play is a very helpful start, but it is only a start. It is necessary, in addition, to see exactly what the nature of this particular play is—what it reveals by its characterization, its plot, its concern or lack of concern with important human problems. The consideration of such matters will be highly relevant to your evaluation of the play.

In addition to the six plays that follow, you might wish to turn back and reconsider those you studied in Part One: Dunsany's *A Night at an Inn* (p. 36) and the selections from Shakespeare's *The Tragedy of Julius Caesar* (p. 18) and *The Tempest* (p. 80).

Sophocles

OEDIPUS THE KING

Sophocles (?496 B.C.–406 B.C.) was one of the great trio of Greek tragic authors; the other two were Aeschylus (525 B.C.–456 B.C.) and Euripides (485 B.C.–406 B.C.). The plays of these three were produced in the age of Pericles (490 B.C.–429 B.C.) or shortly after. The masterpiece of Greek drama, by general agreement, Sophocles' *Oedipus Tyrannus* (425 B.C.), though outstanding, was in many ways a typical product of the Greek period.

Perhaps the most important fact to keep in mind about Greek drama is that it was always closely associated with religious ritual. The tragedies were performed at annual Feasts of Dionysus, in a structure which was dedicated to the god of wine. These dramas used poetry, dancing, and music to recount legends about heroes and gods who were the ancestors of the people of Greece—legends known in detail by playwrights and audiences alike. Naturally, there was a ritualistic quality about plays which unfolded time-hallowed stories.

Although the theater in which *Oedipus* and other tragedies were presented was a temple of Dionysus, it differed greatly from any temple we know today. With its 17,000 seats arranged in semicircular tiers on a hillside, it somewhat resembled a present-day football stadium. From the seats, the spectators looked down on a circular dancing place about sixty feet in diameter—"the orchestra"—in the center of which stood a statue of Dionysus. Beyond this circular space, they saw a stage, perhaps slightly elevated, sixty feet wide but not very deep. Beyond the stage, finally, they saw a "scene building"—a temple which furnished a background and which also served as the actors' dressing room.

The actors, who as a rule appeared only on the stage, naturally differed a great deal from the actors of today because of the nature of the dramas and of the huge open-air theater in which they performed. By padding their flowing robes and by donning shoes which increased their stature, they made themselves both visible and impressive. The colors of their robes at times indicated their station (purple for royalty, for instance), and at times symbolized emotions to be associated with them (dark or dim colors for mourning, for example). They wore masks which made their features distinctive when viewed at a distance and which suggested the emotions of the characters. The masks also increased the actors' height and, like megaphones, added to the carrying power of their voices. The tragedians did not strive, as modern actors do, for lifelike intonations: instead, they declaimed their lines somewhat in the fashion of an old-time orator, and, when they came to highly emotional or lyrical passages,

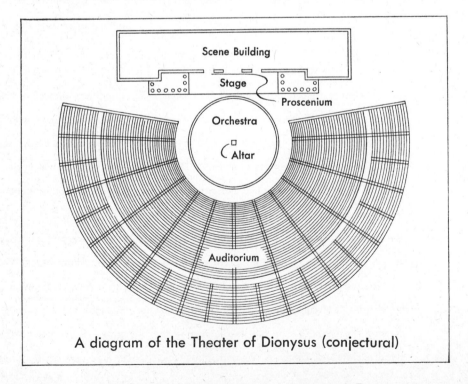

A diagram of the Theater of Dionysus (conjectural)

A performance in the Theater of Dionysus

they sang to the accompaniment of a flute. In some ways, therefore, Greek dramatic presentation was like modern operatic presentation. The method of production, as one would expect, greatly influenced the playwrights. Dramatists characterized not complexly but rather simply, not with subtle details but with broad strokes. They gave the figures in their plays lines which were majestic in diction, formal in movement—closer to oratory or to operatic arias than to lifelike talk. And they kept in mind the kind of scenic background against which all plays had to be presented.

During the whole course of every play, a "chorus" of from twelve to fifteen figures, wearing identical costumes and masks, danced and sang in unison in the orchestra. They were somewhat like a ballet in a modern musical comedy or an opera, for their movements interpreted the action. While the actors recited their lines, the chorus, drawn up in two rows, faced the stage and made interpretive gestures. During choral odes, the chorus faced the audience, sang, and danced about the altar. These odes at times were explanatory, at times narrative, at times philosophical; always, however, the dramatist made them an integral part of his play.

The audience which viewed these opera-like plays was made up of the free population of Athens, with the possible exception of the women of the city. It was a demonstrative group which loudly expressed its approval or disapproval of plays and actors, but it was also, evidently, a discriminating group which appreciated the best plays. It shared the religious beliefs incorporated in the plays, the beliefs, for instance, that overweening pride was one of the greatest of sins, and that sin (whether deliberate or unintentional) inevitably would be punished. It also shared with the dramatist a knowledge of the story which he was dramatizing. Thus, in viewing *Oedipus*, when the king spoke of his world-wide renown, they knew not only that retribution was inevitable: they knew precisely what form it would take—that of a horrible discovery toward which the king moved during the course of the drama.

CHARACTERS

OEDIPUS *the King*	MESSENGER
PRIEST	SECOND MESSENGER
CREON, *the brother-in-law of* OEDIPUS	ANTIGONE ⎱ *daughters of* OEDIPUS
TEIRESIAS	ISMENE ⎰
JOCASTA, *the wife of* OEDIPUS	CHORUS
HERDSMAN	

Scene: In front of the palace of OEDIPUS *at Thebes. To the right of the stage near the altar stands the* PRIEST *with a crowd of children.* OEDIPUS *emerges from the central door.*

OEDIPUS. Children, young sons and daughters of old Cadmus,
  why do you sit here with your suppliant crowns?
  The town is heavy with a mingled burden
  of sounds and smells, of groans and hymns and incense;
  I did not think it fit that I should hear
  of this from messengers but came myself,—
  I Oedipus whom all men call the Great. (*He turns to the* PRIEST)

From David Grene, *Three Greek Tragedies in Translation.* Copyright 1942 by The University of Chicago Press. Used by permission.

You're old and they are young; come, speak for them.
What do you fear or want, that you sit here
suppliant? Indeed I'm willing to give all
that you may need; I would be very hard
should I not pity suppliants like these.
PRIEST. O ruler of my country, Oedipus,
    you see our company around the altar;
    you see our ages; some of us, like these,
    who cannot yet fly far, and some of us
    heavy with age; these children are the chosen
    among the young, and I the priest of Zeus.
    Within the market place sit others crowned
    with suppliant garlands, at the double shrine
    of Pallas and the temple where Ismenus
    gives oracles by fire. King, you yourself
    have seen our city reeling like a wreck
    already; it can scarcely lift its prow
    out of the depths, out of the bloody surf.
    A blight is on the fruitful plants of the earth,
    a blight is on the cattle in the fields.
    a blight is on our women that no children
    are born to them; a God that carries fire,
    a deadly pestilence, is on our town,
    strikes us and spares not, and the house of Cadmus
    is emptied of its people while black Death
    grows rich in groaning and in lamentation.
    We have not come as suppliants to this altar
    because we thought of you as of a God,
    but rather judging you the first of men
    in all the chances of this life and when
    we mortals have to do with more than man.
    You came and by your coming saved our city,
    freed us from tribute which we paid of old
    to the Sphinx, cruel singer. This you did
    in virtue of no knowledge we could give you,
    in virtue of no teaching; it was God
    that aided you, men say, and you are held
    with God's assistance to have saved our lives.
    Now, Oedipus, whom all men call the Greatest,
    here falling at your feet we all entreat you,
    find us some strength for rescue.
    Perhaps you'll hear a wise word from some God,
    perhaps you will learn something from a man
    (for I have seen that for the skilled of practice
    the outcome of their counsels live the most).

Noblest of men, go, and raise up our city,
go,—and give heed. For now this land of ours
calls you its savior since you saved it once.
So, let us never speak about your reign
as of a time when first our feet were set
secure on high, but later fell to ruin.
Raise up our city, save it and raise it up.
Once you have brought us luck with happy omen;
be no less now in fortune.
If you will rule this land, as now you rule it,
better to rule it full of men than empty.
For neither town nor ship is anything
when empty, and none live in it together.

OEDIPUS. Poor children! You have come to me entreating,
but I have known the story before you told it
only too well. I know you are all sick,
yet there is not one of you, sick though you are,
that is as sick as I myself.
Your several sorrows each have single scope
and touch but one of you. My spirit groans
for city and myself and you at once.
You have not roused me like a man from sleep;
know that I have given many tears to this,
gone many ways wandering in thought,
but as I thought I found only one remedy
and that I took. I sent Menoeceus' son
Creon, Jocasta's brother, to Apollo,
to his Pythian temple,
that he might learn there by what act or word
I could save this city. As I count the days,
it vexes me what ails him; he is gone
far longer than he needed for the journey.
But when he comes, then, may I prove a villain,
if I shall not do all the God commands.

PRIEST. Thanks for your gracious words. Your servants here
signal that Creon is this moment coming.

OEDIPUS. His face is bright. O holy Lord Apollo,
grant that his news too may be bright for us
and bring us safety.

PRIEST. It is happy news,
I think, for else his head would not be crowned
with sprigs of fruitful laurel.

OEDIPUS.   We will know soon,
he's within hail. Lord Creon, my good brother,
what is the word you bring us from the God?

(CREON *enters*)

CREON. A good word,—for things hard to bear themselves
   if in the final issue all is well
   I count complete good fortune.

OEDIPUS.   What do you mean?
   What you have said so far
   leaves me uncertain whether to trust or fear.

CREON. If you will hear my news before these others
   I am ready to speak, or else to go within.

OEDIPUS. Speak it to all;
   the grief I bear, I bear it more for these
   than for my own heart.

CREON.   I will tell you, then,
   what I heard from the God.
   King Phoebus in plain words commanded us
   to drive out a pollution from our land,
   pollution grown ingrained within the land;
   drive it out, said the God, not cherish it,
   till it's past cure.

OEDIPUS.   What is the rite
   of purification? How shall it be done?

CREON. By banishing a man, or expiation
   of blood by blood, since it is murder guilt
   which holds our city in this storm of death.

OEDIPUS. Who is this man whose fate the God pronounces?

CREON. My Lord, before you piloted the state
   we had a king called Laius.

OEDIPUS. I know of him by hearsay. I have not seen him.

CREON. The God commanded clearly: let some one
   punish with force this dead man's murderers.

OEDIPUS. Where are they in the world? Where would a trace
   of this old crime be found? It would be hard
   to guess where.

CREON.   The clue is in this land;
   that which is sought is found;
   the unheeded thing escapes:
   so said the God.

OEDIPUS.   Was it at home,
   or in the country that death came upon him,
   or in another country travelling?

CREON. He went, he said himself, upon an embassy,
   but never returned when he set out from home.

OEDIPUS. Was there no messenger, no fellow traveller
   who knew what happened? Such a one might tell
   something of use.

CREON. They were all killed save one. He fled in terror
  and he could tell us nothing in clear terms
  of what he knew, nothing, but one thing only.
OEDIPUS. What was it?
  If we could even find a slim beginning
  in which to hope, we might discover much.
CREON. This man said that the robbers they encountered
  were many and the hands that did the murder
  were many; it was no man's single power.
OEDIPUS. How could a robber dare a deed like this
  were he not helped with money from the city,
  money and treachery?
CREON.   That indeed was thought.
  But Laius was dead and in our trouble
  there was none to help.
OEDIPUS. What trouble was so great to hinder you
  inquiring out the murder of your king?
CREON. The riddling Sphinx induced us to neglect
  mysterious crimes and rather seek solution
  of troubles at our feet.
OEDIPUS. I will bring this to light again. King Phoebus
  fittingly took this care about the dead,
  and you too fittingly.
  And justly you will see in me an ally,
  a champion of my country and the God.
  For when I drive pollution from the land
  I will not serve a distant friend's advantage,
  but act in my own interest. Whoever
  he was that killed the king may readily
  wish to dispatch me with his murderous hand;
  so helping the dead king I help myself.

  Come children, take your suppliant boughs and go;
  up from the altars now. Call the assembly
  and let it meet upon the understanding
  that I'll do everything. God will decide
  whether we prosper or remain in sorrow.
PRIEST. Rise, children—it was this we came to seek,
  which of himself the king now offers us.
  May Phoebus who gave us the oracle
  come to our rescue and stay the plague.
(*Exeunt all but the* CHORUS)
CHORUS
(*Strophe*)
  What is the sweet spoken word of God from the shrine of Pytho rich in gold

that has come to glorious Thebes?
I am stretched on the rack of doubt, and terror and trembling hold
my heart, O Delian Healer, and I worship full of fears
for what doom you will bring to pass, new or renewed in the revolving years.
Speak to me, immortal voice,
child of Golden Hope.

(*Antistrophe*)

First I call on you, Athene, deathless daughter of Zeus,
and Artemis, Earth Upholder,
who sits in the midst of the market place in the throne which men call Fame,
and Phoebus, the Far Shooter, three averters of Fate,
come to us now, if ever before, when ruin rushed upon the state,
you drove destruction's flame away
out of our land.

(*Strophe*)

Our sorrows defy number;
all the ship's timbers are rotten;
taking of thought is no spear for the driving away of the plague.
There are no growing children in this famous land;
there are no women staunchly bearing the pangs of childbirth.
You may see them one with another, like birds swift on the wing,
quicker than fire unmastered,
speeding away to the coast of the Western God.

(*Antistrophe*)

In the unnumbered deaths
of its people the city dies;
those children that are born lie dead on the naked earth
unpitied, spreading contagion of death; and grey haired mothers and wives
everywhere stand at the altar's edge, suppliant moaning;
the hymn to the healing God rings out but with it the wailing voices are
blended.
From these our sufferings grant us, O golden Daughter of Zeus,
glad faced deliverance.

(*Strophe*)

There is no clash of brazen shields but our fight is with the War God,
a War God ringed with the cries of men, a savage God who burns us;
grant that he turn in racing course backwards out of our country's bounds
to the great palace of Amphitrite or where the waves of the Thracian sea
deny the stranger safe anchorage.
Whatsoever escapes the night
at last the light of day revisits;
so smite the War God, Father Zeus,
beneath your thunderbolt,
for you are the Lord of the lightning, the lightning that
carries fire.

(*Antistrophe*)
>   And your unconquered arrow shafts, winged by the golden corded bow,
>   Lycean King, I beg to be at our side for help;
>   and the gleaming torches of Artemis with which she scours the Lycean hills,
>   and I call on the God with the turban of gold, who gave his name to this
>>   country of ours,
>   the Bacchic God with the wine flushed face,
>   Evian One, who travel
>   with the Maenad company,
>   combat the God that burns us
>   with your torch of pine;
>   for the God that is our enemy is a God unhonoured among the Gods.

(OEDIPUS *returns*)
OEDIPUS. For what you ask me—if you will hear my words,
>   and hearing welcome them and fight the plague,
>   you will find strength and lightening of your load.

>   Hark to me; what I say to you, I say
>   as one that is a stranger to the story
>   as stranger to the deed. For I would not
>   be far upon the track if I alone
>   were tracing it without a clue. But now,
>   since after all was finished, I became
>   a citizen among you, citizens—
>   now I proclaim to all the men of Thebes:
>   who so among you knows the murderer
>   by whose hand Laius, son of Labdacus,
>   died—I command him to tell everything
>   to me,—yes, though he fears himself to take the blame
>   on his own head; for bitter punishment
>   he shall have none, but leave this land unharmed.
>   Or if he knows the murderer, another,
>   a foreigner, still let him speak the truth.
>   For I will pay him and be grateful, too.
>   But if you shall keep silence, if perhaps
>   some one of you, to shield a guilty friend,
>   or for his own sake shall reject my words—
>   hear what I shall do then:
>   I forbid that man, whoever he be, my land,
>   my land where I hold sovereignty and throne;
>   and I forbid any to welcome him
>   or cry him greeting or make him a sharer
>   in sacrifice or offering to the Gods,
>   or give him water for his hands to wash.

I command all to drive him from their homes,
since he is our pollution, as the oracle
of Pytho's God proclaimed him now to me.
So I stand forth a champion of the God
and of the man who died.
Upon the murderer I invoke this curse—
whether he is one man and all unknown,
or one of many—may he wear out his life
in misery to miserable doom!
If with my knowledge he lives at my hearth
I pray that I myself may feel my curse.

Even were this no matter of God's ordinance
it would not fit you so to leave it lie,
unpurified, since a good man is dead
and one that was a king. Search it out.
Since I am now the holder of his office,
and have his bed and wife that once was his,
and had his line not been unfortunate
we would have common children—(fortune leaped
upon his head)—because of all these things,
I fight in his defence as for my father,
and I shall try all means to take the murderer
of Laius the son of Labdacus
the son of Polydorus and before him
of Cadmus and before him of Agenor.
Those who do not obey me, may the Gods
grant no crops springing from the ground they plough
nor children to their women! May a fate
like this, or one still worse than this consume them!
For you who these words please, the other Thebans,
may Justice as your ally and all the Gods
live with you, blessing you now and for ever!
CHORUS. As you have held me to my oath, I speak:
  I neither killed the king nor can declare
  the killer; but since Phoebus set the quest
  it is his part to tell who the man is.
OEDIPUS. Right; but to put compulsion on the Gods
  against their will—no man has strength for that.
CHORUS. May I then say what I think second best?
OEDIPUS. If there's a third best. too. spare not to tell it.
CHORUS. I know that what the Lord Teiresias
  sees, is most often what the Lord Apollo
  sees. If you should inquire of this from him
  you might find out most clearly.

OEDIPUS. Even in this my actions have not been sluggard.
   On Creon's word I have sent two messengers
   and why the prophet is not here already
   I have been wondering.
CHORUS.   His skill apart
   there is besides only an old faint story.
OEDIPUS. What is it?
   I seize on every story.
CHORUS.   It was said
   that he was killed by certain wayfarers.
OEDIPUS. I heard that, too, but no one saw the killer.
CHORUS. Yet if he has a share of fear at all,
   his courage will not stand firm, hearing your curse.
OEDIPUS. The man who in the doing did not shrink
   will fear no word.
CHORUS.   Here comes his prosecutor:
   led by your men the godly prophet comes
   in whom alone of mankind truth is native.
(*Enter* TEIRESIAS, *led by a little boy*)
OEDIPUS. Teiresias, you are versed in everything,
   things teachable and things not to be spoken,
   things of the heaven and earth-creeping things.
   You have no eyes but in your mind you know
   with what a plague our city is afflicted.
   My lord, in you alone we find a champion,
   in you alone one that can rescue us.
   Perhaps you have not heard the messengers,
   but Phoebus sent in answer to our sending
   an oracle declaring that our freedom
   from this disease would only come when we
   should learn the names of those who killed King Laius,
   and kill them or expel from our country.
   Do not begrudge us oracles from birds,
   or any other way of prophecy
   within your skill; save yourself and the city,
   save me; redeem the debt of our pollution
   that lies on us because of this dead man.
   We are in your hands; it is the finest task
   to help another when you have means and power.
TEIRESIAS. Alas, how terrible is wisdom when
   it brings no profit to the man that's wise!
   This I knew well, but had forgotten it,
   else I would not have come here.
OEDIPUS.   What is this?
   How sad you are now you have come!

TEIRESIAS. Let me
go home. It will be easiest for us both
to bear our several destinies to the end
if you will follow my advice.

OEDIPUS. You'd rob us
of this your gift of prophecy? You talk
as one who had no care for law nor love
for Thebes who reared you.

TEIRESIAS. Yes, but I see that even your own words
miss the mark; therefore I must fear for mine.

OEDIPUS. For God's sake if you know of anything,
do not turn from us; all of us kneel to you,
all of us here, your suppliants.

TEIRESIAS. All of you here know nothing. I will not
bring to the light of day my troubles, mine—
rather than call them yours.

OEDIPUS. What do you mean?
You know of something but refuse to speak.
Would you betray us and destroy the city?

TEIRESIAS. I will not bring this pain upon us both,
neither on you nor on myself. Why is it
you question me and waste your labour? I
will tell you nothing.

OEDIPUS. You would provoke a stone! Tell us, you villain,
tell us, and do not stand there quietly
unmoved and balking at the final issue.

TEIRESIAS. You blame my temper but you do not see
your own that lives within you; it is me
you chide.

OEDIPUS. Who would not feel his temper rise
at words like these with which you shame our city?

TEIRESIAS. Of themselves things will come, although I hide them
and breathe no word of them.

OEDIPUS. Since they will come
tell them to me.

TEIRESIAS. I will say nothing further.
Against this answer let your temper rage
as wildly as you will.

OEDIPUS. Indeed I am
so angry I shall not hold back a jot
of what I think. For I would have you know
I think you were complotter of the deed
and doer of the deed save in so far
as for the actual killing. Had you had eyes
I would have said alone you murdered him.

TEIRESIAS. Yes? Then I warn you faithfully to keep
   the letter of your proclamation and
   from this day forth to speak no word of greeting
   to these nor me; you are the land's pollution.
OEDIPUS. How shamelessly you started up this taunt!
   How do you think you will escape?
TEIRESIAS.   I have.
   I have escaped; the truth is what I cherish
   and that's my strength.
OEDIPUS.   And who has taught you truth?
   Not your profession surely!
TEIRESIAS.   You have taught me,
   for you have made me speak against my will.
OEDIPUS. Speak what? Tell me again that I may learn it better.
TEIRESIAS. Did you not understand before or would you
   provoke me into speaking?
OEDIPUS.   I did not grasp it,
   not so to call it known. Say it again.
TEIRESIAS. I say you are the murderer of the king
   whose murderer you seek.
OEDIPUS.   Not twice you shall
   say calumnies like this and stay unpunished.
TEIRESIAS. Shall I say more to tempt your anger more?
OEDIPUS. As much as you desire; it will be said
   in vain.
TEIRESIAS. I say that with those you love best
   you live in foulest shame unconsciously
   and do not see where you are in calamity.
OEDIPUS. Do you imagine you can always talk
   like this, and live to laugh at it hereafter?
TEIRESIAS. Yes, if the truth has anything of strength.
OEDIPUS. It has, but not for you; it has no strength
   for you because you are blind in mind and ears
   as well as in your eyes.
TEIRESIAS.   You are a poor wretch
   to taunt me with the very insults which
   every one soon will heap upon yourself.
OEDIPUS. Your life is one long night so that you cannot
   hurt me or any other who sees the light.
TEIRESIAS. It is not fate that I should be your ruin,
   Apollo is enough; it is his care
   to work this out.
OEDIPUS.   Was this your own design
   or Creon's?

TEIRESIAS.   Creon is no hurt to you,
   but you are to yourself.
OEDIPUS. Wealth, sovereignty and skill outmatching skill
   for the contrivance of an envied life,
   great store of jealousy fill your treasury chests,
   if my friend Creon, friend from the first and loyal,
   thus secretly attacks me, secretly
   desires to drive me out and secretly
   suborns this juggling, trick devising quack,
   this wily beggar who has only eyes
   for his own gains, but blindness in his skill.
   For, tell me, where have you seen clear, Teiresias,
   with your prophetic eyes? When the dark singer,
   the sphinx, was in your country, did you speak
   word of deliverance to its citizens?
   And yet the riddle's answer was not the province
   of a chance comer. It was a prophet's task
   and plainly you had no such gift of prophecy
   from birds nor otherwise from any God
   to glean a word of knowledge. But I came,
   Oedipus, who knew nothing, and I stopped her.
   I solved the riddle by my wit alone.
   Mine was no knowledge got from birds. And now
   you would expel me,
   because you think that you will find a place
   by Creon's throne. I think you will be sorry,
   both you and your accomplice, for your plot
   to drive me out. And did I not regard you
   as an old man, some suffering would have taught you
   that what was in your heart was treason.
CHORUS. We look at this man's words and yours, my king,
   and we find both have spoken them in anger.
   We need no angry words but only thought
   how we may best hit the God's meaning for us.
TEIRESIAS. If you are king, at least I have the right
   no less to speak in my defence against you.
   Of that much I am master. I am no slave
   of yours, but Loxias', and so I shall not
   enroll myself with Creon for my patron.
   Since you have taunted me with being blind,
   here is my word for you.
   You have your eyes but see not where you are
   in sin, nor where you live, nor whom you live with.
   Do you know who your parents are? Unknowing

you are an enemy to kith and kin
in death, beneath the earth, and in this life.
A deadly footed, double-striking curse,
from father and mother both, shall drive you forth
out of this land, with darkness on your eyes,
that now have such straight vision. Shall there be
a place will not be harbour to your cries,
a corner of Cithaeron will not ring
in echo to your cries, soon, soon,—
when you shall learn the secret of your marriage,
which steered you to a haven in this house,—
haven no haven, after lucky voyage?
And of the multitude of other evils
establishing a grim equality
between you and your children, you know nothing.
So, muddy with contempt my words and Creon's!
There is no man shall perish as you shall.

OEDIPUS. Is it endurable that I should hear
    such words from him? Go and a curse go with you!
    Quick, home with you! Out of my house at once!

TEIRESIAS. I would not have come either had you not called me.

OEDIPUS. I did not know then you would talk like a fool—
    or it would have been long before I called you.

TEIRESIAS. I am a fool then, as it seems to you—
    but to the parents who have bred you, wise.

OEDIPUS. What parents? Stop! Who are they of all the world?

TEIRESIAS. This day will show your birth and bring your ruin.

OEDIPUS. How needlessly your riddles darken everything.

TEIRESIAS. But it's in riddle answering you are strongest.

OEDIPUS. Yes. Taunt me where you will find me great.

TEIRESIAS. It is this very luck that has destroyed you.

OEDIPUS. I do not care, if it has served this city.

TEIRESIAS. Well, I will go. Come, boy, lead me away.

OEDIPUS. Yes, lead him off. So long as you are here,
    you'll be a stumbling block and a vexation;
    once gone, you will not trouble me again.

TEIRESIAS.   I have said
    what I came here to say not fearing your
    countenance: there is no way you can hurt me.
    I tell you, king, this man, this murderer
    (whom you have long declared you are in search of,
    indicting him in threatening proclamation
    as murderer of Laius)—he is here.
    In name he is a stranger among citizens
    but soon he will be shown to be a citizen

true native Theban, and he'll have no joy
of the discovery: blindness for sight
and beggary for riches his exchange,
he shall go journeying to a foreign country
tapping his way before him with a stick.
He shall be proved father and brother both
to his own children in his house; to her
that gave him birth, a son and husband both;
a fellow sower in his father's bed
with that same father that he murdered.
Go within, reckon that out, and if you find me
mistaken, say I have no skill in prophecy.
(*Exeunt separately* TEIRESIAS *and* OEDIPUS)
CHORUS
(*Strophe*)
   Who is the man proclaimed
   by Delphi's prophetic rock
   as the bloody handed murderer,
   the doer of deeds that none dare name?
   Now is the time for him to run
   with a stronger foot
   than Pegasus
   for the child of Zeus leaps in arms upon him
   with fire and the lightning bolt,
   and terribly close on his heels
   are the Fates that never miss.
(*Antistrophe*)
   Lately from snowy Parnassus
   clearly the voice flashed forth,
   bidding each Theban track him down,
   the unknown murderer.
   In the savage forests he lurks and in
   the caverns like
   the mountain bull.
   He is sad and lonely, and lonely his feet
   that carry him far from the navel of earth;
   but its prophecies, ever living,
   flutter around his head.
(*Strophe*)
   The augur has spread confusion,
   terrible confusion;
   I do not approve what was said
   nor can I deny it.
   I do not know what to say;
   I am in a flutter of foreboding;

I never heard in the present
nor past of a quarrel between
the sons of Labdacus and Polybus,
that I might bring as proof
in attacking the popular fame
of Oedipus, seeking
to take vengeance for undiscovered
death in the line of Labdacus.
(*Antistrophe*)
Truly Zeus and Apollo are wise
and in human things all knowing;
but amongst men there is no
distinct judgment, between the prophet
and me—which of us is right.
One man may pass another in wisdom
but I would never agree
with those that find fault with the king
till I should see the word
proved right beyond doubt. For once
in visible form the Sphinx
came on him and all of us
saw his wisdom and in that test
he saved the city. So he will not be condemned by my mind.
(*Enter* CREON)
CREON. Citizens, I have come because I heard
deadly words spread about me, that the king
accuses me. I cannot take that from him.
If he believes that in these present troubles
he has been wronged by me in word or deed
I do not want to live on with the burden
of such a scandal on me. The report
injures me doubly and most vitally—
for I'll be called a traitor to my city
and traitor also to my friends and you.
CHORUS. Perhaps it was a sudden gust of anger
that forced that insult from him, and no judgment.
CREON. But did he say that it was in compliance
with schemes of mine that the seer told him lies?
CHORUS. Yes, he said that, but why, I do not know.
CREON. Were his eyes straight in his head? Was his mind right
when he accused me in this fashion?
CHORUS. I do not know; I have no eyes to see
what princes do. Here comes the king himself.
(*Enter* OEDIPUS)
OEDIPUS. You, sir, how is it you come here? Have you so much

brazen-faced daring that you venture in
my house although you are proved manifestly
the murder of that man, and though you tried,
openly, highway robbery of my crown?
For God's sake, tell me what you saw in me,
what cowardice or what stupidity,
that made you lay a plot like this against me?
Did you imagine I should not observe
the crafty scheme that stole upon me or
seeing it, take no means to counter it?
Was it not stupid of you to make the attempt,
to try to hunt down royal power without
the people at your back or friends? For only
with the people at your back or money can
the hunt end in the capture of a crown.

CREON. Do you know what you're doing? Will you listen
to words to answer yours, and then pass judgment?

OEDIPUS. You're quick to speak, but I am slow to grasp you,
for I have found you dangerous,—and my foe.

CREON. First of all hear what I shall say to that.

OEDIPUS. At least don't tell me that you are not guilty.

CREON. If you believe you cherish something fine
in obstinacy without brains, you're wrong.

OEDIPUS. And you are wrong if you believe that one,
a criminal, will not be punished only
because he is my kinsman.

CREON.   This is but just——
but tell me, then, of what offense I'm guilty?

OEDIPUS. Did you or did you not urge me to send
to this prophetic mumbler?

CREON.   I did indeed,
and I shall stand by what I told you.

OEDIPUS. How long ago is it since Laius . . . .

CREON. What about Laius? I don't understand.

OEDIPUS. Vanished—died—was murdered?

CREON.   It is long,
a long, long time to reckon.

OEDIPUS.   Was this prophet
in the profession then?

CREON.   He was, and honoured
as highly as he is today.

OEDIPUS. At that time did he say a word about me?

CREON. Never, at least when I was near him.

OEDIPUS. You never made a search for the dead man?

CREON. We searched, indeed, but never learned of anything.

OEDIPUS. Why did our wise old friend not say this then?
CREON. I don't know; and when I know nothing, I
　usually hold my tongue.
OEDIPUS. 　　　　　　　　You know this much,
　and can declare this much if you are loyal.
CREON. What is it? If I know I'll not deny it.
OEDIPUS. That he would not have said that I killed Laius
　had he not met you first.
CREON. 　　　　　　　　You know yourself
　whether he said this, but I demand that I
　should hear as much from you as you from me.
OEDIPUS. Then hear,—I'll not be proved a murderer.
CREON. Well, then. You're married to my sister.
OEDIPUS. 　　　　　　　　　　　　　Yes,
　that I am not disposed to deny.
CREON. 　　　　　　　　You rule
　this country giving her an equal share
　in the government?
OEDIPUS. 　　　　　　Yes, everything she wants
　she has from me.
CREON. 　　　　　And I, as thirdsman to you.
　am rated as the equal of you two?
OEDIPUS. Yes, and it's there you've proved yourself false friend.
CREON. Not if you will reflect on it as I do.
　Consider, first, if you think any one
　would choose to rule and fear rather than rule
　and sleep untroubled by a fear if power
　were equal in both cases. I, at least,
　I was not born with such a frantic yearning
　to be a king—but to do what kings do.
　And so it is with every one who has learned
　wisdom and self-control. As it stands now,
　the prizes are all mine—and without fear.
　But if I were the king myself, I must
　do much that went against the grain.
　How should despotic rule seem sweeter to me
　than painless power and an assured authority?
　I am not so besotted yet that I
　want other honours than those that come with profit.
　Now every man's my pleasure; every man greets me;
　now those who are your suitors fawn on me,—
　success for them depends upon my favour.
　Why should I let all this go to win that?
　My mind would not be traitor if it's wise;
　I am no treason lover. of my nature.

nor would I ever dare to join a plot.
Prove what I say. Go to the oracle
at Pytho and inquire about the answers,
if they are as I told you. For the rest,
if you discover I laid any plot
together with the seer, kill me, I say,
not only by your vote but my own.
But do not charge me on obscure opinion
without some proof to back it. It's not just
lightly to count your knaves as honest men,
nor honest men as knaves. To throw away
an honest friend is, as it were, to throw
your life away, which a man loves the best.
In time you will know all with certainty;
time is the only test of honest men,
one day is space enough to know a rogue.

CHORUS. His words are wise, king, if one fears to fall.
    Those who are quick of temper are not safe.

OEDIPUS. When he that plots against me secretly
    moves quickly, I must quickly counterplot.
    If I wait taking no decisive measure
    his business will be done, and mine be spoiled.

CREON. What do you want to do then? Banish me?

OEDIPUS. No, certainly; kill you, not banish you.

CREON. I do not think that you've your wits about you.

OEDIPUS. For my own interests, yes.

CREON.   But for mine, too,
    you should think equally.

OEDIPUS.   You are a rogue.

CREON. Suppose you do not understand?

OEDIPUS.   But yet
    I must be ruler.

CREON.   Not if you rule badly.

OEDIPUS. O, city, city!

CREON.   I too have some share
    in the city; it is not yours alone.

CHORUS. Stop, my lords! Here—and in the nick of time
    I see Jocasta coming from the house;
    with her help lay the quarrel that now stirs you.

(*Enter* JOCASTA)

JOCASTA. For shame! Why have you raised this foolish squabbling
    brawl? Are you not ashamed to air your private
    griefs when the country's sick? Go in, you, Oedipus,
    and you, too, Creon, into the house. Don't magnify
    your nothing troubles.

CREON.   Sister, Oedipus,
    your husband, thinks he has the right to do
    terrible wrongs—he has but to choose between
    two terrors: banishing or killing me.
OEDIPUS. He's right, Jocasta; for I find him plotting
    with knavish tricks against my person.
CREON. That God may never bless me! May I die
    accursed, if I have been guilty of
    one tittle of the charge you bring against me!
JOCASTA. I beg you, Oedipus, trust him in this,
    spare him for the sake of this his oath to God,
    for my sake, and the sake of those who stand here.
CHORUS. Be gracious, be merciful,
    we beg of you.
OEDIPUS. In what would you have me yield?
CHORUS. He has been no silly child in the past.
    He is strong in his oath now.
    Spare him.
OEDIPUS. Do you know what you ask?
CHORUS. Yes.
OEDIPUS. Tell me then.
CHORUS. He has been your friend before all men's eyes; do not cast
    him away dishonoured on an obscure conjecture.
OEDIPUS. I would have you know that this request of yours
    really requests my death or banishment.
CHORUS. May the Sun God, king of Gods, forbid! May I die without
    God's blessing, without friends' help, if I had any such
    thought. But my spirit is broken by my unhappiness for my
    wasting country; and this would but add troubles amongst
    ourselves to the other troubles.
OEDIPUS. Well, let him go then—if I must die ten times for it,
    or be sent out dishonoured into exile.
    It is your lips that prayed for him I pitied,
    not his; wherever he is, I shall hate him.
CREON. I see you sulk in yielding and you're dangerous
    when you are out of temper; natures like yours
    are justly heaviest for themselves to bear.
OEDIPUS. Leave me alone! Take yourself off, I tell you.
CREON. I'll go, you have not known me, but they have,
    and they have known my innocence. (*Exit*)
CHORUS. Won't you take him inside, lady?
JOCASTA. Yes, when I've found out what was the matter.
CHORUS. There was some misconceived suspicion of a story, and on
    the other side the sting of injustice,

JOCASTA. So, on both sides?

CHORUS. Yes.

JOCASTA. What was the story?

CHORUS. I think it best, in the interests of the country, to leave it
where it ended.

OEDIPUS. You see where you have ended, straight of judgment
although you are, by softening my anger.

CHORUS. Sir, I have said before and I say again—be sure that I would
have been proved a madman, bankrupt in sane council, if I
should put you away, you who steered the country I love
safely when she was crazed with troubles. God grant that
now, too, you may prove a fortunate guide for us.

JOCASTA. Tell me, my lord, I beg of you, what was it
that roused your anger so?

OEDIPUS.   Yes, I will tell you.
I honour you more than I honour them.
It was Creon and the plots he laid against me.

JOCASTA. Tell me—if you can clearly tell the quarrel—

OEDIPUS.   Creon says
that I'm the murderer of Laius.

JOCASTA. Of his own knowledge or on information?

OEDIPUS. He sent this rascal prophet to me, since
he keeps his own mouth clean of any guilt.

JOCASTA. Do not concern yourself about the matter;
listen to me and learn that human beings
have no part in the craft of prophecy.
Of that I'll show you a short proof.
There was an oracle once that came to Laius,—
I will not say that it was Phoebus' own,
but it was from his servants—and it told him
that it was fate that he should die a victim
at the hands of his own son, a son to be born
of Laius and me. But, see now, he,
the king, was killed by foreign highway robbers
at a place where three roads meet—so goes the story;
and for the son—before three days were out
after his birth King Laius pierced his ankles
and by the hands of others cast him forth
upon a pathless hillside. So Apollo
failed to fulfill his oracle to the son,
that he should kill his father, and to Laius
also proved false in that the thing he feared,
death at his son's hands, never came to pass.
So clear in this case were the oracles,

so clear and false. Give them no heed, I say;
what God discovers need of, easily
he shows to us himself.

OEDIPUS.   O dear Jocasta,
as I hear this from you, there comes upon me
a wandering of the soul—I could run mad.

JOCASTA. What trouble is it, that you turn again
and speak like this?

OEDIPUS.   I thought I heard you say
that Laius was killed at a crossroads.

JOCASTA. Yes, that was how the story went and still
that word goes round.

OEDIPUS.   Where is this place, Jocasta,
where he was murdered?

JOCASTA.   Phocis is the country
and the road splits there, one of two roads from Delphi,
another comes from Daulia.

OEDIPUS.   How long ago is this?

JOCASTA. The news came to the city just before
you became king and all men's eyes looked to you.
What is it, Oedipus, that's in your mind?

OEDIPUS. Don't ask me yet—tell me of Laius—
how did he look? How old or young was he?

JOCASTA. He was a tall man and his hair was grizzled
already—nearly white—and in his form
not unlike you.

OEDIPUS.   O God, I think I have
called curses on myself in ignorance.

JOCASTA. What do you mean? I am terrified
when I look at you.

OEDIPUS.   I have a deadly fear
that the old seer had eyes. You'll show me more
if you can tell me one more thing.

JOCASTA.   I will.
I'm frightened,—but if I can understand,
I'll tell you all you ask.

OEDIPUS.   How was his company?
Had he few with him when he went this journey,
or many servants, as would suit a prince?

JOCASTA. In all there were but five, and among them
a herald; and one carriage for the king.

OEDIPUS. It's plain—it's plain—who was it told you this?

JOCASTA. The only servant that escaped safe home.

OEDIPUS. Is he at home now?

JOCASTA. No, when he came home again

and saw you king and Laius was dead,
he came to me and touched my hand and begged
that I should send him to the fields to be
my shepherd and so he might see the city
as far off as he might. So I
sent him away. He was an honest man,
as slaves go, and was worthy of far more
than what he asked of me.
OEDIPUS. O, how I wish that he could come back quickly!
JOCASTA. He can. Why is your heart so set on this?
OEDIPUS. O dear Jocasta, I am full of fears
that I have spoken far too much; and therefore
I wish to see this shepherd.
JOCASTA.   He will come;
but, Oedipus, I think I'm worthy too
to know what is it that disquiets you.
OEDIPUS. It shall not be kept from you, since my mind
has gone so far with its forebodings. Whom
should I confide in rather than you, who is there
of more importance to me who have passed
through such a fortune?
Polybus was my father, king of Corinth,
and Merope, the Dorian, my mother.
I was held greatest of the citizens
in Corinth till a curious chance befell me
as I shall tell you—curious, indeed,
but hardly worth the store I set upon it.
There was a dinner and at it a man,
a drunken man, accused me in his drink
of being bastard. I was furious
but held my temper under for that day.
Next day I went and taxed my parents with it;
they took the insult very ill from him,
the drunken fellow who had uttered it.
So I was comforted for their part, but
still this thing rankled always, for the story
crept about widely. And I went at last
To Pytho, though my parents did not know.
But Phoebus sent me home again unhonoured
in what I came to learn, but he foretold
other and desperate horrors to befall me,
that I was fated to lie with my mother,
and show to daylight an accursed breed
which men would not endure, and I was doomed
to be murderer of the father that begot me.

When I heard this I fled, and in the days
that followed I would measure from the stars
the whereabouts of Corinth—yes, I fled
to somewhere where I should not see fulfilled
the infamies told in that dreadful oracle.
And as I journeyed I came to the place
where, as you say, this king met with his death.
Jocasta, I will tell you the whole truth.
When I was near the branching of the crossroads,
going on foot, I was encountered by
a herald and a carriage with a man in it,
just as you tell me. He that led the way
and the old man himself wanted to thrust me
out of the road by force. I became angry
and struck the coachman who was pushing me.
When the old man saw this he watched his moment,
and as I passed he struck me from his carriage,
full on the head with his two pointed goad.
But he was paid in full and presently
my stick had struck him backwards from the car
and he rolled out of it. And then I killed them
all. If it happened there was any tie
of kinship twixt this man and Laius,
who is then now more miserable than I,
what man on earth so hated by the Gods,
since neither citizen nor foreigner
may welcome me at home or even greet me,
but drive me out of doors? And it is I,
I and no other have so cursed myself.
And I pollute the bed of him I killed
by the hands that killed him. Was I not born evil?
Am I not utterly unclean? I had to fly
and in my banishment not even see
my kindred nor set foot in my own country,
or otherwise my fate was to be yoked
in marriage with my mother and kill my father,
Polybus who begot me and had reared me.
Would not one rightly judge and say that on me
these things were sent by some malignant God?
O no, no, no—O holy majesty
of God on high, may I not see that day!
May I be gone out of men's sight before
I see the deadly taint of this disaster
come upon me.
CHORUS. Sir, we too fear these things. But until you see this man face

to face and hear his story, hope.

OEDIPUS. Yes, I have just this much of hope—to wait until the herdsman comes.

JOCASTA. And when he comes, what do you want with him?

OEDIPUS. I'll tell you; if I find that his story is the same as yours, I at least
will be clear of this guilt.

JOCASTA. Why what so particularly did you learn from my story?

OEDIPUS. You said that he spoke of highway *robbers* who killed Laius. Now if
he uses the same number, it was not I who killed him. One man cannot be
the same as many. But if he speaks of a man travelling alone, then clearly
the burden of the guilt inclines towards me.

JOCASTA. Be sure, at least, that this was how he told the story. He cannot
unsay it now, for every one in the city heard it—not I alone. But, Oedipus,
even if he diverges from what he said then, he shall never prove that the
murder of Laius squares rightly with the prophecy—for Loxias declared that
the king should be killed by his own son. And that poor creature did not
kill him surely,—for he died himself first. So as far as prophecy goes, hence-
forward I shall not look to the right hand or the left.

OEDIPUS. Right. But yet, send some one for the peasant to bring him here; do
not neglect it.

JOCASTA. I will send quickly. Now let me go indoors. I will do nothing except
what pleases you. (*Exeunt*)

CHORUS.

(*Strophe*)

May destiny ever find me
pious in word and deed
prescribed by the laws that live on high
laws begotten in the clear air of heaven,
whose only father is Olympus;
no mortal nature brought them to birth,
no forgetfulness shall lull them to sleep;
for God is great in them and grows not old.

(*Antistrophe*)

Insolence breeds the tyrant, insolence
if it is glutted with a surfeit, unseasonable, unprofitable,
climbs to the roof-top and plunges
sheer down to the ruin that must be,
and there its feet are no service.
But I pray that the God may never
abolish the eager ambition that profits the state.
For I shall never cease to hold the God as our protector.

(*Strophe*)

If a man walks with haughtiness
of hand or word and gives no heed
to Justice and the shrines of Gods

despises—may an evil doom
smite him for his ill-starred pride of heart!—
if he reaps gains without justice
and will not hold from impiety
and his fingers itch for untouchable things.
When such things are done, what man shall contrive
to shield his soul from the shafts of the God?
When such deeds are held in honour,
why should I honour the Gods in the dance?
(*Antistrophe*)
No longer to the holy place,
to the navel of earth I'll go
to worship, nor to Abae
nor to Olympia,
unless the oracles are proved to fit,
for all men's hands to point at.
O Zeus, if you are rightly called
the sovereign lord, all-mastering,
let this not escape you nor your ever-living power!
The oracles concerning Laius
are old and dim and men regard them not.
Apollo is nowhere clear in honour; God's service perishes.
(*Enter* JOCASTA, *carrying garlands*)
JOCASTA. Princes of the land, I have had the thought to go
to the Gods' temples, bringing in my hand
garlands and gifts of incense, as you see.
For Oedipus excites himself too much
at every sort of trouble, not conjecturing,
like a man of sense, what will be from what was,
but he is always at the speaker's mercy,
when he speaks terrors. I can do no good
by my advice, and so I came as suppliant
to you, Lycaean Apollo, who are nearest.
These are the symbols of my prayer and this
my prayer: grant us escape free of the curse.
Now when we look to him we are all afraid;
he's pilot of our ship and he is frightened.
(*Enter a* MESSENGER)
MESSENGER. Might I learn from you, sirs, where is the house of Oedipus? Or
best of all, if you know, where is the king himself?
CHORUS. This is his house and he is within doors. This lady is his wife and
mother of his children.
MESSENGER. God bless you, lady, and God bless your household! God bless
Oedipus' noble wife!
JOCASTA. God bless you, sir, for your kind greeting! What do you want of us

that you have come here? What have you to tell us?

MESSENGER. Good news, lady. Good for your house and for your husband.

JOCASTA. What is your news? Who sent you to us?

MESSENGER. I come from Corinth and the news I bring will give you pleasure. Perhaps a little pain too.

JOCASTA. What is this news of double meaning?

MESSENGER. The people of the Isthmus will choose Oedipus to be their king. That is the rumour there.

JOCASTA. But isn't their king still old Polybus?

MESSENGER. No. He is in his grave. Death has got him.

JOCASTA. Is that the truth? Is Oedipus' father dead?

MESSENGER. May I die myself if it be otherwise!

JOCASTA (*to a servant*). Be quick and run to the King with the news. O oracles of the Gods, where are you now? It was from this man Oedipus fled, lest he should be his murderer! And now he is dead, in the course of nature, and not killed by Oedipus.

(*Enter* OEDIPUS)

OEDIPUS. Dearest Jocasta, why have you sent for me?

JOCASTA. Listen to this man and when you hear reflect what is the outcome of the holy oracles of the Gods.

OEDIPUS. Who is he? What is his message for me?

JOCASTA. He is from Corinth and he tells us that your father Polybus is dead and gone.

OEDIPUS. What's this you say, sir? Tell me yourself.

MESSENGER. Since this is the first matter you want clearly told: Polybus has gone down to death. You may be sure of it.

OEDIPUS. By treachery or sickness?

MESSENGER. A small thing will put old bodies asleep.

OEDIPUS. So he died of sickness, it seems,—poor old man!

MESSENGER. Yes, and of age—the long years he had measured.

OEDIPUS. Ha! Ha! O dear Jocasta, why should one
look to the Pythian hearth? Why should one look
to the birds screaming overhead? They prophesied
that I should kill my father! But he's dead,
and hidden deep in earth, and I stand here
who never laid a hand on spear against him,—
unless perhaps he died of longing for me,
and thus I am his murderer. But they,
the oracles, as they stand—he's taken them
away with him, they're dead as he himself is,
and worthless.

JOCASTA.   That I told you before now.

OEDIPUS. You did, but I was misled by my fear.

JOCASTA. Then lay no more of them to heart, not one.

OEDIPUS. But surely I must fear my mother's bed?

JOCASTA. Why should man fear since chance is all in all
   for him, and he can clearly foreknow nothing?
   Best to live lightly, as one can, unthinkingly.
   As to your mother's marriage bed,—don't fear it.
   Before this, in dreams too, as well as oracles,
   many a man has lain with his own mother.
   But he to whom such things are nothing bears
   his life most easily.
OEDIPUS. All that you say would be said perfectly
   if she were dead; but since she lives I must
   still fear, although you talk so well, Jocasta.
JOCASTA. Still in your father's death there's light of comfort?
OEDIPUS. Great light of comfort; but I fear the living.
MESSENGER. Who is the woman that makes you afraid?
OEDIPUS. Merope, old man, Polybus' wife.
MESSENGER. What about her frightens the queen and you?
OEDIPUS. A terrible oracle, stranger, from the Gods.
MESSENGER. Can it be told? Or does the sacred law
   forbid another to have knowledge of it?
OEDIPUS. O no! Once on a time Loxias said
   that I should lie with my own mother and
   take on my hands the blood of my own father.
   And so for these long years I've lived away
   from Corinth; it has been to my great happiness;
   but yet it's sweet to see the face of parents.
MESSENGER. This was the fear which drove you out of Corinth?
OEDIPUS. Old man, I did not wish to kill my father.
MESSENGER. Why should I not free you from this fear, sir,
   since I have come to you in all goodwill?
OEDIPUS. You would not find me thankless if you did.
MESSENGER. Why, it was just for this I brought the news,—
   to earn your thanks when you had come safe home.
OEDIPUS. No, I will never come near my parents.
MESSENGER.   Son,
   it's very plain you don't know what you're doing.
OEDIPUS. What do you mean, old man? For God's sake, tell me.
MESSENGER. If your homecoming is checked by fears like these.
OEDIPUS. Yes, I'm afraid that Phoebus may prove right.
MESSENGER. The murder and the incest?
OEDIPUS.   Yes, old man;
   that is my constant terror.
MESSENGER.   Do you know
   that all your fears are empty?
OEDIPUS.   How is that,
   if they are father and mother and I their son?

MESSENGER. Because Polybus was no kin to you in blood.
OEDIPUS. What, was not Polybus my father?
MESSENGER. No more than I but just so much.
OEDIPUS. How can
my father be my father as much as one
that's nothing to me?
MESSENGER. Neither he nor I
begat you.
OEDIPUS. Why then did he call me son?
MESSENGER. A gift he took you from these hands of mine.
OEDIPUS. Did he love so much what he took from another's hand?
MESSENGER. His childlessness before persuaded him.
OEDIPUS. Was I a child you bought or found when I
was given to him?
MESSENGER. On Cithaeron's slopes
in the twisting thickets you were found.
OEDIPUS. And why
were you a traveller in those parts?
MESSENGER. I was
in charge of mountain flocks.
OEDIPUS. You were a shepherd?
A hireling vagrant?
MESSENGER. Yes, but at least at that time
the man that saved your life, son.
OEDIPUS. What ailed me when you took me in your arms?
MESSENGER. In that your ankles should be witnesses.
OEDIPUS. Why do you speak of that old pain?
MESSENGER. I loosed you;
the tendons of your feet were pierced and fettered,—
OEDIPUS. My swaddling clothes brought me a rare disgrace.
MESSENGER. So that from this you're called your present name.
OEDIPUS. Was this my father's doing or my mother's?
For God's sake, tell me.
MESSENGER. I don't know, but he
who gave you to me has more knowledge than I.
OEDIPUS. You yourself did not find me then? You took me
from someone else?
MESSENGER. Yes, from another shepherd.
OEDIPUS. Who was he? Do you know him well enough
to tell?
MESSENGER. He was called Laius' man.
OEDIPUS. You mean the king who reigned here in the old days?
MESSENGER. Yes, he was that man's shepherd.
OEDIPUS. Is he alive
still, so that I could see him?

MESSENGER.   You who live here
   would know that best.
OEDIPUS.   Do any of you here
   know of this shepherd whom he speaks about
   in town or in the fields? Tell me. It's time
   that this was found out once for all.
CHORUS. I think he is none other than the peasant
   whom you have sought to see already; but
   Jocasta here can tell us best of that.
OEDIPUS. Jocasta, do you know about this man
   whom we have sent for? Is he the man he mentions?
JOCASTA. Why ask of whom he spoke? Don't give it heed;
   nor try to keep in mind what has been said.
   It will be wasted labour.
OEDIPUS.   With such clues
   I could not fail to bring my birth to light.
JOCASTA. I beg you—do not hunt this out—I beg you,
   if you have any care for your own life.
   What I am suffering is enough.
OEDIPUS.   Keep up
   your heart, Jocasta. Though I'm proved a slave,
   thrice slave, and though my mother is thrice slave,
   you'll not be shown to be of lowly lineage.
JOCASTA. O be persuaded by me, I entreat you;
   do not do this.
OEDIPUS. I will not be persuaded to let be
   the chance of finding out the whole thing clearly.
JOCASTA. It is because I wish you well that I
   give you this counsel—and it's the best counsel.
OEDIPUS. Then the best counsel vexes me, and has
   for some while since.
JOCASTA.   O Oedipus, God help you!
   God keep you from the knowledge of who you are!
OEDIPUS. Here, some one, go and fetch the shepherd for me;
   and let her find her joy in her rich family!
JOCASTA. O Oedipus, unhappy Oedipus!
   that is all I can call you, and the last thing
   that I shall ever call you. (*Exit*)
CHORUS. Why has the queen gone, Oedipus, in wild
   grief rushing from us? I am afraid that trouble
   will break out of this silence.
OEDIPUS. Break out what will! I at least shall be
   willing to see my ancestry, though humble.
   Perhaps she is ashamed of my low birth,
   for she has all a woman's high-flown pride,

But I account myself a child of Fortune,
beneficent Fortune, and I shall not be
dishonoured. She's the mother from whom I spring;
the months, my brothers, marked me, now as small,
and now again as mighty. Such is my breeding,
and I shall never prove so false to it,
as not to find the secret of my birth.

CHORUS.

(*Strophe*)

If I am a prophet and wise of heart
you shall not fail, Cithaeron.
by the limitless sky, you shall not!—
to know at tomorrow's full moon
that Oedipus honours you.
as native to him and mother and nurse at once;
and that you are honoured in dancing by us. as finding favour in sight of
      our king.
Apollo, to whom we cry, find these things pleasing!

(*Antistrophe*)

Who was it bore you, child? One of
the long-lived nymphs who lay with Pan—
the father who treads the hills?
Or was she a bride of Loxias. your mother? The grassy slopes
are all of them dear to him. Or perhaps Cyllene's king
or the Bacchants' God that lives on the tops
of the hills received you a gift from some
one of the Helicon Nymphs, with whom he mostly plays?

(*Enter an* OLD MAN, *led by* OEDIPUS' *servants*)

OEDIPUS. If some one like myself who never met him
may make a guess,—I think this is the herdsman,
whom we were seeking. His old age is consonant
with the other. And besides, the men who bring him
I recognize as my own servants. You
perhaps may better me in knowledge since
you've seen the man before.

CHORUS.   You can be sure
I recognize him. For if Laius
had ever an honest shepherd, this was he.

OEDIPUS. You, sir, from Corinth, I must ask you first,
is this the man you spoke of?

MESSENGER.   This is he
before your eyes.

OEDIPUS.   Old man, look here at me
and tell me what I ask you. Were you ever
a servant of King Laius?

HERDSMAN.   I was,—
   no slave he bought but reared in his own house.
OEDIPUS. What did you do as work? How did you live?
HERDSMAN. Most of my life was spent among the flocks.
OEDIPUS. In what part of the country did you live?
HERDSMAN. Cithaeron and the places near to it.
OEDIPUS. And somewhere there perhaps you knew this man?
HERDSMAN. What was his occupation? Who?
OEDIPUS.   This man here,
   have you had any dealings with him?
HERDSMAN.   No—
   not such that I can quickly call to mind.
MESSENGER. That is no wonder, master. But I'll make him remember what he
   does not know. For I know, that he well knows the country of Cithaeron,
   how he with two flocks, I with one kept company for three years—each year
   half a year—from spring till autumn time and then when winter came I
   drove my flocks to our fold home again and he to Laius' steadings. Well—
   am I right or not in what I said we did?
HERDSMAN. You're right—although it's a long time ago.
MESSENGER. Do you remember giving me a child
   to bring up as my foster child?
HERDSMAN.   What's this?
   Why do you ask this question?
MESSENGER.   Look, old man,
   here he is—here's the man who was that child!
HERDSMAN. Death take you! Won't you hold your tongue?
OEDIPUS.   No, no,
   do not find fault with him, old man. Your words
   are more at fault than his.
HERDSMAN.   O best of masters,
   how do I give offense?
OEDIPUS.   When you refuse
   to speak about the child of whom he asks you.
HERDSMAN. He speaks out of his ignorance, without meaning.
OEDIPUS. If you'll not talk to gratify me, you
   will talk with pain to urge you.
HERDSMAN.   O please, sir,
   don't hurt an old man, sir.
OEDIPUS (*to the* SERVANTS). Here, one of you,
   twist his hands behind him.
HERDSMAN. Why, God help me, why?
   What do you want to know?
OEDIPUS.   You gave a child
   to him,—the child he asked you of?

HERDSMAN.   I did.
  I wish I'd died the day I did.
OEDIPUS.   You will
  unless you tell me truly.
HERDSMAN.   And I'll die
  far worse if I should tell you.
OEDIPUS.   This fellow
  is bent on more delays, as it would seem.
HERDSMAN. O no, no! I have told you that I gave it.
OEDIPUS. Where did you get this child from? Was it your own
  or did you get it from another?
HERDSMAN.   Not
  my own at all; I had it from some one.
OEDIPUS. One of these citizens? or from what house?
HERDSMAN. O master, please—I beg of you, master, please
  don't ask me more.
OEDIPUS.   You're a dead man if I
  ask you again.
HERDSMAN.   It was one of the children
  of Laius.
OEDIPUS. A slave? Or born in wedlock?
HERDSMAN. O God, I am on the brink of frightful speech.
OEDIPUS. And I of frightful hearing. But I must hear.
HERDSMAN. The child was called his child; but she within,
  your wife would tell you best how all this was.
OEDIPUS. *She* gave it to you?
HERDSMAN.   Yes, she did, my lord.
OEDIPUS. To do what with it?
HERDSMAN.   Make away with it.
OEDIPUS. She was so hard—its mother?
HERDSMAN.   Aye, through fear
  of evil oracles.
OEDIPUS.   Which?
HERDSMAN.   They said that he
  should kill his parents.
OEDIPUS.   How was it that you
  gave it away to this old man?
HERDSMAN.   O master,
  I pitied it, and thought that I could send it
  off to another country and this man
  was from another country. But he saved it
  for the most terrible troubles. If you are
  the man he says you are, you're bred to misery.
OEDIPUS. O, O, O, they will all come,

all come out clearly! Light of the sun, let me
look upon you no more after today!
I who first saw the light bred of a match
accursed, and accursed in my living
with them I lived with, cursed in my killing.
(*Exeunt all but the* CHORUS)
CHORUS.
(*Strophe*)
O generations of men, how I
count you as equal with those who live
not at all!
what man, what man on earth wins more
of happiness than a seeming
and after that turning away?
Oedipus, you are my pattern of this,
Oedipus, you and your fate!
Luckless Oedipus, whom of all men
I envy not at all.
(*Antistrophe*)
In as much as he shot his bolt
beyond the others and won the prize
of happiness complete—
O Zeus—and killed and reduced to nought
the hooked taloned maid of the riddling speech,
standing a tower against death for my land:
hence he was called my king and hence
was honoured the highest of all
honours; and hence he ruled
in the great city of Thebes.
(*Strophe*)
But now whose tale is more miserable?
Who is there lives with a savager fate?
Whose troubles so reverse his life as his?
O Oedipus, the famous prince
for whom a great haven
the same both as father and son
sufficed for generation,
how, O how, have the furrows ploughed
by your father endured to bear you, poor wretch,
and hold their peace so long?
(*Antistrophe*)
Time who sees all has found you out
against your will; judges your marriage accursed,
begetter and begot at one in it.

O child of Laius,
would I had never seen you,
I weep for you and cry
a dirge of lamentation.

To speak directly, I drew my breath
from you at the first and so now I lull
my mouth to sleep with your name.
(*Enter a* SECOND MESSENGER)
SECOND MESSENGER. O Princes always honoured by our country,
what deeds you'll hear of and what horrors see
what grief you'll feel. if you as true born Thebans
care for the house of Labdacus's sons.
Phasis nor Ister cannot purge this house,
I think, with all their streams, such things
it hides, such evils shortly will bring forth
into the light. whether they will or not;
and troubles hurt the most
when they prove self-inflicted.
CHORUS. What we had known before did not fall short
of bitter groaning's worth; what's more to tell?
SECOND MESSENGER. Shortest to hear and tell—our glorious queen
Jocasta's dead.
CHORUS.   Unhappy woman! How?
SECOND MESSENGER. By her own hand. The worst of what was done
you cannot know. You did not see the sight.
Yet in so far as I remember it
you'll hear the end of our unlucky queen.
When she came raging into the house she went
straight to her marriage bed, tearing her hair
with both her hands, and crying upon Laius
long dead—Do you remember, Laius,
that night long past which bred a child for us
to send you to your death and leave
a mother making children with her son?
And then she groaned and cursed the bed in which
she brought forth husband by her husband. children
by her own child, an infamous double bond.
How after that she died I do not know,—
for Oedipus distracted us from seeing.
He burst upon us shouting and we looked
to him as he paced frantically around,
begging us always: Give me a sword, I say,
to find this wife no wife, this mother's womb,

this field of double sowing whence I sprang
and where I sowed my children! As he raved
some god showed him the way—none of us there.
Bellowing terribly and led by some
invisible guide he rushed on the two doors,—
wrenching the hollow bolts out of their sockets,
he charged inside. There, there, we saw his wife
hanging, the twisted rope around her neck.
When he saw her, he cried out fearfully
and cut the dangling noose. Then, as she lay,
poor woman, on the ground, what happened after,
was terrible to see. He tore the brooches—
the gold chased brooches fastening her robe—
away from her and lifting them up high
dashed them on his own eyeballs, shrieking out
such things as: they will never see the crime
I have committed or had done upon me!
Dark eyes, now in the days to come look on
forbidden faces, do not recognize
those whom you long for—with such imprecations
he struck his eyes again and yet again
with the brooches. And the bleeding eyeballs gushed
and stained his beard—no sluggish oozing drops
but a black rain and bloody hail poured down.

So it has broken—and not on one head
but troubles mixed for husband and for wife.
The fortune of the days gone by was true
good fortune—but today groans and destruction
and death and shame—of all ills can be named
not one is missing.
CHORUS. Is he now in any ease from pain?
SECOND MESSENGER.   He shouts
for some one to unbar the doors and show him
to all the men of Thebes, his father's killer,
his mother's—no I cannot say the word,
it is unholy—for he'll cast himself,
out of the land, he says, and not remain
to bring a curse upon his house, the curse
he called upon it in his proclamation. But
he wants for strength, aye, and some one to guide him;
his sickness is too great to bear. You, too,
will be shown that. The bolts are opening.
Soon you will see a sight to waken pity
even in the horror of it.

(*Enter the blinded* OEDIPUS)

CHORUS. This is a terrible sight for men to see!
  I never found a worse!
  Poor wretch, what madness came upon you!
  What evil spirit leaped upon your life
  to your ill-luck—a leap beyond man's strength!
  Indeed I pity you, but I cannot
  look at you, though there's much I want to ask
  and much to learn and much to see.
  I shudder at the sight of you.

OEDIPUS. O, O,
  where am I going? Where is my voice
  borne on the wind to and fro?
  Spirit, how far have you sprung?

CHORUS. To a terrible place whereof men's ears
  may not hear, nor their eyes behold it.

OEDIPUS. Darkness!
  Horror of darkness enfolding, resistless, unspeakable visitant sped by an ill
      wind in haste!
  madness and stabbing pain and memory
  of evil deeds I have done!

CHORUS. In such misfortunes it's no wonder
  if double weighs the burden of your grief.

OEDIPUS. My friend,
  you are the only one steadfast, the only one that attends on me;
  you still stay nursing the blind man.
  Your care is not unnoticed. I can know
  your voice, although this darkness is my world.

CHORUS. Doer of dreadful deeds, how did you dare
  so far to do despite to your own eyes?
  what spirit urged you to it?

OEDIPUS. It was Apollo, friends, Apollo,
  that brought this bitter bitterness, my sorrows to completion.
  But the hand that struck me
  was none but my own.
  Why should I see
  whose vision showed me nothing sweet to see?

CHORUS. These things are as you say.

OEDIPUS. What can I see to love?
  What greeting can touch my ears with joy?
  Take me away, and haste—to a place out of the way!
  Take me away, my friends, the greatly miserable,
  the most accursed, whom God too hates
  above all men on earth!

CHORUS. Unhappy in your mind and your misfortune,

would I had never known you!

OEDIPUS. Curse on the man who took
  the cruel bonds from off my legs, as I lay in the field.
  He stole me from death and saved me,
  no kindly service.
  Had I died then
  I would not be so burdensome to friends.

CHORUS. I, too, could have wished it had been so.

OEDIPUS. Then I would not have come
  to kill my father and marry my mother infamously.
  Now I am godless and child of impurity,
  begetter in the same seed that created my wretched self.
  If there is any ill worse than ill,
  that is the lot of Oedipus.

CHORUS. I cannot say your remedy was good;
  you would be better dead than blind and living.

OEDIPUS. What I have done here was best done—don't tell me
  otherwise, do not give me further counsel.
  I do not know with what eyes I could look
  upon my father when I die and go
  under the earth, nor yet my wretched mother—
  those two to whom I have done things deserving
  worse punishment than hanging. Would the sight
  of children, bred as mine are, gladden me?
  No, not these eyes, never. And my city,
  its towers and sacred places of the Gods,
  of these I robbed my miserable self
  when I commanded all to drive *him* out,
  the criminal since proved by God impure
  and of the race of Laius.
  To this guilt I bore witness against myself—
  with what eyes shall I look upon my people?
  No. If there were a means to choke the fountain
  of hearing I would not have stayed my hand
  from locking up my miserable carcase,
  seeing and hearing nothing; it is sweet
  to keep our thoughts out of the range of hurt.

  Cithaeron, why did you receive me? why
  having received me did you not kill me straight?
  And so I had not shown to men my birth.

  O Polybus and Corinth and the house,
  the old house that I used to call my father's—

what fairness you were nurse to, and what foulness
festered beneath! Now I am found to be
a sinner and a son of sinners. Crossroads,
and hidden glade, oak and the narrow way
at the crossroads, that drank my father's blood
offered you by my hands, do you remember
still what I did as you looked on, and what
I did when I came here? O marriage, marriage!
you bred me and again when you had bred
bred children of your child and showed to men
brides, wives and mothers and the foulest deeds
that can be in this world of ours.

Come—it's unfit to say what is unfit
to do.—I beg of you in God's name hide me
somewhere outside your country, yes, or kill me,
or throw me into the sea, to be forever
out of your sight. Approach and deign to touch me
for all my wretchedness, and do not fear.
No man but I can bear my evil doom.
CHORUS. Here Creon comes in fit time to perform
or give advice in what you ask of us.
Creon is left sole ruler in your stead.
OEDIPUS. Creon! Creon! What shall I say to him?
How can I justly hope that he will trust me?
In what is past I have been proved towards him
an utter liar.
(*Enter* CREON)
CREON.   Oedipus, I've come
not so that I might laugh at you nor taunt you
with evil of the past. But if you still
are without shame before the face of men
reverence at least the flame that gives all life,
our Lord the Sun, and do not show unveiled
to him pollution such that neither land
nor holy rain nor light of day can welcome.
(*To a* SERVANT) Be quick and take him in. It is most decent
that only kin should see and hear the troubles
of kin.
OEDIPUS. I beg you, since you've torn me from
my dreadful expectations and have come
in a most noble spirit to a man
that has used you vilely—do a thing for me.
I shall speak for your own good, not for my own.

CREON. What do you need that you would ask of me?
OEDIPUS. Drive me from here with all the speed you can
   to where I may not hear a human voice.
CREON. Be sure, I would have done this had not I
   wished first of all to learn from God the course
   of action I should follow.
OEDIPUS.   But his word
   has been quite clear to let the parricide,
   the sinner, die.
CREON.   Yes, that indeed was said.
   But in the present need we had best discover
   what we should do.
OEDIPUS.   And will you ask about
   a man so wretched?
CREON.   Now even you will trust
   the God.
OEDIPUS. So. I command you—and will beseech you—
   to her that lies inside that house give burial
   as you would have it; she is yours and rightly
   you will perform the rites for her. For me—
   never let this my father's city have me
   living a dweller in it. Leave me live
   in the mountains where Cithaeron is, that's called
   my mountain, which my mother and my father
   while they were living would have made my tomb.
   So I may die by their decree who sought
   indeed to kill me. Yet I know this much:
   no sickness and no other thing will kill me.
   I would not have been saved from death if not
   for some strange evil fate. Well, let my fate
   go where it will.
                  Creon, you need not care
   about my sons; they're men and so wherever
   they are, they will not lack a livelihood.
   But my two girls—so sad and pitiful—
   whose table never stood apart from mine,
   and everything I touched they always shared—
   O Creon, have a thought for them! And most
   I wish that you might suffer me to touch them
   and sorrow with them.
(*Enter* ANTIGONE *and* ISMENE, OEDIPUS' *two daughters*)
   O my lord! O true noble Creon! Can I
   really be touching them, as when I saw?
   What shall I say?

Yes, I can hear them sobbing—my two darlings!
and Creon has had pity and has sent me
what I loved most?
Am I right?

CREON. You're right: it was I gave you this
because I knew from old days how you loved them
as I see now.

OEDIPUS. God bless you for it, Creon,
and may God guard you better on your road
than he did me!
                    O children,
where are you? Come here, come to my hands,
a brother's hands which turned your father's eyes,
those bright eyes you knew once, to what you see,
a father seeing nothing, knowing nothing,
begetting you from his own source of life.
I weep for you—I cannot see your faces—
I weep when I think of the bitterness
there will be in your lives, how you must live
before the world. At what assemblages
of citizens will you make one? to what
gay company will you go and not come home
in tears instead of sharing in the holiday?
And when you're ripe for marriage, who will he be,
the man who'll risk to take such infamy
as shall cling to my children, to bring hurt
on them and those that marry with them? What
curse is not there? "Your father killed his father
and sowed the seed where he had sprung himself
and begot you out of the womb that held him."
These insults you will hear. Then who will marry you?
No one, my children; clearly you are doomed
to waste away in barrenness unmarried.
Son of Menoeceus, since you are all the father
left these two girls, and we, their parents, both
are dead to them—do not allow them wander
like beggars, poor and husbandless.
They are of your own blood.
And do not make them equal with myself
in wretchedness; for you can see them now
so young, so utterly alone, save for you only.
Touch my hand, noble Creon, and say yes.
If you were older, children, and were wiser,
there's much advice I'd give you. But as it is,

let this be what you pray: give me a life
wherever there is opportunity
to live, and better life than was my father's.
CREON. Your tears have had enough of scope; now go within the
house.
OEDIPUS. I must obey, though bitter of heart.
CREON.   In season, all is good.
OEDIPUS. Do you know on what conditions I obey?
CREON.   You tell me them,
and I shall know them when I hear.
OEDIPUS.   That you shall send me out
to live away from Thebes.
CREON. That gift you must ask of the God.
OEDIPUS. But I'm now hated by the Gods.
CREON. So quickly you'll obtain your prayer.
OEDIPUS. You consent then?
CREON. What I do not mean, I do not use to say.
OEDIPUS. Now lead me away from here.
CREON. Let go the children, then, and come.
OEDIPUS. Do not take them from me.
CREON. Do not seek to be master in everything,
for the things you mastered did not follow you throughout your life.
(*As* CREON *and* OEDIPUS *go out*)
CHORUS. You that live in my ancestral Thebes, behold this Oedipus,—
him who knew the famous riddles and was a man most masterful;
not a citizen who did not look with envy on his lot—
See him now and see the breakers of misfortune swallow him!
Look upon that last day always. Count no mortal happy till
he has passed the final limit of his life secure from pain.

Aristotle

from POETICS

The *Poetics* of Aristotle (384–322 B.C.) has remained until the present day the one

discussion of tragedy that no one interested in the subject can afford to overlook.

His central point has become almost an axiom, namely that a tragedy is an imitation

of a serious action which by the evocation of pity and fear effects the purgation of

these emotions. Since Aristotle's main discussion of tragedy occurs in the first half of the *Poetics*, only the first 16 of the 26 sections are reprinted here. Obviously Aristotle

was concerned with Greek tragedy and especially with *Oedipus*. But you will quickly

notice that his principles can be properly and profitably applied in a study of any

tragedy—ancient, Renaissance, or modern.

1   Our subject being Poetry, I propose to speak not only of the art in general but also of its species and their respective capacities; of the structure of plot required for a good poem; of the number and nature of the constituent parts of a poem; and likewise of any other matters in the same line of inquiry. Let us follow the natural order and begin with the primary facts.

Epic poetry and Tragedy, as also Comedy, Dithyrambic poetry, and most flute-playing and lyre-playing, are all, viewed as a whole, modes of imitation. But at the same time they differ from one another in three ways, either by a difference of kind in their means, or by differences in the objects, or in the manner of their imitations.

Just as colour and form are used as means by some, who (whether by art or constant practice) imitate and portray many things by their aid, and the voice is used by others; so also in the above-mentioned group of arts, the means with them as a whole are rhythm, language, and harmony—used, however, either singly or in certain combinations. A combination of harmony and rhythm alone is the means in flute-playing and lyre-playing, and any other arts there may be of the same description, e.g. imitative piping. Rhythm alone, without harmony, is the means in the dancer's imitations; for even he, by the rhythms of his attitudes, may represent men's characters, as well as what they do and suffer. There is further an art which imitates by language alone, without harmony, in prose or in verse, and if in verse, either in some one or in a plurality of metres. This form of imitation is to this day without a name. We have no common name for a mime of Sophron or Xenarchus and a Socratic Conversation; and we should still be without one even if the imitation in the two instances were in trimeters or elegiacs or some other kind of verse—though it is the way with people to tack on 'poet' to the name of a metre, and talk of elegiac-poets and epic-poets, thinking that they call them poets not by reason of the imitative nature of their work, but indiscriminately by reason of the metre they write in. Even if a theory of medicine or physical philosophy be put forth in a metrical form, it is usual to describe the writer in this way; Homer and Empedocles, however, have really nothing in common apart from their metre; so that, if the one is to be called a poet, the other should be termed a physicist rather than a poet. We should be in the same position also, if the imitation in these instances were in all the metres, like the *Centaur* (a rhapsody in a medley of all metres) of Chaeremon; and Chaeremon one has to recognize as a poet. So much, then, as to these arts. There are, lastly, certain other arts, which com-

From *De Poetica*, translated by Ingram Bywater. Reprinted by permission of The Clarendon Press.

bine all the means enumerated. rhythm, melody, and verse, e.g. Dithyrambic and Nomic poetry, Tragedy and Comedy; with this difference, however, that the three kinds of means are in some of them all employed together, and in others brought in separately, one after the other. These elements of difference in the above arts I term the means of their imitation.

2   The objects the imitator represents are actions, with agents who are necessarily either good men or bad—the diversities of human character being nearly always derivative from this primary distinction, since the line between virtue and vice is one dividing the whole of mankind. It follows, therefore, that the agents represented must be either above our own level of goodness, or beneath it, or just such as we are; in the same way as, with the painters, the personages of Polygnotus are better than we are, those of Pauson worse, and those of Dionysius just like ourselves. It is clear that each of the above-mentioned arts will admit of these differences, and that it will become a separate art by representing objects with this point of difference. Even in dancing, flute-playing, and lyre-playing such diversities are possible; and they are also possible in the nameless art that uses language, prose or verse without harmony, as its means; Homer's personages, for instance, are better than we are; Cleophon's are on our own level; and those of Hegemon of Thasos, the first writer of parodies, and Nicochares, the author of the *Diliad*, are beneath it. The same is true of the Dithyramb and the Nome: the personages may be presented in them with the difference exemplified in the . . . of . . . and Argas, and in the Cyclopses of Timotheus and Philoxenus. This difference it is that distinguishes Tragedy and Comedy also; the one would make its personages worse, and the other better, than the men of the present day.

3   A third difference in these arts is in the manner in which each kind of object is represented. Given both the same means and the same kind of object for imitation, one may either (1) speak at one moment in narrative and at another in an assumed character, as Homer does; or (2) one may remain the same throughout, without any such change; or (3) the imitators may represent the whole story dramatically, as though they were actually doing the things described.

As we said at the beginning, therefore, the differences in the imitation of these arts come under three heads, their means, their objects, and their manner.

So that as an imitator Sophocles will be on one side akin to Homer, both portraying good men; and on another to Aristophanes, since both present their personages as acting and doing. This in fact, according to some, is the reason for plays being termed dramas, because in a play the personages act the story. Hence too both Tragedy and Comedy are claimed by the Dorians as their discoveries; Comedy by the Megarians—by those in Greece as having arisen when Megara became a democracy, and by the Sicilian Megarians on the ground that the poet Epicharmus was of their country, and a good deal earlier than Chionides and Magnes; even Tragedy also is claimed by certain of the Peloponnesian Dorians. In support of this claim they point to the words 'comedy' and 'drama'. Their word for the outlying hamlets, they say, is *comae*, whereas Athenians call them *demes*—thus assuming that comedians got the name not from their *comoe* or revels, but from their strolling from hamlet to hamlet, lack of appreciation keeping them out of the city. Their word also for 'to act', they say, is *dran*, whereas Athenians use *prattein*.

So much, then, as to the number and nature of the points of difference in the imitation of these arts.

4 It is clear that the general origin of poetry was due to two causes, each of them part of human nature. Imitation is natural to man from childhood, one of his advantages over the lower animals being this, that he is the most imitative creature in the world, and learns at first by imitation. And it is also natural for all to delight in works of imitation. The truth of this second point is shown by experience: though the objects themselves may be painful to see, we delight to view the most realistic representations of them in art, the forms for example of the lowest animals and of dead bodies. The explanation is to be found in a further fact: to be learning something is the greatest of pleasures not only to the philosopher but also to the rest of mankind, however small their capacity for it; the reason of the delight in seeing the picture is that one is at the same time learning—gathering the meaning of things, e.g. that the man there is so-and-so; for if one has not seen the thing before, one's pleasure will not be in the picture as an imitation of it, but will be due to the execution or colouring or some similar cause. Imitation, then, being natural to us—as also the sense of harmony and rhythm, the metres being obviously species of rhythms—it was through their original aptitude, and by a series of improvements for the most part gradual on their first efforts, that they created poetry out of their improvisations.

Poetry, however, soon broke up into two kinds according to the differences of character in the individual poets; for the graver among them would represent noble actions, and those of noble personages; and the meaner sort the actions of the ignoble. The latter class produced invectives at first, just as others did hymns and panegyrics. We know of no such poem by any of the pre-Homeric poets, though there were probably many such writers among them; instances, however, may be found from Homer downwards, e.g. his *Margites*, and the similar poems of others. In this poetry of invective its natural fitness brought an iambic metre into use; hence our present term 'iambic', because it was the metre of their 'iambs' or invectives against one another. The result was that the old poets became some of them writers of heroic and others of iambic verse. Homer's position, however, is peculiar: just as he was in the serious style the poet of poets, standing alone not only through the literary excellence, but also through the dramatic character of his imitations, so too he was the first to outline for us the general forms of Comedy by producing not a dramatic invective, but a dramatic picture of the Ridiculous; his *Margites* in fact stands in the same relation to our comedies as the *Illiad* and *Odyssey* to our tragedies.

As soon, however, as Tragedy and Comedy appeared in the field, those naturally drawn to the one line of poetry became writers of comedies instead of iambs, and those naturally drawn to the other, writers of tragedies instead of epics, because these new modes of art were grander and of more esteem than the old.

If it be asked whether Tragedy is now all that it need be in its formative elements, to consider that, and decide it theoretically and in relation to the theatres, is a matter for another inquiry.

It certainly began in improvisations—as did also Comedy: the one originating with the authors of the Dithyramb, the other with those of the phallic songs, which still survive as institutions in many of our cities. And its advance after that was little by little, through their improving on whatever they had before them at each stage. It was in fact only after a long series of changes that the movement of Tragedy stopped on its attaining to its natural form. (1) The number of actors was first increased to two by Aeschylus, who curtailed the business of the Chorus, and made the dialogue, or spoken portion, take the leading part in the play. (2) A third actor and scenery were due to Sophocles. (3) Tragedy acquired also its magnitude. Discarding short stories and a ludicrous diction, through its passing out of its satyric stage, it assumed, though only at a late point in its progress, a tone of dignity; and its metre changed then from trochaic to iambic. The reason for their original use of the trochaic tetrameter was that their poetry was satyric and more connected with dancing than it now is. As soon, however, as a spoken part came in, nature herself found the appropriate metre. The iambic, we know, is the most speakable of metres, as is shown by the fact that we very often fall into it in conversation, whereas we rarely talk hexameters, and only when we depart from the speaking tone of voice. (4) Another change was a plurality of episodes or acts. As for the remaining matters, the superadded embellishments and the account of their introduction, these must be taken as said, as it would probably be a long piece of work to go through the details.

5 As for Comedy, it is (as has been observed) an imitation of men worse than the average; worse, however, not as regards any and every sort of fault, but only as regards one particular kind, the Ridiculous, which is a species of the Ugly. The Ridiculous may be defined as a mistake or deformity not productive of pain or harm to others; the mask, for instance, that excites laughter, is something ugly and distorted without causing pain.

Though the successive changes in Tragedy and their authors are not unknown, we cannot say the same of Comedy; its early stages passed unnoticed, because it was not as yet taken up in a serious way. It was only at a late point in its progress that a chorus of comedians was officially granted by the archon; they used to be mere volunteers. It had also already certain definite forms at the time when the record of those termed comic poets begins. Who it was who supplied it with masks, or prologues, or a plurality of actors and the like, has remained unknown. The invented Fable, or Plot, however, originated in Sicily with Epicharmus and Phormis; of Athenian poets Crates was the first to drop the Comedy of invective and frame stories of a general and non-personal nature, in other words, Fables or Plots.

Epic poetry, then, has been seen to agree with Tragedy to this extent, that of being an imitation of serious subjects in a grand kind of verse. It differs from it, however, (1) in that it is in one kind of verse and in narrative form; and (2) in its length—which is due to its action having no fixed limit of time, whereas Tragedy endeavours to keep as far as possible within a single circuit of the sun, or something near that. This, I say, is another point of difference between them, though at first the practice in this respect was just the same in tragedies as in epic poems. They differ also (3) in their constituents, some being common to both and others peculiar to Tragedy—hence a judge of good and bad in Tragedy is a judge of that in epic poetry also. All the parts of the epic are included in Tragedy; but those of Tragedy are not all of them to be found in the Epic.

6 Reserving hexameter poetry and Comedy for consideration hereafter, let us proceed now to the discussion of Tragedy; before doing so, however, we must gather up the definition resulting from what has been said. (A tragedy, then, is the imitation of an action that is serious and also, as having magnitude, complete in itself; in language with pleasurable accessories, each kind brought in separately in the parts of the work; in a dramatic, not in a narrative form; with incidents arousing pity and fear, wherewith to accomplish its catharsis of such emotions.) Here by 'language with pleasurable accessories' I mean that with rhythm and harmony or song superadded; and by 'the kinds separately' I mean that some portions are worked out with verse only, and others in turn with song.

As they act the stories, it follows that in the first place the Spectacle (or stage-appearance of the actors) must be some part of the whole; and in the second Melody and Diction, these two being the means of their imitation. Here by 'Diction' I mean merely this, the compositon of the verses; and by 'Melody', what is too completely understood to require explanation. But further: the subject represented also is an action; and the action involves agents, who must necessarily have their distinctive qualities both of character and thought, since it is from these that we ascribe certain qualities to their actions. There are in the natural order of things, therefore, two causes, Thought and Character, of their actions, and consequently of their success or failure in their lives. Now the action (that which was done) is represented in the play by the Fable or Plot. The Fable, in our present sense of the term, is simply this, the combination of the incidents, or things done in the story; whereas Character is what makes us ascribe certain moral qualities to the agents; and Thought is shown in all they say when proving a particular point or, it may be, enunciating a general truth. There are six parts consequently of every tragedy, as a whole (that is) of such or such quality, viz. a Fable or Plot, Characters, Diction, Thought, Spectacle, and Melody; two of them arising from the means, one from the manner, and three from the objects of the dramatic imitation; and there is nothing else besides these six. Of these, its formative elements, then, not a few of the dramatists have made due use, as every play, one may say, admits of Spectacle, Character, Fable, Diction, Melody, and Thought.

The most important of the six is the combination of the incidents of the story. Tragedy is essentially an imitation not of persons but of action and life, of happiness and misery. All human happiness or misery takes the form of action; the end for which we live is a certain kind of activity, not a quality. Character gives us qualities, but it is in our actions—what we do—that we are happy or the reverse. In a play accordingly they do not act in order to portray the Characters; they include the Characters for the sake of the action. So that it is the action in it, i.e. its Fable or Plot, that is the end and purpose of the tragedy; and the end is everywhere the chief thing. Besides this, a tragedy is impossible without action, but there may be one without Character. The tragedies of most of the moderns are characterless—a defect common among poets of all kinds, and with its counterpart in painting in Zeuxis as compared with Polygnotus; for whereas the latter is strong in character, the work of Zeuxis is devoid of it. And again: one may string together a series of characteristic speeches of the utmost finish as regards Diction and Thought, and yet fail to produce the true tragic effect; but one will have much better success with a tragedy which, however inferior in these respects, has a Plot, a combination of incidents, in it. And again: the most powerful elements of attraction in Tragedy, the Peripeties and Discoveries, are parts of the Plot. A further proof is in the fact that beginners succeed earlier with the Diction and Characters than with the construction of a story; and the same may be said of nearly all the early dramatists. We maintain, therefore, that the first essential, the life and soul, so to speak, of Tragedy is the Plot; and that the Characters come second—compare the parallel in painting, where the most beautiful colours laid on without order will not give one the same pleasure as a simple black-and-white sketch of a portrait. We maintain that Tragedy is primarily an imitation of action, and that it is mainly for the sake of the action that it imitates the personal agents. Third comes the element of Thought, i.e. the power of saying whatever can be said, or what is appropriate to the occasion. This is what, in the speeches in Tragedy, falls under the arts of Politics and Rhetoric; for the older poets make their personages discourse like statesmen, and the modern like rhetoricians. One must not confuse it with Character. Character in a play is that which reveals the moral purpose of the agents, i.e. the sort of thing they seek or avoid, where that is not obvious—hence there is no room for Character in a speech on a purely indifferent subject. Thought, on the other hand, is shown in all they say when proving or disproving some particular point, or enunciating some universal proposition. Fourth among the literary elements is the Diction of the personages, i.e., as before explained, the expression of their thoughts in words, which is practically the same thing with verse as with prose. As for the two remaining parts, the Melody is the greatest of the pleasurable accessories of Tragedy. The Spectacle, though an attraction, is the least artistic of all the parts, and has least to do with the art of poetry. The tragic effect is quite possible without a public performance and actors; and besides, the getting-up of the Spectacle is more a matter for the costumier than the poet.

7 Having thus distinguished the parts, let us now consider the proper construction of the Fable or Plot, as that is at once the first and the most important thing in Tragedy. We have laid it down that a tragedy is an imitation of an action that is complete in itself, as a whole of some magnitude; for a whole may be of no magnitude to speak of. Now a whole is that which has beginning, middle, and end. A beginning is that which is not itself necessarily after anything else, and which has naturally something else after it; an end is that which is naturally after something itself, either as its necessary or usual consequent, and with nothing else after it; and a middle, that which is by nature after one thing and has also another after it. A well-constructed Plot, therefore, cannot either begin or end at any point one likes; beginning and end in it must be of the forms just described. Again: to be beautiful, a living creature, and every whole made up of parts, must not only present a certain order in its arrangement of parts, but also be of a certain definite magnitude. Beauty is a matter of size and order, and therefore impossible either (1) in a very minute creature, since our perception becomes indistinct as it approaches instantaneity; or (2) in a creature of vast size—one, say, 1,000 miles long—as in that case, instead of the object being seen all at once, the unity and wholeness of it is lost to the beholder. Just in the same way, then, as a beautiful whole made up of parts, or a beautiful living creature, must be of some size, but a size to be taken in by the eye, so a story or Plot must be of some length, but of a length to be taken in by the memory. As for the limit of its length, so far as that is relative to public performances and spectators, it does not fall within the theory of poetry. If they had to perform a hundred tragedies, they would be timed by water-clocks, as they are said to have been at one period. The limit, however, set by the actual nature of the thing is this: the longer the story, consistently with its being comprehensible as a whole, the finer it is by reason of its magnitude. As a rough general formula, 'a length which allows of the hero passing by a series of probable or necessary stages from misfortune to happiness, or from happiness to misfortune', may suffice as a limit for the magnitude of the story.

8 The Unity of a Plot does not consist, as some suppose, in its having one man as its subject. An infinity of things befall that one man, some of which it is impossible to reduce to unity; and in like manner there are many actions of one man which cannot be made to form one action. One sees, therefore, the mistake of all the poets who have written a *Heracleid*, a *Theseid*, or similar poems; they suppose that, because Heracles was one man, the story also of Heracles must be one story. Homer, however, evidently understood this point quite well, whether by art or instinct, just in the same way as he excels the rest in every other respect. In writing an *Odyssey*, he did not make

the poem cover all that ever befell his hero—it befell him, for instance, to get wounded on Parnassus and also to feign madness at the time of the call to arms, but the two incidents had no necessary or probable connexion with one another—instead of doing that, he took as the subject of the *Odyssey*, as also of the *Illiad*, an action with a Unity of the kind we are describing. The truth is that, just as in the other imitative arts one imitation is always of one thing, so in poetry the story, as an imitation of action, must represent one action, a complete whole, with its several incidents so closely connected that the transposal or withdrawal of any one of them will disjoin and dislocate the whole. For that which makes no perceptible difference by its presence or absence is no real part of the whole.

9   From what we have said it will be seen that the poet's function is to describe, not the thing that has happened, but a kind of thing that might happen, i.e. what is possible as being probable or necessary. The distinction between historian and poet is not in the one writing prose and the other verse —you might put the work of Herodotus into verse, and it would still be a species of history; it consists really in this, that the one describes the thing that has been, and the other a kind of thing that might be. Hence poetry is something more philosophic and of graver import than history, since its statements are of the nature rather of universals, whereas those of history are singulars. By a universal statement I mean one as to what such or such a kind of man will probably or necessarily say or do—which is the aim of poetry, though it affixes proper names to the characters; by a singular statement, one as to what, say, Alcibiades did or had done to him. In Comedy this has become clear by this time; it is only when their plot is already made up of probable incidents that they give it a basis of proper names, choosing for the purpose any names that may occur to them, instead of writing like the old iambic poets about particular persons. In Tragedy, however, they still adhere to the historic names; and for this reason: what convinces is the possible; now whereas we are not yet sure as to the possibility of that which has not happened, that which has happened is manifestly possible, else it would not have come to pass. Nevertheless even in Tragedy there are some plays with but one or two known names in them, the rest being inventions; and there are some without a single known name, e.g. Agathon's *Antheus*, in which both incidents and names are of the poet's invention; and it is no less delightful on that account. So that one must not aim at a rigid adherence to the traditional stories on which tragedies are based. It would be absurd, in fact, to do so, as even the known stories are only known to a few, though they are a delight none the less to all.

It is evident from the above that the poet must be more the poet of his stories or Plots than of his verses, inasmuch as he is a poet by virtue of the imitative element in his work, and it is actions that he imitates. And if he should come to take a subject from actual history, he is none the less a poet for that; since some historic occurrences may very well be in the probable and possible order of things; and it is in that aspect of them that he is their poet.

Of simple Plots and actions the episodic are the worst. I call a Plot episodic when there is neither probability nor necessity in the sequence of its episodes. Actions of this sort bad poets construct through their own fault, and good ones on account of the players. His work being for public performance, a good poet often stretches out a Plot beyond it capabilities, and is thus obliged to twist the sequence of incident.

Tragedy, however, is an imitation not only of a complete action, but also of incidents arousing pity and fear. Such incidents have the very greatest effect on the mind when they occur unexpectedly and at the same time in consequence of one another; there is more of the marvellous in them then than if they happened of themselves or by mere chance. Even matters of chance seem most marvellous if there is an appearance of design as it were in them; as for instance the statue of Mitys at Argos killed the author of Mitys' death by falling down on him when a looker-on at a public spectacle; for incidents like that we think to be not without a meaning. A Plot, therefore, of this sort is necessarily finer than others.

10 Plots are either simple or complex, since the actions they represent are naturally of this twofold description. The action, proceeding in the way defined, as one continuous whole, I call simple, when the change in the hero's fortunes takes place without Peripety or Discovery; and complex, when it involves one or the other, or both. These should each of them arise out of the structure of the Plot itself, so as to be the consequence, necessary or probable, of the antecedents. There is a great difference between a thing happening *propter hoc* and *post hoc*.

11 A Peripety is the change of the kind described from one state of things within the play to its opposite, and that too in the way we are saying, in the probable or necessary sequence of events; as it is for instance in *Oedipus*: here the opposite state of things is produced by the Messenger, who, coming to gladden Oedipus and to remove his fears as to his mother, reveals the secret of his birth. And in *Lynceus*: just as he is being led off for execution, with Danaus at his side to put him to death, the incidents preceding this bring it about that he is saved and Danaus put to death. A Discovery is, as the very word implies, a change from ignorance to knowledge, and thus to either love or hate, in the personages marked for good or evil fortune. The finest form of Discovery is one attended by Peripeties, like that which goes with the Discovery in *Oedipus*. There are no doubt other forms of it; what we have said may happen in a way in reference to inanimate things, even things of a very casual kind; and it is also possible to discover whether some one has done or not done something. But the form most directly connected with the Plot and the action of the piece is the first-mentioned. This, with a Peripety, will arouse either

pity or fear—actions of that nature being what Tragedy is assumed to represent; and it will also serve to bring about the happy or unhappy ending. The Discovery, then, being of persons, it may be that of one party only to the other, the latter being already known; or both the parties may have to discover themselves. Iphigenia, for instance, was discovered to Orestes by sending the letter; and another Discovery was required to reveal him to Iphigenia.

Two parts of the Plot, then, Peripety and Discovery, are on matters of this sort. A third part is Suffering; which we may define as an action of a destructive or painful nature, such as murders on the stage, tortures, woundings, and the like. The other two have been already explained.

12   The parts of Tragedy to be treated as formative elements in the whole were mentioned in a previous Chapter. From the point of view, however, of its quantity, i.e. the separate sections into which it is divided, a tragedy has the following parts: Prologue, Episode, Exode, and a choral portion, distinguished into Parode and Stasimon; these two are common to all tragedies, whereas songs from the stage and *Commoe* are only found in some. The Prologue is all that precedes the Parode of the chorus; an Episode all that comes in between two whole choral songs; the Exode all that follows after the last choral song. In the choral portion the Parode is the whole first statement of the chorus; a Stasimon, a song of the chorus without anapaests or trochees; a *Commos*, a lamentation sung by chorus and actor in concert. The parts of Tragedy to be used as formative elements in the whole we have already mentioned; the above are its parts from the point of view of its quantity, or the separate sections into which it is divided.

13   The next points after what we have said above will be these: (1) What is the poet to aim at, and what is he to avoid, in constructing his Plots? and (2) What are the conditions on which the tragic effect depends?

We assume that, for the finest form of Tragedy, the Plot must be not simple but complex; and further, that it must imitate actions arousing fear and pity, since that is the distinctive function of this kind of imitation. It follows, therefore, that there are three forms of Plot to be avoided. (1) A good man must not be seen passing from happiness to misery, or (2) a bad man from misery to happiness. The first situation is not fear-inspiring or piteous, but simply odious to us. The second is the most untragic that can be; it has no one of the requisites of Tragedy; it does not appeal either to the human feeling in us, or to our pity, or to our fears. Nor, on the other hand, should (3) an extremely bad man be seen falling from happiness into misery. Such a story may arouse the human feeling in us, but it will not move us to either pity or fear; pity is occasioned by undeserved misfortune, and fear by that of one like ourselves; so that there will be nothing either piteous or fear-inspiring in the situation. There remains, then, the intermediate kind of personage, a man not pre-eminently virtuous and just, whose misfortune, however, is brought upon him not by vice and depravity but by some error of judgement, of the number of those in the enjoyment of great reputation and prosperity; e.g. Oedipus, Thyestes, and the men of note of similar families. The perfect Plot, accordingly, must have a single, and not (as some tell us) a double issue; the change in the hero's fortunes must be not from misery to happiness, but on the contrary from happiness to misery; and the cause of it must lie not in any depravity, but in some great error on his part; the man himself being either such as we have described, or better, not worse, than that. Fact also confirms our theory. Though the poets began by accepting any tragic story that came to hand, in these days the finest tragedies are always on the story of some few houses, on that of Alcmeon, Oedipus, Orestes, Meleager, Thyestes, Telephus, or any others that may have been involved, as either agents or sufferers, in some deed of horror. The theoretically best tragedy, then, has a Plot of this descrip- tion. The critics, therefore, are wrong who blame Euripides for taking this line in his tragedies, and giving many of them an unhappy ending. It is, as we have said, the right line to take. The best proof is this: on the stage, and in the public performances, such plays, properly worked out, are seen to be the most truly tragic; and Euripides, even if his execution be faulty in every other point, is seen to be nevertheless the most tragic certainly of the dramatists. After this comes the construction of Plot which some rank first, one with a double story (like the *Odyssey*) and an opposite issue for the good and the bad per- sonages. It is ranked as first only through the weakness of the audiences; the poets merely follow their public, writing as its wishes dictate. But the pleasure here is not that of Tragedy. It belongs rather to Comedy, where the bitterest enemies in the piece (e.g. Orestes and Aegisthus) walk off good friends at the end, with no slaying of any one by any one.

14 The tragic fear and pity may be aroused by the Spectacle; but they may also be aroused by the very structure and incidents of the play—which is the better way and shows the better poet. The Plot in fact should be so framed that, even without seeing the things take place, he who simply hears the account of them shall be filled with horror and pity at the incidents; which is just the effect that the mere recital of the story in *Oedipus* would have on one. To produce this same effect by means of the Spectacle is less artistic, and requires extraneous aid. Those, however, who make use of the Spectacle to put before us that which is merely monstrous and not productive of fear, are wholly out of touch with Tragedy; not every kind of pleasure should be required of a tragedy, but only its own proper pleasure.

The tragic pleasure is that of pity and fear, and the poet has to produce it by a work of imitation; it is clear, therefore, that the causes should be in- cluded in the incidents of his story. Let us see, then, what kinds of incident strike one as horrible, or rather as piteous. In a deed of this description the parties must necessarily be either friends, or enemies, or indifferent to one another. Now when enemy does it on enemy, there is nothing to move us to pity either in his doing or in his meditating the deed, except so far as the actual pain of the sufferer is concerned; and the same is true when the parties are indifferent to one another. Whenever the tragic deed, however, is done within the family—when murder or the like is done or meditated by brother on brother, by son on father, by mother on son, or son on mother—these are the situations the poet should seek after. The traditional stories, accordingly, must be kept as they are, e.g. the murder of Clytaemnestra by Orestes and of Eriphyle by Alcmeon. At the same time even with these there is something left to the poet himself; it is for him to devise the right way of treating them. Let us explain more clearly what we mean by 'the right way'. The deed of horror may be done by the doer knowingly and consciously, as in the old poets, and in Medea's murder of her children in Euripides. Or he may do it, but in ignorance of his relationship, and discover that afterwards, as does the Oedipus in Sophocles. Here the deed is outside the play; but it may be within it, like the act of the Alcmeon in Astydamas, or that of the Telegonus in *Ulysses Wounded*. A third possibility is for one meditating some deadly injury to another, in ignorance of his relationship, to make the discovery in time to draw back. These exhaust the possibilities, since the deed must necessarily be either done or not done, and either knowingly or unknowingly.

The worst situation is when the personage is with full knowledge on the point of doing the deed, and leaves it undone. It is odious and also (through the absence of suffering) untragic; hence it is that no one is made to act thus except in some few instances, e.g. Haemon and Creon in *Antigone*. Next after this comes the actual perpetration of the deed meditated. A better situation than that, however, is for the deed to be done in ignorance, and the relationship discovered afterwards, since there is nothing odious in it, and the Discovery will serve to astound us. But the best of all is the last; what we have in *Cresphontes*, for example, where Merope, on the point of slaying her son, recognizes him in time; in *Iphigenia*, where sister and brother are in a like position; and in *Helle*, where the son recognizes his mother, when on the point of giving her up to her enemy.

This will explain why our tragedies are restricted (as we said just now) to such a small number of families. It was accident rather than art that led the poets in quest of subjects to embody this kind of incident in their Plots. They are still obliged, accordingly, to have recourse to the families in which such horrors have occurred.

On the construction of the Plot, and the kind of Plot required for Tragedy, enough has now been said.

15 In the Characters there are four points to aim at. First and foremost, that they shall be good. There will be an element of character in the play, if (as has been observed) what a personage says or does reveals a certain moral purpose; and a good element of character, if the purpose so revealed is good. Such goodness is possible in every type of personage, even in a woman or a slave, though the one is perhaps an inferior, and the other a wholly worthless being. The second point is to make them appropriate. The Character before us may be, say, manly; but it is not appropriate in a female Character to be

manly, or clever. The third is to make them like the reality, which is not the same as their being good and appropriate, in our sense of the term. The fourth is to make them consistent and the same throughout; even if inconsistency be part of the man before one for imitation as presenting that form of character, he should still be consistently inconsistent. We have an instance of baseness of character, not required for the story, in the Menelaus in *Orestes*; of the incongruous and unbefitting in the lamentation of Ulysses in *Scylla*, and in the (clever) speech of Melanippe; and of inconsistency in *Iphigenia at Aulis*, where Iphigenia the suppliant is utterly unlike the later Iphigenia. The right thing, however, is in the Characters just as in the incidents of the play to endeavour always after the necessary or the probable; so that whenever such-and-such a personage says or does such-and-such a thing, it shall be the necessary or probable outcome of his character; and whenever this incident follows on that, it shall be either the necessary or the probable consequence of it. From this one sees (to digress for a moment) that the Dénouement also should arise out of the plot itself, and not depend on a stage-artifice, as in *Medea*, or in the story of the (arrested) departure of the Greeks in the *Iliad*. The artifice must be reserved for matters outside the play—for past events beyond human knowledge, or events yet to come, which require to be foretold or announced; since it is the privilege of the Gods to know everything. There should be nothing improbable among the actual incidents. If it be unavoidable, however, it should be outside the tragedy, like the improbability in the *Oedipus* of Sophocles. But to return to the Characters. As Tragedy is an imitation of personages better than the ordinary man, we in our way should follow the example of good portrait-painters, who reproduce the distinctive features of a man, and at the same time, without losing the likeness, make him handsomer than he is. The poet in like manner, in portraying men quick or slow to anger, or with similar infirmities of character, must know how to represent them as such, and at the same time as good men, as Agathon and Homer have represented Achilles.

All these rules one must keep in mind throughout, and, further, those also for such points of stage-effect as directly depend on the art of the poet, since in these too one may often make mistakes. Enough, however, has been said on the subject in one of our published writings.

16 Discovery in general has been explained already. As for the species of Discovery, the first to be noted is (1) the least artistic form of it, of which the poets make most use through mere lack of invention, Discovery by signs or marks. Of these signs some are congenital, like the 'lance-head which the Earth-born have on them', or 'stars', such as Carcinus brings in his *Thyestes*; others acquired after birth—these latter being either marks on the body, e.g. scars, or external tokens, like necklaces, or (to take another sort of instance) the ark in the Discovery in *Tyro*. Even these, however, admit of two uses, a better and a worse; the scar of Ulysses is an instance; the Discovery of him through it is made in one way by the nurse and in another by the swineherds.

A Discovery using signs as a means of assurance is less artistic, as indeed are all such as imply reflection; whereas one bringing them in all of a sudden, as in the *Bath-story*, is of a better order. Next after these are (2) Discoveries made directly by the poet, which are inartistic for that very reason; e.g. Orestes' Discovery of himself in *Iphigenia:* whereas his sister reveals who she is by the letter, Orestes is made to say himself what the poet rather than the story demands. This, therefore, is not far removed from the first-mentioned fault, since he might have presented certain tokens as well. Another instance is the 'shuttle's voice' in the *Tereus* of Sophocles. (3) A third species is Discovery through memory, from a man's consciousness being awakened by something seen. Thus in *The Cyprioe* of Dicaeogenes, the sight of the picture makes the man burst into tears; and in the *Tale of Alcinous*, hearing the harper Ulysses is reminded of the past and weeps; the Discovery of them being the result. (4) A fourth kind is Discovery through reasoning; e.g. in *The Choephoroe;* 'One like me is here; there is no one like me but Orestes; he, therefore, must be here.' Or that which Polyidus the Sophist suggested for *Iphigenia;* since it was natural for Orestes to reflect: 'My sister was sacrificed, and I am to be sacrificed like her.' Or that in the *Tydeus* of Theodectes: 'I came to find a son, and am to die myself.' Or that in *The Phinidae:* on seeing the place the women inferred their fate, that they were to die there, since they had also been exposed there. (5) There is, too, a composite Discovery arising from bad reasoning on the side of the other party. An instance of it is in *Ulysses the False Messenger:* he said he should know the bow—which he had not seen; but to suppose from that that he would know it again (as though he had once seen it) was bad reasoning. (6) The best of all Discoveries, however, is that arising from the incidents themselves, when the great surprise comes about through a probable incident, like that in the *Oedipus* of Sophocles; and also in *Iphigenia;* for it was not improbable that she should wish to have a letter taken home. These last are the only Discoveries independent of the artifice of signs and necklaces. Next after them come Discoveries through reasoning.

Anton Chekhov

THE CHERRY ORCHARD

By the time Chekhov's *The Cherry Orchard* appeared in 1904, the modern theater, in most of its essentials, had come into being. Examples were to be found in all the big cities, not only in Europe and Great Britain but also in the United States. Since that time, some of the architectural fashions have changed, and various experiments have been tried, but most of the important generalizations about the theater hold good for the whole period from the late nineteenth century to the present.

The typical modern theater has an auditorium containing a main floor, two or three horseshoe galleries, and boxes. In general, the prices of seats are determined by the excellence of the view of the stage which they afford. Only those theater-goers who sit in boxes pay high prices for poor (but easily seen) vantage points and thus prolong a generally outmoded aristocratic tradition. The audiences as a rule are made up of the upper and middle economic classes: the laboring class has tended to find its entertainment away from the playhouse. The modern audience contains a much larger proportion of women than any audience in the past. Since the dramatist tries to appeal to his audience, especially in a period when the theater is com-

A performance of The Cherry Orchard

mercialized as it is today, these shifts in the make-up of the audience naturally have influenced dramatic productions.

The stage—the portion of the modern theater building behind the proscenium— has become very complicated because of the liking of present-day audiences for realistic or unusual scenery. Only half or two thirds of the whole area—the part enclosed by painted scenery—is visible, like a picture in a frame, to the audience. Above this five-sided box, in an area extending to the roof of the theater, scenery is lifted and hung, to be lowered when needed. Behind the scene-enclosed area, and to each side, are placed properties and additional scenery. Unless costs prevent, greatly varied and quite elaborate settings and properties may be used in any play. Such extensive changes of scenery are time-consuming, and so the modern theater misses the continuity of action most earlier theaters had, but most contemporary audiences do not find this lack disturbing. The chief modern development, of course, has been in lighting made possible by electricity. By arranging and manipulating lights—footlights, lights in the wings or above the stage, or spotlights located in the gallery, directors can secure realistic or fantastic effects, focus the attention of the audience on details in the setting or parts of the action, and communicate moods or emotions.

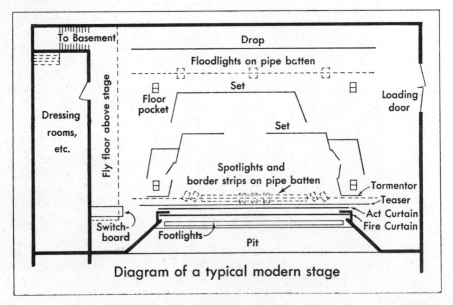

Diagram of a typical modern stage

When *The Cherry Orchard* had its première in 1904, it was played by one of the most influential dramatic companies in the twentieth-century theater—that of the Moscow Art Theater under the guidance of Constantin Stanislavsky. The company aimed for a new sort of realism characterized by meticulous attention to detail in the adaptation of stage settings to the spirit of the play and in the subordination of actors as an ensemble to the demands of the individual drama. Since the group carefully avoided obvious theatricalism, Chekhov's subtle plays were admirable vehicles for such a group. Interestingly, though Chekhov thought this play a comedy, the producer considered it to be a tragedy. This was less of a difficulty than one might expect, however, because the play had some of the aspects of both genres. It pictured the old order, tragically and at the same time comically ineffective, giving place to the new order in Russia. The underplaying of conflict and plot, the nuances of characterization, and the use of symbolism foreshadowed much that was to be typical of the drama a half century later.

CHARACTERS

LUBOV ANDREYEVNA RANEVSKAYA, *a landowner*
ANYA, *her seventeen-year-old daughter*
VARYA, *her adopted daughter, twenty-two years old*
LEONID ANDREYEVICH GAYEV, MME. RANEVSKAYA's *brother*
YERMOLAY ALEXEYEVICH LOPAHIN, *a merchant*
PYOTR SERGEYEVICH TROFIMOV, *a student*
SIMEONOV-PISHCHIK, *a landowner*
CHARLOTTA IVANOVNA, *a governess*
SEMYON YEPIHODOV, *a clerk*
DUNYASHA, *a maid*
FIRS (*pronounced* fierce), *a man-servant, aged eighty-seven*
YASHA, *a young valet*
A Tramp
Stationmaster, Post Office Clerk, Guests, Servants

The action takes place on MME. RANEVSKAYA's *estate.*

Act I

A room that is still called the nursery. One of the doors leads into Anya's room. Dawn, the sun will soon rise. It is May, the cherry trees are in blossom,

From *The Portable Chekhov* translated by Avrahm Yarmolinsky. Copyright 1947 by The Viking Press, Inc., N. Y. Reprinted with their permission.

but it is cold in the orchard; there is a morning frost. The windows are shut. Enter DUNYASHA *with a candle, and* LOPAHIN *with a book in his hand.*

LOPAHIN. The train is in, thank God. What time is it?

DUNYASHA. Nearly two. (*Puts out the candle*) It's light already.

LOPAHIN. How late is the train, anyway? Two hours at least. (*Yawns and stretches*) I'm a fine one! What a fool I've made of myself! I came here on purpose to meet them at the station, and then I went and overslept. I fell asleep in my chair. How annoying! You might have waked me . . .

DUNYASHA. I thought you'd left. (*Listens*) I think they're coming!

LOPAHIN (*listens*). No, they've got to get the luggage, and one thing and another . . . (*Pause*) Lubov Andreyevna spent five years abroad, I don't know what she's like now . . . She's a fine person—lighthearted, simple. I remember when I was a boy of fifteen, my poor father—he had a shop here in the village then—punched me in the face with his fist and made my nose bleed. We'd come into the yard, I don't know what for, and he'd had a drop too much. Lubov Andreyevna, I remember her as if it were yesterday—she was still young and so slim—led me to the wash-basin, in this very room . . . in the nursery. "Don't cry, little peasant," she said, "it'll heal in time for your wedding. . . ." (*Pause*) Little peasant . . . my father was a peasant, it's true, and here I am in a white waistcoat and yellow shoes. A pig in a pastry shop, you might say. It's true I'm rich, I've got a lot of money. . . . But when you look at it closely, I'm a peasant through and through. (*Pages the book*) Here I've been reading this book and I didn't understand a word of it. . . . I was reading it and fell asleep. . . . (*Pause*)

DUNYASHA. And the dogs were awake all night, they feel that their masters are coming.

LOPAHIN. Dunyasha, why are you so—

DUNYASHA. My hands are trembling. I'm going to faint.

LOPAHIN. You're too soft, Dunyasha. You dress like a lady, and look at the way you do your hair. That's not right. One should remember one's place.

(*Enter* YEPIHODOV *with a bouquet; he wears a jacket and highly polished boots that squeak badly. He drops the bouquet as he comes in*)

YEPIHODOV (*picking up the bouquet*). Here, the gardener sent these, said you're to put them in the dining room. (*Hands the bouquet to* DUNYASHA)

LOPAHIN. And bring me some *kvass.*

DUNYASHA. Yes, sir. (*Exits*)

YEPIHODOV. There's a frost this morning—three degrees below—and yet the cherries are all in blossom. I cannot approve of our climate. (*Sighs*) I cannot. Our climate does not activate properly. And, Yermolay Alexeyevich, allow me to make a further remark. The other day I bought myself a pair of boots, and I make bold to assure you, they squeak so that it is really intolerable. What should I grease them with?

LOPAHIN. Oh, get out! I'm fed up with you.

YEPIHODOV. Every day I meet with misfortune. And I don't complain, I've got used to it, I even smile.

(DUNYASHA *enters, hands* LOPAHIN *the kvass*)

YEPIHODOV. I am leaving. (*Stumbles against a chair, which falls over*) There! (*Triumphantly, as it were*) There again, you see what sort of circumstance, pardon the expression. . . . It is absolutely phenomenal! (*Exits*)

DUNYASHA. You know, Yermolay Alexeyevich, I must tell you, Yepihodov has proposed to me.

LOPAHIN. Ah!

DUNYASHA. I simply don't know . . . he's a quiet man, but sometimes when he starts talking, you can't make out what he means. He speaks nicely—and it's touching—but you can't understand it. I sort of like him though, and he is crazy about me. He's an unlucky man . . . every day something happens to him. They tease him about it here . . . they call him, Two-and-Twenty Troubles.

LOPAHIN (*listening*). There! I think they're coming.

DUNYASHA. They *are* coming! What's the matter with me? I feel cold all over.

LOPAHIN. They really are coming. Let's go and meet them. Will she recognize me? We haven't seen each other for five years.

DUNYASHA (*in a flutter*). I'm going to faint this minute. . . . Oh, I'm going to faint!

(*Two carriages are heard driving up to the house.* LOPAHIN *and* DUNYASHA *go out quickly. The stage is left empty. There is a noise in the adjoining rooms.* FIRS, *who had driven to the station to meet* LUBOV ANDREYEVNA RANEVSKAYA, *crosses the stage hurriedly, leaning on a stick. He is wearing an old-fashioned livery and a tall hat. He mutters to himself indistinctly. The hubbub off-stage increases.* A VOICE: "Come, let's go this way." *Enter* LUBOV ANDREYEVNA, ANYA, *and* CHARLOTTA IVANOVNA, *with a pet dog on a leash, all in traveling dresses;* VARYA, *wearing a coat and kerchief;* GAYEV, SIMEONOV-PISHCHIK, LOPAHIN, DUNYASHA *with a bag and an umbrella, servants with luggage. All walk across the room*)

ANYA. Let's go this way. Do you remember what room this is, mamma?

MME. RANEVSKAYA (*joyfully, through her tears*). The nursery!

VARYA. How cold it is! My hands are numb. (*To* MME. RANEVSKAYA) Your rooms are just the same as they were mamma, the white one and the violet.

MME. RANEVSKAYA. The nursery! My darling, lovely room! I slept here when I was a child . . .(*Cries*) And here I am, like a child again! (*Kisses her brother and* VARYA, *and then her brother again*) Varya's just the same as ever, like a nun. And I recognized Dunyasha. (*Kisses* DUNYASHA)

GAYEV. The train was two hours late. What do you think of that? What a way to manage things!

CHARLOTTA (*to* PISHCHIK). My dog eats nuts, too.

PISHCHIK (*in amazement*). You don't say so!

(*All go out, except* ANYA *and* DUNYASHA)

DUNYASHA. We've been waiting for you for hours. (*Takes* ANYA's *hat and coat*)

ANYA. I didn't sleep on the train for four nights and now I'm frozen . . .

DUNYASHA. It was Lent when you left; there was snow and frost, and now . . . My darling! (*Laughs and kisses her*) I have been waiting for you, my sweet, my darling! But I must tell you something . . . I can't put it off another minute . . .

ANYA (*listlessly*). What now?

DUNYASHA. The clerk, Yepihodov, proposed to me, just after Easter.

ANYA. There you are, at it again . . . (*Straightening her hair*) I've lost all my hairpins . . . (*She is staggering with exhaustion*)

DUNYASHA. Really, I don't know what to think. He loves me—he loves me so!

ANYA (*looking towards the door of her room, tenderly*). My own room, my windows, just as though I'd never been away. I'm home! Tomorrow morning I'll get up and run into the orchard. Oh, if I could only get some sleep. I didn't close my eyes during the whole journey—I was so anxious.

DUNYASHA. Pyotr Sergeyevich came the day before yesterday.

ANYA (*joyfully*). Petya!

DUNYASHA. He's asleep in the bath-house. He has settled there. He said he was afraid of being in the way. (*Looks at her watch*) I should wake him, but Miss Varya told me not to. "Don't you wake him," she said.

(*Enter* VARYA *with a bunch of keys at her belt*)

VARYA. Dunyasha, coffee, and be quick . . . Mamma's asking for coffee.

DUNYASHA. In a minute. (*Exits*)

VARYA. Well, thank God, you've come. You're home again. (*Fondling* ANYA) My darling is here again. My pretty one is back.

ANYA. Oh, what I've been through!

VARYA. I can imagine.

ANYA. When we left, it was Holy Week, it was cold then, and all the way Charlotta chattered and did her tricks. Why did you have to saddle me with Charlotta?

VARYA. You couldn't have traveled all alone, darling—at seventeen!

ANYA. We got to Paris, it was cold there, snowing. My French is dreadful. Mamma lived on the fifth floor; I went up there, and found all kinds of Frenchmen, ladies, an old priest with a book. The place was full of tobacco smoke, and so bleak. Suddenly I felt sorry for mamma, so sorry, I took her head in my arms and hugged her and couldn't let go of her. Afterwards mamma kept fondling me and crying . . .

VARYA (*through tears*). Don't speak of it . . . don't.

ANYA. She had already sold her villa at Mentone, she had nothing left, nothing. I hadn't a kopeck left either, we had only just enough to get home. And mamma wouldn't understand! When we had dinner at the stations, she always ordered the most expensive dishes, and tipped the waiters a whole ruble. Charlotta, too. And Yasha kept ordering, too—it was simply awful. You know Yasha's mamma's footman now, we brought him here with us.

VARYA. Yes, I've seen the blackguard.

ANYA. Well, tell me—have you paid the interest?

VARYA. How could we?

ANYA. Good heavens, good heavens!

VARYA. In August the estate will be put up for sale.

ANYA. My God!

(LOPAHIN *peeps in at the door and bleats*)

LOPAHIN. Meh-h-h. (*Disappears*)

VARYA (*through tears*). What I couldn't do to him! (*Shakes her fist threateningly*)

ANYA (*embracing* VARYA, *gently*). Varya, has he proposed to you? (VARYA *shakes her head*) But he loves you. Why don't you come to an understanding? What are you waiting for?

VARYA. Oh, I don't think anything will ever come of it. He's too busy, he has no time for me . . . pays no attention to me. I've washed my hands of him— I can't bear the sight of him. They all talk about our getting married, they all congratulate me—and all the time there's really nothing to it—it's all like a dream. (*In another tone*) You have a new brooch—like a bee.

ANYA (*sadly*). Mamma bought it. (*She goes into her own room and speaks gaily like a child*) And you know, in Paris I went up in a balloon.

VARYA. My darling's home, my pretty one is back! (DUNYASHA *returns with the coffee-pot and prepares coffee.* VARYA *stands at the door of* ANYA's *room*) All day long, darling, as I go about the house, I keep dreaming. If only we could marry you off to a rich man, I should feel at ease. Then I would go into a convent, and afterwards to Kiev, to Moscow . . . I would spend my life going from one holy place to another . . . I'd go on and on . . . What a blessing that would be!

ANYA. The birds are singing in the orchard. What time is it?

VARYA. It must be after two. Time you were asleep, darling. (*Goes into* ANYA's *room*) What a blessing that would be!

(YASHA *enters with a plaid and a traveling bag, crosses the stage*)

YASHA (*finically*). May I pass this way, please?

DUNYASHA. A person could hardly recognize you, Yasha. Your stay abroad has certainly done wonders for you.

YASHA. Hm-m . . . and who are you?

DUNYASHA. When you went away I was that high—(*Indicating with her hand*) I'm Dunyasha—Fyodor Kozoyedev's daughter. Don't you remember?

YASHA. Hm! What a peach! (*He looks round and embraces her. She cries out and drops a saucer.* YASHA *leaves quickly*)

VARYA (*in the doorway, in a tone of annoyance*). What's going on here?

DUNYASHA (*through tears*). I've broken a saucer.

VARYA. Well, that's good luck.

ANYA (*coming out of her room*). We ought to warn mamma that Petya's here.

VARYA. I left orders not to wake him.

ANYA (*musingly*). Six years ago father died. A month later brother Grisha was drowned in the river. . . . Such a pretty little boy he was—only seven. It was

more than mamma could bear, so she went away, went away without looking
back . . . (*Shudders*) How well I understand her, if she only knew! (*Pauses*)
And Petya Trofimov was Grisha's tutor, he may remind her of it all . . .
(*Enter* FIRS, *wearing a jacket and a white waistcoat. He goes up to the
coffee-pot*)

FIRS (*anxiously*). The mistress will have her coffee here. (*Puts on white
gloves*) Is the coffee ready? (*Sternly, to* DUNYASHA) Here, you! And where's
the cream?

DUNYASHA. Oh, my God! (*Exits quickly*)

FIRS (*fussing over the coffee-pot*). Hah! the addlehead! (*Mutters to himself*)
Home from Paris. And the old master used to go to Paris too . . . by carriage.
(*Laughs*)

VARYA. What is it, Firs?

FIRS. What is you pleasure, Miss? (*Joyfully*) My mistress has come home,
and I've seen her at last! Now I can die. (*Weeps with joy*)

(*Enter* MME. RANEVSKAYA, GAYEV, *and* SIMEONOV-PISHCHIK. *The latter is wearing a tight-waisted, pleated coat of fine cloth, and full trousers.* GAYEV, *as he
comes in, goes through the motions of a billiard player with his arms and
body*)

MME. RANEVSKAYA. Let's see, how does it go? Yellow ball in the corner!
Bank shot in the side pocket!

GAYEV. I'll tip it in the corner! There was a time, sister, when you and I used
to sleep in this very room, and now I'm fifty-one, strange as it may seem.

LOPAHIN. Yes, time flies.

GAYEV. Who?

LOPAHIN. I say, time flies.

GAYEV. It smells of patchouli here.

ANYA. I'm going to bed. Good night, mamma. (*Kisses her mother*)

MME. RANEVSKAYA. My darling child! (*Kisses her hands*) Are you happy to be
home? I can't come to my senses.

ANYA. Good night, uncle.

GAYEV (*kissing her face and hands*). God bless you, how like your mother
you are! (*To his sister*) At her age, Luba, you were just like her.

(ANYA *shakes hands with* LOPAHIN *and* PISHCHIK, *then goes out, shutting
the door behind her*)

MME. RANEVSKAYA. She's very tired.

PISHCHIK. Well, it was a long journey.

VARYA (*to* LOPAHIN *and* PISHCHIK). How about it, gentlemen? It's past two
o'clock—isn't it time for you to go?

MME. RANEVSKAYA (*laughs*). You're just the same as ever, Varya. (*Draws
her close and kisses her*) I'll have my coffee and then we'll all go. (FIRS
puts a small cushion under her feet) Thank you, my dear. I've got used to
coffee. I drink it day and night. Thanks, my dear old man. (*Kisses him*)

VARYA. I'd better see if all the luggage has been brought in. (*Exits*)

MME. RANEVSKAYA. Can it really be I sitting here? (*Laughs*) I feel like dancing, waving my arms about. (*Covers her face with her hands*) But maybe I am dreaming! God knows I love my country, I love it tenderly; I couldn't look out of the window in the train, I kept crying so. (*Through tears*) But I must have my coffee. Thank you, Firs, thank you, dear old man. I'm so happy that you're still alive.

FIRS. Day before yesterday.

GAYEV. He's hard of hearing.

LOPAHIN. I must go soon, I'm leaving for Kharkov about five o'clock. How annoying! I'd like to have a good look at you, talk to you . . . You're just as splendid as ever.

PISHCHIK (*breathing heavily*). She's even better-looking. . . . Dressed in the latest Paris fashion. . . . Perish my carriage and all its four wheels. . . .

LOPAHIN. Your brother, Leonid Andreyevich, says I'm a vulgarian and an exploiter. But it's all the same to me—let him talk. I only want you to trust me as you used to. I want you to look at me with your touching, wonderful eyes, as you used to. Dear God! My father was a serf of your father's and grandfather's, but you, you yourself, did so much for me once . . . so much . . . that I've forgotten all about that; I love you as though you were my sister—even more.

MME. RANEVSKAYA. I can't sit still, I simply can't. (*Jumps up and walks about in violent agitation*) This joy is too much for me. . . . Laugh at me, I'm silly! My own darling bookcase! My darling table! (*Kisses it*)

GAYEV. While you were away, nurse died.

MME. RANEVSKAYA (*sits down and takes her coffee*). Yes, God rest her soul; they wrote me about it.

GAYEV. And Anastasy is dead. Petrushka Kossoy has left me and has gone into town to work for the police inspector. (*Takes a box of sweets out of his pocket and begins to suck one*)

PISHCHIK. My daughter Dashenka sends her regards.

LOPAHIN. I'd like to tell you something very pleasant—cheering. (*Glancing at his watch*) I am leaving directly. There isn't much time to talk. But I will put it in a few words. As you know, your cherry orchard is to be sold to pay your debts. The sale is to be on the twenty-second of August; but don't you worry, my dear, you may sleep in peace; there is a way out. Here is my plan. Give me your attention! Your estate is only fifteen miles from the town; the railway runs close by it; and if the cherry orchard and the land along the river bank were cut up into lots and these leased for summer cottages, you would have an income of at least 25,000 rubles a year out of it.

GAYEV. Excuse me. . . . What nonsense.

MME. RANEVSKAYA. I don't quite understand you, Yermolay Alexeyevich.

LOPAHIN. You will get an annual rent of at least ten rubles per acre, and if you advertise at once, I'll give you any guarantee you like that you won't have a square foot of ground left by autumn, all the lots will be snapped up. In short, congratulations, you're saved. The location is splendid—by that deep river. . . . Only, of course, the ground must be cleared . . . all the old buildings, for instance, must be torn down, and this house, too, which is useless, and, of course, the old cherry orchard must be cut down.

MME. RANEVSKAYA. Cut down? My dear, forgive me, but you don't know what you're talking about. If there's one thing that's interesting—indeed, remarkable—in the whole province, it's precisely our cherry orchard.

LOPAHIN. The only remarkable thing about this orchard is that it's a very large one. There's a crop of cherries every other year, and you can't do anything with them; no one buys them.

GAYEV. This orchard is even mentioned in the Encyclopedia.

LOPAHIN (*glancing at his watch*). If we can't think of a way out, if we don't come to a decision, on the twenty-second of August the cherry orchard and the whole estate will be sold at auction. Make up your minds! There's no other way out—I swear. None, none.

FIRS. In the old days, forty or fifty years ago, the cherries were dried, soaked, pickled, and made into jam, and we used to—

GAYEV. Keep still, Firs.

FIRS. And the dried cherries would be shipped by the cartload. It meant a lot of money! And in those days the dried cherries were soft and juicy, sweet, fragrant. . . . They knew the way to do it, then.

MME. RANEVSKAYA. And why don't they do it that way now?

FIRS. They've forgotten. Nobody remembers it.

PISHCHIK (*to* MME. RANEVSKAYA). What's doing in Paris? Eh? Did you eat frogs there?

MME. RANEVSKAYA. I ate crocodiles.

PISHCHIK. Just imagine!

LOPAHIN. There used to be only landowners and peasants in the country, but now these summer people have appeared on the scene. . . . All the towns, even the small ones, are surrounded by these summer cottages; and in another twenty years, no doubt, the summer population will have grown enormously. Now the summer resident only drinks tea on his porch, but maybe he'll take to working his acre, too, and then your cherry orchard will be a rich, happy, luxuriant place.

GAYEV (*indignantly*). Poppycock!

(*Enter* VARYA *and* YASHA)

VARYA. There are two telegrams for you, mamma dear. (*Picks a key from the bunch at her belt and noisily opens an old-fashioned bookcase*) Here they are.

MME. RANEVSKAYA. They're from Paris. (*Tears them up without reading them*) I'm through with Paris.

GAYEV. Do you know, Luba, how old this bookcase is? Last week I pulled out the bottom drawer and there I found the date burnt in it. It was made exactly a hundred years ago. Think of that! We could celebrate its centenary. True, it's an inanimate object, but nevertheless, a bookcase . . .

PISHCHIK (*amazed*). A hundred years! Just imagine!

GAYEV. Yes. (*Tapping it*) That's something. . . . Dear, honored bookcase, hail to you who for more than a century have served the glorious ideals of goodness and justice! Your silent summons to fruitful toil has never weakened in all those hundred years (*through tears*), sustaining, through successive generations of our family, courage and faith in a better future, and fostering in us ideals of goodness and social consciousness. . . . (*Pauses*)

LOPAHIN. Yes . . .

MME. RANEVSKAYA. You haven't changed a bit, Leonid.

GAYEV (*somewhat embarrassed*). I'll play it off the red in the corner! Tip it in the side pocket!

LOPAHIN (*looking at his watch*). Well, it's time for me to go . . .

YASHA (*handing a pill box to* MME. RANEVSKAYA). Perhaps you'll take your pills now.

PISHCHIK. One shouldn't take medicines, dearest lady, they do neither harm nor good. . . . Give them here, my valued friend. (*Takes the pill box, pours the pills into his palm, blows on them, puts them in his mouth, and washes them down with some kvass*) There!

MME. RANEVSKAYA (*frightened*). You must be mad!

PISHCHIK. I've taken all the pills.

LOPAHIN. What a glutton!

(*All laugh*)

FIRS. The gentleman visited us in Easter week, ate half a bucket of pickles, he did . . . (*Mumbles*)

MME. RANEVSKAYA. What's he saying?

VARYA. He's been mumbling like that for the last three years—we're used to it.

YASHA. His declining years!

(CHARLOTTA IVANOVNA, *very thin, tightly laced, dressed in white, a lorgnette at her waist, crosses the stage*)

LOPAHIN. Forgive me, Charlotta Ivanovna, I've not had time to greet you. (*Tries to kiss her hand*)

CHARLOTTA (*pulling away her hand*). If I let you kiss my hand, you'll be wanting to kiss my elbow next, and then my shoulder.

LOPAHIN. I've no luck today. (*All laugh*) Charlotta Ivanovna, show us a trick.

MME. RANEVSKAYA. Yes, Charlotta, do a trick for us.

CHARLOTTA. I don't see the need. I want to sleep. (*Exits*)

LOPAHIN. In three weeks we'll meet again. (*Kisses* MME. RANEVSKAYA's *hand*) Good-by till then. Time's up. (*To* GAYEV) Bye-bye. (*Kisses* PISHCHIK) Bye-bye. (*Shakes hands with* VARYA, *then with* FIRS *and* YASHA) I hate to leave. (*To* MME. RANEVSKAYA) If you make up your mind about the cottages, let me know; I'll get you a loan of 50,000 rubles. Think it over seriously.

VARYA (*crossly*). Will you never go!

LOPAHIN. I'm going, I'm going. (*Exits*)

GAYEV. The vulgarian. But, excuse me . . . Varya's going to marry him, he's Varya's fiancé.

VARYA. You talk too much, uncle dear.

MME. RANEVSKAYA. Well, Varya, it would make me happy. He's a good man.

PISHCHIK. Yes, one must admit, he's a most estimable man. And my Dashenka ... she too says that ... she says ... lots of things. (*Snores; but wakes up at once*) All the same, my valued friend, could you oblige me ... with a loan of 240 rubles? I must pay the interest on the mortgage tomorrow.

VARYA (*alarmed*). We can't, we can't!

MME. RANEVSKAYA. I really haven't any money.

PISHCHIK. It'll turn up. (*Laughs*) I never lose hope, I thought everything was lost, that I was done for, when lo and behold, the railway ran through my land ... and I was paid for it. ... And something else will turn up again, if not today, then tomorrow ... Dashenka will win two hundred thousand ... she's got a lottery ticket.

MME. RANEVSKAYA. I've had my coffee, now let's go to bed.

FIRS (*brushes off* GAYEV; *admonishingly*). You've got the wrong trousers on again. What am I to do with you?

VARYA (*softly*). Anya's asleep. (*Gently opens the window*) The sun's up now, it's not a bit cold. Look, mamma dear, what wonderful trees. And heavens, what air! The starlings are singing!

GAYEV (*opens the other window*). The orchard is all white. You've not forgotten it? Luba? That's the long alley that runs straight, straight as an arrow; how it shines on moonlight nights, do you remember? You've not forgotten?

MME. RANEVSKAYA (*looking out of the window into the orchard*). Oh, my childhood, my innocent childhood. I used to sleep in this nursery—I used to look out into the orchard, happiness waked with me every morning, the orchard was just the same then ... nothing has changed. (*Laughs with joy*) All, all white! Oh, my orchard! After the dark, rainy autumn and the cold winter, you are young again, and full of happiness, the heavenly angels have not left you ... If I could free my chest and my shoulders from this rock that weighs on me, if I could only forget the past!

GAYEV. Yes, and the orchard will be sold to pay our debts, strange as it may seem. ...

MME. RANEVSKAYA. Look! There is our poor mother walking in the orchard ... all in white ... (*Laughs with joy*) It is she!

GAYEV. Where?

VARYA. What are you saying, mamma dear!

MME. RANEVSKAYA. There's no one there, I just imagined it. To the right, where the path turns towards the arbor, there's a little white tree, leaning over, that looks like a woman ...

(TROFIMOV *enters, wearing a shabby student's uniform and spectacles*)

MME. RANEVSKAYA. What an amazing orchard! White masses of blossom, the blue sky ...

TROFIMOV. Lubov Andreyevna! (*She looks round at him*) I just want to pay my respects to you, then I'll leave at once. (*Kisses her hand ardently*) I was told to wait until morning, but I hadn't the patience ... (MME. RANEVSKAYA *looks at him, perplexed*)

VARYA (*through tears*). This is Petya Trofimov.

TROFIMOV. Petya Trofimov, formerly your Grisha's tutor. . . . Can I have changed so much? (MME. RANEVSKAYA *embraces him and weeps quietly*)

GAYEV (*embarrassed*). Don't, don't, Luba.

VARYA (*crying*). I told you, Petya, to wait until tomorrow.

MME. RANEVSKAYA. My Grisha . . . my little boy . . . Grisha . . . my son.

VARYA. What can one do, mamma dear, it's God's will.

TROFIMOV (*softly, through tears*). There . . . there.

MME. RANEVSKAYA (*weeping quietly*). My little boy was lost . . . drowned. Why? Why, my friend? (*More quietly*) Anya's asleep in there, and here I am talking so loudly . . . making all this noise. . . . But tell me, Petya, why do you look so badly? Why have you aged so?

TROFIMOV. A mangy master, a peasant woman in the train called me.

MME. RANEVSKAYA. You were just a boy then, a dear little student, and now your hair's thin—and you're wearing glasses! Is it possible you're still a student? (*Goes towards the door*)

TROFIMOV. I suppose I'm a perpetual student.

MME. RANEVSKAYA (*kisses her brother, then* VARYA). Now, go to bed . . . You have aged, too, Leonid.

PISHCHIK (*follows her*). So now we turn in. Oh, my gout! I'm staying the night here . . . Lubov Andreyevna, my angel, tomorrow morning. . . . I do need 240 rubles.

GAYEV. He keeps at it.

PISHCHIK. I'll pay it back, dear . . . it's a trifling sum.

MME. RANEVSKAYA. All right, Leonid will give it to you. Give it to him, Leonid.

GAYEV. Me give it to him! That's a good one!

MME. RANEVSKAYA. It can't be helped. Give it to him! He needs it. He'll pay it back.

(MME. RANEVSKAYA, TROFIMOV, PISHCHIK, *and* FIRS *go out;* GAYEV, VARYA, *and* YASHA *remain*)

GAYEV. Sister hasn't got out of the habit of throwing money around. (*To* YASHA) Go away, my good fellow, you smell of the barnyard.

YASHA (*with a grin*). And you, Leonid Andreyevich, are just the same as ever.

GAYEV. Who? (*To* VARYA) What did he say?

VARYA (*To* YASHA). Your mother's come from the village; she's been sitting in the servants' room since yesterday, waiting to see you.

YASHA. Botheration!

VARYA. You should be ashamed of yourself!

YASHA. She's all I needed! She could have come tomorrow. (*Exits*)

VARYA. Mamma is just the same as ever; she hasn't changed a bit. If she had her own way, she'd keep nothing for herself.

GAYEV. Yes . . . (*Pauses*) If a great many remedies are offered for some disease, it means it is incurable; I keep thinking and racking my brains; I have many remedies, ever so many, and that really means none. It would be fine if we came in for a legacy; it would be fine if we married off our Anya to a very rich man; or we might go to Yaroslavl and try our luck with our aunt, the Countess. She's very, very rich, you know . . .

VARYA (*weeping*). If only God would help us!

GAYEV. Stop bawling. Aunt's very rich, but she doesn't like us. In the first place, sister married a lawyer who was no nobleman . . . (ANYA *appears in the doorway*) She married beneath her, and it can't be said that her behavior has been very exemplary. She's good, kind, sweet, and I love her, but no matter what extenuating circumstances you may adduce, there's no denying that she has no morals. You sense it in her least gesture.

VARYA (*in a whisper*). Anya's in the doorway.

GAYEV. Who? (*Pauses*) It's queer, something got into my right eye—my eyes are going back on me. . . . And on Thursday, when I was in the circuit court—

(*Enter* ANYA)

VARYA. Why aren't you asleep, Anya?

ANYA. I can't get to sleep, I just can't.

GAYEV. My little pet! (*Kisses* ANYA's *face and hands*) My child! (*Weeps*) You are not my niece, you're my angel! You're everything to me. Believe me, believe—

ANYA. I believe you, uncle. Everyone loves you and respects you . . . but, uncle dear, you must keep still. . . . You must. What were you saying just now about my mother? Your own sister? What made you say that?

GAYEV. Yes, yes . . . (*Covers his face with her hand*) Really, that was awful! Good God! Heaven help me! Just now I made a speech to the bookcase . . . so stupid! And only after I was through, I saw how stupid it was.

VARYA. It's true, uncle dear, you ought to keep still. Just don't talk, that's all.

ANYA. If you could only keep still, it would make things easier for you too.

GAYEV. I'll keep still. (*Kisses* ANYA's *and* VARYA's *hands*) I will. But now about business. On Thursday I was in court; well, there were a number of us there, and we began talking of one thing and another, and this and that, and do you know, I believe it will be possible to raise a loan on a promissory note, to pay the interest at the bank.

VARYA. If only God would help us!

GAYEV. On Tuesday I'll go and see about it again. (*To* VARYA) Stop bawling. (*To* ANYA) Your mamma will talk to Lopahin, and he, of course, will not refuse her . . . and as soon as you're rested, you'll go to Yaroslavl to the Countess, your great-aunt. So we'll be working in three directions at once, and the thing is in the bag. We'll pay the interest—I'm sure of it. (*Puts a candy in his mouth*) I swear on my honor, I swear by anything you like, the estate shan't be sold. (*Excitedly*) I swear by my own happiness! Here's my hand on it, you can call me a swindler and a scoundrel if I let it come to an auction! I swear by my whole being.

ANYA (*relieved and quite happy again*). How good you are, uncle, and how clever! (*Embraces him*) Now I'm at peace, quite at peace, I'm happy.

(*Enter* FIRS)

FIRS (*reproachfully*). Leonid Andreyevich, have you no fear of God? When are you going to bed?

GAYEV. Directly, directly. Go away, Firs, I'll . . . yes, I will undress myself. Now, children, 'nightie-'nightie. We'll consider details tomorrow, but now go to sleep. (*Kisses* ANYA *and* VARYA) I am a man of the 'Eighties; they have nothing good to say of that period nowadays. Nevertheless, in the course of my life I have suffered not a little for my convictions. It's not for nothing that the peasant loves me; one should know the peasant; one should know from which—

ANYA. There you go again, uncle.

VARYA. Uncle dear, be quiet.

FIRS (*angrily*). Leonid Andreyevich!

GAYEV. I'm coming, I'm coming! Go to bed! Double bank shot in the side pocket! Here goes a clean shot . . . (*Exits,* FIRS *hobbling after him*)

ANYA. I am at peace now. I don't want to go to Yaroslavl—I don't like my great-aunt, but still, I am at peace, thanks to uncle. (*Sits down*)

VARYA. We must get some sleep. I'm going now. While you were away something unpleasant happened. In the old servants' quarters there are only the old people, as you know; Yefim, Polya, Yevstigney, and Karp, too. They began letting all sorts of rascals in to spend the night. . . . I didn't say anything. Then I heard they'd been spreading a report that I gave them nothing but dried peas to eat—out of stinginess, you know . . . and it was all Yevstigney's doing. . . . All right, I thought, if that's how it is, I thought, just wait. I sent for Yevstigney. . . . (*Yawns*) He comes. . . . "How's this, Yevstigney?" I say, "You fool . . . " (*Looking at* ANYA) Anichka! (*Pauses*) She's asleep. (*Puts her arm around* ANYA) Come to your little bed. . . . Come . . . (*Leads her*) My darling has fallen asleep. . . . Come.

(*They go out. Far away beyond the orchard a shepherd is piping.* TROFIMOV *crosses the stage and, seeing* VARYA *and* ANYA, *stands still*)

VARYA. Sh! She's asleep . . . asleep . . . Come, darling.

ANYA (*softly, half-asleep*). I'm so tired. Those bells . . . uncle . . . dear. . . . Mamma and uncle . . .

VARYA. Come, my precious, come along. (*They go into* ANYA's *room*)

TROFIMOV (*with emotion*). My sunshine, my spring!

Act II

A meadow. An old, long-abandoned, lopsided little chapel; near it, a well, large slabs, which had apparently once served as tombstones, and an old bench. In the background, the road to the Gayev estate. To one side poplars loom darkly, where the cherry orchard begins. In the distance a row of telegraph poles, and far off, on the horizon, the faint outline of a large city which is seen only in fine, clear weather. The sun will soon be setting. CHARLOTTA, YASHA, *and* DUNYASHA *are seated on the bench.* YEPIHODOV *stands near and plays a guitar. All are pensive.* CHARLOTTA *wears an old peaked cap. She has taken a gun from her shoulder and is straightening the buckle on the strap.*

CHARLOTTA (*musingly*). I haven't a real passport, I don't know how old I am, and I always feel that I am very young. When I was a little girl, my father and mother used to go from fair to fair and give performances, very good ones. And I used to do the *salto mortale,* and all sorts of other tricks. And when papa and mamma died, a German lady adopted me and began to educate me. Very good. I grew up and became a governess. But where I come from and who I am, I don't know. . . . Who were my parents? Perhaps they weren't even married. . . . I don't know. . . . (*Takes a cucumber out of her pocket and eats it*) I don't know a thing. (*Pause*) One wants so much to talk, and there isn't anyone to talk to. . . . I haven't anybody.

YEPIHODOV (*plays the guitar and sings*). "What care I for the jarring world? What's friend or foe to me? . . ." How agreeable it is to play the mandolin.

DUNYASHA. That's a guitar, not a mandolin. (*Looks in a hand mirror and powders her face*)

YEPIHODOV. To a madman in love it's a mandolin. (*Sings*) "Would that the heart were warmed by the fire of mutual love!" (YASHA *joins in*)

CHARLOTTA. How abominably these people sing. Pfui! Like jackals!

DUNYASHA (*to* YASHA). How wonderful it must be though to have stayed abroad!

YASHA. Ah, yes, of course, I cannot but agree with you there. (*Yawns and lights a cigar*)

YEPIHODOV. Naturally. Abroad, everything has long since achieved full perplexion.

YASHA. That goes without saying.

YEPIHODOV. I'm a cultivated man, I read all kinds of remarkable books. And yet I can never make out what direction I should take, what is it that I want, properly speaking. Should I live, or should I shoot myself, properly speaking? Nevertheless, I always carry a revolver about me. . . . Here it is . . . (*Shows revolver*)

CHARLOTTA. I've finished. I'm going. (*Puts the gun over her shoulder*) You are a very clever man, Yepihodov, and a very terrible one; women must be crazy about you. Br-r-r! (*Starts to go*) These clever men are all so stupid; there's no one for me to talk to . . . always alone, alone, I haven't a soul . . . and who I am, and why I am, nobody knows. (*Exits unhurriedly*)

YEPIHODOV. Properly speaking and letting other subjects alone, I must say regarding myself, among other things, that fate treats me mercilessly, like a storm treats a small boat. If I am mistaken, let us say, why then do I wake up this morning, and there on my chest is a spider of enormous dimensions . . . like this . . . (*indicates with both hands*) Again, I take up a pitcher of kvass to have a drink, and in it there is something unseemly to the highest degree, something like a cockroach. (*Pause*) Have you read Buckle? (*Pause*) I wish to have a word with you, Avdotya Fyodorovna, if I may trouble you.

DUNYASHA. Well, go ahead.

YEPIHODOV. I wish to speak with you alone. (*Sighs*)

DUNYASHA (*embarrassed*). Very well. Only first bring me my little cape. You'll find it near the wardrobe. It's rather damp here.

YEPIHODOV. Certainly, ma'am; I will fetch it, ma'am. Now I know what to do with my revolver. (*Takes the guitar and goes off playing it*)

YASHA. Two-and-Twenty Troubles! An awful fool, between you and me. (*Yawns*)

DUNYASHA. I hope to God he doesn't shoot himself! (*Pause*) I've become so nervous, I'm always fretting. I was still a little girl when I was taken into the big house, I am quite unused to the simple life now, and my hands are white, as white as a lady's. I've become so soft, so delicate, so refined, I'm afraid of everything. It's so terrifying; and if you deceive me, Yasha, I don't know what will happen to my nerves. (YASHA *kisses her*)

YASHA. You're a peach! Of course, a girl should never forget herself; and what I dislike more than anything is when a girl don't behave properly.

DUNYASHA. I've fallen passionately in love with you; you're educated—you have something to say about everything. (*Pause*)

YASHA (*yawns*). Yes, ma'am. Now the way I look at it, if a girl loves someone, it means she is immoral. (*Pause*) It's agreeable smoking a cigar in the fresh air. (*Listens*) Someone's coming this way . . . It's our madam and the others. (DUNYASHA *embraces him impulsively*) You go home, as though you'd been to the river to bathe; go by the little path, or else they'll run into you and suspect me of having arranged to meet you here. I can't stand that sort of thing.

DUNYASHA (*coughing softly*). Your cigar's made my head ache.

(*Exits.* YASHA *remains standing near the chapel. Enter* MME. RANEVSKAYA, GAYEV, *and* LOPAHIN)

LOPAHIN. You must make up your mind once and for all—there's no time to lose. It's quite a simple question, you know. Do you agree to lease your land for summer cottages or not? Answer in one word, yes or no; only one word!

MME. RANEVSKAYA. Who's been smoking such abominable cigars here? (*Sits down*)

GAYEV. Now that the railway line is so near, it's made things very convenient. (*Sits down*) Here we've been able to have lunch in town. Yellow ball in the side pocket! I feel like going into the house and playing just one game.

MME. RANEVSKAYA. You can do that later.

LOPAHIN. Only one word! (*Imploringly*) Do give me an answer!

GAYEV (*yawning*). Who?

MME. RANEVSKAYA (*looks into her purse*). Yesterday I had a lot of money and now my purse is almost empty. My poor Varya tries to economize by feeding us just milk soup; in the kitchen the old people get nothing but dried peas to eat, while I squander money thoughtlessly. (*Drops the purse, scattering gold pieces*) You see there they go . . . (*Shows vexation*)

YASHA. Allow me—I'll pick them up. (*Picks up the money*)

MME. RANEVSKAYA. Be so kind, Yasha. And why did I go to lunch in town? That nasty restaurant, with its music and the tablecloth smelling of soap

. . . Why drink so much, Leonid? Why eat so much? Why talk so much? Today again you talked a lot. and all so inappropriately about the 'Seventies, about the decadents. And to whom? Talking to waiters about decadents!

LOPAHIN. Yes.

GAYEV (*waving his hand*). I'm incorrigible; that's obvious. (*Irritably, to* YASHA) Why do you keep dancing about in front of me?

YASHA (*laughs*). I can't hear your voice without laughing—

GAYEV. Either he or I—

MME. RANEVSKAYA. Go away, Yasha; run along.

YASHA (*handing* MME. RANEVSKAYA *her purse*). I'm going, at once. (*Hardly able to suppress his laughter*) This minute. (*Exits*)

LOPAHIN. That rich man, Deriganov, wants to buy your estate. They say he's coming to the auction himself.

MME. RANEVSKAYA. Where did you hear that?

LOPAHIN. That's what they are saying in town.

GAYEV. Our aunt in Yaroslavl has promised to help; but when she will send the money, and how much, no one knows.

LOPAHIN. How much will she send? A hundred thousand? Two hundred?

MME. RANEVSKAYA. Oh, well, ten or fifteen thousand; and we'll have to be grateful for that.

LOPAHIN. Forgive me, but such frivolous people as you are, so queer and unbusinesslike—I never met in my life. One tells you in plain language that your estate is up for sale, and you don't seem to take it in.

MME. RANEVSKAYA. What are we to do? Tell us what to do.

LOPAHIN. I do tell you, every day; every day I say the same thing! You must lease the cherry orchard and the land for summer cottages, you must do it and as soon as possible—right away. The auction is close at hand. Please understand! Once you've decided to have the cottages, you can raise as much money as you like, and you're saved.

MME. RANEVSKAYA. Cottages—summer people—forgive me, but it's all so vulgar.

GAYEV. I agree with you absolutely.

LOPAHIN. I shall either burst into tears or scream or faint! I can't stand it! You've worn me out! (*To* GAYEV) You're an old woman!

GAYEV. Who?

LOPAHIN. An old woman! (*Gets up to go*)

MME. RANEVSKAYA (*alarmed*). No, don't go! Please stay, I beg you, my dear. Perhaps we shall think of something.

LOPAHIN. What is there to think of?

MME. RANEVSKAYA. Don't go, I beg you. With you here it's more cheerful anyway. (*Pause*) I keep expecting something to happen, it's as though the house were going to crash about our ears.

GAYEV (*in deep thought*). Bank shot in the corner. . . . Three cushions in the side pocket. . . .

MME. RANEVSKAYA. We have been great sinners . . .

LOPAHIN. What sins could you have committed?

GAYEV (*putting a candy in his mouth*). They say I've eaten up my fortune in candy! (*Laughs*)

MME. RANEVSKAYA. Oh, my sins! I've squandered money away recklessly, like a lunatic, and I married a man who made nothing but debts. My husband drank himself to death on champagne, he was a terrific drinker. And then, to my sorrow, I fell in love with another man, and I lived with him. And just then—that was my first punishment—a blow on the head: my little boy was drowned here in the river. And I went abroad, went away forever . . . never to come back, never to see this river again . . . I closed my eyes and ran, out of my mind. . . . But he followed me, pitiless, brutal. I bought a villa near Mentone, because he fell ill there; and for three years, day and night, I knew no peace, no rest. The sick man wore me out, he sucked my soul dry. Then last year, when the villa was sold to pay my debts, I went to Paris, and there he robbed me, abandoned me, took up with another woman, I tried to poison myself—it was stupid, so shameful—and then suddenly I felt drawn back to Russia, back to my own country, to my little girl. (*Wipes her tears away*) Lord, Lord! Be merciful, forgive me my sins—don't punish me any more! (*Takes a telegram out of her pocket*) This came today from Paris—he begs me to forgive him, implores me to go back . . . (*Tears up the telegram*) Do I hear music? (*Listens*)

GAYEV. That's our famous Jewish band, you remember? Four violins, a flute, and a double bass.

MME. RANEVSKAYA. Does it still exist? We ought to send for them some evening and have a party.

LOPAHIN (*listens*). I don't hear anything. (*Hums softly*) "The Germans for a fee will Frenchify a Russian." (*Laughs*) I saw a play at the theater yesterday—awfully funny.

MME. RANEVSKAYA. There was probably nothing funny about it. You shouldn't go to see plays, you should look at yourselves more often. How drab your lives are—how full of unnecessary talk.

LOPAHIN. That's true; come to think of it, we do live like fools. (*Pause*) My pop was a peasant, an idiot; he understood nothing, never taught me anything, all he did was beat me when he was drunk, and always with a stick. Fundamentally, I'm just the same kind of blockhead and idiot. I was never taught anything—I have a terrible handwriting, I write so that I feel ashamed before people, like a pig.

MME. RANEVSKAYA. You should get married, my friend.

LOPAHIN. Yes . . . that's true.

MME. RANEVSKAYA. To our Varya, she's a good girl.

LOPAHIN. Yes.

MME. RANEVSKAYA. She's a girl who comes of simple people, she works all day long; and above all, she loves you. Besides, you've liked her for a long time now.

LOPAHIN. Well, I've nothing against it. She's a good girl. (*Pause*)

GAYEV. I've been offered a place in the bank—6,000 a year. Have you heard?

MME. RANEVSKAYA. You're not up to it. Stay where you are.

(FIRS *enters, carrying an overcoat*)

FIRS (*to* GAYEV). Please put this on, sir, it's damp.

GAYEV (*putting it on*). I'm fed up with you, brother.

FIRS. Never mind. This morning you drove off without saying a word. (*Looks him over*)

MME. RANEVSKAYA. How you've aged, Firs.

FIRS. I beg your pardon?

LOPAHIN. The lady says you've aged.

FIRS. I've lived a long time; they were arranging my wedding and your papa wasn't born yet. (*Laughs*) When freedom came I was already head footman. I wouldn't consent to be set free then; I stayed on with the master . . . (*Pause*) I remember they were all very happy, but why they were happy, they didn't know themselves.

LOPAHIN. It was fine in the old days! At least there was flogging!

FIRS (*not hearing*). Of course. The peasants kept to the masters, the masters kept to the peasants; but now they've all gone their own ways, and there's no making out anything.

GAYEV. Be quiet, Firs. I must go to town tomorrow. They've promised to introduce me to a general who might let us have a loan.

LOPAHIN. Nothing will come of that. You won't even be able to pay the interest, you can be certain of that.

MME. RANEVSKAYA. He's raving, there isn't any general. (*Enter* TROFIMOV, ANYA, *and* VARYA)

GAYEV. Here come our young people.

ANYA. There's mamma, on the bench.

MME. RANEVSKAYA (*tenderly*). Come here, come along, my darlings. (*Embraces* ANYA *and* VARYA) If you only knew how I love you both! Sit beside me— there, like that. (*All sit down*)

LOPAHIN. Our perpetual student is always with the young ladies.

TROFIMOV. That's not any of your business.

LOPAHIN. He'll soon be fifty, and he's still a student!

TROFIMOV. Stop your silly jokes.

LOPAHIN. What are you so cross about, you queer bird?

TROFIMOV. Oh, leave me alone.

LOPAHIN (*laughs*). Allow me to ask you, what do you think of me?

TROFIMOV. What I think of you, Yermolay Alexeyevich, is this: you are a rich man who will soon be a millionaire. Well, just as a beast of prey, which devours everything that comes in its way, is necessary for the process of metabolism to go on, so you too are necessary. (*All laugh*)

VARYA. Better tell us something about the planets, Petya.

MME. RANEVSKAYA. No, let's go on with yesterday's conversation.

TROFIMOV. What was it about?

GAYEV. About man's pride.

TROFIMOV. Yesterday we talked a long time, but we came to no conclusion. There is something mystical about man's pride in your sense of the word. Perhaps you're right, from your own point of view. But if you reason simply, without going into subtleties, then what call is there for pride? Is there any sense in it, if man is so poor a thing physiologically, and if, in the great majority of cases, he is coarse, stupid, and profoundly unhappy? We should stop admiring ourselves. We should work, and that's all.

GAYEV. You die, anyway.

TROFIMOV. Who knows? And what does it mean—to die? Perhaps man has a hundred senses, and at his death only the five we know perish, while the other ninety-five remain alive.

MME. RANEVSKAYA. How clever you are, Petya!

LOPAHIN (*ironically*). Awfully clever!

TROFIMOV. Mankind goes forward, developing its powers. Everything that is now unattainable for it will one day come within man's reach and be clear to him; only we must work, helping with all our might those who seek the truth. Here among us in Russia only the very few work as yet. The great majority of the intelligentsia, as far as I can see, seek nothing, do nothing, are totally unfit for work of any kind. They call themselves the intelligentsia, yet they are uncivil to their servants, treat the peasants like animals, are poor students, never read anything serious, do absolutely nothing at all, only talk about science, and have little appreciation of the arts. They are all solemn, have grim faces, they all philosophize and talk of weighty matters. And meanwhile the vast majority of us, ninety-nine out of a hundred, live like savages. At the least provocation—a punch in the jaw, and curses. They eat disgustingly, sleep in filth and stuffiness, bedbugs everywhere, stench and damp and moral slovenliness. And obviously, the only purpose of all our fine talk is to hoodwink ourselves and others. Show me where the public nurseries are that we've heard so much about, and the libraries. We read about them in novels, but in reality they don't exist, there is nothing but dirt, vulgarity, and Asiatic backwardness. I don't like very solemn faces, I'm afraid of them, I'm afraid of serious conversations. We'd do better to keep quiet for a while.

LOPAHIN. Do you know, I get up at five o'clock in the morning, and I work from morning till night; and I'm always handling money, my own and other people's, and I see what people around me are really like. You've only to start doing anything to see how few honest, decent people there are. Sometimes when I lie awake at night, I think: "Oh, Lord, thou hast given us immense forests, boundless fields, the widest horizons, and living in their midst, we ourselves ought really to be giants."

MME. RANEVSKAYA. Now you want giants! They're only good in fairy tales; otherwise they're frightening.

(YEPIHODOV *crosses the stage at the rear, playing the guitar*)

MME. RANEVSKAYA (*pensively*). There goes Yepihodov.

ANYA (*pensively*). There goes Yepihodov.

GAYEV. Ladies and gentlemen, the sun has set.

TROFIMOV. Yes.

GAYEV (*in a low voice, declaiming as it were*). Oh, Nature, wondrous Nature, you shine with eternal radiance, beautiful and indifferent! You, whom we call our mother, unite within yourself life and death! You animate and destroy!

VARYA (*pleadingly*). Uncle dear!

ANYA. Uncle, again!

TROFIMOV. You'd better bank the yellow ball in the side pocket.

GAYEV. I'm silent, I'm silent . . .

(*All sit plunged in thought. Stillness reigns. Only* FIRS's *muttering is audible. Suddenly a distant sound is heard, coming from the sky as it were, the sound of a snapping string, mournfully dying away*)

MME. RANEVSKAYA. What was that?

LOPAHIN. I don't know. Somewhere far away, in the pits, a bucket's broken loose; but somewhere very far away.

GAYEV. Or it might be some sort of bird, perhaps a heron.

TROFIMOV. Or an owl . . .

MME. RANEVSKAYA (*shudders*). It's weird, somehow. (*Pause*)

FIRS. Before the calamity the same thing happened—the owl screeched, and the samovar hummed all the time.

GAYEV. Before what calamity?

FIRS. Before the Freedom.[1] (*Pause*)

MME. RANEVSKAYA. Come, my friends, let's be going. It's getting dark. (*To* ANYA) You have tears in your eyes. What is it, my little one? (*Embraces her*)

ANYA. I don't know, mamma; it's nothing.

TROFIMOV. Somebody's coming.

(*A* Tramp *appears, wearing a shabby white cap and an overcoat. He is slightly drunk*)

TRAMP. Allow me to inquire, will this short-cut take me to the station?

GAYEV. It will. Just follow that road.

TRAMP. My heartfelt thanks. (*Coughing*) The weather is glorious. (*Recites*) "My brother, my suffering brother . . . Go down to the Volga! Whose groans . . . ?" (*To* VARYA) Mademoiselle, won't you spare 30 kopecks for a hungry Russian?

(VARYA, *frightened, cries out*)

LOPAHIN (*angrily*). Even panhandling has its proprieties.

MME. RANEVSKAYA (*scared*). Here, take this. (*Fumbles in her purse*) I haven't any silver . . . never mind, here's a gold piece.

TRAMP. My heartfelt thanks. (*Exits. Laughter*)

VARYA (*frightened*). I'm leaving, I'm leaving . . . Oh, mamma dear, at home the servants have nothing to eat, and you gave him a gold piece!

MME. RANEVSKAYA. What are you going to do with me? I'm such a fool. When we get home, I'll give you everything I have. Yermolay Alexeyevich, you'll lend me some more . . .

---

1. The emancipation of the serfs, proclaimed in 1861.

LOPAHIN. Yes, ma'am.

MME. RANEVSKAYA. Come, ladies and gentlemen, it's time to be going. Oh! Varya, we've settled all about your marriage. Congratulations!

VARYA (*through tears*). Really, mamma, that's not a joking matter.

LOPAHIN. "Aurelia, get thee to a nunnery, go . . ."

GAYEV. And do you know, my hands are trembling: I haven't played billiards in a long time.

LOPAHIN. "Aurelia, nymph, in your orisons, remember me!"

MME. RANEVSKAYA. Let's go, it's almost suppertime.

VARYA. He frightened me! My heart's pounding.

LOPAHIN. Let me remind you, ladies and gentlemen, on the 22nd of August the cherry orchard will be up for sale. Think about that! Think!

(*All except* TROFIMOV *and* ANYA *go out*)

ANYA (*laughs*). I'm grateful to that tramp, he frightened Varya and so we're alone.

TROFIMOV. Varya's afraid we'll fall in love with each other all of a sudden. She hasn't left us alone for days. Her narrow mind can't grasp that we're above love. To avoid the petty and illusory, everything that prevents us from being free and happy—that is the goal and meaning of our life. Forward! Do not fall behind, friends!

ANYA (*strikes her hands together*). How well you speak! (*Pause*) It's wonderful here today.

TROFIMOV. Yes, the weather's glorious.

ANYA. What have you done to me, Petya? Why don't I love the cherry orchard as I used to? I loved it so tenderly. It seemed to me there was no spot on earth lovelier than our orchard.

TROFIMOV. All Russia is our orchard. Our land is vast and beautiful, there are many wonderful places in it. (*Pause*) Think of it, Anya, your grandfather, your great-grandfather and all your ancestors were serf-owners, owners of living souls, and aren't human beings looking at you from every tree in the orchard, from every leaf, from every trunk? Don't you hear voices? Oh, it's terrifying! Your orchard is a fearful place, and when you pass through it in the evening or at night, the old bark on the trees gleams faintly, and the cherry trees seem to be dreaming of things that happened a hundred, two hundred years ago and to be tormented by painful visions. What is there to say? We're at least two hundred years behind, we've really achieved nothing yet, we have no definite attitude to the past, we only philosophize, complain of the blues, or drink vodka. It's all so clear: in order to live in the present, we should first redeem our past, finish with it, and we can expiate it only by suffering, only by extraordinary, unceasing labor. Realize that, Anya.

ANYA. The house in which we live has long ceased to be our own, and I will leave it, I give you my word.

TROFIMOV. If you have the keys, fling them into the well and go away. Be free as the wind.

ANYA (*in ecstasy*). How well you put that!

TROFIMOV. Believe me, Anya, believe me! I'm not yet thirty, I'm young, I'm still a student—but I've already suffered so much. In winter I'm hungry, sick, harassed, poor as a beggar, and where hasn't Fate driven me? Where haven't I been? And yet always, every moment of the day and night, my soul is filled with inexplicable premonitions. . . . I have a premonition of happiness, Anya. . . . I see it already!

ANYA (*pensively*). The moon is rising.

(YEPIHODOV *is heard playing the same mournful tune on the guitar. The moon rises. Somewhere near the poplars* VARYA *is looking for* ANYA *and calling* "Anya, where are you?")

TROFIMOV. Yes, the moon is rising. (*Pause*) There it is, happiness, it's approaching, it's coming nearer and nearer, I can already hear its footsteps. And if we don't see it, if we don't know it, what does it matter? Others will!

VARYA's *voice.* "Anya! Where are you?"

TROFIMOV. That Varya again! (*Angrily*) It's revolting!

ANYA. Never mind, let's go down to the river. It's lovely there.

TROFIMOV. Come on. (*They go*)

VARYA's *voice.* "Anya! Anya!"

Act III

A drawing-room separated by an arch from a ballroom. Evening. Chandelier burning. The Jewish band is heard playing in the anteroom. In the ballroom they are dancing the Grand Rond. PISHCHIK *is heard calling,* "Promenade à une paire." PISHCHIK *and* CHARLOTTA. TROFIMOV *and* MME. RANEVSKAYA, ANYA *and the* Post Office Clerk, VARYA *and the* Stationmaster, *and others, enter the drawing-room in couples.* DUNYASHA *is in the last couple.* VARYA *weeps quietly, wiping her tears as she dances. All parade through drawing-room.* PISHCHIK *calling* "Grand rond, balancez!" *and* "Les cavaliers à genoux et remerciez vos dames!" FIRS *wearing a dress-coat, brings in soda-water on a tray.* PISHCHIK *and* TROFIMOV *enter the drawing-room.*

PISHCHIK. I'm a full-blooded man; I've already had two strokes. Dancing's hard work for me; but as they say, "If you run with the pack, you can bark or not, but at least wag your tail." Still, I'm as strong as a horse. My late lamented father, who would have his joke, God rest his soul, used to say, talking about our origin, that the ancient line of the Simeonov-Pishchiks was descended from the very horse that Caligula had made a senator. (*Sits down*) But the trouble is, I have no money. A hungry dog believes in nothing but meat. (*Snores and wakes up at once*) It's the same with me—I can think of nothing but money.

TROFIMOV. You know, there *is* something equine about your figure.

PISHCHIK. Well, a horse is a fine animal—one can sell a horse.

(*Sound of billiards being played in an adjoining room.* VARYA *appears in the archway*)

TROFIMOV (*teasing her*). Madam Lopahina! Madam Lopahina!

VARYA (*angrily*). Mangy master!

TROFIMOV. Yes, I am a mangy master and I'm proud of it.

VARYA (*reflecting bitterly*). Here we've hired musicians, and what shall we pay them with? (*Exits*)

TROFIMOV (*to* PISHCHIK). If the energy you have spent during your lifetime looking for money to pay interest had gone into something else, in the end you could have turned the world upside down.

PISHCHIK. Nietzsche, the philosopher, the greatest, most famous of men, that colossal intellect, says in his works, that it is permissible to forge banknotes.

TROFIMOV. Have you read Nietzsche?

PISHCHIK. Well . . . Dashenka told me . . . And now I've got to the point where forging banknotes is about the only way out for me. . . . The day after tomorrow I have to pay 310 rubles—I already have 130 . . .(*Feels in his pockets. In alarm*) The money's gone! I've lost my money! (*Through tears*) Where's my money? (*Joyfully*) Here it is! Inside the lining . . . I'm all in a sweat . . .

(*Enter* MME. RANEVSKAYA *and* CHARLOTTA)

MME. RANEVSKAYA (*hums the "Lezginka"*). Why isn't Leonid back yet? What is he doing in town? (*To* DUNYASHA) Dunyasha, offer the musicians tea.

TROFIMOV. The auction hasn't taken place, most likely.

MME. RANEVSKAYA. It's the wrong time to have the band, and the wrong time to give a dance. Well, never mind. (*Sits down and hums softly*)

CHARLOTTA (*hands* PISHCHIK *a pack of cards*). Here is a pack of cards. Think of any card you like.

PISHCHIK. I've thought of one.

CHARLOTTA. Schuffle the pack now. That's right. Give it here, my dear Mr. Pishchik. *Ein, zwei, drei!* Now look for it—it's in your side pocket.

PISHCHIK (*taking the card out of his pocket*). The eight of spades! Perfectly right! Just imagine!

CHARLOTTA (*holding pack of cards in her hands. To* TROFIMOV). Quickly, name the top card.

TROFIMOV. Well, let's see—the queen of spades.

CHARLOTTA. Right! (*To* PISHCHIK) Now name the top card.

PISHCHIK. The ace of hearts.

CHARLOTTA. Right! (*Claps her hands and the pack of cards disappears*) Ah, what lovely weather it is today! (*A mysterious feminine voice which seems to come from under the floor, answers her*). "Oh, yes, it's magnificent weather, madam."

CHARLOTTA. You are my best ideal.

VOICE. "And I find you pleasing too, madam."

STATIONMASTER (*applauding*). The lady ventriloquist, bravo!

PISHCHIK (*amazed*). Just imagine! Enchanting Charlotta Ivanovna, I'm simply in love with you.

CHARLOTTA. In love? (*Shrugs her shoulders*) Are you capable of love? *Guter Mensch, aber schlechter Musikant!*

TROFIMOV (*claps* PISHCHIK *on the shoulder*). You old horse, you!

CHARLOTTA. Attention please! One more trick! (*Takes a plaid from a chair*) Here is a very good plaid; I want to sell it. (*Shaking it out*) Does anyone want to buy it?

PISHCHIK (*in amazement*). Just imagine!

CHARLOTTA. *Ein, zwei, drei!* (*Raises the plaid quickly, behind it stands* ANYA. *She curtsies, runs to her mother, embraces her, and runs back into the ballroom, amidst general enthusiasm*)

MME. RANEVSKAYA (*applauds*). Bravo! Bravo!

CHARLOTTA. Now again! *Ein, zwei, drei!* (*Lifts the plaid; behind it stands* VARYA *bowing*)

PISHCHIK (*running after her*). The rascal! What a woman, what a woman! (*Exits*)

MME. RANEVSKAYA. And Leonid still isn't here. What is he doing in town so long? I don't understand. It must be all over by now. Either the estate has been sold, or the auction hasn't taken place. Why keep us in suspense so long?

VARYA (*trying to console her*). Uncle's bought it, I feel sure of that.

TROFIMOV (*mockingly*). Oh, yes!

VARYA. Great-aunt sent him an authorization to buy it in her name, and to transfer the debt. She's doing it for Anya's sake. And I'm sure that God will help us, and uncle will buy it.

MME. RANEVSKAYA. Great-aunt sent fifteen thousand to buy the estate in her name, she doesn't trust us, but that's not even enough to pay the interest. (*Covers her face with her hands*) Today my fate will be decided, my fate—

TROFIMOV (*teasing* VARYA). Madam Lopahina!

VARYA (*angrily*). Perpetual student! Twice already you've been expelled from the university.

MME. RANEVSKAYA. Why are you so cross, Varya? He's teasing you about Lopahin. Well, what of it? If you want to marry Lopahin, go ahead. He's a good man, and interesting; if you don't want to, don't. Nobody's compelling you, my pet!

VARYA. Frankly, mamma dear, I take this thing seriously; he's a good man and I like him.

MME. RANEVSKAYA. All right then, marry him. I don't know what you're waiting for.

VARYA. But, mamma, I can't propose to him myself. For the last two years everyone's been talking to me about him—talking. But he either keeps silent, or else cracks jokes. I understand; he's growing rich, he's absorbed in business—he has no time for me. If I had money, even a little, say, 100 rubles, I'd throw everything up and go far away—I'd go into a nunnery.

TROFIMOV. What a blessing . . .

VARYA. A student ought to be intelligent. (*Softly, with tears in her voice*) How homely you've grown, Petya! How old you look! (*To* MME. RANEVSKAYA, *with dry eyes*) But I can't live without work, mamma dear; I must keep busy every minute.

(*Enter* YASHA)

YASHA (*hardly restraining his laughter*). Yepihodov has broken a billiard cue. (*Exits*)

VARYA. Why is Yepihodov here? Who allowed him to play billiards? I don't understand these people! (*Exits*)

MME. RANEVSKAYA. Don't tease her, Petya. She's unhappy enough without that.

TROFIMOV. She bustles so—and meddles in other people's business. All summer long she's given Anya and me no peace. She's afraid of a love-affair between us. What business is it of hers? Besides, I've given no grounds for it, and I'm far from such vulgarity. We are above love.

MME. RANEVSKAYA. And I suppose I'm beneath love? (*Anxiously*) What can be keeping Leonid? If I only knew whether the estate has been sold or not. Such a calamity seems so incredible to me that I don't know what to think— I feel lost. . . . I could scream. . . . I could do something stupid. . . . Save me, Petya, tell me something. talk to me!

TROFIMOV. Whether the estate is sold today or not, isn't it all one? That's all done with long ago—there's no turning back, the path is overgrown. Calm yourself, my dear. You mustn't deceive yourself. For once in your life you must face the truth.

MME. RANEVSKAYA. What truth? You can see the truth, you can tell it from falsehood, but I seem to have lost my eyesight, I see nothing. You settle every great problem so boldly, but tell me, my dear boy, isn't it because you're young, because you don't yet know what one of your problems means in terms of suffering? You look ahead fearlessly, but isn't it because you don't see and don't expect anything dreadful, because life is still hidden from your young eyes? You're bolder, more honest, more profound than we are, but think hard, show just a bit of magnanimity, spare me. After all, I was born here, my father and mother lived here, and my grandfather; I love this house. Without the cherry orchard, my life has no meaning for me, and if it really must be sold, then sell me with the orchard. (*Embraces* TROFIMOV, *kisses him on the forehead*) My son was drowned here. (*Weeps*) Pity me, you good, kind fellow!

TROFIMOV. You know, I feel for you with all my heart.

MME. RANEVSKAYA. But that should have been said differently, so differently! (*Takes out her handkerchief—a telegram falls on the floor*) My heart is so heavy today—you can't imagine! The noise here upsets me—my inmost being trembles at every sound—I'm shaking all over. But I can't go into my own room; I'm afraid to be alone. Don't condemn me, Petya. . . . I love you as though you were one of us, I would gladly let you marry Anya—I swear I would—only, my dear boy, you must study—you must take your degree— you do nothing, you let yourself be tossed by Fate from place to place—it's so strange. It's true, isn't it? And you should do something about your beard, to make it grow somehow! (*Laughs*) You're so funny!

TROFIMOV (*picks up the telegram*). I've no wish to be a dandy.

MME. RANEVSKAYA. That's a telegram from Paris. I get one every day. One yesterday and one today. That savage is ill again—he's in trouble again. He begs forgiveness, implores me to go to him, and really I ought to go to Paris to be near him. Your face is stern, Pétya; but what is there to do, my dear boy? What am I to do? He's ill, he's alone and unhappy, and who is to look after him, who is to keep him from doing the wrong thing, who is to give him his medicine on time? And why hide it or keep still about it—I love him! That's clear. I love him, love him! He's a millstone round my neck, he'll drag me to the bottom, but I love that stone, I can't live without it. (*Presses* TROFIMOV's *hand*) Don't think badly of me, Petya, and don't say anything, don't say . . .

TROFIMOV (*through tears*). Forgive me my frankness in heaven's name; but, you know, he robbed you!

MME. RANEVSKAYA. No, no, no, you mustn't say such things! (*Covers her ears*)

TROFIMOV. But he's a scoundrel! You're the only one who doesn't know it. He's a petty scoundrel—a nonentity!

MME. RANEVSKAYA (*controlling her anger*). You are twenty-six or twenty-seven years old, but you're still a schoolboy.

TROFIMOV. That may be.

MME. RANEVSKAYA. You should be a man at your age. You should understand people who love—and ought to be in love yourself. You ought to fall in love! (*Angrily*) Yes, yes! And it's not purity in you, it's prudishness, you're simply a queer fish, a comical freak!

TROFIMOV (*horrified*). What is she saying?

MME. RANEVSKAYA. "I am above love!" You're not above love, but simply, as our Firs says, you're an addlehead. At your age not to have a mistress!

TROFIMOV (*horrified*). This is frightful! What is she saying! (*Goes rapidly into the ballroom, clutching his head*) It's frightful—I can't stand it, I won't stay! (*Exits, but returns at once*) All is over between us! (*Exits into anteroom*)

MME. RANEVSKAYA (*shouts after him*). Petya! Wait! You absurd fellow, I was joking. Petya!

(*Sound of somebody running quickly downstairs and suddenly falling down with a crash.* ANYA *and* VARYA *scream. Sound of laughter a moment later*)

MME. RANEVSKAYA. What's happened?

(ANYA *runs in*)

ANYA (*laughing*). Petya's fallen downstairs! (*Runs out*)

MME. RANEVSKAYA. What a queer bird that Petya is!

(Stationmaster, *standing in the middle of the ballroom, recites Alexey Tolstoy's "Magdalene," to which all listen, but after a few lines, the sound of a waltz is heard from the anteroom and the reading breaks off. All dance.* TROFIMOV, ANYA, VARYA, *and* MME. RANEVSKAYA *enter from the anteroom*)

MME. RANEVSKAYA. Petya, you pure soul, please forgive me. . . . Let's dance.

(*Dances with* PETYA. ANYA *and* VARYA *dance.* FIRS *enters, puts his stick down by the side door.* YASHA *enters from the drawing-room and watches the dancers*)

YASHA. Well, grandfather?

FIRS. I'm not feeling well. In the old days it was generals, barons, and admirals that were dancing at our balls, and now we have to send for the Post Office Clerk and the Stationmaster, and even they aren't too glad to come. I feel kind of shaky. The old master that's gone, their grandfather, dosed everyone with sealing-wax, whatever ailed 'em. I've been taking sealing-wax every day for twenty years or more. Perhaps that's what's kept me alive.

YASHA. I'm fed up with you, grandpop. (*Yawns*) It's time you croaked.

FIRS. Oh, you addlehead! (*Mumbles*)

(TROFIMOV *and* MME. RANEVSKAYA *dance from the ballroom into the drawing-room*)

MME. RANEVSKAYA. *Merci.* I'll sit down a while. (*Sits down*) I'm tired.

(*Enter* ANYA)

ANYA (*excitedly*). There was a man in the kitchen just now who said the cherry orchard was sold today.

MME. RANEVSKAYA. Sold to whom?

ANYA. He didn't say. He's gone. (*Dances off with* TROFIMOV)

YASHA. It was some old man gabbing, a stranger.

FIRS. And Leonid Andreyevich isn't back yet, he hasn't come. And he's wearing his lightweight between-season overcoat; like enough, he'll catch cold. Ah, when they're young they're green.

MME. RANEVSKAYA. This is killing me. Go, Yasha, find out to whom it has been sold.

YASHA. But the old man left long ago. (*Laughs*)

MME. RANEVSKAYA. What are you laughing at? What are you pleased about?

YASHA. That Yepihodov is such a funny one. A funny fellow, Two-and-Twenty Troubles!

MME. RANEVSKAYA. Firs, if the estate is sold, where will you go?

FIRS. I'll go where you tell me.

MME. RANEVSKAYA. Why do you look like that? Are you ill? You ought to go to bed.

FIRS. Yes! (*With a snigger*) Me go to bed, and who's to hand things round? Who's to see to things? I'm the only one in the whole house.

YASHA (*to* MME. RANEVSKAYA). Lubov Andreyevna, allow me to ask a favor of you, be so kind! If you go back to Paris, take me with you, I beg you. It's positively impossible for me to stay here. (*Looking around; sotto voce*) What's the use of talking? You see for yourself, it's an uncivilized country, the people have no morals, and then the boredom! The food in the kitchen's revolting, and besides there's this Firs wanders about mumbling all sorts of inappropriate words. Take me with you, be so kind!

(*Enter* PISHCHIK)

PISHCHIK. May I have the pleasure of a waltz with you, charming lady? (MME. RANEVSKAYA *accepts*) All the same, enchanting lady, you must let me have 180 rubles. . . . You must let me have (*dancing*) just one hundred and eighty rubles. (*They pass into the ballroom*)

YASHA (*hums softly*). "Oh, wilt thou understand the tumult in my soul?"

(*In the ballroom a figure in a gray top hat and checked trousers is jumping about and waving its arms; shouts:* "Bravo, Charlotta Ivanovna!")

DUNYASHA (*stopping to powder her face; to* FIRS). The young miss has ordered me to dance. There are so many gentlemen and not enough ladies. But dancing makes me dizzy, my heart begins to beat fast, Firs Nikolayevich. The Post Office Clerk said something to me just now that quite took my breath away. (*Music stops*)

FIRS. What did he say?

DUNYASHA. "You're like a flower," he said.

YASHA (*yawns*). What ignorance. (*Exits*)

DUNYASHA. "Like a flower!" I'm such a delicate girl. I simply adore pretty speeches.

FIRS. You'll come to a bad end.

(*Enter* YEPIHODOV)

YEPIHODOV (*to* DUNYASHA). You have no wish to see me, Avdotya Fyodorovna . . . as though I was some sort of insect. (*Sighs*) Ah, life!

DUNYASHA. What is it you want?

YEPIHODOV. Indubitably you may be right. (*Sighs*) But of course, if one looks at it from the point of view, if I may be allowed to say so, and apologizing for my frankness, you have completely reduced me to a state of mind. I know my fate. Every day some calamity befalls me, and I grew used to it long ago, so that I look upon my fate with a smile. You gave me your word, and though I—

DUNYASHA. Let's talk about it later, please. But just now leave me alone, I am daydreaming. (*Plays with a fan*)

YEPIHODOV. A misfortune befalls me every day; and if I may be allowed to say so, I merely smile, I even laugh.

(*Enter* VARYA)

VARYA (*to* YEPIHODOV). Are you still here? What an impertinent fellow you are really! Run along, Dunyasha. (*To* YEPIHODOV) Either you're playing billiards and breaking a cue, or you're wandering about the drawing-room as though you were a guest.

YEPIHODOV. You cannot, permit me to remark, penalize me.

VARYA. I'm not penalizing you; I'm just telling you. You merely wander from place to place, and don't do your work. We keep you as a clerk, but Heaven knows what for.

YEPIHODOV (*offended*). Whether I work or whether I walk, whether I eat or whether I play billiards, is a matter to be discussed only by persons of understanding and of mature years.

VARYA (*enraged*). You dare say that to me—you dare? You mean to say I've no understanding? Get out of here at once! This minute!

YEPIHODOV (*scared*). I beg you to express yourself delicately.

VARYA (*beside herself*). Clear out this minute! Out with you!

(YEPIHODOV *goes towards the door,* VARYA *following*)

VARYA. Two-and-Twenty Troubles! Get out—don't let me set eyes on you!

(*Exit* YEPIHODOV. *His voice is heard behind the door:* "I shall lodge a complaint against you!")

VARYA. Oh, you're coming back? (*She seizes the stick left near door by* FIRS) Well, come then . . . come . . . I'll show you . . . Ah, you're coming? You're coming? . . . Come . . . (*Swings the stick just as* LOPAHIN *enters*)

LOPAHIN. Thank you kindly.

VARYA (*angrily and mockingly*). I'm sorry.

LOPAHIN. It's nothing. Thank you kindly for your charming reception.

VARYA. Don't mention it. (*Walks away, looks back and asks softly*) I didn't hurt you, did I?

LOPAHIN. Oh, no, not at all. I shall have a large bump, though.

(*Voices from the ballroom:* "Lopahin is here! Lopahin!")

(*Enter* PISHCHIK)

PISHCHIK. My eyes do see, my ears do hear! (*Kisses* LOPAHIN)

LOPAHIN. You smell of cognac, my dear friends. And we've been celebrating here, too.

(*Enter* MME. RANEVSKAYA)

MME. RANEVSKAYA. Is that you, Yermolay Alexeyevich? What kept you so long? Where's Leonid?

LOPAHIN. Leonid Andreyevich arrived with me. He's coming.

MME. RANEVSKAYA. Well, what happened? Did the sale take place? Speak!

LOPAHIN (*embarrassed, fearful of revealing his joy*). The sale was over at four o'clock. We missed the train—had to wait till half past nine. (*Sighing heavily*) Ugh. I'm a little dizzy.

(*Enter* GAYEV. *In his right hand he holds parcels, with his left he is wiping away his tears*)

MME. RANEVSKAYA. Well, Leonid? What news? (*Impatiently, through tears*) Be quick, for God's sake!

GAYEV (*not answering, simply waves his hand. Weeping, to* FIRS). Here, take these; anchovies, Kerch herrings . . . I haven't eaten all day. What I've been through! (*The click of billiard balls comes through the open door of the billiard room and* YASHA's *voice is heard:* "Seven and eighteen!" GAYEV's *expression changes, he no longer weeps*) I'm terribly tired. Firs, help me change. (*Exits, followed by* FIRS)

PISHCHIK. How about the sale? Tell us what happened.

MME. RANEVSKAYA. Is the cherry orchard sold?

LOPAHIN. Sold.

MME. RANEVSKAYA. Who bought it?

LOPAHIN. I bought it.

(*Pause.* MME. RANEVSKAYA *is overcome. She would fall to the floor, were it not for the chair and table near which she stands.* VARYA *takes the keys from her belt, flings them on the floor in the middle of the drawing-room and goes out*)

LOPAHIN. I bought it. Wait a bit, ladies and gentlemen, please, my head is swimming, I can't talk. (*Laughs*) We got to the auction and Deriganov was there already. Leonid Andreyevich had only 15,000 and straight off Deriganov bid 30,000 over and above the mortgage. I saw how the land lay, got into the fight, bid 40,000. He bid 45,000. I bid fifty-five. He kept adding five thousands, I ten. Well . . . it came to an end. I bid ninety above the mortgage and the estate was knocked down to me. Now the cherry orchard's mine! Mine! (*Laughs uproariously*) Lord! God in Heaven! The cherry orchard's mine! Tell me that I'm drunk—out of my mind—that it's all a dream. (*Stamps his feet*) Don't laugh at me! If my father and my grandfather could rise from their graves and see all that has happened—how their Yermolay, who used to be flogged, their half-literate Yermolay, who used to run about barefoot in winter, how that very Yermolay has bought the most magnificent estate in the world. I bought the estate where my father and grandfather were slaves, where they weren't even allowed to enter the kitchen. I'm asleep— it's only a dream—I only imagine it. . . . It's the fruit of your imagination, wrapped in the darkness of the unknown! (*Picks up the keys, smiling genially*) She threw down the keys, wants to show she's no longer mistress here. (*Jingles keys*) Well, no matter. (*The band is heard tuning up*) Hey, musicians! Strike up! I want to hear you! Come, everybody, and see how Yermolay Lopahin will lay the ax to the cherry orchard and how the trees will fall to the ground. We will build summer cottages there, and our grand-sons and great-grandsons will see a new life here. Music! Strike up!

(*The band starts to play.* MME. RANEVSKAYA *has sunk into a chair and is weeping bitterly*)

LOPAHIN (*reproachfully*). Why, why didn't you listen to me? My dear friend, my poor friend, you can't bring it back now. (*Tearfully*) Oh, if only this were over quickly! Oh, if only our wretched, disordered life were changed!

PISHCHIK (*takes him by the arm; sotto voce*). She's crying. Let's go into the ballroom. Let her be alone. Come. (*Takes his arm and leads him into the ballroom*)

LOPAHIN. What's the matter? Musicians, play so I can hear you! Let me have things the way I want them. (*Ironically*) Here comes the new master, the owner of the cherry orchard. (*Accidentally he trips over a little table, almost upsetting the candelabra*) I can pay for everything.

(*Exits with* PISHCHIK. MME. RANEVSKAYA, *alone, sits huddled up, weeping bitterly. Music plays softly. Enter* ANYA *and* TROFIMOV *quickly.* ANYA *goes to her mother and falls on her knees before her.* TROFIMOV *stands in the doorway*)

ANYA. Mamma, mamma, you're crying! Dear, kind, good mamma, my precious, I love you, I bless you! The cherry orchard is sold, it's gone, that's true, quite true. But don't cry, mamma, life is still before you, you still have your kind, pure heart. Let us go, let us go away from here, darling. We will plant a new orchard, even more luxuriant than this one. You will see it, you will understand, and like the sun at evening, joy—deep, tranquil joy— will sink into your soul, and you will smile, mamma. Come, darling, let us go.

Act IV

Scene as in Act I. No window curtains or pictures, only a little furniture, piled up in a corner, as if for sale. A sense of emptiness. Near the outer door and at the back, suitcases, bundles, etc., are piled up. A door is open on the left and the voices of VARYA *and* ANYA *are heard.* LOPAHIN *stands waiting.* YASHA *holds a tray with glasses full of champagne.* YEPIHODOV *in the anteroom is tying up a box. Behind the scene a hum of voices: peasants have come to say good-by. Voice of* GAYEV: *"Thanks, brothers, thank you."*

YASHA. The country folk have come to say good-by. In my opinion, Yermolay Alexeyevich, they are kindly souls, but there's nothing in their heads. (*The hum dies away. Enter* MME. RANEVSKAYA *and* GAYEV. *She is not crying, but is pale, her face twitches and she cannot speak*)

GAYEV. You gave them your purse, Luba. That won't do! That won't do!

MME. RANEVSKAYA. I couldn't help it! I couldn't! (*They go out*)

LOPAHIN (*calls after them*). Please, I beg you, have a glass at parting. I didn't think of bringing any champagne from town and at the station I could find only one bottle. Please, won't you? (*Pause*) What's the matter, ladies and gentlemen, don't you want any? (*Moves away from the door*) If I'd known, I wouldn't have bought it. Well, then I won't drink any, either. (YASHA *carefully sets the tray down on a chair*) At least you have a glass, Yasha.

YASHA. Here's to the travelers! And good luck to those that stay! (*Drinks*) This champagne isn't the real stuff, I can assure you.

LOPAHIN. Eight rubles a bottle. (*Pause*) It's devilishly cold here.

YASHA. They didn't light the stoves today—it wasn't worth it, since we're leaving. (*Laughs*)

LOPAHIN. Why are you laughing?

YASHA. It's just that I'm pleased.

LOPAHIN. It's October, yet it's as still and sunny as though it were summer. Good weather for building. (*Looks at his watch, and speaks off*) Bear in mind, ladies and gentlemen, the train goes in forty-seven minutes, so you ought to start for the station in twenty minutes. Better hurry up!

(*Enter* TROFIMOV *wearing an overcoat*)

TROFIMOV. I think it's time to start. The carriages are at the door. The devil only knows what's become of my rubbers; they've disappeared. (*Calling off*) Anya! My rubbers are gone. I can't find them.

LOPAHIN. I've got to go to Kharkov. I'll take the same train you do. I'll spend the winter in Kharkov. I've been hanging round here with you, till I'm worn out with loafing. I can't live without work—I don't know what to do with my hands, they dangle as if they didn't belong to me.

TROFIMOV. Well, we'll soon be gone, then you can go on with your useful labors again.

LOPAHIN. Have a glass.

TROFIMOV. No, I won't.

LOPAHIN. So you're going to Moscow now?

TROFIMOV. Yes, I'll see them into town, and tomorrow I'll go on to Moscow.

LOPAHIN. Well, I'll wager the professors aren't giving any lectures, they're waiting for you to come.

TROFIMOV. That's none of your business.

LOPAHIN. Just how many years have you been at the university?

TROFIMOV. Can't you think of something new? Your joke's stale and flat. (*Looking for his rubbers*) We'll probably never see each other again, so allow me to give you a piece of advice at parting: don't wave your hands about! Get out of the habit. And another thing: building bungalows, figuring that summer residents will eventually become small farmers, figuring like that is just another form of waving your hands about. . . . Never mind, I love you anyway; you have fine, delicate fingers, like an artist; you have a fine, delicate soul.

LOPAHIN (*embracing him*). Good-by, my dear fellow. Thank you for everything. Let me give you some money for the journey, if you need it.

TROFIMOV. What for? I don't need it.

LOPAHIN. But you haven't any.

TROFIMOV. Yes, I have, thank you. I got some money for a translation—here it is in my pocket. (*Anxiously*) But where are my rubbers?

VARYA (*from the next room*). Here! Take the nasty things. (*Flings a pair of rubbers onto the stage*)

TROFIMOV. What are you so cross about, Varya? Hm . . . and these are not my rubbers.

LOPAHIN. I sowed three thousand acres of poppies in the spring, and now I've made 40.000 on them, clear profit; and when my poppies were in bloom, what a picture it was! So, as I say, I made 40,000; and I am offering you a loan because I can afford it. Why turn up your nose at it? I'm a peasant—I speak bluntly.

TROFIMOV. Your father was a peasant, mine was a druggist—that proves absolutely nothing whatever. (LOPAHIN *takes out his wallet*) Don't, put that away! If you were to offer me two hundred thousand I wouldn't take it. I'm a free man. And everything that all of you, rich and poor alike, value so highly and hold so dear, hasn't the slightest power over me. It's like so much fluff floating in the air. I can get on without you, I can pass you by, I'm strong and proud. Mankind is moving towards the highest truth, towards the highest happiness possible on earth, and I am in the front ranks.

LOPAHIN. Will you get there?

TROFIMOV. I will. (*Pause*) I will get there, or I will show others the way to get there.

(*The sound of axes chopping down trees is heard in the distance*)

LOPAHIN. Well, good-by, my dear fellow. It's time to leave. We turn up our noses at one another, but life goes on just the same. When I'm working hard, without resting, my mind is easier, and it seems to me that I too know why I exist. But how many people are there in Russia, brother, who exist nobody knows why? Well, it doesn't matter. That's not what makes the wheels go round. They say Leonid Andreyevich has taken a position in the bank, 6,000 rubles a year. Only, of course, he won't stick to it, he's too lazy. . . .

ANYA (*in the doorway*). Mamma begs you not to start cutting down the cherry-trees until she's gone.

TROFIMOV. Really, you should have more tact! (*Exits*)

LOPAHIN. Right away—right away! Those men . . . (*Exits*)

ANYA. Has Firs been taken to the hospital?

YASHA. I told them this morning. They must have taken him.

ANYA (*to* YEPIHODOV *who crosses the room*). Yepihodov, please find out if Firs has been taken to the hospital.

YASHA (*offended*). I told Yegor this morning. Why ask a dozen times?

YEPIHODOV. The aged Firs, in my definitive opinion, is beyond mending. It's time he was gathered to his fathers. And I can only envy him. (*Puts a suitcase down on a hat-box and crushes it*) There now, of course. I knew it! (*Exits*)

YASHA (*mockingly*). Two-and-Twenty Troubles!

VARYA (*through the door*). Has Firs been taken to the hospital?

ANYA. Yes.

VARYA. Then why wasn't the note for the doctor taken too?

ANYA. Oh! Then someone must take it to him. (*Exits*)

VARYA (*from adjoining room*). Where's Yasha? Tell him his mother's come and wants to say good-by.

YASHA (*waves his hand*). She tries my patience.

(DUNYASHA *has been occupied with the luggage. Seeing* YASHA *alone, she goes up to him*)

DUNYASHA. You might just give me one little look, Yasha. You're going away. . . . You're leaving me . . . (*Weeps and throws herself on his neck*)

YASHA. What's there to cry about? (*Drinks champagne*) In six days I shall be in Paris again. Tomorrow we get into an express train and off we go, that's the last you'll see of us. . . . I can scarcely believe it. *Vive la France!* It don't suit me here, I just can't live here. That's all there is to it. I'm fed up with the ignorance here, I've had enough of it. (*Drinks champagne*) What's there to cry about? Behave yourself properly, and you'll have no cause to cry.

DUNYASHA (*powders her face, looking in pocket mirror*). Do send me a letter from Paris. You know I loved you, Yasha, how I loved you! I'm a delicate creature, Yasha.

YASHA. Somebody's coming! (*Busies himself with the luggage; hums softly*)

(*Enter* MME. RANEVSKAYA, GAYEV, ANYA, *and* CHARLOTTA)

GAYEV. We ought to be leaving. We haven't much time. (*Looks at* YASHA) Who smells of herring?

MME. RANEVSKAYA. In about ten minutes we should be getting into the carriages. (*Looks around the room*) Good-by, dear old home, good-by, grandfather. Winter will pass, spring will come, you will no longer be here, they will have torn you down. How much these walls have seen! (*Kisses* ANYA *warmly*) My treasure, how radiant you look! Your eyes are sparkling like diamonds. Are you glad? Very?

ANYA (*gaily*). Very glad. A new life is beginning, mamma.

GAYEV. Well, really, everything is all right now. Before the cherry orchard was sold, we all fretted and suffered; but afterwards, when the question was settled finally and irrevocably, we all calmed down, and even felt quite cheerful. I'm a bank employee now, a financier. The yellow ball in the side pocket! And anyhow, you are looking better Luba, there's no doubt of that.

MME. RANEVSKAYA. Yes, my nerves are better, that's true. (*She is handed her hat and coat*) I sleep well. Carry out my things, Yasha. It's time. (*To* ANYA) We shall soon see each other again, my little girl. I'm going to Paris, I'll live there on the money your great-aunt sent us to buy the estate with— long live Auntie! But that money won't last long.

ANYA. You'll come back soon, soon, mamma, won't you? Meanwhile I'll study, I'll pass my high school examination, and then I'll go to work and help you. We'll read all kinds of books together, mamma, won't we? (*Kisses her mother's hands*) We'll read in the autumn evenings, we'll read lots of books, and a new wonderful world will open up before us. (*Falls into a revery*) Mamma, do come back.

MME. RANEVSKAYA. I will come back, my precious. (*Embraces her daughter. Enter* LOPAHIN *and* CHARLOTTA *who is humming softly*)

GAYEV. Charlotta's happy: she's singing.

CHARLOTTA (*picks up a bundle and holds it like a baby in swaddling-clothes*). Bye, baby, bye. (*A baby is heard crying* "Wah! Wah!") Hush, hush, my pet, my little one. "Wah! Wah!" I'm so sorry for you! (*Throws the bundle down*) You will find me a position, won't you? I can't go on like this.

LOPAHIN. We'll find one for you, Charlotta Ivanovna, don't worry.

GAYEV. Everyone's leaving us. Varya's going away. We've suddenly become of no use.

CHARLOTTA. There's no place for me to live in town, I must go away. (*Hums*) (*Enter* PISHCHIK)

LOPAHIN. There's nature's masterpiece!

PISHCHIK (*gasping*). Oh . . . let me get my breath . . . I'm in agony. . . . Esteemed friends . . . Give me a drink of water. . . .

GAYEV. Wants some money, I suppose. No, thank you . . . I'll keep out of harm's way. (*Exits*)

PISHCHIK. It's a long while since I've been to see you, most charming lady. (*To* LOPAHIN) So you are here . . . glad to see you, you intellectual giant . . . There . . . (*Gives* LOPAHIN *money*) Here's 400 rubles, and I still owe you 840.

LOPAHIN (*shrugging his shoulders in bewilderment*). I must be dreaming . . . Where did you get it?

PISHCHIK. Wait a minute . . . It's hot . . . A most extraordinary event! Some Englishmen came to my place and found some sort of white clay on my land . . . (*To* MME. RANEVSKAYA) And 400 for you . . . most lovely . . . most wonderful . . . (*Hands her the money*) The rest later. (*Drinks water*) A young man in the train was telling me just now that a great philosopher recommends jumping off roofs. "Jump!" says he; "that's the long and the short of it!" (*In amazement*) Just imagine! Some more water!

LOPAHIN. What Englishmen?

PISHCHIK. I leased them the tract with the clay on it for twenty-four years. . . . And now, forgive me, I can't stay. . . . I must be dashing on. . . . I'm going over to Znoikov . . . to Kardamanov . . . I owe them all money . . . (*Drinks water*) Good-by, everybody . . . I'll look in on Thursday . . .

MME. RANEVSKAYA. We're just moving into town; and tomorrow I go abroad.

PISHCHIK (*upset*). What? Why into town? That's why the furniture is like that . . . and the suitcases . . . Well, never mind! (*Through tears*) Never mind . . . Men of colossal intellect, these Englishmen . . . Never mind . . . Be happy. God will come to your help . . . Never mind . . . Everything in this world comes to an end. (*Kisses* MME. RANEVSKAYA's *hand*) If the rumor reaches you that it's all up with me, remember this old . . . horse, and say: Once there lived a certain . . . Simeonov-Pishchik . . . the kingdom of Heaven be his . . . Glorious weather! . . . Yes . . .(*Exits, in great confusion, but at once returns and says in the doorway*) My daughter Dashenka sends her regards. (*Exit*)

MME. RANEVSKAYA. Now we can go. I leave with two cares weighing on me. The first is poor old Firs. (*Glancing at her watch*) We still have about five minutes.

ANYA. Mamma, Firs has already been taken to the hospital. Yasha sent him there this morning.

MME. RANEVSKAYA. My other worry is Varya. She's used to getting up early and working; and now, with no work to do, she is like a fish out of water. She has grown thin and pale, and keeps crying, poor soul. (*Pause*) You know this very well, Yermolay Alexeyevich; I dreamed of seeing her married to you, and it looked as though that's how it would be. (*Whispers to* ANYA, *who nods to* CHARLOTTA *and both go out*) She loves you. You find her attractive. I don't know, I don't know why it is you seem to avoid each other; I can't understand it.

LOPAHIN. To tell you the truth, I don't understand it myself. It's all a puzzle. If there's still time, I'm ready now, at once. Let's settle it straight off, and have done with it! Without you, I feel I'll never be able to propose.

MME. RANEVSKAYA. That's splendid. After all, it will only take a minute. I'll call her at once. . . .

LOPAHIN. And luckily, here's champagne too. (*Looks at the glasses*) Empty! Somebody's drunk it all. (YASHA *coughs*) That's what you might call guzzling . . .

MME. RANEVSKAYA (*animatedly*). Excellent! We'll go and leave you alone. Yasha, *allez!* I'll call her. (*At the door*) Varya, leave everything and come here. Come! (*Exits with* YASHA)

LOPAHIN (*looking at his watch*). Yes . . . (*Pause behind the door, smothered laughter and whispering; at last, enter* VARYA)

VARYA (*looking over the luggage in leisurely fashion*). Strange, I can't find it . . .

LOPAHIN. What are you looking for?

VARYA. Packed it myself, and I don't remember . . . (*Pause*)

LOPAHIN. Where are you going now, Varya?

VARYA. I? To the Ragulins'. I've arranged to take charge there—as housekeeper, if you like.

LOPAHIN. At Yashnevo? About fifty miles from here. (*Pause*) Well, life in this house is ended!

VARYA (*examining luggage*). Where is it? Perhaps I put it in the chest. Yes, life in this house is ended . . . There will be no more of it.

LOPAHIN. And I'm just off to Kharkov—by this next train. I've a lot to do there. I'm leaving Yepihodov here . . . I've taken him on.

VARYA. Oh!

LOPAHIN. Last year at this time it was snowing, if you remember, but now it's sunny and there's no wind. It's cold, though . . . It must be three below.

VARYA. I didn't look. (*Pause*) And besides, our thermometer's broken. (*Pause. Voice from the yard:* "Yermolay Alexeyevich!")

LOPAHIN (*as if he had been waiting for the call*). This minute!

(*Exits quickly.* VARYA *sits on the floor and sobs quietly, her head on a bundle of clothes. Enter* MME. RANEVSKAYA *cautiously*)

MME. RANEVSKAYA. Well? (*Pause*) We must be going.

VARYA (*wiping her eyes*). Yes, it's time, mamma dear. I'll be able to get to the Ragulins' today, if only we don't miss the train.

MME. RANEVSKAYA (*at the door*). Anya, put your things on.

(*Enter* ANYA, GAYEV, CHARLOTTA. GAYEV *wears a heavy overcoat with a hood. Enter servants and coachmen.* YEPIHODOV *bustles about the luggage*)

MME. RANEVSKAYA. Now we can start on our journey.

ANYA (*joyfully*). On our journey!

GAYEV. My friends, my dear, cherished friends, leaving this house forever, can I be silent? Can I at leave-taking refrain from giving utterance to those emotions that now fill my being?

ANYA (*imploringly*). Uncle!

VARYA. Uncle, uncle dear, don't.

GAYEV (*forlornly*). I'll bank the yellow in the side pocket . . . I'll be silent . . .

(*Enter* TROFIMOV, *then* LOPAHIN)

TROFIMOV. Well, ladies and gentlemen, it's time to leave.

LOPAHIN. Yepihodov, my coat.

MME. RANEVSKAYA. I'll sit down just a minute. It seems as though I'd never before seen what the walls of this house were like, the ceilings, and now I look at them hungrily, with such tender affection.

GAYEV. I remember when I was six years old sitting on that window sill on Whitsunday, watching my father going to church.

MME. RANEVSKAYA. Has everything been taken?

LOPAHIN. I think so. (*Putting on his overcoat*) Yepihodov, see that everything's in order.

YEPIHODOV (*in a husky voice*). You needn't worry, Yermolay Alexeyevich.

LOPAHIN. What's the matter with your voice?

YEPIHODOV. I just had a drink of water. I must have swallowed something.

YASHA (*contemptuously*). What ignorance!

MME. RANEVSKAYA. When we're gone, not a soul will be left here.

LOPAHIN. Until the spring.

(VARYA *pulls an umbrella out of a bundle, as though about to hit someone with it.* LOPAHIN *pretends to be frightened*)

VARYA. Come, come, I had no such idea!

TROFIMOV. Ladies and gentlemen, let's get into the carriages—it's time. The train will be in directly.

VARYA. Petya, there they are, your rubbers, by that trunk. (*Tearfully*) And what dirty old things they are!

TROFIMOV (*puts on rubbers*). Let's go, ladies and gentlemen.

GAYEV (*greatly upset, afraid of breaking down*). The train . . . the station . . . Three cushions in the side pocket, I'll bank this one in the corner . . .

MME. RANEVSKAYA. Let's go.

LOPAHIN. Are we all here? No one in there? (*Locks the side door on the left*) There are some things stored here, better lock up. Let us go!

ANYA. Good-by, old house! Good-by, old life!

TROFIMOV. Hail to you, new life!

(*Exit with* ANYA. VARYA *looks round the room and goes out slowly.* YASHA *and* CHARLOTTA *with her dog go out*)

LOPAHIN. And so, until the spring. Go along, friends . . . 'Bye-'bye! (*Exits*)

MME. RANEVSKAYA *and* GAYEV *remain alone. As though they had been waiting for this, they throw themselves on each other's necks, and break into subdued, restrained sobs, afraid of being overheard*)

GAYEV (*in despair*). My sister! My sister!

MME. RANEVSKAYA. Oh, my orchard—my dear, sweet, beautiful orchard! My life, my youth, my happiness—good-by! Good-by! (*Voice of* ANYA, *gay and summoning:* "Mamma!" *Voice of* TROFIMOV, *gay and excited:* "Halloo!")

MME. RANEVSKAYA. One last look at the walls, at the windows . . . Our poor mother loved to walk about this room . . .

GAYEV. My sister, my sister! (*Voice of* ANYA: "Mamma!" *Voice of* TROFIMOV: "Halloo!")

MME. RANEVSKAYA. We're coming.

(*They go out. The stage is empty. The sound of doors being locked, of carriages driving away. Then silence. In the stillness is heard the muffled sound of the ax striking a tree, a mournful, lonely sound.*

(*Footsteps are heard.* FIRS *appears in the doorway on the right. He is dressed as usual in a jacket and white waistcoat and wears slippers. He is ill.*)

FIRS (*goes to the door, tries the handle*). Locked! They've gone . . . (*Sits down on the sofa*) They've forgotten me . . . Never mind . . . I'll sit here a bit . . . I'll wager Leonid Andreyevich hasn't put his fur coat on, he's gone off in his light overcoat . . . (*Sighs anxiously*) I didn't keep an eye on him . . . Ah, when they're young, they're green . . .(*Mumbles something indistinguishable*) Life has gone by as if I had never lived. (*Lies down*) I'll lie

down a while . . . There's no strength left in you, old fellow; nothing is left, nothing. Ah, you addlehead!
(*Lies motionless. A distant sound is heard coming from the sky as it were, the sound of a snapping string mournfully dying away. All is still again, and nothing is heard but the strokes of the ax against a tree far away in the orchard*)

Eugene O'Neill

BOUND EAST FOR CARDIFF

Relatively few dramas produced in America during the twentieth century seem vital one year—let alone ten or twenty—after their first presentation. Only a few such works may be read after plays by Sophocles, Shakespeare, and Chekhov without giving the reader a woeful sense of complete anticlimax. One of the few is *Bound East for Cardiff* (1916), an outstanding work by a playwright generally considered the finest our country has brought forth.

Eugene O'Neill was a product of a movement in the American theater which had begun less than a decade before *Bound East for Cardiff* appeared. Distressed by the commercialization of our theater and stimulated by productions which they had seen in experimental theaters abroad, a number of young playwrights and directors had founded "Little Theaters" or "Art Theaters" in many parts of the country and had begun presenting plays in them. The plays which they staged were often more serious in intention and more experimental in method than those presented in commercial theaters.

Amateur though it was, the movement in time profoundly influenced the commercial stage. It battled against stale techniques. It cultivated a taste on the part of at least some theatergoers for the unusual in playwriting, acting, and producing. And it trained theatrical groups which could satisfy such a taste. One such group was the Provincetown Players, founded in 1915. When this group brought to New York some of its authors, directors, and actors from the Cape Cod fish-house which it had been using for a theater, its dramatic productions won immediate attention and respect. Eugene O'Neill was the most notable playwright active in the Provincetown Players. His first produced play, *Bound East for Cardiff*, was presented in Provincetown in 1916. This was followed by others such as *The Moon of the Caribbees, The Long Voyage Home, Ile,* and *Where the Cross Is Made* before *Beyond the Horizon* and *Emperor Jones*, in 1920, and *Anna Christie*, in 1921, established him as a successful writer for the commercial theater.

Part of an autobiographical sketch indicates the variety of O'Neill's experiences before he became a playwright: "My undergraduate college education was confined to a freshman year at Princeton University, class of 1910. I went with a mining engineer on a gold prospecting trip to Spanish Honduras, Central America. At the end of six months I was invalided home—tropical malarial fever—no gold. After that I became assistant manager of a theatrical company touring the East and Middle West. My first voyage to sea followed: sixty-five days on a Norwegian barque, Boston to Buenos Aires. In Argentina I worked at various occupations—in the draughting department of the Westinghouse Electrical Company, in the wool house of a packing plant in La Plata, in the office of the Singer Sewing Machine Company in Buenos Aires. Followed another voyage at sea, tending mules in a cattle steamer, Buenos Aires to Durban, South Africa, and return. After that a lengthy period of complete destitution in Buenos Aires—'on the beach'—terminated by my signing on as ordinary seaman on a British tramp steamer bound home for New York. My final experience at sea followed soon after this—able seaman on the American Line, New York-Southampton. The next winter I played a part in my father's vaudeville version of *The Count of Monte Cristo*, touring the Far West. Then I worked as reporter on the New London, Connecticut, *Telegraph*. My health broke down, my lungs being affected, and I spent six months in a sanatorium thinking it over. It was in this enforced period of reflection that the urge to write first came to me. The next fall—I was twenty-four— I began my first play—'The Web.' In 1914–1915 I was a student in Professor Baker's

English 47 at Harvard. The summer 1916 I spent at Provincetown. It was during that summer the Provincetown Players, who have made the original productions of nearly all my short plays in New York, were first organized."

The Players' first staging of *Bound East for Cardiff* was assisted by the natural setting of Wharf Theater: a fog was on the harbor and the high tide washed in under the floor of the erstwhile fish-house. George Cram Cook, the dominating figure in the group, played Yank; O'Neill played the Second Mate. Two leading members of the Players testified to the original impact of the play. Said Frank Shay: "The effect produced on us was so strong we all felt instinctively we had had a profound experience." Said Susan Glaspell: "I may see it through memories too emotional, but it seems to me I never sat through a more moving production than *Bound East for Cardiff*." Barrett H. Clark, O'Neill's biographer, asserts, "Of the score of plays written by O'Neill during the first three years [of his career], this is easily the best. . . . An unpretentious episode, moving and tense, yet with hardly a vestige of 'theater' in the conventional sense of the word."

This and three other sea plays in which the same characters appeared were presented as a group in Provincetown and New York in 1924 and were revived in New York in 1929. *Bound East for Cardiff* has since been given frequently.

CHARACTERS

YANK	SCOTTY	IVAN
DRISCOLL	OLSON	THE CAPTAIN
COCKY	PAUL	THE SECOND MATE
DAVIS	SMITTY	

Scene: The seamen's forecastle of the British tramp steamer Glencairn *on a foggy night midway on the voyage between New York and Cardiff. An irregular shaped compartment, the sides of which almost meet at the far end to form a triangle. Sleeping bunks about six feet long, ranged three deep with a space of three feet separating the upper from the lower, are built against the sides. On the right above the bunks three or four port holes can be seen. In front of the bunks, rough wooden benches. Over the bunks on the left, a lamp in a bracket. In the left foreground, a doorway. On the floor near it, a pail with a tin dipper. Oilskins are hanging from a hook near the doorway.*

The far side of the forecastle is so narrow that it contains only one series of bunks.

In under the bunks a glimpse can be had of seachests, suit cases, seaboots, etc., jammed in indiscriminately.

At regular intervals of a minute or so the blast of the steamer's whistle can be heard above all the other sounds.

Five men are sitting on the benches talking. They are dressed in dirty patched suits of dungaree, flannel shirts, and all are in their stocking feet. Four of the men are pulling on pipes and the air is heavy with rancid tobacco smoke. Sitting on the top bunk in the left foreground, a Norwegian, PAUL, *is softly playing some folk song on a battered accordion. He stops from time to time to listen to the conversation.*

In the lower bunk in the rear a dark-haired, hard-featured man is lying apparently asleep. One of his arms is stretched limply over the side of the bunk. His face is very pale, and drops of clammy perspiration glisten on his forehead.

It is nearing the end of the dog watch—about ten minutes to eight in the evening.

COCKY (*a weazened runt of a man. He is telling a story. The others are listening with amused, incredulous faces, interrupting him at the end of each sentence with loud derisive guffaws*). Makin' love to me, she was! It's Gawd's truth! A bloomin' nigger! Greased all over with cocoanut oil, she was. Gawd blimey, I couldn't stand 'er. Bloody old cow, I says; and with that I fetched 'er a biff on the ear wot knocked 'er silly, an'—— (*He is interrupted by a roar of laughter from the others*)

DAVIS (*a middle-aged man with black hair and mustache*). You're a liar, Cocky.

SCOTTY (*a dark young fellow*). Ho-ho! Ye werr neverr in New Guinea in yourr life, I'm thinkin'.

OLSON (*a Swede with a drooping blond mustache—with ponderous sarcasm*). Yust tink of it! You say she wass a cannibal, Cocky?

DRISCOLL (*a brawny Irishman with the battered features of a prizefighter*). How cud ye doubt ut, Ollie? A quane av the naygurs she musta been surely. Who else wud think herself aqual to fallin' in love wid a beauthiful, divil-may-care rake av a man the loike av Cocky? (*A burst of laughter from the crowd*)

COCKY (*indignantly*). Gawd strike me dead if it ain't true, every bleedin' word of it. 'Appened ten year ago come Christmas.

SCOTTY. 'Twas a Christmas dinner she had her eyes on.

DAVIS. He'd a been a tough old bird.

DRISCOLL. 'Tis lucky for both av ye ye escaped; for the quane av the cannibal isles wad 'a died av the belly ache the day after Christmas, divil a doubt av ut. (*The laughter at this is long and loud*)

COCKY (*sullenly*). Blarsted fat 'eads! (*The sick man in the lower bunk in the rear groans and moves restlessly. There is a hushed silence. All the men turn and stare at him*)

DRISCOLL. Ssshh! (*In a hushed whisper*) We'd best not be talkin' so loud and him tryin' to have a bit av a sleep. (*He tiptoes softly to the side of the bunk*) Yank! You'd be wantin' a drink av wather, maybe? (YANK *does not reply.* DRISCOLL *bends over and looks at him*) It's asleep he is, sure enough. His breath is chokin' in his throat loike wather gurglin' in a poipe. (*He comes back quietly and sits down. All are silent, avoiding each other's eyes*)

COCKY (*after a pause*). Pore devil! It's over the side for 'im, Gawd 'elp 'im.

DRISCOLL. Stop your croakin'! He's not dead yet and, praise God, he'll have many a long day yet before him.

SCOTTY (*shaking his head doubtfully*). He's bod, mon, he's verry bod.

DAVIS. Lucky he's alive. Many a man's light woulda gone out after a fall like that.

OLSON. You saw him fall?

DAVIS. Right next to him. He and me was goin' down in number two hold to do some chippin'. He puts his leg over careless-like and misses the ladder and plumps straight down to the bottom. I was scared to look over for a minute, and then I heard him groan and I scuttled down after him. He was hurt bad inside for the blood was drippin' from the side of his mouth. He was groanin' hard, but he never let a word out of him.

COCKY. An' you blokes remember when we 'auled 'im in 'ere? Oh, 'ell, 'e says, oh, 'ell—like that, and nothink else.

OLSON. Did the captain know where he iss hurted?

COCKY. That silly ol' josser! Wot the 'ell would 'e know abaht anythink?

SCOTTY (*scornfully*). He fiddles in his mouth wi' a bit of glass.

DRISCOLL (*angrily*). The divil's own life ut is to be out on the lonely sea wid nothin' betune you and a grave in the ocean but a spindle-shanked, gray-whiskered auld fool the loike av him. 'Twas enough to make a saint shwear to see him wid his gold watch in his hand, tryin' to look as wise as an owl on a tree, and all the toime he not knowin' whether 'twas cholery or the barber's itch was the matther wid Yank.

SCOTTY (*sardonically*). He gave him a dose of salts, na doot?

DRISCOLL. Divil a thing he gave him at all, but looked in the book he had wid him, and shook his head, and walked out widout sayin' a word, the second mate afther him no wiser than himself, God's curse on the two av thim!

COCKY (*after a pause*). Yank was a good shipmate, pore beggar. Lend me four bob in Noo Yark, 'e did.

DRISCOLL (*warmly*). A good shipmate he was and is, none betther. Ye said no more than the truth, Cocky. Five years and more ut is since first I shipped wid him, and we've stuck together iver since through good luck and bad. Fights we've had, God help us, but 'twas only when we'd a bit av drink taken, and we always shook hands the nixt mornin'. Whativer was his was mine, and many's the toime I'd a been on the beach or worse, but for him.

And now—— (*His voice trembles as he fights to control his emotion*) Divil-
take me if I'm not startin' to blubber loike an auld woman, and he not dead
at all, but goin' to live many a long year yet, maybe.

DAVIS. The sleep'll do him good. He seems better now.

OLSON. If he wude eat someting——

DRISCOLL. Wud ye have him be eatin' in his condishun? Sure it's hard enough
on the rest av us wid nothin' the matther wid our insides to be stomachin' the
skoff on this rusty lime-juicer.

SCOTTY (*indignantly*). It's a starvation ship.

DAVIS. Plenty o' work and no food—and the owners ridin' around in carriages!

OLSON. Hash, hash! Stew, stew! Marmalade, py damn! (*He spits disgustedly*)

COCKY. Bloody swill! Fit only for swine is wot I say.

DRISCOLL. And the dishwather they disguise wid the name av tea! And the putty
they call bread! My belly feels loike I'd swalleyed a dozen rivets at the thought
av ut! And sea-biscuit that'd break the teeth av a lion if he had the misfortune to take a bite at one! (*Unconsciously they have all raised their voices,
forgetting the sick man in their sailor's delight at finding something to grum-
ble about*)

PAUL (*swings his feet over the side of his bunk, stops playing his accordion,
and says slowly*): And rot-ten po-tay-toes! (*He starts in playing again. The
sick man gives a groan of pain*)

DRISCOLL (*holding up his hand*). Shut your mouths, all av you. 'Tis a hell av
a thing for us to be complainin' about our guts, and a sick man maybe dyin'
listenin' to us. (*Gets up and shakes his fist at the Norwegian*) God stiffen
you, ye squarehead scut! Put down that organ av yours or I'll break your ugly
face for you. Is that banshee schreechin' fit music for a sick man? (*The
Norwegian puts his accordion in the bunk and lies back and closes his eyes.
DRISCOLL goes over and stands beside* YANK. *The steamer's whistle sounds
particularly loud in the silence*)

DAVIS. Damn this fog! (*Reaches in under a bunk and yanks out a pair of seaboots, which he pulls on*) My lookout next, too. Must be nearly eight bells,
boys. (*With the exception of* OLSON, *all the men sitting up put on oilskins,
sou'westers, seaboots, etc., in preparation for the watch on deck.* OLSON
crawls into a lower bunk on the right)

SCOTTY. My wheel.

OLSON (*disgustedly*). Nothin' but yust dirty weather all dis voyage. I yust can't
sleep when weestle blow. (*He turns his back to the light and is soon fast
asleep and snoring*)

SCOTTY. If this fog keeps up, I'm tellin' ye, we'll no be in Carrdiff for a week
or more.

DRISCOLL. 'Twas just such a night as this the auld Dover wint down. Just about
this toime ut was, too, and we all sittin' round in the fo'castle, Yank beside
me, whin all av a suddint we heard a great slitherin' crash, and the ship
heeled over till we was all in a heap on wan side. What came afther I dis-
remimber exactly, except 'twas a hard shift to get the boats over the side

before the auld teakittle sank. Yank was in the same boat wid me, and sivin morthal days we drifted wid scarcely a drop of wather or a bite to chew on. 'Twas Yank here that held me down whin I wanted to jump into the ocean, roarin' mad wid the thirst. Picked up we were on the same day wid only Yank in his senses, and him steerin' the boat.

COCKY (*protestingly*). Blimey but you're a cheerful blighter, Driscoll! Talkin' abaht shipwrecks in this 'ere blushin' fog. (YANK *groans and stirs uneasily, opening his eyes.* DRISCOLL *hurries to his side*)

DRISCOLL. Are ye feelin' any betther, Yank?

YANK (*in a weak voice*). No.

DRISCOLL. Sure, you must be. You look as sthrong as an ox. (*Appealing to the others*) Am I tellin' him a lie?

DAVIS. The sleep's done you good.

COCKY. You'll be 'avin your pint of beer in Cardiff this day week.

SCOTTY. And fish and chips, mon!

YANK (*peevishly*). What're yuh all lyin' fur? D'yuh think I'm scared to——— (*He hesitates as if frightened by the word he is about to say*)

DRISCOLL. Don't be thinkin' such things! (*The ship's bell is heard heavily tolling eight times. From the forecastle head above the voice of the lookout rises in a long wail: Aaall's welll. The men look uncertainly at* YANK *as if un-decided whether to say good-by or not*)

YANK (*in an agony of fear*). Don't leave me, Drisc! I'm dyin', I tell yuh. I won't stay here alone with every one snorin'. I'll go out on deck. (*He makes a feeble attempt to rise, but sinks back with a sharp groan. His breath comes in wheezy gasps*). Don't leave me, Drisc! (*His face grows white and his head falls back with a jerk*)

DRISCOLL. Don't be worryin', Yank. I'll not move a step out av here—and let that divil av a bosun curse his black head off. You speak a word to the bosun, Cocky. Tell him that Yank is bad took and I'll be stayin' wid him a while yet.

COCKY. Right-o. (COCKY, DAVIS, *and* SCOTTY *go out quietly*)

COCKY (*from the alleyway*). Gawd blimey, the fog's thick as soup.

DRISCOLL. Are ye satisfied now, Yank? (*Receiving no answer, he bends over the still form*) He's fainted, God help him! (*He gets a tin dipper from the bucket and bathes* YANK's *forehead with the water.* YANK *shudders and opens his eyes*)

YANK (*slowly*). I thought I was goin' then. Wha' did yuh wanta wake me up fur?

DRISCOLL (*with forced gayety*). Is it wishful for heaven ye are?

YANK (*gloomily*). Hell, I guess.

DRISCOLL (*crossing himself involuntarily*). For the love av the saints don't be talkin' loike that! You'd give a man the creeps. It's chippin' rust on deck you'll be in a day or two wid the best av us. (YANK *does not answer, but closes his eyes wearily. The seaman who has been on lookout,* SMITTY, *a young Englishman, comes in and takes off his dripping oilskins. While he is doing this the man whose turn at the wheel has been relieved enters. He is a dark burly fellow with a round stupid face. The Englishman steps softly over to* DRISCOLL. *The other crawls into a lower bunk)*

SMITTY (*whispering*). How's Yank?

DRISCOLL. Betther. Ask him yourself. He's awake.

YANK. I'm all right, Smitty.

SMITTY. Glad to hear it, Yank (*He crawls to an upper bunk and is soon asleep)*

IVAN (*The stupid-faced seaman who came in after* SMITTY *twists his head in the direction of the sick man)*. You feel gude, Jank?

YANK (*wearily*). Yes. Ivan.

IVAN. Dot's gude. (*He rolls over on his side and falls asleep immediately)*

YANK (*after a pause broken only by snores—with a bitter laugh*). Good-by and good luck to the lot of you!

DRISCOLL. Is ut painin' you again?

YANK. It hurts like hell—here. (*He points to the lower part of his chest on the left side*) I guess my old pump's busted. Ooohh! (*A spasm of pain contracts his pale features. He presses his hand to his side and writhes on the thin mattress of his bunk. The perspiration stands out in beads on his forehead)*

DRISCOLL (*terrified*). Yank! Yank! What is ut? (*Jumping to his feet*) I'll run for the captain. (*He starts for the doorway)*

YANK (*sitting up in his bunk, frantic with fear*). Don't leave me, Drisc! For God's sake don't leave me alone! (*He leans over the side of his bunk and spits.* DRISCOLL *comes back to him)* Blood! Ugh!

DRISCOLL. Blood again! I'd best be gettin' the captain.

YANK. No, no, don't leave me! If yuh do I'll git up and follow you. I ain't no coward, but I'm scared to stay here with all of them asleep and snorin'. (DRISCOLL, *not knowing what to do, sits down on the bench beside him. He grows calmer and sinks back on the mattress)* The captain can't do me no good, yuh know it yourself. The pain ain't so bad now, but I thought it had me then. It was like a buzz-saw cuttin' into me.

DRISCOLL (*fiercely*). God blarst ut!

(*The* CAPTAIN *and the* SECOND MATE *of the steamer enter the forecastle. The* CAPTAIN *is an old man with gray mustache and whiskers. The* MATE *is clean-shaven and middle-aged. Both are dressed in simple blue uniforms)*

THE CAPTAIN (*taking out his watch and feeling* YANK'S *pulse*). And how is the sick man?

YANK (*feebly*). All right, sir.

THE CAPTAIN. And the pain in the chest?

YANK. It still hurts, sir, worse than ever.

THE CAPTAIN (*taking a thermometer from his pocket and putting it into* YANK'S *mouth*). Here. Be sure and keep this in under your tongue, not over it.

THE MATE (*after a pause*). Isn't this your watch on deck, Driscoll?

DRISCOLL. Yes, sorr, but Yank was fearin' to be alone, and——

THE CAPTAIN. That's all right, Driscoll.

DRISCOLL. Thank ye, sorr.

THE CAPTAIN (*stares at his watch for a moment or so; then takes the ther-*

mometer from YANK'S *mouth and goes to the lamp to read it. His expression grows very grave. He beckons the* MATE *and* DRISCOLL *to the corner near the doorway.* YANK *watches them furtively. The* CAPTAIN *speaks in a low voice to the* MATE). Way up, both of them. (*To* DRISCOLL) Has he been spitting blood again?

DRISCOLL. Not much for the hour just past, sorr, but before that——

THE CAPTAIN. A great deal?

DRISCOLL. Yes, sorr.

THE CAPTAIN. He hasn't eaten anything?

DRISCOLL. No, sorr.

THE CAPTAIN. Did he drink that medicine I sent him?

DRISCOLL. Yes, sorr, but it didn't stay down.

THE CAPTAIN (*shaking his head*). I'm afraid—he's very weak. I can't do anything else for him. It's too serious for me. If this had only happened a week later we'd be in Cardiff in time to——

DRISCOLL. Plaze help him some way, sorr!

THE CAPTAIN (*impatiently*). But, my good man, I'm not a doctor. (*More kindly as he sees* DRISCOLL'S *grief*) You and he have been shipmates a long time?

DRISCOLL. Five years and more, sorr.

THE CAPTAIN. I see. Well, don't let him move. Keep him quiet and we'll hope for the best. I'll read the matter up and send him some medicine, something to ease the pain, anyway. (*Goes over to* YANK) Keep up your courage! You'll be better to-morrow. (*He breaks down lamely before* YANK'S *steady gaze*) We'll pull you through all right—and—hm—well—coming, Robinson? Dammit! (*He goes out hurriedly, followed by the* MATE)

DRISCOLL (*trying to conceal his anxiety*). Didn't I tell you you wasn't half as sick as you thought you was? The Captain'll have you out on deck cursin' and swearin' loike a trooper before the week is out.

YANK. Don't lie, Drisc. I heard what he said, and if I didn't I c'd tell by the way I feel. I know what's goin' to happen. I'm goin' to—— (*He hesitates for a second—then resolutely*) I'm goin' to die, that's what, and the sooner the better!

DRISCOLL (*wildly*). No, and be damned to you, you're not. I'll not let you.

YANK. It ain't no use, Drisc. I ain't got a chance, but I ain't scared. Gimme a drink of water, will yuh, Drisc? My throat's burnin' up. (DRISCOLL *brings the dipper full of water and supports his head while he drinks in great gulps*)

DRISCOLL (*seeking vainly for some word of comfort*). Are ye feelin' more aisy loike now?

YANK. Yes—now—when I know it's all up. (*A pause*) You mustn't take it so hard, Drisc. I was just thinkin' it ain't as bad as people think—dyin'. I ain't never took much stock in the truck them sky-pilots preach. I ain't never had religion; but I know whatever it is what comes after it can't be no worser'n this. I don't like to leave you, Drisc, but—that's all.

DRISCOLL (*with a groan*). Lad, lad, don't be talkin'.

YANK. This sailor life ain't much to cry about leavin'—just one ship after another, hard work, small pay, and bum grub; and when we git into port, just a drunk endin' up in a fight, and all your money gone, and then ship away again. Never meetin' no nice people; never gittin' outa sailor town, hardly, in any port; travellin' all over the world and never seein' none of it; without no one to care whether you're alive or dead. (*With a bitter smile*) There ain't much in all that that'd make yuh sorry to lose it, Drisc.

DRISCOLL (*gloomily*). It's a hell av a life, the sea.

YANK (*musingly*). It must be great to stay on dry land all your life and have a farm with a house of your own with cows and pigs and chickens, 'way in the middle of the land where yuh'd never smell the sea or see a ship. It must be great to have a wife, and kids to play with at night after supper when your work was done. It must be great to have a home of your own, Drisc.

DRISCOLL (*with a great sigh*). It must, surely; but what's the use av thinkin' av ut? Such things are not for the loikes av us.

YANK. Sea-farin' is all right when you're young and don't care, but we ain't chickens no more, and somehow, I dunno, this last year has seemed rotten, and I've had a hunch I'd quit—with you, of course—and we'd save our coin, and go to Canada or Argentine or some place and git a farm, just a small one, just enough to live on. I never told yuh this cause I thought you'd laugh at me.

DRISCOLL (*enthusiastically*). Laugh at you, is ut? When I'm havin' the same thoughts myself, toime afther toime. It's a grand idea and we'll be doin' ut sure if you'll stop your crazy notions—about—about bein' so sick.

YANK (*sadly*). Too late. We shouldn'ta made this trip, and then—— How'd all the fog git in here?

DRISCOLL. Fog?

YANK. Everything looks misty. Must be my eyes gittin' weak, I guess. What was we talkin' of a minute ago? Oh, yes, a farm. It's too late. (*His mind wandering*) Argentine, did I say? D'yuh remember the times we've had in Buenos Aires? The moving pictures in Barracas? Some class to them, d'yuh remember?

DRISCOLL (*with satisfaction*). I do that; and so does the piany player. He'll not be forgettin' the black eye I gave him in a hurry.

YANK. Remember the time we was there on the beach and had to go to Tommy Moore's boarding house to git shipped? And he sold us rotten oilskins and seaboots full of holes, and shipped us on a skysail yarder round the Horn, and took two month's pay for it. And the days we used to sit on the park benches along the Paseo Colon with the vigilantes lookin' hard at us? And the songs at the Sailor's Opera where the guy played ragtime—d'yuh remember them?

DRISCOLL. I do, surely.

YANK. And La Plata—phew, the stink of the hides! I always liked Argentine— all except that booze, caña. How drunk we used to git on that, remember?

DRISCOLL. Cud I forget ut? My head pains me at the menshun av that divil's brew.

YANK. Remember the night I went crazy with the heat in Singapore? And the time you was pinched by the cops in Port Said? And the time we was both locked up in Sydney for fightin'?

DRISCOLL. I do so.

YANK. And that fight on the dock at Cape Town——(*His voice betrays great inward perturbation*)

DRISCOLL (*hastily*). Don't be thinkin' av that now. 'Tis past and gone.

YANK. D'yuh think He'll hold it up against me?

DRISCOLL (*mystified*). Who's that?

YANK. God. They say He sees everything. He must know it was done in fair fight, in self-defense, don't yuh think?

DRISCOLL. Av course. Ye stabbed him, and be damned to him, for the skulkin' swine he was, afther him tryin' to stick you in the back, and you not suspectin'. Let your conscience be aisy. I wisht I had nothin' blacker than that on my sowl. I'd not be afraid av the angel Gabriel himself.

YANK (*with a shudder*). I c'd see him a minute ago with the blood spurtin' out of his neck. Ugh!

DRISCOLL. The fever, ut is, that makes you see such things. Give no heed to ut.

YANK (*uncertainly*). You don't think He'll hold it up agin me—God, I mean.

DRISCOLL. If there's justice in hiven, no! (YANK *seems comforted by this assurance*)

YANK (*after a pause*). We won't reach Cardiff for a week at least. I'll be buried at sea.

DRISCOLL (*putting his hands over his ears*). Ssshh! I won't listen to you.

YANK (*as if he had not heard him*). It's as good a place as any other, I s'pose —only I always wanted to be buried on dry land. But what the hell'll I care—then? (*Fretfully*) Why should it be a rotten night like this with that damned whistle blowin' and people snorin' all round? I wish the stars was out, and the moon, too; I c'd lie out on deck and look at them, and it'd make it easier to go—somehow.

DRISCOLL. For the love av God don't be talkin' loike that!

YANK. Whatever pay's comin' to me yuh can divvy up with the rest of the boys; and you take my watch. It ain't worth much, but it's all I've got.

DRISCOLL. But have ye no relations at all to call your own?

YANK. No, not as I know of. One thing I forgot: You know Fanny the barmaid at the Red Stork in Cardiff?

DRISCOLL. Sure, and who doesn't?

YANK. She's been good to me. She tried to lend me half a crown when I was broke there last trip. Buy her the biggest box of candy yuh c'n find in Cardiff. (*Breaking down—in a choking voice*) It's hard to ship on this voyage I'm goin' on—alone! (DRISCOLL *reaches out and grasps his hand. There is a pause, during which both fight to control themselves*) My throat's like a furnace. (*He gasps for air*) Gimme a drink of water, will yuh, Drisc?

(DRISCOLL *gets him a dipper of water*) I wish this was a pint of beer. Oooohh! (*He chokes, his face convulsed with agony, his hands tearing at his shirt front. The dipper falls from his nerveless fingers*)

DRISCOLL. For the love av God, what is ut, Yank?

YANK (*speaking with tremendous difficulty*). S'long, Drisc! (*He stares straight in front of him with eyes starting from their sockets*) Who's that?

DRISCOLL. Who? What?

YANK (*faintly*). A pretty lady dressed in black. (*His face twitches and his body writhes in a final spasm, then straightens out rigidly*)

DRISCOLL (*pale with horror*). Yank! Yank! Say a word to me for the love av hiven! (*He shrinks away from the bunk, making the sign of the cross. Then comes back and puts a trembling hand on* YANK'S *chest and bends closely over the body*)

COCKY (*from the alleyway*). Oh, Driscoll! Can you leave Yank for arf a mo' and give me a 'and?

DRISCOLL (*with a great sob*). Yank! (*He sinks down on his knees beside the bunk, his head on his hands. His lips move in some half-remembered prayer*)

COCKY (*enters, his oilskins and sou'wester glistening with drops of water*). The fog's lifted. (COCKY *sees* DRISCOLL *and stands staring at him with open mouth.* DRISCOLL *makes the sign of the cross again*)

COCKY (*mockingly*). Sayin' 'is prayers! (*He catches sight of the still figure in the bunk and an expression of awed understanding comes over his face. He takes off his dripping sou'wester and stands, scratching his head*)

COCKY (*in a hushed whisper*). Gawd blimey!

Christopher Fry

A PHOENIX TOO FREQUENT

Eugene O'Neill once said of the reading he did during his apprenticeship as a playwright: "I read about everything I could lay hands on: the Greeks, the Elizabethans—practically all the classics—and of course the moderns. Ibsen and Strindberg, especially Strindberg." The last two authors named were influential not only on the young O'Neill but also upon a vast majority of writers of drama contemporaneous with him. Plays were predominantly realistic and naturalistic—prosaic in their plots and their language. Most authors were much concerned with verisimilitude, with psychological motivation, with social preachments.

Some dramatists, however—including O'Neill at times—were dissatisfied with prevalent aims and methods. They turned to legend and history for settings and stories, attempted to universalize characters and themes, and employed poetic prose or even metrical forms. Authors such as Synge and Yeats in Ireland, for example, and Maxwell Anderson in the United States wrote poetic dramas which were well received by critics and theater-going audiences alike. In very recent times, metrical drama has been given new life by a small but talented group of writers in England. Most notable of these have been two men—T. S. Eliot, already famous as a poet, whose verse plays include *Murder in the Cathedral* and *The Cocktail Party*, and Christopher Fry.

A performance of A Phoenix Too Frequent

Fry's work benefited from a long-standing interest in and association with the stage. He wrote his first play, it is said, at eleven, his first verse play at fourteen. At seventeen he was a teacher for a brief time, and then went into theatrical work—as a member of a repertory company, a cabaret entertainer, an understudy, an actor, and eventually a playwright. His best known verse plays include *The Boy with a Cart*, *The Tower*, *Thursday's Child*, *A Phoenix Too Frequent*, *The Lady's Not for Burning*, and *Venus Observed*.

Fry, like most other authors of dramas in verse, is antirealistic. Says he: "The realistic play is not realistic at all, but just a slice off the top of existence. Writing a realistic play is like meeting a human being for the first time. The realist would observe that this is Mr. So-and-So, that he has a beard and an accent and a mole on his face. But the human being is far more peculiar, something that has gone on since the beginning of time, now miraculously summed up in the strange sort of mysterious creature that stands before us. . . . In my plays I want to look at life—at the commonplaces of existence—as if we had just turned a corner and run into it for the first time." The universal, rather than the particular, in other words, is what he hopes to discover and to convey in his dramas.

Fry's versified plays, like those of Eliot, are in the vein of modern poetry. They are influenced by seventeenth-century authors who are so generally admired and at times imitated by the poets of today: the story of *A Phoenix Too Frequent* came from Jeremy Taylor, the title from Robert Burton. Typically wit and humor are mingled with high seriousness, the humor benefiting from Fry's natural tendency toward playfulness. Typically, too, there are sharp descents from the language of poetry to that of the vernacular. The figures of speech are often startling; sometimes they are rather wild conceits; and the packed lines often take a good deal of thinking about to be understood. And even in a play like the one which follows, the plot of which is essentially that of a comedy, Fry's characters—and Fry himself—are often concerned with very serious implications and problems.

A Phoenix Too Frequent was first produced in the Mercury Theatre in London in the spring of 1946. It was revived in the Arts Theatre, London, in the autumn of the same year. It had its American première in New York in 1950, and since then it has

been frequently presented elsewhere in the United States.

> 'To whom conferr'd a peacock's undecent,
> A squirrel's harsh, a phoenix too frequent.'
> Robert Burton quoting Martial

CHARACTERS

DYNAMENE
DOTO
TEGEUS-CHROMIS

Scene: The tomb of Virilius, near Ephesus; night
Note: The story was got from Jeremy Taylor who had it from Petronius

An underground tomb, in darkness except for the very low light of an oil-lamp.
Above ground the starlight shows a line of trees on which hang the bodies
of several men. It also penetrates a gate and falls on to the first of the steps
which descend into the darkness of the tomb. DOTO *talks to herself in the dark.*

DOTO. Nothing but the harmless day gone into black
Is all the dark is. And so what's my trouble?
Demons is so much wind. Are so much wind.
I've plenty to fill my thoughts. All that I ask
Is don't keep turning men over in my mind,
Venerable Aphrodite. I've had my last one
And thank you. I thank thee. He smelt of sour grass
And was likeable. He collected ebony quoits.
(*An owl hoots near at hand*)
O Zeus! O some god or other, where is the oil?
Fire's from Prometheus. I thank thee. If I
Mean to die I'd better see what I'm doing.
(*She fills the lamp with oil. The flame burns up brightly and shows* DYNAMENE,
beautiful and young, leaning asleep beside a bier)
Honestly, I would rather have to sleep
With a bald bee-keeper who was wearing his boots
Than spend more days fasting and thirsting and crying
In a tomb. I shouldn't have said that. Pretend
I didn't hear myself. But life and death
Is cat and dog in this double-bed of a world.
My master, my poor master, was a man
Whose nose was as straight as a little buttress,
And now he has taken it into Elysium
Where it won't be noticed among all the other straightness.

(*The owl cries again and wakens* DYNAMENE)
   Oh, them owls. Those owls, It's woken her.
DYNAMENE. Ah! I'm breathless. I caught up with the ship
   But it spread its wings, creaking a cry of *Dew,*
   Dew! and flew figurehead foremost into the sun.
DOTO. How crazy, madam.
DYNAMENE.   Doto, draw back the curtains.
   I'll take my barley-water.
DOTO.   We're not at home
   Now, madam. It's the master's tomb.
DYNAMENE.   Of course!
   Oh, I'm wretched. Already I have disfigured
   My vigil. My cynical eyelids have soon dropped me
   In a dream.
DOTO.   But then it's possible, madam, you might
   Find yourself in bed with him again
   In a dream, madam. Was he on the ship?
DYNAMENE. He was the ship.
DOTO.   Oh. That makes it different.
DYNAMENE. He was the ship. He had such a deck, Doto,
   Such a white, scrubbed deck. Such a stern prow,
   Such a proud stern, so slim from port to starboard.
   If ever you meet a man with such fine masts
   Give your life to him, Doto. The figurehead
   Bore his own features, so serene in the brow
   And hung with a little seaweed. O Virilius,
   My husband, you have left a wake in my soul.
   You cut the glassy water with a diamond keel.
   I must cry again.
DOTO.   What, when you mean to join him?
   Don't you believe he will be glad to see you, madam?
   Thankful to see you, I should imagine, among
   Them shapes and shades; all shapes of shapes and all
   Shades of shades, from what I've heard. I know
   I shall feel odd at first with Cerberus,
   Sop or no sop. Still, I know how you feel, madam.
   You think he may find a temptation in Hades.
   I shouldn't worry. It would help him to settle down.
(DYNAMENE *weeps*)
   It would only be *fun,* madam. He couldn't go far
   With a shade.
DYNAMENE.   He was one of the coming men.
   He was certain to have become the most well-organized provost
   The town has known, once they had made him provost.
   He was so punctual, you could regulate

The sun by him. He made the world succumb
To his daily revolution of habit. But who,
In the world he has gone to, will appreciate that?
O poor Virilius! To be a coming man
Already gone—it must be distraction.
Why did you leave me walking about our ambitions
Like a cat in the ruins of a house? Promising husband,
Why did you insult me by dying? Virilius,
Now I keep no flower, except in the vase
Of the tomb.

DOTO.   O poor madam! O poor master!
I presume so far as to cry somewhat for myself
As well. I know you won't mind, madam. It's two
Days not eating makes me think of my uncle's
Shop in the country, where he has a hardware business,
Basins, pots, ewers, and alabaster birds.
He makes you die of laughing. O madam.
Isn't it sad? (*They both weep*)

DYNAMENE.   How could I have allowed you
To come and die of my grief? Doto, it puts
A terrible responsibility on me. Have you
No grief of your own and you could die of?

DOTO.   Not really, madam.

DYNAMENE. Nothing?

DOTO.   Not really. They was all one to me.
Well, all but two was all one to me. And they,
Strange enough, was two who kept recurring.
I could never be sure if they had gone for good
Or not; and so that kept things cheerful, madam.
One always gave a wink before he deserted me,
The other slapped me as it were behind, madam;
Then they would be away for some months.

DYNAMENE.   Oh Doto,
What an unhappy life you were having to lead.

DOTO. Yes, I'm sure. But never mind, madam.
It seemed quite lively then. And now I know
It's what you say; life is more big than a bed
And full of miracles and mysteries like
One man made for one woman, etcetera, etcetera.
Lovely. I feel sung, madam, by a baritone
In mixed company with everyone pleased.
And so I had to come with you here, madam,
For the last sad chorus of me. It's all
Fresh to me. Death's a new interest in life,
If it doesn't disturb you, madam, to have me crying.

It's because of us not having breakfast again.
And the master, of course. And the beautiful world.
And you crying too, madam. Oh—Oh!
DYNAMENE. I can't forbid your crying; but you must cry
On the other side of the tomb. I'm becoming confused.
This is my personal grief and my sacrifice
Of self, solus. Right over there, darling girl.
DOTO. What here?

DYNAMENE.   Now, if you wish, you may cry, Doto.
But our tears are very different. For me
The world is all with Charon, all, all,
Even the metal and plume of the rose garden,
And the forest where the sea fumes overhead
In vegetable tides, and particularly
The entrance to the warm baths in Arcite Street
Where we first met;—all!—the sun itself
Trails an evening hand in the sultry river
Far away down by Acheron. I am lonely,
Virilius. Where is the punctual eye
And where is the cautious voice which made
Balance-sheets sound like Homer and Homer sound
Like balance-sheets? The precision of limbs, the amiable
Laugh, the exact festivity? Gone from the world.
You were the peroration of nature, Virilius.
You explained everything to me, even the extremely
Complicated gods. You wrote them down
In seventy columns. Dear curling calligraphy!
Gone from the world, once and for all. And I taught you
In your perceptive moments to appreciate me.
You said I was harmonious, Virilius,
Moulded and harmonious, little matronal
Ox-eye, your package. And then I would walk
Up and down largely, as it were making my own
Sunlight. What a mad blacksmith creation is
Who blows his furnaces until the stars fly upward
And iron Time is hot and politicians glow
And bulbs and roots sizzle into hyacinth
And orchis, and the sand puts out the lion,
Roaring yellow, and oceans bud with porpoises,
Blenny, tunny and the almost unexisting
Blindfish; throats are cut, the masterpiece
Looms out of labour; nations and rebellions
Are spat out to hang on the wind—and all is gone
In one Virilius, wearing his office tunic,
Checking the pence column as he went.

Where's animation now? What is there that stays
To dance? The eye of the one-eyed world is out. (*She weeps*)
DOTO. I shall try to grieve a little, too.
   It would take lessons, I imagine, to do it out loud
   For long. If I could only remember
   Any one of those fellows without wanting to laugh.
   Hopeless, I am. Now those good pair of shoes
   I gave away without thinking, that's a different—
   Well, I've cried enough about *them*, I suppose.
   Poor madam, poor master.
(TEGEUS *comes through the gate to the top of the steps*)
TEGEUS.   What's your trouble?
DOTO.   Oh!
   Oh! Oh, a man. I thought for a moment it was something
   With harm in it. Trust a man to be where it's dark.
   What is it? Can't you sleep?
TEGEUS.   Now, listen—
DOTO.   Hush!
   Remember you're in the grave. You must go away.
   Madam is occupied.
TEGEUS.   What, here?
DOTO.   Becoming
   Dead. We both are.
TEGEUS.   What's going on here?
DOTO.   Grief.
   Are you satisfied now?
TEGEUS.   Less and less. Do you know
   What the time is?
DOTO.   I'm not interested.
   We've done with all that. Go away. Be a gentleman.
   If we can't be free of men in a grave
   Death's a dead loss.
TEGEUS.   It's two in the morning. All
   I ask is what are women doing down here
   At two in the morning?
DOTO.   Can't you see she's crying?
   Or is she sleeping again? Either way
   She's making arrangements to join her husband.
TEGEUS.   Where?
DOTO. Good god, in the Underworld, dear man. Haven't you learnt
   About life and death?
TEGEUS.   In a manner, yes; in a manner;
   The rudiments. So the lady means to die?
DOTO. For love; beautiful, curious madam.
TEGEUS.   Not curious;

I've had thoughts like it. Death is a kind of love.
Not anything I can explain.

DOTO.   You'd better come in
And sit down.

TEGEUS.   I'd be grateful.

DOTO.   Do. It will be my last
Chance to have company, in the flesh.

TEGEUS.   Do you mean
You're going too?

DOTO.   Oh, certainly I am.
Not anything I can explain.
It all started with madam saying a man
Was two men really, and I'd only noticed one,
One each, I mean. It seems he has a soul
As well as his other troubles. And I like to know
What I'm getting with a man. I'm inquisitive,
I suppose you'd call me.

TEGEUS.   It takes some courage.

DOTO.   Well, yes
And no. I'm fond of change.

TEGEUS.   Would you object
To have me eating my supper here?

DOTO.   Be careful
Of the crumbs. We don't want a lot of squeaking mice
Just when we're dying.

TEGEUS.   What a sigh she gave then.
Down the air like a slow comet.
And now she's all dark again. Mother of me.
How long has this been going on?

DOTO.   Two days.
It should have been three by now, but at first
Madam had difficulty with the Town Council. They said
They couldn't have a tomb used as a private residence.
But madam told them she wouldn't be eating here,
Only suffering, and they thought that would be all right.

TEGEUS. Two of you. Marvellous. Who would have said
I should ever have stumbled on anything like this?
Do you have to cry? Yes, I suppose so. It's all
Quite reasonable.

DOTO.   Your supper and your knees.
That's what's making me cry. I can't bear sympathy
And they're sympathetic.

TEGEUS.   Please eat a bit of something.
I've no appetite left.

DOTO.   And see her go ahead of me?

Wrap it up; put it away. You sex of wicked beards!
It's no wonder you have to shave off your black souls
Every day as they push through your chins.
I'll turn my back on you. It means utter
Contempt. Eat? Utter contempt. Oh, little new rolls!

TEGEUS. Forget it, forget it; please forget it. Remember
I've had no experience of this kind of thing before.
Indeed I'm as sorry as I know how to be. Ssh,
We'll disturb her. She sighed again. O Zeus,
It's terrible! Asleep, and still sighing.
Mourning has made a warren in her spirit,
All that way below. Ponos! the heart
Is the devil of a medicine.

DOTO.   And I don't intend
To turn round.

TEGEUS.   I understand how you must feel.
Would it be—have you any objection
To my having a drink? I have a little wine here.
And, you probably see how it is: grief's in order,
And death's in order, and women—I can usually
Manage that too; but not all three together
At this hour of the morning. So you'll excuse me.
How about you? It would make me more comfortable
If you'd take a smell of it.

DOTO.   One for the road?

TEGEUS. One for the road.

DOTO.   It's the dust in my throat. The tomb
Is so dusty. Thanks, I will. There's no point in dying
Of everything, simultaneous.

TEGEUS.   It's lucky
I brought two bowls. I was expecting to keep
A drain for my relief when he comes in the morning.

DOTO. Are you on duty?

TEGEUS.   Yes.

DOTO.   It looks like it.

TEGEUS.   Well,
Here's your good health.

DOTO.   What good is that going to do me?
Here's to an easy crossing and not too much waiting
About on the bank. Do you have to tremble like that?

TEGEUS. The idea—I can't get used to it.

DOTO.   For a member
Of the forces, you're peculiarly queasy. I wish
Those owls were in Hades—oh no; let them stay where they are.
Have you never had nothing to do with corpses before?

TEGEUS. I've got six of them outside.

DOTO. Morpheus, that's plenty.
What are they doing there?

TEGEUS. Hanging.

DOTO. Hanging?

TEGEUS. On trees.
Five plane trees and a holly. The holly-berries
Are just reddening. Another drink?

DOTO. Why not?

TEGEUS. It's from Samos. Here's—

DOTO. All right. Let's just drink it.
—How did they get in that predicament?

TEGEUS. The sandy-haired fellow said we should collaborate
With everybody; the little man said he wouldn't
Collaborate with anybody; the old one
Said that the Pleiades weren't sisters but cousins
And anyway were manufactured in Lacedaemon.
The fourth said that we hanged men for nothing
The other two said nothing. Now they hang
About at the corner of the night, they're present
And absent, horribly obsequious to every
Move in the air, and yet they keep me standing
For five hours at a stretch.

DOTO. The wine has gone
Down to my knees.

TEGEUS. And up to your cheeks. You're looking
Fresher. If only—

DOTO. Madam? She never would.
Shall I ask her?

TEGEUS. No; no, don't dare, don't breathe it.
This is privilege, to come so near
To what is undeceiving and uncorrupt
And undivided; this is the clear fashion
For all souls, a ribbon to bind the unruly
Curls of living, a faith, a hope, Zeus
Yes, a fine thing. I am human, and this
Is human fidelity, and we can be proud
And unphilosophical.

DOTO. I need to dance
But I haven't the use of my legs.

TEGEUS. No, no, don't dance,
Or, at least, only inwards; don't dance; cry
Again. We'll put a moat of tears
Round her bastion of love, and save
The world. It's something, it's more than something,

It's regeneration, to see how a human cheek
Can become as pale as a pool.

DOTO.   Do you love me, handsome?

TEGEUS. To have found life, after all, unambiguous!

DOTO. Did you say Yes?

TEGEUS.   Certainly; just now I love all men.

DOTO. So do I.

TEGEUS.   And the world is a good creature again.
I'd begun to see it as mildew, verdigris,
Rust, woodrot, or as though the sky had uttered
An oval twirling blasphemy with occasional vistas
In country districts. I was within an ace
Of volunteering for overseas service. Despair
Abroad can always nurse pleasant thoughts of home.
Integrity, by god!

DOTO.   I love all the world
And the movement of the apple in your throat.
So shall you kiss me? It would be better, I should think,
To go moistly to Hades.

TEGEUS.   Hers is the way,
Luminous with sorrow.

DOTO.   Then I'll take
Another little swiggy. I love all men,
Everybody, even you, and I'll pick you
Some outrageous honeysuckle for your helmet,
If only it lived here. Pardon.

DYNAMENE.   Doto. Who is it?

DOTO. Honeysuckle, madam. Because of the bees.
Go back to sleep, madam.

DYNAMENE.   What person is it?

DOTO. Yes, I see what you mean, madam. It's a kind of
Corporal talking to his soul, on a five-hour shift,
Madam, with six bodies. He's been having his supper.

TEGEUS. I'm going. It's terrible that we should have disturbed her.

DOTO. He was delighted to see you so sad, madam.
It has stopped him going abroad.

DYNAMENE.   One with six bodies?
A messenger, a guide to where we go
It is possible he has come to show us the way
Out of these squalid suburbs of life, a shade,
A gorgon, who has come swimming up, against
The falls of my tears (for which in truth he would need
Many limbs) to guide me to Virilius.
I shall go quietly.

TEGEUS.   I do assure you—
  Such clumsiness, such a vile and unforgivable
  Intrusion. I shall obliterate myself
  Immediately.
DOTO.   Oblit—oh, what a pity
  To oblit. Pardon. Don't let him, the nice fellow.
DYNAMENE. Sir: your other five bodies: where are they?
TEGEUS.   Madam—
  Outside; I have them outside. On trees.
DYNAMENE.   Quack!
TEGEUS. What do I reply?
DYNAMENE.   Quack, charlatan!
  You've never known the gods. You came to mock me.
  Doto, this never was a gorgon, never.
  Nor a gentleman either. He's completely spurious.
  Admit it, you creature. Have you even a feather
  Of the supernatural in your system? Have you?
TEGEUS. Some of my relations—
DYNAMENE.   Well?
TEGEUS.   Are dead, I think;
  That is to say I have connexions—
DYNAMENE.   Connexions
  With pickpockets. It's a shameless imposition.
  Does the army provide you with no amusements?
  If I were still of the world, and not cloistered
  In a colourless landscape of winter thought
  Where the approaching Spring is desired oblivion,
  I should write sharply to your commanding officer.
  It should be done, it should be done. If my fingers
  Weren't so cold I would do it now. But they are,
  Horribly cold. And why should insolence matter
  When my colour of life is unreal, a blush on death,
  A partial mere diaphane? I don't know
  Why it should matter. Oafish, non-commissioned
  Young man! The boots of your conscience will pinch for ever
  If life's dignity has any self-protection.
  Oh, I have to sit down. The tomb's going round.
DOTO. Oh, madam, don't give over. I can't remember
  When things were so lively. He looks marvellously
  Marvellously uncomfortable. Go on, madam.
  Can't you, madam? Oh, madam, don't you feel up to it?
  There, do you see her, you acorn-chewing infantryman?
  You've made her cry, you square-bashing barbarian.
TEGEUS. O history, my private history, why

Was I led here? What stigmatism has got
Into my stars? Why wasn't it my brother?
He has a tacit misunderstanding with everybody
And washes in it. Why wasn't it my mother?
She makes a collection of other people's tears
And dries them all. Let them forget I came;
And lie in the terrible black crystal of grief
Which held them, before I broke it. Outside, Tegeus.

DOTO. Hey, I don't think so, I shouldn't say so. Come
Down again, uniform. Do you think you're going
To half kill an unprotected lady and then
Back out upwards? Do you think you can leave her like this?

TEGEUS. Yes, yes, I'll leave her. O directorate of gods,
How can I? Beauty's bit is between my teeth.
She has added another torture to me. Bottom
Of Hades' bottom.

DOTO.   Madam. Madam, the corporal
Has some wine here. It will revive you, madam.
And then you can go at him again, madam.

TEGEUS. It's the opposite of everything you've said,
I swear. I swear by Horkos and the Styx,
I swear by the nine acres of Tityos,
I swear the Hypnotic oath, by all the Titans—
By Koeos, Krios, Iapetos, Kronos, and so on—
By the three Hekatoncheires, by the insomnia
Of Tisiphone, by Jove, by jove, and the dew
On the feet of my boyhood, I am innocent
Of mocking you. Am I a Salmoneus
That, seeing such a flame of sorrow—

DYNAMENE.   You needn't
Labour to prove your secondary education.
Perhaps I jumped to a wrong conclusion, perhaps
I was hasty.

DOTO.   How easy to swear if you're properly educated.
Wasn't it pretty, madam? Pardon.

DYNAMENE.   If I misjudged you
I apologize, I apologize. Will you please leave us?
You were wrong to come here. In a place of mourning
Light itself is a trespasser; nothing can have
The right of entrance except those natural symbols
Of mortality, the jabbing, funeral, sleek-
With-omen raven, the death-watch beetle which mocks
Time: particularly, I'm afraid, the spider
Weaving his home with swift self-generated
Threads of slaughter; and, of course, the worm.

I wish it could be otherwise. Oh dear,
They aren't easy to live with.
DOTO.   Not even a *little* wine, madam?
DYNAMENE. Here, Doto?
DOTO.   Well, on the steps perhaps,
Except it's so draughty.
DYNAMENE.   Doto! Here?
DOTO.   No, madam;
I quite see.
DYNAMENE.   I might be wise to strengthen myself
In order to fast again; it would make me abler
For grief. I will breathe a little of it, Doto.
DOTO. Thank god. Where's the bottle?
DYNAMENE.   What an exquisite bowl.
TEGEUS. Now that it's peacetime we have pottery classes.
DYNAMENE. You made it yourself?
TEGEUS.   Yes. Do you see the design?
The corded god, tied also by the rays
Of the sun, and the astonished ship erupting
Into vines and vine-leaves, inverted pyramids
Of grapes, the uplifted hands of the men (the raiders),
And here the headlong sea, itself almost
Venturing into leaves and tendrils, and Proteus
With his beard braiding the wind, and this
Held by other hands is a drowned sailor—
DYNAMENE. Always, always.
DOTO.   Hold the bowl steady, madam.
Pardon.
DYNAMENE.   Doto, have you been drinking?
DOTO.   Here, madam?
I coaxed some a little way towards my mouth, madam,
But I scarcely swallowed except because I had to. The hiccup
Is from no breakfast, madam, and not meant to be funny.
DYNAMENE. You may drink this too. Oh, how the inveterate body,
Even when cut from the heart, insists on leaf,
Puts out, with a separate meaningless will,
Fronds to intercept the thankless sun.
How it does, oh, how it does. And how it confuses
The nature of the mind.
TEGEUS.   Yes, yes, the confusion;
That's something I understand better than anything.
DYNAMENE. When the thoughts would die, the instincts will set sail
For life. And when the thoughts are alert for life
The instincts will rage to be destroyed on the rocks.
To Virilius it was not so; his brain was an ironing-board

For all crumpled indecision: and I follow him,
The hawser of my world. You don't belong here,
You see; you don't belong here at all.

TEGEUS.   If only
I did. If only you knew the effort it costs me
To mount those steps again into an untrustworthy,
Unpredictable, unenlightened night,
And turn my back on—on a state of affairs,
I can only call it a vision, a hope, a promise,
A—By that I mean loyalty, enduring passion,
Unrecking bravery and beauty all in one.

DOTO. He means you, or you and me; or me. madam.

TEGEUS. It only remains for me to thank you, and to say
That whatever awaits me and for however long
I may be played by this poor musician, existence,
Your person and sacrifice will leave their trace
As clear upon me as the shape of the hills
Around my birthplace. Now I must leave you to your husband.

DOTO. Oh! You, madam.

DYNAMENE.   I'll tell you what I will do.
I will drink with you to the memory of my husband,
Because I have been curt, because you are kind,
And because I'm extremely thirsty. And then we will say
Good-bye and part to go to our opposite corruptions,
The world and the grave.

TEGEUS.   The climax to the vision.

DYNAMENE (*drinking*). My husband, and all he stood for.

TEGEUS.   Stands for.

DYNAMENE.   Stands for.

TEGEUS. Your husband.

DOTO.   The master.

DYNAMENE.   How good it is,
How it sings to the throat, purling with summer.

TEGEUS. It has a twin nature, winter and warmth in one,
Moon and meadow. Do you agree?

DYNAMENE.   Perfectly;
A cold bell sounding in a golden month.

TEGEUS. Crystal in harvest.

DYNAMENE.   Perhaps a nightingale
Sobbing among the pears.

TEGEUS.   In an old autumnal midnight.

DOTO. Grapes.—Pardon. There's some more here.

TEGEUS.   Plenty.
I drink to the memory of your husband.

DYNAMENE.   My husband.

DOTO. The master.

DYNAMENE. He was careless in his choice of wines.

TEGEUS. And yet
Rendering to living its rightful poise is not
Unimportant.

DYNAMENE. A mystery's in the world
Where a little liquid, with flavour, quality, and fume
Can be as no other, can hint and flute our senses
As though a music played in harvest hollows
And a movement was in the swathes of our memory.
Why should scent, why should flavour come
With such wings upon us? Parsley, for instance.

TEGEUS. Seaweed.

DYNAMENE. Lima trees.

DOTO. Horses.

TEGEUS. Fruit in the fire.

DYNAMENE. Do I know your name?

TEGEUS. Tegeus.

DYNAMENE. That's very thin for you,
It hardly covers your bones. Something quite different,
Altogether other. I shall think of it presently.

TEGEUS. Darker vowels, perhaps.

DYNAMENE. Yes, certainly darker vowels.
And your consonants should have a slight angle,
And a certain temperature. Do you know what I mean?
It will come to me.

TEGEUS. Now *your* name—

DYNAMENE. It is nothing
To any purpose. I'll be to you the She
In the tomb. You have the air of a natural-historian
As though you were accustomed to handling birds' eggs,
Or tadpoles, or putting labels on moths. You see?
The genius of dumb things, that they are nameless.
Have I found the seat of the weevil in human brains?
Our names. They make us broody; we sit and sit
To hatch them into reputation and dignity.
And then they set upon us and become despair,
Guilt and remorse. We go where they lead. We dance
Attendance on something wished upon us by the wife
Of our mother's physician. But insects meet and part
And put the woods about them, fill the dusk
And freckle the light and go and come without
A name among them, without the wish of a name
And very pleasant too. Did I interrupt you?

TEGEUS. I forget. We'll have no names then.

DYNAMENE.   I should like
  You to have a name, I don't know why; a small one
  To fill out the conversation.
TEGEUS.   I should like
  You to have a name too, if only for something
  To remember. Have you still some wine in your bowl?
DYNAMENE. Not altogether.
TEGEUS.   We haven't come to the end
  By several inches. Did I splash you?
DYNAMENE.   It doesn't matter.
  Well, here's to my husband's name.
TEGEUS.   Your husband's name.
DOTO. The master.
DYNAMENE.   It was kind of you to come.
TEGEUS. It was more than coming. I followed my future here,
  As we all do if we're sufficiently inattentive
  And don't vex ourselves with questions; or do I mean
  Attentive? If so, attentive to what? Do I sound
  Incoherent?
DYNAMENE.   You're wrong. There isn't a future here,
  Not here, not for you.
TEGEUS.   Your name's Dynamene.
DYNAMENE. Who—Have I been utterly irreverent? Are you—
  Who made you say that? Forgive me the question,
  But are you dark or light? I mean which shade
  Of the supernatural? Or if neither, what prompted you?
TEGEUS. Dynamene—
DYNAMENE.   No, but I'm sure you're the friend of nature,
  It must be so, I think I see little Phoebuses
  Rising and setting in your eyes.
DOTO.   They're not little Phoebuses,
  They're hoodwinks, madam. Your name is on your brooch.
  No little Phoebuses to-night.
DYNAMENE.   That's twice
  You've played me a trick. Oh, I know practical jokes
  Are common on Olympus, but haven't we at all
  Developed since the gods were born? Are gods
  And men both to remain immortal adolescents?
  How tiresome it all is.
TEGEUS.   It was you, each time,
  Who said I was supernatural. When did I say so?
  You're making me into whatever you imagine
  And then you blame me because I can't live up to it.
DYNAMENE. I shall call you Chromis. It has a breadlike sound.
  I think of you as a crisp loaf.

TEGEUS.   And now
    You'll insult me because I'm not sliceable.
DYNAMENE. I think drinking is harmful to our tempers.
TEGEUS. If I seem to be frowning, that is only because
    I'm looking directly into your light: I must look
    Angrily, or shut my eyes.
DYNAMENE.   Shut them.—Oh,
    You have eyelashes! A new perspective of you.
    Is that how you look when you sleep?
TEGEUS.   My jaw drops down.
DYNAMENE. Show me how.
TEGEUS.   Like this.
DYNAMENE.   It makes an irresistible
    Moron of you. Will you waken now?
    It's morning; I see a thin dust of daylight
    Blowing on to the steps.
TEGEUS.   Already? Dynamene,
    You're tricked again. This time by the moon.
DYNAMENE.   Oh well,
    Moon's daylight, then. Doto is asleep.
TEGEUS.   Doto
    Is asleep . . .
DYNAMENE.   Chromis, what made you walk about
    In the night? What, I wonder, made you not stay
    Sleeping wherever you slept? Was it the friction
    Of the world on your mind? Those two are difficult
    To make agree. Chromis—now try to learn
    To answer your name. I won't say Tegeus.
TEGEUS.   And I
    Won't say Dynamene.
DYNAMENE.   Not?
TEGEUS.   It makes you real.
    Forgive me, a terrible thing has happened. Shall I
    Say it and perhaps destroy myself for you?
    Forgive me first, or, more than that, forgive
    Nature who winds her furtive stream all through
    Our reason. Do you forgive me?
DYNAMENE.   I'll forgive
    Anything, if it's the only way I can know
    What you have to tell me.
TEGEUS.   I felt us to be alone;
    Here in a grave, separate from any life,
    I and the only one of beauty, the only
    Persuasive key to all my senses,
    In spite of my having lain day after day

And pored upon the sepals, corolla, stamen, and bracts
Of the yellow bog-iris. Then my body ventured
A step towards interrupting your perfection of purpose
And my own renewed faith in human nature.
Would you have believed that possible?

DYNAMENE.   I have never
Been greatly moved by the yellow bog-iris. Alas,
It's as I said. This place is for none but the spider,
Raven and worms, not for a living man.

TEGEUS. It has been a place of blessing to me. It will always
Play in me, a fountain of confidence
When the world is arid. But I know it is true
I have to leave it, and though it withers my soul
I must let you make your journey.

DYNAMENE.   No.

TEGEUS.   Not true?

DYNAMENE. We can talk of something quite different.

TEGEUS.   Yes, we can!
Oh yes, we will! Is it your opinion
That no one believes who hasn't learned to doubt?
Or, another thing, if we persuade ourselves
To one particular Persuasion, become Sophist,
Stoic, Platonist, anything whatever,
Would you say that there must be areas of soul
Lying unproductive therefore, or dishonoured
Or blind?

DYNAMENE.   No, I don't know.

TEGEUS.   No. It's impossible
To tell. Dynamene, if only I had
Two cakes of pearl-barley and hydromel
I could see you to Hades, leave you with your husband
And come back to the world.

DYNAMENE.   Ambition, I suppose,
Is an appetite particular to man.
What is your definition?

TEGEUS.   The desire to find
A reason for living.

DYNAMENE.   But then, suppose it leads,
As often, one way or another, it does, to death.

TEGEUS. Then that may be life's reason. Oh, but how
Could I bear to return, Dynamene? The earth's
Daylight would be my grave if I had left you
In that unearthly night.

DYNAMENE.   O Chromis——

TEGEUS.   Tell me,
What is your opinion of Progress? Does it, for example,
Exist? Is there ever progression without retrogression?
Therefore is it not true that mankind
Can more justly be said increasingly to Gress?
As the material improves, the craftsmanship deteriorates
And honor and virtue remain the same. I love you,
Dynamene.
DYNAMENE.   Would you consider we go round and round?
TEGEUS. We concertina, I think; taking each time
A larger breath, so that the farther we go out
The farther we have to go in.
DYNAMENE.   There'll come a time.
When it will be unbearable to continue.
TEGEUS. Unbearable.
DYNAMENE.   Perhaps we had better have something
To eat. The wine has made your eyes so quick
I am breathless beside them. It *is*
Your eyes, I think; or your intelligence
Holding my intelligence up above you
Between its hands. Or the cut of your uniform.
TEGEUS. Here's a new roll with honey. In the gods' names
Let's sober ourselves.
DYNAMENE.   As soon as possible.
TEGEUS.   Have you
Any notion of algebra?
DYNAMENE.   We'll discuss you, Chromis.
We will discuss you, till you're nothing but words.
TEGEUS. I? There is nothing, of course, I would rather discuss,
Except—if it would be no intrusion—you, Dynamene.
DYNAMENE. No, you couldn't want to. But your birthplace, Chromis,
With the hills that placed themselves in you for ever
As you say, where was it?
TEGEUS.   My father's farm at Pyxa.
DYNAMENE. There? Could it be there?
TEGEUS.   I was born in the hills
Between showers, a quarter of an hour before milking time.
Do you know Pyxa? It stretches to the crossing of two
Troublesome roads, and buries its back in beechwood,
From which come the white owls of our nights
And the mulling and cradling of doves in the day.
I attribute my character to those shadows
And heavy roots; and my interest in music
To the sudden melodious escape of the young river

Where it breaks from nosing through the cresses and kingcups.
That's honestly so.
DYNAMENE.   You used to climb about
Among the windfallen tower of Phrasidemus
Looking for bees' nests.
TEGEUS.   What? When have I
Said so?
DYNAMENE.   Why, all the children did.
TEGEUS. Yes: but, in the name of light, how do you *know* that?
DYNAMENE. I played there once, on holiday.
TEGEUS.   O Klotho,
Lachesis and Atropos!
DYNAMENE.   It's the strangest chance:
I may have seen, for a moment, your boyhood.
TEGEUS.   I may
Have seen something like an early flower
Something like a girl. If I only could remember how I must
Have seen you. Were you after the short white violets?
Maybe I blundered past you, taking your look,
And scarcely acknowledged how a star
Ran through me, to live in the brooks of my blood for ever.
Or I saw you playing at hiding in the cave
Where the ferns are and the water drips.
DYNAMENE. I was quite plain and fat and I was usually
Hitting someone. I wish I could remember you.
I'm envious of the days and children who saw you
Then. It is curiously a little painful
Not to share your past.
TEGEUS.   How did it come
Our stars could mingle for an afternoon
So long ago, and then forget us or tease us
Or helplessly look on the dark high seas
Of our separation, while time drank
The golden hours? What hesitant fate is that?
DYNAMENE. Time? Time? Why—how old are we?
TEGEUS.   Young,
Thank both our mothers, but still we're older than to-night
And so older than we should be. Wasn't I born
In love with what, only now, I have grown to meet?
I'll tell you something else. I was born entirely
For this reason. I was born to fill a gap
In the world's experience, which had never known
Chromis loving Dynamene.
DYNAMENE.   You are so
Excited, poor Chromis. What is it? Here you sit

With a woman who has wept away all claims
To appearance, unbecoming in her oldest clothes,
With not a trace of liveliness, a drab
Of melancholy, entirely shadow without
A smear of sun. Forgive me if I tell you
That you fall easily into superlatives.

TEGEUS. Very well. I'll say nothing, then. I'll fume
With feeling.

DYNAMENE.   Now you go to the extreme. Certainly
You must speak. You may have more to say. Besides
You might let your silence run away with you
And not say something that you should. And how
Should I answer you then? Chromis, you boy,
I can't look away from you. You use
The lamplight and the moon so skilfully,
So arrestingly, in and around your furrows.
A humorous ploughman goes whistling to a team
Of sad sorrow, to and fro in your brow
And over your arable cheek. Laugh for me. Have you
Cried for women, ever?

TEGEUS.   In looking about for you.
But I have recognized them for what they were.

DYNAMENE. What were they?

TEGEUS.   Never you: never, although
They could walk with bright distinction into all men's
Longest memories, never you, by a hint
Or a faint quality, or at least not more
Than reflectively, stars lost and uncertain
In the sea, compared with the shining salt, the shiners,
The galaxies, the clusters, the bright grain whirling
Over the black threshing-floor of space.
Will you make some effort to believe that?

DYNAMENE.   No, no effort.
It lifts me and carries me. It may be wild
But it comes to me with a charm, like trust indeed,
And eats out of my heart, dear Chromis,
Absurd, disconcerting Chromis. You make me
Feel I wish I could look my best for you.
I wish, at least, that I could believe myself
To be showing some beauty for you, to put in the scales
Between us. But they dip to you, they sink
With masculine victory.

TEGEUS.   Eros, no! No!
If this is less than your best, then never, in my presence,
Be more than your less: never! If you should bring

More to your mouth or to your eyes, a moisture
Or a flake of light, anything, anything fatally
More, perfection would fetch her unsparing rod
Out of pickle to flay me, and what would have been love
Will be the end of me. O Dynamene,
Let me unload something of my lips' longing
On to yours receiving. Oh, when I cross
Like this the hurt of the little space between us
I come a journey from the wrenching ice
To walk in the sun. That is the feeling.

DYNAMENE.   Chromis,
Where am I going? No, don't answer. It's death
I desire, not you.

TEGEUS.   Where is the difference? Call me
Death instead of Chromis. I'll answer to anything.
It's desire all the same, of death in me, or me
In death, but Chromis either way. Is it so?
Do you not love me, Dynamene?

DYNAMENE.   How could it happen?
I'm going to my husband. I'm too far on the way
To admit myself to life again. Love's in Hades.

TEGEUS. Also here. And here are we, not there
In Hades. Is your husband expecting you?

DYNAMENE. Surely, surely?

TEGEUS.   Not necessarily. I,
If I had been your husband, would never dream
Of expecting you. I should remember your body
Descending stairs in the floating light, but not
Descending in Hades. I should say "I have left
My wealth warm on the earth, and, hell, earth needs it."
"Was all I taught her of love," I should say, "so poor
That she will leave her flesh and become shadow?"
"Wasn't our love for each other" (I should continue)
"Infused with life, and life infused with our love?
Very well; repeat me in love, repeat me in life,
And let me sing in your blood for ever."

DYNAMENE. Stop, stop, I shall be dragged apart!
Why should the fates do everything to keep me
From dying honourably? They must have got
Tired of honour in Elysium. Chromis, it's terrible
To be susceptible to two conflicting norths.
I have the constitution of a whirlpool.
Am I actually twirling, or is it just sensation?

TEGEUS. You're still; still as the darkness.

DYNAMENE. What appears
Is so unlike what is. And what is madness
To those who only observe, is often wisdom
To those to whom it happens.

TEGEUS. Are we compelled
To go into all this?

DYNAMENE. Why, how could I return
To my friends? Am I to be an entertainment?

TEGEUS. That's for to-morrow. To-night I need to kiss you,
Dynamene. Let's see what the whirlpool does
Between my arms; let it whirl on my breast. O love,
Come in.

DYNAMENE. I am there before I reach you; my body
Only follows to join my longing which
Is holding you already.—Now I am
All one again.

TEGEUS. I feel as the gods feel:
This is their sensation of life, not a man's:
Their suspension of immortality, to enrich
Themselves with time. O life, O death, O body,
O spirit, O Dynamene.

DYNAMENE. O all
In myself; it so covets all in you,
My care, my Chromis. Then I shall be
Creation.

TEGEUS. You have the skies already;
Out of them you are buffeting me with your gales
Of beauty. Can we be made of dust, as they tell us?
What! dust with dust releasing such a light
And such an apparition of the world
Within one body? A thread of your hair has stung me.
Why do you push me away?

DYNAMENE. There's so much metal
About you. Do I have to be imprisoned
In an armoury?

TEGEUS. Give your hand to the buckles and then
To me.

DYNAMENE. Don't help; I'll do them all myself.

TEGEUS. O time and patience! I want you back again.

DYNAMENE. We have a lifetime. O Chromis, think, think
Of that. And even unfastening a buckle
Is loving. And not easy. Very well,
You can help me. Chromis, what zone of miracle
Did you step into to direct you in the dark

To where I waited, not knowing I waited?

TEGEUS.   I saw

The lamplight. That was only the appearance

Of some great gesture in the bed of fortune.

I saw the lamplight.

DYNAMENE.   But here? So far from life?

What brought you near enough to see lamplight?

TEGEUS.   Zeus,

That reminds me.

DYNAMENE.   What is it, Chromis?

TEGEUS.   I'm on duty.

DYNAMENE. Is it warm enough to do without your greaves?

TEGEUS. Darling loom of magic, I must go back

To take a look at those boys. The whole business

Of guard had gone out of my mind.

DYNAMENE.   What boys, my heart?

TEGEUS. My six bodies.

DYNAMENE.   Chromis, not that joke

Again.

TEGEUS.   No joke, sweet. To-day our city

Held a sextuple hanging. I'm minding the bodies

Until five o'clock. Already I've been away

For half an hour.

DYNAMENE.   What can they do, poor bodies,

In half an hour, or half a century?

You don't really mean to go?

TEGEUS.   Only to make

My conscience easy. Then, Dynamene,

No cloud can rise on love, no hovering thought

Fidget, and the night will be only to *us*.

DYNAMENE. But if every half-hour——

TEGEUS.   Hush, smile of my soul,

My sprig, my sovereign: this is to hold your eyes,

I sign my lips on them both: this is to keep

Your forehead—do you feel the claim of my kiss

Falling into your thought? And now your throat

Is a white branch and my lips two singing birds—

They are coming to rest. Throat, remember me

Until I come back in five minutes. Over all

Here is my parole: I give it to your mouth

To give me again before it's dry. I promise:

Before it's dry, or not long after.

DYNAMENE.   Run,

Run all the way. You needn't be afraid of stumbling.

There's plenty of moon. The fields are blue. Oh, wait,

Wait! My darling. No, not now: it will keep
Until I see you; I'll have it here at my lips.
Hurry.
TEGEUS.   So, long, my haven.
DYNAMENE.   Hurry, hurry! (*Exit* TEGEUS)
DOTO. Yes, madam, hurry; of course. Are we there
Already? How nice. Death doesn't take
Any doing at all. We were gulped into Hades
As easy as an oyster.
DYNAMENE.   Doto!
DOTO.   Hurry, hurry,
Yes, madam.—But they've taken out all my bones.
I haven't a bone left. I'm a Shadow: wonderfully shady
In the legs. We shall have to sit out eternity, madam,
If they've done the same to you.
DYNAMENE.   You'd better wake up.
If you can't go to sleep again, you'd better wake up.
Oh dear.—We're still alive, Doto, do you hear me?
DOTO. You must speak for yourself, madam. I'm quite dead.
I'll tell you how I know. I feel
Invisible. I'm a wraith, madam; I'm only
Waiting to be wafted.
DYNAMENE.   If only you *would* be.
Do you see where you are? Look. Do you see?
DOTO. Yes. You're right, madam. We're still alive.
Isn't it enough to make you swear?
Here we are, dying to be dead,
And where does it get us?
DYNAMENE.   Perhaps you should try to die
In some other place. Yes! Perhaps the air here
Suits you too well. You were sleeping very heavily.
DOTO. And all the time you alone and dying.
I shouldn't have. Has the corporal been long gone,
Madam?
DYNAMENE.   He came and went, came and went,
You know the way.
DOTO.   Very well I do. And went
He should have, come he should never. Oh dear, he must
Have disturbed you, madam.
DYNAMENE.   He could be said
To've disturbed me. Listen; I have something to say to you.
DOTO. I expect so, madam. Maybe I *could* have kept him out
But men are in before I wish they wasn't.
I think quickly enough, but I get behindhand
With what I ought to be saying. It's a kind of stammer

In my way of life, madam.

DYNAMENE.   I have been unkind,
I have sinfully wronged you, Doto.

DOTO.   Never, madam.

DYNAMENE. Oh yes. I was letting you die with me, Doto, without
Any fair reason. I was drowning you
In grief that wasn't yours. That was wrong, Doto.

DOTO. But I haven't got anything against dying, madam.
I may *like* the situation, as far as I like
Any situation, madam. Now if you'd said mangling,
A lot of mangling, I might have thought twice about staying.
We all have our dislikes, madam.

DYNAMENE.   I'm asking you
To leave me, Doto, at once, as quickly as possible,
Now, before—now, Doto, and let me forget
My bad mind which confidently expected you
To companion me to Hades. Now good-bye,
Good-bye.

DOTO.   No, it's not good-bye at all.
I shouldn't know another night of sleep, wondering
How you got on, or what I was missing, come to that.
I should be anxious about you, too. When you belong
To an upper class, the netherworld might come strange.
Now I was born nether, madam, though not
As nether as some. No, it's not good-bye, madam.

DYNAMENE. Oh Doto, go; you must, you must! And if I seem
Without gratitude, forgive me. It isn't so,
It is far, far from so. But I can only
Regain my peace of mind if I know you're gone.

DOTO. Besides, look at the time, madam. Where should I go
At three in the morning? Even if I was to think
Of going; and think of it I never shall.

DYNAMENE. Think of the unmatchable world, Doto.

DOTO.   I do
Think of it, madam. And when I think of it, what
Have I thought? Well, it depends, madam.

DYNAMENE.   I insist,
Obey me! At once! Doto!

DOTO.   Here I sit.

DYNAMENE. What shall I do with you?

DOTO.   Ignore me, madam.
I know my place. I shall die quite unobtrusive.
Oh, look, the corporal's forgotten to take his equipment.

DYNAMENE. Could he be so careless?

DOTO.   I shouldn't hardly have thought so.

Poor fellow. They'll go and deduct it off his credits.
I suppose, madam, I suppose he couldn't be thinking
Of coming back?

DYNAMENE. He'll think of these. He will notice
He isn't wearing them. He'll come; he is sure to come.

DOTO. Oh.

DYNAMENE. I know he will.

DOTO. Oh, oh.
Is that all for to-night, madam? May I go now, madam?

DYNAMENE. Doto! Will you?

DOTO. Just you try to stop me, madam.
Sometimes going is a kind of instinct with me.
I'll leave death to some other occasion.

DYNAMENE. Do,
Doto. Any other time. Now you must hurry.
I won't delay you from life another moment.
Oh, Doto, good-bye.

DOTO. Good-bye. Life is unusual,
Isn't it, madam? Remember me to Cerberus.

(*Re-enter* TEGEUS. DOTO *passes him on the steps*)

DOTO (*as she goes*). You left something behind. Ye gods, what a moon!

DYNAMENE. Chromis, it's true; my lips are hardly dry.
Time runs again; the void is space again;
Space has life again; Dynamene has Chromis.

TEGEUS. It's over.

DYNAMENE. Chromis, you're sick. As white as wool.
Come, you covered the distance too quickly.
Rest in my arms; get your breath again.

TEGEUS. I've breathed one night too many. Why did I see you,
Why in the name of life did I see you?

DYNAMENE. Why?
Weren't we gifted with each other? O heart,
What do you mean?

TEGEUS. I mean that joy is nothing
But the parent of doom. Why should I have found
Your constancy such balm to the world and yet
Find, by the same vision, its destruction
A necessity? We're set upon by love
To make us incompetent to steer ourselves,
To make us docile to fate. I should have known:
Indulgences, not fulfilment, is what the world
Permits us.

DYNAMENE. Chromis, is this intelligible?
Help me to follow you. What did you meet in the fields
To bring about all this talk? Do you still love me?

TEGEUS. What good will it do us? I've lost a body.
DYNAMENE.   A body?
  One of the six? Well, it isn't with them you propose
  To love me; and you couldn't keep it for ever.
  Are we going to allow a body that isn't there
  To come between us?
TEGEUS.   But I'm responsible for it.
  I have to account for it in the morning. Surely
  You see, Dynamene, the horror we're faced with?
  The relatives have had time to cut him down
  And take him away for burial. It means
  A court martial. No doubt about the sentence.
  I shall take the place of the missing man.
  To be hanged, Dynamene! Hanged, Dynamene!
DYNAMENE. No; it's monstrous! Your life is yours, Chromis.
TEGEUS. Anything but. That's why I have to take it.
  At the best we live our lives on loan,
  At the worst in chains. And I was never born
  To have life. Then for what? To be had by it,
  And so are we all. But I'll make it what it is,
  By making it nothing.
DYNAMENE.   Chromis, you're frightening me.
  What are you meaning to do?
TEGEUS.   I have to die,
  Dance of my heart, I have to die, to die,
  To part us, to go to my sword and let it part us.
  I'll have my free will even if I'm compelled to it.
  I'll kill myself.
DYNAMENE.   Oh, no! No, Chromis!
  It's all unreasonable—no such horror
  Can come of a pure accident. Have you hanged?
  How can they hang you for simply not being somewhere?
  How can they hang you for losing a dead man?
  They must have wanted to lose him, or they wouldn't
  Have hanged him. No, you're scaring yourself for nothing
  And making me frantic.
TEGEUS.   It's section six, paragraph
  Three in the Regulations. That's my doom.
  I've read it for myself. And, by my doom,
  Since I have to die, let me die here, in love,
  Promoted by your kiss to tower, in dying,
  High above my birth. For god's sake let me die
  On a wave of life, Dynamene, with an action
  I can take some pride in. How could I settle to death
  Knowing that you last saw me stripped and strangled

On a holly tree? Demoted first and then hanged!
DYNAMENE. Am I supposed to love the corporal
  Or you? It's you I love, from head to foot
  And out to the ends of your spirit. What shall I do
  If you die? How could I follow you? I should find you
  Discussing me with my husband, comparing your feelings,
  Exchanging reactions. Where should I put myself?
  Or am I to live on alone, or find in life
  Another source of love, in memory
  Of Virilius and of you?
TEGEUS.   Dynamene,
  Not that! Since everything in the lives of men
  Is brief to indifference, let our love at least
  Echo and perpetuate itself uniquely
  As long as time allows you. Though you go
  to the limit of age, it won't be far to contain me.
DYNAMENE. It will seem like eternity ground into days and days.
TEGEUS. Can I be certain of you, for ever?
DYNAMENE.   But, Chromis,
  Surely you said——
TEGEUS.   Surely we have sensed
  Our passion to be greater than mortal? Must I
  Die believing it is dying with me?
DYNAMENE.   Chromis,
  You must never die, never! It would be
  An offence against truth.
TEGEUS.   I cannot live to be hanged.
  It would be an offence against life. Give me my sword,
  Dynamene. O Hades, when you look pale
  You take the heart out of me. I could die
  Without a sword by seeing you suffer. Quickly!
  Give me my heart back again with your lips
  And I'll live the rest of my ambitions
  In a last kiss.
DYNAMENE.   Oh, no, no, no!
  Give my blessing to your desertion of me?
  Never, Chromis, never. Kiss you and then
  Let you go? Love you, for death to have you?
  Am I to be made the fool of courts martial?
  Who are they who think they can discipline souls
  Right off the earth? What discipline is that?
  Chromis, love is the only discipline
  And we're the disciples of love. I hold you to that:
  Hold you, hold you.
TEGEUS.   We have no chance. It's determined

In section six, paragraph three, of the Regulations.
That has more power than love. It can snuff the great
Candles of creation. It makes me able
To do the impossible, to leave you, to go from the light
That keeps you.

DYNAMENE.   No!

TEGEUS.   O dark, it does. Good-bye,
My memory of earth, my dear most dear
Beyond every expectation. I was wrong
To want you to keep our vows existent
In the vacuum that's coming. It would make you
A heaviness to the world, when you should be,
As you are, a form of light. Dynamene, turn
Your head away. I'm going to let my sword
Solve all the riddles.

DYNAMENE.   Chromis, I have it! I know!
Virilius will help you.

TEGEUS.   Virilius?

DYNAMENE. My husband. He can be the other body.

TEGEUS. Your husband can?

DYNAMENE.   He has no further use
For what he left of himself to lie with us here.
Is there any reason why he shouldn't hang
On your holly tree? Better, far better, he,
Than you who are still alive, and surely better
Than *idling* into corruption?

TEGEUS.   Hang your husband?
Dynamene, it's terrible, horrible.

DYNAMENE. How little you can understand. I loved
His life not his death. And now we can give his death
The power of life. Not horrible: wonderful!
Isn't it so? That I should be able to feel
He moves again in the world, accomplishing
Our welfare? It's more than my grief could do.

TEGEUS. What can I say?

DYNAMENE.   That you love me; as I love him
And you. Let's celebrate your safety then.
Where's the bottle? There's some wine unfinished in this bowl.
I'll share it with you. Now forget the fear
We were in; look at me, Chromis. Come away
From the pit you nearly dropped us in. My darling,
I give you Virilius.

TEGEUS.   Virilius.
And all that follows.

DOTO (*on the steps, with the bottle*). The master. Both the masters.

Paddy Chayefsky

M A R T Y

Like a modern drama, a television play is presented with a limited number of stage settings and with a few interruptions. But the number of sets which may be used is greater and the interruptions are shorter than in the theater. A background sometimes can be suggested by a few details—a library by some shelves of books, a garden by a flowering plant or two. Such "insert scenes" can be combined with detailed settings so that a studio the size of a storeroom can supply a fair number of different backgrounds. Action may move rapidly from background to background (within limits,

Television performance of Marty

for the action must continue while an actor changes costumes and moves from set to set). The intermissions are relatively short, totaling five minutes, perhaps, in a presentation lasting an hour. Hence there is a continuity of action comparable to that on the Elizabethan stage (Shakespeare's plays are readily adaptable to television).

The audience may be vast—literally millions of people of many backgrounds and classes. Nevertheless, actors who use the exaggerated gestures or facial expressions of the theater seem unnatural on television. For the relationship between actors and audience is comparable to that of intimate drama. The audience is made up of small groups, the screen is close, and there is no problem about seeing details or hearing clearly. Close-ups may be used frequently, and facial expressions can communicate much that would have to be represented by dialog and action on the stage.

But the commercial auspices under which television plays are presented in the United States create some limitations for the writer. The sponsor is eager, naturally enough, to have as large an audience as possible, so situations or incidents which would be likely to offend any sizable number of viewers are taboo. The very fact that the plays are watched in living rooms by families leads to the imposing of more restrictions upon subject matter than are imposed upon dramas in the legitimate

theater. A writer usually submits an outline of his television drama for a reading by the producer and the director of a program. If this is tentatively approved, after a conference and revisions, the outline is scrutinized by the advertising agency in charge of the program and, if again approved, revised. Then the author writes his script, and this, too, is likely to be revised. Moreover, there is a rigid control over the time at the author's disposal: according to the arrangements between sponsor and network, the "half-hour" play will last no more than twenty-two minutes, say, and the "hour" play no more than fifty-three minutes, on the dot—as compared with an hour and twenty minutes for a modern drama. This means that the line or lines of action and the number of incidents must be relatively small. Other limitations result from the nature of the picture-screen; for instance, an author cannot as a rule have more than four or five important characters on camera at one time. These are severe limitations; but dramatic works have always been limited in various ways, and authors still have been able to produce fine works within the limitations. Often because new possibilities and restrictions arise with new production methods or new media, authors necessarily discover fresh areas of life for exploration.

Paddy Chayefsky believes that in his television play *Marty* he has worked in an area which television has helped authors discover—intimate and quite detailed representations of rather commonplace moments in ordinary lives. "The main characters are typical, rather than exceptional," he notes; "the situations are easily identifiable by the audience; and the relationships are as common as common people. . . . I tried to write the dialog as if it had been wire-tapped. I tried to envision the scenes as if a camera had been focused upon the unsuspecting characters and had caught them in an untouched moment of life."

The story as he sees it is a very ordinary love story shown as it really would have happened. It is sound in its psychological depiction of relationships between characters, and it has the aspect of reality. Partly because its characters are so ordinary, partly because it is untheatrical and unexaggerated, with the plot movement from scene to scene gently shaded in a way required in television, it captures and holds the interest and the profound sympathy of members of its audience.

....

Marty, presented on the Philco-Goodyear Playhouse in 1954, was universally praised by critics, and won a number of awards. Adapted as a motion picture in 1955, it was awarded first place in the Cannes Film Festival and was named best production of the year by the Academy of Motion Picture Arts and Sciences.

CHARACTERS

MARTY	YOUNG MAN
CLARA	CRITIC
ANGIE	BARTENDER
MOTHER	TWENTY-YEAR-OLD
AUNT	ITALIAN WOMAN
VIRGINIA	SHORT GIRL
THOMAS	GIRL

Act I

FADE IN: *A butcher shop in the Italian district of New York City. Actually, we fade in on a close-up of a butcher's saw being carefully worked through a side of beef, and we dolly back to show the butcher at work, and then the whole shop. The butcher is a mild-mannered, stout, short, balding young man of thirty-six. His charm lies in an almost indestructible good-natured amiability.*

The shop contains three women customers. One is a young mother with a baby carriage. She is chatting with a second woman of about forty at the door. The customer being waited on at the moment is a stout, elderly Italian woman who is standing on tiptoe, peering over the white display counter, checking the butcher as he saws away.

ITALIAN WOMAN. Your kid brother got married last Sunday, eh, Marty?

MARTY (*absorbed in his work*). That's right, Missus Fusari. It was a very nice affair.

ITALIAN WOMAN. That's the big tall one, the fellow with the mustache.

MARTY (*sawing away*). No, that's my other brother Freddie. My other brother Freddie, he's been married four years already. He lives down on Quincy Street. The one who got married Sunday, that was my little brother Nickie.

ITALIAN WOMAN. I thought he was a big, tall, fat fellow. Didn't I meet him here one time? Big, tall, fat fellow, he tried to sell me life insurance?

MARTY (*sets the cut of meat on the scale, watches its weight register*). No, that's my sister Margaret's husband Frank. My sister Margaret, she's married to the insurance salesman. My sister Rose, she married a contractor. They moved to Detroit last year. And my other sister, Frances, she got married about two and a half years ago in Saint John's Church on Adams Boulevard. Oh, that was a big affair. Well, Missus Fusari, that'll be three dollars. ninety-four cents. How's that with you? (*The Italian woman produces an old leather change purse from her pocketbook and painfully extracts three single dollar bills and ninety-four cents to the penny and lays the money piece by piece on the counter*)

YOUNG MOTHER (*calling from the door*). Hey, Marty, I'm inna hurry.

MARTY (*wrapping the meat, calls amiably back*). You're next right now, Missus Canduso.

(*The old Italian lady has been regarding Marty with a baleful scowl*)

ITALIAN WOMAN. Well, Marty, when you gonna get married? You should be ashamed. All your brothers and sisters, they all younger than you, and they married, and they got children. I just saw your mother inna fruit shop, and she says to me: "Hey, you know a nice girl for my boy Marty?" Watsa matter with you? That's no way. Watsa matter with you? Now, you get married, you hear me what I say?

MARTY (*amiably*). I hear you, Missus Fusari.

(*The old lady takes her parcel of meat, but apparently feels she still hasn't quite made her point*)

ITALIAN WOMAN. My son Frank, he was married when he was nineteen years old. Watsa matter with you?

MARTY. Missus Fusari, Missus Canduso over there, she's inna big hurry, and . . .

ITALIAN WOMAN. You be ashamed of yourself. (*She takes her package of meat, turns, and shuffles to the door and exits.* MARTY *gathers up the money on the counter, turns to the cash register behind him to ring up the sale*)

YOUNG MOTHER. Marty, I want a nice big fat pullet, about four pounds. I hear your kid brother got married last Sunday.

MARTY. Yeah, it was a very nice affair, Missus Canduso.

YOUNG MOTHER. Marty, you oughtta be ashamed. All your kid brothers and sisters, married and have children. When you gonna get married?

(CLOSE-UP: MARTY. *He sends a glance of weary exasperation up to the ceiling. With a gesture of mild irritation, he pushes the plunger of the cash register. It makes a sharp ping.*

(DISSOLVE TO: *Close-up of television set. A baseball game is in progress. Camera pulls back to show we are in a typical neighborhood bar—red leatherette booths—a jukebox, some phone booths. About half the bar stools are occupied by neighborhood folk.* MARTY *enters, pads amiably to one of the booths where a young man of about thirty-odd already sits. This is* ANGIE. MARTY *slides into the booth across from* ANGIE. ANGIE *is a little wasp of a fellow. He has a newspaper spread out before him to the sports pages.* MARTY *reaches over and pulls one of the pages over for himself to read. For a moment the two friends sit across from each other, reading the sports pages. Then* ANGIE, *without looking up, speaks*)

ANGIE. Well, what do you feel like doing tonight?

MARTY. I don't know, Angie. What do you feel like doing?

ANGIE. Well, we oughtta do something. It's Saturday night. I don't wanna go bowling like last Saturday. How about calling up that big girl we picked up inna movies about a month ago in the RKO Chester?

MARTY (*not very interested*). Which one was that?

ANGIE. That big girl that was sitting in front of us with the skinny friend.

MARTY. Oh, yeah.

ANGIE. We took them home alla way out in Brooklyn. Her name was Mary Feeney. What do you say? You think I oughtta give her a ring? I'll take the skinny one.

MARTY. It's five o'clock already, Angie. She's probably got a date by now.

ANGIE. Well, let's call her up. What can we lose?

MARTY. I didn't like her, Angie. I don't feel like calling her up.

ANGIE. Well, what do you feel like doing tonight?

MARTY. I don't know. What do you feel like doing?

ANGIE. Well, we're back to that, huh? I say to you: "What do you feel like doing tonight?" And you say to me: "I don't know, what do you feel like doing?" And then we wind up sitting around your house with a couple of cans of beer, watching Sid Caesar on television. Well, I tell you what I feel like doing. I feel like calling up this Mary Feeney. She likes you.

(MARTY *looks up quickly at this*)

MARTY. What makes you say that?

ANGIE. I could see she likes you.

MARTY. Yeah, sure.

ANGIE (*half rising in his seat*). I'll call her up.

MARTY. You call her up for yourself, Angie. I don't feel like calling her up.

(ANGIE *sits down again. They both return to reading the paper for a moment. Then* ANGIE *looks up again*)

ANGIE. Boy, you're getting to be a real drag, you know that?

MARTY. Angie, I'm thirty-six years old. I been looking for a girl every Saturday night of my life. I'm a little, short, fat fellow, and girls don't go for me, that's all. I'm not like you. I mean, you joke around, and they laugh at you, and you get along fine. I just stand around like a bug. What's the sense of kidding myself? Everybody's always telling me to get married. Get married. Get married. Don't you think I wanna get married? I wanna get married. They drive me crazy. Now, I don't wanna wreck your Saturday night for you, Angie. You wanna go somewhere, you go ahead. I don't wanna go.

ANGIE. Boy, they drive me crazy too. My old lady, every word outta her mouth, when you gonna get married?

MARTY. My mother, boy, she drives me crazy.

(ANGIE *leans back in his seat, scowls at the paper-napkin container.* MARTY *returns to the sports page. For a moment a silence hangs between them. Then . . .*)

ANGIE. So what do you feel like doing tonight?

MARTY (*without looking up*). I don't know. What do you feel like doing?

(*They both just sit,* ANGIE *frowning at the napkin container,* MARTY *at the sports page.*

(*The camera slowly moves away from the booth, looks down the length of the bar, up the wall, past the clock—which reads ten to five—and over to the television screen, where the baseball game is still going on*)

(DISSOLVE SLOWLY TO: *The television screen, now blank. The clock now reads a quarter to six.*

(*Back in the booth,* MARTY *now sits alone. In front of him are three empty beer bottles and a beer glass, half filled. He is sitting there, his face expressionless, but his eyes troubled. Then he pushes himself slowly out of the booth and shuffles to the phone booth; he goes inside, closing the booth door carefully after him. For a moment* MARTY *just sits squatly. Then with some exertion—due to the cramped quarters—he contrives to get a small address book out of his rear pants pocket. He slowly flips through it, finds the page he wants, and studies it, scowling; then he takes a dime from the change he has just received, plunks it into the proper slot, waits for a dial tone . . . then carefully dials a number. . . . He waits. He is beginning to sweat a bit in the hot little booth, and his chest begins to rise and fall deeply*)

MARTY (*with a vague pretense at good diction*). Hello, is this Mary Feeney? . . . Could I please speak to Miss Mary Feeney? . . . Just tell her an old friend . . . (*He waits again. With his free hand he wipes the gathering sweat from his brow*) . . . Oh, hello there, is this Mary Feeney? Hello there, this is Marty Pilletti. I wonder if you recall me . . . Well, I'm kind of a stocky guy. The last time we met was inna movies, the RKO Chester. You was with another girl, and I was with a friend of mine name Angie. This was about a month ago . . . (*The girl apparently doesn't remember him. A sort of panic begins to seize* MARTY. *His voice rises a little*) The RKO Chester on Payne Boulevard. You was sitting in front of us, and we was annoying you, and you got mad, and . . . I'm the fellow who works inna butcher shop . . . come on, you know who I am! . . . That's right, we went to Howard Johnson's and we had hamburgers. You hadda milk shake . . . Yeah, that's right. I'm the stocky one, the heavy-set fellow. . . . Well, I'm glad you recall me, because I hadda swell time that night, and I was just wondering how everything was with you. How's everything? . . . That's swell . . . Yeah, well, I'll tell you why I called . . . I was figuring on taking in a movie tonight, and I was wondering if you and your friend would care to see a movie tonight with me and my friend . . . (*His eyes are closed now*) Yeah, tonight. I know it's pretty late to call for a date, but I didn't know myself till . . . Yeah, I know, well how about . . . Yeah, I know, well maybe next Saturday night. You free next Saturday night? . . . Well, how about the Saturday after that? . . . Yeah, I know . . . Yeah . . . Yeah . . . Oh, I understand, I mean . . . (*He just sits now, his eyes closed, not really listening. After a moment he returns the receiver to its cradle and sits, his shoulders slack, his hands resting listlessly in the lap of his spotted white apron. . . . Then he opens his eyes, straightens himself, pushes the*

*booth door open, and advances out into the bar. He perches on a stool across
the bar from the bartender, who looks up from his magazine)*

BARTENDER. I hear your kid brother got married last week, Marty.

MARTY *(looking down at his hands on the bar)*. Yeah, it was a very nice affair.

BARTENDER. Well, Marty, when you gonna get married?

*(MARTY tenders the bartender a quick scowl, gets off his perch, and starts
for the door—untying his apron as he goes)*

MARTY. If my mother calls up, Lou, tell her I'm on my way home.

*(DISSOLVE TO: MARTY's mother and a young couple sitting around the table in
the dining room of MARTY's home. The young couple—we will soon find out—
are THOMAS, MARTY's cousin, and his wife, VIRGINIA. They have apparently
just been telling the mother some sad news, and the three are sitting around
frowning.*

*(The dining room is a crowded room filled with chairs and lamps, pictures
and little statues, perhaps even a small grotto of little vigil lamps. To the
right of the dining room is the kitchen, old-fashioned, Italian, steaming,
and overcrowded. To the left of the dining room is the living room, furnished
in same fashion as the dining room. Just off the living room is a small bedroom, which is MARTY's. This bedroom and the living room have windows
looking out on front. The dining room has windows looking out to side
alleyway. A stairway in the dining room leads to the second floor.*

(The mother is a round, dark, effusive little woman)

MOTHER *(after a pause)*. Well, Thomas, I knew sooner or later this was gonna
happen. I told Marty. I said: "Marty, you watch. There's gonna be real
trouble over there in your cousin Thomas' house." Because your mother was
here, Thomas, you know?

THOMAS. When was this, Aunt Theresa?

MOTHER. This was one, two, three days ago. Wednesday. Because I went to
the fruit shop on Wednesday, and I came home. And I come arounna back,
and there's your mother sitting onna steps onna porch. And I said: "Catherine, my sister, wadda you doing here?" And she look uppa me, and she
beganna cry.

THOMAS *(to his wife)*. Wednesday. That was the day you threw the milk bottle.

MOTHER. That's right. Because I said to her: "Catherine, watsa matter?"
And she said to me: "Theresa, my daughter-in-law, Virginia, she just threw
the milk bottle at me."

VIRGINIA. Well, you see what happen, Aunt Theresa . . .

MOTHER. I know, I know . . .

VIRGINIA. She comes inna kitchen, and she begins poking her head over my
shoulder here and poking her head over my shoulder there . . .

MOTHER. I know, I know . . .

VIRGINIA. And she begins complaining about this, and she begins complaining
about that. And she got me so nervous, I spilled some milk I was making
for the baby. You see. I was making some food for the baby, and . . .

MOTHER. So I said to her, "Catherine . . ."

VIRGINIA. So, she got me so nervous I spilled some milk. So she said: "You're spilling the milk." She says: "Milk costs twenny-four cents a bottle. Wadda you, a banker?" So I said: "Mama, leave me alone, please. You're making me nervous. Go on in the other room and turn on the television set." So then she began telling me how I waste money, and how I can't cook, and how I'm raising my baby all wrong, and she kept talking about these couple of drops of milk I spilt, and I got so mad, I said: "Mama, you wanna see me really spill some milk?" So I took the bottle and threw it against the door. I didn't throw it at her. That's just something she made up. I didn't throw it anywheres near her. Well, of course, alla milk went all over the floor. The whole twenny-four cents. Well, I was sorry right away, you know, but she ran outta the house.

(*Pause*)

MOTHER. Well, I don't know what you want me to do, Virginia. If you want me, I'll go talk to her tonight.

(THOMAS *and* VIRGINIA *suddenly frown and look down at their hands as if of one mind*)

THOMAS. Well, I'll tell you, Aunt Theresa . . .

VIRGINIA. Lemme tell it, Tommy.

THOMAS. Okay.

VIRGINIA (*leaning forward to the mother*). We want you to do a very big favor for us, Aunt Theresa.

MOTHER. Sure.

VIRGINIA. Aunt Theresa, you got this big house here. You got four bedrooms upstairs. I mean, you got this big house just for you and Marty. All your other kids are married and got their own homes. And I thought maybe Tommy's mother could come here and live with you and Marty.

MOTHER. Well . . .

VIRGINIA. She's miserable living with Tommy and me, and you're the only one that gets along with her. Because I called up Tommy's brother, Joe, and I said: "Joe, she's driving me crazy. Why don't you take her for a couple of years?" And he said: "Oh, no!" I know I sound like a terrible woman . . .

MOTHER. No, Virginia, I know how you feel. My husband, may God bless his memory, his mother, she lived with us for a long time, and I know how you feel.

VIRGINIA (*practically on the verge of tears*). I just can't stand it no more! Every minute of the day! Do this! Do that! I don't have ten minutes alone with my husband! We can't even have a fight! We don't have no privacy! Everybody's miserable in our house!

THOMAS. All right, Ginnie, don't get so excited.

MOTHER. She's right. She's right. Young husband and wife, they should have their own home. And my sister, Catherine, she's my sister, but I gotta admit, she's an old goat. And plenny-a times in my life I feel like throwing the milk bottle at her myself. And I tell you now, as far as I'm concerned, if Catherine wantsa come live here with me and Marty, it's all right with me.

(VIRGINIA *promptly bursts into tears*)

THOMAS (*not far from tears himself, lowers his face*). That's very nice-a you, Aunt Theresa.

MOTHER. We gotta ask Marty, of course, because this is his house too. But he's gonna come home any minute now.

VIRGINIA (*having mastered her tears*). That's very nice-a you, Aunt Theresa.

MOTHER (*rising*). Now, you just sit here. I'm just gonna turn onna small fire under the food. (*She exits into the kitchen*)

VIRGINIA (*calling after her*). We gotta go right away because I promised the baby sitter we'd be home by six, and it's after six now . . .

(*She kind of fades out. A moment of silence.* THOMAS *takes out a cigarette and lights it*)

THOMAS (*calling to his aunt in the kitchen*). How's Marty been lately, Aunt Theresa?

MOTHER (*off in kitchen*). Oh, he's fine. You know a nice girl he can marry? (*She comes back into the dining room, wiping her hands on a kitchen towel*) I'm worried about him, you know? He's thirty-six years old, gonna be thirty-seven in January.

THOMAS. Oh, he'll get married, don't worry, Aunt Theresa.

MOTHER (*sitting down again*). Well, I don't know. You know a place where he can go where he can find a bride?

THOMAS. The Waverly Ballroom. That's a good place to meet girls, Aunt Theresa. That's a kind of big dance hall, Aunt Theresa. Every Saturday night, it's just loaded with girls. It's a nice place to go. You pay seventy-seven cents. It used to be seventy-seven cents. It must be about a buck and a half now. And you go in and you ask some girl to dance. That's how I met Virginia. Nice, respectable place to meet girls. You tell Marty, Aunt Theresa, you tell him: "Go to the Waverly Ballroom. It's loaded with tomatoes."

MOTHER (*committing the line to memory*). The Waverly Ballroom. It's loaded with tomatoes.

THOMAS. Right.

VIRGINIA. You tell him, go to the Waverly Ballroom.

(*There is the sound of a door being unlatched off through the kitchen. The mother promptly rises*)

MOTHER. He's here. (*She hurries into the kitchen. At the porch entrance to the kitchen,* MARTY *has just come in. He is closing the door behind him. He carries his butcher's apron in a bundle under his arm*)

MARTY. Hello, Ma.

(*She comes up to him, lowers her voice to a whisper*)

MOTHER (*whispers*). Marty, Thomas and Virginia are here. They had another big fight with your Aunt Catherine. So they ask me, would it be all right if Catherine come to live with us. So I said, all right with me, but we have to ask you. Marty, she's a lonely old lady. Nobody wants her. Everybody's throwing her outta their house. . . .

MARTY. Sure, Ma, it's okay with me.

(*The mother's face breaks into a fond smile. She reaches up and pats his cheek with genuine affection*)

MOTHER. You gotta good heart. (*Turning and leading the way back to the dining room.* THOMAS *has risen*) He says okay, it's all right Catherine comes here.

THOMAS. Oh, Marty, thanks a lot. That really takes a load offa my mind.

MARTY. Oh, we got plenny-a room here.

MOTHER. Sure! Sure! It's gonna be nice! It's gonna be nice! I'll come over tonight to your house, and I talk to Catherine, and you see, everything is gonna work out all right.

THOMAS. I just wanna thank you people again because the situation was just becoming impossible.

MOTHER. Siddown, Thomas, siddown. All right, Marty, siddown. . . . (*She exits into the kitchen*)

(MARTY *has taken his seat at the head of the table and is waiting to be served.* THOMAS *takes a seat around the corner of the table from him and leans across to him*)

THOMAS. You see, Marty, the kinda thing that's been happening in our house is Virginia was inna kitchen making some food for the baby. Well, my mother comes in, and she gets Virginia so nervous, she spills a couple-a drops . . .

VIRGINIA (*tugging at her husband*). Tommy, we gotta go. I promise the baby sitter six o'clock.

THOMAS (*rising without interrupting his narrative*). So she starts yelling at Virginia, waddaya spilling the milk for. So Virginia gets mad . . . (*His wife is slowly pulling him to the kitchen door*). She says, "You wanna really see me spill milk?" So Virginia takes the bottle and she throws it against the wall. She's got a real Italian temper, my wife, you know that . . . (*He has been tugged to the kitchen door by now*)

VIRGINIA. Marty, I don't have to tell you how much we appreciate what your mother and you are doing for us.

THOMAS. All right, Marty, I'll see you some other time . . . I'll tell you all about it.

MARTY. I'll see you, Tommy.

(THOMAS *disappears into the kitchen after his wife*)

VIRGINIA (*off, calling*). Good-by, Marty!

(*Close in on* MARTY, *sitting at table*)

MARTY. Good-by, Virginia! See you soon! (*He folds his hands on the table before him and waits to be served*)

(*The mother enters from the kitchen. She sets the meat plate down in front of him and herself takes a chair around the corner of the table from him.* MARTY *without a word takes up his knife and fork and attacks the mountain of food in front of him. His mother sits quietly, her hands a little nervous on the table before her, watching him eat. Then . . .*)

MOTHER. So what are you gonna do tonight, Marty?

MARTY. I don't know, Ma. I'm all knocked out. I may just hang arounna house.

(*The mother nods a couple of times. There is a moment of silence. Then . . .*)

MOTHER. Why don't you go to the Waverly Ballroom?

(*This gives* MARTY *pause. He looks up*)

MARTY. What?

MOTHER. I say, why don't you go to the Waverly Ballroom? It's loaded with tomatoes.

(MARTY *regards his mother for a moment*)

MARTY. It's loaded with what?

MOTHER. Tomatoes.

MARTY (*snorts*). Ha! Who told you about the Waverly Ballroom?

MOTHER. Thomas, he told me it was a very nice place.

MARTY. Oh, Thomas. Ma, it's just a big dance hall, and that's all it is. I been there a hundred times. Loaded with tomatoes. Boy, you're funny, Ma.

MOTHER. Marty, I don't want you hang arounna house tonight. I want you to go take a shave and go out and dance.

MARTY. Ma, when are you gonna give up? You gotta bachelor on your hands. I ain't never gonna get married.

MOTHER. You gonna get married.

MARTY. Sooner or later, there comes a point in a man's life when he gotta face some facts, and one fact I gotta face is that whatever it is that women like, I ain't got it. I chased enough girls in my life. I went to enough dances. I got hurt enough. I don't wanna get hurt no more. I just called a girl this afternoon, and I got a real brush-off, boy. I figured I was past the point of being hurt, but that hurt. Some stupid woman who I didn't even wanna call up. She gave me the brush. That's the history of my life. I don't wanna go to the Waverly Ballroom because all that ever happened to me there was girls made me feel like I was a bug. I got feelings, you know. I had enough pain. No, thank you.

MOTHER. Marty . . .

MARTY. Ma, I'm gonna stay home and watch Sid Caesar.

MOTHER. You gonna die without a son.

MARTY. So I'll die without a son.

MOTHER. Put on your blue suit . . .

MARTY. Blue suit, gray suit, I'm still a fat little man. A fat little ugly man.

MOTHER. You not ugly.

MARTY (*his voice rising*). I'm ugly . . . I'm ugly! . . . I'm UGLY!

MOTHER. Marty . . .

MARTY (*crying aloud, more in anguish than in anger*). Ma! Leave me alone! . . . (*He stands abruptly, his face pained and drawn. He makes half-formed gestures to his mother, but he can't find words at the moment. He turns and marches a few paces away, turns to his mother again*) Ma, waddaya want from me?! Waddaya want from me?! I'm miserable enough as it is! Leave me alone! I'll go to the Waverly Ballroom! I'll put onna blue suit and I'll go! And you know what I'm gonna get for my trouble? Heartache! A big night of heartache! (*He sullenly marches back to his seat, sits down, picks*

up his fork, plunges it into the lasagna, and stuffs a mouthful into his mouth; he chews vigorously for a moment. It is impossible to remain angry for long. After a while he is shaking his head and muttering) Loaded with tomatoes . . . boy, that's rich . . . (He plunges his fork in again. Camera pulls slowly away from him and his mother, who is seated—watching him)
FADE OUT.

Act II

FADE IN: *Exterior, three-story building. Pan up to second floor . . . bright neon lights reading "Waverly Ballroom" . . . The large, dirty windows are open; and the sound of a fair-to-middling swing band whooping it up comes out.*

DISSOLVE TO: *Interior, Waverly Ballroom—large dance floor crowded with jitterbugging couples, eight-piece combination hitting a loud kick. Ballroom is vaguely dark, made so by papier-mâché over the chandeliers to create alleged romantic effect. The walls are lined with stags and waiting girls, singly and in small murmuring groups. Noise and mumble and drone.*

DISSOLVE TO: *Live shot—a row of stags along a wall. Camera is looking lengthwise down the row. Camera dollies slowly past each face, each staring out at the dance floor, watching in his own manner of hungry eagerness. Short, fat, tall, thin stags. Some pretend diffidence. Some exhibit patent hunger.*

Near the end of the line, we find MARTY *and* ANGIE, *freshly shaved and groomed. They are leaning against the wall, smoking, watching their more fortunate brethren out on the floor.*

ANGIE. Not a bad crowd tonight, you know?

MARTY. There was one nice-looking one there in a black dress and beads, but she was a little tall for me.

ANGIE (*looking down past* MARTY *along the wall right into the camera*). There's a nice-looking little short one for you right now.

MARTY (*following his gaze*). Where?

ANGIE. Down there. That little one there.

(*The camera cuts about eight faces down, to where the girls are now standing. Two are against the wall. One is facing them, with her back to the dance floor. This last is the one* ANGIE *has in mind. She is a cute little kid, about twenty, and she has a bright smile on—as if the other two girls are just amusing her to death*)

MARTY. Yeah, she looks all right from here.

ANGIE. Well, go on over and ask her. You don't hurry up, somebody else'll grab her.

(MARTY *scowls, shrugs*)

MARTY. Okay, let's go.

(*They slouch along past the eight stags, a picture of nonchalant unconcern. The three girls, aware of their approach, stiffen, and their chatter comes to a halt.* ANGIE *advances to one of the girls along the wall*)

ANGIE. Waddaya say, you wanna dance?

(*The girl looks surprised—as if this were an extraordinary invitation to receive in this place—looks confounded at her two friends, shrugs, detaches herself from the group, moves to the outer fringe of the pack of dancers, raises her hand languidly to dancing position, and awaits* ANGIE *with ineffable boredom.* MARTY, *smiling shyly, addresses the short girl*)

MARTY. Excuse me, would you care for this dance?

(*The short girl gives* MARTY *a quick glance of appraisal, then looks quickly at her remaining friend*)

SHORT GIRL (*not unpleasantly*). Sorry. I just don't feel like dancing just yet.

MARTY. Sure. (*He turns and moves back past the eight stags, all of whom have covertly watched his attempt. He finds his old niche by the wall, leans there. A moment later he looks guardedly down to where the short girl and her friend are. A young, dapper boy is approaching the short girl. He asks her to dance. The short girl smiles, excuses herself to her friend, and follows the boy out onto the floor.* MARTY *turns back to watching the dancers bleakly. A moment later he is aware that someone on his right is talking to him. . . . He turns his head. It is a young man of about twenty-eight*) You say something to me?

YOUNG MAN. Yeah. I was just asking you if you was here stag or with a girl.

MARTY. I'm stag.

YOUNG MAN. Well, I'll tell you. I got stuck onna blind date with a dog, and I just picked up a nice chick, and I was wondering how I'm gonna get ridda the dog. Somebody to take her home, you know what I mean? I be glad to pay you five bucks if you take the dog home for me.

MARTY (*a little confused*). What?

YOUNG MAN. I'll take you over, and I'll introduce you as an old army buddy of mine, and then I'll cut out. Because I got this chick waiting for me out by the hatcheck, and I'll pay you five bucks.

MARTY (*stares at the young man*). Are you kidding?

YOUNG MAN. No, I'm not kidding.

MARTY. You can't just walk off onna girl like that.

(*The young man grimaces impatiently and moves down the line of stags. . . .* MARTY *watches him, still a little shocked at the proposition. About two stags down, the young man broaches his plan to another stag. This stag, frowning and pursing his lips, seems more receptive to the idea. . . . The young man takes out a wallet and gives the stag a five-dollar bill. The stag detaches himself from the wall and, a little ill at ease, follows the young man back past* MARTY *and into the lounge.* MARTY *pauses a moment and then, concerned, walks to the archway that separates the lounge from the ballroom and looks in.*

(*The lounge is a narrow room with a bar and booths. In contrast to the ballroom, it is brightly lighted—causing* MARTY *to squint.*

(*In the second booth from the archway sits a girl, about twenty-eight. Despite the careful grooming that she has put into her cosmetics, she is blatantly* plain. *The young man and the stag are standing, talking to her. She is looking up at the young man, her hands nervously gripping her Coca-Cola glass. We cannot hear what the young man is saying, but it is apparent that he is introducing his new-found army buddy and is going through some cock-and-bull story about being called away on an emergency. The stag is presented as her escort-to-be, who will see to it that she gets home safely. The girl apparently is not taken in at all by this, though she is trying hard not to seem affected.*

(*She politely rejects the stag's company and will get home by herself, thanks for asking anyway. The young man makes a few mild protestations, and then he and the stag leave the booth and come back to the archway from where* MARTY *has been watching the scene. As they pass* MARTY, *we overhear a snatch of dialogue*)

YOUNG MAN. . . . In that case, as long as she's going home alone, give me the five bucks back. . . .

STAG. . . . Look, Mac, you paid me five bucks. I was willing. It's my five bucks. . . .

(*They pass on.* MARTY *returns his attention to the girl. She is still sitting as she was, gripping and ungripping the glass of Coca-Cola in front of her. Her eyes are closed. Then, with a little nervous shake of her head, she gets out of the booth and stands—momentarily at a loss for what to do next. The open fire doors leading out onto the large fire escape catch her eye. She crosses to the fire escape, nervous, frowning, and disappears outside.*)

(MARTY *stares after her, then slowly shuffles to the open fire-escape doorway. It is a large fire escape, almost the size of a small balcony. The girl is standing by the railing, her back to the doorway, her head slunk down on her bosom. For a moment* MARTY *is unaware that she is crying. Then he notices the shivering tremors running through her body and the quivering shoulders. He moves a step onto the fire escape. He tries to think of something to say*)

MARTY. Excuse me, Miss. Would you care to dance?

(*The girl slowly turns to him, her face streaked with tears, her lip trembling. Then, in one of those peculiar moments of simultaneous impulse, she lurches to* MARTY *with a sob, and* MARTY *takes her to him. For a moment they stand in an awkward embrace,* MARTY *a little embarrassed, looking out through the doors to the lounge, wondering if anybody is seeing them. Reaching back with one hand, he closes the fire doors, and then, replacing the hand around her shoulder, he stands stiffly, allowing her to cry on his chest*)

(DISSOLVE TO: *Exterior, apartment door. The mother is standing, in a black coat and a hat with a little feather, waiting for her ring to be answered. The door opens.* VIRGINIA *stands framed in the doorway*)

VIRGINIA. Hello, Aunt Theresa, come in. (*The mother goes into the small foyer.* VIRGINIA *closes the door*)

MOTHER (*in a low voice, as she pulls her coat off*). Is Catherine here?

VIRGINIA (*helps her off with coat, nods—also in a low voice*). We didn't tell her nothing yet. We thought we'd leave it to you. We thought you'd put it like how you were lonely, and why don't she come to live with you. Because that way it looks like she's doing you a favor, insteada we're throwing her out, and it won't be so cruel on her. Thomas is downstairs with the neighbors . . . I'll go call him.

MOTHER. You go downstairs to the neighbors and stay there with Thomas.

VIRGINIA. Wouldn't it be better if we were here?

MOTHER. You go downstairs. I talk to Catherine alone. Otherwise, she's gonna start a fight with you.

(*A shrill, imperious woman's voice from an off-stage room suddenly breaks into the muttered conference in the foyer*)

AUNT (*off*). Who's there?! Who's there?!

(*The mother heads up the foyer to the living room, followed by* VIRGINIA, *holding the mother's coat*)

MOTHER (*calls back*). It's me, Catherine! How you feel?

(*At the end of the foyer, the two sisters meet. The aunt is a spare, gaunt woman with a face carved out of granite. Tough, embittered, deeply hurt type face*)

AUNT. Hey! What are you doing here?

MOTHER. I came to see you. (*The two sisters quickly embrace and release each other*) How you feel?

AUNT. I gotta pain in my left side and my leg throbs like a drum.

MOTHER. I been getting pains in my shoulder.

AUNT. I got pains in my shoulder, too. I have a pain in my hip, and my right arm aches so much I can't sleep. It's a curse to be old. How you feel?

MOTHER. I feel fine.

AUNT. That's nice.

(*Now that the standard greetings are over,* AUNT CATHERINE *abruptly turns and goes back to her chair. It is obviously her chair. It is an old heavy oaken chair with thick armrests. The rest of the apartment is furnished in what is known as "modern"—a piece from* House Beautiful *here, a piece from* Better Homes and Gardens *there.* AUNT CATHERINE *sits, erect and forbidding, in her chair. The mother seats herself with a sigh in a neighboring chair.* VIRGINIA, *having hung the mother's coat, now turns to the two older women. A pause*)

VIRGINIA. I'm going downstairs to the Cappacini's. I'll be up inna little while.

(AUNT CATHERINE *nods expressionlessly.* VIRGINIA *looks at her for a moment, then impulsively crosses to her mother-in-law*)

VIRGINIA. You feel all right?

(*The old lady looks up warily, suspicious of this sudden solicitude*)

AUNT. I'm all right.

(VIRGINIA *nods and goes off to the foyer. The two old sisters sit, unmoving, waiting for the door to close behind* VIRGINIA. *Then the mother addresses herself to* AUNT CATHERINE)

MOTHER. We gotta post card from my son, Nickie, and his bride this morning. They're in Florida inna big hotel. Everything is very nice.

AUNT. That's nice.

MOTHER. Catherine, I want you come live with me in my house with Marty and me. In my house, you have your own room. You don't have to sleep onna couch inna living room like here. (*The aunt looks slowly and directly at the mother*) Catherine, your son is married. He got his own home. Leave him in peace. He wants to be alone with his wife. They don't want no old lady sitting inna balcony. Come and live with me. We will cook in the kitchen and talk like when we were girls. You are dear to me, and you are dear to Marty. We are pleased for you to come.

AUNT. Did they come to see you?

MOTHER. Yes.

AUNT. Did my son Thomas come with her?

MOTHER. Your son Thomas was there.

AUNT. Did he also say he wishes to cast his mother from his house?

MOTHER. Catherine, don't make an opera outta this. The three-a you anna baby live in three skinny rooms. You are an old goat, and she has an Italian temper. She is a good girl, but you drive her crazy. Leave them alone. They have their own life.

(*The old aunt turns her head slowly and looks her sister square in the face. Then she rises slowly from her chair*)

AUNT (*coldly*). Get outta here. This is my son's house. This is where I live. I am not to be cast out inna street like a newspaper.

(*The mother likewise rises. The two old women face each other directly*)

MOTHER. Catherine, you are very dear to me. We have cried many times together. When my husband died, I would have gone insane if it were not for you. I ask you to come to my house because I can make you happy. Please come to my house.

(*The two sisters regard each other. Then* AUNT CATHERINE *sits again in her oaken chair, and the mother returns to her seat. The hardened muscles in the old aunt's face suddenly slacken, and she turns to her sister*)

AUNT. Theresa, what shall become of me?

MOTHER. Catherine . . .

AUNT. It's gonna happen to you. Mark it well. These terrible years. I'm afraida look inna mirror. I'm afraid I'm gonna see an old lady with white hair, like the old ladies inna park, little bundles inna black shawl, waiting for the coffin. I'm fifty-six years old. What am I to do with myself? I have strength in my hands. I wanna cook. I wanna clean. I wanna make dinner for my children. I wanna be of use to somebody. Am I an old dog to lie in fronta the fire till my eyes close? These are terrible years, Theresa! Terrible years!

MOTHER. Catherine, my sister . . .

(*The old aunt stares, distraught, at the mother*)

AUNT. It's gonna happen to you! It's gonna happen to you! What will you do if Marty gets married?! What will you cook?! What happen to alla children tumbling in alla rooms?! Where is the noise?! It is a curse to be a widow! A curse! What will you do if Marty gets married?! What will you do?!

(*She stares at the mother—her deep, gaunt eyes haggard and pained. The mother stares back for a moment, then her own eyes close. The aunt has hit home. The aunt sinks back onto her chair, sitting stiffly, her arms on the thick armrests. The mother sits hunched a little forward, her hands nervously folded in her lap*)

AUNT (*quietly*). I will put my clothes inna bag and I will come to you tomorrow. (*The camera slowly dollies back from the two somber sisters.*

SLOW FADE-OUT.

(CUT TO: *Close-up, intimate,* MARTY *and the girl dancing cheek to cheek. Occasionally the heads of other couples slowly waft across the camera view, temporarily blocking out view of* MARTY *and the girl. Camera stays with them as the slow dance carries them around the floor. Tender scene*)

GIRL. . . . The last time I was here the same sort of thing happened.

MARTY. Yeah?

GIRL. Well, not exactly the same thing. The last time I was up here was about four months ago. Do you see that girl in the gray dress sitting over there?

MARTY. Yeah.

GIRL. That's where I sat. I sat there for an hour and a half without moving a muscle. Now and then, some fellow would sort of walk up to me and then change his mind. I just sat there, my hands in my lap. Well, about ten o'clock, a bunch of kids came in swaggering. They weren't more than seventeen, eighteen years old. Well, they swaggered down along the wall, leering at all the girls. I thought they were kind of cute . . . and as they passed me, I smiled at them. One of the kids looked at me and said: "Forget it, ugly, you ain't gotta chance." I burst out crying. I'm a big crier, you know.

MARTY. So am I.

GIRL. And another time when I was in college . . .

MARTY. I cry alla time. Any little thing. I can recognize pain a mile away. My brothers, my brother-in-laws, they're always telling me what a goodhearted guy I am. Well, you don't get goodhearted by accident. You get kicked around long enough you get to be a real professor of pain. I know exactly how you feel. And I also want you to know I'm having a very good time with you now and really enjoying myself. So you see, you're not such a dog as you think you are.

GIRL. I'm having a very good time too.

MARTY. So there you are. So I guess I'm not such a dog as I think I am.

GIRL. You're a very nice guy, and I don't know why some girl hasn't grabbed you off long ago.

MARTY. I don't know either. I think I'm a very nice guy. I also think I'm a pretty smart guy in my own way.

GIRL. I think you are.

MARTY. I'll tell you some of my wisdom which I thunk up on those nights when I got stood up, and nights like that, and you walk home thinking: "Watsa matter with me? I can't be that ugly." Well, I figure, two people get married, and they gonna live together forty, fifty years. So it's just gotta be more than whether they're good-looking or not. My father was a real ugly man, but my mother adored him. She told me that she used to get so miserable sometimes, like everybody, you know? And she says my father always tried to understand. I used to see them sometimes when I was a kid, sitting in the living room, talking and talking, and I used to adore my old man because he was so kind. That's one of the most beautiful things I have in my life, the way my father and my mother were. And my father was a real ugly man. So it don't matter if you look like a gorilla. So you see, dogs like us, we ain't such dogs as we think we are.

(*They dance silently for a moment, cheeks pressed against each other. Close-ups of each face*)

GIRL. I'm twenty-nine years old. How old are you?

MARTY. Thirty-six.

(*They dance silently, closely. Occasionally the heads of other couples sway in front of the camera, blocking our view of* MARTY *and the girl. Slow, sweet dissolve.*

(DISSOLVE TO: *Interior, kitchen,* MARTY's *home. Later that night. It is dark. Nobody is home. The rear porch door now opens, and the silhouettes of* MARTY *and the girl appear—blocking up the doorway*)

MARTY. Wait a minute. Lemme find the light. (*He finds the light. The kitchen is suddenly brightly lit. The two of them stand squinting to adjust to the sudden glare*) I guess my mother ain't home yet. I figure my cousin Thomas and Virginia musta gone to the movies, so they won't get back till one o'clock, at least.

(*The girl has advanced into the kitchen, a little ill at ease, and is looking around.* MARTY *closes the porch door*)

MARTY. This is the kitchen.

GIRL. Yes, I know.

(MARTY *leads the way into the dining room*)

MARTY. Come on inna dining room. (*He turns on the light in there as he goes. The girl follows him in*) Siddown, take off your coat. You want something to eat? We gotta whole halfa chicken left over from yesterday.

GIRL (*perching tentatively on the edge of a chair*). No, thank you. I don't think I should stay very long.

MARTY. Sure. Just take off your coat a minute.

(*He helps her off with her coat and stands for a moment behind her, looking down at her. Conscious of his scrutiny, she sits uncomfortably, her breasts rising and falling unevenly.* MARTY *takes her coat into the dark living room. The girl sits patiently, nervously.* MARTY *comes back, sits down on another chair. Awkward silence*)

MARTY. So I was telling you, my kid brother Nickie got married last Sunday. . . . That was a very nice affair. And they had this statue of some woman, and they had whisky spouting outta her mouth. I never saw anything so grand in my life. (*The silence falls between them again*) And watta meal. I'm a butcher, so I know a good hunka steak when I see one. That was choice filet, right off the toppa the chuck. A buck-eighty a pound. Of course, if you wanna cheaper cut, get rib steak. That gotta lotta waste on it, but it comes to about a buck and a quarter a pound, if it's trimmed. Listen, Clara, make yourself comfortable. You're all tense.

GIRL. Oh, I'm fine.

MARTY. You want me to take you home, I'll take you home.

GIRL. Maybe that would be a good idea.

(*She stands. He stands, frowning, a little angry—turns sullenly and goes back into the living room for her coat. She stands unhappily. He comes back and wordlessly starts to help her into her coat. He stands behind her, his hands on her shoulders. He suddenly seizes her, begins kissing her on the neck. Camera comes up quickly to intensely intimate close-up, nothing but the heads. The dialogue drops to quick, hushed whispers*)

GIRL. No, Marty, please . . .

MARTY. I like you, I like you, I been telling you all night I like you . . .

GIRL. Marty . . .

MARTY. I just wanna kiss, that's all . . . (*He tries to turn her face to him. She resists*)

GIRL. No . . .

MARTY. Please . . .

GIRL. No . . .

MARTY. Please . . .

GIRL. Marty . . .

(*He suddenly releases her, turns away violently*)

MARTY (*crying out*). All right! I'll take you home! All right! (*He marches a few angry paces away, deeply disturbed. Turns to her*) All I wanted was a lousy kiss! What am I, a leper or something?! (*He turns and goes off into the living room to hide the flush of hot tears threatening to fill his eyes. The girl stands, herself on the verge of tears*)

GIRL (*mutters, more to herself than to him*). I just didn't feel like it, that's all. (*She moves slowly to the archway leading to the living room. MARTY is sitting on the couch, hands in his lap, looking straight ahead. The room is dark except for the overcast of the dining-room light reaching in. The girl goes to the couch, perches on the edge beside him. He doesn't look at her*)

MARTY. Well, that's the history of my life. I'm a little, short, fat, ugly guy. Comes New Year's Eve, everybody starts arranging parties. I'm the guy they gotta dig up a date for. I'm old enough to know better. Let me get a packa cigarettes, and I'll take you home. (*He starts to rise, but doesn't . . . sinks back onto the couch, looking straight ahead. The girl looks at him, her face peculiarly soft and compassionate*)

GIRL. I'd like to see you again, very much. The reason I didn't let you kiss me was because I just didn't know how to handle the situation. You're the kindest man I ever met. The reason I tell you this is because I want to see you again very much. Maybe, I'm just so desperate to fall in love that I'm trying too hard. But I know that when you take me home, I'm going to just lie on my bed and think about you. I want very much to see you again. (MARTY *stares down at his hands in his lap*)

MARTY (*without looking at her*). Waddaya doing tomorrow night?

GIRL. Nothing.

MARTY. I'll call you up tomorrow morning. Maybe we'll go see a movie.

GIRL. I'd like that very much.

MARTY. The reason I can't be definite about it now is my Aunt Catherine is probably coming over tomorrow, and I may have to help out.

GIRL. I'll wait for your call.

MARTY. We better get started to your house because the buses only run about one an hour now.

GIRL. All right. (*She stands*)

MARTY. I'll just get a packa cigarettes.

(*He goes into his bedroom. We can see him through the doorway, opening his bureau drawer and extracting a pack of cigarettes. He comes out again and looks at the girl for the first time. They start to walk to the dining room. In the archway, MARTY pauses, turns to the girl*)

MARTY. Waddaya doing New Year's Eve?

GIRL. Nothing.

(*They quietly slip into each other's arms and kiss. Slowly their faces part, and MARTY's head sinks down upon her shoulder. He is crying. His shoulders shake slightly. The girl presses her cheek against the back of his head. They stand . . . there is the sound of the rear porch door being unlatched. They both start from their embrace. A moment later the mother's voice is heard off in the kitchen*)

MOTHER. Hallo! Hallo, Marty? (*She comes into the dining room, stops at the sight of the girl*) Hallo, Marty, when you come home?

MARTY. We just got here about fifteen minutes ago, Ma. Ma, I want you to meet Miss Clara Davis. She's a graduate of New York University. She teaches history in Benjamin Franklin High School.

(*This seems to impress the mother*)

MOTHER. Siddown, siddown. You want some chicken? We got some chicken in the icebox.

GIRL. No, Mrs. Pilletti, we were just going home. Thank you very much anyway.

MOTHER. Well, siddown a minute. I just come inna house. I'll take off my coat. Siddown a minute. (*She pulls her coat off*)

MARTY. How'd you come home, Ma? Thomas give you a ride?

(*The mother nods*)

MOTHER. Oh, it's a sad business, a sad business. (*She sits down on a dining-room chair, holding her coat in her lap. She turns to the girl, who likewise sits*)

MOTHER. My sister Catherine, she don't get along with her daughter-in-law, so she's gonna come live with us.

MARTY. Oh, she's coming, eh, Ma?

MOTHER. Oh, sure. (*To the girl*) It's a very sad thing. A woman, fifty-six years old, all her life, she had her own home. Now, she's just an old lady, sleeping on her daughter-in-law's couch. It's a curse to be a mother, I tell you. Your children grow up and then what is left for you to do? What is a mother's life but her children? It is a very cruel thing when your son has no place for you in his home.

GIRL. Couldn't she find some sort of hobby to fill out her time?

MOTHER. Hobby! What can she do? She cooks and she cleans. You gotta have a house to clean. You gotta have children to cook for. These are the terrible years for a woman, the terrible years.

GIRL. You mustn't feel too harshly against her daughter-in-law. She also wants to have a house to clean and a family to cook for.

(*The mother darts a quick, sharp look at the girl—then looks back to her hands, which are beginning to twist nervously*)

MOTHER. You don't think my sister Catherine should live in her daughter-in-law's house?

GIRL. Well, I don't know the people, of course, but, as a rule, I don't think a mother-in-law should live with a young couple.

MOTHER. Where do you think a mother-in-law should go?

GIRL. I don't think a mother should depend so much upon her children for her rewards in life.

MOTHER. That's what it says in the book in New York University. You wait till you are a mother. It don't work out that way.

GIRL. Well, it's silly for me to argue about it. I don't know the people involved.

MARTY. Ma, I'm gonna take her home now. It's getting late, and the buses only run about one an hour.

MOTHER (*standing*). Sure.

(*The girl stands*)

GIRL. It was very nice meeting you, Mrs. Pilletti. I hope I'll see you again.

MOTHER. Sure.

(MARTY *and the girl move to the kitchen*)

MARTY. All right, Ma. I'll be back in about an hour.

MOTHER. Sure.

GIRL. Good night, Mrs. Pilletti.

MOTHER. Good night.

(MARTY *and the girl exit into the kitchen. The mother stands, expressionless, by her chair watching them go. She remains standing rigidly even after the porch door can be heard being opened and shut. The camera moves up to a close-up of the mother. Her eyes are wide. She is staring straight ahead. There is fear in her eyes*)

FADE OUT.

Act III

FADE IN: *Film—close-up of church bells clanging away. Pan down church to see typical Sunday morning, people going up the steps of a church and entering. It is a beautiful June morning.*

DISSOLVE TO: *Interior,* MARTY's *bedroom—sun fairly streaming through the curtains.* MARTY *is standing in front of his bureau, slipping his arms into a clean white shirt. He is freshly shaved and groomed. Through the doorway of his bedroom we can see the mother in the dining room, in coat and hat, all set to go to Mass, taking the last breakfast plates away and carrying them into the kitchen. The camera moves across the living room into the dining room. The mother comes out of the kitchen with a paper napkin and begins crumbing the table.*

There is a knock on the rear porch door. The mother leaves her crumbing and goes into the kitchen. Camera goes with her. She opens the rear door to admit AUNT CATHERINE, *holding a worn old European carpetbag. The aunt starts to go deeper into the kitchen, but the mother stays her with her hand.*

MOTHER (*in low, conspiratorial voice*). Hey, I come home from your house last night, Marty was here with a girl.

AUNT. Who?

MOTHER. Marty.

AUNT. Your son Marty?

MOTHER. Well, what Marty you think is gonna be here in this house with a girl?

AUNT. Were the lights on?

MOTHER. Oh, sure. (*Frowns suddenly at her sister*) The girl is a college graduate.

AUNT. They're the worst. College girls are one step from the streets. They smoke like men inna saloon. (*The aunt puts her carpetbag down and sits on one of the wooden kitchen chairs. The mother sits on another*)

MOTHER. That's the first time Marty ever brought a girl to this house. She seems like a nice girl. I think he has a feeling for this girl.

(*At this moment a burst of spirited whistling emanates from* MARTY's *bedroom.*)

(CUT TO: MARTY's *bedroom—*MARTY *standing in front of his mirror, buttoning his shirt or adjusting his tie, whistling a gay tune.*)

(CUT BACK TO: *The two sisters, both their faces turned in the direction of the whistling. The whistling abruptly stops. The two sisters look at each other. The aunt shrugs*)

MOTHER. He been whistling like that all morning.

(*The aunt nods bleakly*)

AUNT. He is bewitched. You will see. Today, tomorrow, inna week, he's gonna say to you: "Hey, Ma, it's no good being a single man. I'm tired running around." Then he's gonna say: "Hey, Ma, wadda we need this old house? Why don't we sell this old house, move into a nicer parta town? A nice little apartment?"

MOTHER. I don't sell this house, I tell you that. This is my husband's house, and I had six children in this house.

AUNT. You will see. A couple-a months, you gonna be an old lady, sleeping onna couch in your daughter-in-law's house.

MOTHER. Catherine, you are a blanket of gloom. Wherever you go, the rain follows. Some day, you gonna smile, and we gonna declare a holiday.

(*Another burst of spirited whistling comes from* MARTY, *off. It comes closer, and* MARTY *now enters in splendid spirits, whistling away. He is slipping into his jacket*)

MARTY (*ebulliently*). Hello, Aunt Catherine! How are you? You going to Mass with us?

AUNT. I was at Mass two hours ago.

MARTY. Well, make yourself at home. The refrigerator is loaded with food. Go upstairs, take any room you want. It's beautiful outside, ain't it?

AUNT. There's a chill. Watch out, you catch a good cold and pneumonia.

MOTHER. My sister Catherine, she can't even admit it's a beautiful day.

(MARTY—*now at the sink, getting himself a glass of water—is examining a piece of plaster that has fallen from the ceiling*)

MARTY (*examining the chunk of plaster in his palm*). Boy, this place is really coming to pieces. (*Turns to mother*) You know, Ma, I think, sometime we oughtta sell this place. The plumbing is rusty—everything. I'm gonna have to replaster that whole ceiling now. I think we oughtta get a little apartment somewheres in a nicer parta town. . . . You all set, Ma?

MOTHER. I'm all set. (*She starts for the porch door. She slowly turns and looks at* MARTY, *and then at* AUNT CATHERINE—*who returns her look. Mother and* MARTY *exit*)

(DISSOLVE TO: *Church. The mother comes out of the doors and down a few steps to where* MARTY *is standing, enjoying the clearness of the June morning*)

MOTHER. In a couple-a minutes nine o'clock Mass is gonna start—in a couple-a minutes . . . (*To passers-by off*) hallo, hallo . . . (*To* MARTY) Well, that was a nice girl last night, Marty. That was a nice girl.

MARTY. Yeah.

MOTHER. She wasn't a very good-looking girl, but she look like a nice girl. I said, she wasn't a very good-looking girl, not very pretty.

MARTY. I heard you, Ma.

MOTHER. She look a little old for you, about thirty-five, forty years old?

MARTY. She's twenny-nine, Ma.

MOTHER. She's more than twenny-nine years old, Marty. That's what she tells you. She looks thirty-five, forty. She didn't look Italian to me. I said, is she an Italian girl?

MARTY. I don't know. I don't think so.

MOTHER. She don't look like Italian to me. What kinda family she come from? There was something about her I don't like. It seems funny, the first time you meet her she comes to your empty house alone. These college girls, they all one step from the streets.

(MARTY *turns, frowning, to his mother*)

MARTY. What are you talkin' about? She's a nice girl.

MOTHER. I don't like her.

MARTY. You don't like her? You only met her for two minutes.

MOTHER. Don't bring her to the house no more.

MARTY. What didn't you like about her?

MOTHER. I don't know! She don't look like Italian to me, plenty nice Italian girls around.

MARTY. Well, let's not get into a fight about it, Ma. I just met the girl. I probably won't see her again. (MARTY *leaves frame*)

MOTHER. Eh, I'm no better than my sister Catherine.

(DISSOLVE TO: *Interior, the bar . . . about an hour later. The after-Mass crowd is there, about six men ranging from twenty to forty. A couple of women in the booths. One woman is holding a glass of beer in one hand and is gently rocking a baby carriage with the other.*)

(*Sitting in the booth of Act I are* ANGIE *and three other fellows, ages twenty, thirty-two, and forty. One of the fellows, aged thirty-two, is giving a critical résumé of a recent work of literature by Mickey Spillane*)

CRITIC. . . . So the whole book winds up, Mike Hammer, he's inna room there with this doll. So he says: "You rat, you are the murderer." So she begins to con him, you know? She tells him how she loves him. And then Bam! He shoots her in the stomach. So she's laying there, gasping for breath, and she says: "How could you do that?" And he says: "It was easy."

TWENTY-YEAR-OLD. Boy, that Mickey Spillane. Boy, he can write.

ANGIE (*leaning out of the booth and looking down the length of the bar, says with some irritation*). What's keeping Marty?

CRITIC. What I like about Mickey Spillane is he knows how to handle women. In one book, he picks up a tomato who gets hit with a car, and she throws a pass at him. And then he meets two beautiful twins, and they throw passes at him. And then he meets some beautiful society leader, and she throws a pass at him, and . . .

TWENTY-YEAR-OLD. Boy, that Mickey Spillane, he sure can write . . .

ANGIE (*looking out, down the bar again*). I don't know watsa matter with Marty.

FORTY-YEAR-OLD. Boy, Angie, what would you do if Marty ever died? You'd die right with him. A couple-a old bachelors hanging to each other like barnacles. There's Marty now.

(ANGIE leans out of the booth)

ANGIE (*calling out*). Hello, Marty, where you been?

(CUT TO: *Front end of the bar.* MARTY *has just come in. He waves back to* ANGIE, *acknowledges another hello from a man by the bar, goes over to the bar, and gets the bartender's attention*)

MARTY. Hello, Lou, gimme change of a half and put a dime in it for a telephone call.

(*The bartender takes the half dollar, reaches into his apron pocket for the change*)

BARTENDER. I hear you was at the Waverly Ballroom last night.

MARTY. Yeah. Angie tell you?

BARTENDER (*picking out change from palm full of silver*). Yeah, I hear you really got stuck with a dog.

(MARTY *looks at him*)

MARTY. She wasn't so bad.

BARTENDER (*extending the change*). Angie says she was a real scrawny-looking thing. Well, you can't have good luck alla time.

(MARTY *takes the change slowly and frowns down at it. He moves down the bar and would make for the telephone booth, but* ANGIE *hails him from the booth*)

ANGIE. Who you gonna call, Marty?

MARTY. I was gonna call that girl from last night, take her to a movie tonight.

ANGIE. Are you kidding?

MARTY. She was a nice girl. I kinda liked her.

ANGIE (*indicating the spot in the booth vacated by the forty-year-old*). Siddown. You can call her later. (MARTY *pauses, frowning, and then shuffles to the booth where* ANGIE *and the other two sit. The critic moves over for* MARTY. *There is an exchange of hellos*)

TWENTY-YEAR-OLD. I gotta girl, she's always asking me to marry her. So I look at that face, and I say to myself: "Could I stand looking at that face for the resta my life?"

CRITIC. Hey, Marty, you ever read a book called *I, the Jury,* by Mickey Spillane?

MARTY. No.

ANGIE. Listen, Marty, I gotta good place for us to go tonight. The kid here, he says, he was downna bazaar at Our Lady of Angels last night and . . .

MARTY. I don't feel like going to the bazaar, Angie. I thought I'd take this girl to a movie.

ANGIE. Boy, you really musta made out good last night.

MARTY. We just talked.

ANGIE. Boy, she must be some talker. She musta been about fifty years old.

CRITIC. I always figger a guy oughtta marry a girl who's twenny years younger than he is, so that when he's forty, his wife is a real nice-looking doll.

TWENTY-YEAR-OLD. That means he'd have to marry the girl when she was one year old.

CRITIC. I never thoughta that.

MARTY. I didn't think she was so bad-looking.

ANGIE. She musta kept you inna shadows all night.

CRITIC. Marty, you don't wanna hang around with dogs. It gives you a bad reputation.

ANGIE. Marty, let's go downna bazaar.

MARTY. I told this dog I was gonna call her today.

ANGIE. Brush her.

(MARTY *looks questioningly at* ANGIE)

MARTY. You didn't like her at all?

ANGIE. A nothing. A real nothing. (MARTY *looks down at the dime he has been nervously turning between two fingers and then, frowning, he slips it into his jacket pocket. He lowers his face and looks down, scowling at his thoughts. Around him, the voices clip along*)

CRITIC. What's playing on Fordham Road? I think there's a good picture in the Loew's Paradise.

ANGIE. Let's go down to Forty-second Street and walk around. We're sure to wind up with something. (*Slowly* MARTY *begins to look up again. He looks from face to face as each speaks*)

CRITIC. I'll never forgive LaGuardia for cutting burlesque outta New York City.

TWENTY-YEAR-OLD. There's burlesque over in Union City. Let's go to Union City . . .

ANGIE. Ah, they're always crowded on Sunday night.

CRITIC. So wadda you figure on doing tonight, Angie?

ANGIE. I don't know. Wadda you figure on doing?

CRITIC. I don't know. (*Turns to the twenty-year-old*) Wadda you figure on doing? (*The twenty-year-old shrugs*)

(*Suddenly* MARTY *brings his fist down on the booth table with a crash. The others turn, startled, toward him.* MARTY *rises in his seat*)

MARTY. "What are you doing tonight?" "I don't know, what are you doing?" Burlesque! Loew's Paradise! Miserable and lonely! Miserable and lonely and stupid! What am I, crazy or something?! I got something good! What am I hanging around with you guys for?! (*He has said this in tones so loud that it attracts the attention of everyone in the bar. A little embarrassed,* MARTY *turns and moves quickly to the phone booth, pausing outside the door to find his dime again.* ANGIE *is out of his seat immediately and hurries after him*)

ANGIE (*a little shocked at* MARTY's *outburst*). Watsa matter with you?

MARTY (*in a low, intense voice*). You don't like her. My mother don't like her. She's a dog, and I'm a fat, ugly little man. All I know is I had a good time last night. I'm gonna have a good time tonight. If we have enough good times together, I'm going down on my knees and beg that girl to marry me. If we make a party again this New Year's, I gotta date for the party. You don't like her, that's too bad. (*He moves into the booth, sits, turns again to* ANGIE, *smiles*) When you gonna get married, Angie? You're thirty-four years old. All your kid brothers are married. You oughtta be ashamed of yourself. (*Still smiling at his private joke, he puts the dime into the slot and then—with a determined finger—he begins to dial*)

FADE OUT.

Edward Albee

THE AMERICAN DREAM

The reputation of Edward Albee, who was born in 1928, has grown steadily since his first play, The Zoo Story, appeared in 1958. The American Dream, Who's Afraid of Virginia Woolf? (1962), and Tiny Alice (1964) are the plays which establish Albee as one of the leading exponents of the techniques of the Theatre of the Absurd.

The Theatre of the Absurd is not so much a new departure as a coalescence of

The Drama
. . . .

678

twentieth-century experimental techniques. The use of eccentric and often abstract settings and of atmospheres pervaded by a sense of inscrutability and madness can be traced at least as far back as the fiction of Kafka. Such writers as James Joyce and Gertrude Stein early in the century experimented with massive distortions of language to produce humor or approximate the meandering monologues of the human mind. The originality of the dramatists of the Theatre of the Absurd is their extension and amalgamation of these techniques which all somehow distort reality.

Critics disagree about the final worth of the Theatre of the Absurd. Some contend that the plays of the movement are too "absurd" because they fail to interpret life. Defenders of the movement maintain that it has a special relevance to the condition of contemporary man—his loss of social and metaphysical identity.

In *The American Dream* Albee has put "absurd" drama in the service of social satire. His own words in the preface to the 1961 edition of the play serve as an excellent introduction to the satiric content of the play:

The play is an examination of the American Scene, an attack on the substitution of artificial for real values in our society, a condemnation of complacency, cruelty, emasculation and vacuity; it is a stand against the fiction that everything in this slipping land of ours is peachy-keen.

CHARACTERS

MOMMY   DADDY   GRANDMA   MRS. BARKER   YOUNG MAN

Scene: A living room. Two armchairs, one toward either side of the stage, facing each other diagonally out toward the audience. Against the rear wall, a sofa. A door, leading out from the apartment, in the rear wall, far stage-right. An archway, leading to other rooms, in the side wall, stage-left.

At the beginning, MOMMY *and* DADDY *are seated in the armchairs,* DADDY *in the armchair stage-left,* MOMMY *in the other.*

Curtain up. A silence. Then:

MOMMY. I don't know what can be keeping them.
DADDY. They're late, naturally.

MOMMY. Of course, they're late; it never fails.

DADDY. That's the way things are today, and there's nothing you can do about it.

MOMMY. You're quite right.

DADDY. When we took this apartment, they were quick enough to have me sign the lease; they were quick enough to take my check for two months' rent in advance . . .

MOMMY. And one month's security . . .

DADDY. . . . and one month's security. They were quick enough to check my references; they were quick enough about all that. But now! But now, try to get the icebox fixed, try to get the doorbell fixed, try to get the leak in the johnny fixed! Just try it . . . they aren't so quick about *that*.

MOMMY. Of course not; it never fails. People think they can get away with anything these days . . . and, of course they can. I went to buy a new hat yesterday. (*Pause*) I said, I went to buy a new hat yesterday.

DADDY. Oh! Yes . . . yes.

MOMMY. Pay attention.

DADDY. I *am* paying attention, Mommy.

MOMMY. Well, be sure you do.

DADDY. Oh, I am.

MOMMY. All right, Daddy; now listen.

DADDY. I'm listening, Mommy.

MOMMY. You're sure!

DADDY. Yes . . . yes, I'm sure, I'm all ears.

MOMMY. (*Giggles at the thought; then*) All right, now. I went to buy a new hat yesterday and I said, "I'd like a new hat, please." And so, they showed me a few hats, green ones and blue ones, and I didn't like any of them, not one bit. What did I say? What did I just say?

DADDY. You didn't like any of them, not one bit.

MOMMY. That's right; you just keep paying attention. And then they showed me one that I did like. It was a lovely little hat, and I said, "Oh, this is a lovely little hat; I'll take this hat; oh my, it's lovely. What color is it?" And they said, "Why, this is beige; isn't it a lovely little beige hat?" And I said, "Oh, it's just lovely." And so, I bought it. (*Stops, looks at* DADDY)

DADDY. (*To show he is paying attention*) And so you bought it.

MOMMY. And so I bought it, and I walked out of the store with the hat right on my head, and I ran spang into the chairman of our woman's club, and she said, "Oh, my dear, isn't that a lovely little hat? Where did you get that lovely little hat? It's the loveliest little hat; I've always wanted a wheat-colored hat *myself*." And, I said, "Why, no, my dear; this hat is beige; beige." And she laughed and said, "Why no, my dear, that's a wheat-colored hat . . . wheat. I know beige from wheat." And I said, "Well, my dear, I know beige from wheat, too." What did I say? What did I just say?

DADDY. (*Tonelessly*) Well, my dear, I know beige from wheat, too.

MOMMY. That's right. And she laughed, and she said, "Well, my dear, they certainly put one over on you. That's wheat if I ever saw wheat. But it's lovely, just the same." And then she walked off. She's a dreadful woman, you don't know her; she has dreadful taste, two dreadful children, a dreadful house, and an absolutely adorable husband who sits in a wheel chair all the time. You don't know him. You don't know anybody, do you? She's just a dreadful woman, but she *is* chairman of our woman's club, so naturally I'm terribly fond of her. So, I went right back into the hat shop, and I said, "Look here; what do you mean selling me a hat that you say is beige, when it's wheat all the time . . . wheat! I can tell beige from wheat any day in the week, but not in this artificial light of yours." They have artificial light, Daddy.

DADDY. Have they!

MOMMY. And I said, "The minute I got outside I could tell that it wasn't a beige hat at all; it was a wheat hat." And they said to me, "How could you tell that when you had the hat on the top of your head?" Well, that made me angry, and so I made a scene right there; I screamed as hard as I could; I took my hat off and I threw it down on the counter, and oh, I made a terrible scene. I said, I made a terrible scene.

DADDY. (*Snapping to*) Yes . . . yes . . . good for you!

MOMMY. And I made an absolutely terrible scene; and they became frightened, and they said, "Oh, madam; oh, madam." But I kept right on, and finally they admitted that they might have made a mistake; so they took my hat into the back, and then they came out again with a hat that looked exactly like it. I took one look at it, and I said, "This hat is wheat-colored; wheat." Well, of course, they said, "Oh, no, madam, this hat is beige; you go outside and see." So, I went outside, and lo and behold, it *was* beige. So I bought it.

DADDY. (*Clearing his throat*) I would imagine that it was the same hat they tried to sell you before.

MOMMY. (*With a little laugh*) Well, of course it was!

DADDY. That's the way things are today; you just can't get satisfaction; you just try.

MOMMY. Well, *I* got satisfaction.

DADDY. That's right, Mommy. *You did* get satisfaction, didn't you?

MOMMY. Why are they so late? I don't know what can be keeping them.

DADDY. I've been trying for two weeks to have the leak in the johnny fixed.

MOMMY. You can't get satisfaction; just try. *I* can get satisfaction, but you can't.

DADDY. I've been trying for two weeks and it isn't so much for my sake; I can always go to the club.

MOMMY. It isn't so much for my sake, either; I can always go shopping.

DADDY. It's really for Grandma's sake.

MOMMY. Of course it's for Grandma's sake. Grandma cries every time she goes to the johnny as it is; but now that it doesn't work it's even worse, it makes Grandma think she's getting feeble-headed.

DADDY. Grandma *is* getting feeble-headed.

MOMMY. Of course Grandma is getting feeble-headed, but not about her johnny-do's.

DADDY. No; that's true. I must have it fixed.

MOMMY. WHY are they so late? I don't know what can be keeping them.

DADDY. When they came here the first time, they were ten minutes early; they were quick enough about it then. (*Enter* GRANDMA *from the archway, stage left. She is loaded down with boxes, large and small, neatly wrapped and tied.*)

MOMMY. Why Grandma, look at you! What *is* all that you're carrying?

GRANDMA. They're boxes. What do they look like?

MOMMY. Daddy! Look at Grandma; look at all the boxes she's carrying!

DADDY. My goodness, Grandma; look at all those boxes.

GRANDMA. Where'll I put them?

MOMMY. Heavens! I don't know. Whatever are they for?

GRANDMA. That's nobody's damn business.

MOMMY. Well, in that case, put them down next to Daddy; there.

GRANDMA. (*Dumping the boxes down, on and around* DADDY's *feet*) I sure wish you'd get the john fixed.

DADDY. Oh, I do wish they'd come and fix it. We hear you . . . for hours . . . whimpering away. . . .

MOMMY. Daddy! What a terrible thing to say to Grandma!

GRANDMA. Yeah. For shame, talking to me that way.

DADDY. I'm sorry, Grandma.

MOMMY. Daddy's sorry, Grandma.

GRANDMA. Well, all right. In that case I'll go get the rest of the boxes. I suppose I deserve being talked to that way. I've gotten so old. Most people think that when you get so old, you either freeze to death, or you burn up. But you don't. When you get so old, all that happens is that people talk to you that way.

DADDY. (*Contrite*) I said I'm sorry, Grandma.

MOMMY. Daddy said he was sorry.

GRANDMA. Well, that's all that counts. People being sorry. Makes you feel better; gives you a sense of dignity, and that's all that's important . . . a sense of dignity. And it doesn't matter if you don't care, or not, either. You got to have a sense of dignity, even if you don't care, 'cause, if you don't have that, civilization's doomed.

MOMMY. You've been reading my book club selections again!

DADDY. How dare you read Mommy's book club selections, Grandma!

GRANDMA. Because I'm old! When you're old you gotta do something. When you get old, you can't talk to people because people snap at you. When you get so old, people talk to you that way. That's why you become deaf, so you won't be able to hear people talking to you that way. And that's why you go and hide under the covers in the big soft bed, so you won't feel the house shaking from people talking to you that way. That's why old people die, eventually. People talk to them that way. I've got to go and get the rest of the boxes. (GRANDMA *exits*)

DADDY. Poor Grandma, I didn't mean to hurt her.

MOMMY. Don't you worry about it; Grandma doesn't know what she means.

DADDY. She knows what she says, though.

MOMMY. Don't you worry about it; she won't know that soon. I love Grandma.

DADDY. I love her, too. Look how nicely she wrapped these boxes.

MOMMY. Grandma has always wrapped boxes nicely. When I was a little girl, I was very poor, and Grandma was very poor, too, because Grandpa was in heaven. And every day, when I went to school, Grandma used to wrap a box for me, and I used to take it with me to school; and when it was lunchtime, all the little boys and girls used to take out their boxes of lunch, and they weren't wrapped nicely at all, and they used to open them and eat their chicken legs and chocolate cakes; and I used to say, "Oh, look at my lovely lunch box; it's so nicely wrapped it would break my heart to open it." And so, I wouldn't open it.

DADDY. Because it was empty.

MOMMY. Oh no. Grandma always filled it up, because she never ate the dinner she cooked the evening before; she gave me all her food for my lunch box the next day. After school, I'd take the box back to Grandma, and she'd open it and eat the chicken legs and chocolate cake that was inside. Grandma used to say, "I love day-old cake." That's where the expression day-old cake came from. Grandma always ate everything a day late. I used to eat all the other little boys' and girls' food at school, because they thought my lunch box was empty. They thought my lunch box was empty, and that's why I wouldn't open it. They thought I suffered from the sin of pride, and since that made them better than me, they were very generous.

DADDY. You were a very deceitful little girl.

MOMMY. We were very poor! But then I married you, Daddy, and now we're very rich.

DADDY. Grandma isn't rich.

MOMMY. No, but you've been so good to Grandma she feels rich. She doesn't know you'd like to put her in a nursing home.

DADDY. I wouldn't!

MOMMY. Well, heaven knows, *I* would! I can't stand it, watching her do the cooking and the housework, polishing the silver, moving the furniture. . . .

DADDY. She likes to do that. She says it's the least she can do to earn her keep.

MOMMY. Well, she's right. You can't live off people. I can live off you, because I married you. And aren't you lucky all I brought with me was Grandma. A lot of women I know would have brought their whole families to live off you. All I brought was Grandma. Grandma is all the family I have.

DADDY. I feel very fortunate.

MOMMY. You should. I have a right to live off of you because I married you, and because I used to let you get on top of me and bump your uglies; and I have a right to all your money when you die. And when you do, Grandma and I can live by ourselves . . . if she's still here. Unless you have her put away in a nursing home.

DADDY. I have no intention of putting her in a nursing home.

MOMMY. Well, I wish somebody would do something with her!

DADDY. At any rate, you're very well provided for.

MOMMY. You're my sweet Daddy; that's very nice.

DADDY. I love my Mommy. (*Enter* GRANDMA *again, laden with more boxes*)

GRANDMA. (*Dumping the boxes on and around* DADDY's *feet*) There; that's the lot of them.

DADDY. They're wrapped so nicely.

GRANDMA. (*To* DADDY) You won't get on my sweet side that way . . .

MOMMY. Grandma!

GRANDMA. . . . telling me how nicely I wrap boxes. Not after what you said: how I whimpered for hours. . . .

MOMMY. Grandma!

GRANDMA. (*To* MOMMY) Shut up! (*To* DADDY) You don't have any feelings, that's what's wrong with you. Old people make all sorts of noises, half of them they can't help. Old people whimper, and cry, and belch, and make great hollow rumbling sounds at the table; old people wake up in the middle of the night screaming, and find out they haven't even been asleep; and when old people *are* asleep, they try to wake up, and they can't . . . not for the longest time.

MOMMY. Homilies, homilies!

GRANDMA. And there's more, too.

DADDY. I'm really very sorry, Grandma.

GRANDMA. I know you are, Daddy; it's Mommy over there makes all the trouble. If you'd listened to me, you wouldn't have married her in the first place. She was a tramp and a trollop and a trull to boot, and she's no better now.

MOMMY. Grandma!

GRANDMA. (*To* MOMMY) Shut up! (*To* DADDY) When she was no more than eight years old she used to climb up on my lap and say, in a sickening little voice, "When I gwo up, I'm going to mahwy a wich old man; I'm going to set my wittle were end right down in a tub o' butter, that's what I'm going to do." And I warned you, Daddy; I told you to stay away from her type. I told you to. I did.

MOMMY. You stop that! You're my mother, not his!

GRANDMA. I am?

DADDY. That's right, Grandma. Mommy's right.

GRANDMA. Well, how would you expect somebody as old as I am to remember a thing like that? You don't make allowances for people. I want an allowance. I want an allowance!

DADDY. All right, Grandma; I'll see to it.

MOMMY. Grandma! I'm ashamed of you.

GRANDMA. Humf! It's a fine time to say that. You should have gotten rid of me a long time ago if that's the way you feel. You should have had Daddy set me up in business somewhere . . . I could have gone into the fur business, or I could have been a singer. But no; not you. You wanted me around so you could sleep in my room when Daddy got fresh. But now it isn't important, because Daddy doesn't want to get fresh with you any more, and I don't blame him. You'd rather sleep with me, wouldn't you, Daddy?

MOMMY. Daddy doesn't want to sleep with anyone. Daddy's been sick.

DADDY. I've been sick. I don't even want to sleep in the apartment.

MOMMY. You see? I told you.

DADDY. I just want to get everything over with.

MOMMY. That's right. Why are they so late? Why can't they get here on time?

GRANDMA. (*An owl*) Who? Who? . . . Who? Who?

MOMMY. You know, Grandma.

GRANDMA. No, I don't.

MOMMY. Well, it doesn't really matter whether you do or not.

DADDY. Is that true?

MOMMY. Oh, more or less. Look how pretty Grandma wrapped these boxes.

GRANDMA. I didn't really like wrapping them; it hurt my fingers, and it frightened me. But it had to be done.

MOMMY. Why, Grandma?

GRANDMA. None of your damn business.

MOMMY. Go to bed.

GRANDMA. I don't want to go to bed. I just got up. I want to stay here and watch. Besides . . .

MOMMY. Go to bed.

DADDY. Let her stay up, Mommy; it isn't noon yet.

GRANDMA. I want to watch; besides . . .

DADDY. Let her watch, Mommy.

MOMMY. Well all right, you can watch; but don't you dare say a word.

GRANDMA. Old people are very good at listening; old people don't like to talk; old people have colitis and lavender perfume. Now I'm going to be quiet.

DADDY. She never mentioned she wanted to be a singer.

MOMMY. Oh, I forgot to tell you, but it was ages ago. (*The doorbell rings*) Oh, goodness! Here they are!

GRANDMA. Who? Who?

MOMMY. Oh, just some people.

GRANDMA. The van people? Is it the van people? Have you finally done it? Have you called the van people to come and take me away?

DADDY. Of course not, Grandma.

GRANDMA. Oh, don't be too sure. She'd have you carted off too, if she thought she could get away with it.

MOMMY. Pay no attention to her, Daddy. (*An aside to* GRANDMA) My God, you're ungrateful! (*The doorbell rings again*)

DADDY. (*Wringing his hands*) Oh dear; oh dear.

MOMMY. (*Still to* GRANDMA) Just you wait; I'll fix your wagon. (*Now to* DADDY) Well, go let them in Daddy. What are you waiting for?

DADDY. I think we should talk about it some more. Maybe we've been hasty . . . a little hasty, perhaps. (*Doorbell rings again*) I'd like to talk about it some more.

MOMMY. There's no need. You made up your mind; you were firm; you were masculine and decisive.

DADDY. We might consider the pros and the . . .

MOMMY. I won't argue with you; it has to be done; you were right. Open the door.

DADDY. But I'm not sure that . . .

MOMMY. Open the door.

DADDY. Was I firm about it?

MOMMY. Oh, so firm; so firm.

DADDY. And was I decisive?

MOMMY. SO decisive! Oh, I shivered.

DADDY. And masculine? Was I really masculine?

MOMMY. Oh, Daddy, you were so masculine; I shivered and fainted.

GRANDMA. Shivered and fainted, did she? Humf!

MOMMY. You be quiet.

GRANDMA. Old people have a right to talk to themselves; it doesn't hurt the gums, and it's comforting. (*Doorbell rings again*)

DADDY. I shall now open the door.

MOMMY. WHAT a masculine Daddy! Isn't he a masculine Daddy?

GRANDMA. Don't expect me to say anything. Old people are obscene.

MOMMY. Some of your opinions aren't so bad. You know that?

DADDY. (*Backing off from the door*) Maybe we can send them away.

MOMMY. Oh, look at you! You're turning into jelly; you're indecisive; you're a woman.

DADDY. All right. Watch me now; I'm going to open the door. Watch. Watch!

MOMMY. We're watching; we're watching.

GRANDMA. *I'm* not.

DADDY. Watch now; it's opening. (*He opens the door*) It's open! (MRS. BARKER *steps into the room*) Here they are!

MOMMY. Here they are!

GRANDMA. Where?

DADDY. Come in. You're late. But, of course, we expected you to be late; we were saying that we expected you to be late.

MOMMY. Daddy, don't be rude! We were saying that you just can't get satisfaction these days, and we were talking about you, of course. Won't you come in?

MRS. BARKER. Thank you. I don't mind if I do.

MOMMY. We're very glad that you're here, late as you are. You do remember us, don't you? You were here once before. I'm Mommy, and this is Daddy, and that's Grandma, doddering there in the corner.

MRS. BARKER. Hello, Mommy; hello, Daddy; and hello there, Grandma.

DADDY. Now that you're here, I don't suppose you could go away and maybe come back some other time.

MRS. BARKER. Oh no; we're much too efficient for that. I said, hello there, Grandma.

MOMMY. Speak to them, Grandma.

GRANDMA. I don't see them.

DADDY. For shame, Grandma; they're here.

MRS. BARKER. Yes, we're here, Grandma. I'm Mrs. Barker. I remember you; don't you remember me?

GRANDMA. I don't recall. Maybe you were younger, or something.

MOMMY. Grandma! What a terrible thing to say!

MRS. BARKER. Oh now, don't scold her, Mommy; for all she knows she may be right.

DADDY. Uh . . . Mrs. Barker, is it? Won't you sit down?

MRS. BARKER. I don't mind if I do.

MOMMY. Would you like a cigarette, and a drink, and would you like to cross your legs?

MRS. BARKER. You forget yourself, Mommy; I'm a professional woman. But I will cross my legs.

DADDY. Yes, make yourself comfortable.

MRS. BARKER. I don't mind if I do.

GRANDMA. Are they still here?

MOMMY. Be quiet, Grandma.

MRS. BARKER. Oh, we're still here. My, what an unattractive apartment you have!

MOMMY. Yes, but you don't know what a trouble it is. Let me tell you . . .

DADDY. I was saying to Mommy . . .

MRS. BARKER. Yes, I know. I was listening outside.

DADDY. About the icebox, and . . . the doorbell . . . and the . . .

MRS. BARKER. . . . and the johnny. Yes, we're very efficient; we have to know everything in our work.

DADDY. Exactly what do you do?

MOMMY. Yes, what is your work?

MRS. BARKER. Well, my dear, for one thing, I'm chairman of your woman's club.

MOMMY. Don't be ridiculous. I was talking to the chairman of my woman's club just yester— Why, so you are. You remember, Daddy, the lady I was telling you about? The lady with the husband who sits in the *swing?* Don't you remember?

DADDY. No . . . no . . . .

MOMMY. Of course you do. I'm so sorry, Mrs. Barker. I would have known you anywhere, except in this artificial light. And look! You have a hat just like the one I bought yesterday.

MRS. BARKER. (*With a little laugh*) No, not really; this hat is cream.

MOMMY. Well, my dear, that may look like a cream hat to you, but I can . . .

MRS. BARKER. Now, now; you seem to forget who I am.

MOMMY. Yes, I do, don't I? Are you sure you're comfortable? Won't you take off your dress?

MRS. BARKER. I don't mind if I do. (*She removes her dress*)

MOMMY. There. You must feel a great deal more comfortable.

MRS. BARKER. Well, I certainly *look* a great deal more comfortable.

DADDY. I'm going to blush and giggle.

MOMMY. Daddy's going to blush and giggle.

MRS. BARKER. (*Pulling the hem of her slip above her knees*) You're lucky to have such a man for a husband.

MOMMY. Oh, don't I know it!

DADDY. I just blushed and giggled and went sticky wet.

MOMMY. Isn't Daddy a caution, Mrs. Barker?

MRS. BARKER. Maybe if I smoked . . . ?

MOMMY. Oh, that isn't necessary.

MRS. BARKER. I don't mind if I do.

MOMMY. No; no, don't. Really.

MRS. BARKER. I don't mind . . .

MOMMY. I won't have you smoking in my house, and that's that! You're a professional woman.

DADDY. Grandma drinks AND smokes; don't you, Grandma?

GRANDMA. No.

MOMMY. Well, now, Mrs. Barker; suppose you tell us why you're here.

GRANDMA. (*As* MOMMY *walks through the boxes*) The boxes . . . the boxes . . .

MOMMY. Be quiet, Grandma.

DADDY. What did you say, Grandma?

GRANDMA. (*As* MOMMY *steps on several of the boxes*) The boxes, damn it!

MRS. BARKER. Boxes; she said boxes. She mentioned the boxes.

DADDY. What about the boxes, Grandma? Maybe Mrs. Barker is here because of the boxes. Is that what you meant, Grandma?

GRANDMA. I don't know if that's what I meant or not. It's certainly not what I *thought* I meant.

DADDY. Grandma is of the opinion that . . .

MRS. BARKER. Can we assume that the boxes are for us? I mean, can we assume that you had us come here for the boxes?

MOMMY. Are you in the habit of receiving boxes?

DADDY. A very good question.

MRS. BARKER. Well, that would depend on the reason we're here. I've got my fingers in so many little pies, you know. Now, I can think of one of my little activities in which we are in the habit of receiving *baskets;* but more in a literary sense than really. We *might* receive boxes, though, under very special circumstances. I'm afraid that's the best answer I can give you.

DADDY. It's a very interesting answer.

MRS. BARKER. *I* thought so. But, does it help?

MOMMY. No; I'm afraid not.

DADDY. I wonder if it might help us any if I said I feel misgivings, that I have definite qualms.

MOMMY. Where, Daddy?

DADDY. Well, mostly right here, right around where the stitches were.

MOMMY. Daddy had an operation, you know.

MRS. BARKER. Oh, you poor Daddy! I didn't know; but then, how could I?

GRANDMA. You might have asked; it wouldn't have hurt you.

MOMMY. Dry up, Grandma.

GRANDMA. There you go. Letting your true feelings come out. Old people aren't dry enough, I suppose. My sacks are empty, the fluid in my eyeballs is all caked on the inside edges, my spine is made of sugar candy, I breathe ice; but you don't hear me complain. Nobody hears old people complain because people think that's all old people do. And *that's* because old people are gnarled and sagged and twisted into the shape of a complaint. (*Signs off*) That's all.

MRS. BARKER. What was wrong, Daddy?

DADDY. Well, you know how it is: the doctors took out something that was there and put in something that wasn't there. An operation.

MRS. BARKER. You're very fortunate, I should say.

MOMMY. Oh, he is; he is. All his life, Daddy has wanted to be a United States Senator; but now . . . why now he's changed his mind, and for the rest of his life he's going to want to be Governor . . . it would be nearer the apartment, you know.

MRS. BARKER. You *are* fortunate, Daddy.

DADDY. Yes, indeed; except that I get these qualms now and then, definite ones.

MRS. BARKER. Well, it's just a matter of things settling; you're like an old house.

MOMMY. Why Daddy, thank Mrs. Barker.

DADDY. Thank you.

MRS. BARKER. Ambition! That's the ticket. I have a brother who's very much like you, Daddy . . . ambitious. Of course, he's a great deal younger than you; he's even younger than I am . . . if such a thing is possible. He runs a little newspaper. Just a little newspaper . . . but he runs it. He's chief cook and bottle washer of that little newspaper, which he calls *The Village Idiot*. He has such a sense of humor; he's so self-deprecating, so modest. And he'd never admit it himself, but he *is* the Village Idiot.

MOMMY. Oh, I think that's just grand. Don't you think so, Daddy?

DADDY. Yes, just grand.

MRS. BARKER. My brother's a dear man, and he has a dear little wife, whom he loves, dearly. He loves her so much he just can't get a sentence out without mentioning her. He wants everybody to know he's married. He's really a stickler on that point; he can't be introduced to anybody and say hello without adding, "Of course, I'm married." As far as I'm concerned, he's the chief exponent of Woman Love in this whole country; he's even been written up in psychiatric journals because of it.

DADDY. Indeed!

MOMMY. Isn't that lovely.

MRS. BARKER. Oh, I think so. There's too much woman hatred in this country, and that's a fact.

GRANDMA. Oh, I don't know.

MOMMY. Oh, I think that's just grand. Don't you think so, Daddy?

DADDY. Yes, just grand.

GRANDMA. In case anybody's interested . . .

MOMMY. Be quiet, Grandma.

GRANDMA. Nuts!

MOMMY. Oh, Mrs. Barker, you *must* forgive Grandma. She's rural.

MRS. BARKER. I don't mind if I do.

DADDY. Maybe Grandma has something to say.

MOMMY. Nonsense. Old people have nothing to say; and if old people *did* have something to say, nobody would listen to them. (*To* GRANDMA) You see? I can pull that stuff just as easy as you can.

GRANDMA. Well, you got the rhythm, but you don't really have the quality. Besides, you're middle-aged.

MOMMY. I'm proud of it!

GRANDMA. Look. I'll show you how it's really done. Middle-aged people think they can do anything, but the truth is that middle-aged people can't do most things as well as they used to. Middle-aged people think they're special because they're like everybody else. We live in the age of deformity. You see? Rhythm *and* content. You'll learn.

DADDY. I do wish I weren't surrounded by women; I'd like some men around here.

MRS. BARKER. You can say that again!

GRANDMA. I don't hardly count as a woman, so can I say my piece?

MOMMY. Go on. Jabber away.

GRANDMA. It's very simple; the fact is, these boxes don't have anything to do with why this good lady is come to call. Now, if you're interested in knowing why these boxes *are* here . . .

DADDY. I'm sure that must be all very true, Grandma, but what does it have to do with why . . . pardon me, what is that name again?

MRS. BARKER. Mrs. Barker.

DADDY. Exactly. What does it have to do with why . . . that name again?

MRS. BARKER. Mrs. Barker.

DADDY. Precisely. What does it have to do with why what's-her-name is here?

MOMMY. They're here because we asked them.

MRS. BARKER. Yes. That's why.

GRANDMA. Now if you're interested in knowing why these boxes *are* here . . .

MOMMY. Well, nobody *is* interested!

GRANDMA. You can be as snippety as you like for all the good it'll do you.

DADDY. You two will have to stop arguing.

MOMMY. I don't argue with her.

DADDY. It will just have to stop.

MOMMY. Well, why don't you call a van and have her taken away?

GRANDMA. Don't bother; there's no need.

DADDY. No, now, perhaps I can go away myself. . . .

MOMMY. Well, one or the other; the way things are now it's impossible. In the first place, it's too crowded in this apartment. (*To* GRANDMA) And it's you that takes up all the space, with your enema bottles, and your Pekinese, and God-only-knows-what-else . . . and now all these boxes. . . .

GRANDMA. These boxes are . . .

MRS. BARKER. I've never heard of enema *bottles.* . . .

GRANDMA. She means enema bags, but she doesn't know the difference. Mommy comes from extremely bad stock. And besides, when Mommy was born . . . well, it was a difficult delivery, and she had a head shaped like a banana.

MOMMY. You ungrateful— Daddy? Daddy, you see how ungrateful she is after all these years, after all the things we've done for her? (*To* GRANDMA) One of these days you're going away in a van; that's what's going to happen to you!

GRANDMA. Do tell!

MRS. BARKER. Like a banana?

GRANDMA. Yup, just like a banana.

MRS. BARKER. My word!

MOMMY. You stop listening to her; she'll say anything. Just the other night she called Daddy a hedgehog.

MRS. BARKER. She didn't!

GRANDMA. That's right, baby; you stick up for me.

MOMMY. I don't know where she gets the words; on the television, maybe.

MRS. BARKER. Did you really call him a hedgehog?

GRANDMA. Oh look; what difference does it make whether I did or not?

DADDY. Grandma's right. Leave Grandma alone.

MOMMY. (*To* DADDY) How dare you!

GRANDMA. Oh, leave her alone, Daddy; the kid's all mixed up.

MOMMY. You see? I told you. It's all those television shows. Daddy, you go right into Grandma's room and take her television and shake all the tubes loose.

DADDY. Don't mention tubes to me.

MOMMY. Oh! Mommy forgot! (*To* MRS. BARKER) Daddy has tubes now, where he used to have tracts.

MRS. BARKER. Is that a fact!

GRANDMA. I know why this dear lady is here.

MOMMY. You be still.

MRS. BARKER. Oh, I do wish you'd tell me.

MOMMY. No! No! That wouldn't be fair at all.

DADDY. Besides, she knows why she's here; she's here because we called them.

MRS. BARKER. La! But that still leaves me puzzled. I know I'm here because you called us, but I'm such a busy girl, with this committee and that committee, and the Responsible Citizens Activities I indulge in.

MOMMY. Oh my; busy, busy.

MRS. BARKER. Yes, indeed. So I'm afraid you'll have to give me some help.

MOMMY. Oh, no. No, you must be mistaken. I can't believe we asked you here to give you any help. With the way taxes are these days, and the way you can't get satisfaction in ANYTHING . . . no, I don't believe so.

DADDY. And if you need help . . . why, I should think you'd apply for a Fulbright Scholarship. . . .

MOMMY. And if not that . . . why, then a Guggenheim Fellowship. . . .

GRANDMA. Oh, come on; why not shoot the works and try for the Prix de Rome. (*Under her breath to* MOMMY *and* DADDY) Beasts!

MRS. BARKER. Oh, what a jolly family. But let me think. I'm knee-deep in work these days; there's the Ladies' Auxiliary Air Raid Committee, for one thing; how do you feel about air raids?

MOMMY. Oh, I'd say we're hostile.

DADDY. Yes, definitely; we're hostile.

MRS. BARKER. Then, you'll be no help there. There's too much hostility in the world these days as it is; but I'll not badger you! There's a surfeit of badgers as well.

GRANDMA. While we're at it, there's been a run on old people, too. The Department of Agriculture, or maybe it wasn't the Department of Agriculture—anyway, it was some department that's run by a girl—put out figures showing that ninety per cent of the adult population of the country is over eighty years old . . . or eighty per cent is over ninety years old . . .

MOMMY. You're such a liar! You just finished saying that everyone is middle-aged.

GRANDMA. I'm just telling you what the government says . . . that doesn't have anything to do with what . . .

MOMMY. It's that television! Daddy, go break her television.

GRANDMA. You won't find it.

DADDY. (Wearily getting up) If I must . . . I must.

MOMMY. And don't step on the Pekinese; it's blind.

DADDY. It may be blind, but Daddy isn't. (*He exits, through the archway, stage left*)

GRANDMA. You won't find *it*, either.

MOMMY. Oh, I'm so fortunate to have such a husband. Just think; I could have a husband who was poor, or argumentative, or a husband who sat in a wheel chair all day . . . OOOOHHHH! *What* have I said? What *have* I said?

GRANDMA. You said you could have a husband who sat in a wheel . . .

MOMMY. I'm mortified! I could die! I could cut my tongue out! I could . . .

MRS. BARKER. (*Forcing a smile*) Oh, now . . . now . . . don't think about it . . .

MOMMY. I could . . . why, I could . . .

MRS. BARKER. . . . don't think about it . . . really. . . .

MOMMY. You're quite right. I won't think about it, and that way I'll forget that I ever said it, and that way it will be all right. (*Pause*) There . . . I've forgotten. Well, now, now that Daddy is out of the room we can have some girl talk.

MRS. BARKER. I'm not sure that I . . .

MOMMY. You *do* want to have some girl talk, don't you?

MRS. BARKER. I was going to say I'm not sure that I wouldn't care for a glass of water. I feel a little faint.

MOMMY. Grandma, go get Mrs. Barker a glass of water.

GRANDMA. Go get it yourself. I quit.

MOMMY. Grandma loves to do little things around the house; it gives her a false sense of security.

GRANDMA. I quit! I'm through!

MOMMY. Now, you be a good Grandma, or you know what will happen to you. You'll be taken away in a van.

GRANDMA. You don't frighten me. I'm too old to be frightened. Besides . . .

MOMMY. WELL! I'll tend to you later. I'll hide your teeth . . . I'll . . .

GRANDMA. Everything's hidden.

MRS. BARKER. I *am* going to faint. I *am*.

MOMMY. Good heavens! I'll go myself. (*As she exits, through the archway, stage-left*) I'll fix you, Grandma. I'll take care of you later. (*She exits*)

GRANDMA. Oh, go soak your head. (*To* MRS. BARKER) Well, dearie, how do you feel?

MRS. BARKER. A little better, I think. Yes, much better, thank you, Grandma.

GRANDMA. That's good.

MRS. BARKER. But . . . I feel so lost . . . not knowing why I'm here . . . and, on top of it, they say I was here before.

GRANDMA. Well, you were. You weren't *here*, exactly, because we've moved around a lot, from one apartment to another, up and down the social ladder like mice, if you like similes.

MRS. BARKER. I don't . . . particularly.

GRANDMA. Well, then, I'm sorry.

MRS. BARKER. (*Suddenly*) Grandma, I feel I can trust you.

GRANDMA. Don't be too sure; it's every man for himself around this place. . . .

MRS. BARKER. Oh . . . is it? Nonetheless, I really do feel that I can trust you. *Please* tell me why they called and asked us to come. I implore you!

GRANDMA. Oh my; that feels good. It's been so long since anybody implored me. Do it again. Implore me some more.

MRS. BARKER. You're your daughter's mother, all right!

GRANDMA. Oh, I don't mean to be hard. If you won't implore me, then beg me, or ask me, or entreat me . . . just anything like that.

MRS. BARKER. You're a dreadful old woman!

GRANDMA. You'll understand some day. Please!

MRS. BARKER. Oh, for heaven's sake! . . . I implore you . . . I beg you . . . I beseech you!

GRANDMA. Beseech! Oh, that's the nicest word I've heard in ages. You're a dear, sweet woman. . . . You . . . beseech . . . me. I can't resist that.

MRS. BARKER. Well, then . . . please tell me why they asked us to come.

GRANDMA. Well, I'll give you a hint. That's the best I can do, because I'm a muddleheaded old woman. Now listen, because it's important. Once upon a time, not too very long ago, but a long enough time ago . . . oh, about twenty years ago . . . there was a man very much like Daddy, and a woman very much like Mommy, who were married to each other, very much like Mommy and Daddy are married to each other; and they lived in an apartment very much like one that's very much like this one, and they lived there with an old woman who was very much like yours truly, only younger, because it was some time ago; in fact, they were all somewhat younger.

MRS. BARKER. How fascinating!

GRANDMA. Now, at the same time, there was a dear lady very much like you, only younger then, who did all sorts of Good Works. . . . And one of the

Good Works this dear lady did was in something very much like a volunteer capacity for an organization very much like the Bye-Bye Adoption Service, which is nearby and which was run by a terribly deaf old lady very much like the Miss Bye-Bye who runs the Bye-Bye Adoption Service nearby.

MRS. BARKER. How enthralling!

GRANDMA. Well, be that as it may. Nonetheless, one afternoon this man, who was very much like Daddy, and this woman who was very much like Mommy came to see this dear lady who did all the Good Works, who was very much like you, dear, and they were very sad and very hopeful, and they cried and smiled and bit their fingers, and they said all the most intimate things.

MRS. BARKER. How spellbinding! What did they say?

GRANDMA. Well, it was very sweet. The woman, who was very much like Mommy, said that she and the man who was very much like Daddy had never been blessed with anything very much like a bumble of joy.

MRS. BARKER. A what?

GRANDMA. A bumble; a bumble of joy.

MRS. BARKER. Oh, like bundle.

GRANDMA. Well, yes; very much like it. Bundle, bumble; who cares? At any rate, the woman, who was very much like Mommy, said that they wanted a bumble of their own, but that the man, who was very much like Daddy, couldn't have a bumble; and the man, who was very much like Daddy, said that yes, they had wanted a bumble of their own, but that the woman, who was very much like Mommy, couldn't have one, and that now they wanted to buy something very much like a bumble.

MRS. BARKER. How engrossing!

GRANDMA. Yes. And the dear lady, who was very much like you, said something that was very much like, "Oh, what a shame; but take heart . . . I think we have just the bumble *for* you." And, well, the lady, who was very much like Mommy, and the man, who was very much like Daddy, cried and smiled and bit their fingers, and said some more intimate things, which were totally irrelevant but which were pretty hot stuff, and so the dear lady, who was very much like you, and who had something very much like a penchant for pornography, listened with something very much like enthusiasm. "Whee," she said. "Whoooopeeeeee!" But that's beside the point.

MRS. BARKER. I suppose *so*. But how gripping!

GRANDMA. Anyway . . . they *bought* something very much like a bumble, and they took it away with them. But . . . things didn't work out very well.

MRS. BARKER. You mean there was trouble?

GRANDMA. You got it. (*With a glance through the archway*) But, I'm going to have to speed up now because I think I'm leaving soon.

MRS. BARKER. Oh. Are you really?

GRANDMA. Yup.

MRS. BARKER. But old people don't go anywhere; they're either taken places, or put places.

GRANDMA. Well, this old person is different. Anyway . . . things started going badly.

MRS. BARKER. Oh yes. Yes.

GRANDMA. Weeeeellll . . . in the first place, it turned out the bumble didn't look like either one of its parents. That was enough of a blow, but things got worse. One night, it cried its heart out, if you can imagine such a thing.

MRS. BARKER. Cried its heart out! Well!

GRANDMA. But that was only the beginning. Then it turned out it only had eyes for its Daddy.

MRS. BARKER. For its Daddy! Why, any self-respecting woman would have gouged those eyes right out of its head.

GRANDMA. Well, she did. That's exactly what she did. But then, it kept its nose up in the air.

MRS. BARKER. Ufggh! How disgusting!

GRANDMA. That's what they thought. But *then,* it began to develop an interest in its you-know-what.

MRS. BARKER. In its you-know-what! Well! I hope they cut its hands off at the wrists!

GRANDMA. Well, yes, they did that eventually. But first, they cut off its you-know-what.

MRS. BARKER. A much better idea!

GRANDMA. That's what they thought. But after they cut off its you-know-what, it *still* put its hands under the covers, *looking* for its you-know-what. So, finally, they *had* to cut off its hands at the wrists.

MRS. BARKER. Naturally!

GRANDMA. And it was such a resentful bumble. Why, one day it called its Mommy a dirty name.

MRS. BARKER. Well, I hope they cut its tongue out!

GRANDMA. Of course. And then, as it got bigger, they found out all sorts of terrible things about it, like: it didn't have a head on its shoulders, it had no guts, it was spineless, its feet were made of clay . . . just dreadful things.

MRS. BARKER. Dreadful!

GRANDMA. So you can understand how they became discouraged.

MRS. BARKER. I certainly can! And what did they do?

GRANDMA. What did they do? Well, for the last straw, it finally up and died; and you can imagine how *that* made them feel, their having paid for it, and all. So, they called up the lady who sold them the bumble in the first place and told her to come right over to their apartment. They wanted satisfaction; they wanted their money back. That's what they wanted.

MRS. BARKER. My, my, my.

GRANDMA. How do you like *them* apples?

MRS. BARKER. My, my, my.

DADDY. (*Off stage*) Mommy! I can't find Grandma's television, and I can't find the Pekinese, either.

MOMMY. (*Off stage*) Isn't that funny! And I can't find the water.

GRANDMA. Heh, heh, heh. I told them everything was hidden.

MRS. BARKER. Did you hide the water, too?

GRANDMA. (*Puzzled*) No. No, I didn't do *that*.

DADDY. (*Off stage*) The truth of the matter is, I can't even find Grandma's room.

GRANDMA. Heh, heh, heh.

MRS. BARKER. My! You certainly did hide things, didn't you?

GRANDMA. Sure, kid, sure.

MOMMY. (*Sticking her head in the room*) Did you ever hear of such a thing, Grandma? Daddy can't find your television, and he can't find the Pekinese, and the truth of the matter is he can't even find your room.

GRANDMA. I told you. I hid everything.

MOMMY. Nonsense, Grandma! Just wait until I get my hands on you. You're a troublemaker . . . that's what you are.

GRANDMA. Well, I'll be out of here pretty soon, baby.

MOMMY. Oh, you don't know how right you are! Daddy's been wanting to send you away for a long time now, but I've been restraining him. I'll tell you one thing, though . . . I'm getting sick and tired of this fighting, and I might just let him have his way. Then you'll see what'll happen. Away you'll go; in a van, too. I'll let Daddy call the van man.

GRANDMA. I'm way ahead of you.

MOMMY. How can you be so old and so smug at the same time? You have no sense of proportion.

GRANDMA. You just answered your own question.

MOMMY. Mrs. Barker, I'd much rather you came into the kitchen for that glass of water, what with Grandma out here, and all.

MRS. BARKER. I don't see what Grandma has to do with it; and besides, I don't think you're very polite.

MOMMY. You seem to forget that you're a guest in this house . . .

GRANDMA. Apartment!

MOMMY. Apartment! And that you're a professional woman. So, if you'll be so good as to come into the kitchen, I'll be more than happy to show you where the water is, and where the glass is, and then you can put two and two together, if you're clever enough. (*She vanishes*)

MRS. BARKER. (*After a moment's consideration*) I suppose she's right.

GRANDMA. Well, that's how it is when people call you up and ask you over to do something for them.

MRS. BARKER. I suppose you're right, too. Well, Grandma, it's been very nice talking to you.

GRANDMA. And I've enjoyed listening. Say, don't tell Mommy or Daddy that I gave you that hint, will you?

MRS. BARKER. Oh, dear me, the hint! I'd forgotten about it, if you can imagine such a thing. No, I won't breathe a word of it to them.

GRANDMA. I don't know if it helped you any . . .

MRS. BARKER. I can't tell, yet. I'll have to . . . what *is* the word I want? . . . I'll have to relate it . . . that's it . . . I'll have to relate it to certain things that I *know*, and . . . draw . . . conclusions. . . . What I'll really have to do is to see if it applies to anything. I mean, after all, I *do* do volunteer work for an adoption service, but it isn't very much *like* the Bye-Bye Adoption Service . . . it *is* the Bye-Bye Adoption Service . . . and while I can remember Mommy and Daddy coming to see me, oh, about twenty years ago, about buying a bumble, I can't quite remember anyone very much *like* Mommy and Daddy coming to see me about buying a bumble. Don't you see? It really presents quite a problem. . . . I'll have to think about it . . . mull it . . . but at any rate, it was truly first-class of you to try to help me. Oh, will you still be here after I've had my drink of water?

GRANDMA. Probably . . . I'm not as spry as I used to be.

MRS. BARKER. Oh. Well, I won't say good-by then.

GRANDMA. No. Don't. (MRS. BARKER *exits through the archway*) People don't say good-by to old people because they think they'll frighten them. Lordy! If they only knew how awful "hello" and "my, you're looking chipper" sounded, they wouldn't say those things either. The truth is, there isn't much you *can* say to old people that doesn't sound just terrible. (*The doorbell rings*) Come on in! (*The* YOUNG MAN *enters.* GRANDMA *looks him over*) Well, now, aren't you a breath of fresh air!

YOUNG MAN. Hello there.

GRANDMA. My, my, my. Are you the van man?

YOUNG MAN. The what?

GRANDMA. The van man. The van man. Are you come to take me away?

YOUNG MAN. I don't know what you're talking about.

GRANDMA. Oh. (*Pause*) Well. (*Pause*) My, my, aren't you something!

YOUNG MAN. Hm?

GRANDMA. I said, my, my, aren't you something.

YOUNG MAN. Oh. Thank you.

GRANDMA. You don't sound very enthusiastic.

YOUNG MAN. Oh, I'm . . . I'm used to it.

GRANDMA. Yup . . . yup. You know, if I were about a hundred and fifty years younger I could go for you.

YOUNG MAN. Yes, I imagine so.

GRANDMA. Unh-hunh . . . will you look at those muscles!

YOUNG MAN. (*Flexing his muscles*) Yes, they're quite good, aren't they?

GRANDMA. Boy, they sure are. They natural?

YOUNG MAN. Well the basic structure was there, but I've done some work, too . . . you know, in a gym.

GRANDMA. I'll bet you have. You ought to be in the movies, boy.

YOUNG MAN. I know.

GRANDMA. Yup! Right up there on the old silver screen. But I suppose you've heard that before.

YOUNG MAN. Yes, I have.

GRANDMA. You ought to try out for them . . . the movies.

YOUNG MAN. Well, actually, I may have a career there yet. I've lived out on the

West Coast almost all my life . . . and I've met a few people who . . . might be able to help me. I'm not in too much of a hurry, though. I'm almost as young as I look.

GRANDMA. Oh, that's nice. And will you look at that face!

YOUNG MAN. Yes, it's quite good, isn't it? Clean-cut, midwest farm boy type, almost insultingly good-looking in a typically American way. Good profile, straight nose, honest eyes, wonderful smile . . .

GRANDMA. Yup. Boy, you know what you are, don't you? You're the American Dream, that's what you are. All those other people, they don't know what they're talking about. You . . . *you* are the American Dream.

YOUNG MAN. Thanks.

MOMMY. (*Off stage*) Who rang the doorbell?

GRANDMA. (*Shouting off-stage*) The American Dream!

MOMMY. (*Off stage*) What? What was that, Grandma?

GRANDMA. (*Shouting*) The American Dream! The American Dream! Damn it!

DADDY. (*Off stage*) How's that, Mommy?

MOMMY. (*Off stage*) Oh, some gibberish; pay no attention. Did you find Grandma's room?

DADDY. (*Off stage*) No. I can't even find Mrs. Barker.

YOUNG MAN. What was all that?

GRANDMA. Oh, that was just the folks, but let's not talk about them, honey; let's talk about you.

YOUNG MAN. All right.

GRANDMA. Well, let's see. If you're not the van man, what are you doing here?

YOUNG MAN. I'm looking for work.

GRANDMA. Are you! Well, what kind of work?

YOUNG MAN. Oh, almost anything . . . almost anything that pays. I'll do almost anything for money.

GRANDMA. Will you . . . will you? Hmmmm. I wonder if there's anything you could do around here?

YOUNG MAN. There might be. It looked to be a likely building.

GRANDMA. It's always looked to be a rather unlikely building to me, but I suppose you'd know better than I.

YOUNG MAN. I can sense these things.

GRANDMA. There *might* be something you could do around here. Stay there! Don't come any closer.

YOUNG MAN. Sorry.

GRANDMA. I don't mean I'd *mind*. I don't know whether I'd mind, or not. . . . But it wouldn't look well; it would look just *awful*.

YOUNG MAN. Yes; I suppose so.

GRANDMA. Now, stay there, let me concentrate. What could you do? The folks have been in something of a quandary around here today, sort of a dilemma, and I wonder if you mightn't be some help.

YOUNG MAN. I hope so . . . if there's money in it. Do you have any money?

GRANDMA. Money! Oh, there's more money around here than you'd know what to do with.

YOUNG MAN. I'm not so sure.

GRANDMA. Well, maybe not. Besides, I've got money of my own.

YOUNG MAN. You have?

GRANDMA. Sure. Old people quite often have lots of money; more often than most people expect. Come here, so I can whisper to you . . . not too close. I might faint.

YOUNG MAN. Oh, I'm sorry.

GRANDMA. It's all right, dear. Anyway . . . have you ever heard of that big baking contest they run? The one where all the ladies get together in a big barn and bake away?

YOUNG MAN. I'm . . . not . . . sure. . . .

GRANDMA. Not so close. Well, it doesn't matter whether you've heard of it or not. The important thing is—and I don't want anybody to hear this . . . the folks think I haven't been out of the house in eight years—the important thing is that I won first prize in that baking contest this year. Oh, it was in all the papers; not under my own name, though. I used a *nom de boulangère;* I called myself Uncle Henry.

YOUNG MAN. Did you?

GRANDMA. Why not? I didn't see any reason not to. I look just as much like an old man as I do like an old woman. And you know what I called it . . . what I won for?

YOUNG MAN. No. What did you call it?

GRANDMA. I called it Uncle Henry's Day-Old Cake.

YOUNG MAN. That's a very nice name.

GRANDMA. And it wasn't any trouble, either. All I did was go out and get a store-bought cake, and keep it around for a while, and then slip it in, unbeknownst to anybody. Simple.

YOUNG MAN. You're a very resourceful person.

GRANDMA. Pioneer stock.

YOUNG MAN. Is all this true? Do you want me to believe all this?

GRANDMA. Well, you can believe it or not . . . it doesn't make any difference to me. All *I* know is, Uncle Henry's Day-Old Cake won me twenty-five thousand smackerolas.

YOUNG MAN. Twenty-five thou—

GRANDMA. Right on the old loggerhead. Now . . . how do you like them apples?

YOUNG MAN. Love 'em.

GRANDMA. I thought you'd be impressed.

YOUNG MAN. Money talks.

GRANDMA. Hey! You look familiar.

YOUNG MAN. Hm? Pardon?

GRANDMA. I said, you look familiar.

YOUNG MAN. Well, I've done some modeling.

GRANDMA. No . . . no. I don't mean that. You look familiar.

YOUNG MAN. Well, I'm a type.

GRANDMA. Yup; you sure are. Why do you say you'd do anything for money . . . if you don't mind my being nosy?

YOUNG MAN. No, no. It's part of the interviews. I'll be happy to tell you. It's that I have no talents at all, except what you see . . . my person; my body, my face. In every other way I am incomplete, and I must therefore . . . compensate.

GRANDMA. What do you mean, incomplete? You look pretty complete to me.

YOUNG MAN. I think I can explain it to you, partially because you're very old, and very old people have perceptions they keep to themselves, because if they expose them to other people . . . well, you know what ridicule and neglect are.

GRANDMA. I do, child, I do.

YOUNG MAN. Then listen. My mother died the night that I was born, and I never knew my father; I doubt my mother did. But, I wasn't alone, because lying with me . . . in the placenta . . . there was someone else . . . my brother . . . my twin.

GRANDMA. Oh, my child.

YOUNG MAN. We were identical twins . . . he and I . . . not fraternal . . . identical; we were derived from the same ovum; and in *this*, in that we were twins not from separate ova but from the same one, we had a kinship such as you cannot imagine. We . . . we felt each other breathe . . . his heartbeats thundered in my temples . . . mine in his . . . our stomachs ached and we cried for feeding at the same time . . . are you old enough to understand?

GRANDMA. I think so, child; I think I'm nearly old enough.

YOUNG MAN. I hope so. But we were separated when we were still very young, my brother, my twin and I . . . inasmuch as you can separate one being. We were torn apart . . . thrown to opposite ends of the continent. I don't know what became of my brother . . . to the rest of myself . . . except that, from time to time, in the years that have passed, I have suffered losses . . . that I can't explain. A fall from grace . . . a departure of innocence . . . loss . . . loss. How can I put it to you? All right; like this: Once . . . it was as if all at once my heart . . . became numb . . . almost as though I . . . almost as though . . . just like that . . . it had been wrenched from my body . . . and from that time I have been unable to love. Once . . . I was asleep at the time . . . I awoke, and my eyes were burning. And since that time I have been unable to see anything, *anything*, with pity, with affection . . . with anything but . . . cool disinterest. And my groin . . . even there . . . since one time . . . one specific agony . . . since then I have not been able to *love* anyone with my body. And even my hands . . . I cannot touch another person and feel love. And there is more . . . there are more losses, but it all comes down to this: I no longer have the capacity to feel anything. I have no emotions. I have been drained, torn asunder . . . disemboweled. I have, now, only my person . . . my body, my face. I use what I have . . . I let people love me . . . I accept the syntax around me, for while I know I cannot relate . . . I know I must be related *to*. I let people love me . . . I let people touch me . . . I let them draw pleasure from my groin . . . from my presence . . . from the fact of me . . . but, that is all it comes to. As I told you, I am incomplete . . . I can feel nothing. I can feel nothing. And so . . . here I am . . . as you see me. I am . . . but this . . . what you see. And it will always be thus.

GRANDMA. Oh, my child; my child. (*Long pause; then*) I was mistaken . . . before. I don't know you from somewhere, but I knew . . . once . . . someone very much like you . . . or, very much as perhaps you were.

YOUNG MAN. Be careful; be very careful. What I have told you may not be true. In my profession . . .

GRANDMA. Shhhhhh. (*The* YOUNG MAN *bows his head, in acquiescence*) Someone . . . to be more precise . . . who might have turned out to be very much like you might have turned out to be. And . . . unless I'm terribly mistaken . . . you've found yourself a job.

YOUNG MAN. What are my duties?

MRS. BARKER. (*Off stage*) Yoo-hoo! Yoo-hoo!

GRANDMA. Oh-oh. You'll . . . you'll have to play it by ear, my dear . . . unless I get a chance to talk to you again. I've got to go into my act, now.

YOUNG MAN. But, I . . .

GRANDMA. Yoo-hoo!

MRS. BARKER. (*Coming through archway*) Yoo-hoo . . . oh, there you are, Grandma. I'm glad to see somebody. I can't find Mommy or Daddy. (*Double takes*) Well . . . who's this?

GRANDMA. This? Well . . . un . . . oh, this is the . . . uh . . . the van man. That's who it is . . . the van man.

MRS. BARKER. So! It's true! They *did* call the van man. They *are* having you carted away.

GRANDMA. (*Shrugging*) Well, you know. It figures.

MRS. BARKER. (*To* YOUNG MAN) How dare you cart this poor old woman away!

YOUNG MAN. (*After a quick look at* GRANDMA, *who nods*) I do what I'm paid to do. I don't ask any questions.

MRS. BARKER. (*After a brief pause*) Oh. (*Pause*) Well, you're quite right, of course, and I shouldn't meddle.

GRANDMA. (*To* YOUNG MAN) Dear, will you take my things out to the van? (*She points to the boxes*)

YOUNG MAN. (*After only the briefest hesitation*) Why certainly.

GRANDMA. (*As the* YOUNG MAN *takes up half the boxes, exits by the front door*) Isn't that a nice young van man?

MRS. BARKER. (*Shaking her head in disbelief, watching the* YOUNG MAN *exit*) Unh-hunh . . . some things have changed for the better. I remember when I had *my* mother carted off . . . the van man who came for her wasn't anything near as nice as this one.

GRANDMA. Oh, did you have your mother carted off, too?

MRS. BARKER. (*Cheerfully*) Why certainly! Didn't you?

GRANDMA. (*Puzzling*) No . . . no, I didn't. At least, I can't remember. Listen dear; I got to talk to you for a second.

MRS. BARKER. Why certainly, Grandma.

GRANDMA. Now, listen.

MRS. BARKER. Yes, Grandma. Yes.

GRANDMA. Now listen carefully. You got this dilemma here with Mommy and Daddy . . .

MRS. BARKER. Yes! I wonder where they've gone to?

GRANDMA. They'll be back in. Now, LISTEN!

MRS. BARKER. Oh, I'm sorry.

GRANDMA. Now, you got this dilemma here with Mommy and Daddy, and I think I got the way out for you. (*The* YOUNG MAN *re-enters through the front door*) Will you take the rest of my things out now, dear? (*To* MRS. BARKER, *while the* YOUNG MAN *takes the rest of the boxes, exits again by the front door*) Fine. Now listen, dear. (*She begins to whisper in* MRS. BARKER's *ear*)

MRS. BARKER. Oh! Oh! Oh! I don't think I could . . . do you really think I could? Well, why not? What a wonderful idea . . . what an absolutely wonderful idea!

GRANDMA. Well, yes, I thought it was.

MRS. BARKER. And you so old!

GRANDMA. Heh, heh, heh.

MRS. BARKER. Well, I think it's absolutely marvelous, anyway. I'm going to find Mommy and Daddy right now.

GRANDMA. Good. You do that.

MRS. BARKER. Well, now. I think I will say good-by. I can't thank you enough. (*She starts to exit through the archway*)

GRANDMA. You're welcome. Say it!

MRS. BARKER. Huh? What?

GRANDMA. Say good-by.

MRS. BARKER. Oh. Good-by. (*She exits*) Mommy! I say, Mommy! Daddy!

GRANDMA. Good-by. (*By herself now, she looks about*) Ah me. (*Shakes her head*) Ah me. (*Takes in the room*) Good-by. (*The* YOUNG MAN *re-enters*)

GRANDMA. Oh, hello, there.

YOUNG MAN. All the boxes are outside.

GRANDMA. (*A little sadly*) I don't know why I bother to take them with me. They don't have much in them . . . some old letters, a couple of regrets . . . Pekinese . . . blind at that . . . the television . . . my Sunday teeth . . . eighty-six years of living . . . some sounds . . . a few images, a little garbled by now . . . and, well . . . (*She shrugs*) . . . you know . . . the things one accumulates.

YOUNG MAN. Can I get you . . . a cab, or something?

GRANDMA. Oh no, dear . . . thank you just the same. I'll take it from here.

YOUNG MAN. And what shall I do now?

GRANDMA. Oh, you stay here, dear. It will all become clear to you. It will be explained. You'll understand.

YOUNG MAN. Very well.

GRANDMA. (*After one more look about*) Well . . .

YOUNG MAN. Let me see you to the elevator.

GRANDMA. Oh . . . that *would* be nice, dear. (*They both exit by the front door, slowly*) (*Enter* MRS. BARKER, *followed by* MOMMY *and* DADDY)

MRS. BARKER. . . . and I'm happy to tell you that the whole thing's settled. Just like that.

MOMMY. Oh, we're so glad. We were afraid there might be a problem, what with delays, and all.

DADDY. Yes, we're very relieved.

MRS. BARKER. Well, now; that's what professional women are for.

MOMMY. Why . . . where's Grandma? Grandma's not here! Where's Grandma? And look! The boxes are gone, too. Grandma's gone, and so are the boxes. She's taken off, and she's stolen something! Daddy!

MRS. BARKER. Why, Mommy, the van man was here.

MOMMY. (*Startled*) The what?

MRS. BARKER. The van man. The van man was here. (*The lights might dim a little, suddenly*)

MOMMY. (*Shakes her head*) No, that's impossible.

MRS. BARKER. Why, I saw him with my own two eyes.

MOMMY. (*Near tears*) No, no, that's impossible. No. There's no such thing as the van man. There is no van man. We . . . we made him up. Grandma? Grandma?

DADDY. (*Moving to* MOMMY) There, there, now.

MOMMY. Oh Daddy . . . where's Grandma?

DADDY. There, there, now. (*While* DADDY *is comforting* MOMMY, GRANDMA *comes out, stage right, near the footlights*)

GRANDMA. (*To the audience*) Shhhhh! I want to watch this. (*She motions to* MRS. BARKER *who, with a secret smile, tiptoes to the front door and opens it. The* YOUNG MAN *is framed therein. Lights up full again as he steps into the room*)

MRS. BARKER. Surprise! Surprise! Here we are!

MOMMY. What? What?

DADDY. Hm? What?

MOMMY. (*Her tears merely sniffles now*) What surprise?

MRS. BARKER. Why, I told you. The surprise I told you about.

DADDY. You . . . you know, Mommy.

MOMMY. Sur . . . prise?

DADDY. (*Urging her to cheerfulness*) You remember, Mommy; why we asked . . . uh . . . what's-her-name to come here?

MRS. BARKER. Mrs. Barker, if you don't mind.

DADDY. Yes. Mommy? You remember now? About the bumble . . . about wanting satisfaction?

MOMMY. (*Her sorrow turning into delight*) Yes. Why yes! Of course! Yes! Oh, how wonderful!

MRS. BARKER. (*To the* YOUNG MAN) This is Mommy.

YOUNG MAN. How . . . how do you do?

MRS. BARKER. (*Stage whisper*) Her name's Mommy.

YOUNG MAN. How . . . how do you do, Mommy?

MOMMY. Well! Hello there!

MRS. BARKER. (*To the* YOUNG MAN) And that is Daddy.

YOUNG MAN. How do you do, sir?

DADDY. How do you do?

MOMMY. (*Herself again, circling the* YOUNG MAN, *feeling his arm, poking him*) Yes, sir! Yes, sirree! Now this is more like it. Now this is a great deal more like it! Daddy! Come see. Come see if this isn't a great deal more like it.

DADDY. I . . . I can see from here, Mommy. It does look a great deal more like it.

MOMMY. Yes, sir. Yes sirree! Mrs. Barker, I don't know *how* to thank you.

MRS. BARKER. Oh, don't worry about that. I'll send you a bill in the mail.

MOMMY. What this really calls for is a celebration. It calls for a drink.

MRS. BARKER. Oh, what a nice idea.

MOMMY. There's some sauterne in the kitchen.

YOUNG MAN. I'll go.

MOMMY. Will you? Oh, how nice. The kitchen's through the archway there. (*As the* YOUNG MAN *exits: to* MRS. BARKER) He's very nice. Really top notch; much better than the other one.

MRS. BARKER. I'm glad you're pleased. And I'm glad everything's all straightened out.

MOMMY. Well, at least we know why we sent for you. We're glad that's cleared up. By the way, what's his name?

MRS. BARKER. Ha! Call him whatever you like. He's yours. Call him what you called the other one.

MOMMY. Daddy? What did we call the other one?

DADDY. (*Puzzles*) Why . . .

YOUNG MAN. (*Re-entering with a tray on which are a bottle of sauterne and five glasses*) Here we are!

MOMMY. Hooray! Hooray!

MRS. BARKER. Oh, good!

MOMMY. (*Moving to the tray*) So, let's— Five glasses? Why five? There are only four of us. Why five?

YOUNG MAN. (*Catches* GRANDMA'*s eye;* GRANDMA *indicates she is not there*) Oh, I'm sorry.

MOMMY. You must learn to count. We're a wealthy family, and you must learn to count.

YOUNG MAN. I will.

MOMMY. Well, everybody take a glass. (*They do*) And we'll drink to celebrate. To satisfaction! Who says you can't get satisfaction these days!

MRS. BARKER. What dreadful sauterne!

MOMMY. Yes, isn't it? (*To* YOUNG MAN, *her voice already a little fuzzy from the wine*) You don't know how happy I am to see you! Yes sirree. Listen, that time we had with . . . with the other one. I'll tell you about it some time. (*Indicates* MRS. BARKER) After she's gone. She was responsible for all the trouble in the first place. I'll tell you all about it. (*Sidles up to him a little*) Maybe . . . maybe later tonight.

YOUNG MAN. (*Not moving away*) Why yes. That would be very nice.

MOMMY. (*Puzzles*) Something familiar about you . . . you know that? I can't quite place it. . . .

GRANDMA. (*Interrupting to audience*) Well, I guess that just about wraps it up. I mean, for better or worse, this is a comedy, and I don't think we'd better go any further. No, definitely not. So, let's leave things as they are right now . . . while everybody's happy . . . while everybody's got what he wants . . . or everybody's got what he thinks he wants. Good night, dears.

Poetry

If you have read Part One in this book, you have learned already that poetry has much in common with fiction and drama. For the sake of emphasizing this fact, we might briefly review the aspects of craftsmanship considered there in relationship to poetry.[1]

Action. If anything, the action in poetry is more diverse than it is in fiction and drama. At one extreme, the poet may do nothing more than observe a duck

---

1. You would do well to also review the discussion of point of view on page 91.

flying against a crimson evening sky; at the other, he may detail the heroic and bloody activities of a ten-year war. Action is especially important in narrative and epic poetry.

Characterization. Characterization also is a matter of first importance in narrative and epic poetry, and in dramatic monologs like Browning's "My Last Duchess." Ordinarily you do not associate problems of characterization with lyric poetry unless you consider how the poem characterizes the intrusive author. (See p. 55.) In that sense, characterization becomes an important aspect of many lyrical poems.

Setting. Setting, too, exhibits great range. It may be set forth in great detail, as in Coleridge's "The Rime of the Ancient Mariner." Or it may be omitted completely, as in a philosophical poem like Emerson's "Brahma." Background is especially prominent in lyric poems developing atmosphere or mood. Poe's "The City in the Sea" (p. 774) is a good example of this.

Language. There are certain differences between the ways that poets and prose writers select and arrange their words, differences that we shall consider shortly. In the main, however, these are less marked than many suppose. Possibly you have heard about "poetic diction" or "poetic license" and have developed the notion that poets use a special language. To support this belief you can point to words like "e'er," "thou," and "swain." It is true that at one time poets did employ terms which were not so commonly seen in prose, but there was rarely a significant difference, and today there is—in most poetry—none at all. Miss Marguerite Wilkinson claims in her *New Voices,* "No good poet of today wants a license for any unfair dealings with words." By their employment of words in context, poets often pack more meaning and emotion into them than prose writers do, but the words themselves are the ones you know already, and probably the ones you use daily.

Certainly, too, the function of words in poetry is the same as in prose. They body forth the action, characters, settings—images of all kinds. They withhold or give emphasis, emotional colorations, and interpretations.

When we add to these matters of craftsmanship their effects in terms of *tone, atmosphere,* and *meaning,* and find that these achievements are substantially the same in poetry and in prose, you may well ask what makes poetry a distinctive literary form. What special characteristics does it have? More specifically, what should you look for as you read poetry that you have not already been looking for in prose? The answer lies especially in five characteristics: *rhythm, sound patterns, compactness, figurativeness,* and *emotional intensity,* the last being the result of the first four. We shall consider them in that order.

RHYTHM

Poetry is distinct from prose not because poetry has rhythm but because it has a more regular rhythm than prose. We need not explain what rhythm is since you already know that from dancing and listening to music. Nor do we need to elaborate much on the thesis that rhythm is part of everyday life. You need only to recall the beating of your own heart to recognize that rhythm is, in fact, a necessity of life. Doubtless you will be quick to admit, too, that you have characteristic rhythms for doing even the simplest things, that you take greater satisfaction out of smooth, rhythmic performances than jerky ones. In short, rhythm is natural to you and gives you pleasure. If this is so in general, it should be so in poetry also. You should find that the rhythms of poetry are natural and pleasurable.

Traditionally, English poetry (but not Anglo-Saxon) has based its rhythm upon accent. Whereas in prose accented and unaccented syllables occur in irregular fashion throughout a sentence, in poetry they create a relatively regular pattern. Notice the difference:

Prose:

My father, a mountaineer, in addition to swinging a hard fist, was very quick on his feet. Unfortunately, however, he stammered.

Poetry:

My father, he was a mountaineer,
His fist was a knotty hammer;
He was quick on his feet as running deer
And he spoke with a Yankee stammer.[1]

If you mark all the accented syllables in these two examples you will discover that whereas there is no pattern in the prose passage, the stanza of verse has four accents in the first and third lines, three accents in the second and fourth, and that unaccented syllables combine with accented ones to form a pattern.

Regular rhythmical arrangement like this is usually called *meter*. In English there are four conventional types of meter, each being distinguished from the others by the number and accent of syllables. By far the most popular, and probably the most natural to English expression, is called *iambic*. The basic unit, or foot, of iambic has one unaccented and one accented syllable (‿ /).

| The shades | of night | were fall | ing fast |

Just the reverse of iambic meter is the *trochaic*, each foot of which contains an accented and an unaccented syllable (/ ‿). Ordinarily the trochaic rhythm is slower than the iambic, thus creating a heavier and more dignified beat, as in the following example:

| Swift of | foot was | Hia | watha |

Anapestic meter contains in each foot two unaccented syllables and one accented (‿ ‿ /). Sprightly and frolicsome in rhythm, this meter is usually best adapted to relatively light subjects.

| For the moon | never beams | without bring | ing me dreams |

1. Stephen Vincent Benét, "The Ballad of William Sycamore."

Dactylic meter reverses the anapestic ($/\,\smile\,\smile$). It is considerably slower and often is employed to create a mood of strangeness.

| Thís is the | fórest pri | mévāl |

"Scanning" a line of poetry consists of seeing what the metrical units are and how many of them occur in the line. A one-foot line is called a monometer line, a two-foot line dimeter, and others in progression up to a seven-foot line are called, respectively, trimeter, tetrameter, pentameter, hexameter, and heptameter. Thus the anapestic line quoted above is a tetrameter, and the dactylic line a trimeter. Such scanning is valuable not only that you may see the prevailing pattern of lines and stanzas but also that you may see diversions from the patterns.

For few poets use the same type of foot throughout a poem, since the result would be too monotonous. To achieve variety and, even more important, to achieve emphasis or onomatopoeia, they use *substitute feet*. These may be feet of the sort we have considered (e.g., the trochaic foot in "This is the forest primeval") or they may be feet of a sort used only as substitutes, perhaps the *spondee* ($//$), two accented syllables, or the *pyrrhus* ($\smile\,\smile$), two unaccented syllables. Keats offers an example of the former in the line,

| The háre | limped trém | bling thróugh | the fró | zen gráss. |

wherein the spondaic second foot serves to emphasize and to imitate the uneven progress of the hare in a stanza describing a bitter chill night. Paradoxical as it may seem, you will find that one of the chief insights you get from observing a poem's rhythmic pattern derives from considering where and why the poet deviates from that pattern.

Many modern poets have come to believe that none of these metrical schemes is adequate for what they have to say. Rhythm, they assert, must be organic, must rise naturally out of mood and content and must not be a regularized system imposed upon them. As a result, they write what is called *free verse*, poetry which follows no systemized metrical pattern. At its worst such poetry seems like nothing so much as bad prose; at its best it achieves a variety and subtlety of rhythm quite beyond the possibilities of the more conventional methods. One of the best examples of free verse in this book is Whitman's "When Lilacs Last in the Dooryard Bloom'd" (p. 782).

SOUND PATTERNS

As we have seen, English rhythm is largely a matter of accent patterns. Corresponding to these are certain sound patterns, the most obvious and familiar of which is rhyme. Rhyme adds melody, creates harmony, and gives finish to line endings. Most important, it distinguishes parts of a poem by setting them off from one another. The following sonnet by Wordsworth exemplifies this last point especially well.

William Wordsworth,   IT IS A BEAUTEOUS EVENING,
CALM AND FREE

It is a beauteous evening, calm and free,
   The holy time is quiet as a Nun
   Breathless with adoration; the broad sun
Is sinking down in its tranquility;
The gentleness of heaven broods o'er the Sea;   5
   Listen! the mighty Being is awake,
   And doth with his eternal motion make
A sound like thunder—everlastingly.
Dear Child! dear Girl! that walkest with me here,
   If thou appear untouched by solemn thought,   10
   Thy nature is not therefore less divine:
Thou liest in Abraham's bosom all the year;
   And worship'st at the Temple's inner shrine,
   God being with thee when we know it not.

The rhyme scheme here is like that of the Petrarchan sonnet: *abba, acca, def, dfe*. According to this pattern, the first eight lines are distinct from the last six, with each of these divisions being subdivided into two equal parts. Notice how the sense of the poem corresponds. The first eight lines describe the scene; the last six evaluate the child's and, incidentally, the poet's reaction to the scene. The first half of the first division deals with evening and sun, the second with the sea. The first half of the second division suggests the child's apparent indifference to the scene; the second half accounts for this attitude. What is clear, therefore, is that rhyme can be a valuable clue to meaning.

But when all this is said, the fact still remains that much great poetry has been written without rhyme. Consequently, though rhyme is valuable and delightful for many reasons, it is not indispensable to all kinds of verse.

Other prominent sound patterns are alliteration, assonance, onomatopoeia, and cacophony. Some of these have already been illustrated in this text (p. 78) and are defined in the Glossary and Index of Critical Terms. Nevertheless, it should be pointed out here, briefly, that these devices are peculiarly valuable to the poet since like rhyme they help create the mood which he feels an essential part of his experience. What is especially important to him is that they do this quickly. Notice how in a single line Coleridge gives you a sense of a curse simply by repeating the "s" sound until he gets a sustained hiss:

Seven days, seven nights, I saw that curse.

To get the full effect of these sound patterns you should read poetry aloud. Try it with Poe's "The City in the Sea" (p. 776) and notice how much sound contributes to your awareness and your pleasure.

COMPACTNESS

Whereas the prose writer within sensible limits may be as discursive as he wishes, the poet should never be so. Because of the limitation of his form, the poet must choose his material with especial care and screen his language for all useless words. This careful selection and sifting result in compactness and consequently the necessity for thoughtful, sensitive reading.

At first glance you may question what the selection of material has to do with compactness of expression. The answer can be discovered by examining the poet's purpose and his medium. The poet's purpose is to communicate experience in as vivid and memorable a fashion as possible. If he is a good poet, he is admirably equipped to do this, for he has the faculty, as Elizabeth Drew shows, of revealing things in relationships which in normal experience are hidden. Especially, he is sensitive to the *quality* of experience. Let us try to clarify this with a simple example. Undoubtedly, you have had that sore, empty feeling that comes at the time of the death of someone dear to you. You continue with your daily tasks, but your mood is different, and somehow the tasks themselves take on a new quality. Now the poet would be interested in this special quality, and he would try to communicate it by selecting the details which most powerfully suggest it.

To be sure, this is what the prose writer does also. But the job of the poet is a harder one. The prose writer may achieve his effect by an accumulation of details—hundreds of them, if he wishes. The poet, however, is held down by the shortness of his form. Possibly he has room for only five details, possibly three, possibly only one. Every detail, therefore, must be supremely right.

Compactness also results from the way poets use words. Like anyone else, they use them first for meaning. But because of the space limitations of the poetic form, they frequently try to pack more meaning into them than prose writers do. Often they have words operating at several levels of meaning at the same time. The example has already been cited (p. 117) of Whitman's "Passage to India," in which the word "passage" refers not only to the physical trip to the Orient, but to the race's circling back to the land of its origin, the mind's journey from the world of science to the world of intuitive insight, and the soul's flight to God.

The poet selects his words, again with probably more care than the prose writer, for their connotations, the moods and associations which they stir up in us. This is not surprising since it is through the connotations of words that the poet can best communicate the quality of his experience within the few lines at his command. He does this, first, by using a great many concrete words. Among concrete words, the poet then chooses those which give him the precise quality that he wants. Even so simple a poem as Edgar Allan Poe's "The Bells" gives us a chance to observe this. In it Poe set for himself the little exercise of catching the quality of four different kinds of bells. Notice the key words he uses with each. In meaning, the words within each group are not too dissimilar; in connotation they are quite different:

> Silver bells: *tinkle, tintinnabulation, jingling*
> Golden bells: *ring, rhyming, chiming*

> Bronze bells: *shriek, clamor, clanging*
> Iron bells: *tolling, moaning, groaning.*

What this comes down to is that in poetry compactness with words is not so much a matter of cutting away needless ones as packing the useful ones with all the meaning and emotion possible. Those learning to write freshman themes can, after practice, eliminate deadwood, but only someone highly sensitive to the potentialities of words can make every one count to the utmost.

The implications of all this for the reader are clear. He must realize that competent poetry is too compact for skimming. He must realize that each detail, each word—literally each word—is important.

FIGURATIVENESS

In discussing details under the heading of compactness, we made no attempt to distinguish between the literal and the figurative. This now should be done, since one of the most outstanding characteristics of poetry is its extensive use of metaphors, similes, personifications, and other figures of speech.

Of all these figures, metaphors and similes are by far the most important. Through the images they create, the poet can catch the quality of the experience he is after far more quickly and vividly than he can by describing his thought or his action literally. You can see why this is so. Metaphors and similes are concrete: they create images which appeal to your senses. Therefore, when well chosen they are easily visualized and remembered. When well phrased, they are richly connotative. Being comparisons, they fuse the original experience with other experiences, thus compounding the physical, emotional, and even intellectual values.

All of this would contradict a popular notion that similes and metaphors are extraneous decorations which can be lopped off without undue loss to meaning or emotion. Figures of speech can be such if they are simply tacked on for no purpose other than to show the poet's cleverness. But when well used they are structural necessities, and often are more essential than a literal statement would be. One must constantly keep in mind that the poet is anxious to convey his sense of meaning and quality of experience and to do it in considerably less space than the prose writer. For this purpose metaphors and similes are indispensable. How quickly or well, for instance, could a literal prose definition of the word "presentiment" carry the quiet foreboding suggested in Emily Dickinson's metaphor:

> Presentiment is that long shadow on the lawn
> Indicative that suns go down;
> The notice to the startled grass
> That darkness is about to pass.

And notice how Coleridge conveys the sense of complete inactivity, first by the metaphor "stuck" and second by the simile of the painting:

> Day after day, day after day,
> We stuck, nor breath nor motion:
> As idle as a painted ship
> Upon a painted ocean.

Through another figure, personification, poets can achieve a startling vividness often quite beyond the potentialities of more conventional statements. In "Grass," for example, Sandburg creates an effect that no disquisition on the transitoriness of life could hope to achieve. Here are the first lines:

> Pile the bodies high at Austerlitz and Waterloo.
> Shovel them under and let me work:
> I am the Grass; I cover all.

Other figures, too, create images and symbols; you can look them up in the Glossary under such headings as hyperbole and synecdoche. Intentionally we have repeated here much about figures of speech which we discussed earlier (pp. 74-75) in order to emphasize the fact that though figures are the tools of all imaginative writers they are especially useful to the poet. In poetry, therefore, you can expect to find them used more extensively and, on the whole, more brilliantly.

EMOTIONAL INTENSITY

If rhythm, sound patterns, compactness, and figures of speech are all handled in a craftsmanlike way, the inevitable result is that the poem will make a stronger emotional impact upon the reader than any equivalent passage in prose can do. The truth of this is almost self-evident. Rhythm heightens feelings almost always; think of one of the simplest kinds, the beat of a drum. Sound patterns add tone values; compactness keeps the material from being thinned out through careless selection or through pale and useless words; figures make the subject vivid and memorable. The most intense realizations of human experiences, therefore, when stated verbally, must almost inevitably find expression in poetry. Prose cannot do them justice.

Except for rhyme, no one of these characteristics which we have discussed is peculiar to poetry. There is simply a difference in degree. This means that there is no sharp line between prose and poetry. One merges into the other as the rhythm becomes more regular, the imagery more vivid, the statement more compact, and the emotion more intense. You cannot measure the difference with a pair of literary calipers, but you can feel it as you read.

If you are to read poetry well, you must know, then, what its characteristics are and what the poet is attempting to do. You must not expect the fully developed situations of the novel, the play, or even the short story. Rather, you should look for sudden bursts of insight into some corner of human experience. More important, possibly, you should look forward to sharing briefly in the experience itself. For it is part of the magic of poetry that at one and the same time it can tell you about experience and make you feel its peculiar significance.

In the following section we have tried to show you the characteristic types of poetry which have been written in the English language. All of the selections included here were originally written in English except the Psalms from the Bible. These are included because they have been read as much or more in America and England than our original verse, and because the Bible has had so profound an effect upon our native poets. The poems are arranged chronologically so that you can see how tastes and forms have changed even though the basic characteristics have remained constant.

In addition to these poems, you might wish to turn back and reconsider those you studied in Parts One, Two, and Three: "Frankie and Johnny" (p. 34), Browning's "My Last Duchess" (p. 55), "The Laboratory" (p. 181), and "The Bishop Orders His Tomb at Saint Praxed's Church" (p. 222), Keats' "To Autumn" (p. 71) and "On First Looking into Chapman's Homer" (p. 184), a verse translation from Homer's *Odyssey* (p. 84), Frost's "Storm-Fear" (p. 86) and "Stopping by Woods on a Snowy Evening" (p. 140), Rossetti's "After Death" (p. 97), Dickinson's "The Last Night That She Lived" (p. 98), Auden's "Musée Des Beaux Arts" (p. 100), Shapiro's "Auto Wreck" (p. 100), Arnold's "Palladium" (p. 113), Whitman's "When I Heard the Learn'd Astronomer" (p. 116), Eliot's "The Love Song of J. Alfred Prufrock" (p. 130), Masefield's "Cargoes" (p. 146), Herrick's "Upon Julia's Clothes" (p. 149), MacLeish's "Ars Poetica" (p. 151), Coleridge's "Kubla Khan" (p. 194), Kipling's "Recessional" (p. 213), and the excerpts from Vergil's *Aeneid* (p. 313).

Hebrew Lyrics

PSALM 1

Blessed is the man that walketh not in the counsel of the ungodly,
Nor standeth in the way of sinners,
Nor sitteth in the seat of the scornful.
But his delight is in the law of the Lord;
And in his law doth he meditate day and night.   5
And he shall be like a tree planted by the rivers of water,
That bringeth forth his fruit in his season,
His leaf also shall not wither;
And whatsoever he doeth shall prosper.
The ungodly are not so;   10
But are like the chaff which the wind driveth away.

Therefore the ungodly shall not stand in the judgment,
Nor sinners in the congregation of the righteous.
For the Lord knoweth the way of the righteous:
But the way of the ungodly shall perish.   15

PSALM 23

The Lord is my shepherd; I shall not want.
He maketh me to lie down in green pastures;
He leadeth me beside the still waters.
He restoreth my soul:
He leadeth me in the paths of righteousness for his name's sake.   5
Yea, though I walk through the valley of the shadow of death,
I will fear no evil; for thou art with me:
Thy rod and thy staff, they comfort me.
Thou preparest a table before me in the presence of mine enemies:
Thou anointest my head with oil; my cup runneth over.   10
Surely goodness and mercy shall follow me all the days of my life:
And I will dwell in the house of the Lord for ever.

PSALM 24

The earth is the Lord's, and the fulness thereof;
The world, and they that dwell therein.
For he hath founded it upon the seas,
And established it upon the floods.
Who shall ascend into the hill of the Lord?   5
Or who shall stand in his holy place?
He that hath clean hands, and a pure heart;
Who hath not lifted up his soul unto vanity, nor sworn deceitfully.
He shall receive the blessing from the Lord,
And righteousness from the God of his salvation.   10
This is the generation of them that seek him,
That seek thy face, O Jacob.
Lift up your heads, O ye gates;
And be ye lift up, ye everlasting doors:
And the King of glory shall come in.   15
Who is this King of glory?
The Lord strong and mighty,
The Lord mighty in battle.

Lift up your heads, O ye gates;
Even lift them up, ye everlasting doors: 20
And the King of glory shall come in.
Who is this King of glory?
The Lord of hosts,
He is the King of glory.

PSALM 100

Make a joyful noise unto the Lord all ye lands.
Serve the Lord with gladness:
Come before his presence with singing.
Know ye that the Lord he is God:
It is he that hath made us, and not we ourselves;   5
We are his people, and the sheep of his pasture.
Enter into his gates with thanksgiving,
And into his courts with praise:
Be thankful unto him, and bless his name.
For the Lord is good;   10
His mercy is everlasting;
And his truth endureth to all generations.

PSALM 121

I will lift up mine eyes unto the hills:
From whence cometh my help.
My help cometh from the Lord,
Which made heaven and earth.
He will not suffer thy foot to be moved.   5
He that keepeth thee will not slumber.
Behold, he that keepeth Israel
Shall neither slumber nor sleep.
The Lord is thy keeper:
The Lord is thy shade upon thy right hand.   10
The sun shall not smite thee by day,
Nor the moon by night.
The Lord shall preserve thee from all evil;
He shall preserve thy soul.
The Lord shall preserve thy going out and thy coming in,   15
From this time forth and even for evermore.

Ballads

Anonymous

SIR PATRICK SPENS

The king sits in Dunfermline toune
    Drinking the blude-red wine:
"O whar will I get guid sailor,
    To sail this schip of mine?"

Up and spak an eldern knicht,   5
    Sat at the kings richt kne:
"Sir Patrick Spens is the best sailor
    That sails upon the se."

The king has written a braid letter,
    And signed it wi his hand,   10
And sent it to Sir Patrick Spens,
    Was walking on the sand.

The first line that Sir Patrick red,
    A loud lauch lauched he;
The next line that Sir Patrick red,   15
    The teir blinded his ee.

"O wha is this has don this deid,
    This ill deid don to me,
To send me out this time o' the yeir,
    To sail upon the se!   20

"Mak hast, mak haste, my mirry men all,
    Our guid schip sails the morne":
"O say na sae, my master deir,
    For I feir a deadlie storme.

"Late late yestreen I saw the new moone,   25
    Wi the auld moone in hir arme,
And I feir, I feir, my deir master,
    That we will cum to harme."

O our Scots nobles wer richt laith
   To weet their cork-heild schoone;   30
Bot lang owre a' the play wer playd,
   Thair hats they swam aboone.

O lang, lang may their ladies sit,
   Wi thair fans into their hand,
Or eir they se Sir Patrick Spens   35
   Cum sailing to the land.

O lang, lang may the ladies stand,
   Wi thair gold kems in their hair,
Waiting for thair ain deir lords,
   For they'll see thame na mair.   40

Haf owre, haf owre to Aberdour,
   It's fiftie fadom deip,
And thair lies guid Sir Patrick Spens,
   Wi the Scots lords at his feit.

Anonymous

THE THREE RAVENS

There were three ravens sat on a tree,
   Downe a downe, hay down, hay downe
There were three ravens sat on a tree,
   With a downe
There were three ravens sat on a tree,   5
They were as blacke as they might be.
   With a downe derrie, derrie, derrie, downe, downe.

The one of them said to his mate,
"Where shall we our breakfast take?"

"Downe in yonder greene field,   10
There lies a knight slain under his shield.

"His hounds they lie downe at his feete,
So well they can their master keepe.

"His haukes they flie so eagerly,
There's no fowle dare him come nie."   15

Downe there comes a fallow doe,
As great with yong as she might goe.

She lift up his bloudy hed,
And kist his wounds that were so red.

She got him up upon her backe,   20
And carried him to earthen lake.

She buried him before the prime,
She was dead herselfe ere even-song time.

God send every gentleman
Such haukes, such hounds, and such a leman.   25

Anonymous

THE TWA CORBIES

As I was walking all alane,
I heard twa corbies making a mane;
The tane unto the t'other say,
"Where sall we gang and dine to-day?"

"In behint yon auld fail dyke,   5
I wot there lies a new slain knight;
And naebody kens that he lies there,
But his hawk, his hound, and lady fair.

"His hound is to the hunting gane,
His hawk to fetch the wild-fowl hame,   10
His lady's ta'en another mate,
So we may mak our dinner sweet.

"Ye'll sit on his white hause-bane,
And I'll pike out his bonny blue een;
Wi' ae lock o' his gowden hair   15
We'll theek our nest when it grows bare.

"Mony a one for him makes mane,
But nane sall ken where he is gane;
O'er his white banes, when they are bare,
The wind sall blaw for evermair."   20

Geoffrey Chaucer

from THE CANTERBURY TALES

The Canterbury Tales is usually considered the first great poem indigenous to England. Even the earlier works of Chaucer himself are more French and Italian than English. But here the foreign elements are assimilated, and the work is native in both material and tone. "The Prologue," parts of which are given here, introduces the persons who are making a pilgrimage to the shrine of Thomas à Becket in Canterbury. In the main part of the poem each pilgrim tells a story, the tales varying from the most pious of moralities to the bawdiest kind of roughhouse.

The language is the East Midland dialect of Late Middle English. Most of the words you can recognize because of their resemblance to modern English. The footnotes will help you with the others.

> Whan that Aprille with his shoures soote
> The droghte of Marche hath percéd to the roote,
> And bathed every veyne in swich licour,
> Of which vertu engendred is the flour;
> Whan Zephirus eek with his swete breeth   5
> Inspiréd hath in every holt and heeth
> The tendre croppes, and the yonge sonne
> Hath in the Ram his halfe cours y-ronne,
> And smale fowles maken melodye,
> That slepen al the night with open yë,   10
> (So priketh hem nature in hir corages),
> Than longen folk to goon on pilgrimages
> (And palmers for to seken straunge strondes)
> To ferne halwes, couthe in sondry londes;
> And specially, from every shires ende   15
> Of Engelond, to Caunterbury they wende,
> The holy blisful martir for to seke,
> That hem hath holpen, whan that they were seke.
>   Bifel that, in that sesoun on a day,
> In Southwerk at the Tabard as I lay   20

1. *soote*, sweet. 5. *eek*, also. 6. *holt*, wood. 8. *halfe cours y-ronne*, after April 11. 11. *corages*, spirit, heart. 14. *ferne*, distant. *halwes*, shrines. *couthe*, known. 17. *martir*, Thomas à Becket. 18. *seke*, sick.

Redy to wenden on my pilgrimage
To Caunterbury with ful devout corage,
At night was come in-to that hostelrye
Wel nyne and twenty in a companye,
Of sondry folk, by aventure y-falle   25
In felawshipe, and pilgrims were they alle,
That toward Caunterbury wolden ryde;
The chambres and the stables weren wyde,
And wel we weren esed atte beste.
And shortly, whan the sonne was to reste,   30
So hadde I spoken with hem everichon,
That I was of hir felawshipe anon,
And made forward erly for to ryse,
To take our wey, ther as I yow devyse.
  But natheles, whyl I have tyme and space,   35
Ere that I ferther in this tale pace,
Me thinketh it acordaunt to resoun,
To telle yow al the condicioun
Of ech of hem, so as it semed me,
And whiche they weren, and of what degree;   40
And eek in what array that they were inne:
And at a knight than wol I first biginne.

  A KNIGHT ther was, and that a worthy man,
That fro the tyme that he first bigan
To ryden out, he loved chivalrye,   45
Trouthe and honour, fredom and curteisye.
Ful worthy was he in his lordes werre,
And therto hadde he riden (no man ferre)
As wel in cristendom as hethenesse,
And ever honoured for his worthinesse.   50
  At Alisaundre he was, whan it was wonne;
Ful ofte tyme he hadde the bord bigonne
Aboven alle naciouns in Pruce.
In Lettow hadde he reysed and in Ruce,
No cristen man so ofte of his degree.   55
In Gernade at the sege eek hadde he be
Of Algezir, and riden in Belmarye.
At Lyeys was he, and at Satalye,
Whan they were wonne; and in the Grete See

---

29. *atte beste,* in the best manner possible. **32.** *hir,* their. **46.** *fredom,* liberality. **48.** *ferre,* farther. **49.** *hethenesse,* heathen lands. **51.** *Alisaundre,* Alexandria. **52.** *bord bigonne,* sat at the head of the table. **53.** *Pruce,* Prussia. **54.** *Lettow,* Lithuania. *Ruce,* Russia. **56.** *Gernade,* Granada, Spain. **57.** *Algezir,* Algeciras. *Belmarye,* Benmarin, Morocco. **58.** *Lyeys,* Lyas in Armenia. *Satalye,* Atalia in Asia Minor.

At many a noble aryve hadde he be.   60
At mortal batailles hadde he been fiftene,
And foughten for our feith at Tramissene
In listes thryes, and ay slayn his foo.
This ilke worthy knight hadde been also
Sometyme with the lord of Palatye,   65
Ageyn another hethen in Turkye:
And everemore he hadde a sovereyn prys,
And though that he were worthy, he was wys,
And of his port as meek as is a mayde.
He nevere yet no vileinye ne sayde   70
In al his lyf, un-to no maner wight.
He was a verray parfit gentil knight.
But for to tellen yow of his array,
His hors were goode, but he was nat gay.
Of fustian he weréd a gipoun   75
Al bismoteréd with his habergeoun,
For he was late y-come from his viage,
And wente for to doon his pilgrimage.

　　With him there was his sone, a yong SQUYER,
A lovyere, and a lusty bacheler,   80
With lokkes crulle, as they were leyd in presse.
Of twenty yeer of age he was, I gesse.
Of his stature he was of evene lengthe,
And wonderly deliver, and greet of strengthe.
And he had been somtyme in chivachye,   85
In Flaundres, in Artoys, and Picardye,
And born him wel, as of so litel space,
In hope to stonden in his lady grace.
Embrouded was he, as it were a mede
Al ful of fresshe floures, whyte and rede.   90
Singinge he was, or floytinge, al the day;
He was as fresh as is the month of May.
Short was his goune, with sleves longe and wyde.
Wel coude he sitte on hors, and faire ryde.
He coude songes make and wel endyte,   95
Juste and eek daunce, and wel purtreye and wryte.
So hote he lovede, that by nightertale
He sleep namore than doth a nightingale.

62. *Tramissene*, Tlemçen in Algeria. 64. *ilke*, same. 65. *Palatye*, Balat, Turkey. 70. *vileinye*, rudeness. 71. *wight*, person. 75. *gipoun*, short doublet worn under armor. 76. *bismoteréd*, besmirched. *habergeoun*, coat of mail. 81. *lokkes crulle*, curly hair. 84. *deliver*, quick, active. 85. *chivachye*, cavalry raids. 91. *floytinge*, whistling, playing the flute. 96. *juste*, joust. *purtreye*, draw. 97. *nightertale*, nighttime.

Curteys he was, lowly, and servisable,
And carf biforn his fader at the table.   100

Ther was also a Nonne, a PRIORESSE,
That of hir smyling was ful simple and coy,
Hir gretteste ooth was but by seÿnt Loy;   120
And she was cleped madame Eglentyne.
Ful wel she song the service divyne,
Entuned in hir nose ful semely;
And Frensh she spak ful faire and fetisly,
After the scole of Stratford atte Bowe,   .   125
For Frensh of Paris was to hir unknowe.
At mete wel y-taught was she with-alle;
She leet no morsel from hir lippes falle,
Ne wette hir fingres in hir sauce depe.
Wel coude she carie a morsel, and wel kepe,   130
That no drope ne fille up-on hir brest.
In curteisye was set ful muche hir lest.
Hir over lippe wyped she so clene,
That in hir coppe was no ferthing sene
Of grece, whan she dronken hadde hir draughte.   135
Ful semely after hir mete she raughte,
And sikerly she was of greet disport,
And ful plesaunt, and amiable of port,
And peyned hir to countrefete chere
Of court, and been estatlich of manere,   140
And to ben holden digne of reverence.
But, for to speken of hir conscience,
She was so charitable and so pitous,
She wolde wepe, if that she sawe a mous
Caught in a trappe, if it were deed or bledde.   145
Of smale houndes had she, that she fedde
With rosted flesh, or milk and wastel breed.
But sore weep she if oon of hem were deed,
Or if men smoot it with a yerde smerte:
And al was conscience and tendre herte.   150
Ful semely hir wimpel pinched was;
Hir nose tretys; hir eyen greye as glas;
Hir mouth ful smal, and ther-to softe and reed;
But sikerly she hadde a fair forheed;
It was almost a spanne brood, I trowe;   155

---

121. *cleped,* called, named. **124.** *fetisly,* handsomely. **130.** *kepe,* care, notice. **132.** *lest,* desire. **136.** *raughte,* reached. **137.** *sikerly,* surely. **139.** *peyned,* took pains. *countrefete,* imitate. *chere,* expressions, behavior. **141.** *digne,* worthy. **142.** *conscience,* tender feelings. **149.** *yerde smerte,* smartly with a stick. **152.** *tretys,* well-formed.

For, hardily, she was nat undergrowe.
Ful fetis was hir cloke, as I was war.
Of smal coral aboute hir arm she bar
A peire of bedes, gauded al with grene;
And ther-on heng a broche of gold ful shene,   160
On which ther was first write a crowned A,
And after, *Amor vincit omnia.*

   A FRERE ther was, a wantown and a merye,
A limitour, a ful solempne man.
In alle the ordres foure is noon that can   210
So muche of daliaunce and fair langage.
He hadde maad ful many a mariage
Of yonge wommen, at his owne cost.
Un-to his ordre he was a noble post.
Ful wel biloved and famulier was he   215
With frankeleyns over-al in his contree,
And eek with worthy wommen of the toun:
For he had power of confessioun,
As seyde him-self, more than a curat,
For of his ordre he was licentiat.   220
Ful swetely herde he confessioun,
And plesaunt was his absolucioun;
He was an esy man to yeve penaunce
Ther as he wiste to han a good pitaunce;
For unto a povre ordre for to yive   225
Is signe that a man is wel y-shrive.
For if he yaf, he dorste make avaunt,
He wiste that a man was repentaunt.
For many a man so hard is of his herte,
He may nat wepe al-thogh him sore smerte.   230
Therfore, in stede of weping and preyeres,
Men moot yeve silver to the povre freres.
His tipet was ay farsed ful of knyves
And pinnes, for to yeven faire wyves.
And certeinly he hadde a mery note;   235
Wel coude he singe and pleyen on a rote.
Of yeddinges he bar utterly the prys.
His nekke whyt was as the flour-de-lys;

---

157. *war,* aware. 208. *wantown,* sportive, lascivious. 209. *limitour,* a friar licensed to beg within certain limits. *solempne,* pompous. 220. *licentiat,* a person licensed by the Pope. 223. *yeve,* give. 224. *ther as,* where. *wiste,* knew. *pitaunce,* pittance. 226. *y-shrive,* confessed. 227. *yaf,* gave. *avaunt,* boast. 233. *tipet,* cape. *farsed,* stuffed. 234. *yeven,* give. 236. *rote,* a stringed instrument. 237. *yeddinges,* songs. *utterly,* entirely. *prys,* worth.

There-to he strong was as a champioun.
He knew the tavernes wel in every toun,   240
And everich hostiler and tappestere
Bet than a lazar or a beggestere;
For un-to swich a worthy man as he
Acorded nat, as by his facultee,
To have with seke lazars aqueyntaunce.   245
It is nat honest, it may nat avaunce
For to delen with no swich poraille,
But al with riche and sellers of vitaille.
And over-al, ther as profit sholde aryse,
Curteys he was, and lowly of servyse.   250
Ther nas no man nowher so vertuous.
He was the beste beggere in his hous;
For thogh a widwe hadde noght a sho,
So plesaunt was his "*In principio*,"
Yet wolde he have a ferthing, er he wente.   255
His purchas was wel bettre than his rente.
And rage he coude, as it were right a whelpe.
In love-dayes ther coude he muchel helpe.
For ther he was nat lyk a cloisterer,
With a thredbar cope as is a povre scoler,   260
But he was lyk a maister or a pope.
Of double worsted was his semi-cope,
That rounded as a belle out of the presse.
Somwhat he lipsed, for his wantownesse,
To make his English swete up-on his tonge;   265
And in his harping, whan that he had songe,
His eyen twinkled in his heed aright,
As doon the sterres in the frosty night.
This worthy limitour was cleped Huberd.

A good WYF was ther of bisyde BATHE,   445
But she was som-del deef, and that was scathe.
Of clooth-making she hadde swiche an haunt,
She passed hem of Ypres and of Gaunt.
In al the parisshe wyf ne was ther noon
That to th' offring bifore hir sholde goon;   450
And if ther dide, certeyn, so wrooth was she,

239. *champioun*, wrestler. **241.** *tappestere*, tapster. **242.** *bet*, better. *lazar*, leper. *beggestere*,
beggar. **244.** *facultee*, official position. **246.** *avaunce*, be profitable. **247.** *poraille*, poor
people. **249.** *over-al*, everywhere. **256.** *purchas*, gain. *rente*, income. **257.** *rage*, frolic. **259.**
cloisterer, one restricted to a cloister. **262.** *semi-cope*, short outer coat. **268.** *doon*, do.
446. *som-del*, somewhat. *scathe*, shame. **447.** *haunt*, skill. **448.** *passed hem*, surpassed them.
450. *goon*, go.

That she was out of alle charitee.
Hir coverchiefs ful fyne were of ground;
I dorste swere they weyeden ten pound
That on a Sonday were upon hir heed.   455
Hir hosen weren of fyn scarlet reed,
Ful streite y-teyd, and shoos ful moiste and newe.
Bold was hir face, and fair, and reed of hewe.
She was a worthy womman al hir lyve,
Housbondes at chirche-dore she hadde fyve,   460
Withouten other companye in youthe;
But thereof nedeth nat to speke as nouthe.
And thryes hadde she been at Jerusalem;
She hadde passed many a straunge streem;
At Rome she hadde been, and at Boloigne,   465
In Galice at seint Jame, and at Coloigne.
She coude muche of wandring by the weye:
Gat-tothed was she, soothly for to seye.
Up-on an amblere esily she sat,
Y-wimpled wel, and on hir heed an hat   470
As brood as is a bokeler or a targe;
A foot-mantel aboute hir hipes large,
And on hir feet a paire of spores sharpe.
In felawschip wel coude she laughe and carpe.
Of remedyes of love she knew perchaunce,   475
For she coude of that art the olde daunce.

The MILLER was a stout carl, for the nones,   545
Ful big he was of braun, and eek of bones;
That proved wel, for over-al ther he cam,
At wrastling he wolde have alwey the ram.
He was short-sholdred, brood, a thikke knarre,
Ther nas no dore that he nolde heve of harre,   550
Or breke it, at a renning, with his heed.
His berd as any sowe or fox was reed,
And ther-to brood, as though it were a spade.
Up-on the cop right of his nose he hade
A werte, and ther-on stood a tuft of heres,   555
Reed as the bristles of a sowes eres;
His nose-thirles blake were and wyde.
A swerd and bokeler bar he by his syde;

453. *ground*, texture. 462. *nouthe*, now. 467. *coude*, knew. 471. *targe*, shield. 472. *foot-mantel*, cloth worn over skirt when riding. 476. *the olde daunce*, all about it. 545. *for the nones*, loosely translated "to be sure." 547. *over-al*, everywhere. 549. *knarre*, knave. 550. *harre*, hinges. 554. *cop*, top. 557. *nose-thirles*, nostrils.

His mouth as greet was as a greet forneys.
He was a janglere and a goliardeys,   560
And that was most of sinne and harlotryes.
Wel coude he stelen corn, and tollen thryes,
And yet he hadde a thombe of gold, pardee.
A whyt cote and blew hood wered he.
A baggepype wel coude he blowe and sowne,   565
And therwithal he broghte us out of towne.

William Shakespeare

WHEN ICICLES HANG BY THE WALL

When icicles hang by the wall,
  And Dick the shepherd blows his nail,
And Tom bears logs into the hall,
  And milk comes frozen home in pail,
When blood is nipped and ways be foul,   5
Then nightly sings the staring owl,
"Tu-whit, tu-who!" A merry note,
While greasy Joan doth keel the pot.

When all aloud the wind doth blow,
  And coughing drowns the parson's saw,   10
And birds sit brooding in the snow,
  And Marian's nose looks red and raw,
When roasted crabs hiss in the bowl,
Then nightly sings the staring owl,
"Tu-whit, tu-who!" A merry note,   15
While greasy Joan doth keel the pot.
    —from *Love's Labour's Lost* (1590-1592; 1598)

O MISTRESS MINE

O mistress mine, where are you roaming?
O, stay and hear; your true love's coming,

559. *forneys*, furnace. **560.** *janglere*, chatterer. *goliardeys*, buffoon, jester. **561.** *harlotryes*, lewd jokes. **562.** *tollen thryes*, take toll three times, i.e., charge excessively. **563.** *a thombe of gold.* There is an old proverb that an honest miller has a thumb of gold. In other words, the miller was honest according to his lights.

That can sing both high and low.
Trip no further, pretty sweeting,
Journeys end in lovers meeting,   5
    Every wise man's son doth know.

What is love? 'Tis not hereafter;
Present mirth hath present laughter;
    What's to come is still unsure.
In delay there lies no plenty;   10
Then come kiss me, sweet and twenty,
    Youth's a stuff will not endure.
         —from *Twelfth Night* (1599-1601; 1623)

BLOW, BLOW, THOU WINTER WIND

Blow, blow, thou winter wind,
Thou art not so unkind
    As man's ingratitude;
Thy tooth is not so keen,
Because thou art not seen,   5
    Although thy breath be rude.
Heigh-ho! sing, heigh-ho! unto the green holly:
Most friendship is feigning, most loving mere folly:
    Then, heigh-ho, the holly!
    This life is most jolly.   10

Freeze, freeze, thou bitter sky,
That dost not bite so nigh
    As benefits forgot:
Though thou the waters warp,
Thy sting is not so sharp   15
    As friend remember'd not
Heigh-ho! sing, & c.
         —from *As You Like It* (1600)

SONNET 18

Shall I compare thee to a summer's day?
Thou art more lovely and more temperate:
Rough winds do shake the darling buds of May,
And summer's lease hath all too short a date:
Sometime too hot the eye of heaven shines,   5
And often is his gold complexion dimmed;

And every fair from fair sometime declines,
By chance or nature's changing course untrimmed;
But thy eternal summer shall not fade,
Nor lose possession of that fair thou owest;   10
Nor shall Death brag thou wander'st in his shade,
When in eternal lines to time thou growest:
So long as men can breathe, or eyes can see,
So long lives this, and this gives life to thee. (1609)

SONNET 29

When, in disgrace with fortune and men's eyes,
I all alone beweep my outcast state,
And trouble deaf heaven with my bootless cries,
And look upon myself, and curse my fate,
Wishing me like to one more rich in hope,   5
Featured like him, like him with friends possessed,
Desiring this man's art and that man's scope,
With what I most enjoy contented least;
Yet in these thoughts myself almost despising,
Haply I think on thee—and then my state,   10
Like to the lark at break of day arising
From sullen earth, sings hymns at heaven's gate;
   For thy sweet love remembered such wealth brings
   That then I scorn to change my state with kings. (1609)

SONNET 30

When to the sessions of sweet silent thought
I summon up remembrance of things past,
I sigh the lack of many a thing I sought,
And with old woes new wail my dear time's waste.
Then can I drown an eye, unused to flow,   5
For precious friends hid in death's dateless night,
And weep afresh love's long since canceled woe,
And moan the expense of many a vanished sight.
Then can I grieve at grievances foregone,
And heavily from woe to woe tell o'er   10
The sad account of fore-bemoanéd moan,
Which I new pay as if not paid before.
   But if the while I think on thee, dear friend,
   All losses are restored and sorrows end. (1609)

SONNET 73

That time of year thou mayst in me behold
When yellow leaves, or none, or few, do hang
Upon those boughs which shake against the cold,
Bare ruined choirs, where late the sweet birds sang.
In me thou see'st the twilight of such day   5
As after sunset fadeth in the west,
Which by and by black night doth take away,
Death's second self, that seals up all in rest.
In me thou see'st the glowing of such fire
That on the ashes of his youth doth lie,   10
As the death-bed whereon it must expire,
Consumed with that which it was nourished by.
   This thou perceivest, which makes thy love more strong,
   To love that well which thou must leave ere long. (1609)

SONNET 94

They that have power to hurt and will do none,
That do not do the thing they most do show,
Who, moving others, are themselves as stone,
Unmoved, cold and to temptation slow;
They rightly do inherit heaven's graces   5
And husband nature's riches from expense;
They are the lords and owners of their faces,
Others but stewards of their excellence.
The summer's flower is to the summer sweet,
Though to itself it only live and die,   10
But if that flower with base infection meet,
The basest weed outbraves his dignity:
   For sweetest things turn sourest by their deeds;
   Lilies that fester smell far worse than weeds. (1609)

SONNET 129

The expense of spirit in a waste of shame
Is lust in action; and till action, lust
Is perjured, murderous, bloody, full of blame,
Savage, extreme, rude, cruel, not to trust;
Enjoy'd no sooner but despised straight;   5
Past reason hunted; and no sooner had,

Past reason hated, as a swallowed bait,
On purpose laid to make the taker mad:
Mad in pursuit, and in possession so;
Had, having, and in quest to have, extreme;   10
A bliss in proof, and proved, a very woe;
Before, a joy proposed; behind, a dream.
    All this the world well knows; yet none knows well
    To shun the heaven that leads men to this hell. (1609)

SONNET 146

Poor soul, the center of my sinful earth—
Fool'd by these rebel powers that thee array,
Why dost thou pine within and suffer dearth,
Painting thy outward walls so costly gay?
Why so large cost, having so short a lease,   5
Dost thou upon thy fading mansion spend?
Shall worms, inheritors of this excess,
Eat up thy charge? Is this thy body's end?
Then, soul, live thou upon thy servant's loss,
And let that pine to aggravate thy store;   10
Buy terms divine in 'selling hours of dross;
Within be fed, without be rich no more:
    So shalt thou feed on Death, that feeds on men,
    And Death once dead, there's no more dying then. (1609)

Renaissance and Seventeenth-Century Poems

Sir Thomas Wyatt

THEY FLEE FROM ME

They flee from me that sometime did me seek
    With naked foot, stalking in my chamber.
I have seen them gentle, tame, and meek,
    That now are wild, and do not remember

That sometime they put themselves in danger   5
To take bread at my hand; and now they range
Busily seeking with a continual change.

Thankèd be fortune, it hath been otherwise
    Twenty times better; but once in special,
In thin array, after a pleasant guise,   10
    When her loose gown from her shoulders did fall,
    And she me caught in her arms long and small,
Therewith all sweetly did me kiss
And softly said, '*Dear heart, how like you this?*'

It was no dream; I lay broad waking: 15
    But all is turned, through my gentleness,
Into a strange fashion of forsaking;
    And I have leave to go of her goodness,
    And she also to use newfangleness.
But since that I so kindly am served,   20
I would fain know what she hath deserved. (1557)

John Donne

SONG

Go and catch a falling star,
    Get with child a mandrake root,
Tell me where all past years are,
    Or who cleft the devil's foot;
Teach me to hear mermaids singing,   5
Or to keep off envy's stinging,
        And find
        What wind
Serves to advance an honest mind.

If thou be'st born to strange sights,   10
    Things invisible to see,
Ride ten thousand days and nights
    Till Age snow white hairs on thee;
Thou, when thou return'st, wilt tell me
All strange wonders that befell thee,   15
        And swear
        No where
Lives a woman true and fair.

If thou find'st one, let me know;
    Such a pilgrimage were sweet.   20
Yet do not, I would not go,
    Though at next door we might meet.
Though she were true when you met her,
And last till you write your letter,
      Yet she   25
      Will be
False, ere I come, to two or three. (1633)

LOVE'S ALCHEMY

Some that have deeper digg'd love's mine than **I**,
Say, where his centric happiness doth lie.
    I have lov'd, and got, and told,
But should I love, get, tell, till I were old,
I should not find that hidden mystery;   5
      Oh, 'tis imposture all.
And as no chemic yet th' elixir got,
      But glorifies his pregnant pot,
      If by the way to him befall
Some odoriferous thing, or medicinal,   10
    So, lovers dream a rich and long delight,
    But get a winter-seeming summer's night.
Our ease, our thrift, our honor, and our day,
Shall we, for this vain bubble's shadow pay?
      Ends love in this, that my man   15
Can be as happy as I can, if he can
Endure the short scorn of a bridegroom's play?
      That loving wretch that swears,
'Tis not the bodies marry, but the minds,
      Which he in her angelic finds,
      Would swear as justly, that he hears,   20
In that day's rude hoarse minstrelsy, the spheres.
    Hope not for mind in women; at their best
    Sweetness and wit they are, but mummy, possest. (1633)

Ben Jonson

AN EPITAPH ON SALATHIEL PAVY

Weep with me, all you that read
This little story;

And know, for whom a tear you shed
  Death's self is sorry.
'Twas a child that so did thrive   5
  In grace and feature,
As heaven and nature seemed to strive
  Which owned the creature.
Years he numbered scarce thirteen
  When fates turned cruel,   10
Yet three filled zodiacs had he been
  The stage's jewel;
And did act, what now we moan,
  Old men so duly,
As sooth, the Parcae thought him one,   15
  He played so truly.
So, by error, to his fate
  They all consented,
But viewing him since, alas, too late!
  They have repented;   20
And have sought, to give new birth,
  In baths to steep him;
But being so much too good for earth,
  Heaven vows to keep him. (1603)

HYMN TO DIANA

Queen and Huntress, chaste and fair,
  Now the sun is laid to sleep,
Seated in thy silver chair
  State in wonted manner keep:
    Hesperus entreats thy light,   5
    Goddess excellently bright.

Earth, let not thy envious shade
  Dare itself to interpose;
Cynthia's shining orb was made
  Heaven to clear when day did close: 10
    Bless us then with wishéd sight,
    Goddess excellently bright.

Lay thy bow of pearl apart
  And thy crystal-shining quiver;
Give unto the flying hart   15
  Space to breathe, how short soever:
    Thou that mak'st a day of night,
    Goddess excellently bright. (1600)

Robert Herrick

CORINNA'S GOING A-MAYING

Get up, get up for shame, the blooming morn
Upon her wings presents the god unshorn.
  See how Aurora throws her fair
  Fresh-quilted colors through the air:
  Get up, sweet slug-a-bed, and see   5
  The dew bespangling herb and tree.
Each flower has wept and bowed toward the east
Above an hour since: yet you not dressed;
  Nay! not so much as out of bed?
  When all the birds have matins said   10
  And sung their thankful hymns, 't is sin,
  Nay, profanation, to keep in,
Whenas a thousand virgins on this day
Spring, sooner than the lark, to fetch in May.

Rise, and put on your foliage, and be seen   15
To come forth, like the springtime, fresh and green,
  And sweet as Flora. Take no care
  For jewels for your gown or hair:
  Fear not; the leaves will strew
  Gems in abundance upon you: 20
Besides, the childhood of the day has kept,
Against you come, some orient pearls unwept;
  Come and receive them while the light
  Hangs on the dew-locks of the night:
  And Titan on the eastern hill   25
  Retires himself, or else stands still
Till you come forth. Wash, dress, be brief in praying:
Few beads are best when once we go a-Maying.

Come, my Corinna, come; and, coming mark
How each field turns a street, each street a park   30
  Made green and trimmed with trees; see how
  Devotion gives each house a bough
  Or branch: each porch, each door ere this
  An ark, a tabernacle is,
Made up of white-thorn, neatly interwove;   35
As if here were those cooler shades of love.
  Can such delights be in the street

And open fields and we not see 't?
Come, we'll abroad; and let's obey
   The proclamation made for May: 40
And sin no more, as we have done, by staying;
But, my Corinna, come, let's go a-Maying.

There's not a budding boy or girl this day
But is got up, and gone to bring in May.
   A deal of youth, ere this, is come   45
   Back, and with white-thorn laden home.
   Some have dispatched their cakes and cream
   Before that we have left to dream:
And some have wept, and wooed, and plighted troth,
And chose their priest, ere we can cast off sloth: 50
   Many a green-gown has been given;
   Many a kiss, both odd and even:
   Many a glance too has been sent
   From out the eye, love's firmament;
Many a jest told of the keys betraying   55
This night, and locks picked, yet we're not a-Maying.

Come, let us go while we are in our prime;
And take the harmless folly of the time.
   We shall grow old apace, and die
   Before we know our liberty.   60
   Our life is short, and our days run
   As fast away as does the sun;
And, as a vapor or a drop of rain,
Once lost, can ne'er be found again,
   So when or you or I are made   65
   A fable, song, or fleeting shade,
   All love, all liking, all delight
   Lies drowned with us in endless night.
Then while time serves, and we are but decaying,
Come, my Corinna, come let's go a-Maying. (1648)   70

George Herbert

VIRTUE

Sweet day, so cool, so calm, so bright,
   The bridal of the earth and sky;

The dew shall weep thy fall to-night,
    For thou must die.

Sweet rose, whose hue, angry and brave,   5
    Bids the rash gazer wipe his eye,
Thy root is ever in its grave,
    And thou must die.

Sweet spring, full of sweet days and roses,
    A box where sweets compacted lie,   10
My music shows ye have your closes,
    And all must die.

Only a sweet and virtuous soul,
    Like seasoned timber, never gives,
But though the whole world turn to coal,   15
    Then chiefly lives. (1630-1633)

Thomas Carew

SONG

Ask me no more where Jove bestows,
When June is past, the fading rose;
For in your beauty's orient deep
These flowers, as in their causes, sleep.

Ask me no more whither do stray   5
The golden atoms of the day;
For in pure love heaven did prepare
Those powders to enrich your hair.

Ask me no more whither doth haste
The nightingale when May is past;   10
For in your sweet, dividing throat
She winters and keeps warm her note.

Ask me no more where those stars 'light
That downwards fall in dead of night;
For in your eyes they sit, and there   15
Fixéd become as in their sphere.

Ask me no more if east or west
The phoenix builds her spicy nest;

For unto you at last she flies,
And in your fragrant bosom dies. (1640)   20

John Milton

ON SHAKESPEARE

What needs my Shakespeare for his honored bones
The labour of an age in piled stones?
Or that his hallowed reliques should be hid
Under a star-ypointing pyramid?
Dear son of memory, great heir of fame,   5
What need'st thou such weak witness of thy name?
Thou in our wonder and astonishment
Hast built thyself a livelong monument.
For whilst, to the shame of slow-endeavoring art
Thy easy numbers flow, and that each heart   10
Hath from the leaves of thy unvalued book
Those Delphic lines with deep impression took,
Then thou, our fancy of itself bereaving,
Dost make *us* marble with too much conceiving,
And so sepúlchred in such pomp dost lie   15
That kings for such a tomb would wish to die. (1632)

ON HIS HAVING ARRIVED
AT THE AGE OF TWENTY-THREE

How soon hath Time, the subtle thief of youth,
   Stol'n on his wing my three-and-twentieth year!
   My hasting days fly on with full career,
   But my late spring no bud or blossom shew'th.
Perhaps my semblance might deceive the truth,   5
   That I to manhood am arriv'd so near,
   And inward ripeness doth much less appear,
   That some more timely-happy spirits indu'th.
Yet it be less or more, or soon or slow,
   It shall be still in strictest measure ev'n,   10
   To that same lot, however mean or high,
Toward which Time leads me, and the will of Heav'n;
   All is, if I have grace to use it so,
   As ever in my great Taskmaster's eye. (1645)

ON THE LATE
MASSACRE IN PIEDMONT

Avenge, O Lord, Thy slaughtered saints, whose bones
Lie scattered on the Alpine mountains cold;
Even them who kept Thy truth so pure of old
When all our fathers worshiped stocks and stones,
Forget not: in Thy book record their groans   5
Who were Thy sheep, and in their ancient fold
Slain by the bloody Piedmontese, that rolled
Mother with infant down the rocks. Their moans
The vales redoubled to the hills, and they
To heaven. Their martyred blood and ashes sow   10
O'er all the Italian fields, where still doth sway
The triple Tyrant, that from these may grow
A hundredfold, who, having learnt Thy way,
Early may fly the Babylonian woe. (1655; 1673)

ON HIS DECEASED WIFE

Methought I saw my late espoused saint
Brought to me like Alcestis from the grave,
Whom Jove's great son to her glad husband gave,
Rescued from death by force though pale and faint.
Mine as whom washed from spot of child-bed taint,   5
Purification in the old law did save,
And such, as yet once more I trust to have
Full sight of her in Heaven without restraint,
Came vested all in white, pure as her mind.
Her face was veiled, yet to my fancied sight,   10
Love, sweetness, goodness, in her person shined,
So clear, as in no face with more delight.
But O, as to embrace me she inclined,
I waked, she fled, and day brought back my night. (1658; 1673)

Andrew Marvell

TO HIS COY MISTRESS

Had we but world enough, and time,
This coyness, lady, were no crime.

We would sit down, and think which way
To walk, and pass our long love's day.
Thou by the Indian Ganges' side   5
Shouldst rubies find: I by the tide
Of Humber would complain. I would
Love you ten years before The Flood,
And you should, if you please, refuse
Till the conversion of the Jews;   10
My vegetable love should grow
Vaster than empires and more slow;
An hundred years should go to praise
Thine eyes, and on thy forehead gaze;
Two hundred to adore each breast,   15
But thirty thousand to the rest;
An age at least to every part,
And the last age should show your heart.
For, lady, you deserve this state;
Nor would I love at lower rate.   20

But at my back I always hear
Time's wingéd chariot hurrying near;
And yonder all before us lie
Deserts of vast eternity.
Thy beauty shall no more be found,   25
Nor in thy marble vault shall sound
My echoing song; then worms shall try
That long preserved virginity;
And your quaint honor turn to dust,
And into ashes all my lust: 30
The grave's a fine and private place,
But none, I think, do there embrace.

Now therefore, while the youthful hue
Sits on thy skin like morning dew,
And while thy willing soul transpires   35
At every pore with instant fires,
Now let us sport us while we may,
And now, like amorous birds of prey,
Rather at once our time devour
Than languish in his slow-chapped power,   40
Let us roll all our strength and all
Our sweetness up into one ball,
And tear our pleasures with rough strife
Thorough the iron gates of life:
Thus, though we cannot make our sun   45
Stand still, yet we will make him run. (c. 1650; 1681)

BERMUDAS

Where the remote Bermudas ride
In the ocean's bosom unespied,
From a small boat that rowed along
The listening winds received this song:

"What should we do but sing His praise   5
That led us through the watery maze
Unto an isle so long unknown,
And yet far kinder than our own?
Where He the huge sea-monsters wracks
That lift the deep upon their backs,   10
He lands us on a grassy stage,
Safe from the storms' and prelates' rage.
He gave us this eternal spring
Which here enamels everything,
And sends the fowls to us in care   15
On daily visits through the air.
He hangs in shades the orange bright
Like golden lamps in a green night,
And does in the pomegranates close
Jewels more rich than Ormus shows.   20
He makes the figs our mouths to meet
And throws the melons at our feet;
But apples plants of such a price,
No tree could ever bear them twice.
With cedars chosen by His hand   25
From Lebanon He stores the land;
And makes the hollow seas that roar
Proclaim the ambergris on shore.
He cast (of which we rather boast)
The Gospel's pearl upon our coast;   30
And in these rocks for us did frame
A temple where to sound His name.
Oh, let our voice His praise exalt
Till it arrive at heaven's vault,
Which thence, perhaps, rebounding may   35
Echo beyond the Mexique bay!"

Thus sung they in the English boat
A holy and a cheerful note;
And all the way, to guide their chime,
With falling oars they kept the time. (1681)   40

Henry Vaughan

THE WORLD

I saw Eternity the other night,
Like a great ring of pure and endless light,
   All calm, as it was bright;
And round beneath it, Time, in hours, days, years,
   Driven by the spheres   5
Like a vast shadow moved; in which the world
   And all her train were hurled.
The doting lover in his quaintest strain
   Did there complain;
Near him, his lute, his fancy, and his flights,   10
   Wit's sour delights,
With gloves, and knots, the silly snares of pleasure,
   Yet his dear treasure,
All scattered lay, while he his eyes did pour
   Upon a flower.   15

The darksome statesman, hung with weights and woe,
Like a thick midnight-fog moved there so slow,
   He did not stay, nor go;
Condemning thoughts, like sad eclipses, scowl
   Upon his soul,   20
And clouds of crying witnesses without
   Pursued him with one shout.
Yet digged the mole, and lest his ways be found,
   Worked under ground,
Where he did clutch his prey; but one did see   25
   That policy;
Churches and altars fed him; perjuries
   Were gnats and flies;
It rained about him blood and tears, but he
   Drank them as free.   30

The fearful miser on a heap of rust
Sat pining all his life there, did scarce trust
   His own hands with the dust,
Yet would not place one piece above, but lives
   In fear of thieves.   35
Thousands there were as frantic as himself,
   And hugged each one his pelf;

The downright epicure placed heaven in sense,
 And scorned pretense;
While others, slipped into a wide excess,   40
 Said little less;
The weaker sort, slight, trivial wares enslave,
 Who think them brave;
And poor, despised Truth sat counting by
 Their victory.   45

Yet some, who all this while did weep and sing,
And sing and weep, soared up into the ring;
 But most would use no wing.
O fools, said I, thus to prefer dark night
 Before true light!   50
To live in grots and caves, and hate the day
 Because it shows the way,
The way, which from this dead and dark abode
 Leads up to God;
A way where you might tread the sun, and be   55
 More bright than he!
But, as I did their madness so discuss,
 One whispered thus
"This ring the Bridegroom did for none provide,
 But for his bride." (1650)   60

Restoration and Eighteenth-Century Poems

John Dryden

A SONG FOR ST. CECILIA'S DAY

From harmony, from heavenly harmony,
 This universal frame began:
 When Nature underneath a heap
  Of jarring atoms lay,

And could not heave her head,   5
The tuneful voice was heard from high:
   "Arise, ye more than dead."

Then cold and hot and moist and dry
   In order to their stations leap,
    And Music's power obey.   10
From harmony, from heavenly harmony,
    This universal frame began:
   From harmony to harmony
Through all the compass of the notes it ran,
The diapason closing full in Man.   15

What passion cannot Music raise and quell!
   When Jubal struck the chorded shell,
  His listening brethren stood around,
   And wondering, on their faces fell
To worship that celestial sound.   20
Less than a god they thought there could not dwell
 Within the hollow of that shell
 That spoke so sweetly and so well.
What passion cannot Music raise and quell!

  The trumpet's loud clangor   25
   Excites us to arms
With shrill notes of anger
  And mortal alarms.
  The double, double, double beat
   Of the thundering drum   30
   Cries: "Hark! the foes come;
Charge, charge, 'tis too late to retreat!"

The soft complaining flute
   In dying notes discovers
   The woes of hopeless lovers,   35
Whose dirge is whispered by the warbling lute.
   Sharp violins proclaim
Their jealous pangs and desperation,
Fury, frantic indignation,
Depth of pains, and height of passion,   40
   For the fair, disdainful dame.

But oh! what art can teach,
What human voice can reach
   The sacred organ's praise?

Notes inspiring holy love,   45
Notes that wing their heavenly ways
   To mend the choirs above.
Orpheus could lead the savage race;
And trees unrooted left their place,
     Sequacious of the lyre;   50
But bright Cecilia raised the wonder higher:
When to her organ vocal breath was given,
An angel heard, and straight appeared,
     Mistaking earth for heaven.

Grand Chorus

As from the power of sacred lays   55
   The spheres began to move,
And sung the great Creator's praise
   To all the blessed above;
So when the last and dreadful hour
This crumbling pageant shall devour,   60
The trumpet shall be heard on high,
The dead shall live, the living die,
And music shall untune the sky. (1687)

Matthew Prior

TO A CHILD OF QUALITY

Five years old, MDCCIV, the author then forty

Lords, knights, and squires, the numerous band
   That wear the fair Miss Mary's fetters,
Were summoned by her high command,
   To show their passions by their letters.

My pen among the rest I took,   5
   Lest those bright eyes that cannot read
Should dart their kindling fires, and look
   The power they have to be obeyed.

Nor quality nor reputation
   Forbid me yet my flame to tell;   10
Dear five years old befriends my passion,
   And I may write till she can spell.

For while she makes her silkworms beds
    With all the tender things I swear,
Whilst all the house my passion reads   15
    In papers round her baby hair,

She may receive and own my flame,
    For, though the strictest prudes should know it,
She'll pass for a most virtuous dame,
    And I for an unhappy poet.   20

Then too, alas! when she shall tear
    The lines some younger rival sends,
She'll give me leave to write, I fear,
    And we shall still continue friends.

For, as our different ages move,   25
    'Tis so ordained, (would Fate but mend it!)
That I shall be past making love,
    When she begins to comprehend it. (1704)

Jonathan Swift

DESCRIPTION OF A CITY SHOWER

   Careful observers may foretell the Hour
(By sure Prognostics) when to dread a Show'r:
While Rain depends, the pensive Cat gives o'er
Her Frolics, and pursues her Tail no more.
Returning Home at Night, you'll find the Sink   5
Strike your offended Sense with double Stink.
If you be wise, then go not far to Dine;
You'll spend in Coach-hire more than save in Wine.
A coming Show'r your shooting Corns presage,
Old Aches throb, your hollow Tooth will rage.   10
Saunt'ring in Coffee-house is Dulman seen;
He damns the Climate, and complains of Spleen.

   Meanwhile the South, rising with dabbled Wings,
A sable Cloud athwart the Welkin flings,
That swill'd more Liquor than it could contain,   15
And like a Drunkard gives it up again.
Brisk Susan whips her Linen from the Rope,
While the first drizzling Show'r is born aslope,
Such is that Sprinkling which some careless Quean
Flirts on you from her Mop, but not so clean.   20

You fly, invoke the Gods; then turning, stop
To rail; she, singing, still whirls on her Mop.
Not yet the Dust had shunn'd th' unequal Strife
But, aided by the Wind, fought still for Life;
And wafted with its Foe by violent Gust.   25
'Twas doubtful which was Rain, and which was Dust.
Ah! where must needy Poet seek for Aid,
When Dust and Rain at once his Coat invade,
His only Coat, where Dust, confus'd with Rain,
Roughen the Nap and leave a mingled Stain.   30

   Now in contiguous Drops the Flood comes down,
Threat'ning with Deluge this Devoted Town.
To Shops in Crowds the daggled Females fly,
Pretend to cheapen Goods, but nothing buy.
The Templer spruce, while ev'ry Spout's a-broach,   35
Stays till 'tis fair, yet seems to call a Coach.
The tuck'd-up Sempstress walks with hasty Strides,
While Streams run down her oil'd Umbrella's Sides.
Here various Kinds of various Fortunes led
Commence Acquaintance underneath a Shed.   40
Triumphant Tories and desponding Whigs
Forget their Feuds, and join to save their Wigs.

   Box'd in a Chair the Beau impatient sits,
While Spouts run clatt'ring o'er the Roof by Fits;
And ever and anon with frightful Din   45
The Leather sounds; he trembles from within.
So when Troy Chair-men bore the Wooden Steed,
Pregnant with Greeks, impatient to be freed,
(Those Bully Greeks, who, as the Moderns do,
Instead of paying Chair-men, run them thro'.)   50
Laoco'n struck the Outside with his Spear,
And each imprison'd Hero quak'd for Fear.

   Now from all Parts the swelling Kennels flow,
And bear their Trophies with them as they go:
Filth of all Hues and Odours seem to tell   55
What Street they sail'd from, by their Sight and Smell.
They, as each Torrent drives, with rapid Force
From Smithfield, or St. Pulchre's shape their Course,
And in huge Confluent join at Snow-Hill Ridge,
Fall from the Conduit prone to Holborn-Bridge.   60
Sweepings from Butchers' Stalls, Dung, Guts, and Blood,
Drown'd Puppies, stinking Sprats, all drench'd in Mud,
Dead Cats and Turnip-Tops come tumbling down the Flood. (1710)

Alexander Pope

ELEGY TO THE MEMORY
OF AN UNFORTUNATE LADY

What beck'ning ghost, along the moonlight shade
Invites my steps, and points to yonder glade?
'Tis she!—but why that bleeding bosom gored,
Why dimly gleams the visionary sword?
O, ever beauteous, ever friendly! tell,   5
Is it, in Heav'n, a crime to love too well?
To bear too tender or too firm a heart,
To act a lover's or a Roman's part?
Is there no bright reversion in the sky
For those who greatly think, or bravely die?   10
    Why bade ye else, ye Pow'rs! her soul aspire
Above the vulgar flight of low desire?
Ambition first sprung from your blest abodes;
The glorious fault of angels and of gods;
Thence to their images on earth it flows,   15
And in the breasts of kings and heroes glows.
Most souls, 'tis true, but peep out once an age,
Dull sullen pris'ners in the body's cage:
Dim lights of life, that burn a length of years,
Useless, unseen, as lamps in sepulchres;   20
Like Eastern kings a lazy state they keep,
And close confined to their own palace, sleep.
    From these perhaps (ere Nature bade her die)
Fate snatch'd her early to the pitying sky.
As into air the purer spirits flow,   25
And sep'rate from their kindred dregs below,
So flew the soul to its congenial place,
Nor left one virtue to redeem her race.
    But thou, false guardian of a charge too good!
Thou, mean deserter of thy brother's blood!   30
See on these ruby lips the trembling breath,
These cheeks now fading at the blast of Death:
Cold is that breast which warm'd the world before,
And those love-darting eyes must roll no more.
Thus, if eternal Justice rules the ball,   35
Thus shall your wives, and thus your children fall;
On all the line a sudden vengeance waits,

And frequent hearses shall besiege your gates.
There passengers shall stand, and pointing say
(While the long fun'rals blacken all the way),   40
'Lo! these were they whose souls the Furies steel'd
And cursed with hearts unknowing how to yield.'
Thus unlamented pass the proud away,
The gaze of fools, and pageant of a day!
So perish all whose breast ne'er learn'd to glow   45
For others' good, or melt at others' woe!
    What can atone (O ever-injured shade!)
Thy fate unpitied, and thy rites unpaid?
No friend's complaint, no kind domestic tear
Pleased thy pale ghost, or graced thy mournful bier.   50
By foreign hands thy dying eyes were closed,
By foreign hands thy decent limbs composed,
By foreign hands thy humble grave adorn'd,
By strangers honor'd, and by strangers mourn'd!
What though no friends in sable weeds appear,   55
Grieve for an hour, perhaps, then mourn a year,
And bear about the mockery of woe
To midnight dances, and the public show?
What though no weeping Loves thy ashes grace,
Nor polish'd marble emulate thy face?   60
What though no sacred earth allow thee room,
Nor hallow'd dirge be mutter'd o'er thy tomb?
Yet shall thy grave with rising flow'rs be drest,
And the green turf lie lightly on thy breast:
There shall the morn her earliest tears bestow,   65
There the first roses of the year shall blow;
While angels with their silver wings o'ershade
The ground now sacred by thy reliques made.
    So peaceful rests, without a stone, a name,
What once had beauty, titles, wealth, and fame.   70
How loved, how honor'd once, avails thee not,
To whom related, or by whom begot;
A heap of dust alone remains of thee,
'Tis all thou art, and all the proud shall be!
    Poets themselves must fall, like those they sung,   75
Deaf the praised ear, and mute the tuneful tongue.
Ev'n he, whose soul now melts in mournful lays,
Shall shortly want the gen'rous tear he pays;
Then from his closing eyes thy form shall part,
And the last pang shall tear thee from his heart;   80
Life's idle business at one gasp be o'er,
The Muse forgot, and thou beloved no more! (1717)

Thomas Gray

ELEGY WRITTEN IN
A COUNTRY CHURCHYARD

The curfew tolls the knell of parting day,
    The lowing herd winds slowly o'er the lea,
The plowman homeward plods his weary way,
    And leaves the world to darkness and to me.

Now fades the glimmering landscape on the sight,   5
    And all the air a solemn stillness holds,
Save where the beetle wheels his droning flight,
    And drowsy tinklings lull the distant folds;

Save that from yonder ivy-mantled tower
    The moping owl does to the moon complain   10
Of such, as wandering near her secret bower,
    Molest her ancient solitary reign.

Beneath those rugged elms, that yew-tree's shade,
    Where heaves the turf in many a moldering heap,
Each in his narrow cell for ever laid,   15
    The rude forefathers of the hamlet sleep.

The breezy call of incense-breathing morn,
    The swallow twittering from the straw-built shed,
The cock's shrill clarion, or the echoing horn,
    No more shall rouse them from their lowly bed.   20

For them no more the blazing hearth shall burn,
    Or busy housewife ply her evening care:
No children run to lisp their sire's return,
    Or climb his knees the envied kiss to share.

Oft did the harvest to their sickle yield,   25
    Their furrow oft the stubborn glebe has broke;
How jocund did they drive their team afield!
    How bowed the woods beneath their sturdy stroke!

Let not Ambition mock their useful toil,
    Their homely joys, and destiny obscure;   30

Nor Grandeur hear with a disdainful smile,
  The short and simple annals of the poor.

The boast of heraldry, the pomp of power,
  And all that beauty, all that wealth e'er gave,
Awaits alike the inevitable hour.   35
  The paths of glory lead but to the grave.

Nor you, ye proud, impute to these the fault,
  If Memory o'er their tomb no trophies raise,
Where through the long-drawn aisle and fretted vault
  The pealing anthem swells the note of praise.   40

Can storied urn or animated bust
  Back to its mansion call the fleeting breath?
Can Honor's voice provoke the silent dust,
  Or Flattery soothe the dull cold ear of Death?

Perhaps in this neglected spot is laid   45
  Some heart once pregnant with celestial fire;
Hands, that the rod of empire might have swayed,
  Or waked to ecstasy the living lyre.

But Knowledge to their eyes her ample page
  Rich with the spoils of time did ne'er unroll;   50
Chill Penury repressed their noble rage,
  And froze the genial current of the soul.

Full many a gem of purest ray serene,
  The dark unfathomed caves of ocean bear:
Full many a flower is born to blush unseen   55
  And waste its sweetness on the desert air.

Some village Hampden, that with dauntless breast
  The little tyrant of his fields withstood;
Some mute inglorious Milton here may rest,
  Some Cromwell guiltless of his country's blood.   60

The applause of listening senates to command,
  The threats of pain and ruin to despise,
To scatter plenty o'er a smiling land,
  And read their history in a nation's eyes,

Their lot forbade: nor circumscribed alone   65
  Their growing virtues, but their crimes confined;

Forbade to wade through slaughter to a throne,
 And shut the gates of mercy on mankind,

The struggling pangs of conscious truth to hide,
 To quench the blushes of ingenuous shame,   70
Or heap the shrine of Luxury and Pride
 With incense kindled at the Muse's flame.

Far from the madding crowd's ignoble strife,
 Their sober wishes never learned to stray;
Along the cool sequestered vale of life   75
 They kept the noiseless tenor of their way.

Yet even these bones from insult to protect,
 Some frail memorial still erected nigh,
With uncouth rhymes and shapeless sculpture decked,
 Implores the passing tribute of a sigh.   80

Their name, their years, spelt by the unlettered muse,
 The place of fame and elegy supply;
And many a holy text around she strews,
 That teach the rustic moralist to die.

For who to dumb Forgetfulness a prey,   85
 This pleasing anxious being e'er resigned,
Left the warm precincts of the cheerful day,
 Nor cast one longing lingering look behind?

On some fond breast the parting soul relies,
 Some pious drops the closing eye requires;   90
Ev'n from the tomb the voice of Nature cries,
 Ev'n in our ashes live their wonted fires.

For thee, who mindful of the unhonored dead
 Dost in these lines their artless tale relate;
If chance, by lonely contemplation led,   95
 Some kindred spirit shall inquire thy fate,

Haply some hoary-headed swain may say,
 "Oft have we seen him at the peep of dawn
Brushing with hasty steps the dews away
 To meet the sun upon the upland lawn.   100

"There at the foot of yonder nodding beech
 That wreathes its old fantastic roots so high,

His listless length at noontide would he stretch,
    And pore upon the brook that babbles by.

"Hard by yon wood, now smiling as in scorn,   105
    Muttering his wayward fancies he would rove,
Now drooping, woeful wan, like one forlorn,
    Or crazed with care, or crossed in hopeless love.

"One morn I missed him on the customed hill,
    Along the heath and near his favorite tree;   110
Another came; nor yet beside the rill,
    Nor up the lawn, nor at the wood was he;

"The next with dirges due in sad array
    Slow through the church-way path we saw him borne.
Approach and read (for thou can'st read) the lay,   115
    Graved on the stone beneath yon aged thorn."

The Epitaph
Here rests his head upon the lap of earth
    A youth to fortune and to fame unknown.
Fair Science frowned not on his humble birth,
    And Melancholy marked him for her own.   120

Large was his bounty, and his soul sincere,
    Heaven did a recompense as largely send:
He gave to Misery all he had, a tear,
    He gained from Heaven ('twas all he wished) a friend.

No farther seek his merits to disclose,   125
    Or draw his frailties from their dread abode,
(There they alike in trembling hope repose)
    The bosom of his Father and his God. (1751)

William Collins

ODE

Written in the beginning of the year 1746

How sleep the brave who sink to rest
By all their country's wishes bless'd!

When Spring, with dewy fingers cold,
Returns to deck their hallow'd mould,
She there shall dress a sweeter sod   5
Than Fancy's feet have ever trod.

By fairy hands their knell is rung;
By forms unseen their dirge is sung;
There Honour comes, a pilgrim gray,
To bless the turf that wraps their clay;   10
And Freedom shall awhile repair,
To dwell a weeping hermit there! (1747)

William Blake

THE TIGER

Tiger! Tiger! burning bright
In the forests of the night,
What immortal hand or eye
Could frame thy fearful symmetry?

In what distant deeps or skies   5
Burnt the fire of thine eyes?
On what wings dare he aspire?
What the hand dare seize the fire?

And what shoulder, and what art,
Could twist the sinews of thy heart?   10
And when thy heart began to beat,
What dread hand? and what dread feet?

What the hammer? what the chain?
In what furnace was thy brain?
What the anvil? what dread grasp   15
Dare its deadly terrors clasp?

When the stars threw down their spears,
And watered heaven with their tears,
Did he smile his work to see?
Did he who made the Lamb make thee?   20

Tiger! Tiger! burning bright
In the forests of the night,
What immortal hand or eye
Dare frame thy fearful symmetry? (1794)

LONDON

I wander through each chartered street.
Near where the chartered Thames does flow,
And mark in every face I meet
Marks of weakness, marks of woe.

In every cry of every man,   5
In every infant's cry of fear,
In every voice, in every ban,
The mind-forged manacles I hear:

How the chimney-sweeper's cry
Every blackening church appalls,   10
And the hapless soldier's sigh
Runs in blood down palace walls.

But most, through midnight streets I hear
How the youthful harlot's curse
Blasts the new-born infant's tear,   15
And blights with plagues the marriage hearse. (1794)

Robert Burns

THE DEIL'S AWA
WI' TH' EXCISEMAN

Chorus

The deil's awa, the deil's awa,
    The deil's awa wi' th' Exciseman;
He's danc'd awa, he's danc'd awa,
    He's danc'd awa wi' th' Exciseman!

The deil cam fiddlin thro' the town   5
  And danc'd awa wi' th' Exciseman.
And ilka wife cries: "Auld Mahoun,
  I wish you luck o' the prize, man!

"We'll mak our maut, we'll brew our drink,
  We'll laugh, sing, and rejoice, man;   10
And monie braw thanks to the meikle black deil,
  That danc'd awa wi' th' Exciseman."

There's threesome reels, there's foursome reels,
  There's hornpipes and strathspeys, man;
But the ae best dance e'er cam to the land   15
  Was *The Deil's Awa wi' th' Exciseman.*

Chorus

The deil's awa, the deil's awa,
  The deil's awa wi' th' Exciseman;
He's danc'd awa, he's danc'd awa,
  He's danc'd awa wi' th' Exciseman! (1792)   20

O, WERT THOU
IN THE CAULD BLAST

O wert thou in the cauld blast
  On yonder lea, on yonder lea,
My plaidie to the angry airt,
  I'd shelter thee, I'd shelter thee.
Or did misfortune's bitter storms   5
  Around thee blaw, around thee blaw,
Thy bield should be my bosom,
  To share it a', to share it a'.

Or were I in the wildest waste,
  Sae black and bare, sae black and bare,   10
The desert were a paradise,
  If thou wert there, if thou wert there.
Or were I monarch o' the globe,
  Wi' thee to reign, wi' thee to reign,
The brightest jewel in my crown   15
  Wad be my queen, wad be my queen. (1796; 1800)

Nineteenth=Century Poems

William Wordsworth

THE WORLD IS
TOO MUCH WITH US

The world is too much with us; late and soon,
Getting and spending, we lay waste our powers:
Little we see in Nature that is ours;
We have given our hearts away, a sordid boon!
The sea that bares her bosom to the moon;   5
The winds that will be howling at all hours,
And are up-gathered now like sleeping flowers;
For this, for everything, we are out of tune;
It moves us not.—Great God! I'd rather be
A Pagan suckled in a creed outworn;   10
So might I, standing on this pleasant lea,
Have glimpses that would make me less forlorn;
Have sight of Proteus rising from the sea;
Or hear old Triton blow his wreathéd horn. (1806; 1807)

LONDON, 1802

Milton! thou shouldst be living at this hour:
England hath need of thee: she is a fen
Of stagnant waters: altar, sword, and pen,
Fireside, the heroic wealth of hall and bower,
Have forfeited their ancient English dower   5
Of inward happiness. We are selfish men:
Oh! raise us up, return to us again;
And give us manners, virtue, freedom, power.
Thy soul was like a Star, and dwelt apart:
Thou hadst a voice whose sound was like the sea,   10
Pure as the naked heavens, majestic, free;
So didst thou travel on life's common way
In cheerful godliness; and yet thy heart
The lowliest duties on herself did lay. (1802; 1807)

O D E

Intimations of immortality from recollections of early childhood

I

There was a time when meadow, grove, and stream,
 The earth, and every common sight,
  To me did seem
  Appareled in celestial light,
The glory and the freshness of a dream.   5
It is not now as it hath been of yore;—
  Turn wheresoe'er I may,
   By night or day,
The things which I have seen I now can see no more.

II

  The Rainbow comes and goes,   10
  And lovely is the Rose;
  The Moon doth with delight
Look round her when the heavens are bare;
  Waters on a starry night
  Are beautiful and fair;   15
 The sunshine is a glorious birth;
 But yet I know, where'er I go,
That there hath passed away a glory from the earth.

III

Now, while the birds thus sing a joyous song,
  And while the young lambs bound   20
   As to the tabor's sound,
To me alone there came a thought of grief:
A timely utterance gave that thought relief,
  And I again am strong:
The cataracts blow their trumpets from the steep;   25
No more shall grief of mine the season wrong;
I hear the Echoes through the mountains throng,
The Winds come to me from the fields of sleep,
  And all the earth is gay;
   Land and sea   30
  Give themselves up to jollity,
  And with the heart of May
  Doth every Beast keep holiday;—
   Thou Child of Joy,
Shout round me, let me hear thy shouts, thou happy Shepherd-boy! 35

IV

Ye blessèd Creatures, I have heard the call
   Ye to each other make; I see
The heavens laugh with you in your jubilee;
   My heart is at your festival,
   My head hath its coronal,   40
The fulness of your bliss, I feel—I feel it all.
   Oh, evil day! if I were sullen
   While Earth herself is adorning,
    This sweet May-morning,
   And the Children are culling   45
    On every side,
   In a thousand valleys far and wide,
Fresh flowers; while the sun shines warm,
And the Babe leaps up on his Mother's arm—
   I hear, I hear, with joy I hear!   50
   —But there's a Tree, of many, one,
A single Field which I have looked upon,
Both of them speak of something that is gone:
   The Pansy at my feet
   Doth the same tale repeat: 55
Whither is fled the visionary gleam?
Where is it now, the glory and the dream?

V

Our birth is but a sleep and a forgetting:
The Soul that rises with us, our life's Star,
   Hath had elsewhere its setting,   60
   And cometh from afar:
   Not in entire forgetfulness,
   And not in utter nakedness,
But trailing clouds of glory do we come
   From God, who is our home: 65
Heaven lies about us in our infancy!
Shades of the prison-house begin to close
   Upon the growing Boy,
But he beholds the light, and whence it flows
   He sees it in his joy;   70
The Youth, who daily farther from the east
   Must travel, still is Nature's priest,
   And by the vision splendid
   Is on his way attended;
At length the Man perceives it die away,   75
And fade into the light of common day,

VI

Earth fills her lap with pleasures of her own;
Yearnings she hath in her own natural kind,
And even with something of a Mother's mind,
     And no unworthy aim,   80
     The homely Nurse doth all she can
To make her Foster-child, her Inmate Man,
     Forget the glories he hath known,
And that imperial palace whence he came.

VII

Behold the Child among his new-born blisses,   85
A six years' Darling of a pigmy size!
See, where 'mid work of his own hand he lies,
Fretted by sallies of his mother's kisses,
With light upon him from his father's eyes!
See, at his feet, some little plan or chart,   90
Some fragment from his dream of human life,
Shaped by himself with newly-learnéd art;
     A wedding or a festival,
     A mourning or a funeral,
      And this hath now his heart,   95
     And unto this he frames his song:
     Then will he fit his tongue
To dialogues of business, love, or strife;
     But it will not be long
     Ere this be thrown aside,   100
     And with new joy and pride
The little Actor cons another part;
Filling from time to time his "humorous stage"
With all the Persons, down to palsied Age,
That Life brings with her in her equipage;   105
     As if his whole vocation
     Were endless imitation.

VIII

Thou, whose exterior semblance doth belie
     Thy Soul's immensity;
Thou best Philosopher, who yet dost keep   110
Thy heritage, thou Eye among the blind,
That, deaf and silent, read'st the eternal deep,
Haunted forever by the eternal mind—
     Mighty Prophet! Seer blest!
     On whom those truths do rest,   115
Which we are toiling all our lives to find,
In darkness lost, the darkness of the grave;

Thou, over whom thy Immortality
Broods like the Day, a Master o'er a Slave,
A Presence which is not to be put by;   120
Thou little Child, yet glorious in the might
Of heaven-born freedom on thy being's height,
Why with such earnest pains dost thou provoke
The years to bring the inevitable yoke,
Thus blindly with thy blessedness at strife?   125
Full soon thy Soul shall have her earthly freight,
And custom lie upon thee with a weight,
Heavy as frost, and deep almost as life!

IX

    Oh, joy! that in our embers
    Is something that doth live,   130
    That nature yet remembers
    What was so fugitive!
The thought of our past years in me doth breed
Perpetual benediction: not indeed
For that which is most worthy to be blest;   135
Delight and liberty, the simple creed
Of Childhood, whether busy or at rest,
With new-fledged hope still fluttering in his breast—
    Not for these I raise
    The song of thanks and praise;   140
    But for those obstinate questionings
    Of sense and outward things,
    Falling from us, vanishings;
    Blank misgivings of a Creature
Moving about in worlds not realized,   145
High instincts before which our mortal nature
Did tremble like a guilty thing surprised:
    But for those first affections,
    Those shadowy recollections,
    Which, be they what they may,   150
Are yet the fountain light of all our day,
Are yet a master light of all our seeing;
  Uphold us, cherish, and have power to make
Our noisy years seem moments in the being
Of the eternal Silence: truths that wake,   155
    To perish never;
Which neither listlessness, nor mad endeavor,
    Nor Man nor Boy,
Nor all that is at enmity with joy,
Can utterly abolish or destroy!   160

Hence in a season of calm weather
    Though inland far we be,
Our Souls have sight of that immortal sea
    Which brought us hither,
    Can in a moment travel thither,   165
And see the Children sport upon the shore,
And hear the mighty waters rolling evermore.

              X

Then sing, ye Birds, sing, sing a joyous song!
    And let the young Lambs bound
    As to the tabor's sound!   170
We in thought will join your throng,
    Ye that pipe and ye that play,
    Ye that through your hearts today
    Feel the gladness of the May!
What though the radiance which was once so bright   175
Be now forever taken from my sight,
  Though nothing can bring back the hour
Of splendor in the grass, of glory in the flower;
    We will grieve not, rather find
    Strength in what remains behind;   180
    In the primal sympathy
    Which having been must ever be;
    In the soothing thoughts that spring
    Out of human suffering;
    In the faith that looks through death,   185
In years that bring the philosophic mind.

              XI

And O, ye Fountains, Meadows, Hills, and Groves,
Forebode not any severing of our loves!
Yet in my heart of hearts I feel your might;
I only have relinquished one delight   190
To live beneath your more habitual sway.
I love the Brooks which down their channels fret,
Even more than when I tripped lightly as they;
The innocent brightness of a new-born Day
    Is lovely yet;   195
The Clouds that gather round the setting sun
Do take a sober coloring from an eye
That hath kept watch o'er man's mortality.
Another race hath been, and other palms are won.
Thanks to the human heart by which we live,   200
Thanks to its tenderness, its joys, and fears,
To me the meanest flower that blows can give
Thoughts that do often lie too deep for tears. (1803-1806; 1807)

George Gordon, Lord Byron

THE DESTRUCTION OF SENNACHERIB

The Assyrian came down like the wolf on the fold,
And his cohorts were gleaming in purple and gold;
And the sheen of their spears was like stars on the sea,
When the blue wave rolls nightly on deep Galilee.

Like the leaves of the forest when Summer is green, 5
That host with their banners at sunset were seen:
Like the leaves of the forest when Autumn hath blown,
That host on the morrow lay withered and strown.

For the Angel of Death spread his wings on the blast,
And breathed in the face of the foe as he passed; 10
And the eyes of the sleepers waxed deadly and chill,
And their hearts but once heaved, and forever grew still!

And there lay the steed with his nostril all wide,
But through it there rolled not the breath of his pride;
And the foam of his gasping lay white on the turf, 15
And cold as the spray of the rock-beating surf.

And there lay the rider distorted and pale,
With the dew on his brow, and the rust on his mail:
And the tents were all silent—the banners alone—
The lances unlifted—the trumpet unblown. 20

And the widows of Ashur are loud in their wail,
And the idols are broke in the temple of Baal;
And the might of the Gentile, unsmote by the sword,
Hath melted like snow in the glance of the Lord! (1815)

SONG OF SAUL

BEFORE HIS LAST BATTLE

Warriors and chiefs! should the shaft or the sword
Pierce me in leading the host of the Lord,
Heed not the corse, though a king's, in your path:
Bury your steel in the bosoms of Gath!

Thou who art bearing my buckler and bow,   5
Should the soldiers of Saul look away from the foe,
Stretch me that moment in blood at thy feet!
Mine be the doom which they dared not to meet.

Farewell to others, but never we part,
Heir to my royalty, son of my heart!   10
Bright is the diadem, boundless the sway,
Or kingly the death, which awaits us today! (1815)

Percy Bysshe Shelley

OZYMANDIAS

I met a traveler from an antique land
Who said: "Two vast and trunkless legs of stone
Stand in the desert. Near them, on the sand,
Half sunk, a shattered visage lies, whose frown,
And wrinkled lip, and sneer of cold command,   5
Tell that its sculptor well those passions read
Which yet survive, stamped on these lifeless things,
The hand that mocked them, and the heart that fed:
And on the pedestal these words appear:
'My name is Ozymandias, king of kings: 10
Look on my works, ye Mighty, and despair!'
Nothing beside remains. Round the decay
Of that colossal wreck, boundless and bare
The lone and level sands stretch far away." (1817; 1818)

ODE TO THE WEST WIND

I

O wild west wind, thou breath of Autumn's being,
Thou, from whose unseen presence the leaves dead
Are driven, like ghosts from an enchanter fleeing,

Yellow, and black, and pale, and hectic red,
Pestilence-stricken multitudes: O thou,   5
Who chariotest to their dark wintry bed

The wingéd seeds, where they lie cold and low,
Each like a corpse within its grave, until
Thine azure sister of the Spring shall blow

Her clarion o'er the dreaming earth, and fill   10
(Driving sweet buds like flocks to feed in air)
With living hues and odors plain and hill:

Wild Spirit, which art moving everywhere;
Destroyer and preserver; hear, oh, hear!

II

Thou on whose stream, mid the steep sky's commotion,   15
Loose clouds like earth's decaying leaves are shed,
Shook from the tangled boughs of Heaven and Ocean,

Angels of rain and lightning: there are spread
On the blue surface of thine aëry surge,
Like the bright hair uplifted from the head   20

Of some fierce Maenad, even from the dim verge
Of the horizon to the zenith's height,
The locks of the approaching storm. Thou dirge

Of the dying year, to which this closing night
Will be the dome of a vast sepulcher,   25
Vaulted with all thy congregated might

Of vapors, from whose solid atmosphere
Black rain, and fire, and hail will burst: oh, hear!

III

Thou who didst waken from his summer dreams
The blue Mediterranean, where he lay,   30
Lulled by the coil of his crystalline streams,

Beside a pumice isle in Baiae's bay,
And saw in sleep old palaces and towers
Quivering within the wave's intenser day,

All overgrown with azure moss and flowers   35
So sweet, the sense faints picturing them! Thou
For whose path the Atlantic's level powers

Cleave themselves into chasms, while far below
The sea-blooms and the oozy woods which wear
The sapless foliage of the ocean, know   40

Thy voice, and suddenly grow gray with fear,
And tremble and despoil themselves: oh, hear!

IV

If I were a dead leaf thou mightest bear,
If I were a swift cloud to fly with thee;
A wave to pant beneath thy power, and share   45

The impulse of thy strength, only less free
Than thou, O uncontrollable! If even
I were as in my boyhood, and could be

The comrade of thy wanderings over Heaven,
As then, when to outstrip thy skyey speed   50
Scarce seemed a vision; I would ne'er have striven

As thus with thee in prayer in my sore need.
Oh, lift me as a wave, a leaf, a cloud!
I fall upon the thorns of life! I bleed!

A heavy weight of hours has chained and bowed   55
One too like thee: tameless, and swift, and proud.

V

Make me thy lyre, even as the forest is:
What if my leaves are falling like its own!
The tumult of thy mighty harmonies

Will take from both a deep, autumnal tone,   60
Sweet though in sadness. Be thou, Spirit fierce,
My spirit! Be thou me, impetuous one!

Drive my dead thoughts over the universe
Like withered leaves to quicken a new birth!
And, by the incantation of this verse,   65

Scatter, as from an unextinguished hearth
Ashes and sparks, my words among mankind!
Be through my lips to unawakened earth

The trumpet of a prophecy! O Wind,
If Winter comes, can Spring be far behind? (1819; 1820)   70

John Keats

ODE TO A NIGHTINGALE

My heart aches, and a drowsy numbness pains
My sense, as though of hemlock I had drunk,

Or emptied some dull opiate to the drains
   One minute past, and Lethe-wards had sunk:
'Tis not through envy of thy happy lot,   5
   But being too happy in thine happiness—
      That thou, light-wingéd Dryad of the trees,
        In some melodious plot
   Of beechen green, and shadows numberless,
      Singest of summer in full-throated ease.   10

O, for a draught of vintage, that hath been
   Cooled a long age in the deep-delvéd earth,
Tasting of Flora and the country green,
   Dance, and Provençal song, and sunburnt mirth!
O for a beaker full of the warm South,   15
   Full of the true, the blushful Hippocrene,
      With beaded bubbles winking at the brim,
        And purple-stainéd mouth;
   That I might drink, and leave the world unseen,
      And with thee fade away into the forest dim: 20

Fade far away, dissolve, and quite forget
   What thou among the leaves hast never known,
The weariness, the fever, and the fret
   Here, where men sit and hear each other groan;
Where palsy shakes a few, sad, last gray hairs,   25
   Where youth grows pale, and specter-thin, and dies;
      Where but to think is to be full of sorrow
        And leaden-eyed despairs,
   Where Beauty cannot keep her lustrous eyes,
      Or new Love pine at them beyond tomorrow.   30

Away! away! for I will fly to thee,
   Not charioted by Bacchus and his pards,
But on the viewless wings of Poesy,
   Though the dull brain perplexes and retards:
Already with thee! tender is the night,   35
And haply the Queen-Moon is on her throne,
   Clustered around by all her starry Fays;
      But here there is no light,
Save what from heaven is with the breezes blown
   Through verdurous glooms and winding mossy ways.   40

I cannot see what flowers are at my feet,
   Nor what soft incense hangs upon the boughs,
But, in embalméd darkness, guess each sweet

Wherewith the seasonable month endows
The grass, the thicket, and the fruit-tree wild;   45
  White hawthorn, and the pastoral eglantine;
    Fast fading violets covered up in leaves;
     And mid-May's eldest child.
  The coming musk-rose, full of dewy wine,
    The murmurous haunt of flies on summer eves.   50

Darkling I listen; and, for many a time,
  I have been half in love with easeful Death,
Called him soft names in many a muséd rime,
  To take into the air my quiet breath;
Now more than ever seems it rich to die,   55
  To cease upon the midnight with no pain,
    While thou art pouring forth thy soul abroad
     In such an ecstasy!
  Still wouldst thou sing, and I have ears in vain—
    To thy high requiem become a sod.   60

Thou wast not born for death, immortal Bird!
  No hungry generations tread thee down;
The voice I hear this passing night was heard
  In ancient days by emperor and clown:
Perhaps the self-same song that found a path   65
  Through the sad heart of Ruth, when, sick for home,
    She stood in tears amid the alien corn;
     The same that oft-times hath
  Charmed magic casements, opening on the foam
    Of perilous seas, in faery lands forlorn.   70

Forlorn! the very word is like a bell
  To toll me back from thee to my sole self,
Adieu! the fancy cannot cheat so well
  As she is famed to do, deceiving elf.
Adieu! adieu! thy plaintive anthem fades   75
  Past the near meadows, over the still stream,
    Up the hillside; and now 'tis buried deep
     In the next valley glades:
  Was it a vision, or a waking dream?
    Fled is that music—Do I wake or sleep? (1819)   80

ODE ON A GRECIAN URN

Thou still unravished bride of quietness,
  Thou foster-child of Silence and slow Time,

Sylvan historian, who canst thus express
 A flowery tale more sweetly than our rime:
What leaf-fringed legend haunts about thy shape   5
  Of deities or mortals, or of both,
   In Tempe or the dales of Arcady?
  What men or gods are these? What maidens loth?
What mad pursuit? What struggle to escape?
   What pipes and timbrels? What wild ecstasy?   10

Heard melodies are sweet, but those unheard
 Are sweeter; therefore, ye soft pipes, play on;
Not to the sensual ear, but, more endeared,
  Pipe to the spirit ditties of no tone:
Fair youth, beneath the trees, thou canst not leave   15
  Thy song, nor ever can those trees be bare;
   Bold Lover, never, never canst thou kiss,
Though winning near the goal—yet, do not grieve;
  She cannot fade, though thou hast not thy bliss,
  Forever wilt thou love, and she be fair!   20

Ah, happy, happy boughs! that cannot shed
 Your leaves, nor ever bid the Spring adieu;
And, happy melodist, unwearièd,
  Forever piping songs forever new.
More happy love! more happy, happy love!   25
  Forever warm and still to be enjoyed,
   Forever panting, and forever young;
All breathing human passion far above,
  That leaves a heart high-sorrowful and cloyed,
   A burning forehead, and a parching tongue.   30

Who are these coming to the sacrifice?
 To what green altar, O mysterious priest,
Lead'st thou that heifer lowing at the skies,
  And all her silken flanks with garlands dressed?
What little town by river or seashore,   35
  Or mountain-built with peaceful citadel,
   Is emptied of this folk, this pious morn?
And, little town, thy streets forevermore
  Will silent be; and not a soul to tell
   Why thou art desolate, can e'er return.   40

O Attic shape! Fair attitude! with brede
 Of marble men and maidens overwrought,
With forest branches and the trodden weed;

Thou, silent form, dost tease us out of thought
As doth eternity: Cold Pastoral!   45
    When old age shall this generation waste,
        Thou shalt remain, in midst of other woe
Than ours, a friend to man, to whom thou say'st,
    "Beauty is truth, truth beauty,—that is all
        Ye know on earth, and all ye need to know." (1819; 1820)   50

ODE ON MELANCHOLY

No, no! go not to Lethe, neither twist
    Wolf's-bane, tight-rooted, for its poisonous wine;
Nor suffer thy pale forehead to be kissed
    By nightshade, ruby grape of Proserpine;
Make not your rosary of yew-berries,   5
    Nor let the beetle, nor the death-moth be
        Your mournful Psyche, nor the downy owl
A partner in your sorrow's mysteries;
    For shade to shade will come too drowsily,
        And drown the wakeful anguish of the soul.   10

But when the melancholy fit shall fall
    Sudden from heaven like a weeping cloud,
That fosters the droop-headed flowers all,
    And hides the green hill in an April shroud;
Then glut thy sorrow on a morning rose,   15
    Or on the rainbow of the salt sand-wave,
        Or on the wealth of globéd peonies;
Or if thy mistress some rich anger shows,
    Emprison her soft hand, and let her rave,
        And feed deep, deep upon her peerless eyes.   20

She dwells with Beauty—Beauty that must die;
    And Joy, whose hand is ever at his lips
Bidding adieu; and aching Pleasure nigh,
    Turning to poison while the bee-mouth sips:
Ay, in the very temple of Delight   25
    Veiled Melancholy has her sovran shrine,
        Though seen of none save him whose strenuous tongue
    Can burst Joy's grape against his palate fine;
His soul shall taste the sadness of her might,
    And be among her cloudy trophies hung. (1819; 1820)   30

ODE TO PSYCHE

O Goddess! hear these tuneless numbers, wrung
    By sweet enforcement and remembrance dear,
And pardon that thy secrets should be sung
    Even into thine own soft-conchéd ear:
Surely I dreamt today, or did I see   5
    The wingéd Psyche with awakened eyes?
I wandered in a forest thoughtlessly,
    And, on the sudden, fainting with surprise,
Saw two fair creatures, couchéd side by side
      In deepest grass, beneath the whisp'ring roof   10
      Of leaves and trembled blossoms, where there ran
        A brooklet, scarce espied:

'Mid hushed, cool-rooted flowers, fragrant-eyed,
    Blue, silver-white, and budded Tyrian,
They lay calm-breathing on the bedded grass;   15
    Their arms embracéd, and their pinions too;
    Their lips touched not, but had not bade adieu,
As if disjoinéd by soft-handed slumber,
And ready still past kisses to outnumber
      At tender eye-dawn of aurorean love: 20
      The wingéd boy I knew;
    But who wast thou, O happy, happy dove?
      His Psyche true!

O latest born and loveliest vision far
    Of all Olympus' faded hierarchy!   25
Fairer than Phoebe's sapphire-regioned star,
    Or Vesper, amorous glowworm of the sky;
Fairer than these, though temple thou hast none,
      Nor altar heaped with flowers;
Nor virgin-choir to make delicious moan   30
      Upon the midnight hours;
No voice, no lute, no pipe, no incense sweet
    From chain-swung censer teeming;
No shrine, no grove, no oracle, no heat
    Of pale-mouthed prophet dreaming.   35

O brightest! though too late for antique vows,
    Too, too late for the fond believing lyre,
When holy were the haunted forest boughs,
    Holy the air, the water, and the fire;
Yet even in these days so far retired   40

From happy pieties, thy lucent fans,
Fluttering among the faint Olympians,
I see, and sing, by my own eyes inspired.
So let me be thy choir, and make a moan
   Upon the midnight hours;   45
Thy voice, thy lute, thy pipe, thy incense sweet
   From swingéd censer teeming;
Thy shrine, thy grove, thy oracle, thy heat
   Of pale-mouthed prophet dreaming.

Yes, I will be thy priest, and build a fane   50
   In some untrodden region of my mind,
Where branchéd thoughts, new grown with pleasant pain,
   Instead of pines shall murmur in the wind:
Far, far around shall those dark-clustered trees
   Fledge the wild-ridgéd mountains steep by steep;   55
And there by zephyrs, streams, and birds, and bees,
   The moss-lain Dryads shall be lulled to sleep;
And in the midst of this wide quietness
A rosy sanctuary will I dress
With the wreathéd trellis of a working brain,   60
   With buds, and bells, and stars without a name,
With all the gardener Fancy e'er could feign,
   Who, breeding flowers, will never breed the same;
And there shall be for thee all soft delight
   That shadowy thought can win,   65
A bright torch, and a casement ope at night,
   To let the warm Love in! (1819; 1820)

William Cullen Bryant

TO THE FRINGED GENTIAN

Thou blossom bright with autumn dew,
And colored with the heaven's own blue,
That openest when the quiet light
Succeeds the keen and frosty night;

Thou comest not when violets lean   5
O'er wandering brooks and springs unseen,
Or columbines, in purple dressed,
Nod o'er the ground-bird's hidden nest.

Thou waitest late, and com'st alone,
When woods are bare and birds are flown,   10
And frosts and shortening days portend
The aged year is near his end.

Then doth thy sweet and quiet eye
Look through its fringes to the sky,
Blue—blue—as if that sky let fall   15
A flower from its cerulean wall.

I would that thus, when I shall see
The hour of death draw near to me,
Hope, blossoming within my heart,
May look to heaven as I depart. (1829)   20

Ralph Waldo Emerson

THE RHODORA:

On Being Asked, Whence Is the Flower?

In May, when sea-winds pierced our solitudes,
I found the fresh rhodora in the woods,
Spreading its leafless blooms in a damp nook,
To please the desert and the sluggish brook.
The purple petals, fallen in the pool,   5
Made the black water with their beauty gay;
Here might the red-bird come his plumes to cool,
And court the flower that cheapens his array.
Rhodora! if the sages ask thee why
This charm is wasted on the earth and sky,   10
Tell them, dear, that if eyes were made for seeing,
Then Beauty is its own excuse for being:
Why thou wert there, O rival of the rose!
I never thought to ask, I never knew:
But, in my simple ignorance, suppose   15
The self-same Power that brought me there brought you. (1834; 1839)

EACH AND ALL

Little thinks, in the field, yon red-cloaked clown
Of thee from the hill-top looking down;

The heifer that lows in the upland farm,
Far-heard, lows not thine ear to charm;
The sexton, tolling his bell at noon,
Deems not that great Napoleon
Stops his horse, and lists with delight,
Whilst his files sweep round yon Alpine height;
Nor knowest thou what argument
Thy life to thy neighbor's creed has lent.
All are needed by each one;
Nothing is fair or good alone.
I thought the sparrow's note from heaven,
Singing at dawn on the alder bough;
I brought him home, in his nest, at even;
He sings the song, but it cheers not now,
For I did not bring home the river and sky;—
He sang to my ear,—they sang to my eye.
The delicate shells lay on the shore;
The bubbles of the latest wave
Fresh pearls to their enamel gave,
And the bellowing of the savage sea
Greeted their safe escape to me.
I wiped away the weeds and foam,
I fetched my sea-born treasures home;
But the poor, unsightly, noisome things
Had left their beauty on the shore
With the sun and the sand and the wild uproar.
The lover watched his graceful maid,
As 'mid the virgin train she strayed,
Nor knew her beauty's best attire
Was woven still by the snow-white choir.
At last she came to his hermitage,
Like the bird from the woodlands to the cage;—
The gay enchantment was undone,
A gentle wife, but fairy none.
Then I said, "I covet truth;
Beauty is unripe childhood's cheat;
I leave it behind with the games of youth":—
As I spoke, beneath my feet
The ground-pine curled its pretty wreath,
Running over the club-moss burrs;
I inhaled the violet's breath;
Around me stood the oaks and firs;
Pine-cones and acorns lay on the ground;
Over me soared the eternal sky,
Full of light and of deity;

Again I saw, again I heard,
The rolling river, the morning bird;—
Beauty through my senses stole; 50
I yielded myself to the perfect whole. (1834?; 1839)

DAYS

Daughters of Time, the hypocritic Days,
Muffled and dumb like barefoot dervishes,
And marching single in an endless file,
Bring diadems and fagots in their hands.
To each they offer gifts after his will, 5
Bread, kingdoms, stars, and sky that holds them all.
I, in my pleached garden, watched the pomp,
Forgot my morning wishes, hastily
Took a few herbs and apples, and the Day
Turned and departed silent. I, too late, 10
Under her solemn fillet saw the scorn. (1852?; 1857)

Edgar Allan Poe

TO HELEN

Helen, thy beauty is to me
  Like those Nicean barks of yore,
That gently, o'er a perfumed sea,
  The weary, wayworn wanderer bore
  To his own native shore. 5

On desperate seas long wont to roam,
  Thy hyacinth hair, thy classic face,
Thy Naiad airs, have brought me home
  To the glory that was Greece
And the grandeur that was Rome. 10

Lo! in yon brilliant window-niche
  How statue-like I see thee stand,

The agate lamp within thy hand!
Ah, Psyche, from the regions which
Are Holy Land! (1831)   15

THE CITY IN THE SEA

Lo! Death has reared himself a throne
In a strange city lying alone
Far down within the dim West,
Where the good and the bad and the worst and the best
Have gone to their eternal rest.   5
There shrines and palaces and towers
(Time-eaten towers that tremble not)
Resemble nothing that is ours.
Around, by lifting winds forgot,
Resignedly beneath the sky   10
The melancholy waters lie.

No rays from the holy heaven come down
On the long night-time of that town;
But light from out the lurid sea
Streams up the turrets silently,   15
Gleams up the pinnacles far and free:
Up domes, up spires, up kingly halls;
Up fanes, up Babylon-like walls,
Up shadowy long-forgotten bowers
Of sculptured ivy and stone flowers,   20
Up many and many a marvelous shrine
Whose wreathed friezes intertwine
The viol, the violet, and the vine.

Resignedly beneath the sky
The melancholy waters lie.   25
So blend the turrets and shadows there
That all seem pendulous in air,
While from a proud tower in the town
Death looks gigantically down.

There open fanes and gaping graves   30
Yawn level with the luminous waves;
But not the riches there that lie
In each idol's diamond eye,—
Not the gayly-jewelled dead,
Tempt the waters from their bed;   35

For no ripples curl, alas,
Along that wilderness of glass;
No swellings tell that winds may be
Upon some far-off happier sea;
No heavings hint that winds have been   40
On seas less hideously serene!

But lo, a stir is in the air!
The wave—there is a movement there!
As if the towers had thrust aside,
In slightly sinking, the dull tide;   45
As if their tops had feebly given
A void within the filmy Heaven!
The waves have now a redder glow,
The hours are breathing faint and low;
And when, amid no earthly moans,   50
Down, down that town shall settle hence,
Hell, rising from a thousand thrones,
Shall do it reverence. (1831; 1845)

Alfred, Lord Tennyson

TITHONUS

The woods decay, the woods decay and fall,
The vapors weep their burthen to the ground,
Man comes and tills the field and lies beneath,
And after many a summer dies the swan.
Me only cruel immortality   5
Consumes: I wither slowly in thine arms,
Here at the quiet limit of the world,
A white-hair'd shadow roaming like a dream
The ever-silent spaces of the East,
Far-folded mists, and gleaming halls of morn.   10

Alas! for this gray shadow, once a man—
So glorious in his beauty and thy choice,
Who madest him thy chosen, that he seem'd
To his great heart none other than a God!
I ask'd thee, "Give me immortality."   15

Then didst thou grant mine asking with a smile,
Like wealthy men who care not how they give.
But thy strong Hours indignant work'd their wills,
And beat me down and marr'd and wasted me
And tho' they could not end me, left me maim'd   20
To dwell in presence of immortal youth,
Immortal age beside immortal youth,
And all I was, in ashes. Can thy love,
Thy beauty, make amends, tho' even now,
Close over us, the silver star, thy guide,   25
Shines in those tremulous eyes that fill with tears
To hear me? Let me go: take back thy gift:
Why should a man desire in any way
To vary from the kindly race of men,
Or pass beyond the goal of ordinance   30
Where all should pause, as is most meet for all?

   A soft air fans the cloud apart; there comes
A glimpse of that dark world where I was born.
Once more the old mysterious glimmer steals
From thy pure brows, and from thy shoulders pure,   35
And bosom beating with a heart renew'd.
Thy cheek begins to redden thro' the gloom,
Thy sweet eyes brighten slowly close to mine,
Ere yet they blind the stars, and the wild team
Which love thee, yearning for thy yoke, arise,   40
And shake the darkness from their loosen'd manes,
And beat the twilight into flakes of fire.

   Lo! ever thus thou growest beautiful
In silence, then before thine answer given
Departest, and thy tears are on my cheek.   45
   Why wilt thou ever scare me with thy tears,
And make me tremble lest a saying learnt,
In days far-off, on that dark earth, be true?
"The Gods themselves cannot recall their gifts."

   Ay me! ay me! with what another heart   50
In days far-off, and with what other eyes
I used to watch—if I be he that watch'd—
The lucid outline forming round thee; saw
The dim curls kindle into sunny rings;
Changed with thy mystic change, and felt my blood   55
Glow with the glow that slowly crimson'd all
Thy presence and thy portals, while I lay,

Mouth, forehead, eyelids, growing dewy-warm
With kisses balmier than half-opening buds
Of April, and could hear the lips that kiss'd   60
Whispering I knew not what of wild and sweet,
Like that strange song I heard Apollo sing,
While Ilion like a mist rose into towers.

　　Yet hold me not for ever in thine East:
How can my nature longer mix with thine?   65
Coldly thy rosy shadows bathe me, cold
Are all thy lights, and cold my wrinkled feet
Upon thy glimmering thresholds, when the steam
Floats up from those dim fields about the homes
Of happy men that have the power to die,   70
And grassy barrows of the happier dead.
Release me, and restore me to the ground;
Thou seëst all things, thou wilt see my grave:
Thou wilt renew thy beauty morn by morn;
I earth in earth forget these empty courts,   75
And thee returning on thy silver wheels. (c. 1842; 1860)

Robert Browning

SOLILOQUY OF
THE SPANISH CLOISTER

Gr-r-r—there go, my heart's abhorrence!
　　Water your damned flower-pots, do!
If hate killed men, Brother Lawrence,
　　God's blood, would not mine kill you!
What? your myrtle-bush wants trimming?   5
　　Oh, that rose has prior claims—
Needs its leaden vase filled brimming?
　　Hell dry you up with its flames!

At the meal we sit together:
　　Salve tibi! I must hear   10
Wise talk of the kind of weather,

Sort of season, time of year:
Not a plenteous cork-crop: scarcely
  Dare we hope oak-galls, I doubt:
What's the Latin name for "parsley"?   15
  What's the Greek name for Swine's Snout?

Whew! We'll have our platter burnished,
  Laid with care on our own shelf!
With a fire-new spoon we're furnished,
  And a goblet for ourself,   20
Rinsed like something sacrificial
  Ere 'tis fit to touch our chaps—
Marked with L for our initial!
  (He-he! There his lily snaps!)

Saint, forsooth! While brown Dolores   25
  Squats outside the Convent bank
With Sanchicha, telling stories,
  Steeping tresses in the tank,
Blue-black, lustrous, thick like horsehairs,
  —Can't I see his dead eye glow,   30
Bright as 'twere a Barbary corsair's?
  (That is, if he'd let it show!)

When he finishes refection,
  Knife and fork he never lays
Cross-wise, to my recollection,   35
  As do I, in Jesu's praise.
I the Trinity illustrate,
  Drinking watered orange-pulp—
In three sips the Arian frustrate;
  While he drains his at one gulp.   40

Oh, those melons! If he's able
  We're to have a feast! so nice!
One goes to the Abbot's table,
  All of us get each a slice.
How go on your flowers? None double?   45
  Not one fruit-sort can you spy?
Strange!—And I, too, at such trouble
  Keep them close-nipped on the sly!

There's a great text in Galatians,
  Once you trip on it, entails   50
Twenty-nine distinct damnations,

One sure, if another fails:
If I trip him just a-dying,
    Sure of heaven as sure can be,
Spin him round and send him flying   55
    Off to hell, a Manichee?

Or, my scrofulous French novel
    On gray paper with blunt type!
Simply glance at it, you grovel
    Hand and foot in Belial's gripe: 60
If I double down its pages
    At the woeful sixteenth print,
When he gathers his greengages,
    Ope a sieve and slip it in't?

Or, there's Satan!—one might venture   65
    Pledge one's soul to him, yet leave
Such a flaw in the indenture
    As he'd miss till, past retrieve,
Blasted lay that rose-acacia
    We're so proud of! *Hy, Zy, Hine.* . . .   70
'St, there's Vespers! *Plena, gratiâ,*
    Ave, Virgo! Gr-r-r—you swine! (1842)

Walt Whitman

ONE'S-SELF I SING

One's-self I sing, a simple separate person,
Yet utter the word Democratic, the word En-Masse.

Of physiology from top to toe I sing,
Not physiognomy alone nor brain alone is worthy for the Muse,
    I say the Form complete is worthier far,
The Female equally with the Male I sing.   5

Of Life immense in passion, pulse, and power,
Cheerful, for freest action form'd under the laws divine,
The Modern Man I sing. (1867; 1871)

ONCE I PASS'D
THROUGH A POPULOUS CITY

Once I pass'd through a populous city imprinting my brain for future use
   with its shows, architecture, customs, traditions,
Yet now of all that city I remember only a woman I casually met there
   who detain'd me for love of me,
Day by day and night by night we were together—all else has long been
   forgotten by me,
I remember I say only that woman who passionately clung to me,
Again she holds me by the hand, I must not go,   5
I see her close beside me with silent lips sad and tremulous. (1860; 1867)

I SAW IN LOUISIANA
A LIVE-OAK GROWING

I saw in Louisiana a live-oak growing,
All alone stood it and the moss hung down from the branches,
Without any companion it grew there uttering joyous leaves of dark green,
And its look, rude, unbending, lusty, made me think of myself,
But I wonder'd how it could utter joyous leaves standing alone there with-
   out its friend near, for I knew I could not,   5
And I broke off a twig with a certain number of leaves upon it, and
   twined around it a little moss,
And brought it away, and I have placed it in sight in my room,
It is not needed to remind me as of my own dear friends,
(For I believe lately I think of little else than of them,)
Yet it remains to me a curious token, it makes me think of manly love;   10
For all that, and though the live-oak glistens there in Louisiana solitary in
   a wide flat space,
Uttering joyous leaves all its life without a friend, a lover near,
I know very well I could not. (1860)

WHEN LILACS LAST
IN THE DOORYARD BLOOM'D

I

When lilacs last in the dooryard bloom'd,
And the great star early droop'd in the western sky in the night,
I mourn'd, and yet shall mourn with ever-returning spring.

Ever-returning spring, trinity sure to me you bring,
Lilac blooming perennial and drooping star in the west,   5
And thought of him I love.

II

O powerful western fallen star!
O shades of night—O moody, tearful night!
O great star disappear'd—O the black murk that hides the star!
O cruel hands that hold me powerless—O helpless soul of me!   10
O harsh surrounding cloud that will not free my soul.

III

In the dooryard fronting an old farm-house near the white-wash'd palings,
Stands the lilac-bush, tall-growing with heart-shaped leaves of rich green,
With many a pointed blossom rising delicate, with the perfume strong I
    love,
With every leaf a miracle—and from this bush in the dooryard,   15
With delicate-color'd blossoms and heart-shaped leaves of rich green,
A sprig with its flower I break.

IV

In the swamp in secluded recesses,
A shy and hidden bird is warbling a song.

Solitary the thrush,   20
The hermit withdrawn to himself, avoiding the settlements,
Sings by himself a song.

Song of the bleeding throat,
Death's outlet song of life (for well dear brother I know,
If thou wast not granted to sing thou would'st surely die).   25

V

Over the breast of the spring, the land, amid cities,
Amid lanes and through old woods, where lately the violets peep'd from
    the ground, spotting the gray débris,
Amid the grass in the fields each side of the lanes, passing the endless
    grass;
Passing the yellow-spear'd wheat, every grain from its shroud in the dark-
    brown fields uprisen,
Passing the apple-tree blows of white and pink in the orchards,   30
Carrying a corpse to where it shall rest in the grave,
Night and day journeys a coffin.

VI

Coffin that passes through lanes and streets,
Through day and night with the great cloud darkening the land,
With the pomp of the inloop'd flags, with the cities draped in black,   35
With the show of the States themselves as of crape-veil'd women standing,
With processions long and winding and the flambeaus of the night,

With the countless torches lit, with the silent sea of faces and the unbared
heads,
With the waiting depot, the arriving coffin, and the somber faces,
With dirges through the night, with the thousand voices rising strong and
solemn,   40
With all the mournful voices of the dirges pour'd around the coffin,
The dim-lit churches and the shuddering organs—where amid these you
journey,
With the tolling tolling bell's perpetual clang,
Here, coffin that slowly passes,
I give you my sprig of lilac.   45

VII

(Nor for you, for one alone,
Blossoms and branches green to coffins all I bring.
For fresh as the morning, thus would I carol a song to you O sane and
sacred death.

All over bouquets of roses,
O death, I cover you over with roses and early lilies,   50
But mostly and now the lilac that blooms the first,
Copious I break, I break the sprigs from the bushes.
With loaded arms I come, pouring for you,
For you and the coffins all of you O death.)

VIII

O western orb sailing the heaven,   55
Now I know what you must have meant as a month since I walk'd,
As I walk'd in silence the transparent shadowy night,
As I saw you had something to tell as you bent to me night after night,
As you droop'd from the sky low down as if to my side (while the other
stars all look'd on),
As we wander'd together the solemn night (for something I know not
what kept me from sleep),   60
As the night advanced, and I saw on the rim of the west how full you
were of woe,
As I stood on the rising ground in the breeze in the cold transparent night,
As I watch'd where you pass'd and was lost in the netherward black of the
night,
As my soul in its trouble dissatisfied sank, as where you sad orb,
Concluded, dropt in the night, and was gone.   65

IX

Sing on there in the swamp,
O singer bashful and tender, I hear your notes, I hear your call,
I hear, I come presently, I understand you,
But a moment I linger, for the lustrous star has detain'd me,
The star my departing comrade holds and detains me.   70

X

O how shall I warble myself for the dead one there I loved?
And how shall I deck my song for the large sweet soul that has gone?
And what shall my perfume be for the grave of him I love?

Sea-winds blown from east and west,
Blown from the Eastern sea and blown from the Western sea till there on
    the prairies meeting: 75
These and with these and the breath of my chant,
I'll perfume the grave of him I love.

XI

O what shall I hang on the chamber walls?
And what shall the pictures be that I hang on the walls,
To adorn the burial-house of him I love?   80

Pictures of growing spring and farms and homes,
With the Fourth-month eve at sundown, and the gray smoke lucid and
    bright,
With floods of the yellow gold of the gorgeous, indolent, sinking sun,
    burning, expanding the air,
With the fresh sweet herbage under foot, and the pale green leaves of the
    trees prolific,
In the distance the flowing glaze, the breast of the river, with a wind-
    dapple here and there;   85
With ranging hills on the banks, with many a line against the sky, and
    shadows;
And the city at hand with dwellings so dense, and stacks of chimneys,
And all the scenes of life and the workshops, and the workmen homeward
    returning.

XII

Lo, body and soul—this land,
My own Manhattan with spires, and the sparkling and hurrying tides,
    and the ships,   90
The varied and ample land, the South and the North in the light—Ohio's
    shores and flashing Missouri,
And ever the far-spreading prairies cover'd with grass and corn.
Lo, the most excellent sun so calm and haughty,
The violet and purple morn with just-felt breezes,
The gentle soft-born measureless light,   95
The miracle spreading bathing all, the fulfill'd noon,
The coming eve delicious, the welcome night and the stars,
Over my cities shining all, enveloping man and land.

XIII

Sing on, sing on you gray-brown bird,
Sing from the swamps, the recesses, pour your chant from the bushes;   100
Limitless out of the dusk, out of the cedars and pines.

Sing on dearest brother, warble your reedy song,
Loud human song, with voice of uttermost woe.

O liquid and free and tender!
O wild and loose to my soul—O wondrous singer!   105
You only I hear—yet the star holds me (but will soon depart,)
Yet the lilac with mastering odor holds me.

XIV

Now while I sat in the day and look'd forth,
In the close of the day with its light and the fields of spring, and the
    farmers preparing their crops,
In the large unconscious scenery of my land with its lakes and forests,   110
In the heavenly aerial beauty (after the perturb'd winds and the storms,)
Under the arching heavens of the afternoon swift passing, and the voices
    of children and women,
The many-moving sea-tides, and I saw the ships how they sail'd,
And the summer approaching with richness, and the fields all busy with
    labor,
And the infinite separate houses, how they all went on, each with its
    meals and minutia of daily usages;   115
And the streets how their throbbings throbb'd, and the cities pent—lo,
    then and there,
Falling upon them all and among them all, enveloping me with the rest,
Appear'd the cloud, appear'd the long black trail;
And I knew death, its thought, and the sacred knowledge of death.

Then with the knowledge of death as walking one side of me,   120
And the thought of death close-walking the other side of me,
And I in the middle as with companions, and as holding the hands of
    companions,
I fled forth to the hiding receiving night that talks not,
Down to the shores of the water, the path by the swamp in the dimness,
To the solemn shadowy cedars and ghostly pines so still.   125

And the singer so shy to the rest receiv'd me,
The gray-brown bird I know receiv'd us comrades three,
And he sang the carol of death, and a verse for him I love.

From deep secluded recesses,
From the fragrant cedars and the ghostly pines so still,   130
Came the carol of the bird.

And the charm of the carol rapt me,
As I held as if by their hands my comrades in the night;
And the voice of my spirit tallied the song of the bird.

Come lovely and soothing death,   135
Undulate round the world, serenely arriving, arriving,
In the day, in the night, to all, to each,
Sooner or later delicate death.

Prais'd be the fathomless universe,
For life and joy, and for objects and knowledge curious,   140
And for love, sweet love—but praise! praise! praise!
For the sure-enwinding arms of cool-enfolding death.

Dark mother always gliding near with soft feet,
Have none chanted for thee a chant of fullest welcome?
Then I chant it for thee, I glorify thee above all,   145
I bring thee a song that when thou must indeed come, come unfalteringly.

Approach strong deliveress,
When it is so, when thou hast taken them, I joyously sing the dead,
Lost in the loving floating ocean of thee,
Laved in the flood of thy bliss O death.   150

From me to thee glad serenades,
Dances for thee I propose saluting thee, adornments and feastings for thee,
And the sights of the open landscape and the high-spread sky are fitting,
And life and the fields, and the huge and thoughtful night.

The night in silence under many a star,   155
The ocean shore and the husky whispering wave whose voice I know,
And the soul turning to thee O vast and well-veil'd death,
And the body gratefully nestling close to thee.

Over the tree-tops I float thee a song,
Over the rising and sinking waves, over the myriad fields and the prairies wide, 160
Over the dense-pack'd cities all and the teeming wharves and ways,
I float this carol with joy, with joy to thee O death!

XV

To the tally of my soul,
Loud and strong kept up the gray-brown bird,
With pure, deliberate notes spreading filling the night.   165

Loud in the pines and cedars dim,
Clear in the freshness moist and the swamp-perfume,
And I with my comrades there in the night.

While my sight that was bound in my eyes unclosed,
As to long panoramas of visions.   170

I saw askant the armies;
And I saw as in noiseless dreams hundreds of battle-flags,
Borne through the smoke of the battles and pierc'd with missiles I saw
   them,
And carried hither and yon through the smoke, and torn and bloody,
And at last but a few shreds left on the staffs (and all in silence,)   175
And the staffs all splinter'd and broken.
I saw battle-corpses, myriads of them,
And the white skeletons of young men, I saw them,
I saw the débris and débris of all the slain soldiers of the war,
But I saw they were not as was thought,   180
They themselves were fully at rest, they suffer'd not,
The living remain'd and suffer'd, the mother suffer'd,
And the wife and the child and the musing comrade suffer'd,
And the armies that remain'd suffer'd.

XVI

Passing the visions, passing the night,   185
Passing, unloosing the hold of my comrades' hands,
Passing the song of the hermit bird and the tallying song of my soul,
Victorious song, death's outlet song, yet varying ever-altering song,
As low and wailing, yet clear the notes, rising and falling, flooding the
   night,
Sadly sinking and fainting, as warning and warning, and yet again burst-
   ing with joy,   190
Covering the earth and filling the spread of the heaven,
As that powerful psalm in the night I heard from recesses,
Passing, I leave thee lilac with heart-shaped leaves,
I leave thee there in the dooryard blooming, returning with spring.

I cease from my song for thee,   195
From my gaze on thee in the west, fronting the west, communing with thee,
O comrade lustrous with silver face in the night.

Yet each I keep and all, retrievements out of the night,
The song, the wondrous chant of the gray-brown bird,
The tallying chant, the echo arous'd in my soul,   200
With the lustrous and drooping star with the countenance full of woe,
With the holders holding my hand hearing the call of the bird,
Comrades mine and I in the midst, and their memory ever to keep, for
   the dead I loved so well,
For the sweetest, wisest soul of all my days and lands—and this for his
   dear sake;
Lilac and star and bird twined with the chant of my soul,   205
There in the fragrant pines and the cedars dusk and dim. (1865; 1881)

Matthew Arnold

DOVER BEACH

The sea is calm tonight,
The tide is full, the moon lies fair
Upon the straits;—on the French coast the light
Gleams and is gone; the cliffs of England stand,
Glimmering and vast, out in the tranquil bay.   5
Come to the window, sweet is the night-air!
Only, from the long line of spray
Where the sea meets the moon-blanched land,
Listen! you hear the grating roar
Of pebbles which the waves draw back, and fling,   10
At their return, up the high strand,
Begin, and cease, and then again begin,
With tremulous cadence slow, and bring
The eternal note of sadness in.

Sophocles long ago   15
Heard it on the Aegean, and it brought
Into his mind the turbid ebb and flow
Of human misery; we
Find also in the sound a thought,
Hearing it by this distant northern sea.   20

The Sea of Faith
Was once, too, at the full, and round earth's shore
Lay like the folds of a bright girdle furled.
But now I only hear
Its melancholy, long, withdrawing roar,   25
Retreating, to the breath
Of the night-wind, down the vast edges drear
And naked shingles of the world.

Ah, love, let us be true
To one another! for the world, which seems   30
To lie before us like a land of dreams,
So various, so beautiful, so new,
Hath really neither joy, nor love, nor light,
Nor certitude, nor peace, nor help for pain;
And we are here as on a darkling plain   35
Swept with confused alarms of struggle and flight,
Where ignorant armies clash by night. (1867)

George Meredith

LUCIFER IN STARLIGHT

On a starred night Prince Lucifer uprose.
Tired of his dark dominion, swung the fiend
Above the rolling ball, in cloud part screened,
Where sinners hugged their specter of repose.
Poor prey to his hot fit of pride were those.   5
And now upon his western wing he leaned,
Now his huge bulk o'er Afric's sands careened,
Now the black planet shadowed Arctic snows.
Soaring through wider zones that pricked his scars
With memory of the old revolt from Awe,   10
He reached a middle height, and at the stars,
Which are the brain of heaven, he looked, and sank.
Around the ancient track marched, rank on rank,
The army of unalterable law. (1883)

Christina Rossetti

A BIRTHDAY

My heart is like a singing bird
  Whose nest is in a watered shoot;
My heart is like an apple-tree
  Whose boughs are bent with thick-set fruit;
My heart is like a rainbow shell   5
  That paddles in a halcyon sea;
My heart is gladder than all these
  Because my love is come to me.

Raise me a dais of silk and down;
  Hang it with vair and purple dyes;   10
Carve it in doves and pomegranates,
  And peacocks with a hundred eyes;
Work it in gold and silver grapes,

In leaves and silver fleurs-de-lys;
Because the birthday of my life   15
Is come, my love is come to me. (1857)

Emily Dickinson

THERE'S A
CERTAIN SLANT OF LIGHT

There's a certain slant of light,
On winter afternoons,
That oppresses, like the weight
Of cathedral tunes.

Heavenly hurt it gives us;   5
We can find no scar,
But internal difference
Where the meanings are.

None may teach it anything,
'Tis the seal, despair,—   10
An imperial affliction
Sent us of the air.

When it comes, the landscape listens,
Shadows hold their breath;
When it goes, 'tis like the distance   15
On the look of death. (1890)

THE CHARIOT

Because I could not stop for Death,
He kindly stopped for me;
The carriage held but just ourselves
And Immortality.

We slowly drove, he knew no haste,   5
And I had put away
My labor and my leisure too,
For his civility.

We passed the school where children played
At wrestling in a ring;   10
We passed the fields of gazing grain,
We passed the setting sun.

We paused before a house that seemed
A swelling of the ground;
The roof was scarcely visible,   15
The cornice but a mound.

Since then 't is centuries; but each
Feels shorter than the day
I first surmised the horses' heads
Were toward eternity. (1890)   20

I NEVER SAW A MOOR

I never saw a moor,
I never saw the sea;
Yet know I how the heather looks,
And what a wave must be.

I never spoke with God,   5
Nor visited in heaven;
Yet certain am I of the spot
As if the chart were given. (1890)

Contemporary Poems

Thomas Hardy

THE DARKLING THRUSH

I leant upon a coppice gate
When Frost was specter-gray,
And Winter's dregs made desolate

The weakening eye of day.
The tangled bine-stems scored the sky   5
  Like strings of broken lyres,
And all mankind that haunted night
  Had sought their household fires.

The land's sharp features seemed to be
  The Century's corpse outleant,   10
His crypt the cloudy canopy,
  The wind his death-lament.
The ancient pulse of germ and birth
  Was shrunken hard and dry,
And every spirit upon earth   15
  Seemed fervorless as I.

At once a voice arose among
  The bleak twigs overhead
In a full-hearted evensong
  Of joy illimited;   20
An aged thrush, frail, gaunt, and small,
  In blast-beruffled plume,
Had chosen thus to fling his soul
  Upon the growing gloom.

So little cause for carolings   25
  Of such ecstatic sound
Was written on terrestrial things
  Afar or nigh around,
That I could think there trembled through
  His happy good-night air   30
Some blessed Hope, whereof he knew
  And I was unaware. (1900)

IN TIME OF
'THE BREAKING OF NATIONS'

I

Only a man harrowing clods
  In a slow silent walk
With an old horse that stumbles and nods
  Half asleep as they stalk.

II

    Only thin smoke without flame   5
       From the heaps of couch-grass;
    Yet this will go onward the same
       Though Dynasties pass.

III

    Yonder a maid and her wight
       Come whispering by: 10
    War's annals will cloud into night
       Ere their story die. (1915)

Gerard Manley Hopkins

THE HABIT OF PERFECTION

Elected Silence, sing to me
And beat upon my whorléd ear;
Pipe me to pastures still and be
The music that I care to hear.

Shape nothing, lips; be lovely-dumb—   5
It is the shut, the curfew sent
From there where all surrenders come
Which only makes you eloquent.

Be shelléd, eyes, with double dark
And find the uncreated light;   10
This ruck and reel which you remark
Coils, keeps, and teases simple sight.

Palate, the hutch of tasty lust,
Desire not to be rinsed with wine;
The can must be so sweet, the crust   15
So fresh that come in fasts divine!

Nostrils, your careless breath that spend
Upon the stir and keep of pride,
What relish shall the censers send
Along the sanctuary side!   20

"The Habit of Perfection" and "I Wake and Feel the Fell of Dark" reprinted from *The Poems of Gerard Manley Hopkins* by permission of the Hopkins family and the Oxford University Press.

O feel-of-primrose hands, O feet
That want the yield of plushy sward,
But you shall walk the golden street
And you unhouse and house the Lord.

And, Poverty, be thou the bride   25
And now the marriage feast begun,
And lily-colored clothes provide
Your spouse not labored-at nor spun. (1866; 1918)

I WAKE AND FEEL
THE FELL OF DARK

I wake and feel the fell of dark, not day.
What hours, O what black hours we have spent
This night! what sights you, heart, saw; ways you went!
And more must, in yet longer light's delay.
　　With witness I speak this. But where I say   5
Hours I mean years, mean life. And my lament
Is cries countless, cries like dead letters sent
To dearest him that lives alas! away.
　　I am gall, I am heartburn. God's most deep decree
Bitter would have me taste: my taste was me;   10
Bones built in me, flesh filled, blood brimmed the curse.
　　Selfyeast of spirit a dull dough sours. I see
The lost are like this, and their scourge to be
As I am mine, their sweating selves; but worse. (1886; 1918)

A. E. Housman

THE TRUE LOVER

The lad came to the door at night,
　　When lovers crown their vows,
And whistled soft and out of sight
　　In shadow of the boughs.

"The True Lover" and "To an Athlete Dying Young" from *A Shropshire Lad* by A. E.
Housman. By permission of the publishers, Henry Holt and Company, Inc., The Society of
Authors as the Literary Representative of the Trustees of the Housman estate, and Messrs.
Jonathon Cape, Ltd., publishers of his *Collected Poems*.

"I shall not vex you with my face   5
   Henceforth, my love, for aye;
So take me in your arms a space
   Before the east is grey.

"When I from hence away am past
   I shall not find a bride,   10
And you shall be the first and last
   I ever lay beside."

She heard and went and knew not why;
   Her heart to his she laid;
Light was the air beneath the sky   15
   But dark under the shade.

"Oh do you breathe, lad, that your breast
   Seems not to rise and fall,
And here upon my bosom prest
   There beats no heart at all?"   20

"Oh loud, my girl, it once would knock,
   You should have felt it then;
But since for you I stopped the clock
   It never goes again."

"Oh lad, what is it, lad, that drips   25
   Wet from your neck on mine?
What is it falling on my lips,
   My lad, that tastes of brine?"

"Oh like enough 'tis blood, my dear,
   For when the knife has slit   30
The throat across from ear to ear
   'Twill bleed because of it."

Under the stars the air was light
   But dark below the boughs,
The still air of the speechless night,   35
   When lovers crown their vows. (1896)

TO AN ATHLETE DYING YOUNG

The time you won your town the race
We chaired you through the market-place;

Man and boy stood cheering by,
And home we brought you shoulder-high.

Today, the road all runners come,   5
Shoulder-high we bring you home,
And set you at your threshold down,
Townsman of a stiller town.

Smart lad, to slip betimes away
From fields where glory does not stay   10
And early though the laurel grows
It withers quicker than the rose.

Eyes the shady night has shut
Cannot see the record cut,
And silence sounds no worse than cheers   15
After earth has stopped the ears.

Now you will not swell the rout
Of lads that wore their honors out,
Runners whom renown outran
And the name died before the man.   20

So set, before its echoes fade,
The fleet foot on the sill of shade,
And hold to the low lintel up
The still-defended challenge-cup.

And round that early-laureled head   25
Will flock to gaze the strengthless dead,
And find unwithered on its curls
The garland briefer than a girl's. (1895; 1896)

William Butler Yeats

SAILING TO BYZANTIUM

That is no country for old men. The young
In one another's arms, birds in the trees
—Those dying generations—at their song,

The salmon-falls, the mackerel-crowded seas,
Fish, flesh, or fowl, commend all summer long   5
Whatever is begotten, born, and dies.
Caught in that sensual music all neglect
Monuments of unageing intellect.

An aged man is but a paltry thing,
A tattered coat upon a stick, unless   10
Soul clap its hands and sing, and louder sing
For every tatter in its mortal dress,
Nor is there singing school but studying
Monuments of its own magnificence;
And therefore I have sailed the seas and come   15
To the holy city of Byzantium.

O sages standing in God's holy fire
As in the gold mosaic of a wall,
Come from the holy fire, perne in a gyre,
And be the singing-masters of my soul.   20
Consume my heart away; sick with desire
And fastened to a dying animal
It knows not what it is; and gather me
Into the artifice of eternity.

Once out of nature I shall never take   25
My bodily form from any natural thing,
But such a form as Grecian goldsmiths make
Of hammered gold and gold enameling
To keep a drowsy Emperor awake;
Or set upon a golden bough to sing   30
To lords and ladies of Byzantium
Of what is past, or passing, or to come. (1928)

AMONG SCHOOL CHILDREN

I

I walk through the long schoolroom questioning;
A kind old nun in a white hood replies;
The children learn to cipher and to sing,
To study reading-books and history,
To cut and sew, be neat in everything   5
In the best modern way—the children's eyes

In momentary wonder stare upon
A sixty-year-old smiling public man.

II

I dream of a Ledaean body, bent
Above a sinking fire, a tale that she   10
Told of a harsh reproof, or trivial event
That changed some childish day to tragedy—
Told, and it seemed that our two natures blent
Into a sphere from youthful sympathy,
Or else, to alter Plato's parable,   15
Into the yolk and white of one shell.

III

And thinking of that fit of grief or rage
I look upon one child or t'other there
And wonder if she stood so at that age—
For even daughters of the swan can share   20
Something of every paddler's heritage—
And had that color upon cheek or hair,
And thereupon my heart is driven wild:
She stands before me as a living child.

IV

Her present image floats into the mind—   25
Did Quattrocento finger fashion it
Hollow of cheek as though it drank the wind
And took a mess of shadows for its meat?
And I though never of Ledaean kind
Had pretty plumage once—enough of that,   30
Better to smile on all that smile, and show
There is a comfortable kind of old scarecrow.

V

What youthful mother, a shape upon her lap
Honey of generation had betrayed,
And that must sleep, shriek, struggle to escape   35
As recollection or the drug decide,
Would think her son, did she but see that shape
With sixty or more winters on its head,
A compensation for the pang of his birth,
Or the uncertainty of his setting forth?   40

VI

Plato thought nature but a spume that plays
Upon a ghostly paradigm of things;
Solider Aristotle played the taws
Upon the bottom of a king of kings;
World-famous golden-thighed Pythagoras   45
Fingered upon a fiddle-stick or strings

What a star sang and careless Muses heard:
Old clothes upon old sticks to scare a bird.

VII

Both nuns and mothers worship images,
But those the candles light are not as those   50
That animate a mother's reveries,
But keep a marble or a bronze repose.
And yet they too break hearts—O Presences
That passion, piety or affection knows,
And that all heavenly glory symbolize—   55
O self-born mockers of man's enterprise;

VIII

Labor is blossoming or dancing where
The body is not bruised to pleasure soul,
Nor beauty born out of its own despair,
Nor blear-eyed wisdom out of midnight oil.   60
O chestnut tree, great rooted blossomer,
Are you the leaf, the blossom or the bole?
O body swayed to music, O brightening glance,
How can we know the dancer from the dance? (1903)

Edwin Arlington Robinson

MINIVER CHEEVY

Miniver Cheevy, child of scorn,
　　Grew lean while he assailed the seasons;
He wept that he was ever born,
　　And he had reasons.

Miniver loved the days of old   5
　　When swords were bright and steeds were prancing.
The vision of a warrior bold
　　Would set him dancing.

Miniver sighed for what was not,
　　And dreamed, and rested from his labors;   10
He dreamed of Thebes and Camelot,
　　And Priam's neighbors.

Miniver mourned the ripe renown
　　That made so many a name so fragrant:

He mourned Romance, now on the town,   15
    And Art, a vagrant.

Miniver loved the Medici,
    Albeit he had never seen one;
He would have sinned incessantly
    Could he have been one.   20

Miniver cursed the commonplace
    And eyed a khaki suit with loathing;
He missed the mediæval grace
    Of iron clothing.

Miniver scorned the gold he sought,   25
    But sore annoyed was he without it;
Miniver thought, and thought, and thought,
    And thought about it.

Miniver Cheevy, born too late,
    Scratched his head and kept on thinking: 30
Miniver coughed, and called it fate,
    And kept on drinking. (1907)

Walter de la Mare

THE LISTENERS

"Is there anybody there?" said the Traveller,
    Knocking on the moonlit door;
And his horse in the silence champed the grasses
    Of the forest's ferny floor:
And a bird flew up out of a turret,   5
    Above the Traveller's head:
And he smote upon the door again a second time;
    "Is there anybody there?" he said.
But no one descended to the Traveller;
    No head from the leaf-fringed sill   10
Leaned over and looked into his grey eyes,
    Where he stood perplexed and still.
But only a host of phantom listeners
    That dwelt in the lone house then

Stood listening in the quiet of the moonlight   15
    To that voice from the world of men:
Stood thronging the faint moonbeams on the dark stair,
    That goes down to the empty hall,
Hearkening in an air stirred and shaken
    By the lonely Traveller's call.   20
And he felt in his heart their strangeness,
    Their stillness answering his cry,
While his horse moved, cropping the dark turf,
    'Neath the starred and leafy sky;
For he suddenly smote on the door, even   25
    Louder, and lifted his head:—
"Tell them I came, and no one answered,
    That I kept my word," he said.
Never the least stir made the listeners,
    Though every word he spake   30
Fell echoing through the shadowiness of the still house
    From the one man left awake:
Aye, they heard his foot upon the stirrup,
    And the sound of iron on stone,
And how the silence surged softly backward,   35
    When the plunging hoofs were gone. (1912)

Robert Frost

AFTER APPLE-PICKING

My long two-pointed ladder's sticking through a tree
Toward heaven still,
And there's a barrel that I didn't fill
Beside it, and there may be two or three
Apples I didn't pick upon some bough.   5
But I am done with apple-picking now.
Essence of winter sleep is on the night,
The scent of apples: I am drowsing off.
I cannot rub the strangeness from my sight
I got from looking through a pane of glass   10
I skimmed this morning from the drinking trough
And held against the world of hoary grass.
It melted, and I let it fall and break.

But I was well
Upon my way to sleep before it fell,   15
And I could tell
What form my dreaming was about to take.
Magnified apples appear and disappear,
Stem end and blossom end,
And every fleck of russet showing clear.   20
My instep arch not only keeps the ache,
It keeps the pressure of a ladder-round.
I feel the ladder sway as the boughs bend.
And I keep hearing from the cellar bin
The rumbling sound   25
Of load on load of apples coming in.
For I have had too much
Of apple-picking: I am overtired
Of the great harvest I myself desired.
There were ten thousand thousand fruit to touch,   30
Cherish in hand, lift down, and not let fall.
For all
That struck the earth,
No matter if not bruised or spiked with stubble,
Went surely to the cider-apple heap   35
As of no worth.
One can see what will trouble
This sleep of mine, whatever sleep it is.
Were he not gone,
The woodchuck could say whether it's like his   40
Long sleep, as I describe its coming on,
Or just some human sleep. (1913; 1914)

John Masefield

ON GROWING OLD

Be with me, Beauty, for the fire is dying,
My dog and I are old, too old for roving,
Man, whose young passion sets the spindrift flying
Is soon too lame to march, too cold for loving.

I take the book and gather to the fire,   5
Turning old yellow leaves; minute by minute,

The clock ticks to my heart; a withered wire
Moves a thin ghost of music in the spinet.

I cannot sail your seas, I cannot wander
Your cornland, nor your hill-land nor your valleys,   10
Ever again, nor share the battle yonder
Where the young knight the broken squadron rallies.

Only stay quiet while my mind remembers
The beauty of fire from the beauty of embers.
Beauty, have pity, for the strong have power,   15
The rich their wealth, the beautiful their grace,
Summer of man its sunlight and its flower,
Springtime of man all April in a face.

Only, as in the jostling in the Strand,
Where the mob thrusts or loiters or is loud   20
The beggar with the saucer in his hand
Asks only a penny from the passing crowd,

So, from this glittering world with all its fashion,
Its fire and play of men, its stir, its march,
Let me have wisdom, Beauty, wisdom and passion,   25
Bread to the soul, rain where the summers parch.

Give me but these, and though the darkness close
Even the night will blossom as the rose. (1922)

Vachel Lindsay

THE LEADEN-EYED

Let not young souls be smothered out before
They do quaint deeds and fully flaunt their pride.
It is the world's one crime its babes grow dull,
Its poor are ox-like, limp and leaden-eyed.
Not that they starve, but starve so dreamlessly;   5
Not that they sow, but that they seldom reap;
Not that they serve, but have no gods to serve;
Not that they die, but that they die like sheep. (1912)

Sara Teasdale

THE LONG HILL

I must have passed the crest a while ago
    And now I am going down—
Strange to have crossed the crest and not to know,
    But the brambles were always catching the hem of my gown.

All the morning I thought how proud I should be   5
    To stand there straight as a queen,
Wrapped in the wind and the sun with the world under me—
    But it's no use now to think of turning back,

It was nearly level along the beaten track
    And the brambles caught in my gown—   10
But it's no use now to think of turning back,
    The rest of the way will be only going down. (1920)

Elinor Wylie

VELVET SHOES

Let us walk in the white snow
    In a soundless space;
With footsteps quiet and slow,
    At a tranquil pace,
    Under veils of white lace.   5

I shall go shod in silk,
    And you in wool,
White as a white cow's milk,
    More beautiful
    Than the breast of a gull.   10

We shall walk through the still town
    In a windless peace;
We shall step upon white down,
    Upon silver fleece,
    Upon softer than these.   15

We shall walk in velvet shoes:
  Wherever we go
Silence will fall like dews
  On white silence below.
  We shall walk in the snow. (1921) 20

Leonard Bacon

AN AFTERNOON
IN ARTILLERY WALK

(Mary Milton loquitur)

I think it is his blindness makes him so.
He is so angry, and so querulous.
Yes, Father! I will look in Scaliger.
Yes, Cousin Phillips took the notes—I think—
May all the evil angels fly away   5
With Cousin Phillips to the Serbonian Bog,
Wherever that may be. And here am I
Locked in with him the livelong afternoon.
There's Anne gone limping with that love of hers,
Her master-carpenter, and Deborah   10
Stolen away. Yes, Father, 'tis an aleph
But the Greek glose on't in the Septuagint
Is something that I cannot quite make out.
The letter's rubbed.
        Oh, thus to wear away   15
My soul and body with this dry-as-dust
This tearer-up of words, this plaguey seeker
After the things that no man understands.
'Tis April. I am seventeen years old,
And Abram Clark will come a-courting me.   20
Oh what a Hell a midday house can be!
Dusty and bright and dumb and shadowless,
Full of this sunshot dryness, like the soul
Of this old pedant here. I will not bear
Longer this tyranny of death in life   25
That drains my spirit like a succubus.
I am too full of blood and life for this—
This dull soul-gnawing discipline he sets

Upon our shoulders, the sad characters.
Chapter on chapter, blank and meaningless.   30
Now by the May-pole merry-makers run,
And the music throbs and pulses in light limbs,
And the girls' kirtles are lifted to the knee.
Ah would that I were blowsy with the heat,
Being bussed by some tall fellow, and kissing him   35
On his hot red lips—some bully royalist
With gold in's purse and lace about his throat
And a long rapier for the Puritans.
Or I would wander by some cool yew-hedge,
Dallying with my lover all the afternoon,   40
And then to cards and supper—cinnamon,
Some delicate pastry, and an amber wine
Burning on these lips that know a year-long lent.
Then to the theatre, and Mistress Nell
That the king's fond of. Mayhap gentlemen   45
About would praise me, and I should hear them buzz,
And feel my cheek grow warm beneath my mask,
And glance most kindly—
      I was in a muse
I have the paper, father, and the pens.   50
Now for the damnable dictation. So!
"High—on a throne—of royal state—which far
Outshone—the wealth of Ormus"—S or Z?
How should I know the letter?—*"and of Ind.*   55
Or where—the gorgeous East—with richest hand
Showers—on her kings—barbaric—pearl and gold.
Satan exalted sate." (1927)

Marianne Moore

POETRY

I, too, dislike it: there are things that are important beyond all this fiddle.
  Reading it, however, with a perfect contempt for it, one discovers in
  it after all, a place for the genuine.
    Hands that can grasp, eyes
      that can dilate, hair that can rise   5
        if it must, these things are important not because a

high-sounding interpretation can be put upon them but because they are
  useful. When they become so derivative as to become unintelligible,
  the same thing may be said for all of us, that we
    do not admire what 10
      we cannot understand: the bat
        holding on upside down or in quest of something to

eat, elephants pushing, a wild horse taking a roll, a tireless wolf under
  a tree, the immovable critic twitching his skin like a horse that feels a
    flea, the base-
  ball fan, the statistician— 15
    nor is it valid
      to discriminate against 'business documents and

school-books'; all these phenomena are important. One must make a dis-
    tinction
  however: when dragged into prominence by half poets, the result is not
    poetry,
  nor till the poets among us can be 20
    'literalists of
    the imagination'—above
      insolence and triviality and can present

for inspection, 'imaginary gardens with real toads in them,' shall we have
  it. In the meantime, if you demand on the one hand, 25
  the raw material of poetry in
    all its rawness and
    that which is on the other hand
      genuine, you are interested in poetry. (1935)

John Crowe Ransom

BELLS FOR

JOHN WHITESIDE'S DAUGHTER

There was such speed in her little body,
And such lightness in her footfall,
It is no wonder that her brown study
Astonishes us all.

Her wars were bruited in our high window.   5
We looked among orchard trees and beyond,
Where she took arms against her shadow,
Or harried unto the pond

The lazy geese, like a snow cloud
Dripping their snow on the green grass,   10
Tricking and stopping, sleepy and proud,
Who cried in goose, Alas,

For the tireless heart within the little
Lady with rod that made them rise
From their noon apple-dreams, and scuttle   15
Goose-fashion under the skies!

But now go the bells, and we are ready;
In one house we are sternly stopped
To say we are vexed at her brown study,
Lying so primly propped. (1923)   20

T. S. Eliot

SWEENEY AMONG THE NIGHTINGALES

ὤμοι πέπληγμαι καιρίαν πληγὴν ἔσω.[1]

Apeneck Sweeney spreads his knees
Letting his arms hang down to laugh,
The zebra stripes along his jaw
Swelling to maculate giraffe.

The circles of the stormy moon   5
Slide westward toward the River Plate,
Death and the Raven drift above
And Sweeney guards the hornèd gate.

Gloomy Orion and the Dog
Are veiled; and hushed the shrunken seas;   10
The person in the Spanish cape
Tries to sit on Sweeney's knees

1. Alas! I am stricken by a timely blow within (from the drama *Agamemnon* of Aeschylus).

Slips and pulls the table cloth
Overturns a coffee-cup,
Reorganized upon the floor   15
She yawns and draws a stocking up;

The silent man in mocha brown
Sprawls at the window-sill and gapes;
The waiter brings in oranges
Bananas, figs and hothouse grapes;   20

The silent vertebrate in brown
Contracts and concentrates, withdraws;
Rachel *née* Rabinovitch
Tears at the grapes with murderous paws;

She and the lady in the cape   25
Are suspect, thought to be in league;
Therefore the man with heavy eyes
Declines the gambit, shows fatigue,

Leaves the room and reappears
Outside the window, leaning in,   30
Branches of wistaria
Circumscribe a golden grin;

The host with someone indistinct
Converses at the door apart,
The nightingales are singing near   35
The Convent of the Sacred Heart,

And sang within the bloody wood
When Agamemnon cried aloud,
And let their liquid siftings fall
To stain the stiff dishonoured shroud. (1919) 40

Archibald MacLeish

YOU, ANDREW MARVELL

And here face down beneath the sun,
And here upon earth's noonward height,

To feel the always coming on,
The always rising of the night.

To feel creep up the curving east   5
The earthly chill of dusk and slow
Upon those under lands the vast
And ever-climbing shadow grow,

And strange at Ecbatan the trees
Take leaf by leaf the evening, strange,   10
The flooding dark about their knees,
The mountains over Persia change,

And now at Kermanshah the gate,
Dark, empty, and the withered grass,
And through the twilight now the late   15
Few travellers in the westward pass.

And Baghdad darken and the bridge
Across the silent river gone,
And through Arabia the edge
Of evening widen and steal on,   20

And deepen on Palmyra's street
The wheel rut in the ruined stone,
And Lebanon fade out and Crete
High through the clouds and overblown,

And over Sicily the air   25
Still flashing with the landward gulls,
And loom and slowly disappear
The sails above the shadowy hulls,

And Spain go under and the shore
Of Africa, the gilded sand,   30
And evening vanish and no more
The low pale light across that land,

Nor now the long light on the sea—
And here face downward in the sun
To feel how swift, how secretly,   35
The shadow of the night comes on. . . . (1926; 1930)

Hart Crane

AT MELVILLE'S TOMB

Often beneath the wave, wide from this ledge
The dice of drowned men's bones he saw bequeath
An embassy. Their numbers as he watched,
Beat on the dusty shore and were obscured.

And wrecks passed without sounds of bells,   5
The calyx of death's bounty giving back
A scattered chapter, livid hieroglyph,
The portent wound in corridors of shells.

Then in the circuit calm of one vast coil,
Its lashings charmed and malice reconciled,   10
Frosted eyes there were that lifted altars;
And silent answers crept across the stars.

Compass, quadrant and sextant contrive
No farther tides . . . High in the azure steeps
Monody shall not wake the mariner.   15
This fabulous shadow only the sea keeps. (1930)

Léonie Adams

COUNTRY SUMMER

Now the rich cherry whose sleek wood
And top with silver petals traced,
Like a strict box its gems encased,
Has spilt from out that cunning lid,
All in an innocent green round,   5
Those melting rubies which it hid;
With moss ripe-strawberry-encrusted,
So birds get half, and minds lapse merry
To taste that deep-red lark's-bite berry,
And blackcap-bloom is yellow-dusted.   10

The wren that thieved it in the eaves
A trailer of the rose could catch
To her poor droopy sloven thatch,
And side by side with the wren's brood,—
O lovely time of beggars' luck—   15
Opens the quaint and hairy bud.
And full and golden is the yield
Of cows that never have to house,
But all night nibble under boughs,
Or cool their sides in the moist field.   20

Into the rooms flow meadow airs,
The warm farm-baking smell blows round;
Inside and out and sky and ground
Are much the same; the wishing star,
Hesperus, kind and early-born,   25
Is risen only finger-far.
All stars stand close in summer air,
And tremble, and look mild as amber;
When wicks are lighted in the chamber
You might say stars were settling there.   30

Now straightening from the flowery hay,
Down the still light the mowers look;
Or turn, because their dreaming shook,
And they waked half to other days,
When left alone in yellow-stubble,   85
The rusty-coated mare would graze.
Yet thick the lazy dreams are born;
Another thought can come to mind,
But like the shivering of the wind,
Morning and evening in the corn. (1926; 1929)   40

W. H. Auden

SEPTEMBER 1, 1939

I sit in one of the dives
On Fifty-Second Street
Uncertain and afraid

As the clever hopes expire
Of a low dishonest decade: 5
Waves of anger and fear
Circulate over the bright
And darkened lands of the earth,
Obsessing our private lives;
The unmentionable odour of death   10
Offends the September night.

Accurate scholarship can
Unearth the whole offence
From Luther until now
That has driven a culture mad,   15
Find what occurred at Linz,
What huge imago made
A psychopathic god:
I and the public know
What all schoolchildren learn,   20
Those to whom evil is done
Do evil in return.

Exiled Thucydides knew
All that a speech can say
About Democracy,   25
And what dictators do,
The elderly rubbish they talk
To an apathetic grave;
Analysed all in his book,
The enlightenment driven away,   30
The habit-forming pain,
Mismanagement and grief:
We must suffer them all again.

Into this neutral air
Where blind skyscrapers use   35
Their full height to proclaim
The strength of Collective Man,
Each language pours its vain
Competitive excuse:
But who can live for long   40
In an euphoric dream;
Out of the mirror they stare,
Imperialism's face
And the international wrong.

Faces along the bar   45
Cling to their average day:
The lights must never go out,
The music must always play,
All the conventions conspire
To make this fort assume   50
The furniture of home;
Lest we should see where we are,
Lost in a haunted wood,
Children afraid of the night
Who have never been happy or good.   55

The windiest militant trash
Important Persons shout
Is not so crude as our wish:
What mad Nijinsky wrote
About Diaghilev   60
Is true of the normal heart;
For the error bred in the bone
Of each woman and each man
Craves what it cannot have,
Not universal love   65
But to be loved alone.

From the conservative dark
Into the ethical life
The dense commuters come,
Repeating their morning vow;   70
"I *will* be true to the wife,
I'll concentrate more on my work,"
And helpless governors wake
To resume their compulsory game:
Who can release them now,   75
Who can reach the deaf,
Who can speak for the dumb?

All I have is a voice
To undo the folded lie,
The romantic lie in the brain   80
Of the sensual man-in-the-street
And the lie of Authority
Whose buildings grope the sky:
There is no such thing as the State
And no one exists alone;   85
Hunger allows no choice

To the citizen or the police;
We must love one another or die.

Defenceless under the night
Our world in stupour lies;   90
Yet dotted everywhere,
Ironic points of light
Flash out wherever the Just
Exchange their messages:
May I, composed like them   95
Of Eros and of dust,
Beleaguered by the same
Negation and despair,
Show an affirming flame. (1940)

Stephen Spender

THE EXPRESS

After the first powerful plain manifesto
The black statement of pistons, without more fuss
But gliding like a queen, she leaves the station.
Without bowing and with restrained unconcern
She passes the houses which humbly crowd outside, 5
The gasworks and at last the heavy page
Of death, printed by gravestones in the cemetery.
Beyond the town there lies the open country
Where, gathering speed, she acquires mystery,
The luminous self-possession of ships on ocean. 10
It is now she begins to sing—at first quite low
Then loud, and at last with a jazzy madness—
The song of her whistle screaming at curves,
Of deafening tunnels, brakes, innumerable bolts.
And always light, aerial, underneath 15
Goes the elate meter of her wheels.
Steaming through metal landscape on her lines
She plunges new eras of wild happiness

Where speed throws up strange shapes, broad curves
And parallels clean like the steel of guns.   20
At last, further than Edinburgh or Rome,
Beyond the crest of the world, she reaches night
Where only a low streamline brightness
Of phosphorus on the tossing hills is white.
Ah, like a comet through flames she moves entranced   25
Wrapt in her music no bird song, no, nor bough
Breaking with honey buds, shall ever equal. (1933)

Dylan Thomas

TWENTY-FOUR YEARS

Twenty-four years remind the tears of my eyes.
(Bury the dead for fear that they walk to the grave in labour.)
In the groin of the natural doorway I crouched like a tailor
Sewing a shroud for a journey
By the light of the meat-eating sun.   5
Dressed to die, the sensual strut begun,
With my red veins full of money,
In the final direction of the elementary town
I advance for as long as forever is. (1939)

Robert Lowell

THE HOLY INNOCENTS

Listen, the hay-bells tinkle as the cart
Wavers on rubber tires along the tar
And cindered ice below the burlap mill
And ale-wife run. The oxen drool and start
In wonder at the fenders of a car   5

And blunder hugely up St. Peter's hill.
These are the undefiled by woman—their
Sorrow is not the sorrow of this world:
King Herod shrieking vengeance at the curled
Up knees of Jesus choking in the air,   10

A king of speechless clods and infants. Still
The world out-Herods Herod; and the year,
The nineteen-hundred forty-fifth of grace,
Lumbers with losses up the clinkered hill
Of our purgation; and the oxen near   15
The worn foundations of their resting place,
The holy manger where their bed is corn
And holly torn for Christmas. If they die,
As Jesus, in the harness, who will mourn?
Lamb of the shepherds, Child, how still you lie. (1946)   20

Isabella Gardner

THAT "CRANING OF THE NECK"

The primary word is I-Thou. The primary word I-Thou can only be spoken with
the whole being. The primary word I-It can never be spoken with the whole being.
Martin Buber

Birthdays from the ocean one desert april noon
I rode through the untouching and no-odored air
astride an english saddle on a western mare
through the resisting tow-colored grass and the dune-
less sand. Under me swam a stream strange in that dried   5
country. A "great blue heron" stood still in the tide-
less water and when I saw him there my heart daz-
zled. I whispered the mare to move quietly as
Indians move, I reined her with a catpaw hand
and my breathless feet crouched into the stirrups and   10
I prayed her through cactus mesquite and cattlebones
to the water's edge where the tall bird fished the stones.
The listening heron expanded with despair
unloosed unwilling wings, heaved from water into air.
O he hated to fly he flapped with a splayed pain-   15
ful motion. Deliberate as a weathervane

he plodded through the air that touched the fishful water.
I followed him silently giving no quarter
all that afternoon. He never flew far from me
we kept meeting past each cape and estuary   20
but he always heaved doggedly out of touch. I
only wanted to stare myself into him to try
and thou him till we recognized and became each
other. We were both fishing. But I could not reach
his eye. He fled in puzzled ponderous pain   25
and I at last rode home, conspicuous as Cain,
yet ashamed of a resigned demeaning pity
that denied us both. I returned to the city
and visited the zoo, fished on a concrete shore,
took children to aquariums, and rode no more.   30
I found that the encyclopedia says "A
gregarious bird . . ." No one spoke that desert day,
not one word. That fisher who heaved to dodge my eye
has damned himself an It and I shall never fly. (1955)

Richard Wilbur

BEASTS

Beasts in their major freedom
Slumber in peace tonight. The gull on his ledge
Dreams in the guts of himself the moon-plucked waves below,
And the sunfish leans on a stone, slept
    By the lyric water,   5

In which the spotless feet
Of deer make dulcet splashes, and to which
The ripped mouse, safe in the owl's talon, cries
Concordance. Here there is no such harm
    And no such darkness   10

As the selfsame moon observes
Where, warped in window-glass, it sponsors now
The werewolf's painful change. Turning his head away
On the sweaty bolster, he tries to remember
    The mood of manhood,   15

But lies at last, as always,
Letting it happen, the fierce fur soft to his face,
Hearing with sharper ears the wind's exciting minors,
The leaves' panic, and the degradation
Of the heavy streams.   20

Meantime, at high windows
Far from thicket and pad-fall, suitors of excellence
Sigh and turn from their work to construe again the painful
Beauty of heaven, the lucid moon
And the risen hunter,   25

Making such dreams for men
As told will break their hearts as always, bringing
Monsters into the city, crows on the public statues,
Navies fed to the fish in the dark
Unbridled waters. (1956)   30

Donald Justice

VARIATIONS ON
A THEME FROM JAMES

"large, loose, baggy monsters"

I

It's not a landscape from too near.
Like sorrows, they require some distance
Not to bulk larger than they are.
The risk is, backing off too far.
Once we have found a middle ground,   5
The warts, the pimples disappear.
There's but a shagginess remains,
An olive or a purple haze,
Which has at least that saving grace
Of average faces, average hills,   10
A nice, unshaven atmosphere.

II

Whatever goats are climbing there,
Being all invisible,
Animate objects of a will

Contemplative without desire,   15
Suffer no vertigo at all,
But climb until *our* spirits tire,
Or dine forever, or until
The speculative garbage fail,
Tin cans and comic books, which small,   20
Imaginary campers there
Forgot against this very hour.

                    III
Such art has nature in her kind
That in the shaping of a hill
She will take care to leave behind   25
Some few abutments here and there,
Something to cling to, just in case.
A taste more finical and nice
Would comb out kink and curl alike.
But oh ye barbers at your trade,   30
What more beguiles us? Your coiffures?
Or gold come waterfalling down? (1958)

Glossary and Index of Critical Terms

Abstract, apart from particular persons, places, and things. Thus, *life* and *firmness* are abstract when considered apart from a person who is alive or a thing which is firm. 73f.

Accent, the stress given a syllable because of its length, sound, position, nature, or meaning. 706

Act, a division of a drama which, as a rule, marks off a stage in the development of the action. In the modern theater, its beginning and conclusion are indicated by the raising and lowering of the curtain. 507f.

Action, that which occurs during the course of a narrative. 30-45. See also *patterns of,* 32-33; *probable action,* 47; *relationship to characters,* 47, 89; *relationship to language,* 73-74; *relationship to tone,* 89; *in poetry,* 704-705

Alexandrine, a line of poetry regularly consisting of six iambic feet with a caesura or break after the third.

Allegory, an expanded metaphor in the form of a narrative, using characters, action, and other elements to expound a concept. 302, 303f., 341

Alliteration, a juxtaposed repetition of consonant sounds, usually at the beginnings of words.
And how the silence surged softly backward

Analogy, a comparison. Usually the term is applied to a figurative rather than a literal comparison.

Anapest, 706

Angle of vision, 91

Antagonist, 48

Anticlimax, a descent which is in comic or distressing contrast with an earlier climax.

Antithesis, a contrast, heightened by the arrangement of the opposing elements.

Apologue, a short piece of fiction designed to communicate a moral or practical truth.

Archetype, 196-205, 320-323

Artistry in details, 140-145

Assonance, strictly speaking, a repetition of vowel sounds. Often, however, the term is used to indicate any repetition of sounds not exact enough to be classified as rhyme.
There open fanes and gaping graves

Atmosphere, 59-60, 95-109

Attractive character, one toward whom the reader is generally sympathetic. 48, 110f., 509

Background, the setting against which the events in an imaginative work take place. 58, 705

Ballad, a simple and often tragic story told in verse. Conventionally the ballad appears in four-line stanzas of alternating iambic tetrameter and trimeter. The folk ballad is usually distinguished from the literary ballad, the former being often of indeterminate origin and usually concerned with physical action of a vigorous and melancholy sort. The latter is written as an imitation of the folk ballad and is usually more sophisticated, more concerned with the psychological and moral implications of the action rather than the action itself.

Blank verse, unrhymed iambic pentameter.

Cacophony, harsh and unpleasing sound.

Caesura, a pause or break, demanded by the sense, coming within a line of poetry.

Catharsis, a term used by Aristotle to describe the proper effect of tragedy—"a purging of pity and terror."

Center of consciousness, 91

Characteristics, 46

Characterization, 46, 47-48, 58-59, 705

Characters, 45-57, 338ff. See also *antagonist; attractive; complex,* 46; *confidant; developing; foil; functions of,* 46, 47-48; *hero; heroine; in drama,* 506; *protagonist; raisonneur; related to action,* 47; *relationship between,* 115; *simple,* 46; *stock; type,* 509; *unattractive; villain,* 48, 177, 509

Choric narrator, 94

Chorus, (1) in Greek drama, 513f.; (2) in poetry, a stanzaic refrain repeated after each verse of the lyric.

Classicism, often defined as the golden mean between *romanticism* and *realism*. Based on the tenets of Greek art and literature, it stresses such characteristics as beauty and simplicity of form, restraint of emotion, and clarity of statement.

Climax, a point of complete development or a point of reversal in a series of related happenings. Some critics define "climax" as the point in reading or seeing a work where the reader or spectator experiences the highest emotional reaction. 33

Closed couplet, a couplet in which an idea is completely expressed. Ordinarily the punctuation at the end of a closed couplet is a colon, semicolon, or period.
True wit is nature to advantage dressed,
What oft was thought, but ne'er so well express'd.
See also *heroic couplet.*

Coincidence, an incident in a series of events

which can only be accounted for as accidental or fortuitous.

Comedy, 509f. See also *manners, comedy of.*

Complication, a situation which forces a character in a narrative to react.

Concrete, that which is experienced through or appeals to the senses. 74ff., 86, 341, 709f.

Confidant, a character to whom another character expresses his thoughts and feelings.

Conflict, the interplay between opposing forces in a narrative. 33, 115f., 509ff.

Connotation, an experience, feeling, attitude, or association suggested by a word. 74, 77, 709

Consistency, see *internal consistency,* 145-149

Convention, an artistic practice generally accepted as a substitute for a more natural and realistic mode of expression. A good example is the lowering of the curtain during a play to indicate the passing of time. 507

Couplet, two successive lines of poetry which rhyme. Usually they are of about the same length. See *closed couplet* and *heroic couplet.*

Dactyl, 707

Denotation, the dictionary or scientific meaning of a word, irrespective of its associations. 74

Denouement, literally, the untying; hence, the untangling of the threads of a plot, the solution or outcome of a series of happenings. See *action,* 30-45

Description, discourse designed to re-create human experience in words. Often the term is applied more narrowly to that discourse which attempts to re-create for the imagination the outward aspects of a person, place, or thing. 58

Developing character, one whose characteristics undergo change in the course of a narrative. 58f., 148

Dialogue, the presentation, in direct discourse, of conversation between two or more characters. 46, 77f.

Diction, the language employed in a work. See *language,* 73-87

Didacticism, obvious preachiness or moralizing in literary works.

Distance, 341-342

Drama, imaginative narrative designed to be performed by actors before an audience. 505-677. See also *acts in,* 507-508; *closet,* 505; *experimental,* 608f.; *foreshadowing; Greek,* 511ff.; *parts in,* 508-509; *relationship to audience, to theater,* 506, 568ff., 651ff.; *representation of,* 505f.; *scenes in,* 507-508; *tone in,* 508-509; *treatment of,* 505f.

Dramatic, descriptive of an action—in drama, fiction, or poetry—in a way which is concrete and direct rather than summarized; also sometimes used to signify the emotional quality of action involving conflicts. 86

Dramatic irony, a device by which the audience is made aware of the outcome of a situation before the characters in the play come to realize it.

Elegy, a poem soberly and philosophically treating of death. Its parts often involve (1) a lamentation, (2) a discussion of the philosophical implications, and (3) an affirmation of belief, resulting in consolation.

Emotional impact, 191-205

Emphasis, 73f., 340-341

Enveloping action, that part of a narrative at the beginning and perhaps at the end which introduces a narrator and unfolds the circumstances under which the story is told; often called *frame.* Examples are the opening paragraphs of *Heart of Darkness* (237), or the *Prologue* to *The Canterbury Tales* (718).

Epic, a narrative poem dealing with action of heroic proportions. Usually the chief characters are national heroes, either real or mythical. Familiar epics are the Greek *Iliad* and *Odyssey,* the Latin *Aeneid,* the German *Nibelungenlied,* the Finnish *Kalevala,* and the Anglo-Saxon *Beowulf.*

Epigram, 172-174

Episode, an event in a narrative which is complete in itself and which may or may not be loosely connected with the main line of action. 510

Escape, 177-182

Euphony, a verbal effect which is pleasing to the ear.

Evaluation, a thoughtful appraisal. In literary criticism the term implies an appraisal reached through the use of standards which are themselves clear and valid. 137-234

Evaluation, standards of: *artistry in details,* 140-145; *biography,* 182-191; *escape,* 177-182; *internal consistency,* 145-171; *literary mode,* 171-176; *morality,* 219-228; *myth,* 205-210; *philosophy,* 228-234; *psychology,* 191-205; *society,* 210-219

Exposition, explanation; in fiction and drama specifically the explanation of the situation and character which is necessary for an understanding of what takes place.

Expressionism, a dramatic mode in which the author conveys meanings, not by literal realism, but by fantastic or psychological symbolism; e.g., O'Neill's *The Hairy Ape* and the dream scenes in *Emperor Jones.*

Fable, a narrative, usually about animals, designed to make clear a moral truth. Sometimes the term applies to the action or plot of a literary work, usually a play, an epic, or a narrative poem.

Farce, 510

Fiction, the interpretation of life in an imaginative narrative, 2-30, 338. See also *adventure,* 177; *detective,* 177; *romantic,* 177

Figures of speech, rhetorical devices designed to appeal to the reader's senses and intellect in such a way as to heighten his perception of the essential quality of the experience described. Figures which appeal primarily to the senses are simile, metaphor, personification, synecdoche, metonymy, hyperbole, litotes, allegory, fable, apologue, and parable; those which appeal primarily to the intellect are analogy, antithesis, and irony. 74-75, 78, 86, 710f.

Focus, the centering of attention by the author upon a certain element or certain elements of literary work. A figurative term for emphasis. 340

Focus of narration, the point of view. 91ff.

Foil character, a character whose qualities contrast to, and thus illuminate, the nature of another character.

Foot, metrical, 706f.

Foreshadowing, the pointing forward to an incident in an imaginative work; an intimation to the reader of what is to follow. 507f.

Form, in literature a species of production, such as fiction, drama, or poetry; or a subspecies, such as the novel, one-act play, or sonnet. The term is also used to designate the arrangement or structure of a work as distinct from its content, or to designate everything that appears on the printed page as distinct from what went through the author's mind or goes through the reader's. 171-176, 338

Frame, see *enveloping action.*

Free verse, 707

Freudians, authors and critics who believe that life should be interpreted in literature in terms of the psychology of Sigmund Freud (1856-1939). 191ff.

Functional, applies to details in characterization, action, and other elements in a work which are useful to other elements or to the unity of the work as a whole. Thus some characterizations motivate action, and some actions contribute to total meaning. 58

Genre, 171-176

Hero, the chief attractive male character in an imaginative work; the male protagonist. 48, 177, 302, 509f.

Heroic couplet, a couplet in which the metrical form is iambic pentameter.

A heap of dust alone remains of thee,
'Tis all thou art, and all the proud shall be!

Heroine, the chief attractive feminine character in an imaginative work; the feminine protagonist. 48, 177, 302, 509f.

Hyperbole, an extravagant exaggeration, as a rule deliberately planned with an eye to its effect.

Iambus, 706

Imagery, concrete details which stimulate the senses. Often the term is employed more narrowly to designate figurative details as distinct from literal ones. 710

Imagism, the type of poetry which is intended to do no more than present small, sharp pictures with special attention to mass, line, and color.

Impressionism, in literature the mode of writing in which the author describes an object or experience, not in clear terms of its reality as he knows or thinks it is, but in terms of his immediate, often momentary sensory reactions to it.

Inconsistency, 510

Inevitability, in a literary work, the relating of character and action in such a way as to convince the reader that the action is the only possible one under the circumstances presented. 509

Insights, see *morality,* 219-228; *philosophy,* 228-234; *psychology,* 191-205; *society,* 210-219

Intrusive narrator, 92

Irony, discourse in which the author or speaker says the opposite of what he feels in a way implying his true attitude. See *dramatic irony.* 111f.

Italian sonnet, see *sonnet.*

Language, 73-87, 141; *poetic,* 705

Litotes, a deliberate understatement for the sake of effect. The opposite of hyperbole.

Manners, comedy of, a comedy which shows and satirizes the manners and conventions of contemporary upper-class society.

Marxists, critics and authors who believe that literature should interpret life in accordance with the social and economic doctrines of Karl Marx (1818-1883). 211

Meanings, 109-135, 339; in poetry, 709; related to character, 48

Melodrama, 510

Metaphor, an implied comparison. 112, 113, 710

Metaphysical poetry, poetry characterized by subtleties of thought and expression. Most frequently the term is applied to the work of seventeenth-century poets like Donne and Herbert.

Meter, 706f.

Metonymy, a figure of speech using an associated idea for the one meant, as a cause for an effect,

an effect for a cause, the container for the thing contained, an attribute of an object for the object itself.
Along the lawn, where scatter'd hamlets rose,
Unwieldy wealth *and* cumbrous pomp *repose.*
Mode, 171-176
Monologue, the direct representation of the speech or thought of a single character; e.g., *My Last Duchess,* 55
Motivation, the depiction of the personalities and of the circumstances acting upon them in an imaginative work which makes certain actions of theirs probable or inevitable. 507
Myth, 205-210
Naturalism, an extreme form of realism which emphasizes scientific aspects of heredity and environment, and which is relatively very frank in its presentation of unpleasant details.
Novel, 175
Objective presentation, with regard to the author, a presentation which involves a minimum of the overt expression of the author's feelings; see *point of view,* 341f.; with regard to the character, the objective or dramatic point of view. 507
Obligatory scene, the scene in which the main conflict in a literary work reaches a decisive stage. It is called "obligatory" since ordinarily the author is obliged to give dramatic treatment to this important action.
Ode, a formal, dignified, and elaborate poem written for a special purpose and often for a special occasion. The *regular* or *Pindaric* ode, designed to be chanted by a chorus, has three parts: the strophe, antistrophe, and epode. The *stanzaic* or *Horatian* ode breaks with this formality but is written in regular stanzas. The *irregular* ode follows no set pattern. 514
Omniscience, the point of view of an author who sees and records what is going on in the hearts and minds of all the characters. 92f.
Onomatopoeia, a device by which sound is suited to the sense. 76f.
Ottava rima, see *stanza.*
Parable, a brief fictional work which concretely illustrates an abstract idea or ideas; for example, Christ's parable of the prodigal son.
Paradox, a statement which is or which seems to be self-contradictory.
Pentameter, 707
Persona, 94
Personality, (1) of authors, 88, 89, 183; (2) of characters, 45-46
Personal narrative, narrative written in the first person. See *point of view,* 93f.
Personification, a figure of speech in which human qualities are attributed to inanimate objects or to abstract qualities. 711
Petrarchan sonnet, 708. See also *sonnet.*
Phantasy, the process of creating mental images, or a pattern of such images appearing in a literary work. 191ff.
Plot, the patterned sequence of action which makes up an imaginative narrative. The term is variously defined, sometimes as the structure of action, sometimes as a series of stages in a conflict, etc. 32, 58-59, 505. See also *action,* 30-45
Poetry, 76, 141f., 146f., 704-819
Point of view, 91-95, 341-344
Primitivists, authors and critics who believe that the primitive and universal emotions related to physical pleasure or pain are those most significant both in life and art.
Privilege, 92f.
Prosody, the science or art of metrical structure. More specifically the term is used to designate a particular theory or practice in versification, like Keats' *prosody.*
Protagonist (from a Greek word meaning "first contestant"), the leading figure in a narrative. 48, 509
Pyrrhus, 707
Raisonneur, a character in a drama or fictional work who voices and supports the attitude of the author concerning the problem which is involved.
Realism, variously defined, has been characterized by James Weber Linn and Houghton Taylor, in *A Foreword to Fiction,* as "the tendency to accept in *some way* the limitations which actual circumstances put on human desires and motives, and to portray *some* of the effects of these circumstances." They continue, "One must say *some* because no realist, even the apparently most unselective, can make clear all the kinds of limitation at once. But if the novelist shows even one aspect of the confining power of actuality, if he shows in any way how life actually affects people, what feelings and motives they actually have, he is to that extent a realist."
Reliability, 342f.
Reporter, 92
Resolution of plot, see *denouement.*
Reversal, 33, 47
Rhyme, similarity in the terminal sounds of words. By nature, rhyme can be perfect (cloud, proud), imperfect (woman, human), apparent (gone, bone), and identical (*light,* used in two senses). According to the placement of words in poetry, rhyme can be tail or terminal (words at the ends of lines rhyming), internal (word

within a line rhyming with end word), and initial (beginning words rhyming). Any of these can, in turn, be masculine (ending on an accented syllable), or feminine (ending on an unaccented syllable). 141, 707f.

Rhythm, the cadence created chiefly by the accent pattern, though other elements like sound values and sentence structure are contributory causes. 76-77; in poetry, 86, 705-707, 711

Rime royal, see *stanza.*

Romance, 175-176, 301-304

Romanticism, the opposite of realism in the sense that it is a tendency to avoid accepting the limitations which actual circumstances put on human desires and motives. Contrary to realism, romanticism stresses the exotic rather than the ordinary, the individual rather than society as a whole, the subjective rather than the objective, the idealistic rather than the skeptical, a disregard for laws and conventions rather than a resignation to them in the belief that they are irresistible.

Run-on line, a line of poetry in which the sense flows without stop to the succeeding line. A run-on line is easily recognized by the absence of any end punctuation.

Satire, a witty or humorous criticism, in fiction, drama, or poetry, of some individual, class, institution, or idea.

Scene, in drama, a division of an act or of a whole play which indicates (1) a stage in the action, (2) a shift in place, or (3) a change in the number of actors on the stage. 507-508. As background, see *setting,* 57-72

Scène à faire, see *obligatory scene.*

Selection, 31-32, 71, 74, 709

Sensibility, 88, 91ff., 343

Sentences, 76-77, 78

Sentimentalism, excessive emotional response—on the part of a character, the author, or the reader —to life or to an imaginative work or some element in an imaginative work.

Setting, 57-72, 339, 341, 705

Shakespearian sonnet, see *sonnet.*

Short story, 338-505

Sibilants, sounds which resemble hissing. In English the sibilants are *s, z, sh, zh, ch,* and *j.* 76

Simile, a stated comparison, usually distinguishable because of the presence of the word *like* or *as.* 75, 710f.

Soliloquy, a speech revealing the thoughts and feelings of a character in a play, and usually delivered when the character is alone on the stage. 507

Sonnet, a short, formalized, lyrical poem containing fourteen lines and written in iambic pentameter. The *Italian* or *Petrarchan* sonnet contains an octet (eight lines) rhyming *abba abba,* and a sestet (six lines) most frequently rhyming *cde cde* or *cdc dcd.* The *English* or *Shakespearian* sonnet contains three quatrains and a couplet, and rhymes *abab cdcd efef gg.* A variation on this is the *Spenserian* sonnet, which rhymes *abab bcbc cdcd ee.* Much of the skill in writing sonnets is in making thought breaks correspond with rhyme breaks. 708

Spenserian sonnet, see *sonnet.*

Spenserian stanza, a nine-line stanza rhyming *ababbcbcc.* The first eight lines are iambic pentameter; the last is iambic hexameter or an Alexandrine.

Spondee, 707

Stanza, a group of lines composing a division within a poem. Usually these divisions are relatively short and have the same pattern. The most familiar stanzas are the *quatrain* (four lines), *quintain* (five lines), *sextain* (six lines), and *octave* (eight lines). A few special forms are the *heroic stanza* (an iambic pentameter quatrain with alternate lines rhyming), *ballad stanza* (alternating tetrameter and trimeter iambic lines which form a quatrain rhyming *abcb*), *rime royal* (a seven-line stanza of iambic pentameter rhyming *ababbcc*), and *ottava rima* (an iambic pentameter octave rhyming *abababcc*). 141f., 146

Stock character, one conventionally associated with certain types of dramas or scenes; e.g., the villain in the old-fashioned melodrama who threatens to foreclose the mortgage.

Structure, the selection, arrangement, and handling of details and elements in an imaginative work which give the work the form and unity it has. 141f., 149

Style, variously defined, a term used to signify (1) the language of an author, (2) the distinctive handling of language by an author, (3) the distinctive craftsmanship in general of an imaginative artist. 84, 89

Subjective presentation, presentation which stresses the author's reaction to his material rather than the material itself.

Suspense, (1) the excited interest of reader or spectator in what will happen next, (2) the quality or form of the work which excites such an interest.

Symbol, anything used to represent something else, as a word is used to represent an idea. In literature the term usually refers to a concrete image employed to designate an abstract quality or concept. 112f.

Synecdoche, a figure of speech in which a part is used for a whole or a whole for a part. *The world is too much with us*
Tale, 302
Technique, the craftsmanship employed by the author to give a literary work form and significance.
Tetrameter, 707
Theatre of the Absurd, 677f.
Theme, 117, 341
Thesis, the theme, proposition, or central idea.
Threnody, a poem in which the poet somberly writes of death and of its implications.
Tone, 88-91, 111, 339
Tone-color, the effect achieved by the arrangement of sounds. Chiefly it is dependent upon the natural pitch of vowel sounds and upon the emotional responses which we make to different sounds. Poe's *The Bells* is an exercise in tone-color. For words quoted from it, see 709f. See also 76f., 141

Tragedy, 508f.
Triteness, the quality of an artistic work which derives from the author's using phrasings or materials which have been used in other works until the reader has become tired of encountering them.
Trochee, 706
Unattractive character, one toward whom the reader is generally unsympathetic. 48
Unities, dramatic, elements in drama wrongly ascribed to Aristotle and rigidly prescribed by French classicists. These include unity of time (a twenty-four-hour period), of place (one setting), and of action (one main action).
Unity, the quality achieved by an artistic work when everything in it is so interrelated as to form a complete whole. 32f., 147, 338, 339-340
Verse, a line or stanza of poetry. The term also designates poetry in general.
Versification, the art or science of metrical composition.

Index of Titles and Authors